ESSAYS IN HONOR OF AMAN ULLAH

ADVANCES IN ECONOMETRICS

Series Editors: Thomas B. Fomby,
R. Carter Hill, Ivan Jeliazkov,
Juan Carlos Escanciano,
Eric Hillebrand, David Jacho-Chávez,
Daniel L. Millimet, Rodney Strachan

Recent Volumes:

Volume 27A: Missing Data Methods: Cross-Sectional Methods and Applications – Edited by David M. Drukker

Volume 27B: Missing Data Methods: Time-Series Methods and Applications – Edited by David M. Drukker

Volume 28: DSGE Models in Macroeconomics: Estimation, Evaluation and New Developments – Edited by Nathan Balke, Fabio Canova, Fabio Milani and Mark Wynne

Volume 29: Essays in Honor of Jerry Hausman – Edited by Badi H. Baltagi, Whitney Newey, Hal White and R. Carter Hill

Volume 30: 30th Anniversary Edition – Edited by Dek Terrell and Daniel Millmet

Volume 31: Structural Econometric Models – Edited by Eugene Choo and Matthew Shum

Volume 32: VAR Models in Macroeconomics — New Developments and Applications: Essays in Honor of Christopher A. Sims – Edited by Thomas B. Fomby, Lutz Kilian and Anthony Murphy

Volume 33: Essays in Honor of Peter C. B. Phillips – Edited by Thomas B. Fomby, Yoosoon Chang and Joon Y. Park

Volume 34: Bayesian Model Comparison – Edited by Ivan Jeliazkov and Dale J. Poirier

Volume 35: Dynamic Factor Models – Edited by Eric Hillebrand and Siem Jan Koopman

ADVANCES IN ECONOMETRICS VOLUME 36

ESSAYS IN HONOR OF AMAN ULLAH

EDITED BY

GLORIA GONZÁLEZ-RIVERA

Department of Economics, University of California Riverside, Riverside, CA, USA

R. CARTER HILL

Department of Economics, Louisiana State University, Baton Rouge, LA, USA

TAE-HWY LEE

Department of Economics, University of California Riverside, Riverside, CA, USA

Emerald

United Kingdom – North America – Japan
India – Malaysia – China

Emerald Group Publishing Limited
Howard House, Wagon Lane, Bingley BD16 1WA, UK

First edition 2016

British Library Cataloguing in Publication Data
A catalogue record for this book is available from the British Library

ISBN: 978-1-78560-787-5
ISSN: 0731-9053 (Series)

Printed and bound by CPI Group (UK) Ltd, Croydon, CR0 4YY

CONTENTS

PART V
ISSUES IN ECONOMETRIC THEORY

PART VI
NONPARAMETRIC AND SEMIPARAMETRIC METHODS

LIST OF CONTRIBUTORS

Aziza Aipenova	Department of Mechanics and Mathematics, Kazakh National University, Almaty, Kazakhstan
Yonghong An	Department of Economics, Texas A&M University, College Station, TX, USA
Badi H. Baltagi	Department of Economics and Center for Policy Research, Syracuse University, New York, Syracuse, USA
Yong Bao	Department of Economics, Purdue University, West Lafayette, IN, USA
Alexander Chudik	Federal Reserve Bank of Dallas, Dallas, TX, USA
Yanqin Fan	Department of Economics, University of Washington, Seattle, WA, USA
Jean-Jacques Forneron	Department of Economics, Columbia University, New York, NY, USA
Amos Golan	Department of Economics and Info-Metrics Institute, American University, Washington, DC, USA; Santa Fe Institute, Santa Fe, NM, USA
Emmanuel Guerre	School of Economics and Finance, Queen Mary, University of London, London, UK
Ai Han	Academy of Mathematics and Systems Science, Chinese Academy of Sciences, Beijing, People's Republic of China
Matthew Harding	Sanford School of Public Policy and Department of Economics, Duke University, Durham, NC, USA

Jerry Hausman	Department of Economics, Massachusetts Institute of Technology, Cambridge, MA, USA
Daniel J. Henderson	Department of Economics, University of Alabama, Tuscaloosa, AL, USA
Yongmiao Hong	Department of Economics and Department of Statistical Sciences, Cornell University, Ithaca, NY, USA
Cheng Hsiao	Department of Economics, University of Southern California, Los Angeles, CA, USA; WISE, Xiamen University, China
Yulia Kotlyarova	Department of Economics, Dalhousie University, Halifax, NS, Canada
Dong Li	School of Economic, Political and Policy Sciences, The University of Texas at Dallas, Dallas, TX, USA
Qi Li	Department of Economics, Texas A&M University, College Station, TX, USA
Long Liu	Department of Economics, College of Business, University of Texas, San Antonio, San Antonio, TX, USA
Robin L. Lumsdaine	Kogod School of Business and Info-Metrics Institute, American University, Washington, DC, USA; National Bureau of Economic Research (NBER), Cambridge, MA, USA
Esfandiar Maasoumi	Department of Economics, Emory University, Atlanta, GA, USA
Carlos Martins-Filho	Department of Economics, University of Colorado at Boulder, Boulder, CO, USA
Kamiar Mohaddes	Faculty of Economics and Girton College, University of Cambridge, Cambridge, UK

Kairat Mynbaev — International School of Economics, Kazakh-British Technical University, Almaty, Kazakhstan

Serena Ng — Department of Economics, Columbia University, New York, NY, USA

Christopher J. Palmer — Haas School of Business, University of California, Berkeley, Berkeley, CA, USA

Christopher F. Parmeter — Department of Economics, University of Miami, Miami, FL, USA

M. Hashem Pesaran — Department of Economics & USC Dornsife INET, University of Southern California, Los Angeles, CA, USA

Peter C. B. Phillips — Department of Economics, Yale University, New Haven, CT, USA

Jeffrey S. Racine — Department of Economics and Graduate Program in Statistics, McMaster University, Hamilton, ON, Canada

Mehdi Raissi — International Monetary Fund, Washington, DC, USA

Eric Renault — Department of Economics, Brown University, Providence, RI, USA

Marcia M. A. Schafgans — Department of Economics, London School of Economics, London, UK

Daniela Scidá — Department of Economics, Brown University, Providence, RI, USA

Liangjun Su — School of Economics, Singapore Management University, Singapore, Singapore

Shouyang Wang — Academy of Mathematics and Systems Science, Chinese Academy of Sciences, Beijing, People's Republic of China

Ximing Wu Department of Agricultural Economics, Texas A&M University, College Station, TX, USA

Xin Yun Academy of Mathematics and Systems Science, Chinese Academy of Sciences, Beijing, People's Republic of China

Yonghui Zhang School of Economics, Renmin University, Beijing, People's Republic of China

Yu Yvette Zhang Department of Agricultural Economics, Texas A&M University, College Station, TX, USA

Yifeng Zhu Department of Economics, Emory University, Atlanta, GA, USA

Victoria Zinde-Walsh Department of Economics, McGill University, Montréal, QC, Canada

INTRODUCTION

The 36th volume of *Advances in Econometrics* in honor of Aman Ullah is a collection of 19 articles contributed by his former students, colleagues, and academic friends, covering a wide range of issues in econometrics. The volume mostly draws upon the works presented at the conference that took place at the historic Mission Inn in Riverside California on March 13–15, 2015.

The volume is organized into six parts. Part I. Tribute (one article) includes a review that pays tribute to the professional career of Aman Ullah. The remaining 18 articles of the volume are organized into five parts corresponding to five general econometrics topics to which Ullah has contributed extensively over the course of his career. These are: Part II. Panel Data Models (four articles), Part III. Finite Sample Econometrics (two articles), Part IV. Information and Entropy (three articles), Part V. Issues in Econometric Theory (three articles), and Part VI. Nonparametric and Semiparametric Methods (six articles). We follow a similar ordering of these six parts to that of the conference program. In each part, the order of articles is alphabetical according to the first author's last name.

"PART I. TRIBUTE" CONSISTS OF A REVIEW ARTICLE

The article "A Selective Review of Aman Ullah's Contributions to Econometrics" by Yong Bao, Yanqin Fan, Liangjun Su, and Victoria Zinde-Walsh provides a historical account of Aman Ullah's contributions to a wide spectrum of econometrics. The main specialization of each of the four author guides his/her own account on how Ullah has contributed to robust inference, finite sample theory, nonparametrics and semiparametrics, and panel and spatial models. On robust inference, the article reviews Aman's early works with his thesis advisor Professor Nagar that go back to the early 1970s, then discusses the double-k class estimators in the late 1970s, and his continuous effort in pursuing robustness of statistics with respect to distributional assumptions in the 1980s. The second section reviews Aman's contributions to finite sample theory in econometrics and his approaches to addressing the exact theory and approximations for a wide range of statistics in various econometrics and statistics models. The third section presents a brief review of some of Aman's works in several sub-areas: nonparametric regression and its derivatives, consistent model specification testing, nonparametric IV and simultaneous equations models, and combined estimation or model averaging. The last section discusses Aman's contributions to panel and spatial models such as seemingly unrelated regressions, parametric, semiparametric and nonparametric panel data models and spatial models.

"PART II. PANEL DATA MODELS" CONSISTS OF THE FOLLOWING FOUR ARTICLES

In "Semiparametric Estimation of Partially Linear Varying Coefficient Panel Data Models," the authors Yonghong An, Cheng Hsiao, and Dong Li estimate a partially linear varying coefficient fixed effect panel data model that consists of a parametric linear part and a nonparametric varying coefficient part. By estimating the model with the series method, the authors show that the parametric component can be estimated at the $\sqrt{N}$-rate and the nonparametric component can be consistently estimated at the standard nonparametric rate. They extend the model to allow endogeneity in the parametric component and establish the asymptotic properties of the semiparametric instrumental variable estimators.

In "Testing for Spatial Lag and Spatial Error Dependence in a Fixed Effects Panel Data Model Using Double Length Artificial Regressions," Badi H. Baltagi and Long Liu consider a battery of tests in a model where the fixed effects are first eliminated using the method in Lee and Yu (2010). The derivations of the tests are then similar to those derived for a cross-section spatial regression model (Baltagi & Li, 2001). This article revisits the joint and conditional Lagrange Multiplier tests derived by Debarsy and Ertur (2010) for a fixed effects spatial lag regression model with spatial auto-regressive error, and derives these tests using artificial double length regressions. These tests and their corresponding LM tests are compared using an empirical example and a Monte Carlo simulation.

Alexander Chudik, Kamiar Mohaddes, M. Hashem Pesaran, and Mehdi Raissi contribute the article "Long-Run Effects in Large Heterogeneous Panel Data Models with Cross-Sectionally Correlated Errors." They develop a cross-sectionally augmented distributed lag (CS-DL) approach to the estimation of long-run effects in large dynamic heterogeneous panel data models with cross-sectionally dependent errors, as a complementary method to cross-sectionally augmented ARDL specifications. The asymptotic distribution of the CS-DL estimator is derived under coefficient heterogeneity in the case where the time dimension (T) and the cross-section dimension (N) are both large. The CS-DL approach is compared with more standard panel data estimators that are based on autoregressive distributed lag (ARDL) specifications. It is shown that unlike the ARDL-type estimator, the CS-DL estimator is robust to misspecification of dynamics and error serial correlation. The theoretical results are illustrated with small sample evidence obtained by means of Monte Carlo simulations, which suggest that the performance of the CS-DL approach is often superior to the alternative panel ARDL estimates, particularly when T is not too large and lies in the range of 30–50.

In "Semiparametric Estimation of Partially Linear Dynamic Panel Data Models with Fixed Effects," Liangjun Su and Yonghui Zhang consider a semiparametric model where the linear part includes either exogenous or endogenous variables or both, and the nonparametric part includes the lagged-dependent variable and some other exogenous variables. Two types of estimation methods are proposed for the first-differenced model. The asymptotic properties of the estimators are investigated when N tends to infinity and the time period T is fixed. Moreover, they propose a specification test for the linearity of the nonparametric component. The performance of the proposed estimators is evaluated via Monte Carlo simulations. The proposed semiparametric estimator is applied to model the relationship between economic growth, intellectual property right protection, and initial economic conditions.

"PART III. FINITE SAMPLE ECONOMETRICS" CONSISTS OF THE FOLLOWING TWO ARTICLES

In "Finite-Sample Bias of the Conditional Gaussian Maximum Likelihood Estimator in ARMA Models," Yong Bao derives the finite-sample bias of the conditional Gaussian maximum likelihood estimator in ARMA models when the error follows some unknown non-normal distribution. The general procedure relies on writing down the score function and its higher-order derivative matrices in terms of quadratic forms in the non-normal error vector. Evaluation of the bias can then be straightforwardly conducted. For the special case of ARMA(1,1), the bias results are further simplified and compared with the existing results in Tanaka (1984). Simulations results confirm that the new bias formula works well in approximating the true finite-sample bias of the Gaussian maximum likelihood estimator under both normal and non-normal distributions.

In "Finite Sample Bias Corrected IV Estimation for Weak and Many Instruments," Matthew Harding, Jerry Hausman and Christopher J. Palmer explore the use of double k-class estimators in scenarios involving weak and/or many instruments and show that there is a scope for gain. They consider the finite sample distribution of the 2SLS estimator and derive bounds on its exact bias in the presence of weak and/or many instruments. They contrast the behavior of the exact bias expressions and the asymptotic expansions popular in the literature, including a consideration of the no-moment problem exhibited by many Nagar-type estimators. After deriving a finite sample unbiased k-class estimator, they introduce two new IV estimators, both in the double k-class estimator. These estimators require choosing the k_2 parameter in a data-driven way. For one of the estimators, k_2 is chosen to correct for the 2SLS bias, and for the other, k_2 is such that minimizes the MSE. Monte Carlo simulations show that these new estimators outperform 2SLS and the Fuller estimators in terms of mean bias and MSE.

"PART IV. INFORMATION AND ENTROPY" CONTAINS THE FOLLOWING THREE ARTICLES

Although in principle prior information can significantly improve inference, incorporating incorrect prior information will bias the estimates of any inferential analysis. This fact deters many scientists from incorporating prior information into their inferential analyses. In the article "On the Construction of Prior Information – An Info-Metrics Approach," Amos Golan and Robin L. Lumsdaine discuss three different, yet complimentary, approaches for constructing prior information with an application to the social sciences where prior information is often hard to come by and very hard to justify or validate. Within an info-metrics framework, they borrow concepts and philosophical reasoning from the natural sciences, where experiments are more regularly conducted and prior information is often used in inferential analysis, despite being nontrivial to specify what that information is and how to quantify it.

In "The Wage Premium of Naturalized Citizenship," Esfandiar Maasoumi and Yifeng Zhu analyze the earning gap between naturalized citizens and noncitizens. Over many years, they find a positive gap characterized by a tent shape across the wage distribution. They focus on a normalized entropy measure of the gap between distributions, and they compare it with conventional measures at the mean, median, and other quantiles. In addition, naturalized citizen earnings (at least) second-order stochastically dominate non-citizen earnings in many of the recent years. They construct two counterfactual distributions to further examine the potential sources of the earning gap, the wage structure effect and the composition effect. Both of these sources contribute to the gap, but the composition effect, while diminishing somewhat after 2005, accounts for about 3/4 of the gap. The unconditional quantile regression (based on the Recentered Influence Function), and conditional quantile regressions confirm that naturalized citizens have generally higher wages, although the gap varies for different income groups in many years.

Built on the earlier contributions by Geweke (1982), Gourieroux, Monfort and Renault (1987), and Schreiber (2000), who measure causality in the context of Markov processes, Eric Renault and Daniela Scida, in their article "Causality and Markovianity: Information Theoretic Measures," reconsider the problem of causality measurement using the Kullback measure of divergence of a casual model from a noncausal counterpart. They specially focus on the design of measures that disentangle the measurement of markovianity and the measurement of Granger causality. This disentangling leads to revisit the equivalence between the Sims and Granger concepts of non-causality and the Log-Likelihood Ratio tests for each of them. The article draws attention to an important point neglected in the literature; namely, that for finite-order Markovian processes, Granger causality implies testing for non-nested hypotheses.

"PART V. ISSUES IN ECONOMETRIC THEORY" CONSISTS OF THE FOLLOWING THREE ARTICLES

In "A Likelihood-Free Reverse Sampler of the Posterior Distribution," Jean-Jacques Forneron and Serena Ng examine properties of an optimization-based sampler that employs auxiliary simulation, summary statistics, and resampling to approximate a posterior distribution for which inference may be hindered by the intractability of the likelihood function. This article extends Forneron and Ng (2014), which focused on the case of exact identification, to the overidentified case. It further provides additional insights into the reverse sampler, which is shown to be an importance sampler when the importance ratio is equal to the determinant or volume of the Jacobian matrix of the importance density transformation. By a change of variable argument, the output is a number of draws from the desired posterior distribution. Optimization always results in acceptable draws. Hence, when the minimum distance problem is not too difficult to solve, combining importance sampling with optimization can be much faster than the method of Approximate Bayesian Computation that by-passes optimization.

In "A Vector Autoregressive Moving Average Model for Interval-Valued Time Series Data," Ai Han, Yongmiao Hong, Shouyang Wang, and Xin Yun propose an Interval-valued Vector Autoregressive Moving Average (IVARMA) model that captures cross-dependence dynamics among multivariate interval-valued time series. It is an important extension to the traditional point-valued VARMA model and univariate autoregressive conditional interval model. They develop a minimum distance estimation method to estimate the parameters of an IVARMA model, and establish consistency, asymptotic normality, and asymptotic efficiency of the proposed estimator. A two-stage minimum distance estimator is shown to be asymptotically most efficient among the class of minimum-distance estimators. Simulation studies showcase the superiority of their estimators in finite sample performance.

In "Inference in Near-Singular Regression," Peter C. B. Phillips considers stationary time series regression models with near-collinear regressors and introduces new normalization techniques to develop the asymptotic theory for regression estimates and test statistics in cases where the signal matrix is nearly singular in finite samples and is asymptotically degenerate. When the regressors are exogenous, he develops the limit theory for the OLS estimator and test statistics. When the regressors are endogenous, he derives the limit theory for the corresponding 2SLS estimator, Wald test statistic, and some overidentification test. It is shown that near-singular designs of the type considered in the article are not completely fatal to least squares inference, but will inevitably involve size distortion except in special Gaussian cases. In the endogenous case, IV estimation is inconsistent and both the block Wald test and the Sargan overidentification test are conservative, biasing these tests in favor of the null.

"PART VI. NONPARAMETRIC AND SEMIPARAMETRIC METHODS" CONSISTS OF THE FOLLOWING SIX ARTICLES

In "Multivariate Local Polynomial Estimators: Uniform Boundary Properties and Asymptotic Linear Representation," Yanqin Fan and Emmanuel Guerre study the asymptotic bias and variance of a general class of multivariate local polynomial estimators of M-regression functions, which include the conditional mean and the conditional quantile functions as special cases. The focus is on the asymptotic bias and variance properties on the boundary and over the whole compact support of the multivariate covariate under a minimal assumption on the support. The support assumption ensures that the vicinity of the support boundary will be visited by the multivariate covariate. They show that, like in the univariate case, multivariate local polynomial estimators have good bias and variance properties near the boundary. They also establish asymptotic normality near the boundary and the optimal uniform convergence rate over the whole support. They obtain a uniform linearization result for the local polynomial quantile regression, and demonstrate that, with the uniformity results, the trimming practice in the local polynomial regression to avoid the boundary effect is unnecessary.

In "Model Averaging over Nonparametric Estimators," Daniel Henderson and Christopher F. Parmeter consider model-averaging methods for nonparametric regression. They combine up to eight nonparametric estimators of the mean function that differ in terms of their choices of kernel (Gaussian or Epanechnikov), bandwidth (least squares cross validation or AIC), and polynomial order (local constant or local linear). The authors propose two averaging schemes based on least-squares weights and cross-validation weights. They provide Monte Carlo evidence showing that model averaging based on either scheme nearly always results in more efficient estimators of the mean function than estimation based on any given choice of kernel, bandwidth and polynomial order. They also provide an empirical application of the proposed estimators.

In "Smoothness: Bias and Efficiency of Nonparametric Kernel Estimators," Yulia Kotlyarova, Marcia M. A. Schafgans, and Victoria Zinde-Walsh provide smoothness conditions for kernel-based estimators that ensure that the asymptotic rate at which the bias goes to zero is determined by the kernel order. In a finite sample, the leading term in the expansion of the bias may provide a poor approximation. The authors explore the relationship between smoothness and bias in a kernel estimator framework. They provide estimators for the degree of the smoothness and the bias and demonstrate that a linearly combined estimator constructed from different kernel functions and bandwidths can lead to estimators with reduced asymptotic mean-square error relative to the individual estimator at the optimal bandwidth. The higher-order kernels can reduce bias given some smoothness assumptions, but when these are violated non-standard results can arise. They examine the finite-sample performance of a combined estimator that minimizes the trace of the MSE of a linear combination of individual kernel estimators for a multimodal density. The combined estimator provides a robust alternative to individual estimators that protects against uncertainty about the degree of smoothness.

In "A Class of Nonparametric Density Derivative Estimators Based on Global Lipschitz Conditions," Kairat Mynbaev, Carlos Martins-Filho, and Aziza Aipenova show that the estimators for derivatives associated with a density function can be useful in identifying its modes and inflection points. In addition, these estimators play an important role in plug-in methods associated with bandwidth selection in nonparametric kernel density estimation. They extend the nonparametric class of density estimators proposed by Mynbaev and Martins-Filho (2010) to the estimation of m-order density derivatives when some smoothness conditions (the higher order Lipschitz conditions) on the density are imposed. Contrary to some existing derivative estimators, the proposed estimators have a full asymptotic characterization, including uniform consistency and asymptotic normality. An expression for the optimal bandwidth that minimizes an asymptotic approximation for the estimators' integrated squared error is provided. A Monte Carlo study sheds light on the finite sample performance of the estimators and contrasts it with that of density derivative estimators based on the classical Rosenblatt–Parzen approach.

Recent developments in shape-constrained nonparametric regression allow practitioners to impose constraints on local polynomial estimators thereby ensuring that the resulting estimates are consistent with underlying theory. In "Local Polynomial Derivative Estimation: Analytic or Taylor?," Jeffrey S. Racine considers the impact of using local polynomial Taylor-based derivative estimates for shape-constrained estimation, and cautions practitioners that these derivatives may be internally inconsistent with the estimated regression function. He points out that the analytic derivative estimator has the advantage to maintain internal consistency between the regression function and derivative estimates when there is a shape constraint but the Taylor-based derivative estimator enjoys a smaller mean-squared error. In such cases, the author suggests that practitioners might prefer to instead use analytic derivatives along the lines of those proposed in the local constant setting by Rilstone and Ullah (1989).

In "A Simple Consistent Nonparametric Estimator of the Lorenz Curve," Yu Yvette Zhang, Ximing Wu, and Qi Li propose a nonparametric estimator of the Lorenz curve that satisfies its theoretical properties, including monotonicity and convexity. They extend the integral transformation idea proposed by Ramsay (1998) to the estimation of the Lorenz curve, where a constrained problem is successfully transformed into an unconstrained one, which is estimated nonparametrically. The authors utilize splines to facilitate the numerical implementation of their estimator and to provide a parametric representation of the constructed Lorenz curve. They conduct Monte Carlo simulations to demonstrate the superior performance of the proposed estimator. They apply the method to estimate the Lorenz curve of the U.S. household income distribution and calculate the Gini index based on the estimated Lorenz curve.

Gloria González-Rivera
R. Carter Hill
Tae-Hwy Lee
Editors

ACKNOWLEDGMENTS

A conference in honour of Aman Ullah took place at Riverside Mission Inn on March 13–15, 2015 to celebrate his long and productive academic career. We would like to thank the following sponsors for their support (in alphabetical order): editors of *Advances in Econometrics*, Emerald Group Publishing Ltd., Info-Metrics Institute of American University, International Association for Applied Econometrics (IAAE) and the University of California Riverside's College of Humanities Arts and Social Sciences, Department of Economics, Department of Statistics, School of Business Administration and School of Public Policy.

We also like to express our thanks to the following UC-Riverside staff: Damaris Carlos, Gary Kuzas, Mark Manalang, Tanya Wine (and Mark Wine) and Patricia Winkler, and two of our graduate students: Bai Huang and Najrin Khanom. Their hard work and dedication before, during, and after the event made our work much easier.

This AIE volume is a collection of papers, most of them presented at the conference, on topics in which Aman Ullah has made major contributions – nonparametric and semiparametric econometrics, finite sample econometrics, shrinkage methods, information/entropy econometrics, model specification testing, robust inference and panel/spatial models. Each paper was rigorously refereed by two or three experts. We would like to thank the following reviewers for their critical and constructive reviews (in alphabetical order): Deniz Baglan (Howard University), Yong Bao (Purdue University), Martin Burda (University of Toronto), Zongwu Cai (University of Kansas), Matias Cattaneo (University of Michigan), John Chao (University of Maryland), Juan Carlos Escanciano (Indiana University), Yanqin Fan (University of Washington), Jiti Gao (Monash University), Amos Golan (American University), William Greene (New York University), Daniel Henderson (University of Alabama), Eric Hillebrand (University of Aarhus), Cheng Hsiao (University of Southern California), Emma Iglesias (University of Coruña), Atsushi Inoue (Vanderbilt University), David Jacho-Chavez (Emory University), Ivan Jeliazkov (University of California, Irvine), Fei Jin (Shanghai University of Finance and Economics), Degui Li (University of York), Dong Li

(University of Texas Dallas), Qi Li (Texas A&M), Wei Lin (Capital University of Economics and Business), Chu-An Liu (Academia Sinica), Essie Maasoumi (Emory University), Ron Mittelhammer (Washington State University), Kusum Mundra (Rutgers University), Kelley Pace (Louisiana State University), Christopher Parmeter (University of Miami), Hashem Pesaran (University of Southern California), Jeff Racine (McMaster University), Chris Skeels (University of Melbourne), Xiaojun Song (Peking University), Liangjun Su (Singapore Management University), Yuying Sun (Chinese Academy of Sciences), Abderrahim Taamouti (Durham University), Yundong Tu (Peking University), Aman Ullah (University of California, Riverside), Alan Wan (City University of Hong Kong), Ying Wang (Peking University), Ximing Wu (Texas A&M University), Ke-Li Xu (Texas A&M University), Jui-Chung Ray Yang (University of Southern California), Zhenlin Yang (Singapore Management University) and Yonghui Zhang (Renmin University).

We would also like to thank the following participants, who made presentations and/or chaired sessions: Deniz Baglan (Howard University), Anil Bera (University of Illinois), Tom Fomby (Southern Methodist University), Yan Ge (Central University of Finance and Economics), Xiao Huang (Kennesaw State University), Wei Lin (Capital University of Economics and Business), Ruixuan Liu (Emory University), Xiangdong Long (Bank of Communications Schroder Fund Management), Shujie Ma (University of California, Riverside), Kusum Mundra (Rutgers University), Xiaojun Song (Peking University), Yundong Tu (Peking University), Yun Wang (University of International Business and Economics) and Jie Wei (Huazhong University of Science and Technology).

PHOTOS

At Riverside Mission Inn on March 13–15, 2015.

Aman Ullah on March 14, 2015, 3.1415, the π day.

PART I
TRIBUTE

A SELECTIVE REVIEW OF AMAN ULLAH'S CONTRIBUTIONS TO ECONOMETRICS

Yong Bao[a], Yanqin Fan[b], Liangjun Su[c] and Victoria Zinde-Walsh[d]

[a]*Department of Economics, Purdue University, West Lafayette, IN, USA*
[b]*Department of Economics, University of Washington, Seattle, WA, USA*
[c]*School of Economics, Singapore Management University, Singapore*
[d]*Department of Economics, McGill University, CIREQ, Montréal, Canada*

ABSTRACT

This paper examines Aman Ullah's contributions to robust inference, finite sample econometrics, nonparametrics and semiparametrics, and panel and spatial models. His early works on robust inference and finite sample theory were mostly motivated by his thesis advisor, Professor Anirudh Lal Nagar. They eventually led to his most original rethinking of many statistics and econometrics models that developed into the monograph Finite Sample Econometrics published in 2004. His desire to relax distributional and functional-form assumptions lead him in the direction of nonparametric estimation and he summarized his views in his most influential textbook Nonparametric Econometrics (with Adrian Pagan) published in 1999 that

Essays in Honor of Aman Ullah
Advances in Econometrics, Volume 36, 3–43

ISSN: 0731-9053/doi:10.1108/S0731-905320160000036001

has influenced a whole generation of econometricians. His innovative contributions in the areas of seemingly unrelated regressions, parametric, semiparametric and nonparametric panel data models, and spatial models have also inspired a larger literature on nonparametric and semiparametric estimation and inference and spurred on research in robust estimation and inference in these and related areas.

Keywords: Finite sample theory; hypothesis testing; nonparametrics; panel data models; robust inference; semiparametrics

JEL classifications: C01; C10; C12; C13; C14; C21; C23

1. INTRODUCTION

Aman Ullah remained a leading scholar in the field of econometrics for the last four decades. His contributions cover a wide spectrum of econometrics that includes robust inference, finite sample theory, nonparametrics and semiparametrics, panel and spatial models, applied microeconometrics, financial econometrics, among others. He is best known for two of his advanced books, namely, *Nonparametric Econometrics* (1999, with Adrian Pagan) and *Finite Sample Econometrics* (2004). The former remains one of the most influential textbooks in nonparametrics that helps to educate generations of econometricians in nonparametric and semiparametric methods and provides an authoritative reference for applied researchers. So far it has received 1,649 citations in Google Scholar. The latter is a monograph that summarizes many of his own significant contributions to the subject of finite sample theory and provides a solid introduction to this difficult and important field.

The main purpose of this paper is to provide a historical account of Aman Ullah's contributions to econometrics which we hope can help readers understand the importance of his works. Given the wide range of research areas Aman Ullah has been engaged in and the formidable list of publications he has produced, it seems impossible for us to review all of his contributions to econometrics. As representatives of his students, colleagues, coauthors, and friends, we decided to do a selective survey on his contributions. In particular, we shall focus on four areas to which Aman Ullah has contributed most. They are robust inference, finite sample econometrics, nonparametrics and semiparametrics, and panel and spatial models. By limiting the scope of our task to these areas, we try to provide a clear account of how Aman Ullah's ideas and works influenced generations of econometricians.

The rest of this paper is organized as follows. We review Aman Ullah's contributions to robust inference in Section 2 and his contributions to finite sample econometrics in Section 3. Section 4 focuses on his contributions to nonparametric and semiparametric methods in econometrics. Section 5 reviews his contributions to panel and spatial models. Final remarks are contained in Section 6.

2. ROBUST INFERENCE

In this section, we review Aman Ullah's contributions to robust inference. We first review his early works with his thesis advisor, Professor Anirudh Lal Nagar, that go back to the early 1970s. Then, we discuss the double-*k* class of estimators he proposed in the late 1970s and his continuous effort in pursuing robustness of statistics with respect to distributional assumptions in the 1980s.

2.1. Indian Statistical Tradition and Beyond

With his thesis supervisor, Professor Anirudh Lal Nagar, Aman Ullah in the 1970s developed a number of exact results and results on approximations to moments of various estimators, in particular, for two-stage least squares (2SLS) estimators. These formulas for the moments of the 2SLS estimators are classical results in the instrumental variables literature. Their works appeared initially in Nagar and Ullah (1970, 1973) and then in Ullah and Nagar (1974). The papers derived expansions for the moment functionals and provided both new results and also methodological developments in obtaining high-level expansions of complicated ratios. Many clever technical tools to replace difficult and costly integration with differentiation in application to moments were designed then and continued to be developed by Aman in his subsequent works.

Aman worked on applying and further generalizing these approaches in a number of directions. From moments of ratios in normal variables to moments under non-normality, to providing exact and approximate distributions, he summarized and generalized the state of knowledge and our understanding of distributional properties of the "econometric functionals". His earlier works such as Ullah (1974) on the sampling distribution of Stein's shrinkage estimator and Ullah and Ullah (1978) on properties of the double-*k* class shrinkage estimators, as well as many papers that followed, extended the methods to suit the specific applications.

This work eventually led to the most original and general rethinking of many econometric statistics that developed into the book *Finite Sample Econometrics* published in 2004. However, the ideas behind this book formed over many years and had their origin in the early work of Aman.

2.2. *Double-k Class Shrinkage Estimators and Ridge Estimators*

The issues of efficient estimation and improvements to the unbiased least squares and maximum likelihood estimators in linear regression led to proposals to consider Stein-rule and -related estimators. Aman Ullah pursued the problem of evaluation of moments of these estimators. His approach was to develop a general view of classes of such estimators. Ullah and Ullah (1978) provided a new unified view of a class of such shrinkage estimators as the double-*k* class with

$$\tilde{b}_{k_1,k_2} = \left[1 - \frac{k_1 \hat{u}'\hat{u}}{y'y - k_2 \hat{u}'\hat{u}}\right] b,$$

where y is the vector of the dependent variable, $\hat{u}$ the residual vector, and b the least squares estimator. This class contains all Stein-type and many related estimators. The paper derived the moments of the estimators where the expansions were skillfully applied. This led to new insights into the dependence of the moments on the parameters (k's) of the estimators and the characteristics of the model.

It then turned out that the double-*k* class also generalizes another important class of estimators: shrinkage and ridge. Shrinkage estimators can be defined as

$$\hat{\beta} = \left[1 + \frac{k\hat{u}'\hat{u}}{b'Bb}\right] b,$$

where B is a weight matrix. These estimators can also be seen as a special case of double-*k* class.

The Stein-type estimators have the potential to improve efficiency. Shrinkage and ridge estimators (Ullah, Vinod, & Kadiyala, 1981; Vinod & Ullah, 1981; Vinod, Ullah, & Kadiyala, 1981) can also be used to protect from possible ill-posedness in regression estimation. The results that provided sampling distributions and test statistics for these estimators in Ullah, Carter, and Srivastava (1984) were a particularly important early breakthroughs for this class. This paper is notable in that it used small σ approximation, arguing that in finite samples the asymptotic approximation may be poor and alternative approximations such as the small σ could provide an improvement. Exploration of different approximations (asymptotic, small σ, Laplace) to provide better finite and small sample distributions continued in Aman's further work and was summarized in Ullah (2004).

2.3. *Robustness Against Distributional Assumptions*

Aman Ullah pursued the idea of robustness of statistics with respect to distributional assumptions by seeking classes of underlying distributions over which distributional properties of the statistics remain the same. Establishing such robustness properties is an important step in reducing sensitivity to misspecification.

He considered the widely used classical asymptotic tests: Wald (W), likelihood ratio (LR), and somewhat misnamed – as it is usually employed in Rao score form – Lagrange multiplier (LM) statistic. All these have the same χ^2 asymptotic distribution in a classical linear regression, yet their finite sample distributions differ. An attempt to order them via first-order expansion worked in the Gaussian case (see, e.g., Evans & Savin, 1982) and raised the possibility of declaring W to be the most conservative and LM the most liberal of these tests. But could that result be extended beyond Gaussian distributions? How robust was it to different error distributions?

Ullah and Zinde-Walsh (1984) worked out the results for the class of t-distributions and discovered that there the ranking of the tests developed in the Gaussian case did not hold and could be reversed. The Wald and LM statistics were very sensitive to the particular distribution; the LR statistic remained numerically the same and thus was robust over the class of t-distributions. A related question concerned deriving the exact distribution of the F statistic over this class of multivariate t-distributions under the null as well as under the alternative; and this problem was solved by Ullah and Phillips (1986).

Characteristically of Aman's broad scientific approach he asked the question how much farther could the results be generalized. The class of multivariate t-distributions belongs to the general class of spherical distributions where the distribution depends only on the length of the random vector but not on the direction and is uniform over spheres in the multidimensional space. Ullah and Zinde-Walsh (1985) derived the properties of the estimators and test statistics under the class of general spherical distributions; the LR statistic remained unchanged. The class of elliptical distributions (an example is a correlated multivariate normal) generalizes spherical classes; none of the statistics including LR can exhibit robustness over this class. However, it is possible to derive robust bounds for the statistic; this was done in Ullah and Zinde-Walsh (1988).

It was this desire to relax distributional assumptions that compelled Aman to examine other approaches and, in particular, led him in the direction of nonparametric kernel estimation. Characteristically, he systematized the knowledge and summarized his views in the influential book *Nonparametric Econometrics* (1999) with Adrian Pagan, which is familiar to all who work in this field.

3. FINITE SAMPLE ECONOMETRICS

This section reviews Aman Ullah's contributions to finite sample econometrics. We first give a brief account of the need for finite sample theory in econometrics.

Then we discuss his approaches to addressing the exact theory and approximations for a wide range of statistics in various econometrics and statistics models.

3.1. A Brief Account

The need for finite sample theory arises on many occasions. For example, the first-order asymptotic theory may indicate that several estimators are asymptotically equivalent, but for practical purpose, one has to make a choice as to which estimator is to be used, and this is typically guided by their performance in finite samples. Newey and Smith (2004) compared the asymptotically equivalent generalized method of moments (GMM) and generalized empirical likelihood (GEL) estimators and suggested that GEL should be favored on the consideration of its relative smaller finite sample bias. It may also happen that different asymptotic distributions can arise, depending on how the data are sampled. But in reality, one is faced with only the observable sample data and has to decide on an asymptotic distribution to be used. In the framework of spatial data, one needs to distinguish between the so-called infill, expanding, and double asymptotics. The same applies to the continuous time models. In panel data models, one needs to distinguish between the so called "large N", "large T", and "large N and large T" asymptotics. Even if one pins down a specific estimator and a specific asymptotic distribution, it may still happen that the resulting inference gives rise to very misleading results for small or even moderately large samples.

Fisher (1921, 1922) and Cramér (1946) laid down the foundations of statistical finite sample theory on exact distributions and moments that are valid for any sample size. Haavelmo (1947) and Anderson and Rubin (1949) brought the exact theory into econometrics, followed by Hurwicz (1950), Basmann (1961), Richardson (1968), and Phillips (1983), among others. However, all these exact distribution and moments results were complicated to obtain and they were mainly for the structural equation estimators. Nagar (1959) pioneered the work on obtaining the approximate moments, followed by Sargan (1975) and Phillips (1980) on developing the Edgeworth approximate distributions to econometric estimators. Nagar's approximate moments, however, were essentially based on the stochastic Taylor series expansion and the moments were derived based on this by taking term-by-term expectations. Srinivasan (1970) questioned the validity of such approximate moments, in the absence of the conditions of validity of stochastic expansions and when the exact moments are not known. Sargan (1974) was the first to establish the conditions under which Nagar's general stochastic expansion procedure is valid, and hence the approximate moments exist. Previous to this, Nagar and Ullah (1970, 1973) tried to demonstrate that the Nagar's approximate moments for the 2SLS estimator are indeed the approximation of the exact moments which exist under certain conditions. But this result, among the other papers at that time, was for the 2SLS estimator in the case of a structural equation with one right-hand endogenous variable. Ullah and Nagar (1974) were then the first to develop the exact moment result for the 2SLS estimator for the case of two endogenous variables on the right-hand side, and a decade later Hillier, Kinal, and Srivastava (1984) extended the exact moment results in the presence of a finite number (greater than two) of right-hand endogenous variables. Overall, in this area of finite sample econometrics, Aman Ullah has made substantial contributions, with his very first publication appearing in 1970 and a monograph on this subject in 2004. He has published more than 40 articles on finite sample econometrics, with both exact and approximate results. Within this process, he has developed unified approaches to studying finite sample econometrics and in this section, we review his contributions over the years. Here, we discuss his approaches to addressing the exact theory and approximations for a wide range of econometric estimators and statistics in various models.

3.2. The Exact Theory

For the classical linear regression model, the exact properties of the ordinary least squares estimator are well established. The focus here is on nonclassical models. We first discuss Aman Ullah's approach to deriving the exact moments of econometric estimators and statistics, and then the method of deriving the exact distribution.

3.2.1. Exact moments

Suppose $\boldsymbol{y}$ is an $n \times 1$ normal random vector with mean $\boldsymbol{\mu}$ and covariance matrix $\boldsymbol{\Sigma}$. Ullah (1990) showed that for vector-valued analytic functions of $\boldsymbol{y}$, denoted by $h(\boldsymbol{y})$ and $g(\boldsymbol{y})$, if their expectations $\mathrm{E}(h(\boldsymbol{y}))$ and $\mathrm{E}(h(\boldsymbol{y})g(\boldsymbol{y}))$ exist, then one can conveniently derive the expectations via a nonstochastic operator $d(\boldsymbol{\mu}, \boldsymbol{\Sigma}) \equiv \boldsymbol{d} = \boldsymbol{\mu} + \boldsymbol{\Sigma}(\partial/\partial\boldsymbol{\mu})$ such that

$$\mathrm{E}(h(\boldsymbol{y})) = h(\boldsymbol{d}), \quad \mathrm{E}(h(\boldsymbol{y})g(\boldsymbol{y})) = h(\boldsymbol{d})\mathrm{E}(g(\boldsymbol{y})). \tag{1}$$

This is a very smart way of deriving the expectations, as it replaces the complicated integration with partial derivative. It provides a unified and simple technique for obtaining exact moments of various special cases of the functions $h(\boldsymbol{y})$ and $g(\boldsymbol{y})$, since many estimators and statistics can be written directly as functions of the sample data $\boldsymbol{y}$.[1] In fact, early in Ullah and Nagar (1974), this operator was utilized implicitly to derive the exact mean of the 2SLS estimator of the structural parameters in an equation with three endogenous variables, also see the applications in Ullah (1974), Ullah and Ullah (1978), Vinod et al. (1981), and Ullah and Maasoumi (1986). The result (1) also provides a recurrence relationship among the higher moments of $h(\boldsymbol{y})$. For example, suppose $h(\cdot)$ is a scalar function, then

$$\mathrm{E}(h^r(\boldsymbol{y})) = h^{r-1}(\boldsymbol{d})h(\boldsymbol{d}) = h^{r-1}(\boldsymbol{d})\mathrm{E}(h(\boldsymbol{y})). \tag{2}$$

Note that many econometric estimators and statistics can be written as or related to quadratic forms in $\boldsymbol{y}$. Applying this operator $\boldsymbol{d}$, Bao and Ullah (2010) derived very neat results for $\mathrm{E}(\prod_{i=1}^{p} \boldsymbol{y}'\boldsymbol{A}_i\boldsymbol{y})$, where $\boldsymbol{A}_i$ are $n \times n$ nonstochastic symmetric matrices. For the ratio of quadratic forms, $\boldsymbol{y}'\boldsymbol{A}_1\boldsymbol{y}/\boldsymbol{y}'\boldsymbol{A}_2\boldsymbol{y}$, where $\boldsymbol{A}_2$ is positive definite, on the other hand, one can apply the following:

$$\begin{aligned}\mathrm{E}\left[\left(\frac{\boldsymbol{y}'\boldsymbol{A}_1\boldsymbol{y}}{\boldsymbol{y}'\boldsymbol{A}_2\boldsymbol{y}}\right)^r\right] &= (\boldsymbol{d}'\boldsymbol{A}_1\boldsymbol{d})^r\mathrm{E}[(\boldsymbol{y}'\boldsymbol{A}_2\boldsymbol{y})^{-r}] \\ &= (\boldsymbol{d}'\boldsymbol{A}_1\boldsymbol{d})^r\frac{1}{\Gamma(r)}\int_0^\infty t^{r-1}|\boldsymbol{A}_0|^{-1/2}\exp\left(-\frac{1}{2}\boldsymbol{\mu}'\boldsymbol{A}_0^*\boldsymbol{\mu}\right)\mathrm{d}t. \end{aligned} \tag{3}$$

where $\boldsymbol{A}_0 = \boldsymbol{I} + 2t\boldsymbol{\Sigma}\boldsymbol{A}_2$ and $\boldsymbol{A}_0^* = 2t\boldsymbol{A}_2\boldsymbol{A}_0^{-1}$. If further $\boldsymbol{\mu} = 0$, $\boldsymbol{\Sigma} = \boldsymbol{I}$, and $\boldsymbol{A}_2 = \boldsymbol{I}$, then

$$\mathrm{E}\left[\left(\frac{\boldsymbol{y}'\boldsymbol{A}_1\boldsymbol{y}}{\boldsymbol{y}'\boldsymbol{y}}\right)^r\right] = \frac{\mathrm{E}\left[(\boldsymbol{y}'\boldsymbol{A}_1\boldsymbol{y})^r\right]}{\mathrm{E}\left[(\boldsymbol{y}'\boldsymbol{y})^r\right]} = \frac{\sum_{i=0}^{r-1}\binom{r-1}{i}2^i i!\,\mathrm{tr}(\boldsymbol{A}_1^{i+1})}{\prod_{i=0}^{r-1}(n+2i)}. \tag{4}$$

When $\boldsymbol{y}$ follows some specific non-normal distribution, one may still be able to explore an operator that is similar to the operator $\boldsymbol{d}$ in the normal case that can help derive the moments of a function of $\boldsymbol{y}$. Ullah (2004) discussed binomial, Poisson, gamma, exponential, and mixture distributions. More generally, suppose each component y_i has an Edgeworth/Gram–Charlier density

$$f(y_i) = \sum_{j=0}^{\infty} c_j\left(\frac{\mathrm{d}}{\mathrm{d}y_i}\right)^j f\left(y_i|\mu_i, \sigma_i^2\right), \tag{5}$$

where $f\left(y_i|\mu_i, \sigma_i^2\right)$ denotes the normal density with mean μ_i and variance σ_i^2. Davis (1976) rewrote this flexible density function as $f(y_i) = \mathrm{E}_{w_i}f(y_i|\mu_i + w_i, \sigma_i^2)$, where w_i is a pseudovariate with mean and variance 0, and higher order cumulants the same as those of y_i. Then one can evaluate $\mathrm{E}(h(\boldsymbol{y}))$ by combining the $\boldsymbol{d}$ operator of Ullah and this technique of Davis as follows:

$$\mathrm{E}(h(\boldsymbol{y})) = \mathrm{E}_{\boldsymbol{w}}(\mathrm{E}(h(\boldsymbol{y})|\boldsymbol{w})), \tag{6}$$

where $\mathrm{E}(h(\boldsymbol{y})|\boldsymbol{w})$ denotes the expectation of $h(\boldsymbol{y})$ when $\boldsymbol{y}$ has a normal density with mean $\boldsymbol{\mu} + \boldsymbol{w}$ and variance $\boldsymbol{I}$. In other words, one can use a two-step procedure to derive the expectation: first one derives the expectation of $h(\boldsymbol{y})$ using the operator $d(\boldsymbol{\mu} + \boldsymbol{w}, \boldsymbol{I})$, which will be in terms of the pseudovector $\boldsymbol{w}$, and then take another round of expectation with respect to $\boldsymbol{w}$. Peters (1989) used this technique to examine the exact moments of the least squares (LS) estimator in the first-order autoregressive (AR) model.

Bao and Ullah (2010) derived the expectation of non-normal quadratic forms up to order 4. The results are in terms of functions of the matrices involved and the cumulants of the distribution up to order 8. These results on moments of quadratic forms may be of their own interest, but they are also frequently used in deriving the approximate moments (to be discussed later) of many estimators and statistics.

3.2.2. *Exact distribution*

A general technique to derive the exact distribution of $h(\boldsymbol{y})$ is to invoke the inversion theorem. Suppose the characteristic function of (the scalar function) $h(\boldsymbol{y})$ is $\varphi(t) = \mathrm{E}[\exp(\mathrm{i}th(\boldsymbol{y}))]$ with $\mathrm{i} = \sqrt{-1}$, then the density function of $x = h(y)$ is

$$f(x) = \frac{1}{2\pi}\int_{-\infty}^{\infty} \exp(-\mathrm{i}tx)\varphi(t)\mathrm{d}t \tag{7}$$

and the distribution function is

$$F(x) = \frac{1}{2} - \frac{1}{\pi}\int_{0}^{\infty} \frac{\mathrm{Im}[\exp(-\mathrm{i}tx)\varphi(t)]}{t}\mathrm{d}t. \tag{8}$$

When $h(\boldsymbol{y})$ is a ratio, the distribution function becomes

$$F(x) = \frac{1}{2} - \frac{1}{\pi}\int_{0}^{\infty} \frac{\mathrm{Im}[\varphi(t, -tx)]}{t}\mathrm{d}t, \tag{9}$$

where $\varphi(\cdot, \cdot)$ denotes the joint characteristic function of the numerator and denominator in defining the ratio.

In general, to apply Eqs. (7) and (8) (or (9)), not only one needs to know the explicit form of $\varphi(t)$, which is typically not available unless one specifies explicitly the distribution of $\boldsymbol{y}$, but also the integral needs to be evaluated, which may be implemented via numerical integration. Bao, Ullah, and Wang (2015) used Eq. (9) to evaluate the exact finite sample distribution of the LS estimator of the mean reversion parameter in continuous time Ornstein–Uhlenbeck processes.

3.3. Approximations

The exact moments and distribution in general are difficult, if not impossible, to derive unless one makes some strong assumptions about the specific functional form of $h(\boldsymbol{y})$ as well as the distribution of $\boldsymbol{y}$. In light of this, approximation methods have been developed and Aman Ullah has made very important contributions in this line of research.

3.3.1. Approximate moments

Nagar (1959) popularized the so-called large-n approximation to obtain the approximate moments by implementing the asymptotic expansion of the sampling error (of the statistic and the parameter of interest) such that the successive terms in the expansions are in order of powers of the sample size n in probability. To fix ideas, suppose $\hat{\boldsymbol{\beta}} = h(\boldsymbol{y})$ for $\boldsymbol{\beta} = h(\boldsymbol{\mu})$, where $\boldsymbol{\beta}$ is $p \times 1$ and $\boldsymbol{\mu} = \mathrm{E}(\boldsymbol{y})$. Write $\boldsymbol{y} = \boldsymbol{\mu} + \boldsymbol{u}$. Then a kth-order Taylor series expansion of $h(\boldsymbol{y})$ at $\boldsymbol{y} = \boldsymbol{\mu}$ yields

$$\hat{\boldsymbol{\beta}} - \boldsymbol{\beta} = \sum_{i=1}^{k} \frac{1}{i!} \nabla_i (\otimes^i \boldsymbol{u}) + \boldsymbol{r}_{k+1}, \tag{10}$$

where $\nabla_1 = \partial h(\boldsymbol{y})/\partial \boldsymbol{y}'|_{\boldsymbol{y}=\boldsymbol{\mu}}$ is $p \times n$, $\otimes^1 \boldsymbol{u} = \boldsymbol{u}$, $\nabla_i = \partial \nabla_{i-1}|_{\boldsymbol{y}=\boldsymbol{\mu}}$ is $p \times n^i$, $\otimes^i \boldsymbol{u} = \boldsymbol{u} \otimes (\otimes^{i-1} \boldsymbol{u})$, $i > 1$, and $\boldsymbol{r}_{k+1}$ is the remainder term. If one can rearrange the terms in the expansion such that $\hat{\boldsymbol{\beta}} - \boldsymbol{\beta}$ is rewritten as the sum of $\boldsymbol{\xi}_{-i/2}$, where $\boldsymbol{\xi}_{-i/2}$ collect terms of $O_P(n^{-i/2})$ that depend on the orders of $\nabla_i(\otimes^i \boldsymbol{u})$, then one may immediately define the approximate moments of $\hat{\boldsymbol{\beta}} - \boldsymbol{\beta}$. For example, the mean-squared error (MSE) $\mathrm{E}[(\hat{\boldsymbol{\beta}} - \boldsymbol{\beta})(\hat{\boldsymbol{\beta}} - \boldsymbol{\beta})']$ may be approximated by $\mathrm{E}(\boldsymbol{\xi}_{-1/2}\boldsymbol{\xi}'_{-1/2} + \boldsymbol{\xi}_{-1}\boldsymbol{\xi}'_{-1} + \boldsymbol{\xi}_{-1/2}\boldsymbol{\xi}'_{-1} + \boldsymbol{\xi}_{-1}\boldsymbol{\xi}'_{-1/2} + \boldsymbol{\xi}_{-1/2}\boldsymbol{\xi}'_{-3/2} + \boldsymbol{\xi}_{-3/2}\boldsymbol{\xi}'_{-1/2})$ and the approximation error is $o(n^{-2})$. Based on this type of expansion, Nagar and Ullah (1970, 1973) derived the approximate moments of the 2SLS estimator in linear simultaneous equation models. Gupta and Ullah (1970) developed the approximate moments of Wald's estimator in the simple linear regression model, and Srivastava, Srivastava, and Ullah (1995) conducted a comparative study of the efficiency properties, via the approximate second moments, of the coefficient of determination and its adjusted version in linear regression models under non-normality. Srivastava and Ullah (1995) compared the efficiency properties of several estimators in terms of their approximate second moments in pooled regressions. Also see Ullah and Huang (2006) on the second-order bias and MSE of the feasible generalized least squares (FGLS) estimators in random-effects panel model with non-normal errors, Bao and Ullah (2006) on the second-order bias and variance of the estimated Sharpe ratio for non-i.i.d. return series, Qian and Ullah (2008) on the approximate bias and MSE of FGLS estimator in paired data models, and Bao, Ullah, and Zhang (2014) on moment approximations for the LS estimator in unit root models with non-normal errors.

When $\hat{\boldsymbol{\beta}}$ is obtained via the moment condition, as considered in Rilstone, Srivastava, and Ullah (1996),

$$\hat{\boldsymbol{\beta}} = \arg_{\boldsymbol{\beta}} \{\psi(\boldsymbol{\beta}; \boldsymbol{y}) = 0\}, \tag{11}$$

it is implicitly a nonlinear function of the data $\boldsymbol{y}$. This includes the (quasi) maximum likelihood ((Q)ML), (generalized) method of moments, (nonlinear) LS estimators, and other extremum estimators. Under the assumptions that $\hat{\boldsymbol{\beta}}$ is $\sqrt{n}$-consistent and that the moment function is smooth enough, a stochastic expansion of $\hat{\boldsymbol{\beta}}$ around $\boldsymbol{\beta}$ is as follows:

$$\hat{\boldsymbol{\beta}} - \boldsymbol{\beta} = \boldsymbol{\xi}_{-1/2} + \boldsymbol{\xi}_{-1} + \boldsymbol{\xi}_{-3/2} + O_P(n^{-2}), \tag{12}$$

where

$$\begin{aligned}
\boldsymbol{\xi}_{-1/2} &= \boldsymbol{\mathcal{F}}^{-1}\boldsymbol{\psi}, \\
\boldsymbol{\xi}_{-1} &= \boldsymbol{\mathcal{F}}^{-1}(\boldsymbol{\mathcal{H}} + \boldsymbol{\mathcal{F}})\boldsymbol{\xi}_{-1/2} + \frac{1}{2}\boldsymbol{\mathcal{F}}^{-1}\boldsymbol{\mathcal{D}}(\boldsymbol{\xi}_{-1/2} \otimes \boldsymbol{\xi}_{-1/2}), \\
\boldsymbol{\xi}_{-3/2} &= \boldsymbol{\mathcal{F}}^{-1}(\boldsymbol{\mathcal{H}} + \boldsymbol{\mathcal{F}})\boldsymbol{\xi}_{-1} + \frac{1}{2}\boldsymbol{\mathcal{F}}^{-1}\left(\frac{\partial \boldsymbol{\mathcal{H}}}{\partial \boldsymbol{\beta}'} - \boldsymbol{\mathcal{D}}\right)(\boldsymbol{\xi}_{-1/2} \otimes \boldsymbol{\xi}_{-1/2}) \\
&\quad + \frac{1}{2}\boldsymbol{\mathcal{F}}^{-1}\boldsymbol{\mathcal{D}}(\boldsymbol{\xi}_{-1/2} \otimes \boldsymbol{\xi}_{-1} + \boldsymbol{\xi}_{-1} \otimes \boldsymbol{\xi}_{-1/2}) \\
&\quad + \frac{1}{6}\boldsymbol{\mathcal{F}}^{-1}\mathrm{E}\left(\frac{\partial \boldsymbol{\mathcal{D}}}{\partial \boldsymbol{\beta}'}\right)(\boldsymbol{\xi}_{-1/2} \otimes \boldsymbol{\xi}_{-1/2} \otimes \boldsymbol{\xi}_{-1/2}),
\end{aligned}$$

in which $\boldsymbol{\psi} = \psi(\boldsymbol{\beta})$, $\boldsymbol{\mathcal{H}} = \mathcal{H}(\boldsymbol{\beta}) = \partial\psi(\boldsymbol{\beta})/\partial\boldsymbol{\beta}'$ is $p \times p$, $\boldsymbol{\mathcal{F}} = \mathcal{F}(\boldsymbol{\beta}) = -\mathrm{E}(\mathcal{H}(\boldsymbol{\beta}))$, $\boldsymbol{\mathcal{D}} = \mathcal{D}(\boldsymbol{\beta}) = \mathrm{E}(\partial\mathcal{H}(\boldsymbol{\beta})/\partial\boldsymbol{\beta}')$ is $p \times p^2$, and $\partial\mathcal{D}/\partial\boldsymbol{\beta}'$ is $p \times p^3$. When $\hat{\boldsymbol{\beta}}$ is the maximum likelihood estimator (MLE), $\boldsymbol{\psi}$ is the score function, $\boldsymbol{\mathcal{H}}$ is the Hessian matrix, and $\boldsymbol{\mathcal{F}}$ is the information matrix.[2] Based on the expansion (12), Rilstone et al. (1996) derived the second-order bias (up to the order $O(n^{-1})$) and MSE (up to the order $O(n^{-2})$) of $\hat{\boldsymbol{\beta}}$ when the data consist of i.i.d. observations. Rilstone and Ullah (2002) applied Eq. (12) to develop the second-order bias of Heckman's sample selection estimator.

It was further observed in Bao and Ullah (2007b) that the expansion (12) is in fact also valid for time series models and they utilized the expansion to derive the large sample second-order biases and MSEs of the parameter estimators in the AR, moving average, vector AR, and absolute AR models. In deriving these approximate moments, the moments of quadratic forms (see the previous subsection) were utilized, as the stochastic terms in the expansion (12) are in terms of quadratic forms in the error vector in the models. Bao and Ullah (2004) applied the expansion (12) to develop the second-order bias of a value-at-risk estimator when the parameters are estimated by the method of QML. Bao and Ullah (2009b) extended the expansion further to higher orders to derive the approximate bias and MSE, up to $O(n^{-5/2})$ and $O(n^{-3})$, respectively.

Bao and Ullah (2007a) also applied the expansion (12) to the MLE in the spatial AR model. The expectations of the stochastic terms in the large-n expansion of the MLE were evaluated in Bao and Ullah (2007a) via the top order invariant polynomial approach of Smith (1989). But it turns out, as recognized in Bao and Ullah (2010), that these moments of ratio are in fact equal to the ratio of moments,

$$\mathrm{E}\left[\frac{\prod_{i=1}^{r}\left(\boldsymbol{v}'\boldsymbol{A}_i\boldsymbol{v}\right)^{k_i}}{(\boldsymbol{v}'\boldsymbol{v})^k}\right] = \frac{\mathrm{E}\left[\prod_{i=1}^{r}\left(\boldsymbol{v}'\boldsymbol{A}_i\boldsymbol{v}\right)^{k_i}\right]}{\mathrm{E}\left[(\boldsymbol{v}'\boldsymbol{v})^k\right]} = \frac{\mathrm{E}\left[\prod_{i=1}^{r}\left(\boldsymbol{v}'\boldsymbol{A}_i\boldsymbol{v}\right)^{k_i}\right]}{\prod_{i=0}^{k-1}(n+2i)}, \tag{13}$$

where $\boldsymbol{v} \sim \mathrm{N}(0, \boldsymbol{I})$, k_i are nonnegative integers and $\sum_{i=1}^{r} k_i = k$. One can see that Eq. (13) generalizes Eq. (4).

When there are exogenous regressors included in the spatial autoregression model and the error term in non-normal, Bao (2013) derived the second-order bias of the quasi maximum likelihood estimator (QMLE) of the full parameter vector, including the coefficients of the exogenous regressors, the spatial AR coefficient, and the error variance. Based on the expansion (12), which is valid regardless of the distribution of $\boldsymbol{y}$, Bao (2013) presented the second bias of the QMLE $\hat{\boldsymbol{\beta}}$ conveniently as

$$\mathrm{B}(\hat{\boldsymbol{\beta}}) = \mathcal{F}^{-1}\mathcal{E}\mathrm{vec}(\mathcal{F}^{-1}) + \frac{1}{2}\mathcal{F}^{-1}\mathcal{D}(\mathcal{F}^{-1}\otimes\mathcal{F}^{-1})\mathrm{vec}(\mathcal{P}) + o(n^{-1}), \tag{14}$$

where $\mathcal{E} = \mathrm{E}(\mathcal{H}\otimes\boldsymbol{\psi}')$ and $\mathcal{P} = \mathrm{E}(\boldsymbol{\psi}\boldsymbol{\psi}')$. Bao (2013) used the results from Bao and Ullah (2010) on non-normal quadratic forms to evaluate the second-order bias of the QMLE. Bao, Ullah, Wang, and Yu (2015) used Eq. (14) to derive the approximate bias of the LS estimator of the mean reversion parameter in continuous-time Lévy processes.

Bao and Ullah (2009a) utilized the expansion (12) further to approximate the skewness and excess kurtosis coefficients of $\sqrt{n}(\hat{\beta}_i - \beta_i)$ (the ith element of $\sqrt{n}(\hat{\boldsymbol{\beta}} - \boldsymbol{\beta})$), up to $O(n^{-1/2})$ and $O(n^{-1})$, respectively. Their skewness result generalizes several expressions that are given in McCullagh (1987) and Linton (1997) in the context of MLE. Given the skewness and kurtosis results, one may follow the lines of Rothenberg (1984, see Eq. (16)) to use the two standardized measures to construct an Edgeworth-type approximation to the distribution of a nonlinear estimator. But as pointed out by Bao and Ullah (2009a), it is still an open question as to whether the Edgeworth distribution is a valid approximation to the true distribution of a general class of (nonlinear) estimators $\hat{\boldsymbol{\beta}}$.

In contrast to the Nagar-type expansion that expresses the various terms as power series of the sample size, the small-σ expansion proposed by Kadane (1971) for the normal case and later explored by Ullah, Srivastava, and Roy (1995) expresses the successive terms in power series of σ in probability, where σ is the standard deviation of the data. Consider again $\hat{\boldsymbol{\beta}}=h(\boldsymbol{y})$ for $\boldsymbol{\beta}=h(\boldsymbol{\mu})$, where $\boldsymbol{\mu}=\mathrm{E}(\boldsymbol{y})$, $\boldsymbol{y}=\boldsymbol{\mu}+\boldsymbol{u}$, $\boldsymbol{u}=\sigma\boldsymbol{v}$. Obviously, from Eq. (10), one can put equivalently

$$\hat{\boldsymbol{\beta}}-\boldsymbol{\beta}=\sum_{i=1}^{k}\sigma^{i}\frac{1}{i!}\nabla_{i}(\otimes^{i}\boldsymbol{v})+\boldsymbol{r}_{k+1}=\sum_{i=1}^{k}\sigma^{i}\boldsymbol{\zeta}_{i}+\boldsymbol{r}_{k+1}, \tag{15}$$

where $\boldsymbol{\zeta}_i=(i!)^{-1}\nabla_i(\otimes^i\boldsymbol{v})$. If σ is small and close to zero, the expansion (15) can be regarded as an asymptotic expansion where the terms are in decreasing order of magnitude in σ. Thus, one can retain the first few terms in the expansion and study the properties of $\hat{\boldsymbol{\beta}}-\boldsymbol{\beta}$ based on the truncated sum. For example, one may define the approximate MSE of $\hat{\boldsymbol{\beta}}$, up to $O(\sigma^4)$, as $\sigma^2\mathrm{E}(\boldsymbol{\zeta}_1\boldsymbol{\zeta}_1')+\sigma^3[\mathrm{E}(\boldsymbol{\zeta}_1\boldsymbol{\zeta}_2')+\mathrm{E}(\boldsymbol{\zeta}_2\boldsymbol{\zeta}_1')]+\sigma^4[\mathrm{E}(\boldsymbol{\zeta}_2\boldsymbol{\zeta}_2')+\mathrm{E}(\boldsymbol{\zeta}_1\boldsymbol{\zeta}_3')+\mathrm{E}(\boldsymbol{\zeta}_3\boldsymbol{\zeta}_1')]$. In deriving the approximate moments of the double-k class estimator, Ullah and Ullah (1978) used the "large-θ" expansion, where θ is inversely related to σ^2. As pointed out by them, their approximate results were identical to those that could arise under the small-σ expansion. In a similar fashion, Ullah and Maasoumi (1986) developed the approximate bias and MSE of the LS estimator in a first-order dynamic regression with exogenous regressors.

We note that the small-σ and the large-n approximations share the same spirit by applying the Taylor series expansion to the function $h(\boldsymbol{y})$ at $\boldsymbol{y}=\boldsymbol{\mu}$. The performance of the small-σ approximation relies on σ being small, whereas the large-n approximation depends on n being large, as their names suggest. Ullah (1980) analyzed the dominance condition based on the approximate large-n and small-σ MSEs of the adaptive ridge estimator in comparison with the LS estimator in linear regressions. Further note that neither approximation makes distributional assumptions on the data $\boldsymbol{y}$, and Ullah, Srivastava, and Chandra (1983) derived the approximate moments of the shrinkage estimator by following the small-σ expansion under the presence of non-normality. Also see Ullah and Srivastava (1994) in developing the small-σ approximate moments of ratio of non-normal quadratic forms and Ullah and Breunig (1995) in deriving the small-σ bias of standard errors of the LS residual.

3.3.2. Approximate distribution

Suppose we focus on the scalar case. Define z be the rescaled estimator such that $z=(\hat{\beta}-\beta)/\sqrt{\mathrm{E}(\xi_{-1/2}^2)}=\xi_0^*+\xi_{-1/2}^*+\xi_{-1}^*+O_P(n^{-3/2})$, where $\xi_{-i/2}^*=\xi_{-(i+1)/2}/\sqrt{\mathrm{E}(\xi_{-1/2}^2)}=O_P(n^{-i/2})$ and $\xi_0^*\to \mathrm{N}(0,1)$. Let $\mathrm{E}(z)=a_1/\sqrt{n}$ and $\mathrm{Var}(z)=1+a_2/n$, where a_1 and a_2 are nonstochastic terms of $O(1)$. Define $z^*=(z-\mathrm{E}(z))/\sqrt{\mathrm{Var}(z)}$, which has zero mean, unit variance. Write $\mathrm{E}(z^{*3})=a_3/\sqrt{n}$ and $\mathrm{E}(z^{*3})=3+a_4/n$, where a_3 and a_4 are nonstochastic terms of $O(1)$. Rothenberg (1984) showed that an approximation to the distribution of z may be written as

$$F(z)=\Phi\left(z+\frac{\lambda_1+\lambda_2 z^2}{6\sqrt{n}}+\frac{\lambda_3 z+\lambda_4 z^3}{72n}\right)+o(n^{-1}), \tag{16}$$

where $\Phi(\cdot)$ denotes the standard normal distribution function, $\lambda_1=a_3-6a_1$, $\lambda_2=-a_3$, $\lambda_3=9a_4-14a_3^2-36a_2+24a_1a_3$, and $\lambda_4=8a_3^2-3a_4$. This is known as an Edgeworth approximation to the distribution of z. It requires the large-n first four moments of z that follow from the expansion $z=\xi_0^*+\xi_{-1/2}^*+\xi_{-1}^*+O_P(n^{-3/2})$. Alternatively, one can first obtain the characteristic function of the stochastic expansion $\xi_0^*+\xi_{-1/2}^*+\xi_{-1}^*$ and then use the inversion theorem to derive the approximate distribution. In this setup, Ullah (1982) derived the Edgeworth distribution of the Stein-rule estimator.

If one follows the small-σ expansion, namely, $z=\zeta_0^*+\sigma\zeta_1^*+\sigma^2\zeta_2^*+O_P(\sigma^3)$, where $\zeta_i^*=\zeta_{i+1}/\sqrt{\sigma^2\mathrm{E}(\zeta_1^2)}$, then the characteristic function of z is

$$\begin{aligned}\varphi(t) &= \mathrm{E}\{\exp[it(\zeta_0^*+\sigma\zeta_1^*+\sigma^2\zeta_2^*+O_P(\sigma^3))]\}\\ &= \mathrm{E}\{\exp(it\zeta_0^*)\exp[it(\sigma\zeta_1^*+\sigma^2\zeta_2^*+O_P(\sigma^3))]\}\\ &= \mathrm{E}\left\{\exp(it\zeta_0^*)\left[1+\sigma it\zeta_1^*+\sigma^2\left(it\zeta_2^*-\frac{t^2}{2}\zeta_1^*\right)+O_P(\sigma^3)\right]\right\}\\ &= \mathrm{E}[\exp(it\zeta_0^*)]+\sigma\mathrm{E}[it\zeta_1^*\exp(it\zeta_0^*)]+\sigma^2\mathrm{E}\left[\left(it\zeta_2^*-\frac{t^2}{2}\zeta_1^*\right)\exp(it\zeta_0^*)\right]\\ &\quad +O_P(\sigma^3).\end{aligned} \tag{17}$$

If $\boldsymbol{v}\sim\mathrm{N}(0,\boldsymbol{I})$, then by applying the inversion theorem (7) and using Ullah's operator $\boldsymbol{d}$, the approximation to the density function of z, up to $O(\sigma)$, is

$$f(z)=\phi(z)\left\{1+\sigma\frac{z}{2\sqrt{\nabla_1'\nabla_1}}\left[\mathrm{tr}(\boldsymbol{H})+(z^2-3)\frac{\nabla_1'\boldsymbol{H}\nabla_1}{\nabla_1'\nabla_1}\right]\right\}+O(\sigma^2), \tag{18}$$

where $\phi(\cdot)$ denotes the standard normal density distribution function and $\boldsymbol{H}=(\partial^2 h(\boldsymbol{y}))/\partial\boldsymbol{y}\partial\boldsymbol{y}'|_{\boldsymbol{y}=\boldsymbol{\mu}}$. Carter, Srivastava, Srivastava, and Ullah (1990) used both the large-n and small-σ Edgeworth approximations to study the finite sample distributions of the Stein-rule estimator and the associated F statistic.

Kundhi and Rilstone (2013) used the expansion (12) to develop the Edgeworth expansion for the distribution of the scalar t-statistic $\hat{z}=\boldsymbol{\tau}'\sqrt{n}(\hat{\boldsymbol{\beta}}-\boldsymbol{\beta})/\sqrt{\boldsymbol{\tau}'\hat{\boldsymbol{V}}\boldsymbol{\tau}}$, where $\boldsymbol{\tau}$ is a vector of constants and $\hat{\boldsymbol{V}}$ is a consistent estimator of $\boldsymbol{V}=n\mathrm{E}(\boldsymbol{\xi}_{-1/2}\boldsymbol{\xi}_{-1/2}')$. They focused on the case when the data are i.i.d. and derived the first three cumulants of a statistic that is equivalent to $\hat{z}$ (up to $O_P(n^{-1/2})$). By plugging these cumulants, Kundhi and Rilstone (2013) were able to derive the Type 1 Edgeworth approximation to the distribution of $\hat{z}$, up to $O(n^{-1/2})$. They showed that the approximation is valid by verifying the conditions in Bhattacharya and Ghosh (1978). For the more general case of nonlinear estimators with non-i.i.d. data, as emphasized in Bao and Ullah (2009a), however, it is still an open question regarding its validity.

4. NONPARAMETRIC AND SEMIPARAMETRIC ECONOMETRICS

Aman's interest in robust methods for estimation and inference in econometrics models has led him to pursue work in nonparametric and semiparametric econometrics. Since late 1980s, Aman has published three books: Ullah (1988c), Pagan and Ullah (1999), and Racine, Su, and Ullah (2014); and more than 50 papers in nonparametric and semiparametric econometrics.

Aman has initiated and produced influential work addressing a broad range of issues in nonparametric and semiparametric econometrics including estimation of response coefficients, consistent model specification testing, nonparametric estimation and inference in structural models, nonparametric time series and financial time series models, combined estimation or model averaging, and nonparametric panel data models. This section presents a brief review of some of Aman's works in four subareas: nonparametric regression and its derivatives, consistent model specification testing, nonparametric IV and simultaneous equations models, and combined estimation. His contributions in panel data models including nonparametric and semiparametric panel models will be reviewed in the next section.

Like his works in other areas, Aman proposed many original ideas in nonparametric econometrics in his early works and has subsequently developed them with his students and coauthors. We begin this section by reviewing one of the oldest and most commonly used nonparametric estimators, the Nadaraya–Watson kernel estimator.

4.1. Nonparametric Regression and Its Derivatives

Consider the following regression:

$$Y = R(X) + U, \quad \mathrm{E}(U|X) = 0, \tag{19}$$

where Y is the dependent variable, $X \in \mathbb{R}^p$ is the covariate vector, and U is the error term.

In parametric econometrics, the regression function $R(\cdot)$ is assumed to be known apart from a finite number of unknown parameters such as in the linear regression model where $R(x) = x'\beta$. Estimating $R(x)$ or its derivatives is then equivalent to estimating the parameter β for which OLS or FGLS is well developed and easily implementable. However, consistency of parametric estimators such as OLS or FGLS depends critically on the correct specification of the parametric regression model and thus is not robust to potential model misspecification. In contrast, nonparametric methods such as local smoothing-based approaches and global sieve-based methods are robust to such potential functional-form misspecification. Since most of Aman's work exploits local smoothing approach, this section focuses exclusively on kernel smoothing methods.

4.1.1. The Nadaraya–Watson Kernel estimator

Suppose a random sample $\{(Y_i, X_i')\}_{i=1}^n$ from Eq. (19) is available. Nadaraya (1964) and Watson (1964) constructed the kernel regression estimator:

$$\hat{R}(x) = \frac{(nh^p)^{-1} \sum_{i=1}^n Y_i K\left(\frac{X_i - x}{h}\right)}{\hat{f}(x)}, \tag{20}$$

where $K(\cdot)$ is a kernel function, $h \equiv h_n \to 0$ is a bandwidth, and

$$\hat{f}(x) = \frac{1}{nh^p} \sum_{i=1}^n K\left(\frac{X_i - x}{h}\right) \tag{21}$$

is the kernel estimator of the density function of the covariate X.

It is now well known that under minimal conditions, $\hat{R}(x)$ is consistent with convergence rate $(nh^p)^{-1/2}$ and asymptotically normally distributed; see, for example, Prakasa Rao (1983) and Bierens (1987).

Instead of using the plug-in approach and

$$R(x) = \frac{\int yf(y,x)\,\mathrm{d}y}{f(x)}$$

to construct $\hat{R}(x)$ as in Nadaraya (1964) and Watson (1964), Ullah (1988a) proposed a novel weighted LS method:

$$\hat{R}(x) = \arg\min_{a} \sum_{i=1}^{n} (Y_i - a)^2 K\left(\frac{X_i - x}{h}\right). \tag{22}$$

This alternative construction has its intuitive appeal giving rise to the alternative name of the Nadaraya–Watson estimator, namely, the local-constant regression. It is the simplest member of the class of local polynomial regressions. Moreover, the weighted LS construction suggests naturally more efficient nonparametric estimators of $R(x)$ for non-i.i.d. errors via "generalized LS" principle, see Su and Ullah (2007) for random-effect panel models and Su, Ullah, and Wang (2013) for general error covariance, both of which will be reviewed in the next section.

4.1.2. Estimation of derivatives of $R(x)$

In most applications in economics, the derivatives of $R(x)$ are the parameters of interest. For instance, the vector of first-order derivatives of $R(x)$, known as the response coefficients in econometrics, measures the ceteris paribus effects of the covariates; the matrix of second-order derivatives of $R(x)$ measures the shape of the regression surface. Aman is among the first researchers to study nonparametric estimation of derivatives of $R(x)$.

Let $\beta(x) = \partial R(x)/\partial x$ and $\beta^{(j)}(x) = \partial\beta^{(j-1)}(x)/\partial x$, $j = 1, 2, \ldots$. Ullah (1988a, 1988b) proposed estimators of $\beta(x)$ and $\beta^{(j)}(x)$ based on $\hat{R}(x)$, see also Rilstone and Ullah (1989). For example, these papers propose to estimate $\beta(x)$ by

$$\hat{\beta}(x) = \left(\frac{\hat{R}(x + hl_j) - \hat{R}(x - hl_j)}{2h}\right)_{j=1}^{p}$$

and establish its asymptotic properties, where l_j is the column vector of dimension p with all elements zero except the jth element taking the value one. Moreover, we note that the first derivative of $R(x)$ is a functional coefficient (varying coefficient) which varies with x. Su, Murtazashvili, and Ullah (2013) have developed nonparametric functional derivative $\beta(Z)$ in the model

$$Y = R(X, Z) + U = X'\beta(Z) + U,$$

where Z is a vector of continuous as well as discrete variables and X is endogenous. The estimation of the second-order derivatives of $R(x)$ and its applications for studying the shape of the demand curve were studied in McMillan, Ullah, and Vinod (1989). Alternative estimators of $R(x)$ and of its derivatives can be obtained directly from local polynomial regression, see Fan and Gijbels (1996). In addition to estimating derivatives of $R(x)$ evaluated at a given value of the covariate, it is known that average derivative estimators have important applications in semi-parametric index models; see Powell, Stock, and Stoker (1989), Li, Lu, and Ullah (2003), among many other subsequent works.

4.2. *Consistent Model Specification Testing*

The rate of convergence of $\hat{R}(x)$ reveals its practical limitation in many economic applications involving a large number of covariates. This, together with the practical appeal of simple linear regression motivated the development of consistent model specification tests. Consider testing the correct specification of a linear regression, namely,

$$\begin{aligned} H_0 &: \Pr\left(R(X) = X'\beta\right) = 1 \quad \text{for some } \beta \in \mathcal{B} \text{ against} \\ H_1 &: \Pr\left(R(X) = X'\beta\right) < 1 \quad \text{for all } \beta \in \mathcal{B}. \end{aligned}$$

Ullah (1985) was the first to propose a test statistic which compares the parametric residual sum of squares with the nonparametric one, see also Ullah (1988a). The asymptotic null distribution of this test statistic was established in Fan and Li (2002) and Dette (1999).

Consistent model specification testing was an active research area in the 1990s. In addition to comparing residual sums of squares, other test statistics were also constructed; see Fan (1994) for testing parametric density function using integrated squared differences between a parametric estimator and a nonparametric estimator of the density function, Zheng (1996) for testing parametric regression, and Fan and Li (1996) for testing semiparametric specification and omitted variables in nonparametric regression using kernel-weighted quadratic forms in residuals from the null model.

One common feature shared by all the smoothing-based consistent tests is that the null asymptotic distributions of the corresponding test statistics are determined by appropriate degenerate U-statistics with kernels depending on the sample size n. These degenerate U-statistics are such that when normalized by $\sqrt{n}$, they approach zero in probability. This phenomenon was referred to as the degeneracy problem in the early literature on consistent model specification testing. Fan and Li (1996), Zheng (1996), and Hong and White (1995) are the first ones to explore CLTs for degenerate U-statistics in, for example, Hall (1984) to establish asymptotic null distributions of their test statistics without resorting to any ad hoc solution such as sample splitting. Fan and Li (1999) extend the CLT in Hall (1984) to dependent mixing processes which is employed in many subsequent works on consistent model specification testing in time series models such as Fan and Ullah (1999a) and Lee and Ullah (2001). In addition to testing specifications of density function or regression function, Su and Ullah (2013) develop consistent tests for conditional heteroskedasticity: Su, Tu, and Ullah (2015) develop tests for additively separable structural models; see Section 4.3.2 for details.

4.3. Nonparametric IV and Triangular Simultaneous Equations Model

4.3.1. Nonparametric IV

Relative to other areas in nonparametric and semiparametric econometrics, the area of nonparametric and semiparametric IV is relatively new and is still a very active research area, see Newey and Powell (1989, 2003), Florens (2003), Hall and Horowitz (2005), Ai and Chen (2003), Darolles, Fan, Florens, and Renault (2011), Santos (2012), among others. It is interesting to note that the subject of nonparametric IV was touched upon in Ullah (1988a), who states that "Suppose (19) is a single equation out of the system of M simultaneous equation model, where X is now referred as a vector of right-hand endogenous variables. Let W be the vector of stochastic exogenous variables (instruments) which appear in the remaining $M-1$ equations." So $\mathrm{E}(U|X)\neq 0$ but $\mathrm{E}(U|W)=0$ and the proper conditioning leads to

$$Y=g(W)+V, \quad V=U+R(X)-g(W),$$

where

$$g(W)=\mathrm{E}(R(X)|W) \quad \text{such that } \mathrm{E}(V|W)=0.$$

Note that $g(W)=\mathrm{E}(Y|W)$ and

$$g(W)=\int R(x)\,\mathrm{d}F(x|W), \tag{23}$$

where $F(\cdot|W)$ denotes the conditional distribution function of X given $W=w$. Equation (23) is a Fredholm integral equation of the first kind and R is the solution to this integral equation. Identification, estimation, and inference in nonparametric IV models have been addressed in Newey and Powell (1989, 2003), Florens (2003), Hall and Horowitz (2005), Ai and Chen (2003), Darolles et al. (2011), among others. It is now known that estimating R via Eq. (23) is an ill-posed inverse problem and regularization of some sort has to be used. Without the completeness condition for point identification of $R(\cdot)$, Santos (2012) provides inference methods under partial identification of $R(\cdot)$.

4.3.2. Nonparametric triangular simultaneous equations model
Building on Newey, Powell, and Vella (1999), Su and Ullah (2008) provide an alternative estimator of $R(\cdot)$ in the nonparametric triangular simultaneous equations model below:

$$\begin{aligned} Y &= R(X, W_1) + U, \quad W = \left(W_1', W_2'\right)', \\ X &= h(W) + \epsilon, \quad \mathrm{E}(\epsilon|W) = 0, \quad \mathrm{E}(U|W,\epsilon) = \mathrm{E}(U|\epsilon). \end{aligned}$$

It is based on the following additive representation of $\mathrm{E}(Y|X, W_1, \epsilon)$:

$$\mathrm{E}(Y|X, W_1, \epsilon) = R(X, W_1) + \mathrm{E}(U|\epsilon). \tag{24}$$

Under the identification condition in Newey et al. (1999), R is identified up to an additive constant. Su and Ullah (2008) propose a three-step estimator of R based on local polynomial estimators of h, $\mathrm{E}(Y|X, W_1, \epsilon)$, and marginal integration. They also establish asymptotic properties of their estimator.

Nonparametric models with additive errors have been extended to allow for nonadditive errors. Consider the following nonseparable model:

$$Y = m(X, U), \tag{25}$$

where, among other conditions, $m(x, \cdot)$ is assumed to be strictly increasing for each $x \in \mathcal{X}$ and X is independent of U given Z. The identification and estimation of Eq. (25) are studied in Matzkin (2003), Hoderlein, Su, White, and Yang (2016), among others. The fundamental result leading to identification of m exploits the strict monotonicity of $m(x, \cdot)$:

$$m(x, u) = G^{-1}\left(G(u|\overline{x}, z)\,|x, z\right) \text{ and} \tag{26}$$

$$U = G^{-1}\left(G(Y|X, z)\,|\overline{x}, z\right) \quad \text{for all } z \in \mathcal{Z}, \tag{27}$$

where $\overline{x}$ is such that $m(\overline{x}, u) = u$ for all $u \in \mathcal{U}$ and $G(\cdot|x, z)$ is the conditional CDF of Y given $X = x$ and $Z = z$. Plug-in estimators are proposed in Matzkin (2003) and Hoderlein et al. (2016) based on Eqs. (26) and (27).

Su et al. (2015) propose a test for an additive error structure against model (25) by noting that under the null hypothesis of an additive error structure and the maintained assumptions in their paper, the structural function m in Eq. (25) satisfies:

$$\Pr\left(\frac{\partial m(X,U)}{\partial u}=1\right)=1.$$

A weighted integrated squared difference between a nonparametric estimator of $\partial m(\cdot,\cdot)/\partial u$ and 1 is used to construct the test. The specific nonparametric estimator they use is the local constant version of that in Hoderlein et al. (2016) based on Eqs. (26) and (27).

4.4. *Combined Estimation*

Fan and Ullah (1999b) present a systematic study of an additively combined estimator of the regression function $R(\cdot)$ in Eq. (19). The combined estimator studied in Fan and Ullah (1999b) takes the following form:

$$\tilde{R}(x)=\hat{\lambda}R(x;\hat{\beta})+(1-\hat{\lambda})\hat{R}(x),$$

where

$$\hat{\lambda}=\frac{n^{-1}\sum_{i=1}^{n}\left[\hat{f}^{(i)}(X_i)R(X_i;\hat{\beta})-\hat{R}^{(i)}(X_i)\right]\hat{f}^{(i)}(X_i)\left[Y_i-R(X_i;\hat{\beta})\right]}{n^{-1}\sum_{i=1}^{n}\left[\hat{f}^{(i)}(X_i)R(X_i;\hat{\beta})-\hat{R}^{(i)}(X_i)\right]^2},$$

in which $\hat{f}^{(i)}(X_i)$ is the leave-one-out kernel estimator of the density function of the covariate evaluated at X_i, $\hat{R}^{(i)}(X_i)$ is the leave-one-out kernel estimator of $R(X_i)$, and $R(x;\hat{\beta})$ is a parametric estimator based on the parametric specification $R(x;\beta)$ of $R(x)$. The asymptotic properties established in Fan and Ullah (1999b) for correct parametric specification, incorrect parametric specification, and approximately correct parametric specification confirm the intuition that by making use of the information in the parametric model, the combined estimator will never perform worse than the nonparametric estimator in terms of convergence rate and it will perform as well as the parametric estimator under correct parametric specification.

An alternative method to additive combination is multiplication combination. It is based on the expression

$$R(x)=R(x;\beta)\left[\frac{R(x)}{R(x;\beta)}\right]$$

so the ratio $\left[\frac{R(x)}{R(x;\beta)}\right]$ acts as a nonparametric correction factor. A multiplicatively combined estimator of $R(x)$ is given by $R(x;\hat{\beta})$ multiplied by a nonparametric estimator of the correction factor. Mishra, Su, and Ullah (2010), Long, Su, and Ullah (2011), and Dungey, Long, Ullah, and Wang (2014) exploit the idea of multiplicative combination to construct combined estimators of conditional variance, conditional covariance, and conditional duration in financial time series models. They also establish asymptotic properties of their estimators. Nonparametric kernel estimators of conditional variance and conditional covariance were first proposed in Ullah (1988b).

It is worth pointing out that the combined estimators in these works are examples of model averaging estimators that are now popular in the econometrics literature.

5. PANEL AND SPATIAL MODELS

This section discusses Aman Ullah's contributions to panel and spatial models. These include his contributions in the areas of seemingly unrelated regressions, parametric, semiparametric and nonparametric panel data models, and spatial models.

5.1. *Seemingly Unrelated Regression*

Zellner's (1962) seemingly unrelated regressions (SUR) have been widely studied in theory and used in practice. He assumed that the regression coefficients remain constant over the sample observations. Singh and Ullah (1974) considered estimating the set of M SUR when the regression coefficients are random:

$$y_{it} = \beta_{it}' X_{it} + u_{it}, \tag{28}$$

$$\beta_{it} = \bar{\beta}_i + \varepsilon_{it}, \tag{29}$$

where $i = 1, \ldots, M$, $t = 1, \ldots, T$, X_{it} is a $k_i \times 1$ vector of independent variables, β_{it} is a $k_i \times 1$ vector of random coefficients with mean $\bar{\beta}_i$, and u_{it} is the error term. The fact that the coefficients in linear regression models may not be constant across cross section, time series, or panel is well documented and analyzed in the book by Raj and Ullah (2012). Plugging Eq. (29) into Eq. (28) yields

$$y_{it} = \bar{\beta}_i' X_{it} + w_{it}, \tag{30}$$

where $w_{it} = u_{it} + \varepsilon_{it}' X_{it}$, or in matrix form

$$\mathbf{y} = \mathbf{X}\bar{\beta} + \mathbf{w}, \tag{31}$$

where, for example, $\mathbf{X} = \text{diag}(X_1, \ldots, X_M)$ with $X_i = (X_{i1}, \ldots, X_{iT})'$ is an $MT \times k$ matrix, $k = \sum_{i=1}^{M} k_i$, and $\bar{\beta} = (\bar{\beta}_1, \ldots, \bar{\beta}_M)'$. Under the standard assumptions for random coefficient models (mainly, $\text{E}\left(u_{it}\varepsilon_{it}\right) = 0$, $\text{E}\left(u_{it}u_{js}\right) = \sigma_{ij}\mathbf{1}\left\{t = s\right\}$, $\text{E}(\varepsilon_{it,\lambda}\varepsilon_{js,\lambda'}) = \delta_{ij,\lambda}\mathbf{1}\left\{t = s, \lambda = \lambda'\right\}$ with $\mathbf{1}\left\{\cdot\right\}$ being the usual indicator function), Aitken's generalized least squares (GLS) estimator of $\bar{\beta}$ is given by

$$\widehat{\bar{\beta}}_{\text{GLS}} = \left(\mathbf{X}'\Omega^{-1}\mathbf{X}\right)^{-1}\mathbf{X}'\Omega^{-1}\mathbf{y},$$

and Zellner's (1962) SUR estimator is given by

$$\widehat{\bar{\beta}}_{\text{SUR}} = \left(\mathbf{X}'\Sigma^{-1}\mathbf{X}\right)^{-1}\mathbf{X}'\Sigma^{-1}\mathbf{y},$$

where $\Omega = \text{E}\left(\mathbf{w}\mathbf{w}'\right)$, and $\Sigma = \Sigma_c \otimes I_T$, and $\Sigma_c = \left\{\sigma_{ij}\right\}_{i,j=1}^{M}$. Singh and Ullah (1974) proposed an FGLS estimator by estimating the elements of Ω based on the first-stage OLS estimators of single equations and demonstrated that it is asymptotically equivalent to $\widehat{\bar{\beta}}_{\text{GLS}}$ and is thus more efficient than the SUR estimator $\widehat{\bar{\beta}}_{\text{SUR}}$.

Zellner's (1962) two-step GLS estimators of SUR models require the nonsingularity of the estimated variance-covariance (VC) matrix of the errors in the SUR system. However, in many applications in economics, business, and management, the assumption of nonsingularity may be violated, such as in the estimation of demand systems and of cost functions. A common procedure is to drop an arbitrary equation and then estimate the remaining equations. Takada, Ullah, and Chen (1995) proposed an alternative solution to the problem where the two-step GLS estimators are obtained by perturbing the singular VC matrix, by adding a ridge-type positive scalar constant to the diagonal elements of the singular matrix. They considered two choices of the ridge parameter γ. One is to set $\gamma = h^2 \int z^2 K\left(z\right)\, \text{d}z$ with $h = 1.06T^{-1/5}$ and $K\left(\cdot\right)$ being the standard normal density function. The other is to set $\gamma = k/[T\text{tr}\left(\Sigma_c^{+}\right)]$, where Σ_c^{+} is the generalized inverse of Σ_c such that

$$\text{tr}\left(\Sigma_c^{+}\right) = \text{tr}\left(\Sigma_{c,11}^{-1}\right) - \iota_{M-1}'\Sigma_{c,11}^{-1}\iota_{M-1}/M,$$

$\Sigma_{c,11}$ is any principal $(M-1) \times (M-1)$ submatrix of Σ_c, and ι_{M-1} is an $(M-1) \times 1$ vector of ones. Ullah and Racine (1992) found that the estimator based on the first choice of ridge-parameter outperforms both the OLS and Zellner's SUR estimators in terms of MSE. Takada et al. (1995) found that the two choices of ridge parameters work approximately equally well in both the simulation study and the empirical problem they considered.

Over the last 15 years or so, various parametric, semiparametric, and nonparametric methods have been proposed to model conditional covariances and correlations (e.g., Engle, 2002). Even if the unconditional correlations are constant over the observations, the conditional correlations may still vary over the observations with respect to variables in the conditioning set. Also, an unconditional uncorrelated process may still be a conditionally correlated process (see, Anatolyev, 2002). In many models, the conditional correlations arise because of conditional covariances and/or conditional heteroskedasticity. In nonparametric SUR or VAR models, it is the conditional covariance that plays an important role. For this reason, Su and Ullah (2009) considered the system of M nonparametric regression equations

$$Y_{it} = m_i (X_{it}) + u_{it}, \quad i = 1, \ldots, M, \; t = 1, \ldots, T, \tag{32}$$

where m_i, $i = 1, \ldots, M$, are unknown smooth regression functions, $u_t = (u_{1t}, \ldots, u_{Mt})'$ are random disturbances such that $\mathrm{E}\,(u_{it}|X_{it}) = 0$ and $\mathrm{E}\left(u_t u_t'|X_t\right) = \Sigma\,(X_t)$ with X_t being the disjoint union of $X_{1t}, \ldots, X_{Mt}$. They were interested in testing the null hypothesis

$$\mathbb{H}_0 : \text{all off-diagonal elements of } \Sigma\,(X_t) \text{ are zero a.s.}, \tag{33}$$

that is, the $U_{it}'s$ are conditionally uncorrelated given X_t. Let $\sigma_{kl}\,(X_t)$ denote the (k, l)th element of $\Sigma\,(X_t)$ and $f\,(x)$ denote the density function of X_t. They considered the functional

$$\Gamma = \sum_{k=1}^{M-1} \sum_{l=k+1}^{M} \int \sigma_{kl}^2\,(x)\, f^2\,(x)\, \mathrm{d}x, \tag{34}$$

which is zero if and only if $\mathbb{H}_0$ holds. They propose a test statistic based upon a kernel estimator of Γ and established its asymptotic distribution under the null hypothesis and a sequence of Pitman local alternatives. They also discussed how to modify their test to test for conditional homoskedasticity.

5.2. *Panel Data Models*

Aman's contributions to panel data models overlap with his contributions to the finite sample theory and nonparametric and semiparametric econometrics. Here we review his distinctive works on parametric, semiparametric, and nonparametric panel data models. See also the survey paper Su and Ullah (2011) for additional discussions.

5.2.1. Parametric panel data models

Aman Ullah's work on parametric panel data models is motivated from his insight into the finite sample properties of estimators and test statistics in the panel framework.

Ullah and Huang (2006) considered the finite sample properties of the FGLS estimator for the random-effects panel data model with non-normal errors:

$$y_{it} = X_{it}'\beta + \varepsilon_{it}, \quad \varepsilon_{it} = \alpha_i + u_{it}, \quad i = 1, \dots N, \ t = 1, \dots, T,$$

where X_{it} is a $p \times 1$ vector of strictly exogenous regressors, β is a $p \times 1$ vector of coefficients, α_i's are random effects (RE), and u_{it} is the idiosyncratic error term. They derived the bias and MSE of the FGLS estimator $\hat{\beta}_{\text{FGLS}}$ up to the orders $O\left(N^{-1}\right)$ and $O\left(N^{-2}\right)$, respectively. They found that the leading bias term depends only on the skewness coefficient and the MSE depends only on the kurtosis coefficient. The $O\left(N^{-1}\right)$ order of bias vanishes for symmetric distributions or for other distributions satisfying certain restriction.

Pesaran, Ullah, and Yamagata (2008) proposed a bias-adjusted version of Breusch and Pagan's (1980, BP hereafter) LM test statistic for testing cross-sectional independence (uncorrrelation in fact) in the error terms. They considered the model

$$y_{it} = X_{it}'\beta_i + \varepsilon_{it}, \quad i = 1, \dots, N, \ t = 1, \dots, T,$$

where X_{it} is a $p \times 1$ vector of strictly exogenous regressors, β_i's are defined on a compact set, and for each i, the error term ε_{it} are i.i.d. $N\left(0, \sigma_i^2\right)$ over t. The null of interest is $\mathbb{H}_0 : \text{Cov}\left(\varepsilon_{it}, \varepsilon_{jt}\right) = 0$ for all t and $i \neq j$. The LM test statistic is given by

$$\text{LM}_{NT} = T \sum_{i=1}^{N-1} \sum_{j=i+1}^{N} \hat{\rho}_{ij}^2, \tag{35}$$

where $\hat{\rho}_{ij}$ denotes the sample estimate of the pairwise correlation of the residuals based on the OLS time series regression of y_{it} on X_{it}. It is well known that this LM statistic is asymptotically χ^2 $(N(N-1)/2)$ when N keeps fixed as $T \to \infty$, and the test tends to exhibit substantial size distortions for large N and small T.

Under the normality assumption, Pesaran et al. (2008) showed that

$$\mu_{Tij} \equiv \mathrm{E}\left[(T-p)\,\hat{\rho}_{ij}^2\right] = \frac{1}{T-p}\mathrm{tr}\left[\mathrm{E}\left(M_i M_j\right)\right],$$
$$\upsilon_{Tij}^2 \equiv \mathrm{Var}\left[(T-p)\,\hat{\rho}_{ij}^2\right] = \left\{\mathrm{tr}\left[\mathrm{E}\left(M_i M_j\right)\right]\right\}^2 a_{1T} + 2\mathrm{tr}\left\{\mathrm{E}\left[\left(M_i M_j\right)^2\right]\right\} a_{2T},$$

where $M_i = I_T - X_i\left(X_i' X_i\right)^{-1} X_i'$, $a_{1T} = a_{2T} - \frac{1}{(T-p)^2}$, and $a_{2T} = 3\left[\frac{(T-p-8)(T-p+2)+24}{(T-p+2)(T-p-2)(T-p-4)}\right]^2$. They defined the bias-adjusted LM statistic as

$$\mathrm{LM}_{adj} = \sqrt{\frac{2}{N(N-1)}}\sum_{i=1}^{N-1}\sum_{j=i+1}^{N}\frac{T\hat{\rho}_{ij}^2 - \mu_{Tij}}{\upsilon_{Tij}} \tag{36}$$

and showed that LM_{adj} converges in distribution to $N(0,1)$ by passing $T\to\infty$ first and then letting $N\to\infty$.

5.2.2. *Partially linear panel data models with REs*

Aman Ullah has a great interest in efficient estimation of partially linear panel data models with REs. Li and Ullah (1998) considered the estimation of the following partially linear panel data models with an one-way error component structure

$$y_{it} = X_{it}'\beta_0 + m\left(Z_{it}\right) + \varepsilon_{it}, \tag{37}$$
$$\varepsilon_{it} = \alpha_i + u_{it}, \tag{38}$$

where X_{it} and Z_{it} are of dimensions $p\times 1$ and $q\times 1$, respectively, β_0 is a $p\times 1$ vector of unknown parameters, $m(\cdot)$ is an unknown smooth function, α_i are REs, and u_{it} are the idiosyncratic error terms. In matrix notation, Eq. (38) can be written as

$$\varepsilon = \left(I_N \otimes \iota_T\right)\alpha + u,$$

where $u = \left(u_{11},\ldots,u_{1T},\ldots,u_{N1},\ldots,u_{NT}\right)'$, and $\alpha = (\alpha_1,\ldots,\alpha_N)'$. Under the standard assumptions on RE (mainly, α_i are i.i.d. $\left(0,\sigma_\alpha^2\right)$, u_{it} are i.i.d. $\left(0,\sigma_u^2\right)$, and α_i and u_{jt} are mutually independent of each other), we have

$$\Omega \equiv \mathrm{E}\left(\varepsilon\varepsilon'\right) = \sigma_\alpha^2\left(I_N \otimes \iota_T\right) + \sigma_u^2 I_{NT}$$
$$= I_N \otimes \left[\sigma_1^2 J_T + \sigma_u^2 \mathrm{E}_T\right] \equiv I_N \otimes \Sigma, \tag{39}$$

where $J_T = \iota_T \iota_T' / T$, $E_T = I_T - J_T$, and $\sigma_1^2 = T\sigma_\alpha^2 + \sigma_u^2$. Taking conditional expectation with respect to Z_{it} on both sides of Eq. (37) and subtracting yield

$$y_{it} - \mathrm{E}\left(y_{it} | Z_{it}\right) = \left[X_{it} - \mathrm{E}\left(X_{it} | y_{it}\right)\right]' \beta_0 + \varepsilon_{it}, \quad (40)$$

provided $\mathrm{E}\left(\varepsilon_{it} | Z_{it}\right) = 0$. Let $\tilde{y}_{it} = y_{it} - \mathrm{E}\left(y_{it} | Z_{it}\right)$ and $\tilde{X}_{it} = X_{it} - \mathrm{E}\left(X_{it} | y_{it}\right)$. Let $\tilde{X} = (\tilde{X}_{11}, \ldots, \tilde{X}_{1T}, \ldots, \tilde{X}_{N1}, \ldots, \tilde{X}_{NT})'$ and similarly define $\tilde{y}$. The OLS estimator of β from Eq. (40) is given by $\tilde{\beta}_{\mathrm{OLS}} = \left(\tilde{X}'\tilde{X}\right)^{-1} \tilde{X}'\tilde{y}$, and the GLS estimator of β is given by $\tilde{\beta}_{\mathrm{GLS}} = \left(\tilde{X}'\Omega^{-1}\tilde{X}\right)^{-1} \tilde{X}'\Omega^{-1}\tilde{y}$, where $\Omega^{-1} = I_N \otimes [(1/\sigma_1^2)J_T + \left(1/\sigma_u^2\right) E_T] \equiv I_N \otimes \Sigma^{-1}$. Neither estimator is feasible. Following the lead of Robinson (1988), Li and Ullah (1998) suggested to estimate the conditional expectations by the kernel method and use a trimming function to handle the random denominator issue. They first obtained the feasible OLS estimator, based on which one could estimate σ_u^2 and σ_1^2 to construct a consistent estimate of Σ^{-1}. They obtained the FGLS estimator and established its asymptotic distribution. They also discussed the case for which the regressor of the parametric component is correlated with the error, and propose a GLS-type IV (GLS-IV) semiparametric estimator. They showed that their estimator for the finite-dimensional parameter is asymptotically efficient.

Nevertheless, the GLS-IV estimator in Li and Ullah (1998) did not make full use of the one-way error component structure and reduces to a semiparametric IV-OLS estimator in the case of just identification. In view of this, Berg, Li, and Ullah (2000) proposed a new semiparametric GLS-IV estimator and a new semiparametric IV-Within estimator that are more efficient than the ones considered in Li and Stengos (1996) and Li and Ullah (1998).

5.2.3. Nonparametric panels with REs

Ullah and Roy (1998) considered nonparametric panel data models with REs:

$$y_{it} = m(X_{it}) + \alpha_i + u_{it}, \quad i = 1, \ldots, N, \;\; t = 1, \ldots, T, \quad (41)$$

where X_{it}, α_i, u_{it} are as defined before, and $m(\cdot)$ is an unknown smooth function. A local linear approximation of the model (41) can be written as

$$\begin{aligned} y_{it} &\approx m(x) + (X_{it} - x)'\beta(x) + \alpha_i + u_{it} \\ &= X_{it}(x)'\delta(x) + \alpha_i + u_{it}, \end{aligned} \quad (42)$$

where X_{it} is "close" to x, $X_{it}(x)=(1\ (X_{it}-x)')'$, $\beta(x)=\partial m(x)/\partial x$, and $\delta(x)=(m(x)\,\beta(x)')'$. In a vector form, we can write

$$Y \approx \mathbf{X}(x)\,\delta(x)+\varepsilon,$$

where $Y=(y_{11},\ldots,y_{1T},\ldots,y_{N1},\ldots,y_{NT})'$, and $\mathbf{X}(x)=(X_{11}(x),\ldots,X_{1T}(x),\ldots,X_{N1}(x),\ldots,X_{NT}(x))'$. Let $K_h(x)=h^{-p}K\,(x/h)$, where K is a kernel function and $h\equiv h\,(N,T)$ is a bandwidth parameter. Then the LLLS estimator of $\delta(x)$ is obtained by choosing δ to minimize

$$[Y-\mathbf{X}(x)\delta]'\,\mathbf{K}\,(x)\,[Y-\mathbf{X}(x)\delta],$$

where $\mathbf{K}(x)=\mathrm{diag}(K_h(X_{11}-x),\ldots,K_h(X_{1T}-x),\ldots,K_h(X_{N1}-x),\ldots,K_h(X_{NT}-x))$ is an $NT\times NT$ diagonal matrix. The solution to this minimization problem is given by

$$\hat{\delta}(x)=\left[\mathbf{X}(x)'\mathbf{K}(x)\mathbf{X}(x)\right]^{-1}\mathbf{X}(x)'\mathbf{K}(x)Y. \tag{43}$$

Denote the first component of $\hat{\delta}(x)$ as $\hat{m}(x)$ which estimates $m\,(x)$.

Clearly, the estimator in Eq. (43) ignores the information on Ω defined in Eq. (39). To incorporate this, Henderson and Ullah (2005) defined a weighted LLLS estimator of $\delta(x)$ by choosing δ to minimize

$$[Y-\mathbf{X}(x)\delta)]'\,\mathbf{W}(x)\,[Y-\mathbf{X}(x)\delta)],$$

which gives

$$\hat{\delta}_{\mathbf{W}}(x)=\left[\mathbf{X}(x)'\mathbf{W}(x)\mathbf{X}(x)\right]^{-1}\mathbf{X}(x)'\mathbf{W}(x)Y, \tag{44}$$

where $\mathbf{W}(x)$ is a kernel-based weight matrix. Lin and Carroll (2000) consider $\mathbf{W}(x)=\mathbf{K}(x)^{1/2}\Omega^{-1}\mathbf{K}(x)^{1/2}$ and $\mathbf{W}(x)=\Omega^{-1}\mathbf{K}(x)$, and Ullah and Roy (1998) suggest $\mathbf{W}(x)=\Omega^{-1/2}\mathbf{K}(x)\Omega^{-1/2}$. When Ω is a diagonal matrix, these choices of $\mathbf{W}(x)$ are the same.

For an operational estimate, we need to estimate Ω. For this purpose, define

$$\hat{\sigma}_1^2=\frac{T}{N}\sum_{i=1}^{N}\bar{\hat{\varepsilon}}_i^2,\quad \hat{\sigma}_u^2=\frac{1}{N(T-1)}\sum_{i=1}^{N}\sum_{t=1}^{T}\left(\hat{\varepsilon}_{it}-\bar{\hat{\varepsilon}}_i\right)^2,$$

where $\bar{\hat{\varepsilon}}_i=T^{-1}\sum_{t=1}^{T}\hat{\varepsilon}_{it}$ and $\hat{\varepsilon}_{it}=y_{it}-\hat{m}(X_{it})$ is the LLLS residual. Noting that $\hat{\sigma}_1^2$ and $\hat{\sigma}_u^2$ estimate $\sigma_1^2=T\sigma_\alpha^2+\sigma_u^2$ and σ_u^2, respectively, we can estimate σ_α^2 by $\hat{\sigma}_\alpha^2=\frac{1}{T}\left(\hat{\sigma}_1^2-\hat{\sigma}_u^2\right)$. With these estimates, Henderson and Ullah (2005) obtained an estimate $\hat{\Omega}$ of Ω with σ_α^2 and σ_u^2 replaced by $\hat{\sigma}_\alpha^2$ and $\hat{\sigma}_u^2$, respectively. The operational estimator of $\delta(x)$ is given by

$$\hat{\delta}_{\widehat{\mathbf{W}}}(x) = \left[\mathbf{X}(x)'\widehat{\mathbf{W}}(x)\mathbf{X}(x)\right]^{-1}\mathbf{X}(x)'\widehat{\mathbf{W}}(x)Y, \tag{45}$$

where $\widehat{\mathbf{W}}(x)$ is $\mathbf{W}(x)$ with Ω replaced by $\widehat{\Omega}$. However, Lin and Carroll (2000) demonstrated that one cannot achieve asymptotic improvement over the LLLS estimator by such weighted LLLS estimation. Henderson and Ullah (2014) also found similar observations in their Monte Carlo study by comparing these weighted estimators. They also showed that the following two-step estimator of Ruckstuhl, Welsh, and Carroll (2000) is more efficient than the above weighted estimators as well as the conventional LLLS estimator.

To obtain a more efficient estimator, Su and Ullah (2007) wrote Eq. (41) in vector form:

$$Y = \mathbf{m}(X) + \varepsilon, \tag{46}$$

where $X = (X_{11}, \ldots, X_{1T}, \ldots, X_{N1}, \ldots, X_{NT})'$, $\mathbf{m}(X) = (m\,(X_{11}), \ldots, m\,(X_{1T}), \ldots, m\,(X_{N1}), \ldots, m\,(X_{NT}))'$, $\varepsilon = \alpha \otimes \iota_T + U$, $U = (u_{11}, \ldots, u_{1T}, \ldots, u_{N1}, \ldots, u_{NT})'$. Multiplying both sides of Eq. (46) by $\tau\Omega^{-\frac{1}{2}}$ yields

$$\tau\Omega^{-\frac{1}{2}}Y = \tau\Omega^{-\frac{1}{2}}\mathbf{m}(X) - \mathbf{m}(X) + \mathbf{m}(X) + \tau\Omega^{-\frac{1}{2}}\varepsilon$$

or

$$Y^* = \mathbf{m}(X) + \tau\Omega^{-\frac{1}{2}}\varepsilon, \tag{47}$$

where $Y^* = \tau\Omega^{-\frac{1}{2}}Y + (I_{NT} - \tau\Omega^{-\frac{1}{2}})\mathbf{m}(X)$ is the transformed variable and $\Omega^{-\frac{1}{2}}\varepsilon$ has an identity VC matrix. However, Y^* is not observed. Su and Ullah (2007) proposed a feasible estimator based on this transformed model via a two-step procedure. In the first step, one runs the LLLS regression Y on X to obtain the estimate $\hat{m}(x)$ of $m(x)$ at each data point and the residuals, based on which we can obtain consistent estimate $\hat{\Omega}$ of Ω as discussed above. This gives $\hat{Y}^* = \tau\hat{\Omega}^{-\frac{1}{2}}Y + (I_{NT} - \tau\hat{\Omega}^{-\frac{1}{2}})\widehat{\mathbf{m}}(X)$, where $\widehat{\mathbf{m}}(X) = (\hat{m}\,(X_{11}), \ldots, \hat{m}\,(X_{1T}), \ldots, \hat{m}\,(X_{N1}), \ldots, \hat{m}\,(X_{NT}))'$. In the second step, we run the LLLS regression of $\hat{Y}^*$ on X. Su and Ullah (2007) established the asymptotic property of this type of two-step estimators. Some related works include Ruckstuhl et al. (2000), Martins-Filho and Yao (2009), and Su, Ullah, et al. (2013) in the panel, SUR, or single-equation framework.

5.2.4. Nonparametric panel data model with fixed effects

Ullah and Roy (1998) also considered the estimation of Eq. (41) when α_i's are treated as fixed effects. Taking the time-average of both sides of Eq. (42) yields

$$\bar{y}_{i\cdot} \approx m\,(x) + (\bar{X}_{i\cdot} - x)'\beta(x) + \alpha_i + \bar{u}_{i\cdot},$$

where, for example, $\bar{X}_{i\cdot} = T^{-1}\sum_{t=1}^{T} X_{it}$. The within-group transformation of the model becomes

$$y_{it} - \bar{y}_{i\cdot} \approx (\bar{X}_{i\cdot} - x)'\beta(x) + (u_{it} - \bar{u}_{i\cdot})\,,$$

Ullah and Roy (1998) proposed to estimate the derivative vector $\beta(x)$ by the minimizing the following objective function

$$\sum_{i=1}^{N}\sum_{t=1}^{T}\left[y_{it} - \bar{y}_{i\cdot} - (\bar{X}_{i\cdot} - x)'\beta(x)\right]^2 K_h\,(X_{it} - x)\,.$$

Apparently, this method cannot estimate the nonparametric regression function itself. They also considered kernel estimation of the first-differenced model, but the asymptotic theory has not been fully established and understood until 2010s; see, for example, Su and Lu (2013) and the references therein.

Motivated by the least squares dummy variable (LSDV) estimation in the panel literature, Su and Ullah (2007) considered profile least squares (PLS) estimation of partially linear panel data models with fixed effects:

$$\begin{aligned} y_{it} &= X_{it}'\beta_0 + m\,(Z_{it}) + \varepsilon_{it}, \quad i = 1, \ldots, N, \;\; t = 1, \ldots, T, \\ \varepsilon_{it} &= \alpha_i + u_{it}. \end{aligned}$$

They assume $\sum_{i=1}^{N}\alpha_i = 0$ (so that $\alpha_1 = -\sum_{i=2}^{N}\alpha_i$) for the purpose of identification and X_{it} is strictly exogenous for expositional simplicity. Let $\alpha = (\alpha_2, \ldots, \alpha_N)'$, $\theta = (\alpha', \beta')'$ $D = (I_N \otimes \iota_T)\,d_N$, and $d_N = [-\iota_{N-1}\; I_{N-1}]'$. Their PLS is comprised of two stages:

Stage 1. Given θ, we can estimate $M\,(z) = \left(m\,(z)\,, h\partial m\,(z)\,/\partial z'\right)'$ by

$$\begin{aligned} M_\theta\,(z) = \arg\min_{M \in \mathbb{R}^{q+1}} &(Y - D\alpha - X\beta - Z\,(z)\,M)'\,\mathbf{K}_H\,(z) \\ &\times (Y - D\alpha - X\beta - Z\,(z)\,M)\,, \end{aligned} \tag{48}$$

where the $NT \times (q+1)$ matrix $Z\,(z)$ is a stack of $Z_{it}\,(z) = [1, (Z_{it} - z)'\,/\,h]'$. Define the smoothing operator by $S\,(z) = [Z\,(z)'\,\mathbf{K}_h\,(z)\,Z\,(z)\,]^{-1} Z\,(z)'\,\mathbf{K}_h\,(z)$. Then

$$M_\theta\,(z) = S\,(z)\,(Y - D\alpha - X\beta)\,.$$

In particular, the estimator for $m(z)$ is given by $m_\theta(z) = s(z)' (Y - D\alpha - X\beta)$, where $s(z)' = e_1' S(z)$, and $e_1 = (1, 0, \ldots, 0)'$ is a $(q+1) \times 1$ vector.

Stage 2. The parameter θ is then estimated as

$$\hat{\theta} = \arg\min_{\theta} (Y - D\alpha - X\beta - m_\theta(Z))' (Y - D\alpha - X\beta - m_\theta(Z)), \quad (49)$$

where $m_\theta(Z) = (m_\theta(z_{11}), \ldots, m_\theta(z_{1T}), \ldots, m_\theta(z_{nT}))'$. Using the formula for partitioned regression, we obtain

$$\hat{\beta} = \left[X^{*\prime} M^* X^*\right]^{-1} X^{*\prime} M^* Y^*,$$

$$\hat{\alpha} \equiv \left(\hat{\alpha}_2, \ldots, \hat{\alpha}_N\right)' = \left[D^{*\prime} D^*\right]^{-1} D^{*\prime}(Y^* - X^*\hat{\beta}),$$

where $D^* = (I_{NT} - \mathbf{S}) D$, $Y^* = (I_{NT} - \mathbf{S}) Y$, $X^* = (I_{NT} - \mathbf{S}) X$, $M^* = I_{NT} - D^* \left[D^{*\prime} D^*\right]^{-1} D^{*\prime}$, $\mathbf{S} = (s_{11}, \ldots, s_{1T}, \ldots, s_{N1}, \ldots, s_{NT})'$, and $s_{it} = s(z_{it})$. The estimator for α_1 is then given by $\hat{\alpha}_1 = -\sum_{i=2}^{N} \hat{\alpha}_i$, and the PLS estimator of $M(z)$ is $\hat{M}(z) = M_{\hat{\theta}}(z) = S(z)(Y - D\hat{\alpha} - X\hat{\beta})$.

This procedure has motivated many subsequent studies; see Henderson, Carroll, and Li (2008), Sun, Carroll, and Li (2009), Chen, Gao, and Li (2012), and Lin, Li, and Sun (2014), to name just a few.

5.2.5. Applied work

Aman Ullah has also made significant contributions to the applied parametric, semiparametric, and nonparametric cross-section, time series, and panel data models. They are in applied micro and financial econometrics areas. Appelbaum and Ullah (1984) provided a measure of degree of a firm risk aversion and a direct test for the risk aversion hypothesis. This was implemented for the U.S. textile data, and they have found that the risk aversion behavior of this industry was statistically insignificant during 1947–1971. After this, the work on the empirical behavior of firm under uncertainty was further explored in Appelbaum and Ullah (1997). In this, using nonparametric estimates of the first four conditional moments of unknown price distribution, an empirical model with production decision under output price uncertainty was analyzed. It was found that for the U.S. printing and publishing, stone, clay, and glass industries, the higher moments play a significant role in determining input and output decisions. Also, the risk neutrality was rejected. These empirical papers were based on the micro-theory models developed by Batra and Ullah (1974) in which they examine the behavior of the long-run equilibrium model of competitive firm maximizing expected utility and facing input-hiring decisions under conditions of price uncertainty. Also, see Ratti and Ullah (1976) for firms facing production uncertainty. In another empirical paper, Khanna, Mundra, and Ullah (1999) studied a different question related to the behavior of firms. That is, they estimated a stochastic frontier model using panel data for the electricity generating industry in India. They investigated the impact of distributional and functional-form assumptions on technical inefficiency and the sources of inefficiency by using maximum likelihood, GLS, and semiparametric – GLS approaches and by incorporating firm-specific inefficiency effects in the cost function itself. The inefficiency was found to be high perhaps because of public ownership. While the above were the applied micro-based papers, Pagan and Ullah (1988) studied a semi-parametric time series regression model with risk (conditional variance) as one of the explanatory variables. This variable was estimated by the nonparametric method for the U.S./Canada exchange market. The effect of price uncertainty upon production was analyzed, and the U.S./Canada exchange market was not found to be efficient. It is after the publication of this paper, Pagan and Ullah thought about writing and developing a book on nonparametric econometrics, which was published in 1999. In a panel context, Kumar and Ullah (2000) proposed a semiparametric model to study a general relationship with varying coefficients and develop a local linear IV method to estimate the smooth varying coefficients. They applied their method to estimate the speed of convergence of a panel of cross-countries per capita output. Ullah and Mundra (2002) considered a semiparametric panel data model in the spirit of Robinson (1988) and applied it to study the effect of immigrants "home link" hypothesis on the U.S. bilateral trade follows.

There are two recent applied papers by Mohanty and Ullah (2012a, 2012b) on the economics of family and happiness, the subjects extensively studied in psychology and sociology but recently emerging in economics literature. In Mohanty and Ullah (2012a), using U.S. NLS 79 data, it is shown that happiness affects the worker's wage not only directly, but also indirectly through its direct effect on years of schooling. Further, in Mohanty and Ullah (2012b), it has been confirmed for the US data that the true effect of workers growing up in intact families on wage increase may be much larger than what has been envisaged so far in the literature, and this higher wages may partly be attributed to their higher level of adulthood happiness. On the other hand, in Su, Murtazashvili, et al. (2013), without taking happiness variable in the model, an impact on return to schooling has been investigated with respect to a functional coefficient (varying coefficient) semiparametric model with and without schooling as an endogenous variable. The return to schooling is considered as an unknown function of experience, marital status, citizenship status, unionization, and whether one is in government job or not, and data used are on Australian females. Some interesting results on the impact of experience on return to schooling have been found. In particular, they found that ignoring schooling to be endogenous provided underestimation of returns to schooling.

5.3. Spatial Models

Bao and Ullah (2007a) considered the following purely AR spatial model:

$$Y_n = \rho W_n Y_n + V_n, \tag{50}$$

where Y_n is an $n \times 1$ vector of observations on the dependent spatial variable, $W_n Y_n$ denotes the spatially lagged dependent variable for a known weight matrix W_n, V_n is an $n \times 1$ vector of i.i.d. Gaussian errors with zero mean and variance σ^2, and ρ is the spatial AR parameter. Using the expansion (12), they derived the second-order bias and MSE of the MLE of ρ, up to the order $O\left(n^{-1}\right)$ and $O\left(n^{-2}\right)$, respectively, under both cases of known and unknown σ^2.

Mynbaev and Ullah (2008) derived the asymptotics of the OLS estimator for the purely AR spatial model in Eq. (50). They showed that under their assumptions, the OLS estimator is inconsistent, and the identification conditions used in the early literature on spatial econometrics for proving the consistency of QML and method of moment (MM) estimators do not hold. Consequently, the QML and MM estimators are not consistent either. They proposed a new two-step estimator based on the OLS estimator which improves over the OLS estimator.

6. CONCLUDING REMARKS

In this paper, we have reviewed Aman's contributions to econometrics. We focused on four areas to which he has contributed most, which are also of the authors' specializations. In common with many of Aman's students, we owe our interests in econometrics research to Aman. What attracted us to his approach is his deeply mathematically grounded general methodology and also meticulous and clever derivations of results. What propels Aman's thinking is his own view of the problem and its importance rather than the prevailing fashion; his approach is well thought out and worked out with depth and skill.

Aman is a gentle and understanding mentor and a great pedagogue. In a flash, he can present practically any area on econometrics in a logical and clear fashion. He once told Vicky that if he were woken from sleep and told to lecture on a particular topic, it would be no problem at all for him. He outlines the outstanding problems and proposes a research direction – it is all totally clear to him. He is very patient with the less quick thinkers and is a great guide.

Scientific genealogy is a fascinating if somewhat incestious subject. If one's students are offspring, one could easily have "grand-children" and sometimes they could be older than the parent; if co-authors are siblings, they could also be your "children" or even "grand-children." Aman has amassed an amazing family of econometricians who he has mentored and who have made substantial contributions to the progress in econometrics.

NOTES

1. As pointed out by Ullah (1990), when $\boldsymbol{\mu} = \mathbf{0}$, to apply the operator $\boldsymbol{d}$, one needs to first consider $\boldsymbol{\mu} \neq \mathbf{0}$ in deriving $h(\boldsymbol{d})$ and then substitute $\boldsymbol{\mu} = \mathbf{0}$ in the final result.

2. In Rilston et al. (1996), the moment condition was defined as a sample average, so were its derivatives. But even if without scaling, one can still apply the expansion (12) to derive the approximate moments. This is because, for example, $\boldsymbol{\xi}_{-1/2} = \mathcal{F}^{-1}\boldsymbol{\psi} = (\mathcal{F}/n)^{-1}(\boldsymbol{\psi}/n)$.

ACKNOWLEDGMENTS

We thank the co-editors for their invitation to write this survey paper to summarize Aman Ullah's most important contributions in the four areas of econometrics reviewed in this paper. Special thanks to Aman Ullah for his interest in our work and for sharing his thoughts on the writings. We also thank the organizers, sponsors, and participants of the Advances in Econometrics conference held at the Riverside Mission Inn on March 14–15, 2015. Su gratefully acknowledges the Singapore Ministry of Education for Academic Research Fund under grant number MOE2012-T2-2-021.

REFERENCES

Ai, C., & Chen, X. (2003). Efficient estimation of models with conditional moment restrictions containing unknown functions. *Econometrica*, *71*, 1795–1843.

Anatolyev, S. (2002). Conditional and unconditional correlatedness and heteroskedasticity. *Econometric Theory*, *18*, 820–821.

Anderson, T., & Rubin, H. (1949). Estimation of the parameters of a single equation in a complete system of stochastic equation. *Annals of Mathematical Statistics*, *20*, 46–63.

Appelbaum, E., & Ullah, A. (1984). An empirical test of risk aversion hypothesis. *Pakistan Journal of Applied Economics*, *3*, 57–64.

Appelbaum, E., & Ullah, A. (1997). Estimation of moments and production decision under uncertainty. *Review of Economics and Statistics*, *9*, 631–637.

Bao, Y. (2013). Finite sample bias of the QMLE in spatial autoregressive models. *Econometric Theory*, *29*, 68–88.

Bao, Y., & Ullah, A. (2004). Bias of a value-at-risk estimator. *Finance Research Letters*, *1*, 241–249.

Bao, Y., & Ullah, A. (2006). Moments of the estimated Sharpe ratio when the observations are not IID. *Finance Research Letters*, *3*, 49–56.

Bao, Y., & Ullah, A. (2007a). Finite sample properties of maximum likelihood estimator in spatial models. *Journal of Econometrics*, *137*, 396–413.

Bao, Y., & Ullah, A. (2007b). The second-order bias and mean squared error of estimators in time series models. *Journal of Econometrics*, *140*, 650–669.

Bao, Y., & Ullah, A. (2009a). On skewness and kurtosis of econometric estimators. *Econometrics Journal*, *12*, 232–247.

Bao, Y., & Ullah, A. (2009b). Higher-order bias and MSE of nonlinear estimators. *Pakistan Journal of Statistics*, *25*, 287–294.

Bao, Y., & Ullah, A. (2010). Expectation of quadratic forms in normal and nonnormal variables with applications. *Journal of Statistical Planning and Inference*, *140*, 1193–1205.

Bao, Y., Ullah, A., & Wang, Y. (2015). The distribution of the mean reversion estimator in the Ornstein-Uhlenbeck process. *Econometric Reviews*, forthcoming.

Bao, Y., Ullah, A., Wang, Y., & Yu, J. (2015). Bias in the estimation of mean reversion in continuous-time Lévy processes. *Economics Letters*, *134*, 16–19.

Bao, Y., Ullah, A., & Zhang, R. (2014). Moment approximation for least-squares estimator in first-order regression models with unit root and nonnormal errors. *Advances in Econometrics*, *33*, 65–92.

Basmann, R. (1961). Note on the exact finite sample frequency functions of generalized classical linear estimators in two leading overidentified cases. *Journal of the American Statistical Association*, *56*, 619–636.

Batra, R., & Ullah, A. (1974). Competitive firm and the theory of input demand under price uncertainty. *Journal of Political Economy*, *82*, 537–548.

Berg, M. D., Li, Q., & Ullah, A. (2000). Instrumental variable estimation of semiparametric dynamic panel data models: Monte Carlo results on several new and existing estimators. In B. H. Baltagi, T. B. Fomby, & R. C. Hill (Eds.), *Nonstationary panels, panel cointegration and dynamic panels* (pp. 297–315). Amsterdam: Elsevier Science Inc.

Bhattacharya, R. N., & Ghosh, J. K. (1978). On the validity of the formal Edgeworth expansion. *Annals of Statistics*, *6*, 434–451.

Bierens, H. J. (1987). Kernel estimators of regression functions. In T. F. Bewley (Ed.), *Advances in econometrics – Fifth world congress* (Vol. I, pp. 99–144). New York, NY: Cambridge University Press.

Breusch, T. S., & Pagan, A. R. (1980). The Lagrange multiplier test and its applications to model specification tests in econometrics. *Review of Economic Studies*, *47*, 239–253.

Carter, R. A. L., Srivastava, M. S., Srivastava, V. K., & Ullah, A. (1990). Unbiased estimation of the MSE matrix of Stein-rule estimators, confidence ellipsoids, and hypothesis testing. *Econometric Theory*, *6*, 63–74.

Chen, J., Gao, J., & Li, D. (2012). A new diagnostic test for cross-section uncorrelatedness in nonparametric panel data models. *Journal of Econometrics*, *71*, 71–85.

Cramér, H. (1946). *Mathematical methods of statistics*. Princeton, NJ: Princeton University Press.

Darolles, S., Fan, Y., Florens, J., & Renault, E. (2011). Nonparametric instrumental regression. *Econometrica*, *79*, 1541–1565.

Davis, A. W. (1976). Statistical distributions in univariate and multivariate Edgeworth populations. *Biometrika*, *63*, 661–670.

Dette, H. (1999). A consistent test for the functional form of a regression based on a difference of variance estimators. *Annals of Statistics*, *27*, 1012–1040.

Dungey, M., Long, X., Ullah, A., & Wang, Y. (2014). A semiparametric conditional duration model. *Economics Letters*, *124*, 362–366.

Engle, R. F. (2002). Dynamic conditional correlation – A dimple class of multivariate GARCH models. *Journal of Business & Economic Statistics*, *20*, 339–350.

Evans, G. B. A., & Savin, N. E. (1982). Conflict among the criteria revisited: The W, LR, and LM tests. *Econometrica*, *50*, 737–748.

Fan, J., & Gijbels, I. (1996). *Local polynomial modeling and its applications*. London: Chapman & Hall.

Fan, Y. (1994). Testing the goodness-of-fit of a parametric density function by kernel method. *Econometric Theory*, *10*, 316–356.

Fan, Y., & Li, Q. (1996). Consistent model specification tests: Omitted variables and semiparametric functional forms. *Econometrica*, *64*, 865–890.

Fan, Y., & Li, Q. (1999). Central limit theorem for degenerate U-Statistics of absolutely regular processes with applications to model specification testing. *Journal of Nonparametric Statistics*, *10*, 245–271.

Fan, Y., & Li, Q. (2002). A consistent model specification test based on the kernel sum of squares of residuals. *Econometric Reviews*, *21*, 337–352.

Fan, Y., & Ullah, A. (1999a). On goodness-of-fit tests for weakly dependent processes using kernel method. *Journal of Nonparametric Statistics*, *11*, 337–360.

Fan, Y., & Ullah, A. (1999b). Asymptotic normality of a combined regression estimator. *Journal of Multivariate Analysis*, *71*, 191–240.

Fisher, R. A. (1921). On the probable error of a coefficient of correlation deduced from a small sample. *Metron*, *1*, 3–32.

Fisher, R. A. (1922). The goodness of fit of regression formulae and the distribution of regression coefficients. *Journal of the Royal Statistical Society*, *85*, 597–612.

Florens, J.-P. (2003). Inverse problems and structural econometrics: The example of instrumental variables. In M. Dewatripont, L. P. Hansen, & S. J. Turnovsky (Eds.), *Advances in economics and econometrics: Theory and applications* (pp. 284–311). New York, NY: Cambridge University Press.

Gupta, Y. P., & Ullah, A. (1970). A note on the moments of the Wald's estimator. *Statistica Neerlandica*, *24*, 109–123.

Haavelmo, T. (1947). Methods of measuring the marginal propensity to consume. *Journal of the American Statistical Association*, *42*, 105–122.

Hall, P. (1984). Central limit theorem for integrated square error of multivariate nonparametric density estimators. *Journal of Multivariate Analysis*, *14*, 1–16.

Hall, P., & Horowitz, J. (2005). Nonparametric methods for inference in the presence of instrumental variables. *Annals of Statistics*, *33*, 2904–2929.

Henderson, D. J., Carroll, R. J., & Li, Q. (2008). Nonparametric estimation and testing of fixed effects panel data models. *Journal of Econometrics*, *144*, 257–275.

Henderson, D. J., & Ullah, A. (2005). A nonparametric random effects estimator. *Economics Letters*, *88*, 403–407.

Henderson, D. J., & Ullah, A. (2014). Nonparametric estimation in a one-way error component model: A Monte Carlo analysis. *Statistical Paradigms*, *14*, 213–237.

Hillier, G. H., Kinal, T. W., & Srivastava, V. K. (1984). On the moments of ordinary least squares and instrumental variables estimators in a general structural equation. *Econometrica*, *52*, 185–202.

Hoderlein, S., Su, L., White, H., & Yang, T. (2016). Testing for monotonicity in unobservables under unconfoundedness. *Journal of Econometrics*, forthcoming.

Hong, Y., & White, H. (1995). Consistent specification testing via nonparametric series regression. *Econometrica*, *63*, 1133–1159.

Hurwicz, L. (1950). Least square bias in time series. In T. Koopmans (Ed.), *Statistical inference in dynamic economic models* (pp. 365–383). New York, NY: Wiley.

Kadane, J. B. (1971). Comparison of k-class estimators when the disturbances are small. *Econometrica, 39*, 723–737.

Khanna, M., Mundra, K., & Ullah, A. (1999). Parametric and semi-parametric estimation of the effect of firm attributes on efficiency: The electricity generating industry in India. *Journal of International Trade & Economic Developments, 8*, 419–436.

Kumar, S., & Ullah, A. (2000). Semiparametric varying parameter panel data models: An application to estimation of speed of convergence. *Advances in Econometrics, 14*, 109–128.

Kundhi, G., & Rilstone, P. (2013). Edgeworth and saddlepoint expansions for nonlinear estimators. *Econometric Theory, 5*, 1057–1078.

Lee, T., & Ullah, A. (2001). Nonparametric bootstrap tests for neglected nonlinearity in time series regression models. *Journal of Nonparametric Statistics, 13*, 425–451.

Li, Q., Lu, X., & Ullah, A. (2003). Multivariate local polynomial regression for estimating average derivatives. *Journal of Nonparametric Statistics, 15*, 607–624.

Li, Q., & Stengos, T. (1996). Semiparametric estimation of partially linear panel data models. *Journal of Econometrics, 71*, 289–397.

Li, Q., & Ullah, A. (1998). Estimating partially linear panel data models with one-way error components. *Econometric Reviews, 17*, 145–166.

Lin, X., & Carroll, R. J. (2000). Nonparametric function estimation for clustered data when the predictor is measured without/with error. *Journal of the American Statistical Association, 95*, 520–534.

Lin, Z., Li, Q., & Sun, Y. (2014). A consistent nonparametric test of parametric regression functional form in fixed effects panel data models. *Journal of Econometrics, 178*, 167–179.

Linton, O. (1997). An asymptotic expansion in the GARCH(1,1) model. *Econometric Theory, 13*, 558–581.

Long, X., Su, L., & Ullah, A. (2011). Estimation and forecasting of dynamic conditional covariance: A semiparametric multivariate model. *Journal of Business Economics & Statistics, 29*, 109–125.

Martins-Filho, C., & Yao, F. (2009). Nonparametric regression estimation with general parametric error covariance. *Journal of Multivariate Analysis, 100*, 309–333.

Matzkin, R. (2003). Nonparametric estimation of nonadditive random functions. *Econometrica, 71*, 1339–1375.

McCullagh, P. (1987). *Tensor methods in statistics.* London: Chapman & Hall.

McMillan, J. A., Ullah, A., & Vinod, H. D. (1989). Estimation of the shape of the demand curve by nonparametric kernel methods. In B. Raj (Ed.), *Advances in econometrics and modelling* (pp. 85–92). Boston, MA: Kluwer Academic Publishers.

Mishra, S., Su, L., & Ullah, A. (2010). Semiparametric estimator of time series conditional variance. *Journal of Business Economics & Statistics, 28*, 256–274.

Mohanty, M., & Ullah, A. (2012a). Direct and indirect effects of happiness on wage: A simultaneous equations approach. *Journal of Socio-Economics, 41*, 143–152.

Mohanty, M., & Ullah, A. (2012b). Why does growing up in an intact family during childhood lead to higher earnings during adulthood in the United States? *American Journal of Economics and Sociology, 71*, 662–694.

Mynbaev, K. T., & Ullah, A. (2008). Asymptotic distribution of the OLS estimator for a purely autoregressive spatial model. *Journal of Multivariate Analysis*, 99, 245–277.

Nadaraya, E. (1964). On regression estimators. *Theory of Probability and Applications, 9*, 157–159.

Nagar, A. L. (1959). The bias and moment matrix of the general k-class estimators of the parameters in simultaneous equations. *Econometrica, 27*, 575–595.

Nagar, A. L., & Ullah, A. (1970). On Nagar's approximates to moments of the two stage least squares estimation. *Indian Economic Review, 5*, 69–80.

Nagar, A. L., & Ullah, A. (1973). Note on approximate skewness and kurtosis of the two-stage least squares estimator. *Indian Economic Review, 8*, 69–80.

Newey, W. K., & Powell, J. (1989). *Instrumental variable estimation of nonparametric models*. Working Paper. MIT.

Newey, W. K., & Powell, J. (2003). Instrumental variable estimation of nonparametric models. *Econometrica*, *71*, 1565–1578.

Newey, W. K., Powell, J., & Vella, F. (1999). Nonparametric estimation of triangular simultaneous equations models. *Econometrica*, *67*, 565–603.

Newey, W. K., & Smith, R. J. (2004). Higher order properties of GMM and generalized empirical likelihood estimators. *Econometrica*, *72*, 219–255.

Pagan, A., & Ullah, A. (1988). Econometric analysis of models involving risk terms. *Journal of Applied Econometrics*, 3, 87–105.

Pagan, A., & Ullah, A. (1999). *Nonparametric econometrics*. New York, NY: Cambridge University Press.

Pesaran, M. H., Ullah, A., & Yamagata, T. (2008). A bias-adjusted LM test of error cross-section independence. *Econometrics Journal*, *11*, 105–127.

Peters, T. A. (1989). The exact moments of OLS in dynamic regression models with non-normal errors. *Journal of Econometrics*, *40*, 279–305.

Phillips, P. C. B. (1980). Finite sample theory and the distribution of alternative estimators of the marginal propensity to consume. *Review of Economic Studies*, *47*, 183–224.

Phillips, P. C. B. (1983). Exact small sample theory in simultaneous equations models. In Z. Griliches & M. Intriligator (Eds.), *Handbook of econometrics* (Vol. 1, pp. 449–516). Amsterdam: North Holland.

Powell, J. L., Stock, J. H., & Stoker, T. M. (1989). Semiparametric estimation of index coefficients. *Econometrica*, *57*, 1403–1430.

Prakasa Rao, B. L. S. (1983). *Nonparametric functional estimation*. New York, NY: Academic Press.

Qian, W., & Ullah, A. (2008). Estimation and finite sample bias and MSE of FGLS estimator of paired data model. In S. Shalabh & C. Heumann (Eds.), *Recent advances in linear models and related areas* (pp. 59–78). Heidelberg: Physica-Verlag.

Racine, J., Su, L., & Ullah, A. (2014). *Handbook of applied nonparametric and semiparametric econometrics*. New York, NY: Oxford University Press.

Raj, B., & Ullah, A. (2012). *Econometrics: A varying coefficients approach*. Routledge: Routledge Revival. First published in 1981 by Croom Helm, UK.

Ratti, R., & Ullah, A. (1976). Uncertainty in production and the competitive firm. *Southern Economic Journal*, *42*, 703–710.

Richardson, D. H. (1968). The exact distribution of a structural estimator. *Journal of the American Statistical Association*, *63*, 1214–1226.

Rilstone, P., Srivastava, V. K., & Ullah, A. (1996). The second-order bias and mean squared error of nonlinear estimators. *Journal of Econometrics*, *75*, 369–395.

Rilstone, P., & Ullah, A. (1989). Nonparametric estimation of response coefficients. *Communications in Statistics – Theory and Methods*, *18*, 2615–2627.

Rilstone, P., & Ullah, A. (2002). Sampling bias in Heckman's sample selection estimator. In Y. P. Chaubey (Ed.), *Recent advances in statistical methods* (pp. 263–273). Hackensack, NJ: World Scientific.

Robinson, P. M. (1988). Root-N consistent semiparametric regression. *Econometrica*, *56*, 931–954.

Rothenberg, T. J. (1984). Approximating the distributions of econometric estimators and test statistics. In Z. Griliches & M. Intriligator (Eds.), *Handbook of econometrics* (Vol. 2, pp. 881–893). Amsterdam: North Holland.

Ruckstuhl, A. F., Welsh, A. H., & Carroll, R. J. (2000). Nonparametric function estimation of the relationship between two repeatedly measured variables. *Statistica Sinica*, *10*, 51–71.

Santos, A. (2012). Inference in nonparametric instrumental variables with partial identification. *Econometrica*, *80*, 213–275.

Sargan, J. (1974). The validity of Nagar's expansion for the moments of econometric estimators. *Econometrica*, *42*, 169–176.

Sargan, J. (1975). Gram-Charlier approximations applied to t ratios of k-class estimators. *Econometrica*, *43*, 326–346.

Singh, B., & Ullah, A. (1974). Estimation of seemingly unrelated regressions with random coefficients. *Journals of the American Statistical Association*, *69*, 191–195.

Smith, M. D. (1989). On the expectation of a ratio of quadratic forms in normal variables. *Journal of Multivariate Analysis*, *31*, 244–257.

Srinivasan, T. N. (1970). Approximations to finite sample moments of estimators whose exact sampling distributions are unknown. *Econometrica*, *38*, 533–541.

Srivastava, A. K., Srivastava, V. K., & Ullah, A. (1995). The coefficient of determination and its adjusted version in linear regression models. *Econometric Reviews*, *14*, 229–240.

Srivastava, V. K., & Ullah, A. (1995). Efficiency properties of some estimators in pooling time-series and cross-section data. *Journal of Quantitative Economics*, *11*, 63–76.

Su, L., & Lu, X. (2013). Nonparametric dynamic panel data models: Kernel estimation and specification testing. *Journal of Econometrics*, *176*, 112–133.

Su, L., Murtazashvili, I., & Ullah, A. (2013). Local linear GMM estimation of functional coefficient IV models with application to the estimation of rate of return to schooling. *Journal of Business & Economic Statistics*, *31*, 184–207.

Su, L., Tu, Y., & Ullah, A. (2015). Testing additive separability of error term in nonparametric structural models. *Econometric Reviews*, *34*, 1056–1087.

Su, L., & Ullah, A. (2006). Profile likelihood estimation of partially linear panel data models with fixed effects. *Economics Letters*, *92*, 75–81.

Su, L., & Ullah, A. (2007). More efficient estimation of nonparametric panel data models with random effects. *Economics Letters*, *96*, 375–380.

Su, L., & Ullah, A. (2008). Local polynomial estimation of nonparametric simultaneous equations models. *Journal of Econometrics*, *144*, 193–218.

Su, L., & Ullah, A. (2009). Testing conditional uncorrelatedness. *Journal of Business & Economic Statistics*, *27*, 18–29.

Su, L., & Ullah, A. (2011). Nonparametric and semiparametric panel econometric models: Estimation and testing. In A. Ullah & D. E. A. Giles (Eds.), *Handbook of empirical economics and finance* (pp. 455–497). New York, NY: Taylor & Francis Group.

Su, L., & Ullah, A. (2013). A nonparametric goodness-of-fit-based test for conditional heteroskedasticity. *Econometric Theory*, *29*, 187–212.

Su, L., Ullah, A., & Wang, Y. (2013). Nonparametric regression estimation with general parametric error covariance: A more efficient two-step estimator. *Empirical Economics*, *45*, 1009–1024.

Sun, Y., Carroll, R. J., & Li, D. (2009). Semiparametric estimation of fixed effects panel data varying coefficient models. *Advances in Econometrics*, *25*, 101–130.

Takada, H., Ullah, A., & Chen, Y.-M. (1995). Estimation of the seemingly unrelated regression model when the error covariance matrix is singular. *Journal of Applied Statistics*, *22*, 517–530.

Ullah, A. (1974). On the sampling distribution of improved estimators for coefficients in linear regression. *Journal of Econometrics*, *2*, 143–150.

Ullah, A. (1980). The exact, large-sample and small-disturbance conditions of dominance of biased estimators in linear models. *Economics Letters*, *6*, 339–344.

Ullah, A. (1982). The approximate distribution of the Stein-rule estimator. *Economics Letters*, *10*, 305–308.

Ullah, A. (1985). Specification analysis of econometric models. *Journal of Quantitative Economics, 1*, 187–210.
Ullah, A. (1988a). Nonparametric estimation and hypothesis testing in econometric models. *Empirical Economics, 13*, 223–249.
Ullah, A. (1988b). Nonparametric estimation of econometric functionals. *Canadian Journal of Economics, 21*, 625–658.
Ullah, A. (1988c). *Semi parametric and nonparametric econometrics.* Heidelberg: Physica-Verlag.
Ullah, A. (1990). Finite sample econometrics: A unified approach. In R. A. L. Carter, J. Dutta, & A. Ullah (Eds.), *Contributions to econometric theory and application* (pp. 242–292). New York, NY: Springer-Verlag.
Ullah, A., (2004). *Finite Sample Econometrics*. New York, NY: Oxford University Press.
Ullah, A., & Breunig, R. (1995). On the bias of the standard errors of the LS residual and the regression coefficients under normal and non-normal errors. *Econometric Theory, 13*, 896–897.
Ullah, A., Carter, R. A. L., & Srivastava, V. K. (1984). The sample distribution of shrinkage estimators and their F-ratios in regression model. *Journal of Econometrics, 25*, 109–122.
Ullah, A., & Huang, X. (2006). Finite sample properties of FGLS estimator for random-effects model under non-normality. In B. H. Baltagi (Ed.), *Panel data econometrics: Theoretical contributions and empirical applications* (pp. 67–89). Amsterdam: Elsevier Science.
Ullah, A., & Maasoumi, E. (1986). Moments of OLS estimators in an autoregressive moving average model with explanatory variables. *Economics Letters, 21*, 265–269.
Ullah, A., & Mundra, K. (2002). Semiparametric panel data estimation: An application to immigrants' homelink effect on U.S. producer trade flows. In A. Ullah, A. Wan, & A. Chaturvedi (Eds.), *Handbook of applied econometrics and statistical inference* (pp. 591–608). New York, NY: Marcel Dekker.
Ullah, A., & Nagar, A. L. (1974). The exact mean of the two stage least squares estimator of the structural parameters in the equation having three endogenous variables. *Econometrica, 42*, 749–758.
Ullah, A., & Phillips, P. C. B. (1986). Distribution of the F-ratio. *Econometric Theory, 2*, 449–452.
Ullah, A., & Racine, J. (1992). Smooth improved estimators of econometric parameters. In W. E. Griffith, H. Lütkepohl, & M. E. Bock (Eds.), *Readings in econometric theory and practice: A volume in honor of George Judge* (pp. 197–213). New York, NY: North Holland.
Ullah, A., & Roy, N. (1998). Nonparametric and semiparametric econometrics of panel data. In A. Ullah & D. E. A. Giles (Eds.), *Handbook of applied economic statistics* (pp. 579–604). New York, NY: Marcel Dekker.
Ullah, A., & Srivastava, V. K. (1994). Moments of the ratio of quadratic forms in non-normal variables with econometric examples. *Journal of Econometrics, 62*, 129–141.
Ullah, A., Srivastava, V. K., & Chandra, R. (1983). Properties of shrinkage estimators when the disturbances are not normal. *Journal of Econometrics, 21*, 389–402.
Ullah, A., Srivastava, V. K., & Roy, N. (1995). Moments of the function of non-normal random vector with applications to econometric estimators and test statistics. *Econometric Reviews, 14*, 459–471.
Ullah, A., & Ullah, S. (1978). Double k-class estimators of coefficients in linear regression. *Econometrica, 46*, 705–722.
Ullah, A., Vinod, H. D., & Kadiyala, R. K. (1981). A family of improved shrinkage factors for the ordinary ridge estimators. *Economic Studies Quarterly, 32*, 164–175.
Ullah, A., & Zinde-Walsh, V. (1984). On the robustness of LM, LR and W Tests in regression models. *Econometrica, 52*, 1055–1066.
Ullah, A., & Zinde-Walsh, V. (1985). Estimation and testing in a regression model with spherically symmetric errors. *Economics Letters, 2*, 127–132.

Ullah, A., & Zinde-Walsh, V. (1988). On robustness of tests in linear models with elliptical error distribution. In I. MacNeill & G. Umphrey (Eds.), *The times series and econometric modelling* (pp. 235–251). Holland: Reidell Press.

Vinod, H. D., & Ullah, A. (1981). *Recent advances in regression methods*. New York, NY: Marcel Dekkar.

Vinod, H. D., Ullah, A., & Kadiyala, K. (1981). Evaluation of the mean squared error of certain generalized ridge estimators using confluent hypergeometric functions. *Sankhya: The Indian Journal of Statistics, Series B*, *43*, 1–14.

Watson, G. S. (1964). Smooth regression analysis. *Sankhya: The Indian Journal of Statistics, Series A*, *26*, 175–184.

Zellner, A. (1962). An efficient estimation of seemingly unrelated regression equations and tests of aggregation bias. *Journals of the American Statistical Association*, *57*, 500–509.

Zheng, J. X. (1996). A consistent test of functional form via nonparametric estimation techniques. *Journal of Econometrics*, *75*, 263–289.

PART II
PANEL DATA MODELS

SEMIPARAMETRIC ESTIMATION OF PARTIALLY LINEAR VARYING COEFFICIENT PANEL DATA MODELS

Yonghong An[a], Cheng Hsiao[b,c] and Dong Li[d]

[a] *Department of Economics, Texas A&M University, College Station, TX, USA*

[b] *Department of Economics, University of Southern California, Los Angeles, CA, USA*

[c] *Wang Yanan Institute for Studies in Economics (WISE), Xiamen University, Xiamen, China*

[d] *School of Economic, Political and Policy Sciences, The University of Texas at Dallas, Richardson, TX, USA*

ABSTRACT

This paper considers the problem of estimating a partially linear varying coefficient fixed effects panel data model. Using the series method, we establish the root N normality for the estimator of the parametric component; and we show that the unknown function can be consistently estimated at the standard nonparametric rate. Furthermore, we extend the model to allow endogeneity in the parametric component and establish the asymptotic properties of the semiparametric instrumental variable estimators.

Keywords: Partially linear; varying coefficient; semiparametric; panel data

JEL classifications: C14; C23

Essays in Honor of Aman Ullah
Advances in Econometrics, Volume 36, 47–65

ISSN: 0731-9053/doi:10.1108/S0731-905320160000036011

1. INTRODUCTION

Panel data models become very popular in recent years. While most of the empirical applications focus on parametric models, there have been some recent attempts to study non/semiparametric panel data models. A fully nonparametric model often suffers from the "curse of dimensionality." Semi-parametric models, while maintaining flexible functional forms, are less likely to suffer from the curse of dimensionality because some variables enter the model parametrically.

In this paper we will consider a partially linear varying coefficient panel data model with fixed effects. We use the standard approach of taking the first difference to eliminate the fixed effects similar to Arellano and Bond (1991). This results in a semiparametric additive model with the restriction that the two additive functions have the same functional form. Series estimation method, instead of the kernel method, is used because of its advantages. The series method can generally keep the additivity property and it is easier to impose structure/restrictions (see Dechevsky & Penez, 1997). It is also computationally convenient because the results can be summarized by a few coefficients. Of course the series method has its disadvantages, such as potentially erroneous extrapolation to areas with few data points.

Recently, semiparametric estimation of additive models and additive partially linear models has received much attention, see Linton and Nielson (1995), Newey (1994), Fan and Li (1996), Fan, Härdle, and Mammen (1998), Sperlich, Tjøstheim, and Yang (2002), and Li (2000), to mention a few.

The additive regression model partly avoids the "curse of dimensionality" problem which circumvents the estimation of a fully nonparametric regression model. Linton and Nielsen (1995), Newey (1994), and Tjøstheim and Auestad (1994) proposed to estimate additive models using the kernel marginal integration method. Li (2000), on the other hand, used the series method to estimate an additive partially linear model.

Consider the following example of the Cobb–Douglas production function. Suppose that we have three inputs – land, capital, and labor – in a production process. Another input, Research & Development (R&D), may affect the productivity of capital and labor, but not that of land. In this case, capital and labor enter the model with coefficients being nonparametric functions of R&D, while ln *Land* enters the model as a parametric linear component: $\ln y = \beta_0 + \beta_1(R\&D) \cdot \ln K + \beta_2(R\&D) \cdot \ln L + \beta_3 \ln Land$. Li, Huang, Li, and Fu (2002) considered a cross-sectional version of the model without the linear component using the nonparametric kernel method. This paper extends the model to a partially linear varying coefficient panel data model with fixed effects. The complication is that the kernel method is not desirable in this case (we will explain more on this point later in the paper). Thus, we propose to use the series method to estimate the model and establish the asymptotic properties of the estimators in this paper. We will establish the root N normality for the estimator of the parametric component. We will also show that the unknown function can be consistently estimated at the standard nonparametric rate. Furthermore, we extend the model to allow endogeneity in the parametric component and establish the semiparametric instrumental variable asymptotic properties of the estimators.

Baltagi and Li (2002) considered a partially linear panel data model using the series method. Henderson, Carroll, and Li (2008) considered a fully nonparametric panel data model using the kernel method. Zhou and Liang (2009) and Cai and Xiong (2012) both considered a (cross-sectional) model without the panel structure or the fixed effect. Cai and Li (2008) considered a panel data model (without fixed effects) using local linear fitting. Huang, Wu, and Zhou (2004) studied the varying coefficient panel data model without the parametric component or the fixed effects. Sun, Carroll, and Li (2010) considered a fixed effects varying coefficient panel data model (without the parametric linear component) using local linear regressions and kernel-based weights. Sun et al. (2010) removed the fixed effects through the LSDV approach and can be problematic when N is large. This paper considers a partially linear varying coefficient panel data model with fixed effects. Our model can nest most of these models except that in Henderson et al. (2008) (the latter is a fully nonparametric model). The current paper can be considered either a complement or an extension to Cai and Li (2008), Zhou and Liang (2009), and Cai and Xiong (2012). Su and Lu (2013) considered a nonparametric dynamic panel data model using the kernel estimation based on a Fredholm integral equation of the second kind. Qian and Wang (2012) studied semiparametric panel data models using marginal integration instead. Other related research include Chen, Gao, and Li (2012), Yao and Zhang (2015), and Su and Ullah (2006). Baltagi (2008) and Su and Ullah (2011) and Sun, Zhang, and Li (2015) provided excellent reviews of recent developments in nonparametric and semiparametric panel data models.

This paper is organized as follows. We will present the model in Section 2. The main results, including the endogeneity case, are reported in Section 3. Section 4 concludes the paper.

2. THE MODEL

Consider the following semiparametric partially linear varying coefficient panel data model:

$$y_{it} = x_{it}'\gamma + z_{it}'\beta(w_{it}) + u_{it}, \quad i = 1, \ldots, N; \ \ t = 1, \ldots, T, \tag{1}$$

where x_{it} is a $q \times 1$ vector of random variables, γ is a $q \times 1$ vector of unknown parameters, z_{it} is of dimension $d \times 1$, $w_{it} = (w_{it,1}, \ldots, w_{it,r})$ is of dimension $r \times 1$, and $\beta(\cdot)=(\beta_1(\cdot),\ldots,\beta_d(\cdot))'$ is a $d \times 1$ vector of unknown varying coefficient functions, $u_{it}=\mu_i+\nu_{it}$ is the one-way error component disturbance satisfying $E(\nu_{it}|w_{it},x_{it},z_{it})=0.$[1] μ_i's are fixed effects, ν_{it} are assumed to be i.i.d. $(0,\sigma_\nu^2)$.

The asymptotic theory in this paper assumes a finite value of T while letting the number of individuals N approach infinity. This is typical in micropanel data models.

First differencing Eq. (1) to eliminate the fixed effects, we obtain

$$y_{it}-y_{i,t-1}=(x'_{it}-x'_{i,t-1})\gamma+(z'_{it}\beta(w_{it})-z'_{i,t-1}\beta(w_{i,t-1}))+\nu_{it}-\nu_{i,t-1}. \quad (2)$$

We will not use the kernel method to estimate the above model for the following two reasons. The kernel method suffers from the "curse of dimensionality" because both z_{it} and $z_{i,t-1}$ enter the model nonparametrically – any non-iterative kernel estimation methods (e.g., Li & Stengos, 1996) would double the dimensions of the nonparametric component, the second term on the right-hand side. Also, the non-iterative kernel estimation method generally cannot recover the unknown function $\beta(\cdot)$ because it ignores the additive structure in $z'_{it}\beta(w_{it})-z'_{i,t-1}\beta(w_{i,t-1})$. Su and Lu (2013), and Rodriguez-Poo and Soberon (2014), however, proposed a locally linear kernel estimator after a Taylor expansion. They are able to recover the unknown function at the cost that the estimator has a slower convergence rate. Then they try to recover the convergence rate by using some backfitting algorithms.

We will propose the series estimation method instead as a complementary approach to the kernel method. We approximate the varying coefficient function $\beta_l(w)$ by a linear combination of k_l base functions:

$$p_l^{k_l}(w)'\alpha_l^{k_l} = [p_{l1}(w),\ldots,p_{lk_l}(w)]\begin{bmatrix}\alpha_{l1}\\ \vdots \\ \alpha_{lk_l}\end{bmatrix}, \quad (3)$$

where $p_l^{k_l}(w)=[p_{l1}(w),\ldots,p_{lk_l}(w)]'$ is a $k_l \times 1$ vector of base functions and $\alpha_l^{k_l}=(\alpha_{l1},\ldots,\alpha_{lk_l})'$ is a $k_l \times 1$ vector of unknown parameters. The approximation functions $p_l^{k_l}(w)$ have the property that, as k_l grows, there is a linear combination of $p_l^{k_l}(w)$ that can approximate any smooth function $\beta_l(w)$ arbitrarily well in the sense that the approximation mean-square error can be arbitrarily small. Examples of base functions include B-splines and sieve bases. Power series are generally not desirable because they are too sensitive to outliers.

Define the $K \times 1$ matrices $p^K(w_{it})=(p_1^{k_1}(w_{it})',\ldots,p_d^{k_d}(w_{it})')'$ and $\alpha=(\alpha_1^{k_1\prime},\ldots,\alpha_d^{k_d\prime})'$, where $K=\sum_{l=1}^d k_l$. Thus, we use a linear combination of

K functions, $p^K(w_{it})'\alpha$, to approximate $\beta(w_{it})$:

$$p^K(w_{it})\alpha = \sum_{j=1}^{d} p_j^{k_j}(w_{it})'\alpha_j^{k_j}. \tag{4}$$

Similarly, we can use $p^K(w_{i,t-1})'\alpha$ to approximate $\beta(w_{i,t-1})$.

Hence, we can rewrite Eq. (2) as:

$$y_{it} - y_{i,t-1} = (x'_{it} - x'_{i,t-1})\gamma + (z'_{it}p^K(w_{it}) - z'_{i,t-1}p^K(w_{i,t-1}))'\alpha + \text{error}_{it}, \tag{5}$$

where $\text{error}_{it} = (z'_{it}\beta(w_{it}) - z'_{i,t-1}\beta(w_{i,t-1})) - (z'_{it}p^K(w_{it}) - z'_{i,t-1}p^K(w_{i,t-1}))'\alpha + \nu_{it} - \nu_{i,t-1}$.

Equation (2) can be written in matrix form as

$$Y = X\gamma + G + \nu - \nu_{-1}, \tag{6}$$

where

$$Y = \begin{bmatrix} \vdots \\ y_{it} - y_{i,t-1} \\ \vdots \end{bmatrix}, \quad X = \begin{bmatrix} \vdots \\ x_{it} - x_{i,t-1} \\ \vdots \end{bmatrix},$$
$$G = \begin{bmatrix} \vdots \\ z'_{it}\beta(w_{it}) - z'_{i,t-1}\beta(w_{i,t-1}) \\ \vdots \end{bmatrix}, \tag{7}$$

and a typical element of $\nu - \nu_{-1}$ is $\nu_{it} - \nu_{i,t-1}$.

Equation (5) can be similarly written as

$$Y = X\gamma + P\alpha + \text{Error}, \tag{8}$$

where

$$P = \begin{bmatrix} \vdots \\ z'_{it}p^K(w_{it}) - z'_{i,t-1}p^K(w_{i,t-1}) \\ \vdots \end{bmatrix}. \tag{9}$$

Let $\hat{\gamma}$ and $\hat{\alpha}$ be the least-square estimators from Eq. (8). $\beta_l(w)$ can be approximated by $\hat{\beta}_l(w) = p_l^{k_l}(w)'\hat{\alpha}_l^{k_l}$, $l = 1, \ldots, d$. We will establish the $\sqrt{N}$-normality for $\hat{\gamma}$, the parameter in the parametric component, and the rate of convergence for $\hat{\beta}_l(w)$, the varying coefficient in the nonparametric component. While the series method proposed in this paper can reserve the additive structure of the first differenced nonparametric component to avoid the "curse of dimensionality" suffered by the kernel method, we cannot obtain the asymptotic normality for the nonparametric component that usually can be obtained using the kernel method.[2]

3. MAIN RESULTS

We will first introduce some definitions and assumptions.

Definition 1. *A function $\xi(z_{it}, z_{i,t-1}; w_{it}, w_{i,t-1})$ is said to belong to an additive class of functions $\mathcal{G}$ ($\xi \in \mathcal{G}$) if $\xi(z_{it}, z_{i,t-1}; w_{it}, w_{i,t-1}) = z_{it}'\beta(w_{it}) - z_{i,t-1}'\beta(w_{i,t-1})$, $\beta(\cdot)$ is twice differentiable in the interior of its support $\mathcal{S}$, which is a compact subset of $\mathbb{R}^r$, and $E[\beta^2(w)] < \infty$.*

For any scalar or vector function $R(z, w)$, we use the notation of $E_{\mathcal{G}}(R(z, w))$ to denote the projection of $R(z, w)$ onto the additive functional space $\mathcal{G}$ (under the L_2-norm). That is, $E_{\mathcal{G}}(R(z, w))$ is an element that belongs to $\mathcal{G}$, which has an additive structure, and it is the closest function to $R(z, w)$ among all the functions in $\mathcal{G}$. More specifically, we have

$$
\begin{aligned}
&E\{[R(z_{it}, w_{it}) - E_{\mathcal{G}}(R(z_{it}, w_{it}))][R(z_{it}, w_{it}) - E_{\mathcal{G}}(R(z_{it}, w_{it}))]'\} \\
&\quad = \inf_{\xi \in \mathcal{G}} E\{[R(z_{it}, w_{it}) - \xi(z_{it}, w_{it})][R(z_{it}, w_{it}) - \xi(z_{it}, w_{it})]'\}, \qquad (10)
\end{aligned}
$$

where the infimum is in the sense that

$$
\begin{aligned}
&E\{[R(z_{it}, w_{it}) - E_{\mathcal{G}}(R(z_{it}, w_{it}))][R(z_{it}, w_{it}) - E_{\mathcal{G}}(R(z_{it}, w_{it}))]'\} \\
&\quad \leq E\{[R(z_{it}, w_{it}) - \xi(z_{it}, w_{it})][R(z_{it}, w_{it}) - \xi(z_{it}, w_{it})]'\}, \qquad (11)
\end{aligned}
$$

for all $\xi \in \mathcal{G}$, where for square matrices A and B, $A \leq B$ means that $A - B$ is negative semidefinite.

Define $\theta(z, w) = E(X|Z = z, W = w)$. We will use $h(z, w)$ to denote the projection of $\theta(z, w)$ onto $\mathcal{G}$, that is, $h(z, w) = E_{\mathcal{G}}(\theta(z, w))$. Note that the series method proposed in this paper can deal with the case where z_{it} and $z_{i,t-1}$ have overlapping variables. For example, z_{it} can have current and lagged exogenous variables.

Assumption 1.

(i) We assume that $(Y_{it}, X_{it}, Z_{it}, W_{it})$'s are independent across individuals, that is, (Y_i, X_i, Z_i, W_{it}) are independent and identically distributed as (Y_1, X_1, Z_1, W_1), where $Y_i = (Y_{i1}, \ldots, Y_{iT})'$, X_i, W_i, and Z_i are similarly

defined; (ii) The support of (X_1, Z_1, W_1) *is a compact subset of* $\mathbb{R}^{q+r+d}$*; (iii)* $\theta(z,w)$ *and* $Var(Y_1|X_1 = x, Z_1 = z, W_1 = w)$ *are both bounded functions on the support of* (X_1, Z_1, W_1)*.*

Assumption 2.
(i) For every K, there is a nonsingular matrix B such that for $P^K(w) = B\,p^k(w)$*: the smallest eigenvalue of* $E[P^K(W_{it})P^K(W_{it})']$ *is bounded away from zero uniformly in K; (ii) There is a sequence of constants* $\zeta_0(K)$ *satisfying* $\sup \| P^K(w) \| \le \zeta_0(K)$ *and* $K = K(N)$ *such that* $(\zeta_0(K))^2 K/N \to 0$ *as* $N \to \infty$*.*

Assumption 3.
(i) There exist some $\delta(>0)$, $\alpha_\beta = \alpha_\beta(K)$, $\sup |z'\beta(w) - P^K(w)\alpha_\beta| = O(K^{-\delta})$ *as* $K \to \infty$*; (ii)* $\sqrt{N}K^{-\delta} \to 0$ *and* $N \to \infty$*.*

Assumption 1 is quite standard in the additive models so that we can use laws of large numbers and the central limit theorems to examine the asymptotic properties of our proposed estimators. Assumption 2 ensures that $P'P$ is asymptotically nonsingular. Newey (1997) gave some primitive conditions for power series and splines such that Assumptions 2 and 3 hold. Assumption 3 is similar to the counterpart assumptions in the kernel method. When $N \to \infty$, we want $K \to \infty$ so that the bias would converge to zero. But we want K to converge to ∞ slower so that the variance term would converge to zero as well.

Define $M = P(P'P)^- P'$, where $(A)^-$ denotes any symmetric generalized inverse of A. Note that $P'P$ is nonsingular with probability one under the assumptions given in the paper. Define $\tilde{A} = MA$. Premultiplying Eq. (6) by M yields

$$\tilde{Y} = \tilde{X}\gamma + \tilde{G} + \tilde{u}. \tag{12}$$

Subtracting Eq. (12) from Eq. (6) leads to

$$Y - \tilde{Y} = (X - \tilde{X})\gamma + (G - \tilde{G}) + (u - \tilde{u}). \tag{13}$$

We estimate γ by least-squares regression of $Y - \tilde{Y}$ on $X - \tilde{X}$:

$$\hat{\gamma} = [(X - \tilde{X})'(X - \tilde{X})]^-(X - \tilde{X})'(Y - \tilde{Y}). \tag{14}$$

Plug Eq. (13) into Eq. (14), we have

$$\begin{aligned}\hat{\gamma} &= [(X - \tilde{X})'(X - \tilde{X})]^-(X - \tilde{X})'(Y - \tilde{Y}) \\ &= \gamma + [(X - \tilde{X})'(X - \tilde{X})]^-(X - \tilde{X})'(G - \tilde{G} + U - \tilde{U}).\end{aligned} \tag{15}$$

$\beta(w)$ is estimated by $\hat{\beta}(w) = p^K(w)'\hat{\alpha}$ where $\hat{\alpha}$ is given by

$$\hat{\alpha} = (P'P)^{-}P'(Y - X\hat{\gamma}). \tag{16}$$

The intuition is straightforward: we first remove the nonparametric component by projecting and differencing; obtain the coefficients in the parametric component; move the estimated parametric component to the left-hand side (since it has a root-N rate); estimate the nonparametric component using the series method.

Next, we establish the asymptotic properties of the proposed estimators $\hat{\gamma}$ and $\hat{\beta}(\cdot)$.

Theorem 1. *Define* $\epsilon_{it} = X_{it} - h(Z_{it}, W_{it})$, *where* $h(Z_{it}, W_{it}) = E_{\mathcal{G}}(\theta(Z_{it}, W_{it}))$ *with* $\theta(Z_{it}, W_{it}) = E(X_{it}|Z_{it}, W_{it})$ *are defined above. Assume that* $\Phi \stackrel{def}{=} \frac{1}{T}\sum_{t=1}^{T} E(\epsilon_{it}\epsilon_{it}')$ *is positive definite, then we have (i)* $\sqrt{N}(\hat{\gamma} - \gamma) \to N(0, \Sigma)$ *in distribution, where* $\Sigma = \Phi^{-1}\Omega\Phi^{-1}$, $\Omega = \frac{1}{T}\sum_t E[\sigma_u^2(X_{it}, Z_{it}, W_{it})\epsilon_{it}\epsilon_{it}']$ *and* $\sigma_u^2(X_{it}, Z_{it}, W_{it}) = E(U_{it}^2|X_{it} = x, Z_{it} = z, W_{it} = w)$; *(ii) A consistent estimator of* Σ *is given by* $\hat{\Sigma} = \hat{\Phi}^{-1}\hat{\Omega}\hat{\Phi}^{-1}$, *where* $\hat{\Phi} = (NT)^{-1}\sum_i\sum_t(X_{it} - \tilde{X}_{it})(X_{it} - \tilde{X}_{it})'$, $\hat{\Omega} = (NT)^{-1}\sum_i\sum_t \hat{U}_{it}^2(X_{it} - \tilde{X}_{it})(X_{it} - \tilde{X}_{it})'$, $\hat{U}_{it} = Y_{it} - X_{it}'\hat{\gamma} - Z_{it}\hat{\beta}(W_{it})$.

The proof is given in the appendix.

Theorem 1 establishes the $\sqrt{N}$-consistency and asymptotic normality of $\hat{\gamma}$. The next theorem establishes the consistency for the nonparametric component estimator.

Theorem 2. *Under Assumptions 1–3, we have*

(i) $\sup_{w\in\mathcal{S}}\left|\hat{\beta}(w) - \beta(w)\right| = O_p(\zeta_0(K))(\sqrt{K}/\sqrt{N} + K^{-\delta})$;

(ii) $N^{-1}(\hat{\beta}(w) - \beta(w))^2 = O_p(K/N + K^{-2\delta})$;

(iii) $\int(\hat{\beta}(w) - \beta(w))^2 dF(w) = O_p(K/N + K^{-2\delta})$, *where* $F(.)$ *is the cumulative distribution function of* W.

The first two theorems are based on the assumption that X is exogenous. In econometric applications, X may include endogenous variables. For example, a lagged-dependent variable or other endogenous variables may be part of X. The estimators proposed in this paper can be extended to allow this possibility. Note that we only allow endogeneity in the parametric part, not the nonparametric part. Ai and Chen (2003) proposed an estimator based on moment conditions in a partially linear model (without fixed effects) in which there is endogeneity in the nonparametric component. However, we assume no endogeneity in the nonparametric component in this paper.

Now instead of using the OLS-type estimator as given in Eq. (14), we use an instrumental variable (IV) semiparametric estimation method. We assume that there exists a $q \times 1$ vector instrument variables Q_{it} that identifies the model, such that $E(v_{it} - v_{i,t-1}|Q_{it}) = 0$ and $Cov(Q_{it}, X_{it}) \neq 0$. Hence, we can estimate γ by the following IV method:

$$\begin{aligned}\hat{\gamma}_{IV} &= [(Q - \tilde{Q})'(X - \tilde{X})]^{-}(Q - \tilde{Q})'(Y - \tilde{Y}) \\ &= \gamma + [(Q - \tilde{Q})'(X - \tilde{X})]^{-}(Q - \tilde{Q})'[(G - \tilde{G}) + (U - \tilde{U})]. \qquad (17)\end{aligned}$$

$\beta(w)$ is estimated by $\hat{\beta}(w)_{IV} = p^K(w)'\hat{\alpha}_{IV}$ where $\hat{\alpha}_{IV}$ is given by

$$\hat{\alpha}_{IV} = (P'P)^{-}P'(Y - X\hat{\gamma}_{IV}). \qquad (18)$$

We have the following theorem for the IV estimators:

Theorem 3. *Define* $\epsilon_{it} = Q_{it} - E_{\mathcal{G}}(Q_{it})$, $\tau_{it} = X_{it} - E_{\mathcal{G}}(X_{it})$, *and assume that* $\Psi \stackrel{def}{=} \frac{1}{T}\sum_{t=1}^{T} E(\epsilon_{it}\tau_{it}')$ *is positive definite, we have (i)* $\sqrt{N}(\hat{\gamma}_{IV} - \gamma) \to N(0, \Upsilon)$ *in distribution, where* $\Upsilon = \Psi^{-1}\Lambda\Psi^{-1}$, $\Lambda = \frac{1}{T}\sum_t E[\sigma_u^2(Z_{it})\epsilon_{it}\epsilon_{it}']$ *and* $\sigma_u^2(Z_{it}) = E(U_{it}^2|Z_{it} = z)$; *(ii) A consistent estimator of* Υ *is given by* $\hat{\Upsilon} = \hat{\Psi}^{-1}\hat{\Lambda}\hat{\Psi}^{-1}$, *where* $\hat{\Psi} = (NT)^{-1}\sum_i\sum_t (W_{it} - \tilde{W}_{it})(X_{it} - \tilde{X}_{it})'$, $\hat{\Lambda} = (NT)^{-1}\sum_i\sum_t \hat{U}_{it}^2(Q_{it} - \tilde{Q}_{it})(Q_{it} - \tilde{Q}_{it})'$, *and* $\hat{U}_{it} = Y_{it} - X_{it}\hat{\gamma}_{IV} - Z_{it}'\hat{\beta}(W_{it})$.

The proof of Theorem 3 is similar to the proof of Theorem 1, a sketchy proof is given in the appendix.

Once we have established the asymptotic normality of $\hat{\gamma}_{IV}$, the consistency of the nonparametric component can be established, similar to the results in Theorem 2.

In practice one has to choose K, the smoothing parameter in the series method. This is very much like choosing the bandwidth parameter in the kernel method. Some popular methods to choose K include the Mallows' C_L or C_p method, the generalized cross-validation method, and the leave-one-out cross-validation method. Li (1987) showed that the three methods are asymptotically equivalent.

4. CONCLUSION

In this paper, we consider a partially linear varying coefficient panel data model with fixed effects. Using the series method, we establish the root N normality result for the estimator of the parametric component, and we show that the unknown function can be consistently estimated at the standard nonparametric rate.

The asymptotic theory depends on N being large while T is fixed. We also extend the model to allow endogeneity in the parametric component. To further extend the results to allow endogeneity in both the parametric and the nonparametric components along the lines of Ai and Chen (2003) is left for a future project.

One drawback of the first difference approach is the efficiency loss due to the serial correlation introduced by the first difference (Arellano and Bond, 1991). Efficiency loss may also come from heteroscedasticity. While it is possible to take the particular error component structure into account by applying GMM or GLS types of estimation, the derivation can be tedious and will be left for future research.

NOTES

1. We will allow endogeneity (such as lag-dependent variable) in the regression later in this paper.
2. We thank an anonymous referee for raising this point.

ACKNOWLEDGMENTS

The authors thank the editors and two anonymous referees for helpful comments. Hsiao acknowledges partial research support by China NSF Grant No. #71131008. Any remaining errors are our own.

REFERENCES

Arellano, M., & Bond, S. (1991). Some tests of specification for panel data: Monte Carlo evidence and an application to employment equations. *Review of Economic Studies*, *58*, 277–297.

Ai, C., & Chen, X. (2003). Efficient estimation of models with conditional moment restrictions containing unknown functions. *Econometrica*, *71*, 1795–1843.

Baltagi, B. H. (2008). *Econometric analysis of panel data* (4th ed.). Chichester: Wiley.

Baltagi, B. H., & Li, D. (2002). Series estimation of partially linear panel data models with fixed effects. *Annals of Economics and Finance*, *3*, 103–116.

Cai, Z., & Li, Q. (2008). Nonparametric estimation of varying coefficient dynamic panel models. *Econometric Theory*, *24*, 1321–1342.

Cai, Z., & Xiong, H. (2012). Partially varying coefficient instrumental variables models. *Statistica Neerlandica*, *66*, 85–110.

Chen, J., Gao, J., & Li, D. (2012). Semiparametric trending panel data models with cross-sectional dependence. *Journal of Econometrics*, *171*, 71–85.

Dechevsky, L., & Penez, S. (1997). On shape-preserving probabilistic wavelet approximators. *Stochastic Analysis and Applications*, *15*, 187–215.

Fan, J., Härdle, W., & Mammen, E. (1998). Direct estimation of low dimensional components in additive models. *Annals of Statistics*, *26*, 943–971.

Fan, Y., & Li, Q. (1996). *On estimating additive partially linear models*. Unpublished manuscript.

Henderson, D. J., Carroll, R. J., & Li, Q. (2008). Nonparametric estimation and testing of fixed effects panel data models. *Journal of Econometrics*, *144*, 257–275.

Huang, J. Z., Wu, C. O., & Zhou, L. (2004). Polynomial spline estimation and inference for varying coefficient models with longitudinal data. *Statistica Sinica*, *14*, 763–788.

Li, K. C. (1987). Asymptotic optimality for C_p, C_L, cross-validation, and generalized cross-validation: Discrete index set. *Annals of Statistics*, *15*, 958–975.

Li, Q. (2000). Efficient estimation of additive partially linear models. *International Economic Review*, *41*, 1073–1092.

Li, Q., & Stengos, T. (1996). Semiparametric estimation of partially linear panel data models. *Journal of Econometrics*, *71*, 389–397.

Li, Q., Huang, C. J., Li, D., & Fu, T.-T. (2002). Semiparametric smooth coefficient models. *Journal of Business and Economic Statistics*, *20*, 412–422.

Linton, O. B., & Nielsen, J. P. (1995). A kernel method of estimating structured nonparametric regression based on marginal integration. *Biometrika*, *82*, 91–100.

Newey, W. K. (1994). Kernel estimation of partial means in a general variance estimator. *Econometric Theory*, *10*, 233–253.

Newey, W. K. (1997). Convergence rates and asymptotic normality for series estimators. *Journal of Econometrics*, *79*, 147–168.

Qian, J., & Wang, L. (2012). Estimating semiparametric panel data models by marginal integration. *Journal of Econometrics*, *167*, 483–493.

Rodriguez-Poo, J. M., & Soberon, A. (2014). Direct semi-parametric estimation of fixed effects panel data varying coefficient models. *The Econometrics Journal*, *17*, 107–138.

Sperlich, S., Tjøstheim, D., & Yang, L. (2002). Nonparametric estimation and testing of interaction in additive models. *Econometric Theory*, *18*, 197–251.

Su, L., & Lu, X. (2013). Nonparametric dynamic panel data models: Kernel estimation and specification testing. *Journal of Econometrics*, *176*, 112–133.

Su, L., & Ullah, A. (2006). Profile likelihood estimation of partially linear panel data models with fixed effects. *Economics Letters*, *92*, 75–81.

Su, L., & Ullah, A. (2011). Nonparametric and semiparametric panel econometric models: Estimation and testing. In A. Ullah & D. E. A. Giles (Eds.), *Handbook of empirical economics and finance* (pp. 455–497). New York, NY: Taylor & Francis Group.

Sun, Y., Carroll, R. J., & Li, D. (2010). Semiparametric estimation of fixed effects panel data varying coefficient models. In Q. Li & J. S. Racine (Eds.), *Nonparametric econometric methods* (Vol. 24, pp. 101–129). Advances in Econometrics. Bingley, UK: Emerald Group Publishing Limited.

Sun, Y., Zhang, Y. Y., & Li, Q. (2015). Nonparametric panel data regression models. In B. H. Baltagi (Ed.), *The Oxford handbook of panel data econometrics* (pp. 285–324). Oxford: Oxford University Press.

Tjøstheim, D., & Auestad, B. H. (1994). Nonparametric identification of nonlinear time series: Projections. *Journal of American Statistical Association*, *89*, 1398–1409.

Yao, F., & Zhang, J. (2015). Efficient kernel-based semiparametric IV estimation with an application to resolving a puzzle on the estimation of the return to schooling. *Empirical Economics*, *48*, 253–281.

Zhou, Y., & Liang, H. (2009). Statistical inference for semiparametric varying-coefficient partially linear models with generated regressors. *Annals of Statistics*, *37*, 427–458.

APPENDIX A: PROOF OF LEMMAS

Here, we prove some lemmas which will be utilized in the proofs of theorems.

We define $S_{A,B}=n^{-1}A'B=n^{-1}\sum_i A_iB_i'$ and $S_A=S_{A,A}$.

Lemma 1. $P'P/(NT)-I=O_p(\zeta_0(K)\sqrt{K}/\sqrt{N})$.

Proof. See the proof of Theorem 1 in Newey (1997, pp. 161–162). ■

We use $\mathbf{1}$ to denote an indicator function that takes value one if $(P'P)$ is invertible and zero otherwise. Whenever we have $(P'P)^{-1}$, it should be understood as $\mathbf{1}(P'P)^{-1}$ and since $Prob(\mathbf{1}=1)\to 1$ almost surely, we will often omit the indicator function $\mathbf{1}$.

Lemma 2. $\|\tilde{\alpha}_f-\alpha_f\|=O_p(K^{-\delta})$, *where* $\tilde{\alpha}_f=(P'P)^{-}P'f$, α_f *satisfies Assumption (3), for* $f=\beta$ *or* $f=h_{(s)}$ $(s=1,\ldots,q)$.

Proof. We have

$$\begin{aligned}
\mathbf{1}\left\|\tilde{\alpha}_f-\alpha_f\right\| &\overset{def}{=}\mathbf{1}\left\|(P'P)^{-}P'(f-P\alpha_f)\right\| \\
&=\mathbf{1}\{(f-P\alpha_f)'P(P'P)^{-1}(P'P/(NT))^{-1}P'(f-P\alpha_f)/(NT)\}^{1/2} \\
&=\mathbf{1}O_p(1)\{(f-P\alpha_f)'P(P'P)^{-1}P'(f-P\alpha_f)/(NT)\}^{1/2} \\
&\leq O_p(1)\{(f-P\alpha_f)'(f-P\alpha_f)/(NT)\}^{1/2}=O_p(K^{-\delta}), \qquad \text{(A.1)}
\end{aligned}$$

by Lemma 1, Assumption 3, and the fact that $P(P'P)^{-1}P'$ is idempotent. So $\|\tilde{\alpha}_f-\alpha_f\|=O_p(K^{-\delta})$ since $Prob(\mathbf{1}=1)\to 1$. ■

Lemma 3. *Define* $\eta_{it}=\theta(Z_{it},W_{it})-h(Z_{it},W_{it})$ *where* $h(z,w)=E_{\mathcal{G}}(\theta(z,w))$. η *is a column vector with typical elements* η_{it}. $P'\eta/(NT)=O_p(\zeta_0(K)/\sqrt{N})=o_p(1)$.

Proof. Note that $E(P_{it}\eta_{it})=0$ since $p^K(.)\in\mathcal{G}$ and $\eta(.)\perp\mathcal{G}$. Define $P_i=(P_{i1}',\ldots,P_{iT}')'$ and $\eta_i=(\eta_{i1},\ldots,\eta_{iT})'$. In this case,

$$\begin{aligned}
E\left\|P'\eta/(NT)\right\|^2 &=(NT)^{-2}E(\eta'PP'\eta) \\
&=(NT)^{-2}E\left\{\left(\sum_i \eta_i'P_i\right)\left(\sum_j P_j'\eta_j\right)\right\} \\
&=(NT)^{-2}E\left(\sum_i\sum_j \eta_i'P_iP_j'\eta_j\right) \\
&=(NT)^{-2}\left\{E\left(\sum_i \eta_i'P_iP_i'\eta_i\right)+E\left(\sum_i\sum_{j\neq i}\eta_i'P_iP_j'\eta_j\right)\right\}
\end{aligned}$$

$$
\begin{aligned}
&= (NT)^{-2}\sum\nolimits_i E(\eta_i' P_i P_i' \eta_i) + 0 = N^{-1}T^{-2}E(tr(P_i P_i' \eta_i \eta_i'))\\
&= N^{-1}T^{-2} tr(E(P_i P_i' \eta_i \eta_i'))\\
&\leq N^{-1}T^{-2} C\, tr(E(P_i P_i')) = N^{-1}T^{-2}C \sum_{t=1}^{T}\sum_{l=1}^{K} E(P_{it,l}^2)\\
&\leq N^{-1}T^{-1}C(\zeta_0(K))^2 = O((\zeta_0^2(K))^2/N),
\end{aligned}
$$

by Assumption 2. Hence, $P'\eta/(NT) = O_p(\zeta_0(K)/\sqrt{N}) = o_p(1)$. ■

Lemma 4. *$S_{f-\tilde{f}} = O_p(K^{-2\delta}) = o_p(N^{-1/2})$, where $f = \beta$ or $f = h$.*

Proof. Note that $\tilde{f} \equiv P\tilde{\beta}_f$, so that

$$
\begin{aligned}
S_{f-\tilde{f}} &= N^{-1}\left\| f - \tilde{f} \right\|^2 \leq N^{-1}\left\| f - P\alpha_f \right\|^2 + \left\| P(\alpha_f - \tilde{\alpha}_f) \right\|^2\\
&= N^{-1}\left\| f - P\alpha_f \right\|^2 + T(\alpha_f - \tilde{\alpha}_f)'\{P'P/(NT)\}(\alpha_f - \tilde{\alpha}_f)\\
&= O(K^{-2\delta}) + O_p(K^{-2\delta})\\
&= O_p(K^{-2\delta}),
\end{aligned}
$$

by Assumption 3, Lemmas 1 and 2. ■

Lemma 5. *(i) $S_{\tilde{a}} = O_p(K/N)$, for $a = U$ or v; (ii) $S_{\tilde{\eta}} = o_p(1)$.*

Proof.

(i) Similar to the proof of Theorem 1 in Newey (1997), for $a = v$, we have

$$
\begin{aligned}
E(S_{\tilde{v}}|Z) &= (NT)^{-1}E\{v'P(P'P)^{-1}P'v|Z\}\\
&= (NT)^{-1}tr[P(P'P)^{-1}P'E(vv'|Z)]\\
&\leq (NT)^{-1}C\, tr[P(P'P)^{-1}P']\\
&= O(K/N),
\end{aligned}
$$

which implies $S_{\tilde{v}} = O_p(K/N)$. It is similar for $a = u$.

(ii) $S_{\tilde{\eta}} = (NT)^{-1}\tilde{\eta}'\tilde{\eta} = (\eta'P/(NT))(P'P/(NT))^{-1}(P'\eta/(NT)) = O_p(\zeta_0^2(K)K/N) = o_p(1)$ by Lemmas 1 and 3. ■

Lemma 6. *For any $T \times T$ matrix $A = (a_{ts})$ in which elements are bounded $|a_{ts}| \leq M < \infty$, there is a constant C such that $CI_T - A$ is positive definite.*

Proof. Let $C = \bar{M}T$ for some $\bar{M} > M$ (recall T is a fixed value). Then for any vector $x \neq 0$,

$$x'(CI_T - A)x = Cx'x - x'Ax = \bar{M}T\sum_{t=1}^{T} x_t^2 - \sum_{t=1}^{T}\sum_{s=1}^{T} a_{ts}x_t x_s$$
$$\geq \bar{M}T\sum_{t=1}^{T} x_t^2 - \frac{M}{2}\sum_{t=1}^{T}\sum_{s=1}^{T}(x_t^2 + x_s^2) > 0. \quad \blacksquare$$

APPENDIX B: PROOF OF THEOREM 1

Recall that $\theta(Z_{it}, W_{it}) = E(X_{it}|Z_{it}, W_{it})$, $v_{it} = X_{it} - \theta(Z_{it}, W_{it})$, $\epsilon_{it} = X_{it} - h(Z_{it}, W_{it})$, and $\eta_{it} = \theta(Z_{it}, W_{it}) - h(Z_{it}, W_{it})$ where $h(z, w) = E_{\mathcal{G}}(\theta(z, w))$.

We will use the following short-hand notations: $\theta_{it} = \theta(Z_{it}, W_{it})$, $\beta_{it} = \beta(W_{it})$, $h_{it} = h(Z_{it}, W_{it})$. Hence, $v_{it} = X_{it} - \theta_{it}$, $\epsilon_{it} = X_{it} - h_{it}$, and $\eta_{it} = \theta_{it} - h_{it}$. θ is the $NT \times k_1$ matrix with typical element θ_{it}. h, G, η, ϵ, v, and U are similarly defined.

From the definitions, we have $X = \eta + v + h$ and $\tilde{X} = \tilde{\eta} + \tilde{v} + \tilde{h}$. Subtracting these two equalities yields

$$X - \tilde{X} = \eta - \tilde{\eta} + v - \tilde{v} + h - \tilde{h}. \tag{B.1}$$

Note that if $S_{X-\tilde{X}}^{-1}$ exists, we have

$$\sqrt{N}(\hat{\gamma} - \gamma) = S_{X-\tilde{X}}^{-1}\sqrt{N}S_{X-\tilde{X},G-\tilde{G}+U-\tilde{U}}. \tag{B.2}$$

We need to show the followings: (i) $S_{X-\tilde{X}} = \Phi + o_p(1)$, (ii) $S_{X-\tilde{X},G-\tilde{G}} = o_p(N^{-1/2})$, (iii) $S_{X-\tilde{X},\tilde{U}} = o_p(N^{-1/2})$, and (iv) $\sqrt{N}S_{X-\tilde{X},U} \to N(0, \Omega)$ in distribution.

(i) Proof of $S_{X-\tilde{X}} = \Phi + o_p(1)$.
From Eq. (B.1) we have $S_{X-\tilde{X}} = S_{(\eta+v)+(h-\tilde{h})-\tilde{\eta}-\tilde{v}} = S_{\eta+v} + S_{(h-\tilde{h})-\tilde{\eta}-\tilde{v}} + 2S_{(\eta+v),(h-\tilde{h})-\tilde{\eta}-\tilde{v}}$.

First, we have

$$S_{\eta+v} = (NT)^{-1}\sum_{i,t}(\eta_{it}+v_{it})(\eta_{it}+v_{it})' = (NT)^{-1}\sum_i\sum_t \epsilon_{it}\epsilon_{it}'$$
$$= N^{-1}\sum_i\left(T^{-1}\sum_t \epsilon_{it}\epsilon_{it}'\right) = \Phi + o_p(1),$$

by the Law of Large Numbers.

Second, $S_{(h-\tilde{h})-\tilde{\eta}-\tilde{v}} \leq 2S_{(h-\tilde{h})} + 4S_{\tilde{\eta}} + 4S_{\tilde{v}} = o_p(1)$ by Lemmas 4 and 5.

Finally, $S_{(\eta+v),(h-\tilde{h})-\tilde{\eta}-\tilde{v}} \leq (S_{\eta+v}S_{(h-\tilde{h})-\tilde{\eta}-\tilde{v}})^{1/2} = [O_p(1)o_p(1)]^{1/2} = o_p(1)$ by the above results.

(ii) Proof of $S_{X-\tilde{X},G-\tilde{G}} = o_p(N^{-1/2})$.

By Eq. (B.1), we have

$$S_{X-\tilde{X},G-\tilde{G}} = S_{\eta-\tilde{\eta}+v-\tilde{v}+h-\tilde{h},G-\tilde{G}}$$
$$= S_{\eta+v,G-\tilde{G}} + S_{h-\tilde{h},G-\tilde{G}} - S_{\tilde{v},G-\tilde{G}} - S_{\tilde{\eta},G-\tilde{G}}. \tag{B.3}$$

For these four terms, we have

(1) $S_{\eta+v,G-\tilde{G}} \leq \{S_{\eta+v}S_{G-\tilde{G}}\}^{1/2} = O_p(K^{-\delta})$ by Lemma 4 and $S_{\eta+v} = O_p(1)$.
(2) $S_{h-\tilde{h},G-\tilde{G}} \leq \{S_{h-\tilde{h}}S_{G-\tilde{G}}\}^{1/2} = O_p(K^{-2\delta})$ by Lemma 4.
(3) $S_{\tilde{v},G-\tilde{G}} \leq \{S_{\tilde{v}}S_{G-\tilde{G}}\}^{1/2} = o_p(1)O_p(K^{-\delta})$ by Lemmas 4 and 5.
(4) $S_{\tilde{\eta},G-\tilde{G}} \leq \{S_{\tilde{\eta}}S_{G-\tilde{G}}\}^{1/2} = o_p(1)O_p(K^{-\delta})$ by Lemmas 4 and 5.

(iii) Proof of $S_{X-\tilde{X},\tilde{U}} = o_p(N^{-1/2})$.
By Eq. (B.1), $S_{X-\tilde{X},\tilde{U}} = S_{\eta-\tilde{\eta}+v-\tilde{v}+h-\tilde{h},\tilde{U}} = S_{\eta,\tilde{U}} + S_{v,\tilde{U}} + S_{h-\tilde{h},\tilde{U}} - S_{\tilde{v},\tilde{U}} - S_{\tilde{\eta},\tilde{U}}$. We consider these five terms separately.

(1) We have

$$E[\|S_{\eta,\tilde{U}}\|^2|Z,W] = (NT)^{-2}E[U'P(P'P)^{-1}P'\eta\eta'P(P'P)^{-1}P'U|Z,W]$$
$$= (NT)^{-2}tr[P(P'P)^{-1}P'\eta\eta'P(P'P)^{-1}P'E(UU'|Z)]$$
$$\leq C(NT)^{-2}tr(\tilde{\eta}\tilde{\eta}') = C(NT)^{-1}tr(S_{\tilde{\eta}}) = o_p(N^{-1}),$$

by Lemma 5. Hence, $S_{\eta,\tilde{U}} = O_p(N^{-1/2})$.

(2) We have

$$\begin{aligned}&E[\|S_{v,\tilde{U}}\|^2|X,Z,W]\\&=(NT)^{-2}tr[P(P'P)^{-1}P'vv'P(P'P)^{-1}P'E(UU'|X,Z,W)]\\&\leq C(NT)^{-2}tr(\tilde{v}\tilde{v}')=C(NT)^{-1}tr(S_{\tilde{v}})=O(K/N^2),\end{aligned}$$

by Lemma 5.

(3) $S_{h-\tilde{h},\tilde{U}} \leq \{S_{h-\tilde{h}}S_{\tilde{U}}\}^{1/2} = O_p(K^{-\delta})O_p(\sqrt{K}/\sqrt{N})$ by Lemmas 4 and 5.

(4) $S_{\tilde{v},\tilde{U}} \leq \{S_{\tilde{v}}S_{\tilde{U}}\}^{1/2} = O_p(K/N)$ by Lemma 5.

(5) We have

$$\begin{aligned}E[\|S_{\tilde{\eta},\tilde{U}}\|^2|Z,W] &= (NT)^{-2}tr[P(P'P)^{-1}P'\eta\eta'P(P'P)^{-1}P'E(UU'|Z)]\\&\leq C(NT)^{-2}tr(\tilde{\eta}\tilde{\eta}')=C(NT)^{-1}tr(S_{\tilde{\eta}})=o_p(N^{-1}),\end{aligned}$$

by Lemma 5. Hence, $S_{\tilde{\eta},\tilde{U}} = o_p(N^{-1/2})$.

(iv) Proof of $\sqrt{N}S_{X-\tilde{X},U} \to N(0,\Omega)$ in distribution.
$S_{X-\tilde{X},U} = S_{\eta-\tilde{\eta}+v-\tilde{v}+h-\tilde{h},U} = S_{\eta+v,U} + S_{h-\tilde{h},U} - S_{\tilde{v},U} - S_{\tilde{\eta},U}$. We consider them separately.

(1) $\sqrt{N}S_{\eta+v,U} = \sqrt{N}S_{\eta+v,U} = \sqrt{N}\sum_i(\eta_i + v_i)u_i' \to N(0,\Omega)$ by Levi-Lindberg central limit theorem.

(2) We have

$$\begin{aligned}E\left[\|S_{h-\tilde{h},U}\|^2|Z\right] &= (NT)^{-2}tr[(h-\tilde{h})(h-\tilde{h})'E(UU'|Z)]\\&\leq C(NT)^{-1}tr[(h-\tilde{h})(h-\tilde{h})'/NT]\\&= C(NT)^{-1}tr(S_{h-\tilde{h}})=o_p(N^{-1}),\end{aligned}$$

by Lemmas 4 and 5. Hence, $S_{h-\tilde{h},U} = o_p(N^{-1/2})$.

(3) Similarly, we have

$$E[\|S_{\tilde{v},U}\|^2|Z,W] \leq C(NT)^{-1}tr[S_{\tilde{v}}] = o_p(N^{-1}),$$

by Lemma 5. Hence, $S_{\tilde{v},U} = o_p(N^{-1/2})$.

(4) We have

$$E[\|S_{\tilde{\eta},U}\|^2|Z,W] \leq C(NT)^{-1}tr[S_{\tilde{\eta}}] = o_p(N^{-1})$$

by Lemma 5. Hence, $S_{\tilde{\eta},U} = o_p(N^{-1/2})$.

(i)–(iv) above imply that $\sqrt{N}(\hat{\gamma}-\gamma)=\Phi^{-1}N(0,\Omega)+o_p(1)\to N(0,\Phi^{-1}\Omega\Phi^{-1})$.

Proof of $\hat{\Sigma}=\Sigma+o_p(1)$.
$\hat{\Phi}\equiv S_{X-\tilde{X}}=\Phi+o_p(1)$ is proved in (i) of Theorem 1.

Similarly, we can prove that $\hat{\Omega}=\Omega+o_p(1)$. Notice that $\hat{\gamma}-\gamma=O_p(N^{-1/2})$ and $\hat{G}-G=o_p(1)$. It is easy to prove that $\hat{u}_{it}=u_{it}+o_p(1)$. Also, we know that $h_{it}-\tilde{h}_{it}=o_p(1)$, $\tilde{v}_{it}=o_p(1)$ and $\tilde{\eta}_{it}=o_p(1)$. Hence $X_{it}-\tilde{X}_{it}=\epsilon_{it}+o_p(1)$. These results lead to $\hat{\Omega}=\Omega+o_p(1)$ by a law of large numbers.

APPENDIX C: PROOF OF THEOREM 2

This theorem is almost the same as Theorem 1 in Newey (1997) and Theorem 4.1 in Newey (1994) except that our estimator $\hat{\beta}$ has an extra term $X(\gamma-\hat{\gamma})$. It suffices to show that the contribution of this extra term is asymptotically negligible. One would expect this to be true because $(\gamma-\hat{\gamma})=O_p(N^{-1/2})$ which has a smaller order than that of the nonparametric series estimation convergence rate.

We have

$$\begin{aligned}\hat{\alpha} &= (P'P)^{-}P'(Y-X\hat{\gamma})=(P'P)^{-}P'[(Y-X\gamma)-X(\hat{\gamma}-\gamma)]\\ &= \alpha_g+(P'P)^{-}P'[(G-P\alpha_g)+U]-(P'P)^{-}P'X(\hat{\gamma}-\gamma)\\ &= \alpha_g+D_{1N}-D_{2N}(\hat{\gamma}-\gamma),\end{aligned}\tag{C.1}$$

where $D_{1N}=(P'P)^{-}P'[(G-P\alpha_g)+U]$ and $D_{2N}=(P'P)^{-}P'X$. $\|D_{1N}\|=O_p(K^{-\delta}+\sqrt{K}/\sqrt{N})$ was proved by Theorem 4.1 in Newey (1994).

Next we will show that $D_{2N}(\hat{\gamma}-\gamma)=O_p(N^{-1/2})$.

$$\begin{aligned}\|D_{2N}\|^2 &= \left\|(P'P)^{-}P'(\eta+v+h)\right\|^2=\left\|\tilde{\alpha}_\eta+\tilde{\alpha}_v+\tilde{\alpha}_h\right\|^2\\ &\le C\left(\left\|\tilde{\alpha}_\eta\right\|^2+\|\tilde{\alpha}_v\|^2+\|\tilde{\alpha}_h\|^2\right)\\ &= O_p\left(\frac{1}{N}\left\{\|\tilde{\eta}\|^2+\|\tilde{v}\|^2+\left\|\tilde{h}\right\|^2\right\}\right)=N^{-1}\{O_p(\|h\|^2)+o_p(1)\}\\ &= O_p(1).\end{aligned}$$

So $D_{2N}(\hat{\gamma}-\gamma)=O_p(\hat{\gamma}-\gamma)=O_p(1/\sqrt{N})$ which has an order smaller than $O_p(\sqrt{K}/\sqrt{N})$. Thus, $\left\|\hat{\alpha}-\alpha_g\right\|=O_p(K^{-\delta}+\sqrt{K}/\sqrt{N})$ as in Newey (1997). The rest of proofs (to prove (i)–(iii) in our Theorem 2) follows the same arguments as in the proofs of Theorem 1 in Newey (1997) for (i) and that of Theorem 4.1 in Newey (1994) for (ii) and (iii).

APPENDIX D: PROOF OF THEOREM 3

Note that

$$\hat{\gamma}_{IV} = \gamma + [(Q - \tilde{Q})'(X - \tilde{X})]^{-1}(Q - \tilde{Q})'[(G - \tilde{G}) + (U - \tilde{U})]. \qquad \text{(D.1)}$$

So we have

$$\sqrt{N}(\hat{\gamma}_{IV} - \gamma) = S^{-1}_{(Q-\tilde{Q}),(Y_{-1}-\tilde{Y}_{-1})}\sqrt{N}S_{(Q-\tilde{Q}),(G-\tilde{G})+(U-\tilde{U})}. \qquad \text{(D.2)}$$

We will show the followings: (i) $S_{(Q-\tilde{Q}),(X-\tilde{X})} = \Psi + o_p(1)$; (ii) $S_{(Q-\tilde{Q}),(G-\tilde{G})} = o_p(N^{-1/2})$; (iii) $S_{(Q-\tilde{Q}),\tilde{U}} = o_p(N^{-1/2})$; and (iv) $\sqrt{N}S_{(Q-\tilde{Q}),U} \to N(0,\Lambda)$ in distribution.

(i) Proof of $S_{(Q-\tilde{Q}),(X-\tilde{X})} = \Psi + o_p(1)$.
Let $Q = [Q - E_{\mathcal{G}}(Q)] + E_{\mathcal{G}}(Q) = \epsilon + h$. Then $\tilde{Q} = \tilde{\epsilon} + \tilde{h}$. Let $X = [X - E_{\mathcal{G}}(X)] + E_{\mathcal{G}}(X) = \tau + \varkappa$. Then $\tilde{X} = \tilde{\tau} + \tilde{\varkappa}$. Follow the proof in Theorem 1, we have

$$S_{(Q-\tilde{Q}),(X-\tilde{X})} = S_{\epsilon+(h-\tilde{h}-\tilde{\epsilon}),\tau+(\varkappa-\tilde{\varkappa}-\tilde{\tau})} = \frac{1}{T}\sum_{t=1}^{T} E(\epsilon_{it}\tau'_{it}) + o_p(1) = \Psi + o_p(1). \qquad \text{(D.3)}$$

(ii) Proof of $S_{(Q-\tilde{Q}),(G-\tilde{G})} = o_p(N^{-1/2})$.
The proof is similar to that in Theorem 1 and thus omitted.

(iii) Proof of $S_{(Q-\tilde{Q}),\tilde{U}} = o_p(N^{-1/2})$.
The proof is similar to that in Theorem 1 and thus omitted.

(iv) Proof of $\sqrt{N}S_{(Q-\tilde{Q}),U} \to N(0,\Lambda)$ in distribution.
$S_{(Q-\tilde{Q}),U} = S_{\epsilon+(h-\tilde{h}-\tilde{\epsilon}),U} = S_{\epsilon,U} + S_{(h-\tilde{h}),U} - S_{\tilde{\epsilon},U}$. We consider them separately.

(1) We have $\sqrt{N}S_{\epsilon,U} = \sqrt{N}\sum_i \epsilon_i u'_i \to N(0,\Lambda)$ by Levi-Lindberg central limit theorem.

(2) We have

$$E\left[\left\| S_{(h-\tilde{h}),U} \right\|^2 Q, Z\right] = (NT)^{-2} tr[(h-\tilde{h})(h-\tilde{h})' E(UU'|Z)]$$
$$\leq C(NT)^{-1} tr(S_{h-\tilde{h}}) = o_p(N^{-1}),$$

by Lemmas 4 and 5. Hence, $S_{(h-\tilde{h}),U} = o_p(N^{-1/2})$.

(3) Similar to that in the proof of Theorem 1, $S_{\tilde{\epsilon},U} = o_p(N^{-1/2})$.

So we have $\sqrt{N} S_{(Q-\tilde{Q}),U} \to N(0, \Lambda)$ in distribution.

From (i)–(iv), we have $\sqrt{N}(\hat{\gamma}_{IV} - \gamma) \to N(0, \Psi^{-1}\Lambda\Psi^{-1})$ in distribution.

TESTING FOR SPATIAL LAG AND SPATIAL ERROR DEPENDENCE IN A FIXED EFFECTS PANEL DATA MODEL USING DOUBLE LENGTH ARTIFICIAL REGRESSIONS

Badi H. Baltagi[a] and Long Liu[b]

[a] *Department of Economics and Center for Policy Research, Syracuse University, Syracuse, NY, USA*

[b] *Department of Economics, University of Texas at San Antonio, San Antonio, TX, USA*

ABSTRACT

This paper revisits the joint and conditional Lagrange multiplier tests derived by Debarsy and Ertur (2010) for a fixed effects spatial lag regression model with spatial autoregressive error, and derives these tests using artificial double length regressions (DLR). These DLR tests and their corresponding LM tests are compared using an empirical example and a Monte Carlo simulation.

Keywords: Double length regression; spatial lag dependence; spatial error dependence; artificial regressions; panel data; fixed effects

JEL classifications: C12; C21; R15

Essays in Honor of Aman Ullah
Advances in Econometrics, Volume 36, 67–84

ISSN: 0731-9053/doi:10.1108/S0731-905320160000036012

1. INTRODUCTION

Davidson and MacKinnon (1984, 1988, 1993) proposed double length regressions (DLR) as a useful tool for deriving LM tests. These DLRs are computationally simple and outperform their outer product gradient (OPG) regression counterparts. They have been applied in econometrics by Baltagi (1999) to test linear versus log-linear regressions with AR(1) disturbances. Also by Baltagi and Li (2001) to test for spatial dependence in a cross-section regression model and by Le and Li (2008), who applied it to test for functional form and spatial error dependence, to mention a few. Recently, Baltagi and Liu (2014) extended the Baltagi and Li (2001) paper by deriving the DLR tests corresponding to the joint and conditional LM tests of spatial lag and spatial error in a cross-section regression model. Testing for spatial dependence in a cross-section regression has been extensively studied by Anselin (1988a, 1988b, 2001), Anselin and Bera (1998), Anselin, Bera, Florax, and Yoon (1996), and Krämer (2005), to mention a few. The presence of spatial correlation can render inference using ordinary least-squares misleading, see Krämer (2003), also, Mynbaev and Ullah (2008), who derive the asymptotic distribution of the OLS estimator in a spatial autoregressive model.[1] Anselin et al. (1996) consider a spatial autoregressive cross-section regression model with spatial autoregressive disturbances and derive a series of Lagrange multiplier (LM) tests. These are called the joint, conditional, and marginal LM tests for spatial lag and spatial error dependence. In fact, Baltagi and Li (2001) derived the DLR counterpart for the marginal LM tests for spatial lag and spatial error considered by Anselin et al. (1996) and illustrated these tests using Anselin's (1988b) empirical example relating crime to housing values and income for 49 neighborhoods in Columbus, Ohio in 1980. Monte Carlo experiments showed that these DLR tests have similar performance to their LM counterparts.

This paper focuses on similar tests but in the context of a spatial panel data model, see Lee and Yu (2010a) and Baltagi (2011) for recent surveys.[2] In fact, Baltagi, Song, and Koh (2003) derived the joint LM test for spatial error correlation as well as random country effects. Additionally, they derived conditional LM tests, which test for random country effects given the presence of spatial error correlation. Also, spatial error correlation given the presence of random country effects. These conditional LM tests are an alternative to the one directional LM tests that test for random country effects ignoring the presence of spatial error correlation or the one directional LM tests for spatial error correlation ignoring the presence of random country effects. Baltagi and Liu (2008) derived a joint LM test which simultaneously tests for the absence of spatial lag dependence and random individual effects. The joint LM statistic is the sum of two standard LM statistics. The first one tests for the absence of spatial lag dependence ignoring the random individual effects, and the second one tests for the absence of random individual effects ignoring the spatial lag dependence. Baltagi and Liu (2008) also derived two conditional LM tests. The first one tests for the absence of random individual effects allowing for the possible presence of spatial lag dependence. The second one tests for the absence of spatial lag dependence allowing for the possible presence of random individual effects. Debarsy and Ertur (2010) derived LM and LR tests designed to discriminate between spatially autocorrelated disturbances versus a spatially lagged dependent variable in the context of a fixed effects spatial panel data model. Following Lee and Yu (2010b), they combine a spatial lag model with a spatially autocorrelated disturbances in a fixed effects spatial panel data setting. They derive joint, marginal as well as conditional LM and LR tests, under the assumption of normality of the disturbances. They investigate the performance of these tests using Monte Carlo experiments. This paper derives the DLR tests corresponding to the joint and conditional LM tests for spatial lag and spatial error considered by Debarsy and Ertur (2010). It illustrates these tests using an empirical example and investigates the performance of these tests using Monte Carlo experiments.

This paper is organized as follows: Section 2 derives the DLR for the presence of spatial lag and error dependence in the context of a fixed effects panel data model. Our suggested DLR tests and their corresponding LM tests are compared using an illustrative example in Section 3 and a Monte Carlo simulation in Section 4. Section 5 concludes this paper.

2. THE SPATIAL DEPENDENCE MODEL

Consider the spatial lag panel data regression model

$$y_t = \rho W y_t + X_t\beta + \mu + v_t, \qquad t = 1, \ldots, T, \tag{1}$$

with spatial autoregressive remainder errors

$$v_t = \lambda M v_t + \epsilon_t, \qquad t = 1, \ldots, T, \tag{2}$$

where $y_t' = (y_{t1}, \ldots, y_{tN})$ is a vector of observations on the dependent variable for N regions or households observed at time $t = 1, \ldots, T$. X_t is an $N \times k$ matrix of observations on k explanatory variables. We assume X_t to be of full column rank and its elements are assumed to be asymptotically bounded in absolute value. β is a $k \times 1$ vector of parameters. ρ and λ are scalar spatial autoregressive coefficients with $|\rho| < 1$ and $|\lambda| < 1$. W and M are known $N \times N$ row-normalized spatial weight matrices whose diagonal elements are zero and summation of each row is 1. W and M also satisfy the condition that $(I - \lambda M)$ and $(I - \rho W)$ are nonsingular.

$\mu' = (\mu_1, \ldots, \mu_N)$ where μ_i denote the ith individual's fixed effect. These μ_i's are time-invariant random variables that are possibly correlated with the explanatory variables. $v_t' = (v_{t1}, \ldots, v_{tN})$ is a vector of remainder disturbances that follow a first-order spatial autoregressive model. $\epsilon_t' = (\epsilon_{t1}, \ldots, \epsilon_{tN})$ and ϵ_{ti} is i.i.d. over t and i and is assumed to be $N(0, \sigma_\epsilon^2)$. Normality is needed for the derivation of the DLR, see Davidson and MacKinnon (1993).

Define $E_T = I_T - \bar{J}_T$, where I_T is an identity matrix of dimension T, $\bar{J}_T = J_T/T$ and J_T is a matrix of ones of dimension T, see Baltagi (2013). Lee and Yu (2010a, 2010b) define $\left[F_{T,T-1}, \frac{1}{\sqrt{T}}\iota_T\right]$ as the orthonormal matrix of the eigenvectors of the demeaning operator, with $F_{T,T-1}$ the $T \times (T-1)$ matrix of eigenvectors of E_T corresponding to eigenvalues equal to 1. ι_T is a vector of ones of dimension T. Define the transformed $N \times (T-1)$ matrix $\left(y_1^*, \ldots, y_{T-1}^*\right) = (y_1, \ldots, y_T) F_{T,T-1}$. Equivalently, this can be written as:

$$y^* = \begin{pmatrix} y_1^* \\ \vdots \\ y_{T-1}^* \end{pmatrix} = \left(F_{T,T-1}' \otimes I_N\right) \begin{pmatrix} y_1 \\ \vdots \\ y_T \end{pmatrix},$$

where y^* is of dimension $N(T-1) \times 1$, I_N is an identity matrix of dimension N, and $\otimes$ denotes the Kronecker product. One can see that the transformed sample is shrunk by one time period. Similarly, define X_t^*, v_t^*, and ϵ_t^* for $t = 1, \ldots, T-1$. The benchmark model in Eq. (1) becomes:

$$y_t^* = \rho W y_t^* + X_t^* \beta + v_t^*, \quad \text{for } t = 1, \ldots, T-1, \tag{3}$$

and

$$v_t^* = \lambda M v_t^* + \epsilon_t^*, \quad \text{for } t = 1, \ldots, T-1. \tag{4}$$

Rewrite Eq. (3) in matrix form as

$$y^* = \rho\left(I_{T-1} \otimes W\right) y^* + X^* \beta + v^*, \tag{5}$$

and

$$v^* = \lambda\left(I_{T-1} \otimes M\right) v^* + \epsilon^*, \tag{6}$$

where X^* is $N(T-1) \times k$, β is $k \times 1$, and ε^* is $N(T-1) \times 1$. I_{T-1} is an identity matrix of dimension $T-1$. This follows from the fact that $\left(F_{T,T-1}' \otimes I_N\right)\left(I_T \otimes W\right) = \left(F_{T,T-1}' \otimes W\right) = \left(I_{T-1} \otimes W\right)\left(F_{T,T-1}' \otimes I_N\right)$. A similar result obtains when we replace W by M. The observations are ordered with t being the slow running index and i the fast running index, that is, $y^{*\prime} = \left(y_{11}, \ldots, y_{1N}, \ldots, y_{(T-1),1}, \ldots, y_{(T-1),N}\right)$. X^*, v^*, and ϵ^* are similarly defined.

Model (5) can be rewritten as

$$(I_{T-1} \otimes BA)\, y^* - (I_{T-1} \otimes B)\, X^* \beta = \epsilon^*, \tag{7}$$

where $A = I_N - \rho W$ and $B = I_N - \lambda M$. This yields the following representation for the itth observation:

$$f_{it}\left(y^*_{it}, \varphi\right) = \frac{1}{\sigma_\epsilon} \epsilon^*_{it}, \qquad i = 1, \ldots, N; \qquad t = 1, \ldots, T-1, \tag{8}$$

where

$$\begin{aligned} f_{it}\left(y^*_{it}, \varphi\right) = \frac{1}{\sigma_\epsilon} \Bigg[& y^*_{it} - \rho \sum_{s=1}^{N} w_{is} y^*_{st} - \lambda \sum_{j=1}^{N} m_{ij} y^*_{jt} + \rho\lambda \sum_{j=1}^{N} \left(m_{ij} \sum_{s=1}^{N} w_{js} y^*_{st} \right) \\ & - \left(x^*_{it} - \lambda \sum_{j=1}^{N} m_{ij} x^*_{jt} \right)' \beta \Bigg], \end{aligned} \tag{9}$$

with $\varphi' = \left[\beta', \sigma^2_\epsilon, \rho, \lambda\right]$.

Under the normality assumption, we have $\frac{1}{\sigma_\epsilon} \epsilon^*_{it} \sim NID\,(0, 1)$ and hence the log-likelihood function of Eq. (7) is given by

$$\begin{aligned} L\left(y^*, \varphi\right) = & -\frac{N(T-1)}{2} \ln 2\pi - \frac{N(T-1)}{2} \ln \sigma^2_\epsilon + (T-1) \ln |A| \\ & + (T-1) \ln |B| - \frac{1}{2\sigma^2_\epsilon} \left[(I_{T-1} \otimes BA)\, y^* - (I_{T-1} \otimes B)\, X^* \beta \right]' \\ & \times \left[(I_{T-1} \otimes BA)\, y^* - (I_{T-1} \otimes B)\, X^* \beta \right]. \end{aligned} \tag{10}$$

Ord (1975) shows that $\ln|A| = \ln|I_N - \rho W| = \sum_{i=1}^{N} \ln(1 - \rho\omega_i)$, where ω_i's are the eigenvalues of W. Similarly, $\ln|B| = \ln|I_N - \lambda M| = \sum_{i=1}^{N} \ln(1 - \lambda\eta_i)$, where η_i's are the eigenvalues of M. As shown in Lemma 1 of Li, Yu, and Bai (2013), all the eigenvalues of a row normalized spatial weight matrix are real numbers. The Jacobian term can be rewritten as

$$
\begin{aligned}
&-\frac{N(T-1)}{2}\ln\sigma_\epsilon^2+(T-1)\ln|A|+(T-1)\ln|B| \\
&=(T-1)\sum_{i=1}^{N}\ln(1-\rho\omega_i)+(T-1)\sum_{i=1}^{N}\ln(1-\lambda\eta_i)-\frac{N(T-1)}{2}\ln\sigma_\epsilon^2 \\
&=(T-1)\sum_{i=1}^{N}k_{it}\left(y_{it}^*,\varphi\right), \qquad (11)
\end{aligned}
$$

where

$$
\begin{aligned}
k_{it}\left(y_{it}^*,\varphi\right)=\ln(1-\rho\omega_i)+\ln(1-\lambda\eta_i)-\frac{1}{2}\ln\sigma_\epsilon^2,\quad i=1,\ldots,N,& \\
t=1,\ldots,T-1.& \qquad (12)
\end{aligned}
$$

For the purpose of deriving the DLR, the contribution of the ith observation to the log-likelihood function can be written as

$$
l_{it}\left(y_{it}^*,\varphi\right)=-\frac{1}{2}\ln(2\pi)-\frac{1}{2}f_{it}^2\left(y_{it}^*,\varphi\right)+k_{it}\left(y_{it}^*,\varphi\right). \qquad (13)
$$

Defining $F_{itj}\left(y_{it}^*,\varphi\right)=\partial f_{it}\left(y_{it}^*,\varphi\right)/\partial\varphi_j$ and $K_{ijt}\left(y_{it}^*,\varphi\right)=\partial k_{it}\left(y_{it}^*,\varphi\right)/\partial\varphi_j$, then $F(y^*,\varphi)$ and $K(y^*,\varphi)$ are matrices with typical elements $F_{itj}\left(y_{it}^*,\varphi\right)$ and $K_{itj}\left(y_{it}^*,\varphi\right)$. Similarly, let $f(y^*,\varphi)$ be the vector with typical elements $f_{it}\left(y_{it}^*,\varphi\right)$.

For $F(y^*,\varphi)$, the typical elements are

$$
\frac{\partial f_{it}\left(y_{it}^*,\varphi\right)}{\partial\beta'}=-\frac{1}{\sigma_\epsilon}\left(x_{it}^*-\lambda\sum_{j=1}^{N}m_{ij}x_{jt}^*\right)', \qquad (14)
$$

$$
\begin{aligned}
\frac{\partial f_{it}\left(y_{it}^*,\varphi\right)}{\partial\sigma_\epsilon}=-\frac{1}{\sigma_\epsilon^2}\Bigg[&y_{it}^*-\rho\sum_{s=1}^{N}w_{is}y_{st}^*-\lambda\sum_{j=1}^{N}m_{ij}y_{jt}^* \\
&+\rho\lambda\sum_{j=1}^{N}\left(m_{ij}\sum_{s=1}^{N}w_{js}y_{st}^*\right)-\left(x_{it}^*-\lambda\sum_{j=1}^{N}m_{ij}x_{jt}^*\right)'\beta\Bigg],
\end{aligned}
$$

$$\frac{\partial f_{it}\left(y_{it}^{*},\varphi\right)}{\partial\rho}=-\frac{1}{\sigma_{\epsilon}}\left[\sum_{s=1}^{N}w_{is}y_{st}^{*}-\lambda\sum_{j=1}^{N}\left(m_{ij}\sum_{s=1}^{N}w_{js}y_{st}^{*}\right)\right],$$

$$\frac{\partial f_{it}\left(y_{it}^{*},\varphi\right)}{\partial\lambda}=-\frac{1}{\sigma_{\epsilon}}\left[\sum_{j=1}^{N}m_{ij}y_{jt}^{*}-\rho\sum_{j=1}^{N}\left(m_{ij}\sum_{s=1}^{N}w_{js}y_{st}^{*}\right)-\sum_{j=1}^{N}m_{ij}x_{jt}^{*\prime}\beta\right].$$

For $K\left(y^{*},\varphi\right)$, the typical elements are

$$\begin{aligned}\frac{\partial k_{it}\left(y_{it}^{*},\varphi\right)}{\partial\beta'}&=0,\\ \frac{\partial k_{it}\left(y_{it}^{*},\varphi\right)}{\partial\sigma_{\epsilon}}&=-\frac{1}{\sigma_{\epsilon}},\\ \frac{\partial k_{it}\left(y_{it}^{*},\varphi\right)}{\partial\rho}&=-\frac{\omega_{i}}{1-\rho\omega_{i}},\\ \frac{\partial k_{it}\left(y_{it}^{*},\varphi\right)}{\partial\lambda}&=-\frac{\eta_{i}}{1-\lambda\eta_{i}}.\end{aligned} \tag{15}$$

The DLR can be written as an artificial regression with $2N\left(T-1\right)$ observations:

$$\begin{bmatrix}f\left(y^{*},\varphi\right)\\ \iota_{N(T-1)}\end{bmatrix}=\begin{bmatrix}-F\left(y^{*},\varphi\right)\\ K\left(y^{*},\varphi\right)\end{bmatrix}b+\text{residuals}, \tag{16}$$

where $\iota_{N(T-1)}$ denotes a vector of ones of dimension $N\left(T-1\right)$. The basic result in Davidson and MacKinnon (1984) is that the information matrix can be expressed as

$$\Im\left(y^{*},\varphi\right)=\operatorname*{plim}_{N\to\infty}\left[\frac{1}{N}\left(F\left(y^{*},\varphi\right)'F\left(y^{*},\varphi\right)+K\left(y^{*},\varphi\right)'K\left(y^{*},\varphi\right)\right)\right]. \tag{17}$$

Another important observation is that the gradient of the log-likelihood function can be written as

$$g\left(y^{*},\varphi\right)\equiv\frac{\partial\ln L\left(y^{*},\varphi\right)}{\partial\varphi}=-F\left(y^{*},\varphi\right)'f\left(y^{*},\varphi\right)+K\left(y^{*},\varphi\right)'\iota_{N(T-1)}. \tag{18}$$

The LM test statistic in score form is given by

$$g\left(y^{*},\tilde{\varphi}\right)'\left[N\Im\left(y^{*},\tilde{\varphi}\right)\right]^{-1}g\left(y^{*},\tilde{\varphi}\right), \tag{19}$$

where $g\left(y^*,\tilde{\varphi}\right)$ is the gradient evaluated at the restricted estimates. The DLR variant of the LM test then uses a consistent estimate of the information matrix under the null of the form

$$\frac{1}{N}\left(F\left(y^*,\tilde{\varphi}\right)'F\left(y^*,\tilde{\varphi}\right)+K\left(y^*,\tilde{\varphi}\right)'K\left(y^*,\tilde{\varphi}\right)\right). \tag{20}$$

In this case, the LM test coincides with the explained sum of squares from the DLR regression in Eq. (16). Equation (16) evaluated at the restricted estimates can be written as

$$\mathcal{Y}=\mathcal{X}b+\text{residuals}, \tag{21}$$

where $\mathcal{Y}=\begin{bmatrix} f\left(y^*,\tilde{\varphi}\right) \\ \iota_{N(T-1)} \end{bmatrix}$ and $\mathcal{X}=\begin{bmatrix} -F\left(y^*,\tilde{\varphi}\right) \\ K\left(y^*,\tilde{\varphi}\right) \end{bmatrix}$. Since the OLS estimator of b is $\left(\mathcal{X}'\mathcal{X}\right)^{-1}\mathcal{X}'\mathcal{Y}$, the explained sum of squares from the DLR regression is $\mathcal{Y}'\mathcal{X}\left(\mathcal{X}'\mathcal{X}\right)^{-1}\mathcal{X}'\mathcal{Y}$. Note that the residual sum of squares of the above artificial regression is $\mathcal{Y}'\left[I-\mathcal{X}\left(\mathcal{X}'\mathcal{X}\right)^{-1}\mathcal{X}'\right]\mathcal{Y}$ and $\mathcal{Y}'\mathcal{Y}=f\left(y^*,\tilde{\varphi}\right)'f\left(y^*,\tilde{\varphi}\right)+\iota_{N(T-1)'}\iota_{N(T-1)}=2N(T-1)$. Therefore, the DLR test statistics can be alternatively computed as $2N(T-1)$ minus the residual sum of squares of the above artificial regressions. This DLR test is computationally simple and requires only the eigenvalues of W. These eigenvalues are also needed for ML estimation and the LM test.

2.1. *Joint DLR Test for $H_0^a:\lambda=\rho=0$*

Under $H_0^a:\rho=\lambda=0$, the restricted MLEs are the OLS estimates of the following transformed panel data regression:

$$y^*=X^*\beta+\epsilon^*, \qquad t=1,\ldots,T-1 \tag{22}$$

In this case, $\tilde{\beta}=\left(X^{*\prime}X^*\right)^{-1}X^{*\prime}y^*$, $\tilde{\sigma}_\epsilon^2=\frac{1}{N(T-1)}\tilde{e}^{*\prime}\tilde{e}^*$ with $\tilde{e}^*$ denoting the OLS residuals of this transformed panel data regression. Using these restricted ML estimates $\tilde{\varphi}'=\left[\tilde{\beta}',\tilde{\sigma}_\epsilon^2,\tilde{\rho},\tilde{\lambda}\right]$ with $\tilde{\rho}=\tilde{\lambda}=0$, we run the following $2N\left(T-1\right)$ observations artificial regression:

$$\begin{bmatrix} \frac{1}{\tilde{\sigma}_\epsilon}\tilde{e}^* \\ \iota_{N(T-1)} \end{bmatrix}=\begin{bmatrix} \frac{1}{\tilde{\sigma}_\epsilon}X^* & \frac{1}{\tilde{\sigma}_\epsilon^2}\tilde{e}^* & \frac{1}{\tilde{\sigma}_\epsilon}\left(I_{T-1}\otimes W\right)y^* & \frac{1}{\tilde{\sigma}_\epsilon}\left(I_{T-1}\otimes M\right)\tilde{e}^* \\ 0 & -\frac{1}{\tilde{\sigma}_\epsilon}\iota_{N(T-1)} & -\iota_{T-1}\otimes\omega & -\iota_{T-1}\otimes\eta \end{bmatrix}b$$
$$+\text{residuals}, \tag{23}$$

where $\omega = (\omega_1, \ldots, \omega_N)'$ are the eigenvalues of W, and $\eta = (\eta_1, \ldots, \eta_N)'$ are the eigenvalues of M. $\iota_{N(T-1)}$ and ι_{T-1} are vector of ones of dimension $N(T-1)$ and $T-1$, respectively. The explained sum of squares from the DLR in Eq. (23) will provide an asymptotically valid test statistic for H_0^a. This should be asymptotically distributed as χ_2^2 under the null.[3] It can alternatively be computed as $2N(T-1)$ minus the residual sum of squares of the above artificial regression.[4]

2.2. Conditional DLR Test for $H_0^b : \rho = 0$ (Allowing an Unrestricted Estimate of λ)

Under $H_0^b : \rho = 0$ (allowing an unrestricted estimate of λ), the restricted model is a panel data transformed regression with first-order spatial autoregressive disturbances:

$$\begin{aligned} y^* &= X^*\beta + \upsilon^*, \\ \upsilon^* &= \lambda\left(I_{T-1} \otimes M\right)\upsilon^* + \epsilon^*. \end{aligned} \tag{24}$$

Let $\hat{\beta}$, $\hat{\lambda}$, and $\hat{\sigma}_\epsilon^2$ denote the MLEs of β, λ, and σ_ϵ^2, respectively, under this restricted model. Using these restricted ML estimates $\hat{\varphi}' = \left[\hat{\beta}', \hat{\sigma}_\epsilon^2, \hat{\rho}, \hat{\lambda}\right]$ with $\hat{\rho} = 0$, we run the following $2N(T-1)$ observations artificial regression:

$$\begin{bmatrix} \frac{1}{\hat{\sigma}_\epsilon}\hat{e}^* \\ \iota_{N(T-1)} \end{bmatrix} = \begin{bmatrix} \frac{1}{\hat{\sigma}_\epsilon}\left(I_{T-1} \otimes \hat{B}\right)X^* & \frac{1}{\hat{\sigma}_\epsilon^2}\hat{e}^* & \frac{1}{\hat{\sigma}_\epsilon}\left(I_{T-1} \otimes W\hat{B}\right)y^* & \frac{1}{\hat{\sigma}_\epsilon}\left(I_{T-1} \otimes M\right)\hat{u}^* \\ 0 & -\frac{1}{\hat{\sigma}_\epsilon}\iota_{N(T-1)} & -\iota_{T-1} \otimes \omega & -\iota_{T-1} \otimes \eta^* \end{bmatrix} b + \text{residuals}, \tag{25}$$

where $\hat{e}^* = \left(I_{T-1} \otimes \hat{B}\right)\hat{\upsilon}^*$ with $\hat{B} = I_N - \hat{\lambda}M$ and $\hat{\upsilon}^* = y^* - X^*\hat{\beta}$, $\omega = (\omega_1, \ldots, \omega_N)'$ and $\eta^* = \left(\frac{\eta_1}{1-\hat{\lambda}\eta_1}, \ldots, \frac{\eta_N}{1-\hat{\lambda}\eta_N}\right)'$. The explained sum of squares from the DLR in Eq. (25) will provide an asymptotically valid test statistic for H_0^b. This should be asymptotically distributed as χ_1^2 under the null. It can alternatively be computed as $2N(T-1)$ minus the residual sum of squares of the above artificial regression.

2.3. *Conditional DLR Test for $H_0^c: \lambda = 0$ (Allowing an Unrestricted Estimate of ρ)*

Under $H_0^c: \lambda = 0$ (allowing an unrestricted estimate of ρ), the restricted model is a panel spatial autoregressive regression model of order one:

$$y^* = \rho \left(I_{T-1} \otimes W \right) y^* + X^* \beta + \epsilon^*. \tag{26}$$

Let $\bar{\beta}$, $\bar{\rho}$, and $\bar{\sigma}_\epsilon^2$ denote the MLEs of β, ρ, and σ_ϵ^2, respectively, under this restricted model. Using these restricted ML estimates $\bar{\varphi}' = \left[\bar{\beta}', \bar{\sigma}_\epsilon^2, \bar{\rho}, \bar{\lambda} \right]$ with $\bar{\lambda} = 0$, we run the following $2N(T-1)$ observations artificial regression:

$$\begin{bmatrix} \frac{1}{\bar{\sigma}_\epsilon} \bar{e}^* \\ \iota_{N(T-1)} \end{bmatrix} = \begin{bmatrix} \frac{1}{\bar{\sigma}_\epsilon} X^* & \frac{1}{\bar{\sigma}_\epsilon^2} \bar{e}^* & \frac{1}{\bar{\sigma}_\epsilon} \left(I_{T-1} \otimes W \right) y^* & \frac{1}{\bar{\sigma}_\epsilon} \left(I_{T-1} \otimes M \right) \bar{e}^* \\ 0 & -\frac{1}{\bar{\sigma}_\epsilon} \iota_{N(T-1)} & -\iota_{T-1} \otimes \omega^* & -\iota_{T-1} \otimes \eta \end{bmatrix} b$$
$$+ \text{residuals}, \tag{27}$$

where $\bar{e}^* = \left(I_{T-1} \otimes \bar{A} \right) y^* - X^* \hat{\beta}$ with $\bar{A} = I_N - \bar{\rho} W$, $\omega^* = \left(\frac{\omega_1}{1 - \bar{\rho}\omega_1}, \ldots, \frac{\omega_N}{1 - \bar{\rho}\omega_N} \right)'$ and $\eta = (\eta_1, \ldots, \eta_N)'$. The explained sum of squares from the DLR in Eq. (27) will provide an asymptotically valid test statistic for H_0^c. This should be asymptotically distributed as χ_1^2 under the null. It can alternatively be computed as $2N(T-1)$ minus the residual sum of squares of the above artificial regression.

3. EMPIRICAL ILLUSTRATION

Following Munnell (1990), Baltagi and Pinnoi (1995) considered the Cobb–Douglas production function relationship investigating the contribution of different types of public infrastructure on private production. Their regression model is as follows:

$$\log(Y) = \alpha + \beta_1 \log(K_1) + \beta_2 \log(K_2) + \beta_3 \log(L) + \beta_4 \log(Unemp) + u,$$

where Y is gross state product, K_1 is public capital that includes highways and streets, water and sewer facilities and other public buildings and structures. K_2 is the private capital stock based on the Bureau of Economic Analysis national stock estimates, L is the labor input measured as employment in nonagricultural payrolls. *Unemp* is the state unemployment rate included to capture business cycle effects. This panel consists of annual observations for 48 contiguous states over the period 1970–1986. The weighting matrix $W = M$ has elements different from zero if two states are neighbors. According to the queen contiguity matrix,

Table 1. Empirical Test Results.

	Statistic	p-value
$H_0^a : \lambda = \rho = 0$		
$\text{LM}_{\lambda\rho}$	243.405	0.000
$\text{DLR}_{\lambda\rho}$	191.157	0.000
$H_0^b : \rho = 0$ (allowing an unrestricted estimate of λ)		
$\text{LM}_{\rho\mid\lambda}$	5.960	0.015
$\text{DLR}_{\rho\mid\lambda}$	6.133	0.013
$H_0^c : \lambda = 0$ (allowing an unrestricted estimate of ρ)		
$\text{LM}_{\lambda\mid\rho}$	34.326	0.000
$\text{DLR}_{\lambda\mid\rho}$	34.495	0.000

Arizona and Colorado are considered neighbors. This weighting matrix has been row-normalized. Table 1 compares the results from applying the DLR statistics derived in this paper with their LM counterparts derived by Debarsy and Ertur (2010). The DLR statistics are computed as $2N\,(T-1)$ minus the residual sum of squares from Eqs. (23), (25) and (27). As we can see from the table, for all hypotheses considered, the DLR and its LM counterpart are close and provide the same decision. The joint test and conditional tests reject the absence of spatial dependence.

4. MONTE CARLO SIMULATION

This section investigates the small sample performance of the DLR and LM tests. Following Debarsy and Ertur (2010), we generate the data using the model in Eq. (1) with one regressor x_{it} generated by $x_{it} = 0.1t + 0.5x_{i,t-1} + z_{it}$ with $z_{it} \overset{i.i.d.}{\sim} U\,[-5, 5]$. The true parameters are as follows: $\beta = 3$, while ρ and λ varied over the range $(-0.8, -0.5, -0.2, 0, 0.2, 0.5, 0.8)$. The sample size chosen is ($N = 49$; $T = 10$). The weighting matrix $W = M$ is a row-normalized Rook-type of order 2. The individual specific effects are $\mu_i \overset{i.i.d.}{\sim} U\,[-5, 5]$ and the disturbances are $\epsilon_{it} \overset{i.i.d.}{\sim} N\,(0, 1)$. We performed 1,000 replications. It is worth pointing out that the eigenvalues of W need only to be computed once. Table 2 shows the simulation results. The size of the joint DLR and LM tests for $H_0^a : \rho = \lambda = 0$, using the 5% critical value of a χ_2^2, is 5.8% and 5.5%, respectively. The simulations are performed using a 2.83-GHz processor desktop computer with 2 GB of RAM and running Windows 7 Enterprise, Service Pack 1. Computation time of the simulation results is shown in Table 3. For the joint test, DLR computation time in seconds is more much shorter than LM. For conditional tests, the computation

Table 2. Simulation Results.

ρ	λ	$LM_{\lambda\rho}$	$DLR_{\lambda\rho}$	$LM_{\rho\|\lambda}$	$DLR_{\rho\|\lambda}$	$LM_{\lambda\|\rho}$	$DLR_{\lambda\|\rho}$
−0.8	−0.8	1.000	1.000	1.000	1.000	1.000	1.000
	−0.5	1.000	1.000	1.000	1.000	0.953	0.961
	−0.2	1.000	1.000	1.000	1.000	0.338	0.369
	0	1.000	1.000	1.000	1.000	0.038	0.039
	0.2	1.000	1.000	1.000	1.000	0.406	0.378
	0.5	1.000	1.000	1.000	1.000	0.994	0.994
	0.8	1.000	1.000	1.000	1.000	1.000	1.000
−0.5	−0.8	1.000	1.000	1.000	1.000	1.000	1.000
	−0.5	1.000	1.000	1.000	1.000	0.953	0.960
	−0.2	1.000	1.000	1.000	1.000	0.319	0.354
	0	1.000	1.000	1.000	1.000	0.045	0.046
	0.2	1.000	1.000	1.000	1.000	0.432	0.405
	0.5	0.999	0.999	1.000	1.000	0.994	0.994
	0.8	1.000	1.000	0.999	0.999	1.000	1.000
−0.2	−0.8	1.000	1.000	0.881	0.888	1.000	1.000
	−0.5	1.000	1.000	0.839	0.852	0.964	0.971
	−0.2	0.994	0.999	0.803	0.808	0.288	0.327
	0	0.797	0.825	0.724	0.726	0.056	0.060
	0.2	0.586	0.584	0.689	0.692	0.427	0.407
	0.5	0.988	0.985	0.574	0.575	0.989	0.988
	0.8	1.000	1.000	0.520	0.522	1.000	1.000
0	−0.8	1.000	1.000	0.060	0.060	1.000	1.000
	−0.5	0.993	0.995	0.049	0.049	0.971	0.975
	−0.2	0.362	0.418	0.049	0.049	0.344	0.382
	0	0.058	0.055	0.048	0.049	0.063	0.064
	0.2	0.569	0.523	0.049	0.049	0.435	0.408
	0.5	0.999	0.999	0.070	0.072	0.992	0.989
	0.8	1.000	1.000	0.049	0.047	1.000	1.000
0.2	−0.8	1.000	1.000	0.922	0.920	1.000	1.000
	−0.5	0.934	0.946	0.869	0.869	0.969	0.978
	−0.2	0.754	0.754	0.808	0.813	0.362	0.388
	0	0.909	0.898	0.741	0.747	0.047	0.048
	0.2	0.996	0.996	0.672	0.678	0.406	0.376
	0.5	1.000	1.000	0.568	0.567	0.991	0.990
	0.8	1.000	1.000	0.575	0.570	1.000	1.000
0.5	−0.8	1.000	1.000	1.000	1.000	1.000	1.000
	−0.5	1.000	1.000	1.000	1.000	0.976	0.979
	−0.2	1.000	1.000	1.000	1.000	0.351	0.377
	0	1.000	1.000	1.000	1.000	0.046	0.041
	0.2	1.000	1.000	1.000	1.000	0.417	0.396
	0.5	1.000	1.000	0.997	0.998	0.989	0.988
	0.8	1.000	1.000	1.000	1.000	1.000	1.000
0.8	−0.8	1.000	1.000	0.999	0.997	1.000	1.000
	−0.5	1.000	1.000	1.000	1.000	0.989	0.990
	−0.2	1.000	1.000	1.000	1.000	0.379	0.396
	0	1.000	1.000	1.000	1.000	0.040	0.042
	0.2	1.000	1.000	1.000	1.000	0.454	0.434
	0.5	1.000	1.000	1.000	1.000	0.993	0.992
	0.8	1.000	1.000	1.000	1.000	1.000	1.000

Note: 1,000 replications.

Table 3. Computation Time of Simulation Results.

ρ	λ	$LM_{\lambda\rho}$	$DLR_{\lambda\rho}$	$LM_{\rho\|\lambda}$	$DLR_{\rho\|\lambda}$	$LM_{\lambda\|\rho}$	$DLR_{\lambda\|\rho}$
−0.8	−0.8	154.60	41.94	542.95	539.57	673.19	675.59
	−0.5	148.48	30.53	544.75	542.49	674.80	675.94
	−0.2	148.80	30.47	544.40	542.10	674.16	678.12
	0	148.25	30.30	544.70	541.72	673.82	675.95
	0.2	148.26	30.59	545.35	543.84	674.69	676.14
	0.5	147.86	30.64	544.80	542.94	676.17	676.93
	0.8	148.26	30.64	544.74	542.79	674.67	677.79
−0.5	−0.8	148.47	30.68	546.33	542.01	675.76	679.71
	−0.5	148.74	30.84	547.64	544.32	673.79	676.17
	−0.2	148.17	30.51	544.94	541.81	673.86	677.78
	0	148.08	30.44	544.64	542.35	674.36	676.28
	0.2	148.40	30.57	546.45	541.84	673.88	676.43
	0.5	196.23	30.67	545.19	541.97	684.14	687.69
	0.8	150.58	31.00	552.47	550.78	679.82	687.33
−0.2	−0.8	148.87	31.25	548.63	544.34	677.87	693.14
	−0.5	149.06	30.53	546.89	545.52	675.74	678.69
	−0.2	148.59	30.77	546.10	543.35	677.67	678.02
	0	148.48	30.53	546.45	543.23	675.36	678.24
	0.2	148.53	31.41	546.88	561.44	674.94	677.40
	0.5	149.51	30.52	545.38	542.27	674.32	676.56
	0.8	148.40	30.65	545.27	566.47	744.56	677.72
0	−0.8	148.16	30.32	545.14	542.01	674.10	676.78
	−0.5	148.28	30.53	546.05	541.98	674.27	676.84
	−0.2	148.44	30.34	545.13	542.47	675.45	676.98
	0	148.17	30.31	545.08	541.71	673.98	677.48
	0.2	148.16	30.29	544.86	541.79	674.01	676.61
	0.5	148.19	30.52	546.13	542.79	674.62	676.86
	0.8	148.41	30.33	545.12	542.29	674.92	676.40
0.2	−0.8	148.61	30.69	545.20	542.12	674.49	677.77
	−0.5	157.19	43.37	555.58	547.00	682.05	684.23
	−0.2	150.21	31.62	552.50	560.22	698.88	731.89
	0	275.49	30.71	545.99	541.87	682.82	687.41
	0.2	150.31	32.19	563.30	553.04	685.14	680.04
	0.5	149.47	31.19	554.56	571.71	738.19	715.10
	0.8	148.28	30.83	542.95	543.64	675.61	677.32
0.5	−0.8	147.90	31.00	543.07	543.73	676.69	679.20
	−0.5	148.28	30.84	554.07	555.43	686.90	678.99
	−0.2	147.67	30.96	542.35	541.09	673.85	675.77
	0	147.46	30.66	541.37	541.43	675.33	676.45
	0.2	148.01	30.93	542.52	542.56	675.55	677.72
	0.5	148.01	30.85	542.45	542.84	675.54	676.97
	0.8	147.95	30.98	542.45	543.11	675.06	676.42
0.8	−0.8	147.82	30.89	542.15	542.72	679.29	693.55
	−0.5	151.58	31.00	542.62	542.97	675.73	677.56
	−0.2	148.22	30.90	547.90	550.36	685.30	678.20
	0	147.76	31.06	544.35	544.20	677.93	676.78
	0.2	148.03	30.94	543.32	543.01	675.34	677.74
	0.5	148.01	31.01	542.88	542.76	675.22	677.35
	0.8	148.16	30.87	544.19	544.46	676.66	678.98

Notes: The simulation is performed using a 2.83 GHz processor desktop computer with 2 GB of RAM and running Windows 7 Enterprise, Service Pack 1. 1,000 replications. Unit in seconds.

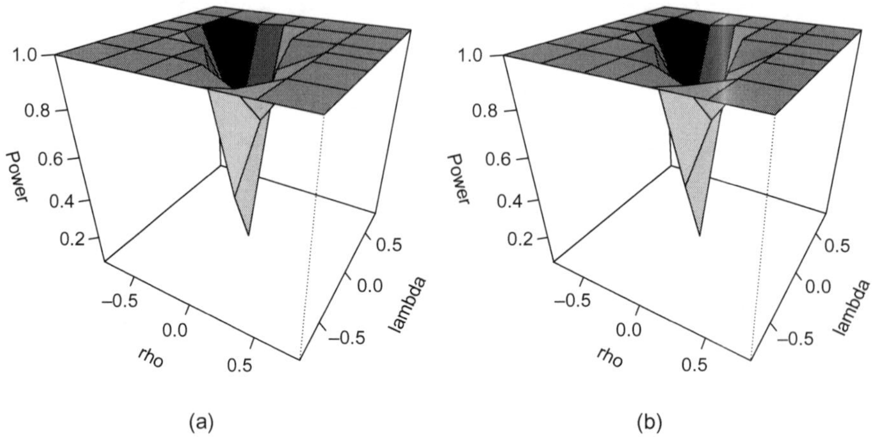

Fig. 1. Test for $H_0^a : \lambda = \rho = 0$. (a) LM Test and (b) DLR Test.

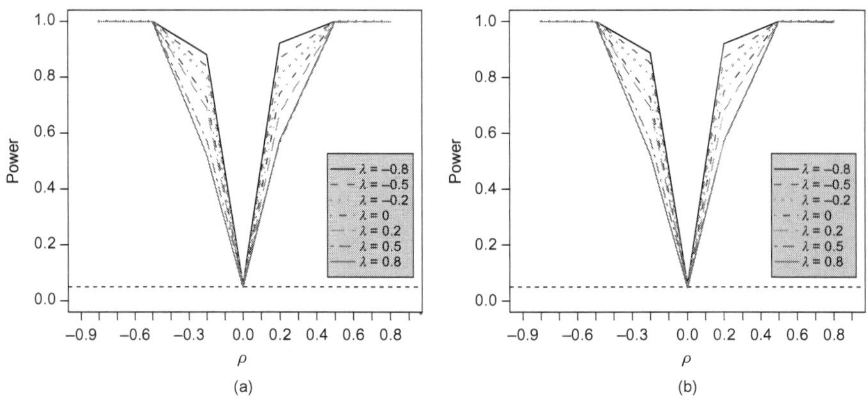

Fig. 2. Test for $H_0^b : \rho = 0$ (Allowing an Unrestricted Estimate of λ). (a) LM Test and (b) DLR Test.

the time for the LM and DLR is similar. Fig. 1 plots the corresponding power of the joint DLR and LM tests for $H_0^a : \rho = \lambda = 0$. The size of the conditional LM test for $H_0^b : \rho = 0$ (allowing an unrestricted estimate of λ), using the 5% critical value of a χ_1^2, varies between 4.8% and 7.0% depending on the value of λ, while that of the corresponding DLR test varies between 4.7% and 7.2% depending on the value of λ. Fig. 2 plots the corresponding power of the conditional LM test for $H_0^b : \rho = 0$ (allowing an unrestricted estimate of λ). Similarly, the size of the conditional LM test for $H_0^c : \lambda = 0$ (allowing an unrestricted estimate of ρ), using the 5% critical

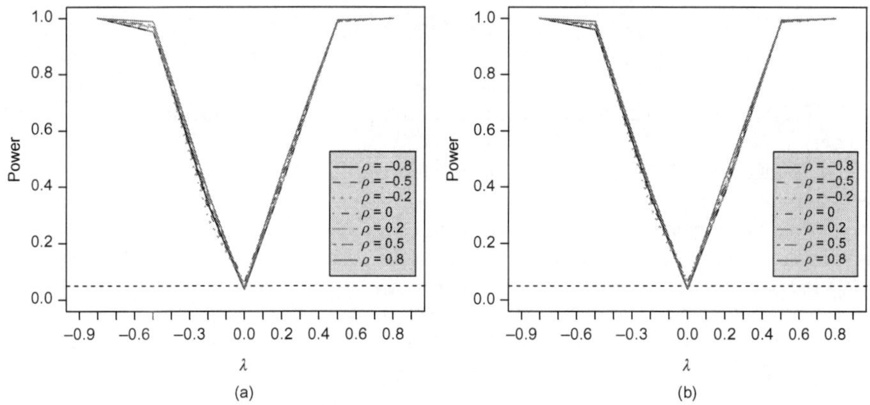

Fig. 3. Test for $H_0^c: \lambda = 0$ (Allowing an Unrestricted Estimate of ρ). (a) LM Test and (b) DLR Test.

value of a χ_1^2, varies between 3.8% and 6.3% depending on the value of ρ, while that of the corresponding DLR test varies between 3.9% and 6.4% depending on the value of ρ. Fig. 3 plots the corresponding power of the conditional LM test for $H_0^c: \lambda = 0$ (allowing an unrestricted estimate of ρ). As clear from the figures, the joint and conditional DLR and LM tests yield similar small sample performance in the Monte Carlo experiments.

5. CONCLUSION

This paper derives three artificial DLR tests corresponding to the LM tests derived by Debarsy and Ertur (2010) for the fixed effects spatial lag regression model with spatial autoregressive error. The first DLR jointly tests for zero spatial lag dependence as well as zero spatial autoregressive error in a fixed effects panel data model. The second DLR conditionally tests for zero spatial lag dependence allowing for spatial error dependence. While the third DLR conditionally tests for zero spatial error dependence allowing for spatial lag dependence. The proposed tests are illustrated using the productivity puzzle empirical example by Munnell (1990). In addition, Monte Carlo experiments show that the small sample performance of these DLR tests have similar performance to their corresponding LM counterparts. Furthermore, it would be nice if the normality assumption of the disturbances can be relaxed, though this is beyond the scope of this paper.

NOTES

1. Few finite sample studies exist in this literature, most notably Bao and Ullah (2007), who study the finite sample properties of the maximum likelihood estimator in spatial models.

2. Baltagi and Pirotte (2010) show that inference can be misleading if spatial dependence is ignored in spatial panel models.

3. In spatial models, the functional form changes with the sample size, that is, the functions F and K should have a sample size subscript. As a result, Slutsky's Lemma no longer applies and replacing the true parameter values φ with consistent estimates in Eq. (1) above does not necessarily lead to a consistent estimate of the information matrix. When F and K have the same functional form in different sample sizes, their continuity would guarantee this. Here, we need some stronger assumptions on the functions or require that the estimates are converging in a stronger sense (e.g., almost surely). Also, the standard LM tests are derived under the normality and homoskedasticity assumptions of the regression disturbances. Hence, they may not be robust against non-normality or heteroskedasticity of the disturbances. Baltagi and Yang (2013) applied the technique in Born and Breitung (2011) and introduced general methods to modify the standard LM tests so that they become robust against heteroskedasticity and non-normality. This is beyond the scope of this paper, though. We acknowledge this limitation in this paper and thank the referee for pointing it out.

4. It is important to point out that the asymptotic distribution of our test statistics is not explicitly derived in this paper. There is no proof in the literature that the LM tests are asymptotically χ^2 under the null. Given the simulations below, they most likely are but we cannot say under what assumptions this holds. These are likely to hold under a similar set of primitive assumptions developed by Kelejian and Prucha (2001) for the Moran-I test.

ACKNOWLEDGMENTS

We dedicate this paper in honor of Aman Ullah's many contributions to econometrics. We would like to thank two anonymous referees for their helpful comments and suggestions.

REFERENCES

Anselin, L. (1988a). *Spatial econometrics: Methods and models.* Dordrecht: Kluwer Academic Publishers.

Anselin, L. (1988b). Lagrange multiplier test diagnostics for spatial dependence and spatial heterogeneity. *Geographical Analysis*, *20*, 1–17.

Anselin, L. (2001). Rao's score tests in spatial econometrics. *Journal of Statistical Planning and Inference*, *97*, 113–139.

Anselin, L., & Bera, A. (1998). Spatial dependence in linear regression models with an introduction to spatial econometrics. In A. Ullah & D. E. A. Giles (Eds.), *Handbook of applied economic statistics*. New York, NY: Marcel Dekker.

Anselin, L., Bera, A., Florax, R., & Yoon, M. (1996). Simple diagnostic tests for spatial dependence. *Regional Science and Urban Economics*, *26*, 77–104.

Baltagi, B. H. (1999). Double length regressions for linear and log-linear regressions with AR(1) disturbances. *Statistical Papers*, *40*, 199–209.

Baltagi, B. H. (2011). Spatial panels. In A. Ullah & D. E. A. Giles (Eds.), *The handbook of empirical economics and finance* (pp. 435–454). Boca Raton, FL: Chapman & Hall.

Baltagi, B. H. (2013). *Econometric analysis of panel data*. New York, NY: Wiley.

Baltagi, B. H., & Li, D. (2001). Double length artificial regressions for testing spatial dependence. *Econometric Reviews*, *20*, 31–40.

Baltagi, B. H., & Liu, L. (2008). Testing for random effects and spatial lag dependence in panel data models. *Statistics and Probability Letters*, *78*, 3304–3306.

Baltagi, B. H., & Liu, L. (2014). Testing for spatial lag and spatial error dependence using double length artificial regressions. *Statistical Papers*, *55*(2), 477–486.

Baltagi, B. H., & Pinnoi, N. (1995). Public capital stock and state productivity growth: Further evidence from an error components model. *Empirical Economics*, *20*, 351–359.

Baltagi, B. H., & Pirotte, A. (2010). Panel data inference under spatial dependence. *Economic Modelling*, *27*, 1368–1381.

Baltagi, B. H., Song, S. H., & Koh, W. (2003). Testing panel data regression models with spatial error correlation. *Journal of Econometrics*, *117*, 123–150.

Baltagi, B. H., & Yang, Z. (2013). Heteroskedasticity and nonnormality robust LM tests for spatial dependence. *Regional Science and Urban Economics*, *43*(5), 725–739.

Bao, Y., & Ullah, A. (2007). Finite sample properties of maximum likelihood estimator in spatial models. *Journal of Econometrics*, *137*(2), 396–413.

Born, B., & Breitung, J. (2011). Simple regression based tests for spatial dependence. *Econometrics Journal*, *14*, 330–342.

Davidson, R., & MacKinnon, J. G. (1984). Model specification tests based on artificial linear regressions. *International Economic Review*, *25*, 485–502.

Davidson, R., & MacKinnon, J. G. (1988). Double-length artificial regression. *Oxford Bulletin of Economics and Statistics*, *50*, 203–217.

Davidson, R., & MacKinnon, J. G. (1993). *Estimation and inference in econometrics*. Oxford: Oxford University Press.

Debarsy, N., & Ertur, C. (2010). Testing for spatial autocorrelation in a fixed effects panel data model. *Regional Science and Urban Economics*, *40*(6), 453–470.

Kelejian, H. H., & Prucha, I. R. (2001). On the asymptotic distribution of the Moran I test with applications. *Journal of Econometrics*, *104*, 219–257.

Krämer, W. (2003). The robustness of the F-test to spatial autocorrelation among regression disturbances. *Statistica*, *3*, 435–440.

Krämer, W. (2005). Finite sample power of Cliff-Ord-type tests for spatial disturbance correlation in linear regression. *Journal of Statistical Planning and Inference*, *128*, 489–496.

Le, C., & Li, D. (2008). Double-length regression tests for testing functional forms and spatial error dependence. *Economics Letters*, *101*, 253–257.

Lee, L. F., & Yu, J. (2010a). Some recent developments in spatial panel data models. *Regional Science and Urban Economics*, *40*, 255–271.

Lee, L. F., & Yu, J. (2010b). Estimation of spatial autoregressive panel data models with fixed effects. *Journal of Econometrics*, *154*, 165–185.

Li, M., Yu, D., & Bai, P. (2013). A note on the existence and uniqueness of quasi-maximum likelihood estimators for mixed regressive, spatial autoregression models. *Statistics & Probability Letters*, *83*(2), 568–572.

Munnell, A. (1990). Why has productivity growth declined? Productivity and public investment. *New England Economic Review*, *30*, 3–22.

Mynbaev, K. T., & Ullah, A. (2008). Asymptotic distribution of the OLS estimator for a purely autoregressive spatial model. *Journal of Multivariate Analysis*, *99*(2), 245–277.

Ord, J. (1975). Estimation methods for models of spatial interaction. *Journal of the American Statistical Association*, *70*, 120–126.

LONG-RUN EFFECTS IN LARGE HETEROGENEOUS PANEL DATA MODELS WITH CROSS-SECTIONALLY CORRELATED ERRORS

Alexander Chudik[a], Kamiar Mohaddes[b], M. Hashem Pesaran[c,d] and Mehdi Raissi[e]

[a]*Federal Reserve Bank of Dallas, Dallas, TX, USA*
[b]*Faculty of Economics and Girton College, University of Cambridge, Cambridge, UK*
[c]*Department of Economics & USC Dornsife INET, University of Southern California, Los Angeles, CA, USA*
[d]*Trinity College, Cambridge, UK*
[e]*International Monetary Fund, Washington, DC, USA*

ABSTRACT

This paper develops a cross-sectionally augmented distributed lag (CS-DL) approach to the estimation of long-run effects in large dynamic heterogeneous panel data models with cross-sectionally dependent errors. The asymptotic distribution of the CS-DL estimator is derived under coefficient heterogeneity in the case where the time dimension (T) *and the cross-section dimension* (N) *are both large. The CS-DL approach is compared with more*

Essays in Honor of Aman Ullah
Advances in Econometrics, Volume 36, 85–135

ISSN: 0731-9053/doi:10.1108/S0731-905320160000036013

standard panel data estimators that are based on autoregressive distributed lag (ARDL) specifications. It is shown that unlike the ARDL-type estimator, the CS-DL estimator is robust to misspecification of dynamics and error serial correlation. The theoretical results are illustrated with small sample evidence obtained by means of Monte Carlo simulations, which suggest that the performance of the CS-DL approach is often superior to the alternative panel ARDL estimates, particularly when T *is not too large and lies in the range of 30–50.*

Keywords: Long-run relationships; estimation and inference; panel distributed lags; large dynamic heterogeneous panels; cross-section dependence

JEL classifications: C23

1. INTRODUCTION

Estimation of long-run effects is of great importance in economics. The concept of 'long-run relations' is typically associated with the steady-state solution of a structural macroeconomic model. Often the same long-run relations can also be obtained from arbitrage conditions within and across markets. As a result, many long-run relationships in economics are free of particular model assumptions; examples being purchasing power parity, uncovered interest parity and the Fisher inflation parity. Other long-run relations, such as those between macroeconomic aggregates like consumption and income, output and investment, and technological progress and real wages, are less grounded in arbitrage and hence are more controversial, but still form a major part of what is generally agreed-upon in empirical macroeconomic modelling. This is in contrast to the analysis of short-run effects, which are model specific and subject to identification problems.

This paper is concerned with the estimation and inference of long-run effects using dynamic panel data models where the time dimension (T) and the cross-section dimension (N) are both relatively large. Such panels are becoming increasingly available and cover countries, counties, regions, industries and firms, and typically feature dynamics in the form of lagged-dependent variables, slope heterogeneity (at least in the case of short-run coefficients), as well as cross-sectionally dependent innovations. These three key features complicate estimation and inference.

Earlier literature on the estimation of long-run effects using panel data, such as the pooled mean group approach (Pesaran, Shin, and Smith, 1999), the panel dynamic OLS approach (Mark and Sul 2003) and the panel fully modified OLS approach (Pedroni 2001), allow for lagged-dependent variables and heterogeneity of short-run dynamics, but they do not allow for error cross-section dependence. Wrongly assuming that errors are cross-sectionally independently distributed leads to incorrect inference and in some cases inconsistent estimates, depending on the nature of the error cross-section dependence. For example, when cross-section dependence is due to the presence of unobserved common factors, parameter inconsistency arises if the factors and the regressors are correlated.

The problem of error cross-section dependence has been addressed in the literature primarily in the context of panel data models without lagged-dependent variables. See, for example, the common correlated effects (CCE) approach of Pesaran (2006), or the interactive fixed effects (IFE) estimator of Bai (2009). A survey of the recent literature is provided by Chudik and Pesaran (2015a). Two exceptions are Song (2013), who extends Bai's approach to allow for lagged-dependent variables and coefficient heterogeneity, and Chudik and Pesaran (2015b), who extend the CCE approach to allow for weakly exogenous regressors (including lagged-dependent variables).[1] Both approaches rely on the estimation of unit-specific ARDL specifications, appropriately augmented with cross-section averages to filter out the effects of the unobserved common factors, from which long-run effects can be indirectly estimated. We refer to this approach as cross-sectionally augmented ARDL or CS-ARDL in short. The main drawback of computing the long-run coefficients from CS-ARDL specifications is that due to the inclusion of lagged-dependent variables in the regressions often quite a large time dimension is required for satisfactory small sample performance, especially if the sum of the AR coefficients in the ARDL specifications are close to unity. In the case of heterogenous slope specifications, the CS-ARDL estimates of the long-run coefficients could also be sensitive to outlier estimates of the long-run effects for individual cross-section units.

This paper makes a theoretical contribution to the econometric analysis of the long run by proposing a new approach to the estimation of long-run coefficients in dynamic heterogeneous panels with cross-sectionally dependent errors. The approach is based on a distributed lag representation that does not include lags of the dependent variable, and allows for residual factor error structure and weak cross-section dependence of idiosyncratic errors. Similar to CCE estimators proposed by Pesaran (2006), the individual regressions are augmented with cross-section averages to deal with the effects of common factors. We derive the asymptotic distribution of the proposed cross-sectionally augmented distributed lag (or CS-DL for short) mean group and pooled estimators under the coefficient heterogeneity and large time and cross-section dimensions. By means of Monte Carlo experiments, we also investigate the consequences of various departures from our maintained assumptions on the small sample properties of CS-DL estimators by allowing for unit roots in the factors and/or in the regressors, breaks in the error processes, and homogeneity of long-run coefficients. We also investigate whether the use of CS-DL estimates of long-run coefficients can improve the estimation of short-run coefficients.

The main advantage of the proposed CS-DL approach is its robustness to dynamic misspecification and its small sample performance, which is often better compared to estimating unit-specific CS-ARDL specifications, under a variety of settings investigated in the Monte Carlo experiments when T is moderately large ($30 \leq T \leq 50$). Furthermore, the imposition of CS-DL estimates of long-run coefficients can substantially improve the estimates of short-run coefficients. Last but not least, the CS-DL approach does not require the rank condition required by the CS-ARDL approach, which ensures that the cross-section averages approximate the space of the unobserved factors arbitrarily well, as $N \rightarrow \infty$, if it is assumed that the factor loadings in the equation for the dependent variable are independently distributed from factor loadings in the equations for regressors. In the case when the rank condition and the independence of factor loadings do not hold, it is possible to consider augmentation by principal components instead of cross-section averages, but the derivation of asymptotic results is more complicated in the case of principal components and lies outside the scope of this paper.

Despite these important advantages, the CS-DL approach should be seen as complementary and not as superior to the CS-ARDL approach. The main drawback is that, unlike the panel CS-ARDL approach, the CS-DL approach does not allow for feedback effects from the dependent variable onto the regressors. However, a careful investigation of the size of the small sample bias due to the presence of such feedback effects suggests that the CS-DL approach can still outperform the CS-ARDL approach when T is moderately large. The relative merits of different approaches are carefully documented in the paper, and our main conclusion is that the CS-DL approach is a valuable complementary method for estimating long-run effects in panels where the time dimension is moderately large.

The remainder of this paper is organized as follows. Section 2 shows how long-run coefficients can be derived from vector autoregressive models, and discuss alternative estimation approaches. Section 3 introduces the CS-DL approach to the estimation of long-run relationships. Section 4 investigates the relative small sample performance of CS-DL and CS-ARDL estimators, using Monte Carlo experiments. Section 5 offers some concluding remarks. Mathematical derivations are provided in an appendix.

A brief word on notation: All vectors are column vectors represented by bold lower case letters, and matrices are represented by bold upper case letters. $\varrho(\mathbf{A})$ is the spectral radius of the $n \times n$ matrix, $\mathbf{A} = (a_{ij})$, $\|\mathbf{A}\| = \sqrt{\varrho(\mathbf{A}'\mathbf{A})}$ is the spectral norm of $\mathbf{A}$.[2] $\|\mathbf{A}\|_\infty$ and $\|\mathbf{A}\|_1$, defined by $\|\mathbf{A}\|_\infty = \max_{1 \leq i \leq n} \Sigma_{j=1}^{n} |a_{ij}|$ and $\|\mathbf{A}\|_1 = \max_{1 \leq j \leq n} \Sigma_{i=1}^{n} |a_{ij}|$, are maximum row sum matrix and column sum matrix norms, respectively. $a_n = O(b_n)$ denotes the deterministic sequence, $\{a_n\}$ is at most of order b_n. Convergence in probability and convergence in distribution are denoted by $\overset{p}{\rightarrow}$ and $\overset{d}{\rightarrow}$, respectively. $(N, T) \overset{j}{\rightarrow} \infty$ denotes joint asymptotics in N and T, with N and $T \rightarrow \infty$, in no particular order. We use K to denote a positive fixed constant that does not vary with N or T.

2. ESTIMATION OF LONG-RUN OR LEVEL RELATIONSHIPS IN ECONOMICS

The estimation of long-run relations can be carried out with or without constraining the short-run dynamics. In this section, we focus on the estimation of long-run relations without restricting the short-run dynamics and we assume that there exists a single long-run relationship between the dependent variable, y_t, and a set of regressors.[3] For illustrative purposes, suppose that there is one regressor x_t and suppose that $\mathbf{z}_t = (y_t, x_t)'$ is jointly determined by the following vector autoregression of order 1, VAR(1):

$$\mathbf{z}_t = \mathbf{\Phi z}_{t-1} + \mathbf{e}_t, \tag{1}$$

where $\mathbf{\Phi} = (\phi_{ij})$ is a 2×2 matrix of unknown parameters, and $\mathbf{e}_t = \left(e_{yt}, e_{xt}\right)'$ is a two-dimensional vector of reduced-form errors. Denoting the covariance of e_{yt} and e_{xt} by $\omega Var\,(e_{xt})$, we can write

$$e_{yt} = E\left(e_{yt}\,|e_{xt}\right) + u_t = \omega e_{xt} + u_t, \tag{2}$$

where by construction u_t is uncorrelated with e_{xt}, namely, $E\,(u_t\,|e_{xt}) = 0$. Substituting (2) for e_{yt}, the equation for the dependent variable y_t in Eq. (1) is

$$y_t = \phi_{11} y_{t-1} + \phi_{12} x_{t-1} + \omega e_{xt} + u_t. \tag{3}$$

Using the equation for the regressor x_t in Eq. (1), we obtain the following expression for e_{xt}:

$$e_{xt} = x_t - \phi_{21} y_{t-1} - \phi_{22} x_{t-1},$$

and substituting this expression for e_{xt} back in Eq. (3) yields the following *conditional* model for y_t:

$$y_t = \varphi y_{t-1} + \beta_0 x_t + \beta_1 x_{t-1} + u_t, \tag{4}$$

where

$$\varphi = \phi_{11} - \omega\phi_{21}, \quad \beta_0 = \omega, \quad \beta_1 = \phi_{12} - \omega\phi_{22}. \tag{5}$$

Note that u_t is uncorrelated with the regressor x_t and its lagged values by construction. (4) is ARDL(1,1) representation of y_t conditional on x_t, and the short-run coefficients φ, β_0 and β_1 can be directly estimated from Eq. (4) by least squares regardless whether $\mathbf{z}_t$ is integrated of order one, $I(1)$ for short, or stationary, $I(0)$. See Pesaran and Shin (1999) for a related discussion. Model (4) can also be written in the form of the error-correction model,

$$\Delta y_t = -(1-\varphi)(y_{t-1} - \theta x_{t-1}) + \beta_0 \Delta x_t + u_t,$$

or as the following level relationship

$$y_t = \theta x_t + \alpha(L)\Delta x_t + \tilde{u}_t, \tag{6}$$

where $\tilde{u}_t = (1-\varphi L)^{-1} u_t$, $\alpha(L) = \sum_{\ell=0}^{\infty} \alpha_\ell L^\ell$, $\alpha_\ell = -\sum_{s=\ell+1}^{\infty} \delta_s$, for $\ell = 0, 1, 2, \ldots$, and

$$\delta(L) = \sum_{\ell=0}^{\infty} \delta_\ell L^\ell = (1-\varphi L)^{-1}(\beta_0 + \beta_1 L).$$

The level coefficient, θ, is defined by

$$\theta = \frac{\beta_0 + \beta_1}{1-\varphi}.$$

Note that if $\mathbf{z}_t$ is $I(1)$ then $(1, -\theta)'$ is the cointegrating vector and the level relation (6) is also cointegrating.

The level coefficient θ can still be motivated as the long-run outcome of a counterfactual exercise even if $\mathbf{z}_t$ is stationary. One possible counterfactual is to consider the effects of a permanent shock to the x_t process on y_t in the long run. Let

$$g_{yt} = \lim_{s\to\infty} E\left(y_{t+s} - \mu_{y,t+s} \middle| \mathcal{I}_{t-1}, e_{x,t+h} = \sigma_x, \text{ for } h = 0, 1, 2, \ldots\right),$$

and similarly

$$g_{xt} = \lim_{s\to\infty} E\left(x_{t+s} - \mu_{x,t+s} \middle| \mathcal{I}_{t-1}, e_{x,t+h} = \sigma_x, \text{ for } h = 0, 1, 2, \ldots\right),$$

where μ_{yt} and μ_{xt}, respectively, are the deterministic components of y_t and x_t (in the current illustrative example deterministic components are zero) and $\mathcal{I}_t$ is the set containing all information up to the period t. Using Eq. (1) and noting that

$E\left(e_{yt}\left|e_{xt}\right.\right)=\omega e_{xt}$, we obtain $g_{yt}=g_y$, $g_{xt}=g_x$,[4]

$$\mathbf{g}=\begin{pmatrix} g_y \\ g_x \end{pmatrix}=(\mathbf{I}_2-\mathbf{\Phi})^{-1}\begin{pmatrix} \omega \\ 1 \end{pmatrix}\sigma_x=\begin{pmatrix} -\frac{\omega+\phi_{12}-\omega\phi_{22}}{\phi_{11}+\phi_{22}-\phi_{11}\phi_{22}+\phi_{12}\phi_{21}-1} \\ -\frac{\omega\phi_{21}-\phi_{11}+1}{\phi_{11}+\phi_{22}-\phi_{11}\phi_{22}+\phi_{12}\phi_{21}-1} \end{pmatrix}\sigma_x,$$

and

$$\frac{g_y}{g_x}=\frac{\omega+\phi_{12}-\omega\phi_{22}}{1-(\phi_{11}-\omega\phi_{21})},$$

which upon using Eq. (5) yields, $g_y=\theta g_x$, namely, the long-run impact of a permanent change in the mean of x on y is given by θ. Note that only in the special case when the reduced-form errors are uncorrelated ($\omega=0$), is the short-run coefficient β_0 in the ARDL model (4) equal to 0 and the long-run coefficient θ reduces to $\phi_{12}/\left(1-\phi_{11}\right)$. But, in general, when $\omega\neq 0$, the short-run coefficient β_0 is non-zero and contemporaneous values of the regressor should not be excluded from Eq. (4). In the stationary case with regressors not strictly exogenous, θ depends also on the parameters of the x_t process and the estimation of θ should therefore be based on Eq. (4).

An alternative way to show that θ is equal to the ratio g_y/g_x is to consider the ARDL representation (4) for the future period $t+s$, given the information at time $t-1$. We first note that

$$y_{t+s}=\varphi y_{t+s-1}+\beta_0 x_{t+s}+\beta_1 x_{t+s-1}+u_{t+s},$$

and after taking the conditional expectation with respect to $\{\mathcal{I}_{t-1}, e_{x,t+h}=\sigma_x,$ for $h=0,1,2,\ldots\}$, taking limits as $s\to\infty$, and noting that in the stationary case $g_{yt}=g_y$ and $g_{xt}=g_x$, we obtain

$$g_y=\varphi g_y+\beta_0 g_x+\beta_1 g_x,$$

and hence

$$\frac{g_y}{g_x}=\frac{\beta_0+\beta_1}{1-\varphi}=\theta,$$

as desired.

Regardless of whether the variables are $I(1)$, or $I(0)$, or whether the regressors are exogenous or not, the level coefficient θ is well defined and can be consistently estimated. The rates of convergence and the asymptotic distribution of the ARDL estimates of θ in the case of $I(1)$ regressors are established in Pesaran and Shin (1999). See, in particular, their Theorem 3.3.

2.1. Two Approaches to the Estimation of Long-Run Effects

Consider now the problem of the estimation of long-run effects in heterogeneous dynamic panels with a multi-factor error structure. Let y_{it} be the dependent variable of the ith cross-section unit, $\mathbf{x}_{it}$ be the $k \times 1$ vector of unit-specific regressors, and consider the following panel $ARDL(p_{yi}, p_{xi})$ specification:

$$y_{it} = \sum_{\ell=1}^{p_{yi}} \varphi_{i\ell} y_{i,t-\ell} + \sum_{\ell=0}^{p_{xi}} \boldsymbol{\beta}_{i\ell}' \mathbf{x}_{i,t-\ell} + u_{it}, \tag{7}$$

$$u_{it} = \boldsymbol{\gamma}_i' \mathbf{f}_t + \varepsilon_{it}, \tag{8}$$

for $i = 1, 2, \ldots, N$ and $t = 1, 2, \ldots, T$, where $\mathbf{f}_t$ is an $m \times 1$ vector of unobserved common factors, and p_{yi} and p_{xi} are the lag orders chosen to be sufficiently long so that u_{it} is a serially uncorrelated process across all i. The vector of long-run coefficients is then given by

$$\boldsymbol{\theta}_i = \frac{\sum_{\ell=0}^{p_{xi}} \boldsymbol{\beta}_{i\ell}}{1 - \sum_{\ell=1}^{p_{yi}} \varphi_{i\ell}}. \tag{9}$$

There are two approaches to estimating the long-run coefficients. One approach, already considered in the literature, is to estimate the individual short-run coefficients $\{\varphi_{i\ell}\}$ and $\{\boldsymbol{\beta}_{i\ell}\}$ in the ARDL relation (7) and then compute the estimates of long-run effects using formula (9) with the short-run coefficients replaced by their estimates $\{\hat{\varphi}_{i\ell}\}$ and $\{\hat{\boldsymbol{\beta}}_{i\ell}\}$. We shall refer to this approach as the 'ARDL approach to the estimation of long-run effects'. The advantage of this approach is that the estimates of short-run coefficients are also obtained. But when the focus is on the long-run coefficients, $\boldsymbol{\theta}_i$ can be estimated *directly* without first estimating the short-run coefficients. This is possible by observing that the ARDL model (7) can be written as

$$y_{it} = \boldsymbol{\theta}_i \mathbf{x}_{it} + \boldsymbol{\alpha}_i' (L) \Delta \mathbf{x}_{it} + \tilde{u}_{it}, \tag{10}$$

where

$$\boldsymbol{\theta}_i = \boldsymbol{\delta}_i (1), \quad \boldsymbol{\delta}_i (L) = \varphi_i^{-1} (L) \boldsymbol{\beta}_i (L) = \sum_{\ell=0}^{\infty} \boldsymbol{\delta}_{i\ell} L^{\ell},$$

$$\varphi_i (L) = 1 - \sum_{\ell=1}^{p_{yi}} \varphi_{i\ell} L^{\ell}, \quad \boldsymbol{\beta}_i (L) = \sum_{\ell=0}^{p_{xi}} \boldsymbol{\beta}_{i\ell} L^{\ell}$$

and

$$\boldsymbol{\alpha}_i (L) = -\sum_{\ell=0}^{\infty} \sum_{s=\ell+1}^{\infty} \boldsymbol{\delta}_{is} L^{\ell}, \quad \tilde{u}_{it} = \varphi_i (L)^{-1} u_{it}.$$

We shall refer to the direct estimation of $\boldsymbol{\theta}_i$ based on the distributed lag representation (10) as the 'distributed lag (DL) approach to the estimation of long-run effects'. Under the usual assumptions on the roots of $\varphi_i(L)$ falling strictly outside the unit circle, the coefficients of $\boldsymbol{\alpha}_i(L)$ are exponentially decaying; and it is possible to show that, in the absence of feedback effects from lagged values of y_{it} onto the regressors $\mathbf{x}_{it}$, a consistent estimate of $\boldsymbol{\theta}_i$ can be obtained directly based on the least-squares regression of y_{it} on $\mathbf{x}_{it}$ and $\left\{\Delta \mathbf{x}_{i,t-\ell}\right\}_{\ell=0}^{p}$, where the truncation lag order p is chosen appropriately as an increasing function of the sample size. But, when the feedback effects from the lagged values of the dependent variable to the regressors are present, $\tilde{u}_{it}$ will be correlated with $\mathbf{x}_{it}$ and the DL approach would no longer be consistent. Note that strict exogeneity is, however, not necessarily required for the consistency of the DL approach, since arbitrary correlations amongst the individual reduced-form innovations in $\mathbf{e}_t$ are still allowed. Using the individual long-run estimates, $\hat{\boldsymbol{\theta}}_i$, consistent estimates of the average long-run effects can be obtained as $\bar{\hat{\boldsymbol{\theta}}} = N^{-1}\sum_{i=1}^{N}\hat{\boldsymbol{\theta}}_i$.

2.2. *Pros and Cons of the Two Approaches to the Estimation of Long-Run Effects*

Consider first the ARDL approach, where the estimates of long-run effects are computed based on the estimates of the short-run coefficients in Eq. (7). In the case where the unobserved common factors are serially uncorrelated and are also uncorrelated with the regressors, the long-run coefficients can be estimated consistently from the Ordinary Least Squares (OLS) estimates of the short-run coefficients, irrespective of whether the regressors are strictly exogenous or jointly determined with y_{it}, in the sense that $\mathbf{z}_{it} = \left(y_{it}, \mathbf{x}_{it}'\right)'$ follows a VAR model. The long-run estimates are also consistent irrespective of whether the underlying variables are $I(0)$ or $I(1)$. These robustness properties are clearly important in empirical research. However, the ARDL approach has also a number of drawbacks. The sampling uncertainty could be large especially when the speed of convergence towards the long-run relation is rather slow and the time dimension is not sufficiently long. This is readily apparent from Eq. (9) since even a small change to $1 - \sum_{\ell=1}^{p_{yi}}\hat{\varphi}_{i\ell}$ could have a large impact on the estimates of $\boldsymbol{\theta}_i$ when $\sum_{\ell=1}^{p_{yi}}\hat{\varphi}_{i\ell}$ is close to unity. In this respect, a correct specification of the lag orders could be quite important for the performance of the ARDL estimates of $\boldsymbol{\theta}_i$. Underestimating the lag orders leads to inconsistent estimates, whilst overestimating the lag orders could result in a loss of efficiency and low power when the ARDL long-run estimates are used for inference.

In the more general case when the unobserved common factors are correlated with the regressors, then the LS estimation of the ARDL model is no longer consistent and the effects of unobserved common factors need to be taken into account. There are two possible estimators developed in the literature so far for this case:[5] a principal-components based approach by Song (2013), who extends the IFE estimator of Bai (2009) to the dynamic heterogeneous panels, and the dynamic CCE mean group estimator suggested by Chudik and Pesaran (2015b). A recent overview of these methods is provided in Chudik and Pesaran (2015a). These estimators have been proposed (so far) only for stationary panels, and are subject to the small T bias of the ARDL approach discussed above. Bias correction techniques can also be used, but overall they do not seem to be effective when the speed of adjustment to the steady state is slow.[6]

The main merit of the DL approach proposed in this paper is its robustness along a number of important dimensions, and the fact that it tends to exhibit better small sample performance as compared to the panel ARDL estimates when the time dimension T is not very large. Specifically, (i) it is robust to the possibility of unit roots in regressors and/or factors, (ii) it is applicable irrespective of whether the short- and/or long-run coefficients are heterogenous or homogeneous, (iii) it is robust to an arbitrary degree of serial correlation in ε_{it} and $\mathbf{f}_t$,[7] (iv) it does not require knowledge of the number of unobserved common factors under certain conditions, and (v) it continues to be valid under weak cross-section dependence in the idiosyncratic errors, ε_{it}. These robustness properties are very important considerations in applied research. In addition, the CS-DL approach does not require specifying the individual lag orders, p_{yi} and p_{xi}, and is robust to possible breaks in ε_{it}. The main drawback of the CS-DL approach, however, is that $\tilde{u}_{it} = \varphi_i (L)^{-1} u_{it}$ will be correlated with $\mathbf{x}_{it}$ when there are feedback effects from lagged values of y_{it} onto the regressors, $\mathbf{x}_{it}$. This correlation in turn introduces a bias even when N and T are sufficiently large, and therefore the CS-DL estimation of the long-run effects is consistent only in the case when the feedback effects (or reverse causality) are not present. The second drawback is that the small sample performance is very good only when the eigenvalues of $\varphi_i (L)$ are not close to the unit circle. We will provide small sample evidence on the two approaches by means of Monte Carlo experiments in Section 4.

3. CS-DL APPROACH TO ESTIMATION OF MEAN LONG-RUN COEFFICIENTS

3.1. The ARDL Panel Data Model

To simplify the exposition, we consider the panel ARDL data model (7) with $p_{yi} = 1$ and $p_{xi} = 0$

$$y_{it} = \varphi_i y_{i,t-1} + \boldsymbol{\beta}_i' \mathbf{x}_{it} + \boldsymbol{\gamma}_i' \mathbf{f}_t + \varepsilon_{it}. \tag{11}$$

To allow for correlation between the m unobserved factors, $\mathbf{f}_t$, and the k observed regressors, $\mathbf{x}_{it}$, we assume that the latter is generated according to the following factor model:

$$\mathbf{x}_{it} = \mathbf{\Gamma}_i' \mathbf{f}_t + \mathbf{v}_{it}, \tag{12}$$

for $i = 1, 2, \ldots, N$ and $t = 1, 2, \ldots, T$, where $\mathbf{\Gamma}_i$ is an $m \times k$ matrix of factor loadings, and $\mathbf{v}_{it}$ are the idiosyncratic components of $\mathbf{x}_{it}$ which are assumed to be distributed independently of the idiosyncratic errors, ε_{it}. The panel data model (11) and (12) is identical to the model considered by Pesaran (2006), with the exception that the lagged-dependent variable is included in Eq. (11). We have also omitted observed common effects and deterministics (such as intercepts and time trends) from Eq. (11) to simplify the exposition. Introducing these terms and additional lags of the dependent variable and regressors complicates notations but does not pose additional technical difficulties.

We are interested in the estimation of the mean long-run coefficients $\boldsymbol{\theta} = E(\boldsymbol{\theta}_i)$, where $\boldsymbol{\theta}_i$, $i = 1, 2, \ldots, N$, are the cross-section-specific long-run coefficients defined by Eq. (9), which for $p_{yi} = 1$ and $p_{xi} = 0$ reduces to

$$\boldsymbol{\theta}_i = \frac{\boldsymbol{\beta}_i}{1 - \varphi_i}. \tag{13}$$

We postulate the following assumptions.

Assumption 1. (*Individual specific errors*).
Individual-specific errors ε_{it} and $\mathbf{v}_{jt'}$ are independently distributed for all i, j, t and t'. ε_{it} follows a linear stationary process with absolute summable autocovariances (uniformly in i),

$$\varepsilon_{it} = \sum_{\ell=0}^{\infty} \alpha_{\varepsilon i\ell} \zeta_{i,t-\ell}, \tag{14}$$

for $i = 1, 2, \ldots, N$, where the vector of innovations $\boldsymbol{\zeta}_t = (\zeta_{1t}, \zeta_{2t}, \ldots, \zeta_{Nt})'$ is spatially correlated according to

$$\boldsymbol{\zeta}_t = \mathbf{R}\boldsymbol{\varsigma}_t,$$

in which the elements of ς_t, ς_{it}, are independently and identically distributed (IID) with zero means, unit variances and finite fourth-order cumulants. Matrix $\mathbf{R}$ has bounded maximum column and row sum matrix norms, namely, $\|\mathbf{R}\|_\infty < K$ and $\|\mathbf{R}\|_1 < K$. In particular,

$$Var(\varepsilon_{it}) = \sigma_{\zeta i}^2 \sum_{\ell=0}^{\infty} \alpha_{\varepsilon i\ell}^2 = \sigma_i^2 \leq K < \infty, \tag{15}$$

for $i = 1, 2, \ldots, N$, where $\sigma^2_{\zeta i} = Var(\zeta_{it})$. $\mathbf{v}_{it}$ follows a linear stationary process with absolute summable autocovariances uniformly in i,

$$\mathbf{v}_{it} = \sum_{\ell=0}^{\infty} \mathbf{S}_{i\ell} \boldsymbol{\nu}_{i,t-\ell}, \tag{16}$$

for $i = 1, 2, \ldots, N$, where $\boldsymbol{\nu}_{it}$ is a $k \times 1$ vector of IID random variables, with mean zero, variance matrix $\mathbf{I}_k$, and finite fourth-order cumulants. In particular,

$$\|\text{Var}(\mathbf{v}_{it})\| = \left\| \sum_{\ell=0}^{\infty} \mathbf{S}_{i\ell}\mathbf{S}'_{i\ell} \right\| = \|\boldsymbol{\Sigma}_{vi}\| \leq K < \infty, \tag{17}$$

for $i = 1, 2, \ldots, N$.

Assumption 2. (*Unobserved common factors*).
The $m \times 1$ vector of unobserved common factors, $\mathbf{f}_t = (f_{1t}, f_{2t}, \ldots, f_{mt})'$, is covariance stationary with absolute summable autocovariances, and it is distributed independently of $\varsigma_{it'}$ and $\mathbf{v}_{it'}$ for all i, t and t'. Fourth moments of $f_{\ell t}$, for $\ell = 1, 2, \ldots, m$, are bounded.

Assumption 3. (*Factor loadings*).
The factor loadings, $\boldsymbol{\gamma}_i$, and $\boldsymbol{\Gamma}_i$, are independently and identically distributed across i, and of the common factors $\mathbf{f}_t$, for all i and t, with fixed means $\boldsymbol{\gamma}$ and $\boldsymbol{\Gamma}$, respectively, and bounded second moments. In particular,

$$\boldsymbol{\gamma}_i = \boldsymbol{\gamma} + \boldsymbol{\eta}_{\gamma i}, \; \boldsymbol{\eta}_{\gamma i} \sim \text{IID}\left(\underset{m\times 1}{\mathbf{0}}, \boldsymbol{\Omega}_{\gamma} \right), \quad \text{for } i = 1, 2, \ldots, N,$$

and

$$vec(\boldsymbol{\Gamma}_i) = vec(\boldsymbol{\Gamma}) + \boldsymbol{\eta}_{\Gamma i}, \; \boldsymbol{\eta}_{\Gamma i} \sim IID\left(\underset{km\times 1}{\mathbf{0}}, \boldsymbol{\Omega}_{\Gamma} \right), \quad \text{for } i = 1, 2, \ldots, N,$$

where $\boldsymbol{\Omega}_{\gamma}$ and $\boldsymbol{\Omega}_{\Gamma}$ are $m \times m$ and $km \times km$ symmetric nonnegative definite matrices, $\|\boldsymbol{\gamma}\| < K$, $\left\|\boldsymbol{\Omega}_{\gamma}\right\| < K$, $\|\boldsymbol{\Gamma}\| < K$, and $\|\boldsymbol{\Omega}_{\Gamma}\| < K$.

Assumption 4. (*Long-run coefficients*).
The long-run coefficients, $\boldsymbol{\theta}_i$, defined in Eq. (13), follow the random coefficient model

$$\boldsymbol{\theta}_i = \boldsymbol{\theta} + \boldsymbol{\upsilon}_i, \quad \boldsymbol{\upsilon}_i \sim IID\left(\underset{k\times 1}{\mathbf{0}}, \boldsymbol{\Omega}_\theta\right), \quad \text{for } i = 1, 2, \ldots, N, \tag{18}$$

where $\|\boldsymbol{\theta}\| < K$, $\|\boldsymbol{\Omega}_\theta\| < K$, $\boldsymbol{\Omega}_\theta$ is $k \times k$ symmetric nonnegative definite matrix, and the random deviations $\boldsymbol{\upsilon}_i$ are independently distributed of $\boldsymbol{\gamma}_j$, $\boldsymbol{\Gamma}_j$, ς_{jt}, $\mathbf{v}_{jt}$ and $\mathbf{f}_t$ for all i, j and t. The coefficients of the lagged dependent variable, φ_i, are distributed with a support strictly inside the unit circle.

The polynomial $1 - \varphi_i L$ is invertible under Assumption 4, and multiplying Eq. (11) by $(1 - \varphi_i L)^{-1}$ we obtain

$$\begin{aligned} y_{it} &= (1 - \varphi_i L)^{-1} \boldsymbol{\beta}_i' \mathbf{x}_{it} + (1 - \varphi_i L)^{-1} \boldsymbol{\gamma}_i' \mathbf{f}_t + (1 - \varphi_i L)^{-1} \varepsilon_{it} \\ &= \boldsymbol{\theta}_i \mathbf{x}_{it} + \boldsymbol{\alpha}_i'(L) \Delta \mathbf{x}_{it} + \boldsymbol{\gamma}_i' \tilde{\mathbf{f}}_{it} + \tilde{\varepsilon}_{it}, \quad \text{for } i = 1, 2, \ldots, N, \end{aligned} \tag{19}$$

where $\Delta \mathbf{x}_{it} = \mathbf{x}_{it} - \mathbf{x}_{i,t-1}$, $\alpha_i(L) = -\sum_{\ell=0}^{\infty} \left[\varphi_i^{\ell+1} (1 - \varphi_i)^{-1} \boldsymbol{\beta}_i\right] L^\ell$, $\tilde{\mathbf{f}}_{it} = (1 - \varphi_i L)^{-1} \mathbf{f}_t$, and $\tilde{\varepsilon}_{it} = (1 - \varphi_i L)^{-1} \varepsilon_{it}$. The DL specification in Eq. (19) does not include the lagged values of the dependent variable, and as a result the CCE estimation procedure can be applied to Eq. (19) directly. The regression of y_{it} on $\mathbf{x}_{it}$ is estimated by augmenting the individual regressions by differences of unit-specific regressors $\mathbf{x}_{it}$ and their lags, in addition to augmentation with cross-section averages that take care of the effects of unobserved common factors. It is important to note that the CCE procedure continues to be applicable despite the fact that the errors, $\tilde{\varepsilon}_{it}$, are serially correlated (see Pesaran, 2006).

Let $\mathbf{w} = (w_1, w_2, \ldots, w_N)'$ be an $N \times 1$ vector of weights that satisfies the following 'granularity' conditions:

$$\|\mathbf{w}\| = O\left(N^{-\frac{1}{2}}\right), \tag{20}$$

$$\frac{w_i}{\|\mathbf{w}\|} = O\left(N^{-\frac{1}{2}}\right) \text{ uniformly in } i, \tag{21}$$

and the normalization condition

$$\sum_{i=1}^{N} w_i = 1. \tag{22}$$

Define the cross-section averages $\bar{\mathbf{z}}_{wt} = \left(y_{wt}, \bar{\mathbf{x}}'_{wt}\right)' = \sum_{i=1}^{N} w_i \mathbf{z}_{it}$, and consider augmenting the regressions of y_{it} on $\mathbf{x}_{it}$ and the current and lagged values of $\Delta \mathbf{x}_{it}$, with the following set of cross-section averages, $\mathcal{S}_{Npt} = \bar{\mathbf{z}}_{wt} \cup \left\{\Delta \bar{\mathbf{x}}_{w,t-\ell}\right\}_{\ell=0}^{p}$. Cross-section averages approximate the unobserved common factors arbitrarily well if

$$\vartheta_{fNp} = \mathbf{f}_t - E\left(\mathbf{f}_t | \mathcal{S}_{Npt}\right) \xrightarrow{p} \mathbf{0}, \tag{23}$$

uniformly in t, as N and $p \xrightarrow{j} \infty$. Sufficient conditions for result (23) to hold are given by Assumptions 1–4 and if the rank condition $rank\,(\mathbf{\Gamma}) = m$ holds. Different sets of cross-section averages could also be considered. For example, if the set of cross-section averages is defined as $\mathcal{S}_{Np_{\bar{z}}t} = \{\bar{\mathbf{z}}_{wt-\ell}\}_{\ell=0}^{p_{\bar{z}}}$, then the sufficient condition for Eq. (23) to hold under Assumption 1–4 would be the usual rank condition $rank\,(\mathbf{C}) = m$, where $\mathbf{C} = (\boldsymbol{\gamma}, \mathbf{\Gamma})$. Using covariates to enlarge the set of cross-section averages could also be considered, as in Chudik and Pesaran (2015b). The rank condition can be relaxed in the case where $\boldsymbol{\gamma}_i$ and $\mathbf{\Gamma}_i$ are independently distributed.[8] In this case, the asymptotic variance of the CCE estimator does depend on the rank condition, nevertheless the CS-DL estimators are consistent and the proposed non-parametric estimators of the covariance matrix of the CS-DL estimators given below continue to be valid regardless of whether the rank condition holds.

More formally, let $\mathbf{y}_i = \left(y_{i,p+1}, y_{i,p+2}, \ldots, y_{i,T}\right)'$, $\mathbf{X}_i = \left(\mathbf{x}_{i,p+1}, \mathbf{x}_{i,p+2}, \ldots, \mathbf{x}_{i,T}\right)'$, $\bar{\mathbf{Z}}_w = \left(\bar{\mathbf{z}}_{w,p+1}, \bar{\mathbf{z}}_{w,p+2}, \ldots, \bar{\mathbf{z}}_{w,T}\right)'$,

$$\underset{(T-p)\times pk}{\Delta \mathbf{X}_{ip}} = \begin{pmatrix} \Delta \mathbf{x}'_{i,p+1} & \Delta \mathbf{x}'_{i,p} & \cdots & \Delta \mathbf{x}'_{i2} \\ \Delta \mathbf{x}'_{i,p+2} & \Delta \mathbf{x}'_{i,p+1} & \cdots & \Delta \mathbf{x}'_{i3} \\ \vdots & \vdots & & \vdots \\ \Delta \mathbf{x}'_{iT} & \Delta \mathbf{x}'_{i,T-1} & \cdots & \Delta \mathbf{x}'_{i,T-p+1} \end{pmatrix},$$

$\Delta \bar{\mathbf{X}}_{wp} = \sum_{i=1}^{N} w_i \Delta \mathbf{X}_{ip}$, $\mathbf{Q}_{wi} = \left(\bar{\mathbf{Z}}_w, \Delta \bar{\mathbf{X}}_{wp}, \Delta \mathbf{X}_{ip}\right)$, and define the projection matrix

$$\mathbf{M}_{qi} = \mathbf{I}_{T-p} - \mathbf{Q}_{wi}\left(\mathbf{Q}'_{wi}\mathbf{Q}_{wi}\right)^{+}\mathbf{Q}'_{wi}, \tag{24}$$

for $i = 1, 2, \ldots, N$, where $p = p(T)$ is a chosen non-decreasing truncation lag function such that $0 \leq p < T$, and $\mathbf{A}^{+}$ is the Moore–Penrose pseudo-inverse of $\mathbf{A}$. We use the Moore–Penrose pseudo-inverse as opposed to the standard inverse in Eq. (24) because the column vectors of $\mathbf{Q}_{wi}$ could be asymptotically (as $N \to \infty$) linearly dependent.

The CS-DL mean group estimator of the long-run coefficients is given by

$$\widehat{\boldsymbol{\theta}}_{MG} = \frac{1}{N}\sum_{i=1}^{N}\widehat{\boldsymbol{\theta}}_i, \tag{25}$$

where

$$\widehat{\boldsymbol{\theta}}_i = \left(\mathbf{X}_i'\mathbf{M}_{qi}\mathbf{X}_i'\right)^{-1}\mathbf{X}_i'\mathbf{M}_{qi}\mathbf{y}_i. \tag{26}$$

The CS-DL-pooled estimator of the long-run coefficients is

$$\widehat{\boldsymbol{\theta}}_P = \left(\sum_{i=1}^{N} w_i\mathbf{X}_i'\mathbf{M}_{qi}\mathbf{X}_i\right)^{-1}\sum_{i=1}^{N} w_i\mathbf{X}_i'\mathbf{M}_{qi}\mathbf{y}_i. \tag{27}$$

Estimators $\widehat{\boldsymbol{\theta}}_{MG}$ and $\widehat{\boldsymbol{\theta}}_P$ differ from the mean group and pooled CCE estimator developed in Pesaran (2006), which only allows for the inclusion of a fixed number of regressors, whilst the CS-DL-type estimators include p lags of $\Delta\mathbf{x}_{it}$ and their cross-section averages, where p increases with T, albeit at a slower rate.

In addition to Assumptions 1–4, we shall also require Assumption 5 to hold. This assumption ensures that $\widehat{\boldsymbol{\theta}}_{MG}$ and $\widehat{\boldsymbol{\theta}}_P$ and their asymptotic distributions are well defined.

Assumption 5.

(a) The matrix $\lim_{N,T,p\xrightarrow{j}\infty}\sum_{i=1}^{N} w_i\boldsymbol{\Sigma}_i = \boldsymbol{\Psi}^*$ *exists and is nonsingular, and* $\sup_{i,p}\left\|\boldsymbol{\Sigma}_i^{-1}\right\| < K$, *where* $\boldsymbol{\Sigma}_i = p\lim T^{-1}\mathbf{X}_i'\mathbf{M}_{hi}\mathbf{X}_i$, *and* $\mathbf{M}_{hi}$ *is defined in Eq. (A.3).*

(b) Denote the tth row of matrix $\widetilde{\mathbf{X}}_i = \mathbf{M}_{hi}\mathbf{X}_i$ *by* $\widetilde{\mathbf{x}}_{it}' = (\widetilde{x}_{i1t}, \widetilde{x}_{i2t}, \ldots, \widetilde{x}_{ikt})$. *The individual elements of* $\widetilde{\mathbf{x}}_{it}$ *have uniformly bounded fourth moments, namely there exists a positive constant* $K < \infty$ *such that* $E\left(\widetilde{x}_{ist}^4\right) < K$, *for any* $t = 1, 2, \ldots, T$, $i = 1, 2, \ldots, N$ *and* $s = 1, 2, \ldots, k$.

(c) There exists T_0 *such that for all* $T \geq T_0$, $\left(\sum_{i=1}^{N} w_i\mathbf{X}_i'\mathbf{M}_{qi}\mathbf{X}_i/T\right)^{-1}$ *exists.*

(d) There exists N_0, T_0 *and* $p_0 = p(T_0)$ *such that for all* $N \geq N_0$, $T \geq T_0$ *and* $p \geq p_0$, *the* $k \times k$ *matrices* $\left(\mathbf{X}_i'\mathbf{M}_{qi}\mathbf{X}_i/T\right)^{-1}$ *exist for all i, uniformly.*

Our main findings are summarized in the following theorems.

Theorem 1. **(*Asymptotic distribution of* $\widehat{\boldsymbol{\theta}}_{MG}$).** *Suppose* y_{it}, *for* $i = 1, 2, \ldots, N$ *and* $t = 1, 2, \ldots, T$ *are generated according to the panel data model (11)–(12), Assumptions 1–5 hold, and* $(N, T, p)\xrightarrow{j}\infty$ *such that* $\sqrt{N}p\rho^p \to 0$, *for any* *constant* $0<\rho<1$ *and* $p^3/T \to \varkappa$, $0<\varkappa<\infty$. *Then, if rank* $(\boldsymbol{\Gamma}) = m$ *we have*

$$\sqrt{N}\left(\widehat{\boldsymbol{\theta}}_{MG} - \boldsymbol{\theta}\right) \xrightarrow{d} N\left(\mathbf{0}, \boldsymbol{\Omega}_{\theta}\right), \tag{28}$$

where $\boldsymbol{\Omega}_{\theta} = Var\left(\boldsymbol{\theta}_i\right)$ *and* $\widehat{\boldsymbol{\theta}}_{MG}$ *is given by Eq. (25). If rank* $(\boldsymbol{\Gamma}) \neq m$ *and* $\boldsymbol{\gamma}_i$ *is independently distributed of* $\boldsymbol{\Gamma}_i$, *we have*

$$\sqrt{N}\left(\widehat{\boldsymbol{\theta}}_{MG} - \boldsymbol{\theta}\right) \xrightarrow{d} N\left(\mathbf{0}, \boldsymbol{\Sigma}_{MG}\right), \tag{29}$$

where

$$\boldsymbol{\Sigma}_{MG} = \boldsymbol{\Omega}_{\theta} + \lim_{p,N\to\infty}\left[\frac{1}{N}\sum_{i=1}^{N}\boldsymbol{\Sigma}_i^{-1}\mathbf{Q}_{ifp}\boldsymbol{\Omega}_{\gamma p}\mathbf{Q}'_{ifp}\boldsymbol{\Sigma}_i^{-1}\right], \tag{30}$$

in which $\boldsymbol{\Omega}_{\gamma p} = Var(\boldsymbol{\gamma}_{ip})$, $\boldsymbol{\gamma}_{ip} = (\boldsymbol{\gamma}'_i, \varphi_i\boldsymbol{\gamma}'_i, \varphi_i^2\boldsymbol{\gamma}'_i, \ldots, \varphi_i^p\boldsymbol{\gamma}'_i)'$, $\boldsymbol{\Sigma}_i = p\lim T^{-1}\mathbf{X}'_i \mathbf{M}_{hi}\mathbf{X}_i$ *and* $\mathbf{Q}_{ifp} = p\lim T^{-1}\mathbf{X}'_i\mathbf{M}_{hi}\mathbf{F}_p$. *In both cases, the asymptotic variance of* $\widehat{\boldsymbol{\theta}}_{MG}$ *can be consistently estimated nonparametrically by*

$$\widehat{\boldsymbol{\Sigma}}_{MG} = \frac{1}{N-1}\sum_{i=1}^{N}\left(\widehat{\boldsymbol{\theta}}_i - \widehat{\boldsymbol{\theta}}_{MG}\right)\left(\widehat{\boldsymbol{\theta}}_i - \widehat{\boldsymbol{\theta}}_{MG}\right)'. \tag{31}$$

Theorem 2. ***(Asymptotic distribution of*** $\widehat{\boldsymbol{\theta}}_P$***).*** *Suppose* y_{it}, *for* $i = 1, 2, \ldots, N$ *and* $t = 1, 2, \ldots, T$ *are generated by the panel data model (11)–(12), Assumptions 1–5 hold, and* $(N, T, p) \xrightarrow{j} \infty$, *such that* $\sqrt{N}p\rho^p \to 0$, *for any constant* $0<\rho<1$ *and* $p^3/T \to \varkappa$, $0<\varkappa<\infty$. *Then, if* $\boldsymbol{\gamma}_i$ *is independently distributed of* $\boldsymbol{\Gamma}_i$, *we have*

$$\left(\sum_{i=1}^{N} w_i^2\right)^{-1/2}\left(\widehat{\boldsymbol{\theta}}_P - \boldsymbol{\theta}\right) \xrightarrow{d} N\left(\mathbf{0}, \boldsymbol{\Sigma}_P\right), \tag{32}$$

where $\widehat{\boldsymbol{\theta}}_P$ *is given by Eq. (27),*

$$\boldsymbol{\Sigma}_P = \boldsymbol{\Psi}^{*-1}\mathbf{R}^*\boldsymbol{\Psi}^{*-1}, \quad \boldsymbol{\Psi}^* = \lim_{p,N\to\infty}\sum_{i=1}^{N} w_i\boldsymbol{\Sigma}_i, \tag{33}$$

$$\mathbf{R}^* = \mathbf{R}^*_\theta + \mathbf{R}^*_\gamma, \quad \mathbf{R}^*_\theta = \lim_{p,N\to\infty} \frac{1}{N}\sum_{i=1}^{N} \widetilde{w}_i^2 \mathbf{\Sigma}_i \mathbf{\Omega}_\theta \mathbf{\Sigma}_i,$$

$$\mathbf{R}^*_\gamma = \lim_{p,N\to\infty} \frac{1}{N}\sum_{i=1}^{N} \widetilde{w}_i^2 \mathbf{Q}_{ifp} \mathbf{\Omega}_{\gamma p} \mathbf{Q}'_{ifp},$$

$\mathbf{\Omega}_\theta = Var(\boldsymbol{\theta}_i)$, $\mathbf{\Omega}_{\gamma p} = Var(\boldsymbol{\gamma}_{ip})$, $\boldsymbol{\gamma}_{ip} = (\boldsymbol{\gamma}'_i, \varphi_i\boldsymbol{\gamma}'_i, \varphi_i^2\boldsymbol{\gamma}'_i, \ldots, \varphi_i^p\boldsymbol{\gamma}'_i)'$, $\mathbf{\Sigma}_i = p\lim T^{-1}\mathbf{X}'_i\mathbf{M}_{hi}\mathbf{X}_i$, $\mathbf{Q}_{ifp} = p\lim T^{-1}\mathbf{X}'_i\mathbf{M}_{hi}\mathbf{F}_p$ and $\widetilde{w}_i = \sqrt{N}w_i\left(\sum_{i=1}^N w_i^2\right)^{-1/2}$. If rank $(\mathbf{\Gamma}) = m$, then $\boldsymbol{\gamma}_i$ is no longer required to be independently distributed of $\mathbf{\Gamma}_i$ and Eq. (32) continues to hold with $\mathbf{\Sigma}_P = \mathbf{\Psi}^{*-1}\mathbf{R}^*_\theta\mathbf{\Psi}^{*-1}$. In both cases, $\mathbf{\Sigma}_P$ can be consistently estimated by $\hat{\mathbf{\Sigma}}_P$ defined by Eq. (A.25).

Theorems 1–2 establish asymptotic distributions of $\widehat{\boldsymbol{\theta}}_{MG}$ and $\widehat{\boldsymbol{\theta}}_P$ under slope heterogeneity. These theorems distinguish between cases where the rank condition that ensures Eq. (23) is satisfied or not. Under the former, unobserved common factors can be approximated by cross-section averages when N is large and regardless of whether $\boldsymbol{\gamma}_i$ is correlated with $\mathbf{\Gamma}_i$, $\widehat{\boldsymbol{\theta}}_{MG}$ and $\widehat{\boldsymbol{\theta}}_P$ are consistent and asymptotically normal. In the latter case, where the unobserved common factors cannot be approximated by cross-section averages when N is large, then so long as $\boldsymbol{\gamma}_i$ and $\mathbf{\Gamma}_i$ are independently distributed, both $\widehat{\boldsymbol{\theta}}_{MG}$ and $\widehat{\boldsymbol{\theta}}_P$ continue to be consistent and asymptotically normal, but the asymptotic variance also depends on unobserved common factors and their loadings. In both (full rank or rank deficient) cases, the asymptotic variance of the CS-DL estimators can be estimated consistently using the same non-parametric formulae as in the full-rank case.

There are several departures from the assumptions of these theorems that might be of interest in applied work, such as the consequences of breaks in the error processes, ε_{it}, possibility of unit roots in factors and/or regressor specific components, and situations where some or all coefficients are homogeneous over the cross-section units. These theoretical extensions are outside the scope of this paper, but we investigate the robustness of the proposed CS-DL estimator to such departures by means of Monte Carlo simulations in the next section.

4. MONTE CARLO EXPERIMENTS

This section investigates the small sample properties of the CS-DL estimators and compares them with the estimates obtained from the panel ARDL approach using the dynamic CCEMG estimator of the short-run coefficients advanced in Chudik and Pesaran (2015b), which we denote by CS-ARDL. First, we present results from the baseline experiments with heterogeneous slopes (long- and short-run coefficients), and then we document the small sample performance of the alternative estimators under various deviations from the baseline experiments, including robustness of the estimators to the introduction of unit roots in the regressors or factors, possible breaks in the idiosyncratic error processes, and the consequences of feedback effects from lagged values of y_{it} onto $\mathbf{x}_{it}$. Second, we investigate whether it is possible to improve on the estimation of short-run coefficients, provided the model is correctly specified, by imposing CS-DL estimates of the long-run coefficients.

We start with a brief summary of the estimation methods and a description of the data-generating processes (DGP). Then we present findings on the estimation of the mean long-run coefficient and on the extent to which estimates of the short-run coefficients can be improved by using the CS-DL estimators of the long-run effects.

4.1. Estimation Methods

The CS-DL estimators are based on the following auxiliary regressions:

$$y_{it} = c_{yi} + \boldsymbol{\theta}_i'\mathbf{x}_{it} + \sum_{\ell=0}^{p-1} \boldsymbol{\delta}_{i\ell}' \Delta \mathbf{X}_{i,t-\ell} + \sum_{\ell=0}^{p_{\bar{y}}} \omega_{y,i\ell}\bar{y}_{t-\ell} + \sum_{\ell=0}^{p_{\bar{x}}} \omega_{x,i\ell}'\bar{\mathbf{x}}_{t-\ell} + e_{it}, \tag{34}$$

where $\bar{\mathbf{x}}_t = N^{-1}\sum_{i=1}^{N}\mathbf{x}_{it}$, $\bar{y}_t = N^{-1}\sum_{i=1}^{N} y_{it}$, $p_{\bar{x}}$ is set equal to the integer part of $T^{1/3}$, denoted as $[T^{1/3}]$, $p = p_{\bar{x}}$ and $p_{\bar{y}}$ is set to 0. We consider both CS-DL mean group and pooled estimators based on Eq. (34).

The CS-ARDL estimator is based on the following regressions:

$$y_{it} = c_{yi}^* + \sum_{\ell=1}^{p_y} \varphi_{i\ell} y_{i,t-\ell} + \sum_{\ell=0}^{p_x} \boldsymbol{\beta}_{i\ell}'\mathbf{x}_{i,t-\ell} + \sum_{\ell=0}^{p_{\bar{z}}} \boldsymbol{\psi}_{i\ell}'\bar{\mathbf{z}}_{t-\ell} + e_{it}^*, \tag{35}$$

where $\bar{\mathbf{z}}_t = (\bar{y}_t, \bar{\mathbf{x}}_t')'$, $p_{\bar{z}} = [T^{1/3}]$ and two options for the remaining lag orders are considered: ARDL(2,1) specification, $p_y = 2$ and $p_x = 1$, and ARDL(1,0) specification, $p_y = 1$ and $p_x = 0$. The CS-ARDL estimates of the individual mean level coefficient are then given by

$$\hat{\boldsymbol{\theta}}_{CS-ARDL,i} = \frac{\sum_{\ell=0}^{p_x} \hat{\boldsymbol{\beta}}_{i\ell}}{1 - \sum_{\ell=1}^{p_y} \hat{\varphi}_{i\ell}}, \tag{36}$$

where the estimates of the short-run coefficients $(\hat{\varphi}_{i\ell}, \hat{\boldsymbol{\beta}}_{i\ell})$ are based on Eq. (35). The mean long-run effects are estimated as $N^{-1}\sum_{i=1}^{N}\hat{\boldsymbol{\theta}}_{CS-ARDL,i}$ and the inference is based on the usual non-parametric estimator of asymptotic variance of the mean group estimator.

4.2. *Data-Generating Process*

The dependent variable and regressors are generated using the following ARDL(2,1) panel data model with factor error structure,

$$y_{it} = c_{yi} + \varphi_{i1} y_{i,t-1} + \varphi_{i2} y_{i,t-2} + \beta_{i0} x_{it} + \beta_{i1} x_{i,t-1} + u_{it},\ u_{it} = \boldsymbol{\gamma}_i' \mathbf{f}_t + \varepsilon_{it}, \quad (37)$$

and

$$x_{it} = c_{xi} + \kappa_{yi} y_{i,t-1} + \boldsymbol{\gamma}_{xi}' \mathbf{f}_t + v_{it}. \quad (38)$$

We generate y_{it}, x_{it} for $i = 1, 2, \ldots, N$, and $t = -99, \ldots, 0, 1, 2, \ldots, T$ with the starting values $y_{i,-101} = y_{i,-100} = 0$, and discard the first 100 observations ($t = -99, -48, \ldots, 0$) to reduce the effects of the initial values on the outcomes. The individual effects are generated as $c_{iy} \sim IIDN(1, 1)$, and $c_{xi} = c_{yi} + \varsigma_{c_x i}$, where $\varsigma_{c_x i} \sim IIDN(0, 1)$, thus allowing for dependence between x_{it} and c_{yi}.[9]

We consider three cases depending on the heterogeneity/homogeneity of the slopes:

- (heterogeneous slopes - baseline) $\varphi_{i1} = (1 + \varkappa_{\varphi i}) \eta_{\varphi i}$, $\varphi_{i2} = -\varkappa_{\varphi i} \eta_{\varphi i}$, $\varkappa_{\varphi i} \sim IIDU(0.2, 0.3)$, $\eta_{\varphi i} \sim IIDU(0, \varphi_{\max})$. The long-run coefficients are generated as $\theta_i \sim IIDN(1, 0.2^2)$ and the regression coefficient are generated as $\beta_{i0} = \varkappa_{\beta i} \eta_{\beta i}$, $\beta_{i1} = (1 - \varkappa_{\beta i}) \eta_{\beta i}$, where $\eta_{\beta i} = \theta_i / (1 - \varphi_{i1} - \varphi_{i2})$ and $\varkappa_{\beta i} \sim IIDU(0, 1)$.
- (homogeneous long-run, heterogenous short-run slopes) $\theta_i = 1$ for all i and the remaining coefficients $(\varphi_{i1}, \varphi_{i2}, \beta_{i0}, \beta_{i1})$ are generated as in the previous fully heterogeneous case.
- (homogeneous long- and short-run slopes) $\varphi_{i1} = 1.15\varphi_{\max}/2$, $\varphi_{i2} = -0.15\varphi_{\max}/2$, $\theta_i = 1$ and $\beta_{i0} = \beta_{i1} = 0.5/(1 - \varphi_{\max}/2)$.

We also consider the case of ARDL(1,0) panel model by setting $\varkappa_{\varphi i} = 0$ and $\varkappa_{\beta i} = 1$ for all i, which gives $\varphi_{i2} = \beta_{i1} = 0$ for all i. We consider three values for $\varphi_{\max} = 0.6, 0.8$ or 0.9.

The unobserved common factors in $\mathbf{f}_t$ and the unit-specific components, v_{it}, are generated as independent AR(1) processes:

$$f_{t\ell} = \rho_{f\ell} f_{t-1,\ell} + \varsigma_{ft\ell},\ \varsigma_{ft\ell} \sim IIDN(0, \sigma^2_{\varsigma f\ell}), \quad (39)$$

$$v_{it} = \rho_{xi} v_{i,t-1} + \nu_{it},\ \nu_{it} \sim IIDN(0, \sigma^2_{\nu i}), \quad (40)$$

for $i = 1, 2, \ldots, N$, $\ell = 1, 2, \ldots, m$, and for $t = -99, \ldots, 0, 1, 2, \ldots, T$ with the starting values $f_{\ell,-100} = 0$, and $v_{i,-100} = 0$. The first 100 time observations

$(t = -99, -48, \ldots, 0)$ are discarded. We consider three possibilities for the AR(1) coefficients $\rho_{f\ell}$ and ρ_{xi}:

- (stationary baseline) $\rho_{xi} \sim IIDU\,[0.0.95]$, $\sigma_{vi}^2 = 1 - \rho_{xi}^2$ for all i; $\rho_{f\ell} = 0.6$, and $\sigma_{\varsigma f\ell}^2 = 1 - \rho_{f\ell}^2$ for $\ell = 1, 2, \ldots, m$.
- (nonstationary factors) $\rho_{xi} \sim IIDU\,[0.0.95]$, $\sigma_{vi}^2 = 1 - \rho_{xi}^2$ for all i; and $\rho_{f\ell} = 1$, $\sigma_{\varsigma f\ell}^2 = 0.1^2$ for $\ell = 1, 2, \ldots, m$.
- (nonstationary regressors and stationary factors) $\rho_{xi} = 1$, $\sigma_{vi}^2 = 0.1^2$ for all i; and $\rho_{f\ell} = 0.6$, $\sigma_{\varsigma f\ell}^2 = 1 - \rho_{f\ell}^2$, for $\ell = 1, 2, \ldots, m$.

We consider also two options for the feedback coefficients κ_{yi}: no feedback effects, $\kappa_{yi} = 0$ for all i, and with feedback effects, $\kappa_{yi} \sim IIDU\,(0, 0.2)$.

Factor loadings are generated as

$$\gamma_{i\ell} \sim IIDN\left(\gamma_\ell, 0.2^2\right) \quad \text{and} \quad \gamma_{xi\ell} \sim IIDN\left(\gamma_{x\ell}, 0.2^2\right),$$

for $\ell = 1, 2, \ldots, m$, and $i = 1, 2, \ldots, N$. Also, without loss of generality, the means of factor loadings are calibrated so that $Var\left(\boldsymbol{\gamma}_i'\mathbf{f}_t\right) = Var\left(\boldsymbol{\gamma}_{xi}'\mathbf{f}_t\right) = 1$ in the stationary case. We set $\gamma_\ell = \sqrt{b_\gamma}$, and $\gamma_{x\ell} = \sqrt{\ell b_x}$, for $\ell = 1, 2, \ldots, m$, where $b_\gamma = 1/m - 0.2^2$, and $b_x = 2/\left[m\,(m+1)\right] - 2/\,(m+1)\,0.2^2$. This ensures that the contribution of the unobserved factors to the variance of y_{it} does not rise with m in the stationary case. We consider $m = 2$ or 3 unobserved common factors.

Finally, the idiosyncratic errors, ε_{it}, are generated to be heteroskedastic, weakly cross-sectionally dependent and serially correlated. Specifically,

$$\varepsilon_{it} = \rho_{\varepsilon i}\varepsilon_{i,t-1} + \zeta_{it}, \tag{41}$$

where $\boldsymbol{\zeta}_t = (\zeta_{1t}, \zeta_{2t}, \ldots, \zeta_{Nt})'$ are generated using the following spatial autoregressive model (SAR):

$$\boldsymbol{\zeta}_t = a_\epsilon \mathbf{S}_\epsilon \boldsymbol{\zeta}_t + \boldsymbol{\varsigma}_t, \tag{42}$$

in which the elements of $\boldsymbol{\varsigma}_t$ are drawn as $IIDN\left[0, \frac{1}{2}\sigma_i^2\left(1 - \rho_{\varepsilon i}^2\right)\right]$, with σ_i^2 obtained as independent draws from $\chi^2(2)$ distribution,

$$\mathbf{S}_\epsilon = \begin{pmatrix} 0 & 1 & 0 & 0 & \ldots & 0 \\ \frac{1}{2} & 0 & \frac{1}{2} & 0 & & 0 \\ 0 & \frac{1}{2} & 0 & \ddots & & \vdots \\ 0 & 0 & \ddots & \ddots & \frac{1}{2} & 0 \\ \vdots & & & \frac{1}{2} & 0 & \frac{1}{2} \\ 0 & 0 & \ldots & 0 & 1 & 0 \end{pmatrix},$$

and the spatial autoregressive parameter is set to $a_\epsilon = 0.6$. Note that $\{\epsilon_{it}\}$ is cross-sectionally weakly dependent for $|a_\epsilon| < 1$. We consider $\rho_{\varepsilon i} = 0$ for all i or $\rho_{\varepsilon i} \sim IIDU(0, 0.8)$. We also consider the possibility of breaks in ε_{it} by generating for each i random break points $b_i \in \{1, 2, \ldots, T\}$ and

$$\begin{aligned} \varepsilon_{it} &= \rho^a_{\varepsilon i}\varepsilon_{i,t-1} + \zeta_{it}, \quad \text{for } t = 1, 2, \ldots, b_i \\ \varepsilon_{it} &= \rho^b_{\varepsilon i}\varepsilon_{i,t-1} + \zeta_{it}, \quad \text{for } t = b_i + 1, b_i + 2, \ldots, T, \end{aligned}$$

where $\rho^a_{\varepsilon i}, \rho^b_{\varepsilon i} \sim IIDU(0, 0.8)$, and $\boldsymbol{\zeta}_t = (\zeta_{1t}, \zeta_{2t}, \ldots, \zeta_{Nt})'$ is generated using SAR model (42) with $\varsigma_{it} \sim IIDN\left[0, \frac{1}{2}\sigma_i^2\left(1 - \rho^{a2}_{\varepsilon i}\right)\right]$.

The above DGP is more general than the other DGPs used in MC experiments in the literature and allows the factors and regressors to be correlated and persistent. The above DGPs also include models with unit roots, breaks in the error processes, and allows for correlated individual effects. To summarize, we consider the following cases:

1. (Three options for heterogeneity of coefficients) heterogeneous baseline, homogeneous long-run with heterogeneous short-run and both long-and short-run homogeneous,
2. (Two options for lags) ARDL(2,1) baseline, and ARDL(1,0) model where $\varkappa_{\varphi i} = 0$ and $\varkappa_{\beta i} = 1$ for all i, which gives $\varphi_{i2} = \beta_{i1} = 0$ for all i.
3. (Three options for $\varphi_{\max}$) $\varphi_{\max} = 0.6$ (baseline), 0.8, or 0.9
4. (Three options for the persistence of factors and regressors) stationary baseline, I(1) factors, or I(1) regressor specific components v_{it},
5. (Two options for the number of factors) full-rank case baseline $m = 2$, or rank-deficient case $m = 3$,
6. (Three options for the persistence of idiosyncratic errors) serially uncorrelated baseline $\rho_{\varepsilon i} = 0$, $\rho_{\varepsilon i} \sim IIDU(0, 0.8)$, or breaks in the error process.
7. (Two options for feedback effects) $\kappa_{yi} = 0$ for all i (baseline), or $\kappa_{yi} \sim IIDU(0, 0.2)$.

Due to the large number of possible cases (648 in total), we only consider baseline experiments and various departures from the baseline. We consider the following combinations of sample sizes: $N, T \in \{30, 50, 100, 150, 200\}$, and set the number of replications to $R = 2{,}000$, in the case of all experiments.

4.3. Monte Carlo Findings on the Estimation of Mean Long-Run Coefficients

The results for the baseline DGP are summarized in Table 1. This table shows that both CS-DL estimators (MG and pooled) perform well in the baseline experiments. This table also shows that the CS-ARDL approach does not perform well when T

Table 1. Monte Carlo Estimates of Bias, RMSE, Size and Power for Estimation of Long-Run Coefficients (θ) for the Baseline Experiment.

	Bias ($\times100$)					Root-Mean-Square Errors ($\times100$)					Size (5% level, $H_0:\theta=1$)					Power (5% level, $H_1:\theta=1.2$)				
(N,T)	30	50	100	150	200	30	50	100	150	200	30	50	100	150	200	30	50	100	150	200
CS-DL mean group ($p_{\bar{y}}=0$, $p_{\bar{x}}=[T^{1/3}]$ and $p=p_{\bar{x}}-1$)																				
30	−0.65	−0.49	0.04	−0.11	−0.15	16.88	11.24	8.55	7.34	6.44	6.35	6.15	7.75	5.80	6.40	28.30	50.20	70.30	80.10	87.15
50	−1.12	−1.00	−0.34	−0.12	−0.03	13.19	8.83	6.33	5.82	4.92	5.90	6.15	5.25	6.45	5.20	39.45	70.20	89.10	93.45	97.80
100	−1.32	−0.92	−0.09	−0.11	0.15	9.66	6.25	4.49	4.03	3.56	5.95	6.30	5.55	4.50	5.45	62.95	92.45	99.50	99.75	100.00
150	−1.19	−0.96	−0.11	0.16	−0.05	7.91	5.24	3.78	3.38	2.94	5.90	6.50	5.90	6.25	5.75	79.45	98.20	99.85	100.00	100.00
200	−1.06	−0.75	−0.24	−0.07	0.03	6.70	4.38	3.17	2.86	2.47	5.60	6.00	4.85	5.10	4.50	88.65	99.80	100.00	100.00	100.00
CS-DL pooled ($p_{\bar{y}}=0$, $p_{\bar{x}}=[T^{1/3}]$ and $p=p_{\bar{x}}-1$)																				
30	−0.40	−0.19	0.16	−0.08	−0.04	15.31	10.44	8.12	7.10	6.41	6.95	6.60	7.20	6.95	6.50	33.75	53.65	73.15	82.45	88.25
50	−0.93	−1.00	−0.29	−0.16	−0.06	11.47	8.31	6.08	5.55	4.80	6.00	6.70	5.70	6.00	4.60	47.05	75.50	91.40	94.80	97.80
100	−1.09	−0.83	−0.13	−0.10	0.14	8.17	5.88	4.26	3.90	3.53	5.85	6.35	5.20	4.60	5.80	74.20	95.10	99.75	99.90	99.95
150	−1.02	−0.72	−0.09	0.11	−0.02	6.83	4.82	3.55	3.28	2.87	5.90	6.10	5.80	5.95	5.55	87.60	98.95	99.95	100.00	100.00
200	−0.81	−0.68	−0.22	−0.06	0.03	5.89	4.11	3.04	2.74	2.43	5.25	5.70	5.20	5.15	5.05	94.55	99.95	100.00	100.00	100.00
Based on CS-ARDL estimates of short-run coefficients (ARDL(2,1) specifications with $p_{\bar{z}}=[T^{1/3}]$)																				
30	−10.40	−3.87	−1.73	−1.38	−0.88	361.68	20.62	7.59	6.24	5.54	10.75	9.80	9.45	8.25	7.50	39.95	66.05	86.05	94.10	96.00
50	3.72	−3.96	−2.12	−1.30	−1.00	182.36	9.56	5.83	4.89	4.32	10.45	12.75	8.10	7.65	6.55	45.40	81.30	98.00	98.90	99.70
100	17.57	−4.03	−2.02	−1.39	−0.83	966.97	7.31	4.34	3.58	3.16	12.90	13.90	10.05	8.45	8.05	61.30	96.40	100.00	100.00	100.00
150	−9.46	−3.93	−2.03	−1.20	−1.07	159.90	6.46	3.84	3.03	2.68	13.65	18.45	12.05	9.45	8.95	67.60	99.50	100.00	100.00	100.00
200	11.29	−3.97	−2.15	−1.42	−1.01	678.37	6.66	3.52	2.79	2.31	13.90	20.10	13.10	11.05	7.70	71.00	99.40	100.00	100.00	100.00
Based on CS-ARDL estimates of short-run coefficients (ARDL(1,0) specifications with $p_{\bar{z}}=[T^{1/3}]$)																				
30	−23.29	−26.91	−23.58	−22.66	−22.01	274.46	28.91	24.83	23.77	22.99	58.05	75.70	85.90	90.40	91.95	86.10	98.00	99.90	100.00	100.00
50	−27.78	−27.49	−23.95	−22.72	−22.28	109.97	28.68	24.70	23.36	22.83	73.20	90.75	97.25	98.60	99.25	92.00	99.80	100.00	100.00	100.00
100	−31.85	−27.64	−24.18	−22.94	−22.21	62.82	28.23	24.54	23.26	22.50	87.75	99.45	100.00	100.00	100.00	96.10	100.00	100.00	100.00	100.00
150	−30.11	−27.60	−24.01	−22.82	−22.34	81.52	28.02	24.26	23.05	22.53	93.35	99.90	100.00	100.00	100.00	97.20	100.00	100.00	100.00	100.00
200	−31.20	−27.73	−24.20	−22.96	−22.40	50.42	28.04	24.39	23.12	22.55	94.25	100.00	100.00	100.00	100.00	97.30	100.00	100.00	100.00	100.00

Notes: The dependent variable and regressors are generated according to Eqs. (37)–(38) with correlated individual effects, and with cross-sectionally weakly dependent and serially correlated heteroskedastic idiosyncratic innovations generated according to Eqs. (41)–(42) with $a_\varepsilon=0.6$. The knowledge of lag orders is not used in the estimation stage and the integer part of $T^{1/3}$ gives $3,3,4,5$ and 5 for $T=30, 50, 100, 150$ and 200, respectively.
DGP is an ARDL(2,1) model with heterogeneous coefficients, $\varphi_{\max}=0.6$, stationary regressors, $m=2$ factors, no feedback effects and $\rho_{\varepsilon i}=0$.

is not large (<50). The problems arising when $\sum_{\ell=1}^{p_y} \hat{\varphi}_{i\ell}$ is close to unity could be one of the explanations behind the inferior performance of the CS-ARDL approach when T is not large. Also, CS-ARDL estimates that are based on misspecified lag orders are inconsistent, as to be expected. In contrast, the consistency of the CS-DL estimators does not depend on knowing the correct lag specifications of the underlying ARDL model.

Next, we investigate robustness of the results to different assumptions regarding slope heterogeneity. Table 2 presents findings for the experiment that depart from the baseline DGP by assuming homogeneous long-run slopes, while allowing the short-run slopes to be heterogeneous. Table 3 gives the results when both long- and short-run slopes are homogeneous. These results show that the CS-DL estimators continue to have good size and power properties in all these cases.

Experiments based on the ARDL(1,0) specification (as the DGP) are summarized in Table 4. CS-DL estimators continue to perform well, showing their robustness to the underlying ARDL specification.

The effects of increasing the value of $\varphi_{\max}$ on the properties of the various estimators are summarized in Tables 5 (for $\varphi_{\max} = 0.8$) and 6 (for $\varphi_{\max} = 0.9$). The small sample performance of the CS-DL estimators deteriorates as $\varphi_{\max}$ moves closer to unity, as to be expected. Tables 5–6 show that the small sample performances of different estimators deteriorate substantially for values of $\varphi_{\max}$ close to unity. This is partly due to an inappropriate lag truncation. It can take a large lag order for the truncation bias to be negligible when the largest eigenvalue of the dynamic specification (given by the lags of the dependent variable) is close to one. We see quite a substantial bias when $\varphi_{\max} = 0.9$. Therefore, it is important that the CS-DL approach is used when the speed of convergence towards equilibrium is not too slow and/or T is sufficiently large so that biases arising from the approximation of dynamics by DL functions can be controlled.

The robustness of the results to the number of unobserved factors (m) is investigated in Table 7. This table provides a summary in the case of $m = 3$ factors, which represents the rank-deficient case. It is interesting to note that despite the failure of the rank condition, the CS-DL estimators continue to perform well (the results are almost unchanged as compared with those in Table 1), while the CS-ARDL estimates are affected by two types of biases (the time series bias and the bias due to rank deficiency) that seem to apply in opposite directions.

The robustness of the results to the presence of unit roots in the unobserved factors and the regressors are examined in Tables 8 and 9, respectively. As can be seen the CS-DL estimators continue to perform well when factors contain unit roots. Table 9, on the other hand, shows large RMSE and low power for $T = 30$ and 50, when the idiosyncratic errors have unit roots. But, interestingly enough, the reported size is correct and biases are very small for all sample sizes.

Table 2. Monte Carlo Estimates of Bias, RMSE, Size and Power for Estimation of Long-Run Coefficients (θ) in the Homogeneous Case.

	Bias ($\times 100$)					Root-Mean-Square Errors ($\times 100$)					Size (5% level, $H_0: \theta = 1$)					Power (5% level, $H_1: \theta = 1.2$)				
(N,T)	30	50	100	150	200	30	50	100	150	200	30	50	100	150	200	30	50	100	150	200
CS-DL mean group ($p_{\bar{y}} = 0$, $p_{\bar{x}} = [T^{1/3}]$ and $p = p_{\bar{x}} - 1$)																				
30	−1.59	−0.63	0.00	−0.05	0.01	16.55	10.27	7.40	6.21	5.31	6.00	5.30	6.40	5.25	5.85	30.85	55.85	78.45	88.30	95.05
50	−1.49	−0.95	−0.34	−0.02	−0.11	12.92	8.04	5.89	4.97	4.22	5.25	5.85	6.55	5.60	6.30	41.75	74.65	93.15	97.30	99.55
100	−0.96	−0.55	−0.20	0.02	0.02	9.16	5.76	4.09	3.53	3.02	5.10	5.70	5.40	5.10	5.70	64.90	94.40	99.75	100.00	100.00
150	−1.06	−0.83	−0.18	0.00	−0.10	7.63	4.94	3.35	2.88	2.41	5.45	6.50	5.45	5.35	5.35	79.55	98.70	100.00	100.00	100.00
200	−1.10	−0.77	0.02	−0.02	−0.08	6.47	4.22	2.87	2.52	2.10	4.60	5.95	5.20	5.30	5.00	89.70	99.90	100.00	100.00	100.00
CS-DL pooled ($p_{\bar{y}} = 0$, $p_{\bar{x}} = [T^{1/3}]$ and $p = p_{\bar{x}} - 1$)																				
30	−0.97	−0.42	−0.04	−0.08	0.04	14.33	9.31	6.81	5.83	4.92	7.00	5.55	6.75	5.50	5.95	36.45	62.00	84.30	91.90	97.00
50	−1.01	−0.83	−0.29	−0.02	−0.09	11.07	7.38	5.40	4.59	3.91	5.90	5.20	6.20	5.30	6.85	49.75	80.45	95.50	98.15	99.75
100	−0.72	−0.51	−0.16	0.00	0.05	7.87	5.32	3.76	3.21	2.76	5.30	5.70	5.45	5.60	5.80	76.25	96.60	99.85	100.00	100.00
150	−0.80	−0.61	−0.14	0.05	−0.08	6.55	4.36	3.06	2.59	2.24	6.00	6.05	5.40	5.05	5.15	89.55	99.80	100.00	100.00	100.00
200	−0.95	−0.67	0.04	−0.03	−0.07	5.49	3.83	2.59	2.29	1.91	5.00	6.35	5.10	5.60	5.25	96.15	100.00	100.00	100.00	100.00
Based on CS-ARDL estimates of short-run coefficients (ARDL(2,1) specifications with $p_{\bar{z}} = [T^{1/3}]$)																				
30	−0.25	−3.59	−1.80	−1.24	−0.80	284.59	10.67	6.61	5.00	4.10	10.90	9.90	10.00	8.30	7.90	41.75	72.45	92.20	98.40	99.65
50	−8.02	−3.87	−2.03	−1.39	−1.03	85.61	8.89	5.21	4.08	3.37	10.80	11.10	9.65	9.75	8.55	50.70	85.65	99.35	99.90	100.00
100	−3.69	−3.87	−2.17	−1.38	−0.95	154.40	6.94	4.03	3.01	2.45	12.25	14.85	12.45	10.05	9.10	62.05	97.65	100.00	100.00	100.00
150	−0.25	−3.94	−2.11	−1.37	−1.06	90.79	6.27	3.51	2.60	2.12	14.05	18.10	14.80	12.30	11.75	67.95	99.50	100.00	100.00	100.00
200	−1.53	−3.98	−2.06	−1.37	−1.05	320.07	5.75	3.16	2.39	1.92	15.25	22.55	16.25	14.25	12.15	71.90	99.70	100.00	100.00	100.00
Based on CS-ARDL estimates of short-run coefficients (ARDL(1,0) specifications with $p_{\bar{z}} = [T^{1/3}]$)																				
30	−30.79	−27.20	−23.78	−22.80	−22.12	55.20	28.90	24.89	23.63	22.85	62.55	81.15	91.10	96.25	98.30	87.00	98.90	100.00	100.00	100.00
50	−32.12	−27.63	−24.23	−23.14	−22.57	47.11	28.66	24.88	23.66	23.00	76.85	94.25	99.05	99.75	100.00	94.25	99.90	100.00	100.00	100.00
100	−34.77	−27.78	−24.41	−23.21	−22.57	252.97	28.33	24.72	23.46	22.79	89.85	99.60	99.95	100.00	100.00	96.65	100.00	100.00	100.00	100.00
150	−32.53	−27.88	−24.35	−23.16	−22.62	36.50	28.27	24.56	23.33	22.76	92.55	99.90	100.00	100.00	100.00	96.90	100.00	100.00	100.00	100.00
200	−33.96	−27.90	−24.38	−23.16	−22.63	53.98	28.17	24.54	23.28	22.75	94.35	99.85	100.00	100.00	100.00	97.05	99.95	100.00	100.00	100.00

Notes: The dependent variable and regressors are generated according to Eqs. (37)–(38) with correlated individual effects, and with cross-sectionally weakly dependent and serially correlated heteroskedastic idiosyncratic innovations generated according to Eqs. (41)–(42) with $a_\varepsilon = 0.6$. The knowledge of lag orders is not used in the estimation stage and the integer part of $T^{1/3}$ gives $3, 3, 4, 5$ and 5 for $T = 30, 50, 100, 150$ and 200, respectively.

DGP is an ARDL(2,1) model with homogeneous long-run coefficients, heterogeneous short-run coefficients, $\varphi_{\max} = 0.6$, stationary regressors, $m = 2$ factors, no feedback effects and $\rho_{\varepsilon i} = 0$.

Table 3. Monte Carlo Estimates of Bias, RMSE, Size and Power for Estimation of Long-Run Coefficients (θ) in the Case of Homogeneous Short-Run Coefficients.

	Bias ($\times 100$)					Root-Mean-Square Errors ($\times 100$)					Size (5% level, $H_0:\theta=1$)					Power (5% level, $H_1:\theta=1.2$)				
(N,T)	30	50	100	150	200	30	50	100	150	200	30	50	100	150	200	30	50	100	150	200
CS-DL mean group ($p_{\bar{y}}=0$, $p_{\bar{x}}=[T^{1/3}]$ and $p=p_{\bar{x}}-1$)																				
30	−2.20	−1.52	−0.09	−0.34	−0.35	19.01	12.19	8.55	7.37	6.14	7.25	6.00	6.40	5.75	5.70	27.80	49.20	69.05	80.30	90.00
50	−2.23	−1.69	−0.51	0.17	0.05	14.93	9.35	6.85	5.79	4.84	6.10	5.45	6.30	6.55	5.60	35.95	67.20	86.15	92.40	97.25
100	−2.24	−1.84	−0.36	−0.21	0.06	10.55	6.93	4.68	4.01	3.33	6.10	7.15	5.45	5.10	4.90	59.10	89.95	98.75	99.90	100.00
150	−1.98	−1.99	−0.47	−0.11	−0.03	8.79	5.82	3.91	3.35	2.66	6.30	7.30	6.50	5.35	4.20	75.35	98.00	99.95	100.00	100.00
200	−2.22	−1.86	−0.35	−0.20	−0.01	7.94	4.96	3.38	2.85	2.38	6.70	6.90	5.25	4.75	4.80	84.40	99.65	100.00	100.00	100.00
CS-DL pooled ($p_{\bar{y}}=0$, $p_{\bar{x}}=[T^{1/3}]$ and $p=p_{\bar{x}}-1$)																				
30	−1.94	−1.39	−0.03	−0.35	−0.44	16.68	10.97	7.95	6.83	5.81	7.05	6.00	6.55	6.20	5.85	32.40	54.20	74.35	84.85	93.15
50	−1.96	−1.45	−0.40	0.16	0.02	12.88	8.70	6.29	5.36	4.43	6.80	6.65	6.25	6.60	5.45	44.55	72.80	89.75	95.50	98.75
100	−2.00	−1.66	−0.31	−0.16	0.04	9.10	6.34	4.37	3.70	3.07	6.25	6.10	6.20	5.35	5.25	70.55	93.50	99.30	99.95	100.00
150	−1.68	−1.62	−0.43	−0.08	−0.04	7.61	5.22	3.57	3.05	2.48	6.40	7.10	6.00	4.95	4.05	84.15	99.25	100.00	100.00	100.00
200	−1.94	−1.61	−0.31	−0.19	−0.04	6.76	4.50	3.13	2.59	2.20	6.95	6.55	5.05	3.95	4.45	92.70	99.75	100.00	100.00	100.00
Based on CS-ARDL estimates of short-run coefficients (ARDL(2,1) specifications with $p_{\bar{z}}=[T^{1/3}]$)																				
30	−14.08	−3.81	−1.92	−1.59	−1.26	310.27	12.81	7.66	6.02	5.04	10.50	10.45	9.20	9.40	9.35	32.50	61.25	84.10	95.30	98.25
50	−4.56	−4.15	−2.14	−1.35	−1.00	242.69	10.59	6.20	4.72	3.98	10.15	11.85	9.80	8.75	8.95	37.90	76.00	96.15	99.50	99.75
100	2.62	−4.32	−2.28	−1.51	−1.11	203.52	8.24	4.61	3.48	2.88	10.70	14.15	11.60	9.35	9.25	47.05	93.10	99.85	100.00	100.00
150	−3.39	−4.50	−2.35	−1.56	−1.12	163.77	7.29	4.09	3.03	2.43	9.90	18.25	14.30	12.10	9.25	51.30	98.35	100.00	100.00	100.00
200	−13.55	−4.32	−2.31	−1.64	−1.18	298.99	6.58	3.71	2.77	2.22	11.40	21.30	15.50	14.05	11.80	56.00	99.45	100.00	100.00	100.00
Based on CS-ARDL estimates of short-run coefficients (ARDL(1,0) specifications with $p_{\bar{z}}=[T^{1/3}]$)																				
30	−14.02	−10.86	−6.61	−5.78	−5.30	53.22	15.60	9.81	8.21	7.30	24.60	25.10	22.30	22.70	23.35	58.60	82.10	94.65	98.45	99.90
50	−15.83	−11.12	−7.07	−5.88	−5.26	67.84	14.14	9.05	7.41	6.59	30.70	34.25	30.60	31.40	33.65	71.95	93.60	99.90	99.95	100.00
100	−8.04	−11.36	−7.41	−6.14	−5.54	407.90	12.88	8.38	6.88	6.20	41.55	53.15	51.55	52.70	56.60	83.55	99.55	100.00	100.00	100.00
150	−15.24	−11.63	−7.51	−6.24	−5.54	43.70	12.68	8.17	6.77	5.99	50.75	68.95	68.25	70.15	72.20	88.85	100.00	100.00	100.00	100.00
200	−14.75	−11.53	−7.54	−6.33	−5.62	37.89	12.32	8.03	6.70	5.94	56.55	79.15	79.75	82.75	84.60	90.60	99.95	100.00	100.00	100.00

Notes: The dependent variable and regressors are generated according to Eqs. (37)–(38) with correlated individual effects, and with cross-sectionally weakly dependent and serially correlated heteroskedastic idiosyncratic innovations generated according to Eqs. (41)–(42) with $a_\varepsilon=0.6$. The knowledge of lag orders is not used in the estimation stage and the integer part of $T^{1/3}$ gives $3,3,4,5$ and 5 for $T=30,50,100,150$ and 200, respectively.

DGP is an ARDL(2,1) model with homogeneous short-run coefficients, $\varphi_{\max}=0.6$, stationary regressors, $m=2$ factors, no feedback effects and $\rho_{\varepsilon i}=0$.

Table 4. Monte Carlo Estimates of Bias, RMSE, Size and Power for Estimation of Long-Run Coefficients (θ) in the Case of ARDL(1,0) Model.

	Bias ($\times 100$)					Root-Mean-Square Errors ($\times 100$)					Size (5% level, $H_0:\theta=1$)					Power (5% level, $H_1:\theta=1.2$)				
(N,T)	30	50	100	150	200	30	50	100	150	200	30	50	100	150	200	30	50	100	150	200
CS-DL mean group ($p_{\bar{y}}=0$, $p_{\bar{x}}=[T^{1/3}]$ and $p=p_{\bar{x}}-1$)																				
30	−2.81	−2.34	−1.01	−0.45	−0.51	16.57	10.87	7.93	7.39	6.40	7.00	6.50	5.60	6.80	6.35	34.90	59.65	77.10	82.55	88.80
50	−2.77	−2.29	−0.96	−0.53	−0.57	13.13	8.64	6.25	5.48	5.04	7.30	6.50	6.25	5.45	6.40	47.70	77.20	92.30	95.45	98.20
100	−2.34	−2.30	−0.99	−0.44	−0.57	8.99	6.39	4.51	3.97	3.57	5.90	7.15	6.05	4.90	5.75	71.20	96.00	99.65	99.90	100.00
150	−2.50	−2.18	−1.04	−0.52	−0.52	7.94	5.21	3.71	3.21	2.95	7.10	7.35	6.10	4.90	5.80	85.10	99.45	100.00	100.00	100.00
200	−2.95	−2.36	−1.08	−0.51	−0.57	7.05	4.73	3.37	2.88	2.57	8.25	8.55	7.70	6.50	5.70	94.55	99.90	100.00	100.00	100.00
CS-DL pooled ($p_{\bar{y}}=0$, $p_{\bar{x}}=[T^{1/3}]$ and $p=p_{\bar{x}}-1$)																				
30	−2.50	−2.03	−0.98	−0.38	−0.55	14.54	10.27	7.74	7.23	6.34	6.60	7.20	6.10	6.65	5.90	39.80	62.10	79.85	82.80	89.35
50	−2.58	−2.10	−0.81	−0.51	−0.52	11.58	8.08	6.09	5.31	4.95	6.85	6.50	6.15	5.75	5.60	55.75	81.10	93.30	96.45	98.40
100	−2.08	−2.14	−0.88	−0.37	−0.54	7.97	6.04	4.31	3.89	3.51	5.70	7.25	6.15	5.40	6.10	80.65	96.75	99.80	99.95	100.00
150	−2.40	−1.92	−0.92	−0.49	−0.46	6.89	4.88	3.54	3.10	2.90	7.25	7.10	5.80	5.10	5.55	93.30	99.70	100.00	100.00	100.00
200	−2.69	−2.14	−0.96	−0.44	−0.49	6.22	4.39	3.22	2.75	2.53	8.25	7.75	6.75	6.05	5.60	98.45	100.00	100.00	100.00	100.00
Based on CS-ARDL estimates of short-run coefficients (ARDL(2,1) specifications with $p_{\bar{z}}=[T^{1/3}]$)																				
30	−20.46	−3.19	−1.79	−1.05	−0.78	1,278.76	10.93	7.21	6.12	5.43	9.95	9.10	7.80	7.70	6.80	39.75	66.70	87.80	93.50	96.25
50	−9.43	−3.23	−1.59	−1.12	−0.88	356.48	8.81	5.55	4.70	4.34	8.95	9.90	7.20	7.25	6.60	48.55	81.60	97.10	99.15	99.70
100	−2.25	−3.30	−1.72	−1.13	−0.96	99.43	6.69	4.25	3.42	3.11	9.05	12.20	9.20	6.95	7.60	58.00	97.15	99.95	100.00	100.00
150	−34.29	−2.95	−1.83	−1.15	−0.87	819.84	5.85	3.63	2.94	2.65	11.15	11.85	10.50	8.60	8.60	65.35	98.90	100.00	100.00	100.00
200	−2.09	−3.32	−1.76	−1.18	−0.93	101.18	6.98	3.22	2.59	2.30	11.70	16.50	10.80	8.95	7.70	70.55	99.45	100.00	100.00	100.00
Based on CS-ARDL estimates of short-run coefficients (ARDL(1,0) specifications with $p_{\bar{z}}=[T^{1/3}]$)																				
30	−6.54	−4.05	−1.86	−0.96	−0.64	19.35	9.58	6.56	5.50	4.98	13.80	12.15	9.75	8.60	6.90	62.55	82.50	93.95	96.85	98.10
50	−6.10	−4.52	−1.89	−1.25	−0.89	26.10	8.02	5.05	4.35	4.04	17.55	14.40	9.00	7.40	6.65	76.65	95.00	99.25	99.75	99.85
100	−18.34	−4.40	−2.12	−1.38	−1.04	537.53	6.50	4.06	3.21	2.91	23.30	19.50	12.10	8.55	7.80	90.55	99.85	100.00	100.00	100.00
150	−11.14	−4.26	−2.27	−1.43	−1.01	129.28	5.75	3.58	2.83	2.51	32.05	23.20	15.65	11.10	9.65	95.65	99.90	100.00	100.00	100.00
200	−7.45	−4.62	−2.21	−1.46	−1.11	11.91	5.73	3.25	2.59	2.24	36.55	31.35	17.45	12.40	9.95	97.30	100.00	100.00	100.00	100.00

Notes: The dependent variable and regressors are generated according to Eqs. (37)–(38) with correlated individual effects, and with cross-sectionally weakly dependent and serially correlated heteroskedastic idiosyncratic innovations generated according to Eqs. (41)–(42) with $a_{\varepsilon}=0.6$. The knowledge of lag orders is not used in the estimation stage and the integer part of $T^{1/3}$ gives $3, 3, 4, 5$ and 5 for $T=30, 50, 100, 150$ and 200, respectively.
DGP is an ARDL(1,0) model with heterogeneous coefficients, $\varphi_{\max}=0.6$, stationary regressors, $m=2$ factors, no feedback effects and $\rho_{\varepsilon i}=0$.

Table 5. Monte Carlo Estimates of Bias, RMSE, Size and Power for Estimation of Long-Run Coefficients (θ) in the Case of $\phi_{\max} = 0.8$.

	Bias (×100)					Root-Mean-Square Errors (×100)					Size (5% level, $H_0: \theta = 1$)					Power (5% level, $H_1: \theta = 1.2$)				
(N, T)	30	50	100	150	200	30	50	100	150	200	30	50	100	150	200	30	50	100	150	200
CS-DL mean group ($p_{\bar{y}} = 0$, $p_{\bar{x}} = [T^{1/3}]$ and $p = p_{\bar{x}} - 1$)																				
30	−5.95	−5.68	−2.87	−1.19	−1.86	21.83	14.77	10.87	9.28	8.23	7.70	8.65	7.45	5.75	6.90	28.35	51.30	63.45	66.20	79.25
50	−6.32	−5.87	−2.92	−1.59	−1.70	17.52	12.12	8.42	7.36	6.68	7.90	9.45	6.90	6.60	6.50	40.50	70.75	82.50	86.35	92.55
100	−6.47	−5.47	−3.03	−1.81	−1.67	13.09	9.40	6.46	5.24	4.83	9.35	12.35	8.85	5.85	7.70	65.10	91.90	98.25	98.95	99.70
150	−6.24	−5.60	−2.95	−1.65	−1.70	11.21	8.34	5.55	4.40	4.07	10.55	13.85	9.40	6.25	8.50	80.95	98.45	99.95	99.85	99.95
200	−6.32	−5.68	−3.08	−1.66	−1.68	10.26	7.94	5.05	4.00	3.55	12.30	18.90	10.70	8.05	8.10	90.40	99.65	100.00	100.00	100.00
CS-DL pooled ($p_{\bar{y}} = 0$, $p_{\bar{x}} = [T^{1/3}]$ and $p = p_{\bar{x}} - 1$)																				
30	−5.46	−5.46	−2.49	−1.12	−1.73	19.66	13.97	10.21	8.88	7.85	7.20	7.75	7.45	5.90	6.50	32.70	55.50	65.80	69.15	81.85
50	−5.54	−5.31	−2.80	−1.29	−1.52	15.73	11.23	8.01	7.04	6.45	8.00	8.75	6.45	6.35	6.70	44.60	73.95	84.45	87.80	93.65
100	−6.04	−5.03	−2.78	−1.64	−1.48	11.81	8.76	6.07	4.98	4.68	10.20	10.65	8.65	6.20	7.95	72.05	94.20	98.50	99.10	99.70
150	−5.61	−5.12	−2.63	−1.46	−1.54	10.06	7.77	5.20	4.19	3.86	9.95	13.25	10.20	6.90	7.70	86.00	98.80	99.95	99.85	99.95
200	−5.78	−5.05	−2.70	−1.47	−1.56	9.20	7.19	4.72	3.79	3.41	12.45	17.45	10.35	7.05	7.55	94.60	99.75	100.00	100.00	100.00
Based on CS-ARDL estimates of short-run coefficients (ARDL(2,1) specifications with $p_{\bar{z}} = [T^{1/3}]$)																				
30	−12.89	−5.14	−2.82	−1.50	−1.28	786.15	19.34	9.43	7.65	6.69	10.85	11.55	8.90	7.35	7.60	35.00	55.00	74.90	82.50	90.00
50	−2.09	−8.46	−2.72	−1.69	−1.29	394.84	187.62	7.57	6.04	5.40	11.55	10.80	9.15	8.00	7.45	37.90	68.50	89.35	95.00	97.90
100	−30.77	−5.24	−2.87	−2.08	−1.45	768.23	19.56	5.70	4.55	4.04	11.50	14.75	10.10	9.15	9.00	44.10	85.50	98.85	99.75	100.00
150	−15.09	−4.79	−2.98	−1.96	−1.47	375.14	18.01	5.25	3.85	3.37	12.30	16.90	14.00	10.65	9.30	46.45	92.40	99.50	100.00	100.00
200	−1.15	−6.97	−3.07	−1.96	−1.47	229.52	69.18	4.68	3.59	2.98	12.30	22.20	15.75	12.30	9.85	49.15	95.30	100.00	100.00	100.00
Based on CS-ARDL estimates of short-run coefficients (ARDL(1,0) specifications with $p_{\bar{z}} = [T^{1/3}]$)																				
30	−26.96	−31.57	−23.02	−21.56	−20.97	145.97	203.84	24.91	23.16	22.29	48.25	60.65	70.50	74.85	79.35	72.25	89.15	98.15	99.60	99.70
50	−25.05	−27.49	−23.46	−21.76	−21.08	424.65	29.74	24.99	22.68	21.90	57.20	76.25	87.55	91.00	94.00	77.80	96.45	99.70	100.00	100.00
100	−35.41	−27.96	−23.42	−22.14	−21.19	148.21	32.71	24.01	22.60	21.62	68.30	92.05	98.20	99.70	99.75	84.25	98.30	100.00	100.00	100.00
150	−96.09	−27.09	−23.65	−22.06	−21.17	2,622.39	41.48	24.07	22.37	21.46	72.70	96.05	99.85	99.95	100.00	85.90	99.10	100.00	100.00	100.00
200	−30.44	−28.11	−23.68	−21.92	−21.27	248.48	30.67	24.00	22.18	21.48	73.70	97.70	100.00	100.00	100.00	85.25	98.95	100.00	100.00	100.00

Notes: The dependent variable and regressors are generated according to Eqs. (37)–(38) with correlated individual effects, and with cross-sectionally weakly dependent and serially correlated heteroskedastic idiosyncratic innovations generated according to Eqs. (41)–(42) with $a_\varepsilon = 0.6$. The knowledge of lag orders is not used in the estimation stage and the integer part of $T^{1/3}$ gives 3, 3, 4, 5 and 5 for $T = 30, 50, 100, 150$ and 200, respectively.

DGP is an ARDL(2,1) model with heterogeneous coefficients, $\varphi_{\max} = 0.8$, stationary regressors, $m = 2$ factors, no feedback effects and $\rho_{\varepsilon i} = 0$.

Table 6. Monte Carlo Estimates of Bias, RMSE, Size and Power for Estimation of Long-Run Coefficients (θ) in the Case of $\phi_{\max} = 0.9$.

	Bias ($\times 100$)					Root Mean Square Errors ($\times 100$)					Size (5% level, $H_0: \theta = 1$)					Power (5% level, $H_1: \theta = 1.2$)				
(N,T)	30	50	100	150	200	30	50	100	150	200	30	50	100	150	200	30	50	100	150	200
CS-DL mean group ($p_{\bar{y}} = 0$, $p_{\bar{x}} = [T^{1/3}]$ and $p = p_{\bar{x}} - 1$)																				
30	−12.05	−11.37	−6.94	−4.56	−4.89	27.31	19.55	14.78	12.60	11.66	9.00	9.85	9.75	8.05	9.45	31.80	53.15	61.35	63.65	73.00
50	−11.64	−10.52	−6.96	−4.69	−4.71	22.01	16.59	12.23	10.16	9.21	9.15	13.45	11.15	7.85	10.40	41.40	69.35	80.35	79.80	89.90
100	−12.19	−10.74	−6.77	−4.77	−4.63	18.30	14.13	9.85	7.95	7.19	16.35	21.95	16.95	11.60	13.30	67.65	92.05	97.05	96.85	99.45
150	−11.60	−10.76	−6.67	−4.79	−4.63	15.71	13.28	8.88	7.07	6.48	19.90	31.35	22.20	15.05	17.95	84.40	98.20	99.70	99.45	100.00
200	−11.87	−10.66	−6.58	−4.88	−4.77	15.17	12.52	8.22	6.67	6.15	24.00	38.55	27.40	19.25	22.05	92.45	99.80	99.95	100.00	100.00
CS-DL pooled ($p_{\bar{y}} = 0$, $p_{\bar{x}} = [T^{1/3}]$ and $p = p_{\bar{x}} - 1$)																				
30	−11.26	−10.51	−6.36	−4.21	−4.53	24.79	18.53	14.13	12.10	11.24	9.00	10.00	9.75	8.25	9.35	34.00	55.35	63.80	65.80	74.20
50	−10.81	−9.80	−6.44	−4.41	−4.45	20.53	15.76	11.48	9.76	8.83	9.60	13.35	10.95	8.35	9.35	47.60	71.95	81.60	82.50	91.20
100	−11.12	−9.97	−6.24	−4.39	−4.29	16.72	13.31	9.26	7.47	6.85	15.10	20.80	15.20	11.10	13.00	73.60	92.65	97.50	97.55	99.20
150	−10.72	−10.13	−6.22	−4.53	−4.33	14.51	12.54	8.31	6.71	6.13	19.60	30.10	20.00	14.40	17.05	88.05	98.60	99.65	99.70	99.85
200	−10.97	−9.94	−6.18	−4.53	−4.41	14.03	11.76	7.82	6.30	5.81	25.35	35.70	26.10	17.80	22.55	94.70	99.80	99.90	99.95	100.00
Based on CS-ARDL estimates of short-run coefficients (ARDL(2,1) specifications with $p_{\bar{z}} = [T^{1/3}]$)																				
30	−21.58	−6.64	−3.38	−1.70	−1.36	438.72	121.05	12.25	9.96	8.51	11.25	11.05	8.35	8.00	7.25	29.00	46.80	61.95	69.25	76.05
50	4.94	−5.49	−3.31	−2.27	−1.61	922.24	34.12	9.95	7.80	6.81	10.25	10.70	8.70	7.55	7.60	32.30	57.05	75.60	85.50	90.60
100	8.35	−3.40	−3.87	−2.43	−1.82	770.17	112.28	7.72	5.92	5.01	10.95	13.90	11.85	9.55	8.00	35.55	71.20	94.40	97.10	99.25
150	−22.01	−7.03	−3.45	−2.61	−1.84	513.85	91.47	6.40	5.07	4.24	10.65	16.85	11.95	11.30	8.75	35.85	78.90	97.40	99.75	99.80
200	41.07	−4.61	−3.61	−2.70	−1.92	2,063.94	127.98	5.90	4.57	3.80	12.45	17.90	14.55	12.30	10.25	38.60	82.55	99.35	100.00	100.00
Based on CS-ARDL estimates of short-run coefficients (ARDL(1,0) specifications with $p_{\bar{z}} = [T^{1/3}]$)																				
30	21.99	−27.42	−22.99	−20.75	−20.04	1,921.14	70.72	26.25	23.39	22.18	40.55	51.10	57.40	60.25	63.65	60.40	80.05	90.60	94.50	97.40
50	−40.53	−25.17	−23.32	−21.48	−20.71	238.17	219.25	25.35	22.96	21.99	46.45	61.40	71.85	78.45	82.15	65.90	87.55	96.65	98.90	99.65
100	−93.36	−34.65	−23.62	−21.97	−21.09	3,030.40	242.83	27.18	22.76	21.72	54.20	75.05	92.25	93.50	97.30	72.30	91.90	99.55	99.80	100.00
150	−33.97	−33.48	−23.56	−21.88	−20.96	472.17	329.85	24.24	22.39	21.39	55.15	81.65	96.60	99.15	99.60	71.60	93.60	99.85	100.00	99.95
200	−37.78	−14.74	−23.75	−22.07	−21.10	247.78	701.23	24.30	22.42	21.41	59.35	86.65	98.80	99.90	100.00	73.45	94.25	100.00	100.00	100.00

Notes: The dependent variable and regressors are generated according to Eqs. (37)–(38) with correlated individual effects, and with cross-sectionally weakly dependent and serially correlated heteroskedastic idiosyncratic innovations generated according to Eqs. (41)–(42) with $a_{\varepsilon} = 0.6$. The knowledge of lag orders is not used in the estimation stage and the integer part of $T^{1/3}$ gives $3, 3, 4, 5$ and 5 for $T = 30, 50, 100, 150$ and 200, respectively.
DGP is an ARDL(2,1) model with heterogeneous coefficients, $\varphi_{\max} = 0.9$, stationary regressors, $m = 2$ factors, no feedback effects and $\rho_{\varepsilon i} = 0$.

Table 7. Monte Carlo Estimates of Bias, RMSE, Size and Power for Estimation of Long-Run Coefficients (θ) in the Case of $m = 3$ Factors.

	Bias (×100)					Root-Mean-Square Errors (×100)					Size (5% level, $H_0: \theta = 1$)					Power (5% level, $H_1: \theta = 1.2$)				
(N,T)	30	50	100	150	200	30	50	100	150	200	30	50	100	150	200	30	50	100	150	200
CS-DL mean group ($p_{\bar{y}} = 0$, $p_{\bar{x}} = [T^{1/3}]$ and $p = p_{\bar{x}} - 1$)																				
30	−1.85	−1.02	0.00	−0.01	−0.02	17.23	11.03	8.20	7.45	6.63	6.70	6.15	6.90	5.75	6.40	29.80	51.70	68.05	78.05	85.25
50	−0.79	−0.63	−0.24	0.03	0.10	12.90	8.79	6.68	5.77	5.04	4.90	6.55	6.35	6.20	5.05	38.65	67.25	85.85	92.70	96.60
100	−1.00	−0.94	−0.23	0.09	−0.15	9.57	6.23	4.73	4.12	3.72	5.70	5.40	5.55	5.20	5.35	61.05	92.80	99.10	99.60	99.95
150	−1.19	−0.88	−0.02	0.00	−0.06	7.77	5.03	3.73	3.34	2.92	6.05	4.85	5.15	5.40	4.60	78.45	98.30	99.90	100.00	100.00
200	−0.99	−0.78	−0.03	−0.03	0.09	6.62	4.50	3.23	2.88	2.61	5.00	5.60	5.20	4.85	4.90	89.15	99.60	100.00	100.00	100.00
CS-DL pooled ($p_{\bar{y}} = 0$, $p_{\bar{x}} = [T^{1/3}]$ and $p = p_{\bar{x}} - 1$)																				
30	−1.59	−0.79	0.08	−0.04	0.01	15.07	10.40	7.96	7.15	6.57	7.05	6.40	7.05	5.95	6.45	34.10	54.25	72.20	80.00	86.40
50	−0.91	−0.57	−0.17	0.03	0.11	11.51	8.27	6.44	5.57	4.93	5.65	6.50	6.55	5.50	5.00	47.50	71.95	88.25	93.90	97.65
100	−1.01	−0.88	−0.21	0.10	−0.16	8.33	5.78	4.51	3.97	3.58	5.55	5.85	5.50	5.35	5.20	72.30	94.90	99.55	99.85	100.00
150	−0.90	−0.72	−0.04	0.00	−0.07	6.78	4.73	3.61	3.28	2.88	6.20	5.15	5.70	5.35	4.80	87.25	99.10	100.00	100.00	100.00
200	−0.96	−0.63	−0.05	0.01	0.08	5.79	4.19	3.08	2.81	2.55	5.25	6.30	5.10	5.40	5.60	94.80	99.85	100.00	100.00	100.00
Based on CS-ARDL estimates of short-run coefficients (ARDL(2,1) specifications with $p_{\bar{z}} = [T^{1/3}]$)																				
30	−5.34	−2.54	−0.89	−0.10	0.34	144.86	11.33	7.34	6.29	5.65	9.10	8.80	7.80	6.70	7.15	37.10	61.60	83.70	88.95	93.35
50	−5.60	−2.52	−1.03	−0.20	0.23	157.20	9.36	5.91	4.86	4.28	9.20	9.80	8.10	6.20	5.85	44.65	76.50	94.60	98.05	99.40
100	−0.04	−3.29	−1.21	−0.23	−0.07	83.58	10.20	4.28	3.43	3.10	9.65	11.05	7.85	6.65	6.25	56.30	95.20	100.00	100.00	100.00
150	−4.99	−2.93	−0.94	−0.44	0.01	94.15	7.97	3.48	2.82	2.54	11.80	13.50	8.20	4.80	5.40	64.25	98.65	99.95	100.00	100.00
200	7.81	1.08	−1.01	−0.36	0.08	383.41	178.92	3.08	2.51	2.23	12.10	15.05	8.15	6.75	6.55	67.70	99.60	100.00	100.00	100.00
Based on CS-ARDL estimates of short-run coefficients (ARDL(1,0) specifications with $p_{\bar{z}} = [T^{1/3}]$)																				
30	−24.61	−25.74	−22.19	−20.87	−20.48	271.79	27.83	23.55	22.09	21.54	57.05	70.00	81.45	84.80	86.65	84.95	97.50	99.85	99.95	100.00
50	−29.47	−25.95	−22.39	−21.20	−20.52	39.80	27.22	23.27	21.90	21.18	70.30	88.00	94.45	97.15	98.05	91.90	99.65	100.00	100.00	100.00
100	−30.85	−26.44	−22.73	−21.26	−20.94	37.04	27.17	23.16	21.63	21.28	85.75	98.60	100.00	99.95	100.00	96.20	99.95	100.00	100.00	100.00
150	−31.83	−26.42	−22.46	−21.61	−20.86	48.65	26.97	22.76	21.85	21.08	89.95	99.95	99.95	100.00	100.00	96.05	99.95	100.00	100.00	100.00
200	−29.13	−26.22	−22.55	−21.46	−20.80	108.14	26.59	22.77	21.66	20.97	91.85	99.85	100.00	100.00	100.00	96.20	100.00	100.00	100.00	100.00

Notes: The dependent variable and regressors are generated according to Eqs. (37)–(38) with correlated individual effects, and with cross-sectionally weakly dependent and serially correlated heteroskedastic idiosyncratic innovations generated according to Eqs. (41)–(42) with $a_\varepsilon = 0.6$. The knowledge of lag orders is not used in the estimation stage and the integer part of $T^{1/3}$ gives 3, 3, 4, 5 and 5 for $T = 30, 50, 100, 150$ and 200, respectively.
DGP is an ARDL(2,1) model with heterogeneous coefficients, $\varphi_{\max} = 0.6$, stationary regressors, $m = 3$ factors, no feedback effects and $\rho_{\varepsilon i} = 0$.

Table 8. Monte Carlo Estimates of Bias, RMSE, Size and Power for Estimation of Long-Run Coefficients (θ) in the Case of Unit Roots in Factors.

	Bias ($\times 100$)					Root-Mean-Square Errors ($\times 100$)					Size (5% level, $H_0: \theta = 1$)					Power (5% level, $H_1: \theta = 1.2$)				
(N, T)	30	50	100	150	200	30	50	100	150	200	30	50	100	150	200	30	50	100	150	200
CS-DL mean group ($p_{\bar{y}} = 0$, $p_{\bar{x}} = [T^{1/3}]$ and $p = p_{\bar{x}} - 1$)																				
30	−1.04	−1.04	−0.14	0.06	0.05	16.26	11.33	8.28	7.27	6.55	5.65	6.85	6.60	5.95	6.55	28.50	53.25	71.45	78.30	86.40
50	−0.84	−0.84	−0.30	0.20	−0.16	12.76	8.51	6.56	5.79	5.18	5.15	4.85	5.35	6.40	5.70	38.25	70.50	87.65	92.80	97.10
100	−1.42	−0.99	−0.04	0.03	−0.14	9.37	6.29	4.55	4.05	3.62	5.30	5.50	5.10	5.55	5.40	63.55	92.60	98.75	99.80	100.00
150	−1.15	−0.91	−0.14	−0.08	0.01	7.87	5.26	3.73	3.31	2.91	5.90	6.40	4.75	4.95	4.90	78.30	98.10	99.95	100.00	100.00
200	−1.14	−0.79	−0.21	−0.03	0.03	6.79	4.43	3.24	2.90	2.50	5.50	4.95	5.20	5.10	4.95	88.00	99.65	100.00	100.00	100.00
CS-DL pooled ($p_{\bar{y}} = 0$, $p_{\bar{x}} = [T^{1/3}]$ and $p = p_{\bar{x}} - 1$)																				
30	−0.69	−0.78	−0.15	0.09	0.04	14.53	10.66	8.01	7.04	6.47	6.25	6.75	6.80	6.15	7.20	33.10	57.20	72.95	80.50	88.00
50	−0.69	−0.81	−0.27	0.19	−0.24	11.42	7.97	6.17	5.62	5.06	5.05	5.25	5.80	6.40	5.60	45.45	74.10	90.60	94.15	97.55
100	−1.17	−0.80	−0.05	0.02	−0.09	8.25	5.77	4.38	4.03	3.60	5.40	5.55	5.80	5.65	5.60	72.60	95.00	99.50	99.90	100.00
150	−0.94	−0.82	−0.14	−0.05	0.03	6.98	4.88	3.55	3.20	2.85	6.05	5.90	5.70	5.15	5.40	86.00	98.90	100.00	100.00	100.00
200	−0.98	−0.70	−0.20	−0.01	0.01	5.96	4.15	3.16	2.83	2.48	5.60	5.45	5.60	5.40	5.20	94.05	99.90	100.00	100.00	100.00
Based on CS-ARDL estimates of short-run coefficients (ARDL(2,1) specifications with $p_{\bar{z}} = [T^{1/3}]$)																				
30	14.28	−3.42	−1.78	−0.89	−0.48	760.36	14.43	7.34	6.04	5.47	9.40	10.10	8.35	6.75	7.20	38.75	66.45	88.85	93.30	96.40
50	−3.16	−3.92	−2.23	−1.19	−0.94	106.12	9.21	6.14	4.87	4.52	11.35	10.70	10.25	7.65	8.40	49.10	83.25	96.90	99.25	99.55
100	−9.23	−5.09	−2.62	−1.63	−1.20	293.70	7.95	4.67	3.75	3.31	15.00	18.15	12.30	9.90	8.40	65.15	97.95	100.00	100.00	100.00
150	−12.59	−5.44	−2.95	−1.97	−1.39	395.28	7.37	4.33	3.35	2.78	18.40	25.50	18.25	13.50	8.80	73.35	99.55	100.00	100.00	100.00
200	−5.66	−5.90	−3.07	−2.04	−1.47	91.39	7.55	4.15	3.13	2.56	21.95	34.35	22.30	16.80	11.60	77.50	99.90	100.00	100.00	100.00
Based on CS-ARDL estimates of short-run coefficients (ARDL(1,0) specifications with $p_{\bar{z}} = [T^{1/3}]$)																				
30	−28.65	−26.01	−22.78	−21.75	−21.38	43.69	28.01	24.09	22.81	22.34	54.90	72.60	84.75	89.45	91.55	84.60	97.80	99.90	100.00	100.00
50	−30.99	−26.05	−23.52	−21.99	−21.78	80.99	27.34	24.34	22.65	22.38	67.60	87.65	96.40	98.10	99.00	89.65	99.60	100.00	100.00	100.00
100	−32.82	−27.17	−23.82	−22.65	−21.99	69.50	27.81	24.20	22.98	22.28	86.30	99.45	100.00	100.00	100.00	95.80	99.95	100.00	100.00	100.00
150	−26.37	−27.61	−24.12	−22.92	−22.31	175.08	28.01	24.37	23.13	22.50	92.10	99.95	100.00	100.00	100.00	96.95	100.00	100.00	100.00	100.00
200	−32.57	−27.95	−24.27	−22.94	−22.32	41.83	28.25	24.46	23.11	22.46	93.85	100.00	100.00	100.00	100.00	96.45	100.00	100.00	100.00	100.00

Notes: The dependent variable and regressors are generated according to Eqs. (37)–(38) with correlated individual effects, and with cross-sectionally weakly dependent and serially correlated heteroskedastic idiosyncratic innovations generated according to Eqs. (41)–(42) with $a_\varepsilon = 0.6$. The knowledge of lag orders is not used in the estimation stage and the integer part of $T^{1/3}$ gives 3, 3, 4, 5 and 5 for $T = 30, 50, 100, 150$ and 200, respectively.
DGP is an ARDL(2,1) model with heterogeneous coefficients, $\varphi_{\max} = 0.6$, unit roots in factors, $m = 2$ factors, no feedback effects and $\rho_{\varepsilon i} = 0$.

Table 9. Monte Carlo Estimates of Bias, RMSE, Size and Power for Estimation of Long-Run Coefficients (θ) in the Case of Unit Roots in Regressor Specific Components.

	Bias ($\times 100$)					Root-Mean-Square Errors ($\times 100$)					Size (5% level, $H_0: \theta = 1$)					Power (5% level, $H_1: \theta = 1.2$)				
(N,T)	30	50	100	150	200	30	50	100	150	200	30	50	100	150	200	30	50	100	150	200
CS-DL mean group ($p_{\bar{y}} = 0$, $p_{\bar{x}} = [T^{1/3}]$ and $p = p_{\bar{x}} - 1$)																				
30	−2.99	0.37	0.25	0.33	−0.13	65.72	32.60	15.74	10.52	8.06	5.70	5.00	5.45	5.70	5.65	7.85	11.45	29.45	52.30	72.85
50	−0.20	0.66	−0.40	0.24	0.20	51.19	26.47	12.29	8.26	6.42	5.45	6.40	6.00	5.25	5.30	8.30	14.55	42.20	69.35	87.30
100	−0.76	−0.50	−0.09	0.11	0.09	37.01	18.87	9.00	5.88	4.44	4.70	5.65	6.00	5.00	4.45	9.40	22.00	64.90	91.60	99.05
150	−0.85	−0.17	−0.25	−0.06	0.08	30.36	15.18	7.17	4.76	3.72	4.55	5.35	5.80	4.90	5.45	10.75	27.15	81.85	98.60	99.90
200	0.15	−0.14	−0.18	−0.17	0.18	27.24	13.26	6.28	4.21	3.15	5.90	5.55	5.40	6.00	5.00	12.25	34.05	89.65	99.60	100.00
CS-DL pooled ($p_{\bar{y}} = 0$, $p_{\bar{x}} = [T^{1/3}]$ and $p = p_{\bar{x}} - 1$)																				
30	−1.75	0.62	−0.04	−0.01	−0.06	47.00	24.71	12.38	9.06	7.13	5.20	5.60	6.50	7.40	6.70	8.95	14.60	40.85	64.45	78.95
50	−0.67	0.37	0.00	−0.01	0.02	36.30	19.19	9.39	6.88	5.64	4.95	5.40	5.70	6.45	6.30	10.40	20.25	57.30	82.95	93.15
100	−0.92	−0.95	−0.24	−0.01	−0.01	27.06	13.97	6.90	4.75	4.01	6.15	5.90	5.85	4.95	5.10	14.50	35.45	84.50	98.25	99.50
150	−1.09	−0.34	−0.08	−0.13	0.13	21.26	11.24	5.47	3.98	3.31	4.70	5.55	4.75	5.45	4.85	16.95	46.00	95.00	99.75	100.00
200	−0.05	−0.11	−0.03	−0.10	0.07	18.94	9.81	4.74	3.45	2.76	4.95	5.45	5.00	5.05	5.20	20.10	55.20	98.25	100.00	100.00
Based on CS-ARDL estimates of short-run coefficients (ARDL(2,1) specifications with $p_{\bar{z}} = [T^{1/3}]$)																				
30	11.59	−2.76	−0.64	−0.09	−0.27	1,487.96	52.46	15.63	10.51	8.10	5.00	5.80	5.60	5.70	6.00	7.30	12.85	31.35	55.35	73.00
50	−28.86	−0.82	−0.92	−0.12	−0.02	1,128.77	27.42	12.19	8.26	6.34	4.60	6.10	6.70	5.80	5.60	7.95	14.95	44.25	70.55	88.30
100	−6.61	−1.86	−0.68	−0.24	−0.12	361.66	19.50	9.00	5.77	4.47	4.70	5.10	6.35	5.25	5.80	8.75	22.25	67.60	93.20	99.20
150	−61.57	−1.90	−0.82	−0.28	−0.11	2,620.58	16.18	7.17	4.67	3.67	4.05	5.40	5.50	4.95	5.80	10.05	30.85	83.80	99.00	99.95
200	2.04	−1.54	−0.68	−0.41	0.00	336.21	14.05	6.24	4.21	3.12	5.05	5.25	5.45	5.55	4.90	11.10	36.55	91.45	99.70	100.00
Based on CS-ARDL estimates of short-run coefficients (ARDL(1,0) specifications with $p_{\bar{z}} = [T^{1/3}]$)																				
30	−14.85	−9.27	−4.73	−2.76	−2.30	146.76	36.98	17.15	11.44	8.94	6.65	6.45	6.85	7.05	7.30	12.20	17.30	38.80	58.70	76.15
50	−18.57	−8.15	−4.38	−2.42	−1.79	136.51	28.29	13.16	8.92	6.79	6.80	7.15	7.35	6.70	6.15	12.90	22.80	53.80	76.50	91.50
100	−16.57	−8.00	−3.42	−2.03	−1.39	72.70	20.94	9.73	6.19	4.75	6.60	7.90	7.75	6.75	7.15	16.30	33.75	76.10	95.75	99.40
150	−12.87	−7.13	−3.19	−1.80	−1.24	85.37	17.40	7.87	5.12	3.91	8.00	7.75	7.90	6.95	7.00	19.85	43.15	89.60	99.30	100.00
200	−16.82	−6.73	−2.89	−1.82	−1.04	346.63	15.13	6.99	4.62	3.33	8.45	7.75	8.35	7.75	6.15	23.20	51.75	95.40	99.90	100.00

Notes: The dependent variable and regressors are generated according to Eqs. (37)–(38) with correlated individual effects, and with cross-sectionally weakly dependent and serially correlated heteroskedastic idiosyncratic innovations generated according to Eqs. (41)–(42) with $a_\varepsilon = 0.6$. The knowledge of lag orders is not used in the estimation stage and the integer part of $T^{1/3}$ gives 3, 3, 4, 5 and 5 for $T = 30, 50, 100, 150$ and 200, respectively.
DGP is an ARDL(2,1) model with heterogeneous coefficients, $\varphi_{\max} = 0.6$, unit roots in v_{it}, $m = 2$ factors, no feedback effects and $\rho_{\varepsilon i} = 0$.

The robustness of the CS-DL estimators to the patterns of residual serial correlation is investigated in Table 10, while Table 11 presents results on the robustness of CS-DL estimators to possible breaks in the error processes. As can be seen, and as predicted by the theory, the CS-DL estimators are robust to both of these departures from the baseline scenario, whereas the CS-ARDL approach is not. Recall, the CS-ARDL approach requires the lag orders to be correctly specified, and does not allow for residual serial correlation and/or breaks in the error processes, whilst CS-DL does.

Last but not least, the consequences of feedback effects from y_{it} to the regressors, x_{it}, is documented in Table 12. This table shows that the CS-ARDL approach is consistent regardless of the feedback effects, provided the lag orders are correctly specified, again as predicted by the theory. But a satisfactory performance (in terms of bias and size of the test) for the CS-ARDL approach requires T to be sufficiently large. On the other hand, in the presence of feedbacks, the CS-DL estimators are inconsistent and show positive bias even for T sufficiently large. But the bias due to feedback effects seems to be quite small; between -0.02 and 0.06, and the CS-DL estimators tend to outperform the CS-ARDL estimators when $T \leq 50$, even when the underlying ARDL model is correctly specified.

4.4. *Monte Carlo Findings on the Improvement in Estimation of Short-Run Coefficients*

As a final exercise, we consider if it is possible to improve on the estimation of the short-run coefficients by imposing the CS-DL estimates of the long run, before estimating the short-run coefficients. We consider the experiment that departs from the baseline model by assuming a homogeneous long-run coefficient, whilst all the short-run slopes are allowed to be heterogeneous, and use the ARDL(1,0) as the DGP. More specifically, we impose the CS-DL pooled estimator of the long-run coefficient, $\hat{\theta}_P$, when estimating the short-run coefficients using the CS-ARDL approach. In particular, we estimate the following unit-specific regressions:

$$\Delta y_{it} = c_{yi}^{*} + \lambda_i \left(y_{i,t-1} - \hat{\theta}_P x_{it} \right) + \sum_{\ell=0}^{p_{\bar{z}}} \boldsymbol{\delta}_{i\ell}' \bar{\mathbf{z}}_{t-\ell} + \varepsilon_{it}^{*}, \tag{43}$$

for $i = 1, 2, \ldots, N$, and the resulting mean group estimator of $E(\varphi_{i1}) = 1 + E(\lambda_i)$ is denoted by

$$\tilde{\varphi}_{1,MG} = N^{-1} \sum_{i=1}^{N} \tilde{\varphi}_{i1}, \; \tilde{\varphi}_{i1} = 1 - \tilde{\lambda}_i,$$

Table 10. Monte Carlo Estimates of Bias, RMSE, Size and Power for Estimation of Long-Run Coefficients (θ) in the Case of Serially Correlated Idiosyncratic Errors.

	Bias (×100)					Root-Mean-Square Errors (×100)					Size (5% level, $H_0: \theta = 1$)					Power (5% level, $H_1: \theta = 1.2$)				
(N,T)	30	50	100	150	200	30	50	100	150	200	30	50	100	150	200	30	50	100	150	200
CS-DL mean group ($p_{\bar{y}} = 0$, $p_{\bar{x}} = [T^{1/3}]$ and $p = p_{\bar{x}} - 1$)																				
30	−1.11	−0.45	−0.21	0.01	0.12	21.91	14.75	11.44	10.33	8.89	7.05	6.00	5.40	6.25	5.55	20.20	31.40	47.00	53.70	64.15
50	−0.29	−1.04	0.08	−0.15	−0.04	16.85	11.71	8.88	7.89	6.96	5.25	6.20	5.95	5.00	5.95	24.05	46.65	64.10	71.85	82.20
100	−1.22	−0.75	−0.11	0.03	0.08	12.21	8.14	6.04	5.55	4.97	4.80	5.05	4.85	4.45	5.90	43.90	72.35	90.05	94.50	97.70
150	−1.21	−1.04	−0.07	0.09	−0.03	10.05	6.90	5.22	4.65	4.16	5.05	5.40	5.55	5.35	6.65	58.00	86.40	96.80	99.15	99.70
200	−1.28	−0.80	0.05	0.01	−0.08	8.62	5.89	4.56	3.99	3.45	5.40	5.25	6.25	5.45	4.15	70.00	94.45	99.05	99.95	100.00
CS-DL pooled ($p_{\bar{y}} = 0$, $p_{\bar{x}} = [T^{1/3}]$ and $p = p_{\bar{x}} - 1$)																				
30	−0.86	−0.35	−0.06	−0.12	0.22	20.29	14.11	11.03	10.01	8.71	6.85	6.30	6.25	6.20	6.30	24.05	33.80	49.75	58.05	67.25
50	−0.35	−0.97	0.10	−0.11	−0.05	15.46	11.22	8.51	7.57	6.73	5.70	5.95	5.10	5.60	5.55	28.65	50.00	67.10	75.40	83.80
100	−1.11	−0.57	−0.11	0.08	0.15	11.05	7.75	5.89	5.28	4.75	5.30	4.50	4.65	5.00	4.55	49.65	75.05	91.10	95.30	98.35
150	−1.00	−0.77	−0.07	0.02	−0.05	9.06	6.50	5.02	4.43	4.01	5.20	5.45	5.55	4.90	6.00	66.10	90.00	97.60	99.45	99.75
200	−1.01	−0.52	0.00	0.04	−0.05	7.93	5.59	4.35	3.82	3.36	5.95	5.30	5.70	4.60	4.75	76.15	95.40	99.60	100.00	100.00
Based on CS-ARDL estimates of short-run coefficients (ARDL(2,1) specifications with $p_{\bar{z}} = [T^{1/3}]$)																				
30	−15.73	22.36	16.11	16.50	17.10	1,331.93	276.49	20.13	19.44	19.45	6.85	14.05	31.85	40.85	50.60	9.65	10.65	11.80	11.75	11.80
50	−1.80	13.61	16.51	16.65	17.00	568.06	81.68	19.19	18.46	18.44	7.50	20.60	46.55	61.45	71.70	8.95	11.60	11.20	12.80	11.60
100	43.49	16.66	15.91	16.56	17.04	1,184.81	34.38	17.18	17.47	17.81	10.55	36.15	72.45	88.25	94.65	7.80	10.90	12.10	12.80	14.00
150	21.78	16.67	16.16	16.54	16.87	382.97	38.39	17.12	17.17	17.40	11.05	47.10	88.60	96.60	99.05	7.10	14.00	16.20	15.60	15.90
200	15.42	−93.00	16.23	16.65	16.86	323.97	4,968.11	16.94	17.14	17.26	13.40	57.50	95.35	99.35	99.90	5.85	13.25	17.45	17.80	17.90
Based on CS-ARDL estimates of short-run coefficients (ARDL(1,0) specifications with $p_{\bar{z}} = [T^{1/3}]$)																				
30	16.40	−6.69	16.36	17.54	18.91	697.94	880.16	23.81	22.65	23.23	6.75	7.70	17.15	24.65	30.80	17.05	15.95	12.15	10.70	9.60
50	−20.75	12.88	15.81	17.78	18.31	2,302.74	61.28	23.24	20.87	21.06	4.45	9.05	23.80	38.50	44.45	15.95	16.20	11.95	8.50	8.80
100	48.11	12.90	15.75	18.12	18.87	1,567.80	164.94	41.04	22.77	20.28	5.10	11.70	46.05	66.15	75.90	17.95	17.55	11.35	8.55	6.65
150	26.90	12.79	16.79	17.82	18.81	1,050.80	491.93	18.79	18.97	19.79	3.85	16.40	63.75	83.05	91.10	15.30	18.55	11.85	8.90	8.05
200	0.27	−25.36	16.89	16.07	18.58	354.88	1,004.96	19.27	84.64	19.27	3.65	20.55	79.10	92.90	96.70	16.75	17.85	11.20	9.20	7.35

Notes: The dependent variable and regressors are generated according to Eqs. (37)–(38) with correlated individual effects, and with cross-sectionally weakly dependent and serially correlated heteroskedastic idiosyncratic innovations generated according to Eqs. (41)–(42) with $a_\varepsilon = 0.6$. The knowledge of lag orders is not used in the estimation stage and the integer part of $T^{1/3}$ gives 3, 3, 4, 5 and 5 for $T = 30, 50, 100, 150$ and 200, respectively.
DGP is an ARDL(2,1) model with heterogeneous coefficients, $\varphi_{\max} = 0.6$, stationary regressors, $m = 2$ factors, no feedback effects and $\rho_{\varepsilon i} \sim IIDU(0, 0.8)$.

Table 11. Monte Carlo Estimates of Bias, RMSE, Size and Power for Estimation of Long-Run Coefficients (θ) in the Case of Breaks in Errors.

	Bias ($\times 100$)					Root-Mean-Square Errors ($\times 100$)					Size (5% level, $H_0: \theta = 1$)					Power (5% level, $H_1: \theta = 1.2$)				
(N,T)	30	50	100	150	200	30	50	100	150	200	30	50	100	150	200	30	50	100	150	200
CS-DL mean group ($p_{\bar{y}} = 0$, $p_{\bar{x}} = [T^{1/3}]$ and $p = p_{\bar{x}} - 1$)																				
30	−1.72	−1.26	0.09	0.11	0.25	18.91	12.45	9.88	9.03	7.86	7.20	6.45	6.60	6.05	6.15	25.55	44.75	59.60	64.90	72.45
50	−0.83	−0.82	−0.08	0.09	0.05	14.33	10.13	7.55	6.75	6.27	4.90	6.25	5.75	4.80	5.85	33.70	58.60	78.05	83.05	87.85
100	−1.00	−0.91	−0.08	0.10	−0.06	10.50	7.00	5.23	5.00	4.37	5.30	5.15	4.75	5.70	4.95	54.90	85.70	95.85	96.95	99.20
150	−0.88	−0.90	−0.10	0.05	−0.05	8.57	5.62	4.43	4.01	3.63	6.00	5.35	6.05	4.50	4.75	71.40	95.80	99.25	99.70	100.00
200	−0.63	−0.85	−0.29	0.00	−0.01	7.47	4.92	3.72	3.36	3.12	5.50	5.00	4.90	4.55	4.70	80.85	98.15	100.00	100.00	100.00
CS-DL pooled ($p_{\bar{y}} = 0$, $p_{\bar{x}} = [T^{1/3}]$ and $p = p_{\bar{x}} - 1$)																				
30	−1.57	−1.05	0.01	0.15	0.10	16.82	12.04	9.49	8.78	7.74	7.10	7.10	6.60	6.70	6.80	30.20	48.15	61.50	66.10	74.70
50	−1.13	−0.72	−0.04	0.10	0.06	12.71	9.34	7.25	6.48	6.09	4.80	6.20	5.70	5.05	5.75	41.60	63.65	80.55	84.65	89.50
100	−0.90	−0.78	−0.15	0.03	−0.02	9.11	6.53	5.03	4.80	4.27	5.55	5.45	4.80	5.65	5.50	63.95	89.15	96.85	98.20	99.55
150	−0.83	−0.79	−0.03	0.09	−0.03	7.40	5.37	4.23	3.86	3.52	5.45	5.75	5.55	4.70	4.75	81.20	96.60	99.40	99.85	99.95
200	−0.65	−0.78	−0.27	−0.01	−0.05	6.61	4.71	3.59	3.25	3.01	5.20	4.75	4.90	4.50	4.60	87.80	99.35	99.95	100.00	100.00
Based on CS-ARDL estimates of short-run coefficients (ARDL(2,1) specifications with $p_{\bar{z}} = [T^{1/3}]$)																				
30	6.24	6.67	9.59	11.95	14.00	143.70	16.06	14.00	14.80	16.05	5.15	7.90	20.45	33.40	47.30	19.30	28.25	32.35	24.85	19.80
50	10.20	7.71	9.03	11.55	13.95	111.76	19.37	11.73	13.27	15.25	5.70	11.20	24.55	46.10	68.65	21.30	33.45	41.95	32.90	22.50
100	30.94	7.07	9.19	11.58	13.88	514.17	26.38	10.71	12.48	14.59	6.45	13.35	44.50	75.60	91.90	24.45	50.40	57.90	48.75	35.30
150	24.76	7.07	8.80	11.62	13.67	876.89	15.90	9.83	12.24	14.13	7.50	18.80	58.30	89.95	98.20	25.80	57.75	74.45	62.40	47.05
200	1.98	6.22	8.85	11.51	13.76	403.92	28.52	9.58	11.97	14.12	7.80	22.55	70.15	96.35	99.70	28.30	66.50	84.55	73.25	54.60
Based on CS-ARDL estimates of short-run coefficients (ARDL(1,0) specifications with $p_{\bar{z}} = [T^{1/3}]$)																				
30	−28.03	−10.64	−5.13	−1.40	2.17	411.57	21.22	12.54	10.55	10.34	25.20	21.75	13.05	8.55	6.90	54.20	64.00	67.10	60.45	52.10
50	−15.90	−9.72	−5.33	−1.90	2.08	78.66	20.38	11.70	8.89	8.24	28.55	23.30	14.90	9.95	6.65	59.20	75.90	82.00	76.55	65.05
100	−30.60	−11.17	−5.39	−1.63	2.16	353.77	28.48	9.12	5.93	6.09	34.05	33.95	20.45	8.00	6.95	69.50	89.50	95.20	94.20	86.30
150	−15.01	381.68	−5.79	−1.55	2.13	497.45	17,476	7.85	5.01	5.18	38.45	41.60	26.80	8.50	7.75	74.20	93.75	98.75	97.80	94.45
200	−14.40	−11.21	−5.69	−1.72	2.24	123.28	26.47	7.33	4.61	4.59	41.95	49.25	30.75	9.95	8.20	76.90	95.45	99.60	99.55	98.75

Notes: The dependent variable and regressors are generated according to Eqs. (37)–(38) with correlated individual effects, and with cross-sectionally weakly dependent and serially correlated heteroskedastic idiosyncratic innovations generated according to Eqs. (41)–(42) with $a_\varepsilon = 0.6$. The knowledge of lag orders is not used in the estimation stage and the integer part of $T^{1/3}$ gives 3, 3, 4, 5 and 5 for $T = 30, 50, 100, 150$ and 200, respectively.

DGP is an ARDL(2,1) model with heterogeneous coefficients, $\varphi_{\max} = 0.6$, stationary regressors, $m = 2$ factors, no feedback effects and breaks in errors.

Table 12. Monte Carlo Estimates of Bias, RMSE, Size and Power for Estimation of Long-Run Coefficients (θ) in the Case of Feedback Effects.

	Bias (×100)					Root-Mean-Square Errors (×100)					Size (5% level, $H_0:\theta=1$)					Power (5% level, $H_1:\theta=1.2$)				
(N,T)	30	50	100	150	200	30	50	100	150	200	30	50	100	150	200	30	50	100	150	200
CS-DL mean group ($p_{\bar{y}}=0$, $p_{\bar{x}}=[T^{1/3}]$ and $p=p_{\bar{x}}-1$)																				
30	−1.51	2.38	5.10	5.74	5.84	16.20	10.51	9.35	9.16	8.54	6.00	6.60	12.50	15.70	18.20	32.55	43.95	53.10	57.00	65.75
50	−1.45	2.38	5.11	5.48	6.06	12.54	8.54	7.91	7.68	7.79	6.50	8.10	14.45	19.00	25.55	45.25	62.35	70.55	77.40	81.15
100	−0.97	2.85	5.16	5.61	6.05	8.88	6.34	6.70	6.85	6.93	5.80	7.90	23.30	31.85	43.05	69.00	85.35	92.80	95.60	97.85
150	−1.23	2.64	5.05	5.68	6.15	7.50	5.41	6.12	6.45	6.76	5.80	8.70	30.90	46.05	59.55	84.60	95.60	98.90	99.50	99.90
200	−1.46	2.55	4.91	5.61	6.03	6.57	4.72	5.75	6.26	6.50	6.30	9.90	37.55	55.20	71.25	92.90	98.75	99.90	99.95	100.00
CS-DL pooled ($p_{\bar{y}}=0$, $p_{\bar{x}}=[T^{1/3}]$ and $p=p_{\bar{x}}-1$)																				
30	2.28	4.73	6.80	7.10	7.00	14.57	10.87	10.37	10.04	9.43	7.25	8.90	17.20	19.90	21.25	30.75	40.75	45.90	50.95	57.55
50	2.26	4.83	6.77	6.89	7.40	11.41	9.10	8.96	8.75	8.94	6.55	10.70	21.25	26.60	33.25	41.50	54.60	61.40	69.95	72.05
100	2.96	5.30	6.89	7.10	7.42	8.53	7.65	8.07	8.11	8.17	7.20	16.60	37.05	47.05	58.10	61.00	75.60	85.40	89.95	92.90
150	2.70	5.07	6.72	7.20	7.50	7.21	6.83	7.55	7.84	8.03	8.05	20.65	50.65	63.80	75.60	76.60	90.55	95.50	97.85	98.55
200	2.47	5.10	6.68	7.15	7.36	6.21	6.40	7.30	7.68	7.78	7.60	25.45	62.00	75.80	85.45	87.80	95.70	99.05	99.50	99.80
Based on CS-ARDL estimates of short-run coefficients (ARDL(2,1) specifications with $p_{\bar{z}}=[T^{1/3}]$)																				
30	−49.31	−6.64	−2.84	−1.50	−1.23	1,613.71	11.90	7.13	6.12	5.29	17.15	14.35	8.40	8.70	7.50	54.75	80.05	93.55	95.05	97.95
50	15.94	−7.02	−3.05	−2.03	−1.28	1,208.10	10.96	6.01	4.85	4.27	19.45	19.25	11.10	8.95	7.75	65.05	93.30	99.15	99.90	99.70
100	−17.83	−6.54	−3.06	−2.00	−1.50	120.30	9.22	4.83	3.81	3.25	26.80	26.90	15.40	12.55	10.15	78.50	99.35	100.00	100.00	100.00
150	−14.20	−6.84	−3.24	−2.06	−1.45	127.42	8.28	4.40	3.27	2.74	32.55	35.75	21.15	13.70	9.90	82.20	99.90	100.00	100.00	100.00
200	−17.89	−7.08	−3.39	−2.15	−1.57	283.24	8.22	4.28	3.15	2.56	37.60	47.30	27.80	19.30	12.55	83.90	99.85	100.00	100.00	100.00
Based on CS-ARDL estimates of short-run coefficients (ARDL(1,0) specifications with $p_{\bar{z}}=[T^{1/3}]$)																				
30	−37.31	−29.77	−24.72	−23.08	−22.33	236.77	31.59	25.86	24.09	23.27	74.60	86.65	91.90	93.30	94.25	93.00	99.70	100.00	100.00	100.00
50	−39.45	−29.96	−25.01	−23.50	−22.67	100.20	30.98	25.63	24.07	23.19	88.15	97.15	99.00	99.55	99.80	96.60	100.00	100.00	100.00	100.00
100	−38.09	−30.16	−25.06	−23.56	−22.75	60.47	30.71	25.39	23.86	23.02	94.90	99.80	100.00	100.00	100.00	97.70	99.95	100.00	100.00	100.00
150	−37.23	−30.28	−25.21	−23.61	−22.85	52.96	30.76	25.43	23.80	23.03	95.80	99.85	100.00	100.00	100.00	97.80	99.90	100.00	100.00	100.00
200	−39.43	−30.46	−25.40	−23.73	−22.89	54.51	30.72	25.56	23.88	23.03	95.80	99.90	100.00	100.00	100.00	97.85	99.95	100.00	100.00	100.00

Notes: The dependent variable and regressors are generated according to Eqs. (37)–(38) with correlated individual effects, and with cross-sectionally weakly dependent and serially correlated heteroskedastic idiosyncratic innovations generated according to Eqs. (41)–(42) with $a_\varepsilon=0.6$. The knowledge of lag orders is not used in the estimation stage and the integer part of $T^{1/3}$ gives 3, 3, 4, 5 and 5 for $T=30, 50, 100, 150$ and 200, respectively.

DGP is an ARDL(2,1) model with heterogeneous coefficients, $\varphi_{\max}=0.6$, stationary regressors, $m=2$ factors, $\kappa_{yi}\sim IIDU(0,0.2)$, and $\rho_{\varepsilon i}=0$.

Table 13. Monte Carlo Estimates of Bias, RMSE, Size and Power for Estimation of $\varphi_1 = E(\varphi_{i1})$.

	Bias (×100)					Root-Mean-Square Errors (×100)					Size (5% level, $H_0: \varphi_1 = 0.3$)					Power (5% level, $H_1: \varphi_1 = 0.4$)				
(N,T)	30	50	100	150	200	30	50	100	150	200	30	50	100	150	200	30	50	100	150	200
Imposing CS-DL pooled estimate of long-run coefficient																				
30	−8.38	−4.35	−1.90	−1.01	−0.86	10.26	6.22	4.18	3.68	3.64	51.45	27.60	12.50	9.10	9.35	96.25	95.00	93.45	90.70	90.80
50	−8.89	−4.78	−2.13	−1.36	−0.98	10.00	5.88	3.55	3.13	2.86	70.70	42.25	16.15	12.35	9.25	99.50	99.70	99.60	98.85	99.10
100	−9.27	−4.92	−2.30	−1.49	−1.15	9.85	5.51	3.10	2.44	2.24	91.55	64.60	24.90	15.75	11.70	100.00	100.00	100.00	100.00	100.00
150	−9.36	−5.10	−2.40	−1.48	−1.16	9.79	5.48	2.92	2.18	1.97	98.15	82.40	36.15	19.75	14.55	100.00	100.00	100.00	100.00	100.00
200	−9.37	−5.09	−2.36	−1.55	−1.10	9.72	5.40	2.76	2.08	1.74	99.15	89.95	45.75	24.10	16.00	100.00	100.00	100.00	100.00	100.00
Infeasible estimator: Imposing knowledge of long run coefficients																				
30	−7.95	−4.01	−1.77	−0.94	−0.78	9.48	5.73	4.00	3.53	3.53	48.40	23.30	11.55	8.25	8.50	97.25	95.85	93.10	91.65	91.15
50	−8.42	−4.41	−1.98	−1.29	−0.88	9.31	5.43	3.38	3.01	2.77	70.60	36.55	14.45	11.00	8.00	99.80	99.85	99.65	98.90	99.20
100	−8.73	−4.50	−2.13	−1.44	−1.07	9.21	5.05	2.91	2.36	2.15	93.00	60.65	22.30	14.25	10.85	100.00	100.00	100.00	100.00	100.00
150	−8.77	−4.67	−2.21	−1.41	−1.08	9.13	5.03	2.71	2.10	1.88	98.20	77.70	31.50	18.25	13.00	100.00	100.00	100.00	100.00	100.00
200	−8.83	−4.67	−2.18	−1.48	−1.01	9.12	4.95	2.57	2.00	1.65	99.30	86.65	38.80	22.30	14.10	100.00	100.00	100.00	100.00	100.00
Unconstrained CS-ARDL approach																				
30	−12.76	−6.34	−2.78	−1.58	−1.20	13.99	7.73	4.63	3.83	3.70	74.60	42.30	16.65	10.75	10.50	99.30	98.15	95.80	93.50	92.40
50	−13.34	−6.79	−3.04	−1.96	−1.37	14.11	7.59	4.14	3.40	3.01	92.00	63.95	24.05	14.95	10.55	99.95	99.95	99.80	99.30	99.60
100	−13.71	−6.96	−3.22	−2.13	−1.57	14.12	7.38	3.82	2.87	2.47	99.45	88.25	40.65	23.45	15.25	100.00	100.00	100.00	100.00	100.00
150	−13.77	−7.14	−3.30	−2.09	−1.59	14.10	7.41	3.68	2.63	2.23	99.85	96.95	57.80	30.35	21.40	100.00	100.00	100.00	100.00	100.00
200	−13.83	−7.13	−3.27	−2.17	−1.52	14.10	7.35	3.56	2.56	2.02	100.00	99.55	67.90	40.00	23.70	100.00	100.00	100.00	100.00	100.00

Notes: The dependent variable and regressors are generated according to Eqs. (37)–(38) with correlated individual effects, and with cross-sectionally weakly dependent and serially correlated heteroskedastic idiosyncratic innovations generated according to Eqs. (41)–(42) with $a_\varepsilon = 0.6$.
DGP is an ARDL(1,0) model with homogeneous long-run coefficients, heterogeneous short-run coefficients, $\varphi_{\max} = 0.6$, stationary regressors, $m = 2$ factors, no feedback effects and $\rho_{\varepsilon i} = 0$.

where $\tilde{\lambda}_i$ is the least-square estimate of λ_i based on Eq. (43). The results of these experiments are summarized in Table 13. Imposing the CS-DL pooled estimator of the long-run coefficient improves the small sample properties of the short-run estimates substantially, about 80–90% reduction of the difference between the RMSE of the infeasible CS-ARDL estimator and the RMSE of the unconstrained estimator, when $T = 30$.

5. CONCLUDING REMARKS

Estimation of long-run effects is an important task in economics. This often requires a large time dimension for panel data models with slope heterogeneity, lagged-dependent variables, and cross-sectionally correlated innovations. This paper proposes a CS-DL approach to the estimation of long-run effects as a complementary method to cross-sectionally augmented ARDL specifications. Based on a series of Monte Carlo simulations, we show the robustness of panel CS-ARDL estimates to the endogeneity problem. We also show that the CS-DL estimators are robust to residual serial correlation, breaks in error processes and misspecifications of dynamics. However, unlike the CS-ARDL approach, the CS-DL procedure could be subject to simultaneity bias. Nevertheless, the extensive Monte Carlo experiments reported in the paper suggest that the endogeneity bias of the CS-DL approach is more than compensated for by its better small sample performance as compared to the CS-ARDL procedure when the time dimension is not very large. CS-ARDL seems to dominate CS-DL only if the time dimension is sufficiently large and the underlying ARDL model is correctly specified.

NOTES

1. Moon and Weidner (2016) also allow for lagged dependent variables, but do not allow for coefficient heterogeneity.
2. Note that if $\mathbf{x}$ is a vector, then $\|\mathbf{x}\| = \sqrt{\varrho(\mathbf{x}'\mathbf{x})} = \sqrt{\mathbf{x}'\mathbf{x}}$ corresponds to the Euclidean length of the vector $\mathbf{x}$.
3. The problem of the estimation and inference in the case of multiple long-run relations is further complicated by the identification problem and simultaneous determination of variables. The case of multiple long-run relations is discussed, for example, in Pesaran (1997).
4. Note that, in the stationary case, $\sum_{\ell=0}^{\infty} \mathbf{\Phi}^{\ell} = (\mathbf{I}_2 - \mathbf{\Phi})^{-1}$.
5. Also related is the quasi maximum likelihood estimator for dynamic panels by Moon and Weidner (2016), but this estimator has been developed only for panels with homogeneous slope coefficients.

6. Chudik and Pesaran (2015b) consider the application of two bias correction procedures to dynamic CCE-type estimators, but find that they do not fully eliminate the bias.

7. Note that $\boldsymbol{\theta}_i$ is identified even when ε_{it} is serially correlated.

8. Correlation of $\boldsymbol{\gamma}_i$ and $\boldsymbol{\Gamma}_i$ could introduce a bias in the CCE estimates in the case where $\mathbf{C}$ is rank deficient. See Sarafidis and Wansbeek (2012) and Section 29.4 in (Pesaran, 2015).

9. Unlike in the case of panel data models with short T, estimation methods considered in this paper do not require any restrictions on the way the individual effects, c_{yi} and c_{xi}, are generated, and the MC results are unlikely to depend significantly on the ways individual effects are generated. To illustrate this point we have also carried out a number of experiments where we use a spatial scheme to generate correlated individual effects, and found little change in the small sample results. Details and findings for these experiments are available from the authors upon request.

ACKNOWLEDGEMENTS

We are grateful to Ron Smith and participants at the Conference in Honor of Aman Ullah held on 13–14 March 2015 at UC Riverside for constructive comments and suggestions. We would also like to thank the editors and two anonymous referees for helpful suggestions. The views expressed in this paper are those of the authors and do not necessarily represent those of Federal Reserve Bank of Dallas, the Federal Reserve System, the International Monetary Fund or IMF policy. Hashem Pesaran acknowledges financial support under ESRC Grant No. ES/I031626/1.

REFERENCES

Bai, J. (2009). Panel data models with interactive fixed effects. *Econometrica*, *77*, 1229–1279. Retrieved from http://www.jstor.org/stable/40263859

Chudik, A., & Pesaran, M. H. (2015a). Large panel data models with cross-sectional dependence: A survey. In B. Baltagi (Ed.), *The Oxford handbook on panel data*. Oxford: Oxford University Press. Retrieved from http://ukcatalogue.oup.com/product/9780199940042.do

Chudik, A., & Pesaran, M. H. (2015b). Common correlated effects estimation of heterogeneous dynamic panel data models with weakly exogenous regressors. *Journal of Econometrics*, *188*, 393–420. Retrieved from http://www.cesifo-group.de/DocDL/cesifo1_wp4232.pdf

Mark, N. C., & Sul, D. (2003). Cointegration vector estimation by panel DOLS and long-run money demand. *Oxford Bulletin of Economics and Statistics*, *65*(5). 655–680. doi:10.1111/j.1468-0084.2003.00066.x

Moon, H. R., & Weidner, M. (2016). Dynamic linear panel regression models with interactive fixed effects. Econometric Theory. Forthcoming. doi:10.1017/S0266466615000328. Retrieved from http://journals.cambridge.org/article_S0266466615000328

Pedroni, P. (2001). Fully modified OLS for heterogeneous cointegrated panels. *Advances in Econometrics*, *15*, 93–130. Retrieved from http://www.emeraldinsight.com/doi/abs/10.1016/S0731-9053%2800%2915004-2.

Pesaran, M. H. (1997). The role of economic theory in modelling the long run. *Economic Journal*, *107*, 178–191. Retrieved from http://www.jstor.org/stable/2235280

Pesaran, M. H. (2006). Estimation and inference in large heterogeneous panels with multifactor error structure. *Econometrica*, *74*, 967–1012. Retrieved from http://www.jstor.org/stable/3805914

Pesaran, M. H. (2015). *Time series and panel data econometrics*. Oxford: Oxford University Press.

Pesaran, M. H., & Chudik, A. (2014). Aggregation in large dynamic panels. *Journal of Econometrics*, *178*, 273–285. doi:10.1016/j.jeconom.2013.08.027

Pesaran, M. H., & Shin, Y. (1999). An autoregressive distributed lag modelling approach to cointegration analysis. In S. Strom (Ed.), *Econometrics and economic theory in 20th century: The Ragnar Frisch Centennial Symposium* (pp. 371–413). Cambridge: Cambridge University Press.

Pesaran, M. H., Shin, Y., & Smith, R. P. (1999). Pooled mean group estimation of dynamic heterogeneous panels. *Journal of the American Statistical Association*, *94*, 621–634. doi: 10.1080/01621459.1999.10474156

Sarafidis, V., & Wansbeek, T. (2012). Cross-sectional dependence in panel data analysis. *Econometric Reviews*, *31*, 483–531. doi:10.1080/07474938.2011.611458

Song, M. (2013, January). Asymptotic theory for dynamic heterogeneous panels with cross-sectional dependence and its applications. Mimeo. Retrieved from http://economics.missouri.edu/seminars/files/2013/20130124.pdf

APPENDIX

We start by briefly summarizing the notations used in this paper, and introduce new notations which will prove useful in the proofs provided below. We use $\langle \mathbf{a}, \mathbf{b} \rangle = \mathbf{a}'\mathbf{b}$ to denote the inner product (corresponding to the Euclidean norm) of vectors $\mathbf{a}$ and $\mathbf{b}$. $\|\mathbf{A}\|_\infty = \max_{1 \leq i \leq n} \sum_{j=1}^{n} |a_{ij}|$ and $\|\mathbf{A}\|_1 = \max_{1 \leq j \leq n} \sum_{i=1}^{n} |a_{ij}|$ denote the maximum row sum matrix and column sum matrix norms of $\mathbf{A} \in \mathbb{M}^{n \times n}$, respectively, where $\mathbb{M}^{n \times n}$ is the space of real-valued $n \times n$ matrices. $\|\mathbf{A}\| = \sqrt{\varrho(\mathbf{A}'\mathbf{A})}$ is the spectral norm of $\mathbf{A}$, $\varrho(\mathbf{A})$ is the spectral radius of $\mathbf{A}$, $Col(\mathbf{A})$ denotes the space spanned by the column vectors of $\mathbf{A}$, and $\mathbf{A}^+$ is the Moore–Penrose pseudoinverse of $\mathbf{A}$. Note that $\|\mathbf{a}\| = \sqrt{\varrho(\mathbf{a}'\mathbf{a})} = \sqrt{\mathbf{a}'\mathbf{a}}$ corresponds to the Euclidean length of vector $\mathbf{a}$.

Let $\mathbf{z}_{it} = (y_{it}, \mathbf{x}'_{it})'$, $\bar{\mathbf{z}}_{wt} = (\bar{y}_{wt}, \bar{\mathbf{x}}'_{wt})' = \sum_{i=1}^{N} w_i \mathbf{z}_{it}$, $\Delta = (1 - L)$, L is the lag operator,

$$\underset{T-p\times 1}{\mathbf{y}_i} = \begin{pmatrix} y_{i,p+1} \\ y_{i,p+2} \\ \vdots \\ y_{iT} \end{pmatrix}, \quad \underset{T-p\times k}{\mathbf{X}_i} = \begin{pmatrix} \mathbf{x}'_{i,p+1} \\ \mathbf{x}'_{i,p+2} \\ \vdots \\ \mathbf{x}'_{iT} \end{pmatrix},$$

$$\underset{(T-p)\times pk}{\Delta\mathbf{X}_{ip}} = \begin{pmatrix} \Delta\mathbf{x}'_{i,p+1} & \Delta\mathbf{x}'_{i,p} & \cdots & \Delta\mathbf{x}'_{i2} \\ \Delta\mathbf{x}'_{i,p+2} & \Delta\mathbf{x}'_{i,p+1} & \cdots & \Delta\mathbf{x}'_{i3} \\ \vdots & \vdots & & \vdots \\ \Delta\mathbf{x}'_{iT} & \Delta\mathbf{x}'_{i,T-1} & \cdots & \Delta\mathbf{x}'_{i,T-p+1} \end{pmatrix},$$

$$\underset{(T-p)\times k+1}{\bar{\mathbf{Z}}_w} = \begin{pmatrix} \bar{\mathbf{z}}'_{w,p+1} \\ \bar{\mathbf{z}}'_{w,p+2} \\ \vdots \\ \bar{\mathbf{z}}'_{wT} \end{pmatrix}, \quad \underset{(T-p)\times pk}{\Delta\bar{\mathbf{X}}_{wp}} = \begin{pmatrix} \Delta\bar{\mathbf{x}}'_{w,p+1} & \Delta\bar{\mathbf{x}}'_{w,p} & \cdots & \Delta\bar{\mathbf{x}}'_{w2} \\ \Delta\bar{\mathbf{x}}'_{w,p+2} & \Delta\bar{\mathbf{x}}'_{w,p+1} & \cdots & \Delta\bar{\mathbf{x}}'_{w3} \\ \vdots & \vdots & & \vdots \\ \Delta\bar{\mathbf{x}}'_{wT} & \Delta\bar{\mathbf{x}}'_{w,T-1} & \cdots & \Delta\bar{\mathbf{x}}'_{w,T-p+1} \end{pmatrix},$$

$$\underset{T-p\times k}{\mathbf{V}_i} = \begin{pmatrix} \mathbf{v}'_{i,p+1} \\ \mathbf{v}'_{i,p+2} \\ \vdots \\ \mathbf{v}'_{iT} \end{pmatrix}$$

$\mathbf{Q}_{wi} = (\mathbf{Q}_w, \Delta\mathbf{X}_{ip})$, $\mathbf{Q}_w = (\bar{\mathbf{Z}}_w, \Delta\bar{\mathbf{X}}_{wp})$,

$$\mathbf{M}_{qi} = \mathbf{I}_{T-p} - \mathbf{Q}_{wi}\left(\mathbf{Q}'_{wi}\mathbf{Q}_{wi}\right)^{+}\mathbf{Q}'_{wi}, \tag{A.1}$$

$$\boldsymbol{\gamma}_{ip} = \left(\boldsymbol{\gamma}_i', \varphi_i \boldsymbol{\gamma}_i', \varphi_i^2 \boldsymbol{\gamma}_i', \dots, \varphi_i^p \boldsymbol{\gamma}_i'\right)',$$

$$\underset{T-p\times m(p+1)}{\mathbf{F}_p} = \left(\mathbf{F}_{(0)}, \mathbf{F}_{(1)}, \dots, \mathbf{F}_{(p)}\right), \quad \underset{T-p\times m}{\mathbf{F}_{(\ell)}} \begin{pmatrix} \mathbf{f}_{p+1-\ell}' \\ \mathbf{f}_{p+2-\ell}' \\ \vdots \\ \mathbf{f}_{T-\ell}' \end{pmatrix},$$

$$\text{for } \ell = 0, 1, 2, \dots, p, \text{ and } \boldsymbol{\varepsilon}_i = \begin{pmatrix} \varepsilon_{i,p+1} \\ \varepsilon_{i,p+2} \\ \vdots \\ \varepsilon_{iT} \end{pmatrix}. \tag{A.2}$$

Using the above notations, the model for the dependent variable can be written as

$$\mathbf{y}_i = \mathbf{X}_i \boldsymbol{\theta}_i + \Delta \mathbf{X}_{ip} \boldsymbol{\alpha}_{ip} + \mathbf{F}_p \boldsymbol{\gamma}_{ip} + \boldsymbol{\vartheta}_i + \boldsymbol{\varepsilon}_i,$$

for $i = 1, 2, \dots, N$, where $\boldsymbol{\alpha}_{ip}$ is a $pk \times 1$ vector containing the first p coefficients vectors of the polynomial $\alpha_i(L)$ stacked into one single column vector, $\boldsymbol{\vartheta}_i = \left(\vartheta_{i,p+1}, \vartheta_{i,p+1}, \dots, \vartheta_{i,T}\right)'$, and

$$\vartheta_{it} = \sum_{\ell=p+1}^{\infty} \varphi_i^{\ell+1} \left(\boldsymbol{\beta}_i' \Delta \mathbf{x}_{i,t-\ell+1} + \boldsymbol{\gamma}_i' f_{t-\ell}\right),$$

for $i = 1, 2, \dots, N$ and $t = p+1, p+2, \dots, T$. The model for regressors can be written as

$$\mathbf{X}_i = \mathbf{F}_{(0)} \boldsymbol{\Gamma}_i + \mathbf{V}_i,$$

for $i = 1, 2, \dots, N$.

Define also the following projection matrix:

$$\underset{T-p\times T-p}{\mathbf{M}_{hi}} = \mathbf{I}_{T-p} - \mathbf{H}_{wi} \left(\mathbf{H}_{wi}' \mathbf{H}_{wi}\right)^{+} \mathbf{H}_{wi}', \tag{A.3}$$

in which

$$\underset{T-p\times k(p+2)+1}{\mathbf{H}_{wi}} = \left(\mathbf{H}_w, \Delta \mathbf{X}_{ip}\right), \quad \underset{T-p\times k(p+1)+1}{\mathbf{H}_w} = \begin{pmatrix} \mathbf{h}_{wp,p+1}' \\ \mathbf{h}_{w,p+2}' \\ \vdots \\ \mathbf{h}_{wp,T}' \end{pmatrix},$$

and

$$\underset{k(p+1)+1\times 1}{\mathbf{h}_{wpt}} = \begin{pmatrix} \bar{\boldsymbol{\theta}}_w' \bar{\boldsymbol{\Gamma}}_w' + (1-L)\,\boldsymbol{\alpha}_w'(L)\,\bar{\boldsymbol{\Gamma}}_w' + \boldsymbol{\gamma}_w'(L) \\ \bar{\boldsymbol{\Gamma}}_w' \\ (1-L)\,\bar{\boldsymbol{\Gamma}}_w' \\ L\,(1-L)\,\bar{\boldsymbol{\Gamma}}_w' \\ \vdots \\ L^{p-1}(1-L)\,\bar{\boldsymbol{\Gamma}}_w' \end{pmatrix} \mathbf{f}_t,$$

where

$$\bar{\boldsymbol{\theta}}_w = \sum_{i=1}^{N} w_i \boldsymbol{\theta}_i, \quad \bar{\boldsymbol{\Gamma}}_w = \sum_{i=1}^{N} w_i \boldsymbol{\Gamma}_i, \quad \boldsymbol{\alpha}_w(L) = \sum_{i=1}^{N} w_i \boldsymbol{\alpha}_i(L), \quad \boldsymbol{\gamma}_w(L) = \sum_{i=1}^{N} w_i \boldsymbol{\gamma}_i(L),$$

and $\boldsymbol{\gamma}_i(L) = \sum_{\ell=0}^{\infty} \varphi_i^l \boldsymbol{\gamma}_i L^l$.

A.1. Proofs of Theorems

Proof of Theorem 1. We have

$$\begin{aligned} \sqrt{N}\left(\widehat{\boldsymbol{\theta}}_{MG} - \boldsymbol{\theta}\right) &= \frac{1}{\sqrt{N}} \sum_{i=1}^{N} \boldsymbol{\upsilon}_{\theta i} + \frac{1}{\sqrt{N}} \sum_{i=1}^{N} \widehat{\boldsymbol{\Psi}}_{iT}^{-1} \frac{\mathbf{X}_i' \mathbf{M}_{qi} \mathbf{F}_p \boldsymbol{\gamma}_{ip}}{T} \\ &+ \frac{1}{\sqrt{N}} \sum_{i=1}^{N} \widehat{\boldsymbol{\Psi}}_{iT}^{-1} \frac{\mathbf{X}_i' \mathbf{M}_{qi} \boldsymbol{\vartheta}_i}{T} + \frac{1}{\sqrt{N}} \sum_{i=1}^{N} \widehat{\boldsymbol{\Psi}}_{iT}^{-1} \frac{\mathbf{X}_i' \mathbf{M}_{qi} \boldsymbol{\varepsilon}_i}{T} \end{aligned} \qquad \text{(A.4)}$$

where $\widehat{\boldsymbol{\Psi}}_{iT} = T^{-1}\mathbf{X}_i'\mathbf{M}_{qi}\mathbf{X}_i$,

$$\underset{T-p\times m(p+1)}{\mathbf{F}_p} = \begin{pmatrix} \mathbf{f}_{p+1}' & \mathbf{f}_p' & \cdots & \mathbf{f}_1' \\ \vdots & \vdots & & \vdots \\ \mathbf{f}_T' & \mathbf{f}_{T-1}' & \cdots & \mathbf{f}_{T-p}' \end{pmatrix},$$

$\boldsymbol{\gamma}_{ip} = \left(\boldsymbol{\gamma}_i', \varphi_i \boldsymbol{\gamma}_i', \ldots, \varphi_i^p \boldsymbol{\gamma}_i'\right)'$, $\boldsymbol{\vartheta}_i = \left(\vartheta_{i,p+1}, \vartheta_{i,p+1}, \ldots, \vartheta_{i,T}\right)'$, and

$$\vartheta_{it} = \sum_{\ell=p+1}^{\infty} \varphi_i^{\ell+1} \left(\boldsymbol{\beta}_i' \Delta \mathbf{x}_{i,t-\ell+1} + \boldsymbol{\gamma}_i' f_{t-\ell}\right).$$

Consider the asymptotics $(N, T, p) \xrightarrow{j} \infty$ such that $\sqrt{N} p\rho^p \to 0$, for any constant $0 < \rho < 1$ and $p^3/T \to \varkappa$, $0 < \varkappa < \infty$. In what follows we establish convergence of the individual terms on the right side of Eq. (A.4).

It follows from Eq. (A.26) of Lemma 1 and Eq. (A.27) of Lemma 2 that

$$\widehat{\mathbf{\Psi}}_{\Xi,iT} - \mathbf{\Sigma}_i = o_p\left(N^{-1/2}\right) \text{ uniformly in } i. \tag{A.5}$$

Eqs.(A.5), (A.28) of Lemma 2, and Eq. (A.30) of Lemma 3 imply

$$\frac{1}{\sqrt{N}} \sum_{i=1}^{N} \widehat{\mathbf{\Psi}}_{iT}^{-1} \frac{\mathbf{X}_i' \mathbf{M}_{qi} \boldsymbol{\varepsilon}_i}{T} \xrightarrow{p} \underset{k\times 1}{\mathbf{0}}. \tag{A.6}$$

Consider now the second term on the right side of Eq. (A.4), which involves common factors and their loadings. In the previous literature on CCE estimators, Pesaran (2006) established the asymptotic results for the term involving factors and their loadings in the expression for his CCEMG estimator by focusing on the properties of the matrix (using Pesaran's, 2006, notations) $\mathbf{X}_i' \bar{\mathbf{M}}_w \mathbf{F}/T$, see Eq. (40) in Pesaran (2006), in the full-rank case, and by exploring the relation (still using Pesaran's, 2006, notations) $\mathbf{M}_q \mathbf{F} \bar{\mathbf{C}}_w = \mathbf{0}$, see Pesaran (2006, p. 979), in the rank-deficient case. But unlike in the set-up of Pesaran (2006), the dimension of $\mathbf{X}_i' \mathbf{M}_{qi} \mathbf{F}_p / T$ in this paper increases with the sample size, and furthermore $\mathbf{M}_{hi} \mathbf{F}_p \overline{\boldsymbol{\gamma}}_{wp}$ is not necessarily zero since $\mathbf{F}_p \overline{\boldsymbol{\gamma}}_{wp}$ (due to the truncation lag p) does not necessarily belong to the linear space spanned by the column vectors of $\mathbf{H}_{wi}$. We therefore focus on the elements of the vector $\mathbf{X}_i' \mathbf{M}_{qi} \mathbf{F}_p \boldsymbol{\gamma}_{ip} / T$ below, which has fixed (finite) dimensions, and we also take advantage of the exponential decay of certain coefficients below. Using Eq. (A.5), boundedness of $\mathbf{\Sigma}_i^{-1}$ (by Assumption 5), and the result (A.29) of Lemma 2 we obtain

$$\frac{1}{\sqrt{N}} \sum_{i=1}^{N} \left(\frac{\mathbf{X}_i' \mathbf{M}_{qi} \mathbf{X}_i}{T} \right)^{-1} \frac{\mathbf{X}_i' \mathbf{M}_{qi} \mathbf{F}_p}{T} \boldsymbol{\gamma}_{ip}$$
$$- \frac{1}{\sqrt{N}} \sum_{i=1}^{N} \left(\frac{\mathbf{X}_i' \mathbf{M}_{hi} \mathbf{X}_i}{T} \right)^{-1} \frac{\mathbf{X}_i' \mathbf{M}_{hi} \mathbf{F}_p}{T} \boldsymbol{\gamma}_{ip} \xrightarrow{p} \underset{k\times 1}{\mathbf{0}}.$$

Vector $\boldsymbol{\gamma}_{ip}$ can be written as $\boldsymbol{\gamma}_{ip} = \left(\overline{\boldsymbol{\gamma}}_{wp} - \overline{\boldsymbol{\eta}}_{\gamma wp}\right) + \boldsymbol{\eta}_{\gamma ip}$, and

$$T^{-1} \mathbf{X}_i' \mathbf{M}_{hi} \mathbf{F}_p \boldsymbol{\gamma}_{ip} = T^{-1} \mathbf{X}_i' \mathbf{M}_{hi} \mathbf{F}_p \overline{\boldsymbol{\gamma}}_{wp} + T^{-1} \mathbf{X}_i' \mathbf{M}_{hi} \mathbf{F}_p \left(\boldsymbol{\eta}_{\gamma ip} - \overline{\boldsymbol{\eta}}_{\gamma wp}\right).$$

Note again that $\mathbf{F}_p\bar{\boldsymbol{\gamma}}_{wp}$ does not necessarily belong to the linear space spanned by the column vectors of $\mathbf{H}_{wi}$ due to the truncation lag p. But Assumption 4 constrains the support of φ_i to fall strictly within the unit circle, which implies that there exists a positive constant $\rho < 1$ such that $|\varphi_i| < \rho < 1$ for all possible realizations of the random variable φ_i. Therefore, under Assumptions 3-4, the coefficients in the polynomials $\boldsymbol{\alpha}_w(L) = \sum_{i=1}^N w_i \boldsymbol{\alpha}_i(L)$ and $\boldsymbol{\gamma}_w(L) = \sum_{i=1}^N w_i \boldsymbol{\gamma}_i(L)$, where $\boldsymbol{\alpha}_i(L) = \sum_{\ell=0}^\infty \varphi_i^{\ell+1}(1-\varphi_i)^{-1}\boldsymbol{\beta}_i L^\ell$ and $\boldsymbol{\gamma}_i(L) = \sum_{\ell=0}^\infty \varphi_i^l \boldsymbol{\gamma}_i L^l$, decay exponentially to zero[10] and we have

$$\bar{\boldsymbol{\gamma}}_w'(L,p)\mathbf{f}_t - E\left[\bar{\boldsymbol{\gamma}}_w'(L,p)\mathbf{f}_t \left|\mathbf{h}_{wpt}\right.\right] = O_p(\rho^p), \tag{A.7}$$

uniformly in t, where $\bar{\boldsymbol{\gamma}}_w(L,p) = \sum_{\ell=0}^p \sum_{i=1}^N w_i \varphi_i^\ell \boldsymbol{\gamma}_i L^\ell$ is the truncated polynomial of $\bar{\boldsymbol{\gamma}}_w(L)$ featuring only orders up to L^p. Using the properties of orthogonal projectors, we obtain[11]

$$\left\|\mathbf{M}_{hi}\mathbf{F}_p\bar{\boldsymbol{\gamma}}_{wp}\right\| \leq \left\|\mathbf{F}_p\bar{\boldsymbol{\gamma}}_{wp} - \mathbf{H}_{wi}\mathbf{c}\right\|, \tag{A.8}$$

for any $k(p+1)+1 \times 1$ vector $\mathbf{c}$. Let $\mathbf{c}$ be defined by $E\left[\bar{\boldsymbol{\gamma}}_w'(L,p)\mathbf{f}_t \left|\mathbf{h}_{wpt}\right.\right] = \mathbf{c}'\mathbf{h}_{wpt}$. Then it follows from Eq. (A.7) that the individual elements of $T-p \times 1$ vector $\left(\mathbf{F}_p\bar{\boldsymbol{\gamma}}_{wp} - \mathbf{H}_{wi}\mathbf{c}\right)$ are uniformly $O_p(\rho^p)$ and using Eq. (A.8) we have

$$\left\|\mathbf{M}_{hi}\mathbf{F}_p\bar{\boldsymbol{\gamma}}_{wp}\right\| = O_p\left[(T-p)^{1/2}\rho^p\right].$$

Now using Cauchy–Schwarz inequality, we obtain[12]

$$T^{-1}\mathbf{X}_i'\mathbf{M}_{hi}\mathbf{F}_p\bar{\gamma}_{wp} = O_p(\rho^p). \tag{A.9}$$

Noting that $\sqrt{N}\rho^p \to 0$, and using Eq. (A.5) and boundedness of $\boldsymbol{\Sigma}_i^{-1}$ (by Assumption 5) we have

$$\frac{1}{\sqrt{N}}\sum_{i=1}^N \left(\frac{\mathbf{X}_i'\mathbf{M}_{hi}\mathbf{X}_i}{T}\right)^{-1} \frac{\mathbf{X}_i'\mathbf{M}_{hi}\mathbf{F}_p}{T}\bar{\boldsymbol{\gamma}}_{wp} \xrightarrow{p} \mathbf{0},$$

and it then follows that

$$\frac{1}{\sqrt{N}}\sum_{i=1}^N \widehat{\boldsymbol{\Psi}}_{\Xi,iT}^{-1}\frac{\mathbf{X}_i'\mathbf{M}_{qi}\mathbf{F}_p}{T}\boldsymbol{\gamma}_{ip}$$
$$-\frac{1}{\sqrt{N}}\sum_{i=1}^N \left(\frac{\mathbf{X}_i'\mathbf{M}_{hi}\mathbf{X}_i}{T}\right)^{-1} \frac{\mathbf{X}_i'\mathbf{M}_{hi}\mathbf{F}_p}{T}\left(\boldsymbol{\eta}_{\gamma ip} - \bar{\boldsymbol{\eta}}_{\gamma wp}\right) \xrightarrow{p} \underset{k\times 1}{\mathbf{0}}. \tag{A.10}$$

Now consider the term $\frac{1}{\sqrt{N}}\sum_{i=1}^{N}\left(\frac{\mathbf{X}_i'\mathbf{M}_{hi}\mathbf{X}_i}{T}\right)^{-1}\frac{\mathbf{X}_i'\mathbf{M}_{hi}\mathbf{F}_p}{T}\overline{\boldsymbol{\eta}}_{\gamma wp}$. Let us denote individual columns of $\mathbf{F}_p$ as $\mathbf{f}_{p,[j]}$, for $j=1,2,\ldots,m\,(p+1)$, and individual elements of $\overline{\boldsymbol{\eta}}_{\gamma wp}$ and $\overline{\boldsymbol{\gamma}}_{wp}$ as $\overline{\eta}_{\gamma wp,j}$ and $\overline{\gamma}_{wp,j}$, respectively, for $j=1,2,\ldots,m\,(p+1)$. $\mathbf{F}_p\overline{\boldsymbol{\eta}}_{\gamma wp}$ thus can be written as $\sum_{j=1}^{mp}\mathbf{f}_{p,[j]}\overline{\eta}_{\gamma wp,j}$. Let

$$\pi_j = \frac{\overline{\eta}_{\gamma wp,j}}{\gamma_{p,j}+\overline{\eta}_{\gamma wp,j}},$$

where $\gamma_{p,j}$ is the j-th element of the vector $E\left(\boldsymbol{\gamma}_{ip}\right)$. Note that $p\lim_{N\to\infty}\pi_j=1$ if $\gamma_{p,j}=0$ and $p\lim_{N\to\infty}\pi_j=0$ if $\gamma_{p,j}\neq 0$. Expression $\mathbf{F}_p\overline{\boldsymbol{\eta}}_{ywp}$ can now be written as $\mathbf{F}_p\overline{\boldsymbol{\eta}}_{ywp}=\sum_{j=1}^{m(p+1)}\mathbf{f}_{p,[j]}\overline{\gamma}_{wp,j}\pi_j$ and

$$\frac{\mathbf{X}_i'\mathbf{M}_{hi}\mathbf{F}_p}{T}\overline{\boldsymbol{\eta}}_{ywp} = \sum_{j=1}^{m(p+1)}\frac{\mathbf{X}_i'\mathbf{M}_{hi}\mathbf{f}_{p,[j]}}{T}\overline{\gamma}_{wp,j}\pi_j.$$

Using the same arguments as in the derivation of Eq. (A.9), we obtain $\frac{\mathbf{X}_i'\mathbf{M}_{hi}\mathbf{f}_{p,[j]}}{T}\overline{\gamma}_{wp,j}=O_p\left(\rho^p\right)$, and using the properties of π_j we have

$$\sum_{j=1}^{mp}\frac{\mathbf{X}_i'\mathbf{M}_{hi}\mathbf{f}_{p,[j]}}{T}\overline{\gamma}_{wp,j}\pi_j = O_p\left(p\rho^p\right).$$

But $\sqrt{N}p\rho^p\to 0$, and therefore

$$\sqrt{N}\frac{\mathbf{X}_i'\mathbf{M}_{hi}\mathbf{F}_p}{T}\overline{\boldsymbol{\eta}}_{ywp}\overset{p}{\to}\underset{k\times 1}{\mathbf{0}}. \tag{A.11}$$

Using this result in Eq. (A.10) together with Eq. (A.5) and the boundedness of $\left\|\boldsymbol{\Sigma}_i^{-1}\right\|$, we obtain

$$\frac{1}{\sqrt{N}}\sum_{i=1}^{N}\widehat{\boldsymbol{\Psi}}_{\Xi,iT}^{-1}\frac{\mathbf{X}_i'\mathbf{M}_{qi}\mathbf{F}_p}{T}\boldsymbol{\gamma}_i-\frac{1}{\sqrt{N}}\sum_{i=1}^{N}\left(\frac{\mathbf{X}_i'\mathbf{M}_{hi}\mathbf{X}_i}{T}\right)^{-1}\frac{\mathbf{X}_i'\mathbf{M}_{hi}\mathbf{F}_p}{T}\boldsymbol{\eta}_{\gamma ip}\overset{p}{\to}\underset{k\times 1}{\mathbf{0}}. \tag{A.12}$$

Consider now the third term on the right side of Eq. (A.4). Let $\tilde{\mathbf{x}}_{it}$ denote the column $(t-p)$ of the matrix $\mathbf{X}_i'\mathbf{M}_{qi}$, for $t=p+1,p+2,\ldots,T$. We have

$\tilde{\mathbf{x}}_{it} = O_p(1)$ uniformly in i, $\widehat{\boldsymbol{\Psi}}_{iT}^{-1} = O_p(1)$ uniformly in i, and

$$E\left|\sqrt{N}\vartheta_{it}\right| \leq \sqrt{N} \sum_{\ell=p+1}^{\infty} |\varphi_i|^{\ell+1} E\left|\boldsymbol{\beta}_i' \Delta \mathbf{x}_{i,t-\ell+1} + \boldsymbol{\gamma}_i' f_{t-\ell}\right| < K\sqrt{N}\rho^p, \quad \text{(A.13)}$$

uniformly in i and t. It follows that $E\left|\sqrt{N}\vartheta_{it}\right| \xrightarrow{p} 0$ as $\sqrt{N}\rho^p \to 0$,

$$\frac{1}{T}\sum_{t=1}^{T} \tilde{\mathbf{x}}_{it}\vartheta_{it} \xrightarrow{p} 0 \text{ uniformly in } i, \quad \text{(A.14)}$$

and

$$\frac{1}{N}\sum_{i=1}^{N} \widehat{\boldsymbol{\Psi}}_{iT}^{-1} \left(\frac{\mathbf{X}_i' \mathbf{M}_{qi} \left(\sqrt{N}\vartheta_i\right)}{T} \right) \xrightarrow{p} \underset{k\times 1}{\mathbf{0}}. \quad \text{(A.15)}$$

Using Eqs. (A.6), (A.12) and (A.15) in Eq. (A.4), we obtain

$$\sqrt{N}\left(\widehat{\boldsymbol{\theta}}_{MG} - \boldsymbol{\theta}\right) \overset{d}{\sim} \boldsymbol{\vartheta}_{\theta i},$$

where

$$\boldsymbol{\vartheta}_{\theta i} = \frac{1}{\sqrt{N}}\sum_{i=1}^{N} \boldsymbol{\upsilon}_i + \frac{1}{\sqrt{N}}\sum_{i=1}^{N} \left(\frac{\mathbf{X}_i' \mathbf{M}_{hi} \mathbf{X}_i}{T} \right)^{-1} \frac{\mathbf{X}_i' \mathbf{M}_{hi} \mathbf{F}_p}{T} \boldsymbol{\eta}_{\gamma ip}, \quad \text{(A.16)}$$

and recall that $\boldsymbol{\upsilon}_i$ and $\boldsymbol{\eta}_{\gamma ip}$ are independently distributed across i. It now follows that when $\boldsymbol{\eta}_{\gamma i}$ is independently distributed from $\boldsymbol{\Gamma}_i$ and regardless of whether the rank condition holds, $\sqrt{N}\left(\widehat{\boldsymbol{\theta}}_{MG} - \boldsymbol{\theta}\right) \xrightarrow{d} N\left(\underset{k\times 1}{\mathbf{0}}, \boldsymbol{\Sigma}_{MG}\right)$, where

$$\boldsymbol{\Sigma}_{MG} = \boldsymbol{\Omega}_\theta + \lim_{p,N\to\infty} \left[\frac{1}{N}\sum_{i=1}^{N} \boldsymbol{\Sigma}_i^{-1} \mathbf{Q}_{ifp} \boldsymbol{\Omega}_{\gamma p} \mathbf{Q}_{ifp}' \boldsymbol{\Sigma}_i^{-1} \right], \quad \text{(A.17)}$$

in which $\boldsymbol{\Omega}_\theta = Var(\boldsymbol{\theta}_i)$, $\boldsymbol{\Omega}_{\gamma p} = Var(\boldsymbol{\gamma}_{ip})$, $\boldsymbol{\gamma}_{ip} = \left(\boldsymbol{\gamma}_i', \varphi_i \boldsymbol{\gamma}_i', \ldots, \varphi_i^p \boldsymbol{\gamma}_i'\right)'$, $\boldsymbol{\Sigma}_i = p\lim T^{-1}\mathbf{X}_i'\mathbf{M}_{hi}\mathbf{X}_i$ and $\mathbf{Q}_{ifp} = p\lim T^{-1}\mathbf{X}_i'\mathbf{M}_{hi}\mathbf{F}_p$. When the rank condition stated in assumptions of Theorem 1 holds then $\mathbf{Q}_{ifp} = \underset{k\times m(p+1)}{\mathbf{0}}$, and therefore even if $\boldsymbol{\eta}_{\gamma i}$ is correlated with $\boldsymbol{\Gamma}_i$, $\sqrt{N}\left(\widehat{\boldsymbol{\theta}}_{MG} - \boldsymbol{\theta}\right) \overset{d}{\sim} \frac{1}{\sqrt{N}}\sum_{i=1}^{N} \boldsymbol{\upsilon}_i$. Consistency of the nonparametric estimator can be established in the same way as in Chudik and Pesaran (2015b). ■

Proof of Theorem 2. Consider

$$\left(\sum_{i=1}^{N} w_i^2\right)^{-1/2} \left(\widehat{\boldsymbol{\theta}}_P - \boldsymbol{\theta}\right) = \left(\sum_{i=1}^{N} w_i \frac{\mathbf{X}_i'\mathbf{M}_{qi}\mathbf{X}_i}{T}\right)^{-1} \times \frac{1}{\sqrt{N}} \sum_{i=1}^{N} \widetilde{w}_i \frac{\mathbf{X}_i'\mathbf{M}_{qi}\left(\mathbf{X}_i\mathbf{v}_i + \mathbf{F}_p\boldsymbol{\gamma}_{ip} + \boldsymbol{\vartheta}_i + \boldsymbol{\varepsilon}_i\right)}{T}, \tag{A.18}$$

where $\boldsymbol{\vartheta}_i$ is defined in Eq. (A.4), $\widetilde{w}_i = \sqrt{N} w_i \left(\sum_{i=1}^{N} w_i^2\right)^{-1/2}$, and, by granularity conditions (20)–(21) there exists a constant $K < \infty$ (independent of i and N), such that

$$|\widetilde{w}_i| = \left| \sqrt{N} w_i \left(\sum_{i=1}^{N} w_i^2\right)^{-1/2} \right| < K. \tag{A.19}$$

We focus on the individual terms on the right side of Eq. (A.18) below and assume that $(N, T, p) \xrightarrow{j} \infty$ such that $\sqrt{N} p \rho^p \to 0$ for any constant $0 < \rho < 1$ and $p^3/T \to \varkappa$, $0 < \varkappa < \infty$.

Using results (A.26) of Lemma 1 we have

$$\sum_{i=1}^{N} w_i \frac{\mathbf{X}_i'\mathbf{M}_{qi}\mathbf{X}_i}{T} - \sum_{i=1}^{N} w_i \boldsymbol{\Sigma}_{iq} \xrightarrow{p} \underset{k\times 1}{\mathbf{0}},$$

for any weights $\{w_i\}$ satisfying granularity conditions (20)–(21). The limit $\lim_{N\to\infty} \sum_{i=1}^{N} w_i \boldsymbol{\Sigma}_{iq} = \boldsymbol{\Psi}^*$ exists by Assumption 5 and furthermore, by the same assumption, $\boldsymbol{\Psi}^*$ is nonsingular. It therefore follows that

$$\left(\sum_{i=1}^{N} w_i \frac{\mathbf{X}_i'\mathbf{M}_{qi}\mathbf{X}_i}{T}\right)^{-1} \xrightarrow{p} \boldsymbol{\Psi}^{*-1}. \tag{A.20}$$

Noting that $\boldsymbol{\gamma}_{ip}$ can be written as $\boldsymbol{\gamma}_{ip} = \overline{\boldsymbol{\gamma}}_{wp} + \boldsymbol{\eta}_{ip} - \overline{\boldsymbol{\eta}}_{wp}$, and using Eqs. (A.9), (A.11), (A.19) and $\sqrt{N}\rho^p \to 0$ we obtain[13]

$$\frac{1}{\sqrt{N}} \sum_{i=1}^{N} \widetilde{w}_i \frac{\mathbf{X}_i' \mathbf{M}_{qi} \mathbf{F}_p}{T} \boldsymbol{\gamma}_{ip} - \frac{1}{\sqrt{N}} \sum_{i=1}^{N} \widetilde{w}_i \frac{\mathbf{X}_i' \mathbf{M}_{qi} \mathbf{F}_p}{T} \boldsymbol{\eta}_{ip} \overset{p}{\to} \underset{k\times 1}{\mathbf{0}}. \tag{A.21}$$

Equations (A.14) and (A.19) imply

$$\frac{1}{\sqrt{N}} \sum_{i=1}^{N} \widetilde{w}_i \frac{\mathbf{X}_i' \mathbf{M}_{qi} \boldsymbol{\vartheta}_i}{T} \overset{p}{\to} \underset{k\times 1}{\mathbf{0}}. \tag{A.22}$$

Result (A.28) of Lemma 2 and result (A.30) of Lemma 3 establish

$$\sqrt{N} \frac{\mathbf{X}_i' \mathbf{M}_{qi} \boldsymbol{\varepsilon}_i}{T} \overset{p}{\to} \underset{k\times 1}{\mathbf{0}} \text{ uniformly in } i,$$

and therefore (noting that $\widetilde{w}_i$ is uniformly bounded in i, see Eq. (A.19)),

$$\frac{1}{\sqrt{N}} \sum_{i=1}^{N} \widetilde{w}_i \frac{\mathbf{X}_i' \mathbf{M}_{qi} \boldsymbol{\varepsilon}_i}{T} = \frac{1}{N} \sum_{i=1}^{N} \widetilde{w}_i \left(\sqrt{N} \frac{\mathbf{X}_i' \mathbf{M}_{qi} \boldsymbol{\varepsilon}_i}{T} \right) \overset{p}{\to} \underset{k\times 1}{\mathbf{0}}. \tag{A.23}$$

Using Eqs. (A.20), (A.21), (A.22), (A.23) and result (A.27) of Lemma 2 in (A.18), we obtain

$$\left(\sum_{i=1}^{N} w_i^2 \right)^{-1/2} \left(\widehat{\boldsymbol{\theta}}_P - \boldsymbol{\theta} \right) \overset{d}{\sim} \boldsymbol{\Psi}^{*-1} \frac{1}{\sqrt{N}} \sum_{i=1}^{N} \widetilde{w}_i \frac{\mathbf{X}_i' \mathbf{M}_{hi} \left(\mathbf{X}_i \mathbf{v}_i + \mathbf{F}_p \boldsymbol{\eta}_{ip} \right)}{T}.$$

Assumption 5 is sufficient for the bounded second moments of $\mathbf{X}_i' \mathbf{M}_{hi} \mathbf{X}_i / T$ and $\mathbf{X}_i' \mathbf{M}_{hi} \mathbf{F}_p / T$. In particular, condition $E\left(\widetilde{x}_{ist}^4\right) < K$, for $s = 1, 2, \ldots, k$, is sufficient for the bounded second moment of $\mathbf{X}_i' \mathbf{M}_{hi} \mathbf{X}_i / T$. To see this note that

$$\frac{\mathbf{X}_i' \mathbf{M}_{hi} \mathbf{X}_i}{T} = \frac{1}{T} \sum_{t=1}^{T} \widetilde{\mathbf{x}}_{it} \widetilde{\mathbf{x}}_{it}',$$

and, by Minkowski's inequality,

$$\left\| \frac{1}{T} \sum_{t=1}^{T} \widetilde{x}_{ist} \widetilde{x}_{ipt} \right\|_{L_2} \leq \frac{1}{T} \sum_{t=1}^{T} \left\| \widetilde{x}_{ist} \widetilde{x}_{ipt} \right\|_{L_2},$$

for any $s, p = 1, 2, \ldots, k$. But by Cauchy–Schwarz inequality, we have $E\left(\widetilde{x}_{ist}^2 \widetilde{x}_{ipt}^2\right) \leq \left[E\left(\widetilde{x}_{ist}^4\right) E\left(\widetilde{x}_{ipt}^4\right)\right]^{1/2}$, and therefore bounded fourth moments of the elements of $\widetilde{\mathbf{x}}_{it}$ are sufficient for the existence of an upper bound for the second moments of $\mathbf{X}_i'\mathbf{M}_{hi}\mathbf{X}_i/T$. Similar arguments can be used to establish that $\mathbf{X}_i'\mathbf{M}_{hi}\mathbf{F}_p/T$ has bounded second moments. Note also that $\mathbf{v}_i$ and $\boldsymbol{\eta}_{ip}$ are independently distributed across i; and, independently distributed of $\mathbf{M}_{hi}$, $\mathbf{F}_p$ and, assuming that $\boldsymbol{\gamma}_i$ is independently distributed of $\boldsymbol{\Gamma}_i$, also $\mathbf{X}_i$. It therefore follows, using similar arguments as in Lemma 4 of Pesaran (2006), that

$$\left(\sum_{i=1}^{N} w_i^2\right)^{-1/2} \left(\widehat{\boldsymbol{\theta}}_P - \boldsymbol{\theta}\right) \xrightarrow{d} N\left(\mathbf{0}, \boldsymbol{\Sigma}_P\right),$$

where

$$\boldsymbol{\Sigma}_P = \boldsymbol{\Psi}^{*-1}\mathbf{R}^*\boldsymbol{\Psi}^{*-1}, \tag{A.24}$$

in which

$$\boldsymbol{\Psi}^* = \lim_{p,N\to\infty} \sum_{i=1}^{N} w_i \boldsymbol{\Sigma}_i,\ \mathbf{R}^* = \lim_{p,N\to\infty} \frac{1}{N} \sum_{i=1}^{N} \widetilde{w}_i^2 \left(\boldsymbol{\Sigma}_i \boldsymbol{\Omega}_\theta \boldsymbol{\Sigma}_i + \mathbf{Q}_{ifp} \boldsymbol{\Omega}_{\gamma p} \mathbf{Q}_{ifp}'\right),$$

$\boldsymbol{\Omega}_\theta = Var(\boldsymbol{\theta}_i)$, $\boldsymbol{\Omega}_{\gamma p} = Var\left(\boldsymbol{\gamma}_{ip}\right)$, $\boldsymbol{\gamma}_{ip} = \left(\boldsymbol{\gamma}_i', \varphi_i \boldsymbol{\gamma}_i', \ldots, \varphi_i^p \boldsymbol{\gamma}_i'\right)'$, $\boldsymbol{\Sigma}_i = p \lim T^{-1}\mathbf{X}_i'\mathbf{M}_{hi}\mathbf{X}_i$ and $\mathbf{Q}_{ifp} = p \lim T^{-1}\mathbf{X}_i'\mathbf{M}_{hi}\mathbf{F}_p$. $\boldsymbol{\Sigma}_P$ can be estimated as

$$\widehat{\boldsymbol{\Sigma}}_P = \left(\sum_{i=1}^{N} w_i^2\right) \hat{\boldsymbol{\Psi}}^{*-1} \hat{\mathbf{R}}^* \hat{\boldsymbol{\Psi}}^{*-1}, \tag{A.25}$$

where

$$\hat{\boldsymbol{\Psi}}^* = \sum_{i=1}^{N} w_i \left(\frac{\mathbf{X}_i'\mathbf{M}_{qi}\mathbf{X}_i}{T}\right),$$

and

$$\hat{\mathbf{R}}^* = \frac{1}{N-1} \sum_{i=1}^{N} \tilde{w}_i^2 \left(\frac{\mathbf{X}_i'\mathbf{M}_{qi}\mathbf{X}_i}{T}\right) \left(\widehat{\boldsymbol{\theta}}_i - \widehat{\boldsymbol{\theta}}_{MG}\right) \left(\widehat{\boldsymbol{\theta}}_i - \widehat{\boldsymbol{\theta}}_{MG}\right)' \left(\frac{\mathbf{X}_i'\mathbf{M}_{qi}\mathbf{X}_i}{T}\right).$$

When the rank condition holds, then the column vectors of $\mathbf{F}_p$ belong to the space spanned by the column vectors of $\mathbf{H}_w$, and therefore regardless of whether $\boldsymbol{\eta}_{\gamma i}$ is correlated with $\boldsymbol{\Gamma}_i$ or not, $\left(\sum_{i=1}^{N} w_i^2\right)^{-1/2} \left(\widehat{\boldsymbol{\theta}}_P - \boldsymbol{\theta}\right) \xrightarrow{d} N\left(\mathbf{0}, \boldsymbol{\Sigma}_P\right)$ in the full rank case with $\boldsymbol{\Sigma}_P$ reduced to $\boldsymbol{\Psi}^{*-1}\mathbf{R}_{\theta}^{*}\boldsymbol{\Psi}^{*-1}$ and $\mathbf{Q}_{if} = \underset{k\times m(p+1)}{\mathbf{0}}$. Consistency of $\widehat{\boldsymbol{\Sigma}}_P$ can be established using similar arguments as in Pesaran (2006). ■

A.2. Lemmas

Lemma 1. *Suppose Assumptions 1–5 hold and* $(N, T, p) \xrightarrow{j} \infty$ *such that* $p^3/T \to \varkappa$, $0 < \varkappa < \infty$. *Then,*

$$\frac{\mathbf{X}_i'\mathbf{M}_{hi}\mathbf{X}_i}{T} \xrightarrow{p} \boldsymbol{\Sigma}_i, \quad \textit{uniformly in } i. \tag{A.26}$$

Proof. Let $\boldsymbol{\xi}_{hit}'$ denote the individual rows of $\mathbf{M}_{hi}\mathbf{X}_i$ so that

$$\frac{\mathbf{X}_i'\mathbf{M}_{hi}\mathbf{X}_i}{T} = \frac{T-p}{T}\frac{1}{T-p}\sum_{t=p+1}^{T}\boldsymbol{\xi}_{hit}\boldsymbol{\xi}_{hit}'.$$

Ergodicity in mean of $\boldsymbol{\xi}_{hit}$ has been established in Chudik and Pesaran (2015b, Lemma A3). This completes the proof of Eq. (A.26). ■

Lemma 2. *Suppose Assumptions 1–5 hold and* $(N, T, p) \xrightarrow{j} \infty$ *such that* $p^3/T \to \varkappa$, $0 < \varkappa < \infty$. *Then,*

$$\sqrt{N}\frac{\mathbf{X}_i'\mathbf{M}_{qi}\mathbf{X}_i}{T} - \sqrt{N}\frac{\mathbf{X}_i'\mathbf{M}_{hi}\mathbf{X}_i}{T} \xrightarrow{p} \underset{k\times k}{\mathbf{0}}, \quad \textit{uniformly in } i. \tag{A.27}$$

$$\sqrt{N}\frac{\mathbf{X}_i'\mathbf{M}_{qi}\boldsymbol{\varepsilon}_i}{T} - \sqrt{N}\frac{\mathbf{X}_i'\mathbf{M}_{hi}\boldsymbol{\varepsilon}_i}{T} \xrightarrow{p} \underset{k\times 1}{\mathbf{0}}, \quad \textit{uniformly in } i. \tag{A.28}$$

$$\left\|\sqrt{N}\frac{\mathbf{X}_i'\mathbf{M}_{qi}\mathbf{F}_p}{T} - \sqrt{N}\frac{\mathbf{X}_i'\mathbf{M}_{hi}\mathbf{F}_p}{T}\right\|_1 \xrightarrow{p} 0, \quad \textit{uniformly in } i. \tag{A.29}$$

Proof. Results (A.27) and (A.28) can be established in the same way as Chudik and Pesaran (2015b, results A.21 and A.22 of Lemma A6). Consider now Eq. (A.29). $\mathbf{F}_p$ can be written as $\mathbf{F}_p = \left[\mathbf{F}_{(0)}, \mathbf{F}_{(1)}, \ldots, \mathbf{F}_{(p)}\right]$, where $\mathbf{F}_{(\ell)} = \left(\mathbf{f}_{p+1-\ell}, \mathbf{f}_{p+2-\ell}, \ldots, \mathbf{f}_{T-\ell}\right)'$ for $\ell = 0, 1, 2, \ldots, p$. Using the same arguments as in Chudik and Pesaran (2015b, results A.23 of Lemma A6), it can be shown that

$$\sqrt{N}\frac{\mathbf{X}_i'\mathbf{M}_{qi}\mathbf{F}_{(\ell)}}{T} - \sqrt{N}\frac{\mathbf{X}_i'\mathbf{M}_{hi}\mathbf{F}_{(\ell)}}{T} \xrightarrow{p} \underset{k\times m}{\mathbf{0}},$$

uniformly in i and ℓ. This is sufficient for Eq. (A.29) to hold. ■

Lemma 3. *Suppose Assumptions 1–5 hold and* $(N, T, p) \xrightarrow{j} \infty$ *such that* $p^3/T \to \varkappa$, $0 < \varkappa < \infty$. *Then,*

$$\frac{1}{\sqrt{N}} \sum_{i=1}^{N} \frac{\mathbf{X}_i' \mathbf{M}_{hi} \boldsymbol{\varepsilon}_i}{T} \xrightarrow{p} \underset{k \times 1}{\mathbf{0}}, \quad \textit{uniformly in i.} \tag{A.30}$$

Proof. Results (A.27) can be established in the same way as Chudik and Pesaran (2015b, results A.26). ■

SEMIPARAMETRIC ESTIMATION OF PARTIALLY LINEAR DYNAMIC PANEL DATA MODELS WITH FIXED EFFECTS

Liangjun Su[a] and Yonghui Zhang[b]

[a]*School of Economics, Singapore Management University, Singapore*

[b]*School of Economics, Renmin University of China, Beijing, People's Republic of China*

ABSTRACT

In this paper, we study a partially linear dynamic panel data model with fixed effects, where either exogenous or endogenous variables or both enter the linear part, and the lagged-dependent variable together with some other exogenous variables enter the nonparametric part. Two types of estimation methods are proposed for the first-differenced model. One is composed of a semiparametric GMM estimator for the finite-dimensional parameter θ *and a local polynomial estimator for the infinite-dimensional parameter* m *based on the empirical solutions to Fredholm integral equations of the second kind, and the other is a sieve IV estimate of the parametric and nonparametric components jointly. We study the asymptotic properties for these two types of estimates when the number of individuals* N *tends to* ∞ *and the time period* T *is fixed. We also propose a specification test for the linearity of the nonparametric component based on a weighted square distance between the parametric estimate under the linear restriction and the semiparametric*

Essays in Honor of Aman Ullah
Advances in Econometrics, Volume 36, 137–204

ISSN: 0731-9053/doi:10.1108/S0731-905320160000036014

estimate under the alternative. Monte Carlo simulations suggest that the proposed estimators and tests perform well in finite samples. We apply the model to study the relationship between intellectual property right (IPR) protection and economic growth, and find that IPR has a non-linear positive effect on the economic growth rate.

Keywords: Fredholm integral equation; generated covariate; GMM; local polynomial regression; partially linear model; Sieve method

JEL classifications: C14; C33; C36

1. INTRODUCTION

Recently nonparametric panel models have received a lot of attention. The increasing popularity of nonparametric approach to panel data modelling largely comes from its flexibility in exploring hidden structures and its robustness to model misspecification which often occurs under a parametric setting. On the other hand, a fully nonparametric model usually suffers from the notorious problem of 'curse of dimensionality' when the dimension of the nonparametric covariates is high, and it becomes very difficult to interpret a nonparametric estimator in empirical applications when the dimension is larger than two. To overcome these shortcomings, many semiparametric models have also been proposed in the panel data literature as a compromise between nonparametric and parametric specifications. By imposing different structures on the unknown functions, various semiparametric models such as additive models, partially linear models, single-index models, transformation models and varying-coefficient models have been studied extensively in the literature. For example, Chen, Gao, and Li (2012) consider partially linear panel data models where the time trend enters the nonparametric component; Chen, Gao, and Li (2013a; 2013b) and Dong, Gao, and Peng (2015a) study the estimation of panel data models with different single-index structures; Dong, Gao, and Peng (2015b) consider a partially linear panel data model with cross-sectional dependence and non-stationarity; Feng, Gao, Peng, and Zheng (2015) consider the estimation of varying-coefficient panel data models. For recent selective overviews, see Su and Ullah (2011), Chen, Li, and Gao (2013) and Sun, Zhang, and Li (2015).

In this paper, we focus on the following partially linear dynamic panel data model with fixed effects

$$Y_{it} = Z_{it}'\theta_0 + m\left(Y_{i,t-1}, X_{it}\right) + \alpha_i + \varepsilon_{it}, \tag{1}$$

$i = 1, \ldots, N, t = 1, \ldots, T$, where Y_{it} is the scalar-dependent variable for individual i at time period t, Z_{it} is a $d_z \times 1$ vector of regressors that enter the linear component of the model, θ_0 is an unknown parameter that takes value on the compact parameter space $\Theta \subset \mathbb{R}^{d_z}$, $m(\cdot)$ is an unknown smooth function defined on $\mathbb{R}^{d_x+1}$, X_{it} is a $d_x \times 1$ vector of regressors that enter the nonparametric component $m(\cdot)$ together with the lagged-dependent variable, $Y_{i,t-1}$, α_i's are unobserved individual effects and ε_{it}'s are idiosyncratic error terms. The subscript '0' in θ_0 indicates the true parameter value. Clearly, $Y_{i,t-1}$ is correlated with the fixed effect α_i. We also allow Z_{it} and X_{it} to be correlated with α_i. As in Baltagi and D. Li (2002), Baltagi and Q. Li (2002) and Yao and Zhang (2015), we allow Z_{it} or a subset of Z_{it} to be endogenous and assume the existence of a $d_v \times 1$ vector of instrumental variables (IVs) V_{it} where $d_v \geq d_z$.[1] Also like them, we restrict X_{it} to be exogenous to avoid the ill-posed inverse problem. The latter problem can be addressed by extending the estimation procedure of Ai and Chen (2003), Chen and Pouzo (2012), or Florens, Johannes, and Van Bellegem (2012) to the panel setting but is certainly beyond the scope of this paper. We are interested in the estimation of θ_0 and $m(\cdot)$ under large N and small T.

Since Engle, Granger, Rice, and Weiss (1986) and Robinson (1988), partially linear models have been widely studied and applied in the econometrics literature. In the panel framework, partially linear structures have also attracted a lot of attention. For example, Li and Stengos (1996) and Li and Ullah (1998) consider kernel estimation of partially linear panel data models with random effects where the endogenous variables appear in the linear component; Baltagi and D. Li (2002) and Baltagi and Q. Li (2002), respectively, propose series and kernel estimation of partially linear dynamic panel models with fixed effects where the lagged-dependent variables enter the model linearly; Su and Ullah (2006a) study profile likelihood kernel estimation of partially linear *static* panel data models with fixed effects; Baglan (2010) considers series estimation of partially linear dynamic panel data models with fixed effects where the lagged-dependent variable enters the model linearly; Qian and Wang (2012) consider kernel estimation of nonparametric component in a fixed effect partially linear *static* panel data model via marginal integration. To the best of our knowledge, so far endogeneity and lagged-dependent variables have been allowed to enter the partially linear panel data models only through the linear component. It remains unclear whether one can allow both to enter the nonparametric component of the model. In this paper, our goal is less ambitious in the sense that we only allow lagged-dependent variables to enter the nonparametric component. The endogenous variables, if present, only enter the linear component of the model. Despite this less ambitious goal, the inclusion of lagged-dependent variables in the nonparametric component turns out to be sufficiently technically challenging and the introduction of endogeneity in the linear component further complicates the issue to a great deal.

Despite the existence of a large literature on nonparametric panel data models, there is a lack of satisfactory development in nonparametric and semiparametric panel data models where a lagged-dependent variable enters the nonparametric component of the model. The few exceptions include Su and Lu (2013) and Lee (2014), who consider kernel and sieve estimation of nonparametric dynamic panel data models, respectively. Su and Lu (2013) also document the empirical evidence of non-linear effects of lagged-dependent variables in the economic growth literature. This paper contributes to the literature by allowing lagged-dependent variables to enter the nonparametric component in panel data models.

For notational simplicity, let $\underline{\xi}_{it} \equiv \left(\xi_{it}, \xi_{i,t-1}, \ldots, \xi_{i1}\right)$, where $\xi = Y, X, Z$, or V. Following Su and Lu (2013), we assume that $E(\varepsilon_{it}|\underline{Y}_{i,t-1}, \underline{X}_{it}, \underline{V}_{it}) = 0$ and consider the first-differenced model

$$\Delta Y_{it} = \Delta Z_{it}'\theta_0 + m\left(Y_{i,t-1}, X_{it}\right) - m\left(Y_{i,t-2}, X_{i,t-1}\right) + \Delta\varepsilon_{it}, \tag{2}$$

where, for example, $\Delta Y_{it} \equiv Y_{it} - Y_{i,t-1}$. Clearly, the first-differenced model in Eq. (2) exhibits some important features. First, Eq. (2) still has a partially linear structure with a linear component $(\Delta Z_{it}'\theta_0)$ and two additive nonparametric components $\left(m\left(Y_{i,t-1}, X_{it}\right) \text{ and } m\left(Y_{i,t-2}, X_{i,t-1}\right)\right)$. Second, the two additive nonparametric components share the same functional form which should be incorporated in the estimation procedure. In fact, as we show below, this feature, in conjunction with the martingale difference sequence (m.d.s.) type of conditions on ε_{it}, implies that $m(\cdot)$ implicitly solves a class of Fredholm integral equations of the second kind indexed by the finite-dimensional parameter θ. Third, the error term $\Delta\varepsilon_{it}$ follows a *non-invertible* moving average process of order 1 (MA(1)) and is correlated with both $Y_{i,t-1}$ and ΔZ_{it} in general. Despite the fact that it is hard to apply this last feature to improve efficiency as in Xiao, Linton, Carroll, and Mammen (2003), Su and Ullah (2006b) and Gao, Lu, and Tjøstheim (2006), it invalidates the traditional kernel estimation based on either marginal integration or backfitting method because of the endogeneity issue in the first-differenced model. In addition, the presence of the linear component ΔZ_{it} in Eq. (2) makes our model different from that in Su and Lu (2013) and complicates our estimation procedures and asymptotic analysis substantially.

In this paper, we propose two estimation procedures, both of which take into account all the features mentioned above. The first one comprises the semiparametric GMM estimation of θ_0 and kernel estimation of $m(\cdot)$ based on the empirical solutions to Fredholm integral equations of the second kind. The second one estimates both the parametric and nonparametric component at a single step via the sieve IV method. As remarked later on, our methods can be used to estimate models with both individual and time fixed effects.

Under some fairly general and mild conditions that allow for the nonstationarity of $(Y_{i,t-1}, Z_{it}, V_{it}, X_{it}, \varepsilon_{it})$ along the time dimension and conditional heteroskedasticity among ε_{it}, we show that both types of estimates of the finite dimensional parameter have the usual parametric convergence rates and follow asymptotic normal distributions. We also derive the uniform convergence rates for the nonparametric estimates over a compact support and establish their asymptotic normal distributions by passing N to infinity and keeping T fixed as in typical micro-panel data models. Based on our estimators, we also propose a nonparametric test for the linearity of the nonparametric component. We examine the finite sample performance of our estimators and tests through Monte Carlo simulations. We apply the proposed model to study the relationship between economic growth, its lagged value, and intellectual property right (IPR) protection. We find substantial non-linearity in the relationship between a country's economic growth rate and its lagged value and a positive non-linear relationship between economic growth rate and IPR protection.

The rest of this paper is organized as follows. In Section 2 we introduce the semiparametric GMM estimation of θ and kernel estimation of m based on a Fredholm integral equation of the second kind and study the asymptotic properties of these estimators. In Section 3 we discuss the sieve IV estimation of θ and m and derive the asymptotic properties of our proposed estimators. In Section 4, we propose a nonparametric test for the linearity of the nonparametric component. In Section 5 we conduct a small set of Monte Carlo simulations to evaluate the finite sample performance of our estimators and tests. We apply our method to a real data set in Section 6. Final remarks are contained in Section 7. All technical details are relegated to the appendix.

Throughout this paper, we restrict our attention to a balanced panel. We use $i = 1, \ldots, N$ to denote individuals and $t = 1, \ldots, T$ to denote time. All asymptotic theories are established by passing N to infinity and holding T as a fixed constant. For natural numbers a and b, we use $\mathbf{I}_a$ to denote an $a \times a$ identity matrix, $\mathbf{0}_{a \times b}$ an $a \times b$ matrix of zeros, and l_a an $a \times 1$ vector of ones. Let $T_l \equiv T - l$ for $l = 1, 2$. For conformable vectors u and v, we use u/v to denote element-wise division. For a real matrix B, let $\|B\| \equiv \sqrt{\operatorname{tr}(B'B)}$ denote its Frobenius norm and $\|B\|_{\text{sp}} \equiv \sqrt{\lambda_{\max}(B'B)}$ its spectral norm, where $\lambda_{\max}(\cdot)$ is the largest eigenvalue of '$\cdot$'. Let $\mathbf{P}_B \equiv B(B'B)^- B$ and $\mathbf{M}_B \equiv \mathbf{I} - \mathbf{P}_B$ where $(\cdot)^-$ denotes the Moore–Penrose generalized inverse and $\mathbf{I}$ is a conformable identity matrix. Let $\stackrel{P}{\to}$ and $\stackrel{D}{\to}$ signify convergence in probability and distribution, respectively.

2. SEMIPARAMETRIC GMM ESTIMATION OF θ AND KERNEL ESTIMATION OF m

In this section, we first outline the idea for the semiparametric GMM estimation of θ and kernel estimation of $m(\cdot)$ based on the empirical solution to a Fredholm integral equation of the second kind and then present the estimation details. We also derive the convergence rates for the proposed estimators and establish their asymptotic normal distributions.

2.1. Basic Idea

Note that $E(\varepsilon_{it}|\underline{Y}_{i,t-1}, \underline{X}_{it}, \underline{V}_{it}) = 0$. By the law of iterated expectations, we have $E(\varepsilon_{it}|\underline{Y}_{i,t-1}, \underline{X}_{it}) = 0$. Based on this observation, we obtain the following conditional moment conditions:

$$E\left[\Delta Y_{it} - \Delta Z_{it}'\theta_0 - m\left(Y_{i,t-1}, X_{it}\right) + m\left(Y_{i,t-2}, X_{i,t-1}\right)|\underline{U}_{i,t-2}\right] = 0, \quad (3)$$

$i = 1, \ldots, N,\ t = 3, \ldots, T,$ where $\underline{U}_{i,t-2} \equiv (U_{i,t-2}, U_{i,t-3}, \ldots, U_{i1})$ and $U_{it} \equiv \left(Y_{it}, X_{i,t+1}'\right)'$. Clearly, for large t the conditioning information set $\underline{U}_{i,t-2}$ contains a large number of valid IVs for the local nonparametric identification of $m(\cdot)$. But for both technical reasons and practical concerns, it seems unrealistic to use all variables in $\underline{U}_{i,t-2}$ in nonparametric regressions. To avoid the curse of dimensionality problem, we consider only a small number of IVs that are measurable with respect to the σ-algebra generated by $\underline{U}_{i,t-2}$. In this paper, we only use $U_{i,t-2}$ and leave the optimal choice of IVs for the estimation of the nonparametric component as future research.

To proceed, we define some notation. Let $\mathcal{U}$ be a compact subset of $\mathbb{R}^{d_x+1}$.[2] We assume that $U_{i,t-2}$ has a positive density on $\mathcal{U}$ and denote the conditional probability density function (PDF) of $U_{i,t-1}$ given that $U_{i,t-2}$ lies in $\mathcal{U}$ as $f_{t-2}(\cdot)$. Similarly, we use $f_{t-1|t-2}(\cdot|\cdot)$ to denote the conditional PDF of $U_{i,t-1}$ given $U_{i,t-2}$, conditionally on $U_{i,t-2} \in \mathcal{U}$. Let

$$n \equiv \sum_{i=1}^{N}\sum_{t=3}^{T} \mathbf{1}\left(U_{i,t-2} \in \mathcal{U}\right) \quad \text{and} \quad n_{t-2} \equiv \sum_{i=1}^{N} \mathbf{1}\left(U_{i,t-2} \in \mathcal{U}\right) \quad \text{for } t \in \{3, \ldots, T\},$$

where $\mathbf{1}(\cdot)$ is the usual indicator function. By the Kinchin law of large numbers (LLN), $n_{t-2}/N \xrightarrow{P} p_{t-2} \equiv P\left(U_{i,t-2} \in \mathcal{U}\right)$ and $n/N \xrightarrow{P} \sum_{t=3}^{T} p_{t-2} \equiv p$. Let $r_{t|t-2}^{[y]}(u) \equiv E(-\Delta Y_{it}|U_{i,t-2} = u)$ and $r_{t|t-2}^{[z]}(u) \equiv E\left(-\Delta Z_{it}|U_{i,t-2} = u\right)$. Define

$$f(u) \equiv \sum_{t=3}^{T} \frac{p_{t-2}}{p} f_{t-2}(u), \quad f(\bar{u}|u) \equiv \sum_{t=3}^{T} \frac{p_{t-2}}{p} f_{t-1|t-2}(\bar{u}|u), \quad (4)$$

$$r_y(u) \equiv \sum_{t=3}^{T} \frac{p_{t-2}}{p} r_{t|t-2}^{[y]}(u),$$

$$r_z(u) \equiv \sum_{t=3}^{T} \frac{p_{t-2}}{p} r_{t|t-2}^{[z]}(u) \quad \text{and} \quad r_\theta(u) \equiv r_y(u) - \theta' r_z(u) \tag{5}$$

where we suppress the dependence of p, $f(u)$, $f(\bar{u}|u)$, $r_y(u)$, $r_z(u)$ and $r_\theta(u)$ on T.

Equation (3) implies that

$$\begin{aligned} m(u) &= E\left[m\left(U_{i,t-1}\right)|U_{i,t-2}=u\right] + E\left(-\Delta Y_{it}|U_{i,t-2}=u\right), \\ &\quad - \theta_0' E\left(-\Delta Z_{it}|U_{i,t-2}=u\right) \\ &= \int m(\bar{u})\, f_{t-1|t-2}(\bar{u}|u)\, d\bar{u} + r_{t|t-2}^{[y]}(u) - \theta_0' r_{t|t-2}^{[z]}(u) \ \text{ for } t=3,\ldots,T. \end{aligned} \tag{6}$$

Multiplying both sides of Eq. (6) by p_{t-2}/p and summing up over $t=3,\ldots,T$ yields

$$m(u) = \int m(\bar{u})\, f(\bar{u}|u)\, d\bar{u} + \left[r_y(u) - \theta_0' r_z(u)\right]. \tag{7}$$

Under certain regularity conditions, for any $\theta \in \Theta$ there exists a unique solution $m_\theta(u)$ to a Fredholm integral equation of the second kind in an infinite-dimensional Hilbert space $\mathcal{L}_2(f)$:

$$m_\theta = \mathcal{A} m_\theta + r_\theta, \tag{8}$$

where $\mathcal{A}$: $\mathcal{L}_2(f) \to \mathcal{L}_2(f)$ is a bounded linear operator defined by

$$\mathcal{A} m(u) \equiv \int m(\bar{u})\, f(\bar{u}|u)\, d\bar{u} \quad \text{for } u \in \mathcal{U} \tag{9}$$

and $\mathcal{L}_2(f)$ is a Hilbert space with norm $\|m\|_2 \equiv [\int_{\mathcal{U}} m(u)^2 f(u)\, du]^{1/2}$. Let $\mathcal{I}$ be the identity operator. Under some conditions to be specified later on, $\mathcal{I} - \mathcal{A}$ is invertible and

$$\sup_{\|m\|_2 \le 1} \left\|(\mathcal{I} - \mathcal{A})^{-1} m\right\|_2 < \infty. \tag{10}$$

Then given θ, the unique solution to Eq. (8) is given by

$$m_\theta = (\mathcal{I} - \mathcal{A})^{-1}\left(r_y - \theta' r_z\right) = m_y - \theta' m_z, \tag{11}$$

where $m_y \equiv (\mathcal{I} - \mathcal{A})^{-1} r_y$ and $m_z \equiv (\mathcal{I} - \mathcal{A})^{-1} r_z$ are solutions to

$$m(u) = \mathcal{A} m(u) + r_y(u) \quad \text{and} \quad m(u) = \mathcal{A} m(u) + r_z(u), \ \text{respectively.} \tag{12}$$

To facilitate the theoretical study, we will consider the following auxiliary first-differenced models:

$$\begin{aligned} \Delta Y_{it} &= m_y\left(U_{i,t-1}\right) - m_y\left(U_{i,t-2}\right) + \eta_{y,it}, \\ \Delta Z_{it,l} &= m_{z_l}\left(U_{i,t-1}\right) - m_{z_l}\left(U_{i,t-2}\right) + \eta_{z_l,it}, \quad l = 1, \ldots, d_z, \end{aligned} \tag{13}$$

where $Z_{it,l}$ and z_l denote the lth element in Z_{it} and z, respectively, the error terms $\eta_{y,it}$ and $\eta_{z_l,it}$ satisfy $E\left(\eta_{y,it}|U_{i,t-2}\right) = 0$ and $E\left(\eta_{z_l,it}|U_{i,t-2}\right) = 0$. It is easy to see that under these moment conditions, m_y and $m_z \equiv (m_{z_1}, \ldots, m_{z_{d_z}})'$ are the solutions to the Fredholm integral equations of the second kind in Eq. (12).

Apparently, m_θ is linear in θ. Given the estimates $\hat{m}_y(u)$ and $\hat{m}_z(u)$ of $m_y(u)$ and $m_z(u)$, we can estimate $m_\theta(u)$ by $\hat{m}_\theta(u) \equiv \hat{m}_y(u) - \theta'\hat{m}_z(u)$ for any $\theta \in \Theta$. Below, we first introduce how one can obtain the kernel estimates $\hat{m}_y(u)$ and $\hat{m}_z(u)$ based on local polynomial regressions, and then study the semiparametric GMM estimation of θ based on some identification conditions.

2.2. *Semiparametric GMM Estimation*

2.2.1. *Kernel estimation of $m_y(u)$ and $m_z(u)$*

Now we consider how to estimate $m_y(u)$ and $m_z(u)$ as the solutions to the two equations in Eq. (12). Assume that nonparametric estimates of r_y, r_z and $\mathcal{A}$ are given by $\hat{r}_y$, $\hat{r}_z$ and $\widehat{\mathcal{A}}$, respectively. Then the plug-in estimators $\hat{m}_y$ and $\hat{m}_z$ are given by the solutions to

$$\hat{m}_y = \widehat{\mathcal{A}}\hat{m}_y + \hat{r}_y \quad \text{and} \quad \hat{m}_z = \widehat{\mathcal{A}}\hat{m}_z + \hat{r}_z, \tag{14}$$

respectively.

Here we consider the local polynomial estimates of r_y, r_z and $\mathcal{A}$. Let $u \equiv \left(y, x'\right)' \equiv \left(u_0, u_1, \ldots, u_{d_x}\right)'$ be a $(d_x + 1) \times 1$ vector, where x is $d_x \times 1$ and y is a scalar. Let $\boldsymbol{j} \equiv (j_0, j_1, \ldots, j_{d_x})'$ be a $(d_x + 1)$-vector of non-negative integers. Following Masry (1996), we adopt the notation: $u^{\boldsymbol{j}} \equiv \boldsymbol{\Pi}_{i=0}^{d_x} u_i^{j_i}$, $\boldsymbol{j}! \equiv \boldsymbol{\Pi}_{i=1}^{d_x} j_i!$, $|\boldsymbol{j}| \equiv \sum_{i=0}^{d_x} j_i$, and $\sum_{0 \le |\boldsymbol{j}| \le q} \equiv \sum_{k=0}^{q} \sum_{j_0=0}^{k} \cdots \sum_{\substack{j_{d_x}=0 \\ j_0+j_1+\ldots+j_{d_x}=k}}^{k}$. Let $g_l \equiv (l + d_x)!/(l!d_x!)$ be the number of distinct $(d_x + 1)$-tuples $\boldsymbol{j}$ with $|\boldsymbol{j}| = l$. Let $G \equiv \sum_{l=0}^{q} g_l$. Let $\mu_h(\cdot) = \mu(\cdot/h)$, where μ is a stacking function such that $\mu_h\left(U_{i,t-2} - u\right)$ denotes a $G \times 1$ vector that stacks $\left(\left(U_{i,t-2} - u\right)/h\right)^{\boldsymbol{j}}$, $0 \le |\boldsymbol{j}| \le q$, in lexicographic order (e.g. $\mu_h(u) = (1, (u/h)')'$ when $q = 1$).

To estimate $r_y(u)$, we consider the following minimization problem:

$$\min_{\beta} \sum_{i=1}^{N} \sum_{t=3}^{T} \left[-\Delta Y_{it} - \sum_{0 \leq |\mathbf{j}| \leq q} \beta_{\mathbf{j}}' \left(\left(U_{i,t-2} - u \right) / h \right)^{\mathbf{j}} \right]^2 \times K_h \left(U_{i,t-2} - u \right) \mathbf{1} \left(U_{i,t-2} \in \mathcal{U} \right), \quad (15)$$

where $\boldsymbol{\beta}$ stacks the $\beta_{\mathbf{j}}$'s $(0 \leq |\mathbf{j}| \leq q)$ in lexicographic order, $K_h(u) = h_0^{-1} k(y/h_0) \Pi_{j=1}^{d_x} h_j^{-1} k(x_j/h_j)$ for $u \equiv (y, x')'$, k is a univariate PDF, and $h = (h_0, h_1, \ldots, h_{d_x})'$ is a bandwidth sequence that shrinks to zero as $N \to \infty$. Note that in Eq. (15) we use an indicator function $\mathbf{1}(\cdot)$ to handle the non-compact support of $U_{i,t-2}$. Like Mammen, Linton, and Nielsen (1999), Mammen, Støve, and Tjøstheim (2009) and Su and Lu (2013), our estimators only use observations in the estimation of $r_y(u)$ if the covariates $U_{i,t-2}$ lie in a compact set $\mathcal{U}$ on $\mathbb{R}^{d_x+1}$. This device greatly facilitates the asymptotic analysis of our estimator in the case of infinite support for $U_{i,t-2}$; it is not needed if $U_{i,t-2}$ is compactly supported.

Let $\hat{r}_y(u)$ denotes the first element of the solution to the above minimization problem. Then

$$\hat{r}_y(u) = -e_1' [S_{NT}(u)]^{-1} \frac{1}{n} \sum_{i=1}^{N} \sum_{t=3}^{T} \mathbf{1}_{it} K_h \left(U_{i,t-2} - u \right) \mu_h \left(U_{i,t-2} - u \right) \Delta Y_{it}$$

$$= \frac{-1}{n} \sum_{i=1}^{N} \sum_{t=3}^{T} \mathcal{K}_{it}(u) \Delta Y_{it} \quad (16)$$

where

$$S_{NT}(u) \equiv \frac{1}{n} \sum_{i=1}^{N} \sum_{t=3}^{T} \mathbf{1}_{it} K_h \left(U_{i,t-2} - u \right) \mu_h \left(U_{i,t-2} - u \right) \mu_h \left(U_{i,t-2} - u \right)', \quad (17)$$

$$\mathcal{K}_{it}(u) \equiv \mathbf{1}_{it} e_1' S_{NT}(u)^{-1} \mu_h \left(U_{i,t-2} - u \right) K_h \left(U_{i,t-2} - u \right). \quad (18)$$

$e_1 \equiv (1, 0, \ldots, 0)'$ is a $G \times 1$ vector with 1 in the first position and zeros elsewhere, and $\mathbf{1}_{it} \equiv \mathbf{1}\left(U_{i,t-2} \in \mathcal{U} \right)$. Similarly, we can estimate $\mathcal{A}m_y(u)$ by $\widehat{\mathcal{A}m}_y(u) = n^{-1} \sum_{i=1}^{N} \sum_{t=3}^{T} \mathcal{K}_{it}(u) m_y(U_{i,t-1})$.

In terms of numerical algorithm, if Eq. (10) is satisfied, it is well known that the first part of Eq. (12) implies that $m_y = (\mathcal{I} - \mathcal{A})^{-1} r_y = \sum_{j=0}^{\infty} \mathcal{A}^j r_y$. Rust (2000) discusses several methods to solve an integral equation, including both iterative and noniterative methods; see also Linton and Mammen (2005) and

Darolles, Fan, Florens, and Renault (2011) for related discussions. The iterative method relies on the observation (e.g. Theorem 2.10 in Kress, 1997) that the sequence of approximations

$$m_y^{(l)} = \mathcal{A} m_y^{(l-1)} + r_y, \quad l = 1, 2, \ldots, \tag{19}$$

is ultimately close to the truth from any starting point $m_y^{(0)}$. As in Su and Lu (2013), the initial estimator can be constructed based on the sieve IV method detailed in Section 3. If $\widehat{\mathcal{A}}$ and $\hat{r}_y$ are sufficiently close to $\mathcal{A}$ and r_y, respectively, then

$$\hat{m}_y^{(l)} = \widehat{\mathcal{A}} \hat{m}_y^{(l-1)} + \hat{r}_y, \quad l = 1, 2, \ldots \tag{20}$$

is close to m_y. The noniterative method involves solving a linear system of equations. Using the local polynomial estimates to replace the unknown conditional expectations in Eq. (12) yields

$$\hat{m}_y(u) - \frac{1}{n} \sum_{j=1}^{N} \sum_{s=3}^{T} \mathcal{K}_{js}(u)\, \hat{m}_y\left(U_{j,s-1}\right) = -\frac{1}{n} \sum_{j=1}^{N} \sum_{s=3}^{T} \mathcal{K}_{js}(u)\, \Delta Y_{js}. \tag{21}$$

Evaluating Eq. (21) at $u = U_{i,t-1}$, $i = 1, \ldots, N$, $t = 2, \ldots, T$, yields the following linear system of equations with NT_2 equations and NT_2 unknowns:

$$\hat{\mathcal{M}}_y - \mathcal{K} \hat{\mathcal{M}}_y = -\mathcal{K}\mathcal{Y}, \tag{22}$$

where $\hat{\mathcal{M}}_y \equiv \left[\hat{m}_y(U_{12}), \ldots, \hat{m}_y\left(U_{1,T-1}\right), \ldots, \hat{m}_y(U_{N2}), \ldots, \hat{m}_y\left(U_{N,T-1}\right)\right]'$, $\mathcal{Y} \equiv (\Delta Y_{13}, \ldots, \Delta Y_{1T}, \ldots, \Delta Y_{N3}, \ldots, \Delta Y_{NT})'$, $\mathcal{Z} \equiv \left[\Delta Z_{13}', \ldots, \Delta Z_{1T}', \ldots, \Delta Z_{N3}', \ldots \Delta Z_{NT}'\right]'$ and

$$\mathcal{K} \equiv \frac{1}{n} \begin{bmatrix} \mathcal{K}_{13}(U_{12}) & \ldots & \mathcal{K}_{NT}(U_{12}) \\ \vdots & \ddots & \vdots \\ \mathcal{K}_{13}\left(U_{N,T-1}\right) & \ldots & \mathcal{K}_{NT}\left(U_{N,T-1}\right) \end{bmatrix}.$$

The solution to the above linear system of equations is given by $\hat{\mathcal{M}}_y = -\left(\mathbf{I}_{NT_2} - \mathcal{K}\right)^{-} \mathcal{K}\mathcal{Y}$. Then we can obtain $\hat{m}_y(u)$ based on Eq. (21) for any $u \in \mathcal{U}$. The iterative and noniterative estimators are asymptotically equivalent. Nevertheless, the noniterative estimator involves the inversion of an $NT_2 \times NT_2$ matrix which may not be stable if NT_2 is large, say, $NT_2 \geq 1{,}000$. For further discussions, see Section 3.3 in Linton and Mammen (2005).

By the same algorithms (iterative and noniterative), we can obtain the estimate $\hat{m}_z \equiv (\hat{m}_{z_1}, \ldots, \hat{m}_{z_{d_z}})$ of $m_z \equiv (m_{z_1}, \ldots, m_{z_{d_z}})$. Then we have the $\hat{m}_\theta \equiv \hat{m}_y - \theta' \hat{m}_z$ as the estimate of $m_\theta = m_y - \theta' m_z$ for any given $\theta \in \Theta$.

2.2.2. *Semiparametric GMM estimation of* θ

Now we turn to the estimation of θ. Let $\Delta\varepsilon_{it}(\theta) = \Delta Y_{it} - \Delta Z_{it}'\theta - [m_\theta(U_{i,t-1}) - m_\theta(U_{i,t-2})]$. Then by Eq. (11),

$$\begin{aligned} \Delta\varepsilon_{it}(\theta) &= [\Delta Y_{it} - m_y(U_{i,t-1}) + m_y(U_{i,t-2})] \\ &\quad - \theta'[\Delta Z_{it} - m_z(U_{i,t-1}) + m_z(U_{i,t-2})] \\ &= \eta_{y,it} - \theta'\eta_{z,it}, \end{aligned} \tag{23}$$

where $\eta_{y,it} \equiv \Delta Y_{it} - \Delta m_{y,it}$, $\eta_{z,it} \equiv \Delta Z_{it} - \Delta m_{z,it}$, $\Delta m_{a,it} = m_{a,it} - m_{a,i,t-1}$, and $m_{a,it} \equiv m_a(U_{i,t-1})$ for $a = y$, z, and θ. Note that $\Delta\varepsilon_{it} = \Delta\varepsilon_{it}(\theta_0)$. In principle we can obtain an infeasible estimate of θ by considering the regression of $\eta_{y,it}$ on $\eta_{z,it}$. Difficulty arises because of the endogeneity issue. To see this, observe that

$$\begin{aligned} &E(\Delta\varepsilon_{it}\eta_{z,it}) \\ &= E(\varepsilon_{it}Z_{it}) + E(\varepsilon_{i,t-1}Z_{i,t-1}) - E(\varepsilon_{i,t-1}Z_{it}) + E[\varepsilon_{i,t-1}m_z(U_{i,t-1})] \\ &\quad - E(\varepsilon_{it}Z_{i,t-1}) - E[\varepsilon_{it}m_z(U_{i,t-2})] + E[\varepsilon_{i,t-1}m_z(U_{i,t-2})] \\ &\quad - E[\varepsilon_{it}m_z(U_{i,t-1})] \\ &= E(\varepsilon_{it}Z_{it}) + E(\varepsilon_{i,t-1}Z_{i,t-1}) - E(\varepsilon_{i,t-1}Z_{it}) - E(\varepsilon_{it}Z_{i,t-1}) \\ &\quad + E[\varepsilon_{i,t-1}m_z(U_{i,t-1})], \end{aligned}$$

where we use the fact that $E[\varepsilon_{it}m_z(U_{i,t-s})] = 0$ for any $s \geq 1$ under the m.d.s. condition that $E(\varepsilon_{it}|\underline{Y}_{i,t-1}, \underline{X}_{it}, \underline{V}_{it}) = 0$. Note that each of the five terms in the last expression is typically non-vanishing if Z_{it} contains endogenous regressors. Even if Z_{it} is strictly exogenous, we have $E(\Delta\varepsilon_{it}\eta_{z,it}) = E[\varepsilon_{i,t-1}m_z(U_{i,t-1})] \neq 0$ because of the dynamic nature of the model. Thus, $E(\Delta\varepsilon_{it}\eta_{z,it}) \neq 0$ in general and we need to find a $d_w \times 1$ vector W_{it} of IVs to consistently estimate θ, where $d_w \geq d_z$. We need W_{it} to be orthogonal to $\Delta\varepsilon_{it}$ and correlated with $\eta_{z,it}$. Given the m.d.s. assumption, the set of valid IVs could be very large, which is particularly true if T is large. But it seems extremely difficult to address the optimal choice of IVs here. Given the IV V_{it} for Z_{it} such that $E(V_{it}\varepsilon_{it}) = 0$ and $E(V_{it}Z_{it}') \neq 0$, in this paper we simply recommend choosing $W_{it} \equiv (V_{i,t-1}', U_{i,t-2}')'$ as the IVs for

$\eta_{z,it}$ and leave the efficient choice of IVs for future research.[3] Note that

$$E\left(\Delta\varepsilon_{it} W_{it}\right) = 0. \tag{24}$$

Let $\varsigma_{it} = (\Delta Y_{it}, \Delta Z_{it}', U_{i,t-1}', U_{i,t-2}', W_{it}')'$ and $\hat{\xi}(\cdot) = \left(\hat{m}_y(\cdot), \hat{m}_z(\cdot)\right)$. Let $\hat{\eta}_{y,it} = \Delta Y_{it} - \hat{m}_{y,it} + \hat{m}_{y,i,t-1}$ and $\hat{\eta}_{z,it} = \Delta Z_{it} - \hat{m}_{z,it} + \hat{m}_{z,i,t-1}$, where $\hat{m}_{a,it} = \hat{m}_a\left(U_{i,t-1}\right)$ for $a = y$ and z. Let $\tilde{\mathbf{1}}_{it} = \mathbf{1}\left(U_{i,t-1} \in \mathcal{U}\right) \mathbf{1}\left(U_{i,t-2} \in \mathcal{U}\right)$ and $\tilde{W}_{it} = \tilde{\mathbf{1}}_{it} W_{it}$. By Eqs. (23) and (24), we define the semiparametric GMM estimator $\hat{\theta}_{gmm}$ of θ_0 as the solution

$$\hat{\theta}_{gmm} = \arg\min_{\theta\in\Theta} \left\| Q_{NT}\left(\theta, \hat{\xi}\right) \right\|_{A_{NT}}$$

where $\|b\|_{A_{NT}} = b' A_{NT} b$ for a $d_w \times 1$ vector b, A_{NT} is a $d_w \times d_w$ matrix that is symmetric and asymptotically positive definite (p.d.), $Q_{NT}(\theta, \xi) = \frac{1}{\tilde{n}} \sum_{i=1}^{N} \sum_{t=3}^{T} q(\varsigma_{it}, \theta, \xi)$, $\xi(\cdot) = (m_y(\cdot), m_{z_1}(\cdot), \ldots, m_{z_{d_z}}(\cdot))$, $\tilde{n} = \sum_{i=1}^{N} \sum_{t=3}^{T} \tilde{\mathbf{1}}_{it}$, and

$$\begin{aligned} q\left(\varsigma_{it}, \theta, \xi\right) &= \left(\eta_{y,it} - \theta' \eta_{z,it}\right) \tilde{W}_{it} \\ &= \left\{ \left[\Delta Y_{it} - m_y\left(U_{i,t-1}\right) + m_y\left(U_{i,t-2}\right)\right] \right. \\ &\quad \left. - \theta' \left[\Delta Z_{it} - m_z\left(U_{i,t-1}\right) + m_z\left(U_{i,t-2}\right)\right] \right\} \tilde{\mathbf{1}}_{it} W_{it}. \end{aligned}$$

Note that $q(\varsigma_{it}, \theta, \hat{\xi}) = \left(\hat{\eta}_{y,it} - \theta' \hat{\eta}_{z,it}\right) \tilde{W}_{it}$ and we have restricted our attention to those observations with $U_{i,t-1} \in \mathcal{U}$ and $U_{i,t-2} \in \mathcal{U}$ in the above procedure for some technical reasons. Apparently

$$\hat{\theta}_{gmm} = \left(\hat{\boldsymbol{\eta}}_z' \tilde{\mathbf{W}} A_{NT} \tilde{\mathbf{W}}' \hat{\boldsymbol{\eta}}_z\right)^{-1} \hat{\boldsymbol{\eta}}_z' \tilde{\mathbf{W}} A_{NT} \tilde{\mathbf{W}}' \hat{\boldsymbol{\eta}}_y, \tag{25}$$

where $\tilde{\mathbf{W}} \equiv (\tilde{W}_1', \ldots, \tilde{W}_N')'$, $\tilde{W}_i \equiv (\tilde{W}_{i3}, \ldots, \tilde{W}_{iT})'$, $\hat{\boldsymbol{\eta}}_a \equiv (\hat{\eta}_{a,1}', \ldots, \hat{\eta}_{a,N}')'$, and $\hat{\eta}_{a,i} \equiv (\hat{\eta}_{a,i3}, \ldots, \hat{\eta}_{a,iT})'$ for $a = y$ and z. In case $A_{NT} = \left(\frac{1}{\tilde{n}} \tilde{\mathbf{W}}' \tilde{\mathbf{W}}\right)^{-1}$, $\hat{\theta}_{gmm}$ becomes the two-stage least squares (2SLS) estimator:

$$\hat{\theta}_{2SLS} = \left(\hat{\boldsymbol{\eta}}_z' \mathbf{P}_{\tilde{W}} \hat{\boldsymbol{\eta}}_z\right)^{-1} \hat{\boldsymbol{\eta}}_z' \mathbf{P}_{\tilde{W}} \hat{\boldsymbol{\eta}}_y, \tag{26}$$

where $\mathbf{P}_{\tilde{\mathbf{W}}} \equiv \tilde{\mathbf{W}}(\tilde{\mathbf{W}}'\tilde{\mathbf{W}})^{-1}\tilde{\mathbf{W}}'$. Let $\eta_{a,i} \equiv (\eta_{a,i3}, \ldots, \eta_{a,iT})'$, and $\boldsymbol{\eta}_a \equiv (\eta_{a,1}', \ldots, \eta_{a,N}')'$ for $a = y$ and z. Then the infeasible semiparametric GMM estimator of θ_0 is given by

$$\tilde{\theta}_{gmm} = \left(\boldsymbol{\eta}_z' \tilde{\mathbf{W}} A_{NT} \tilde{\mathbf{W}}' \boldsymbol{\eta}_z\right)^{-1} \boldsymbol{\eta}_z' \tilde{\mathbf{W}} A_{NT} \tilde{\mathbf{W}}' \boldsymbol{\eta}_y. \tag{27}$$

Under some regularity conditions, both $\hat{\theta}_{gmm}$ and $\tilde{\theta}_{gmm}$ are asymptotic normal but with different asymptotic variances.

2.2.3. *Final estimation of m (u)*

Up to now, we have suppressed the dependence of all feasible estimates ($\hat{m}_y$, $\hat{m}_z$, $\hat{\theta}_{gmm}$) on the bandwidth vector $h = (h_0, h_1, \ldots, h_{d_x})$. As we shall see, to obtain the usual $\sqrt{\bar{n}}$-consistency of $\hat{\theta}_{gmm}$, we require the use of undersmoothing bandwidth (see Assumption A.6). For the estimation of the nonparametric object $m(u)$, we still follow the literature and recommend the use of the optimal rate of bandwidth sequence. To avoid confusion, we use $b = (b_0, b_1, \ldots, b_{d_x})$ to denote such a bandwidth sequence. Accordingly, we use $\hat{m}_y^b$ and $\hat{m}_z^b$ to denote $\hat{m}_y$ and $\hat{m}_z$ when the bandwidth h is replaced by b.

Plugging the estimator $\hat{\theta}_{gmm}$ into $\hat{m}_\theta(u)$, we obtain the estimate of $m(u)$ by

$$\hat{m}^b_{\hat{\theta}_{gmm}}(u) \equiv \hat{m}^b_y(u) - \hat{m}^b_z(u)' \hat{\theta}_{gmm}$$

for any $u \in \mathcal{U}$.

Note that $m(\cdot)$ is identified only upon to a location shift in Eq. (2). Under some assumptions (A.1(i) and (ii)) in the next subsection, we have $E\left[m\left(U_{i,t-1}\right)\right] = E(Y_{it} - Z'_{it}\theta_0)$. This motivates us to recenter $\hat{m}^b_{\hat{\theta}_{gmm}}(u)$ to obtain

$$\hat{m}^b_{\hat{\theta}_{gmm}}(u) + \frac{1}{NT_1} \sum_{i=1}^{N} \sum_{t=2}^{T} \left[Y_{it} - Z'_{it}\hat{\theta}_{gmm} - \hat{m}^b_{\hat{\theta}_{gmm}}\left(U_{i,t-1}\right)\right].$$

2.3. *Asymptotic Properties of $\hat{\theta}_{IV}$ and $\hat{m}_{\hat{\theta}_{IV}}(u)$*

Let $Y_i \equiv (Y_{i1}, \ldots, Y_{iT})'$. Similarly, we define Z_i, V_i, X_i or ε_i. Recall that $\eta_{y,it} = \Delta Y_{it} - \Delta m_{y,it}$, $E\left(\eta_{y,it}|U_{i,t-2}\right) = 0$, $\eta_{z,it} = \Delta Z_{it} - \Delta m_{z,it}$ and $E\left(\eta_{z,it}|U_{i,t-2}\right) = 0$. Let $\sigma^2_{\varepsilon,t-2}(u) \equiv \mathrm{Var}(\Delta\varepsilon_{it}|U_{i,t-2} = u)$, $\sigma^2_{y,t-2}(u) \equiv \mathrm{Var}(\eta_{y,it}|U_{i,t-2} = u)$ and $\sigma^2_{z_l,t-2}(u) \equiv \mathrm{Var}(\eta_{z_l,it}|U_{i,t-2} = u)$ for $l = 1, \ldots, d_z$. Let $\bar{q} = q$ if q is odd and $q + 1$ if q is even. We make the following assumptions on $\{Y_{it}, X_{it}, Z_{it}, V_{it}, \alpha_i, \varepsilon_{it}\}$, the function of interest m, the kernel function k and the bandwidth h.

Assumptions.
A.1.

(i) $(Y_i, X_i, Z_i, V_i, \alpha_i, \varepsilon_i)$, $i = 1, \ldots, N$, *are IID.* $E(\alpha_i) = 0$.
(ii) $E\left(\varepsilon_{it}|\underline{Y}_{i,t-1}, \underline{X}_{it}, \underline{V}_{it}\right) = 0$.
(iii) The PDF $f(\cdot)$ *is uniformly bounded and bounded below from 0 on* $\mathcal{U}$.

(iv) $\left\| m_y \right\|_2 \leq C_y$, $\max_{1\leq l\leq d_z} \left\| m_{z_l} \right\|_2 \leq C_z$ *for some* C_y, $C_z < \infty$, *where* m_{z_l} *is the lth element of* m_z.

(v) $\int_{\mathcal{U}} [m(\bar{u}) - m(u)]^2 f(u) f(\bar{u}|u) d\bar{u}du > 0$ *for all* $m \in \mathcal{L}_2(f)$ *with* $m \neq 0$.

(vi) $\int_{\mathcal{U}} \int \left[\frac{f(\bar{u}|u)}{f(\bar{u})}\right]^2 f(\bar{u}) f(u) d\bar{u}du < \infty$.

(vii) $\sup_{\|m\|_2\leq 1} \sup_{u\in\mathcal{U}} \int |m(\bar{u})| f(\bar{u}|u) d\bar{u} < \infty$.

A.2.

(i) *For* $t = 3, \ldots, T$, $f_{t-2}(\cdot)$ *has all* $(\bar{q}+1)$*th partial derivatives which are uniformly continuous on* $\mathcal{U}$.

(ii) $m_y(\cdot)$ *and* $m_z(\cdot)$ *have all* $(\bar{q}+1)$*th partial derivatives which are uniformly continuous on* $\mathcal{U}$.

(iii) *For* $t = 3, \ldots, T, \sigma^2_{\varepsilon,t-2}(\cdot), \sigma^2_{y,t-2}(\cdot)$, *and* $\sigma^2_{z_l,t-2}(\cdot), l = 1, \ldots, d_z$, *have all second order partial derivatives which are uniformly continuous on* $\mathcal{U}$.

A.3. *The kernel function* $k: \mathbb{R} \to \mathbb{R}$ *is a symmetric and continuous PDF that has a compact support.*

A.4. *Let* $h! \equiv \Pi_{l=0}^{d_x} h_l$ *and* $\|h\|^2 \equiv \sum_{l=0}^{d_x} h_l^2$. *As* $N \to \infty$, T *is fixed,* $\|h\| \to 0$, $Nh!/\log N \to \infty$, $N\|h\|^{2(\bar{q}+1)} h! \to C \in [0, \infty)$.

Assumptions A.1–A.4 parallel Assumptions A.1–A.4 in Su and Lu (2013). A.1(i) rules out cross-sectional dependence among $\{X_i, Z_i, V_i, \alpha_i, \varepsilon_i\}$ but allow *non-stationarity* along the time dimension for the time series $\{Y_{it}, X_{it}, Z_{it}, V_{it}, \varepsilon_{it}\}_{t=1}^T$. The latter means that the observed data can have time-varying marginal or transition density functions. A.1(ii) imposes sequential exogeneity on (X_{it}, V_{it}). A.1(iii) requires that $f(\cdot)$ be well behaved on $\mathcal{U}$ as in typical local polynomial regressions. A.1(iv) imposes the finite second moment on $m\left(U_{i,t-1}\right)$ so that $\mathcal{L}_2(f)$ is well defined. A.1(v) imposes assumptions on the functional forms of the regression function $m(\cdot)$ and the mixture densities $f(\cdot)$ and $f(\cdot|\cdot)$. It ensures that the operator $\mathcal{I} - \mathcal{A}$ is one-to-one and Eq. (10) is satisfied. A.1(vi) implies that there is not much dependence between $U_{i,t-1}$ and $U_{i,t-2}$ under the mixture transition density $f(\cdot|\cdot)$ and it ensures that the operator $\mathcal{A}$ is Hilbert–Schmidt and a fortiori compact (see Carrasco, Florens, & Renault, 2007, for further discussions). A.1(vii) also imposes some restriction on the operator $\mathcal{A}$ and can be easily satisfied. For example, if $\int m(u)^2 f(u) du < \infty$ and $\sup_{u\in\mathcal{U}} \int f(\bar{u}|u)^2 / f(\bar{u}) d\bar{u} < \infty$, A.1(vii) holds by Cauchy–Schwarz inequality.

A.2 mainly specifies the smoothness conditions on f_{t-2}, m_y, m_z, $\sigma^2_{\varepsilon,t-2}$, $\sigma^2_{y,t-2}$, and $\sigma^2_{z_l,t-2}$. A.3 requires that the kernel k be compactly supported. This assumption can be relaxed at the cost of lengthy arguments. A.4 specifies conditions on the choice of bandwidth sequences and the local polynomial order q. Note that we shall use the fact that the bias for the qth-order local polynomial regression is of order $O(\|h\|^{q+1})$ if q is odd and $O(\|h\|^{q+2})$ if q is even when the kernel function k is symmetric. See Li and Racine (2007, pp. 90–91).

Let $Dm_{\theta,it}(u) \equiv m_\theta\left(U_{i,t-2}\right) - m_\theta(u) - \sum_{1\le|\mathbf{j}|\le q} \frac{1}{\mathbf{j}!} m_\theta^{(\mathbf{j})}(u)\left(U_{i,t-2} - u\right)^{\mathbf{j}}$. Define

$$B_{\theta,NT}(u) \equiv \frac{1}{n}\sum_{i=1}^{N}\sum_{t=3}^{T} \bar{\mathcal{K}}_{it}(u)\, Dm_{\theta,it}(u)$$

$$\text{and} \quad V_{\theta,NT}(u) \equiv \frac{1}{n}\sum_{i=1}^{N}\sum_{t=3}^{T} \bar{\mathcal{K}}_{it}(u)\, \eta_{\theta,it}, \tag{28}$$

where

$$\bar{\mathcal{K}}_{it}(u) \equiv e_1'\left[\bar{S}_{NT}(u)\right]^{-1} \mathbf{1}_{it} K_h\left(U_{i,t-2} - u\right) \mu_h\left(U_{i,t-2} - u\right), \tag{29}$$

and $\bar{S}_{NT}(u) \equiv E\left[S_{NT}(u)\right]$. Note that the non-stochastic term $\bar{S}_{NT}(u)$ is used in the definition of $V_{\theta,NT}(u)$ and $B_{\theta,NT}(u)$ to facilitate the asymptotic analysis. Analogously, define $B_{a,NT}(u)$ and $V_{a,NT}(u)$ with θ in the definitions of $B_{\theta,NT}(u)$ and $V_{\theta,NT}(u)$ being replaced by a for $a = y, z_1, \ldots, z_{d_z}$. By the standard local polynomial regression theory (e.g. Masry, 1996; Hansen, 2008), we have $\sup_{\theta\in\Theta}\sup_{u\in\mathcal{U}}\left|V_{\theta,NT}(u)\right| = O_P[(\log n)^{1/2}\ (nh!)^{-1/2}]$ and $\sup_{\theta\in\Theta}\sup_{u\in\mathcal{U}}\left|B_{\theta,NT}(u)\right| = O_P(\|h\|^{\bar{q}+1})$. Similar results hold for $B_{a,NT}(u)$ and $V_{a,NT}(u)$ with $a = y, z_1, \ldots, z_{d_z}$.

The following theorem characterizes the Bahadur-type representations of $\hat{m}_a(u)$, $a = y, z_1, \ldots, z_{d_z}$, and $\hat{m}_\theta(u)$ with a uniform control on the higher order terms that are asymptotically negligible in later study.

Theorem 1. *Suppose Assumptions A.1–A.4 hold. Then*

(i) $\sup_{u\in\mathcal{U}}\left|\hat{m}_a(u) - m_a(u) - (\mathcal{I} - \mathcal{A})^{-1} V_{a,NT}(u) - (\mathcal{I} - \mathcal{A})^{-1} B_{a,NT}(u)\right| = O_P\left(\nu_n^2\right)$ *for* $a = y, z_1, \ldots, z_{d_z}$,

(ii) $\sup_{\theta\in\Theta}\sup_{u\in\mathcal{U}}\left|\hat{m}_\theta(u) - m_\theta(u) - (\mathcal{I} - \mathcal{A})^{-1} V_{\theta,NT}(u) - (\mathcal{I} - \mathcal{A})^{-1} B_{\theta,NT}(u)\right| = O_P\left(\nu_n^2\right)$,

where $\nu_n \equiv (nh!)^{-1/2}(\log n)^{1/2} + \|h\|^{\bar{q}+1}$.

Remark 1. *The result in Theorem 1(i) is analogous to that in Theorem 2.1 in Su and Lu (2013) for the case* $a = y$. *In particular, the terms* $(\mathcal{I} - \mathcal{A})^{-1} V_{y,NT}(u)$ *and* $(\mathcal{I} - \mathcal{A})^{-1} B_{y,NT}(u)$ *signify the asymptotic variance and bias of* $\hat{m}_y(u)$, *respectively. In terms of our notation, Su and Lu (2013) show that*

$$\sup_{u\in\mathcal{U}}\left|\hat{m}_y(u)-m_y(u)-V_{y,NT}(u)-(\mathcal{I}-\mathcal{A})^{-1}B_{y,NT}(u)\right|$$
$$=O_P\left[n^{-1/2}(\log n)^{1/2}+\nu_n^2\right],$$

where the asymptotic bias term has the same structure as ours but the variance term is different from ours. Observing that $(\mathcal{I}-\mathcal{A})^{-1}=\mathcal{I}+\mathcal{A}(\mathcal{I}-\mathcal{A})^{-1}$, *the variance term in Theorem 1(i) for the case* $a=y$ *can be decomposed into two terms*

$$(\mathcal{I}-\mathcal{A})^{-1}V_{y,NT}(u)=V_{y,NT}(u)+\mathcal{A}(\mathcal{I}-\mathcal{A})^{-1}V_{y,NT}(u). \tag{30}$$

The first term $V_{y,NT}(u)$ *stands for the usual variance term for local polynomial regression that is* $O_P[(nh!)^{-1/2}]$ *for each* $u\in\mathcal{U}$ *and* $O_P[(nh!)^{-1/2}(\log n)^{1/2}]$ *uniformly in* $u\in\mathcal{U}$. *The second term* $\mathcal{A}(\mathcal{I}-\mathcal{A})^{-1}\times V_{y,NT}(u)$ *appears frequently in kernel estimation based on solving a Fredholm integral equation of the second kind (see, e.g. Linton & Mammen, 2005; Su & Lu, 2013), and it is* $O_P(n^{-1/2})$ *for each* $u\in\mathcal{U}$ *and* $O_P[n^{-1/2}(\log n)^{1/2}]$ *uniformly in* $u\in\mathcal{U}$ *(see also condition (B4b) in the proof of Theorem 1(i)). Apparently, the second term is of smaller order than the first term and has been ignored by Su and Lu (2013) in their study of kernel estimation of nonparametric dynamic panel data models. We keep the second term in Eq. (30) because it contributes to the asymptotic variance of our semiparametric GMM estimator* $\hat{\theta}_{gmm}$ *of* θ *despite the fact it does not contribute to the asymptotic variance of our nonparametric estimator* $\hat{m}_{\hat{\theta}_{gmm}}(u)$ *of* $m(u)$. *As in Su and Lu (2013), the asymptotic bias term in Theorem 1(i) reflects the fact that the bias accumulates during the iteration.*

To study the asymptotic normality of $\hat{\theta}_{gmm}$, we need to introduce more notation. Let $Q_{NT,wz}\equiv\tilde{n}^{-1}\sum_{i=1}^{N}\sum_{t=3}^{T}W_{it}\eta'_{z,it}\tilde{\mathbf{1}}_{it}$ and $Q_{wz}\equiv E\left(Q_{NT,wz}\right)$. Define the operator $\mathcal{L}(\bar{u},u)$ by

$$(\mathcal{I}-\mathcal{A})^{-1}m(u)=\int_{\mathcal{U}}\mathcal{L}(u,\bar{u})\,m(\bar{u})\,f(\bar{u})\,d\bar{u}. \tag{31}$$

Let $\bar{\mathcal{L}}(v,u)\equiv\int_{\mathcal{U}}\mathcal{L}(u,\bar{u})\mathbf{1}(v\in\mathcal{U})\,e_1'\bar{S}_{NT}(\bar{u})^{-1}\mu_h(v-\bar{u})K_h(v-\bar{u})\,d\bar{u}$. Note that $\bar{\mathcal{L}}(v,u)\equiv\int_{\mathcal{U}}\mathcal{L}(u,\bar{u})\times\mathbf{1}(v\in\mathcal{U})K_h(v-\bar{u})\,d\bar{u}$ in case $q=1$.

Let $\chi_{a,i} = (U'_{i1}, \ldots, U'_{iT}, \; W'_{i3}, \ldots, W'_{iT}, \; \eta_{a,i3}, \ldots, \eta_{a,iT})'$. For $a = y, z_1, \ldots, z_{d_z}$, define

$$\varphi_1\left(\chi_{a,i}\right) = \frac{-N(N-1)}{2n\tilde{n}} \sum_{s=3}^{T} \sum_{t=3}^{T} E_j \left[\left[\bar{\mathcal{L}}\left(U_{it}, U_{j,s-1}\right) - \bar{\mathcal{L}}\left(U_{it}, U_{j,s-2}\right) \right] \tilde{\mathbf{1}}_{js} W_{js} \right] \eta_{a,it} \tag{32}$$

where E_j denotes expectation with respect to variables indexed by j. Let $\varphi_{1,z}(\chi_{z,i}) = (\varphi_1(\chi_{z_1,i}), \ldots, \varphi_1(\chi_{z_{d_z},i}))$. Note that $\varphi_1(\chi_{y,i})$ and $\varphi_{1,z}(\chi_{z,i})$ are of dimensions $d_w \times 1$ and $d_w \times d_z$, respectively, and they reflect the estimation errors by replacing $\eta_{y,it}$ and $\eta_{z,it}$ in Eq. (23) by their respective kernel estimates $\hat{\eta}_{y,it}$ and $\hat{\eta}_{z,it}$.

We add the following assumptions.

A.5.

(i) As $N \to \infty$, $A_{NT} \xrightarrow{P} A > 0$ *and* $Q_{NT,wz} \xrightarrow{P} Q_{wz}$. Q_{wz} *has full rank* d_z.

(ii) $\max_{3 \le t \le T} E \left\| \tilde{W}_{it} \right\| < \infty$.

(iii) $\frac{1}{\sqrt{\tilde{n}}} \tilde{\mathbf{W}}' \Delta \boldsymbol{\varepsilon} + \frac{\sqrt{\tilde{n}}}{N} \sum_{i=1}^{N} [\varphi_1(\chi_{y,i}) - \varphi_{1,z}(\chi_{z,i})\theta_0] \xrightarrow{D} N(0, \Omega_0)$.

A.6. *As* $N \to \infty$, $N \|h\|^{2(\bar{q}+1)} \to 0$ *and* $N(h!)^2/(\log N)^2 \to \infty$.

A.5(i) and (ii) are standard in the GMM literature. If one chooses $A_{NT} = (\tilde{n}^{-1}\tilde{\mathbf{W}}'\tilde{\mathbf{W}})^{-1}$, we could require $Q_{NT,w} \equiv \tilde{n}^{-1} \sum_{i=1}^{N} \sum_{t=3}^{T} W_{it} W'_{it} \tilde{\mathbf{1}}_{it} \xrightarrow{P} E\left(Q_{NT,w}\right) > 0$. A.5(iii) is a high-level condition. Let $\xi_{i,N} = \sum_{t=3}^{T} \tilde{W}_{it} \boldsymbol{\Delta} \varepsilon_{it} + \left[\varphi_1\left(\chi_{y,i}\right) - \varphi_{1,z}\left(\chi_{z,i}\right)\theta_0\right]$. Under our large N and fixed T framework, one set of sufficient conditions for A.5(iii) is: (i) $\xi_{i,N}$ are independent across i with $E\left(\xi_{i,N}\right) = 0$; (ii) $E\|\xi_i\|^{2+\delta} < C$ for some $C < \infty$ and some $\delta > 0$. The zero mean restriction can be easily verified. The main complication lies in the verification of the moment conditions on $\varphi_1\left(\chi_{y,i}\right)$ and $\varphi_{1,z}\left(\chi_{z,i}\right)$, where we find it is difficult to obtain more primitive conditions. The term $[\varphi_1(\chi_{y,i}) - \varphi_{1,z}(\chi_{z,i})\theta_0]$ indicates the effect of parameter estimation error (PEE) because of the use of $\hat{\eta}_{a,it}$, $a = y$ and z, in the semiparametric estimation of θ. The first part of A.6 requires the use of an undersmoothing bandwidth for the nonparametric estimates in order to eliminate the impact of their asymptotic biases on the second-stage parametric estimates, and the second part is needed to ensure $\tilde{n}\nu_n^2 = o_P(1)$.

The following theorem establishes the asymptotic normality of $\hat{\theta}_{gmm}$.

Theorem 2. *Under Assumptions A.1–A.6, we have*

$$\sqrt{\tilde{n}}\left(\hat{\theta}_{gmm} - \theta_0\right) \xrightarrow{d} N\left(0, \left(Q'_{wz} A Q_{wz}\right)^{-1} Q'_{wz} A \Omega_0 A Q_{wz} \left(Q'_{wz} A Q_{wz}\right)^{-1}\right).$$

Remark 2. *We prove the above theorem based on the explicit formula for the semiparametric GMM estimator* $\hat{\theta}_{gmm}$ *and Theorem 1. As expected,* $\hat{\theta}_{gmm}$ *converges to* θ_0 *at the usual parametric rate* $\tilde{n}^{1/2}$ *but with the asymptotic variance different from that of its infeasible version* $\tilde{\theta}_{gmm}$ *because it is standard to show that*

$$\sqrt{\tilde{n}}\left(\tilde{\theta}_{gmm}-\theta_0\right)\xrightarrow{d}N\left(0,\left(Q_{wz}'AQ_{wz}\right)^{-1}Q_{wz}'A\Omega_0^{\dagger}AQ_{wz}\left(Q_{wz}'AQ_{wz}\right)^{-1}\right)$$

where $\Omega_0^{\dagger}\equiv\lim_{N\to\infty}\frac{1}{\tilde{n}}\mathrm{Var}(\tilde{\mathbf{W}}'\Delta\boldsymbol{\varepsilon})$. *To make inference, we need to obtain consistent estimates of* Q_{wz} *and* Ω_0. *Apparently, we can estimate* Q_{wz} *by* $Q_{NT,wz}$. *The estimation of* Ω_0 *is quite involved. We follow Chen, Linton, and Van Keilegom (2003) and Mammen, Rothe, and Schienle (2015) and recommend the use of bootstrapping for practical purpose. The procedure is standard and detailed in these papers.*

Remark 3. *Alternatively, we can establish the above result based on the literature on semiparametric estimation with nonparametrically generated covariates; see Newey (1994), Ahn (1997), Chen et al. (2003), Ichimura and Lee (2010), Kong, Linton, and Xia (2010), Hahn and Ridder (2013), Escanciano, Jacho-Chávez, and Lewbel (2014), Mammen, Rothe, and Schienle (2015), among others. Under certain conditions, these authors show that the estimator* $\hat{\theta}_{gmm}$ *exhibits the following representation:*

$$\begin{aligned}\sqrt{\tilde{n}}\left(\hat{\theta}_{gmm}-\theta_0\right) &= -\left(Q_{NT}^{\theta\prime}A_{NT}Q_{NT}^{\theta}\right)^{-1}Q_{NT}^{\theta\prime}A_{NT}\\ &\quad\times\left\{\frac{1}{\sqrt{\tilde{n}}}\sum_{i=1}^{N}\sum_{t=3}^{T}q\left(\varsigma_{it},\theta_0,\xi_0\right)+\sqrt{\tilde{n}}Q_{NT}^{\xi}[\hat{\xi}-\xi_0]\right\}\\ &\quad+O_P\left(\left\|\hat{\xi}-\xi_0\right\|_{\Xi}^{2}\right)+o_P(1). \qquad (33)\end{aligned}$$

Here, Q_{NT}^{θ} *denotes the ordinary derivative of* $Q_{NT}(\theta,\xi)$ *with respect to* θ *evaluated at the true value* (θ_0,ξ_0)*;* $Q_{NT}^{\xi}[\bar{\xi}]\equiv Q_{NT}^{\xi}(\theta_0,\xi_0)\left[\bar{\xi}\right]$ *denotes the pathwise derivative of* $Q_{NT}(\theta_0,\xi)$ *at* ξ_0 *in the direction* $\bar{\xi}$*, that is,* $Q_{NT}^{\xi}[\bar{\xi}]\equiv\lim_{\tau\to0}\left[Q_{NT}\left(\theta_0,\xi_0+\tau\bar{\xi}\right)-Q_{NT}\left(\theta_0,\xi_0\right)\right]/\tau$ *for any* $\bar{\xi}$ *such that* $\xi_0+\tau\bar{\xi}\in\Xi$ *for* $|\tau|$ *sufficiently small;* $\|\cdot\|_{\Xi}$ *denotes the pseudo-norm induced by the sup-norm on a suitable class of smooth functions* Ξ*. That is,* *for any* $\xi = (m_y, m_{z_1}, \ldots, m_{z_{d_z}}) \in \Xi$,

$$\|\xi\|_{\Xi} \equiv \sup_{u \in \mathcal{U}} \left|m_y(u)\right| + \sup_{u \in \mathcal{U}} \sum_{j=1}^{d_z} \left|m_{z_j}(u)\right|.$$

Noting that $Q_{NT}^{\theta} = -Q_{NT,wz}$ *and* $\sum_{i=1}^{N} \sum_{t=3}^{T} q(\varsigma_{it}, \theta_0, \xi_0) = \tilde{\mathbf{W}}' \Delta \boldsymbol{\varepsilon}$ *in out setup, the representation in (33) implies that* $\hat{\theta}_{gmm}$ *is* $\sqrt{\tilde{n}}$*-consistent and asymptotically normal with asymptotic variance* $\left(Q_{wz}' A Q_{wz}\right)^{-1} Q_{wz}' A \Omega_0 A Q_{wz} \left(Q_{wz}' A Q_{wz}\right)^{-1}$ *provided*

$$\left\|\hat{\xi} - \xi_0\right\|_{\Xi} = o_P\left(\tilde{n}^{-1/4}\right) \tag{34}$$

and

$$\frac{1}{\sqrt{\tilde{n}}} \tilde{\mathbf{W}}' \Delta \boldsymbol{\varepsilon} + \sqrt{\tilde{n}} Q_{NT}^{\xi} [\hat{\xi} - \xi_0] \xrightarrow{D} N(0, \Omega_0). \tag{35}$$

Verifying Eq. (34) is straightforward given the uniform convergence results in Theorem 1. To verify Eq. (35), we can readily calculate the path derivative of $Q_{NT}(\theta_0, \xi)$ *at* ξ_0 *to obtain*

$$\sqrt{\tilde{n}} Q_{NT}^{\xi} [\hat{\xi} - \xi_0] = \frac{1}{\sqrt{\tilde{n}}} \sum_{i=1}^{N} \sum_{t=1}^{T} \tilde{W}_{it} \left[\left(-\delta_{y,it} + \delta_{y,i,t-1}\right) - \left(-\delta_{z,it} + \delta_{z,i,t-1}\right)' \theta_0 \right] \tag{36}$$

where $\delta_{a,it} = \hat{m}_a\left(U_{i,t-1}\right) - m_a\left(U_{i,t-1}\right)$ *for* $a = y$ *and* z*. Under our conditions that include the use of undersmoothing bandwidth* h*, we can apply Theorem 1 and show that*

$$\sqrt{\tilde{n}} Q_{NT}^{\xi} [\hat{\xi} - \xi_0] = \frac{\sqrt{\tilde{n}}}{N} \sum_{i=1}^{N} [\varphi_1(\chi_{y,i}) - \varphi_{1,z}(\chi_{z,i})\theta_0] + o_P(1)$$

where both $\varphi_1\left(\chi_{y,i}\right)$ *and* $\varphi_{1,z}\left(\chi_{z,i}\right)$ *have zero mean and are square-integrable.*

We did not use the above arguments in our proof for two reasons. First, we have explicit formula for our semiparametric GMM estimator and their asymptotic distribution can be established by following standard asymptotic tools without resorting to the empirical process theory. Second, to apply the results in papers such as Newey (1994) and Chen et al. (2003), we have to limit our attention to a particular class of smooth functions (e.g. Ξ *is the popular nonparametric function class studied in detail in* *van der Vaart & Wellner, 1996, p. 154), and verify that the corresponding non-parametric estimates, $\hat{m}_a$, $a = y, z_1, \ldots, z_d$, also belong to this class with probability tending to one. It is well known such a verification can be extremely difficult even in applications that are involved with standard kernel estimates (e.g. local polynomial quantile regression estimates). This is indeed the case here because $\hat{m}_a$'s do not possess a closed-form expression and we are unable to verify that they belong to the same function class as their population truth. See Escanciano et al. (2014) for further discussions.*

Given the asymptotic normality result of $\hat{\theta}_{gmm}$ in the above theorem, we establish the uniform convergence and point-wise asymptotic normality of $\hat{m}^b_{\hat{\theta}_{gmm}}(u)$ in the following theorem.

Theorem 4. *Suppose Assumptions A.1–A.6 hold. Suppose that Assumption A.4 is also satisfied with h replaced by $b = (b_0, b_1, \ldots, b_{d_x})$. Then*

(i) $\sup_{u \in \mathcal{U}} \left| \hat{m}^b_{\hat{\theta}_{gmm}}(u) - m(u) \right| = O_P((nb!)^{-1/2}(\log n)^{1/2} + \|b\|^{\bar{q}+1})$;
(ii) for any $u \in$interior$(\mathcal{U})$,

$$\sqrt{nb!}\left[\hat{m}^b_{\hat{\theta}_{gmm}}(u) - m(u) - (\mathcal{I} - \mathcal{A})^{-1} B_0(u)\right]$$
$$\xrightarrow{d} N\left(0, \frac{\sigma_0^2(u)}{f(u)} e_1' \mathbb{S}^{-1} \mathbb{K} \mathbb{S}^{-1} e_1\right),$$

where $B_0(u) \equiv e_1' \mathbb{S}^{-1} \sum_{|\mathbf{j}| = \bar{q}+1} (\mathbf{j}!)^{-1} m^{(\mathbf{j})}(u) \int K(w) \mu_h(w) (w \odot b)^{\mathbf{j}} dw$, $\mathbb{S} \equiv [f(u)]^{-1} \lim_{N \to \infty} E[\bar{S}_{NT}(u)]$, $\mathbb{K} \equiv \int K(\bar{u})^2 \mu(\bar{u}) \mu(\bar{u})' d\bar{u}$, *and* $\sigma_0^2(u) = \sum_{t=3}^{T} (p_{t-2}/p) f_{t-2}(u) \sigma^2_{\varepsilon,t-2}(u)$.

Remark 4. *The above results are as expected. Since the parametric estimate $\hat{\theta}_{gmm}$ converges to θ_0 at the usual parametric rate, it has no asymptotic impact on the estimation of the nonparametric component $m(u)$. As in Su and Lu (2013), the asymptotic bias and variance formulae in Theorem 4 exhibit complicated forms because of the allowance of a general order of local polynomial regressions and the use of different bandwidths for different covariates. In the special case where $q = 1$, one can easily verify that*

$$\mathbb{S} = \begin{pmatrix} 1 & \mathbf{0}_{1 \times (d_x+1)} \\ \mathbf{0}_{(d_x+1) \times 1} & \mathbf{I}_{d_x+1} \int v^2 k(v) dv \end{pmatrix}$$

$$\text{and} \quad \mathbb{K} = \begin{pmatrix} \left[\int k(v)^2 dv\right]^{d_x+1} & \mathbf{0}_{1 \times (d_x+1)} \\ \mathbf{0}_{(d_x+1) \times 1} & \mathbf{I}_{d_x+1} \left[\int v^2 k(v)^2 dv\right]^{d_x+1} \end{pmatrix}.$$

Then the asymptotic variance simplifies to $\frac{\sigma_0^2(u)}{f(u)}[\int k(v)^2 dv]^{d_x+1}$ *and* $B_0(u) = \frac{1}{2}\sum_{l=0}^{d_x} b_l^2 \frac{\partial^2 m(u)}{\partial u_l^2} \int v^2 k(v)\, dv$.

Remark 5. *From Theorem 4, we can see that the asymptotic variance of the estimator* $\hat{m}^b_{\hat{\theta}_{gmm}}(u)$ *shares the same structure as that of a typical local polynomial estimator of either* m *in the model*

$$\Delta Y_{it} - \theta_0' \Delta Z_{it} = m\left(U_{i,t-1}\right) - m\left(U_{i,t-2}\right) + \Delta\varepsilon_{it} \tag{37}$$

by pretending the other one and the finite-dimensional parameter θ_0 *are known. Nevertheless, the asymptotic bias of* $\hat{m}^b_{\hat{\theta}_{gmm}}(u)$ *is different from the case where one of the two* m*'s and* θ_0 *are known in Eq. (37) since the operator* $(\mathcal{I} - \mathcal{A})^{-1}$ *signifies the accumulated bias. Since the error term* $\Delta\varepsilon_{it}$ *in Eq. (37) follows an MA(1) process, it is interesting to explore such an MA(1) structure and propose a more efficient estimate of* $m(u)$. *But because the process* $\{\Delta\varepsilon_{it}, t \geq 2\}$ *is not invertible, the techniques developed in Xiao et al. (2003) and Su and Ullah (2006b) are not applicable here.*

Remark 6. *Interestingly, our method can also be applied to estimate the partially linear model with both individual and time fixed effects:*

$$Y_{it} = Z_{it}'\theta_0 + m\left(Y_{i,t-1}, X_{it}\right) + \alpha_i + \omega_t + \varepsilon_{it}, \tag{38}$$

where the new term ω_t *indicates unobserved time effect. The first-differenced model now becomes*

$$\begin{aligned} \Delta Y_{it} &= \Delta Z_{it}^{\dagger\prime}\theta_0^{\dagger} + D_t'\omega + m\left(Y_{i,t-1}, X_{it}\right) - m\left(Y_{i,t-2}, X_{i,t-1}\right) + \Delta\varepsilon_{it} \\ &= \Delta Z_{it}^{\dagger\prime}\theta_0^{\dagger} + m\left(Y_{i,t-1}, X_{it}\right) - m\left(Y_{i,t-2}, X_{i,t-1}\right) + \Delta\varepsilon_{it} \end{aligned} \tag{39}$$

where $\omega = (\omega_1, \ldots, \omega_T)'$, $\theta_0^{\dagger} = (\theta_0^{\dagger\prime}, \omega')'$, $\Delta Z_{it}^{\dagger} = (\Delta Z_{it}', D_t')'$, *and* D_t *is a* $T \times 1$ *vector with* 1 *and* -1 *in its* t *and* $(t-1)$*th positions, respectively, for* $t = 2, \ldots, T$. *Then one can apply the method proposed in this section to estimate both* $m(\cdot)$ *and* $\theta_0^{\dagger}$ *jointly.*

3. SIEVE IV ESTIMATION

In this section, we consider sieve IV estimation of θ and m.

3.1. Estimation

Since $m(\cdot)$ is unknown, we propose to estimate $m(\cdot)$ and θ jointly by the method of sieves (see, e.g. Chen, 2007). To proceed, let $\{p_l(u),\ l = 1, 2, \ldots\}$ denote a sequence of known basis functions that can well approximate any square-integrable function of u. Let $L \equiv L_N$ be some integer such that $L \to \infty$ as $N \to \infty$. Let $p^L(u) \equiv (p_1(u), p_2(u), \ldots, p_L(u))'$ be the $L \times 1$ vector of basis functions. Let $p_{i,t-1} \equiv p^L(U_{i,t-1})$, $\Delta p_{i,t-1} \equiv p_{i,t-1} - p_{i,t-2}$, $\Delta p_i \equiv (\Delta p_{i2}, \ldots, \Delta p_{i,T-1})'$, and $\Delta \mathbf{p} \equiv (\Delta p_1', \Delta p_2', \ldots, \Delta p_N')'$. Obviously, we suppress the dependence of p_{it}, Δp_{it}, Δp_i and $\Delta \mathbf{p}$ on L, N, or T. In particular, Δp_i and $\Delta \mathbf{p}$ are of dimension $T_2 \times L$ and $NT_2 \times L$, respectively.

Under fairly weak conditions, we can approximate $m\left(U_{i,t-1}\right) - m\left(U_{i,t-2}\right)$ in Eq. (3) by $\beta_m' \Delta p_{i,t-1}$ for some $L \times 1$ vector β_m. This motivates us to consider the following model:

$$\Delta Y_{it} = \Delta Z_{it}' \theta_0 + \beta_m' \Delta p_{i,t-1} + \Delta \varepsilon_{it} + R_{it}, \tag{40}$$

where $R_{it} \equiv m\left(U_{i,t-1}\right) - m\left(U_{i,t-2}\right) - \beta_m' \Delta p_{i,t-1}$ signifies the sieve approximation error. Note that $\Delta p_{i,t-1}$ is correlated with $\Delta \varepsilon_{it}$ and that ΔZ_{it} may be correlated with $\Delta \varepsilon_{it}$ too unless Z_{it} is strictly exogenous. To estimate θ and β_m in the above model consistently, we run the regression of ΔY_{it} on ΔZ_{it} and $\Delta p_{i,t-1}$ by using a $d_{\bar{w}} \times 1$ vector $\bar{W}_{it}$ as the IV for $\Delta p_{i,t-1}$ and ΔZ_{it}, where $d_{\bar{w}} \geq d_z + L$. Note that a variety of measurable functions of $\underline{U}_{i,t-2}$ can serve as valid instruments for $\Delta p_{i,t-1}$. Following the lead of Anderson and Hsiao (1982), in the simulations and applications below we choose $\bar{W}_{it} \equiv (V_{i,t-1}', p_{i,t-2}')'$ when Z_{it} is endogenous and can be implemented by V_{it} and $\bar{W}_{it} \equiv \left(\Delta Z_{it}', p_{i,t-2}'\right)'$ when Z_{it} is strictly exogenous. We assume that $d_{\bar{w}} \leq cL$ for some $c > 1$.

Let $\bar{W}_i \equiv (\bar{W}_{i3}, \ldots, \bar{W}_{iT})'$, $\bar{\mathbf{W}} \equiv (\bar{W}_1', \bar{W}_2', \ldots, \bar{W}_N')'$, $\Delta Y_i \equiv (\Delta Y_{i3}, \ldots, \Delta Y_{iT})'$, and $\Delta \mathbf{Y} \equiv (\Delta Y_1', \Delta Y_2', \ldots, \Delta Y_N')'$. Similarly, define R_i and $\mathbf{R}$. Then the sieve IV/2SLS estimate of $\left(\theta', \beta_m'\right)'$ is given by[4]

$$\left(\hat{\theta}_{sieve}', \hat{\beta}_m'\right)' \equiv \left[(\Delta \mathbf{Z}, \Delta \mathbf{p})' \mathbf{P}_{\bar{\mathbf{W}}} (\Delta \mathbf{Z}, \Delta \mathbf{p})\right]^{-} (\Delta \mathbf{Z}, \Delta \mathbf{p})' \mathbf{P}_{\bar{\mathbf{W}}} \Delta \mathbf{Y}$$

where $\mathbf{P}_{\bar{\mathbf{W}}} \equiv \bar{\mathbf{W}}(\bar{\mathbf{W}}'\bar{\mathbf{W}})^{-}\bar{\mathbf{W}}'$. Let $\mathbf{Y}_w \equiv \mathbf{P}_{\bar{\mathbf{W}}} \Delta \mathbf{Y}$, $\mathbf{Z}_w \equiv \mathbf{P}_{\bar{\mathbf{W}}} \Delta \mathbf{Z}$ and $\mathbf{p}_w \equiv \mathbf{P}_{\bar{\mathbf{W}}} \Delta \mathbf{p}$. By the formula for partitioned regressions, we have

$$\hat{\beta}_m = \left(\mathbf{p}_w' \mathbf{M}_{\mathbf{Z}_w} \mathbf{p}_w\right)^{-1} \mathbf{p}_w' \mathbf{M}_{\mathbf{Z}_w} \mathbf{Y}_w \text{ and } \hat{\theta}_{sieve} = \left(\mathbf{Z}_w' \mathbf{M}_{\mathbf{p}_w} \mathbf{Z}_w\right)^{-1} \mathbf{Z}_w' \mathbf{M}_{\mathbf{p}_w} \mathbf{Y}_w.$$

Then we can estimate $m\,(u)$ by $\hat{m}_{sieve}\,(u) \equiv \hat{\beta}_m' p^L(u)$. We recenter $\hat{m}_{sieve}\,(u)$ as follows:

$$\hat{m}_{sieve}\,(u) + \frac{1}{NT_1} \sum_{i=1}^{N} \sum_{t=2}^{T} \left[Y_{it} - Z_{it}' \hat{\theta}_{sieve} - \hat{m}_{sieve} \left(U_{i,t-1} \right) \right].$$

3.2. *Asymptotic Properties of $\hat{\theta}_{sieve}$ and $\hat{m}_{sieve}$*

To apply the method of sieves, we assume that $m\,(u)$ satisfies some smoothness conditions. Let $\mathcal{X} \equiv \mathcal{Y} \times \mathcal{X}_1 \subset \mathbb{R} \times \mathbb{R}^{d_x}$ be the support of $(Y_{i,t-1}, X_{it})$. Early literature (e.g. de Jong, 2002; Newey, 1997) requires compact support implicitly or explicitly. To allow for the unboundedness of $\mathcal{X}$, we follow Chen, Hong, and Tamer (2005), Su and Jin (2012) and Lee (2014) and use a weighted sup-norm metric defined as

$$\|m\|_{\infty,\varpi} \equiv \sup_{u \in \mathcal{X}} |m\,(u)| \left[1 + \|u\|^2\right]^{-\varpi/2} \quad \text{for some } \varpi \geq 0. \tag{41}$$

If $\varpi = 0$, the norm defined in Eq. (41) is the usual sup-norm that is suitable for the case of compact support.

Recall that a typical smoothness assumption requires that a function $m : \mathcal{X} \to \mathbb{R}$ belong to a Hölder space. Let $\boldsymbol{\alpha} \equiv (\alpha_1, \ldots, \alpha_{d_x+1})'$ denote a $(d_x + 1)$-vector of non-negative integers and $|\boldsymbol{\alpha}| \equiv \sum_{l=1}^{d_x+1} \alpha_l$. For any $u = (u_1, \ldots, u_{d_x+1})$, the $|\boldsymbol{\alpha}|$th derivative of $m : \mathcal{X} \to \mathbb{R}$ is denoted as $\nabla^{\boldsymbol{\alpha}} m(u) \equiv \partial^{|\boldsymbol{\alpha}|} m(u) / (\partial u_1^{\alpha_1} \ldots \partial u_{d_x+1}^{\alpha_d})$. The Hölder space $\Lambda^\gamma(\mathcal{X})$ of order $\gamma > 0$ is a space of functions $m : \mathcal{X} \to \mathbb{R}$ such that the first $\lceil \gamma \rceil$ derivatives are bounded, and the $\lceil \gamma \rceil$th derivatives are Hölder continuous with the exponent $\gamma - \lceil \gamma \rceil \in (0, 1]$. Define the Hölder norm:

$$\|m\|_{\Lambda^\gamma} \equiv \sup_{u \in \mathcal{X}} |m\,(u)| + \max_{|\boldsymbol{\alpha}| = \lceil \gamma \rceil} \sup_{u \neq u^*} \frac{|\nabla^{\boldsymbol{\alpha}} m(u) - \nabla^{\boldsymbol{\alpha}} m(u^*)|}{\|u - u^*\|^{\gamma - \lceil \gamma \rceil}}.$$

The following definition is adopted from Chen et al. (2005).

Definition 1. *Let $\Lambda^\gamma(\mathcal{X}, \varpi) \equiv \left\{ m : \mathcal{X} \to \mathbb{R} \text{ such that } m(\cdot)[1 + ||\cdot||^2]^{-\varpi/2} \in \Lambda^\gamma(\mathcal{X}) \right\}$ denote a weighted Hölder space of functions. A weighted Hölder ball with radius c is*

$$\Lambda_c^\gamma(\mathcal{X}, \varpi) \equiv \left\{ m \in \Lambda^\gamma(\mathcal{X}, \varpi) : \left\| m(\cdot)[1 + ||\cdot||^2]^{-\varpi/2} \right\|_{\Lambda^\gamma} \leq c < \infty \right\}.$$

Function $m(\cdot)$ is said to be $H(\gamma, \varpi)$-smooth on $\mathcal{X}$ if it belongs to a weighted Hölder ball $\Lambda_c^\gamma(\mathcal{X}, \varpi)$ for some $\gamma > 0$, $c > 0$ and $\varpi \geq 0$.

To proceed, we define some additional notation. Let $Q_{NT,\bar{w}z} \equiv N^{-1}T_2^{-1}\sum_{i=1}^{N}\sum_{t=3}^{T}\bar{W}_{it}\Delta Z_{it}'$, $Q_{NT,\bar{w}} \equiv N^{-1}T_2^{-1}\sum_{i=1}^{N}\sum_{t=3}^{T}\bar{W}_{it}\bar{W}_{it}'$, and $Q_{NT,\bar{w}p} \equiv N^{-1}T_2^{-1}\sum_{i=1}^{N}\sum_{t=3}^{T}\bar{W}_{it}\Delta p_{it}'$. Let $Q_{\bar{w}z} \equiv E(Q_{NT,\bar{w}z})$, $Q_w \equiv E(Q_{NT,\bar{w}})$, and $Q_{\bar{w}p} \equiv E(Q_{NT,\bar{w}p})$. Define

$$
\begin{aligned}
Q_1 &\equiv Q_{\bar{w}z}'Q_{\bar{w}}^{-1}Q_{\bar{w}z} - Q_{\bar{w}z}'Q_{\bar{w}}^{-1}Q_{\bar{w}p}\left(Q_{\bar{w}p}'Q_{\bar{w}}^{-1}Q_{\bar{w}p}\right)^{-1}Q_{\bar{w}p}'Q_{\bar{w}}^{-1}Q_{\bar{w}z},\\
Q_2 &\equiv Q_{\bar{w}z}'Q_{\bar{w}}^{-1} - Q_{\bar{w}z}'Q_{\bar{w}}^{-1}Q_{\bar{w}p}\left(Q_{\bar{w}p}'Q_{\bar{w}}^{-1}Q_{\bar{w}p}\right)^{-1}Q_{\bar{w}p}'Q_{\bar{w}}^{-1},\\
Q_3 &\equiv Q_{\bar{w}p}'Q_{\bar{w}}^{-1}Q_{\bar{w}p} - Q_{\bar{w}p}'Q_{\bar{w}}^{-1}Q_{\bar{w}z}\left(Q_{\bar{w}z}'Q_{\bar{w}}^{-1}Q_{\bar{w}z}\right)^{-1}Q_{\bar{w}z}'Q_{\bar{w}}^{-1}Q_{\bar{w}p}, \text{ and}\\
Q_4 &\equiv Q_{\bar{w}p}'Q_{\bar{w}}^{-1} - Q_{\bar{w}p}'Q_{\bar{w}}^{-1}Q_{\bar{w}z}\left(Q_{\bar{w}z}'Q_{\bar{w}}^{-1}Q_{\bar{w}z}\right)^{-1}Q_{\bar{w}z}'Q_{\bar{w}}^{-1}.
\end{aligned}
$$

Let $Q_{pp,\alpha} \equiv \int_{u\in\mathcal{X}} p^L(u)\,p^L(u)'\,\alpha(u)\,du$ where $\alpha(u)$ is a non-negative weight function.

To establish the large sample properties of $\hat{\theta}_{sieve}$, we need the following assumptions.

A.7.

(i) $m(\cdot)$ *is* $H(\gamma,\varpi)$*-smooth on* $\mathcal{X}$ *for some* $\gamma > (d_x+1)/2$ *and* $\varpi \geq 0$.

(ii) For any $H(\gamma,\varpi)$*-smooth function* $m(u)$*, there exists a linear combination of basis functions* $\Pi_{\infty,L}m \equiv \beta_m' p^L(\cdot)$ *in the sieve space* $\mathcal{G}_L \equiv \{m(\cdot) = \alpha' p^L(\cdot)\}$ *such that* $\left\|m - \Pi_{\infty,L}m\right\|_{\infty,\varpi} = O\left(L^{-\gamma/(d_x+1)}\right)$ *for some* $\bar{\varpi} > \varpi + \gamma$.

(iii) $\operatorname{plim}_{(N,T)\to\infty}(NT_1)^{-1}\sum_{i=1}^{N}\sum_{t=2}^{T}\left(1+\|U_{i,t-1}\|^2\right)^{\bar{\varpi}}\alpha\left(U_{i,t-1}\right) < \infty$.

(iv) There are a sequence of constants $\zeta_0(L)$ *and compact sets* $\mathcal{U}_N$ *satisfying that* $\sup_{u\in\mathcal{U}_N}\|u\| = O(\zeta_0(L)^{1/\bar{\varpi}})$, $\sup_{u\in\mathcal{U}_N}\left\|p^L(u)\right\| \leq \zeta_0(L)$*, and* $\zeta_0(L)^2 L/N \to 0$ *as* $N\to\infty$.

A.8.

(i) $\sup_{2\leq t\leq T} E\|\chi_{it}\|^4 \leq C < \infty$ *for* $\chi_{it} = Z_{it}, \bar{W}_{it}$*, and* p_{it}.

(ii) $Q_{NT,\bar{w}} \xrightarrow{P} Q_{\bar{w}} > 0$, $Q_{NT,\bar{w}z} \xrightarrow{P} Q_{\bar{w}z}$*, and* $Q_{NT,\bar{w}p} \xrightarrow{P} Q_{\bar{w}p}$. $(Q_{\bar{w}z}, Q_{\bar{w}p})$ *has full rank* $d_z + L$.

(iii) $\Omega_1 \equiv Var[T_2^{-1/2}\sum_{t=3}^{T}\bar{W}_{1t}\Delta\varepsilon_{1t}] > 0$.

(iv) There exist positive constants $\underline{c}_{Q_1}, \bar{c}_{Q_1}, \underline{c}_{Q_3}$ *and* $\bar{c}_{Q_3}$ *such that* $0 < \underline{c}_{Q_l} \leq \lambda_{\min}(Q_l) \leq \bar{c}_{Q_l} < \infty$ *for* $l = 1, 3$.

(v) $\lambda_{\max}\left(Q_{pp,\alpha}\right) < \infty$.

A.9. *As* $N\to\infty$, $L^3/N \to 0, \sqrt{N}L^{-\gamma/(d_x+1)} \to 0$.

Assumptions A.7(i)–(iii) are widely assumed in the literature on sieve estimation when an infinite support is allowed; see Chen et al. (2005), Su and Jin (2012),

Lee (2014) and Su and Zhang (2015). A.7(iv) is needed to obtain the uniform convergence rate for the sieve estimate $\hat{m}_{sieve}(u)$ over a possibly divergent sequences of compact sets. A.8(i) imposes moment conditions on Z_{it}, $\bar{W}_{it}$, and p_{it}. A.8(ii) and (iii) are standard (see, e.g. Newey, 1997). A.8(iv) is a high-level assumption. A.9 imposes further restrictions on L to control the sieve approximation bias and variance.

We establish the asymptotic normality of $\hat{\theta}_{sieve}$ in the following theorem.

Theorem 7. *Suppose Assumptions A.1(i) and (ii) and A.7–A.9 hold. Then* $\sqrt{NT_2}(\hat{\theta}_{sieve} - \theta_0) \xrightarrow{d} N(0, Q_1^{-1} Q_2 \Omega_1 Q_2' Q_1^{-1})$.

Remark 7. *The above theorem gives the asymptotic distribution of* $\hat{\theta}_{sieve}$. *The sieve IV estimation uses all observations in the estimation procedure and it is easier to implement than the kernel-based semiparametric GMM estimation. Nevertheless, it seems difficult to make a theoretical comparison between the two types of estimates. We compare them only through Monte Carlo simulations.*

The following theorem reports the convergence rates and asymptotic normality of $\hat{m}_{sieve}(u)$.

Theorem 8. *Suppose Assumptions A.1(i) and (ii) and A.7–A.9 hold. Suppose* $\left\| p^L(u) \right\| \geq c > 0$. *Then*

(i) $\int \left[\hat{m}_{sieve}(u) - m(u)\right]^2 \alpha(u)\, du = O_P\left(L/N + L^{-2\gamma/(d_x+1)}\right)$,

(ii) $\frac{1}{NT_1} \sum_{i=1}^{N} \sum_{t=2}^{T} \left[\hat{m}_{sieve}(U_{i,t-1}) - m(U_{i,t-1})\right]^2 = O_P\left(L/N + L^{-2\gamma/(d_x+1)}\right)$,

(iii) $\sup_{u \in \mathcal{U}_N} \left|\hat{m}_{sieve}(u) - m(u)\right| = O_P(\zeta_0(L)(\sqrt{L/N} + L^{-\gamma/(d_x+1)}))$,

(iv) $\sqrt{NT_2} A_L(u)^{-1/2} \left[\hat{m}_{sieve}(u) - m(u)\right] \xrightarrow{d} N(0,1)$,

where $A_L(u) \equiv p^L(u)' Q_3^{-1} Q_4 \Omega_1 Q_4' Q_3^{-1} p^L(u)$.

Remark 8. *Following Newey (1997), we can also study the consistency and asymptotic normality of the plug-in estimates of linear or non-linear functionals of m. The argument is standard and we do not repeat it to save space. To improve the finite sample performance of the nonparametric estimate, we can treat* $\hat{\theta}_{sieve}$ *as the true value* θ_0 *and then apply the method in Su and Lu (2013) to re-estimate the unknown function* $m(u)$. *Given* $\hat{\theta}_{sieve}$, *we can solve the following integral equation:*

$$m(u) = \mathcal{A}m(u) + \left[r_y(u) - \hat{\theta}_{sieve}' r_z(u)\right]. \tag{42}$$

Solving the empirical integral equation gives the new local polynomial estimator $\hat{m}(u)$ *of* $m(u)$, *which can be written as* $\hat{m}^b_{\hat{\theta}_{sieve}}(u)$ *using notation defined in Section 2 when the bandwidth is chosen to be b and the same kernel function is used as before. We denote these estimators as* $\hat{m}_{s,iter}$ *and* $\hat{m}_{s,noniter}$ *when iterative and noniterative algorithms are used, respectively. It is trivial to show that both estimators have the same asymptotic distribution as* $\hat{m}^b_{\hat{\theta}_{gmm}}(u)$ *given in Theorem 4.*

Remark 9. *Once we obtain the estimators* $\hat{m}_{s,iter}$ *and* $\hat{m}_{s,noniter}$, *we can update the estimates of* θ *by treating* $\hat{m}_{s,iter}$ *or* $\hat{m}_{s,noniter}$ *as the true unknown function* m *by IV or OLS method based on the following first differenced models:*

$$\Delta Y_{it} - \left[\hat{m}_{s,iter}\left(U_{i,t-1}\right) - \hat{m}_{s,iter}\left(U_{i,t-2}\right)\right] = \Delta Z_{it}'\theta_0 + \Delta\varepsilon_{it} \tag{43}$$

or

$$\Delta Y_{it} - \left[\hat{m}_{s,noniter}\left(U_{i,t-1}\right) - \hat{m}_{s,noniter}\left(U_{i,t-2}\right)\right] = \Delta Z_{it}'\theta_0 + \Delta\varepsilon_{it}. \tag{44}$$

When Z_{it} *is endogenous, one could use the same IV as before, that is, we can use a subvector of* $\bar{W}_{it}$ *that corresponds to the IV for* ΔZ_{it}. *If* Z_{it} *is strictly exogenous, then OLS regression will yield consistent estimates of* θ. *But because* $m(\cdot)$ *can only be estimated sufficiently well on compact sets, we only use observations for which both* $U_{i,t-1}$ *and* $U_{i,t-2}$ *lie on* $\mathcal{U}$ *in the above regression. We denote these two estimates of* θ *as* $\hat{\theta}_{s,iter}$ *or* $\hat{\theta}_{s,noniter}$, *respectively. Following the proof of Theorem 2, we can readily establish their* $\sqrt{N}$*-consistency and asymptotic normality under some regularity conditions. We omit the details to save space.*

4. TESTING FOR THE LINEARITY OF THE UNKNOWN NONPARAMETRIC COMPONENT

In this section, we maintain the correct specification of the partially linear panel data model and consider testing the linearity of the nonparametric component $m(\cdot)$ in the partially linear model. The null hypothesis is

$$\mathbb{H}_0 : m\left(U_{i,t-1}\right) = \upsilon_0 + \gamma_0' U_{i,t-1} \quad \text{a.s. for some } \left(\upsilon_0, \gamma_0'\right)' \in \Upsilon \subset \mathbb{R}^{d_x+2}$$

where $i = 1, \ldots, N,\ t = 2, \ldots, T$ and Υ is a compact subset of $\mathbb{R}^{d_x+2}$. The alternative hypothesis is given by

$$\mathbb{H}_1 : \Pr\left[m\left(U_{i,t-1}\right) = \upsilon + \gamma' U_{i,t-1}\right] < 1 \quad \text{for } \forall \ \left(\upsilon, \gamma'\right)' \in \Upsilon \text{ for some } t = 2, \ldots, T.$$

There are several tests for linearity in nonparametric panel data models. Lee (2013) proposes a residual-based test to check the validity of the linear *dynamic* models with both large N and T and her test requires the consistent estimation of the generalized spectral derivatives which is impossible for fixed T. In the spirit of Härdle and Mammen (1993), Su and Lu (2013) introduce a nonparametric test for linearity in nonparametric *dynamic* panel data models by comparing two estimates, that is, the restricted estimate under $\mathbb{H}_0$ and the unrestricted estimate under $\mathbb{H}_1$ when N is large and T is fixed, and Lin, Li, and Sun (2014) propose a similar test for a linear functional form in *static* panel data models when both N and T are large. This idea is also used in Su and Zhang (2015), who propose a test for linear functional form in nonparametric *dynamic* panel data model with *interactive* fixed effects when both N and T are large. In addition, Li, Xu, and Jin (2011) propose a test for linearity of nonparametric component in a cross-sectional partially linear model and propose to obtain the p-value by using fiducial method. Nevertheless, to the best of our knowledge, there is no test for linearity of nonparametric component in partially linear dynamic panel data models with fixed effects.

Following Su and Lu (2013), we consider the smooth functional:

$$\Gamma \equiv \int_{\mathcal{U}} \left[m(u) - \upsilon_0 - u'\gamma_0\right]^2 a(u)\, f(u)\, du,$$

where $a(u)$ is a user-specified non-negative weighting function with compact support $\mathcal{U}$. Clearly, we have $\Gamma = 0$ under $\mathbb{H}_0$ and generally $\Gamma > 0$ under $\mathbb{H}_1$. This motivates us to propose a test based on Γ. Under $\mathbb{H}_0$, we estimate the following linear panel data model:

$$Y_{it} = Z'_{it}\theta_0 + \upsilon_0 + \gamma'_0 U_{i,t-1} + \alpha_i + \varepsilon_{it}$$

by applying the usual IV/GMM method to the first-differenced model. For example, if Z_{it} and X_{it} are strictly exogenous, we can follow Anderson and Hsiao (1982) or Arellano and Bond (1991) to obtain the IV/GMM estimates of θ and γ. Let $(\breve{\theta}, \breve{\gamma})$ be the IV/GMM estimate. Then we can estimate υ by $\breve{\upsilon} = \frac{1}{NT_2}\sum_{i=1}^{N}\sum_{t=3}^{T}\left(Y_{it} - Z'_{it}\breve{\theta} - U'_{i,t-1}\breve{\gamma}\right)$ under the identification restriction that $E(\alpha_i) = E(\varepsilon_{it}) = 0$. Then we have two natural test statistics

$$\Gamma_{NT,1} = \frac{1}{NT_1}\sum_{i=1}^{N}\sum_{t=2}^{T}\left[\hat{m}\left(U_{i,t-1}\right) - \breve{\upsilon} - U'_{i,t-1}\breve{\gamma}\right]^2 a\left(U_{i,t-1}\right),$$

and

$$\Gamma_{NT,2} = \frac{1}{NT_1} \sum_{i=1}^{N} \sum_{t=2}^{T} \left[\hat{\theta}' Z_{it} + \hat{m}\left(U_{i,t-1}\right) - Z_{it}' \breve{\theta} - \breve{\upsilon} - U_{i,t-1}' \breve{\gamma} \right]^2 a\left(U_{i,t-1}\right),$$

where $a(\cdot)$ is a non-negative weight function, $\hat{\theta}$ is either one of the two estimates ($\hat{\theta}_{gmm}$ and $\hat{\theta}_{\text{sieve}}$) discussed above, $\hat{m}$ is either one of the four estimates: $\hat{m}_{gmm,iter}$, $\hat{m}_{gmm,noniter}$, $\hat{m}_{s,iter}$, and $\hat{m}_{s,noniter}$. We do not recommend the use of $\hat{m}_{sieve}$ because simulations indicate that it tends to be outperformed by the other four estimates.

Note that all parametric estimates have the usual parametric convergence rate under the null hypotheses. Following the asymptotic results in Sections 2 and 3 and the analysis in Su and Lu (2013), one can easily show that $\Gamma_{NT,1}$ and $\Gamma_{NT,2}$ are asymptotically equivalent under the null, and after being suitably normalized, they share the same asymptotic normal null distribution as the corresponding test statistic Γ_{NT} in Su and Lu (2013):

$$\left(NT_1 (b!)^{1/2} \Gamma_{NT,s} - \mathbb{B}_{NT}\right) \xrightarrow{D} N\left(0, \sigma_0^2\right) \quad \text{for } s = 1, 2 \text{ under } \mathbb{H}_0,$$

where $\mathbb{B}_{NT}$ and σ_0^2 are as defined in Su and Lu (2013, eqns. (3.7) and (3.8)). Under $\mathbb{H}_0$, we can consistently estimate them by $\hat{\mathbb{B}}_{NT}$ and $\hat{\sigma}_{NT}^2$ whose formulae are also given in the latter paper. The feasible test statistics are then given by

$$J_{NT,s} \equiv \left(NT_1 (b!)^{1/2} \Gamma_{NT,s} - \hat{\mathbb{B}}_{NT}\right) \Big/ \sqrt{\hat{\sigma}_{NT}^2}, \quad s = 1, 2,$$

which are asymptotically distributed as $N(0, 1)$ under the null. Following Su and Lu (2013), one can also study the local power properties of $J_{NT,1}$ and $J_{NT,2}$ and demonstrate that they can detect local alternatives converging to the null at the usual nonparametric rate $(NT_1)^{-1/2} (b!)^{-1/4}$. The global consistency of the tests can also be established, following almost identical arguments as used in Su and Lu (2013). We omit the details to save space.

Remark 10. (***Specification test for the partially linear model***). *One might also be interested in testing for the correct specification of the partially linear model. For simplicity, assume that Z_{it} is also sequentially exogenous and $E\left(\varepsilon_{it} | Z_{it}, U_{i,t-1}, \alpha_i\right) = 0$. In this case, the null and alternative hypotheses are*

$$\mathbb{H}_0' : E\left(Y_{it} | Z_{it}, U_{i,t-1}, \alpha_i\right) = Z_{it}' \theta_0 + m_0\left(U_{i,t-1}\right) + \alpha_i$$
$$\textit{a.s. for some } \theta_0 \in \Theta \in \mathbb{R}^{d_z} \textit{ and } m_0 \in \mathcal{M},$$

and

$$\mathbb{H}_1' : Pr\left[E\left(Y_{it}|Z_{it}, U_{i,t-1}, \alpha_i\right) = Z_{it}'\theta + m\left(U_{i,t-1}\right) + \alpha_i\right] < 1$$
$$\text{for all } \theta \in \Theta \in \mathbb{R}^{d_z} \text{ and } m \in \mathcal{M}$$

where $\mathcal{M}$ is certain class of smooth functions. There are several possible ways to conduct the tests. For example, one may follow Fan and Li (1996) and construct a residual-based kernel-smooth test. For another example, one may follow Delgado and González-Manteiga (2001) and Li, Hsiao, and Zinn (2003) and consider a residual-based non-smooth test via the use of empirical process theory. Alternatively, one may consider a weighted square-distance-based test by comparing the semiparametric estimate of the regression function under the null with the purely nonparametric estimate under the alterative. Such ideas have been frequently applied in the nonparametric literature to construct specification tests for parametric or semiparametric models in either cross section or time series studies. A major problem that pertains to our panel data model is that the fixed effects α_i's cannot be consistently estimated in the case of fixed T and thus it is difficult to construct a test based on the estimated residuals. That motivates Su and Lu (2013) to take the third approach mentioned above. Apparently, this approach is also problematic if $d_z + d_x + 1$, the dimension of $(Z_{it}, U_{i,t-1})$, is high because it is then hard to estimate the nonparametric function under the alternative. Of course, other approaches to specification tests are also typically subject to the 'curse of dimensionality'. It remains an open question how to derive a practical test in this framework and we leave it for future research.

Remark 11. (***A bootstrap version of the test***). *It is well known that nonparametric tests based on their asymptotic normal null distributions may perform poorly in finite samples. As an alternative, people frequently rely on bootstrap p-values to make inference. Below, we propose a recursive bootstrap procedure to obtain the bootstrap p-values for our test. Let J_{NT} be one of $J_{NT,1}$ and $J_{NT,2}$ defined above. The procedure goes as follows:*

1. *Estimate the restricted model under $\mathbb{H}_0$ and obtain the residuals $\breve{\varepsilon}_{it} = Y_{it} - Z_{it}'\breve{\theta} - \breve{\upsilon} - \left(Y_{i,t-1}, X_{it}'\right)\breve{\gamma}$, where $\breve{\theta}$, $\breve{\upsilon}$, and $\breve{\gamma}$ are the IV or GMM estimates of θ, υ, and θ, under the null. Calculate the test statistic J_{NT} based on the original sample $\{Y_{it}, X_{it}, Z_{it}, V_{it}\}$. Let $\breve{\alpha}_i \equiv \bar{\breve{\varepsilon}}_i \equiv T^{-1}\sum_{t=1}^{T}\breve{\varepsilon}_{it}$.*
2. *Obtain the bootstrap error $\varepsilon_{it}^* = \left(\breve{\varepsilon}_{it} - \bar{\breve{\varepsilon}}_{\cdot t}\right)\epsilon_{it}$ for $i = 1, 2, \ldots, N$ and $t = 2, \ldots, T$, where $\bar{\breve{\varepsilon}}_{\cdot t} \equiv N^{-1}\sum_{i=1}^{N}\breve{\varepsilon}_{it}$ and ϵ_{it}'s are IID across both i and t and follow a two-point distribution: $\epsilon_{it} = (1 - \sqrt{5})/2$ with probability*

$(1+\sqrt{5})/2\sqrt{5}$ and $\epsilon_{it}=(\sqrt{5}+1)/2$ with probability $(\sqrt{5}-1)/2\sqrt{5}$. Generate the bootstrap analogue Y_{it}^{*} of Y_{it} as

$$Y_{it}^{*}=Z_{it}'\breve{\theta}+\breve{\upsilon}+\left(Y_{i,t-1}^{*},X_{it}'\right)\breve{\gamma}+\breve{\alpha}_i+\varepsilon_{it}^{*}$$
$$\text{for } i=1,2,\ldots,N \text{ and } t=2,\ldots,T,$$

where $Y_{i1}^{*}=Y_{i1}$.

3. *Given the bootstrap resample $\{Y_{it}^{*},X_{it},Z_{it},V_{it}\}$, estimate both the restricted (linear) and unrestricted (semiparametric) first-differenced model and calculate the bootstrap test statistic J_{NT}^{*} analogously to J_{NT}.*
4. *Repeat steps 2 and 3 for B times and index the bootstrap test statistics as $\{J_{NT,l}^{*}\}_{l=1}^{B}$. The bootstrap p-value is calculated by $p^{*}\equiv B^{-1}\sum_{l=1}^{B}\mathbf{1}(J_{NT,l}^{*}>J_{NT})$.*

Note that we impose the null hypothesis of linear dynamic panel data models in step 2. Conditional on the data, $\left(Y_{it}^{*},\varepsilon_{it}^{*}\right)$ are independently but not identically distributed (INID) across i, and ε_{it}^{*} are also independently distributed across t. So we need to resort to the CLT for second-order U-statistics with INID data (e.g. de Jong, 1987) to justify the asymptotic validity of the above bootstrap procedure. See Su and Lu (2013) for more discussions.

5. SIMULATIONS

In this section, we conduct a small set of Monte Carlo simulations to examine the finite sample performance of our proposed estimators and test statistics.

5.1. Data Generating Processes

We first consider the following three data generating processes (DGPs) where both Z_{it} and X_{it} are strictly exogenous:

DGP 1: $Y_{it}=0.5Z_{it}+0.25Y_{i,t-1}+X_{it}+\alpha_i+\varepsilon_{it}$;
DGP 2: $Y_{it}=0.5Z_{it}+\phi\left(Y_{i,t-1}\right)+X_{it}^{2}+\alpha_i+\varepsilon_{it}$;
DGP 3: $Y_{it}=0.5Z_{it}+\phi(Y_{i,t-1}-Y_{i,t-1}^{2})[1.5+\phi(X_{it})]+\alpha_i+\varepsilon_{it}$;

where $\phi(\cdot)$ is the standard normal PDF, ε_{it} are IID $N(0,1)$ across both i and t, α_i are IID $U(-1/2,1/2)$, $X_{it}=0.25\alpha_i+\varepsilon_{x,it}$ with $\{\varepsilon_{x,it}\}$ being IID $N(0,1)$ across both i and t and independent of $\{\alpha_i\}$ and $\{\varepsilon_{it}\}$, $Z_{it}=0.25\alpha_i+\varepsilon_{z,it}$ with $\{\varepsilon_{z,it}\}$ being IID $N(0,1)$ and independent of $\{\alpha_i,\varepsilon_{x,it},\varepsilon_{it}\}$. DGP 1 is a linear dynamic panel data model, whereas DGPs 2–3 specify partially linear dynamic panel data models.

The lagged-dependent variable $Y_{i,t-1}$ and regressor X_{it} enter the model additively in DGP 2 and multiplicatively in DGP 3.

Next, we consider another three DGPs with exogenous X_{it} but endogenous Z_{it}:

DGP 4: $Y_{it} = 0.5Z_{it} + 0.25Y_{i,t-1} + X_{it} + \alpha_i + \varepsilon_{it}$;
DGP 5: $Y_{it} = 0.5Z_{it} + \phi\left(Y_{i,t-1}\right) + X_{it}^2 + \alpha_i + \varepsilon_{it}$;
DGP 6: $Y_{it} = 0.5Z_{it} + \phi(Y_{i,t-1} - Y_{i,t-1}^2)\,[1.5 + \phi(X_{it})] + \alpha_i + \varepsilon_{it}$;

where the regression functions parallel those in DGPs 1–3 in order, $\{\alpha_i, X_{it}\}$ are generated in the same way as in DGPs 1–3, the endogenous regressor Z_{it} is generated according to

$$Z_{it} = 0.25\alpha_i + V_{it} + \varepsilon_{z,it},$$

$\left(\varepsilon_{it}, \varepsilon_{z,it}\right)$ are IID draws from $N\left(\begin{pmatrix}0\\0\end{pmatrix}, \begin{pmatrix}1 & 0.3\\0.3 & 1\end{pmatrix}\right)$, and V_{it} are IID $N(0,1)$ and independent of $\{\varepsilon_{it}, \varepsilon_{z,it}\}$.

Obviously, m is defined as follows: $m(y,x) = 0.25y + x$ in DGPs 1 and 4, $m(y,x) = \phi(y) + x^2$ in DGPs 2 and 5, and $m(y,x) = \phi(y - y^2)\,[1.5 + \phi(x)]$ in DGPs 3 and 6. All the six DGPs are used to evaluate the performance of our estimates and tests for the linearity of the function $m(\cdot)$. In the case of testing for the non-linearity of $m(\cdot)$, DGPs 1 and 4 are used for the size study and all the other four DGPs are for power comparisons.

5.2. *Implementation*

In the estimation, we consider the following estimates for θ and $m(\cdot)$:

1. $\hat{\theta}_{gmm,iter}$ and $\hat{m}_{gmm,iter}$: semiparametric GMM estimate of θ and local quadratic estimate of m, respectively; both are based on the local quadratic estimates of $m_y(u)$ and $m_z(u)$ via the iterative algorithm. We choose $W_{it} = (\Delta Z_{it}, U_{i,t-2}')'$ in DGPs 1–3 and $W_{it} = (V_{i,t-1}, U_{i,t-2}')'$ in DGPs 4–6.
2. $\hat{\theta}_{gmm,noniter}$ and $\hat{m}_{gmm,noniter}$: semiparametric GMM estimate of θ and local quadratic estimate of m, respectively; both are based on the local quadratic estimates of $m_y(u)$ and $m_z(u)$ via the noniterative algorithm. We choose $W_{it} = (\Delta Z_{it}, U_{i,t-2}')'$ in DGPs 1–3 and $W_{it} = (V_{i,t-1}, U_{i,t-2}')'$ in DGPs 4–6.
3. $\hat{\theta}_{sieve}$ and $\hat{m}_{sieve}$: sieve IV estimates of θ and m, respectively. We choose $\bar{W}_{it} = (\Delta Z_{it}, p_{i,t-2}')'$ in DGPs 1–3 and $\bar{W}_{it} = (V_{i,t-1}, p_{i,t-2}')'$ in DGPs 4–6.
4. $\hat{m}_{s,iter}$ and $\hat{m}_{s,noniter}$: local quadratic estimates of m by finding the empirical solution to Eq. (42) through the iterative and noniterative algorithms, respectively. See Remark 8.
5. $\hat{\theta}_{s,iter}$ and $\hat{\theta}_{s,noniter}$: IV or OLS estimates of θ by running the regression in Eqs. (43) and (44), respectively. See Remark 9 for more details.

To obtain $\hat{\theta}_{gmm,iter}$ or $\hat{\theta}_{gmm,noniter}$, we consider the semiparametric 2SLS estimates of θ by setting $A_{NT} = (\frac{1}{\tilde{n}}\tilde{\mathbf{W}}'\tilde{\mathbf{W}})^{-1}$. Note that when a local polynomial regression is called upon, we always apply the local quadratic regression so that $q=2$. For all iterative local quadratic estimates of the nonparametric components, we follow Su and Lu (2013) and choose the sieve-IV estimates as the initial estimates. For the sieve estimates, we choose the cubic B-spline as the sieve basis and include the tensor product terms to approximate the bivariate function $m(y,x)$. Along each dimension of the covariate in $m(\cdot)$, we let $L_0 = \lfloor (NT_2)^{1/4} \rfloor + 1$ and choose L_0 sieve approximating terms, where $\lfloor a \rfloor$ denotes the integer part of a.[5] For the convergence criterion in the iterative algorithms, we terminate the procedure if

$$\frac{\sum_{j=1}^{J}\left[m_a^{(l+1)}(u_j) - m_a^{(l)}(u_j)\right]^2}{\sum_{j=1}^{J}\left[m_a^{(l)}(u_j)\right]^2 + 0.0001} < 0.001, \qquad a = y,\ z_1, \ldots, z_{d_z},$$

where u_j, $j = 1, \ldots, J$, are the J evaluation points. In practice, researchers can choose the evaluation points on their own. Here we let the number of evaluation points be 625, with 25 grid points along each dimension. For each DGP, the evaluation points are fixed across replications and approximately evenly distributed between 0.2 quantile and 0.8 quantile of the data points. A similar convergence criterion is used in the literature; see Nielsen and Sperlich (2005), Henderson, Carroll, and Li (2008), Mammen et al. (2009) and Su and Lu (2013), to name just a few. In the specification test, we choose the data points on $\mathcal{U}$ as the evaluation points.

For both estimation and testing, we need to choose the kernel function and the bandwidth sequence. We use the Epanechnikov kernel $k(z) = 0.75\left(1 - z^2\right)\mathbf{1}(|z| \le 1)$ and choose the bandwidths by Silverman's 'rule of thumb': $h = 2.35 S_U (NT_2)^{-1/[2(q+2)-0.5]}$ and $b = 2.35 S_U (NT_2)^{-1/[2(q+2)+d_x+1]}$ where $d_x = 1$, $q = 2$, $S_U = (S_Y, S_X)$, and S_Y and S_X denote the sample standard deviation of $\left\{Y_{i,t-1}\right\}$ and $\{X_{it}\}$, respectively. Note that h satisfies the undersmoothing requirement, and b has the optimal rate for local quadratic regressions. Admittedly, these choices of bandwidth sequences are usually not optimal for either the estimation or the testing issue. There is a room to improve the performance of our estimates and tests by developing a data-driven rule for the selection of 'optimal' bandwidth sequences. It is well known that a bandwidth that is optimal for the estimation problem is typically not optimal for the testing problems. One has to separately consider these two issues. Given the complication of our kernel estimates, we do not address these issues in this paper and leave them for future research.

In the sieve IV estimates discussed in Section 3, we also use cubic B-spline, choose $L_0 = \lfloor (NT_2)^{1/4} \rfloor + 1$ sieve approximating terms along each dimension of the covariates in $m(\cdot)$, and include the tensor product terms in the approximation.

Also, we need to choose the compact set $\mathcal{U}$. For this, we trim out the data on the two-sided 5% tails along each dimension in $U_{i,t-1}$ or $U_{i,t-2}$. This trimming is also used for implementing our tests, in which case the weight function $a(\cdot)$ is an indicator function: it takes value 1 if $U_{i,t-1}$ lies in $\mathcal{U}$ and 0 otherwise. We only consider the testing results for $J_{NT,1}$ defined in Section 4 by comparing the semiparametric estimates of $m(\cdot)$ with its Anderson–Hsiao-type IV estimate under the linear null hypothesis. Given the poor performance of $\hat{m}_{sieve}$ in simulations, we only consider the other four estimates of $m(\cdot)$: $\hat{m}_{gmm,iter}$, $\hat{m}_{gmm,noniter}$, $\hat{m}_{s,iter}$, and $\hat{m}_{s,noniter}$, and denote the corresponding J-test statistics as $J_{gmm,iter}$, $J_{gmm,noniter}$, $J_{s,iter}$, and $J_{s,noniter}$, respectively.

For the (N, T) pair, we consider $N = 25, 50, 100$ and $T = 4, 6$. For each scenario, the number of replications is 1,000 for the estimation. For the test, we use 500 replications and 200 bootstrap resamples for the size study and 250 replications and 200 bootstrap resamples for the power study.

5.3. Estimation and Testing Results

Table 1 reports the bias (Bias) and root mean-squared error (RMSE) of various estimates of θ. We summarize the findings from Table 1. First, for all DGPs under investigation, the RMSEs decrease as either N or T increases and are roughly halved as N is quadrupled. Second, for the linear DGPs (DGPs 1 and 4), $\hat{\theta}_{s,iter}$ and $\hat{\theta}_{s,noniter}$ tend to have smaller RMSEs than $\hat{\theta}_{sieve}$, $\hat{\theta}_{gmm,iter}$, and $\hat{\theta}_{gmm,noniter}$. Third, for non-linear DGPs, $\hat{\theta}_{sieve}$ usually has the smallest RMSE but largest bias among all estimates under study, $\hat{\theta}_{s,iter}$ and $\hat{\theta}_{s,noniter}$ tend to have smaller RMSE than $\hat{\theta}_{gmm,iter}$ and $\hat{\theta}_{gmm,noniter}$ when N is small.

Table 2 presents the median and mean RMSEs for the estimates of the nonparametric component m. Clearly, we can see that both median and mean RMSEs of $\hat{m}_{sieve}$ are much larger than those of other estimates. $\hat{m}_{s,iter}$ and $\hat{m}_{s,noniter}$ can improve the original sieve IV estimate $\hat{m}_{sieve}$ significantly. As expected, $\hat{m}_{s,iter}$ and $\hat{m}_{s,noniter}$ have similar performance as $\hat{m}_{gmm,iter}$ and $\hat{m}_{gmm,noniter}$ for most DGPs. Note that in DGPs 2 and 5, both $\hat{m}_{gmm,iter}$ and $\hat{m}_{s,iter}$ have much larger median and mean RMSEs than their noniterative analogues, which may be caused by the bad convergence of the iterative algorithm. In empirical applications, both estimates based on iterative and noniterative algorithms can be reported. When there is a large difference between the two estimates, we recommend the use of the noniterative algorithm when NT_2 is not excessively large (e.g. $NT_2 < 1,000$) and that of the iterative algorithm otherwise.

Table 1. Estimation Results for θ.

			$\hat{\theta}_{gmm,iter}$		$\hat{\theta}_{gmm,noniter}$		$\hat{\theta}_{sieve}$		$\hat{\theta}_{s,iter}$		$\hat{\theta}_{s,noniter}$	
DGP	T	N	Bias	RMSE	Bias	RMSE	Bias	RMSE	Bias	RMSE	Bias	RMSE
1	4	25	−0.035	0.195	−0.033	0.195	−0.089	0.236	−0.043	0.185	−0.041	0.184
		50	−0.027	0.136	−0.026	0.137	−0.049	0.150	−0.028	0.129	−0.028	0.129
		100	−0.035	0.097	−0.035	0.097	−0.024	0.094	−0.034	0.095	−0.095	0.095
	6	25	−0.026	0.134	−0.025	0.134	−0.043	0.147	−0.029	0.128	−0.028	0.128
		50	−0.027	0.094	−0.027	0.094	−0.019	0.095	−0.027	0.090	−0.027	0.090
		100	−0.029	0.070	−0.028	0.069	−0.015	0.066	−0.027	0.067	−0.027	0.067
2	4	25	0.009	0.285	0.006	0.266	−0.071	0.239	−0.000	0.260	−0.002	0.242
		50	0.007	0.201	0.007	0.189	−0.035	0.155	0.002	0.187	0.004	0.176
		100	0.003	0.134	0.001	0.122	−0.014	0.097	0.001	0.129	0.001	0.118
	6	25	0.005	0.203	0.002	0.190	−0.027	0.154	0.003	0.188	0.000	0.177
		50	0.009	0.140	0.004	0.129	−0.001	0.098	0.007	0.132	0.005	0.123
		100	0.002	0.095	−0.003	0.088	−0.004	0.065	0.001	0.091	0.002	0.086
3	4	25	0.000	0.181	0.001	0.184	−0.099	0.234	−0.015	0.174	−0.016	0.174
		50	0.006	0.127	0.006	0.130	−0.061	0.158	0.000	0.123	−0.001	0.124
		100	0.000	0.086	0.000	0.086	−0.030	0.100	−0.001	0.085	−0.002	0.085
	6	25	0.004	0.132	0.004	0.132	−0.047	0.155	−0.001	0.127	−0.001	0.128
		50	0.003	0.088	0.002	0.088	−0.022	0.096	0.000	0.085	0.001	0.085
		100	0.000	0.061	0.001	0.061	−0.013	0.067	0.000	0.060	0.000	0.060
4	4	25	−0.075	0.297	−0.070	0.298	0.059	0.180	0.095	0.159	0.096	0.161
		50	−0.065	0.197	−0.062	0.194	0.051	0.137	0.081	0.129	0.082	0.129
		100	−0.068	0.145	−0.067	0.146	0.030	0.104	0.036	0.095	0.036	0.095
	6	25	−0.060	0.182	−0.058	0.182	0.072	0.147	0.086	0.132	0.087	0.132
		50	−0.051	0.133	−0.050	0.134	0.035	0.104	0.046	0.099	0.045	0.099
		100	−0.059	0.104	−0.058	0.103	0.019	0.073	0.017	0.071	0.018	0.072
5	4	25	0.014	0.371	0.011	0.367	0.080	0.183	0.145	0.237	0.143	0.228
		50	−0.002	0.246	0.002	0.230	0.078	0.149	0.122	0.195	0.129	0.193
		100	0.003	0.172	−0.004	0.162	0.045	0.110	0.082	0.157	0.092	0.163
	6	25	0.011	0.243	0.011	0.229	0.091	0.156	0.123	0.201	0.134	0.202
		50	0.011	0.171	0.009	0.160	0.059	0.115	0.102	0.170	0.111	0.174
		100	0.004	0.115	0.000	0.106	0.033	0.078	0.064	0.124	0.073	0.130
6	4	25	0.009	0.236	0.007	0.244	0.056	0.171	0.135	0.185	0.134	0.185
		50	0.000	0.161	0.001	0.159	0.047	0.137	0.120	0.154	0.120	0.154
		100	0.001	0.111	0.000	0.112	0.029	0.105	0.083	0.117	0.081	0.116
	6	25	0.014	0.151	0.014	0.152	0.075	0.148	0.128	0.163	0.127	0.163
		50	0.007	0.108	0.006	0.108	0.042	0.105	0.092	0.121	0.091	0.120
		100	−0.002	0.073	−0.002	0.073	0.020	0.074	0.063	0.087	0.062	0.086

Table 3 gives the empirical rejection frequency for our proposed tests. From this table, we can see that the levels behave reasonably well for DGPs 1 and 4. All the four tests are slightly undersized for DGP 1 and oversized for DGP 4. DGPs 2–3 and 5–6 examine the empirical power of our tests. The powers of all four tests are reasonably good.

Table 2. Estimation Results for m (RMSE).

			$\hat{m}_{gmm,iter}$		$\hat{m}_{gmm,noniter}$		$\hat{m}_{sieve}$		$\hat{m}_{s,iter}$		$\hat{m}_{s,noniter}$	
DGP	T	N	Median	Mean	Median	Mean	Median	Mean	Median	Mean	Median	Mean
1	4	25	0.410	0.390	0.392	0.369	0.751	0.732	0.399	0.381	0.408	0.384
		50	0.320	0.304	0.310	0.295	0.625	0.614	0.311	0.295	0.320	0.307
		100	0.250	0.241	0.246	0.236	0.444	0.437	0.245	0.235	0.253	0.241
	6	25	0.306	0.289	0.294	0.278	0.633	0.618	0.297	0.284	0.298	0.285
		50	0.243	0.233	0.235	0.224	0.441	0.439	0.236	0.227	0.239	0.229
		100	0.190	0.184	0.186	0.179	0.362	0.354	0.186	0.179	0.189	0.184
2	4	25	0.707	0.680	0.438	0.412	0.712	0.690	0.459	0.432	0.457	0.430
		50	0.621	0.602	0.324	0.311	0.611	0.590	0.353	0.336	0.341	0.320
		100	0.543	0.540	0.244	0.231	0.437	0.429	0.278	0.264	0.254	0.239
	6	25	0.594	0.581	0.320	0.305	0.608	0.597	0.344	0.329	0.323	0.305
		50	0.515	0.504	0.240	0.228	0.434	0.423	0.271	0.258	0.247	0.234
		100	0.454	0.449	0.179	0.173	0.359	0.356	0.211	0.203	0.184	0.178
3	4	25	0.381	0.364	0.377	0.351	0.703	0.679	0.378	0.356	0.380	0.358
		50	0.302	0.291	0.301	0.288	0.597	0.578	0.304	0.291	0.306	0.296
		100	0.236	0.227	0.234	0.227	0.440	0.437	0.235	0.230	0.236	0.229
	6	25	0.293	0.280	0.292	0.276	0.604	0.589	0.295	0.282	0.292	0.281
		50	0.231	0.220	0.230	0.221	0.432	0.423	0.232	0.225	0.231	0.223
		100	0.181	0.174	0.182	0.175	0.360	0.353	0.183	0.175	0.184	0.177
4	4	25	0.397	0.375	0.404	0.380	0.727	0.698	0.388	0.370	0.395	0.375
		50	0.313	0.296	0.312	0.296	0.625	0.613	0.304	0.292	0.312	0.301
		100	0.243	0.234	0.245	0.238	0.445	0.439	0.238	0.233	0.245	0.238
	6	25	0.302	0.290	0.300	0.286	0.623	0.611	0.291	0.277	0.292	0.277
		50	0.239	0.232	0.236	0.230	0.431	0.423	0.232	0.224	0.236	0.236
		100	0.190	0.183	0.189	0.181	0.365	0.360	0.185	0.177	0.188	0.181
5	4	25	0.717	0.690	0.455	0.425	0.704	0.672	0.450	0.431	0.453	0.425
		50	0.633	0.617	0.338	0.318	0.613	0.602	0.348	0.335	0.342	0.325
		100	0.544	0.536	0.254	0.242	0.441	0.427	0.278	0.268	0.259	0.246
	6	25	0.601	0.592	0.334	0.315	0.603	0.589	0.341	0.325	0.328	0.312
		50	0.523	0.518	0.248	0.238	0.424	0.415	0.268	0.256	0.250	0.239
		100	0.461	0.454	0.184	0.178	0.357	0.354	0.212	0.205	0.186	0.179
6	4	25	0.367	0.352	0.381	0.370	0.710	0.687	0.369	0.353	0.372	0.363
		50	0.288	0.276	0.295	0.290	0.622	0.595	0.292	0.280	0.294	0.281
		100	0.223	0.216	0.232	0.223	0.428	0.421	0.230	0.221	0.231	0.224
	6	25	0.287	0.270	0.296	0.281	0.616	0.606	0.292	0.272	0.288	0.270
		50	0.228	0.219	0.233	0.222	0.433	0.426	0.232	0.220	0.232	0.217
		100	0.179	0.174	0.181	0.177	0.359	0.354	0.181	0.176	0.181	0.177

Table 3. Empirical Rejection Frequency.

			$J_{s,iter}$			$J_{s,noniter}$			$J_{gmm,iter}$			$J_{gmm,noniter}$		
DGP	T	N	1%	5%	10%	1%	5%	10%	1%	5%	10%	1%	5%	10%
1	4	25	0.008	0.042	0.074	0.012	0.036	0.066	0.008	0.034	0.056	0.010	0.036	0.064
		50	0.012	0.032	0.060	0.008	0.030	0.056	0.008	0.026	0.038	0.006	0.032	0.070
		100	0.008	0.040	0.058	0.002	0.024	0.060	0.008	0.028	0.060	0.002	0.020	0.062
	6	25	0.012	0.040	0.060	0.010	0.040	0.080	0.016	0.036	0.062	0.008	0.042	0.086
		50	0.006	0.042	0.084	0.010	0.044	0.084	0.008	0.050	0.092	0.012	0.036	0.080
		100	0.010	0.058	0.088	0.014	0.046	0.086	0.014	0.036	0.086	0.018	0.036	0.078
2	4	25	0.020	0.116	0.192	0.100	0.268	0.392	0.004	0.024	0.060	0.076	0.236	0.376
		50	0.080	0.276	0.472	0.364	0.592	0.696	0.024	0.056	0.132	0.316	0.556	0.696
		100	0.380	0.676	0.792	0.804	0.932	0.980	0.064	0.192	0.312	0.804	0.952	0.980
	6	25	0.168	0.396	0.584	0.464	0.708	0.840	0.112	0.260	0.400	0.416	0.716	0.836
		50	0.376	0.712	0.848	0.932	0.992	1.000	0.308	0.542	0.692	0.900	0.992	1.000
		100	0.572	0.840	0.996	0.992	0.996	1.000	0.760	0.920	0.956	1.000	1.000	1.000
3	4	25	0.024	0.100	0.184	0.016	0.056	0.128	0.032	0.100	0.204	0.020	0.052	0.120
		50	0.104	0.212	0.300	0.052	0.160	0.268	0.104	0.232	0.316	0.048	0.164	0.244
		100	0.152	0.288	0.392	0.116	0.224	0.312	0.136	0.276	0.416	0.124	0.228	0.292
	6	25	0.080	0.200	0.296	0.052	0.168	0.288	0.088	0.220	0.336	0.028	0.144	0.264
		50	0.144	0.288	0.420	0.112	0.248	0.360	0.136	0.320	0.420	0.096	0.232	0.316
		100	0.360	0.584	0.688	0.284	0.528	0.612	0.416	0.572	0.708	0.244	0.420	0.624
4	4	25	0.032	0.070	0.130	0.026	0.066	0.116	0.034	0.070	0.136	0.028	0.078	0.120
		50	0.018	0.046	0.088	0.020	0.052	0.102	0.020	0.068	0.114	0.018	0.062	0.110
		100	0.018	0.066	0.100	0.014	0.054	0.104	0.014	0.048	0.110	0.028	0.074	0.126
	6	25	0.024	0.060	0.114	0.024	0.074	0.102	0.032	0.078	0.116	0.024	0.060	0.122
		50	0.016	0.050	0.122	0.014	0.058	0.098	0.020	0.060	0.104	0.020	0.062	0.112
		100	0.012	0.060	0.112	0.020	0.072	0.108	0.022	0.078	0.116	0.016	0.076	0.124
5	4	25	0.020	0.108	0.236	0.076	0.240	0.364	0.012	0.024	0.056	0.084	0.232	0.312
		50	0.100	0.288	0.432	0.280	0.512	0.688	0.020	0.072	0.124	0.244	0.484	0.624
		100	0.276	0.576	0.728	0.700	0.868	0.928	0.048	0.128	0.248	0.656	0.860	0.932
	6	25	0.040	0.204	0.396	0.396	0.628	0.752	0.012	0.084	0.184	0.324	0.588	0.732
		50	0.188	0.424	0.600	0.824	0.972	0.984	0.088	0.240	0.328	0.792	0.932	0.972
		100	0.544	0.856	0.904	0.980	1.000	1.000	0.268	0.532	0.724	0.984	1.000	1.000
6	4	25	0.052	0.108	0.176	0.036	0.076	0.104	0.044	0.092	0.144	0.020	0.068	0.108
		50	0.064	0.180	0.284	0.056	0.144	0.236	0.104	0.208	0.316	0.044	0.120	0.224
		100	0.148	0.292	0.472	0.096	0.220	0.328	0.156	0.304	0.424	0.112	0.216	0.340
	6	25	0.048	0.192	0.288	0.056	0.140	0.244	0.088	0.208	0.276	0.036	0.152	0.248
		50	0.196	0.380	0.496	0.132	0.344	0.448	0.196	0.400	0.536	0.116	0.260	0.420
		100	0.388	0.708	0.776	0.336	0.592	0.700	0.384	0.636	0.776	0.312	0.544	0.672

6. AN EMPIRICAL APPLICATION: THE IMPACT OF IPR PROTECTION ON ECONOMIC GROWTH

6.1. Motivation

In this section, we apply the partially linear dynamic panel data model to study the classical question of how IPR protection affects economic growth. IPRs, as the rights to use and sell knowledge and inventions, with the aim of guaranteeing adequate returns for innovators and creators, has played a central role in the long-standing debates concerning economic policy. In forming a decision on how to protect IPR, there is a typical trade-off: if IPR protection is stronger, only the owner of knowledge design will use it and the impact on economic growth will be smaller; if IPR protection is weaker, the diffusion or transfer of knowledge and technology will be accelerated and the adopters will benefit without paying adequate costs. This could cause higher economic growth, but at the same time weaken the incentive of innovation and then reduce the growth enhancement. Many theoretic growth models have discussed this topic, but the conclusions are ambiguous. Some advocate stronger IPR protection reform and the others oppose to this. For instance, Dinopoulos and Segerstrom (2010) develop an endogenous economic growth model to evaluate the effect of stronger IPR protection in developing countries, and conclude that stronger IPR protection in the South promotes innovation in the global economy and explains faster growth rate of some developing countries. In some North–South trade models, Branstetter, Fisman, and Foley (2006) and Glass and Wu (2007) support a similar view that patent reform increases the economic growth rate permanently. However, Furukawa (2007) proves that IPR cannot increase economic growth in an endogenous growth model with costless imitation, whereas Eicher and Garcia-Peñalosa (2008) show that the relationship between IPR and economic growth is ambiguous. From another side, there is also no conclusive result from a large body of empirical studies. For example, Chen and Puttitanun (2005) find a positive effect for developing countries, Park and Ginarte (1997) and Kanwar and Evenson (2003) discover a general positive effect; Groizard, Foster, and Greenaway (2009) and Falvey et al. (2009) find an ambiguous relationship. In addition, there are also some studies on the non-linear relationship between IPR protection and economic growth; see Furukawa (2007) and Panagopoulos (2009) for an inverted-U relationship, Chen and Puttitanun (2005) for a U-shape relationship between optimal IPR and economic growth for developing countries, and Falvey et al. (2009) for a nonlinear relationship which depends on other variables such as the level of development, the imitative ability and the market size of the importing country. In summary, from the theoretical or empirical point of view, there is no conclusive relationship between IPR and economic growth. Note that most of the empirical studies on this question use linear models and exclude dynamic nature. In this section, we reinvestigate this topic using our proposed partially linear dynamic panel data models that allow general nonlinearity of unknown form for the lagged-dependent variable and IPR and the usual linearity of control variables.

6.2. *Data and Variables*

The data set includes 93 countries or regions for the years 1975–2005. We examine the five-year economic growth rate. Let $\Delta \ln GDP_{it} = \ln GDP_{i,s_t} - \ln GDP_{i,s_t-5}$ denote the growth rate of country i over the tth five-year period, where GDP_{i,s_t} and GDP_{i,s_t-5} denote the real GDP per capita for country i in the end year s_t and the starting year $s_t - 5$, respectively. For example, $s_1 = 1980$ and $\Delta \ln GDP_{i1} = \ln GDP_{i,1980} - \ln GDP_{i,1975}$. We include two more sets of regressors other than the lagged growth rate ($\Delta \ln GDP_{i,t-1}$). The first set includes IPR (IPR_{it}), the variable of our main interest, measured by the updated Ginarte–Park index of patent rights (Park, 2008), which enters the model together with $\Delta \ln GDP_{i,t-1}$ nonparametrically. The second set includes linear control variables $(Z_{1,it}, \cdots, Z_{9,it}) = (FDI_{it}, FDI_{it}^2, Schooling_{it}, Invest_{it}, GonvC_{it}, Institutions_{it}, Openness_{it}, POP_{it}, INF_{it})$, where FDI_{it} denotes the inward FDI inflows as a share of GDP and FDI_{it}^2 is its squared term, $Schooling_{it}$ denotes the average of human capital measured as percentage of secondary school enrollment in total population, $Invest_{it}$ denotes the domestic investment measured by gross capital formation as a share of GDP, $GonvC_{it}$ denotes the general government final consumption expenditure as a share of GDP, $Institutions_{it}$ is a measure of market distortions, as proxied by the Fraser Institute' Index of Legal Structure and Security of Property Rights, $Openness_{it}$ is measured by imports plus exports as a share of GDP, POP_{it} is the population growth rate, and INF_{it} denotes the inflation measured by percentage change in the GDP deflator. Following the literature on economic growth, we take five-year averages of annual values for IPR_{it} and all the control variables. For the list of countries/regions and the sources of all variables, see Appendix 7. Table 4 provides summary statistics on the data set. From Table 4 we see that the five-year GDP growth rates (non-annualized) range from −53.44% to 55.93%. There is also considerable variation in the five-year average IPR with the smallest value 0 and the largest value 4.88. The summary statistics for control variables are also listed in the table.

Table 4. Descriptive Statistics (93 Countries, 1975–2005).

Variable	Mean	Median	Std. Deviation	Max	Min
GDP growth	0.0846	0.0884	0.1430	0.5593	−0.5344
IPR	2.5683	2.3850	1.1016	4.8800	0.0000
FDI	0.0183	0.0101	0.0253	0.2079	−0.0335
Domestic investment	0.2116	0.2097	0.0625	0.5182	0.0248
Schooling	0.2766	0.2545	0.1689	0.7523	0.0053
Government consumption	0.1553	0.1494	0.0572	0.4036	0.0409
Population growth rate	0.0177	0.0187	0.0111	0.0631	−0.0464
Institutions	5.4397	5.3800	2.0275	9.6200	1.1400
Openness	5.9992	6.1350	2.2893	9.7200	0.0000
Inflation	0.3942	0.0799	2.6733	48.2871	−0.0673

6.3. *Estimation Results*

We consider the following partially linear dynamic panel data model with fixed effects:

$$\begin{aligned}\Delta \ln GDP_{it} &= m\left(\Delta \ln GDP_{i,t-1}, IPR_{it}\right) + \theta_1 FDI_{it} + \theta_2 FDI_{it}^2 \\ &\quad + \theta_3 Schooling_{it} + \theta_4 Invest_{it} + \theta_5 GonvC_{it} + \theta_6 Institutions_{it} \\ &\quad + \theta_7 Openness_{it} + \theta_8 POP_{it} + \theta_9 INF_{it} + \alpha_i + \varepsilon_{it},\end{aligned}$$

$i = 1, \ldots, 93, t = 2, \ldots, 6$. For both the estimation and testing, we follow the details in Section 5.2 and consider five estimates for the parametric component, five estimates for the nonparametric component, and four test statistics to test the linearity or quadraticity of the nonparametric component. To make inferences on the estimated parameters, we also report the t-values based on bootstrap standard errors (s.e.'s) where we resample the N individual countries with replacement to form 400 bootstrap resamples. The details of implementation of our estimation and tests are the same as in the simulations.

Table 5 presents the semiparametric estimation results for the parametric part and the parametric estimation results based on Anderson–Hsiao estimator. We report five semiparametric estimates, $\hat{\theta}_{sieve}$, $\hat{\theta}_{s,iter}$ $\hat{\theta}_{s,noniter}$, $\hat{\theta}_{gmm,iter}$, and $\hat{\theta}_{gmm,noniter}$ as explained in Section 5.2. The numbers in parentheses are the t-values based on the bootstrap s.e.'s when 400 bootstrap resamples are used. We also report the linear and quadratic estimates $\hat{\theta}_{linear}$ and $\hat{\theta}_{quadratic}$ in the last two columns. Their bootstrap t-values are given in the parentheses based on 400 wild bootstrap resamples with the estimated parametric functional forms being imposed in the bootstrap world. We summarize the main findings as follows. First, we can see

Table 5. Estimation Results of the Parametric Part.

Dependent Variable: Five-Year Per Capita GDP Growth Rate							
Var.\Coeff. est.	$\hat{\theta}_{sieve}$	$\hat{\theta}_{s,iter}$	$\hat{\theta}_{s,noniter}$	$\hat{\theta}_{gmm,iter}$	$\hat{\theta}_{gmm,noniter}$	$\hat{\theta}_{linear}$	$\hat{\theta}_{quadratic}$
FDI	0.3882 (0.8692)	0.6254 (1.6878)	0.6417 (1.7245)	0.5176 (1.2643)	0.5574 (1.3236)	2.3772 (4.9943)	2.3875 (4.9363)
FDI^2	−0.5619 (−2.1829)	−0.3876 (−0.9849)	−0.4907 (−1.2886)	−0.4074 (−1.2252)	−0.4876 (−1.5242)	−7.1854 (−2.8423)	−7.3474 (−2.8347)
Schooling	0.0050 (0.0274)	−0.1367 (−0.6889)	−0.0747 (−0.4031)	−0.1245 (−0.6149)	−0.0827 (−0.4157)	0.3041 (2.2252)	0.2987 (2.2043)
Investment	0.9915 (3.3873)	0.8973 (3.5642)	0.9018 (3.4605)	0.8746 (3.1676)	0.9144 (3.3107)	1.0011 (4.3078)	1.0017 (4.2820)
GonvC	−1.0128 (−3.0822)	−1.0427 (−3.4668)	−1.0181 (−3.3812)	−1.0843 (−3.4157)	−0.9291 (−2.9157)	−0.8670 (−2.9374)	−0.8808 (−2.9478)
Institutions	0.0000 (0.0014)	0.0035 (0.4465)	0.0026 (0.3172)	0.0035 (0.4060)	0.0030 (0.3396)	0.0073 (1.1756)	0.0073 (1.1654)
Openness	0.0003 (0.0393)	−0.0044 (−0.6566)	−0.0030 (−0.4359)	−0.0060 (−0.8376)	−0.0048 (−0.6764)	0.0021 (0.3807)	0.0023 (0.4151)
Inflation	−0.0022 (−0.2752)	−0.0023 (−0.2709)	−0.0026 (−0.3078)	−0.0027 (−0.2562)	−0.0028 (−0.2811)	−0.0045 (−3.2430)	−0.0045 (−3.2569)
Population	−0.8022 (−1.5938)	−1.0487 (−1.4287)	−0.9330 (−0.9484)	−1.0934 (−1.6077)	−0.9765 (−1.4023)	−0.4786 (−0.4481)	−0.4951 (−0.4590)
Lag of growth rate	–	–	–	–	–	0.0155 (0.2411)	0.0193 (0.3000)
IPR	–	–	–	–	–	−0.0250 (−1.9342)	−0.0402 (−0.9043)
IPR^2	–	–	–	–	–	–	0.0029 (0.3793)

Note: The numbers in parentheses are the t-values based on bootstrap standard errors.

that the estimated results are quite robust among all estimating procedures but $\hat{\theta}_{sieve}$. Second, for the semiparametric estimates, only the estimated coefficients for *Investment* and *GonvC* are *significant* at the 5% significance level. Third, most control variables are not significant at the 5% level possibly due to the inclusion of the lagged-dependent variable in the model. Forth, there are large differences between parametric and semiparametric estimates for the control variables *FDI*, FDI^2, *Schooling*, *Institutions*, *Openness* and *POP*. Sixth, we find negative but insignificant effects of IPR protection on economic growth rate in both the linear and quadratic models at the 5% level. Last, we see an insignificant U-shape relationship between IPR and economic growth rate in the quadratic model, which is similar to the findings in Chen and Puttitanun (2005).

In Fig. 1, we plot the estimated surface of $m(\cdot,\cdot)$ to present the relationship between the economic growth rate and IPR and the lagged five-year growth rate as well. Apparently, as in the simulation the sieve estimate in Fig. 1(a) is quite different from the other four estimates. Fig. 1(b)–(e) clearly demonstrate the existence of a nonlinear relationship between economic growth rate and IPR protection and the lagged growth rate. In sharp contrast to the parametric estimation results, it seems that there exists a (basically) positive association between the economic growth rate and the IPR protection, which is conformable with many empirical studies and implies that the positive effects of IPR dominate its negative effects.

Fig. 2 present the estimated two-dimensional relationships between economic growth rate and its lag and IPR. Since the sieve estimate is less accurate as shown in the simulation, we only report the other four estimates for the nonparametric component. Fig. 2(a), (c) and (e) presents the relationships between economic growth rate and its lag when IPR is fixed at its 0.25, 0.5 and 0.75 sample quantiles, respectively. Specifically, they show the estimates of $m(\cdot; IPR_{0,25})$, $m(\cdot; IPR_{0,5})$, and $m(\cdot; IPR_{0,75})$, where IPR_α is the αth empirical quantile of data $\{IPR_{it}\}$. We summarize the main findings as follows. First, we can see clearly a significant non-linear relationships between economic growth rate and its lag, and the shapes of $\hat{m}(\cdot; IPR_\alpha)$, $\alpha = 0.25$, 0.5 and 0.75 are drastically different. It seems that the patterns of dynamics in economic growth rate vary with the change of the level of IPR protection. Fig. 2(b), (d) and (f) gives the estimated relationships between economic growth rate and IPR when the lagged growth rate is fixed at its 0.25, 0.5 and 0.75 sample quantiles, respectively. From this column, we first find slight non-linear relationships between economic growth rate and IPR. Second, it seems that IPR protection has a global positive impact on economic growth rate, which contradicts the findings in the parametric models. Third, for all the three estimated curves, their first-order derivatives neither monotonically decrease nor increase as IPR increases, which implies the relationships between IPR and economic growth rate is neither inverted-U-shaped nor U-shaped. Figs. 3 and 4 report the 90%

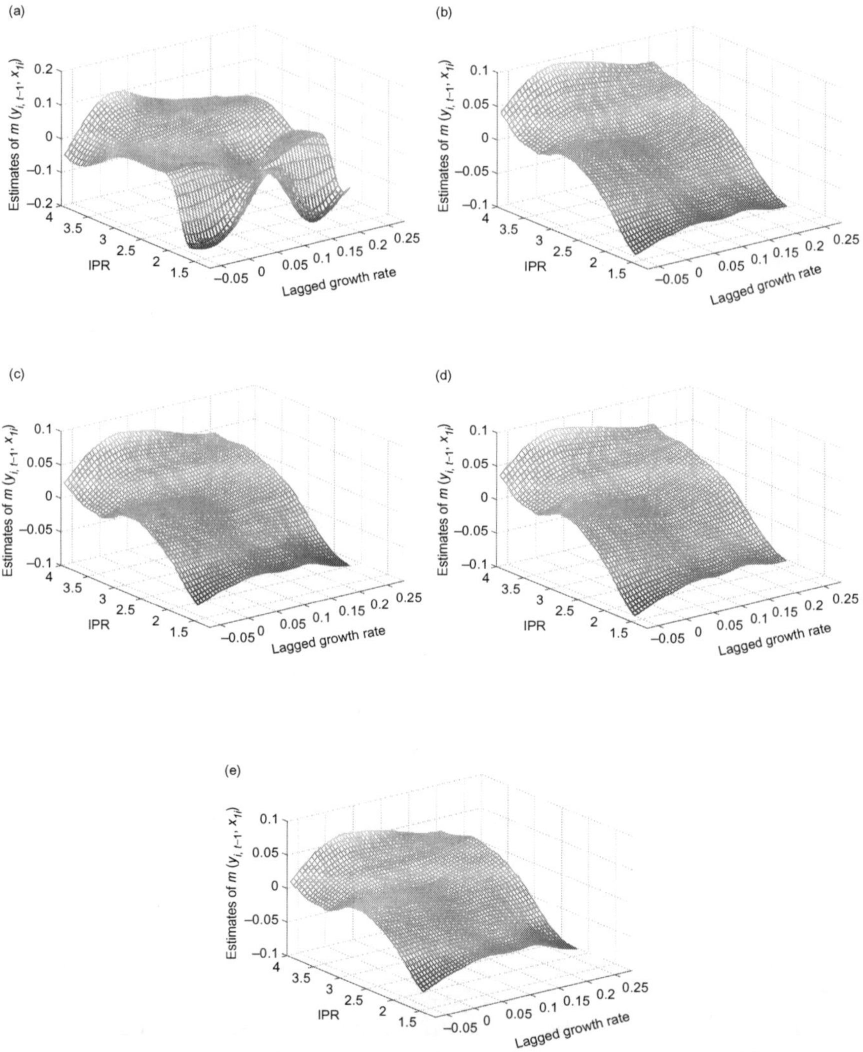

Fig. 1. 3-D Plots of Estimated Relationship between the Economic Growth Rate and the Lagged Growth Rate ($y_{i,t-1}$) and IPR (x_{it}). (a) Sieve; (b) Sieve Iterative; (c) Sieve Noniterative; (d) Semiparametric GMM Iterative; and (e) Semiparametric GMM Noniterative.

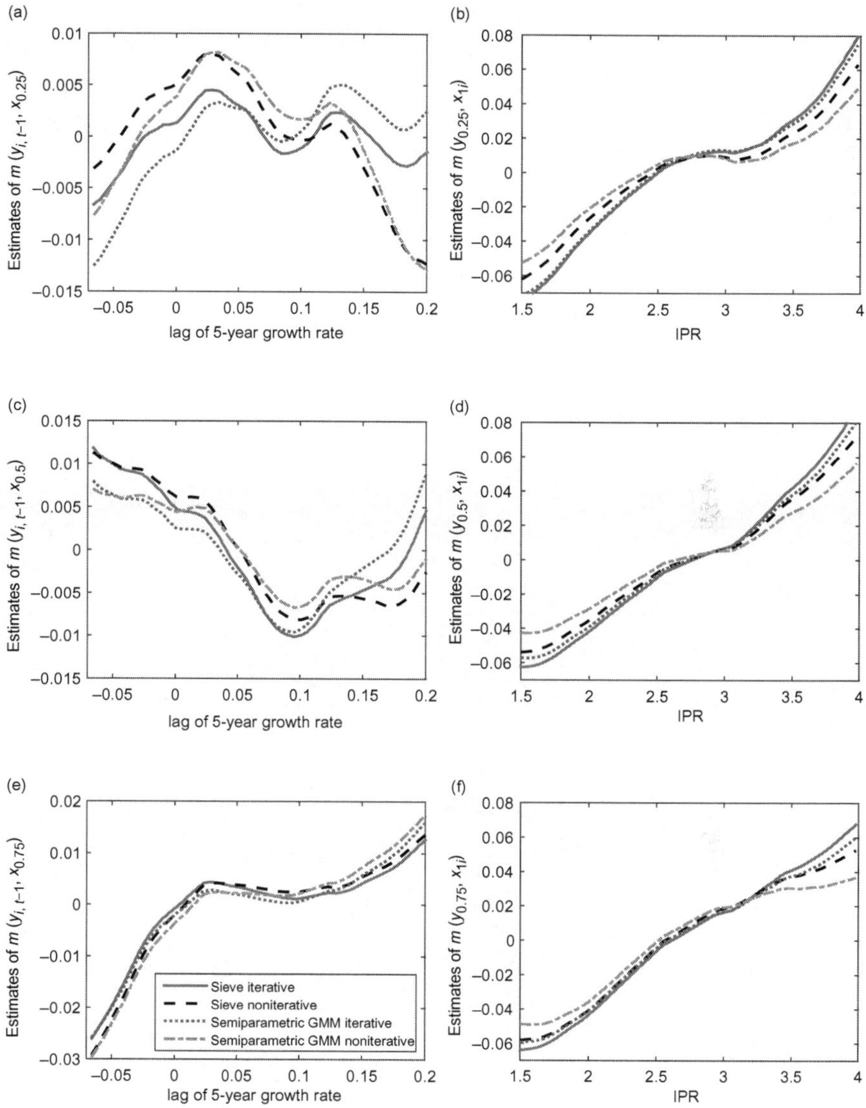

Fig. 2. 2-D Plots of Estimated Relationship between the Economic Growth Rate and the Lagged Growth Rate ($y_{i,t-1}$) and IPR (x_{it}). (a) Five-Year Growth Rate and Its Lag; (b) Five-Year Growth Rate and IPR; (c) Five-Year Growth Rate and Its Lag; (d) Five-Year Growth Rate and IPR; (e) Five-Year Growth Rate and Its Lag; and (f) Five-Year Growth Rate and IPR.

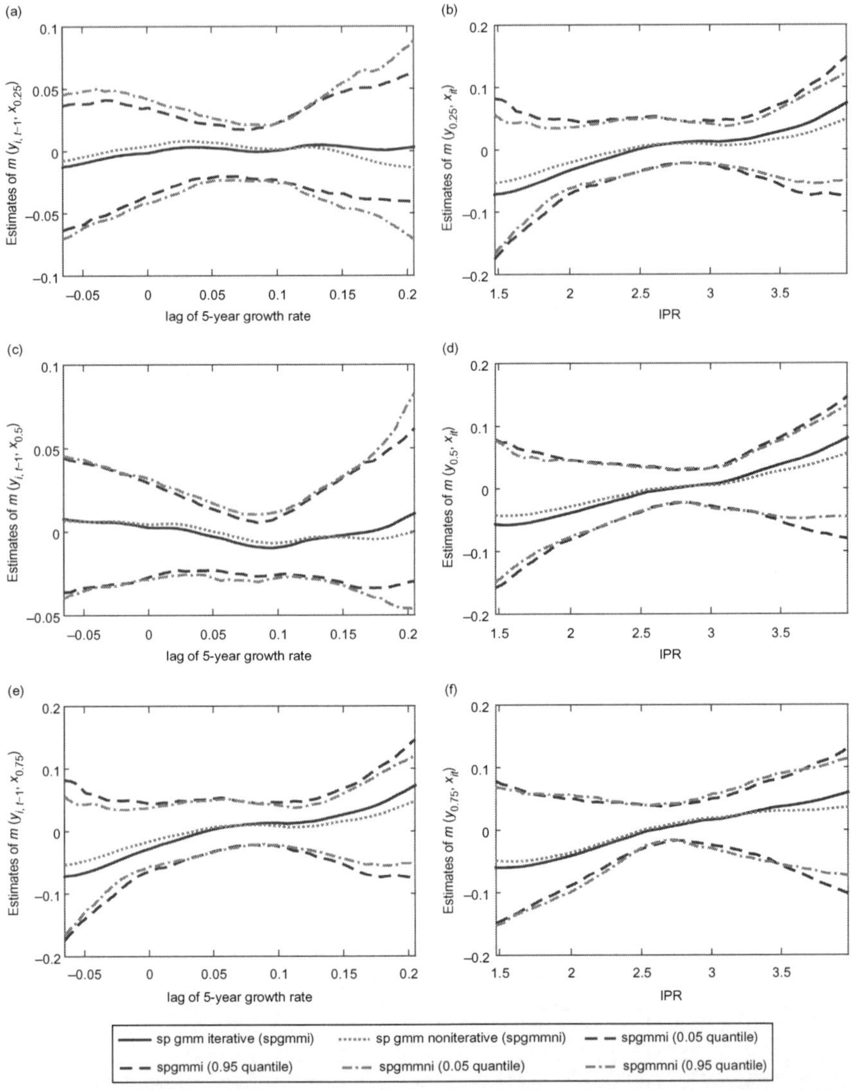

Fig. 3. Ninety Percent Confidence Bands for the Semiparametric GMM Estimates of the Nonparametric Components at Various Quantiles. (a) Five-Year Growth Rate and Its Lag; (b) Five-Year Growth Rate and IPR; (c) Five-Year Growth Rate and Its Lag; (d) Five-Year Growth Rate and IPR; (e) Five-Year Growth Rate and Its Lag; and (f) Five-Year Growth Rate and IPR.

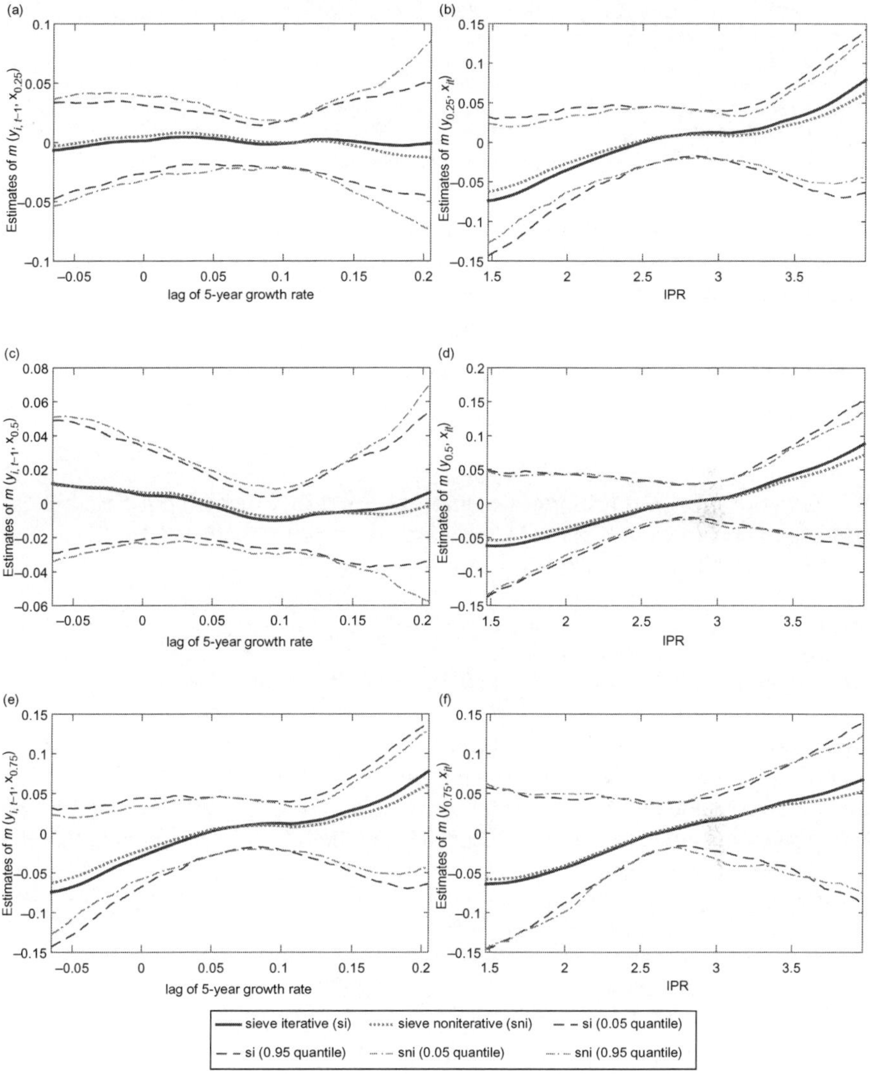

Fig. 4. Ninety Percent Confidence Bands for the Sieve Estimates of the Nonparametric Components at Various Quantiles. (a) Five-Year Growth Rate and Its Lag; (b) Five-Year Growth Rate and IPR; (c) Five-Year Growth Rate and Its Lag; (d) Five-Year Growth Rate and IPR; (e) Five-Year Growth Rate and Its Lag; and (f) Five-Year Growth Rate and IPR.

Table 6. Bootstrap p-Values Based on 2,000 Bootstrap Resamples.

Test Statistics	$J_{s,iter}$	$J_{s,noniter}$	J_{iter}	$J_{noniter}$
Linear function (H_0 vs. H_1)	0.0055	0.0075	0.0575	0.0110
Quadratic function (H_0' vs. H_1')	0.0075	0.0070	0.0560	0.0105

pointwise confidence bands for the semiparametric GMM and sieve estimates of the nonparametric component, respectively, based on 400 bootstraps. As usual, these bands seem to be wide given the fact the effective number of observations used in our estimation is given by $NT_2 = 93 \times (6 - 2) = 372$, which is not very large.

6.4. Specification Test Results

Based on our proposed testing procedure, we can test two commonly used linear and quadratic functional form specifications. The null hypotheses for linear and quadratic functional forms can be stated as follows:

$$H_0 : m\left(Y_{i,t-1}, IPR_{it}\right) = \rho Y_{i,t-1} + \theta IPR_{it} \quad \text{for some } (\rho, \theta) \in \mathbb{R}^2,$$
$$H_0' : m\left(Y_{i,t-1}, IPR_{it}\right) = \rho Y_{i,t-1} + \theta_1 IPR_{it} + \theta_2 IPR_{it}^2 \quad \text{for some } (\rho, \theta_1, \theta_2) \in \mathbb{R}^3.$$

Table 6 reports the bootstrap p-values for our test $J_{NT,1}$ for different estimation procedures based on 2,000 bootstrap resamples. We can reject either H_0 or H_0' at the 5% significance level for the $J_{s,iter}$, $J_{s,noniter}$ and $J_{noniter}$ statistics and at the 10% significance level for the J_{iter} statistic. In general, we can conclude that the nonparametric component $m(\cdot, \cdot)$ is neither linear nor quadratic in IPR at least at the 10% significance level.

7. CONCLUSION

This paper provides two types of estimates of partially linear dynamic panel models where the lagged-dependent variable enters the nonparametric component. One is based on the solutions to a class of Fredholm integral equations of the second kind and the other is based on the sieve approximation. We prove the asymptotic normality for the estimates of the parametric component and uniform consistency and asymptotic normality for the estimates of the nonparametric component. We also consider a specification test for the linearity of the nonparametric component based on the weighted squared distance between the semiparametric and parametric estimates. Monte Carlo simulations show that our estimators and tests perform reasonably well in finite samples. We illustrate our methods with an empirical application on economic growth and find a positive non-linear relationship between the IPR protection and economic growth rate.

There are several interesting topics for further research. First, we do not address the choice of optimal IVs in this paper. Since we need IVs for the estimation of both the parametric and nonparametric components, we need a separate consideration of the choice of IVs for the estimation of the nonparametric component and the parametric component. Due to the nature of our first approach, we choose the IV for the nonparametric component as $U_{i,t-2}$ in order to derive a Fredholm integral equation of the second kind. More researches are needed to consider the optimal choice of IV for nonparametric estimation despite the fact that it is only relatively well studied how to choose optimal IVs for the parametric estimation. Second, we do not allow the endogenous regressors to enter the nonparametric component to avoid the ill-posed inverse problem. It is of great interest to allow the endogenous regressors to enter the nonparametric component in the panel data framework. We leave these for future research.

ACKNOWLEDGMENTS

The authors thank the editors, three referees, Aman Ullah, and the participants at the AIE Conference in Honor of Aman Ullah for valuable comments. Su gratefully acknowledges the Singapore Ministry of Education for Academic Research Fund under Grant Number MOE2012-T2-2-021 and the funding support provided by the Lee Kong Chian Fund for Excellence. Zhang gratefully acknowledges the Renmin University of China for Academic Research Fund under Grant Number 14XNF045.

NOTES

1. When some variables in Z_{it} are exogenous, we choose themselves as their IVs.

2. The reason to introduce $\mathcal{U}$ is to handle the non-compact support of $U_{i,t-2}$. If one is willing to assume that $U_{i,t-2}$ has compact support, then one can take $\mathcal{U}$ as the support of $U_{i,t-2}$.

3. Even if Z_{it} is strictly exogenous so that $V_{it} = Z_{it}$, we still need IVs for $\eta_{z,it}$ because of the appearance of the lagged dependent variable in $m_z\left(Y_{i,t-1}, X_{it}\right)$. In this case, we can use either $\left(Z_{it}', U_{i,t-2}'\right)'$ or $\left(\Delta Z_{it}', U_{i,t-2}'\right)'$ as IVs for $\eta_{z,it}$.

4. More generally, we can consider the sieve GMM estimate defined by: $(\hat{\theta}_{sieve}', \hat{\beta}_m')' = [\,(\Delta\mathbf{Z}, \Delta\mathbf{p})'\,\bar{\mathbf{W}}\bar{A}_{NT}\bar{\mathbf{W}}'\,\,(\Delta\mathbf{Z}, \Delta\mathbf{p})\,]^{-}\,\,(\Delta\mathbf{Z},\Delta\mathbf{p})'\,\bar{\mathbf{W}}\bar{A}_{NT}\bar{\mathbf{W}}'\Delta\mathbf{Y}$, $\bar{A}_{NT}$ is a $d_{\bar{w}} \times d_{\bar{w}}$

weight matrix that is symmetric and asymptotically positive definite. The asymptotic properties are similar to the 2SLS estimator but the notation is slightly more complicated. So we decide to focus on the sieve 2SLS estimation here.

5. We also apply $L_0 = \lfloor c(NT_2)^{1/4} \rfloor + 1$ for different values of c (0.5, 1, 2) and find our iterative estimates are quite robust to the choice of c.

6. Define the operator $\mathcal{L}^{\dagger}$ by $\mathcal{A}(\mathcal{I}-\mathcal{A})^{-1} m(u) = \int_{\mathcal{U}} \mathcal{L}^{\dagger}(u, \bar{u}) m(\bar{u}) f(\bar{u}) d\bar{u}$. Strictly speaking, Linton and Mammen (2005, p. 281) show that $\mathcal{L}^{\dagger}(u, \bar{u})$ satisfies the square integrability condition. The result for $\mathcal{L}$ follows from the fact that $(\mathcal{I}-\mathcal{A})^{-1} = \mathcal{I} + \mathcal{A}(\mathcal{I}-\mathcal{A})^{-1}$ and that we restrict the integration to be done over the compact set $\mathcal{U}$.

REFERENCES

Ahn, H. (1997). Semiparametric estimation of a single-index model with nonparametrically generated regressors. *Econometric Theory, 13*, 3–31.

Ai, C., & Chen, X. (2003). Efficient estimation of models with conditional moment restrictions containing unknown functions. *Econometrica, 71*, 1795–1843.

Anderson, T. W., & Hsiao, C. (1982). Formulation and estimation of dynamic models using panel data. *Journal of Econometrics, 18*, 47–82.

Arellano, M., & Bond, S. (1991). Some tests of specification for panel data: Monte Carlo evidence and an application to employment equations. *Reviews of Economic Studies, 58*, 277–297.

Baglan, D. (2010). *Efficient estimation of a partially linear dynamic panel data model with fixed Effects: Application to unemployment dynamics in the U.S.* Working Paper, Department of Economics, Howard University.

Baltagi, B. H., & Li, D. (2002). Series estimation of partially linear panel data models with fixed effects. *Annals of Economic and Finance, 3*, 103–116.

Baltagi, B. H., & Li, Q. (2002). On instrumental variable estimation of semiparametric dynamic panel data models. *Economics Letters, 76*, 1–9.

Barro, R. J., & Lee, J. W. (2013). A new data set of educational attainment in the world, 1950–2010. *Journal of Development Economics, 104*, 184–198.

Bernstein, D. S. (2005). *Matrix mathematics: Theory, facts, and formulas with application to linear systems theory.* Princeton, NJ: Princeton University Press.

Branstetter, L. G., Fisman, R., & Foley, F. C. (2006). Do stronger intellectual property rights increase international technology transfer? Empirical evidence from US firm-level panel data? *The Quarterly Journal of Economics, 121*, 321–349.

Carrasco, M., Florens, J. P., & Renault, E. (2007). Linear inverse problems in structural econometrics estimation based on spectral decomposition and regularization. In J. J. Heckman & E. Leamer (Eds.), *Handbook of econometrics* (Vol. 6, pp. 5633–5751). Amsterdam: North Holland.

Chen, J., Gao, J., & Li, D. (2012). Semiparametric trending panel data models with cross-sectional dependence. *Journal of Econometrics, 171*, 71–85.

Chen, J., Gao, J., & Li, D. (2013a). Estimation in partially linear single-index panel data models with fixed effects. *Journal of Business & Economic Statistics, 31*, 315–330.

Chen, J., Gao, J., & Li, D. (2013b). Estimation in a single-index panel data model with heterogeneous link functions. *Econometric Reviews, 33*, 928–955.

Chen, J., Li, D., & Gao, J. (2013). *Non- and semi-parametric panel data models: A selective review.* Working Paper No. 18/13, University of York.

Chen, X. (2007). Large sample sieve estimation of semi-nonparametric models. In J. J. Heckman & E. Leamer (eds), *Handbook of econometrics* (Vol. 6, pp. 5549–5632), Amsterdam: North Holland.

Chen, X., Hong, H., & Tamer E. (2005). Measurement error models with auxiliary data. *Review of Economic Studies 72*, 343–366.

Chen, X., Linton, O., & Van Keilegom, I. (2003). Estimation of semiparametric models when the criterion function is not smooth. *Econometrica, 71*, 1591–1608.

Chen, X., & Pouzo, D. (2012). Estimation of nonparametric conditional moment models with possibly nonsmooth generalized residuals. *Econometrica, 80*, 277–321.

Chen, Y., & Puttitanun, T. (2005). Intellectual property rights and innovation in developing countries. *Journal of Development Economics, 78*, 474–493.

Darolles, S., Fan, Y., Florens, J., & Renault, E. (2011). Nonparametric instrumental regression. *Econometrica, 79*, 1541–1565.

de Jong, P. (1987). A central limit theorem for generalized quadratic forms. *Probability Theory and Related Fields, 75*, 261–277.

de Jong, R. M. (2002). A note on 'Convergence rates and asymptotic normality for series estimators': Uniform convergence rates. *Journal of Econometrics, 111*, 1–9.

Delgado, M. A., & González-Manteiga, W. (2001). Significance testing in nonparametric regression based on the bootstrap. *Annals of Statistics, 29*, 1469–1507.

Dinopoulos, E., & Segerstrom, P. (2010). Intellectual property rights, multinational firms and economic growth. *Journal of Development Economics, 92*, 13–27.

Dong, C., Gao, J., & Peng, B. (2015a). Semiparametric single-index panel data models with cross-sectional dependence. *Journal of Econometrics, 188*(1), 301–312.

Dong, C., Gao, J., & Peng, B. (2015b). *Partially linear panel data models with cross-sectional dependence and nonstationarity*. Working Paper No. 07/15, Monash University.

Eicher, T., & Garcia-Peñalosa, C. (2008). Endogenous strength of intellectual property rights: Implications for economic development and growth. *European Economic Review, 52*, 237–258.

Engle, R. F., Granger, C., Rice, J., & Weiss, A. (1986). Semiparametric estimates of the relation between weather and electricity sales. *Journal of the American Statistical Association, 81*, 310–320.

Escanciano, J., Jacho-Chávez, D., & Lewbel, A. (2014). Uniform convergence of weighted sums of non and semiparametric residuals for estimation and testing. *Journal of Econometrics, 178*, 426–473.

Falvey, R., Foster, N., & Greenaway, D. (2009). Trade, imitative ability and intellectual property rights. *Review World Economics, 145*, 373–404.

Fan, Y., & Li, Q. (1996). Consistent model specification tests: Omitted variables and semiparametric functional forms. *Econometrica, 64*, 865–890.

Feng, G., Gao, J., Peng, B., & Zheng, X. (2015). *A varying coefficient panel data model with fixed effects: Theory and an application to the US commercial banks*. Working Paper No. 09/15, Monash University.

Florens, J. P., Johannes, J., & Van Bellegem, S. (2012). Instrumental regression in partially linear models. *The Econometrics Journal, 15*, 304–324.

Furukawa, Y. (2007). The protection of intellectual property rights and endogenous growth: Is stronger always better? *Journal of Economic Dynamic & Control, 31*, 3644–3670.

Gao, J., Lu, Z., & Tjøstheim, D. (2006). Estimation in semiparametric spatial regression. *Annals of Statistics, 34*, 1395–1435.

Glass, A. J., & Wu, X. (2007). Intellectual property rights and quality improvement. *Journal of Development Economics, 82*, 393–415.

Groizard, J. L. (2009). Technology trade. *Journal of Development Studies, 45*, 1526–1544.

Gwartney, J., Hall, D., Joshua, C., & Lawson, R. (2010). 2010 economic freedom dataset. *Economic Freedom Network.*

Hahn, J., & Ridder, G. (2013). Asymptotic variance for semiparametric estimators with generated regressors. *Econometrica, 81*, 315–340.

Hansen, B. E. (2008). Uniform convergence rates for kernel estimation with dependent data. *Econometric Theory, 24*, 726–748.

Härdle, W., & Mammen, E. (1993). Comparing nonparametric versus parametric regression fits. *Annals of Statistics, 21*, 1926–1947.

Henderson, D. J., Carroll, R. J., & Li, Q. (2008). Nonparametric estimation and testing of fixed effects panel data models. *Journal of Econometrics, 144*, 257–275.

Ichimura, H., & Lee, S. (2010). Characterization of the asymptotic distribution of semiparametric M-estimators. *Journal of Econometrics, 159*, 252–266.

Kanwar, S., & Evenson, R. (2003). Does intellectual property protection spur technological change? *Oxford Economic Papers, 55*, 235–285.

Kong, E., Linton, O., & Xia, Y. (2010). Uniform Bahadur representation for local polynomial estimates of M-regression and its application to the additive model. *Econometric Theory, 26*, 1529–1564.

Kress, R. (1997). *Linear integral equation*. New York, NY: Springer.

Lee, A. J. (1990). *U-statistics: Theory and practice*. New York, NY: Marcel Dekker.

Lee, Y. (2014). Nonparametric estimation of dynamic panel models with fixed effects. *Econometric Theory, 30*, 1315–1347.

Lee, Y.-J. (2013). Testing a linear dynamic panel data model against nonlinear alternatives. *Journal of Econometrics, 178*, 146–166.

Li, Q., Hsiao, C., & Zinn, J. (2003). Consistent specification tests for semiparametric/nonparametric models based on series estimation methods. *Journal of Econometrics, 112*, 295–325.

Li, Q., & Racine, J. (2007). *Nonparametric econometrics: Theory and practice*. Princeton, NJ: Princeton University Press.

Li, Q., & Stengos, T. (1996). Semiparametric estimation of partially linear panel data models. *Journal of Econometrics, 71*, 289–397.

Li, Q., & Ullah, A. (1998). Estimating partially panel data models with one-way error components. *Econometric Reviews, 17*, 145–166.

Li, N., Xu, X., & Jin, P. (2011). Testing the linearity in partially linear models. *Journal of Nonparametric Statistics, 23*, 99–114.

Lin, Z., Li, Q., & Sun, Y. (2014). A consistent nonparametric test of parametric regression functional form in fixed effects panel data models. *Journal of Econometrics, 178*, 167–179.

Linton O. B., & Mammen, E. (2005). Estimating semiparametric ARCH(∞) model by kernel smoothing methods. *Econometrica, 73*, 771–836.

Mammen, E., Linton, O. B., & Nielsen, J. P. (1999). The existence and asymptotic properties of a backfitting projection algorithm under weak conditions. *Annals of Statistics, 27*, 1443–1490.

Mammen, E., Rothe, C., & Schienle, M. (2015). Semiparametric estimation with generated covariates. Forthcoming in *Econometric Theory.*

Mammen, E., Støve, B., & Tjøstheim, D. (2009). Nonparametric additive models for panels of time series. *Econometric Theory 25*, 442–481.

Mammen, E., & Yu, K. (2009). Nonparametric estimation of noisy integral equations of the second kind. *Journal of the Korean Statistical Society, 38*, 99–110.

Masry, E. (1996). Multivariate local polynomial regression for time series: Uniform strong consistency rates. *Journal of Time Series Analysis, 17*, 571–599.

Newey, W. K. (1994). The asymptotic variance of semiparametric estimators. *Econometrica, 62*, 1349–1382.

Newey, W. K. (1997). Convergence rates and asymptotic normality for series estimators. *Journal of Econometrics, 79*, 147–168.

Nielsen, J. P., & Sperlich, S. (2005). Smooth backfitting in practice. *Journal of the Royal Statistical Society, Series B, 67*, 43–61.

Panagopoulos, A. (2009). Revisiting the link between knowledge spillovers and growth: An intellectual property perspective. *Economics of Innovation and New Technology, 18*, 533–546.

Park, W. G. (2008). International patent protection: 1965–2005. *Research Policy 37*, 761–766.

Park, W. G., & Ginarte, J. C. (1997). Intellectual property rights and economic growth. *Contemporary Economic Policy*, *15*, 51–61.

Qian, J., & Wang, L. (2012). Estimating semiparametric panel data models by marginal integration. *Journal of Econometrics, 167*, 483–493.

Robinson, P. M. (1988). Root-n-consistent semiparametric regression. *Econometrica, 56*, 931–954.

Rust, J. (2000). *Nested fixed point algorithm documentation manual.* Version 6, Yale University.

Su, L., & Jin, S. (2012). Sieve estimation of panel data models with cross section dependence. *Journal of Econometrics, 169*, 34–47.

Su, L., & Lu, X. (2013). Nonparametric dynamic panel data models: Kernel estimation and specification testing. *Journal of Econometrics, 176*, 112–133.

Su, L., & Ullah, A. (2006a). Profile likelihood estimation of partially linear panel data models with fixed effects. *Economics Letters, 92*, 75–81.

Su, L., & Ullah, A. (2006b). More efficient estimation in nonparametric regression with nonparametric autocorrelated errors. *Econometric Theory, 22*, 98–126.

Su, L., & Ullah, A. (2011). Nonparametric and semiparametric panel econometric models: Estimation and testing. In A. Ullah & D. E. A. Giles (Eds). *Handbook of empirical economics and finance* (pp. 455–497). New York, NY: Taylor & Francis Group.

Su, L., & Zhang, Y. (2015). *Nonparametric dynamic panel data models with interactive fixed effects: Sieve estimation and specification testing*. Working Paper, School of Economics, Singapore Management University.

Sun, Y., Zhang, Y. Y. & Li, Q. (2015). Nonparametric panel data regression models. In B. H. Baltagi (Ed.), *The Oxford handbook of panel data econometrics* (pp. 285–324). Oxford: Oxford University Press.

Van der Vaart, A., & Wellner, J. A. (1996). *Weak convergence and empirical processes with applications to statistics*. New York, NY: Springer.

Xiao, Z., Linton, O. B., Carroll, R. J., & Mammen, E. (2003). More efficient local polynomial estimation in nonparametric regression with autocorrelated errors. *Journal of American Statistical Association, 98*, 980–992.

Yao, F., & Zhang, J. (2015). Efficient kernel-based semiparametric IV estimation with an application to resolving a puzzle on the estimation of the return to schooling. *Empirical Economics, 48*, 253–281.

APPENDIX A. PROOF OF THE RESULTS IN SECTIONS 2 AND 3

Proof of Theorem 1. The proof follows from that of Theorem 2.1 in Su and Lu (2013, **SL** hereafter) closely. The major difference is that we also maintain the second-order variance term that plays an important role in the determination of the asymptotic variance of our parametric estimator but not in that of our nonparametric estimator. Let $|m|_\infty \equiv \sup_{u\in\mathcal{U}} |m(u)|$. Let $\Delta_n \equiv (nh!)^{-1/2}$ and $\nu_n \equiv \Delta_n(\log n)^{1/2} + \|h\|^{\bar{q}+1}$. We prove the first part of the theorem by verifying the conditions in Mammen and Yu (2009):

(B1) $\sup_{\|m\|_2\le 1} |\mathcal{A}m|_\infty < \infty$;
(B2) $\sup_{\|m\|_2\le 1} \left\|(\mathcal{I}-\mathcal{A})^{-1} m\right\|_2 < \infty$;
(B3) $\sup_{\|m\|_2\le 1} \left|(\widehat{\mathcal{A}}-\mathcal{A})m\right|_\infty = O_P(\nu_n)$; and
(B4) For each $a \in \{y, z_1, \ldots, z_{d_z}\}$, there exists a decomposition $\hat{r}_a - r_a + (\widehat{\mathcal{A}} - \mathcal{A})m_a = V_{a,NT} + B_{a,NT} + R_{a,NT}$ with random functions $V_{a,NT}$, $B_{a,NT}$ and $R_{a,NT}$ such that: (B4a) $||V_{a,NT}||_2 = O_P(\Delta_n)$, (B4b) $|\mathcal{A}(\mathcal{I}-\mathcal{A})^{-1} V_{a,NT}|_\infty = O_P(\sqrt{\log n/n})$, (B4c) $||B_{a,NT}||_2 = O_P(\|h\|^{\bar{q}+1})$, and (B4d) $\left|R_{a,NT}\right|_\infty = O_P[\Delta_n(\log n)^{1/2}\nu_n]$.

To see this, we focus on the case $a = y$ in the theorem and in (B4) since all the other cases can be proved similarly. Using $\mathcal{A}^{-1} - \mathcal{C}^{-1} = \mathcal{A}^{-1}(\mathcal{C}-\mathcal{A})\mathcal{C}^{-1}$ and $(\mathcal{I}-\mathcal{A})^{-1} = \mathcal{I} + \mathcal{A}(\mathcal{I}-\mathcal{A})^{-1}$, we have

$$\begin{aligned}
\hat{m}_y - m_y &= (\mathcal{I}-\widehat{\mathcal{A}})^{-1}\hat{r}_y - (\mathcal{I}-\mathcal{A})^{-1} r_y \\
&= (\mathcal{I}-\widehat{\mathcal{A}})^{-1}(\hat{r}_y - r_y) + [(\mathcal{I}-\widehat{\mathcal{A}})^{-1} - (\mathcal{I}-\mathcal{A})^{-1}] r_y \\
&= (\mathcal{I}-\widehat{\mathcal{A}})^{-1}\left[(\hat{r}_y - r_y) + (\widehat{\mathcal{A}}-\mathcal{A})(\mathcal{I}-\mathcal{A})^{-1} r_y\right] \\
&= (\mathcal{I}-\widehat{\mathcal{A}})^{-1}\left[(\hat{r}_y - r_y) + (\widehat{\mathcal{A}}-\mathcal{A}) m_y\right] \\
&= (\mathcal{I}-\widehat{\mathcal{A}})^{-1}\left[V_{y,NT} + B_{y,NT} + R_{y,NT}\right] \\
&= V_{y,NT} + \mathcal{A}(\mathcal{I}-\mathcal{A})^{-1} V_{y,NT} + (\mathcal{I}-\mathcal{A})^{-1} B_{y,NT} \\
&\quad + \mathcal{D}_1 V_{y,NT} + \mathcal{D}_2 B_{y,NT} + (\mathcal{I}-\widehat{\mathcal{A}})^{-1} R_{y,NT}, \qquad (A.1)
\end{aligned}$$

where $\mathcal{D}_1 \equiv \widehat{\mathcal{A}}(\mathcal{I}-\widehat{\mathcal{A}})^{-1} - \mathcal{A}(\mathcal{I}-\mathcal{A})^{-1}$, $\mathcal{D}_2 \equiv (\mathcal{I}-\widehat{\mathcal{A}})^{-1} - (\mathcal{I}-\mathcal{A})^{-1}$, and the fifth equality follows from (A.2) below. Following the proof of Theorem 5 in Mammen et al. (2009), we can show that

$$\begin{aligned}
|\mathcal{D}_1 V_{y,NT}|_\infty &= O_P(\nu_n \Delta_n) \text{ by (B2), (B3), (B4a) and (B4b),} \\
\left|\mathcal{D}_2 B_{y,NT}\right|_\infty &= O_P(\nu_n \left\|h\right\|^{\bar{q}+1}) \text{ by (B2), (B3) and (B4c),} \\
|(\mathcal{I}-\widehat{\mathcal{A}})^{-1} R_{y,NT}|_\infty &= O_P[\Delta_n (\log n)^{1/2} \nu_n] \text{ by (B2), (B3) and (B4d).}
\end{aligned}$$

With these results, by the fact that $(\mathcal{I}-\mathcal{A})^{-1} = \mathcal{I} + \mathcal{A}(\mathcal{I}-\mathcal{A})^{-1}$ and Minkowski inequality, we have

$$\begin{aligned}
&\left|\hat{m}_y - m_y - (\mathcal{I}-\mathcal{A})^{-1} V_{y,NT} - (\mathcal{I}-\mathcal{A})^{-1} B_{y,NT}\right|_\infty \\
&\leq \left|\mathcal{D}_1 V_{y,NT}\right|_\infty + \left|\mathcal{D}_2 B_{y,NT}\right|_\infty + \left|(\mathcal{I}-\widehat{\mathcal{A}})^{-1} R_{y,NT}\right|_\infty \\
&= O_P\left(\nu_n \Delta_n + \nu_n \left\|h\right\|^{\bar{q}+1} + \Delta_n (\log n)^{1/2} \nu_n\right) = O_P\left(\nu_n^2\right).
\end{aligned}$$

That is, the first part of Theorem 1 holds for $a = y$. Analogously, it holds for $a = z_1, \ldots, z_{d_z}$. Noting that $\hat{m}_\theta(u) - m_\theta(u) = \hat{m}_y(u) - m_y(u) - \theta'\left[\hat{m}_z(u) - m_z(u)\right]$, $V_{\theta,NT}(u) = V_{y,NT}(u) - \theta' V_{z,NT}(u)$, and $B_{\theta,NT}(u) = B_{y,NT}(u) - \theta' B_{z,NT}(u)$, we have by Minkowski and Cauchy–Schwarz inequalities and the fact that Θ is compact

$$\begin{aligned}
&\sup_{\theta\in\Theta}\sup_{u\in\mathcal{U}} \left|\hat{m}_\theta(u) - m_\theta(u) - (\mathcal{I}-\mathcal{A})^{-1} V_{\theta,NT}(u) - (\mathcal{I}-\mathcal{A})^{-1} B_{\theta,NT}(u)\right| \\
&\leq \sup_{u\in\mathcal{U}} \left|\hat{m}_y(u) - m_y(u) - (\mathcal{I}-\mathcal{A})^{-1} V_{y,NT}(u) - (\mathcal{I}-\mathcal{A})^{-1} B_{y,NT}(u)\right| \\
&\quad + \sup_{\theta\in\Theta} \left\|\theta\right\| \\
&\quad \times \sup_{u\in\mathcal{U}} \left\|\hat{m}_z(u) - m_z(u) - (\mathcal{I}-\mathcal{A})^{-1} V_{z,NT}(u) - (\mathcal{I}-\mathcal{A})^{-1} B_{z,NT}(u)\right\| \\
&= O_P\left(\nu_n^2\right) + O_P\left(\nu_n^2\right) = O_P\left(\nu_n^2\right).
\end{aligned}$$

Thus, the second part of Theorem 1 also follows.

Now, we verify (B1)–(B4). Apparently, Assumption A.1(vii) ensures (B1). By the discussion of Assumption A.1(v) in **SL**, Assumption A.1(v) implies (B2).

To verify (B3), letting $\bar{m}_a(u) \equiv \mathcal{A}m_a(u)$, we have the following bias-variance decomposition:

$$
\begin{aligned}
(\widehat{\mathcal{A}} - \mathcal{A})m_a(u) &= \frac{1}{n}\sum_{i=1}^{N}\sum_{t=3}^{T}\mathcal{K}_{it}(u)\, m_a(U_{i,t-1}) - \bar{m}_a(u) \\
&= \frac{1}{n}\sum_{i=1}^{N}\sum_{t=3}^{T}\mathcal{K}_{it}(u)\left[m_a(U_{i,t-1}) - \bar{m}_a\left(U_{i,t-2}\right)\right] \\
&\quad + \frac{1}{n}\sum_{i=1}^{N}\sum_{t=3}^{T}\mathcal{K}_{it}(u)\left[\bar{m}_a\left(U_{i,t-2}\right) - \bar{m}_a(u)\right] \\
&\equiv A_{a,1NT}(u) + A_{a,2NT}(u), \text{ say,}
\end{aligned}
$$

where in the second equation we use the fact that $\frac{1}{n}\sum_{i=1}^{N}\sum_{t=3}^{T}\mathcal{K}_{it}(u) = 1$ because $S_{NT}(u)\, S_{NT}(u)^{-1} = \mathbf{I}_G$. By the same fact, $A_{a,2NT}(u) = \frac{1}{n}\sum_{i=1}^{N}\sum_{t=3}^{T}\mathcal{K}_{it}(u)$ $D\bar{m}_{a,it}(u)$, where $D\bar{m}_{a,it}(u) \equiv \bar{m}_a\left(U_{i,t-2}\right) - \bar{m}_a(u) - \sum_{1\le|\mathbf{j}|\le q}\frac{1}{\mathbf{j}!}\bar{m}_a^{(\mathbf{j})}(u)$ $\left(U_{i,t-2} - u\right)^{\mathbf{j}}$. Using the arguments as used in Masry (1996) and Hansen (2008), we can readily show that $\sup_{u\in\mathcal{U}}\left|A_{a,1NT}(u)\right| = O_P[\Delta_n(\log n)^{1/2}]$ and $\sup_{u\in\mathcal{U}}\left|A_{a,2NT}(u)\right| = O_P(\|h\|^{\bar{q}+1})$. Consequently, (B3) follows. Noting that $\Delta Y_{it} = m_y\left(U_{i,t-1}\right) - m_y\left(U_{i,t-2}\right) + \eta_{y,it}$ and $r_y(u) + \bar{m}_y(u) = m_y(u)$ (see Eqs. (12) and (13)), we have

$$
\begin{aligned}
&\hat{r}_y(u) - r_y(u) + \widehat{\mathcal{A}}m_y(u) - \mathcal{A}m_y(u) \\
&= \frac{1}{n}\sum_{i=1}^{N}\sum_{t=3}^{T}\mathcal{K}_{it}(u)\left[-\Delta Y_{it} + m_y\left(U_{i,t-1}\right)\right] - \left[r_y(u) + \bar{m}_y(u)\right] \\
&= \frac{1}{n}\sum_{i=1}^{N}\sum_{t=3}^{T}\mathcal{K}_{it}(u)\left\{\left[m_y\left(U_{i,t-2}\right) - \eta_{y,it}\right] - m_y(u)\right\} \\
&= \frac{-1}{n}\sum_{i=1}^{N}\sum_{t=3}^{T}\mathcal{K}_{it}(u)\,\eta_{y,it} + \frac{1}{n}\sum_{i=1}^{N}\sum_{t=3}^{T}\mathcal{K}_{it}(u)\left[m_y\left(U_{i,t-2}\right) - m_y(u)\right] \\
&= \frac{-1}{n}\sum_{i=1}^{N}\sum_{t=3}^{T}\mathcal{K}_{it}(u)\,\eta_{y,it} + \frac{1}{n}\sum_{i=1}^{N}\sum_{t=3}^{T}\mathcal{K}_{it}(u)\,\mathcal{D}m_{y,it}(u) \\
&= V_{y,NT}(u) + B_{y,NT}(u) + R_{y,NT}(u),
\end{aligned}
\qquad (A.2)
$$

where

$$B_{y,NT}(u) \equiv \frac{1}{n}\sum_{i=1}^{N}\sum_{t=3}^{T}\bar{\mathcal{K}}_{it}(u)\,Dm_{y,it}(u),$$

$$V_{y,NT}(u) \equiv \frac{1}{n}\sum_{i=1}^{N}\sum_{t=3}^{T}\bar{\mathcal{K}}_{it}(u)\,\eta_{y,it},$$

$$R_{y,NT}(u) = e_1'\{[S_{NT}(u)]^{-1} - [\bar{S}_{NT}(u)]^{-1}\}[R_{y,1NT}(u) + R_{y,2NT}(u)], \quad \text{(A.3)}$$

$Dm_{y,it}(u) \equiv m_y(U_{i,t-2}) - m_y(u) - \sum_{1\le|\mathbf{j}|\le q}\frac{1}{\mathbf{j}!}m_y^{(\mathbf{j})}(u)(U_{i,t-2}-u)^{\mathbf{j}}$, $R_{y,1NT}(u) = \frac{-1}{n}\sum_{i=1}^{N}\sum_{t=3}^{T}\mathbf{1}_{it}K_h(U_{i,t-2}-u)\,\mu_h(U_{i,t-2}-u)\,\eta_{y,it}$, and $R_{y,2NT}(u) = \frac{1}{n}\sum_{i=1}^{N}\sum_{t=3}^{T}\mathbf{1}_{it}K_h(U_{i,t-2}-u)\,\mu_h(U_{i,t-2}-u)\,Dm_{y,it}(u)$. Using the above decomposition and following **SL**, one can readily verify conditions (B4a)–(B4d). ■

Proof of Theorem 2. We make the following decomposition:

$$\begin{aligned}
\hat{\theta}_{gmm} - \theta_0 &= (\tilde{\theta}_{gmm} - \theta_0) \\
&\quad + \left(\hat{\boldsymbol{\eta}}_z'\tilde{\mathbf{W}}A_{NT}\tilde{\mathbf{W}}'\hat{\boldsymbol{\eta}}_z\right)^{-}\hat{\boldsymbol{\eta}}_z'\tilde{\mathbf{W}}A_{NT}\tilde{\mathbf{W}}'\hat{\boldsymbol{\eta}}_y \\
&\quad - \left(\boldsymbol{\eta}_z'\tilde{\mathbf{W}}A_{NT}\tilde{\mathbf{W}}'\boldsymbol{\eta}_z\right)^{-}\boldsymbol{\eta}_z'\tilde{\mathbf{W}}A_{NT}\tilde{\mathbf{W}}'\boldsymbol{\eta}_y \\
&= (\tilde{\theta}_{gmm} - \theta_0) + \left(\boldsymbol{\eta}_z'\tilde{\mathbf{W}}A_{NT}\tilde{\mathbf{W}}'\boldsymbol{\eta}_z\right)^{-} \\
&\quad \times\left(\hat{\boldsymbol{\eta}}_z'\tilde{\mathbf{W}}A_{NT}\tilde{\mathbf{W}}'\hat{\boldsymbol{\eta}}_y - \boldsymbol{\eta}_z'\tilde{\mathbf{W}}A_{NT}\tilde{\mathbf{W}}'\boldsymbol{\eta}_y\right) \\
&\quad + \left[\left(\hat{\boldsymbol{\eta}}_z'\tilde{\mathbf{W}}A_{NT}\tilde{\mathbf{W}}'\hat{\boldsymbol{\eta}}_z\right)^{-} - \left(\boldsymbol{\eta}_z'\tilde{\mathbf{W}}A_{NT}\tilde{\mathbf{W}}'\boldsymbol{\eta}_z\right)^{-}\right]\boldsymbol{\eta}_z'\tilde{\mathbf{W}}A_{NT}\tilde{\mathbf{W}}'\boldsymbol{\eta}_y \\
&\quad + \left[\left(\hat{\boldsymbol{\eta}}_z'\tilde{\mathbf{W}}A_{NT}\tilde{\mathbf{W}}'\hat{\boldsymbol{\eta}}_z\right)^{-} - \left(\boldsymbol{\eta}_z'\tilde{\mathbf{W}}A_{NT}\tilde{\mathbf{W}}'\boldsymbol{\eta}_z\right)^{-}\right] \\
&\quad \times\left(\hat{\boldsymbol{\eta}}_z'\tilde{\mathbf{W}}A_{NT}\tilde{\mathbf{W}}'\hat{\boldsymbol{\eta}}_y - \boldsymbol{\eta}_z'\tilde{\mathbf{W}}A_{NT}\tilde{\mathbf{W}}'\boldsymbol{\eta}_y\right) \\
&\equiv (\tilde{\theta}_{gmm} - \theta_0) + B_1 + B_2 + B_3, \text{ say.}
\end{aligned}$$

Let $\Delta\boldsymbol{\varepsilon} \equiv (\Delta\varepsilon_1, \ldots, \Delta\varepsilon_N)'$ where $\Delta\varepsilon_i \equiv (\Delta\varepsilon_{i3}, \ldots, \Delta\varepsilon_{iT})'$. It suffices to prove the theorem by showing that

(i) $\frac{1}{\tilde{n}^2}\hat{\boldsymbol{\eta}}_z'\tilde{\mathbf{W}}A_{NT}\tilde{\mathbf{W}}'\hat{\boldsymbol{\eta}}_z = Q_{wz}'AQ_{wz} + o_P(1)$,
(ii) $\sqrt{\tilde{n}}(\tilde{\theta}_{gmm} - \theta_0) = (Q_{wz}'AQ_{wz})^{-1}Q_{wz}'A\frac{1}{\sqrt{\tilde{n}}}\tilde{\mathbf{W}}'\Delta\boldsymbol{\varepsilon} + o_P(1)$,

(iii) $\sqrt{\tilde{n}}B_1 = \left(Q'_{wz}AQ_{wz}\right)^{-1} \frac{\sqrt{\tilde{n}}}{N}\sum_{i=1}^{N}[Q'_{wz}A\varphi_1\left(\chi_{y,i}\right) + \varphi_{1,z}\left(\chi_{z,i}\right)' AQ_{wz}\theta_0] + o_P(1)$,
(iv) $\sqrt{\tilde{n}}B_2 = -\left(Q'_{wz}AQ_{wz}\right)^{-1} \frac{\sqrt{\tilde{n}}}{N}\sum_{i=1}^{N}[Q'_{wz}A\varphi_{1,z}\left(\chi_{z,i}\right) + \varphi_{1,z}\left(\chi_{z,i}\right)' AQ_{wz}]\theta_0 + o_P(1)$, and
(v) $\sqrt{\tilde{n}}B_3 = o_P(1)$,

because these results, in conjunction with Slutsky lemma, the continuous mapping theorem, and Assumption A.5(iii), imply that

$$\begin{aligned}\sqrt{\tilde{n}}\left(\hat{\theta}_{gmm} - \theta_0\right) &= \left(Q'_{wz}AQ_{wz}\right)^{-1} Q'_{wz}A\left\{\frac{1}{\sqrt{\tilde{n}}}\tilde{\mathbf{W}}'\Delta\boldsymbol{\varepsilon} + \frac{\sqrt{\tilde{n}}}{N}\sum_{i=1}^{N}[\varphi_1(\chi_{y,i}) - \varphi_{1,z}(\chi_{z,i})\theta_0]\right\} \\ &\quad + o_P(1) \\ &\xrightarrow{D} N\left(0, \left(Q'_{wz}AQ_{wz}\right)^{-1} Q'_{wz}A\Omega_0 AQ_{wz}\left(Q'_{wz}AQ_{wz}\right)^{-1}\right).\end{aligned}$$

We first show (i). By Theorem 1, Remark 1 and Assumption A.6, we have that uniformly in $u \in \mathcal{U}$,

$$\hat{m}_a(u) - m_a(u) = (\mathcal{I} - \mathcal{A})^{-1} V_{a,NT}(u) + o_P(n^{-1/2}) \text{ for } a = y,\ z, \text{ and} \tag{A.4}$$

$$\hat{m}_a(u) - m_a(u) = O_P(\nu_n) \text{ for } a = y,\ z. \tag{A.5}$$

It follows that $\max_{i,t}\tilde{\mathbf{1}}_{it}\left\|\Delta m_{a,it} - \Delta\hat{m}_{a,it}\right\| = O_P(\nu_n)$ for $a = y$ and z. Noting that $\hat{\eta}_{z,it} - \eta_{z,it} = \Delta m_{z,it} - \Delta\hat{m}_{z,it}$, we have by Assumption A.5(ii) and Markov inequality

$$\begin{aligned}\left\|\frac{1}{\tilde{n}}\left(\hat{\boldsymbol{\eta}}_z - \boldsymbol{\eta}_z\right)'\tilde{\mathbf{W}}\right\| &\le \frac{1}{\tilde{n}}\sum_{i=1}^{N}\sum_{t=3}^{T}\tilde{\mathbf{1}}_{it}\left\|\Delta m_{z,it} - \Delta\hat{m}_{z,it}\right\|\left\|W_{it}\right\| \\ &\le \max_{i,t}\tilde{\mathbf{1}}_{it}\left\|\Delta m_{a,it} - \Delta\hat{m}_{a,it}\right\|\frac{1}{\tilde{n}}\sum_{i=1}^{N}\sum_{t=3}^{T}\left\|W_{it}\right\|\tilde{\mathbf{1}}_{it} = O_P(\nu_n).\end{aligned} \tag{A.6}$$

With this result, one can readily show that $\frac{1}{\tilde{n}^2}\hat{\boldsymbol{\eta}}'_z\tilde{\mathbf{W}}A_{NT}\tilde{\mathbf{W}}'\hat{\boldsymbol{\eta}}_z = \frac{1}{\tilde{n}^2}\boldsymbol{\eta}'_z\tilde{\mathbf{W}}A_{NT}\tilde{\mathbf{W}}'\boldsymbol{\eta}_z + o_P(1)$. Then (i) follows by noticing that

$$\frac{1}{\tilde{n}^2}\boldsymbol{\eta}'_z\tilde{\mathbf{W}}A_{NT}\tilde{\mathbf{W}}'\boldsymbol{\eta}_z \xrightarrow{P} Q'_{wz}AQ_{wz} > 0 \tag{A.7}$$

by Assumption A.5(i) and Slutsky lemma.

For (ii), by Eq. (26) and the fact that $\eta_{y,it} = \theta_0' \eta_{z,it} + \Delta\varepsilon_{it}$ we have

$$\sqrt{\tilde{n}}\left(\tilde{\theta}_{gmm} - \theta_0\right) = \left(\frac{1}{\tilde{n}^2}\boldsymbol{\eta}_z'\tilde{\mathbf{W}}A_{NT}\tilde{\mathbf{W}}'\boldsymbol{\eta}_z\right)^{-1}\frac{1}{\tilde{n}}\boldsymbol{\eta}_z'\tilde{\mathbf{W}}A_{NT}\frac{1}{\sqrt{\tilde{n}}}\tilde{\mathbf{W}}'\Delta\boldsymbol{\varepsilon}.$$

Then (ii) follows by Eq. (A.7), Assumption A.5(i) and the fact that $\frac{1}{\sqrt{\tilde{n}}}\tilde{\mathbf{W}}'\Delta\boldsymbol{\varepsilon} = O_P(1)$.

To show (iii), let the operator $\mathcal{L}(\bar{u}, u)$ be as defined in Eq. (31). As in Linton and Mammen (2005, p. 821), we can show that $\int_{\mathcal{U}}\int_{\mathcal{U}} \mathcal{L}(u, \bar{u})^2 m(\bar{u}) f(\bar{u}) f(u)\, d\bar{u}du < \infty$ under Assumptions A.1(iv)–(vi) and

$$\begin{aligned}
&(\mathcal{I} - \mathcal{A})^{-1} V_{y,NT}(u) \\
&= \int_{\mathcal{U}} \mathcal{L}(u, \bar{u}) \frac{1}{n} \sum_{i=1}^{N}\sum_{t=3}^{T} \mathbf{1}_{it} e_1' \bar{S}_{NT}(\bar{u})^{-1} \mu_h\left(U_{i,t-2} - \bar{u}\right) K_h\left(U_{i,t-2} - \bar{u}\right) d\bar{u}\eta_{y,it} \\
&= \frac{1}{n}\sum_{i=1}^{N}\sum_{t=3}^{T} \bar{\mathcal{L}}\left(U_{i,t-2}, u\right)\eta_{y,it}, \qquad \text{(A.8)}
\end{aligned}$$

where $\bar{\mathcal{L}}(v, u) \equiv \int_{\mathcal{U}} \mathcal{L}(u, \bar{u})\mathbf{1}(v \in \mathcal{U}) e_1' \bar{S}_{NT}(\bar{u})^{-1} \mu_h(v - \bar{u}) K_h(v - \bar{u})\, d\bar{u}$.[6] Next, we make the following decomposition:

$$\begin{aligned}
&\frac{1}{\tilde{n}^{3/2}}\left(\hat{\boldsymbol{\eta}}_z'\tilde{\mathbf{W}}A_{NT}\tilde{\mathbf{W}}'\hat{\boldsymbol{\eta}}_y - \boldsymbol{\eta}_z'\tilde{\mathbf{W}}A_{NT}\tilde{\mathbf{W}}'\boldsymbol{\eta}_y\right) \\
&= \frac{1}{\tilde{n}^{3/2}}\boldsymbol{\eta}_z'\tilde{\mathbf{W}}A_{NT}\tilde{\mathbf{W}}'(\hat{\boldsymbol{\eta}}_y - \boldsymbol{\eta}_y) + \frac{1}{\tilde{n}^{3/2}}(\hat{\boldsymbol{\eta}}_z - \boldsymbol{\eta}_z)'\tilde{\mathbf{W}}A_{NT}\tilde{\mathbf{W}}'\boldsymbol{\eta}_y \\
&\quad + \frac{1}{\tilde{n}^{3/2}}(\hat{\boldsymbol{\eta}}_z - \boldsymbol{\eta}_z)'\tilde{\mathbf{W}}A_{NT}\tilde{\mathbf{W}}'(\hat{\boldsymbol{\eta}}_y - \boldsymbol{\eta}_y) \\
&\equiv I_1 + I_2 + I_3, \text{ say.}
\end{aligned}$$

Apparently, by Eq. (A.6) and Assumptions A.5(i) and A.6, $I_3 = \sqrt{\tilde{n}}\,O_P(\nu_n^2) = o_P(1)$. To study I_1 and I_2, we resort to the results in Eqs. (A.4) and (A.8) and the theory for second-order U-statistics. For $a = y, z_1, \ldots, z_{d_z}$, define

$$\begin{aligned}\varphi^0\left(\chi_{a,i}, \chi_{a,j}\right) &= -\frac{N(N-1)}{n\tilde{n}} \sum_{s=3}^{T} \sum_{t=3}^{T} \left[\bar{\mathcal{L}}\left(U_{j,s-2}, U_{i,t-1}\right) - \bar{\mathcal{L}}\left(U_{j,s-2}, U_{i,t-2}\right)\right] \\ &\quad \times \tilde{\mathbf{1}}_{it} W_{it} \eta_{a,js}, \\ \varphi\left(\chi_{a,i}, \chi_{a,j}\right) &= \left[\varphi^0\left(\chi_{a,i}, \chi_{a,j}\right) + \varphi^0\left(\chi_{a,j}, \chi_{a,i}\right)\right]/2,\end{aligned}$$

where $\chi_{a,i} = (U_{i1}', \ldots, U_{i,T-1}', W_{i3}', \ldots, W_{iT}', \ \eta_{a,i3}, \ldots, \eta_{a,iT})'$. Let $\varphi_1\left(\chi_{a,i}\right) = E\left[\varphi\left(\chi_{a,i}, \chi_{a,j}\right) | \chi_{a,i}\right]$ and $\varphi_2(\chi_{a,i}, \ \chi_{a,j}) = \varphi\left(\chi_{a,i}, \chi_{a,j}\right) - \varphi_1\left(\chi_{a,i}\right) - \varphi_1\left(\chi_{a,j}\right) + E\left[\varphi_1\left(\chi_{a,i}\right)\right]$ for any $i \neq j$. It is easy to verify that φ_1 is as given in Eq. (32) and $E\left[\varphi_1\left(\chi_{a,i}\right)\right] = 0$. By Eqs. (A.4) and (A.8),

$$\begin{aligned}&\frac{1}{\sqrt{\tilde{n}}} \tilde{\mathbf{W}}'(\hat{\boldsymbol{\eta}}_y - \boldsymbol{\eta}_y) \\ &\quad = -\frac{1}{\sqrt{\tilde{n}}} \sum_{i=1}^{N} \sum_{t=3}^{T} \left(\Delta \hat{m}_{y,it} - \Delta m_{y,it}\right) \tilde{\mathbf{1}}_{it} W_{it} \\ &\quad = -\frac{1}{\sqrt{\tilde{n}}} \sum_{i=1}^{N} \sum_{t=3}^{T} \left[\left(\hat{m}_{y,it} - m_{y,it}\right) - \left(\hat{m}_{y,i,t-1} - m_{y,i,t-1}\right)\right] \tilde{\mathbf{1}}_{it} W_{it} \\ &\quad = -\frac{1}{\sqrt{\tilde{n}}} \sum_{i=1}^{N} \sum_{t=3}^{T} \left[\frac{1}{n} \sum_{j=1}^{N} \sum_{s=3}^{T} \left[\bar{\mathcal{L}}\left(U_{j,s-2}, U_{i,t-1}\right) - \bar{\mathcal{L}}\left(U_{j,s-2}, U_{i,t-2}\right)\right] \eta_{y,js}\right] \\ &\qquad \times \tilde{\mathbf{1}}_{it} W_{it} + o_P(1) \\ &\quad = \sqrt{\tilde{n}} \mathcal{V}_{y,NT} + o_P(1)\end{aligned}$$

where

$$\begin{aligned}&\mathcal{V}_{y,NT} \\ &\quad = -\frac{1}{n\tilde{n}} \sum_{j=1}^{N} \sum_{i=1}^{N} \sum_{s=3}^{T} \sum_{t=3}^{T} \left[\bar{\mathcal{L}}\left(U_{j,s-2}, U_{i,t-1}\right) - \bar{\mathcal{L}}\left(U_{j,s-2}, U_{i,t-2}\right)\right] \tilde{\mathbf{1}}_{it} W_{it} \eta_{y,js} \\ &\quad = \frac{2}{N(N-1)} \sum_{1 \leq i < j \leq N} \varphi\left(\chi_{y,i}, \chi_{y,j}\right) + \frac{1}{n\tilde{n}} \sum_{i=1}^{N} \varphi\left(\chi_{y,i}, \chi_{y,i}\right) \\ &\quad \equiv \mathcal{V}_{y,NT1} + \mathcal{V}_{y,NT2}, \text{ say,}\end{aligned}$$

By Markov inequality, we can readily show that $\mathcal{V}_{y,NT2} = O_P(N^{-1})$. Let $\mathcal{H}^{(1)}_{y,NT} = \frac{1}{N}\sum_{i=1}^{N}\varphi_1(\chi_{y,i})$ and $\mathcal{H}^{(2)}_{y,NT} = \frac{1}{N(N-1)}\sum_{1\le i<j\le N}\varphi_2(\chi_{y,i},\chi_{y,j})$. By Hoeffding decomposition (e.g. Lee, 1990, p. 26), $\mathcal{V}_{y,NT1} = 2\mathcal{H}^{(1)}_{y,NT} + \mathcal{H}^{(2)}_{y,NT}$. By straightforward moment calculations, $E\left\|\mathcal{H}^{(2)}_{y,NT}\right\|^2 = O(N^{-2})$. So $\mathcal{H}^{(2)}_{y,NT} = O_P(N^{-1}) = o_P(\tilde{n}^{-1/2})$. Then we have $\frac{1}{\sqrt{\tilde{n}}}\tilde{\mathbf{W}}(\hat{\eta}_y - \eta_y) = \sqrt{\tilde{n}}\mathcal{V}_{y,NT1} + o_P(1) = \frac{\sqrt{\tilde{n}}}{N}\sum_{i=1}^{N}\varphi_1(\chi_{y,i}) + o_P(1)$ and

$$I_1 = \frac{1}{\tilde{n}}\boldsymbol{\eta}_z'\tilde{\mathbf{W}}A_{NT}\frac{1}{\tilde{n}^{1/2}}\tilde{\mathbf{W}}'\left(\hat{\boldsymbol{\eta}}_y - \boldsymbol{\eta}_y\right) = Q_{wz}'A\frac{\sqrt{\tilde{n}}}{N}\sum_{i=1}^{N}\varphi_1(\chi_{y,i}) + o_P(1).$$

By the same token we can show that $\frac{1}{\tilde{n}^{1/2}}\left(\hat{\boldsymbol{\eta}}_z - \boldsymbol{\eta}_z\right)'\tilde{\mathbf{W}} = \frac{\sqrt{\tilde{n}}}{N}\sum_{i=1}^{N}\varphi_{1,z}(\chi_{z,i}) + o_P(1)$, where $\varphi_{1,z}(\chi_{z,i}) = (\varphi_1(\chi_{z_1,i}),\ldots,\varphi_1(\chi_{z_{d_z},i}))$ is a $d_w \times d_z$ matrix. Using $\eta_{y,it} = \theta_0'\eta_{z,it} + \Delta\varepsilon_{it}$ again, we can readily show that $\frac{1}{\tilde{n}}\tilde{\mathbf{W}}'\boldsymbol{\eta}_y = \frac{1}{\tilde{n}}\tilde{\mathbf{W}}'\boldsymbol{\eta}_z\theta_0 + \frac{1}{\tilde{n}}\tilde{\mathbf{W}}'\Delta\boldsymbol{\varepsilon} = Q_{wz}\theta_0 + o_P(1)$. It follows that $I_2 = \frac{1}{\tilde{n}^{1/2}}\left(\hat{\boldsymbol{\eta}}_z - \boldsymbol{\eta}_z\right)'\tilde{\mathbf{W}}A_{NT}\frac{1}{\tilde{n}}\tilde{\mathbf{W}}'\boldsymbol{\eta}_y = \frac{\sqrt{\tilde{n}}}{N}\sum_{i=1}^{N}\varphi_{1,z}(\chi_{z,i})'AQ_{wz}\theta_0 + o_P(1)$. Consequently,

$$\begin{aligned}&\frac{1}{\tilde{n}^{3/2}}\left(\hat{\boldsymbol{\eta}}_z'\tilde{\mathbf{W}}A_{NT}\tilde{\mathbf{W}}'\hat{\boldsymbol{\eta}}_y - \boldsymbol{\eta}_z'\tilde{\mathbf{W}}A_{NT}\tilde{\mathbf{W}}'\boldsymbol{\eta}_y\right)\\&\quad= \frac{\sqrt{\tilde{n}}}{N}\sum_{i=1}^{N}\left[Q_{wz}'A\varphi_1(\chi_{y,i}) + \varphi_{1,z}(\chi_{z,i})'AQ_{wz}\theta_0\right] + o_P(1),\end{aligned}$$

and (iii) follows.

Now, we show (iv). By the fact that $A_1^{-1} - A_2^{-1} = A_1^{-1}(A_2 - A_1)A_2^{-1}$ for any two conformable non-singular matrices A_1 and A_2 and that $\eta_{y,it} = \theta_0'\eta_{z,it} + \Delta\varepsilon_{it}$, we have

$$\begin{aligned}\sqrt{\tilde{n}}B_2 &= \hat{\Phi}_{NT}^{-1}\sqrt{\tilde{n}}\left(\Phi_{NT} - \hat{\Phi}_{NT}\right)\theta_0\\&\quad+ \hat{\Phi}_{NT}^{-1}\sqrt{\tilde{n}}\left(\Phi_{NT} - \hat{\Phi}_{NT}\right)\Phi_{NT}^{-1}\frac{1}{\tilde{n}^2}\boldsymbol{\eta}_z'\tilde{\mathbf{W}}A_{NT}\tilde{\mathbf{W}}'\Delta\boldsymbol{\varepsilon}\\&\equiv I_4 + I_5,\ \text{say},\end{aligned}$$

where $\hat{\Phi}_{NT} = \frac{1}{\tilde{n}^2}\hat{\boldsymbol{\eta}}_z'\tilde{\mathbf{W}}A_{NT}\tilde{\mathbf{W}}'\hat{\boldsymbol{\eta}}_z$ and $\Phi_{NT} = \frac{1}{\tilde{n}^2}\boldsymbol{\eta}_z'\tilde{\mathbf{W}}A_{NT}\tilde{\mathbf{W}}'\boldsymbol{\eta}_z$. By arguments as used in the derivation of (i) and (iii), we can readily show that

$$I_4 = -\left(Q_{wz}'AQ_{wz}\right)^{-1}\frac{\sqrt{\tilde{n}}}{N}\sum_{i=1}^{N}\left[Q_{wz}'A\varphi_{1,z}(\chi_{z,i}) + \varphi_{1,z}(\chi_{z,i})'AQ_{wz}\right]\theta_0 + o_P(1)$$

$$\text{and} \quad I_5 = O_P(1)\, O_P(1)\, O_P(1)\, O_P(\tilde{n}^{-1/2}) = o_P(1).$$

Then (iv) follows.

Lastly, noting that $\frac{1}{\tilde{n}}\tilde{\mathbf{W}}'\hat{\boldsymbol{\eta}}_a - \frac{1}{\tilde{n}}\tilde{\mathbf{W}}'\boldsymbol{\eta}_a = O_P(\nu_n)$ for $a = y$ and z, we can readily show that $\sqrt{\tilde{n}}B_3 = \sqrt{\tilde{n}}\,O_P(\nu_n^2) = o_P(1)$ by Slutsky lemma and Assumptions A.5(i) and A.6. This completes the proof of the theorem. ■

Proof of Theorem 4. Let $\hat{m}^b_{\theta_0}(u) \equiv \hat{m}^b_y(u) - \theta_0'\hat{m}^b_z(u)$. Let $B_y(u)$, $B_z(u)$, and $B_\theta(u)$ be analogously defined as $B_0(u)$ in Theorem 4 with m being replaced by $m_y(u)$, $m_z(u)$, and $m_\theta(u)$, respectively. In view of the fact that $m_{\theta_0}(u) = m(u)$ and $B_{\theta_0}(u) = B_0(u)$, we have

$$\begin{aligned}
&\sqrt{nb!}[\hat{m}^b_{\hat{\theta}_{gmm}}(u) - m(u) - (\mathcal{I} - \mathcal{A})^{-1} B_0(u)] \\
&= \sqrt{nb!}[\hat{m}^b_{\theta_0}(u) - m_{\theta_0}(u) - (\mathcal{I} - \mathcal{A})^{-1} B_{\theta_0}(u)] \\
&\quad + \sqrt{nb!}[\hat{m}^b_{\hat{\theta}_{gmm}}(u) - \hat{m}_{\theta_0}(u)].
\end{aligned}$$

It suffices to prove the theorem by showing that (i) $\sqrt{nb!}[\hat{m}^b_{\theta_0}(u) - m_{\theta_0}(u) - (\mathcal{I} - \mathcal{A})^{-1} B_{\theta_0}(u)] \xrightarrow{d} N\left(0, \frac{\sigma_0^2(u)}{f(u)} e_1'\mathbb{S}^{-1}\mathbb{K}\mathbb{S}^{-1}e_1\right)$, (ii) $\sup_{u\in\mathcal{U}} |\hat{m}^b_{\theta_0}(u) - m_{\theta_0}(u)| = O_P\left((nb!)^{-1/2}(\log n)^{1/2} + \|b\|^{\bar{q}+1}\right)$, (iii) $\sup_{u\in\mathcal{U}} \left\|(\mathcal{I} - \mathcal{A})^{-1} B_0(u)\right\| = O_P\left(\|b\|^{\bar{q}+1}\right)$, and (iv) $\sqrt{nb!}\sup_{u\in\mathcal{U}} |\hat{m}^b_{\hat{\theta}_{gmm}}(u) - \hat{m}^b_{\theta_0}(u)| = o_P(1)$.

Noting that $\hat{m}^b_{\theta_0}(u) - m_{\theta_0}(u) = [\hat{m}^b_y(u) - m_y(u)] - \theta_0'\left[\hat{m}^b_z(u) - m_z(u)\right]$, $B_{\theta_0}(u) = B_y(u) - \theta_0' B_z(u)$, and $\Delta\varepsilon_{it}(\theta_0) = \eta_{y,it} - \theta_0'\eta_{z,it} = \Delta\varepsilon_{it}$, the proof of (i)–(iii) follows straightforward from that of Theorems 2.1 and 2.2 in **SL**. Noting that $\hat{m}^b_\theta(u) = \hat{m}^b_y(u) - \theta'\hat{m}^b_z(u)$ for $\theta = \hat{\theta}_{gmm}$ and θ_0, we have by Theorems 1 and 2

$$\begin{aligned}
\sqrt{nb!}\sup_{u\in\mathcal{U}} |\hat{m}^b_{\hat{\theta}_{gmm}}(u) - \hat{m}^b_{\theta_0}(u)| &\le \sqrt{nb!}\left\|\hat{\theta}_{gmm} - \theta_0\right\| \sup_{u\in\mathcal{U}} \left|\hat{m}^b_z(u)\right| \\
&= -\sqrt{nb!}\left\|\hat{\theta}_{gmm} - \theta_0\right\| \left(\sup_{u\in\mathcal{U}} |m_z(u)| + o_P(1)\right) \\
&= \sqrt{nb!}O_P(\tilde{n}^{-1/2})O_P(1) = o_P(1).
\end{aligned}$$

Thus (iv) follows. ■

Proof of Theorem 7. Noting that $\mathbf{Y}_w = \mathbf{Z}_w\theta_0 + \mathbf{p}_w\beta + \mathbf{P}_{\bar{\mathbf{W}}}\Delta\boldsymbol{\varepsilon} + \mathbf{P}_{\bar{\mathbf{W}}}\mathbf{R}$ and $\mathbf{M}_{\mathbf{p}_w}\mathbf{p}_w = 0$, we have

$$\begin{aligned}
\hat{\theta}_{sieve} - \theta_0 &= \left(\mathbf{Z}_w'\mathbf{M}_{\mathbf{p}_w}\mathbf{Z}_w\right)^{-}\mathbf{Z}_w'\mathbf{M}_{\mathbf{p}_w}\mathbf{Y}_w - \theta_0 \\
&= \left(\mathbf{Z}_w'\mathbf{M}_{\mathbf{p}_w}\mathbf{Z}_w\right)^{-}\mathbf{Z}_w'\mathbf{M}_{\mathbf{p}_w}\mathbf{P}_{\bar{\mathbf{W}}}\Delta\boldsymbol{\varepsilon} + \left(\mathbf{Z}_w'\mathbf{M}_{\mathbf{p}_w}\mathbf{Z}_w\right)^{-}\mathbf{Z}_w'\mathbf{M}_{\mathbf{p}_w}\mathbf{P}_{\bar{\mathbf{W}}}\mathbf{R}.
\end{aligned}$$

It suffices to prove the theorem by showing that (i) $Q_{1,NT} \equiv \frac{1}{NT_2}\mathbf{Z}_w'\mathbf{M}_{\mathbf{p}_w}\mathbf{Z}_w \stackrel{P}{\to} Q_1 > 0$, (ii) $R_{NT} \equiv \frac{1}{NT_2}\mathbf{Z}_w'\mathbf{M}_{\mathbf{p}_w}\mathbf{P}_{\bar{\mathbf{W}}}\mathbf{R} = o_P(N^{-1/2})$, and (iii) $\frac{1}{\sqrt{NT_2}}\mathbf{Z}_w'\mathbf{M}_{\mathbf{p}_w}\mathbf{P}_{\bar{\mathbf{W}}}\Delta\boldsymbol{\varepsilon} \stackrel{D}{\to} N\left(0, Q_2\Omega_1 Q_2'\right)$.

To show (i), note that $Q_{1,NT} = \frac{1}{NT_2}\mathbf{Z}_w'\mathbf{Z}_w - \frac{1}{NT_2}\mathbf{Z}_w'\mathbf{P}_{\mathbf{p}_w}\mathbf{Z}_w = \frac{1}{NT_2}\Delta\mathbf{Z}'\mathbf{P}_{\bar{\mathbf{W}}}\Delta\mathbf{Z} - \frac{1}{NT_2}\Delta\mathbf{Z}'\mathbf{P}_{\bar{\mathbf{W}}}\Delta\mathbf{p}\left(\Delta\mathbf{p}'\mathbf{P}_{\bar{\mathbf{W}}}\Delta\mathbf{p}\right)^{-}\Delta\mathbf{p}'\mathbf{P}_{\bar{\mathbf{W}}}\Delta\mathbf{Z}$. By Assumptions A.1(i) and A.8(i) and Chebyshev inequality, one can readily show that

$$\left\|\frac{1}{NT_2}\bar{\mathbf{W}}'\Delta\mathbf{Z} - Q_{\bar{w}z}\right\| = O_P\left(\sqrt{L/N}\right), \quad \left\|\frac{1}{NT_2}\bar{\mathbf{W}}'\Delta\mathbf{p} - Q_{\bar{w}p}\right\| = O_P\left(L/\sqrt{N}\right),$$
$$\left\|\frac{1}{NT_2}\bar{\mathbf{W}}'\bar{\mathbf{W}} - Q_{\bar{w}}\right\| = O_P\left(L/\sqrt{N}\right). \tag{A.9}$$

By Eq. (A.9), the triangle inequality, the submultiplicative property of Frobenius norm and Assumption A.8, we can readily show that

$$\frac{1}{NT_2}\Delta\mathbf{Z}'\mathbf{P}_{\bar{\mathbf{W}}}\Delta\mathbf{Z} = \frac{\Delta\mathbf{Z}'\bar{\mathbf{W}}}{NT_2}\left(\frac{\bar{\mathbf{W}}'\bar{\mathbf{W}}}{NT_2}\right)^{-}\frac{\bar{\mathbf{W}}'\Delta\mathbf{Z}}{NT_2} = Q_{\bar{w}z}'Q_{\bar{w}}^{-1}Q_{\bar{w}z} + O_P\left(\frac{L}{\sqrt{N}}\right).$$

Similarly, $\frac{1}{NT_2}\Delta\mathbf{Z}'\mathbf{P}_{\bar{\mathbf{W}}}\Delta\mathbf{p} = Q_{\bar{w}z}'Q_{\bar{w}}^{-1}Q_{\bar{w}p} + O_P(L/\sqrt{N})$ and $\frac{1}{NT_2}\Delta\mathbf{p}'\mathbf{P}_{\bar{\mathbf{W}}}\Delta\mathbf{p} = Q_{\bar{w}p}'Q_{\bar{w}}^{-1}Q_{\bar{w}p} + O_P(L/\sqrt{N})$. It follows that $Q_{1,NT} \stackrel{P}{\to} Q_{\bar{w}z}'Q_{\bar{w}}^{-1}Q_{\bar{w}z} - Q_{\bar{w}z}'Q_{\bar{w}}^{-1} Q_{\bar{w}p}\left(Q_{\bar{w}p}'Q_{\bar{w}}^{-1}Q_{\bar{w}p}\right)^{-1}Q_{\bar{w}p}'Q_{\bar{w}}^{-1}Q_{\bar{w}z} = Q_1 > 0$.

Next, we show (ii). By the submultiplicative property of the spectral norm, the fact that $\|\mathbf{P}_{\bar{\mathbf{W}}}\|_{\text{sp}} = 1$ and that $\|\mathbf{M}_{\mathbf{p}_w}\|_{\text{sp}} = 1$, we have

$$\begin{aligned}
\|R_{NT}\|_{\text{sp}}^2 &= \frac{1}{(NT_2)^2}\left\|\mathbf{Z}_w'\mathbf{M}_{\mathbf{p}_w}\mathbf{P}_{\bar{\mathbf{W}}}\mathbf{R}\right\|_{\text{sp}}^2 \le \frac{1}{(NT_2)^2}\|\mathbf{Z}_w\|_{\text{sp}}^2\|\mathbf{R}\|^2 \\
&= \lambda_{\max}\left(\frac{1}{NT_2}\mathbf{Z}_w'\mathbf{Z}_w\right)\frac{1}{NT_2}\|\mathbf{R}\|^2 \le \lambda_{\max}\left(\frac{1}{NT_2}\Delta\mathbf{Z}'\Delta\mathbf{Z}\right)\frac{1}{NT_2}\|\mathbf{R}\|^2 \\
&= O_P(1)\,O_P\left(L^{-2\gamma/(1+d_x)}\right)
\end{aligned}$$

where we use the fact that $\frac{1}{NT_2}\|\mathbf{R}\|^2 = O_P\left(L^{-2\gamma/(1+d_x)}\right)$ under Assumptions A.1(i) and A.7 by arguments as used in the proof of Lemma A.2 in Su and Jin (2012). Then by Chebyshev inequality and Assumptions A.8 and A.9, $\sqrt{N}\|R_{NT}\| = O_P(\sqrt{N}L^{-\gamma/(1+d_x)}) = o_P(1)$.

Now, we show (iii). Let $Q_{2,NT} \equiv \mathbf{Z}_w'\mathbf{M}_{\mathbf{p}_w}\bar{\mathbf{W}}(\bar{\mathbf{W}}'\bar{\mathbf{W}})^{-}$. Using $\mathbf{M}_{\mathbf{p}_w} = \mathbf{I}_{NT_2} - \mathbf{P}_{\bar{\mathbf{W}}}\Delta\mathbf{p}\left(\Delta\mathbf{p}'\mathbf{P}_{\bar{\mathbf{W}}}\Delta\mathbf{p}\right)^{-}\Delta\mathbf{p}'\mathbf{P}_{\bar{\mathbf{W}}}$, $\mathbf{Z}_w = \mathbf{P}_{\bar{\mathbf{W}}}\Delta\mathbf{Z}$, and $\mathbf{P}_{\bar{\mathbf{W}}}\bar{\mathbf{W}} = \bar{\mathbf{W}}$, we have

$Q_{2,NT} = [\Delta\mathbf{Z}'\bar{\mathbf{W}} - \Delta\mathbf{Z}' P_{\bar{W}} \Delta\mathbf{p} \left(\Delta\mathbf{p}'\mathbf{P}_{\bar{W}}\Delta\mathbf{p}\right)^{-} \Delta\mathbf{p}'\bar{\mathbf{W}}] \left(\bar{\mathbf{W}}'\bar{\mathbf{W}}\right)^{-}$. Using Eq. (A.9), we can readily show that

$$\begin{aligned}
&\left\| Q_{2,NT} - Q_2 \right\| \\
&= \left\| \left[\frac{\Delta\mathbf{Z}'\bar{\mathbf{W}}}{NT_2} - \frac{\Delta\mathbf{Z}'\mathbf{P}_{\bar{\mathbf{W}}}\Delta\mathbf{p}}{NT_2} \left(\frac{\Delta\mathbf{p}'\mathbf{P}_{\bar{\mathbf{W}}}\Delta\mathbf{p}}{NT_2} \right)^{-} \frac{\Delta\mathbf{p}'\bar{\mathbf{W}}}{NT_2} \right] \left(\frac{\bar{\mathbf{W}}'\bar{\mathbf{W}}}{NT_2} \right)^{-} - Q_2 \right\| \\
&= O_P\left(L/\sqrt{N}\right)
\end{aligned}$$

where $Q_2 = [Q'_{\bar{w}z} - Q'_{\bar{w}z} Q_{\bar{w}}^{-1} Q_{\bar{w}p} (Q'_{\bar{w}p} Q_{\bar{w}}^{-1} Q_{\bar{w}p})^{-1} Q'_{\bar{w}p}] Q_{\bar{w}}^{-1}$. It follows that $|| \left(Q_{2,NT} - Q_2\right) \frac{1}{\sqrt{NT_2}} \bar{\mathbf{W}}' \Delta\boldsymbol{\varepsilon} || \leq || Q_{2,NT} - Q_2 || \frac{1}{\sqrt{NT_2}} \left\| \bar{\mathbf{W}}' \Delta\boldsymbol{\varepsilon} \right\| = O_P(L/\sqrt{N})$ $O_P(\sqrt{L}) = o_P(1)$ as $\frac{1}{\sqrt{NT_2}} \left\| \bar{\mathbf{W}}' \Delta\boldsymbol{\varepsilon} \right\| = O_P(\sqrt{L})$ by Chebyshev inequality. Consequently, we can apply the Liapounov CLT to obtain

$$\begin{aligned}
\frac{1}{\sqrt{NT_2}} \mathbf{Z}'_w \mathbf{M}_{\mathbf{p}_w} \mathbf{P}_{\bar{\mathbf{W}}} \Delta\boldsymbol{\varepsilon} &= \frac{1}{\sqrt{NT_2}} Q_2 \bar{\mathbf{W}} \Delta\boldsymbol{\varepsilon} + \left(Q_{2,NT} - Q_2\right) \frac{1}{\sqrt{NT_2}} \bar{\mathbf{W}} \Delta\boldsymbol{\varepsilon} \\
&= \frac{1}{\sqrt{NT_2}} Q_2 \bar{\mathbf{W}} \Delta\boldsymbol{\varepsilon} + o_P(1) \xrightarrow{D} N\left(0, Q_2 \Omega_1 Q'_2\right)
\end{aligned}$$

where we use the fact that $\lambda_{\max}\left(Q_2 \Omega_1 Q'_2\right) < \infty$ by Assumption A.8. ■

Proof of Theorem 8.

(i) Using $\hat{\beta}_m = \left(\mathbf{p}'_w \mathbf{M}_{\mathbf{Z}_w} \mathbf{p}_w\right)^{-} \mathbf{p}'_w \mathbf{M}_{\mathbf{Z}_w} \mathbf{Y}_w$ and $\mathbf{M}_{\mathbf{Z}_w} \mathbf{Y}_w = \mathbf{M}_{\mathbf{Z}_w} (\mathbf{p}_w \beta_m + \mathbf{P}_{\bar{\mathbf{W}}} \Delta\boldsymbol{\varepsilon} + \mathbf{P}_{\bar{\mathbf{W}}} \mathbf{R})$, we have with probability approaching 1 (w.p.a.1)

$$\begin{aligned}
&\hat{m}_{sieve}(u) - m(u) \\
&= p^L(u)' \hat{\beta}_m - m(u) = p^L(u)' \left(\mathbf{p}'_w \mathbf{M}_{\mathbf{Z}_w} \mathbf{p}_w\right)^{-} \mathbf{p}'_w \mathbf{M}_{\mathbf{Z}_w} \mathbf{Y}_w - m(u) \\
&= p^L(u)' \left(\mathbf{p}'_w \mathbf{M}_{\mathbf{Z}_w} \mathbf{p}_w\right)^{-} \mathbf{p}'_w \mathbf{M}_{\mathbf{Z}_w} \mathbf{P}_{\bar{\mathbf{W}}} \Delta\boldsymbol{\varepsilon} \\
&\quad + p^L(u)' \left(\mathbf{p}'_w \mathbf{M}_{\mathbf{Z}_w} \mathbf{p}_w\right)^{-} \mathbf{p}'_w \mathbf{M}_{\mathbf{Z}_w} \mathbf{P}_{\bar{\mathbf{W}}} \mathbf{R} + \left[p^L(u)' \beta_m - m(u)\right] \\
&\equiv D_{NT,1}(u) + D_{NT,2}(u) + D_{NT,3}(u), \text{ say,}
\end{aligned} \tag{A.10}$$

where we use the fact that $\frac{1}{NT_2} \mathbf{p}'_w \mathbf{M}_{\mathbf{Z}_w} \mathbf{p}_w$ is asymptotically nonsingular (see Eq. (A.14)). Then by Cauchy–Schwarz inequality,

$\int \left[\hat{m}_{sieve}(u) - m(u)\right]^2 \alpha(u)\, du \leq 3 \sum_{j=1}^{3} \int D_{NT,j}(u)^2 \alpha(u)\, du$. By Assumptions A.1 and A.8 and Eq. (A.9), one can readily show that

$$\begin{aligned}
\left\| \frac{1}{NT_2} \Delta \mathbf{p}' \mathbf{P}_{\bar{\mathbf{W}}} \Delta \mathbf{p} - Q'_{\bar{w}p} Q_{\bar{w}}^{-1} Q_{\bar{w}p} \right\| &= O_P\left(L/\sqrt{N}\right), \\
\left\| \frac{1}{NT_2} \Delta \mathbf{p}' \mathbf{P}_{\bar{\mathbf{W}}} \Delta \mathbf{Z} - Q'_{\bar{w}p} Q_{\bar{w}}^{-1} Q_{\bar{w}z} \right\| &= O_P\left(L/\sqrt{N}\right), \\
\left\| \frac{1}{NT_2} \Delta \mathbf{Z}' \mathbf{P}_{\bar{\mathbf{W}}} \Delta \mathbf{Z} - Q'_{\bar{w}z} Q_{\bar{w}}^{-1} Q_{\bar{w}z} \right\| &= O_P\left(L/\sqrt{N}\right). \qquad \text{(A.11)}
\end{aligned}$$

Let $Q_{3,NT} \equiv \frac{1}{NT_2} \mathbf{p}'_w \mathbf{M}_{\mathbf{Z}_w} \mathbf{p}_w$. Then we can apply the triangle inequality and the fact that $\mathbf{p}'_w \mathbf{M}_{\mathbf{Z}_w} \mathbf{p}_w = \mathbf{p}'_w \mathbf{p}_w - \mathbf{p}'_w \mathbf{Z}_w \left(\mathbf{Z}'_w \mathbf{Z}_w\right)^- \mathbf{Z}'_w \mathbf{p}_w = \Delta \mathbf{p}' \mathbf{P}_{\bar{\mathbf{W}}} \Delta \mathbf{p} - \Delta \mathbf{p}' \mathbf{P}_{\bar{\mathbf{W}}} \Delta \mathbf{Z} \left(\Delta \mathbf{Z}' \mathbf{P}_{\bar{\mathbf{W}}} \Delta \mathbf{Z}\right)^- \Delta \mathbf{Z}' \mathbf{P}_{\bar{\mathbf{W}}} \Delta \mathbf{p}$ to obtain

$$\left\| Q_{3,NT} - Q_3 \right\| = O_P(L/\sqrt{N}) \qquad \text{(A.12)}$$

where $Q_3 \equiv Q'_{\bar{w}p} Q_{\bar{w}}^{-1} Q_{\bar{w}p} - Q'_{\bar{w}p} Q_{\bar{w}}^{-1} Q_{\bar{w}z} \left(Q'_{\bar{w}z} Q_{\bar{w}}^{-1} Q_{\bar{w}z}\right)^{-1} Q'_{\bar{w}z} Q_{\bar{w}}^{-1} Q_{\bar{w}p} > 0$ under Assumption A.8. This implies that w.p.a.1

$$\lambda_{\max}\left(\frac{1}{NT_2} \mathbf{p}'_w \mathbf{M}_{\mathbf{Z}_w} \mathbf{p}_w\right) \leq \lambda_{\max}(Q_3) + O_P(L/\sqrt{N}) \leq 2\lambda_{\max}(Q_3) \qquad \text{(A.13)}$$

and

$$\lambda_{\min}\left(\frac{1}{NT_2} \mathbf{p}'_w \mathbf{M}_{\mathbf{Z}_w} \mathbf{p}_w\right) \geq \lambda_{\min}(Q_3) - O_P(L/\sqrt{N}) \geq \frac{1}{2}\lambda_{\min}(Q_3). \qquad \text{(A.14)}$$

By the rotational property of the trace operator and the fact that $\mathrm{tr}(AB) \leq \mathrm{tr}(A)\, \lambda_{\max}(B)$ for any symmetric matrix B and p.s.d. matrix A

(e.g. Bernstein, 2005, p. 275),

$$\begin{aligned}
&\int D_{NT,1}(u)^2 \alpha(u)\, du \\
&= \operatorname{tr}\left[\left(\mathbf{p}_w' \mathbf{M}_{\mathbf{Z}_w} \mathbf{p}_w\right)^- \mathbf{p}_w' \mathbf{M}_{\mathbf{Z}_w} \mathbf{P}_{\bar{\mathbf{W}}} \Delta\boldsymbol{\varepsilon} \Delta\boldsymbol{\varepsilon}' \mathbf{P}_{\bar{\mathbf{W}}} \mathbf{M}_{\mathbf{Z}_w} \mathbf{p}_w \left(\mathbf{p}_w' \mathbf{M}_{\mathbf{Z}_w} \mathbf{p}_w\right)^- Q_{pp,\alpha} \right] \\
&\le \lambda_{\max}\left(Q_{pp,\alpha}\right) \\
&\quad \times \operatorname{tr}\left[\mathbf{p}_w' \mathbf{M}_{\mathbf{Z}_w} \mathbf{P}_{\bar{\mathbf{W}}} \Delta\boldsymbol{\varepsilon} \Delta\boldsymbol{\varepsilon}' \mathbf{P}_{\bar{\mathbf{W}}} \mathbf{M}_{\mathbf{Z}_w} \mathbf{p}_w \; \left(\mathbf{p}_w' \mathbf{M}_{\mathbf{Z}_w} \mathbf{p}_w\right)^- \left(\mathbf{p}_w' \mathbf{M}_{\mathbf{Z}_w} \mathbf{p}_w\right)^- \right] \\
&\le \lambda_{\max}\left(Q_{pp,\alpha}\right) c_{1NT}^{-2} \frac{1}{(NT_2)^2} \operatorname{tr}\left(\mathbf{p}_w' \mathbf{M}_{\mathbf{Z}_w} \mathbf{P}_{\bar{\mathbf{W}}} \Delta\boldsymbol{\varepsilon} \Delta\boldsymbol{\varepsilon}' \mathbf{P}_{\bar{\mathbf{W}}} \mathbf{M}_{\mathbf{Z}_w} \mathbf{p}_w \right) \\
&= \lambda_{\max}\left(Q_{pp,\alpha}\right) c_{1NT}^{-2} \frac{1}{(NT_2)^2} \\
&\quad \times \operatorname{tr}\left(\bar{\mathbf{W}}' \Delta\boldsymbol{\varepsilon} \Delta\boldsymbol{\varepsilon}' \bar{\mathbf{W}} (\bar{\mathbf{W}}'\bar{\mathbf{W}})^- \bar{\mathbf{W}}' \mathbf{M}_{\mathbf{Z}_w} \mathbf{p}_w \mathbf{p}_w' \mathbf{M}_{\mathbf{Z}_w} \bar{\mathbf{W}} (\bar{\mathbf{W}}'\bar{\mathbf{W}})^- \right) \\
&\le \lambda_{\max}\left(Q_{pp,\alpha}\right) c_{1NT}^{-2} c_{2NT} \frac{1}{(NT_2)^2} \operatorname{tr}\left(\bar{\mathbf{W}}' \Delta\boldsymbol{\varepsilon} \Delta\boldsymbol{\varepsilon}' \bar{\mathbf{W}} \right).
\end{aligned}$$

where $Q_{pp,\alpha} = \int p^L(u)\, p^L(u)' \alpha(u)\, du$, $c_{1NT} = \lambda_{\min}(\frac{1}{NT_2} \mathbf{p}_w' \mathbf{M}_{\mathbf{Z}_w} \mathbf{p}_w)$, and $c_{2NT} = \lambda_{\max}((\bar{\mathbf{W}}'\bar{\mathbf{W}})^- \bar{\mathbf{W}}' \mathbf{M}_{\mathbf{Z}_w} \mathbf{p}_w \mathbf{p}_w' \mathbf{M}_{\mathbf{Z}_w} \bar{\mathbf{W}} (\bar{\mathbf{W}}'\bar{\mathbf{W}})^-) = O_P(1)$ by results in Eqs. (A.9) and (A.11). In addition, $\operatorname{tr}(\bar{\mathbf{W}}' \Delta\boldsymbol{\varepsilon} \Delta\boldsymbol{\varepsilon}' \bar{\mathbf{W}}) = O_P(L/N)$ by straightforward expectation calculations and Markov inequality. It follows that $\int D_{NT,1}(u)^2 \alpha(u)\, du = O_P(L/N)$. Analogously, noting that $\lambda_{\max}\left(\mathbf{P}_{\bar{\mathbf{W}}}\right) = 1$ and $\frac{1}{NT_2} \|\mathbf{R}\|^2 = O_P\left(L^{-2\gamma/(d_x+1)}\right)$ by Assumptions A.1 and A.7 and Lemma A.2 of Su and Jin (2012), we have

$$\begin{aligned}
&\int D_{NT,2}(u)^2 \alpha(u)\, du \\
&\le \lambda_{\max}\left(Q_{pp,\alpha}\right) c_{1NT}^{-2} \frac{1}{(NT_2)^2} \operatorname{tr}\left(\mathbf{p}_w' \mathbf{M}_{\mathbf{Z}_w} \mathbf{P}_{\bar{\mathbf{W}}} \mathbf{R} \mathbf{R}' \mathbf{P}_{\bar{\mathbf{W}}} \mathbf{M}_{\mathbf{Z}_w} \mathbf{p}_w \right) \\
&= \lambda_{\max}\left(Q_{pp,\alpha}\right) c_{1NT}^{-2} \frac{1}{(NT_2)^2} \operatorname{tr}\left(\mathbf{P}_{\bar{\mathbf{W}}} \mathbf{R} \mathbf{R}' \mathbf{P}_{\bar{\mathbf{W}}} \mathbf{M}_{\mathbf{Z}_w} \mathbf{p}_w \mathbf{p}_w' \mathbf{M}_{\mathbf{Z}_w} \right) \\
&\le \lambda_{\max}\left(Q_{pp,\alpha}\right) c_{1NT}^{-2} c_{3NT} \frac{1}{NT_2} \operatorname{tr}\left(\mathbf{P}_{\bar{\mathbf{W}}} \mathbf{R} \mathbf{R}' \mathbf{P}_{\bar{\mathbf{W}}} \right) \\
&\le \lambda_{\max}\left(Q_{pp,\alpha}\right) c_{1NT}^{-2} c_{3NT} \frac{1}{NT_2} \operatorname{tr}\left(\mathbf{R} \mathbf{R}' \right) \\
&= O(1)\, O_P(1)\, O_P(1)\, O_P\left(L^{-2\gamma/(d_x+1)}\right) = O_P\left(L^{-2\gamma/(d_x+1)}\right),
\end{aligned}$$

where $c_{3NT} = \lambda_{\max}\left(\frac{1}{NT_2}\mathbf{M}_{\mathbf{Z}_w}\mathbf{p}_w\mathbf{p}_w'\mathbf{M}_{\mathbf{Z}_w}\right) = \lambda_{\max}\left(\frac{1}{NT_2}\mathbf{p}_w'\mathbf{M}_{\mathbf{Z}_w}\mathbf{p}_w\right) = O_P(1)$ by (A.13) and the fact that $\lambda_{\max}\left(B'B\right) = \lambda_{\max}\left(BB'\right)$ for any real matrix B. In addition, $\int D_{NT,3}(u)^2\,\alpha(u)\,du = O_P\left(L^{-2\gamma/(d_x+1)}\right)$ by Assumption A.7 and standard arguments (see, e.g. Chen et al., 2005; Su and Jin, 2012). It follows that $\int\left[\hat{m}_{sieve}(u) - m(u)\right]^2\alpha(u)\,du = O_P\left(L/N + L^{-2\gamma/(d_x+1)}\right)$.

(ii) The proof is analogous to that in part (i) and thus omitted.

(iii) The proof parallels that of part (i). The major difference is that now we also need to use Assumption A.7(iv) and restrict our attention to the sequence of compact subsets $\{\mathcal{U}_N\}$ of $\mathcal{X}$ that is expanding at controllable rate. To appreciate this, we focus on the analysis of $D_{NT,2}(u)$ and $D_{NT,3}(u)$. As in the proof of (i), we can show that $\left\|\left(\mathbf{p}_w'\mathbf{M}_{\mathbf{Z}_w}\mathbf{p}_w\right)^{-}\mathbf{p}_w'\mathbf{M}_{\mathbf{Z}_w}\mathbf{P}_{\bar{\mathbf{W}}}\mathbf{R}\right\| = O_P(L^{-\gamma/(d_x+1)})$. Then by Cauchy–Schwarz inequality and Assumption A.7(iv), $\sup_{u\in\mathcal{U}_N}\left|D_{NT,2}(u)\right| \leq \left\|p^L(u)\right\|\left\|\left(\mathbf{p}_w'\mathbf{M}_{\mathbf{Z}_w}\mathbf{p}_w\right)^{-}\mathbf{p}_w'\mathbf{M}_{\mathbf{Z}_w}\mathbf{P}_{\bar{\mathbf{W}}}\mathbf{R}\right\| = \zeta_0(L)\,O_P(L^{-\gamma/(d_x+1)})$. By Assumptions A.7(ii) and (iv),

$$
\begin{aligned}
&\sup_{u\in\mathcal{U}_N}\left|D_{NT,3}(u)\right| \\
&= \sup_{u\in\mathcal{U}_N}\left|\left[p^L(u)'\beta_m - m(u)\right]\left(1+\|u\|^2\right)^{-\bar{\varpi}/2}\right|\left(1+\|u\|^2\right)^{\bar{\varpi}/2} \\
&\leq \left\|m - \Pi_{\infty,L}m\right\|_{\infty,\bar{\varpi}}\sup_{u\in\mathcal{U}_N}\left(1+\|u\|^2\right)^{\bar{\varpi}/2} = O(L^{-\gamma/(d_x+1)})\zeta_0(L).
\end{aligned}
$$

(iv) By the decomposition in Eq. (A.10), we can prove the theorem by showing that (iv1) $\mathcal{D}_{NT,1} \equiv \sqrt{NT_2}A_L^{-1/2}(u)\,D_{NT,1}(u) \xrightarrow{D} N(0,1)$, (iv2) $\mathcal{D}_{NT,2} \equiv \sqrt{NT_2}A_L^{-1/2}(u)\,D_{NT,2}(u) = o_P(1)$, and (iv3) $\mathcal{D}_{NT,3} \equiv \sqrt{NT_2}A_L^{-1/2}(u)\,D_{NT,3}(u) = o_P(1)$. By the fact that $\left\|p^L(u)\right\| \geq c > 0$ and Assumption A.8,

$$
\begin{aligned}
A_L(u) &= p^L(u)'\,Q_3^{-1}Q_4\Omega_1Q_4'Q_3^{-1}p^L(u) \\
&\geq \lambda_{\min}\left(Q_4\Omega_1Q_4'\right)\lambda_{\min}\left(Q_3^{-1}Q_3^{-1}\right)\left\|p^L(u)\right\| \\
&\geq \lambda_{\min}(\Omega_1)\left[\lambda_{\max}(Q_3)\right]^{-2}\left\|p^L(u)\right\|^2 > 0. \qquad \text{(A.15)}
\end{aligned}
$$

Let $Q_{4,NT} \equiv \mathbf{p}_w'\mathbf{M}_{\mathbf{Z}_w}\bar{\mathbf{W}}(\bar{\mathbf{W}}'\bar{\mathbf{W}})^{-}$. Noting that $\mathbf{p}_w'\mathbf{M}_{\mathbf{Z}_w}\bar{\mathbf{W}} = \mathbf{p}_w'\bar{\mathbf{W}} - \mathbf{p}_w'\mathbf{Z}_w\left(\mathbf{Z}_w'\mathbf{Z}_w\right)^{-}\mathbf{Z}_w'\bar{\mathbf{W}} = \Delta\mathbf{p}'\bar{\mathbf{W}} - \Delta\mathbf{p}'\mathbf{P}_{\bar{\mathbf{W}}}\Delta\mathbf{Z}\left(\Delta\mathbf{Z}'\mathbf{P}_{\bar{\mathbf{W}}}\Delta\mathbf{Z}\right)^{-}\Delta\mathbf{Z}'\bar{\mathbf{W}}$, we can readily apply Eqs. (A.9) and (A.11) to show that

$$\left\| Q_{4,NT} - Q_4 \right\| = O_P\left(L/\sqrt{N}\right) \tag{A.16}$$

where $Q_4 \equiv Q'_{\bar{w}p} Q_{\bar{w}}^{-1} - Q'_{\bar{w}p} Q_{\bar{w}}^{-1} Q_{\bar{w}z} \left(Q'_{\bar{w}z} Q_{\bar{w}}^{-1} Q_{\bar{w}z}\right)^{-1} Q'_{\bar{w}z} Q_{\bar{w}}^{-1}$. Note that

$$\begin{aligned}
\mathcal{D}_{NT,1} &= A_L^{-1/2}(u)\, p^L(u)'\, Q_{3,NT}^{-} Q_{4,NT} \frac{\bar{\mathbf{W}}'\Delta\boldsymbol{\varepsilon}}{\sqrt{NT_2}} \\
&= A_L^{-1/2}(u)'\, p^L(u)'\, Q_3^{-1} Q_4 \frac{\bar{\mathbf{W}}'\Delta\boldsymbol{\varepsilon}}{\sqrt{NT_2}} \\
&\quad + A_L^{-1/2}(u)\, p^L(u)' (Q_{3,NT}^{-} Q_{4,NT} - Q_3^{-1} Q_4) \frac{\bar{\mathbf{W}}'\Delta\boldsymbol{\varepsilon}}{\sqrt{NT_2}} \\
&\equiv \mathcal{D}_{NT,11} + \mathcal{D}_{NT,12}, \text{ say.}
\end{aligned}$$

It is standard to verify the Liapounov conditions and show that $\mathcal{D}_{NT,11} \xrightarrow{D} N(0,1)$. By Eqs. (A.12), (A.16), (A.15), and the fact that $\frac{1}{\sqrt{NT_2}} ||\bar{\mathbf{W}}'\Delta\boldsymbol{\varepsilon}|| = O_P(\sqrt{L})$, $\left|\mathcal{D}_{NT,12}\right| \leq A_L^{-1/2}(u) \left\| p^L(u) \right\|' ||Q_{3,NT}^{-} Q_{4,NT} - Q_3^{-1} Q_4|| \ \frac{1}{\sqrt{NT_2}} \left\| \bar{\mathbf{W}}'\Delta\boldsymbol{\varepsilon} \right\| \leq [\lambda_{\min}(\Omega_1)]^{-1/2} \lambda_{\max}(Q_3) \ \ O_P(L/\sqrt{N}) O_P(\sqrt{L}) = O_P(\sqrt{L^3/N}) = o_P(1)$. Then (iv1) follows.

Next, by the Cauchy–Schwarz inequality, the fact that $a'Ba \leq a'a\lambda_{\max}(B)$ for any vector a and conformable p.s.d. symmetric matrix B, that $\lambda_{\max}\left(C'C\right) = \lambda_{\max}\left(CC'\right)$ for any real matrix C, and that $\lambda_{\max}\left(\mathbf{P}_{\bar{\mathbf{W}}}\right) = 1$, we have

$$\begin{aligned}
\mathcal{D}_{NT,2}^2 &\leq NT_2 c_{NT} \mathbf{R}'\mathbf{P}_{\bar{\mathbf{W}}} \mathbf{M}_{\mathbf{Z}_w} \mathbf{p}_w \left(\mathbf{p}_w' \mathbf{M}_{\mathbf{Z}_w} \mathbf{p}_w\right)^{-} \left(\mathbf{p}_w' \mathbf{M}_{\mathbf{Z}_w} \mathbf{p}_w\right)^{-} \mathbf{p}_w' \mathbf{M}_{\mathbf{Z}_w} \mathbf{P}_{\bar{\mathbf{W}}} \mathbf{R} \\
&\leq c_{NT} \left[\lambda_{\min}\left(Q_{3,NT}\right)\right]^{-2} \frac{1}{NT_2} \mathbf{R}'\mathbf{P}_{\bar{\mathbf{W}}} \mathbf{M}_{\mathbf{Z}_w} \mathbf{p}_w \mathbf{p}_w' \mathbf{M}_{\mathbf{Z}_w} \mathbf{P}_{\bar{\mathbf{W}}} \mathbf{R} \\
&\leq c_{NT} \left[\lambda_{\min}\left(Q_{3,NT}\right)\right]^{-2} \lambda_{\max}\left(\frac{1}{NT_2} \mathbf{M}_{\mathbf{Z}_w} \mathbf{p}_w \mathbf{p}_w' \mathbf{M}_{\mathbf{Z}_w}\right) \mathbf{R}'\mathbf{P}_{\bar{\mathbf{W}}} \mathbf{R} \\
&\leq c_{NT} \left[\lambda_{\min}\left(Q_{3,NT}\right)\right]^{-2} \lambda_{\max}\left(Q_{3,NT}\right) \|\mathbf{R}\|^2 \\
&= O(1)\, O_P(1)\, O_P(1)\, O_P\left(NL^{-2\gamma/(d_x+1)}\right) = o_P(1)
\end{aligned}$$

where $c_{NT} \equiv A_L^{-1}(u)\, p^L(u)'\, p^L(u) \leq [\lambda_{\min}(\Omega_1)]^{-1} [\lambda_{\max}(Q_3)]^2 = O(1)$ by Eq. (A.15) and the next to last equality follows because $N^{-1} \|\mathbf{R}\|^2 = O_P\left(L^{-2\gamma/(d_x+1)}\right)$. Then (iv2) follows. By Eq. (A.15) and

Assumptions A.8(iii) and A.9,

$$
\begin{aligned}
\left|\mathcal{D}_{NT,3}\right| &= \sqrt{NT_2}A_L^{-1/2}(u)\left|\left[p^L(u)'\beta_m - m(u)\right]\left(1+\|u\|^2\right)^{-\bar{\varpi}/2}\right| \\
&\quad \times \left(1+\|u\|^2\right)^{\bar{\varpi}/2} \\
&\leq \sqrt{NT_2}A_L^{-1/2}(u)\left\|m - \Pi_{\infty,L}m\right\|_{\infty,\bar{\varpi}}\left(1+\|u\|^2\right)^{\bar{\varpi}/2} \\
&= O(\sqrt{N}L^{-\gamma/(d_x+1)}) = o(1).
\end{aligned}
$$

Thus, (iv3) follows. ■

APPENDIX B. DATA

B.1. List of Countries/Regions (93)

Algeria, Argentina, Australia, Austria, Bangladesh, Belgium, Benin, Bolivia, Botswana, Brazil, Burundi, Cameroon, Canada, Cyprus, Central African Rep.,

Table B1. Lists of Variables.

Variables	Definition	Source
GDP growth rate	Growth rate of real GDP per capita (constant 2005 prices)	UNCTAD
IPR	Updated GP index of patent rights	Park (2008)
Foreign Direct Investment	Inward FDI flows (US Dollars at current prices and current exchange rates in millions)	UNCTAD
Government consumption	General Government final consumption expenditure as a share of real GDP	UNCTAD
Schooling	Percentage of secondary schooling attained in population	Barro and Lee (2013)
Domestic Investment	Gross capital formation (US Dollars at current prices and current exchange rates in millions)	UNCTAD
Openness	Fraser Institute's Index of Freedom to trade internationally	Fraser Institute (Gwartney, Hall, Joshua, & Lawson, 2010)
Population growth rate	Five-year average annual growth rate	UNCTAD
Inflation	Percentage change in the GDP deflator	World Bank

Chile, China, Colombia, Congo, Costa Rica, Denmark, Dominican Rep., Ecuador, Egypt, El Salvador, Fiji, Finland, France, Gabon, Ghana, Greece, Guatemala, Guyana, Haiti, Honduras, Hong Kong, India, Iceland, Indonesia, Iran, Ireland, Ivory Coast, Israel, Italy, Jamaica, Japan, Jordan, Kenya, Korea (South), Malawi, Malaysia, Mali, Malta, Mauritius, Mexico, Morocco, Nepal, Netherlands, New Zealand, Nicaragua, Niger, Pakistan, Norway, Papua New Guinea, Paraguay, Peru, Philippines, Poland, Portugal, Romania, Rwanda, Senegal, Sierra Leone, Singapore, South Africa, Spain, Sri Lanka, Sweden, Switzerland, Syria, Tanzania, Thailand, Togo, Trinidad & Tobago, Tunisia, Turkey, Uganda, United Kingdom, United States, Uruguay, Venezuela, Zambia, Zimbabwe.

PART III
FINITE SAMPLE ECONOMETRICS

FINITE-SAMPLE BIAS OF THE CONDITIONAL GAUSSIAN MAXIMUM LIKELIHOOD ESTIMATOR IN ARMA MODELS

Yong Bao

Department of Economics, Purdue University, West Lafayette, IN, USA

ABSTRACT

I derive the finite-sample bias of the conditional Gaussian maximum likelihood estimator in ARMA models when the error follows some unknown non-normal distribution. The general procedure relies on writing down the score function and its higher order derivative matrices in terms of quadratic forms in the non-normal error vector with the help of matrix calculus. Evaluation of the bias can then be straightforwardly conducted. I give further simplified bias results for some special cases and compare with the existing results in the literature. Simulations are provided to confirm my simplified bias results.

Keywords: ARMA; conditional Gaussian maximum likelihood estimator; bias

JEL classifications: C32; C12

Essays in Honor of Aman Ullah
Advances in Econometrics, Volume 36, 207–244

ISSN: 0731-9053/doi:10.1108/S0731-905320160000036015

1. INTRODUCTION

The autoregressive moving average (ARMA) model popularized by the classical book of Box and Jenkins (1970) has been a workhorse model for modern time series analysis. Many statistical software packages such as Eviews and STATA have developed built-in functions to estimate ARMA models. More sophisticated models, for example, those with conditional higher moments, can arise if the error term is believed to deviate from the standard i.i.d. assumption. Also, integrated and fractionally integrated ARMA models may be used to model time series with long memory. Yet, the standard stationary ARMA models are still routinely used in applied work, and usually they are regarded as benchmark models against which more complicated models are compared.

The parameters in stationary ARMA models are usually estimated by the approach of maximum likelihood, and in some cases, the least squares may be used. In writing down the sample likelihood function, researchers frequently assume a Gaussian distribution. (And econometricians call the resulting estimator the quasi-maximum likelihood estimator (QMLE) when the true distribution is non-Gaussian.) Asymptotically, under some regularity assumptions, the resulting Gaussian likelihood estimator behaves quite nicely by following the work of White (1994). In particular, the Gaussian likelihood estimator is $\sqrt{T}$-consistent, where T is the sample size, and asymptotically normal.

In finite samples, however, the Gaussian likelihood estimator can be biased. For the special case of the autoregressive (AR) model, the well-known Kendall's (1954) approximate bias formulae $-2\rho/T$ and $(-1+3\rho)/T$ for AR models of order 1 without and with an intercept, respectively, were long recognized in the literature. Bao and Ullah (2007b) showed that Kendall's formulae are also valid under non-normality.[1] For the simple moving average (MA) model of order 1, Bao and Ullah (2007b) derived the approximate bias of the Gaussian likelihood estimator of the MA parameter under non-normality. For some simple ARMA models, the bias results were available in Tanaka (1984) and Cordeiro and Klein (1994) when the error distribution is Gaussian. For the general ARMA models with possible non-Gaussian errors, however, no attempt has been made in the literature to derive the finite-sample bias of the QMLE of the complete set of parameters.

In deriving their bias results, Cordeiro and Klein (1994) followed the approach of Cox and Snell (1968) that is valid for the maximum likelihood estimator (MLE) when the assumed distribution coincides with the true distribution. The approach of Tanaka (1984) shares essentially the same spirit. Most economic and financial data are by nature distributed as non-Gaussian, though researchers are never sure about what non-normal distributions shall be used to describe the data. To deal with non-normality in the data, researchers have adopted strategies that include parametric flexible distributions and semi- and nonparametric distributions. Nevertheless, in terms of estimation and inference, the Gaussian maximum likelihood approach typically fares well asymptotically, and at the same time it does not call for a search for a complicated, and possibly misspecified, non-normal distribution. In finite samples, on the other hand, the Gaussian MLE might behave poorly. So in this paper, I focus on the Gaussian likelihood estimator, or QMLE, in stationary ARMA models and study its finite-sample bias when the data are in fact non-normally distributed.

Bao and Ullah (2007a, 2007b) and Bao (2013) outlined the general methodology to approximate the finite-sample bias based on some stochastic expansion of the moment condition in identifying the parameter vector.[2] The challenge in deriving the finite-sample bias is to work out the expectations involved, especially when the distribution is not normal. Recently, Yang (2015) suggested that when it is not possible to evaluate the expectations, the (residual-based) bootstrap might be used. The trade-off is then it does not enable researchers to have analytical bias expressions and thus the nature of the bias might not be well understood. It should be pointed out that Yang (2015) still follows the approach of Bao and Ullah (2007a, 2007b) and Bao (2013); it is just that in the last step, when one is not able to evaluate the expectations, the bootstrap is called upon to approximate the expectations. In this paper, I show that with the help of matrix calculus as in Bao and Hua (2014) to write down the score function and its higher order derivatives conveniently in terms of non-normal quadratic forms, explicit evaluation of the expectations is possible, and thus one could avoid the bootstrap procedure.[3] In turn, the bias of the Gaussian MLE in ARMA models can be straightforwardly calculated.

The plan of this paper is as follows. In the next section, a brief discussion of the approach to be employed in this paper is discussed. Section 3 derives the general bias result for ARMA models with possible nonzero means and non-normal error distributions. Section 4 applies the result from Section 3 to some specific models and provides further simplified analytical results. Some discrepancy is found between my results and those from Tanaka (1984) for the ARMA(1,1) model. A Monte Carlo study is then provided to demonstrate that my analytical results generally capture the true bias behaviors quite well across different parameter ranges, under both normal and noncentral t distributions. The last section concludes. Technical details are collected in the appendix.

Throughout, vec, rvec, tr, $\otimes$, and $\odot$ denote the column vectorization, row vectorization, trace, Kronecker product, Hadamard (element-by-element) product operators, respectively. Matrix dimension subscripts or superscripts are typically suppressed, unless deemed necessary. $\boldsymbol{I}$, $\mathbf{1}$, $\mathbf{0}$, and $\mathbf{O}$ represent the identity matrix, vector of ones, zero vector, and zero matrix, respectively, and $\boldsymbol{K}_{m,n}$ is the $mn \times mn$ commutation matrix following the definition of Magnus and Neudecker (1979). $[\boldsymbol{A}_s]_{s=1}^{m} = [\boldsymbol{A}_1, \ldots, \boldsymbol{A}_m]$ denotes a matrix of m horizontal blocks $\boldsymbol{A}_s$, where $\boldsymbol{A}_s$ are indexed by s. The ij-th element of a matrix $\boldsymbol{A}$ is denoted by $\{\boldsymbol{A}\}_{ij}$ or a_{ij}.

2. THE APPROXIMATE BIAS

Before I derive the finite-sample bias of the QMLE in ARMA models, it is convenient to present and compare the general approaches of Cox and Snell (1968) and Bao and Ullah (2007a, 2007b) and Bao (2013). I use the following notation: $\mathcal{L} = \mathcal{L}(\boldsymbol{\beta}) = \mathcal{L}(\boldsymbol{\beta}, \boldsymbol{y})$ is the log-likelihood function from a sample $\boldsymbol{y}$ of size T, $\boldsymbol{\beta}$ is a $k \times 1$ parameter vector, $\boldsymbol{\psi} = \psi(\boldsymbol{\beta})$ is the score function, $\boldsymbol{\mathcal{H}} = \mathcal{H}(\boldsymbol{\beta})$ is the Hessian matrix, $\boldsymbol{\mathcal{F}} = \mathcal{F}(\boldsymbol{\beta}) = -\mathrm{E}(\mathcal{H}(\boldsymbol{\beta}))$ is the Fisher information matrix, $\boldsymbol{\mathcal{P}} = \mathrm{E}(\boldsymbol{\psi}\boldsymbol{\psi}')$ is the expectation of the outer product of the score function, $\boldsymbol{\mathcal{D}} = \mathcal{D}(\boldsymbol{\beta}) = \mathrm{E}(\partial\mathcal{H}(\boldsymbol{\beta})/\partial\boldsymbol{\beta}')$ is the expectation of the second-order derivative matrix of the score function, and $\boldsymbol{\mathcal{E}} = \mathrm{E}(\boldsymbol{\mathcal{H}} \otimes \boldsymbol{\psi}')$.[4] Throughout, expectations are taken with respect to the true distribution of the data.

When dealing with the MLE $\hat{\boldsymbol{\beta}}$, Cox and Snell (1968) showed that the large-sample approximation to the bias of its sth component is

$$\mathrm{B}(\hat{\beta}_s) = \sum_{i,j,l=1}^{k} f^{si} f^{jl} \left(e_{ij,l} + \frac{1}{2} d_{ijl} \right) + o(T^{-1}), \tag{1}$$

where $e_{ij,l} = \mathrm{E}[(\partial^2\mathcal{L}/\partial\beta_i\partial\beta_j)(\partial\mathcal{L}/\partial\beta_l)]$, $d_{ijl} = \mathrm{E}(\partial^3\mathcal{L}/\partial\beta_i\partial\beta_j\partial\beta_l)$, f^{ij} is the ij-th element of the inverse of $\boldsymbol{\mathcal{F}}$.[5] It should be emphasized that Cox and Snell's (1968) result is valid for the MLE in the sense that the assumed distribution in defining $\mathcal{L}$ is the same as the actual distribution of the data. When the assumed distribution is Gaussian but the data may be non-Gaussian, as is typically the case for most economic and financial data, then Eq. (1) is not necessarily correct in approximating the finite-sample bias of the resulting Gaussian MLE.

In applying Cox and Snell's (1968) formula to the MLE, one has to derive the approximate bias for each parameter one by one. Recognizing this challenge, Cordeiro and Klein (1994) took a step further by providing a matrix representation,

$$\mathrm{B}(\hat{\boldsymbol{\beta}}) = \boldsymbol{\mathcal{F}}^{-1}\boldsymbol{A}\mathrm{vec}(\boldsymbol{\mathcal{F}}^{-1}) + o(T^{-1}), \tag{2}$$

where $\boldsymbol{A} = (\boldsymbol{A}^{(1)}, \boldsymbol{A}^{(2)}, \ldots, \boldsymbol{A}^{(k)})$ with the $k \times k$ matrix $\boldsymbol{A}^{(s)}$ consisting of $a_{ij}^{(l)} = \partial\mathrm{E}[(\partial^2\mathcal{L}/\partial\beta_i\partial\beta_j)]/\partial\beta_l - d_{ijl}/2$. Note that $\partial\mathrm{E}[(\partial^2\mathcal{L}/\partial\beta_i\partial\beta_j)]/\partial\beta_l = d_{ijl} + e_{ij,l}$ by straightforward calculus, so Eq. (2) is equivalent to

$$\mathrm{B}(\hat{\boldsymbol{\beta}}) = \boldsymbol{\mathcal{F}}^{-1} \left(\boldsymbol{\mathcal{E}} + \frac{1}{2}\boldsymbol{\mathcal{D}} \right) \mathrm{vec}(\boldsymbol{\mathcal{F}}^{-1}) + o(T^{-1}). \tag{3}$$

Bao and Ullah (2007a, 2007b) and Bao (2013) showed that under typical regularity conditions, a valid bias approximation to a large-class of $\sqrt{T}$-consistent estimators, including the QMLE, is given by

$$\begin{aligned}\mathrm{B}(\hat{\boldsymbol{\beta}}) &= \mathcal{F}^{-1}\mathcal{E}\mathrm{vec}(\mathcal{F}^{-1})\\ &\quad + \frac{1}{2}\mathcal{F}^{-1}\mathcal{D}(\mathcal{F}^{-1}\otimes\mathcal{F}^{-1})\mathrm{vec}(\mathcal{P}) + o(T^{-1}).\end{aligned} \tag{4}$$

Comparing Eq. (4) with Eq. (3), one can see immediately that Eq. (4) includes Eq. (3) as a special case, since for the case of MLE, the information equality holds, namely, $\mathcal{F}=\mathcal{P}$, and $(\mathcal{F}^{-1}\otimes\mathcal{F}^{-1})\mathrm{vec}(\mathcal{P})=\mathrm{vec}(\mathcal{F}^{-1}\mathcal{P}\mathcal{F}^{-1})=\mathrm{vec}(\mathcal{F}^{-1})$. For a typical QMLE, the information equality in general does not hold, thus one should not blindly apply Eq. (3) (or Eq. (2), or Eq. (1)) to derive the approximate bias. For MLE, one should of course not take the trouble of replacing $\mathrm{vec}(\mathcal{F}^{-1})$ with $(\mathcal{F}^{-1}\otimes\mathcal{F}^{-1})\mathrm{vec}(\mathcal{P})$, and thus should use Eq. (3) (or Eq. (2), or Eq. (1)) directly. The merit of Eq. (4) is its applicability to a large class of $\sqrt{T}$-consistent estimators, in addition to its ability to jointly evaluating the approximate biases of all the elements of $\hat{\boldsymbol{\beta}}$. In what follows, I use Eq. (4) to derive the finite-sample bias of the QMLE in ARMA models.[6]

A remaining challenge to use Eq. (4) is how to evaluate the expectations involved in $\mathcal{F}$, $\mathcal{P}$, $\mathcal{D}$, $\mathcal{E}$. Recall that for QMLE, the distribution is not normal and usually unknown. One natural option may be to resort to the bootstrap, as suggested by Yang (2015) in the framework of spatial AR models. In addition to its numerical intensity, the bootstrap provides little insight into the nature of the bias. Another option may be to approximate the expectations by numerical simulations. This was employed by Linton (1997) and Iglesias and Phillips (2008) in the context of conditional volatility models. Again, it may mask the nature of the bias structure. It also relies on the distribution assumption in its implementation. In the next section, I show that it is possible to derive and evaluate the approximate bias of the QMLE in ARMA models analytically. This relies on writing down the sample score function as quadratic forms in the non-normal error vector by following the approach of Bao and Hua (2014). I derive the resulting Hessian matrix, third-order derivative matrix, and the Kronecker product matrix of the Hessian and score all in terms of non-normal quadratic forms. With some mild assumption on the moments (up to order 4) of the error term, without complete knowledge of the distribution, I am then able to evaluate analytically these expectations in Eq. (4).

3. THE GENERAL BIAS RESULT OF QMLE IN ARMA(p, q)

I consider the following ARMA(p, q) process:

$$(y_t - \mu) - \sum_{i=1}^{p} \phi_i (y_{t-i} - \mu) = u_t - \sum_{j=1}^{q} \theta_i u_{t-j}, \tag{5}$$

where the u_t is the i.i.d. error term with mean zero, variance σ^2, skewness coefficient γ_1, and excess kurtosis coefficient γ_2. It is assumed that the process is stationary and invertible and the polynomials $1 - \sum_{i=1}^{p} \phi_i z^i$ and $1 - \sum_{i=1}^{q} \theta_i z^i$ do not have common roots. Collect the parameters as $\boldsymbol{\phi} = (\phi_1, \ldots, \phi_p)'$, $\boldsymbol{\theta} = (\theta_1, \ldots, \theta_q)'$, $\boldsymbol{\alpha} = (\mu, \boldsymbol{\phi}', \boldsymbol{\theta}')'$, $\boldsymbol{\beta} = (\boldsymbol{\alpha}', \sigma^2)'$.

The mean of the process is μ, which may or may not known a prior. (If it is known, without loss of generality, it can be assumed to be zero.) In what follows, it is understood that the relevant parts of $\mathcal{F}$, $\mathcal{P}$, $\mathcal{D}$, $\mathcal{E}$ that are associated with μ should be deleted if one is to derive the approximate bias when μ is known.

Following Bao and Hua (2014), I use $\boldsymbol{L}$ to denote a $T \times T$ lag matrix, which has ones on the subdiagonal and zero elsewhere, and $\boldsymbol{L}_r = (\text{vec}(\boldsymbol{L}), \ldots, \text{vec}(\boldsymbol{L}^r))$. If one treats the pre-sample $y_{1-p} = \cdots = y_0 = \mu$, $u_{1-q} = \cdots = u_0 = 0$, then in matrix notation (5) may be written as

$$\boldsymbol{\Phi}(\boldsymbol{y} - \mu \mathbf{1}) = \boldsymbol{\Theta} \boldsymbol{u}, \tag{6}$$

where $\boldsymbol{y} = (y_1, \ldots, y_T)'$, $\boldsymbol{u} = (u_1, \ldots, u_T)'$, $\boldsymbol{\Phi} = \boldsymbol{I} - \sum_{i=1}^{p} \boldsymbol{L}^i \phi_i$ and $\boldsymbol{\Theta} = \boldsymbol{I} - \sum_{i=1}^{q} \boldsymbol{L}^i \theta_i$. The Gaussian conditional sample log-likelihood function, conditional on $y_{1-p} = \cdots = y_0 = \mu$, $u_{1-q} = \cdots = u_0 = 0$, can be written as

$$\mathcal{L}(\boldsymbol{\beta}) = -\frac{T}{2} \log(2\pi) - \frac{T}{2} \log \sigma^2 - \frac{\boldsymbol{u}'\boldsymbol{u}}{2\sigma^2}. \tag{7}$$

Maximizing Eq. (7) with respect to $\boldsymbol{\beta}$ gives the Gaussian MLE, or QMLE, $\hat{\boldsymbol{\beta}}$.[7] Under typical regularity conditions, the QMLE $\hat{\boldsymbol{\beta}}$ is asymptotically normal:

$$\sqrt{T}(\hat{\boldsymbol{\beta}} - \boldsymbol{\beta}) \to N(\mathbf{0}, \boldsymbol{V}), \tag{8}$$

where $\boldsymbol{V} = T\mathcal{F}^{-1}\mathcal{P}\mathcal{F}^{-1}$ is the Huber (1967) sandwich asymptotic covariance.[8]

The score function may be put as

$$\boldsymbol{\psi} = \frac{1}{\sigma^2}\begin{pmatrix} \boldsymbol{u}'\boldsymbol{\Theta}^{-1}\boldsymbol{\Phi}\mathbf{1} \\ \boldsymbol{L}_p'\mathrm{vec}(\boldsymbol{\Phi}^{-1\prime}\boldsymbol{u}\boldsymbol{u}') \\ -\boldsymbol{L}_q'\mathrm{vec}(\boldsymbol{\Theta}^{-1\prime}\boldsymbol{u}\boldsymbol{u}') \\ \dfrac{\boldsymbol{u}'\boldsymbol{u}}{2\sigma^2} - \dfrac{T}{2} \end{pmatrix}. \tag{9}$$

One can easily verify that regardless of the error distribution, $\mathrm{E}(\boldsymbol{\psi}) = \mathbf{0}$. Based on this matrix representation of the score function, the expectation of its outer product, $\boldsymbol{\mathcal{P}} = \mathrm{E}(\boldsymbol{\psi}\boldsymbol{\psi}')$, may be written as

$$\boldsymbol{\mathcal{P}} = \begin{pmatrix} \dfrac{1}{\sigma^2}\mathbf{1}'\boldsymbol{\Phi}'\boldsymbol{\Theta}^{-1\prime}\boldsymbol{\Theta}^{-1}\boldsymbol{\Phi}\mathbf{1} & \mathbf{0}_p' & \mathbf{0}_q' & \dfrac{\gamma_1}{2\sigma^3}\mathbf{1}'\boldsymbol{\Theta}^{-1}\boldsymbol{\Phi}\mathbf{1} \\ \mathbf{0}_p & \boldsymbol{L}_p'(\boldsymbol{\Phi}^{-1}\otimes\boldsymbol{\Phi}^{-1})\boldsymbol{L}_p & -\boldsymbol{L}_p'(\boldsymbol{\Phi}^{-1}\otimes\boldsymbol{\Theta}^{-1})\boldsymbol{L}_q & \mathbf{0}_p \\ \mathbf{0}_q & -\boldsymbol{L}_q'(\boldsymbol{\Theta}^{-1}\otimes\boldsymbol{\Phi}^{-1})\boldsymbol{L}_p & \boldsymbol{L}_q'(\boldsymbol{\Theta}^{-1}\otimes\boldsymbol{\Theta}^{-1})\boldsymbol{L}_q & \mathbf{0}_q \\ \dfrac{\gamma_1}{2\sigma^3}\mathbf{1}'\boldsymbol{\Theta}^{-1}\boldsymbol{\Phi}\mathbf{1} & \mathbf{0}_p' & \mathbf{0}_q' & \dfrac{(\gamma_2+2)T}{4\sigma^4} \end{pmatrix}. \tag{10}$$

The Hessian matrix now becomes

$$\boldsymbol{\mathcal{H}} = \begin{pmatrix} \mathcal{H}_{\mu,\mu} & \mathcal{H}_{\mu,\boldsymbol{\phi}'} & \mathcal{H}_{\mu,\boldsymbol{\theta}'} & \mathcal{H}_{\mu,\sigma^2} \\ \mathcal{H}_{\boldsymbol{\phi},\mu} & \mathcal{H}_{\boldsymbol{\phi},\boldsymbol{\phi}'} & \mathcal{H}_{\boldsymbol{\phi},\boldsymbol{\theta}'} & \mathcal{H}_{\boldsymbol{\phi},\sigma^2} \\ \mathcal{H}_{\boldsymbol{\theta},\mu} & \mathcal{H}_{\boldsymbol{\theta},\boldsymbol{\phi}'} & \mathcal{H}_{\boldsymbol{\theta},\boldsymbol{\theta}'} & \mathcal{H}_{\boldsymbol{\theta},\sigma^2} \\ \mathcal{H}_{\sigma^2,\mu} & \mathcal{H}_{\sigma^2,\boldsymbol{\phi}'} & \mathcal{H}_{\sigma^2,\boldsymbol{\theta}'} & \mathcal{H}_{\sigma^2,\sigma^2} \end{pmatrix}, \tag{11}$$

where

$$\mathcal{H}_{\mu,\mu} = -\frac{1}{\sigma^2}\mathbf{1}'\boldsymbol{\Phi}'\boldsymbol{\Theta}^{-1\prime}\boldsymbol{\Theta}^{-1}\boldsymbol{\Phi}\mathbf{1},$$

$$\mathcal{H}_{\mu,\sigma^2} = \mathcal{H}_{\sigma^2,\mu} = -\frac{1}{\sigma^4}\boldsymbol{u}'\boldsymbol{\Theta}^{-1}\boldsymbol{\Phi}\mathbf{1},$$

$$\mathcal{H}_{\sigma^2,\sigma^2} = \frac{T}{2\sigma^4} - \frac{1}{\sigma^6}\boldsymbol{u}'\boldsymbol{u},$$

$$\mathcal{H}_{\boldsymbol{\phi},\mu} = -\frac{1}{\sigma^2}\boldsymbol{L}_p'\text{vec}(\boldsymbol{\Theta}^{-1\prime}\boldsymbol{u}1') - \frac{1}{\sigma^2}\boldsymbol{L}_p'\text{vec}(\boldsymbol{\Phi}^{-1\prime}\boldsymbol{\Theta}^{-1}\boldsymbol{\Phi}\mathbf{1}\boldsymbol{u}'),$$

$$\mathcal{H}_{\boldsymbol{\theta},\mu} = \frac{1}{\sigma^2}\boldsymbol{L}_q'\text{vec}(\boldsymbol{\Theta}^{-1\prime}\boldsymbol{\Theta}^{-1}\boldsymbol{\Phi}\mathbf{1}\boldsymbol{u}') + \frac{1}{\sigma^2}\boldsymbol{L}_q'\text{vec}(\boldsymbol{\Theta}^{-1\prime}\boldsymbol{u}\mathbf{1}'\boldsymbol{\Phi}'\boldsymbol{\Theta}^{-1\prime}),$$

$$\mathcal{H}_{\boldsymbol{\phi},\sigma^2} = -\frac{1}{\sigma^4}\boldsymbol{L}_p'\text{vec}(\boldsymbol{\Phi}^{-1\prime}\boldsymbol{u}\boldsymbol{u}'),$$

$$\mathcal{H}_{\boldsymbol{\theta},\sigma^2} = \frac{1}{\sigma^4}\boldsymbol{L}_q'\text{vec}(\boldsymbol{\Theta}^{-1\prime}\boldsymbol{u}\boldsymbol{u}'),$$

$$\mathcal{H}_{\boldsymbol{\phi},\boldsymbol{\phi}'} = -\frac{1}{\sigma^2}\boldsymbol{L}_p'(\boldsymbol{\Phi}^{-1}\boldsymbol{u}\boldsymbol{u}' \otimes \boldsymbol{\Phi}^{-1})\boldsymbol{L}_p,$$

$$\mathcal{H}_{\boldsymbol{\phi},\boldsymbol{\theta}'} = \frac{1}{\sigma^2}\boldsymbol{L}_p'(\boldsymbol{\Phi}^{-1}\boldsymbol{u}\boldsymbol{u}' \otimes \boldsymbol{\Theta}^{-1})\boldsymbol{L}_q + \frac{1}{\sigma^2}\boldsymbol{L}_p'(\boldsymbol{\Theta}^{-1}\boldsymbol{u}\boldsymbol{u}' \otimes \boldsymbol{\Phi}^{-1\prime})\boldsymbol{K}_{T,T}\boldsymbol{L}_q,$$

$$\mathcal{H}_{\boldsymbol{\theta},\boldsymbol{\theta}'} = -\frac{1}{\sigma^2}\boldsymbol{L}_q'(\boldsymbol{\Theta}^{-1}\boldsymbol{u}\boldsymbol{u}' \otimes \boldsymbol{\Theta}^{-1})\boldsymbol{L}_q - \frac{2}{\sigma^2}\boldsymbol{L}_q'(\boldsymbol{\Theta}^{-1}\boldsymbol{u}\boldsymbol{u}' \otimes \boldsymbol{\Theta}^{-1\prime})\boldsymbol{K}_{T,T}\boldsymbol{L}_q.$$

Then it follows that the information matrix is

$$\mathcal{F} = \begin{pmatrix} \frac{1}{\sigma^2}\mathbf{1}'\boldsymbol{\Phi}'\boldsymbol{\Theta}^{-1\prime}\boldsymbol{\Theta}^{-1}\boldsymbol{\Phi}\mathbf{1} & \mathbf{0}_p' & \mathbf{0}_q' & 0 \\ \mathbf{0}_p & \boldsymbol{L}_p'(\boldsymbol{\Phi}^{-1} \otimes \boldsymbol{\Phi}^{-1})\boldsymbol{L}_p & -\boldsymbol{L}_p'(\boldsymbol{\Phi}^{-1} \otimes \boldsymbol{\Theta}^{-1})\boldsymbol{L}_q & \mathbf{0}_p \\ \mathbf{0}_q & -\boldsymbol{L}_q'(\boldsymbol{\Theta}^{-1} \otimes \boldsymbol{\Phi}^{-1})\boldsymbol{L}_p & \boldsymbol{L}_q'(\boldsymbol{\Theta}^{-1} \otimes \boldsymbol{\Theta}^{-1})\boldsymbol{L}_q & \mathbf{0}_q \\ 0 & \mathbf{0}_p' & \mathbf{0}_q' & \frac{T}{2\sigma^4} \end{pmatrix}. \tag{12}$$

The third-order derivative of $\psi(\boldsymbol{\beta})$ is defined as a $(p+q+2) \times (p+q+2)^2$ matrix by following the convention of Rilstone et al. (1996), namely, one takes the derivative of each element/block of $\mathcal{H}(\boldsymbol{\beta})$ with respect to $\boldsymbol{\beta}'$. Then I may present

$$\mathcal{D} = (\mathcal{D}_1, \mathcal{D}_2, \mathcal{D}_3, \mathcal{D}_4), \tag{13}$$

where

$$\mathcal{D}_1 = \begin{pmatrix} 0 & \frac{2}{\sigma^2}[\mathrm{vec}(\boldsymbol{\Theta}^{-1\prime}\boldsymbol{\Theta}^{-1}\boldsymbol{\Phi}\mathbf{1}\mathbf{1}')]'\boldsymbol{L}_p & -\frac{2}{\sigma^2}[\mathrm{vec}(\boldsymbol{\Theta}^{-1\prime}\boldsymbol{\Theta}^{-1}\boldsymbol{\Phi}\mathbf{1}\mathbf{1}'\boldsymbol{\Phi}'\boldsymbol{\Theta}^{-1\prime})]'\boldsymbol{L}_q & \frac{1}{\sigma^4}\mathbf{1}'\boldsymbol{\Phi}'\boldsymbol{\Theta}^{-1\prime}\boldsymbol{\Theta}^{-1}\boldsymbol{\Phi}\mathbf{1} \\ \frac{2}{\sigma^2}\boldsymbol{L}_p'\mathrm{vec}(\boldsymbol{\Theta}^{-1\prime}\boldsymbol{\Theta}^{-1}\boldsymbol{\Phi}\mathbf{1}\mathbf{1}') & \mathbf{O}_p & \mathbf{O}_{p\times q} & \mathbf{0}_p \\ -\frac{2}{\sigma^2}\boldsymbol{L}_q'\mathrm{vec}(\boldsymbol{\Theta}^{-1\prime}\boldsymbol{\Theta}^{-1}\boldsymbol{\Phi}\mathbf{1}\mathbf{1}'\boldsymbol{\Phi}'\boldsymbol{\Theta}^{-1\prime}) & \mathbf{O}_{q\times p} & \mathbf{O}_q & \mathbf{0}_q \\ \frac{1}{\sigma^4}\mathbf{1}'\boldsymbol{\Phi}'\boldsymbol{\Theta}^{-1\prime}\boldsymbol{\Theta}^{-1}\boldsymbol{\Phi}\mathbf{1} & \mathbf{0}_p' & \mathbf{0}_q' & 0 \end{pmatrix}.$$

$$\mathcal{D}_2 = \left(\begin{matrix} \frac{2}{\sigma^2}[\mathrm{vec}(\boldsymbol{\Theta}^{-1\prime}\boldsymbol{\Theta}^{-1}\boldsymbol{\Phi}\mathbf{1}\mathbf{1}')]'\boldsymbol{L}_p & \mathbf{0}_{p^2}' \\ \mathbf{O}_p & \mathbf{O}_{p\times p^2} \\ \mathbf{O}_{q\times p} & -[\boldsymbol{L}_q'(\boldsymbol{\Phi}^{-1\prime}\otimes\boldsymbol{\Theta}^{-1\prime}\boldsymbol{L}^{i\prime}\boldsymbol{\Phi}^{-1\prime}+(\boldsymbol{L}^{i\prime}\boldsymbol{\Phi}^{-1\prime}\otimes\boldsymbol{\Theta}^{-1\prime}\boldsymbol{\Phi}^{-1})\boldsymbol{K}_{T,T})\boldsymbol{L}_p]_{i=1}^p \cdots \\ \mathbf{0}_p' & \frac{1}{\sigma^2}\mathrm{rvec}[\boldsymbol{L}_p'(\boldsymbol{\Phi}^{-1}\otimes\boldsymbol{\Phi}^{-1})\boldsymbol{L}_p] \end{matrix}\right.$$

$$\left.\begin{matrix} \mathbf{0}_{pq}' & \mathbf{0}_p' \\ -[\boldsymbol{L}_p'(\boldsymbol{\Phi}^{-1}\otimes\boldsymbol{\Phi}^{-1}\boldsymbol{\Theta}^{-1}\boldsymbol{L}^j+\boldsymbol{\Phi}^{-1}\boldsymbol{\Theta}^{-1}\boldsymbol{L}^j\otimes\boldsymbol{\Phi}^{-1})\boldsymbol{L}_q]_{j=1}^q & \frac{1}{\sigma^2}\boldsymbol{L}_p'(\boldsymbol{\Phi}^{-1}\otimes\boldsymbol{\Phi}^{-1})\boldsymbol{L}_p \\ [\boldsymbol{L}_q'(\boldsymbol{\Theta}^{-1}\otimes\boldsymbol{\Phi}^{-1}\boldsymbol{\Theta}^{-1}\boldsymbol{L}^j+(\boldsymbol{\Phi}^{-1}\boldsymbol{\Theta}^{-1}\otimes\boldsymbol{\Theta}^{-1}\boldsymbol{L}^j)\boldsymbol{K}_{T,T}+2\boldsymbol{\Theta}^{-1}\boldsymbol{\Theta}^{-1}\boldsymbol{L}^j\otimes\boldsymbol{\Phi}^{-1})\boldsymbol{L}_p]_{j=1}^q & -\frac{1}{\sigma^2}\boldsymbol{L}_q'(\boldsymbol{\Theta}^{-1}\otimes\boldsymbol{\Phi}^{-1})\boldsymbol{L}_p \\ -\frac{1}{\sigma^2}\mathrm{rvec}[\boldsymbol{L}_p'(\boldsymbol{\Phi}^{-1}\otimes\boldsymbol{\Theta}^{-1})\boldsymbol{L}_q] & \mathbf{0}_p' \end{matrix}\right),$$

$$\mathcal{D}_3 = \left(\begin{matrix} -\frac{2}{\sigma^2}[\mathrm{vec}(\boldsymbol{\Theta}^{-1\prime}\boldsymbol{\Theta}^{-1}\boldsymbol{\Phi}\mathbf{1}\mathbf{1}'\boldsymbol{\Phi}'\boldsymbol{\Theta}^{-1\prime})]'\boldsymbol{L}_q & \mathbf{0}_{pq}' \\ \mathbf{O}_{p\times q} & -[\boldsymbol{L}_p'(\boldsymbol{\Phi}^{-1}\otimes\boldsymbol{\Phi}^{-1}\boldsymbol{\Theta}^{-1}\boldsymbol{L}^i+(\boldsymbol{\Phi}^{-1}\boldsymbol{\Theta}^{-1}\otimes\boldsymbol{\Phi}^{-1}\boldsymbol{L}^i)\boldsymbol{K}_{T,T})\boldsymbol{L}_q]_{i=1}^p \\ \mathbf{O}_q & [\boldsymbol{L}_q'(\boldsymbol{\Theta}^{-1}\otimes\boldsymbol{\Phi}^{-1}\boldsymbol{\Theta}^{-1}\boldsymbol{L}^i+\boldsymbol{\Theta}^{-1}\boldsymbol{L}^i\boldsymbol{\Theta}^{-1\prime}\otimes\boldsymbol{\Phi}^{-1\prime}+2(\boldsymbol{\Theta}^{-1}\boldsymbol{\Theta}^{-1}\otimes\boldsymbol{\Phi}^{-1}\boldsymbol{L}^i)\boldsymbol{K}_{T,T})\boldsymbol{L}_q]_{i=1}^p \cdots \\ \mathbf{0}_q' & -\frac{1}{\sigma^2}\mathrm{rvec}[\boldsymbol{L}_q'(\boldsymbol{\Theta}^{-1}\otimes\boldsymbol{\Phi}^{-1})\boldsymbol{L}_p] \end{matrix}\right.$$

$$\left.\begin{matrix} \mathbf{0}_{q^2}' & \mathbf{0}_q' \\ [\boldsymbol{L}_p'(\boldsymbol{\Phi}^{-1}\boldsymbol{\Theta}^{-1}\boldsymbol{L}^j\otimes\boldsymbol{\Theta}^{-1}+(\boldsymbol{\Phi}^{-1}\boldsymbol{\Theta}^{-1}\otimes\boldsymbol{\Theta}^{-1}\boldsymbol{L}^j)\boldsymbol{K}_{T,T}+2\boldsymbol{\Phi}^{-1}\otimes\boldsymbol{\Theta}^{-1}\boldsymbol{\Theta}^{-1}\boldsymbol{L}^j)\boldsymbol{L}_q]_{j=1}^q & -\frac{1}{\sigma^2}\boldsymbol{L}_p'(\boldsymbol{\Phi}^{-1}\otimes\boldsymbol{\Theta}^{-1})\boldsymbol{L}_q \\ -2[\boldsymbol{L}_q'(\boldsymbol{\Theta}^{-1}\otimes\boldsymbol{\Theta}^{-1}\boldsymbol{\Theta}^{-1}\boldsymbol{L}^j+\boldsymbol{\Theta}^{-1}\boldsymbol{\Theta}^{-1}\boldsymbol{L}^j\otimes\boldsymbol{\Theta}^{-1}+(\boldsymbol{\Theta}^{-1}\boldsymbol{\Theta}^{-1}\otimes\boldsymbol{\Theta}^{-1}\boldsymbol{L}^j)\boldsymbol{K}_{T,T})\boldsymbol{L}_q]_{j=1}^q & \frac{1}{\sigma^2}\boldsymbol{L}_q'(\boldsymbol{\Theta}^{-1}\otimes\boldsymbol{\Phi}^{-1})\boldsymbol{L}_q \\ \frac{1}{\sigma^2}\mathrm{rvec}[\boldsymbol{L}_q'(\boldsymbol{\Theta}^{-1}\otimes\boldsymbol{\Phi}^{-1})\boldsymbol{L}_q] & \mathbf{0}_q' \end{matrix}\right),$$

$$
\mathcal{D}_4 = \begin{pmatrix}
\frac{1}{\sigma^4}\mathbf{1}'\boldsymbol{\Phi}'\boldsymbol{\Theta}^{-1'}\boldsymbol{\Theta}^{-1}\boldsymbol{\Phi}\mathbf{1} & \mathbf{0}'_p & \mathbf{0}'_q & 0 \\
\mathbf{0}_p & \frac{1}{\sigma^2}\boldsymbol{L}'_p(\boldsymbol{\Phi}^{-1}\otimes\boldsymbol{\Phi}^{-1})\boldsymbol{L}_q & -\frac{1}{\sigma^2}\boldsymbol{L}'_p(\boldsymbol{\Phi}^{-1}\otimes\boldsymbol{\Theta}^{-1})\boldsymbol{L}_q & \mathbf{0}_p \\
\mathbf{0}_q & -\frac{1}{\sigma^2}\boldsymbol{L}'_q(\boldsymbol{\Theta}^{-1}\otimes\boldsymbol{\Phi}^{-1})\boldsymbol{L}_p & \frac{1}{\sigma^2}\boldsymbol{L}'_q(\boldsymbol{\Theta}^{-1}\otimes\boldsymbol{\Theta}^{-1})\boldsymbol{L}_q & \mathbf{0}_q \\
0 & \mathbf{0}'_p & \mathbf{0}'_q & \frac{2T}{\sigma^6}
\end{pmatrix}.
$$

Next, I may write

$$
\mathcal{E} = \begin{pmatrix}
\mathrm{E}(\mathcal{H}_{\mu,\mu}\otimes\boldsymbol{\psi}') & \mathrm{E}(\mathcal{H}_{\mu,\boldsymbol{\phi}'}\otimes\boldsymbol{\psi}') & \mathrm{E}(\mathcal{H}_{\mu,\boldsymbol{\theta}'}\otimes\boldsymbol{\psi}') & \mathrm{E}(\mathcal{H}_{\mu,\sigma^2}\otimes\boldsymbol{\psi}') \\
\mathrm{E}(\mathcal{H}_{\boldsymbol{\phi},\mu}\otimes\boldsymbol{\psi}') & \mathrm{E}(\mathcal{H}_{\boldsymbol{\phi},\boldsymbol{\phi}'}\otimes\boldsymbol{\psi}') & \mathrm{E}(\mathcal{H}_{\boldsymbol{\phi},\boldsymbol{\theta}'}\otimes\boldsymbol{\psi}') & \mathrm{E}(\mathcal{H}_{\boldsymbol{\phi},\sigma^2}\otimes\boldsymbol{\psi}') \\
\mathrm{E}(\mathcal{H}_{\boldsymbol{\theta},\mu}\otimes\boldsymbol{\psi}') & \mathrm{E}(\mathcal{H}_{\boldsymbol{\theta},\boldsymbol{\phi}'}\otimes\boldsymbol{\psi}') & \mathrm{E}(\mathcal{H}_{\boldsymbol{\theta},\boldsymbol{\theta}'}\otimes\boldsymbol{\psi}') & \mathrm{E}(\mathcal{H}_{\boldsymbol{\theta},\sigma^2}\otimes\boldsymbol{\psi}') \\
\mathrm{E}(\mathcal{H}_{\mu,\sigma^2}\otimes\boldsymbol{\psi}') & \mathrm{E}(\mathcal{H}_{\sigma^2,\boldsymbol{\phi}'}\otimes\boldsymbol{\psi}') & \mathrm{E}(\mathcal{H}_{\sigma^2,\boldsymbol{\theta}'}\otimes\boldsymbol{\psi}') & \mathrm{E}(\mathcal{H}_{\sigma^2,\sigma^2}\otimes\boldsymbol{\psi}')
\end{pmatrix}. \quad (14)
$$

where detailed expressions for these expectations are provided in the appendix.

In summary, with Eqs. (10), (12), (13), and (14), one can directly use Eq. (4) to evaluate the finite-sample bias of the full set of the QMLE $\hat{\boldsymbol{\beta}}$ in ARMA models.[9]

4. DEMONSTRATIONS

In this section, I demonstrate that one may be able to further simplify analytically the bias result (4) in terms of model parameters explicitly by working with some simple ARMA models. The details are provided in the appendix.

First consider the ARMA(1,1) model. My bias result following Eq. (4) becomes

$$
\mathrm{B}(\hat{\boldsymbol{\beta}}) = \frac{1}{T}\begin{pmatrix}
0 \\
\dfrac{-\phi(1+\theta^2)\left(2+\phi+\phi^2\right)+\theta\left(1+\phi+5\phi^2+\phi^3\right)}{(\phi-\theta)^2} \\
\dfrac{\theta\left(1+\theta+\theta^2\right)-(\theta+2)\left(1+\theta^2\right)\phi+\theta\left(3+\theta-\theta^2\right)\phi^2}{(\phi-\theta)^2} \\
-3\sigma^2
\end{pmatrix} + o(T^{-1}). \quad (15)
$$

Some interesting observations follow: (i) Up to the order of approximation, $\hat{\mu}$ is unbiased, $\hat{\sigma}^2$ is downward biased, and $\hat{\phi}$ and $\hat{\theta}$ may be severely biased when ϕ

is close to θ. Note that I assume $\phi \neq \theta$ to begin with. When $\phi = \theta$, ARMA(1,1) degenerates into ARMA(0,0) and ϕ and θ are not identified. One can also see this clearly by examining the information matrix $\mathcal{F}$ provided in the appendix, which becomes singular when $\phi = \theta$. (ii) The distribution parameters γ_1 and γ_2 in fact do not appear in the bias result. In other words, Eq. (15) is robust to the distribution assumption of the ARMA(1,1) model, though the general bias result (4) (with $\mathcal{P}$, $\mathcal{F}$, $\mathcal{D}$, $\mathcal{E}$ given by Eqs. (10), (12), (13), and (14), respectively) indicates that the distribution parameters may matter.[10] (iii) If $\theta = 0$ but $\phi \neq 0$, so the true process is AR(1) but the model is estimated as ARMA(1,1), Eq. (15) indicates that the bias of the estimated AR parameter $\hat{\phi}$ in this redundant model is $-[\left(2+\phi+\phi^2\right)/\phi]/T$, standing in contrast to the well-known $-(1+3\phi)/T$ result for the AR(1) regression model. Further, the estimated MA parameter $\hat{\theta}$ is not unbiased: its bias is $-(2/\phi)/T$, standing in contrast to the traditional wisdom in linear regression models that estimating a redundant parameter does not introduce bias for it. One can tell a similar story when $\phi = 0$ but $\theta \neq 0$.

Given the second observation, it follows that my bias result should be the same as that derived by following the approach of Cox and Snell (1968) that deals with the MLE. Surprisingly, little attempt was made in the literature to apply Cox and Snell (1968) to the ARMA(1,1) model, perhaps partly because of the lengthy algebra to be involved to derive the bias for each parameter estimator one by one. The only publication that I am aware of is Tanaka (1984). Tanaka did not provide any detail of his derivation and his bias expressions for ARMA(1,1) is

$$\mathrm{B}(\hat{\boldsymbol{\beta}})_{\text{Tanaka}} = \frac{1}{T}\begin{pmatrix} 0 \\ -\phi - \dfrac{2\phi(1-\phi\theta)^2}{(\phi-\theta)^2} - \dfrac{2(1-\phi\theta)^3}{(\phi-\theta)^3} + \dfrac{3\phi(1-\phi\theta)^4}{(\phi-\theta)^4} - \dfrac{(1-\phi\theta)(1+\phi)}{\phi-\theta} \\ \theta - \dfrac{2(1-\phi\theta)}{\phi-\theta} - \dfrac{4\theta(1-\phi\theta)^2}{(\phi-\theta)^2} + \dfrac{(1-\phi\theta)^3}{(\phi-\theta)^3} + \dfrac{3\theta(1-\phi\theta)^4}{(\phi-\theta)^4} - \dfrac{(1-\phi\theta)(1+\theta)}{\phi-\theta} \\ -3\sigma^2 \end{pmatrix} + o(T^{-1}). \tag{16}$$

As can be seen, there is quite a difference between my derived bias and Tanaka's (1984) regarding $\hat{\phi}$ and $\hat{\theta}$. I am not able to verify directly with Tanaka, so in the following I conduct a Monte Carlo study to assess which one better approximates the finite-sample bias. For a fair comparison, I simulate an ARMA(1,1) with Gaussian errors, in line with Tanaka's (1984) model assumptions. To save space, I provide only the bias results regarding $\hat{\phi}$ and $\hat{\theta}$. (Simulations results confirm very well the unbiasedness of $\hat{\mu}$ and the downward bias $-3\sigma^2/T$ of $\hat{\sigma}^2$.) Table 1 reports the "true" bias (defined as the difference between the estimate and the true

Table 1. Finite-Sample Bias of MLE in ARMA(1,1) with Unknown Mean.

ϕ	θ	$B(\hat{\phi})$ True	$B(\hat{\theta})$ True	$B(\hat{\phi})$	$B(\hat{\theta})$	$B(\hat{\phi})$ Tanaka	$B(\hat{\theta})$ Tanaka
0.3	−0.8	−0.0202	−0.0137	−0.0215	−0.0114	−0.0394	−0.0166
	−0.5	−0.0281	−0.0173	−0.0279	−0.0162	−0.0551	−0.0340
	−0.3	−0.0381	−0.0260	−0.0365	−0.0240	−0.0683	−0.0505
	−0.1	−0.0612	−0.0491	−0.0564	−0.0433	−0.0220	−0.0103
	0	−0.0818	−0.0712	−0.0797	−0.0667	0.2574	0.2704
	0.1	−0.1043	−0.0963	−0.1366	−0.1244	2.4909	2.5573
	0.5	0.0086	0.0370	−0.0019	0.0209	4.4155	3.9187
	0.8	0.0112	0.0411	0.0098	0.0321	0.1212	0.0848
0.8	−0.8	−0.0237	−0.0211	−0.0349	−0.0119	−0.0383	−0.0127
	−0.5	−0.0315	−0.0169	−0.0367	−0.0154	−0.0386	−0.0164
	−0.3	−0.0357	−0.0189	−0.0385	−0.0184	−0.0385	−0.0184
	−0.1	−0.0405	−0.0231	−0.0411	−0.0224	−0.0374	−0.0190
	0	−0.0436	−0.0263	−0.0430	−0.0250	−0.0360	−0.0180
	0.1	−0.0475	−0.0307	−0.0455	−0.0283	−0.0331	−0.0150
	0.3	−0.0613	−0.0464	−0.0538	−0.0389	−0.0145	0.0083
	0.5	−0.0999	−0.0896	−0.0760	−0.0650	0.1160	0.1750

value averaged over 100,000 simulations), followed by the bias calculated from my result (15) and that from Tanaka's (1984) result (16), with $\mu = 1$, $\sigma^2 = 0.5$, and $T = 100$.[11]

Table 1 shows that my bias result (15) in general captures well the true bias behaviors of $\hat{\phi}$ and $\hat{\theta}$ in finite samples. Tanaka's (1984) formula (16) may work well, but there are quite some occasions that it may provide very misleading results and there can be substantial discrepancy between the calculated bias from his formula (16) and the true one.

As mentioned earlier, if the mean parameter μ is known a priori, then the corresponding parts in $\mathcal{P}$, $\mathcal{F}$, $\mathcal{D}$, $\mathcal{E}$ can be deleted to derive the bias of $\hat{\boldsymbol{\beta}} = (\hat{\phi}, \hat{\theta}, \hat{\sigma}^2)'$. Some simple algebra shows that in this case (4) produces the following bias result:

$$\mathrm{B}(\hat{\boldsymbol{\beta}}|\mu) = \frac{1}{T}\begin{pmatrix} -\dfrac{\phi\left(1+\phi^2+\theta^2-4\theta\phi+\theta^2\phi^2\right)}{(\phi-\theta)^2} \\ -\dfrac{\phi+\theta^2\phi-2\theta\phi^2-\theta^3\left(1-\phi^2\right)}{(\phi-\theta)^2} \\ -2\sigma^2 \end{pmatrix} + o(T^{-1}). \tag{17}$$

Table 2. Finite-Sample Bias of MLE in ARMA(1,1) with Known Mean.

ϕ	θ	$B(\hat{\phi})$ True	$B(\hat{\theta})$ True	$B(\hat{\phi})$	$B(\hat{\theta})$	$B(\hat{\phi}\|\mu)$ Tanaka	$B(\hat{\theta}\|\mu)$ Tanaka
0.3	−0.8	−0.0065	−0.0100	−0.0068	−0.0091	−0.0247	−0.0143
	−0.5	−0.0091	−0.0093	−0.0092	−0.0090	−0.0364	−0.0268
	−0.3	−0.0132	−0.0115	−0.0129	−0.0113	−0.0447	−0.0378
	−0.1	−0.0242	−0.0212	−0.0229	−0.0201	0.0114	0.0129
	0	−0.0355	−0.0334	−0.0363	−0.0333	0.3007	0.3037
	0.1	−0.0487	−0.0494	−0.0736	−0.0710	2.5540	2.6107
	0.5	−0.0506	−0.0360	−0.0572	−0.0428	4.3602	3.8549
	0.8	−0.0128	0.0028	−0.0099	0.0047	0.1014	0.0575
0.8	−0.8	−0.0160	−0.0109	−0.0164	−0.0098	−0.0199	−0.0106
	−0.5	−0.0169	−0.0104	−0.0173	−0.0100	−0.0193	−0.0110
	−0.3	−0.0179	−0.0107	−0.0182	−0.0105	−0.0182	−0.0105
	−0.1	−0.0194	−0.0120	−0.0195	−0.0116	−0.0158	−0.0082
	0	−0.0206	−0.0131	−0.0205	−0.0125	−0.0135	−0.0055
	0.1	−0.0222	−0.0148	−0.0218	−0.0139	−0.0094	−0.0005
	0.3	−0.0288	−0.0223	−0.0265	−0.0191	0.0129	0.0280
	0.5	−0.0504	−0.0469	−0.0400	−0.0350	0.1520	0.2050

The bias expressions now are quite different compared with the unknown μ case. They also stand in contrast to the expressions from Tanaka (1984):

$$B(\hat{\boldsymbol{\beta}}|\mu)_{\text{Tanaka}} = \frac{1}{T}\begin{pmatrix} -\phi - \dfrac{2\phi(1-\phi\theta)^2}{(\phi-\theta)^2} - \dfrac{2(1-\phi\theta)^3}{(\phi-\theta)^3} + \dfrac{3\phi(1-\phi\theta)^4}{(\phi-\theta)^4} \\ \theta - \dfrac{2(1-\phi\theta)}{\phi-\theta} - \dfrac{4\theta(1-\phi\theta)^2}{(\phi-\theta)^2} + \dfrac{(1-\phi\theta)^3}{(\phi-\theta)^3} + \dfrac{3\theta(1-\phi\theta)^4}{(\phi-\theta)^4} \\ -2\sigma^2 \end{pmatrix} + o(T^{-1}). \tag{18}$$

Simulations are run again to assess the finite-sample performance of my bias result and compare with that from Tanaka (1984). Similar as before, Table 2 (with the same experiment design as in Table 1 except that μ is not estimated) shows that my bias result performs really well, but Tanaka's (1984) does not seem to work on some occasions.

Finally, since my bias results (15) and (17) are derived for the QMLE, I also conduct an experiment with u_t simulated from a standardized noncentral t distribution with noncentrality parameter 1 and degrees of freedom 10. The results (15) and (17) indicate that the bias of $\hat{\boldsymbol{\beta}}$ should be robust to the distribution specification

Table 3. Finite-Sample Bias of QMLE in ARMA(1,1) with Unknown Mean.

ϕ	θ	$T=100$				$T=200$			
		$B(\hat{\phi})$ True	$B(\hat{\theta})$ True	$B(\hat{\phi})$	$B(\hat{\theta})$	$B(\hat{\phi})$ True	$B(\hat{\theta})$ True	$B(\hat{\phi})$	$B(\hat{\theta})$
0.3	−0.8	−0.0204	−0.0137	−0.0215	−0.0114	−0.0109	−0.0064	−0.0107	−0.0057
	−0.5	−0.0290	−0.0181	−0.0279	−0.0162	−0.0146	−0.0088	−0.0139	−0.0081
	−0.3	−0.0392	−0.0271	−0.0365	−0.0240	−0.0194	−0.0131	−0.0183	−0.0120
	−0.1	−0.0624	−0.0502	−0.0564	−0.0433	−0.0311	−0.0245	−0.0282	−0.0216
	0	−0.0835	−0.0727	−0.0797	−0.0667	−0.0453	−0.0387	−0.0398	−0.0333
	0.1	−0.1065	−0.0982	−0.1366	−0.1244	−0.0731	−0.0679	−0.0683	−0.0622
	0.5	0.0096	0.0381	−0.0019	0.0209	0.0055	0.0166	−0.0010	0.0105
	0.8	0.0114	0.0415	0.0098	0.0321	0.0079	0.0201	0.0049	0.0160
0.8	−0.8	−0.0242	−0.0210	−0.0349	−0.0119	−0.0137	−0.0084	−0.0174	−0.0059
	−0.5	−0.0319	−0.0171	−0.0367	−0.0154	−0.0169	−0.0081	−0.0183	−0.0077
	−0.3	−0.0360	−0.0191	−0.0385	−0.0184	−0.0186	−0.0093	−0.0192	−0.0092
	−0.1	−0.0407	−0.0233	−0.0411	−0.0224	−0.0205	−0.0114	−0.0206	−0.0112
	0	−0.0438	−0.0266	−0.0430	−0.0250	−0.0218	−0.0129	−0.0215	−0.0125
	0.1	−0.0478	−0.0310	−0.0455	−0.0283	−0.0234	−0.0148	−0.0227	−0.0142
	0.3	−0.0617	−0.0467	−0.0538	−0.0389	−0.0288	−0.0211	−0.0269	−0.0194
	0.5	−0.1015	−0.0910	−0.0760	−0.0650	−0.0448	−0.0394	−0.0380	−0.0325

Table 4. Finite-Sample Bias of QMLE in ARMA(1,1) with Known Mean.

ϕ	θ	$T=100$				$T=200$			
		$B(\hat{\phi})$ True	$B(\hat{\theta})$ True	$B(\hat{\phi})$	$B(\hat{\theta})$	$B(\hat{\phi})$ True	$B(\hat{\theta})$ True	$B(\hat{\phi})$	$B(\hat{\theta})$
0.3	−0.8	−0.0067	−0.0099	−0.0068	−0.0091	−0.0037	−0.0050	−0.0034	−0.0046
	−0.5	−0.0099	−0.0100	−0.0092	−0.0090	−0.0051	−0.0050	−0.0046	−0.0045
	−0.3	−0.0144	−0.0127	−0.0129	−0.0113	−0.0072	−0.0063	−0.0065	−0.0056
	−0.1	−0.0256	−0.0226	−0.0229	−0.0201	−0.0134	−0.0116	−0.0114	−0.0101
	0	−0.0369	−0.0346	−0.0363	−0.0333	−0.0215	−0.0194	−0.0182	−0.0167
	0.1	−0.0511	−0.0514	−0.0736	−0.0710	−0.0388	−0.0376	−0.0368	−0.0355
	0.5	−0.0497	−0.0350	−0.0572	−0.0428	−0.0291	−0.0227	−0.0286	−0.0214
	0.8	−0.0126	0.0032	−0.0099	0.0047	−0.0051	0.0024	−0.0050	0.0024
0.8	−0.8	−0.0162	−0.0109	−0.0164	−0.0098	−0.0083	−0.0053	−0.0082	−0.0049
	−0.5	−0.0172	−0.0106	−0.0173	−0.0100	−0.0087	−0.0052	−0.0086	−0.0050
	−0.3	−0.0182	−0.0110	−0.0182	−0.0105	−0.0092	−0.0054	−0.0091	−0.0052
	−0.1	−0.0198	−0.0123	−0.0195	−0.0116	−0.0099	−0.0060	−0.0098	−0.0058
	0	−0.0210	−0.0135	−0.0205	−0.0125	−0.0105	−0.0065	−0.0102	−0.0062
	0.1	−0.0227	−0.0153	−0.0218	−0.0139	−0.0112	−0.0072	−0.0109	−0.0069
	0.3	−0.0292	−0.0225	−0.0265	−0.0191	−0.0139	−0.0102	−0.0132	−0.0096
	0.5	−0.0510	−0.0473	−0.0400	−0.0350	−0.0231	−0.0208	−0.0200	−0.0175

for ARMA(1,1). Tables 3 and 4 report the simulation results (with the same experiment design as in Tables 1 and 2 except the distribution of u_t and the additional $T = 200$). They again reveal the quite remarkable performance of my QMLE bias results (15) and (17) in the presence of a non-Gaussian error distribution.

For completeness, I have also derived the bias results for the QMLE in MA(1), MA(2), AR(1), and AR(2) models, with known or unknown means. Similar to the ARMA(1,1) model, the non-normality parameters γ_1 and γ_2 do not appear in the bias expressions, so my bias results should be the same as those in Tanaka (1984) for the MLE, and it turns out to be the case for these four models. Note that Cordeiro and Klein (1994) verified Tanaka's (1984) results for AR(1), MA(1), and AR(2) under the assumption of normality.

5. CONCLUDING REMARKS

I have derived the finite-sample approximate bias of the conditional Gaussian MLE (or QMLE) in ARMA models. With the help of matrix calculus, I write down the score function and its higher order derivative matrices in terms of quadratic forms in the non-normal error vector. The approximate bias can then be evaluated straightforwardly in terms of model parameters directly. The error distribution may matter to the extent that its third and fourth moments may affect the finite-sample bias of the QMLE. I have worked with the full parameter vector jointly, instead of deriving the bias for each parameter one by one. For a general ARMA model, calculation of the approximate bias of the QMLE in finite samples can be straightforwardly conducted. For specific ARMA models, the general result may be further simplified. I demonstrate this through some simple ARMA models and I find that the bias results are in fact robust to the error distribution. For a specific ARMA(1,1) model, there is a discrepancy between my bias results and those given in Tanaka (1984). Through simulations, I find that my ARMA(1,1) bias formulae work really well in capturing the true bias behaviors of the (Q)MLE. Given the analytical bias result, one may immediately construct a feasible bias-corrected QMLE by replacing the parameters in the bias formula with their consistent estimates. It can be shown that the feasible bias-corrected QMLE is unbiased up to the order of bias approximation. If one is concerned about the bias-variance trade-off in implementing the bias-correction procedure, a very promising route to pursue is the indirect inference method of Phillips and Yu (2009); one may argue that the ultimate purpose of bias-correction is to improve subsequent inferences, and thus it may be more desirable to investigate how to correct the variance/MSE so as to design a corrected t ratio as in Yang (2015). I leave these two issues for future research.

ACKNOWLEDGMENTS

I am grateful to two anonymous referees and Gloria González-Rivera for their constructive feedback. I also thank the participants in the Advances in Econometrics conference (Riverside, CA) for their valuable comments. I am indebted to Aman Ullah for inspiring me to start this line of research.

NOTES

1. When the distribution is normal, the exact moments of the least squares estimator of the AR coefficient can be evaluated, at least numerically, by following the approach of Sawa (1978). When the distribution is non-normal, however, it is typically impossible to derive the exact moments, unless one imposes some specific, possibly misspecified, distributions. Thus, in this paper, I focus on the approximate bias.

2. Earlier works in the literature include Rilstone, Srivastava, and Ullah (1996), Rilstone and Ullah (2002), among others. See Ullah (2004) for an excellent treatment of this subject.

3. The primary motivation of using the bootstrap in Yang (2015) was that for the estimator of parameter of main interest after the other parameters are concentrated out, the score function is in terms of ratios of random variates, and so is the finite-sample bias of the estimator. By imposing a very strong assumption that the moments of these ratios exist, which are typically unverifiable under non-normality, Yang (2015) proceeded to approximate the assumed unkown moments via the bootstrap procedure.

4. Note that here matrix derivatives are defined recursively as in Rilstone et al. (1996), which stands in contrast to, for example, Magnus and Neudecker (1988).

5. In Cox and Snell (1968), f^{ij} was originally defined as the element of $-\mathcal{F}$. Since Eq. (1) involves the product of two f's, using f^{ij} or $-f^{ij}$ is equivalent.

6. Note that in Bao and Ullah (2007a, 2007b) and Bao (2013), $\boldsymbol{\psi}$, $\mathcal{F}$, $\mathcal{H}$, $\mathcal{D}$ are all scaled down by $T^{1/2}$. Obviously, scaling up or down these matrices at the same time by the same factor does not affect the bias formula (4).

7. In this paper, I work with the conditional (Q)MLE so that a nice matrix representation (6) is available. This stands in contrast to the exact MLE. For the finite-sample approximate bias, as the contribution of the initial observations to the sample likelihood function is $o_P(T)$ but the leading terms in $\mathcal{P}$, $\mathcal{F}$, $\mathcal{D}$, $\mathcal{E}$ are all $O(T)$, the exact and conditional MLE's should share the same finite-sample bias features, up to $O(T^{-1})$.

8. From Eqs. (10) and (12) to follow, one can easily see that for the QMLE of $\boldsymbol{\alpha}$, this sandwich form degenerates simply into the inverse of the part of $\mathcal{F}$ associated with $\boldsymbol{\alpha}$.

9. When T is small, one may use directly $\boldsymbol{K}_{T,T}$, which is $T^2 \times T^2$, in $\boldsymbol{D}$ and $\mathcal{E}$. For large T, however, it is advised not to use this matrix of large dimensions, but to replace $\boldsymbol{K}_{T,T}\boldsymbol{L}_r$ by $(\text{vec}(\boldsymbol{L}'), \ldots, \text{vec}(\boldsymbol{L}'^r))$ for $r = p, q$. A Mathematica code is available upon request from the author for implementing the calculation of the finite-sample bias.

10. It is yet to be confirmed whether the robustness result (of the bias to non-normality) can be generalized to any ARMA(p, q) model. In case one is not sure about this, γ_1 and γ_2 may be replaced by their consistent estimates that can be constructed from the sample analogues based on the residuals.

11. I have tried other combinations of μ, σ^2, T, as well as different values of ϕ and θ. The findings are virtually the same. Since I have derived analytically the expectations (i.e., those terms in $\mathcal{F}$, $\mathcal{P}$, $\mathcal{D}$, and $\mathcal{E}$) in the bias approximation, I do not compare with the bootstrap approach of Yang (2015) that replaces the expectations with the bootstrap sample averages. On the other hand, I have experimented with the standard bootstrap approach: Given $\hat{\boldsymbol{\beta}}$ and $\hat{\boldsymbol{u}}$, (i) generate the bootstrap sample $\boldsymbol{y}^* = \hat{\mu}\mathbf{1} + \hat{\boldsymbol{\Phi}}^{-1}\hat{\boldsymbol{\Theta}}\hat{\boldsymbol{u}}^*$ with $\hat{\boldsymbol{u}}^*$ resampled from $\hat{\boldsymbol{u}}$; (ii) re-estimate the model with $\boldsymbol{y}^*$ and denote the QMLE by $\hat{\boldsymbol{\beta}}^{(b)}$; (iii) repeat (i) and (ii) B times;

(iv) approximate the bias by $B^{-1} \sum_{b=1}^{B} \hat{\boldsymbol{\beta}}^{(b)} - \hat{\boldsymbol{\beta}}$. It turns out that the bootstrap approach provides no better bias approximations than my analytical bias results.

REFERENCES

Bao, Y. (2013). Finite sample bias of the QMLE in spatial autoregressive models. *Econometric Theory*, *29*, 68–88.

Bao, Y., & Hua, Y. (2014). On the Fisher information matrix of a vector ARMA process. *Economics Letters*, *123*, 14–16.

Bao, Y., & Ullah, A. (2007a). Finite sample properties of maximum likelihood estimator in spatial models. *Journal of Econometrics*, *137*, 396–413.

Bao, Y., & Ullah, A. (2007b). The second-order bias and mean squared error of estimators in time series models. *Journal of Econometrics*, *140*, 650–669.

Birgé, L. (2014). Model selection for density estimation with L2-loss. *Probability Theory and Related Fields*, *158*, 533–574.

Box, G. E. P., & Jenkins, G. M. (1970). *Time series analysis: Forecasting and control*. San Francisco, CA: Holden-Day.

Cattaneo, J. M. D., Crump, R. K., & Jansson, M. (2014). Bootstrapping density-weighted average derivatives. *Econometric Theory*, *30*, 1135–1164.

Cordeiro, G. M., & Klein, R. (1994). Bias correction in ARMA models. *Statistics and Probability Letters*, *19*, 169–176.

Cox, D. R., & Snell, J. (1968). A general definition of residuals. *Journal of the Royal Statistical Society Series B*, *30*, 248–275.

Huber, P. J. (1967). The behavior of maximum likelihood estimates under nonstandard conditions. *Proceedings of the fifth Berkeley symposium on mathematical statistics and probability* (Vol. 1, pp. 221–233).

Iglesias, E. M., & Phillips, G. D. A. (2008). Finite sample theory of QMLEs in ARCH models with dynamics in the mean equation. *Journal of Time Series Analysis*, *29*, 719–737.

Kendall, M. G. (1954). Note on bias in estimation of autocorrelation. *Biometrika*, *41*, 403–404.

Linton, O. (1997). An asymptotic expansion in the GARCH(1,1) model. *Econometric Theory*, *13*, 558–581.

Magnus, J. R., & Neudecker, H. (1979). The commutation matrix: Some properties and applications. *Annals of Statistics*, *7*, 381–394.

Magnus, J. R., & Neudecker, H. (1988). *Matrix differential calculus with applications in statistics and econometrics*. Chichester, NY: Wiley.

Phillips, P. C. B., & Yu, J. (2009). Maximum likelihood and Gaussian estimation of continuous time models in finance. In T. G. Andersen, R. A. Davis, J.-P. Kreiß, T. Mikosch (Eds.), *Handbook of financial time series* (pp. 497–530). New York, NY: Springer-Verlag.

Rilstone, P., Srivastava, V. K., & Ullah, A. (1996). The second-order bias and mean squared error of nonlinear estimators. *Journal of Econometrics*, *75*, 369–395.

Rilstone, P., & Ullah, A. (2002). Sampling bias in Heckman's sample selection estimator. In Y. P. Chaubey (Ed.), *Recent advances in statistical methods* (pp. 263–273). Hackensack, NJ: World Scientific.

Sawa, T. (1978). The exact moments of the least squares estimator for the autoregressive model. *Journal of Econometrics*, *8*, 159–172.

Tanaka, K. (1984). An asymptotic expansion associated with the maximum likelihood estimators in ARMA models. *Journal of the Royal Statistical Society Series B*, *46*, 58–67.

Ullah, A. (2004). *Finite sample econometrics*. New York, NY: Oxford University Press.
White, H. (1994). *Estimation, inference and specification analysis*. New York, NY: Cambridge University Press.
Yang, Z. (2015). A general method for third-order bias and variance correction on a nonlinear estimator. *Journal of Econometrics*, *186*, 178–200.

APPENDIX

A.1. The Derivative Matrices and Their Expectations

Note that $\boldsymbol{L}$ is strictly lower triangular, so are $\boldsymbol{\Phi}$, $\boldsymbol{\Theta}$, $\boldsymbol{\Phi}^{-1}$, $\boldsymbol{\Theta}^{-1}$, and their powers and products. One can also verify that $\boldsymbol{\Phi}^{-1}\boldsymbol{L}^i = \boldsymbol{L}^i\boldsymbol{\Phi}^{-1}$ (and $\boldsymbol{\Theta}^{-1}\boldsymbol{L}^i = \boldsymbol{L}^i\boldsymbol{\Theta}^{-1}$, $\boldsymbol{\Theta}\boldsymbol{\Phi} = \boldsymbol{\Phi}\boldsymbol{\Theta}$), so that

$$\begin{aligned}
\boldsymbol{\Theta}^{-1}\boldsymbol{L}^i\boldsymbol{\Phi}^{-1}\boldsymbol{\Theta} &= \boldsymbol{\Theta}^{-1}\boldsymbol{L}^i\boldsymbol{\Phi}^{-1}\left(\boldsymbol{I} - \sum_{j=1}^{q}\boldsymbol{L}^j\theta_j\right)\\
&= \boldsymbol{\Theta}^{-1}\boldsymbol{L}^i\boldsymbol{\Phi}^{-1} - \sum_{j=1}^{q}\theta_j\boldsymbol{\Theta}^{-1}\boldsymbol{L}^i\boldsymbol{\Phi}^{-1}\boldsymbol{L}^j\\
&= \boldsymbol{\Theta}^{-1}\boldsymbol{L}^i\boldsymbol{\Phi}^{-1} - \sum_{j=1}^{q}\theta_j\boldsymbol{\Theta}^{-1}\boldsymbol{L}^j\boldsymbol{L}^i\boldsymbol{\Phi}^{-1}\\
&= \boldsymbol{\Theta}^{-1}\left(\boldsymbol{I} - \sum_{j=1}^{q}\boldsymbol{L}^j\theta_i\right)\boldsymbol{L}^i\boldsymbol{\Phi}^{-1}\\
&= \boldsymbol{L}^i\boldsymbol{\Phi}^{-1}.
\end{aligned}$$

From Eq. (6), I can write $\boldsymbol{u} = \boldsymbol{\Theta}^{-1}\ \boldsymbol{\Phi}(\boldsymbol{y} - \boldsymbol{1}\mu)$ and it follows that

$$\begin{aligned}
\frac{\partial \boldsymbol{u}}{\partial \mu} &= -\boldsymbol{\Theta}^{-1}\boldsymbol{\Phi}\boldsymbol{1},\\
\frac{\partial \boldsymbol{u}}{\partial \phi_i} &= \boldsymbol{\Theta}^{-1}\frac{\partial \boldsymbol{\Phi}}{\partial \phi_i}(\boldsymbol{y} - \boldsymbol{1}\mu) = -\boldsymbol{\Theta}^{-1}\boldsymbol{L}^i(\boldsymbol{y} - \boldsymbol{1}\mu) = -\boldsymbol{\Theta}^{-1}\boldsymbol{L}^i\boldsymbol{\Phi}^{-1}\boldsymbol{\Theta}\boldsymbol{u} = -\boldsymbol{\Phi}^{-1}\boldsymbol{L}^i\boldsymbol{u},\\
\frac{\partial \boldsymbol{u}}{\partial \theta_j} &= \frac{\partial \boldsymbol{\Theta}^{-1}}{\partial \theta_j}\boldsymbol{\Phi}(\boldsymbol{y} - \boldsymbol{1}\mu) = \boldsymbol{\Theta}^{-1}\boldsymbol{L}^j\boldsymbol{\Theta}^{-1}\boldsymbol{\Phi}(\boldsymbol{y} - \boldsymbol{1}\mu) = \boldsymbol{\Theta}^{-1}\boldsymbol{L}^j\boldsymbol{u}.
\end{aligned}$$

With these results, I can put the components of the score function as follows (where $\boldsymbol{l}_i = \text{vec}(\boldsymbol{L}^i)$):

$$\begin{aligned}
\frac{\partial \mathcal{L}}{\partial \mu} &= \frac{1}{\sigma^2}\boldsymbol{u}'\boldsymbol{\Theta}^{-1}\boldsymbol{\Phi}\mathbf{1},\\
\frac{\partial \mathcal{L}}{\partial \phi_i} &= \frac{1}{\sigma^2}\boldsymbol{u}'\boldsymbol{\Phi}^{-1}\boldsymbol{L}^i\boldsymbol{u} = \frac{1}{\sigma^2}\boldsymbol{l}_i'\text{vec}(\boldsymbol{\Phi}^{-1\prime}\boldsymbol{u}\boldsymbol{u}'),\\
\frac{\partial \mathcal{L}}{\partial \theta_j} &= -\frac{1}{\sigma^2}\boldsymbol{u}'\boldsymbol{\Theta}^{-1}\boldsymbol{L}^j\boldsymbol{u} = -\frac{1}{\sigma^2}\boldsymbol{l}_j'\text{vec}(\boldsymbol{\Theta}^{-1\prime}\boldsymbol{u}\boldsymbol{u}'),\\
\frac{\partial \mathcal{L}}{\partial \sigma^2} &= \frac{\boldsymbol{u}'\boldsymbol{u}}{2\sigma^4} - \frac{T}{2\sigma^2},
\end{aligned}$$

whose expectations are obviously all equal to zero, regardless of the distribution. (Recall that $\boldsymbol{\Phi}^{-1}\boldsymbol{L}^i$ and $\boldsymbol{\Theta}^{-1}\boldsymbol{L}^j$ are both strictly lower triangular.) To evaluate the expectation of the outer product of the score function, the following results on quadratic forms in the non-normal vector $\boldsymbol{u}$ may be used: for any matrices $\boldsymbol{A}$ and $\boldsymbol{B}$ (of conformable dimensions),

$$\begin{aligned}
\text{E}(\boldsymbol{u}\boldsymbol{u}'\boldsymbol{A}\boldsymbol{u}) &= \gamma_1\sigma^3(\boldsymbol{I}\odot\boldsymbol{A})\mathbf{1},\\
\text{E}(\boldsymbol{u}'\boldsymbol{A}\boldsymbol{u}\boldsymbol{u}'\boldsymbol{B}\boldsymbol{u}) &= \sigma^4[\text{tr}(\boldsymbol{A})\text{tr}(\boldsymbol{B}) + \text{tr}(\boldsymbol{A}\boldsymbol{B}) + \text{tr}(\boldsymbol{A}\boldsymbol{B}') + \gamma_2\text{tr}(\boldsymbol{A}\odot\boldsymbol{B})]. \qquad \text{(A.1)}
\end{aligned}$$

Then it can be shown that $\mathcal{P} = \text{E}(\boldsymbol{\psi}\boldsymbol{\psi}')$ has the following components:

$$\begin{aligned}
\text{E}\left(\frac{\partial \mathcal{L}}{\partial \mu}\frac{\partial \mathcal{L}}{\partial \mu}\right) &= \frac{1}{\sigma^2}\mathbf{1}'\boldsymbol{\Phi}'\boldsymbol{\Theta}^{-1\prime}\boldsymbol{\Theta}^{-1}\boldsymbol{\Phi}\mathbf{1},\\
\text{E}\left(\frac{\partial \mathcal{L}}{\partial \mu}\frac{\partial \mathcal{L}}{\partial \phi_i}\right) &= \frac{1}{\sigma^4}\mathbf{1}'\boldsymbol{\Phi}'\boldsymbol{\Theta}^{-1\prime}\text{E}(\boldsymbol{u}\boldsymbol{u}'\boldsymbol{\Phi}^{-1}\boldsymbol{L}^i\boldsymbol{u}) = 0,\\
\text{E}\left(\frac{\partial \mathcal{L}}{\partial \mu}\frac{\partial \mathcal{L}}{\partial \theta_j}\right) &= -\frac{1}{\sigma^4}\mathbf{1}'\boldsymbol{\Phi}'\boldsymbol{\Theta}^{-1\prime}\text{E}(\boldsymbol{u}\boldsymbol{u}'\boldsymbol{\Theta}^{-1}\boldsymbol{L}^j\boldsymbol{u}) = 0,\\
\text{E}\left(\frac{\partial \mathcal{L}}{\partial \mu}\frac{\partial \mathcal{L}}{\partial \sigma^2}\right) &= \frac{1}{2\sigma^6}\mathbf{1}'\boldsymbol{\Phi}'\boldsymbol{\Theta}^{-1\prime}\text{E}(\boldsymbol{u}\boldsymbol{u}'\boldsymbol{u}) = \frac{\gamma_1}{2\sigma^3}\mathbf{1}'\boldsymbol{\Theta}^{-1}\boldsymbol{\Phi}\mathbf{1},\\
\text{E}\left(\frac{\partial \mathcal{L}}{\partial \phi_{i_1}}\frac{\partial \mathcal{L}}{\partial \phi_{i_2}}\right) &= \frac{1}{\sigma^4}\text{E}(\boldsymbol{u}'\boldsymbol{\Phi}^{-1}\boldsymbol{L}^{i_1}\boldsymbol{u}\boldsymbol{u}'\boldsymbol{\Phi}^{-1}\boldsymbol{L}^{i_2}\boldsymbol{u})\\
&= \text{tr}(\boldsymbol{\Phi}^{-1}\boldsymbol{L}^{i_1}\boldsymbol{\Phi}^{-1\prime}\boldsymbol{L}^{i_2\prime}) = \boldsymbol{l}_{i_1}'(\boldsymbol{\Phi}^{-1}\otimes\boldsymbol{\Phi}^{-1})\boldsymbol{l}_{i_2},
\end{aligned}$$

$$\begin{aligned}
\mathrm{E}\left(\frac{\partial \mathcal{L}}{\partial \phi_i}\frac{\partial \mathcal{L}}{\partial \theta_j}\right) &= -\frac{1}{\sigma^4}\mathrm{E}(\boldsymbol{u}'\boldsymbol{\Phi}^{-1}\boldsymbol{L}^i\boldsymbol{u}\boldsymbol{u}'\boldsymbol{\Theta}^{-1}\boldsymbol{L}^j\boldsymbol{u}) \\
&= -\mathrm{tr}(\boldsymbol{\Phi}^{-1\prime}\boldsymbol{L}^{i_1\prime}\boldsymbol{\Theta}^{-1}\boldsymbol{L}^j) = -\boldsymbol{l}_i'(\boldsymbol{\Phi}^{-1}\otimes\boldsymbol{\Theta}^{-1})\boldsymbol{l}_j, \\
\mathrm{E}\left(\frac{\partial \mathcal{L}}{\partial \phi_i}\frac{\partial \mathcal{L}}{\partial \sigma^2}\right) &= \frac{1}{2\sigma^6}\mathrm{E}(\boldsymbol{u}'\boldsymbol{\Phi}^{-1}\boldsymbol{L}^{i_1}\boldsymbol{u}\boldsymbol{u}'\boldsymbol{u}) = 0, \\
\mathrm{E}\left(\frac{\partial \mathcal{L}}{\partial \theta_{j_1}}\frac{\partial \mathcal{L}}{\partial \theta_{j_2}}\right) &= \frac{1}{\sigma^4}\mathrm{E}(\boldsymbol{u}'\boldsymbol{\Theta}^{-1}\boldsymbol{L}^{j_1}\boldsymbol{u}\boldsymbol{u}'\boldsymbol{\Theta}^{-1}\boldsymbol{L}^{j_2}\boldsymbol{u}) \\
&= \mathrm{tr}(\boldsymbol{\Theta}^{-1\prime}\boldsymbol{L}^{j_1\prime}\boldsymbol{\Theta}^{-1}\boldsymbol{L}^{j_2}) = \boldsymbol{l}_{j_1}'(\boldsymbol{\Theta}^{-1}\otimes\boldsymbol{\Theta}^{-1})\boldsymbol{l}_{j_2}, \\
\mathrm{E}\left(\frac{\partial \mathcal{L}}{\partial \theta_j}\frac{\partial \mathcal{L}}{\partial \sigma^2}\right) &= \frac{1}{2\sigma^6}\mathrm{E}(\boldsymbol{u}'\boldsymbol{\Theta}^{-1}\boldsymbol{L}^j\boldsymbol{u}\boldsymbol{u}'\boldsymbol{u}) = 0, \\
\mathrm{E}\left(\frac{\partial \mathcal{L}}{\partial \sigma^2}\frac{\partial \mathcal{L}}{\partial \sigma^2}\right) &= \frac{(\gamma_2+2)T}{4\sigma^4}.
\end{aligned}$$

By taking the second-order derivative of the log-likelihood function, I collect the following:

$$\begin{aligned}
\frac{\partial^2 \mathcal{L}}{\partial \mu \partial \mu} &= \frac{1}{\sigma^2}\frac{\partial \boldsymbol{u}'\boldsymbol{\Theta}^{-1}\boldsymbol{\Phi}\mathbf{1}}{\partial \mu} = -\frac{1}{\sigma^2}1'\boldsymbol{\Phi}'\boldsymbol{\Theta}^{-1\prime}\boldsymbol{\Theta}^{-1}\boldsymbol{\Phi}\mathbf{1}, \\
\frac{\partial^2 \mathcal{L}}{\partial \mu \partial \phi_i} &= \frac{1}{\sigma^2}\frac{\partial \boldsymbol{u}'\boldsymbol{\Theta}^{-1}\boldsymbol{\Phi}\mathbf{1}}{\partial \phi_i} = -\frac{1}{\sigma^2}(\boldsymbol{u}'\boldsymbol{L}^{i\prime}\boldsymbol{\Phi}^{-1\prime}\boldsymbol{\Theta}^{-1}\boldsymbol{\Phi}\mathbf{1} + \boldsymbol{u}'\boldsymbol{\Theta}^{-1}\boldsymbol{L}^i\mathbf{1}), \\
\frac{\partial^2 \mathcal{L}}{\partial \mu \partial \theta_j} &= \frac{1}{\sigma^2}\frac{\partial \boldsymbol{u}'\boldsymbol{\Theta}^{-1}\boldsymbol{\Phi}\mathbf{1}}{\partial \theta_j} = \frac{1}{\sigma^2}(\boldsymbol{u}'\boldsymbol{L}^{j\prime}\boldsymbol{\Theta}^{-1\prime}\boldsymbol{\Theta}^{-1}\boldsymbol{\Phi}\mathbf{1} + \boldsymbol{u}'\boldsymbol{\Theta}^{-1}\boldsymbol{L}^j\boldsymbol{\Theta}^{-1}\boldsymbol{\Phi}\mathbf{1}), \\
\frac{\partial^2 \mathcal{L}}{\partial \mu \partial \sigma^2} &= -\frac{1}{\sigma^4}\boldsymbol{u}'\boldsymbol{\Theta}^{-1}\boldsymbol{\Phi}\mathbf{1}, \\
\frac{\partial^2 \mathcal{L}}{\partial \phi_{i_1} \partial \phi_{i_2}} &= \frac{1}{\sigma^2}\frac{\partial \boldsymbol{u}'\boldsymbol{\Phi}^{-1}\boldsymbol{L}^{i_1}\boldsymbol{u}}{\partial \phi_{i_2}} \\
&= \frac{1}{\sigma^2}(-\boldsymbol{u}'\boldsymbol{L}^{i_2\prime}\boldsymbol{\Phi}^{-1\prime}\boldsymbol{\Phi}^{-1}\boldsymbol{L}^{i_1}\boldsymbol{u} + \boldsymbol{u}'\boldsymbol{\Phi}^{-1}\boldsymbol{L}^{i_2}\boldsymbol{\Phi}^{-1}\boldsymbol{L}^{i_1}\boldsymbol{u} - \boldsymbol{u}'\boldsymbol{\Phi}^{-1}\boldsymbol{L}^{i_1}\boldsymbol{\Phi}^{-1}\boldsymbol{L}^{i_2}\boldsymbol{u}) \\
&= -\frac{1}{\sigma^2}\boldsymbol{u}'\boldsymbol{L}^{i_2\prime}\boldsymbol{\Phi}^{-1\prime}\boldsymbol{\Phi}^{-1}\boldsymbol{L}^{i_1}\boldsymbol{u}, \\
\frac{\partial^2 \mathcal{L}}{\partial \phi_i \partial \theta_j} &= \frac{1}{\sigma^2}\frac{\partial \boldsymbol{u}'\boldsymbol{\Phi}^{-1}\boldsymbol{L}^i\boldsymbol{u}}{\partial \theta_j} = \frac{1}{\sigma^2}(\boldsymbol{u}'\boldsymbol{L}^{j\prime}\boldsymbol{\Theta}^{-1\prime}\boldsymbol{\Phi}^{-1}\boldsymbol{L}^i\boldsymbol{u} + \boldsymbol{u}'\boldsymbol{\Phi}^{-1}\boldsymbol{L}^i\boldsymbol{\Theta}^{-1}\boldsymbol{L}^j\boldsymbol{u}),
\end{aligned}$$

$$\frac{\partial^2 \mathcal{L}}{\partial \phi_i \partial \sigma^2} = -\frac{1}{\sigma^4}\boldsymbol{u}'\boldsymbol{\Phi}^{-1}\boldsymbol{L}^i\boldsymbol{u},$$

$$\frac{\partial^2 \mathcal{L}}{\partial \theta_{j_1} \partial \theta_{j_2}} = -\frac{1}{\sigma^2}\frac{\partial \boldsymbol{u}'\boldsymbol{\Theta}^{-1}\boldsymbol{L}^{j_1}\boldsymbol{u}}{\partial \theta_{j_2}}$$

$$= -\frac{1}{\sigma^2}\boldsymbol{u}'(\boldsymbol{L}^{j_2\prime}\boldsymbol{\Theta}^{-1\prime}\boldsymbol{\Theta}^{-1}\boldsymbol{L}^{j_1} + \boldsymbol{\Theta}^{-1}\boldsymbol{L}^{j_2}\boldsymbol{\Theta}^{-1}\boldsymbol{L}^{j_1} + \boldsymbol{\Theta}^{-1}\boldsymbol{L}^{j_1}\boldsymbol{\Theta}^{-1}\boldsymbol{L}^{j_2})\boldsymbol{u},$$

$$\frac{\partial^2 \mathcal{L}}{\partial \theta_j \partial \sigma^2} = \frac{1}{\sigma^4}\boldsymbol{u}'\boldsymbol{\Theta}^{-1}\boldsymbol{L}^j\boldsymbol{u},$$

$$\frac{\partial^2 \mathcal{L}}{\partial \sigma^2 \partial \sigma^2} = \frac{T}{2\sigma^4} - \frac{\boldsymbol{u}'\boldsymbol{u}}{\sigma^6}.$$

The information matrix as in Eq. (12) then follows immediately.

Many elements of the expectation of the third-derivative of the log likelihood function are obviously zero. Below I collect those nonzero elements:

$$\mathrm{E}\left(\frac{\partial^3 \mathcal{L}}{\partial \mu \partial \mu \partial \phi_i}\right) = \frac{2}{\sigma^2}\boldsymbol{1}'\boldsymbol{L}^{i\prime}\boldsymbol{\Theta}^{-1\prime}\boldsymbol{\Theta}^{-1}\boldsymbol{\Phi}\boldsymbol{1},$$

$$\mathrm{E}\left(\frac{\partial^3 \mathcal{L}}{\partial \mu \partial \mu \partial \theta_j}\right) = -\frac{2}{\sigma^2}\boldsymbol{1}'\boldsymbol{\Phi}'\boldsymbol{\Theta}^{-1\prime}\boldsymbol{\Theta}^{-1}\boldsymbol{L}^j\boldsymbol{\Theta}^{-1}\boldsymbol{\Phi}\boldsymbol{1},$$

$$\mathrm{E}\left(\frac{\partial^3 \mathcal{L}}{\partial \mu \partial \mu \partial \sigma^2}\right) = \frac{1}{\sigma^4}\boldsymbol{1}'\boldsymbol{\Phi}'\boldsymbol{\Theta}^{-1\prime}\boldsymbol{\Theta}^{-1}\boldsymbol{\Phi}\boldsymbol{1},$$

$$\mathrm{E}\left(\frac{\partial^3 \mathcal{L}}{\partial \phi_{i_1} \partial \phi_{i_2} \partial \theta_j}\right) = -\mathrm{tr}(\boldsymbol{L}^{j\prime}\boldsymbol{\Theta}^{-1\prime}\boldsymbol{L}^{i_2\prime}\boldsymbol{\Phi}^{-1\prime}\boldsymbol{L}^{i_1}\boldsymbol{\Phi}^{-1} + \boldsymbol{L}^{i_2\prime}\boldsymbol{\Phi}^{-1\prime}\boldsymbol{L}^{i_1}\boldsymbol{\Phi}^{-1}\boldsymbol{\Theta}^{-1}\boldsymbol{L}^j),$$

$$\mathrm{E}\left(\frac{\partial^3 \mathcal{L}}{\partial \phi_{i_1} \partial \phi_{i_2} \partial \sigma^2}\right) = \frac{1}{\sigma^2}\mathrm{tr}(\boldsymbol{\Phi}^{-1\prime}\boldsymbol{L}^{i_1\prime}\boldsymbol{\Phi}^{-1}\boldsymbol{L}^{i_2}),$$

$$\mathrm{E}\left(\frac{\partial^3 \mathcal{L}}{\partial \phi_i \partial \theta_{j_1} \partial \theta_{j_2}}\right) = \mathrm{tr}(\boldsymbol{L}^{j_1\prime}\boldsymbol{\Theta}^{-1\prime}\boldsymbol{\Phi}^{-1}\boldsymbol{L}^i\boldsymbol{\Theta}^{-1}\boldsymbol{L}^{j_2} + \boldsymbol{L}^{j_2\prime}\boldsymbol{\Theta}^{-1\prime}\boldsymbol{\Phi}^{-1}\boldsymbol{L}^i\boldsymbol{\Theta}^{-1}\boldsymbol{L}^{j_1}$$

$$+ 2\boldsymbol{L}^{j_1\prime}\boldsymbol{\Theta}^{-1\prime}\boldsymbol{L}^{j_2\prime}\boldsymbol{\Theta}^{-1\prime}\boldsymbol{\Phi}^{-1}\boldsymbol{L}^i),$$

$$\mathrm{E}\left(\frac{\partial^3 \mathcal{L}}{\partial \phi_i \partial \theta_j \partial \sigma^2}\right) = -\frac{1}{\sigma^2}\mathrm{tr}(\boldsymbol{\Phi}^{-1\prime}\boldsymbol{L}^{i\prime}\boldsymbol{\Theta}^{-1}\boldsymbol{L}^j),$$

$$\mathrm{E}\left(\frac{\partial^3 \mathcal{L}}{\partial\theta_{j_1}\partial\theta_{j_2}\partial\theta_{j_3}}\right) = -2\mathrm{tr}(\boldsymbol{L}^{j_3\prime}\boldsymbol{\Theta}^{-1\prime}\boldsymbol{L}^{j_2\prime}\boldsymbol{\Theta}^{-1\prime}\boldsymbol{\Theta}^{-1}\boldsymbol{L}^{j_1} + \boldsymbol{L}^{j_2\prime}\boldsymbol{\Theta}^{-1\prime}\boldsymbol{\Theta}^{-1}\boldsymbol{L}^{j_1}\boldsymbol{\Theta}^{-1}\boldsymbol{L}^{j_3}$$
$$+ \boldsymbol{L}^{j_3\prime}\boldsymbol{\Theta}^{-1\prime}\boldsymbol{\Theta}^{-1}\boldsymbol{L}^{j_2}\boldsymbol{\Theta}^{-1}\boldsymbol{L}^{j_1}),$$
$$\mathrm{E}\left(\frac{\partial^3 \mathcal{L}}{\partial\theta_{j_1}\partial\theta_{j_2}\partial\sigma^2}\right) = \frac{1}{\sigma^2}\mathrm{tr}(\boldsymbol{L}^{j_2\prime}\boldsymbol{\Theta}^{-1\prime}\boldsymbol{\Theta}^{-1}\boldsymbol{L}^{j_1}),$$
$$\mathrm{E}\left(\frac{\partial^3 \mathcal{L}}{\partial\sigma^2\partial\sigma^2\partial\sigma^2}\right) = \frac{2T}{\sigma^6}.$$

To evaluate the various expectations on the right-hand side of Eq. (14), note that for any matrix $\boldsymbol{A}$ of column size m,

$$\boldsymbol{A}\otimes\boldsymbol{\psi}' = (\boldsymbol{\psi}'\otimes\boldsymbol{A})\boldsymbol{K}_{p+q+2,m} = (\psi_\mu\boldsymbol{A}\ \ \psi_{\boldsymbol{\phi}}'\otimes\boldsymbol{A}\ \ \psi_{\boldsymbol{\theta}}'\otimes\boldsymbol{A}\ \ \psi_{\sigma^2}\boldsymbol{A})\boldsymbol{K}_{p+q+2,m}, \qquad \text{(A.2)}$$

where when $m=1$, the commutation matrix $\boldsymbol{K}$ becomes $\boldsymbol{I}$. By following this, the various blocks in $\boldsymbol{\mathcal{E}} = \mathrm{E}(\boldsymbol{\mathcal{H}}\otimes\boldsymbol{\psi}')$ on the right-hand side of Eq. (14) are as follows (obviously, $\mathrm{E}(\mathcal{H}_{\mu,\mu}\otimes\boldsymbol{\psi}') = \mathbf{0}'_{p+q+2}$):

$$\mathrm{E}(\mathcal{H}_{\boldsymbol{\phi},\mu}\otimes\boldsymbol{\psi}') = \mathrm{E}(\mathcal{H}_{\boldsymbol{\phi},\mu}\boldsymbol{\psi}') = \left[\mathrm{E}(\mathcal{H}_{\boldsymbol{\phi},\mu}\psi_\mu)\ \mathrm{E}(\mathcal{H}_{\boldsymbol{\phi},\mu}\psi_{\boldsymbol{\phi}}')\ \mathrm{E}(\mathcal{H}_{\boldsymbol{\phi},\mu}\psi_{\boldsymbol{\theta}}')\ \mathrm{E}(\mathcal{H}_{\boldsymbol{\phi},\mu}\psi_{\sigma^2})\right],$$
$$\mathrm{E}(\mathcal{H}_{\mu,\boldsymbol{\phi}'}\otimes\boldsymbol{\psi}') = \mathrm{rvec}[\mathrm{E}(\mathcal{H}_{\boldsymbol{\phi},\mu}\otimes\boldsymbol{\psi}')],$$
$$\mathrm{E}(\mathcal{H}_{\boldsymbol{\theta},\mu}\otimes\boldsymbol{\psi}') = \mathrm{E}(\mathcal{H}_{\boldsymbol{\theta},\mu}\boldsymbol{\psi}') = \left[\mathrm{E}(\mathcal{H}_{\boldsymbol{\theta},\mu}\psi_\mu)\ \mathrm{E}(\mathcal{H}_{\boldsymbol{\theta},\mu}\psi_{\boldsymbol{\phi}}')\ \mathrm{E}(\mathcal{H}_{\boldsymbol{\theta},\mu}\psi_{\boldsymbol{\theta}}')\ \mathrm{E}(\mathcal{H}_{\boldsymbol{\theta},\mu}\psi_{\sigma^2})\right],$$
$$\mathrm{E}(\mathcal{H}_{\mu,\boldsymbol{\theta}'}\otimes\boldsymbol{\psi}') = \mathrm{rvec}[\mathrm{E}(\mathcal{H}_{\boldsymbol{\theta},\mu}\otimes\boldsymbol{\psi}')],$$
$$\mathrm{E}(\mathcal{H}_{\mu,\sigma^2}\otimes\boldsymbol{\psi}') = \left[\mathrm{E}(\mathcal{H}_{\mu,\sigma^2}\psi_\mu)\ \mathrm{E}(\mathcal{H}_{\mu,\sigma^2}\psi_{\boldsymbol{\phi}}')\ \mathrm{E}(\mathcal{H}_{\mu,\sigma^2}\psi_{\boldsymbol{\theta}}')\ \mathrm{E}(\mathcal{H}_{\mu,\sigma^2}\psi_{\sigma^2})\right],$$
$$\mathrm{E}(\mathcal{H}_{\boldsymbol{\phi},\boldsymbol{\phi}'}\otimes\boldsymbol{\psi}') = \left[\mathrm{E}(\mathcal{H}_{\boldsymbol{\phi},\boldsymbol{\phi}'}\psi_\mu)\ \mathrm{E}(\psi_{\boldsymbol{\phi}}'\otimes\mathcal{H}_{\boldsymbol{\phi},\boldsymbol{\phi}'})\ \mathrm{E}(\psi_{\boldsymbol{\theta}}'\otimes\mathcal{H}_{\boldsymbol{\phi},\boldsymbol{\phi}'})\ \mathrm{E}(\mathcal{H}_{\boldsymbol{\phi},\boldsymbol{\phi}'}\psi_{\sigma^2})\right]\boldsymbol{K}_{p+q+2,p},$$
$$\mathrm{E}(\mathcal{H}_{\boldsymbol{\theta},\boldsymbol{\phi}'}\otimes\boldsymbol{\psi}') = \left[\mathrm{E}(\mathcal{H}_{\boldsymbol{\theta},\boldsymbol{\phi}'}\psi_\mu)\ \mathrm{E}(\psi_{\boldsymbol{\phi}}'\otimes\mathcal{H}_{\boldsymbol{\theta},\boldsymbol{\phi}'})\ \mathrm{E}(\psi_{\boldsymbol{\theta}}'\otimes\mathcal{H}_{\boldsymbol{\theta},\boldsymbol{\phi}'})\ \mathrm{E}(\mathcal{H}_{\boldsymbol{\theta},\boldsymbol{\phi}'}\psi_{\sigma^2})\right]\boldsymbol{K}_{p+q+2,p},$$
$$\mathrm{E}(\mathcal{H}_{\boldsymbol{\phi},\boldsymbol{\theta}'}\otimes\boldsymbol{\psi}') = \left[\mathrm{E}(\mathcal{H}_{\boldsymbol{\phi},\boldsymbol{\theta}'}\psi_\mu)\ \mathrm{E}(\psi_{\boldsymbol{\phi}}'\otimes\mathcal{H}_{\boldsymbol{\phi},\boldsymbol{\theta}'})\ \mathrm{E}(\psi_{\boldsymbol{\theta}}'\otimes\mathcal{H}_{\boldsymbol{\phi},\boldsymbol{\theta}'})\ \mathrm{E}(\mathcal{H}_{\boldsymbol{\phi},\boldsymbol{\theta}'}\psi_{\sigma^2})\right]\boldsymbol{K}_{p+q+2,q},$$
$$\mathrm{E}(\mathcal{H}_{\boldsymbol{\theta},\boldsymbol{\theta}'}\otimes\boldsymbol{\psi}') = \left[\mathrm{E}(\mathcal{H}_{\boldsymbol{\theta},\boldsymbol{\theta}'}\psi_\mu)\ \mathrm{E}(\psi_{\boldsymbol{\phi}}'\otimes\mathcal{H}_{\boldsymbol{\theta},\boldsymbol{\theta}'})\ \mathrm{E}(\psi_{\boldsymbol{\theta}}'\otimes\mathcal{H}_{\boldsymbol{\theta},\boldsymbol{\theta}'})\ \mathrm{E}(\mathcal{H}_{\boldsymbol{\theta},\boldsymbol{\theta}'}\psi_{\sigma^2})\right]\boldsymbol{K}_{p+q+2,q},$$
$$\mathrm{E}(\mathcal{H}_{\boldsymbol{\phi},\sigma^2}\otimes\boldsymbol{\psi}') = \mathrm{E}(\mathcal{H}_{\boldsymbol{\phi},\sigma^2}\boldsymbol{\psi}') = \left[\mathrm{E}(\mathcal{H}_{\boldsymbol{\phi},\sigma^2}\psi_\mu)\ \mathrm{E}(\mathcal{H}_{\boldsymbol{\phi},\sigma^2}\psi_{\boldsymbol{\phi}}')\ \mathrm{E}(\mathcal{H}_{\boldsymbol{\phi},\sigma^2}\psi_{\boldsymbol{\theta}}')\ \mathrm{E}(\mathcal{H}_{\boldsymbol{\phi},\sigma^2}\psi_{\sigma^2})\right],$$
$$\mathrm{E}(\mathcal{H}_{\sigma^2,\boldsymbol{\phi}'}\otimes\boldsymbol{\psi}') = \mathrm{rvec}[\mathrm{E}(\mathcal{H}_{\boldsymbol{\phi},\sigma^2}\otimes\boldsymbol{\psi}')],$$
$$\mathrm{E}(\mathcal{H}_{\boldsymbol{\theta},\sigma^2}\otimes\boldsymbol{\psi}') = \mathrm{E}(\mathcal{H}_{\boldsymbol{\theta},\sigma^2}\boldsymbol{\psi}') = \left[\mathrm{E}(\mathcal{H}_{\boldsymbol{\theta},\sigma^2}\psi_\mu)\ \mathrm{E}(\mathcal{H}_{\boldsymbol{\theta},\sigma^2}\psi_{\boldsymbol{\phi}}')\ \mathrm{E}(\mathcal{H}_{\boldsymbol{\theta},\sigma^2}\psi_{\boldsymbol{\theta}}')\ \mathrm{E}(\mathcal{H}_{\boldsymbol{\theta},\sigma^2}\psi_{\sigma^2})\right],$$
$$\mathrm{E}(\mathcal{H}_{\sigma^2,\boldsymbol{\theta}'}\otimes\boldsymbol{\psi}') = \mathrm{rvec}[\mathrm{E}(\mathcal{H}_{\boldsymbol{\theta},\sigma^2}\otimes\boldsymbol{\psi}')],$$
$$\mathrm{E}(\mathcal{H}_{\sigma^2,\sigma^2}\otimes\boldsymbol{\psi}') = \left[\mathrm{E}(\mathcal{H}_{\sigma^2,\sigma^2}\psi_\mu)\ \mathrm{E}(\mathcal{H}_{\sigma^2,\sigma^2}\psi_{\boldsymbol{\phi}}')\ \mathrm{E}(\mathcal{H}_{\sigma^2,\sigma^2}\psi_{\boldsymbol{\theta}}')\ \mathrm{E}(\mathcal{H}_{\sigma^2,\sigma^2}\psi_{\sigma^2})\right].$$

To evaluate the above expectations, further note that for any conformable vector $\boldsymbol{a}$ and matrix $\boldsymbol{A}$,

$$\mathrm{E}(\boldsymbol{u}\boldsymbol{u}'\boldsymbol{a}\boldsymbol{u}') = \gamma_1\sigma^3\mathrm{Diag}(\boldsymbol{a}), \quad \mathrm{E}(\boldsymbol{u}\boldsymbol{u}'\boldsymbol{A}\boldsymbol{u}\boldsymbol{u}') = \sigma^4[\mathrm{tr}(\boldsymbol{A})\boldsymbol{I} + \boldsymbol{A} + \boldsymbol{A}' + \gamma_2(\boldsymbol{A}\odot\boldsymbol{I})], \qquad \text{(A.3)}$$

where $\mathrm{Diag}(\boldsymbol{a})$ denotes a diagonal matrix with the elements of $\boldsymbol{a}$ on the diagonal and zeros elsewhere. Given this and upon substitution, the expectations can be expressed as follows:

$$\mathrm{E}(\mathcal{H}_{\boldsymbol{\phi},\mu}\psi_{\mu}) = -\frac{2}{\sigma^2}\boldsymbol{L}_p'\mathrm{vec}(\boldsymbol{\Theta}^{-1\prime}\boldsymbol{\Theta}^{-1}\boldsymbol{\Phi}\boldsymbol{1}\boldsymbol{1}'),$$

$$\mathrm{E}(\mathcal{H}_{\boldsymbol{\phi},\mu}\psi_{\boldsymbol{\phi}}') = \mathbf{O}_p,\ \mathrm{E}(\mathcal{H}_{\boldsymbol{\phi},\mu}\psi_{\boldsymbol{\theta}}') = \mathbf{O}_{p\times q},\quad \mathrm{E}(\mathcal{H}_{\boldsymbol{\phi},\mu}\psi_{\sigma^2}) = -\frac{\gamma_1}{2\sigma^3}\boldsymbol{L}_p'\mathrm{vec}(\boldsymbol{\Phi}^{-1\prime}\boldsymbol{\Theta}^{-1}\boldsymbol{\Phi}\boldsymbol{1}\boldsymbol{1}' + \boldsymbol{\Theta}^{-1\prime}\boldsymbol{1}\boldsymbol{1}'),$$

$$\mathrm{E}(\mathcal{H}_{\boldsymbol{\theta},\mu}\psi_{\mu}) = \frac{2}{\sigma^2}\boldsymbol{L}_q'\mathrm{vec}(\boldsymbol{\Theta}^{-1\prime}\boldsymbol{\Theta}^{-1}\boldsymbol{\Phi}\boldsymbol{1}\boldsymbol{1}'\boldsymbol{\Phi}'\boldsymbol{\Theta}^{-1\prime}),\quad \mathrm{E}(\mathcal{H}_{\boldsymbol{\theta},\mu}\psi_{\boldsymbol{\phi}}') = \mathbf{O}_{q\times p},\quad \mathrm{E}(\mathcal{H}_{\boldsymbol{\theta},\mu}\psi_{\boldsymbol{\theta}}') = \mathbf{O}_q,$$

$$\mathrm{E}(\mathcal{H}_{\boldsymbol{\theta},\mu}\psi_{\sigma^2}) = \frac{\gamma_1}{2\sigma^3}\boldsymbol{L}_q'\mathrm{vec}(\boldsymbol{\Theta}^{-1\prime}\boldsymbol{\Theta}^{-1}\boldsymbol{\Phi}\boldsymbol{1}\boldsymbol{1}' + \boldsymbol{\Theta}^{-1\prime}\boldsymbol{1}\boldsymbol{1}'\boldsymbol{\Phi}'\boldsymbol{\Theta}^{-1\prime}),$$

$$\mathrm{E}(\mathcal{H}_{\mu,\sigma^2}\psi_{\mu}) = -\frac{1}{\sigma^4}\boldsymbol{1}'\boldsymbol{\Phi}'\boldsymbol{\Theta}^{-1\prime}\boldsymbol{\Theta}^{-1}\boldsymbol{\Phi}\boldsymbol{1},\quad \mathrm{E}(\mathcal{H}_{\mu,\sigma^2}\psi_{\boldsymbol{\phi}}') = \boldsymbol{0}_p',\quad \mathrm{E}(\mathcal{H}_{\mu,\sigma^2}\psi_{\boldsymbol{\theta}}') = \boldsymbol{0}_q',$$

$$\mathrm{E}(\mathcal{H}_{\mu,\sigma^2}\psi_{\sigma^2}) = -\frac{\gamma_1}{2\sigma^5}\boldsymbol{1}'\boldsymbol{\Theta}^{-1}\boldsymbol{\Phi}\boldsymbol{1},\quad \mathrm{E}(\mathcal{H}_{\boldsymbol{\phi},\boldsymbol{\phi}'}\psi_{\mu}) = -\frac{\gamma_1}{\sigma}\boldsymbol{L}_p'(\boldsymbol{\Phi}^{-1}\mathrm{Diag}(\boldsymbol{\Theta}^{-1}\boldsymbol{\Phi}\boldsymbol{1}) \otimes \boldsymbol{\Phi}^{-1})\boldsymbol{L}_p,$$

$$\mathrm{E}(\psi_{\boldsymbol{\phi}}' \otimes \mathcal{H}_{\boldsymbol{\phi},\boldsymbol{\phi}'}) = -[\boldsymbol{L}_p'(\boldsymbol{\Phi}^{-1}(\boldsymbol{\Phi}^{-1}\boldsymbol{L}^i + \boldsymbol{L}^{i\prime}\boldsymbol{\Phi}^{-1\prime}) \otimes \boldsymbol{\Phi}^{-1})\boldsymbol{L}_p]_{i=1}^{p},$$

$$\mathrm{E}(\psi_{\boldsymbol{\theta}}' \otimes \mathcal{H}_{\boldsymbol{\phi},\boldsymbol{\phi}'}) = [\boldsymbol{L}_p'(\boldsymbol{\Phi}^{-1}(\boldsymbol{\Theta}^{-1}\boldsymbol{L}^j + \boldsymbol{L}^{j\prime}\boldsymbol{\Theta}^{-1\prime}) \otimes \boldsymbol{\Phi}^{-1})\boldsymbol{L}_p]_{j=1}^{q},$$

$$\mathrm{E}(\mathcal{H}_{\boldsymbol{\phi},\boldsymbol{\phi}'}\psi_{\sigma^2}) = -\frac{\gamma_2+2}{2\sigma^2}\boldsymbol{L}_p'(\boldsymbol{\Phi}^{-1} \otimes \boldsymbol{\Phi}^{-1})\boldsymbol{L}_p,\quad \mathrm{E}(\mathcal{H}_{\boldsymbol{\theta},\boldsymbol{\phi}'}\psi_{\mu}) = \frac{\gamma_1}{\sigma}\boldsymbol{L}_q'(\boldsymbol{\Theta}^{-1}\mathrm{Diag}(\boldsymbol{\Theta}^{-1}\boldsymbol{\Phi}\boldsymbol{1}) \otimes \boldsymbol{\Phi}^{-1})\boldsymbol{L}_p,$$

$$\mathrm{E}(\psi_{\boldsymbol{\phi}}' \otimes \mathcal{H}_{\boldsymbol{\theta},\boldsymbol{\phi}'}) = [\boldsymbol{L}_q'(\boldsymbol{\Theta}^{-1}(\boldsymbol{\Phi}^{-1}\boldsymbol{L}^i + \boldsymbol{L}^{i\prime}\boldsymbol{\Phi}^{-1\prime}) \otimes \boldsymbol{\Phi}^{-1} + (\boldsymbol{\Phi}^{-1} \otimes \boldsymbol{\Theta}^{-1\prime}\boldsymbol{\Phi}^{-1}\boldsymbol{L}^i)\boldsymbol{K}_{T,T})\boldsymbol{L}_p]_{i=1}^{p},$$

$$\mathrm{E}(\psi_{\boldsymbol{\theta}}' \otimes \mathcal{H}_{\boldsymbol{\theta},\boldsymbol{\phi}'}) = -[\boldsymbol{L}_q'(\boldsymbol{\Theta}^{-1}(\boldsymbol{\Theta}^{-1}\boldsymbol{L}^j + \boldsymbol{L}^{j\prime}\boldsymbol{\Theta}^{-1\prime}) \otimes \boldsymbol{\Phi}^{-1} + (\boldsymbol{\Phi}^{-1} \otimes \boldsymbol{\Theta}^{-1\prime}\boldsymbol{\Theta}^{-1}\boldsymbol{L}^j)\boldsymbol{K}_{T,T})\boldsymbol{L}_p]_{j=1}^{q},$$

$$\mathrm{E}(\mathcal{H}_{\boldsymbol{\theta},\boldsymbol{\phi}'}\psi_{\sigma^2}) = \frac{\gamma_2+2}{2\sigma^2}\boldsymbol{L}_q'(\boldsymbol{\Theta}^{-1} \otimes \boldsymbol{\Phi}^{-1})\boldsymbol{L}_p,\quad \mathrm{E}(\mathcal{H}_{\boldsymbol{\phi},\boldsymbol{\theta}'}\psi_{\mu}) = \frac{\gamma_1}{\sigma}\boldsymbol{L}_p'(\boldsymbol{\Phi}^{-1}\mathrm{Diag}(\boldsymbol{\Theta}^{-1}\boldsymbol{\Phi}\boldsymbol{1}) \otimes \boldsymbol{\Theta}^{-1})\boldsymbol{L}_q,$$

$$\mathrm{E}(\psi_{\boldsymbol{\phi}}' \otimes \mathcal{H}_{\boldsymbol{\phi},\boldsymbol{\theta}'}) = [\boldsymbol{L}_p'(\boldsymbol{\Phi}^{-1}(\boldsymbol{\Phi}^{-1}\boldsymbol{L}^i + \boldsymbol{L}^{i\prime}\boldsymbol{\Phi}^{-1\prime}) \otimes \boldsymbol{\Theta}^{-1} + (\boldsymbol{\Theta}^{-1}\boldsymbol{L}^{i\prime}\boldsymbol{\Phi}^{-1\prime} \otimes \boldsymbol{\Phi}^{-1\prime})\boldsymbol{K}_{T,T})\boldsymbol{L}_q]_{i=1}^{p},$$

$$\mathrm{E}(\psi_{\boldsymbol{\theta}}' \otimes \mathcal{H}_{\boldsymbol{\phi},\boldsymbol{\theta}'}) = -[\boldsymbol{L}_p'(\boldsymbol{\Phi}^{-1}(\boldsymbol{\Theta}^{-1}\boldsymbol{L}^j + \boldsymbol{L}^{j\prime}\boldsymbol{\Theta}^{-1\prime}) \otimes \boldsymbol{\Theta}^{-1} + (\boldsymbol{\Theta}^{-1}\boldsymbol{L}^{j\prime}\boldsymbol{\Theta}^{-1\prime} \otimes \boldsymbol{\Phi}^{-1\prime})\boldsymbol{K}_{T,T})\boldsymbol{L}_q]_{j=1}^{q},$$

$$\mathrm{E}(\mathcal{H}_{\boldsymbol{\phi},\boldsymbol{\theta}'}\psi_{\sigma^2}) = \frac{\gamma_2+2}{2\sigma^2}\boldsymbol{L}_p'(\boldsymbol{\Phi}^{-1} \otimes \boldsymbol{\Theta}^{-1})\boldsymbol{L}_q,\ \mathrm{E}(\mathcal{H}_{\boldsymbol{\theta},\boldsymbol{\theta}'}\psi_{\mu}) = -\frac{\gamma_1}{\sigma}\boldsymbol{L}_q'(\boldsymbol{\Theta}^{-1}\mathrm{Diag}(\boldsymbol{\Theta}^{-1}\boldsymbol{\Phi}\boldsymbol{1}) \otimes \boldsymbol{\Theta}^{-1})\boldsymbol{L}_q,$$

$$\mathrm{E}(\psi_{\boldsymbol{\phi}}' \otimes \mathcal{H}_{\boldsymbol{\theta},\boldsymbol{\theta}'}) = -[\boldsymbol{L}_q'(\boldsymbol{\Theta}^{-1}(\boldsymbol{\Phi}^{-1}\boldsymbol{L}^i + \boldsymbol{L}^{i\prime}\boldsymbol{\Phi}^{-1\prime}) \otimes \boldsymbol{\Theta} + 2(\boldsymbol{L}^{i\prime}\boldsymbol{\Phi}^{-1\prime}\boldsymbol{\Theta}^{-1} \otimes \boldsymbol{\Theta}^{-1\prime})\boldsymbol{K}_{T,T})\boldsymbol{L}_q]_{i=1}^{p},$$

$$\mathrm{E}(\psi_{\boldsymbol{\theta}}' \otimes \mathcal{H}_{\boldsymbol{\theta},\boldsymbol{\theta}'}) = [\boldsymbol{L}_q'(\boldsymbol{\Theta}^{-1}(\boldsymbol{\Theta}^{-1}\boldsymbol{L}^j + \boldsymbol{L}^{j\prime}\boldsymbol{\Theta}^{-1\prime}) \otimes \boldsymbol{\Theta}^{-1} + 2(\boldsymbol{L}^{j\prime}\boldsymbol{\Theta}^{-1\prime}\boldsymbol{\Theta}^{-1} \otimes \boldsymbol{\Theta}^{-1\prime})\boldsymbol{K}_{T,T})\boldsymbol{L}_q]_{j=1}^{q},$$

$$\mathrm{E}(\mathcal{H}_{\boldsymbol{\theta},\boldsymbol{\theta}'}\psi_{\sigma^2}) = -\frac{\gamma_2+2}{2\sigma^2}\boldsymbol{L}_q'(\boldsymbol{\Theta}^{-1} \otimes \boldsymbol{\Theta}^{-1})\boldsymbol{L}_q,\quad \mathrm{E}(\mathcal{H}_{\boldsymbol{\phi},\sigma^2}\psi_{\mu}) = \boldsymbol{0}_p,\quad \mathrm{E}(\mathcal{H}_{\boldsymbol{\phi},\sigma^2}\psi_{\boldsymbol{\phi}}') = -\frac{1}{\sigma^2}\boldsymbol{L}_p'(\boldsymbol{\Phi}^{-1} \otimes \boldsymbol{\Phi}^{-1})\boldsymbol{L}_p,$$

$$\mathrm{E}(\mathcal{H}_{\boldsymbol{\phi},\sigma^2}\psi_{\boldsymbol{\theta}}') = \frac{1}{\sigma^2}\boldsymbol{L}_p'(\boldsymbol{\Phi}^{-1} \otimes \boldsymbol{\Theta}^{-1})\boldsymbol{L}_q,\quad \mathrm{E}(\mathcal{H}_{\boldsymbol{\phi},\sigma^2}\psi_{\sigma^2}) = \boldsymbol{0}_p,\quad \mathrm{E}(\mathcal{H}_{\boldsymbol{\theta},\sigma^2}\psi_{\mu}) = \boldsymbol{0}_q,$$

$$\mathrm{E}(\mathcal{H}_{\boldsymbol{\theta},\sigma^2}\psi_{\boldsymbol{\phi}}') = \frac{1}{\sigma^2}\boldsymbol{L}_q'(\boldsymbol{\Theta}^{-1} \otimes \boldsymbol{\Phi}^{-1})\boldsymbol{L}_p,\quad \mathrm{E}(\mathcal{H}_{\boldsymbol{\theta},\sigma^2}\psi_{\boldsymbol{\theta}}') = -\frac{1}{\sigma^2}\boldsymbol{L}_q'(\boldsymbol{\Theta}^{-1} \otimes \boldsymbol{\Theta}^{-1})\boldsymbol{L}_q,\quad \mathrm{E}(\mathcal{H}_{\boldsymbol{\theta},\sigma^2}\psi_{\sigma^2}) = \boldsymbol{0}_q,$$

$$\mathrm{E}(\mathcal{H}_{\sigma^2,\sigma^2}\psi_{\mu}) = -\frac{\gamma_1}{\sigma^5}\boldsymbol{1}'\boldsymbol{\Theta}^{-1}\boldsymbol{\Phi}\boldsymbol{1},\quad \mathrm{E}(\mathcal{H}_{\sigma^2,\sigma^2}\psi_{\boldsymbol{\phi}}') = \boldsymbol{0}_p',\quad \mathrm{E}(\mathcal{H}_{\sigma^2,\sigma^2}\psi_{\boldsymbol{\theta}}') = \boldsymbol{0}_q',\quad \mathrm{E}(\mathcal{H}_{\sigma^2,\sigma^2}\psi_{\sigma^2}) = -\frac{T(\gamma_2+2)}{2\sigma^6}.$$

A.2. *Specific ARMA Models*

From the bias formula (4), the $O(T)$ terms in $\mathcal{F}$, $\mathcal{D}$, $\mathrm{E}(\mathcal{H} \otimes \boldsymbol{\psi}')$, $\mathcal{P}$ are needed and terms of lower orders can be ignored to simplify the $O(T^{-1})$ bias. When $p=1$ (or $q=1$), for notational convenience, denote $\boldsymbol{\phi}=\phi_1=\phi$ (or $\boldsymbol{\theta}=\theta_1=\theta$).

A.2.1. *AR(1)*

For $\boldsymbol{\Phi}=\boldsymbol{I}-\phi\boldsymbol{L}$, its inverse $\boldsymbol{\Phi}^{-1}$ is lower triangular with ij-th elements ϕ^{i-j}, $i \geq j$. The 3×3 matrix $\mathcal{F}$ is diagonal with

$$\{\mathcal{F}\}_{11} = \frac{1}{\sigma^2}\mathbf{1}'\boldsymbol{\Phi}'\boldsymbol{\Phi}\mathbf{1} = \frac{T(1-\phi)^2}{\sigma^2} + O(1),$$

$$\{\mathcal{F}\}_{22} = \mathrm{tr}[(\boldsymbol{\Phi}^{-1}\boldsymbol{L})(\boldsymbol{\Phi}^{-1}\boldsymbol{L})'] = \frac{T}{1-\phi^2} + O(1),$$

$$\{\mathcal{F}\}_{33} = \frac{T}{2\sigma^4}.$$

$\mathcal{P}$ has the same diagonals as $\mathcal{F}$, and

$$\{\mathcal{P}\}_{13} = \{\mathcal{P}\}_{31} = \frac{\gamma_1}{2\sigma^3}\mathbf{1}'\boldsymbol{\Phi}\mathbf{1} = \frac{\gamma_1 T(1-\phi)}{2\sigma^3} + O(1), \quad \{\mathcal{P}\}_{33} = \frac{(\gamma_2+2)T}{4\sigma^4}.$$

The 3×9 matrix $\mathcal{D}$ has the following nonzero elements:

$$\{\mathcal{D}\}_{12} = \{\mathcal{D}\}_{14} = \{\mathcal{D}\}_{21} = \frac{2}{\sigma^2}\mathbf{1}'\boldsymbol{L}'\boldsymbol{\Phi}\mathbf{1} = \frac{2T(1-\phi)}{\sigma^2} + O(1),$$

$$\{\mathcal{D}\}_{13} = \{\mathcal{D}\}_{17} = \{\mathcal{D}\}_{31} = \frac{1}{\sigma^4}\mathbf{1}'\boldsymbol{\Phi}'\boldsymbol{\Phi}\mathbf{1} = \frac{T(1-\phi)^2}{\sigma^4} + O(1),$$

$$\{\mathcal{D}\}_{26} = \{\mathcal{D}\}_{28} = \{\mathcal{D}\}_{35} = \frac{1}{\sigma^2}\mathrm{tr}[(\boldsymbol{\Phi}^{-1}\boldsymbol{L})(\boldsymbol{\Phi}^{-1}\boldsymbol{L})'] = \frac{T}{\sigma^2(1-\phi^2)} + O(1),$$

$$\{\mathcal{D}\}_{39} = \frac{2T}{\sigma^6}.$$

The 3×9 matrix $\mathcal{E}$ has the following nonzero elements:

$$\{\mathcal{E}\}_{14} = \{\mathcal{E}\}_{41} = -\frac{2}{\sigma^2}\mathbf{1}'\boldsymbol{L}'\boldsymbol{\Phi}\mathbf{1} = -\frac{2T(1-\phi)}{\sigma^2} + O(1),$$

$$\{\mathcal{E}\}_{16} = \{\mathcal{E}\}_{23} = -\frac{\gamma_1}{2\sigma^3}(\mathbf{1}'\boldsymbol{L}'\boldsymbol{\Phi}^{-1'}\boldsymbol{\Phi}\mathbf{1} + \mathbf{1}'\boldsymbol{L}\mathbf{1}) = -\frac{\gamma_1 T}{\sigma^3} + O(1),$$

$$\{\mathcal{E}\}_{17} = \{\mathcal{E}\}_{31} = -\frac{1}{\sigma^4}\mathbf{1}'\boldsymbol{\Phi}'\boldsymbol{\Phi}\mathbf{1} = -\frac{T(1-\phi)^2}{\sigma^4} + O(1),$$

$$\{\mathcal{E}\}_{19} = \{\mathcal{E}\}_{33} = -\frac{\gamma_1}{2\sigma^5}\mathbf{1}'\boldsymbol{\Phi}1 = -\frac{\gamma_1 T(1-\phi)}{2\sigma^5} + O(1),$$

$$\{\mathcal{E}\}_{24} = -\frac{\gamma_1}{\sigma}\mathrm{tr}[(\boldsymbol{\Phi}^{-1}\boldsymbol{L})\mathrm{Diag}(\boldsymbol{\Phi}\mathbf{1})(\boldsymbol{\Phi}^{-1}\boldsymbol{L})'] = -\frac{\gamma_1 T}{\sigma(1+\phi)} + O(1),$$

$$\{\mathcal{E}\}_{25} = -2\mathrm{tr}[(\boldsymbol{\Phi}^{-1}\boldsymbol{L})^2(\boldsymbol{\Phi}^{-1}\boldsymbol{L})'] = -\frac{2T\phi}{(1-\phi^2)^2} + O(1),$$

$$\{\mathcal{E}\}_{26} = -\frac{\gamma_2+2}{2\sigma^2}\mathrm{tr}[(\boldsymbol{\Phi}^{-1}\boldsymbol{L})(\boldsymbol{\Phi}^{-1}\boldsymbol{L})'] = -\frac{(\gamma_2+2)T}{2\sigma^2(1-\phi^2)} + O(1),$$

$$\{\mathcal{E}\}_{28} = \{\mathcal{E}\}_{35} = -\frac{1}{\sigma^2}\mathrm{tr}[(\boldsymbol{\Phi}^{-1}\boldsymbol{L})(\boldsymbol{\Phi}^{-1}\boldsymbol{L})'] = -\frac{T}{\sigma^2(1-\phi^2)} + O(1),$$

$$\{\mathcal{E}\}_{37} = -\frac{\gamma_1}{\sigma^5}\mathbf{1}'\boldsymbol{\Phi}1 = -\frac{\gamma_1 T(1-\phi)}{\sigma^5} + O(1), \quad \{\mathcal{E}\}_{39} = -\frac{(\gamma_2+2)T}{2\sigma^6}.$$

Upon substitution, one has

$$\mathrm{B}(\hat{\boldsymbol{\beta}}) = \frac{1}{T}\begin{pmatrix} 0 \\ -(1+3\phi) \\ -2\sigma^2 \end{pmatrix} + o(T^{-1}).$$

When μ is known, one can simply delete the elements in $\mathcal{F}$, $\mathcal{P}$, $\mathcal{D}$, and $\mathcal{E}$ that pertain to μ, and this gives

$$B(\hat{\boldsymbol{\beta}}) = \frac{1}{T}\begin{pmatrix} -2\phi \\ -\sigma^2 \end{pmatrix} + o(T^{-1}).$$

A.2.2. MA(1)

For $\boldsymbol{\Theta} = \boldsymbol{I} - \theta\boldsymbol{L}$, its inverse $\boldsymbol{\Theta}^{-1}$ is lower triangular with ij-th elements θ^{i-j}, $i \geq j$. The 3×3 matrix $\mathcal{F}$ is diagonal with

$$\{\mathcal{F}\}_{11} = \frac{1}{\sigma^2}\mathbf{1}'\boldsymbol{\Theta}^{-1\prime}\boldsymbol{\Theta}^{-1}\mathbf{1} = \frac{T}{\sigma^2\,(1-\theta)^2} + O(1),$$

$$\{\mathcal{F}\}_{22} = \mathrm{tr}[(\boldsymbol{\Theta}^{-1}\boldsymbol{L})(\boldsymbol{\Theta}^{-1}\boldsymbol{L})'] = \frac{T}{1-\theta^2} + O(1),$$

$$\{\mathcal{F}\}_{33} = \frac{T}{2\sigma^4}.$$

$\mathcal{P}$ has the same diagonals as $\mathcal{F}$, and

$$\{\mathcal{P}\}_{13} = \{\mathcal{P}\}_{31} = \frac{\gamma_1}{2\sigma^3}\mathbf{1}'\mathbf{\Theta}^{-1}\mathbf{1} = \frac{\gamma_1 T}{2\sigma^3(1-\theta)} + O(1), \quad \{\mathcal{P}\}_{33} = \frac{(\gamma_2+2)T}{4\sigma^4}.$$

The 3×9 matrix $\mathcal{D}$ has the following nonzero elements:

$$\{\mathcal{D}\}_{12} = \{\mathcal{D}\}_{14} = \{\mathcal{D}\}_{21} = -\frac{2}{\sigma^2}\mathbf{1}'\mathbf{\Theta}^{-1\prime}\mathbf{\Theta}^{-1}\boldsymbol{L}\mathbf{\Theta}^{-1}\mathbf{1} = -\frac{2T}{\sigma^2(1-\theta)^3} + O(1),$$

$$\{\mathcal{D}\}_{13} = \{\mathcal{D}\}_{17} = \{\mathcal{D}\}_{31} = \frac{1}{\sigma^4}\mathbf{1}'\mathbf{\Theta}^{-1\prime}\mathbf{\Theta}^{-1}\mathbf{1} = \frac{T}{\sigma^4(1-\theta)^2} + O(1),$$

$$\{\mathcal{D}\}_{25} = -6\mathrm{tr}[(\mathbf{\Theta}^{-1}\boldsymbol{L})^2(\mathbf{\Theta}^{-1}\boldsymbol{L})'] = -\frac{6T\theta}{(1-\theta^2)^2} + O(1),$$

$$\{\mathcal{D}\}_{26} = \{\mathcal{D}\}_{28} = \{\mathcal{D}\}_{35} = \frac{1}{\sigma^2}\mathrm{tr}[(\mathbf{\Theta}^{-1}\boldsymbol{L})(\mathbf{\Theta}^{-1}\boldsymbol{L})'] = \frac{T}{\sigma^2(1-\theta^2)} + O(1),$$

$$\{\mathcal{D}\}_{39} = \frac{2T}{\sigma^2}.$$

The 3×9 matrix $\mathcal{E}$ has the following nonzero elements:

$$\{\mathcal{E}\}_{14} = \{\mathcal{E}\}_{21} = \frac{2}{\sigma^2}\mathbf{1}'\mathbf{\Theta}^{-1\prime}\mathbf{\Theta}^{-1}\boldsymbol{L}\mathbf{\Theta}^{-1}\mathbf{1} = \frac{2T}{\sigma^2(1-\theta)^3} + O(1),$$

$$\{\mathcal{E}\}_{16} = \{\mathcal{E}\}_{23} = \frac{\gamma_1}{2\sigma^3}(\mathbf{1}'\mathbf{\Theta}^{-1\prime}\mathbf{\Theta}^{-1}\boldsymbol{L}1 + \mathbf{1}'\mathbf{\Theta}^{-1}\boldsymbol{L}\mathbf{\Theta}^{-1}\mathbf{1}) = \frac{\gamma_1 T}{\sigma^3(1-\theta)^2} + O(1),$$

$$\{\mathcal{E}\}_{17} = \{\mathcal{E}\}_{31} = -\frac{1}{\sigma^4}\mathbf{1}'\mathbf{\Theta}^{-1\prime}\mathbf{\Theta}^{-1}\mathbf{1} = -\frac{T}{\sigma^4(1-\theta)^2} + O(1),$$

$$\{\mathcal{E}\}_{19} = \{\mathcal{E}\}_{33} = \{\mathcal{E}\}_{37} = -\frac{\gamma_1}{2\sigma^5}\mathbf{1}'\mathbf{\Theta}^{-1}\mathbf{1} = -\frac{\gamma_1 T}{2\sigma^5(1-\theta)} + O(1),$$

$$\{\mathcal{E}\}_{24} = -\frac{\gamma_1}{\sigma}\mathrm{tr}[(\mathbf{\Theta}^{-1}\boldsymbol{L})\mathrm{Diag}(\mathbf{\Theta}^{-1}\mathbf{1})(\mathbf{\Theta}^{-1}\boldsymbol{L})'] = -\frac{\gamma_1 T}{\sigma(1-\theta)(1-\theta^2)} + O(1),$$

$$\{\mathcal{E}\}_{25} = 4\mathrm{tr}[(\mathbf{\Theta}^{-1}\boldsymbol{L})^2(\mathbf{\Theta}^{-1}\boldsymbol{L})'] = \frac{4T\theta}{(1-\theta^2)^2} + O(1),$$

$$\{\mathcal{E}\}_{26} = -\frac{\gamma_2+2}{2\sigma^2}\mathrm{tr}[(\mathbf{\Theta}^{-1}\boldsymbol{L})(\mathbf{\Theta}^{-1}\boldsymbol{L})'] = -\frac{(\gamma_2+2)T}{2\sigma^2(1-\theta^2)} + O(1),$$

$$\{\mathcal{E}\}_{28} = \{\mathcal{E}\}_{35} = -\frac{1}{\sigma^2}\mathrm{tr}[(\mathbf{\Theta}^{-1}\boldsymbol{L})(\mathbf{\Theta}^{-1}\boldsymbol{L})'] = -\frac{T}{\sigma^2(1-\theta^2)} + O(1),$$

$$\{\mathcal{E}\}_{39} = -\frac{T(\gamma_2+2)}{2\sigma^6}.$$

By substitution, one has

$$\mathrm{B}(\hat{\boldsymbol{\beta}}) = \frac{1}{T}\begin{pmatrix} 0 \\ 1+2\theta \\ -2\sigma^2 \end{pmatrix} + o(T^{-1}).$$

When μ is known, by deleting the elements in $\mathcal{F}$, $\mathcal{P}$, $\mathcal{D}$, and $\mathcal{E}$ that pertain to μ, one has

$$B(\hat{\boldsymbol{\beta}}) = \frac{1}{T}\begin{pmatrix} \theta \\ -\sigma^2 \end{pmatrix} + o(T^{-1}).$$

A.2.3. ARMA(1,1)

The 4×4 matrix $\mathcal{F}$ has the following nonzero elements:

$$\{\mathcal{F}\}_{11} = \frac{1}{\sigma^2}\mathbf{1}'\boldsymbol{\Phi}'\boldsymbol{\Theta}^{-1'}\boldsymbol{\Theta}^{-1}\boldsymbol{\Phi}\mathbf{1} = \frac{T\,(1-\phi)^2}{\sigma^2\,(1-\theta)^2} + O(1),$$

$$\{\mathcal{F}\}_{22} = \mathrm{tr}[(\boldsymbol{\Phi}^{-1}\boldsymbol{L})(\boldsymbol{\Phi}^{-1}\boldsymbol{L})'] = \frac{T}{1-\phi^2} + O(1),$$

$$\{\mathcal{F}\}_{23} = \{\mathcal{F}\}_{32} = -\mathrm{tr}[(\boldsymbol{\Phi}^{-1}\boldsymbol{L})(\boldsymbol{\Theta}^{-1}\boldsymbol{L})'] = -\frac{T}{1-\phi\theta} + O(1),$$

$$\{\mathcal{F}\}_{33} = \mathrm{tr}[(\boldsymbol{\Theta}^{-1}\boldsymbol{L})(\boldsymbol{\Theta}^{-1}\boldsymbol{L})'] = \frac{T}{1-\theta^2} + O(1), \quad \{\mathcal{F}\}_{44} = \frac{T}{2\sigma^4}.$$

$\mathcal{P}$ has the same top-left 3×3 block as $\mathcal{F}$, and

$$\{\mathcal{P}\}_{14} = \{\mathcal{P}\}_{41} = \frac{\gamma_1}{2\sigma^3}\mathbf{1}'\boldsymbol{\Theta}^{-1}\boldsymbol{\Phi}\mathbf{1} = \frac{\gamma_1 T(1-\phi)}{2\sigma^3(1-\theta)} + O(1), \quad \{\mathcal{P}\}_{44} = \frac{(\gamma_2+2)T}{4\sigma^4}.$$

The 4×16 matrix $\mathcal{D}$ has the following nonzero elements:

$$\{\mathcal{D}\}_{12} = \{\mathcal{D}\}_{15} = \{\mathcal{D}\}_{21} = \frac{2}{\sigma^2}\mathbf{1}'\boldsymbol{L}'\boldsymbol{\Theta}^{-1'}\boldsymbol{\Theta}^{-1}\boldsymbol{\Phi}\mathbf{1} = \frac{2T(1-\phi)}{\sigma^2(1-\theta)^2} + O(1),$$

$$\{\mathcal{D}\}_{13} = \{\mathcal{D}\}_{19} = \{\mathcal{D}\}_{31} = -\frac{2}{\sigma^2}\mathbf{1}'\boldsymbol{\Phi}'\boldsymbol{\Theta}^{-1'}\boldsymbol{\Theta}^{-1}\boldsymbol{L}\boldsymbol{\Theta}^{-1}\boldsymbol{\Phi}\mathbf{1} = -\frac{2T(1-\phi)^2}{\sigma^2(1-\theta)^3} + O(1),$$

$$\{\mathcal{D}\}_{14} = \{\mathcal{D}\}_{1,13} = \{\mathcal{D}\}_{41} = \frac{1}{\sigma^4}\mathbf{1}'\boldsymbol{\Phi}'\boldsymbol{\Theta}^{-1'}\boldsymbol{\Theta}^{-1}\boldsymbol{\Phi}\mathbf{1} = \frac{T\,(1-\phi)^2}{\sigma^4\,(1-\theta)^2} + O(1),$$

$$\{\mathcal{D}\}_{27} = \{\mathcal{D}\}_{2,10} = \{\mathcal{D}\}_{36} = -2\text{tr}[(\boldsymbol{\Phi}^{-1}\boldsymbol{L})(\boldsymbol{\Theta}^{-1}\boldsymbol{L})(\boldsymbol{\Phi}^{-1}\boldsymbol{L})']$$
$$= -\frac{2T\phi}{(1-\phi^2)(1-\phi\theta)} + O(1),$$
$$\{\mathcal{D}\}_{28} = \{\mathcal{D}\}_{2,14} = \{\mathcal{D}\}_{46} = \frac{1}{\sigma^2}\text{tr}[(\boldsymbol{\Phi}^{-1}\boldsymbol{L})(\boldsymbol{\Phi}^{-1}\boldsymbol{L})'] = \frac{T}{\sigma^2(1-\phi^2)} + O(1),$$
$$\{\mathcal{D}\}_{2,11} = \{\mathcal{D}\}_{37} = \{\mathcal{D}\}_{3,10} = 2\text{tr}[(\boldsymbol{\Phi}^{-1}\boldsymbol{L})(\boldsymbol{\Theta}^{-1}\boldsymbol{L})(\boldsymbol{\Theta}^{-1}\boldsymbol{L})'] + 2\text{tr}[(\boldsymbol{\Theta}^{-1}\boldsymbol{L})^2(\boldsymbol{\Phi}^{-1}\boldsymbol{L})']$$
$$= \frac{2T\theta}{(1-\theta^2)(1-\phi\theta)} + \frac{2T\phi}{(1-\phi\theta)^2} + O(1),$$
$$\{\mathcal{D}\}_{2,12} = \{\mathcal{D}\}_{2,15} = \{\mathcal{D}\}_{38} = \{\mathcal{D}\}_{3,14} = \{\mathcal{D}\}_{47} = \{\mathcal{D}\}_{4,10} = -\frac{1}{\sigma^2}\text{tr}[(\boldsymbol{\Phi}^{-1}\boldsymbol{L})(\boldsymbol{\Theta}^{-1}\boldsymbol{L})']$$
$$= -\frac{T}{\sigma^2(1-\phi\theta)} + O(1),$$
$$\{\mathcal{D}\}_{3,11} = -6\text{tr}[(\boldsymbol{\Theta}^{-1}\boldsymbol{L})^2(\boldsymbol{\Theta}^{-1}\boldsymbol{L})'] = -\frac{6T\theta}{(1-\theta^2)^2} + O(1),$$
$$\{\mathcal{D}\}_{3,12} = \{\mathcal{D}\}_{3,15} = \{\mathcal{D}\}_{4,11} = \frac{1}{\sigma^2}\text{tr}[(\boldsymbol{\Theta}^{-1}\boldsymbol{L})(\boldsymbol{\Theta}^{-1}\boldsymbol{L})'] = \frac{T}{\sigma^2(1-\theta^2)} + O(1),$$
$$\{\mathcal{D}\}_{4,16} = \frac{2T}{\sigma^6}.$$

The 4×16 matrix $\mathcal{E}$ has the following nonzero elements:

$$\{\mathcal{E}\}_{15} = \{\mathcal{E}\}_{21} = -\frac{2}{\sigma^2}\mathbf{1}'\boldsymbol{\Phi}'\boldsymbol{\Theta}^{-1\prime}\boldsymbol{\Theta}^{-1}\boldsymbol{L}\mathbf{1} = -\frac{2T(1-\phi)}{\sigma^2(1-\theta)^2} + O(1),$$
$$\{\mathcal{E}\}_{18} = \{\mathcal{E}\}_{24} = -\frac{\gamma_1}{2\sigma^3}(\mathbf{1}'\boldsymbol{L}'\boldsymbol{\Phi}^{-1\prime}\boldsymbol{\Theta}^{-1}\boldsymbol{\Phi}\mathbf{1} + \mathbf{1}'\boldsymbol{\Theta}^{-1}\boldsymbol{L}\mathbf{1}) = -\frac{\gamma_1 T}{\sigma^3(1-\theta)} + O(1),$$
$$\{\mathcal{E}\}_{19} = \{\mathcal{E}\}_{31} = \frac{2}{\sigma^2}\mathbf{1}'\boldsymbol{\Phi}'\boldsymbol{\Theta}^{-1\prime}\boldsymbol{L}'\boldsymbol{\Theta}^{-1\prime}\boldsymbol{\Theta}^{-1}\boldsymbol{\Phi}\mathbf{1} = \frac{2T(1-\phi)^2}{\sigma^2(1-\theta)^3} + O(1),$$
$$\{\mathcal{E}\}_{1,12} = \{\mathcal{E}\}_{34} = \frac{\gamma_1}{2\sigma^3}(\mathbf{1}'\boldsymbol{L}'\boldsymbol{\Theta}^{-1\prime}\boldsymbol{\Theta}^{-1}\boldsymbol{\Phi}\mathbf{1} + \mathbf{1}'\boldsymbol{\Theta}^{-1}\boldsymbol{L}\boldsymbol{\Theta}^{-1}\boldsymbol{\Phi}\mathbf{1}) = \frac{\gamma_1 T(1-\phi)}{\sigma^3(1-\theta)^2} + O(1),$$
$$\{\mathcal{E}\}_{1,13} = \{\mathcal{E}\}_{41} = -\frac{1}{\sigma^4}\mathbf{1}'\boldsymbol{\Phi}'\boldsymbol{\Theta}^{-1\prime}\boldsymbol{\Theta}^{-1}\boldsymbol{\Phi}\mathbf{1} = -\frac{T(1-\phi)^2}{\sigma^4(1-\theta)^2} + O(1),$$
$$\{\mathcal{E}\}_{1,16} = \{\mathcal{E}\}_{44} = -\frac{\gamma_1}{2\sigma^5}\mathbf{1}'\boldsymbol{\Theta}^{-1}\boldsymbol{\Phi}\mathbf{1} = -\frac{\gamma_1 T(1-\phi)}{2\sigma^5(1-\theta)} + O(1),$$

$$\{\mathcal{E}\}_{25} = -\frac{\gamma_1}{\sigma}\mathrm{tr}[(\boldsymbol{\Phi}^{-1}\boldsymbol{L})\mathrm{Diag}(\boldsymbol{\Theta}^{-1}\boldsymbol{\Phi}\mathbf{1})(\boldsymbol{\Phi}^{-1}\boldsymbol{L})'] = -\frac{\gamma_1 T}{\sigma(1+\phi)(1-\theta)} + O(1),$$

$$\{\mathcal{E}\}_{26} = -2\mathrm{tr}[(\boldsymbol{\Phi}^{-1}\boldsymbol{L})^2(\boldsymbol{\Phi}^{-1}\boldsymbol{L})'] = -\frac{2T\phi}{(1-\phi^2)^2} + O(1),$$

$$\{\mathcal{E}\}_{27} = 2\mathrm{tr}[(\boldsymbol{\Phi}^{-1}\boldsymbol{L})(\boldsymbol{\Theta}^{-1}\boldsymbol{L})(\boldsymbol{\Phi}^{-1}\boldsymbol{L})'] = \frac{2T\phi}{(1-\phi^2)(1-\phi\theta)} + O(1),$$

$$\{\mathcal{E}\}_{28} = -\frac{\gamma_2+2}{2\sigma^2}\mathrm{tr}[(\boldsymbol{\Phi}^{-1}\boldsymbol{L})(\boldsymbol{\Phi}^{-1}\boldsymbol{L})'] = -\frac{(\gamma_2+2)T}{2\sigma^2(1-\phi^2)} + O(1),$$

$$\{\mathcal{E}\}_{29} = \{\mathcal{E}\}_{35} = \frac{\gamma_1}{\sigma}\mathrm{tr}[(\boldsymbol{\Theta}^{-1}\boldsymbol{L})\mathrm{Diag}(\boldsymbol{\Theta}^{-1}\boldsymbol{\Phi}\mathbf{1})(\boldsymbol{\Phi}^{-1}\boldsymbol{L})] = \frac{\gamma_1 T(1-\phi)}{\sigma(1-\theta)(1-\phi\theta)} + O(1),$$

$$\{\mathcal{E}\}_{2,10} = \{\mathcal{E}\}_{36} = 2\mathrm{tr}[(\boldsymbol{\Phi}^{-1}\boldsymbol{L})(\boldsymbol{\Theta}^{-1}\boldsymbol{L})(\boldsymbol{\Phi}^{-1}\boldsymbol{L})'] + \mathrm{tr}[(\boldsymbol{\Phi}^{-1}\boldsymbol{L})^2(\boldsymbol{\Theta}^{-1}\boldsymbol{L})']$$

$$= \frac{2T\phi}{(1-\phi^2)(1-\phi\theta)} + \frac{T\theta}{(1-\phi\theta)^2} + O(1),$$

$$\{\mathcal{E}\}_{2,11} = \{\mathcal{E}\}_{37} = -\mathrm{tr}[(\boldsymbol{\Theta}^{-1}\boldsymbol{L})^2(\boldsymbol{\Phi}^{-1}\boldsymbol{L})'] - 2\mathrm{tr}[(\boldsymbol{\Phi}^{-1}\boldsymbol{L})(\boldsymbol{\Theta}^{-1}\boldsymbol{L})(\boldsymbol{\Theta}^{-1}\boldsymbol{L})']$$

$$= -\frac{T\phi}{(1-\phi\theta)^2} - \frac{2T\theta}{(1-\phi\theta)(1-\theta^2)} + O(1),$$

$$\{\mathcal{E}\}_{2,12} = \{\mathcal{E}\}_{38} = \frac{\gamma_2+2}{2\sigma^2}\mathrm{tr}[(\boldsymbol{\Phi}^{-1}\boldsymbol{L})(\boldsymbol{\Theta}^{-1}\boldsymbol{L})'] = \frac{(\gamma_2+2)T}{2\sigma^2(1-\phi\theta)} + O(1),$$

$$\{\mathcal{E}\}_{2,14} = \{\mathcal{E}\}_{46} = -\frac{1}{\sigma^2}\mathrm{tr}[(\boldsymbol{\Phi}^{-1}\boldsymbol{L})(\boldsymbol{\Phi}^{-1}\boldsymbol{L})'] = -\frac{T}{\sigma^2(1-\phi^2)} + O(1),$$

$$\{\mathcal{E}\}_{2,15} = \{\mathcal{E}\}_{3,14} = \{\mathcal{E}\}_{47} = \{\mathcal{E}\}_{4,10} = \frac{1}{\sigma^2}\mathrm{tr}[(\boldsymbol{\Phi}^{-1}\boldsymbol{L})(\boldsymbol{\Theta}^{-1}\boldsymbol{L})'] = \frac{T}{\sigma^2(1-\phi\theta)} + O(1),$$

$$\{\mathcal{E}\}_{39} = -\frac{\gamma_1}{\sigma}\mathrm{tr}[(\boldsymbol{\Theta}^{-1}\boldsymbol{L})\mathrm{Diag}(\boldsymbol{\Theta}^{-1}\boldsymbol{\Phi}\mathbf{1})(\boldsymbol{\Theta}^{-1}\boldsymbol{L})'] = -\frac{\gamma_1 T(1-\phi)}{\sigma(1-\theta)(1-\theta^2)} + O(1),$$

$$\{\mathcal{E}\}_{3,10} = -2\mathrm{tr}[(\boldsymbol{\Phi}^{-1}\boldsymbol{L})(\boldsymbol{\Theta}^{-1}\boldsymbol{L})(\boldsymbol{\Theta}^{-1}\boldsymbol{L})'] - 2\mathrm{tr}[(\boldsymbol{\Theta}^{-1}\boldsymbol{L})^2(\boldsymbol{\Phi}^{-1}\boldsymbol{L})']$$

$$= -\frac{2T\theta}{(1-\phi\theta)(1-\theta^2)} - \frac{2T\phi}{(1-\phi\theta)^2} + O(1),$$

$$\{\mathcal{E}\}_{3,11} = 4\mathrm{tr}[(\boldsymbol{\Theta}^{-1}\boldsymbol{L})^2(\boldsymbol{\Theta}^{-1}\boldsymbol{L})'] = \frac{4T\theta}{(1-\theta^2)^2} + O(1),$$

$$\{\mathcal{E}\}_{3,12} = -\frac{\gamma_2+2}{2\sigma^2}\mathrm{tr}[(\boldsymbol{\Theta}^{-1}\boldsymbol{L})(\boldsymbol{\Theta}^{-1}\boldsymbol{L})'] = -\frac{(\gamma_2+2)T}{2\sigma^2(1-\theta^2)} + O(1),$$

$$\{\mathcal{E}\}_{3,15} = \{\mathcal{E}\}_{4,11} = -\frac{1}{\sigma^2}\mathrm{tr}[(\boldsymbol{\Theta}^{-1}\boldsymbol{L})(\boldsymbol{\Theta}^{-1}\boldsymbol{L})'] = -\frac{T}{\sigma^2(1-\theta^2)} + O(1),$$

$$\{\mathcal{E}\}_{4,13} = -\frac{\gamma_1}{\sigma^5}\mathbf{1}'\boldsymbol{\Theta}^{-1}\boldsymbol{\Phi}\mathbf{1} = -\frac{\gamma_1 T(1-\phi)}{\sigma^5(1-\theta)} + O(1), \quad \{\mathcal{E}\}_{4,16} = -\frac{T(\gamma_2+2)}{2\sigma^6}.$$

By plugging $\mathcal{D}$, $\mathcal{E}$, $\mathcal{F}$, $\mathcal{P}$ into Eq. (4), the bias result for ARMA(1,1) as presented in Eq. (15) follows. If μ is known, one can simply delete the corresponding elements/blocks of $\mathcal{F}$, $\mathcal{P}$, $\mathcal{D}$, and $\mathcal{E}$ pertaining to μ, the result (17) follows.

A.2.4. AR(2)

For the AR(2) model, $\boldsymbol{\Phi} = \boldsymbol{I} - \phi_1\boldsymbol{L} - \phi_2\boldsymbol{L}^2$. One can easily see that $\boldsymbol{\Phi}\mathbf{1} = (1, 1-\phi_1, 1-\phi_1-\phi_2, \ldots, 1-\phi_1-\phi_2)'$. Also, $\boldsymbol{\Phi}^{-1}$ is lower triangular with 1 on its main diagonal, ϕ_1 on its first subdiagonal, and its ij-th elements follow a second-order difference equation: $\{\boldsymbol{\Phi}^{-1}\}_{ij} = \phi_1\{\boldsymbol{\Phi}^{-1}\}_{i-1,j} + \phi_2\{\boldsymbol{\Phi}^{-1}\}_{i-2,j}, i \geq j+2$.

The 4×4 matrix $\mathcal{F}$ has the following nonzero elements:

$$\{\mathcal{F}\}_{11} = \frac{1}{\sigma^2}\mathbf{1}'\boldsymbol{\Phi}'\boldsymbol{\Phi}\mathbf{1} = \frac{T(1-\phi_1-\phi_2)^2}{\sigma^2} + O(1),$$

$$\{\mathcal{F}\}_{22} = \mathrm{tr}[(\boldsymbol{\Phi}^{-1}\boldsymbol{L})(\boldsymbol{\Phi}^{-1}\boldsymbol{L})'] = \frac{T(1-\phi_2)}{(1+\phi_1-\phi_2)(1+\phi_2)(1-\phi_1-\phi_2)} + O(1),$$

$$\{\mathcal{F}\}_{23} = \{\mathcal{F}\}_{32} = \mathrm{tr}[(\boldsymbol{\Phi}^{-1}\boldsymbol{L})(\boldsymbol{\Phi}^{-1}\boldsymbol{L}^2)']$$

$$= \frac{T\phi_1}{(1+\phi_1-\phi_2)(1+\phi_2)(1-\phi_1-\phi_2)} + O(1),$$

$$\{\mathcal{F}\}_{33} = \mathrm{tr}[(\boldsymbol{\Phi}^{-1}\boldsymbol{L}^2)(\boldsymbol{\Phi}^{-1}\boldsymbol{L}^2)'] = \frac{T(1-\phi_2)}{(1+\phi_1-\phi_2)(1+\phi_2)(1-\phi_1-\phi_2)} + O(1),$$

$$\{\mathcal{F}\}_{44} = \frac{T}{2\sigma^4}.$$

$\mathcal{P}$ has the same top-left 3×3 block as $\mathcal{F}$, and

$$\{\mathcal{P}\}_{14} = \{\mathcal{P}\}_{41} = \frac{\gamma_1}{2\sigma^3}\mathbf{1}'\boldsymbol{\Phi}\mathbf{1} = \frac{\gamma_1 T(1-\phi_1-\phi_2)}{2\sigma^3} + O(1), \quad \{\mathcal{P}\}_{44} = \frac{(\gamma_2+2)T}{4\sigma^4}.$$

The 4×16 matrix $\mathcal{D}$ has the following nonzero elements:

$$\{\mathcal{D}\}_{12} = \{\mathcal{D}\}_{15} = \{\mathcal{D}\}_{21} = \frac{2}{\sigma^2}\mathbf{1}'\boldsymbol{L}'\boldsymbol{\Phi}\mathbf{1} = \frac{2T(1-\phi_1-\phi_2)}{\sigma^2} + O(1),$$

$$\{\mathcal{D}\}_{13} = \{\mathcal{D}\}_{19} = \{\mathcal{D}\}_{31} = \frac{2}{\sigma^2}\mathbf{1}'\boldsymbol{L}'\boldsymbol{L}'\boldsymbol{\Phi}\mathbf{1} = \frac{2T(1-\phi_1-\phi_2)}{\sigma^2} + O(1),$$

$$\{\mathcal{D}\}_{14} = \{\mathcal{D}\}_{1,13} = \{\mathcal{D}\}_{41} = \frac{1}{\sigma^4}\mathbf{1}'\boldsymbol{\Phi}'\boldsymbol{\Phi}\mathbf{1} = \frac{T(1-\phi_1-\phi_2)^2}{\sigma^4} + O(1),$$

$$\{\mathcal{D}\}_{28} = \{\mathcal{D}\}_{2,14} = \{\mathcal{D}\}_{46} = \frac{1}{\sigma^2}\mathrm{tr}[(\boldsymbol{\Phi}^{-1}\boldsymbol{L})(\boldsymbol{\Phi}^{-1}\boldsymbol{L})']$$

$$= \frac{T(1-\phi_2)}{\sigma^2(1+\phi_1-\phi_2)(1+\phi_2)(1-\phi_1-\phi_2)} + O(1),$$

$$\{\mathcal{D}\}_{2,12} = \{\mathcal{D}\}_{2,15} = \{\mathcal{D}\}_{38} = \{\mathcal{D}\}_{3,14} = \{\mathcal{D}\}_{47} = \{\mathcal{D}\}_{4,10} = \frac{1}{\sigma^2}\mathrm{tr}[(\boldsymbol{\Phi}^{-1}\boldsymbol{L})(\boldsymbol{\Phi}^{-1}\boldsymbol{L}^2)']$$

$$= \frac{T\phi_1}{\sigma^2(1+\phi_1-\phi_2)(1+\phi_2)(1-\phi_1-\phi_2)} + O(1),$$

$$\{\mathcal{D}\}_{3,12} = \{\mathcal{D}\}_{3,15} = \{\mathcal{D}\}_{4,11} = \frac{1}{\sigma^2}\mathrm{tr}[(\boldsymbol{\Phi}^{-1}\boldsymbol{L}^2)(\boldsymbol{\Phi}^{-1}\boldsymbol{L}^2)']$$

$$= \frac{T(1-\phi_2)}{\sigma^2(1+\phi_1-\phi_2)(1+\phi_2)(1-\phi_1-\phi_2)} + O(1),$$

$$\{\mathcal{D}\}_{4,16} = \frac{2T}{\sigma^6}.$$

The 4×16 matrix $\mathcal{E}$ has the following nonzero elements:

$$\{\mathcal{E}\}_{15} = \{\mathcal{E}\}_{21} = -\frac{2}{\sigma^2}\mathbf{1}'\boldsymbol{L}'\boldsymbol{\Phi}\mathbf{1} = -\frac{2T(1-\phi_1-\phi_2)}{\sigma^2} + O(1),$$

$$\{\mathcal{E}\}_{18} = \{\mathcal{E}\}_{24} = -\frac{\gamma_1}{2\sigma^3}(\mathbf{1}'\boldsymbol{L}'\boldsymbol{\Phi}^{-1\prime}\boldsymbol{\Phi}\mathbf{1} + \mathbf{1}'\boldsymbol{L}'\mathbf{1}) = -\frac{\gamma_1 T}{\sigma^3} + O(1),$$

$$\{\mathcal{E}\}_{19} = \{\mathcal{E}\}_{31} = -\frac{2}{\sigma^2}\mathbf{1}'\boldsymbol{L}'\boldsymbol{L}'\boldsymbol{\Phi}\mathbf{1} = -\frac{2T(1-\phi_1-\phi_2)}{\sigma^2} + O(1),$$

$$\{\mathcal{E}\}_{1,12} = \{\mathcal{E}\}_{34} = -\frac{\gamma_1}{2\sigma^3}(\mathbf{1}'\boldsymbol{L}'\boldsymbol{L}'\boldsymbol{\Phi}^{-1\prime}\boldsymbol{\Phi}\mathbf{1} + \mathbf{1}'\boldsymbol{L}'\boldsymbol{L}'\mathbf{1}) = -\frac{\gamma_1 T}{\sigma^3} + O(1),$$

$$\{\mathcal{E}\}_{1,13} = \{\mathcal{E}\}_{41} = -\frac{1}{\sigma^4}\mathbf{1}'\boldsymbol{\Phi}'\boldsymbol{\Phi}\mathbf{1} = -\frac{T(1-\phi_1-\phi_2)^2}{\sigma^4} + O(1),$$

$$\{\mathcal{E}\}_{1,16} = \{\mathcal{E}\}_{44} = -\frac{\gamma_1}{2\sigma^5}\mathbf{1}'\boldsymbol{\Phi}\mathbf{1} = -\frac{\gamma_1 T(1-\phi_1-\phi_2)}{2\sigma^5} + O(1),$$

$$\{\mathcal{E}\}_{25} = -\frac{\gamma_1}{\sigma}\mathrm{tr}[(\boldsymbol{\Phi}^{-1}\boldsymbol{L})\mathrm{Diag}(\boldsymbol{\Phi}\mathbf{1})(\boldsymbol{\Phi}^{-1}\boldsymbol{L})'] = -\frac{\gamma_1 T(1-\phi_2)}{\sigma(1+\phi_1-\phi_2)(1+\phi_2)} + O(1),$$

$$\{\mathcal{E}\}_{26} = -2\mathrm{tr}\left[(\boldsymbol{\Phi}^{-1}\boldsymbol{L})^2(\boldsymbol{\Phi}^{-1}\boldsymbol{L})'\right]$$

$$= -\frac{2T\phi_1(1-\phi_2)}{(1+\phi_1-\phi_2)^2(1+\phi_2)(1-\phi_1-\phi_2)^2} + O(1),$$

$$
\begin{aligned}
\{\mathcal{E}\}_{27} &= -2\mathrm{tr}\left[(\mathbf{\Phi}^{-1}\boldsymbol{L}^2)(\mathbf{\Phi}^{-1}\boldsymbol{L})(\mathbf{\Phi}^{-1}\boldsymbol{L})'\right] \\
&= -\frac{2T[\phi_1^2 + \phi_2(1-\phi_2)^2]}{(1+\phi_1-\phi_2)^2(1+\phi_2)^2(1-\phi_1-\phi_2)^2} + O(1), \\
\{\mathcal{E}\}_{28} &= -\frac{\gamma_2+2}{2\sigma^2}\mathrm{tr}\left[(\mathbf{\Phi}^{-1}\boldsymbol{L})(\mathbf{\Phi}^{-1}\boldsymbol{L})'\right] \\
&= -\frac{(\gamma_2+2)T(1-\phi_2)}{2\sigma^2(1+\phi_1-\phi_2)(1+\phi_2)(1-\phi_1-\phi_2)} + O(1), \\
\{\mathcal{E}\}_{29} &= \{\mathcal{E}\}_{35} = -\frac{\gamma_1}{\sigma}\mathrm{tr}[(\mathbf{\Phi}^{-1}\boldsymbol{L})\mathrm{Diag}(\mathbf{\Phi}\mathbf{1})(\mathbf{\Phi}^{-1}\boldsymbol{L}^2)'] \\
&= -\frac{\gamma_1 T\phi_1}{\sigma(1+\phi_1-\phi_2)(1+\phi_2)} + O(1), \\
\{\mathcal{E}\}_{2,10} &= \{\mathcal{E}\}_{36} = -\mathrm{tr}\left[(\mathbf{\Phi}^{-1}\boldsymbol{L})^2(\mathbf{\Phi}^{-1}\boldsymbol{L}^2)'\right] - \mathrm{tr}\left[(\mathbf{\Phi}^{-1}\boldsymbol{L}^2)(\mathbf{\Phi}^{-1}\boldsymbol{L})(\mathbf{\Phi}^{-1}\boldsymbol{L})'\right] \\
&= -\frac{T[1-\phi_2(2-\phi_1^2-\phi_2)]}{(1+\phi_1-\phi_2)^2(1+\phi_2)^2(1-\phi_1-\phi_2)^2} \\
&\quad - \frac{T[\phi_1^2+\phi_2(1-\phi_2)^2]}{(1+\phi_1-\phi_2)^2(1+\phi_2)^2(1-\phi_1-\phi_2)^2} + O(1), \\
\{\mathcal{E}\}_{2,14} &= \{\mathcal{E}\}_{46} = -\frac{1}{\sigma^2}\mathrm{tr}\left[(\mathbf{\Phi}^{-1}\boldsymbol{L})(\mathbf{\Phi}^{-1}\boldsymbol{L})'\right] \\
&= -\frac{T(1-\phi_2)}{\sigma^2(1+\phi_1-\phi_2)(1+\phi_2)(1-\phi_1-\phi_2)} + O(1), \\
\{\mathcal{E}\}_{2,11} &= \{\mathcal{E}\}_{37} = -\mathrm{tr}\left[(\mathbf{\Phi}^{-1}\boldsymbol{L})(\mathbf{\Phi}^{-1}\boldsymbol{L}^2)(\mathbf{\Phi}^{-1}\boldsymbol{L}^2)'\right] - \mathrm{tr}\left[(\mathbf{\Phi}^{-1}\boldsymbol{L}^2)^2(\mathbf{\Phi}^{-1}\boldsymbol{L})'\right] \\
&= -\frac{T\phi_1(1-\phi_2)}{(1+\phi_1-\phi_2)^2(1+\phi_2)(1-\phi_1-\phi_2)^2} \\
&\quad - \frac{T\phi_1[\phi_1^2+2\phi_2(1-\phi_2)]}{(1+\phi_1-\phi_2)^2(1+\phi_2)^2(1-\phi_1-\phi_2)^2} + O(1), \\
\{\mathcal{E}\}_{3,10} &= -2\mathrm{tr}\left[(\mathbf{\Phi}^{-1}\boldsymbol{L})(\mathbf{\Phi}^{-1}\boldsymbol{L}^2)(\mathbf{\Phi}^{-1}\boldsymbol{L}^2)'\right] \\
&= -\frac{2T\phi_1(1-\phi_2)}{(1+\phi_1-\phi_2)^2(1+\phi_2)(1-\phi_1-\phi_2)^2} + O(1), \\
\{\mathcal{E}\}_{2,12} &= \{\mathcal{E}\}_{38} = -\frac{\gamma_2+2}{2\sigma^2}\mathrm{tr}\left[(\mathbf{\Phi}^{-1}\boldsymbol{L})(\mathbf{\Phi}^{-1}\boldsymbol{L}^2)'\right] \\
&= -\frac{(\gamma_2+2)T\phi_1}{2\sigma^2(1+\phi_1-\phi_2)(1+\phi_2)(1-\phi_1-\phi_2)} + O(1),
\end{aligned}
$$

$$\begin{aligned}
\{\mathcal{E}\}_{2,15} &= \{\mathcal{E}\}_{3,14} = \{\mathcal{E}\}_{47} = \{\mathcal{E}\}_{4,10} \\
&= -\frac{1}{\sigma^2}\mathrm{tr}\left[(\boldsymbol{\Phi}^{-1}\boldsymbol{L})(\boldsymbol{\Phi}^{-1}\boldsymbol{L}^2)'\right] \\
&= -\frac{T\phi_1}{\sigma^2(1+\phi_1-\phi_2)(1+\phi_2)(1-\phi_1-\phi_2)} + O(1), \\
\{\mathcal{E}\}_{39} &= -\frac{\gamma_1}{\sigma}\mathrm{tr}[(\boldsymbol{\Phi}^{-1}\boldsymbol{L}^2)\mathrm{Diag}(\boldsymbol{\Phi}\mathbf{1})(\boldsymbol{\Phi}^{-1}\boldsymbol{L}^2)'] \\
&= -\frac{\gamma_1 T(1-\phi_2)}{\sigma(1+\phi_1-\phi_2)(1+\phi_2)} + O(1), \\
\{\mathcal{E}\}_{3,11} &= -2\mathrm{tr}\left[(\boldsymbol{\Phi}^{-1}\boldsymbol{L}^2)^2(\boldsymbol{\Phi}^{-1}\boldsymbol{L}^2)'\right] \\
&= -\frac{2T[\phi_1^2+\phi_2(1-\phi_2)^2]}{(1+\phi_1-\phi_2)^2(1+\phi_2)^2(1-\phi_1-\phi_2)^2} + O(1), \\
\{\mathcal{E}\}_{3,12} &= -\frac{\gamma_2+2}{2\sigma^2}\mathrm{tr}\left[(\boldsymbol{\Phi}^{-1}\boldsymbol{L}^2)(\boldsymbol{\Phi}^{-1}\boldsymbol{L}^2)'\right] \\
&= -\frac{(\gamma_2+2)T(1-\phi_2)}{2\sigma^2(1+\phi_1-\phi_2)(1+\phi_2)(1-\phi_1-\phi_2)} + O(1), \\
\{\mathcal{E}\}_{3,15} &= \{\mathcal{E}\}_{4,11} = -\frac{1}{\sigma^2}\mathrm{tr}\left[(\boldsymbol{\Phi}^{-1}\boldsymbol{L}^2)(\boldsymbol{\Phi}^{-1}\boldsymbol{L}^2)'\right] \\
&= -\frac{T(1-\phi_2)}{\sigma^2(1+\phi_1-\phi_2)(1+\phi_2)(1-\phi_1-\phi_2)} + O(1), \\
\{\mathcal{E}\}_{4,13} &= -\frac{\gamma_1}{\sigma^5}\mathbf{1}'\boldsymbol{\Phi}\mathbf{1} = -\frac{\gamma_1 T(1-\phi_1-\phi_2)}{\sigma^5} + O(1), \\
\{\mathcal{E}\}_{4,16} &= -\frac{T(\gamma_2+2)}{2\sigma^6}.
\end{aligned}$$

By substitution, one has the bias result

$$B(\hat{\boldsymbol{\beta}}) = \frac{1}{T}\begin{pmatrix} 0 \\ -(1+\phi_1+\phi_2) \\ -2(1+2\phi_2) \\ -3\sigma^2 \end{pmatrix} + o(T^{-1}).$$

If μ is known, by deleting all the elements related to μ in $\mathcal{F}$, $\mathcal{P}$, $\mathcal{D}$, and $\mathcal{E}$, one gets

$$B(\hat{\boldsymbol{\beta}}) = \frac{1}{T}\begin{pmatrix} -\phi_1 \\ -(1+3\phi_2) \\ -2\sigma^2 \end{pmatrix} + o(T^{-1}).$$

A.2.5. MA(2)

For the MA(2) model, $\boldsymbol{\Theta} = \boldsymbol{I} - \theta_1 \boldsymbol{L} - \theta_2 \boldsymbol{L}^2$, $\boldsymbol{\Theta}^{-1}$ is lower triangular with 1 on its main diagonal, θ_1 on its first subdiagonal, and its ij-th elements follow a second-order difference equation: $\left\{\boldsymbol{\Theta}^{-1}\right\}_{ij} = \theta_1 \left\{\boldsymbol{\Theta}^{-1}\right\}_{i-1,j} + \theta_2 \left\{\boldsymbol{\Theta}^{-1}\right\}_{i-2,j}$, $i \geq j+2$. The 4×4 matrix $\mathcal{F}$ has the following nonzero elements:

$$
\begin{aligned}
\{\mathcal{F}\}_{11} &= \frac{1}{\sigma^2} \mathbf{1}' \boldsymbol{\Theta}^{-1\prime} \boldsymbol{\Theta}^{-1} \mathbf{1} = \frac{T}{\sigma^2 (1-\theta_1-\theta_2)^2} + O(1), \\
\{\mathcal{F}\}_{22} &= \operatorname{tr}[(\boldsymbol{\Theta}^{-1}\boldsymbol{L})(\boldsymbol{\Theta}^{-1}\boldsymbol{L})'] = \frac{T(1-\theta_2)}{(1+\theta_1-\theta_2)(1+\theta_2)(1-\theta_1-\theta_2)} + O(1), \\
\{\mathcal{F}\}_{23} &= \{\mathcal{F}\}_{32} = \operatorname{tr}[(\boldsymbol{\Theta}^{-1}\boldsymbol{L})(\boldsymbol{\Theta}^{-1}\boldsymbol{L}^2)'] \\
&= \frac{T\theta_1}{(1+\theta_1-\theta_2)(1+\theta_2)(1-\theta_1-\theta_2)} + O(1), \\
\{\mathcal{F}\}_{33} &= \operatorname{tr}[(\boldsymbol{\Theta}^{-1}\boldsymbol{L}^2)(\boldsymbol{\Theta}^{-1}\boldsymbol{L}^2)'] = \frac{T(1-\theta_2)}{(1+\theta_1-\theta_2)(1+\theta_2)(1-\theta_1-\theta_2)} + O(1), \\
\{\mathcal{F}\}_{44} &= \frac{T}{2\sigma^4}.
\end{aligned}
$$

$\mathcal{P}$ has the same top-left 3×3 block as $\mathcal{F}$, and

$$
\{\mathcal{P}\}_{14} = \{\mathcal{P}\}_{41} = \frac{\gamma_1}{2\sigma^3} \mathbf{1}' \boldsymbol{\Theta}^{-1} \mathbf{1} = \frac{\gamma_1 T}{2\sigma^3(1-\theta_1-\theta_2)} + O(1), \quad \{\mathcal{P}\}_{44} = \frac{(\gamma_2+2)T}{4\sigma^4}.
$$

The 4×16 matrix $\mathcal{D}$ has the following nonzero elements:

$$
\begin{aligned}
\{\mathcal{D}\}_{12} = \{\mathcal{D}\}_{15} = \{\mathcal{D}\}_{21} &= -\frac{2}{\sigma^2} \mathbf{1}' \boldsymbol{\Theta}^{-1\prime} \boldsymbol{\Theta}^{-1} \boldsymbol{L} \boldsymbol{\Theta}^{-1} \mathbf{1} \\
&= -\frac{2T}{\sigma^2(1-\theta_1-\theta_2)^3} + O(1), \\
\{\mathcal{D}\}_{13} = \{\mathcal{D}\}_{19} = \{\mathcal{D}\}_{31} &= -\frac{2}{\sigma^2} \mathbf{1}' \boldsymbol{\Theta}^{-1\prime} \boldsymbol{\Theta}^{-1} \boldsymbol{L}^2 \boldsymbol{\Theta}^{-1} \mathbf{1} \\
&= -\frac{2T}{\sigma^2(1-\theta_1-\theta_2)^3} + O(1),
\end{aligned}
$$

$$\{\mathcal{D}\}_{14} = \{\mathcal{D}\}_{1,13} = \{\mathcal{D}\}_{41} = \frac{1}{\sigma^4}\mathbf{1}'\boldsymbol{\Theta}^{-1\prime}\boldsymbol{\Theta}^{-1}\mathbf{1} = \frac{T}{\sigma^4(1-\theta_1-\theta_2)^2} + O(1),$$

$$\begin{aligned}\{\mathcal{D}\}_{26} &= -6\mathrm{tr}[(\boldsymbol{\Theta}^{-1}\boldsymbol{L})^2(\boldsymbol{\Theta}^{-1}\boldsymbol{L})'] \\ &= -\frac{6T\theta_1(1-\theta_2)}{(1+\theta_1-\theta_2)^2(1+\theta_2)(1-\theta_1-\theta_2)^2} + O(1),\end{aligned}$$

$$\begin{aligned}\{\mathcal{D}\}_{27} = \{\mathcal{D}\}_{2,10} = \{\mathcal{D}\}_{36} &= -2\mathrm{tr}[(\boldsymbol{\Theta}^{-1}\boldsymbol{L})^2(\boldsymbol{\Theta}^{-1}\boldsymbol{L}^2)'] \\ &\quad - 4\mathrm{tr}[(\boldsymbol{\Theta}^{-1}\boldsymbol{L})(\boldsymbol{\Theta}^{-1}\boldsymbol{L}^2)(\boldsymbol{\Theta}^{-1}\boldsymbol{L})'] \\ &= -\frac{2T[1-\theta_2(2-\theta_1^2-\theta_2)]}{(1+\theta_1-\theta_2)^2(1+\theta_2)^2(1-\theta_1-\theta_2)^2} \\ &\quad - \frac{4T[\theta_1^2+\theta_2(1-\theta_2)^2]}{(1+\theta_1-\theta_2)^2(1+\theta_2)^2(1-\theta_1-\theta_2)^2} + O(1),\end{aligned}$$

$$\begin{aligned}\{\mathcal{D}\}_{28} = \{\mathcal{D}\}_{2,14} = \{\mathcal{D}\}_{46} &= \frac{1}{\sigma^2}\mathrm{tr}[(\boldsymbol{\Theta}^{-1}\boldsymbol{L})(\boldsymbol{\Theta}^{-1}\boldsymbol{L})'] \\ &= \frac{T(1-\theta_2)}{\sigma^2(1+\theta_1-\theta_2)(1+\theta_2)(1-\theta_1-\theta_2)} + O(1),\end{aligned}$$

$$\begin{aligned}\{\mathcal{D}\}_{2,11} = \{\mathcal{D}\}_{37} = \{\mathcal{D}\}_{3,10} &= -2\mathrm{tr}[(\boldsymbol{\Theta}^{-1}\boldsymbol{L}^2)^2(\boldsymbol{\Theta}^{-1}\boldsymbol{L})'] \\ &\quad - 4\mathrm{tr}[(\boldsymbol{\Theta}^{-1}\boldsymbol{L})(\boldsymbol{\Theta}^{-1}\boldsymbol{L}^2)(\boldsymbol{\Theta}^{-1}\boldsymbol{L}^2)'] \\ &= -\frac{2T\theta_1[\theta_1^2+2\theta_2(1-\theta_2)]}{(1+\theta_1-\theta_2)^2(1+\theta_2)^2(1-\theta_1-\theta_2)^2} \\ &\quad - \frac{4T\theta_1(1-\theta_2)}{(1+\theta_1-\theta_2)^2(1+\theta_2)(1-\theta_1-\theta_2)^2} + O(1),\end{aligned}$$

$$\begin{aligned}\{\mathcal{D}\}_{2,12} &= \{\mathcal{D}\}_{2,15} = \{\mathcal{D}\}_{38} = \{\mathcal{D}\}_{3,14} = \{\mathcal{D}\}_{47} = \{\mathcal{D}\}_{4,10} \\ &= \frac{1}{\sigma^2}\mathrm{tr}[(\boldsymbol{\Theta}^{-1}\boldsymbol{L})(\boldsymbol{\Theta}^{-1}\boldsymbol{L}^2)'] \\ &= \frac{T\theta_1}{\sigma^2(1+\theta_1-\theta_2)(1+\theta_2)(1-\theta_1-\theta_2)} + O(1),\end{aligned}$$

$$\begin{aligned}\{\mathcal{D}\}_{3,11} &= -6\mathrm{tr}[(\boldsymbol{\Theta}^{-1}\boldsymbol{L}^2)^2(\boldsymbol{\Theta}^{-1}\boldsymbol{L}^2)'] \\ &= -\frac{6T[\theta_1^2+\theta_2(1-\theta_2)^2]}{(1+\theta_1-\theta_2)^2(1+\theta_2)^2(1-\theta_1-\theta_2)^2} + O(1),\end{aligned}$$

$$
\begin{aligned}
\{\mathcal{D}\}_{3,12} = \{\mathcal{D}\}_{3,15} = \{\mathcal{D}\}_{4,11} &= \frac{1}{\sigma^2}\mathrm{tr}[(\boldsymbol{\Theta}^{-1}\boldsymbol{L}^2)(\boldsymbol{\Theta}^{-1}\boldsymbol{L}^2)'] \\
&= \frac{T(1-\theta_2)}{\sigma^2(1+\theta_1-\theta_2)(1+\theta_2)(1-\theta_1-\theta_2)} + O(1), \\
\{\mathcal{D}\}_{4,16} &= \frac{2T}{\sigma^6}.
\end{aligned}
$$

The 4×16 matrix $\mathcal{E}$ has the following nonzero elements:

$$
\begin{aligned}
\{\mathcal{E}\}_{15} = \{\mathcal{E}\}_{21} &= \frac{2}{\sigma^2}\mathbf{1}'\boldsymbol{\Theta}^{-1\prime}\boldsymbol{\Theta}^{-1}\boldsymbol{L}\boldsymbol{\Theta}^{-1}\mathbf{1} = \frac{2T}{\sigma^2(1-\theta_1-\theta_2)^3} + O(1), \\
\{\mathcal{E}\}_{18} = \{\mathcal{E}\}_{24} &= \frac{\gamma_1}{2\sigma^3}(\mathbf{1}'\boldsymbol{\Theta}^{-1\prime}\boldsymbol{\Theta}^{-1}\boldsymbol{L}\mathbf{1} + \mathbf{1}'\boldsymbol{\Theta}^{-1}\boldsymbol{L}\boldsymbol{\Theta}^{-1}\mathbf{1}), \\
&= \frac{\gamma_1 T}{\sigma^3(1-\theta_1-\theta_2)^2} + O(1), \\
\{\mathcal{E}\}_{19} = \{\mathcal{E}\}_{31} &= \frac{2}{\sigma^2}\mathbf{1}'\boldsymbol{\Theta}^{-1\prime}\boldsymbol{\Theta}^{-1}\boldsymbol{L}^2\boldsymbol{\Theta}^{-1}\mathbf{1} = \frac{2T}{\sigma^2(1-\theta_1-\theta_2)^3} + O(1), \\
\{\mathcal{E}\}_{1,12} = \{\mathcal{E}\}_{34} &= \frac{\gamma_1}{2\sigma^3}(\mathbf{1}'\boldsymbol{\Theta}^{-1\prime}\boldsymbol{\Theta}^{-1}\boldsymbol{L}^2\mathbf{1} + \mathbf{1}'\boldsymbol{\Theta}^{-1}\boldsymbol{L}^2\boldsymbol{\Theta}^{-1}\mathbf{1}) \\
&= \frac{\gamma_1 T}{\sigma^3(1-\theta_1-\theta_2)^2} + O(1), \\
\{\mathcal{E}\}_{1,13} = \{\mathcal{E}\}_{41} &= -\frac{1}{\sigma^4}\mathbf{1}'\boldsymbol{\Theta}^{-1\prime}\boldsymbol{\Theta}^{-1}\mathbf{1} = -\frac{T}{\sigma^4(1-\theta_1-\theta_2)^2} + O(1), \\
\{\mathcal{E}\}_{1,16} = \{\mathcal{E}\}_{44} &= -\frac{\gamma_1}{2\sigma^5}\mathbf{1}'\boldsymbol{\Theta}^{-1}\mathbf{1} = -\frac{\gamma_1 T}{2\sigma^5(1-\theta_1-\theta_2)} + O(1), \\
\{\mathcal{E}\}_{25} &= -\frac{\gamma_1}{\sigma}\mathrm{tr}[(\boldsymbol{\Theta}^{-1}\boldsymbol{L})\mathrm{Diag}(\boldsymbol{\Theta}^{-1}\mathbf{1})(\boldsymbol{\Theta}^{-1}\boldsymbol{L})'] \\
&= -\frac{\gamma_1 T(1-\theta_2)}{\sigma(1+\theta_2)(1+\theta_1-\theta_2)(1-\theta_1-\theta_2)^2} + O(1), \\
\{\mathcal{E}\}_{26} &= 4\mathrm{tr}[(\boldsymbol{\Theta}^{-1}\boldsymbol{L})^2(\boldsymbol{\Theta}^{-1}\boldsymbol{L})'] = \frac{4T\theta_1(1-\theta_2)}{(1+\theta_1-\theta_2)^2(1+\theta_2)(1-\theta_1-\theta_2)^2} + O(1), \\
\{\mathcal{E}\}_{27} &= 2\mathrm{tr}[(\boldsymbol{\Theta}^{-1}\boldsymbol{L})(\boldsymbol{\Theta}^{-1}\boldsymbol{L}^2)(\boldsymbol{\Theta}^{-1}\boldsymbol{L})'] + 2\mathrm{tr}[(\boldsymbol{\Theta}^{-1}\boldsymbol{L})^2(\boldsymbol{\Theta}^{-1}\boldsymbol{L}^2)'] \\
&= \frac{2T[\theta_1^2+\theta_2(1-\theta_2)^2]}{(1+\theta_1-\theta_2)^2(1+\theta_2)^2(1-\theta_1-\theta_2)^2} \\
&\quad + \frac{2T[1-\theta_2(2-\theta_1^2-\theta_2)]}{(1+\theta_1-\theta_2)^2(1+\theta_2)^2(1-\theta_1-\theta_2)^2} + O(1),
\end{aligned}
$$

$$
\begin{aligned}
\{\mathcal{E}\}_{28} &= -\frac{\gamma_2+2}{2\sigma^2}\operatorname{tr}[(\mathbf{\Theta}^{-1}\boldsymbol{L})(\mathbf{\Theta}^{-1}\boldsymbol{L})'] \\
&= -\frac{(\gamma_2+2)T(1-\theta_2)}{2\sigma^2(1+\theta_1-\theta_2)(1+\theta_2)(1-\theta_1-\theta_2)} + O(1), \\
\{\mathcal{E}\}_{29} &= \{\mathcal{E}\}_{35} = -\frac{\gamma_1}{\sigma}\operatorname{tr}[(\mathbf{\Theta}^{-1}\boldsymbol{L}^2)\operatorname{Diag}(\mathbf{\Theta}^{-1}\mathbf{1})(\mathbf{\Theta}^{-1}\boldsymbol{L})'] \\
&= -\frac{\gamma_1 T\theta_1}{\sigma(1+\theta_2)(1+\theta_1-\theta_2)(1-\theta_1-\theta_2)^2} + O(1), \\
\{\mathcal{E}\}_{2,10} &= \{\mathcal{E}\}_{36} = \operatorname{tr}[(\mathbf{\Theta}^{-1}\boldsymbol{L})^2(\mathbf{\Theta}^{-1}\boldsymbol{L}^2)'] + 3\operatorname{tr}[(\mathbf{\Theta}^{-1}\boldsymbol{L})(\mathbf{\Theta}^{-1}\boldsymbol{L}^2)\left(\mathbf{\Theta}^{-1}\boldsymbol{L}\right)'] \\
&= \frac{T[1-\theta_2(2-\theta_1^2-\theta_2)]}{(1+\theta_1-\theta_2)^2(1+\theta_2)^2(1-\theta_1-\theta_2)^2} \\
&\quad + \frac{3T[\theta_1^2+\theta_2(1-\theta_2)^2]}{(1+\theta_1-\theta_2)^2(1+\theta_2)^2(1-\theta_1-\theta_2)^2} + O(1), \\
\{\mathcal{E}\}_{2,11} &= \{\mathcal{E}\}_{37} = 3\operatorname{tr}[(\mathbf{\Theta}^{-1}\boldsymbol{L})(\mathbf{\Theta}^{-1}\boldsymbol{L}^2)(\mathbf{\Theta}^{-1}\boldsymbol{L}^2)'] + \operatorname{tr}[(\mathbf{\Theta}^{-1}\boldsymbol{L}^2)^2(\mathbf{\Theta}^{-1}\boldsymbol{L})'] \\
&= \frac{3T\theta_1(1-\theta_2)}{(1+\theta_1-\theta_2)^2(1+\theta_2)(1-\theta_1-\theta_2)^2} \\
&\quad + \frac{T\theta_1[\theta_1^2+2\theta_2(1-\theta_2)]}{(1+\theta_1-\theta_2)^2(1+\theta_2)^2(1-\theta_1-\theta_2)^2} + O(1), \\
\{\mathcal{E}\}_{2,12} &= \{\mathcal{E}\}_{38} = -\frac{\gamma_2+2}{2\sigma^2}\operatorname{tr}[(\mathbf{\Theta}^{-1}\boldsymbol{L})(\mathbf{\Theta}^{-1}\boldsymbol{L}^2)'] \\
&= -\frac{(\gamma_2+2)T\theta_1}{2\sigma^2(1+\theta_1-\theta_2)(1+\theta_2)(1-\theta_1-\theta_2)} + O(1), \\
\{\mathcal{E}\}_{2,14} &= \{\mathcal{E}\}_{46} = -\frac{1}{\sigma^2}\operatorname{tr}[(\mathbf{\Theta}^{-1}\boldsymbol{L})(\mathbf{\Theta}^{-1}\boldsymbol{L})'] \\
&= -\frac{T(1-\theta_2)}{\sigma^2(1+\theta_1-\theta_2)(1+\theta_2)(1-\theta_1-\theta_2)} + O(1), \\
\{\mathcal{E}\}_{2,15} &= \{\mathcal{E}\}_{3,14} = \{\mathcal{E}\}_{47} = \{\mathcal{E}\}_{4,10} = -\frac{1}{\sigma^2}\operatorname{tr}[(\mathbf{\Theta}^{-1}\boldsymbol{L})(\mathbf{\Theta}^{-1}\boldsymbol{L}^2)'] \\
&= -\frac{T\theta_1}{\sigma^2(1+\theta_1-\theta_2)(1+\theta_2)(1-\theta_1-\theta_2)} + O(1), \\
\{\mathcal{E}\}_{39} &= -\frac{\gamma_1}{\sigma}\operatorname{tr}[(\mathbf{\Theta}^{-1}\boldsymbol{L}^2)\operatorname{Diag}(\mathbf{\Theta}^{-1}\mathbf{1})(\mathbf{\Theta}^{-1}\boldsymbol{L}^2)'] \\
&= -\frac{\gamma_1 T(1-\theta_2)}{\sigma(1+\theta_2)(1+\theta_1-\theta_2)(1-\theta_1-\theta_2)^2} + O(1),
\end{aligned}
$$

$$\{\mathcal{E}\}_{3,10} = 2\mathrm{tr}[(\boldsymbol{\Theta}^{-1}\boldsymbol{L})(\boldsymbol{\Theta}^{-1}\boldsymbol{L}^2)(\boldsymbol{\Theta}^{-1}\boldsymbol{L}^2)'] + 2\mathrm{tr}[(\boldsymbol{\Theta}^{-1}\boldsymbol{L}^2)^2(\boldsymbol{\Theta}^{-1}\boldsymbol{L})']$$
$$= \frac{2T\theta_1(1-\theta_2)}{(1+\theta_1-\theta_2)^2(1+\theta_2)(1-\theta_1-\theta_2)^2} + \frac{2T\theta_1[\theta_1^2+2\theta_2(1-\theta_2)]}{(1+\theta_1-\theta_2)^2(1+\theta_2)^2(1-\theta_1-\theta_2)^2} + O(1),$$

$$\{\mathcal{E}\}_{3,11} = 4\mathrm{tr}[(\boldsymbol{\Theta}^{-1}\boldsymbol{L}^2)^2(\boldsymbol{\Theta}^{-1}\boldsymbol{L}^2)'] = \frac{4T[\theta_1^2+\theta_2(1-\theta_2)^2]}{(1+\theta_1-\theta_2)^2(1+\theta_2)^2(1-\theta_1-\theta_2)^2} + O(1),$$

$$\{\mathcal{E}\}_{3,12} = -\frac{\gamma_2+2}{2\sigma^2}\mathrm{tr}[(\boldsymbol{\Theta}^{-1}\boldsymbol{L}^2)(\boldsymbol{\Theta}^{-1}\boldsymbol{L}^2)'] = -\frac{(\gamma_2+2)T(1-\theta_2)}{2\sigma^2(1+\theta_1-\theta_2)(1+\theta_2)(1-\theta_1-\theta_2)} + O(1),$$

$$\{\mathcal{E}\}_{3,15} = \{\mathcal{E}\}_{4,11} = -\frac{1}{\sigma^2}\mathrm{tr}[(\boldsymbol{\Theta}^{-1}\boldsymbol{L}^2)(\boldsymbol{\Theta}^{-1}\boldsymbol{L}^2)']$$
$$= -\frac{T(1-\theta_2)}{\sigma^2(1+\theta_1-\theta_2)(1+\theta_2)(1-\theta_1-\theta_2)} + O(1),$$

$$\{\mathcal{E}\}_{4,13} = -\frac{\gamma_1}{\sigma^5}\mathbf{1}'\boldsymbol{\Theta}^{-1}\mathbf{1} = -\frac{\gamma_1 T}{\sigma^5(1-\theta_1-\theta_2)} + O(1),$$

$$\{\mathcal{E}\}_{4,16} = -\frac{T(\gamma_2+2)}{2\sigma^6}.$$

By substitution, one has the bias result

$$B(\hat{\boldsymbol{\beta}}) = \frac{1}{T}\begin{pmatrix} 0 \\ (1+\theta_1+\theta_2) \\ (1+3\theta_2) \\ -3\sigma^2 \end{pmatrix} + o(T^{-1}).$$

If μ is known, by deleting all the elements related to μ in $\mathcal{F}$, $\mathcal{P}$, $\mathcal{D}$, and $\mathcal{E}$, one gets

$$B(\hat{\boldsymbol{\beta}}) = \frac{1}{T}\begin{pmatrix} \theta_1 \\ 2\theta_2 \\ -2\sigma^2 \end{pmatrix} + o(T^{-1}).$$

FINITE SAMPLE BIAS CORRECTED IV ESTIMATION FOR WEAK AND MANY INSTRUMENTS

Matthew Harding[a], Jerry Hausman[b], and Christopher J. Palmer[c]

[a]*Sanford School of Public Policy and Department of Economics, Duke University, Durham, NC, USA*
[b]*Department of Economics, Massachusetts Institute of Technology, Cambridge, MA, USA*
[c]*Haas School of Business, University of California at Berkeley, Berkeley, CA, USA*

ABSTRACT

This paper considers the finite-sample distribution of the 2SLS estimator and derives bounds on its exact bias in the presence of weak and/or many instruments. We then contrast the behavior of the exact bias expressions and the asymptotic expansions currently popular in the literature, including a consideration of the no-moment problem exhibited by many Nagar-type estimators. After deriving a finite-sample unbiased k-class estimator, we introduce a double-k-class estimator based on Nagar (1962) that dominates k-class estimators (including 2SLS), especially in the cases of weak and/or

Essays in Honor of Aman Ullah
Advances in Econometrics, Volume 36, 245–273

ISSN: 0731-9053/doi:10.1108/S0731-905320160000036016

many instruments. We demonstrate these properties in Monte Carlo simulations showing that our preferred estimators outperform Fuller (1977) estimators in terms of mean bias and MSE.

Keywords: Instrumental variables; weak and many instruments; finite sample; k-class estimators

JEL classifications: C31; C13; C15

1. INTRODUCTION

The failure of standard first-order asymptotic theory to provide a reliable guide to estimation in the widely used simultaneous equations model in the presence of weak and/or many instruments has led to renewed interest in the finite sample properties of estimators for these models. Weak instruments refers to the situation where in finite samples the endogenous regressor is only weakly correlated to the instrument set, while the many-instruments case refers to situations where the dimensionality of the instrument set is large relative to the sample size.

Faced with the failure of the traditional asymptotic framework in these models, econometricians have turned their attention to alternative asymptotic frameworks such as higher order expansions (Hahn, Hausman, & Kuersteiner, 2004), local-to-zero asymptotics (Poskitt & Skeels, 2009; Staiger & Stock, 1997), and many/weak instrument (Bekker) asymptotics (Bekker, 1994; Hansen, Hausman, & Newey, 2008). While all these methods have provided valuable insights, we are nevertheless faced with uncertainty as to how successful these approximations can be in the difficult cases of weak and/or many instruments. As with all approximations, we face the choice of how many expansion terms to include before we can be confident in the accuracy of the estimation.

Exact finite sample results on the distribution of instrumental variable estimators (IV) have been known for many years but have largely remained outside the grasp of practitioners due to the lack of computational tools for the evaluation of the complicated functions on which they depend in practical time (Anderson & Sawa, 1979; Nagar, 1959; Richardson, 1968; Richardson & Wu, 1971; Phillips, 1980, 1983; Sawa, 1972). Recent computational advances have removed this constraint, and we are now able to employ the exact finite sample methodology to better understand the statistical behavior of these models in the case of weak and/or many instruments. Still, Hirano and Porter (2015) show that a finite sample unbiased estimate is unattainable without imposing further assumptions on the structure of the problem. As an example of this, Andrews and Armstrong (2015) develop an unbiased estimator when the sign of the first stage is known; although it appears their estimator does not do as well as Fuller (1977), there is no absolute ranking.

In this paper, we approach the problem of estimating simultaneous equations models from the perspective of the exact finite sample properties of these estimators. We consider broad classes of estimators such as the k-class estimators and evaluate their promises and limitations as methods to correctly provide finite sample inference on the structural parameters in simultaneous equations. To contextualize the performance of our estimator, Hahn et al. (2004) demonstrate that with weak instruments, Fuller outperforms LIML. While LIML does not have finite sample moments, which in practice means that it provides very dispersed estimates, Fuller has all moments and removes substantial finite sample bias. In this paper, we consider the "classic" situation of one endogenous variable and homoskedastic normal disturbances and find that our preferred double-k-class estimators typically outperform Fuller estimates in mean bias and MSE and rarely do worse.

In Section 2, we start by considering the exact finite sample bias of the 2SLS estimator and analyze its dependence on the goodness of fit as measured by the concentration parameter in the first-stage regression and the number of instruments employed. We show that the finite sample bias is strictly increasing in the number of instruments K and is always positive for $K > 1$. The bias decreases exponentially with the concentration parameter and is negligible for values of the concentration parameter greater than 60. Furthermore, we show that the maximum finite sample bias for weak and/or many instruments cannot exceed the ratio of the covariance between the first stage and the structural equation and the variance of the first stage.

We also derive the exact finite sample unbiased estimator as a member of the k-class of IV estimators. Additionally, we show that by employing the k-class we face a fundamental trade-off. Estimators that aim to limit the finite sample bias are also estimators which lack finite sample moments and are thus infeasible in practice. We show using a Monte Carlo design that for severe cases of many and weak instruments, there is no member of the k-class that also has moments which can adequately minimize the effect of finite sample bias.

In order to address this problem, we consider a modification of the k-class, originally due to Nagar (1962), which allows for distinct parameters (k_1, k_2) to enter the estimating equations. We use a Monte Carlo design to show that this class of estimator is rich enough to allow for estimators with finite sample moments which are also unbiased and have very attractive MSE properties. We derive the optimal choice of parameters for a set of double-k-class estimators based on 2SLS.

In Section 3, we resurrect the "double-k-class" of estimators and extend Nagar (1962) to consider how finite sample bias and MSE are affected by choice of the double-k-class parameters (k_1, k_2) in the presence of weak and/or many instruments. Section 4 derives double-k-class estimators with certain optimality properties (e.g. in terms of their finite sample bias and MSE) in such circumstances. Section 5 presents Monte Carlo results contrasting the performance of our preferred double-k-class estimators with 2SLS and Fuller. We find that our preferred bias-minimizing double-k-class estimator outperforms 2SLS and Fuller's minimum-bias estimator ("Fuller1") even in the presence of weak and/or many instruments and that our preferred MSE-minimizing double-k-class estimator generally outperforms Fuller's minimum-MSE estimator ("Fuller4") in MSE, especially in many-instrument settings. Section 6 concludes.

2. FINITE SAMPLE BEHAVIOR OF *k*-CLASS ESTIMATORS

We consider the following specification for a system of equations with two endogenous variables y_1 and y_2:

$$\begin{aligned} y_1 &= \beta y_2 + \epsilon = \beta z\pi + w \\ y_2 &= z\pi + v, \end{aligned} \tag{1}$$

where $w = \beta v + \epsilon$. We let y_1 and y_2 be $N \times 1$ vectors of observations on the endogenous variables and denote by z the $N \times K$ matrix of observations on the predetermined (or exogenous) variables. The first equation is the (structural) equation of interest which measures the association between the two endogenous variables while the second equation is more commonly referred to as "the first-stage regression." The number of instruments is $\dim(\pi) = K$.

This system of equations admits the reduced form:

$$(y_1 \quad y_2) = z(\beta\pi \quad \pi) + (w \quad v), \tag{2}$$

where the rows of $(w\ v)$ are independently and identically distributed as $N(0, \Omega)$ for

$$\Omega = \begin{pmatrix} \sigma_{ww} & \sigma_{wv} \\ \sigma_{wv} & \sigma_{vv} \end{pmatrix}. \tag{3}$$

Furthermore, we denote the variance of the error term in the structural equation by $\sigma_{\epsilon\epsilon}$ and the covariance between the structural equation for y_1 and the reduced-form equation for y_2 by $\sigma_{\epsilon v}$.

An important statistic for the finite sample behavior of IV estimators is the concentration parameter μ^2, where

$$\mu^2 = \frac{\pi' z' z \pi}{\sigma_{vv}}. \tag{4}$$

The concentration parameter is a measure of noncentrality and will play a quintessential role in the bias expressions for IV estimators we shall encounter throughout this paper. It is occasionally informative to impose the normalization $\sigma_{\epsilon\epsilon} = \sigma_{vv} = 1$. Using this normalization, a simple approximation of μ^2 is given by:

$$\mu^2 \approx \frac{E(\hat{\pi}' z' z \hat{\pi})}{E(\hat{v}'\hat{v})/(N-K)} = \frac{(N-K)R^2}{1-R^2}, \tag{5}$$

where R^2 is the (theoretical) first-stage coefficient of determination. Note that there is a close connection between the expression above and the first stage F-statistic implying that $\mu^2 \approx KF$ (Buse, 1992; Hansen et al., 2008).

Before proceeding, we need to define the *confluent hypergeometric function* ${}_1F_1$ given by the expansion:

$${}_1F_1(a;b;c) = \sum_{j=1}^{\infty} \frac{(a)_j}{(b)_j} \frac{c^j}{j!}. \tag{6}$$

This function is one of the independent solutions to the differential equation $cd^2q/dc^2 + (b-c)dq/dc - ac = 0$ and is commonly used to characterize the non-central χ^2 distribution. As we shall see, it emerges in the expression for the bias of the 2SLS estimator below. Note that the confluent hypergeometric function is defined in terms of Pochammer's symbol $(a)_j$ corresponding to the ascending factorial (Abadir, 1999):

$$(a)_j = \prod_{k=0}^{j-1} (a+k) = a(a+1)(a+2)\cdots(a+j-1) \quad \text{for } (a)_0 = 1. \tag{7}$$

The series expansion of the confluent hypergeometric function ${}_1F_1(a;b;c)$ converges for all finite c and $a > 0$ and $b > 0$ (Muller, 2001). While analytically attractive, its computation presents a number of numerical challenges for some regions of the parameter space (a, b, c). In particular, the efficient computation of hypergeometric functions has to be addressed with care (Koev and Edelman, 2006).

If we define the commonly used projection operators $P_z = z'(z'z)^{-1}z'$ and $Q_z = I - P_z$, we can derive the 2SLS estimator of β as:

$$\hat{\beta}_{2SLS} = \frac{y_2' P_z y_1}{y_2' P_z y_2}. \tag{8}$$

Recently, econometricians have devoted considerable attention to the behavior of this estimator in the presence of weak and/or many instruments (see Poskitt & Skeels, 2013 for a survey, as well as Hahn & Hausman, 2002a; Hahn et al., 2004; Hansen et al., 2008; Hirano & Porter, 2015; Nelson & Startz, 1990; Staiger & Stock, 1997).

To better understand the issues involved let us consider, the exact finite sample bias of the 2SLS estimator, as derived by Richardson (1968) and Richardson and Wu (1971):

$$E(\hat{\beta}_{2SLS}) = \beta - \left(\beta - \frac{\sigma_{wv}}{\sigma_{vv}}\right) exp\left(-\frac{\mu^2}{2}\right) {}_1F_1\left(\frac{K}{2} - 1; \frac{K}{2}; \frac{\mu^2}{2}\right). \tag{9}$$

Equivalent expressions are also found in Chao and Swanson (2003) and Ullah (2004). Note in particular that since $\sigma_{wv} = \beta\sigma_{vv} + \sigma_{\epsilon v}$, we have

$$E(\hat{\beta}_{2SLS} - \beta) = \frac{\sigma_{\epsilon v}}{\sigma_{vv}} exp\left(-\frac{\mu^2}{2}\right) {}_1F_1\left(\frac{K}{2} - 1; \frac{K}{2}; \frac{\mu^2}{2}\right). \tag{10}$$

The exact finite sample bias of 2SLS is linear in the correlation between the structural equation and the first stage, $\sigma_{\epsilon v}$ and nonlinear in the concentration parameter μ^2 and the number of instruments K. Let us now direct our attention to the nonlinear part of the bias expression which we shall denote by $B(\mu^2, K) = exp(\mu^2/2)_1F_1(K/2 - 1; K/2; \mu^2/2)$.

In Fig. 1, we plot the term $B(\mu^2, K)$ for a range of parameters $\mu^2 \in [0, 70]$ and $K \in \{1, 2, 3, 5, 15, 100\}$ in order to illustrate the effect of weak instruments (low μ^2) and many instruments (high K) on the bias of the 2SLS estimator.[1] Many of the simulations herein hold μ^2 fixed while varying K. Notice that the expression for B does not depend on additional sampling information beyond μ^2 and K. For all values of K the bias term B goes to 0 for values of $\mu^2 > 60$. For low values of μ^2 the weak-instruments bias is compounded in the presence of many instruments. The bias resulting from the use of many instruments is eliminated by high values of the concentration parameter. As Eq. (4) shows, for a given sample size we obtain a high value of the concentration parameter if the value of the first stage R^2 is large. Many instruments can thus be safely used if the first stage is strongly identified by those instruments.

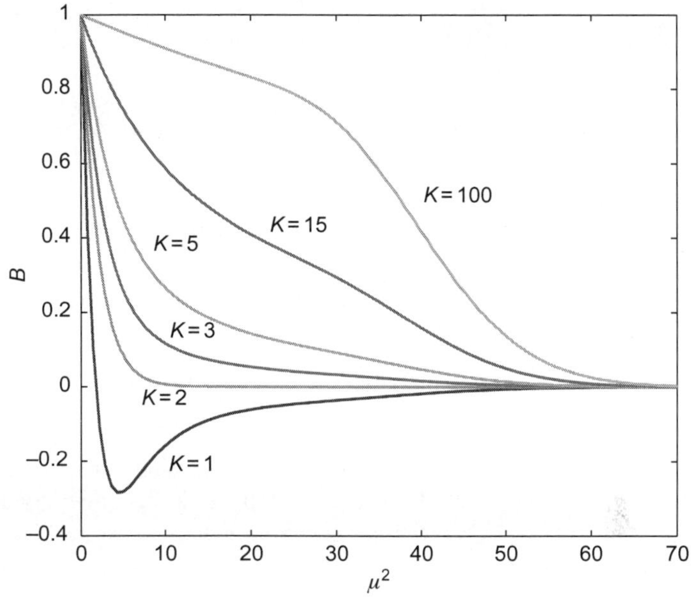

Fig. 1. Finite Sample Bias Term B as a Function of the Concentration Parameter μ^2 for Different Numbers of Instruments K.

Furthermore, notice that for any given value of the concentration parameter, the bias is increasing with the number of instruments (consistent with Owen, 1976), but nevertheless, it remains the case that the bias term B is bounded and less than 1. For $K > 1$ the bias term B is always positive and decreases monotonically with μ^2.[2] The just-identified case allows for both positive and negative bias. In fact, it appears that for most cases with a low first stage R^2, it is safer to choose two weak instruments than a single one. The bias does however increase rapidly as one adds further weak instruments. Recall however that the exact final sample bias for 2SLS is scaled by $\frac{\sigma_{\epsilon v}}{\sigma_{vv}}$ and thus the extent of the correlation between the first stage and the structural equation, $\sigma_{\epsilon v}$ plays a central role.

It is possible to derive the exact bias expression for the 2SLS estimator for the over-identified case with $K = 2$. In this case, we have

$$E(\hat{\beta}_{2SLS} - \beta) = \frac{\sigma_{\epsilon v}}{\sigma_{vv}} exp\left(-\frac{\mu^2}{2}\right), \tag{11}$$

which shows that the bias decreases exponentially with the concentration parameter, thus emphasizing the importance of the first-stage fit. While no equally simple expression can be derived for the just-identified case with $K = 1$, we can nevertheless obtain an approximation for small values of μ^2:

$$E(\hat{\beta}_{2SLS} - \beta) = \frac{\sigma_{\epsilon v}}{\sigma_{vv}} exp\left(-\frac{\mu^2}{2}\right)\left(\mu^2 - \frac{\mu^4}{6}\right) + O\left(\left(\sqrt{\frac{\mu^2}{2}}\right)^5\right) \tag{12}$$

The additional polynomial terms in the bias expression allow for both positive and negative bias at different levels of the concentration parameter.

We can ask how big the bias due to weak and/or many instruments can be by looking at the limits of the term $B(\mu^2, K)$. The bias is strictly increasing in the number of instruments K. Furthermore, we can derive the following limits:

$$\lim_{\mu^2 \to 0} B(\mu^2, K) = \lim_{K \to \infty} B(\mu^2, K) = 1. \tag{13}$$

This implies that the maximum finite sample bias for weak and/or many instruments cannot exceed $\sigma_{\epsilon v}/\sigma_{vv}$. Hahn and Hausman (2002b) show that under no identification $\pi = 0$, the bias of the OLS estimator is approximately equal to $\sigma_{\epsilon v}/\sigma_{vv}$. Thus, the weak-instruments bias of the 2SLS estimator cannot exceed the corresponding OLS bias.

Nagar (1959) derived a large N expansion of the bias in a fairly complicated fashion, while a simpler derivation was given in Hahn and Hausman (2002b). In fact, the same second-order approximation to the bias can be directly obtained from the properties of the bias term $B(\mu^2, K)$ above. Let us consider a large μ^2 approximation of B. Using expression 13.1.4 in Slater (1964) we have:

$$B(\mu^2, K) = 2\frac{\Gamma(K/2)}{\Gamma(K/2 - 1)}\left(\frac{1}{\mu^2}\right) + O\left(\left(\frac{\mu^2}{2}\right)^{-2}\right). \tag{14}$$

But since $\Gamma(K/2) = (K/2 - 1)\Gamma(K/2 - 1)$, we have

$$B(\mu^2, K) = \frac{K - 2}{\mu^2} + O\left(\left(\frac{\mu^2}{2}\right)^{-2}\right). \tag{15}$$

Returning to the 2SLS bias expression we obtain:

$$E(\hat{\beta}_{2SLS} - \beta) \approx \frac{\sigma_{\epsilon v}}{\sigma_{vv}}\frac{K - 2}{\mu^2} = \frac{\sigma_{\epsilon v}}{\sigma_{vv}}\frac{(K - 2)(1 - R^2)}{(N - K)R^2}, \tag{16}$$

where R^2 corresponds to the R^2 of the first stage regression. This expression is basically the same as the approximate bias expression given in Hahn and Hausman (2002a, 2002b) and which can be employed to derive a bias-corrected estimator:

$$\beta_{BC} = \frac{\hat{\beta}_{2SLS} - \frac{\sigma_{wv}}{\sigma_{vv}} B(\mu^2, K)}{1 - B(\mu^2, K)}. \tag{17}$$

In order to operationalize this estimator, one would additionally require an estimate of the concentration parameter μ^2. Since in finite samples this estimator itself will be biased, Hansen et al. (2008) suggest the unbiased estimator $\mu_*^2 = \hat{\mu}^2 - K$.

Alternatively, we can proceed from Eq. (10) and employ the approach of Hahn and Hausman (2002b) by first noting that:

$$\sigma_{\epsilon v} = E\left[\frac{1}{N-K}(y_2' Q_z)(y_1 - y_2\beta)\right]. \tag{18}$$

Then we have,

$$E(\beta_{2SLS}) = \beta + E\left[\frac{N-K}{y_2' Q_z y_2}\left(\frac{1}{N-K} y_2' Q_z y_1 - \frac{1}{N-K} y_2' Q_z y_2 \beta\right) B(\mu^2, K)\right] \tag{19}$$

$$E(\beta_{2SLS}) = E\left[\beta + \frac{y_2' Q_z y_1}{y_2' Q_z y_2} B(\mu^2, K) - \beta B(\mu^2, K)\right]. \tag{20}$$

Hence, we can solve for β as:

$$\beta_{BC} = \frac{y_2' P_z y_1 - \kappa y_2' Q_z y_1}{y_2' P_z y_2 - \kappa y_2' Q_z y_2}, \tag{21}$$

where

$$\kappa = B(\mu^2, K)\frac{y_2' P_z y_2}{y_2' Q_z y_2} = B(\mu^2, K)\frac{\mu^2}{N-K} = B(\mu^2, K)\frac{R^2}{1-R^2}. \tag{22}$$

This estimator has zero finite sample bias by construction. Its actual sample performance however will depend on the extent to which we can accurately determine the concentration parameter in a given sample. The performance of this particular estimator was found to be unreliable in simulations – it greatly outperformed all other estimators apart from infrequent, extreme outliers. Still, it is worth noticing that the finite sample bias-corrected estimator derived above is a member of the Nagar (1959) k-class family of estimators, which generalizes the 2SLS estimator.[3]

Recent work has devoted significant attention to the behavior of k-class estimators. This remarkable class of estimators includes many of the commonly used estimators for simultaneous equations. Thus, using the notation introduced above we obtain the k-class estimator β_{kIV} as:

$$\beta_{kIV} = \frac{y_2' P_z y_1 - k y_2' Q_z y_1}{y_2' P_z y_2 - k y_2' Q_z y_2}, \tag{23}$$

for different values of the parameter k. By setting $k = -1$ we obtain the OLS estimator and $k = 0$ leads to the 2SLS estimator. But other leading estimators can be obtained as a member of the k-class. Thus, LIML corresponds to the estimator with $k = \phi$ where ϕ is set to the smallest eigenvalue of $W'P_z W(W'Q_z W)^{-1}$ for $W = (y_1, y_2)$. The estimator of Fuller (1977) corresponds to $k = \phi - 1/(N - K)$ while the Nagar (1959) estimator corresponds to $k = (K - 2)/(N - K)$.[4]

Sawa (1972) shows that for $k \leq 0$ the k-class estimators have moments, while for $k > 0$ they may not even have the first moment. Unfortunately, the estimators we are interested in such as LIML, Nagar or the exact finite sample unbiased estimator derived above all have values of k greater than 0.[5] While these estimators have the potential to remove the 2SLS finite sample bias by adjusting k away from 0, their practical usefulness is stymied by their lack of moments. As Fuller (1977) realized, however, there is a small region of values of $k > 0$ for which the estimators do in fact have moments. An estimator using a value of $k > 0$ but less than the values of k prescribed by LIML or Nagar will remove some of the finite sample bias while retaining moments. This explains the popularity of Fuller as a solution to the weak and/or many instruments problem.

We do, however, face the question as to how useful k-class estimators ultimately are given that we face a trade-off between bias reduction and the lack of moments. In order to gain further insight into this problem we introduce a simple Monte Carlo simulation design for the model in Eq. (1). For a choice of values for the parameters N, K, ρ and R^2 we simulate the model 50,000 times and estimate the structural parameter β using all the k-class estimators for values of k between $k_l < 0 < k_u$. In practice, we choose 300 values of k on the line $[k_l, k_u]$. Thus, each value of k on this line defines a k-class estimator which is then applied to all the simulated samples. Furthermore, for each value of k we compute the mean bias, MSE, median bias, and interquartile range of the estimates for β.

In order to better understand the finite sample behavior of the k-class estimators, we plot the above summary statistics over a range of k-class estimators for three cases of interest to us: a benign case that does not exhibit weak instruments and employs only a small number of instruments, and two more pathological cases, one with weak instruments and the other with weak *and* many instruments. The Figs. 2–7 below were generated using a typical choice of parameter values, but it is easy to replicate the same qualitative properties for other parameter values falling within the same three cases of interest. Thus, in the simulations we use

$N = 250$ and $\rho = 0.9$. The value of ρ is higher than what we would expect in typical applications. As we have seen from our discussion of the bias earlier on, ρ scales the bias upward. This allows us to better visualize the results in the figures below without changing their interpretation. Lower values of ρ lead to very similar results.

Let us first consider the "normal" case which does not exhibit either weak or many instruments. To simulate this case, we use $K = 5$ and choose a value of $R^2 = 0.3$ for the theoretical first-stage fit. This leads to a value of the concentration parameter of $\mu^2 = 105$ which we deem to be large enough to avoid the weak-instruments problem. We plot our summary statistics for the k-class estimators for $k \in [-0.1, 0.1]$ in Fig. 2. We notice that the mean bias and median bias are monotonically decreasing over the chosen range of k. In particular, note that at the value of $k = 0$ that corresponds to the standard 2SLS estimator, the estimator still has some small amount of finite sample bias of just under 5%. Notice however that if we choose a value of $k = 0.012$ which corresponds to the value recommended by the Nagar estimator, the bias is eliminated altogether. Furthermore, the MSE is small at values of k close to 0, but it increases as k deviates from 0 in either direction. The interquartile range increases with k over this range. Notice that for this range of values of k all the estimators have moments. However, as we increase k away from 0 both the mean bias and the MSE will diverge. This example shows that

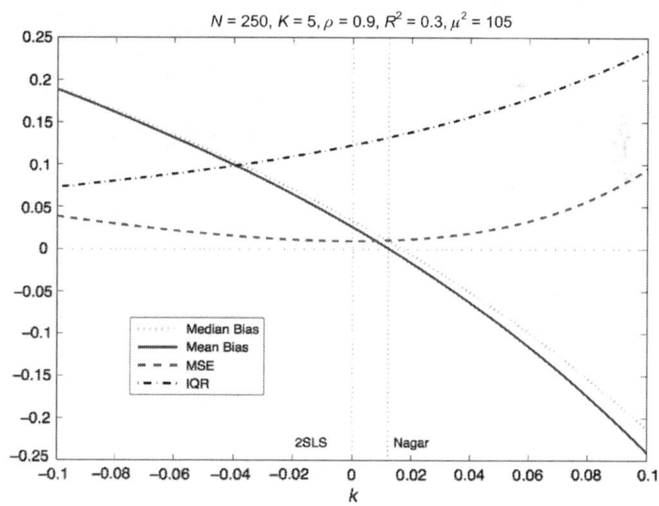

Fig. 2. Monte Carlo Simulation of k-Class Estimators for the "Normal" Case with a High Value of the Concentration Parameter and $K = 5$ Instruments.

the range of values of $k > 0$ for which the estimators have moments is nevertheless large enough to allow for the unbiased estimation of the structural parameter β by employing a member of k-class such as the Nagar estimator or the exact finite sample unbiased estimator derived above. As we decrease k toward -1 which corresponds to the OLS estimator, both the mean bias and MSE will continue to increase but remain bounded.

Let us now turn our attention to the weak (but not many) instruments case. To simulate this case, we use $K = 5$ and choose a value of $R^2 = 0.1$ for the theoretical first-stage fit. This leads to a value of the concentration parameter of $\mu^2 = 27.2$ which we deem to be small enough to lead to the weak-instruments problem. We plot our summary statistics for the k-class estimators for $k \in [-0.1, 0.1]$ in Fig. 3. The 2SLS estimator at $k = 0$ now has substantial finite sample bias of about 15%. Furthermore, perhaps the most striking aspect of this figure is that the estimators lose moments for values of $k > 0$. As k increases the first moment becomes unstable (hence, the oscillations visible in the numerical simulations) and eventually diverges. Similarly, the MSE explodes for the value of k used by the Nagar estimator. Notice however that if we were to choose a value of k less than that prescribed by the Nagar estimator it would still be possible to eliminate most of the finite sample bias of 2SLS. The Fuller estimator does in fact choose such a value of $k > 0$ allowing the estimator to have moments. This is the type of

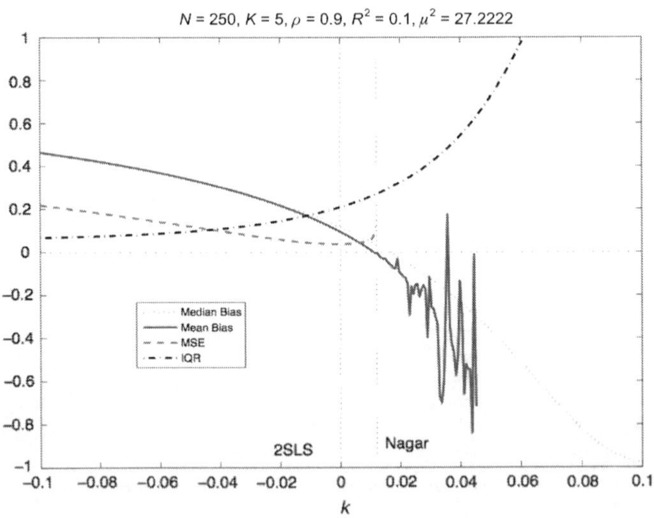

Fig. 3. Monte Carlo Simulation of k-Class Estimators for the Weak-Instruments Case with a Low Value of the Concentration Parameter and $K = 5$ Instruments.

situation for which the Fuller estimator performs very well. Notice however that the interquartile range increases sharply with values of k, which is confirmed in simulations by the fact that the Fuller estimator exhibits a fairly wide distribution relative to the 2SLS estimator.

Finally, let us focus our attention on the weak and many instruments case. To simulate this case we use $K=30$ and choose a value of $R^2=0.1$ for the theoretical first-stage fit. This leads to a value of the concentration parameter of $\mu^2=27.2$ which we deem to be small enough to lead to the weak-instruments problem. The resulting finite sample problem is amplified by the presence of a large number of instruments. We plot our summary statistics for the k-class estimators for $k \in [-0.1, 0.15]$ in Fig. 4. The 2SLS estimator at $k=0$ now has very substantial finite sample bias of at least 45%. As we increase k above 0 the bias decreases but very soon, at value of k of about 0.06 the estimators lose moments. Both the first and second moments diverge rapidly and the interquartile range explodes too. The value of k recommended by the Nagar estimator which would be required to eliminate the bias altogether is well within the "no moments" range of values of k and thus this estimator is no help. Furthermore, notice that an estimator such as Fuller which does have moments cannot remove the bias since the range of values of k for which such a k-class estimator retains moments still corresponds to a bias

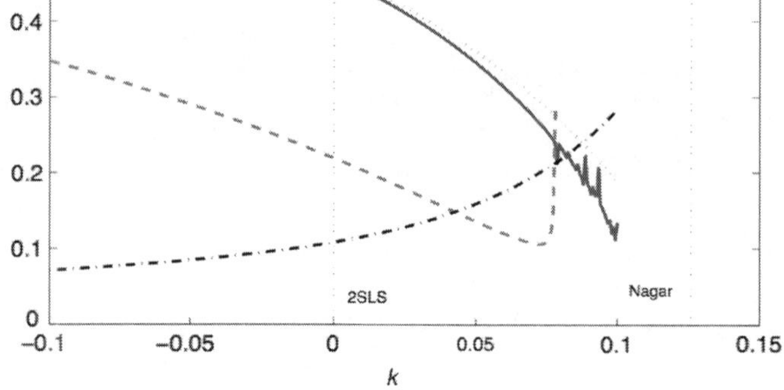

Fig. 4. Monte Carlo Simulation of k-Class Estimators for the Many-Instruments Case with a Low Value of the Concentration Parameter and $K=30$ Instruments.

of at least 30%. There is thus no range of values of k for which a k-class estimator has moments while also successfully removing the bias.

These results, while purely computational in nature, reveal a serious limitation of k-class estimators. Values of the parameters k which would be required to eliminate the finite sample bias due to many weak instruments lie outside the range of values for which this class of estimators has moments. Thus, unfortunately, no member of the k-class can achieve the dual goal of removing bias while maintaining moments.

This is a serious concern that prompts us to investigate alternatives to the k-class of estimators as a solution to the weak and many instruments problem. In the next section, we explore a modification of the k-class due to Nagar (1972) as a solution to the finite sample unbiased estimation of the structural parameters in a system of simultaneous equations.

3. FINITE SAMPLE BIAS CORRECTION IN THE DOUBLE k-CLASS

In the previous section, we have uncovered a fundamental problem with the k-class of estimators for simultaneous equations. The use of a single parameter k to adjust for the finite sample bias in the weak and/or many instruments case is too restrictive and leads to estimators with no moments. To illustrate, consider the 2SLS case with $k=0$, by construction the estimator has moments but also substantial finite sample bias. On the other hand, although the Nagar estimator is second-order unbiased (through an appropriate choice of $k=(K-2)/(N-K)$), for the case where $\pi=0$, it is easy to see that the denominator of the expression for the estimator will also equal 0 in expectation since

$$E\left[y_2'P_zy_2-\frac{K-2}{N-K}(y_2'Q_zy_2)\right]=(K-2)\sigma_{vv}-\frac{K-2}{N-K}(N-K)\sigma_{vv}=0. \quad (24)$$

Intuitively, the k-class is too restrictive since the same parameter k enters both sides of the estimating equations. Manipulating this one parameter we cannot achieve the two goals of reducing bias and estimators with finite sample moments.

In a now largely forgotten contribution, Nagar (1962) suggested a minor change to the estimating equations of IV estimators by allowing for two distinct values of k to enter the expression for the k-class IV estimators:

$$\beta_{2kIV}(k_1,k_2)=\frac{y_2'P_zy_1-k_2y_2'Q_zy_1}{y_2'P_zy_2-k_1y_2'Q_zy_2}. \quad (25)$$

We denote the resulting class of estimators the double-k-class indexed by $(k_1,\ k_2)$. Thus, the case of $k = k_1 = k_2$ becomes a special case on which we hope to improve upon by choosing different values of k_1 and k_2.

We can immediately rewrite Eq. (25) as,

$$\beta_{2kIV}(k_1, k_2) = \beta_{kIV}(k_1) + (k_1 - k_2)\frac{y_2' Q_z y_1}{y_2' P_z y_2 - k_1 y_2' Q_z y_2}, \tag{26}$$

where $\beta_{kIV}(k_1)$ is the k-class IV estimator with a value of $k = k_1$. For any given k-class estimator with $k = k_1$, we can construct a corresponding double-k-class estimator by moving k_2 away from k_1 by some fixed amount. Intuitively, we can see from Eq. (26) that for $k_1 \neq k_2$ the additional term on the right may potentially offset the finite sample bias of the k-class estimator on which it is based.

The double-k-class of IV estimators has received very limited attention over the years (Dwivedi & Srivastava, 1984; Gao & Lahiri, 2002; Nagar, 1962; Srivastava, Agnihotri, & Dwivedi, 1980) and to our knowledge has never been considered as an option for the estimation of systems of equations with weak and/or many instruments. The double-k-class is also a generalization of a now-forgotten class of estimators proposed by Theil (1958) and called the h-class, and which appears to correspond to the case of $k_1 = h^2$ and $k_2 = h$ for a real-valued parameter h.

We first wish to evaluate the finite sample performance of double-k-class estimators using 2SLS as the benchmark, leaving the discussion of the fully general case for future research. Thus, we will look at two particular subsets of the double-k-class,

$$\beta_{2kIV}(\Delta, 0) = \frac{y_2' P_z y_1}{y_2' P_z y_2 - \Delta y_2' Q_z y_2} = \beta_{kIV}(\Delta) + \Delta\frac{y_2' Q_z y_1}{y_2' P_z y_2 - \Delta y_2' Q_z y_2} \tag{27}$$

and

$$\beta_{2kIV}(0, \Delta) = \frac{y_2' P_z y_1 - \Delta y_2' Q_z y_1}{y_2' P_z y_2} = \beta_{2SLS} - \Delta\frac{y_2' Q_z y_1}{y_2' P_z y_2}. \tag{28}$$

We will employ Monte Carlo simulations to show that both of these modifications of 2SLS can be successful in solving the weak and/or many instruments problem for well-chosen values of Δ. Note that these simulations are constructed under the assumption that the underlying parameters are known. In practice some of these parameters themselves need to be estimated and thus the finite sample performance of these estimators will differ. Therefore, in this section, we document that a solution exists, while in the next section we discuss procedures for implementing these solutions in practice.

Let us first consider the baseline case which does not exhibit either weak or many instruments. To simulate this case we use $K = 5$ and choose a value of $R^2 = 0.3$ for the theoretical first stage fit. This leads to a value of the concentration parameter of $\mu^2 = 105$ which we deem to be large enough to avoid the weak-instruments problem. We plot our summary statistics for the double-k-class estimators in Fig. 5. In the left panel, we plot our summary statistics for the double-k-class estimator with $k_1 = \Delta$ and $k_2 = 0$ (Equation 27), while in the second panel, we plot the statistics for the double-k-class estimators with $k_1 = 0$ and $k_2 = \Delta$ (Equation 28). We choose a range of $\Delta \in [-0.1, 0.1]$. We notice that for $\Delta = 0$ which corresponds to the 2SLS case we have a small amount of finite sample bias. This finite sample bias can be removed by choosing a small negative value of k_1 in the left panel or a small positive value of k_2 in the second panel. Furthermore, this can be achieved at a modest cost in MSE, which increases slowly as Δ increases or decreases away from 0. It appears that the resulting estimators maintain moments over the the chosen range on Δ. Notice that a particularly attractive feature of the estimator in Equation 28 is that the bias is linear in Δ while the MSE is quadratic.

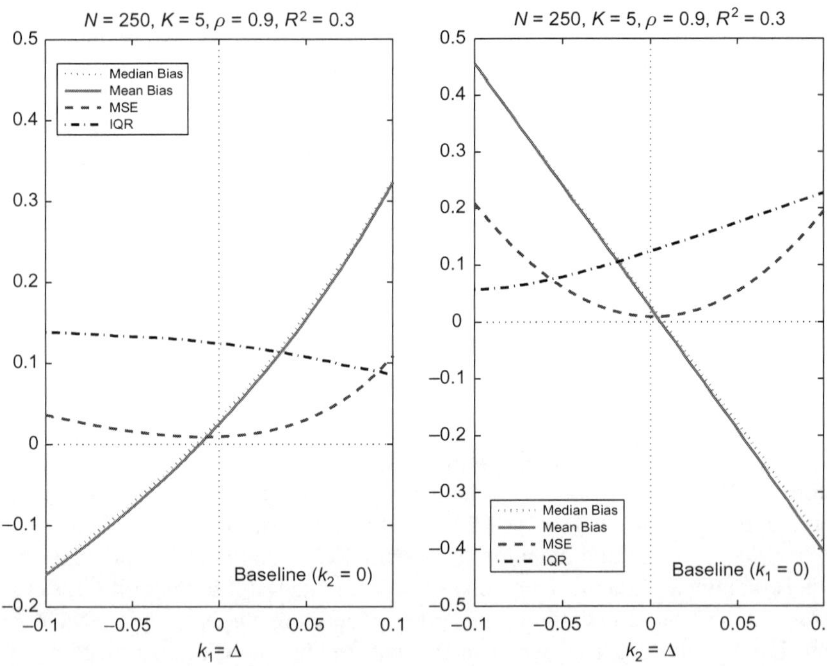

Fig. 5. Monte Carlo Simulation of Double-k-Class Estimators for the "Normal" Case with a High Value of the Concentration Parameter and $K = 5$ Instruments.

Let us now turn our attention to the "weak-instruments" case which does not employ too many instruments. To simulate this case we use $K = 5$ and choose a value of $R^2 = 0.1$ for the theoretical first stage fit. This leads to a value of the concentration parameter of $\mu^2 = 27.2$ which we deem to be small enough to lead to the weak-instruments problem. We plot our summary statistics for the double-k-class estimators in Fig. 6. In the left panel, we plot our summary statistics for the double-k-class estimator with $k_1 = \Delta$ and $k_2 = 0$ (Eq. (27)), while in the second panel we plot the statistics for the double-k-class estimators with $k_1 = 0$ and $k_2 = \Delta$ (Eq. (28)). We choose a range of $\Delta \in [-0.1,\ 0.1]$. We notice that for $\Delta = 0$ which corresponds to the 2SLS case we now have a substantial amount of finite sample bias. This finite sample bias can be removed by choosing a small negative value of k_1 in the left panel or a small positive value of k_2 in the second panel. Furthermore, this can be achieved at a modest cost due to increasing MSE. Notice that while the estimators in the right panel maintain moments for all values of Δ, those in

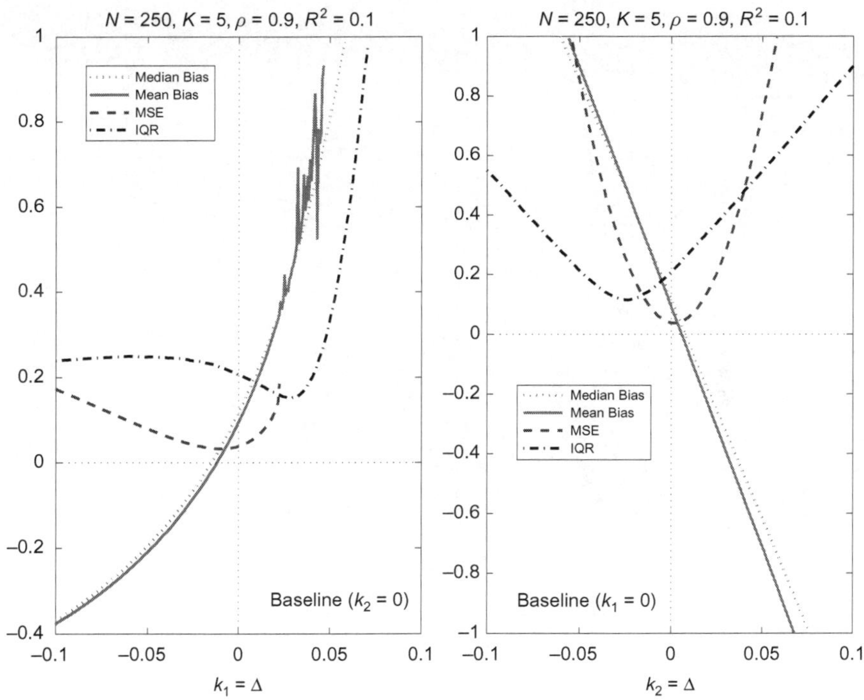

Fig. 6. Monte Carlo Simulation of Double-k-Class Estimators for the "Weak-Instruments" Case with a low Value of the Concentration Parameter and $K = 5$ Instruments.

the left panel do not for $\Delta > 0$. It is important to note, however, that the values of Δ required to address the finite sample bias of 2SLS are such that $\Delta < 0$ and thus we avoid the moment problem as well.

Finally, let us return to the "weak and many instruments" case. As before, we simulate this case using $K = 30$ and set the theoretical first stage $R^2 = 0.1$. We plot our summary statistics for the double-k-class estimators in Fig. 7. In the left panel we plot our summary statistics for the double-k-class estimator with $k_1 = \Delta$ and $k_2 = 0$ (equation 27), while in the second panel we plot the statistics for the double-k-class estimators with $k_1 = 0$ and $k_2 = \Delta$ (Equation 28). We choose a range of $\Delta \in [-0.1, 0.1]$. We note that for $\Delta = 0$, which corresponds to the 2SLS case, we now have a very substantial amount of finite sample bias. This finite sample bias can be removed by choosing a small negative value of k_1 in the left panel or a small positive value of k_2 in the second panel. Furthermore, this can be achieved at a modest cost due to increasing MSE.

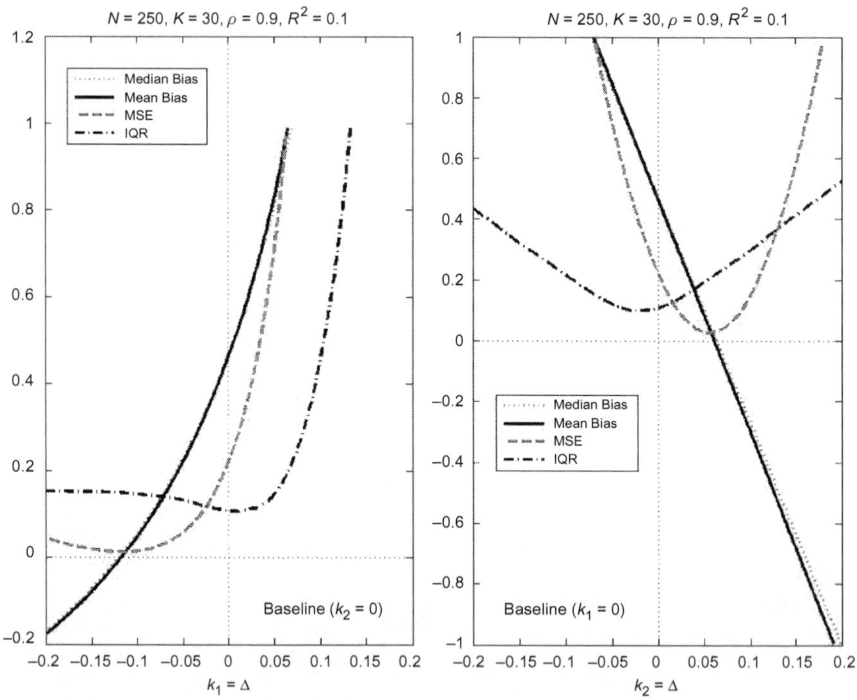

Fig. 7. Monte Carlo Simulation of Double-k-Class Estimators for the "Many Instruments" Case with a Low Value of the Concentration Parameter and $K = 30$ Instruments.

Qualitatively, these three cases are very similar in the sense that for a fixed (finite) sample size, we can find values of Δ for each case such that the bias is completely eliminated while avoiding the no-moments problems of the estimators in the k-class. Having shown that the double-k-class estimators can provide a satisfactory solution to the weak and/or many instruments problem of the baseline 2SLS estimator in theory, we now need to discuss the choice of Δ.

4. OPTIMAL PARAMETER CHOICE FOR DOUBLE k-CLASS ESTIMATORS

Dwivedi and Srivastava (1984) derive the exact finite sample bias expression for the double-k-class estimators. Define $m = N/2$ and $n = (N - K)/2$. As before, denote by μ^2 the first-stage concentration parameter. Then for non-negative integers a, b, c, d we can define,

$$\phi(a, b) = \exp\left(\frac{-\mu^2}{2}\right) \sum_{j=0}^{\infty} \frac{\Gamma(m - n + j - a)}{\Gamma(m - n + j + b)} \frac{(\mu^2/2)^j}{j!} \tag{29}$$

and

$$\psi_d(a; b; c) = \exp\left(\frac{-\mu^2}{2}\right) \sum_{\alpha=0}^{\infty} \sum_{j=0}^{\infty} (d\alpha + 1)(k_1 + 1)^{\alpha} \times \frac{\Gamma(m + j - a - 1)\Gamma(n + \alpha + b)}{\Gamma(m + j + \alpha + c)\Gamma(n)} \frac{(\mu^2/2)^j}{j!}. \tag{30}$$

Then, Dwivedi and Srivastava (1984) show that the bias of the double-k-class is,

$$E(\hat{\beta}_{2kIV}) - \beta = \left(\beta - \frac{\sigma_{wv}}{\sigma_{vv}}\right)\left(\frac{\mu^2}{2}\psi_0(1; 0; 1) - 1\right) + (k_1 - k_2)\frac{\sigma_{wv}}{\sigma_{vv}}\psi_0(1; 0; 1). \tag{31}$$

Furthermore, if $K > 1$ and $k_1 = 0$ we also have,

$$E(\hat{\beta}_{2kIV}) - \beta = \left(\beta - \frac{\sigma_{wv}}{\sigma_{vv}}\right)\left(\frac{\mu^2}{2}\phi(0; 1) - 1\right) - k_2\frac{\sigma_{wv}}{\sigma_{vv}}n\phi(1; 0). \tag{32}$$

4.1. Mean Unbiased Estimation

Using the properties above, for a given value of k_1 we can derive the value of k_2 such that the resulting double-k-class estimator is unbiased. If $k_1 \neq 0$, then,

$$k_2^* = k_1 + \frac{\sigma_{vv}}{\sigma_{wv}}\left(\beta - \frac{\sigma_{wv}}{\sigma_{vv}}\right)\left[\frac{\frac{\mu^2}{2}\psi_0(1;0;1) - 1}{\psi_0(1;0;1)}\right], \tag{33}$$

while if $k_1 = 0$ this reduces to,

$$k_2^* = \frac{\sigma_{vv}}{\sigma_{wv}}\left(\beta - \frac{\sigma_{wv}}{\sigma_{vv}}\right)\left[\frac{\frac{\mu^2}{2}\phi(0;1) - 1}{n\phi(1;0)}\right]. \tag{34}$$

Then, using the fact that

$$-\left[\frac{\frac{\mu^2}{2}\phi(0;1) - 1}{n\phi(1;0)}\right] = \frac{K-2}{N-K}, \tag{35}$$

we have a simplified version of k_2^* that does not require estimating μ^2:

$$k_2^* = -\left(\frac{K-2}{N-K}\right)\frac{\sigma_{vv}}{\sigma_{wv}}\left(\beta - \frac{\sigma_{wv}}{\sigma_{vv}}\right) \tag{36}$$

Notice two facts about the optimal choice of the k_2. First, for a fixed K, k_2^* tends to 0 as $N \to \infty$, a requirement for consistency. Second, k_2^* depends on the unknown value of the structural parameter β. This suggests a two-step estimation approach in order to operationalize this estimator. In the tables, we denote this as the "two-step k_2^*" estimator, which simply estimates σ_{vv}, σ_{wv} from the reduced form and β by Fuller:

$$\hat{k}_2^{2\text{-}step} = -\left(\frac{K-2}{N-K}\right)\frac{\hat{\sigma}_{vv}}{\hat{\sigma}_{wv}}\left(\hat{\beta}_{Fuller} - \frac{\hat{\sigma}_{wv}}{\hat{\sigma}_{vv}}\right) \tag{37}$$

The resulting estimator is the double-k-class estimator with $k_1 = 0$ and $k_2 = \hat{k}_2^{2\text{-}step}$.

4.2. *Minimum MSE Estimation*

Alternatively, we can choose the value of k_2 which minimizes the MSE. Using the expressions in Dwivedi and Srivastava (1984) we can define,

$$\bar{\sigma} = \sigma_{ww} - \frac{\sigma_{wv}^2}{\sigma_{vv}}. \tag{38}$$

Then the parameter choice which minimizes the MSE of the estimator is given by

$$k_2^* = \frac{\frac{\sigma_{wv}}{\sigma_{vv}}\left(\beta - \frac{\sigma_{wv}}{\sigma_{vv}}\right)\left(\frac{\mu^2}{2}\phi(1;1) - \phi(1;0)\right)}{\frac{\bar{\sigma}}{4\sigma_{vv}}\phi(2;0) + \frac{n+1}{2}\left(\frac{\sigma_{wv}}{\sigma_{vv}}\right)^2 \phi(1;0)} \tag{39}$$

Again, note that the optimal choice of k_2 depends on unknown parameters β, σ_{vv}, and σ_{wv} and additionally on μ^2. Mirroring the solution strategy discussed before we can construct a feasible two-step estimator by plugging in the Fuller estimator of β (this time setting the Fuller parameter $\kappa = 4$ so that $k^{Fuller} = \phi - 4/(N-K)$ to minimize MSE) and the using reduced-form estimates of the remaining parameters (bias correcting μ^2 by K) to obtain $\hat{k}_2^{2\text{-}step}(\kappa = 4)$.

5. MONTE CARLO SIMULATIONS

We now explore the finite sample performance of the two feasible double-k-class estimators introduced above that either minimize the bias or MSE. Since these choices are functions of the unknown structural parameter β, the feasible estimators plug in an initial estimate obtained from Fuller's estimator.

Following the simulation design in Hahn and Hausman (2002a), we generate data using the following design with two endogenous variables y_1 and y_2:

$$\begin{aligned} y_1 &= \beta y_2 + \epsilon = \beta z \pi + w \\ y_2 &= z\pi + v, \end{aligned} \tag{40}$$

where $w = \beta v + \epsilon$. We let y_1 and y_2 be $N \times 1$ vectors of observations on the endogenous variables and denote by z the $N \times K$ matrix of K instruments.

If we define:

$$\Omega = \begin{pmatrix} \sigma_{ww} & \sigma_{wv} \\ \sigma_{wv} & \sigma_{vv} \end{pmatrix}, \tag{41}$$

then our design has $\sigma_{vv} = \sigma_{ww} = 1$ and we let $\sigma_{wv} = -0.3$. The parameter of interest β is given by $\beta = 2\sigma_{wv}$, which pins down $\sigma_{\epsilon v} = 0.3$. Each element of $\pi = \sqrt{\frac{\mu^2}{(N-K)K}}$, where μ^2 corresponds to the theoretical concentration parameter

$$\mu^2 = \frac{\pi' z' z \pi}{\sigma_{vv}}. \tag{42}$$

In the Monte Carlo experiments below we consider permutations of $\mu^2 \in \{8, 12, 24, 32\}$, $K \in \{8, 24\}$, and $N \in \{200, 800\}$. Both of the sample sizes we consider are quite small, highlighting the problems with traditional IV estimators in finite samples. The various values of μ^2 and K allow us to consider the case of weak and many instruments, respectively, potentially occurring simultaneously. We use a log normal distribution for the instrumental variables standardized with mean zero and variance one, and the stochastic disturbance is either normally distributed or has a t-distribution with 12 degrees of freedom, again standardized to have mean zero and variance one.

Table 1 reports Monte Carlo simulation results for the data-generating process with normally distributed disturbances. The Panel A reports results for $N = 800$ and the Panel B reports results for $N = 200$, while the left-hand columns display mean bias results and the right-hand columns indicate the MSE of each estimator. Given that the true coefficient is $\beta = -0.6$, the 2SLS mean bias results are large. For example, the mean bias of 2SLS for weak but not many instruments ($\mu^2 = K = 8$) is 0.147, which represents a bias of nearly 25%. Fuller1 (which denotes Fuller's k-class estimator with $k = \phi - 1/(N - K)$) consistently outperforms 2SLS in mean bias, sometimes by an order of magnitude. Our preferred estimator to minimize mean bias is labeled "two-step k_2^* min bias" and is defined in equation (37) above. This estimator uses the Fuller1 estimate of β to construct k_2^* and does not require estimating μ^2. In mean bias, this estimator generally has almost 50% less mean bias than Fuller1, especially in the rows corresponding to weak instruments, and failing to have lower mean bias than Fuller1 only in a few specifications.

Turning to minimum MSE estimation, the Fuller estimator that has been shown to perform best in terms of MSE is $k = \phi - 4/(N - K)$, and we benchmark our results against this estimator, which we label Fuller4. As a general rule, 2SLS has low MSE because its variance is so small despite its location being badly biased. Fuller4, by contrast, has mean bias that is around half of the mean bias of 2SLS but MSE that is up to 20% higher than the MSE of 2SLS. Our preferred estimator for minimizing MSE is labeled "two-step k_2^* min MSE." While this estimator dominates 2SLS in terms of mean bias, it generally has similar or higher mean bias as Fuller4. The MSE comparison between Fuller4 and this optimal double-k-class estimator is more nuanced. When many instruments is an issue (i.e. $K = 24$), the feasible double-k-class estimator has MSE nearly 50% less than Fuller4. When

Table 1. Monte Carlo Results for Normally Distributed.

		Mean Bias					MSE				
μ^2	K	2SLS	Fuller1	Two-step k_2^* min bias	Fuller4	Two-step k_2^* min MSE	2SLS	Fuller1	Two-step k_2^* min bias	Fuller4	Two-step k_2^* min MSE
Panel A: Results with $N = 800$											
8	8	0.147	0.048	0.027	0.122	0.111	0.088	0.246	0.313	0.106	0.141
8	24	0.224	0.076	0.051	0.141	0.205	0.080	0.438	0.564	0.174	0.093
12	8	0.115	0.015	0.008	0.083	0.088	0.066	0.163	0.178	0.080	0.089
12	24	0.199	0.034	0.016	0.099	0.180	0.066	0.301	0.351	0.132	0.072
24	8	0.068	−0.005	0.001	0.037	0.059	0.037	0.064	0.061	0.043	0.040
24	24	0.148	−0.002	−0.005	0.042	0.135	0.041	0.111	0.109	0.066	0.042
32	8	0.053	−0.005	0.001	0.026	0.048	0.029	0.043	0.041	0.033	0.030
32	24	0.126	−0.003	−0.002	0.029	0.117	0.033	0.066	0.063	0.046	0.033
Panel B: Results with $N = 200$											
8	8	0.149	0.048	0.028	0.123	0.115	0.089	0.245	0.318	0.107	0.138
8	24	0.220	0.078	0.054	0.138	0.204	0.079	0.440	0.563	0.177	0.091
12	8	0.116	0.016	0.010	0.085	0.091	0.066	0.163	0.178	0.080	0.086
12	24	0.193	0.038	0.020	0.096	0.177	0.064	0.302	0.344	0.134	0.070
24	8	0.070	−0.002	0.004	0.038	0.061	0.037	0.065	0.061	0.043	0.039
24	24	0.141	0.000	−0.003	0.040	0.131	0.040	0.109	0.106	0.065	0.040
32	8	0.055	−0.002	0.004	0.027	0.050	0.028	0.043	0.040	0.032	0.029
32	24	0.120	−0.003	−0.003	0.027	0.112	0.031	0.065	0.062	0.045	0.031

Notes: This table shows mean bias (left-hand columns) and MSE results (right-hand columns) for estimation of β from 10,000 Monte Carlo simulations using the estimators described in the text. Panel A reports results for $N = 800$ and Panel B reports results for $N = 200$. The data-generating process is described in the text with the true $\beta = -0.6$ and the true $\sigma_{ev} = 0.3$.

Table 2. Monte Carlo Results for Thick-Tailed Errors.

		Mean Bias					MSE				
μ^2	K	2SLS	Fuller1	Two-step k_2^* min bias	Fuller4	Two-step k_2^* min MSE	2SLS	Fuller1	Two-step k_2^* min bias	Fuller4	Two-step k_2^* min MSE
Panel A: Results with $N = 800$											
8	8	0.152	0.053	0.034	0.126	0.116	0.091	0.246	0.339	0.106	0.152
8	24	0.225	0.077	0.055	0.142	0.207	0.081	0.447	0.577	0.177	0.095
12	8	0.120	0.022	0.015	0.089	0.093	0.068	0.165	0.196	0.081	0.097
12	24	0.199	0.032	0.016	0.098	0.181	0.066	0.312	0.362	0.135	0.073
24	8	0.073	0.000	0.005	0.041	0.063	0.037	0.066	0.064	0.044	0.041
24	24	0.148	−0.007	−0.008	0.039	0.135	0.042	0.117	0.114	0.068	0.042
32	8	0.057	0.000	0.005	0.030	0.052	0.029	0.044	0.042	0.033	0.030
32	24	0.126	−0.007	−0.005	0.026	0.116	0.033	0.071	0.066	0.048	0.033
Panel B: Results with $N = 200$											
8	8	0.150	0.052	0.032	0.125	0.117	0.090	0.250	0.331	0.108	0.143
8	24	0.217	0.067	0.038	0.131	0.199	0.077	0.436	0.568	0.171	0.088
12	8	0.119	0.024	0.015	0.088	0.094	0.068	0.169	0.194	0.083	0.093
12	24	0.190	0.026	0.006	0.089	0.174	0.063	0.299	0.348	0.130	0.068
24	8	0.073	0.002	0.007	0.042	0.063	0.038	0.069	0.066	0.045	0.042
24	24	0.140	−0.008	−0.010	0.035	0.129	0.039	0.112	0.109	0.065	0.039
32	8	0.058	0.001	0.006	0.031	0.052	0.030	0.046	0.044	0.034	0.031
32	24	0.118	−0.007	−0.007	0.024	0.110	0.031	0.068	0.064	0.046	0.031

Notes: This table shows mean bias (left-hand columns) and MSE results (right-hand columns) for estimation of β from 10,000 Monte Carlo simulations using the estimators described in the text. Panel A reports results for $N = 800$ and Panel B reports results for $N = 200$. The data-generating process is described in the text with thick-tailed errors (a t-distribution with 12 degrees of freedom), the true $\beta = -0.6$ and the true $\sigma_{ev} = 0.3$.

many instruments are not a problem (i.e. in the $K = 8$ specifications), the two-step double-k-class estimator has mean similar or slightly higher MSE.

To test whether these results rely on the relatively thin tails of the normal distribution, in Table 2, we show Monte Carlo results when the stochastic disturbances have thicker tails, which we simulate by drawing from a t-distribution with 12 degrees of freedom. The results are broadly consistent with Table 1. 2SLS is badly biased, and Fuller1 shows tremendous finite sample bias reduction. Our preferred estimator for minimizing bias almost always dominates Fuller1 in mean bias. While Fuller4 offers a nice alternative to 2SLS in terms of minimizing MSE (mainly because Fuller4 is less badly biased than 2SLS), when many instruments are an issue, the feasible double-k-class estimator that minimizes MSE outperforms Fuller4 in MSE.

6. CONCLUSION

In this paper, we present new tools for addressing the finite sample bias of instrumental variable estimators in the presence of weak and/or many instruments. Currently practitioners have a number of estimators at their disposal, but the most commonly used ones such as 2SLS can suffer from substantial bias. Fuller (1977) performs reasonably well in the case of weak and many instruments but is not unbiased.

We reintroduce Nagar's double-k-class estimators to construct optimal estimators that minimize mean bias or MSE. To do so, we derive the exact finite sample bias of the estimators in terms of hypergeometric functions and employ recent computational advances in the speed with which hypergeometric functions can be evaluated to develop a computationally attractive estimator that weakly dominates k-class estimators, including 2SLS. Monte Carlo results demonstrate that in simulations our estimator has lower mean bias than Fuller and does comparably well for MSE, outperforming Fuller in terms of MSE in the case of many instruments. Additional research may suggest further solutions to the problem of weak and many instruments in the double-k-class of estimators, including generalizing our estimator to accommodate conditional heteroskedasticity or multiple endogenous regressors, and determining whether the optimal double-k-class estimators proposed here also remove asymptotic bias under many/weak instrument (Bekker) asymptotics.

NOTES

1. Note that, in general, the concentration parameter is weakly increasing in K and unless proper normalizations are made to the coefficients, increasing K for a fixed μ^2 shrinks the reduced-form variance. See Section 5 for more details on our simulations data-generating process.

2. Note that these numerical results are consistent with earlier analytical work by Richardson and Wu (1971) and Chao and Swanson (2007). In particular, see Proposition 3.1 of Chao and Swanson (2007).

3. Simulation results for this estimator are not reported in this paper, but are available from the authors. A two-part estimator that uses the β_{BC} when the bias-corrected concentration parameter estimate is positive ($\hat{\mu}^2 - K > 0$) and Fuller otherwise significantly outperforms other estimators in both mean bias and MSE.

4. See Hahn et al. (2004) for a detailed review of the performance of these estimators and their corresponding higher-order bias and MSE approximations. Note however that there is a minor but sometimes confusing difference in the way these estimators are defined in the recent literature (including this paper) relative to the notation employed in earlier research such as Nagar (1959) or Sawa (1972), who define the k parameter as $1 + k$ for the values of k discussed above. Furthermore, it is important to keep in mind that some of the values of k are fixed while others are stochastic, which leads to subtle differences in the way we think about the properties of these estimators.

5. See Kinal (1980) for the definitive treatment of the existence of moments for k-class estimators.

ACKNOWLEDGEMENTS

We are grateful to Tim Armstrong for providing excellent research assistance. Thanks to Plamen Koev for sharing his code for the computation of hypergeometric functions.

REFERENCES

Abadir, K. (1999). An introduction to hypergeometric functions for economists. *Econometric Reviews*, *18*, 287–330.

Anderson, T. W., & Sawa, T. (1979). Evaluation of the distribution function of the two-stage least squares estimate. *Econometrica*, *47*, 163–182.

Andrews, I., & Armstrong, T. B. (2015). Unbiased instrumental variables estimation under known first-stage sign, *mimeo*, 1–36.

Bekker, P. A. (1994). Alternative approximations to the distributions of instrumental variable estimators. *Econometrica*, *62*, 657–681.

Buse, A. (1992). The bias of instrumental variable estimators. *Econometrica: Journal of the Econometric Society*, *60*, 173–180.

Chao, J., & Swanson, N. (2007). Alternative specifications of the bias and MSE of the IV estimator under weak identification with an application to bias correction. *Journal of Econometrics*, *137*, 515–555.

Chuanming, G., & Lahiri, K. (2001). A note on the double k-class estimator in simultaneous equations. *Journal of Econometrics*, *108*, 101–111.

Dwivedi, T. D., & Srivastava, V. K. (1984). Exact finite sample properties of double k-class estimators in simultaneous equations. *Journal of Econometrics*, *25*, 263–283.

Fuller, W. A. (1977). Some properties of a modification of the limited information estimator. *Econometrica*, *45*, 939–953.

Hahn, J., & Hausman, J. A. (2002a). A new specification test for the validity of instrumental variables. *Econometrica*, *70*, 163–189.

Hahn, J., & Hausman, J. A. (2002b). Notes on bias in estimators for simultaneous equation models. *Economics Letters*, *75*, 237–241.

Hahn, J., Hausman, J., & Kuersteiner, G. (2004). Estimation with weak instruments: Accuracy of higher-order bias and MSE approximations. *The Econometrics Journal*, *7*(1), 272–306.

Hansen, C., Hausman, J., & Newey, W. (2008). Estimation with many instrumental variables. *Journal of Business & Economic Statistics*, *26*(4).

Hillier, G., Kinal, T., & Srivastava, V. K. (1984). On the moments of ordinary least squares and instrumental variables estimators in a general structural equation. *Econometrica*, *52*, 185–202.

Hirano, K., & Porter, J. R. (2015). Location properties of point estimators in linear instrumental variables and related models. *Econometric Reviews*, *34*(6–10), 720–733.

Kinal, T. W. (1980). The existence of moments of k-class estimators. *Econometrica: Journal of the Econometric Society*, *48*, 241–249.

Koev, P., & Edelman, A. (2006). The efficient evaluation of the hypergeometric function of a matrix argument. *Mathematics of Computation*, *75*, 833–846.

Muller, K. E. (2001). Computing the confluent hypergeometric function M(a,b,x). *Numerische Mathematik*, *90*, 179–196.

Nagar, A. L. (1959). The bias and moment matrix of the general k-class estimators of the parameters in simultaneous equations. *Econometrica*, *27*, 575–595.

Nagar, A. L. (1962). Double k-class estimators of parameters in simultaneous equations and their small sample properties. *International Economic Review*, *3*, 168–188.

Nelson, C. R., & Startz, R. (1990). Some further results on the exact small sample properties of the instrumental variables estimator. *Econometrica*, *58*, 967–976.

Owen, A. D. (1976). A proof that both the bias and the mean square error of the two-stage least squares estimator are monotonically non-increasing functions of the sample size. *Econometrica*, *44*, 409–411.

Phillips, P. (1980). The exact distribution of instrumental variable estimators in an equation containing n+1 endogenous variables. *Econometrica*, *48*, 861–878.

Phillips, P. C. B. (1983). Exact small sample theory in the simultaneous equations model. *Handbook of Econometrics*, *1*, 449–516.

Poskitt, D. S., & Skeels, C. L. (2013). Inference in the presence of weak instruments: A selected survey. *Foundations and Trends in Econometrics*, *6*(1), 1–102.

Poskitt, D. S., & Skeels, C. L. (2009). Assessing the magnitude of the concentration parameter in a simultaneous equations model. *The Econometrics Journal*, *12*(1), 26–44.

Richardson, D. H. (1968). The exact distribution of a structural coefficient estimator. *Journal of the American Statistical Association*, *63*, 1214–1226.

Richardson, D. H., & Wu, D. M. (1971). A note on the comparison of ordinary and two-stage least squares estimators. *Econometrica*, *39*, 973–981.

Sawa, T. (1969). The exact sampling distribution of ordinary least squares and two-stage least squares estimators. *Journal of the American Statistical Association*, *64*, 923–937.

Sawa, T. (1972). Finite sample properties of the k-class estimators. *Econometrica*, *40*, 653–680.

Slater, L. J. (1964). Confluent hypergeometric functions. In M. Abramowitz & I. A. Stegun (Eds.). *Handbook of mathematical functions*. National Bureau of Standards.

Srinivasan, T. N. (1970). Approximations to finite sample moments of estimators whose exact sampling distributions are unknown. *Econometrica*, *38*, 533–541.

Srivastava, V. K., Agnihotri, B. S., & Dwivedi, T. D. (1980). Dominance of double k-class estimators in simultaneous equations. *Annals of the Institute for Statistical Mathematics*, *32A*, 387–392.

Staiger, D., & James, H. S. (1997). Instrumental variables regression with weak instruments. *Econometrica*, *65*, 557–586.

Theil, H. (1958). Economic forecasts and policy. Amsterdam: North-Holland.

Ullah, A. (2004). *Finite sample econometrics*. Oxford.
Zellner, A. (1963). Estimators for seemingly unrelated regression equations: Some exact finite sample results. *Journal of the American Statistical Association*, *58*, 977–992.

APPENDIX A: DERIVATIONS OF EXPRESSIONS IN SECTION 2

In a few of these derivations, we use the fact that

$$\begin{aligned} B(m,k) &= e^{-m/2}{}_1F_1(k/2-1;k/2;m/2) \\ &= e^{-m/2}e^{m/2}{}_1F_1(k/2-(k/2-1);k/2;-m/2) = {}_1F_1(1;k/2;-m/2). \end{aligned}$$

The second equality is known as Kummar's Transformation (see Eq. (25) in Abadir, 1999).

Part (a)

$$B(m,2) = e^{-m/2}{}_1F_1(0;1;m/2) = e^{-m/2}\sum_{j=0}^{\infty}\frac{(0)_j}{(1)_j}\frac{(m/2)^j}{j!} = e^{-m/2}$$

since the first term of the series is 1 and $(0)_j = 0$ for $j \geq 1$.

Part (b)

$$\begin{aligned} \lim_{k\to\infty} B(m,k) &= \lim_{k\to\infty} {}_1F_1(1;k/2;-m/2) \\ &= \lim_{k\to\infty} 1 + \sum_{j=1}^{\infty}((k/2)_j)^{-1}\frac{(-m/2)^j}{j!} \\ &= 1 + \sum_{j=1}^{\infty}\lim_{k\to\infty}((k/2)_j)^{-1}\frac{(-m/2)^j}{j!} = 1 \end{aligned}$$

Part (c)

$B(m,k)$ is continuous in m, so

$$\lim_{m\to 0} B(m,k) = B(0,k) = e^0{}_1F_1(k/2-1;k/2;0) = 1 \tag{A.1}$$

since hypergeometric functions evaluated at zero are equal to 1, the first term in the infinite series.

Part (d)

When we do the substitution, we get $1 + (1/6)e^{-m/2}(-6 - m)m$ (the last minus sign in this expression is a plus sign in the corresponding equation). To derive this, expand $e^{-m/2}$ as $1 - m/2 + \mathcal{O}(m^2)$. Then

$$\begin{aligned} 1 + (1/6)e^{-m/2}(-6 - m)m &= 1 - (1/6)m(6 + m)(1 - m/2 + \mathcal{O}(m^2)) \\ &= 1 - (1/6)m(6 - 3m + m - m^2/2) + \mathcal{O}(m^3) \\ &= 1 - (1/3)m(3 - m) + \mathcal{O}(m^3). \end{aligned}$$

$B(m, 1)$ can be expanded as

$$\begin{aligned} B(m,1) &= {}_1F_1(1; 1/2; -m/2) = 1 + \frac{1}{1/2}(-m/2) + \frac{1 \cdot 2}{(1/2)(3/2)} \frac{(-m/2)^2}{2} + \mathcal{O}(m^3) \\ &= 1 - m + \frac{2 \cdot 2}{3 \cdot 4} m^2 + \mathcal{O}(m^3) = 1 - (1/3)m(3 - m) + \mathcal{O}(m^3) \end{aligned}$$

so $B(m, 1) = 1 + (1/6)e^{-m/2}(-6 - m)m + \mathcal{O}(m^3)$.

Part (e)

It suffices to show that ${}_1F_1(k/2 - 1; k/2; m/2)$ is strictly increasing in k, which will follow if we can show that each term in the infinite series is strictly increasing in k. The jth term is

$$\frac{(k/2 - 1)_j}{(k/2)_j} \frac{(m/2)^j}{j!} = \frac{k/2 - 1}{k/2 + j - 1} \frac{(m/2)^j}{j!} \tag{A.2}$$

which is strictly increasing in k for $m \geq 0$ since

$$\frac{d}{dk}\left(\frac{k/2 - 1}{k/2 + j - 1}\right) = \frac{(1/2)(k/2 + j - 1) - (k/2 - 1)(1/2)}{(k/2 + j - 1)^2} = \frac{j}{2(k/2 + j - 1)^2} > 0. \tag{A.3}$$

PART IV
INFORMATION AND ENTROPY

ON THE CONSTRUCTION OF PRIOR INFORMATION – AN INFO-METRICS APPROACH

Amos Golan[a,b,c] and Robin L. Lumsdaine[a,d,e]

[a]*Info-Metrics Institute, American University, Washington, DC, USA*
[b]*Department of Economics, American University, Washington, DC, USA*
[c]*Santa Fe Institute, Santa Fe, NM, USA*
[d]*Kogod School of Business, American University, Washington, DC, USA*
[e]*National Bureau of Economic Research (NBER), Cambridge, MA, USA*

ABSTRACT

Although in principle prior information can significantly improve inference, incorporating incorrect *prior information will bias the estimates of any inferential analysis. This fact deters many scientists from incorporating prior information into their inferential analyses. In the natural sciences, where experiments are more regularly conducted, and can be combined with other relevant information, prior information is often used in inferential analysis, despite it being sometimes nontrivial to specify what that information is and how to quantify that information. In the social sciences, however, prior information is often hard to come by and very hard to justify or validate. We review a number of ways to construct such information. This information emerges naturally, either from*

Essays in Honor of Aman Ullah
Advances in Econometrics, Volume 36, 277–314

ISSN: 0731-9053/doi:10.1108/S0731-905320160000036017

fundamental properties and characteristics of the systems studied or from logical reasoning about the problems being analyzed. Borrowing from concepts and philosophical reasoning used in the natural sciences, and within an info-metrics framework, we discuss three different, yet complimentary, approaches for constructing prior information, with an application to the social sciences.

Keywords: Entropy; grouping property; maximum entropy; priors; relative entropy; transformation groups

JEL classifications: C100; C180; C490

1. INTRODUCTION

Essential to any inferential problem is the specification of the information set. Often this is taken to mean the observed information or sample that will be used for our analysis. Such a sample may come from an experiment (usually in the natural sciences) or from data collection (usually in the social and behavioral sciences). Yet an equally important, but often overlooked component is what we will call the prior information. This we define to be everything we know about the system but without the observed sample. It is the information that is available *in advance of* estimation/inference. In particular, prior information can come from anything that potentially influences the specification of a problem but arises outside of the determining system. Examples include: confirmed theory, intuition, elicitation of opinions independent of the data, beliefs, expert judgment, or even previously observed data. Throughout this paper, we remain agnostic as to the *source* of prior information and we will use the terms "prior" and "prior information" interchangeably.

Prior information emerges naturally from fundamental properties and characteristics of the systems studied or from logical reasoning about the problems being analyzed, or even from empirically observing other systems. Yet constructing and quantifying this prior information remains a challenge across all disciplines, especially in the social sciences where priors are often based not on observed phenomena but rather on underlying unobserved beliefs. Regardless of the information used to construct the priors, an essential property of a "good" prior is its invariance to certain sample or parameter spaces (e.g., Kass & Wasserman, 1996). The priors we discuss here have these properties.

In this paper, we provide a number of ways to construct and quantify priors that arise from some fundamental properties of the system or from other logical reasoning. Although each specific problem has to be handled individually, the general frameworks we discuss here are suitable for constructing priors across all disciplines.

Because the prior information we discuss can come from different sources, each setting requires a different specification. But before we start we must emphasize the following. Prior information can significantly improve inference. Incorporating incorrect prior information, however, will bias the estimates of any inferential analysis, *even if the model itself is specified correctly*. This fact deters many scientists from incorporating prior information into their inferential analyses. In the natural sciences, where experiments are more regularly conducted, and can be combined with other relevant information, prior information is often used in inferential analysis, despite it being sometimes nontrivial to specify what that information is and how to quantify that information. In the social sciences, however, such data are often hard to come by and prior information is instead based on the elicitation of opinions or beliefs. Therefore, it is often very hard to justify or validate.

We concentrate here only on priors that can be quantified and are useful for information-theoretic procedures, or at times for Bayesian procedures. We start by reviewing how to incorporate priors into the info-metrics inferential problem, briefly summarizing the maximum entropy formulation with priors, also called cross entropy. Once that goal is achieved, we will show ways to construct these priors. We start with the simpler, yet generic, case of constructing priors for discrete distributions; this can be handled via the grouping property that goes back to Shannon (1948). These priors are used within information-theoretic methods of inference, in other words, they inform our inference about the entire probability distribution and enable us to construct the probability distribution directly. For continuous distributions, the challenge of constructing such priors is much more difficult, in part because the extent to which typical problems that arise in practice are underdetermined is much more severe (i.e., potentially uncountable). We tackle this via the method of transformation groups, championed by Jaynes (1968) and based on the mathematical concept of group theory. This approach works for both discrete and continuous functions but is most often applied to continuous problems. The priors constructed within this approach can be used in *all* inferential methods that accommodate priors, including those that are interested in inference about a specific aspect of the probability distribution (e.g., certain parameters or moments), rather than the whole distribution.

In the final discussion section, we discuss and provide some simple examples using the traditional maximum entropy to construct priors, including a very brief discussion of the challenge of empirical priors (left for further research). The final section concludes.

2. ENTROPY DEFICIENCY: MINIMUM CROSS ENTROPY – A BRIEF SUMMARY

We consider here the problem of inferring a normalized (the probabilities sum up to one), discrete probability distribution from a small number of expectation values. Let $k = 1, 2, \ldots, K$ be an unobserved set of mutually exclusive and together exhaustive alternatives or possible states. Let $\{X_m\}$ be a set of M linearly independent variables (e.g., moments) defined on the K states, where X_m has the value x_{mk} on the state k. Such a situation may arise in the social sciences, for example, when trying to identify an underlying probability distribution of a population (e.g., people in the United States) based on observed data consisting of grouped averages (e.g., Metropolitan Statistical Areas – MSAs, or state-level averages). When $M < K - 1$, the number of unknown quantities exceeds the number of observed moments and therefore the problem is underdetermined. That means that we need to select a criterion that chooses one of the many possible solutions that satisfy the observed moments. Within the info-metrics approach, that criterion is entropy. The entropy we use here is the Boltzmann–Gibbs–Shannon entropy (Shannon, 1948) that was then generalized by Kullback and Leibler (1951). For motivation, reviews and summary of such an approach see, for example, Levine (1980), Levine and Tribus (1979), Golan (2008), and Golan (forthcoming).

The Kullback–Leibler entropy criterion compares two probability distributions in terms of their information and is defined as follows: Let P and Q be two normalized probability distributions of the random variables X and Y respectively. The *relative entropy*, known also as *entropy deficiency*, between these two probability distributions is

$$D(P||Q) = D(X||Y) \equiv \sum_{k=1}^{K} p_k \log(p_k/q_k) \tag{1}$$

where $D(P||Q) \geq 0$ with equality if and only if $p_k = q_k$ for all k. Though the log could be of any base, for the rest of this paper we use the natural log.

The *relative entropy* captures the informational distance between two proper probability distributions, but it is not a true distance as it is not symmetric: $D(P||Q) \neq D(Q||P)$. It reflects the gain in information resulting from the additional information in P relative to Q. It is an information-theoretic distance of P from Q that captures the inefficiency of assuming a priori that the distribution is Q when the correct distribution is P. It captures the overall information loss when using Q to approximate P. We note that in their original work Kullback and Leibler proposed the positive, symmetric information distance of $D(P||Q) + D(Q||P)$.

The continuous version of the relative entropy is

$$D(P||Q) = \int p(x) \log \frac{p(x)}{q(x)} dx \tag{2}$$

If we regard q_k and $q(x)$ as a prior distribution for the discrete or the continuous cases respectively, then we can generalize the maximum entropy formulation to include priors. In that case, rather than maximizing the entropy $H(p) = -\sum_{k=1}^{K} p_k \log p_k$ subject to the observed information, we minimize the entropy deficiency $D(P||Q)$ subject to the same constraints. This is known as the *cross entropy* formulation and is a generalization of Jaynes' (1957a, 1957b) principle of maximum entropy. See Shore and Johnson (1980) and Skilling (1989) for axiomatic derivation. The most important question is naturally, where these included priors are coming from. We discuss that issue in the next two sections, after formalizing the cross entropy. Specifically,

$$\begin{aligned}
&\underset{\{P\}}{Minimize}\, D(P||Q) = \sum_k p_k \log\left(p_k / q_k\right) \\
&subject\ to \\
&y_m = \sum_k p_k f_m(X_k);\ \ k=1,\ldots,K;\ M<K-1 \\
&\sum_k p_k = 1 \\
&p_k \geq 0
\end{aligned} \tag{3}$$

where f_m is a function of the X's (say the m variables or moments $m = 1, \ldots, M$), and the symbols y_m stand for expectation values. We view this set of constraints as *conservation rules* (or *conservation laws*) that must be satisfied. We want to infer p_k, $k = 1, 2, \ldots, K$, the probabilities of the K states. In the linear case, the constraints can be specified in vector notation as $\mathbf{y} = \mathbf{Xp}$, where $\mathbf{y}$ is an M-dimensional vector of expectation values, $\mathbf{X}$ is an $M \times K$ matrix of rank M, and $\mathbf{p}$ is an I-dimensional vector whose components are the unknown probabilities p_k. We note that X_m, or x_{mk}, are the magnitudes of the constraints; the expectations y_m must be within the range of these variables. The $\mathbf{X}$ and y_m (usually called $\mathbf{y}$) are commonly referred to as the *data* and constitute a core part of the input information used in this, and all other, inferential processes.

We have M variables (or moments or constraints) and we know that P is normalized. So all together there are $M+1$ observed pieces of information. Since $M < K-1$, we do not have enough equations to determine P uniquely and an inferential procedure is needed. The cross entropy optimization procedure is the one used here. Constructing the Lagrangian and solving, we get

$$\hat{p}_k = \frac{q_k \exp\left[\sum_{m=1}^{M} \hat{\lambda}_m f_m(X_k)\right]}{\sum_k q_k \exp\left[\sum_{m=1}^{M} \hat{\lambda}_m f_m(X_k)\right]} \equiv \frac{q_k \exp\left[\sum_{m=1}^{M} \hat{\lambda}_m f_m(X_k)\right]}{\Omega\left(\hat{\lambda}_1, \ldots, \hat{\lambda}_M\right)} \tag{4}$$

where the parameters of interest, $\hat{\lambda}_m$, are the inferred Lagrange multipliers associated with the M constraints (moments), $\Omega\left(\hat{\lambda}_1, \ldots, \hat{\lambda}_M\right) \equiv \sum_k q_k \exp\left[\sum_{m=1}^{M} \hat{\lambda}_m f_m(X_k)\right]$ is the normalization factor and "≡" stands for definition.

We note that this is a generalized version of the maximum entropy formulation. See the basic work of Jaynes (1957a) and Levine (1980) as well as extensions in Golan, Judge, and Miller (1996) and related discussion in Cover and Thomas (2006). Specifically, if the priors are uniform (i.e., $q_k = 1/K$ for all k) then this solution is equivalent to the maximal entropy one.

The normalization factor in Eq. (4), Ω, can be expressed as

$$\hat{\lambda}_0 = \log\left[\sum_k q_k \exp\left(\sum_{m=1}^{M} \hat{\lambda}_m f_m(X_k)\right)\right] \tag{5}$$

where $\hat{\lambda}_0$ is the Lagrange multiplier associated with the normalization constraint, $\sum_k p_k = 1$, and is a function of the other M multipliers.[1] The unconstrained, concentrated model (concentrated on the real parameters of interest – the M Lagrange multipliers, λ's) is[2]

$$
\begin{aligned}
\ell(\lambda) &= \sum_k p_k \log(p_k/q_k) + \sum_{m=1}^{M} \lambda_m \left[y_m - \sum_k p_k f_m(X_k) \right] \\
&= \sum_k p_k \log \left[\frac{q_k \exp\left[\sum_{m=1}^{M} \lambda_m f_m(X_k)\right]}{\sum_k q_k \exp\left[\sum_{m=1}^{M} \lambda_m f_m(X_k)\right]} \right] - \sum_k p_k \log(q_k) \\
&\quad + \sum_m \lambda_m \left[y_m - \sum_k p_k f_m(X_k) \right] \\
&= \sum_m \lambda_m y_m - \log\left[\sum_k q_k \exp\left[\sum_{m=1}^{M} \lambda_m f_m(X_k) \right] \right] \\
&= \sum_m \lambda_m y_m - \log[\Omega(\lambda_1, \ldots, \lambda_M)] \qquad (6)
\end{aligned}
$$

We have thus succeeded in transforming the model to be a function solely of the M Lagrange multipliers. The concentrated model (6) is just the dual of the constrained model (3). Maximizing (6) with respect to λ's yields the optimal λ's which in turn enable us to determine the desired p's via Eq. (4).

The traditional maximum entropy solution (where $q_k = 1/K$ for all k) yields the least informed solution out of all those that satisfy the constraints. In contrast, the cross entropy solution yields the solution (probability distribution) *that is closest to the prior distribution* yet still satisfies all of the constraints. The motivation for this formulation, diagnostics and inferential statistics are similar to those of the maximum entropy formulation and are not discussed here.[3] Once we have a way to incorporate priors within the info-metrics inferential problem, we need to turn our attention to determining these priors. This is what we do next.

As noted at the outset, using incorrect priors will result in solutions that may be far from the underlying truth. In statistical terms, the solution will be biased toward the prior. This is especially critical with the type of problems we discuss here that are most often underdetermined. If the priors are correct, or very close to the true priors, the cross entropy solution ensures a minimal bias even for underdetermined problems. Naturally, as with the Bayesian approach, the more data we have, the less impact the priors will have, but in the class of problems we discuss here where the problem is underdetermined and the insufficiency of the amount of data is severe, substantial bias is likely to exist whenever the priors are misspecified.

3. DISCRETE DISTRIBUTIONS: GROUPING PROPERTY

We start with the discrete prior distributions that emerge naturally from the physical properties of the system. We discuss the technical origin of the prior information. We provide here a specific example but one that arises very often in the natural sciences. Consider a set of $k = 1, \ldots, K$ events with associated probabilities $\{p_k\}$ and write its entropy as $-\sum_k p_k \log p_k$. We take the K events to be exhaustive and mutually exclusive so that $\sum_k p_k = 1$. Then, if no additional information is available we will infer that the distribution of maximal entropy is the uniform one, $p_k = 1/K$ where all the possible K events are equally likely. This is what we did in the previous section.

However, there are many situations where this answer is clearly incorrect. As a simple example consider tossing two dice, one black and one white. The two dice are independent of one another. Let k enumerate the sum of the two faces, $k = 2, 3, \ldots, 12$; thus there are $K = 11$ events. Even when the dice are perfectly tossed and are bias free, we expect that intermediate values of the sum, say $k = 6$, 7, or 8, are more probable than the extreme values $k = 2$ or 12. Our reasoning is that since there are 36 possible outcomes (black-white pairs) that map to 11 sums (events), some events correspond to more than one outcome of the experiment. For example, $k = 3$ can result under two scenarios: when the (black, white) faces of the two dice are (1, 2) or when they are (2,1). But the event $k = 2$ can occur only for the single outcome (1, 1) while $k = 4$ corresponds to three possible outcomes (1,3; 2,2; 3,1), etc. Our expectation is that the different results of tossing two independent dice (i.e., the 36 possible paired outcomes) are equally probable. That is, their joint probability is the product of their (individual) marginal probabilities. But if so, the probabilities p_k that the sum of the two faces is k cannot be equal for all values of k. Rather, even when no constraining information is available we expect that $p_k = n_k / \sum_k n_k$ where n_k is the number of ways in which the event k can be realized.

The situation we just described is common in the natural sciences where often the basic symmetry and structure of a problem lead us to be able to figure out the equally probable events. The mathematical tool to describe this symmetry is Shannon's grouping property (Shannon, 1948). A simple version of the grouping property (Cover & Thomas, 2006) is described as follows. Let P be a normalized K-dimensional discrete distribution with entropy $H(P)$. Let Q be a normalized $K-1$-dimensional discrete distribution with entropy $H(Q)$. We define the distribution Q to be the same as P for all elements but the last one. Thus, $q_1 = p_1, \ldots, q_{K-2} = p_{K-2}$ and $q_{K-1} = p_{K-1} + p_K$. The grouping property relates the entropy of P to that of Q with the appropriate weights. Specifically,

$$H(P) = H(Q) + (p_{K-1} + p_K)H\left(\frac{p_{K-1}}{(p_{K-1} + p_K)}, \frac{p_K}{(p_{K-1} + p_K)}\right)$$

Going back to the dice problem, consider the set of all "elementary" outcomes. By elementary we mean that if there are no constraints these outcomes are equally probable. In the case of the dice, this corresponds to all 36 pairs of combinations of the dice (the 36 dots in the left side of Fig. 1). We take the elementary outcomes to be exhaustive so that their probabilities sum to unity. We assume that the elementary outcomes can be grouped into disjoint sets (in this case, the k events) and that every elementary outcome belongs to one and only one set. The set of all elementary outcomes is often called the sample space. The a priori probability of a set number k, $p_k = n_k / \sum_k n_k$, is the number of dots within its boundaries, n_k, divided by the total number of elementary outcomes, that is, 36. A schematic graphical representation is provided in Fig. 1 where each elementary outcome is represented by a dot and a set is a bounded connected region.

In physics, the number n_k is called the "degeneracy" of the event k. It is the number of elementary outcomes that corresponds to the specification of this event. The grouping property allows us to express the entropy of the distribution of events in terms of the distribution $\{p_k\}$ of events k plus a term correcting for the grouping within the different sets. As we did previously, we use the index i to label the elementary outcomes. We can now specify the grouping property as

$$-\sum_i p_i \log p_i = -\sum_k p_k \log p_k + \sum_k p_k H_k \quad (7)$$

where H_k is the entropy of the distribution of events within the set k. It is helpful to view the grouping property as a weighted sum of the entropies of the events, $\sum_k p_k H_k$, plus a correction term for the uncertainty, $-\sum_k p_k \log p_k$. This term is often known as the *mixing entropy*. Unless the k events are themselves elementary, the mixing entropy is only a part of the entropy.

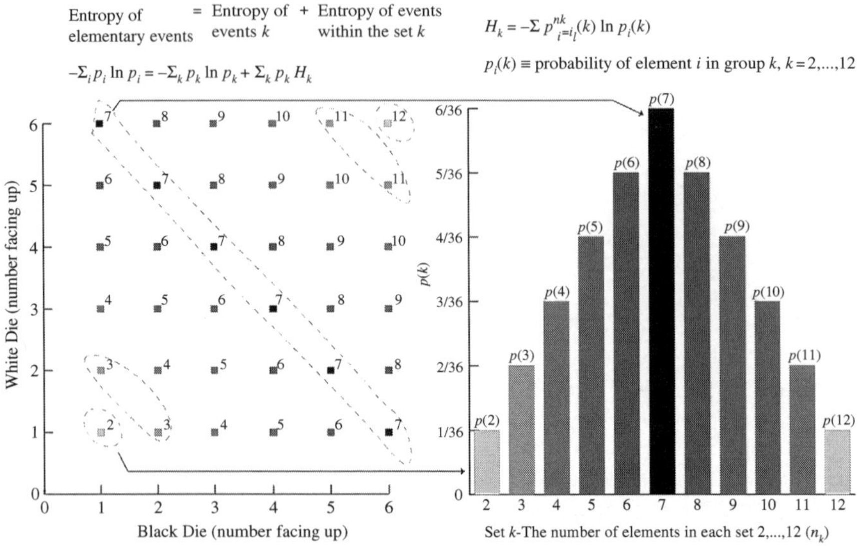

Fig. 1. The Two-Dice Example. *Notes*: A graphical representation of the relationship between elementary outcomes (represented by dots) and events. Each event contains at least one elementary outcome. Events with the same number on their top-right are members of the same set. For example, the two outcomes (1, 2) and (2, 1) are members of the event "$k = 3$" presented as a number on the top-right of each outcome on the left panel. The left panel captures the elementary outcomes – events relationship. Each outcome is a two-dimensional point capturing the number on the top face of each die. Each event is the sum of the numbers on the top faces of the two dice. The right panel shows the probability distribution of the events. The total number of elements in each set is n_k, known as the degeneracy of event k. From Eqs. (7) and later (9), we can calculate the different entropies in this case. The first element of the left-hand side of Eq. (7), the entropy of the elementary elements, $-\sum_i p_i \log p_i$, is 3.584. The first term on the right-hand side, entropy of the events k, $-\sum_k p_k \log p_k$, is 2.270 where the p_k's are 0.028, 0.056, 0.083, 0.111, 0.139, 0.167, 0.139, 0.111, 0.083, 0.056, and 0.028, respectively, for $k = 2, \ldots, 12$ (see right panel). The right-hand side $\sum_k p_k H_k$ is 1.314 (3.584 = 2.27 + 1.314).

Equation (7) is an identity; it is valid whenever we group elementary outcomes into sets (events).

We now discuss the special but quite common circumstance when a special form of the grouping becomes relevant. This is when the experiment can only provide an incomplete resolution of the states of the system. In the two-dice example, this occurs when we are only told the sum of the two faces.

The fundamental inference issue is then that we need to maximize the entropy as given by Eq. (7) without being given any information on the distribution within any one of the groups. When there is complete uncertainty about the distribution within any one of the k groups, the entropy of the distribution within the group must be maximal. This is equivalent to saying that all the n_k states within the group are equally probable. It follows then that $H_k = \log n_k$.

What is the distribution over events k when there are no constraints beyond normalization? We need to maximize Eq. (7) subject only to $\sum_k p_k = 1$. The result is $\log p_k = \log n_k - \lambda_0$ where the Lagrange multiplier λ_0 ensures the normalization (see Eq. (5)). Solving explicitly for λ_0 by using the normalization constraint yields

$$p_k \equiv p_k^0 = \frac{n_k}{\sum_k n_k} \tag{8}$$

We call the distribution $\{p_k^0\}$ the prior distribution. It is the appropriate distribution (i) when there is incomplete resolution of states, and (ii) when there is no additional information, captured in terms of constraints, on the system.

The grouping property (7) expressed now in terms of the prior distribution is

$$\begin{aligned} -\sum_i p_i \log p_i &= -\sum_k p_k \log p_k + \sum_k p_k H_k \\ &= -\sum_k p_k \log p_k + \sum_k p_k \log n_k \\ &= \log\left(\sum_k n_k\right) - \sum_k p_k \log\left(p_k/p_k^0\right) \end{aligned} \tag{9}$$

where the first right-hand side term of the bottom equation is just the entropy of the uniform distribution of dimension K. The structure of Eq. (9) is instructive. If all possible elementary outcomes are equally probable, the entropy should be at its global maximal value. This is the logarithm of the number of possible states. In our case, this is $\log\left(\sum_k n_k\right)$. So the second term in Eq. (9) has to be non-positive. But it is just $D(P||Q)$, the entropy deficiency defined in Eq. (1). It measures by how much the actual distribution deviates from the prior and it vanishes if and only if the prior is the actual distribution. The entropy deficiency is therefore useful in the special but common situation that the theoretical arguments or experimental evidence fail to fully resolve the states.

To demonstrate the more interesting, yet more complex, issue we extend the two-dice example in two ways. First, we look at the symmetric case (fair dice) but increase the number of dice. As the number of dice increases, the ratio of elementary outcomes to events increases, representing higher uncertainty of the possible grouping.[4] This is shown in Fig. 2 for the case of 2, 3, and 5 dice. In that figure, we present the possible events on the same support (x-axis). As expected, as the number of dice increases the location parameters (mean) shifts to the right while the scale parameter (variance) increases. Thus, the case of more than two dice is a straightforward extension of the formulas we derived for the two-dice case, using maximum entropy with equal probabilities for each of the elementary outcomes.

In the second extension of the two-dice example, we keep the number of dice fixed at two, but this time we generate our elementary outcomes under different symmetric and asymmetric scenarios. That is, we assume that the dice may be unfair (with mean different than 3.5) or that the dice have different distributions; they are biased in different ways. In this case, the elementary outcomes have unknown and possibly unequal probabilities. The only things we observe are the event distribution and the means of each die. This is shown in Fig. 3. For comparison, we also show the baseline symmetric two fair dice case (heavy black line). We present five different cases. The first is another symmetric case where the probability of each of the specific numbers on the first die is monotonically increasing ($p_6 > p_5 > \cdots > p_1$), while the second has probabilities that are monotonically decreasing ($p_1 > p_2 > \cdots > p_6$). The slope of the two lines is equal but with opposite signs (Exp A). For this case, suppose one die has a mean of 3, while the other has a mean of 4. The second case (Exp B) also has one increasing and one decreasing probability distribution but this time with different slopes corresponding to means of 3.1 and 4.3. The next case is composed of one fair die (with a mean of 3.5) and one monotonically increasing distribution with a mean of 4.3 (Exp C). The fourth case is two increasing distributions but with different slopes corresponding to means of 4.1 and 4.6, respectively (Exp D). The last case (Exp E) captures two monotonically decreasing distributions: one with a mean of 1.9 and the other

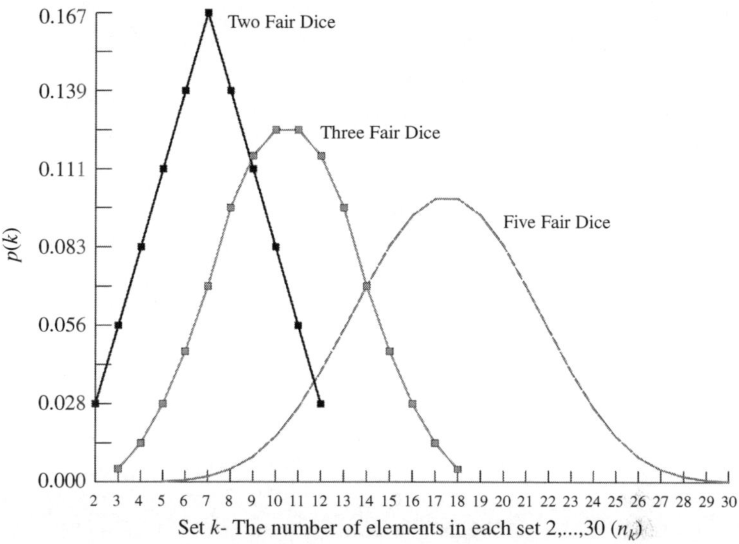

Fig. 2. Symmetric Distributions based on 2, 3, and 5 Fair Dice Presented on the Same Support. *Notes*: The dark line captures the two-dice case. The darker gray is based on 3 fair dice while the light gray distribution is the one resulting from five fair dice. Note the shift (to the right) of the mean and the increase in the variance as the number of dice increases.

with a mean of 2.3. With this information, using maximum entropy, we are able to recover the distribution of the elementary outcomes, subject to the moment conditions on the dice.

These examples capture the more realistic cases where our events of interest are composed of basic elements that were generated by different distributions.

How can these concepts be applied in a social science setting? As a simple analogy equivalent to our baseline two-dice example, consider a finite set (K) of different jobs, that requires a mix of experience (e.g., years in the labor market) and education, defined as categorical variables.[5] We would like to infer the probability distribution of the underlying population, in terms of their combination of experience and education, yet we do not observe these directly. At one end of the (discrete) job spectrum are those that require little experience or education, while at the other end are those that are highly specialized, requiring both large amounts of experience and education. Many jobs require a mix of both. Like the dice example,

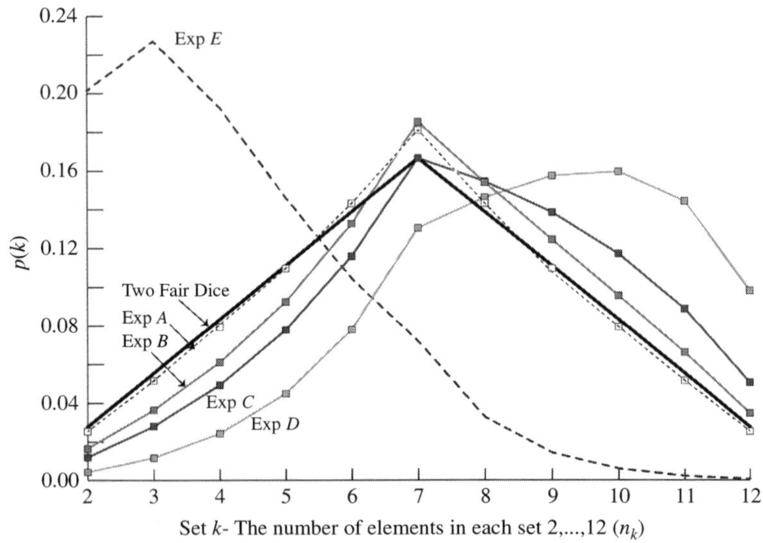

Fig. 3. Symmetric and Asymmetric Distributions Based on Two Dice with Different Means. *Notes*: The symmetric two fair dice ("baseline") case is the heavy black line. Another symmetric case is where the probabilities associated with the faces of the first die are monotonically increasing while the probabilities for the second die are monotonically decreasing but at the same rate. In this case, as with the baseline case, the slope of the two lines is equal but with different signs (Exp *A*, the dashed line). For this experiment, one die has a mean of 3 while the other has a mean of 4. The other scenarios result in asymmetric distributions. Like Exp *A*, Exp *B* also has one increasing and one decreasing distribution but with different slopes (so that the rate of increase/decrease differs), corresponding to means of 3.1 and 4.3 and resulting in an asymmetric distribution. The next scenario is composed of one fair die (with a mean of 3.5) and one monotonically increasing distribution with a mean of 4.3 (Exp *C*). The fourth scenario is composed of two increasing distributions but with different slopes corresponding to means of 4.1 and 4.6, respectively (Exp *D*). The last scenario (Exp *E*) is based on two monotonically decreasing distributions – one with a mean of 1.9 and the other with a mean of 2.3.

therefore, the probability distribution of jobs is not uniform; rather jobs that require a medium level of both experience and education are more prevalent than those that require neither or those that require high levels of both. As described above, our information can provide only a partial (incomplete) resolution of the states of the system. In this case, the grouping property can be useful to identify the probability distribution despite being unable to fully resolve the states.

Just as we were able to extend the two-dice example, we can similarly extend our social science example. First, suppose that there are more than two (categorical) variables that influence a probability distribution of events. One such example is the use of personal credit scores to evaluate the creditworthiness of potential borrowers. These scores typically depend on a (finite) set of criteria, but often the exact function that summarizes these criteria (i.e., the weights that a credit bureau assigns to each criterion to arrive at the score) is not observed; only the probability distribution of the score is observed. As the number of criteria increases, this underdetermined problem becomes more severe; because the number of possible ways to combine the criteria increases exponentially, there is higher uncertainty regarding the possible grouping.

As a second example, suppose we want to infer the distribution of firms' market share in a certain market based on the firms' inputs and outputs. As with the credit score example, this is a complicated problem because in reality firms have many inputs and many outputs. Despite its high dimension, however, the grouping property allows us to construct the priors. But, as with all problems, the resulting prior probability distribution is industry (or country) specific.

In addition, unlike the dice example, in these social science examples it is unlikely that the properties of (1) symmetry (e.g., [3,4] is equivalent to [4,3]) or (2) uniform elementary outcome probability distribution (i.e., each face of the die is equally likely), hold. In the credit score example, the age of the oldest debt is likely to receive a different weight than the type of debt; in addition, the histogram of different ages across borrowers likely differs from the histogram of different debt types that they use. In the firms' market share example, the amount of output produced by a firm with X capital units and Y labor units is likely to differ from that produced by a firm with Y capital units and X labor units; in addition, the distribution of possible amounts of capital may differ from that of possible amounts of labor. Thus, in social science examples, it is likely that the cases where the dice are unfair or each die has a different distribution will be more applicable.

3.1. A Simple Example

In order to demonstrate, in a very simple way, the advantage of using the grouping property when only partial data are observed, we return to the two-dice example presented earlier. We use this simulated example, rather than using real data, because it will be easier to discern the benefits from the results when the true (underlying) distribution is known. There is nothing specific about the choice of dice, however, and we can just as easily think of the dice as representing six different response choices, as described in the social science examples above.

Consider again the two-dice example presented earlier. We only observe the mean value, Y, of the sum of the two dice after tossing the two dice N times.[6] In particular, we do not have any information about the mean of each individual die, nor do we know whether each die is "fair." The degeneracies of the values (i.e., the number of combinations on the two dice, n_k, that correspond to each sum outcome, k, $k = 2, 3, \ldots, 12$) and priors are calculated from Eqs. (7)–(9). We use the maximum entropy procedure (3) to infer the unknown distribution of the 11 outcomes (see Fig. 1). For each of three different levels of the mean value, Y, we estimate two cases. The first is the simple maximum entropy with no priors (which is similar to using uniform priors, 1/11, for each group). In the second case, we use the grouping property to calculate priors and then use those priors within the maximum entropy method. Stated differently, using the exact same two constraints (i.e., the mean value of the N tosses and the maximum entropy normalization that the probabilities sum to one) in each case, we maximize Shannon's entropy in the first case and the bottom part of Eq. (9) – the cross entropy – in the second case.

Fig. 4 presents our results. With an observed mean of 7 ($Y = 7$), the maximum entropy solution with no priors is just the uniform distribution (the gray dashed line) across the 11 groups. In contrast, using the grouping property to calculate the prior distribution, we arrive at a distribution that is symmetric about group 7 (the gray solid line). In this informed case (with priors) we get a solution that is equal to the priors. In addition, this solution is equal to the true (theoretical) distribution in the case when we have two fair dice (i.e., with probability 1/6 that each specific face will be rolled on each die and the theoretical mean of the sum of the two dice equal to 7). Note that in both cases, in the absence of additional information, the resulting distributions are symmetric about the mean.

The next scenario we consider is with an observed mean of $Y = 8$. Because the mean is tilted toward the higher end of the outcome distribution, in this case the maximum entropy (uniform priors) case yields monotonically increasing probabilities (the red dashed line). In contrast, the solution when using the priors derived by employing the grouping property (the red solid line) is closer to both the distribution we derived in the $Y = 7$

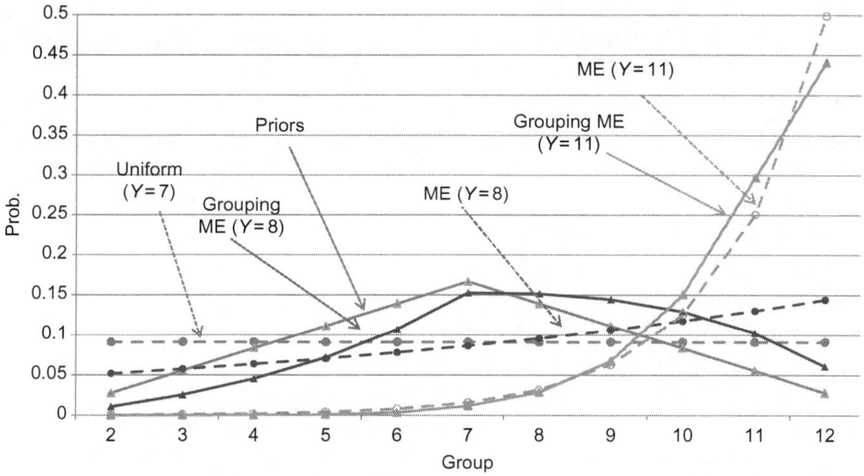

Fig. 4. Estimated Probabilities of the 11 Groups for the Two-Dice Example. *Notes*: Each group consists of all elements of the sum of the two dice. We calculate priors from the grouping property (Eqs. (7) and (9)). Using the observed information in terms of the means of the sum of the two dice (after N tosses) we present three scenarios. Each scenario consists of two cases. The information used in each case is exactly the same. The first case is the maximum entropy estimates where no priors are used (or equivalently the priors of the different groups are equally likely, i.e., we ignore the "grouping property"). The second is the cross entropy case where we maximize Eq. (9) rather than just the entropy. The first scenario (the gray lines, $Y = 7$) is where the observed mean value (Y) is 7. Application of the maximum entropy approach results in a uniform distribution where each group is equally likely (dashed gray line). This is the expected result in the absence of any additional information. If, on the other hand, we use the cross entropy (grouping) model, then the results we obtain are equivalent to the true probability distribution (see gray solid line – labelled 'priors'). The other two scenarios are for $Y = 8$ and $Y = 11$, that is, where the observed mean is either 8 or 11. In both cases, the simple ME estimates (dashed lines) are increasing monotone probabilities while those for the grouping case (solid lines) are always closer to the priors that we have estimated. Due to the symmetry (about $Y = 7$) of the problem we just present here scenarios of $Y \geq 7$. Note that if $Y = 2$ or 12, both the maximum entropy and grouping approaches will yield the correct solution of probability of one on group 2 or 12, respectively.

case and the true distribution when we have two fair dice. The reason for this difference (from the maximum entropy solution) is that the distribution derived using cross entropy and priors constructed via the grouping property takes into account the uncertainty that arises from our observed mean (i.e., the likelihood that we observe a mean of 8 when the true population mean is 7). In this way, the grouping property allows for the possibility that our prior information (the observed mean) is incorrect.

We next consider the case when the observed mean is very far from the mean that might be expected if both dice were fair dice, $Y = 11$. The results are qualitatively similar (see the blue dashed and solid lines), in that again the distribution derived using priors derived by the grouping property is closer to the distribution of two fair dice than the maximum entropy solution. In both cases, however, the probability densities are quite skewed toward the higher outcomes, reflecting the higher observed mean and the likelihood that the dice are not actually fair.

In general, the further is the observed mean value from the true (unbiased) mean ($Y = 7$), assuming the dice are fair, the further are the solutions from the correct ("unobserved") values since the solution will be biased toward the prior information we use. In the case of the maximum entropy solution, the observed information includes the observed mean value (moment) and the uniform (uninformed – and in this specific example, incorrect) priors. Under cross entropy, the observed information includes the same observed moment but more informed (non-uniform) priors. In our example, we construct these priors via the grouping property. Thus, the cross entropy solution is a more informed one. If the priors we use are correct, than the solution has a smaller bias relative to the maximum entropy solution. In all cases in this example, using the priors calculated via the grouping property results in improved solutions. For example, if the two dice are in fact fair dice, the mean-squared error (MSE) for the observed mean of $Y = 7$ is 0.002 and exactly zero, respectively, for the maximum entropy and the cross entropy cases. For $Y = 8$, these are 0.003 and 0.001, respectively, while for $Y = 11$ the MSEs are 0.031 and 0.028, respectively. Note that for $Y = 2$ or $Y = 12$, the solutions of both models (with or without priors) are similar regardless of the model or prior used. This is because in these extreme cases, the probability of groups 2 or 12 is exactly 1.

This example illustrates the potential gain from using the grouping property to construct priors and then estimating the unobserved distribution, using these priors, given incomplete (aggregate level) information versus the simple maximum entropy approach that ignores the uncertainty inherent in our prior information.

So far our discussion about prior information and how to incorporate this within the maximum entropy formulation has concentrated only on inferring discrete probability distributions, where the grouping property can be used. However, the grouping property cannot be applied to continuous distributions where the number of possible events is infinite. We therefore must take a different approach for constructing priors in the continuous case. We do this in the next section.

But before summarizing the approach we take, we emphasize that there is already much discussion in the literature about the requirement to incorporate the correct prior information when estimating continuous parameters arising from different data-generating processes governed by continuous density functions. Constructing these priors is, most often, not trivial. For some classical examples in econometrics, see the seminal work and discussion therein of Shiller (1973), Zellner and Richard (1973) and within general economic modeling, Sims (1980). Within the natural sciences see Jaynes (1968) and Dose (2003), as well as the general summary by Kass and Wasserman (1996) and Dawid (1983). In our discussion below, we concentrate on deriving priors via the logic of transformation (invariance) groups.

4. TRANSFORMATION GROUPS OR TRANSFORMATION INVARIANCE

In this section, we provide a brief summary of one unique way to construct priors, inspired by the work of Jaynes (1968) that is quite different from the commonly used methods. Unlike our earlier discussion that concentrated on discrete priors for information theoretic approaches, the discussion here deals with priors for inference of continuous parameters, and continuous random variables, within all possible inferential methods. We discuss here the principle of group transformation (or transformation invariance) for deriving prior probability distributions. This is particularly useful in situations where it is not possible to reduce the problem via a finite number of groupings and hence the grouping property cannot be employed (i.e., in a continuous problem where the degrees of freedom is infinitely large), although it can also be used for inference in problems with discrete distributions. Our objective here is to introduce readers to this novel way of thinking by (i) highlighting the intuition behind constructing these priors, and (ii) providing a very fundamental idea, via simple examples, of how to construct these priors. Further development of these ideas as they relate to specific economic examples is left for further research.

With this in mind, we now turn our attention to the problem of inferring a (continuous) density function from a small number of expectation values (i.e., from a set of M linearly independent variables, e.g., moments). As with the discrete case discussed above, the problem is underdetermined because M is smaller than the number of possible states, K, but in the continuous case the challenge is greater because K is infinite (and possibly uncountable) – hence the grouping property cannot be used. Instead, we use an alternative approach. The method, known as transformation groups, is based on the mathematical notion of group theory and can be used for both discrete and continuous distributions.[7]

The motivation for this approach is that we want to determine priors for inferential problems involving continuous random variables that reflect our complete uncertainty about the problem and do not alter the fundamental structure of the problem. Unlike with the grouping property where events themselves are transformed (grouped), the method of transformation groups involves not a transformation on events, but rather a transformation of the problem into an equivalent one. This approach is analogous to the idea of introducing a nuisance parameter and then arriving at a solution that is invariant to that parameter. In other words, we want to identify prior information that is invariant under certain transformations and therefore reflects our uncertainty about the quantities of interest.

Though the mathematics can become somewhat complicated, the logic is a simple extension (to problems, rather than events) of Laplace's principle of indifference to the *events*, also known as the "principle of insufficient reason." Laplace's principle of indifference (or insufficient reason) instructs us to assign equal probabilities to all events unless we know that a priori some events are more probable than others. This is also the logic underlying the maximum entropy principle and was straightforward to apply in settings with a finite number of discrete events, as discussed above. But this is practically impossible to do in the continuous case, so one must resort to other approaches, such as transformation groups. With transformation groups, we analogously apply the indifference principle among *problems* (rather than events), assigning equal probabilities to all problems. That is, if the problem is specified carefully, than indifference among similar problems is determined by the specification of the problem and is independent of our possibly misleading prior information. The solution must be invariant to any part of the problem that is not explicitly specified in the statement of the problem.

To demonstrate the idea, we return to our simple, discrete, example. We are given a six-sided die. The only information we have is that it is a cube with six equally sized, square, faces with the numbers 1 through 6 on each face. We want to infer the probability that after rolling the die the uppermost face of the die is 1: $p(1|I)$ where I is the information we have. With the same information we can also infer $p(2|I)$ or in general $p(i|I)$ for $i = 1, 2, \ldots, 6$. But the information we have at hand does not allow us to distinguish between these probabilities. In fact, we can reassign the six numbers on the different faces as we wish, or similarly we can transform the numbers to 7 through 12. Therefore, by Laplace's principle of indifference, it must be that $p(1|I) = p(2|I) = \cdots = p(6|I)$. We also know that $\sum_{i=1}^{6} p(i|I) = 1$. Therefore, it must be that $p(i|I)/\left[\sum_{i=1}^{6} p(i|I)\right] = 1/6$.

Consider now a simple continuous example due to Jaynes (1968). Let $\{x_1, \ldots, x_n\}$ be a sample of n observations generated from a population characterized by a two parameter distribution. We want to infer two population parameters, namely, the mean μ, known also as the location parameter, and the standard deviation σ, known as the scale parameter from an (unknown) density function. We want to estimate the underlying density function with possibly an infinite number of moments, given the two values (an observed mean and an observed standard deviation) that we know. The only other thing we know is that we can characterize a two parameter distribution as

$$p(dx|\mu, \sigma) = f(x; \mu, \sigma)dx = \frac{1}{\sigma}h\left(\frac{x - \mu}{\sigma}\right)dx \tag{10}$$

To improve our density estimation – originally an underdetermined problem – we can make use of this additional structure. But we are worried about introducing a prior distribution that is possibly incorrect, since we know that our inference will depend on that prior distribution. What prior should we choose given our state of complete uncertainty?

To mitigate our concern about introducing a possibly incorrect prior distribution, we want first to construct the most uninformed priors for the two parameters about which we have information and then to incorporate these priors into the density estimation. To do so, we use the transformation group approach.

We start by explicitly specifying the information given to us in the problem. The only thing we know is that our sample came from Eq. (10); therefore the two parameters must be the location and scale parameters. Do we know anything else? For example, would a shift in location make the problem appear different to us? If so, it must be that we have more information about the location than we originally thought. Similarly, would a change of scale make the problem seem different to us? If so, we must have some knowledge about the absolute magnitude of the scale of that problem. Stated in terms of our uncertainty, our complete uncertainty about the location and scale parameters captures our state of knowledge about whether a shift in location or a change in scale, or both, would change that state of knowledge. So, we can use that information to construct unbiased priors that will improve our inference about the problem. To do so, we transform our variables (x, μ, σ) to (x', μ', σ') via the following relationships:

$$\begin{aligned} \mu' &= \mu + c \\ \sigma' &= a\sigma \\ (x' - \mu') &= a(x - \mu) \end{aligned} \tag{11}$$

where $c \in (-\infty, \infty)$ and $a \in (0, \infty)$. We call this transformation group (11). Now, "invariance" means that the sampling distributions of the original and transformed variables must be the same. (We have the same information on both.) Thus, we can now rewrite Eq. (10) in terms of the transformed variables

$$p(dx'|\mu', \sigma') = h(x'; \mu', \sigma')dx' = \frac{1}{\sigma'} h\left(\frac{x' - \mu'}{\sigma'}\right) dx' \tag{12}$$

The transformed prior distribution can then be written as $g(\mu', \sigma')d\mu' d\sigma'$. Using the rules of transformation of variables, the transformation group (11) yields the unique relationship among the two sets of priors:

$$g(\mu', \sigma') = a^{-1} f(\mu, \sigma) \tag{13}$$

We now restate our problem as follows. Consider a sample of n observations $\{x_1', \ldots, x_n'\}$. We want to infer μ' and σ'. If our complete information (i.e., what we know about this new problem) is exactly the same as with the original problem, or stated differently, if our level of uncertainty (i.e., what we do not know) regarding each one of these two problems is exactly the same, then the two problems must be equivalent: they come from the same underlying distribution (population). Therefore, both cases must be inferred with the same (unknown) prior information. This implies that the prior information arising from μ' and σ' must be the same as that on μ and σ. But, if the two equivalent problems are derived from the same prior information, logical consistency requires that the two must have the same prior probabilities. Thus, $f(\cdot)$ and $g(\cdot)$ must be equal:

$$f(\mu,\sigma) = g(\mu',\sigma') = g(\mu,\sigma) \tag{14}$$

for all values of a and c. Combining Eqs. (11), (13), and (14), the functional form of $f(\cdot)$ must satisfy $f(\mu,\sigma) = af(\mu + c, a\sigma)$. This problem has the solution

$$f(\mu,\sigma) \propto \sigma^{-1} \tag{15}$$

Note that this solution is solely due to the transformation group (11) that we employed and not due to our original specification of Eq. (10). In particular, our inference problem could have been solved without specifying (10). Under transformation group (11), the prior for this problem is the known Jeffreys prior (Jeffreys, 1946, 1961). Different transformations will result in different priors as they capture different levels of uncertainties about the unknown parameters.

In discussing this example, we presumed to know nothing about the possible values of the location and scale parameters, that is, applying Laplace's principle of indifference, all were equally likely. Naturally, in most, if not all, problems in practice, we do have some magnitudes in mind. We know something about the possible "coordinates" of the location and magnitude of scale (or other) parameters. Thus, our invariance group does not vary over an infinite range (although it still may correspond to an infinite number of possible values). In this case, we refer to the invariance of both a and c. Such knowledge should be incorporated in the specification of the problem. Information of this type helps to narrow the range of invariance that is required.

We can now relate this to other common problems.

Assume we are indifferent about the possible transformation $\mu' = \mu + a$ where μ is the quantity of interest and a is a constant. Let $p(\mu)d\mu$ be an infinitesimal probability mass for μ in the range $d\mu$. Translation (or "group") invariance implies, in this case, that this mass value remains unchanged if we express it in terms of the translation μ'. In other words,

$$p(\mu)d\mu = p(\mu')d\mu' = p(\mu + a)d\mu$$

where the second equality holds because $d\mu = d\mu'$ since $da = 0$. Now, for the above equality to hold for any a it must be the case that $p(\mu)$ is equal for all values of μ (from $-\infty$ to $+\infty$). As a side point, though it is invariant and convenient, this prior is known in the literature as an "improper" one (e.g., Jeffreys, 1961; Kass & Wasserman, 1996; Lindley, 1973). Therefore, such a prior can be viewed as the limit for $\Delta\mu \to \infty$ of $p(\mu) = 1/\Delta\mu$, where $\Delta\mu$ is a large finite range about the values of interest.

As a second example consider a Poisson process of a random variable X

$$P(x; \lambda t) = \frac{(\lambda t)^x e^{-\lambda t}}{x!}, \quad x = 1, 2, \ldots$$

Without any other information, we must assume that the process is invariant under time scale, t, transformation. Therefore, our prior density on the parameter λ (which is both the mean and variance in this case) must obey $f(\lambda) = qf(q\lambda)$, so the prior density on λ is just $f(\lambda) \propto \lambda^{-1}$. Simply stated, two observers that observe the same process, but count the measurements with watches that run at different rates (t and t^*) must have the same underlying prior density. This is because their measurements for a given time interval are related via $t = qt^*$, their rate constants are related via $\lambda^* t^* = \lambda t$, or $\lambda^* = q\lambda$, and therefore they must be using the same prior information.

Drawing now on an example from economics, consider the distribution of wealth, or GDP, that is characterized as a *scale free* distribution, that is, the distribution is invariant to a change in scaling of the unit of measurement. Scale free distributions can be described via a *power law,* a scenario whereby growth occurs in a manner proportional to the existing level of wealth, giving rise to a "rich get richer" model. A wide variety of natural phenomena across many different disciplines have been shown to exhibit power law features (e.g., Clauset, Shalizi, & Newman, 2009). But, empirically, in most cases such distributions have been shown to behave as power laws only beyond a certain value. This is commonly observed with economic data. Examples include the distribution of GDP across countries or the distribution of wealth within a country.

The power law distribution captures the common occurrence that some measurements are invariant to the choice of the scale. Such a distribution has a wider (right-hand side) tail, meaning that moving farther out the tail is associated with an order of magnitude difference in the level of say, wealth or GDP, or in more general terms a variable X (with values x). Thus, in this case (and in power law cases more generally), an uninformed prior, say uniform, will not work because it will fail to capture the order of magnitude difference that the power law implies. So instead we can use a uniform prior of $\log(x)$, that is transformation invariant, resulting in a prior for X that is proportional to $1/x$. Note the similarity to the first example yielding the Jeffreys prior for the scale parameter. This makes sense as in both cases we are dealing with the scale of the distribution.

The concepts we are describing here are relevant to a wide variety of economic problems, in particular those that involve a structural model, usually specified via a system of (interconnected) equations. Such systems as initially specified are inherently underdetermined and require additional assumptions (a priori restrictions) to "identify" the model. These restrictions are a type of prior information; inference depends critically on the assumption that such information is correct.[8]

To summarize the idea we can view the notion of constructing priors via transformation groups as follows. The Laplace principle of indifference is about events. But choosing priors for a (possibly infinite) set of events is not always possible and may result in choosing inappropriate priors if our intuition misleads us.[9] And even if our intuition is correct, it may differ from that of our neighbor, resulting in two different priors for exactly the same problem. The transformation group, on the other hand, deals with indifference among problems and hence does not suffer from the possible deficiencies of the Laplace principle of indifference about events.[10] The indifference among problems is specified precisely, is independent of personal intuition, and, if specified correctly, has a unique solution.

The prior information we obtain from transformation groups only captures an idealized state of knowledge that is based on the exact specification of the problem. We need that prior information (specifically, we can even think of it as a pre-prior) in order to define an invariant measure on our parameter space. Once we have this invariant measure, other info-metrics procedures can be applied, such as the maximum entropy one, to solve the specific problem.

4.1. Example – Prior for a Straight Line

Consider a straight line (regression) represented with one parameter: $y = \beta x + u$ where y is the dependent variable, x is the independent variable, β is the parameter of interest, and u is a mean zero noise. We do not assume anything else about u. We want to impose minimal structure on β in the sense that all possibilities that are consistent with the observed information are equally likely, as long as they are consistent with the specification of the problem. In the die case above this approach led us to conclude that all faces must have the same probability (because the way the problem was specified there was no reason to suspect any other probability structure). That is, each face of the die could be obtained by a simple "transformation" (i.e., a roll of the die). In the regression context, we similarly argue that the equally likely "space" for the parameter β is in terms of coordinate transformation. To keep the formulation as simple as possible while concentrating on our core topic of interest – a prior for β – from here on we ignore u as it does not affect the transformation. So we specify the problem as $y = \beta x$.

This simple linear regression example is based on the work of Dose (2003), with an application to surface physics by Van Toussaint and Dose (2006). Note that this formulation of the problem concentrates our uncertainty on the parameter of interest, β. In the classical framework, the regression problem is specified in terms of a prior distribution for the error term u; such a specification places uncertainty on the noise, rather than the substance of the problem.

To find a prior with a minimal amount of structure, we consider a second problem with exactly the same information (i.e., the data x and y) as the first. In this case, the transformation group we use is a simple rotation transformation on the axes, that is we transform pairs of data (x, y) to (x', y'). As with the location – scale example above, we have the requirement that the prior $p(\beta)d\beta$ is the same (free of the coordinates) in both problems. That is,

$$p(\beta')d\beta' = p(\beta)d\beta \tag{16}$$

where β' is the parameter of interest in the similar (transformed) problem $y' - \beta' x' = 0$.

In this example, we use the following concept discussed nicely in Dose (2003) that simplifies the transformation process. The overall idea follows on the transformation of variables formula. Any transformation problem from one set of coordinates to another requiring the above equality (16) to hold is captured in the functional form

$$p(\beta) = p(\beta')\left|\frac{\partial \beta'}{\partial \beta}\right| \tag{17}$$

where the right-hand side is the Jacobian.[11] Following Dose (2003) we can simplify this calculation if we use the fact that any finite transformation can be constructed as a sequence of infinitesimal transformations. Therefore, it is sufficient to consider only one of these infinitesimal transformations (of size $\varepsilon > 0$). Let $T_\varepsilon(\beta)$ be that infinitesimal transformation of β to β'. We can rewrite the above transformation as

$$p(\beta) = p(T_\varepsilon(\beta))\left|\frac{\partial T_\varepsilon(\beta)}{\partial \beta}\right|$$

where the right-hand side is a function of ε while the left side is not. Differentiating with respect to ε and equating to zero satisfies our requirement for transformation invariance. Note that the process of getting to the result is similar to what we derived previously, though the current transformation is simpler and more elegant.

Going back to our problem, rather than a location-shift transformation, it makes sense in this case to consider a rotation transformation. Let ω be the angle of rotation between the coordinates (x, y) and the coordinates (x', y'). We can now express this rotation as

$$\begin{aligned} x' &= x\cos\omega - y\sin\omega \cong x - \varepsilon y \\ y' &= x\sin\omega + y\cos\omega \cong \varepsilon x + y \end{aligned}$$

where "$\cong$" stands for approximation. We can now write (x, y) in terms of (x', y'):

$$\begin{aligned} x &= x' + \varepsilon y' \\ y &= -\varepsilon x' + y' \end{aligned} \tag{18}$$

Recalling that $y - \beta x = 0$, we multiply both sides by -1 and substitute the expressions on the right-hand side of Eq. (18) into that equality to get

$$-y + \beta x = \varepsilon x' - y' + \beta(x' + \varepsilon y') = 0$$

We can now represent β' in terms of β. We do so by first grouping the x' and y' terms to get $x'(\beta + \varepsilon) - y'(1 + \beta\varepsilon) = 0$. Dividing both sides by $(1 + \beta\varepsilon)$ and moving y' to the other side we get $\frac{\beta+\varepsilon}{1-\beta\varepsilon}x' = y'$. Recalling that

$\beta' x' = y'$, this implies that $\beta' = (\beta + \varepsilon)/(1 - \beta\varepsilon)$ which is approximately (up to second order in ε) equal to $\beta + \varepsilon(1 + \beta^2)$.

The Jacobian of the transformation $\partial\beta'/\partial\beta$ is $(1 + 2\beta\varepsilon)$. We now differentiate with respect to ε, evaluate this derivative at $\varepsilon = 0$, and equate the result to zero:

$$\frac{d}{d\varepsilon}\{p(\beta + \varepsilon(1 + \beta^2))(1 + 2\beta\varepsilon)\}_{\varepsilon=0} = 0$$

This yields the differential equation

$$p'(\beta^2 + 1) + 2\beta p = 0$$

Solving this equation and making sure the p's are normalized so that they sum to one, yields the desired prior

$$p(\beta) = \frac{1}{\pi}\left(\frac{1}{1 + \beta^2}\right)$$

where the first term on the right-hand side is due to the normalization of the probabilities $p(\beta)$ to sum to one. That is, the factor $1/\pi$ is a consequence of the normalization (Dose, 2003). The intuition is as follows. The coefficient β can be viewed as $\beta = \tan(\omega)$ where ω is the angle of the straight line with respect to the positive x-axis. Therefore, the distribution of ω, specified via Eq. (18) is just $p(\omega) = 1/\pi$ and explains the normalization in the above equation.

Conceptually, the structure of the priors is very simple. The angles (ω) of the straight lines from the x-axis are distributed uniformly, as we expect given the information we had about the problem. Via a change of coordinates, we preserve the uniform distribution by creating a transformation that is linear.

This framework can be extended for analyzing linear and other regressions, including any log transformation of the data, such as the commonly used Cobb–Douglas function. But these extensions are not trivial and involve more than just log-linearizing, or just transforming, the data. Such a problem is outside the scope of this paper which just highlights the potential of priors emerging from the use of transformation groups.

5. DISCUSSION

We have arrived at priors via a procedure that is similar to that of the maximum entropy solution, where the only information imposed is the information that is already well established (from theory or observation) for the particular problem or system with no additional constraints imposed. Stated slightly differently, a prior distribution in our context is the distribution with maximum entropy when constraints that are special to the system at hand are not imposed. The benefits of using such priors are that by reducing the entropic deficiency, we reduce the potential bias that arises from using an incorrect prior. We discuss this in more detail below.

5.1. Maximum Entropy Priors

The principle of Maximum Entropy (Jaynes, 1957a, 1957b) is often used for constructing prior distributions, especially within a Bayesian framework. See for example the discussion in Jaynes (1968), the nice set of papers in Levine and Tribus (1979) and the more recent summary of Dawid (1983) and Kass and Wasserman (1996).

Generally speaking, within the maximum entropy framework, the priors are constructed based solely on universal information, such as that a distribution is characterized only by a scale and location parameters. Or, similarly, the distribution is characterized by an arithmetic, or logarithmic, mean and normalization, which takes us to the exponential or power law distributions respectively. In fact, most of the literature (see references in the previous paragraph) on priors uses the maximum entropy approach to construct the least informed priors that are then used within other statistical approaches. We provide here one simple example.

Let X be a continuous random variable with possible values over the whole real line, $(-\infty, \infty)$, and with the two moments $\int xf(x)dx = \mu$ and $\int (x-\mu)^2 f(x)dx = \sigma^2$. If we maximize the differential entropy, $H(X) = -\int f(x)\log f(x)dx$, subject to these moment constraints and normalization, we get the normal distribution. But it can be derived in a simpler way.

Suppose we know the variance σ^2 but we don't know the mean (though we know that a finite mean must exist if a finite variance exists). Maximizing the differential entropy (i.e., optimizing the Lagrangian) subject to that single constraint $\int (x-\mu)^2 f(x)dx = \sigma^2$ and normalization yields the solution

$$f(x) = \exp\left(-1-\lambda_0-\lambda_1(x-\mu)^2\right) = \frac{\exp\left(-\lambda_1(x-\mu)^2\right)}{\int_{-\infty}^{\infty}\exp\left(-\lambda_1(x-\mu)^2\right)dx}$$

where λ_1 is the Lagrange multiplier associated with the variance constraint and λ_0 is the multiplier associated with the normalization. Substituting this solution into the constraint on σ^2, we can now express the constraint as

$$\int_{-\infty}^{\infty}(x-\mu)^2 f(x)dx - \sigma^2 = 0$$
$$= \int_{-\infty}^{\infty}(x-\mu)^2\frac{\exp\left(-\lambda_1(x-\mu)^2\right)}{\int_{-\infty}^{\infty}\exp\left(-\lambda_1(x-\mu)^2\right)dx} - \sigma^2$$

Solving for λ_1 yields $\lambda_1 = 1/2\sigma^2$ and the resulting normalized density function is

$$f(x) = \frac{1}{\sigma\sqrt{2\pi}}\exp\left(-\frac{(x-\mu)^2}{2\sigma^2}\right)$$

which is the familiar normal density function (see Appendix B for a more detailed derivation). It has the entropy

$$H(f) = -\int f\ln f = -\int f(x)\left[-(x^2/2\sigma^2) - \ln\sqrt{2\pi\sigma^2}\right]$$
$$= \frac{EX^2}{2\sigma^2}+\frac{1}{2}\ln\left(2\pi\sigma^2\right) = \frac{1}{2}+\frac{1}{2}\ln\left(2\pi\sigma^2\right) = \frac{1}{2}\ln e+\frac{1}{2}\ln\left(2\pi\sigma^2\right)$$
$$= \frac{1}{2}\ln\left(2\pi e\sigma^2\right).$$

We have shown that the constraint $\int xf(x)dx = \mu$ is not necessary and that we arrive at the same solution for the density by maximizing the entropy subject only to the variance σ^2 (and normalization). This is because the differential entropy is translational invariant, meaning $H(X + Constant) = H(X)$ for any constant. For more derivations and examples along these lines, see the vast literature on the maximum entropy formulations such as Cover and Thomas (2006), Soofi (2000) or Soofi and Retzer (2002) as well as Golan (forthcoming).

5.2. Empirical Priors

A common problem in the social sciences is that theory often cannot inform our choice of prior information. In these cases we are forced to derive such information empirically. This may come from previous experiments or from other similar systems. This paper emphasizes that we need to use this empirically derived prior information with caution. It is also necessary to confirm the robustness of our results to small changes in this prior information.

Finally, we must connect our discussion to the literature on "perfect" priors constructed from some universal information that characterizes a whole family of problems. In the empirical case, it is harder to construct such priors. What we do in this case here is observe as many possible empirical situations that emerge from similar systems and look for the commonalities. If we find those, we can construct the prior information accordingly and at least mitigate the inferential impact that results from using incorrect prior information. These issues fall outside the scope of the current discussion and are to be further developed in future work.

6. CONCLUDING REMARKS

We discussed two fundamental ways, and mentioned two others, of constructing prior information for use in inferential problems. In each case the fundamental issue is how to do that while using only the information which comes from our understanding of the system, or problem, together with other logical consistency arguments, and without incorporating additional information. Part of the challenge is that each problem is different. Each problem demands understanding of the information known and of the process that takes place. For example, in the grouping property discussion we need to understand both the basic process that generates the elementary outcomes and the process by which these outcomes are transformed into the events (groups) of interest. That information comes from the economics, physics, biology or other properties of the system. But often some of that information (i.e., either the process that generates the elementary outcomes, or the process by which the outcomes are transformed, or both processes) is missing which increases the uncertainty and therefore makes the problem harder to analyze.

Within the transformation group procedure the major issue is what transformation group to use. It must be one that satisfies what we know about the system such that the invariance is in line with the specification of the problem. In this case we usually have less information then in the grouping case.

Under the maximum entropy prior construction we have assumed that we have the exact information about the family of distributions. Imposing the correct moment constraints (e.g., variance for the normal, or normalization for the uniform) allows us to arrive at the needed priors.

In our discussion here we did not touch on all possible ways of constructing prior information. Rather, we concentrated on constructing prior information that is useful for inference about a wide variety of problems and is not well known in the econometrics literature. In addition, we provided a few simple theoretical examples for understanding the theories we discussed, as well as highlighting a few empirical situations where these techniques might be used. Further extensions and empirical applications are the subject of our next paper on this topic.

NOTES

1. For ease of exposition in the equation below, we suppress the dependence of the probabilities, p_i, on the Lagrange multipliers (λ) but emphasize that this dependence is important in being able to transform the constrained model in the way we describe.

2. For the complete derivation, including all intermediate steps, see Appendix A.

3. For a good discussion see Golan (2008), Cover and Thomas (2006) and the references they provide.

4. Generally speaking, if we have d S-sided dice, the number of elementary outcomes is S^d while the number of events is $(S-1)d+1$. Thus, the number of elementary outcomes increases exponentially with the number of dice while the number of events increases only linearly.

5. The analogy is immediate when the two variables consist of six categories each, with each category equally likely, as when the categories are defined by percentile rankings (e.g., 1/6 of the population is in each category). For the purposes of the analogy to the baseline example, the categories are independently determined; in reality, however, we recognize that education and experience may be correlated.

6. The actual number of tosses, N, does not affect the resulting estimated distribution. It does, however affect the confidence interval around these estimates. Here, we are only concerned about the estimated values.

7. Within the context of assigning prior probabilities, the transformation group discussion is based on the work of Jaynes (1968) and on earlier work of Kendall and Moran (1963). It goes back to the mathematical notion of group theory and transformation of variables or transformation of groups. For more recent summary of invariant priors, see Dawid (1983). A nice summary, with many examples, on ways to construct priors, as well as transformation groups, is provided in Kass and Wasserman (1996).

8. For concrete examples underlying our discussion in this paragraph, we refer the reader to the seminal Sims (1980) paper criticizing identification claims in structural macroeconomic models of supply and demand. Specifically, Sims notes that identification of the structural form of a model (derived from economic theory) is usually achieved via some kind of "normalization" (e.g., a reduced form transformation, a triangular decomposition, orthogonalization of the residuals) and that a variety of different normalizations are admissible. The choice of normalization is an example of what we term "prior information." Sims goes further to refer to "the crutch of supposed a priori knowledge," noting that, "… the restrictions imposed in the usual style of identification are neither essential to constructing a model which can perform these functions nor innocuous; an alternative style of identification is available and practical."

9. For example, in the dice case above, it is difficult to choose correct priors for the events (representing the sum of numbers rolled on a set of dice) if we have incorrect priors regarding the "fairness" (or more generally the underlying probability distribution) of each die.

10. Namely, that we may end up with incorrect priors or two different priors for the exact same problem.

11. Although, for simplicity, we use a simple univariate linear example, it should be obvious from Eq. (16) that our discussion can be easily generalized to the multivariate linear regression problem $y = X\boldsymbol{\beta} + u$, where $\boldsymbol{\beta}$ is instead a whole vector of coefficients. In the discussion that follows, the extension to the multivariate problem is immediate (e.g., we can consider an ε ball), although notationally more cumbersome – hence, the reason for focusing our exposition on the univariate case.

ACKNOWLEDGMENTS

This paper has benefitted from discussions with Ansgar Wohlschlegel and conference participants at the Conference of Advances in Econometrics: Essays in Honor of Aman Ullah (13–15 March 2015). We would also like to thank the editors and the reviewers for their very helpful feedback and suggestions. Lumsdaine is grateful for the generous hospitality of both Erasmus University Rotterdam and the University of Portsmouth (UK) during her sabbatical, that facilitated progress on this paper.

REFERENCES

Clauset, A., Shalizi, C. R., & Newman, M. E. J. (2009). Power-law distributions in empirical data. *SIAM Review*, *51*(4), 661–703.

Cover, T. M., & Thomas, J. A. (2006). *Elements of information theory* (2nd ed.). New York, NY: Wiley.

Dawid, A. P. (1983). Invariant prior distributions. In S. Kotz & N. L. Johnson (Eds.), *Encyclopedia of statistical* sciences (pp. 228–236). New York, NY: Wiley.

Dose, V. (2003). Hyperplane priors. In C. J. Williams (Ed.), *Bayesian inference and maximum entropy methods in science and Engineering, Conference. Proceedings*. (Vol. 659, pp. 350–357). Melville, NY: AIP.

Golan, A. (2008). Information and entropy econometrics – A review and synthesis. *Foundations and Trends in Econometrics*, *2*(1–2), 1–145.

Golan, A. (forthcoming). *Foundations of info-metrics*. Oxford: Oxford University Press.

Golan, A., Judge, G., & Miller, D. (1996). *Maximum entropy econometrics: Robust estimation with limited data*. New York, NY: Wiley.

Jaynes, E. T. (1957a). Information theory and statistical mechanics. *Physics Review*, *106*, 620–630.

Jaynes, E. T. (1957b). Information theory and statistical mechanics II. *Physics Review*, *108*, 171–190.

Jaynes, E. T. (1968). Prior probabilities. *IEEE Transactions on Systems Science and Cybernetics*, *4*(3), 227–241.

Jeffreys, H. (1946). An invariant form of the prior probability in estimation problems. *Proceedings of the Royal Society of London, Series A*, *186*, 453–461.

Jeffreys, H. (1961). *Theory of probability* (3rd ed.). London: Oxford University Press.

Kass, R. E., & Wasserman, L. (1996). The selection of prior distributions by formal rules. *Journal of the American Statistical Association*, *91*(435), 1343–1370.

Kendall, M. P., & Moran, P. A. P. (1963). *Geometrical probability*. London: Griffin.

Kullback, S., & Leibler, R. A. (1951). On information and sufficiency. *Annals of Mathematical Statistics*, *22*, 79–86.

Levine, R. D. (1980). An information theoretical approach to inversion problems. *Journal of Physics A*, *13*, 91–108.

Levine, R. D., & Tribus, M. (1979). *The maximum entropy formalism*. Cambridge, MA: MIT Press.

Lindley, D. V. (1973). Discussion of "Marginalization Paradoxes in Bayesian and Structural Inference" by Dawid, Stone and Zidek. *Journal of the Royal Statistical Society: Series B*, *35*, 218–219.

Shannon, C. E. (1948). A mathematical theory of communication. *Bell System Technical Journal*, *27*, 379–423.

Shiller, R. J. (1973). A distributed lag estimator derived from smoothness priors. *Econometrica*, *41*(4), 775–788.

Shore, J. E., & Johnson, R. (1980). Axiomatic derivation of the principle of maximum entropy and the principle of minimum cross entropy. *IEEE Transactions on Information Theory*, *IT-26*(1), 26–37.

Sims, C. A. (1980). Macroeconomics and reality. *Econometrica*, *48*(1), 1–48.

Skilling, J. (1989). The axioms of maximum entropy. In J. Skilling (Ed.), *Maximum entropy and Bayesian methods in science and engineering* (pp. 173–187). Dordrecht: Kluwer Academic.

Soofi, E. S. (2000). Principal information theoretic approaches. *Journal of the American Statistical Association*, *95*(452), 1349–1353.

Soofi, E. S., & Retzer, J. J. (2002). Information indices: Unifications and applications. *Journal of Econometrics*, *107*, 17–40.

Van Toussaint, U., & Dose, V. (2006). Bayesian inference in surface physics. *Applied Physics A*, *82*(2006), 403–413.

Zellner, A., & Richard, J. F. (1973). Use of prior information in the analysis and estimation of Cobb-Douglas production function models. *International Economic Review*, *14*, 107–119.

APPENDIX A: DERIVATION OF THE CONCENTRATED MODEL

We show here the detailed derivation of the concentrated model (6) that transforms the problem from its primal, constrained state (probability space) to its dual (Lagrange multiplier space) unconstrained state.

Taking into account the solution (4) and inserting it into the Lagrangian, but without the normalization constraint that the probabilities sum to one (as it is already satisfied in Eq. (4)), we have

$$
\begin{aligned}
\ell(\lambda) &= \sum_k p_k \ln(p_k/q_k) + \sum_{m=1}^{M} \lambda_m \left[y_m - \sum_k p_k f_m(X_k) \right] \\
&= \sum_k p_k \ln(p_k) - \sum_k p_k \ln(q_k) + \sum_{m=1}^{M} \lambda_m \left[y_m - \sum_k p_k f_m(X_k) \right] \\
&= \sum_k p_k \ln \left[\frac{q_k \exp\left[\sum_{m=1}^{M} \lambda_m f_m(X_k)\right]}{\Omega(\lambda_1, \ldots, \lambda_M)} \right] - \sum_k p_k \ln(q_k) \\
&\quad + \sum_m \lambda_m \left[y_m - \sum_k p_k f_m(X_k) \right] \\
&= \sum_k p_k \ln(q_k) + \sum_k p_k \ln \left[\exp\left[\sum_{m=1}^{M} \lambda_m f_m(X_k) \right] \right] \\
&\quad - \sum_k p_k \ln[\Omega(\lambda_1, \ldots, \lambda_M)] - \sum_k p_k \ln(q_k) + \sum_m \lambda_m \left[y_m - \sum_k p_k f_m(X_k) \right] \\
&= \sum_k p_k \left[\sum_{m=1}^{M} \lambda_m f_m(X_k) \right] + \sum_m \lambda_m \left[y_m - \sum_k p_k f_m(X_k) \right] \\
&\quad - \sum_k p_k \ln[\Omega(\lambda_1, \ldots, \lambda_M)] \\
&= \sum_{k,m} \lambda_m p_k f_m(X_k) + \sum_m \lambda_m y_m - \sum_{m,k} \lambda_m p_k f_m(X_k) \\
&\quad - \sum_k p_k \ln[\Omega(\lambda_1, \ldots, \lambda_M)] \\
&= \sum_{k,m} \lambda_m p_k f_m(X_k) - \sum_{m,k} \lambda_m p_k f_m(X_k) + \sum_m \lambda_m y_m - \ln(\Omega) \sum_k p_k \\
&= \sum_m \lambda_m y_m - \ln[\Omega(\lambda_1, \ldots, \lambda_M)]
\end{aligned}
$$

where in the second line, we express the relative entropy with more explicit notation. The rest just follows our earlier definitions and simple algebra.

The maximum entropy solution is just a special case of the above cross entropy method where the priors are uniform: $q_k = 1/K$ for all $k = 1, \ldots, K$.

APPENDIX B: MAXIMUM ENTROPY AND THE NORMAL DISTRIBUTION

Suppose we only know that a certain continuous random variable has a finite mean, μ and variance σ^2. Using the maximum entropy we write the Lagrangian

$$\ell = -\int f(x) \log f(x)dx + \lambda_0(f(x)dx - 1) + \lambda_1\left(\int xf(x)dx - \mu\right) \\ + \lambda_2\left(\int (x-\mu)^2 f(x)dx - \sigma^2\right)$$

The optimal condition is

$$-\log f(x) - 1 + \lambda_0 + \lambda_1 x + \lambda_2(x-\mu)^2 = 0$$

So

$$f(x) = \exp\left[(\lambda_0 - 1) + \lambda_1 x + \lambda_2(x-\mu)^2\right]$$

Substituting into the three constraints (normalization of probabilities, mean, and variance) to solve for the λ's we get

$$\int \exp\left[(\lambda_0 - 1) + \lambda_1 x + \lambda_2(x-\mu)^2\right]dx = 1$$
$$\int x\exp\left[(\lambda_0 - 1) + \lambda_1 x + \lambda_2(x-\mu)^2\right]dx = \mu$$
$$(x-\mu)^2 \int x^2\exp\left[(\lambda_0 - 1) + \lambda_1 x + \lambda_2(x-\mu)^2\right]dx = \sigma^2$$

And solving we get

$$\lambda_0 = 1 - \frac{1}{4}\log\left(4\pi^2\sigma^4\right)$$
$$\lambda_1 = 0$$
$$\lambda_2 = -\frac{1}{2\sigma^2}$$

Finally, substituting these back into $f(x)$ we have

$$f(x) = \exp\left[(\lambda_0 - 1) + \lambda_1 x + \lambda_2 (x-\mu)^2\right] = \frac{1}{\sqrt{2\pi\sigma}}\exp\left[-\frac{1}{2}\frac{(x-\mu)^2}{\sigma^2}\right]$$

Note that it turns out that we don't need to incorporate the mean to derive the above since $\lambda_1 = 0$.

THE WAGE PREMIUM OF NATURALIZED CITIZENSHIP

Esfandiar Maasoumi and Yifeng Zhu
Department of Economics, Emory University, Atlanta, GA, USA

ABSTRACT

We examine the potential effect of naturalization on the U.S. immigrants' earnings. We find the earning gap between naturalized citizens and noncitizens is positive over many years, with a tent shape across the wage distribution. We focus on a normalized metric entropy measure of the gap between distributions, and compare with conventional measures at the mean, median, and other quantiles. In addition, naturalized citizen earnings (at least) second-order stochastically dominate noncitizen earnings in many of the recent years. We construct two counterfactual distributions to further examine the potential sources of the earning gap, the "wage structure" effect and the "composition" effect. Both of these sources contribute to the gap, but the composition effect, while diminishing somewhat after 2005, accounts for about 3/4 of the gap. The unconditional quantile regression (based on the Recentered Influence Function), and conditional quantile regressions confirm that naturalized citizens have generally higher wages, although the gap varies for different income groups, and has a tent shape in many years.

Keywords: Earning gap; citizenship; stochastic dominance tests; RIF regression; entropy measure; immigration

JEL classifications: C13; J70

Essays in Honor of Aman Ullah
Advances in Econometrics, Volume 36, 315–348

ISSN: 0731-9053/doi:10.1108/S0731-905320160000036018

1. INTRODUCTION

Studies of immigrant wages go back to at least Chiswick (1978). Most studies are concerned with the analysis of earnings differences of immigrants compared with natives (see, e.g., Aldashev, Gernandt, & Thomsen, 2012; Bartolucci, 2014). The earning gap between naturalized citizens and noncitizens has received less attention. Besides political and social rights, citizenship provides economic benefits. Most federal, state, local public sector and certain licensed professional jobs are restricted to citizens. These government jobs are stable and offer higher wages. Most private employers prefer citizenship holders as well, due to the risk of knowingly or inadvertently hiring unauthorized immigrants, and the administrative cost of hiring noncitizens. Second, the 1996 US welfare reform sharply reduced welfare eligibility for noncitizens (permanent residents qualify for these benefits after at least 40 quarters of work with legal status).

In the literature, economists are interested in three main questions related to citizenship's impact on economic benefits to immigrants. (1) How large is the earning gap? (2) How could one separate out the earning gap due to "composition" effect, or human capital characteristics? (3) How to evaluate the changes in the distribution and quantiles of the unconditional (marginal) distribution of immigrant log wages? Our paper proposes to offer some answers to these questions and examines new concepts and techniques for this purpose.

Identification of the "citizenship" effect is more likely by focusing on immigrants alone as a more homogeneous group compared with natives. We also focus on immigrants who are actively in the labor market.

Previous research on wage differentials is often based on certain measures such as means and medians. Sumption and Flamm (2012) reports 50–70% gap for the median annual incomes during the period from 1993 to 2010, and naturalized citizens appear to have weathered the effects of the economic crisis more successfully as the median income fell only by 5% from 2006 to 2010, while the decline of noncitizens' median income is 19%.[1] However, the differences at "representative" parts of the earnings distribution (mean, median, or any percentile) may not be "representative." This type of heterogeneity challenges the status of any scalar measure of the gap, especially simple aggregators like the mean and median, or any single quantile. Maasoumi and Wang (2015) are the first to utilize a normalized metric entropy measure of the wage gap, adapted from Bhattacharay–Matusita–Hellinger, and developed in Granger, Maasoumi, and Racine (2004). They argue this measure is a more comprehensive welfare-theoretic metric of distance between two earnings distributions. This is important for credible complete, "cardinal rankings." For weaker uniform orderings, they proposed stochastic dominance (SD) tests to rank the earnings distributions over large classes of familiar welfare functions. Maasoumi, Pitts, and Wu (2014) implement similar methods for the wage gap between incumbent and newly hired employees. Our paper employs the same entropy measure and SD tests to explore the earning gap between naturalized citizens with noncitizens in the United States from 1994 to 2012. The raw earning gap is often tent shaped in each year, possibly peaking from 1995 to 1997, while the trough appears during 1999–2001. The SD rankings are inferred to a statistical degree of confidence, allowing uniform ranking of naturalized citizens wages over noncitizens for most years. First-order SD rankings before 2003 are not statistically significant (significance level considered is 5%), but we find second-order significant SD for more than half of time after (including) 2003.

Moving beyond raw wages comparisons, we examine which part of the wage gap may be due to differences in the composition effects (human capital characteristics), and due to wage structure (market returns). The latter is considered by some as an indication of "discrimination" in the context of gender or race gaps. Our paper follows the counterfactual analysis proposed by Maasoumi and Wang (2015) by identifying and estimating two types of counterfactual distributions. This provides a decomposition of the gap into the aforementioned components. This decomposition procedure is described in Firpo, Fortin, and Lemieux (2007) and generalizes the Oaxaca-Blinder-type decomposition (at the conditional mean) to the whole distribution.

Based on the counterfactual analysis, the entropy gap estimates suggest a potential very small market structural gap from 1994 to 2012, holding human capital characteristics. SD tests seldom show significant ranking between the (two) noncitizen counterfactual distributions compared with the actual noncitizen wage distributions. Human capital characteristics appear to account for most of the differences in the hourly wage distributions. Entropy estimates quantify the magnitude of this human capital effect over the entire distribution of wages.

Most of the previous studies on the earning gap between naturalized citizens and noncitizens place "citizenship" as an explanatory variable in a Mincer-type earnings regression. Based on a linear (conditional mean) regression analysis, Pastor and Scoggins (2012) find that in 2010, naturalized citizens earned 7.9% on average more than noncitizens after controlling for numerous human capital characteristics. Bratsberg, Ragan, and Nasir (2002) track the same young male immigrants group from 1979 through 1991, showing an average wage gain of around 5.6% from naturalization. These results focus on the coefficient of the citizenship variable in the conditional mean. By contrast, we are interested in possibly heterogeneous effect of citizenship at different quantiles. Our paper examines the effect of changing the proportion of naturalization on the τth quantile of the unconditional distribution of log wages. This kind of analysis follows methods that have been developed only recently, such as in Firpo, Fortin, and Lemieux (2009). The approach consists of running a regression of the Recentered Influence Function (RIF) of the unconditional quantile on desired explanatory variables. For each year from 1994 to 2012, we discover a tent shape for the citizenship effect, implying that this effect is different for different levels of income, and is highest between the median and the 75-th percentile. For comparison, we also implement the traditional conditional quantile regressions (Koenker, 2005; Koenker & Bassett, 1978).[2] The findings from different methods provide a robustness check, and generally agree, but can differ quantitatively at different quantiles.

In Section 2, we will present the methods, data description is provided in Section 3. In Section 4, we provide the results, and conclude our paper in Section 5.

2. EMPIRICAL METHODOLOGY

2.1. *Basic Notation*

Let $\ln(\omega^0)$ and $\ln(\omega^1)$ denote the log wages of naturalized citizens and noncitizens, respectively. We observe a random sample of $N = N_0 + N_1$ immigrants. N_0 and N_1 denote the sample sizes of naturalized citizens and noncitizens, respectively. Let $F_0(y) \equiv Pr[\ln(\omega^0) \leq y]$ represents the cumulative density function (CDF) of $\ln(\omega^0)$ (i.e., the log of earning for naturalized citizens) and $f_0(y)$ is the corresponding probability density function (PDF); $F_1(y)$ and $f_1(y)$ are similarly defined for $\ln(\omega^1)$.

Individual earnings are determined by both observable, X_i, and unobservable characteristics ϵ_i via an unknown wage functions g_d

$$\ln(\omega_i^d) = g_d(X_i^d, \epsilon_i^d), \quad d = 0, 1 \tag{1}$$

The wage gap between naturalized citizens and noncitizens stems from two sources in Eq. (1): (1) differences in the distributions of both observable and unobservable characteristics, X_i^d and ϵ_i^d, respectively; (2) differences in the wage structures, $g_d(\cdot)$.

2.2. *Decision-Theoretics: Entropy as a Distributional Measure of the Earnings Gap*

The need for careful decision/welfare-theoretic understanding of measures of earnings gap has led to a reevaluation of suitable functions of the earnings distributions. A brief review of the issues is given in Maasoumi and Wang (2015). Flexible Evaluative Functions (EFs) that account for different outcomes at different parts of the earnings distribution provide better support for functionals that go beyond the mean and median, any single quantile, or merely reporting a set of quantiles. The classical literature on ideal measures of inequality provides the relevant backdrop and guidance. This literature identifies Entropy measure as "ideal" distribution functions.[3] As argued in Maasoumi and Wang (2015), the "gap" between two distribution is conveniently seen as the distance between the entropies (inequality measures) of the relevant distributions. When "metricness" is further required for distance functions (rather than mere divergence), a metric entropy member of the Generalized Entropy family emerges which is a normalization of the Bhattacharya–Matusita–Hellinger measure proposed by Granger et al. (2004). Other entropy measures can be employed with qualitatively consistent results. But only a metric measure that satisfies the triangularity rule may support coherent statements about respective "distances" amongst three or more distributions.

$$S_\rho = \frac{1}{2}\int_{-\infty}^{\infty}\left(f_1^{\frac{1}{2}} - f_0^{\frac{1}{2}}\right)^2 dy, \qquad (2)$$

This entropy measure possess several properties: (1) it can be applied to discrete and continuous variables;[4] (2) if $f_1 = f_0$, the two distribution are equal, then $S_\rho = 0$, and lies between 0 and 1 as it is normalized; (3) it is a metric, accommodating assessment across multiple distributions because triangularity property is satisfied; (4) it is invariant under continuous and strictly increasing transformation on the underlying variables; and (5) it is dimensionless, accommodating multivariable assessments.

Following Granger et al. (2004), Maasoumi and Racine (2002), and Maasoumi and Wang (2015), we consider a kernel-based implementation of Eq. (2). We use Gaussian kernels and the "normal reference rule-of-thumb" bandwidth ($=1.06 \cdot \min(\sigma_d, \frac{IQR^d}{1.349}) \cdot n^{-\frac{1}{5}}$, where $\sigma_d, d = 0, 1$ is the sample standard deviation of $\ln(\omega_i^d)_{i=1}^{N_d}$, IRQ^d is the interquartile range of the sample d). Interestingly, Gaussian kernels also enjoy an entropic justification as the Maximum Entropy choice when only the first two moments of data are utilized.

The entropy values S_ρ may not be statistically significantly different from 0, thus in this paper, we obtain critical values to test the hypothesis $H_0 : S_\rho = 0$ based on 299 bootstrap resamples. The critical values are reported in Table 1.

2.3. *Stochastic Dominance*

In our paper, we employ statistical tests for the first- and the second-order SD. This is motivated by the fact that there is no universally accepted Evaluation Function, and SD rankings, or lack of them, reveal whether (weak) uniform rankings hold across large classes of EFs, or else, how restrictive such functions need to be to provide (cardinal) complete rankings.

Table 1. Critical Values for Testing of $H_0 : S_\rho = 0$.

Year	Noncitizen versus Naturalized			C1 versus Noncitizen			C2 versus Noncitizen		
	90th	95th	99th	90th	95th	99th	90th	95th	99th
1994	0.29	0.31	0.35	0.32	0.34	0.40	0.34	0.38	0.49
1995	0.34	0.39	0.45	0.23	0.27	0.34	0.27	0.30	0.37
1996	0.34	0.38	0.44	0.51	0.65	0.78	0.35	0.39	0.44
1997	0.33	0.37	0.44	0.52	0.58	0.79	0.30	0.35	0.42
1998	0.29	0.34	0.40	0.28	0.30	0.38	0.28	0.33	0.41
1999	0.26	0.29	0.36	0.46	0.51	0.60	0.39	0.41	0.51
2000	0.26	0.28	0.37	0.30	0.33	0.39	0.56	0.60	0.75
2001	0.22	0.25	0.29	0.21	0.23	0.28	0.27	0.30	0.34
2002	0.18	0.20	0.23	0.22	0.23	0.28	0.24	0.27	0.35
2003	0.19	0.20	0.24	0.37	0.45	0.53	0.23	0.25	0.30
2004	0.18	0.20	0.25	0.19	0.20	0.27	0.26	0.31	0.37
2005	0.20	0.24	0.28	0.23	0.27	0.30	0.21	0.23	0.27
2006	0.16	0.18	0.24	0.25	0.27	0.33	0.24	0.27	0.32
2007	0.25	0.27	0.31	0.26	0.28	0.33	0.27	0.30	0.36
2008	0.21	0.22	0.29	0.19	0.21	0.27	0.27	0.29	0.33
2009	0.19	0.20	0.29	0.17	0.19	0.24	0.19	0.21	0.30
2010	0.18	0.20	0.24	0.17	0.19	0.22	0.27	0.29	0.36
2011	0.21	0.22	0.28	0.25	0.27	0.35	0.28	0.31	0.37
2012	0.21	0.23	0.28	0.24	0.27	0.31	0.22	0.24	0.27

Source: IPUMS CPS (http://cps.ipums.org/cps/).
Notes: The entropy ($\times 100$) 90th, 95th, and 99th percentile critical values under the null of no entropic difference between two wage distributions. C1 is noncitizen counterfactual #1, C2 is noncitizen counterfactual #2. Critical values obtained from 299 bootstrap resamples.

First-Order Dominance: *Naturalized citizen earnings* $(\ln(\omega^0))$ *first-order stochastically dominate noncitizen earnings* $(\ln(\omega^1))$ *(denoted* $\ln(\omega^0)$ *FSD* $\ln(\omega^1)$*) if and only if*

1. $E[u(\ln(\omega^0))] \geq E[u(\ln(\omega^1))]$ *for all* $u \in U_1$ *with strict inequality for some* u;
2. *Or,* $F_0(y) \leq F_1(y)$ *for all* y *with strict inequality for some* y,

where U_1 *denotes the class of all (increasing) von Neumann–Morgenstern-type of social welfare functions* u *such that welfare is increasing in wages (i.e.,* $u' \geq 0$*).*

Second-Order Dominance: *Naturalized citizen earnings* $(\ln(\omega^0))$ *second-order stochastically dominate noncitizen earnings* $(\ln(\omega^1))$ *(denoted* $\ln(\omega^0)$ *SSD* $\ln(\omega^1)$*) if and only if*

1. $E[u(\ln(\omega^0))] \geq E[u(\ln(\omega^1))]$ *for all* $u \in U_2$ *with strict inequality for some* u;
2. *Or,* $\int_{-\infty}^{y} F_0(t)dt \leq \int_{-\infty}^{y} F_1(t)dt$ *for all* y *with strict inequality for some* y,

where U_2 denotes the class of social welfare functions in U_1 such that $u'' \leq 0$ (i.e., concavity).

Then a generalized Kolmogorov–Smirnov test discussed in Linton, Maasoumi, and Whang (2005) and Maasoumi and Heshmati (2000) is used to conduct SD tests. The Kolmogorov–Smirnov test statistics for FSD and SSD are based on empirical counterparts of the following:

$$d = \sqrt{\frac{N_0 N_1}{N_0 + N_1}} \min\{\sup [F_1(y) - F_0(y)], \sup [F_0(y) - F_1(y)]\}, \quad (3)$$

$$s = \sqrt{\frac{N_0 N_1}{N_0 + N_1}} \min \left\{ \sup \int_{-\infty}^{y} [F_1(t) - F_0(t)]dt, \sup \int_{-\infty}^{y} [F_0(t) - F_1(t)]dt \right\}. \quad (4)$$

To estimate these test statistics, we replace CDFs by empirical CDFs (e.g., $\hat{F}_0(y) = \frac{1}{N_0} \sum_{i=1}^{N_0} I(\ln(\omega_i^0) \leq y))$, where $I(\cdot)$ is an indicator function. Additionally, 99 replications of bootstrap technique following the literature (e.g., Maasoumi & Heshmati, 2000; Maasoumi & Wang, 2015), implemented here to obtain the robustness check of the results. If Probability $[d \leq 0]$ is large enough, say 0.95, and $\hat{d} \leq 0$, then FSD is statistically significant. Similar definition for SSD.

2.4. *Counterfactual Distributions*

The identification of contributing components of the earning gap has been mostly conducted by Oaxaca-Blinder regression decompositions at the conditional mean. In our context, we conduct decompositions that are both robust to wage equation specifications and consider the whole distribution of wages. This is done first by inverse probability techniques, describe immediately below, and later by direct quantile regression and RIF regressions. The goal is to separate wage/market structure and the human capital characteristics components. The different techniques of identifying quantiles/distributions provide a check on robustness of findings. The conditional quantile regressions are further limited by functional specification choices.

Consider two counterfactual cases, as follows:

$$\ln(\omega_i^{c1}) = g_0(X_{i1}, \epsilon_{i1}) \quad (\textit{Counterfactual} \quad \textit{Outcome}\#1), \quad (5)$$

$$\ln(\omega_i^{c2}) = g_1(X_{i0}, \epsilon_{i0}) \quad (\textit{Counterfactual} \quad \textit{Outcome}\#2). \quad (6)$$

$F_{c1}(f_{c1})$ represents the corresponding CDF (pdf) of the counterfactual outcome $\ln(\omega_i^{c1})$, thus the differences in the distributions of F_{c1} and F_1 ($\ln(\omega_i^{c1})$ vs $\ln(\omega_i^{1})$)

only come from differences in wage structures or potential discrimination. $F_{c2}(f_{c2})$ represents the corresponding CDF (pdf) of the counterfactual outcome $\ln(\omega_i^{c2})$, as a result, the differences between the distributions of F_{c2} and F_1 ($\ln(\omega_i^{c2})$ vs $\ln(\omega_i^1)$) come from the differences in human capital characteristics.

There are many identification strategies for these two counterfactual distributions. We adopt the common assumptions of Ignorability (Unconfoundedness) and Overlapping Support, as employed by Firpo (2007) and Firpo et al. (2007).

Assumption 1. (*Ignorability*).
Let (D, X, ϵ) have a joint distribution. For all x in X, ϵ is independent of D given $X = x$; D=1 for noncitizens.

Assumption 2. (*Overlapping Support*).
For all x in X, $0 < p(x) = Pr[D = 1|X = x] < 1$, here $p(x)$ is called "propensity-score." In practical, we estimate the propensity score using logistic regression.[5]

Consider the following three inverse probability weighing functions:

$$\omega_1(D) = \frac{D}{p}, \quad \omega_0(D) = \frac{1-D}{1-p}, \quad \omega_c(D, X) = \left(\frac{p(X)}{1-p(X)}\right) \cdot \left(\frac{1-D}{p}\right),$$

here p is the probability that an individual is in group 1.

With these reweighing functions, we transform the marginal distribution of $\ln(\omega)$ to the conditional distributions of $\ln(\omega^1)$ given $D = 1$, $\ln(\omega^0)$ given $D = 0$, and $\ln(\omega^0)$ given $D = 1$.

We can identify F_1, F_0, F_{c1}, and F_{c2} as follows.

Theorem 2.1. *Under Assumptions 1 and 2:*

(1)
$$F_d(y) = \mathbb{E}[\omega_d(D) \cdot \mathbb{I}(\ln(\omega)) \leq y], \quad d = 0, 1. \tag{7}$$

(2)
$$F_{ct}(y) = \mathbb{E}[\omega_{ct}(D, X) \cdot \mathbb{I}(\ln(\omega)) \leq y], \quad t = 1, 2. \tag{8}$$

$\omega_{c2}(D, X) = \omega_c(D, X)$ if we let naturalized citizens to be the treatment group taking dummy value of 1, while $\omega_{c1}(D, X) = \omega_c(D, X)$ if setting noncitizens as the treatment group instead.

2.5. *Decomposition of the Distributional Statistics*

Armed with the conditional distributions $F_d(y), d = 0, 1$ and $F_{ct}(y), t = 0, 1$, we can decompose the wage gap into two parts, as suggested by Firpo et al. (2007).

Let ν be a functional of the conditional joint distribution of $(\ln(\omega)_0, \ln(\omega)_1)|D$, that is, $\nu: \mathcal{F}_\nu \to \mathbb{R}$, and $\mathcal{F}_\nu$ is a class of distribution functions such that $F \in \mathcal{F}_\nu$ if $\|\nu(F)\| < +\infty$. The difference in the ν's between the two groups is called the ν-overall wage gap.

$$\Delta_O^\nu = \nu(F_0) - \nu(F_1) = \nu_0 - \nu_1 \tag{9}$$

Then the difference (9) in wages can be decomposed into two parts:

$$\Delta_O^\nu = (\nu_0 - \nu_{c2}) + (\nu_{c2} - \nu_1) = \Delta_S^\nu + \Delta_X^\nu. \tag{10}$$

The first term Δ_S^ν is the difference in the wage structure, since it is the gap between $g_1(\cdot,\cdot)$ to $g_0(\cdot,\cdot)$ keeping the the distribution of human capital characteristics constant. The second term Δ_X^ν reflects the difference in composition effect. In the last part of this paper, we also provide decompositions of the total difference in mean wages (as in Oaxaca-Blinder decomposition) as well as in at quantiles, based on common index (parametric) specifications. This will provide a check on the consistency of the two different approaches.

2.6. *Unconditional Quantile Partial Effects (UQPE)*

Following the RIF regression method provided by Firpo et al. (2009), we can obtain the effect of increasing the proportion of naturalized immigrants on the τth quantile of the unconditional distribution of $\ln(\omega)$.

$$IF(\ln(\omega); q_\tau; F) = \lim_{\varepsilon \to 0} \frac{q_\tau(F_\varepsilon) - q_\tau(F)}{\varepsilon} = \frac{\tau - \mathbb{I}\{\ln(\omega) \le q_\tau\}}{f(q_\tau)}, \tag{11}$$

$$RIF(\ln(\omega); q_\tau; F) = q_\tau + IF(\ln(\omega); q_\tau; F) = q_\tau + \frac{\tau - \mathbb{I}\{\ln(\omega) \le q_\tau\}}{f(q_\tau)}, \tag{12}$$

where q_τ is the τth quantile. $F_\varepsilon(y) = (1-\varepsilon)F + \varepsilon\delta_y, 0 \le \varepsilon \le 1$ and δ_y is a distribution that only puts mass at the value y. We use $RIF(\ln(\omega); q_\tau)$ instead of $RIF(\ln(\omega); q_\tau; F)$ to simplify the notation.

The Unconditional Quantile Partial Effect (UQPE)

$$\alpha(\tau) = \frac{\partial q_\tau(F_{\ln(\omega), t\cdot G_Y^*})}{\partial t}\Big|_{t=0} = E\left[\frac{dE[RIF(\ln(\omega), q_\tau)|X]}{dX}\right], \tag{13}$$

here, $F_{\ln(\omega), t\cdot G^*_{\ln(\omega)}} = (1-t)\cdot F_{\ln(\omega)} + t\cdot G^*_{\ln(\omega)}$. $G^*_{\ln(\omega)}$ is the counterfactual distribution of $\ln(\omega)$, which can be obtained by replacing $F_X(x)$ with $G_X(x)$. $G_Y^* = \int F_{Y|X}(y|X=x)\cdot dG_X(x)$. The new distribution G_X is the distribution of a random $k \times 1$ vector Z, where $Z_i = X_i$ for $i \neq j$ and $i = 1, \ldots, K$, and $Z_j = X_j + t$, here j is the specific dimension we interested in.

From Eq. (12),

$$RIF(\ln(\omega); q_\tau) = c_{1,\tau} \cdot I\{\ln(\omega) > q_\tau\} + c_{2,\tau},$$

where $c_{1,\tau} = \frac{1}{f(q_\tau)}$, $c_{2,\tau} = q_\tau - c_{1,\tau} \cdot (1 - \tau)$.

Take the expectation,

$$E[RIF(\ln(\omega); q_\tau)|X = x] = c_{1,\tau} \cdot Pr[\ln(\omega) > q_\tau|X = x] + c_{2,\tau},$$

suppose $Pr[\ln(\omega) > q_\tau|X = x]$ is linear in x, then from Eq. (13), we know $\alpha(\tau) = E[\frac{dE[RIF(\ln(\omega), q_\tau)|X]}{dX}]$ is the same as the coefficient of regression RIF on X.

The estimator of RIF is

$$\widehat{RIF}(\ln(\omega); \widehat{q}_\tau) = \widehat{c}_{1,\tau} \cdot \mathbb{I}\{\ln(\omega) > \widehat{q}_\tau\} + \widehat{c}_{2,\tau},$$

here $\widehat{c}_{1,\tau} = \frac{1}{\widehat{f}(\widehat{q}_\tau)}$ and $\widehat{c}_{2,\tau} = \widehat{q}_\tau - \widehat{c}_{1,\tau} \cdot (1 - \tau)$. Then the average marginal effect or the UQPE-$\alpha(\tau)$ could be obtained by regressing $\widehat{RIF}(\ln(\omega); \widehat{q}_\tau)$ on X, we call it RIF-OLS method. Firpo et al. (2009) also mentioned logistic and polynomial series nonparamentric methods; however, the results are very close to the RIF-OLS method for the example in Firpo et al.'s (2009) paper.

3. DATA

In this paper, we examine the 1994–2012 Integrated Public Use Microdata Series, March Current Population Survey (King et al., 2010) (IPUMS-CPS). There are 176,164 observations for the 19 years we considered. The average sample size from 1994 to 2012 is 3,706 for naturalized citizens, and 5,566 for noncitizens. The minimum numbers appeared in 1994 for both groups are 1,663 and 3,209 for naturalized and noncitizens, respectively. This data source contains detailed information on the labor market outcomes such as earnings and other characteristics. Thus, it is widely used in the literature.[6] 1994 is the first year when the citizenship information is collected within immigrants. We restrict our sample to individuals aged 18–64, with at least 20 working weeks and 35 working hours (inclusive) per week in the previous year. Hourly wages less than or equals to $1 are excluded.

We use the log of hourly wages, which is obtained by dividing an individual's wage and salary income by the hours worked in the previous year. This is the standard procedure in the literature (e.g., Maasoumi & Wang, 2015). In our counterfactual analysis, unconditional and conditional quantile regressions, we include age, age squared,[7] education dummies (five education groups: less than high school, high school, some college, college, graduate), current married dummy variable (1 if married and zero otherwise), race dummy (1 if non-white and zero otherwise), region dummies (Northeast, Midwest, South, and West), and three occupations dummies (high-skill for managerial and professional specialty occupations; medium-skill contains technical, sales, and administrative support occupations; low-skill consists of service, farming, forestry and other occupations).

4. EMPIRICAL RESULTS

4.1. Distributional Comparison and Analysis

First we look at the raw differences measured by the Bhattacharya–Matusita–Hellinger entropy, alongside specific quantile (or moment based) differences of the wage gap between naturalized and noncitizens. This is given in Panel A of Table 2. Generally speaking, the $S_\rho \times 100$ gap and 10th, 25th, 50th (Median), 75th, 90th percentile gaps including the mean difference are positive and consistent from 1994 to 2012, indicating that naturalized citizens earn more than noncitizens. In addition, from the Panel A, the gap is not constant at different quantiles. For example, at the 10th quantile, the earning gap is 0.24–0.36, while it is 0.37–0.49 for the 50th quantile. The earning gap increases for above median incomes, and then decreases to 0.21–0.38 for the 90th quantile again. Thus, it seems that the association of citizenship is higher for median and above median wages, and generally lower at both tails. A tent shape.

Continuing with the raw entropy differences, nominal peak appears in 1995–1997, while the trough emerges during the period 1999–2001 (shown in Fig. 1 as well[8]). 2001 is the collapse of the Dot-com bubble. At lower wages (10th quantile), the gap is increasing in the period 2007–2012 compared with the prior period, suggesting the financial crisis may have impacted low income noncitizens more than other income levels. Citizenship may be associated with more stable wages in uncertain economic environments. But this may also be partly due to more active enforcement of immigration laws in some periods.

Fig. 2 displays the empirical CDFs of naturalized citizens and noncitizens in some years. Predominantly, all noncitizens CDFs are to the left of those of naturalized citizens (except Year 1994 when there is a cross at the higher end).[9] These graphical impressions are confirmed statistically. In Table 2, we find generally significant SD of citizen immigrant wages.

As just mentioned, in Panel B of Table 2, we report SD tests based on 99 bootstrap replications. In all the years 1994–2012, naturalized citizen earnings

Table 2. Naturalized Citizen versus Noncitizen Wage Distributions.

Panel A: The Raw Wage Gap

Year	$S_\rho \times 100$	Mean	10th	25th	50th	75th	90th
1994	4.00	0.35	0.29	0.35	0.41	0.39	0.27
1995	5.80	0.41	0.36	0.45	0.49	0.43	0.36
1996	5.59	0.42	0.31	0.41	0.47	0.42	0.38
1997	5.16	0.40	0.29	0.40	0.46	0.48	0.33
1998	4.45	0.37	0.27	0.38	0.44	0.38	0.31
1999	3.75	0.36	0.24	0.33	0.41	0.39	0.32
2000	3.71	0.33	0.25	0.35	0.40	0.37	0.21
2001	3.40	0.32	0.25	0.35	0.37	0.38	0.24
2002	3.90	0.36	0.28	0.33	0.42	0.38	0.26
2003	3.87	0.36	0.27	0.34	0.39	0.36	0.33
2004	4.03	0.36	0.26	0.33	0.43	0.38	0.29
2005	4.18	0.36	0.22	0.38	0.43	0.37	0.29
2006	4.40	0.38	0.26	0.38	0.41	0.46	0.32
2007	3.96	0.37	0.29	0.36	0.39	0.43	0.38
2008	4.33	0.38	0.28	0.39	0.43	0.41	0.35
2009	3.79	0.35	0.30	0.33	0.43	0.36	0.26
2010	4.02	0.36	0.30	0.37	0.43	0.39	0.31
2011	4.02	0.36	0.27	0.36	0.43	0.39	0.31
2012	3.96	0.37	0.30	0.36	0.43	0.42	0.29

Panel B: Stochastic Dominance Tests

Year	OR	$d_{1,max}$	$d_{2,max}$	d	$P[d \leq 0]$	$s_{1,max}$	$s_{2,max}$	s	$P[s \leq 0]$
1994	SSD	0.04	8.44	0.04	0.36	−0.04	250.97	−0.04	0.91
1995	FSD	−0.01	10.50	−0.01	0.30	−0.04	322.73	−0.04	0.77
1996	FSD	−0.04	10.10	−0.04	0.85	−0.04	252.88	−0.04	0.94
1997	SSD	0.00	10.42	0.00	0.28	−0.05	278.53	−0.05	0.68
1998	FSD	−0.01	10.67	−0.01	0.23	−0.04	273.61	−0.04	0.79
1999	FSD	−0.04	9.74	−0.04	0.75	−0.08	236.08	−0.08	0.83
2000	FSD	−0.04	10.45	−0.04	0.76	−0.04	274.21	−0.04	0.86
2001	FSD	−0.05	11.40	−0.05	0.68	−0.05	269.71	−0.05	0.93
2002	FSD	−0.06	12.50	−0.06	0.84	−0.06	322.67	−0.06	0.87
2003	FSD	−0.07	12.61	−0.07	0.94	−0.07	303.39	−0.07	0.98
2004	FSD	−0.08	12.59	−0.08	0.65	−0.09	323.23	−0.09	0.68
2005	FSD	−0.09	12.77	−0.09	0.98	−0.09	298.37	−0.09	1.00
2006	FSD	−0.06	13.41	−0.06	0.55	−0.08	330.51	−0.08	0.57
2007	FSD	−0.06	13.22	−0.06	0.66	−0.07	334.96	−0.07	0.74
2008	FSD	−0.06	13.86	−0.06	0.91	−0.06	328.82	−0.06	1.00
2009	FSD	−0.07	12.83	−0.07	0.92	−0.07	323.90	−0.07	0.98
2010	FSD	−0.02	13.27	−0.02	0.63	−0.06	287.41	−0.06	0.96
2011	FSD	−0.06	13.31	−0.06	0.79	−0.06	273.41	−0.06	0.86
2012	FSD	−0.05	12.67	−0.05	0.83	−0.06	279.47	−0.06	0.98

Source: IPUMS CPS (http://cps.ipums.org/cps/).

Notes: Panel A: Column 2: Entropy wage gap ($\times 100$) is invariant to log transformation. Columns 3–8: conventional measures of the log wage differences. Panel B: OR means observed ranking. $P[d] \leq 0$ and $P[s] \leq 0$ results are based on 99 replications of bootstrap resampling produce.

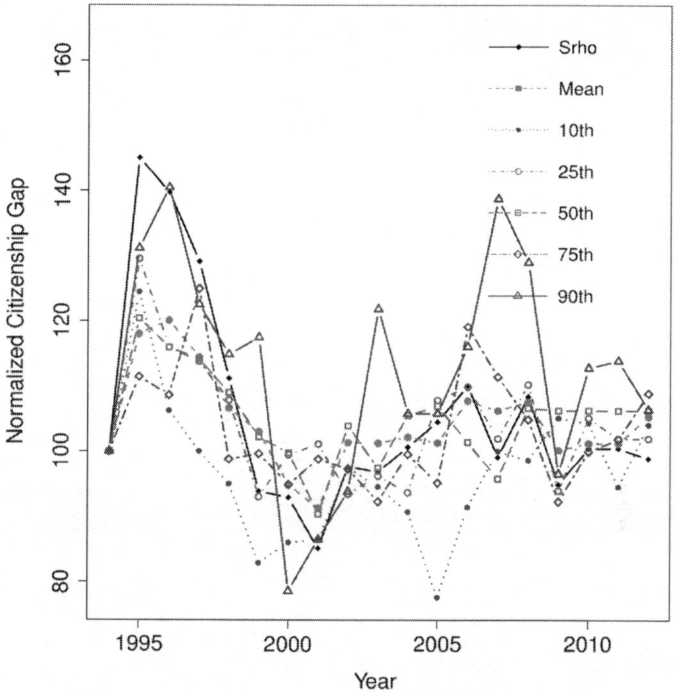

Fig. 1. The Time Trend of Citizenship Wage Gap.

stochastic dominate noncitizen earnings. Furthermore, we find first-order SD except for the years 1994 and 1997. The columns labeled d and s are the Kolmogorov–Smirnov test statistics for FSD and SSD, respectively (Expressions (3–4)), while the columns labeled $P[d \leq 0]$ and $P[s \leq 0]$ report the probabilities of first-order and second-order SD, respectively. From Panel B of Table 2, FSD is only significant in 2005, but SSD is significant for 2003, 2005, 2008–2010, and 2012. In 2011, the probability is 0.86, which is noteworthy. The earnings distribution of naturalized citizens is found to dominate from 2008 to 2012, indicating noncitizens have not faired well during the recent economic recession. Some regulations may have contributed to this outcome. For example, The U.S. Senate agreed on February, 2009 to set restrictions on the hiring of H-1B workers by financial services firms that received federal bailout funds.

4.2. *Counterfactual Analysis*

Comparing noncitizen counterfactual #1 and noncitizen, measures of earning gap and SD tests are displayed in Table 3 and Fig. 3. Other years graphs are in Fig. A.2.

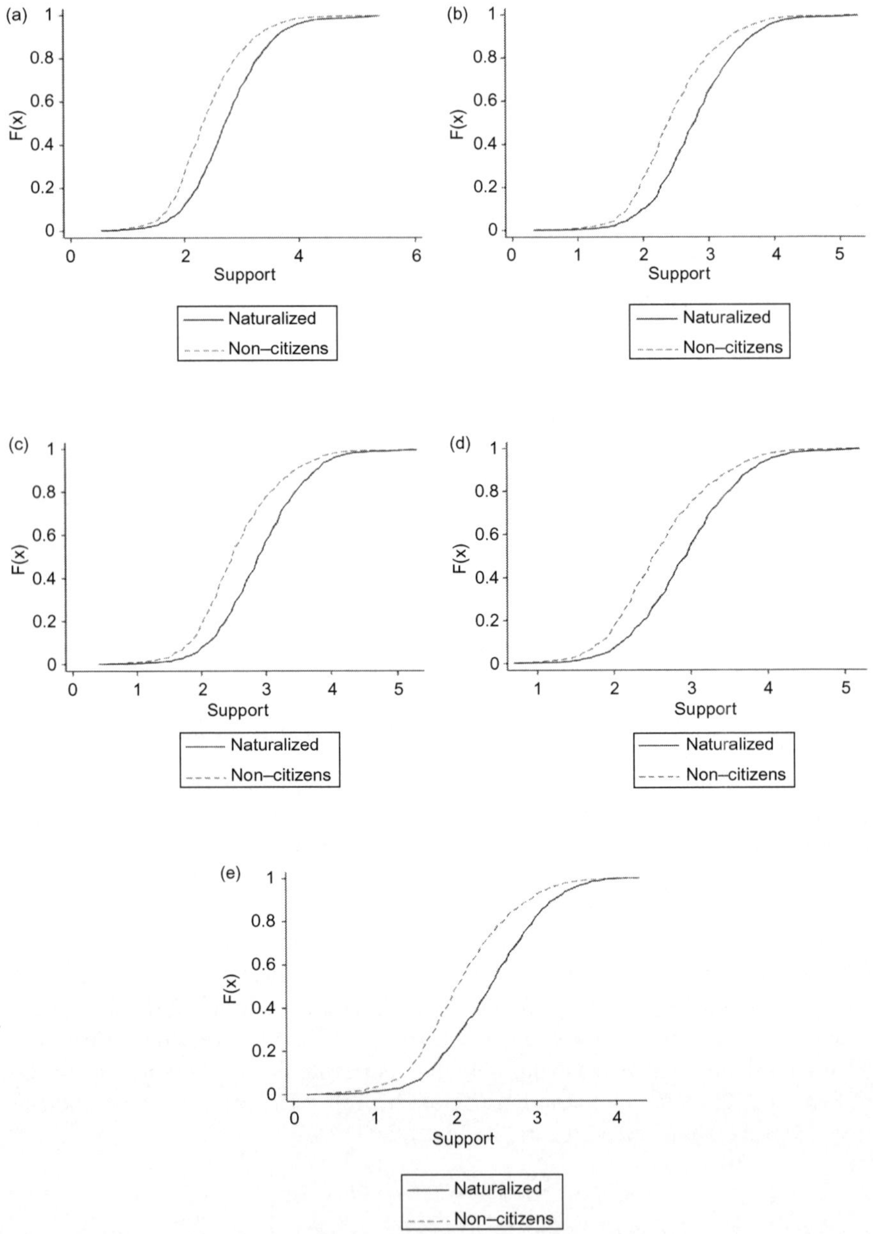

Fig. 2. CDF Comparisons of Naturalized Citizen and Noncitizen. (a) 2003; (b) 2005; (c) 2008; (d) 2009; and (e) 1994.

Table 3. Noncitizen Counterfactual #1 versus Noncitizen Distributions.

Panel A: Measures of Wage Differentials

Year	$S_\rho \times 100$	Mean	10th	25th	50th	75th	90th
1994	0.36	0.07	0.02	0.07	0.09	0.09	0.04
1995	1.23	0.17	0.17	0.15	0.22	0.18	0.12
1996	1.08	0.16	0.14	0.11	0.19	0.22	0.16
1997	1.25	0.14	0.07	0.18	0.21	0.18	0.13
1998	0.75	0.12	0.12	0.12	0.17	0.16	0.07
1999	0.80	0.14	0.06	0.11	0.14	0.17	0.13
2000	0.94	0.13	0.13	0.18	0.14	0.13	0.06
2001	0.68	0.11	0.14	0.13	0.15	0.14	0.03
2002	1.03	0.15	0.12	0.17	0.18	0.16	0.05
2003	0.78	0.12	0.04	0.16	0.17	0.11	0.11
2004	0.77	0.13	0.12	0.13	0.14	0.15	0.05
2005	0.99	0.13	0.08	0.18	0.18	0.13	0.08
2006	0.98	0.14	0.13	0.21	0.15	0.13	0.06
2007	0.90	0.15	0.19	0.16	0.18	0.15	0.13
2008	1.32	0.18	0.17	0.20	0.18	0.16	0.10
2009	0.85	0.14	0.14	0.12	0.16	0.13	0.05
2010	0.81	0.12	0.10	0.13	0.14	0.15	0.07
2011	0.98	0.14	0.08	0.15	0.18	0.14	0.09
2012	0.90	0.14	0.11	0.16	0.18	0.13	0.06

Panel B: Stochastic Dominance Tests

Year	OR	$d_{1,max}$	$d_{2,max}$	d	$P[d \leq 0]$	$s_{1,max}$	$s_{2,max}$	s	$P[s \leq 0]$
1994	SSD	0.06	3.24	0.06	0.06	−0.06	81.49	−0.06	0.94
1995	SSD	0.08	7.29	0.08	0.14	−0.07	212.94	−0.07	0.83
1996	None	0.18	6.48	0.18	0.07	0.14	145.28	0.14	0.40
1997	None	0.98	6.61	0.98	0.00	8.85	143.56	8.85	0.06
1998	SSD	0.18	6.81	0.18	0.00	−0.06	137.12	−0.06	0.77
1999	FSD	−0.06	6.18	−0.06	0.45	−0.06	136.05	−0.06	0.97
2000	SSD	0.13	7.74	0.13	0.07	−0.07	150.75	−0.07	0.45
2001	SSD	0.28	7.79	0.28	0.02	−0.09	137.45	−0.09	0.75
2002	None	0.09	9.70	0.09	0.19	0.42	196.17	0.42	0.36
2003	None	0.26	8.10	0.26	0.14	1.52	152.75	1.52	0.37
2004	FSD	−0.05	8.73	−0.05	0.20	−0.16	172.87	−0.16	0.49
2005	SSD	0.07	9.46	0.07	0.15	−0.08	166.08	−0.08	0.70
2006	FSD	−0.03	9.76	−0.03	0.15	−0.15	190.52	−0.15	0.83
2007	None	0.17	9.28	0.17	0.13	0.53	199.70	0.53	0.29
2008	FSD	−0.03	11.25	−0.03	0.66	−0.11	237.46	−0.11	1.00
2009	FSD	−0.05	8.65	−0.05	0.27	−0.11	185.39	−0.11	0.92
2010	SSD	0.10	9.23	0.10	0.05	−0.09	149.57	−0.09	0.75
2011	SSD	0.02	9.92	0.02	0.17	−0.10	161.76	−0.10	0.73
2012	FSD	−0.01	8.91	−0.01	0.19	−0.10	158.71	−0.10	0.77

Source: IPUMS CPS (http://cps.ipums.org/cps/).
Notes: Panel A: Column 2 is entropy gap (×100). Columns 3–8 report conventional measures of the log wages gap. Panel B: OR means observed ranking. $P[d] \leq 0$ and $P[s] \leq 0$ results are based on 99 replications of bootstrap resampling produce.

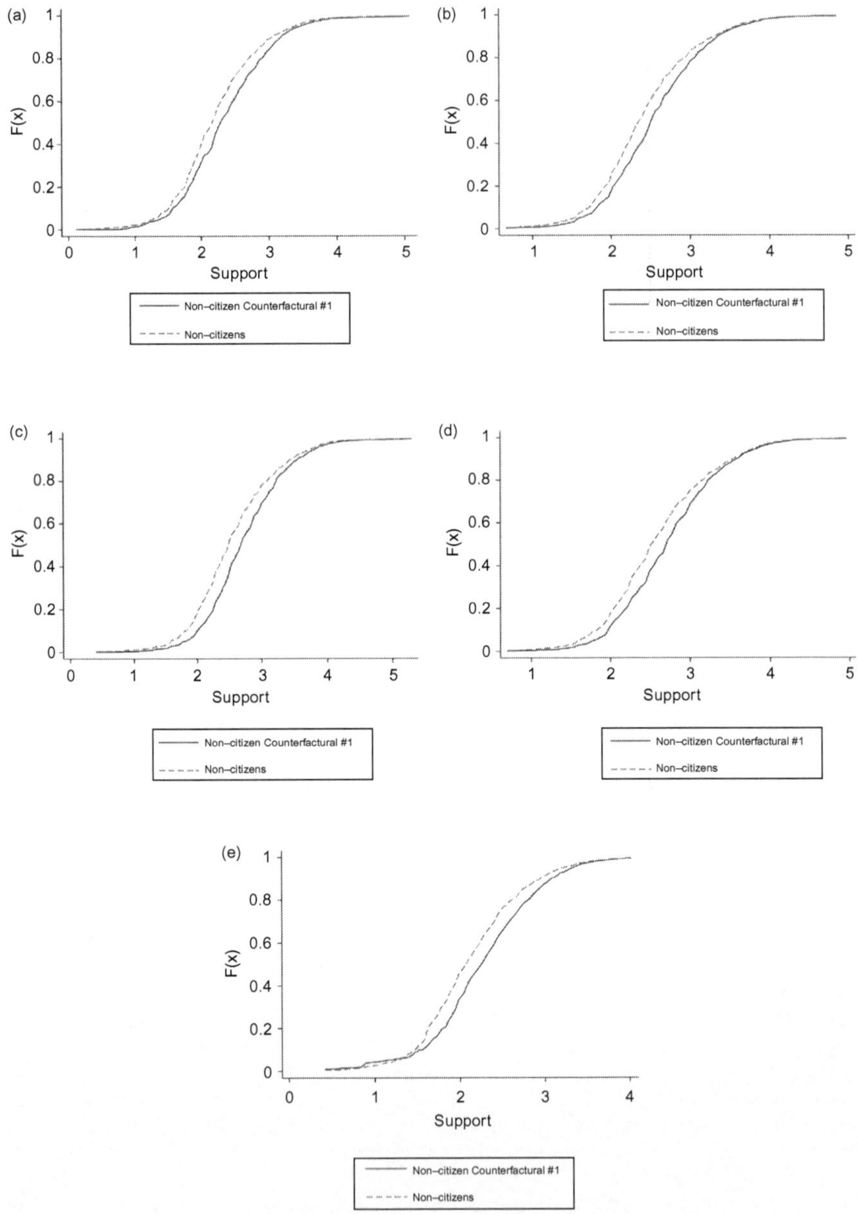

Fig. 3. CDF Comparisons of Noncitizen Counterfactual # 1 and Noncitizen. (a) 1999; (b) 2004; (c) 2008; (d) 2009; and (e) 1997.

Table 4. Noncitizen Counterfactual #2 versus Noncitizen Distributions.

Panel A: Measures of Wage Differentials

Year	$S_\rho \times 100$	Mean	10th	25th	50th	75th	90th
1994	1.62	0.23	0.14	0.18	0.25	0.33	0.24
1995	1.60	0.22	0.15	0.17	0.27	0.29	0.26
1996	1.42	0.21	0.08	0.16	0.21	0.29	0.25
1997	1.61	0.22	0.11	0.17	0.26	0.31	0.24
1998	1.39	0.21	0.10	0.16	0.21	0.27	0.25
1999	1.36	0.21	0.07	0.16	0.22	0.26	0.31
2000	1.71	0.24	0.13	0.16	0.26	0.36	0.31
2001	1.34	0.21	0.14	0.15	0.22	0.30	0.26
2002	1.59	0.23	0.10	0.17	0.26	0.29	0.24
2003	1.33	0.20	0.10	0.15	0.25	0.27	0.24
2004	1.50	0.22	0.13	0.15	0.25	0.29	0.27
2005	1.70	0.24	0.13	0.21	0.30	0.34	0.25
2006	1.65	0.24	0.15	0.22	0.26	0.36	0.30
2007	1.65	0.24	0.17	0.16	0.25	0.27	0.29
2008	1.40	0.22	0.16	0.15	0.22	0.26	0.23
2009	1.28	0.21	0.14	0.15	0.24	0.30	0.20
2010	1.23	0.21	0.10	0.15	0.22	0.29	0.24
2011	1.31	0.22	0.08	0.14	0.24	0.31	0.27
2012	1.11	0.20	0.07	0.13	0.23	0.29	0.18

Panel B: Stochastic Dominance Tests

Year	OR	$d_{1,max}$	$d_{2,max}$	d	$P[d \leq 0]$	$s_{1,max}$	$s_{2,max}$	s	$P[s \leq 0]$
1994	FSD	−0.05	8.05	−0.05	0.48	−0.06	240.58	−0.06	0.64
1995	FSD	−0.06	8.60	−0.06	0.60	−0.06	275.01	−0.06	0.94
1996	FSD	−0.04	7.43	−0.04	0.51	−0.06	190.10	−0.06	0.85
1997	None	0.13	8.70	0.13	0.12	1.00	225.37	1.00	0.16
1998	None	0.15	8.02	0.15	0.11	0.77	219.97	0.77	0.20
1999	None	0.07	8.13	0.07	0.13	0.29	201.42	0.29	0.27
2000	FSD	−0.04	9.64	−0.04	0.62	−0.07	274.66	−0.07	0.78
2001	FSD	−0.07	10.63	−0.07	0.34	−0.08	264.87	−0.08	0.51
2002	FSD	−0.08	12.02	−0.08	0.68	−0.08	308.49	−0.08	0.78
2003	None	0.08	10.37	0.08	0.25	0.08	251.36	0.08	0.45
2004	FSD	−0.05	10.80	−0.05	0.58	−0.07	299.83	−0.07	0.88
2005	FSD	−0.10	11.86	−0.10	0.51	−0.10	293.64	−0.10	0.55
2006	FSD	−0.12	11.94	−0.12	0.95	−0.12	331.67	−0.12	0.97
2007	FSD	−0.11	12.38	−0.11	0.37	−0.11	319.73	−0.11	0.60
2008	FSD	−0.08	11.77	−0.08	0.72	−0.10	287.03	−0.10	0.79
2009	FSD	−0.08	11.13	−0.08	0.31	−0.16	292.81	−0.16	0.42
2010	FSD	−0.11	10.63	−0.11	0.84	−0.11	250.11	−0.11	0.90
2011	FSD	−0.09	10.91	−0.09	0.63	−0.10	250.18	−0.10	0.77
2012	FSD	−0.08	9.92	−0.08	0.64	−0.15	228.67	−0.15	0.84

Source: IPUMS CPS (http://cps.ipums.org/cps/).
Notes: Panel A: Column 2 reports Entropy gap (×100). Columns 3–8 report conventional measures of log wage differences. Panel B: OR means observed ranking. $P[d] \leq 0$ and $P[s] \leq 0$ results are based on 99 replications of bootstrap resampling produce.

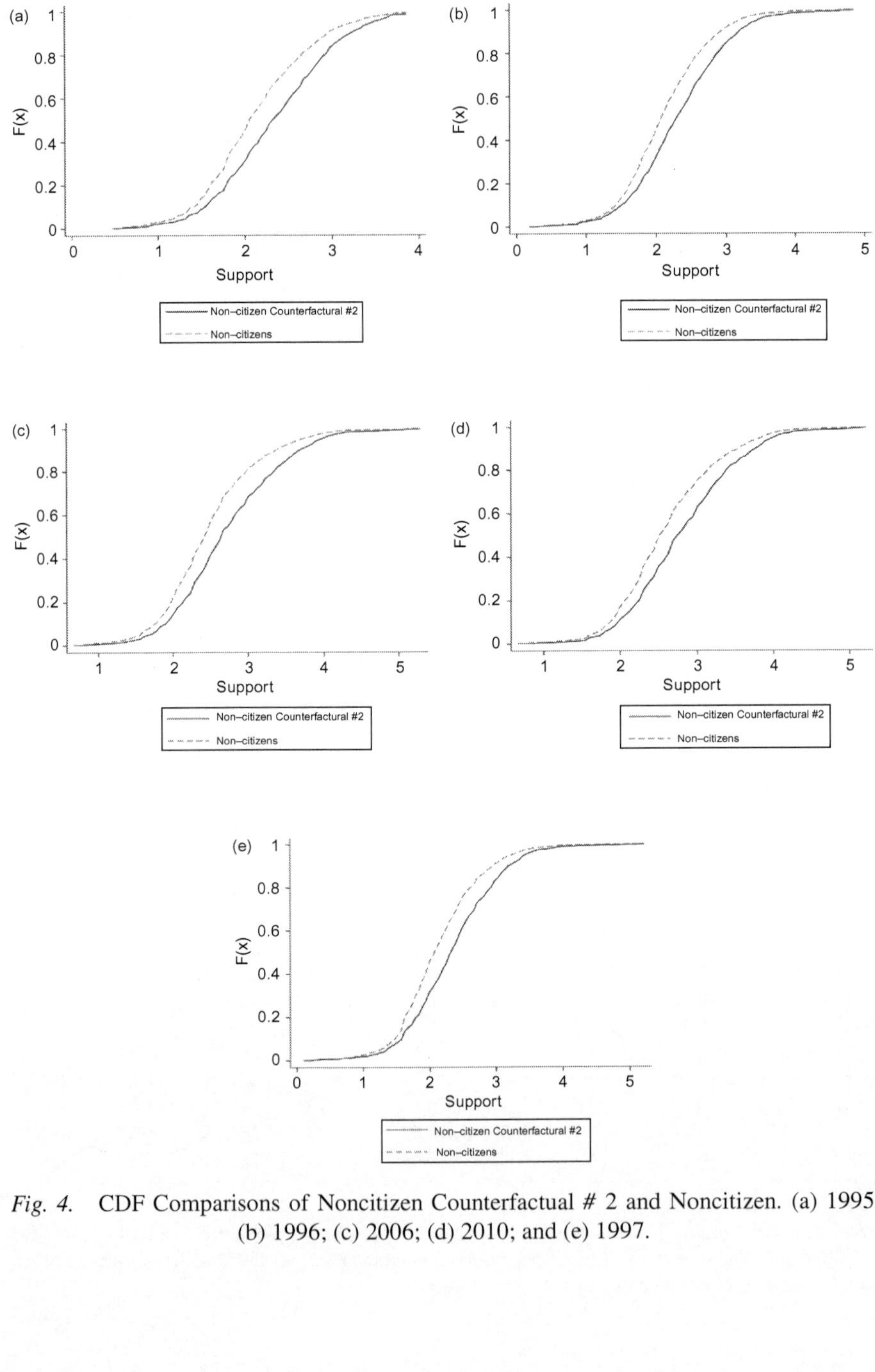

Fig. 4. CDF Comparisons of Noncitizen Counterfactual # 2 and Noncitizen. (a) 1995; (b) 1996; (c) 2006; (d) 2010; and (e) 1997.

Table 5. Wage Gap Decomposition.

Panel A: The Wage Structure Component of the Gap

Year	Mean	10th	25th	50th	75th	90th
1994	0.12	0.14	0.16	0.16	0.08	0.07
1995	0.17	0.20	0.24	0.20	0.14	0.07
1996	0.21	0.25	0.21	0.24	0.18	0.10
1997	0.18	0.18	0.20	0.20	0.16	0.14
1998	0.17	0.18	0.20	0.21	0.12	0.09
1999	0.15	0.17	0.17	0.18	0.15	0.04
2000	0.11	0.10	0.16	0.18	0.05	−0.01
2001	0.10	0.12	0.20	0.16	0.08	0.01
2002	0.12	0.16	0.12	0.11	0.12	0.06
2003	0.15	0.13	0.17	0.16	0.12	0.11
2004	0.12	0.14	0.14	0.13	0.08	0.06
2005	0.11	0.13	0.14	0.11	0.06	0.06
2006	0.11	0.10	0.15	0.13	0.08	−0.01
2007	0.12	0.11	0.18	0.12	0.13	0.09
2008	0.14	0.13	0.22	0.17	0.11	0.09
2009	0.12	0.13	0.17	0.17	0.05	0.05
2010	0.13	0.18	0.19	0.18	0.09	0.05
2011	0.12	0.18	0.20	0.16	0.05	0.01
2012	0.14	0.19	0.21	0.17	0.09	0.07

Panel B: Composition Effect Component of the Gap

Year	Mean	10th	25th	50th	75th	90th
1994	0.23	0.14	0.18	0.25	0.33	0.24
1995	0.22	0.15	0.17	0.27	0.29	0.26
1996	0.21	0.08	0.16	0.21	0.29	0.25
1997	0.22	0.11	0.17	0.26	0.31	0.24
1998	0.21	0.10	0.16	0.21	0.27	0.25
1999	0.21	0.07	0.16	0.22	0.26	0.31
2000	0.24	0.13	0.16	0.26	0.36	0.31
2001	0.21	0.14	0.15	0.22	0.30	0.26
2002	0.23	0.10	0.17	0.26	0.29	0.24
2003	0.20	0.10	0.15	0.25	0.27	0.24
2004	0.22	0.13	0.15	0.25	0.29	0.27
2005	0.24	0.13	0.21	0.30	0.34	0.25
2006	0.24	0.15	0.22	0.26	0.36	0.30
2007	0.24	0.17	0.16	0.25	0.27	0.29
2008	0.22	0.16	0.15	0.22	0.26	0.23
2009	0.21	0.14	0.15	0.24	0.30	0.20
2010	0.21	0.10	0.15	0.22	0.29	0.24
2011	0.22	0.08	0.14	0.24	0.31	0.27
2012	0.20	0.07	0.13	0.23	0.29	0.18

Source: IPUMS CPS (http://cps.ipums.org/cps/).
Notes: Panel A: Column 2: The Standard Oaxaca-Blinder decomposition. Columns 3–7 are quantile "wage structure" source of the earning gap. Panel B: Column 2: Composition effect from the Standard Oaxaca-Blinder decomposition. Columns 3–7, composition effects at quantiles.

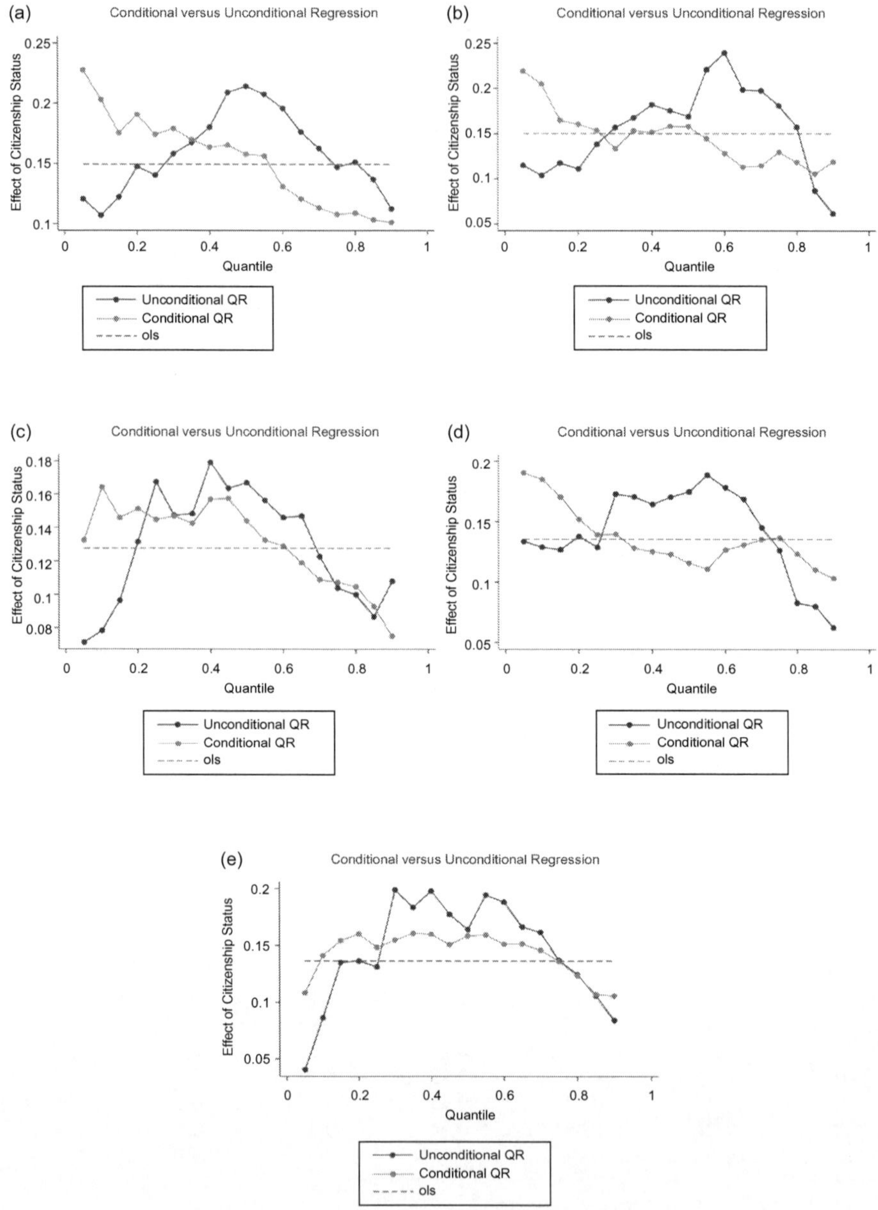

Fig. 5. Unconditional and Conditional Quantile Regression Estimates of the Effect of Citizenship Status on Log Wages. (a) 1995; (b) 1998; (c) 2005; (d) 2009; and (e) 2010.

Table 6. Comparing OLS, Unconditional Quantile Regressions (UQR), and Conditional Quantile Regressions (CQR): Citizenship Status Effect.

Year	OLS	10th Centile		50th Centile		90th Centile	
		UQR	CQR	UQR	CQR	UQR	CQR
1994	0.13	0.08	0.21	0.16	0.13	0.10	0.09
1995	0.15	0.11	0.20	0.21	0.16	0.11	0.10
1996	0.16	0.13	0.21	0.20	0.17	0.16	0.14
1997	0.14	0.07	0.16	0.19	0.17	0.14	0.11
1998	0.15	0.10	0.20	0.17	0.16	0.06	0.12
1999	0.15	0.10	0.14	0.16	0.14	0.09	0.14
2000	0.13	0.08	0.15	0.17	0.15	0.05	0.09
2001	0.12	0.11	0.15	0.15	0.13	0.06	0.08
2002	0.14	0.10	0.16	0.15	0.15	0.06	0.10
2003	0.14	0.06	0.14	0.18	0.14	0.14	0.11
2004	0.13	0.10	0.15	0.17	0.14	0.09	0.08
2005	0.13	0.08	0.16	0.17	0.14	0.11	0.07
2006	0.12	0.09	0.16	0.15	0.12	0.03	0.09
2007	0.13	0.12	0.16	0.17	0.13	0.10	0.09
2008	0.14	0.11	0.16	0.17	0.15	0.09	0.13
2009	0.14	0.13	0.18	0.17	0.12	0.06	0.10
2010	0.14	0.09	0.14	0.16	0.16	0.08	0.11
2011	0.12	0.09	0.14	0.14	0.14	0.04	0.09
2012	0.14	0.11	0.16	0.18	0.16	0.04	0.11

Notes: All robust standard errors (OLS) and bootstrapped standard errors (99 replications) for UQR and CQR are less than 0.01, thus are neglected in this table.

Comparison of F_{c1} and F_1 controls for "human capital characteristics," reflecting wage structure components. From Panel B of Table 3, there is generally no statistically significant first- or second-order SD (except in 1999 and 2008, when probabilities are larger than 0.95). Thus, the noncitizen wage distribution #1 and the counterfactual wage distribution #1 are generally unrankable. Market returns cannot account for the wage gap.

In Panel A of Table 3 entropy gap S_ρ peaks in 2008 (1.32) but is otherwise quite stable and much smaller than the raw values observed in prior tables. This is consistent with the SD tests. Only other, possibly very narrow decision-theoretic definitions of the gap can possibly order these distributions.

Table 4 and Fig. 4 show the comparison results for noncitizen counterfactual #2 and noncitizens. Graphs for remaining years are in Fig. A.3. Here, noncitizen counterfactual #2 represents the corresponding earning distributions, if we use the distribution of the naturalized citizens' human capital instead of noncitizens' while keeping the wage structure unchanged. The gap is generally positive in Panel A,

Table 4, accounting for most of the total gap reported in the raw comparisons. There is no discernible general trend in the human capital/characteristics component of the gap. It is stable around 1.33–1.65, with peaks in 2000 and 2005, and troughs in 2009–2012. In the recent recession years, we find the impact of the "skills gap" is declining amongst immigrants. Accordingly, the entropy gap S_ρ has decreased from 1.70 in 2005 to 1.11 in 2012.

The earnings distributions of noncitizen counterfactual #2 graphically FSD the earnings distributions of noncitizen; see Fig. 4. For FSD, these are not statistically significance except for 2006, as can be seen in Panel B, Table 4 for many years. But there is a fairly strong evidence of statistical SSD. The high probabilities for SSD suggest the likelihood of general third-order SD for all years. This suggests that EFs that are (increasingly) inequality averse would order these two outcomes. Skills matter, especially so with increasing inequality aversion, which values upward mobility at lower wages more highly than at higher wages.

4.3. Decomposition of the Gap in Conditional Means and Quantiles

In this section, we examine alternative methods to the nonparametric distribution-based analysis provided so far. Thus, we reexamine decompositions of the wage gap based on modeling of the conditional means (Mincer-type earnings equations), and conditional quantile regressions. For comparison purposes in this context, we also obtain the corresponding partial effects of "citizenship" on immigrant wages based on the RIF Regressions described in prior sections.

Table 5 reports the gap due to "wage structure" and "composition" effects. These are reported at the mean and select quantiles. The results at the conditional mean are known as the Oaxaca-Blinder decompositions.

4.4. The UQPE and the Conditional Quantile Partial Effect (CQPE) of Citizenship

If citizenship effect is "causal," one may wish to find the partial impact of it on immigrants' wages. In this part, we treat citizenship as a factor contributing to immigrants' income. Firpo et al. (2009) suggests a different measure to obtain UQPE, instead of the coefficient of the factor from the traditional conditional quantile regression. The reason is that the coefficient $\beta_\tau = F^{-1}(\tau|D=1) - F^{-1}(\tau|D=0)$ from a conditional quantile regression is generally different from $dq_\tau(p)/dp$, $p=P[D=1]$. $D=1$ for a citizen immigrant. $p=P[D=1]$ denotes the proportion of naturalized immigrants.

Table 6 and Fig. 5 report unconditional quantile regression estimates (labeled UQR), standard OLS (conditional mean) estimates, and standard (conditional) quantile regression estimates (labeled CQR) of the effect of citizenship status on log wages.[10] The estimates are uniformly positive each year, however, the magnitudes are varied for different quantiles. Although the shape of the UQPE is slightly different every year, it is generally the tent shape, illustrating citizenship is more important to middle and upper middle wages, compared to very low-income and high-incomes. This result also indicates that citizenship increases inequality in the lower tail of the distribution while decreases inequality for the upper tail. For example, in year 2012 in Table 6, the difference between entries for the 50th and the 10th quantiles is 0.07 ($=0.18-0.11$), and the difference between the 90th and the 50th quantiles is -0.14 ($=0.04-0.18$). Thus, a 10% increase in the citizenship rate is associated with an increase of 0.007 in the 50–10 gap, but a decrease of the 90–50 gap by 0.014. For comparison, the CQPE results are also positive, but due to the decreasing magnitudes corresponding with larger quantiles, the increase in citizenship ratio will reduce the conditional earning distribution inequality. Bootstrapped standard errors (for UQR and CQR) and robust OLS standard errors are not reported in Table 6, since the largest value is $0.00358618 < 0.01$.

5. CONCLUSIONS AND FUTURE WORK

In this paper, we implement entropy and SD tests for the comparison of the wage distributions between naturalized and noncitizen immigrants in the United States. We construct two counterfactual wage distributions to clarify the sources of the wage gap. In addition, we obtain the estimate of the UQPE of citizenship. We use CPS data 1994–2012 here. The findings by the two different approaches of inverse probability weighting and quantile regression decompositions are in general agreement. Our main conclusions are as follows:

(1) The wage gap between naturalized and noncitizen is generally stable during 1994–2012, and its has a tent shape, suggesting heterogeneity over the wage distribution.
(2) The Raw Naturalized citizen earnings at least SSD noncitizen earnings for most years.
(3) Decomposition of the gap into "wage structure" and "composition" components reveals that human capital characteristics, and skills (observed or otherwise) are the primary source of the wage gap between immigrants.
(4) When wage outcomes cannot be uniformly ranked, as when characteristics are controlled for, our decision-theoretic approach makes clear that only narrow EFs would rank wage distributions and outcomes. In such cases, the metric

entropy proposed in this paper presents an attractive function of the whole distribution of earnings with a set of weights to different wage earners that is better supported than assessments based on the mean, median, or individual quantiles. Other entropy measures, such as the symmetrized Kullback–Leibler, would provide interesting measures of "divergence," with different underlying welfare functions. The patterns of the gap discovered in this paper are likely to be robust to the choice of entropy functionals.

CPS data do not contain English proficiency information. Neglecting this information may result in overestimates of the effect of "citizenship." Literature on program evaluation that accounts for separate grades in maths and English suggests this is an important distinction. These different skills are also likely differently correlated with length of residency which is often higher for naturalized immigrants.

ACKNOWLEDGMENTS

We thank Jens Hainmueller, Le Wang, Ke Wu, and attendants of the Advanced Microeconometrics seminars at Emory University and Northwestern University Causal Inference Workshop 2014, and conference in honor of Aman Ullah at UC Riverside 2015. We thank reviewers and coeditors for their many constructive comments and suggestions. This research was supported by Professional Development Supports Funds provided by Laney Graduate School, Emory University.

NOTES

1. For immigrants with at least 10 years of residence in the United States.

2. The conditional quantile regression coefficient can be interpreted as the marginal effect of citizenship ratio at the τth quantile of the conditional distribution of log wages. Our unconditional quantile approach, following Firpo et al. (2009), provides the marginal effect on the unconditional τth quantile, averaged over conditioning sets.

3. Earlier literature expositing welfare functions associated with entropy measures includes insightful accounts in Cowell and Kuga (1981) and Cowell (1977).

4. For the discrete variables, $S_\rho = \frac{1}{2}\sum(p_1^{1/2} - p_0^{1/2})^2$.

5. In our paper, we use linear regression, nonparametric regression can be implemented to relieve the parametric functional form restriction.

6. The IPUMS-USA(IPUMS American Community Survey) provides data from 2001 to 2011, including information on English proficiency, but is less complete on education level, and covers fewer years.

7. We include the squared age to reflect the idea that there are declining returns to additional age after some period of time.

8. Fig. 1 shows the plot of the normalized values of S_ρ, mean, 10th, 25th, 50th, 75th, and 90th percentiles.

9. Graphs for other years are in Fig. A.1.
10. Other years graphs are in Fig. A.4.

REFERENCES

Aldashev, A., Gernandt, J., & Thomsen, S. L. (2012). The immigrant-native wage gap in Germany. *Journal of Economics and Statistics (Jahrbuecher fuer Nationaloekonomie und Statistik)*, *232*(5), 490–517.

Bartolucci, C. (2014). Understanding the native – Immigrant wage gap using matched employer-employee data evidence from Germany. *ILR Review*, *67*(4), 1166–1202.

Bratsberg, B., Ragan, J. F., Jr., & Nasir, Z. M. (2002). The effect of naturalization on wage growth: A panel study of young male immigrants. *Journal of Labor Economics*, *20*(3), 568–597.

Chiswick, B. R. (1978). The effect of Americanization on the earnings of foreign-born men. *Journal of Political Economy*, *86*(5), 897–921.

Cowell, F. A. (1977). Measuring inequality. Londres: P. Alan Publishers.

Cowell, F. A., & Kuga, K. (1981). Additivity and the entropy concept: An axiomatic approach to inequality measurement. *Journal Economic Theory*, *25*(1), 131–143.

Firpo, S. (2007). Efficient semiparametric estimation of quantile treatment effects. *Econometrica*, *75*(1), 259–276.

Firpo, S., Fortin, N., & Lemieux, T. (2007, June). *Decomposing wage distributions using recentered influence function regressions*. University of British Columbia.

Firpo, S., Fortin, N. M., & Lemieux, T. (2009). Unconditional quantile regressions. *Econometrica*, *77*(3), 953–973.

Granger, C., Maasoumi, E., & Racine, J. S. (2004). A dependence metric for possibly nonlinear processes. *Journal of Time Series Analysis*, *25*(5), 649–669.

King, M., Ruggles, S., Alexander, J. T., Flood, S., Genadek, K., Schroeder, M. B., & Vick, R. (2010). *Integrated public use microdata series, current population survey: Version 3.0.[machine-readable database]* (p. 20). University of Minnesota, Minneapolis, MN.

Koenker, R. (2005). Quantile regression (Vol. 38). Cambridge: Cambridge University Press.

Koenker, R., & Bassett, G., Jr. (1978). Regression quantiles. *Econometrica*, *46*(1), 33–50.

Linton, O., Maasoumi, E., & Whang, Y. J. (2005). Consistent testing for stochastic dominance under general sampling schemes. *The Review of Economic Studies, 72*(3), 735–765.

Maasoumi, E., & Heshmati, A. (2000). Stochastic dominance amongst Swedish income distributions. *Econometric Reviews*, *19*(3), 287–320.

Maasoumi, E., Pitts, M., & Wu, K. (2014). The gap between the conditional wage distributions of incumbents and the newly hired employees: Decomposition and uniform ordering. *Essays in Honor of Peter CB Phillips* (Advances in Econometrics, Vol. 33, pp. 587–612). Bingley, UK: Emerald Group Publishing Limited.

Maasoumi, E., & Racine, J. S. (2002). Entropy and predictability of stock market returns. *Journal of Econometrics*, *107*(1), 291–312.

Maasoumi, E., & Wang, L. (2015). *The gender earnings gap between earnings distributions*. Working Paper, Department of Economics, Emory University.

Pastor, M., & Scoggins, J. (2012). *Citizen gain: The economic benefits of naturalization for immigrants and the economy*. Los Angeles: Center for the Study of Immigrant Integration, University of Southern California.

Sumption, M., & Flamm, S. (2012). The economic value of citizenship for immigrants in the United States. Migration Policy Institute, Washington, DC.

APPENDIX

In this appendix, we provide the other years CDF Comparisons between different groups, and unconditional, conditional quantile regression estimates of the effect of citizenship status on log wages.

A.1. CDF Comparisons

Fig. A.1 shows the empirical CDFs of naturalized citizens and noncitizens in other years different from years shown in the main text. Figs. A.2 and A.3 display the empirical CDFs comparison results for noncitizen counterfactual #1 versus noncitizen and noncitizen counterfactual #2 versus noncitizens, respectively.

A.2. Unconditional and Conditional Quantile Regression Estimates

Fig. A.4 shows the unconditional and conditional quantile regression estimates of the effect of citizenship status on log wages in other years from 1994 to 2012.

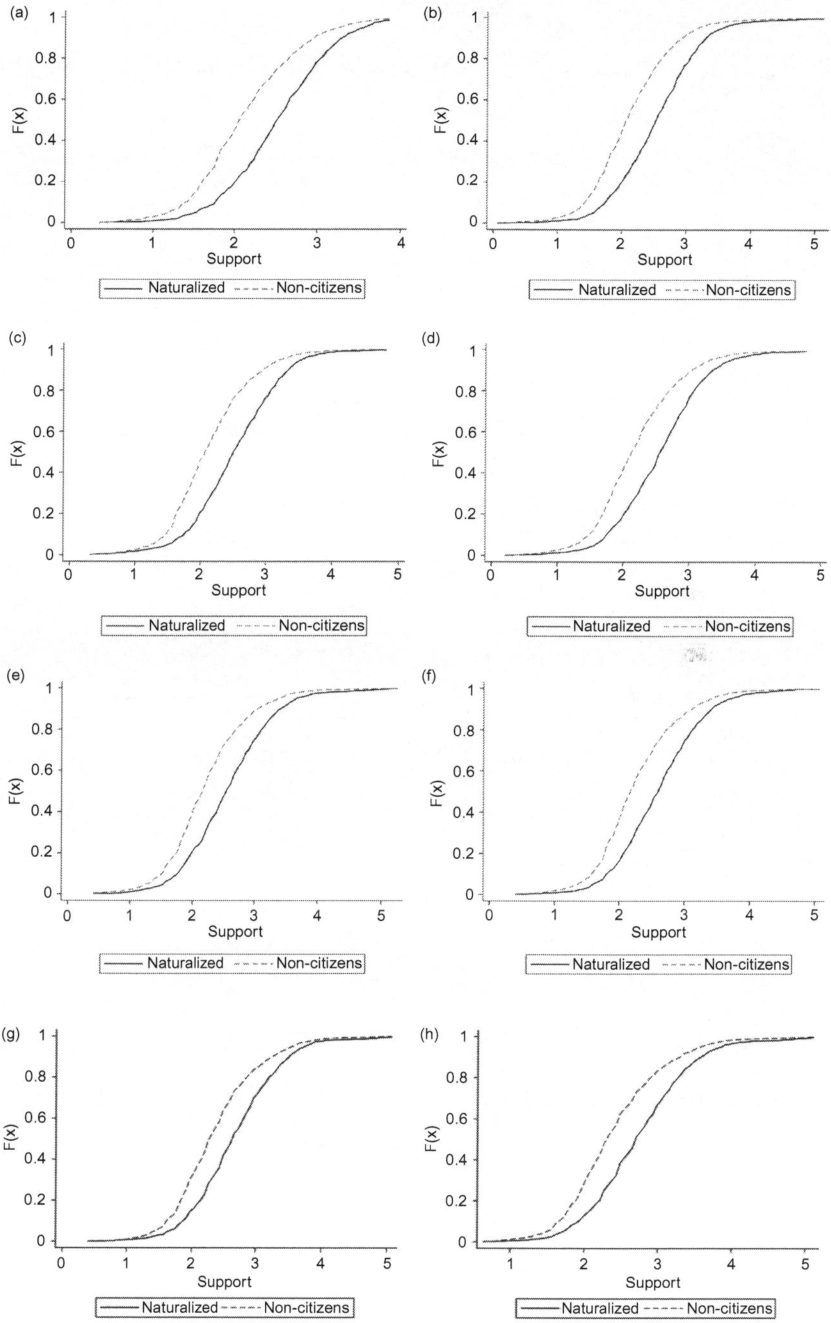

Fig. A.1. CDF Comparisons of Naturalized Citizen and Noncitizen (1994–2012). (a) 1995; (b) 1996; (c) 1997; (d) 1998; (e) 1999; (f) 2000; (g) 2001; (h) 2002; (i) 2004; (j) 2006; (k) 2007; (l) 2010; (m) 2011; and (n) 2012.

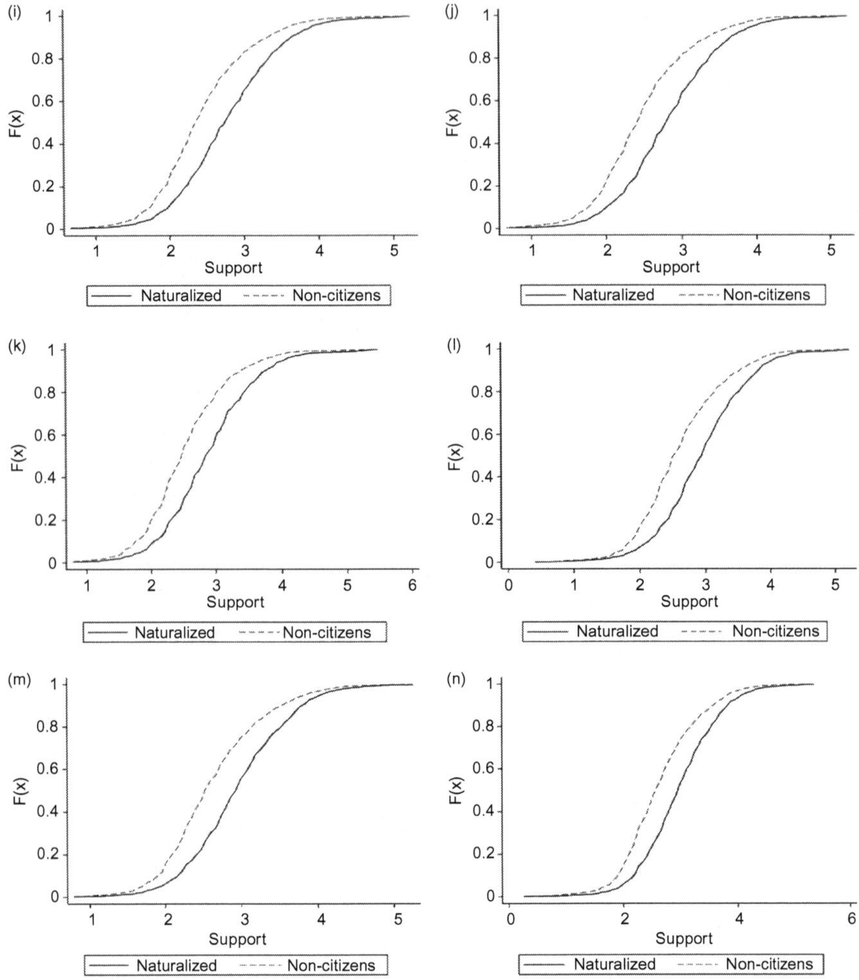

Fig. A.1. (*Continued*)

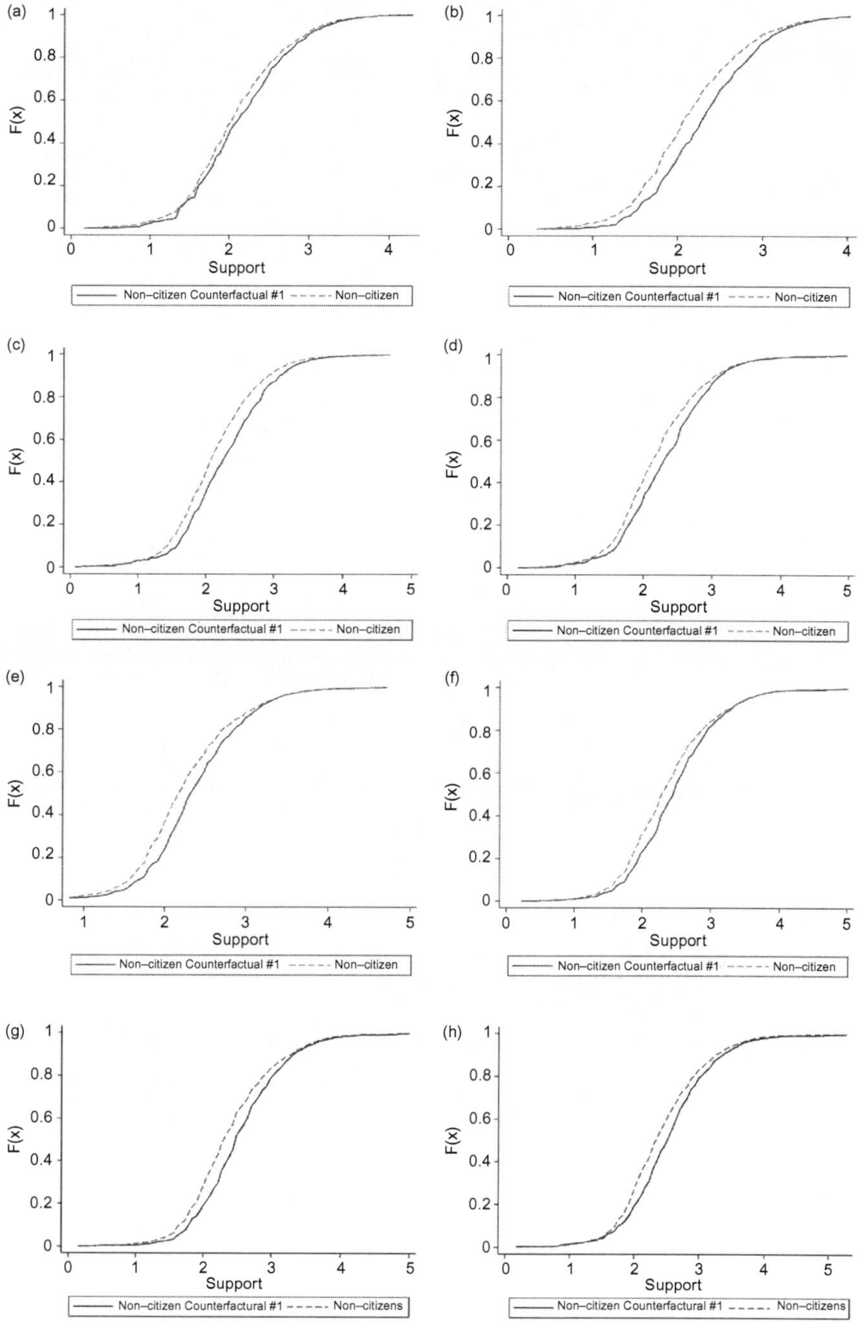

Fig. A.2. CDF Comparisons of Noncitizen Counterfactual # 1 and Noncitizen (1994–2012). (a) 1994; (b) 1995; (c) 1996; (d) 1998; (e) 2000; (f) 2001; (g) 2002; (h) 2003; (i) 2005; (j) 2006; (k) 2007; (l) 2010; (m) 2011; and (n) 2012.

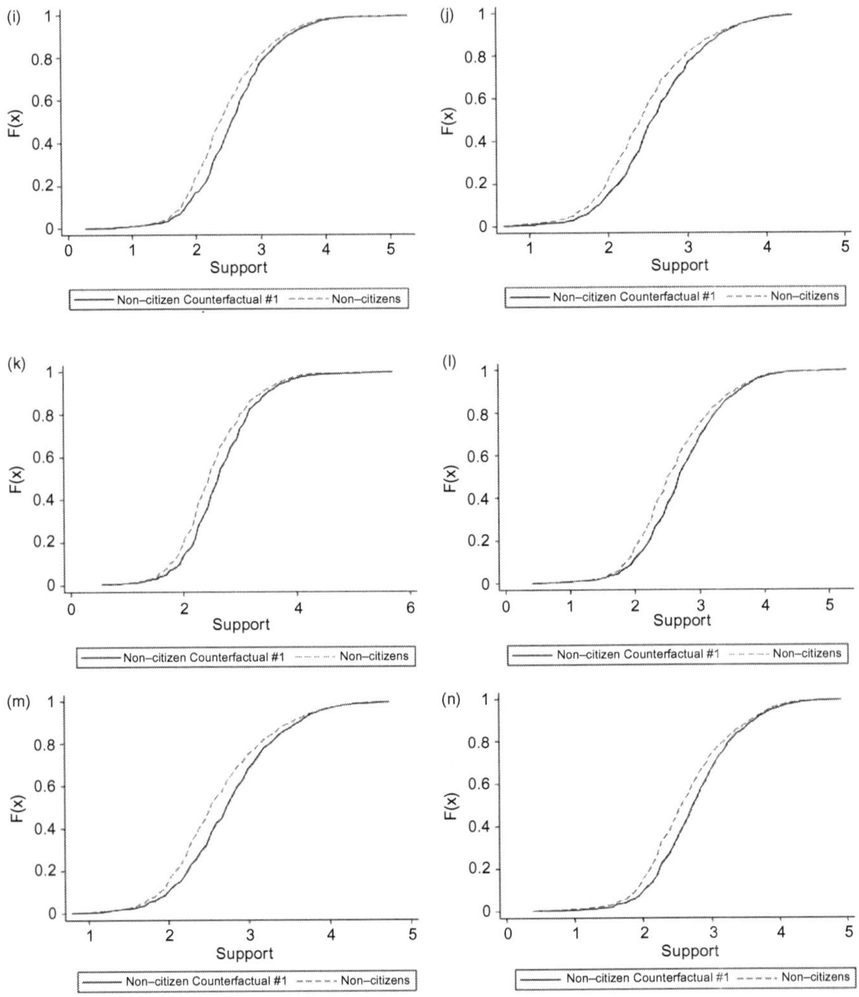

Fig. A.2. (*Continued*)

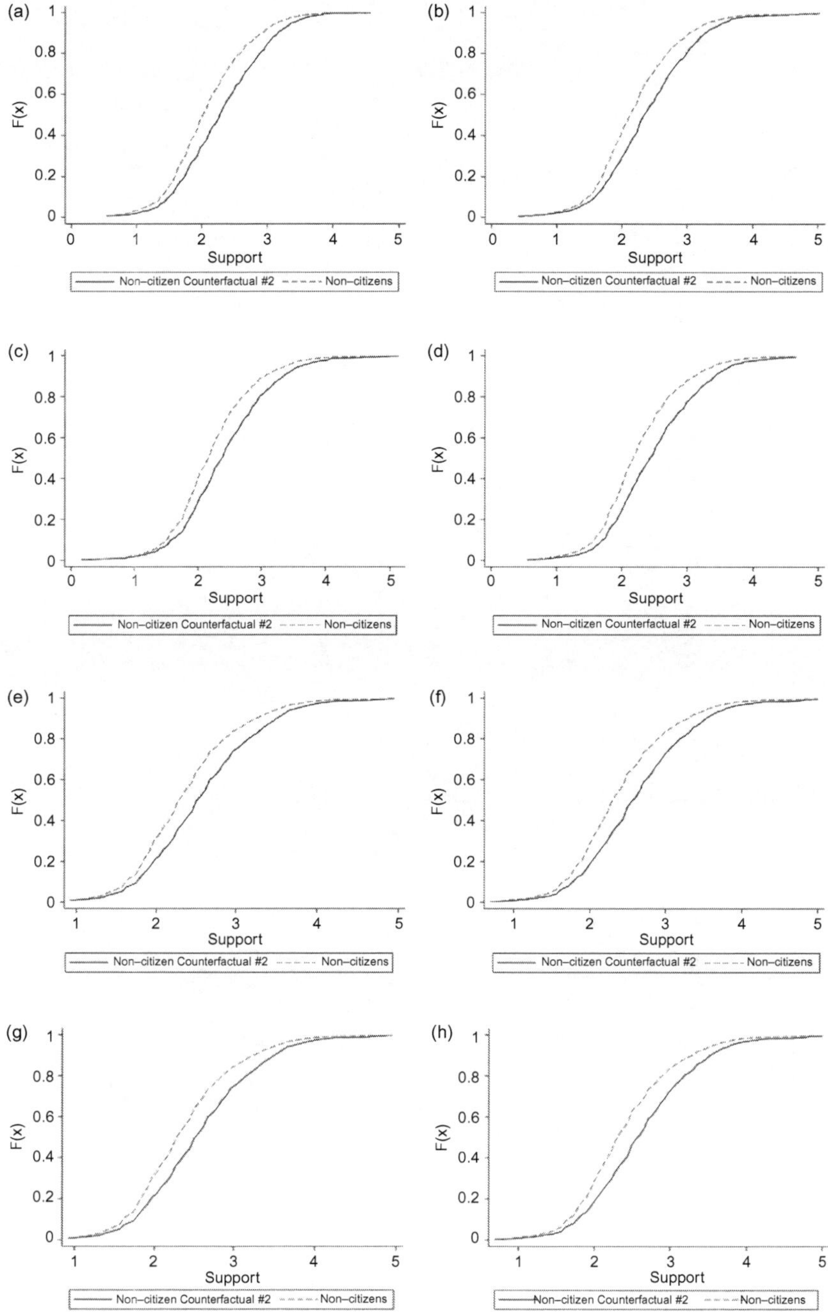

Fig. A.3. CDF Comparisons of Noncitizen Counterfactual # 2 and Noncitizen (1994–2012). (a) 1994; (b) 1998; (c) 1999; (d) 2000; (e) 2001; (f) 2002; (g) 2003; (h) 2004; (i) 2005; (j) 2007; (k) 2008; (l) 2009; (m) 2011; and (n) 2012.

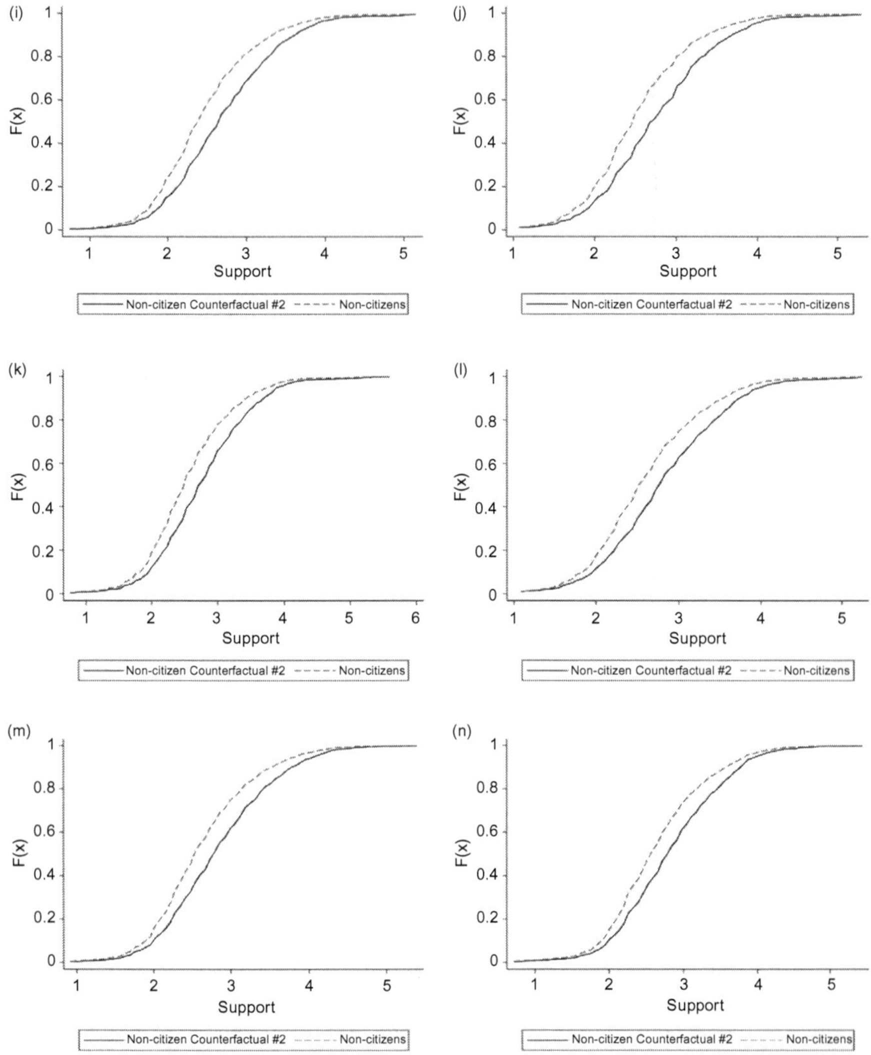

Fig. A.3. *(Continued)*

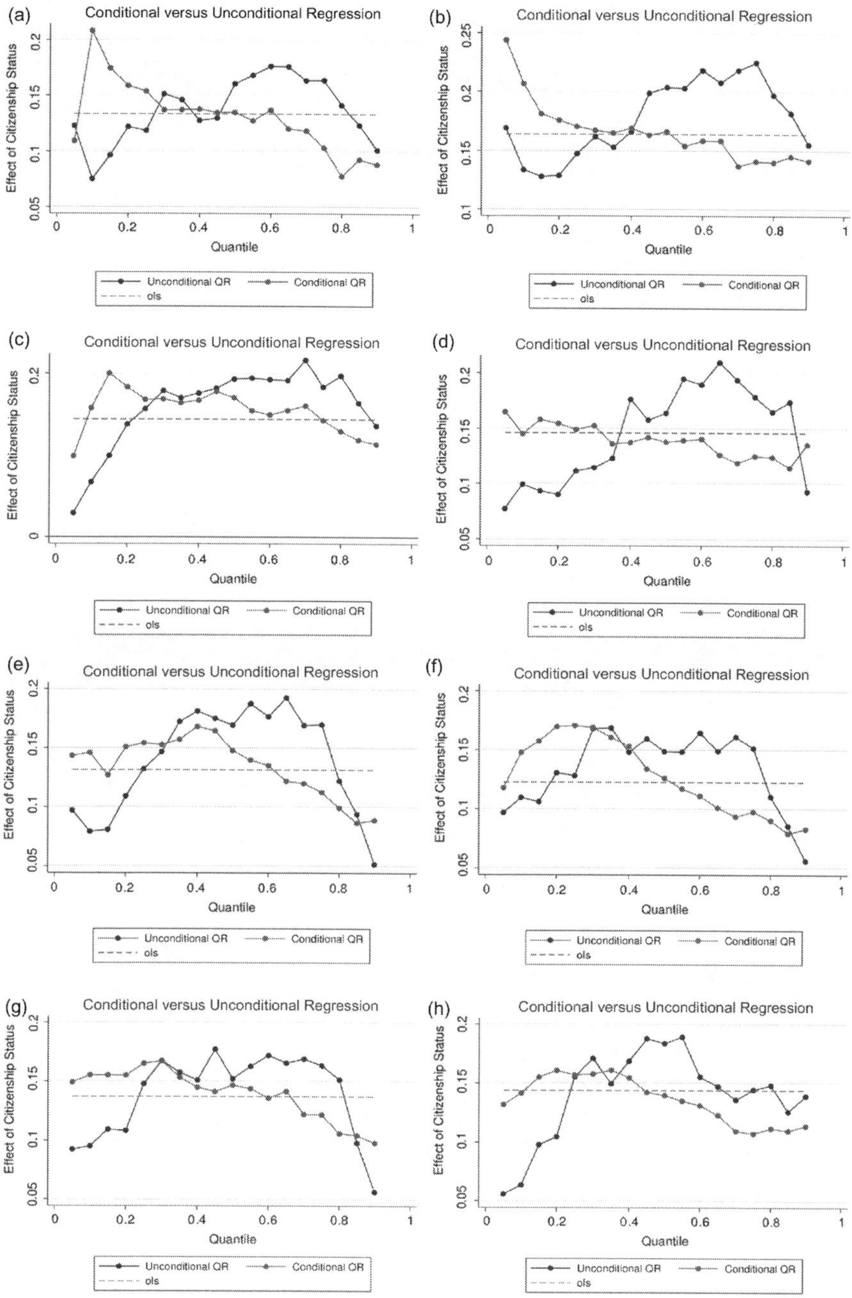

Fig. A.4. Unconditional and Conditional Quantile Regression Estimates of the Effect of Citizenship Status on Log Wages (1994–2012). (a) 1994; (b) 1996; (c) 1997; (d) 1999; (e) 2000; (f) 2001; (g) 2002; (h) 2003; (i) 2004; (j) 2006; (k) 2007; (l) 2008; (m) 2011; (n) 2012.

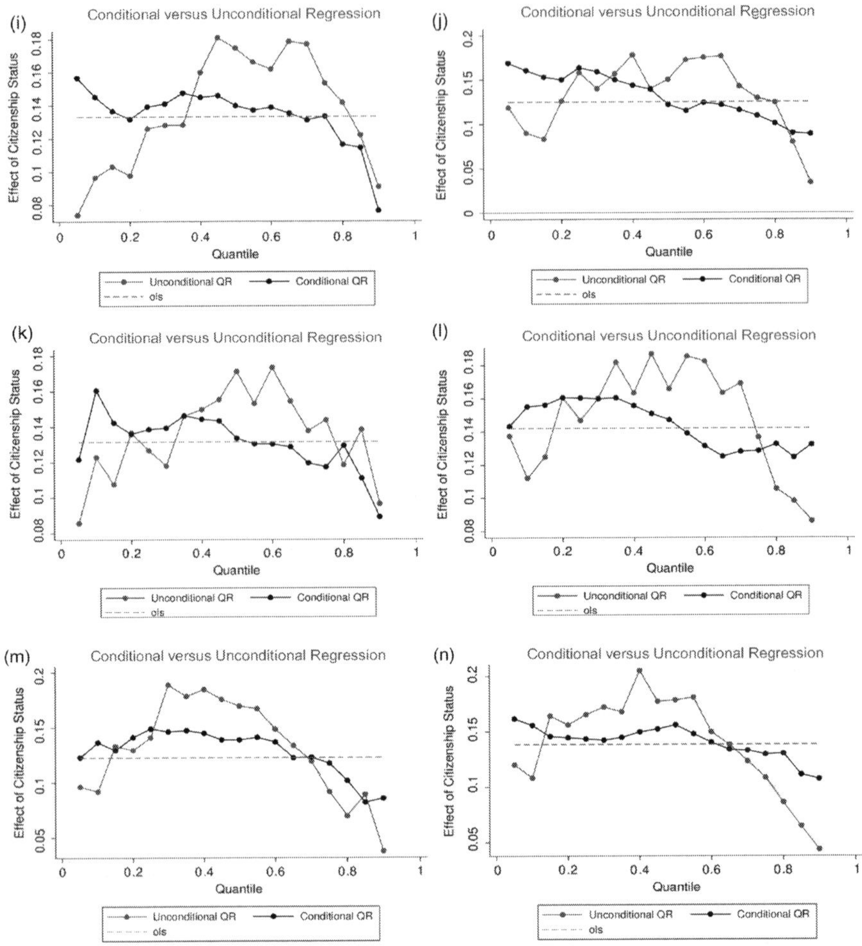

Fig. A.4. (*Continued*)

CAUSALITY AND MARKOVIANITY: INFORMATION THEORETIC MEASURES

Eric Renault and Daniela Scidá
Department of Economics, Brown University, Providence, RI, USA

ABSTRACT

Many Information Theoretic Measures have been proposed for a quantitative assessment of causality relationships. While Gouriéroux, Monfort, and Renault (1987) had introduced the so-called "Kullback Causality Measures," extending Geweke's (1982) work in the context of Gaussian VAR processes, Schreiber (2000) has set a special focus on Granger causality and dubbed the same measure "transfer entropy." Both papers measure causality in the context of Markov processes. One contribution of this paper is to set the focus on the interplay between measurement of (non)-markovianity and measurement of Granger causality. Both of them can be framed in terms of prediction: how much is the forecast accuracy deteriorated when forgetting some relevant conditioning information? In this paper we argue that this common feature between (non)-markovianity and Granger causality has led people to overestimate the amount of causality because what they consider as a causality measure may also convey a measure of the amount of (non)-markovianity. We set a special focus on the design of measures that properly disentangle these two components. Furthermore, this disentangling

Essays in Honor of Aman Ullah
Advances in Econometrics, Volume 36, 349–385

ISSN: 0731-9053/doi:10.1108/S0731-905320160000036019

leads us to revisit the equivalence between the Sims and Granger concepts of noncausality and the log-likelihood ratio tests for each of them. We argue that Granger causality implies testing for non-nested hypotheses.

Keywords: Granger causality; Sims causality; Kullback information; Markov property; likelihood ratio test; non-nested hypotheses

JEL classifications: C01; C12; C32; C53

1. INTRODUCTION

As first raised by Geweke (1982, p. 304), using measures of causality is important, beyond testing for independence or unidirectional causality, because "in the typical case in which the hypothesis of independence ... is not literally entertained," it requires that one be able to measure the actual degree of causality. We argue in this paper that this measurement issue should be adjusted according to the goal of the study. On the one hand, following Sims (1972, p. 540), one may want to question "the practice of making causal interpretations of distributed lag regressions of income on money" or, more generally, to make an economic interpretation of the evidence of some degree of causality. While, on the other hand, one may simply want to choose a forecasting formula, in the spirit of Hoel (1947). The former objective entails a measure of causality that may be different from the one needed for the latter objective.

According to this duality of objectives, we emphasize that two alternative measures of causality may be relevant, depending upon the question at stake. The difference is actually due to a new point of view on causality measurement. The main contribution of our new approach is to disentangle the measure of Granger causality with a measure of non-Markovianity.

Geweke's (1982) measure of linear feedback has been path-breaking and led to a very general Kullback causality measure proposed by Gouriéroux, Monfort, and Renault 1987 (GMR throughout) for a general process under the maintained assumption that (X, Y) is a Markov process of order p. This Kullback causality measure has been more recently dubbed "transfer entropy" by Schreiber (2000). Even though this framework has a very general validity, we question in this paper a maintained point of view shared by Geweke (1982), GMR, as well as Schreiber (2000), and summarized as follows by GMR (p. 390): "despite the fact that the process X does not have a marginal autoregressive representation of order p, the marginal regression has to be performed after a truncation at **this order** p."

We introduce the bold notation for the definition of "**this order** p" because it encapsulates our difference with the former literature.

We stress that obviously if (X, Y) is jointly Markov of order p, it is also Markov of order $(p + r)$ for any positive number r. While this non-uniqueness of Markov order is immaterial for statistical inference about the joint process (X, Y), it is crucial when stating as GMR (p. 390) that "the marginal regression has to be performed after a truncation at this order p." We note that when the marginal regression is performed after a truncation at order $(p + r)$, increasing r could dramatically reduce the Granger causality measure. Of course, when Y does not cause X in the Granger sense, X is itself Markov of order p. This is the reason why Geweke (1982, p. 309) notes that the auto-regression of X on p of its own lags is constrained maximum likelihood (constrained by the non-causality hypothesis) so that the proposed causality measure corresponds to the likelihood ratio test.

However, we argue that, when measuring causality, we precisely have in mind a case where causality is at play, so that X is not marginally a Markov process of order p. There is no reason to perform a regression of X on only p (or even $p + r$) of its own lags. Increasing r decreases the causality measure and it is only for r tending to infinity that we rightly assess the degree of causality. The overestimated causality measure obtained by a marginal regression on $(p + r)$ lags encapsulates not only the right causality measure, but also a measure of "non-Markovianity." That is, how far the process X is from being Markov of order $(p + r)$. While, generalizing Geweke (1982), GMR prove asymptotic equivalence between their Kullback causality measure and the aforementioned likelihood ratio test statistic, this equivalence is valid only under the null hypothesis of non-causality. In contrast, we consider, like Geweke (1982, p. 304), that it is precisely in the typical case in which the hypothesis of noncausality is "not literally entertained" that the causality measure is useful. Hence, one needs to revisit the measure proposed by Geweke (1982) and generalized by GMR.

The main innovation of this paper is to revisit the issue of causality measure in a framework of non-nested hypotheses. We argue that, when the process (X, Y) is assumed to be Markov of order p, assessing the degree of Granger causality from Y to X is not equivalent to comparing the probability distributions of X given p lagged values, including and not including lagged values of Y. When lagged values of Y are not included, the probability distribution of X given its own lagged values should rather include $(p + r)$ lags, with a large r. Since the Kullback contrast is not endowed with the symmetry property of a genuine distance, considering two non-nested models leads to two possible candidates for a causality measure: either the DGP (Data Generating Process) corresponds to the model where having only p lags of X is compensated by including p lags of Y, or it corresponds to the model where not including lagged values of Y is compensated by having $p + r$, instead of p, lagged values of X. In the former case, the causality measure is given by the Kullback contrast between the DGP and the closest candidate distribution without causality, evaluated at the DGp. In the latter case, one works the other way round by maintaining the assumption that the process X alone is Markov of order $(p+r)$. That is, one wonders what is the probability distribution the closest to the DGP, when allowing for only p lags on the distribution of X given the past but adding past p values of Y to the conditioning information. The Kullback contrast computed in this manner provides an alternative causality measure.

These two alternative causality measures correspond to the two possible strategies for the Cox procedure of modified likelihood ratio (MLR) principle for testing non-nested hypotheses. The first approach tests whether the null hypothesis "(X, Y) Markov of order p" can be rejected by considering the performance of a forecasting equation where X can be forecasted from $(p+r)$ of its own lags. We argue that this first point of view is better suited for addressing the issue of the choice of a forecasting formula, in the spirit of Hoel (1947). When the Kullback measure takes a large value, it means that a large number of lagged values of X is not sufficient to mimic the actual predicting distribution of X given p lagged values of X and Y jointly. Following Hoel's (1947) terminology, the multivariate framework allowing for the forecast of X by using not only its own past but also the past of other variables Y can be seen as "the new forecasting formula," while working only with the past of X is the "old formula." Then, it is natural to make the null hypothesis correspond to the new formula. Typically we have in mind circumstances in which the new formula has some advantages in terms of parsimony because $[p. \dim(Y)] < [r. \dim(X)]$.

The second approach tests whether the null hypothesis "X Markov of order $(p+r)$" can be rejected by considering the performance for forecasting X of an alternative model for (X, Y) that is jointly Markov of order p. Rejecting the null hypothesis in this context provides evidence of Granger causality from Y to X that is even more compelling than the standard likelihood ratio test computed with the constrained version of a parametric model for a process (X, Y) jointly Markov of order p. In fact, in this situation, the Cox MLR test statistic tells us that not only the p lagged values of Y have significant coefficients when the forecasting formula includes p lagged values of X, but also they are significant if one adds a large number r of lagged values of X. Therefore, our second Kullback causality measure and the associated Cox test is better suited when the question at stake is really the theoretical question of non-causality from Y to X (see, e.g., the discussion in Sims, 1972).

As extensively discussed by Pesaran and Weeks (2001), the dual aspect of tests for non-nested hypotheses leads to two different interpretations: model choice for the purpose of decision making or testing for the empirical validity of a theoretical prediction. The former interpretation, and thus our first causality measure, is more about decision making: choosing the best forecasting formula. By contrast, the second causality measure is really assessing the amount of causality from Y to X, in the sense of a theoretical statement.

Besides the aforementioned existing causality measures, as well as the application in econometrics of the Cox principle for MLR (see, e.g., Fisher & McAleer, 1981; Gouriéroux & Monfort, 1994; Pesaran, 1982), the methodology set forth in this paper is also related to the concept of "asymmetric VAR" as put forward by Hsiao (1979, 1981) and Keating (2000). The idea of asymmetric VAR is to identify different lag orders for different variables entering a multivariate autoregressive process. The latter authors have precisely stated the importance of this approach for causality testing. For instance Keating (2000, p. 2) emphasizes that "each equation of a bivariate VAR could have 3 lags of output and 6 lags of money," which is analogous to us having a larger number $(p + r)$ of lags for the candidate exogenous variables X.

Finally, it is worth noting that the mutual implications between non-Markovianity and causality that has obliged us to cautiously derive a strategy of non-nested hypotheses is immaterial in the context of Sims non-causality. It has been documented in the literature that Sims and Granger noncausality are not fully equivalent for at least two reasons: role of initial variables (Chamberlain, 1982; Florens & Mouchart, 1982) as well as the impact of a third variable Z included in the forecasting environment (Dufour & Tessier, 1993). While the introduction of a third variable (or a set of variables) Z in the environment is beyond the scope of this paper, we revisit the role of initial values in the context of causality measures. It sheds more light on the interpretation of the nonequivalence pointed out by Chamberlain (1982) and Florens and Mouchart (1982), but also on the role of the Markov assumption in discussing this equivalence (see also Florens, Mouchart, & Rolin, 1993).

This paper is organized as follows. In Section 2, we revisit the Kullback causality measures for Sims and Granger noncausality (from Y to X) as already introduced by GMR. However, in contrast with these authors, we do not maintain any Markov assumption. This allows us to characterize the difference between the two concepts and their measures through a concept and a measure of initiation of X by Y. In Section 3, we analyze extensively the impact of the Markov assumption on our causality measures. More generally, we document the possible overestimation of causality measures due to the discrepancy between a true value and a pseudo-true value. Besides the theoretical definition of the measures, we describe their sample counterparts and their connection with a Cox procedure for testing non-nested hypotheses. The asymmetry of the Cox procedure leads us to explicitly disentangle two testing strategies, depending on whether the focus of interest is the choice of a practical forecasting formula or really an empirical assessment of some theoretical statement on noncausality. For sake of illustration we provide in Section 4 some numerical evidence of the overestimation of Granger causality due to a confusion with non-Markovianity. Finally, Section 5 provides some concluding remarks and sketches some paths for extensions. The main mathematical proofs are gathered in the appendix.

2. INFORMATION THEORETIC CAUSALITY MEASURES

2.1. General Framework

We consider a multivariate discrete time process that starts at time $t=-\varpi$ and is denoted by $\{Z_t; t \geq -\varpi\}$. Each component Z_t is partitioned into two subvectors, X_t and Y_t, whose ranges are respectively $\Re(X)$ and $\Re(Y)$, some subsets of Euclidean spaces; the range of Z_t is $\Re(X) \times \Re(Y)$. Vectors $(X'_{t+h}, X'_{t+h-1}, \ldots, X'_t)', (Y'_{t+h}, Y'_{t+h-1}, \ldots, Y'_t)'$ and $(Z'_{t+h}, Z'_{t+h-1}, \ldots, Z'_t)'$ are denoted by X_t^{t+h}, Y_t^{t+h} and Z_t^{t+h}, respectively. The probability distribution of the process $\{Z_t; t \geq -\varpi\}$ is defined by:

(i) The probability distribution of the initial vector $Z^0_{-\varpi}$ which is assumed to have a probability density function $f_0\left(z^0_{-\varpi}\right) = f_0\left(x^0_{-\varpi}, y^0_{-\varpi}\right)$ with respect to a product measure $\otimes_{i=0}^{\varpi}\mu(dz_{-i})$ where $\mu(dz)$ is itself a product measure $\mu_x(dx) \times \mu_y(dy)$ on $\Re(X) \times \Re(Y)$;
(ii) The conditional probability distributions of Z_t given $Z_{-\varpi}^{t-1}$, for any $t \geq 1$, which are assumed to have a p.d.f. $f_{0t}\left(z_t | z_{-\varpi}^{t-1}\right)$ with respect to μ (which, for notational simplicity, is assumed to be the same for all t).

The joint p.d.f. of $Z^t_{-\varpi}$ with respect to $\otimes_{i=-\varpi}^{t}\mu(dz_i)$ is:

$$f_{0t}\left(z^t_{-\varpi}\right) = f_0\left(z^0_{-\varpi}\right) \prod_{i=1}^{t} f_{0i}\left(z_i | z_{-\varpi}^{i-1}\right)$$

Note that the notation $f_{0t}\left(z_t | z_{-\varpi}^{t-1}\right)$ allows the process $\{Z_t; t \geq -\varpi\}$ to be non-stationary. For instance, even in the case of a Markov process of order $p \leq \varpi + 1$, that is, the case when

$$f_{0t}\left(z_t | z_{-\varpi}^{t-1}\right) = f_{0t}\left(z_t | z_{-p+1}^{t-1}\right),$$

the transition density $f_{0t}(z_t \mid z_{-p+1}^{t-1})$ may depend on t. In order to accommodate nonstationarity, our definitions below of noncausality depend on the range of observations, namely $t = 1, \ldots, T$, on top of possibly some conditioning initial values $t = 0, -1, \ldots, -\varpi$. In other words, every time we write "Y does not cause X" in some sense, the reader should understand that "Y does not cause X between dates $(-\varpi)$ and T."

2.2. *Kullback Measure of Sims Causality*

Following Chamberlain's (1982) extension of Sims' (1972) concept of noncausality, we first define:

Definition 1 (*Sims noncausality*). *Y does not cause X in the Sims sense (Y.NCS.X) if, for all* $t = 1, \ldots, T$:

$$f_{0t}\left(y_t | x_{-\varpi}^T, y_{-\varpi}^{t-1}\right) = f_{0t}\left(y_t | x_{-\varpi}^t, y_{-\varpi}^{t-1}\right),$$

Following GMR, we define a Kullback measure of causality from Y to X, in the Sims sense, by considering the set of all possible p.d.f.s $f_t\left(z_{-\varpi}^t\right)$, $t = 1, 2, \ldots, T$, for which, possibly by contrast with the Data Generating Process (DGP) $f_{0t}\left(z_{-\varpi}^t\right)$, $t = 1, 2, \ldots, T$, there is no causality in the Sims sense from Y to X:

$$HS[Y \nrightarrow X] = \{f_T(\cdot);\ Y.NCS.X\}$$

with, by definition,

$$f_T\left(z_{-\varpi}^T\right) = f\left(z_{-\varpi}^0\right) \prod_{t=1}^{T} f_t\left(z_t | z_{-\varpi}^{t-1}\right)$$

Then, we can define a discrepancy between the DGP and the noncausality hypothesis in the Sims sense by solving the program:

$$\begin{cases} \text{Min} \dfrac{1}{T} \mathbb{E}_0 \log \left(\dfrac{f_{0T}\left(z_{-\varpi}^T\right)}{f_T\left(z_{-\varpi}^T\right)} \right) \\ \text{s.t.} \quad f_T(\cdot) \in HS[Y \nrightarrow X] \end{cases} \tag{1}$$

We define our Kullback measure of Sims causality from Y to X, denoted by $CS_{Y \to X}(T)$, as the value of the minimization program (1). We can show that:

Proposition 1. *The value of the program* (1) *is:*

$$CS_{Y\to X}(T) = \frac{1}{T}\sum_{t=1}^{T}\mathbb{E}_0 \log\left(\frac{f_{0t}\left(y_t|x_{-\varpi}^{T}, y_{-\varpi}^{t-1}\right)}{f_{0t}\left(y_t|x_{-\varpi}^{t}, y_{-\varpi}^{t-1}\right)}\right)$$

The notation $CS_{Y\to X}(T)$ stresses that the Sims causality measure depends on the range $\{1, 2, \ldots, T\}$ of observations, while the initial date $(-\varpi)$ is considered throughout as given.

Then, obviously:

Corollary 1.

$$CS_{Y\to X}(T) \geq 0$$
$$CS_{Y\to X}(T) = 0 \Leftrightarrow Y.NCS.X$$

2.3. *Initiation of* X *by* Y

The Sims noncausality property allows the econometrician to write down a model in which endogenous variables y_t are explained by predetermined variables, that comprises past endogenous variables, $y_{-\varpi}^{t-1}$, as well as past and present exogenous variables, $x_{-\varpi}^{t}$. However, in order to fully specify the conditional probability distribution of the observed path z_1^T given the initial values $z_{-\varpi}^{0}$, it also takes a specification of the initiation of the observed path x_1^T of exogenous variables by possibly the endogenous ones $y_{-\varpi}^{0}$. This is obvious from the following decomposition where both the roles of Sims noncausality and initiation are displayed in bold notations:

$$\frac{f_T\left(z_{-\varpi}^{T}\right)}{f_0\left(z_{-\varpi}^{0}\right)} = f_T\left(x_1^T|x_{-\varpi}^{0}, \mathbf{y}_{-\varpi}^{0}\right)\prod_{t=1}^{T} f_t\left(y_t|x_{-\varpi}^{\mathbf{T}}, y_{-\varpi}^{t-1}\right) \tag{2}$$

While Sims noncausality is about some simplification of the second part of the RHS of Eq. (2), the initiation issue arises from the first part. We then define:

Definition 2 (*Non-initiation*). *Y does not initiate X (Y.NI.X) if:*

$$f_T\left(x_1^T|x_{-\varpi}^{0}, y_{-\varpi}^{0}\right) = f_T\left(x_1^T|x_{-\varpi}^{0}\right)$$

Similar to the methodology of causality measurement described above, we will define a Kullback measure of initiation of X by Y by considering the set of all possible p.d.f. $f_t\left(z_{-\varpi}^t\right)$, $t=1,2,\ldots,T$, for which, possibly by contrast with the DGP $f_{0t}\left(z_{-\varpi}^t\right)$, $t=1,2,\ldots,T$, there is no such initiation:

$$HIN[Y \nrightarrow X]=\{f_T(\cdot);\ Y.NI.X\}$$

Then, we can characterize a discrepancy between the DGP and the non-initiation hypothesis by solving the program:

$$\begin{cases} \text{Min}\dfrac{1}{T}\mathbb{E}_0 \log\left(\dfrac{f_{0T}\left(z_{-\varpi}^T\right)}{f_T\left(z_{-\varpi}^T\right)}\right) \\ \text{s.t.} \quad f_T(\cdot)\in HIN[Y \nrightarrow X] \end{cases} \tag{3}$$

We define our Kullback measure of initiation of X by Y, denoted by $CIN_{Y\to X}(T)$, as the value of the minimization program (3). We can show that:

Proposition 2. *The value of the program* (3) *is:*

$$CIN_{Y\to X}(T)=\frac{1}{T}\sum_{t=1}^{T}\mathbb{E}_0 \log\left(\frac{f_{0t}\left(x_t|x_{-\varpi}^{t-1},y_{-\varpi}^0\right)}{f_{0t}\left(x_t|x_{-\varpi}^{t-1}\right)}\right)$$

Then, obviously:

Corollary 2.

$$\begin{aligned} CIN_{Y\to X}(T) &\geq 0 \\ CIN_{Y\to X}(T) &= 0 \Leftrightarrow Y.NI.X \end{aligned}$$

It is worth noting that $CIN_{Y\to X}(T)$ is a Cesaro mean of a sequence u_t with

$$u_t=\mathbb{E}_0 \log\left(\frac{f_{0t}(x_t\,|x_{-\varpi}^{t-1},y_{-\varpi}^0)}{f_{0t}(x_t\,|x_{-\varpi}^{t-1})}\right)$$

Following Chamberlain (1982), we consider the following condition (R):

Condition (R).

$$\lim_{t=\infty} u_t=0$$

Under regularity conditions, our Condition (R) is equivalent to condition (R) introduced by Chamberlain (1982, p. 571). Chamberlain (1982, p. 571) notes that "condition (R) requires that the current effect of y's from the distant past vanishes; similar assumptions are routine in the analysis of aggregate time-series data." Even though stationarity is not a maintained assumption for us, Condition (R) is obviously related to the concept of ergodicity. From the aforementioned Cesaro mean argument, we deduce that:

Proposition 3. *Under Condition (R):*

$$\lim_{T=\infty} CIN_{Y\to X}(T) = 0$$

It is worth noting that more often than not, at least in a stationary environment, this limit will be a decreasing limit because the sequence u_t itself should be nonincreasing. To see that, imagine the case of a process $\{Z_t;\ t \geq -\varpi\}$ that is stationary Gaussian. Then, the question is akin to the behavior of a function:

$$h(n) = \mathbb{E}\log\left(\frac{f\,(Z|X_1, X_2, \ldots, X_n, Y)}{f\,(Z|X_1, X_2, \ldots, X_n)}\right), \quad n = 1, 2, \ldots, N \tag{4}$$

when p.d.f.s are computed from the joint Gaussian distribution of a vector $(Z, X_1, X_2, \ldots, X_N, Y)'$. Obviously, the difference between the numerator and the denominator in Eq. (4) is fully explained by the informational content of the difference:

$$Y - \mathbb{E}[Y\,|X_1, X_2, \ldots, X_n]$$

Thus, this difference should obviously be reduced when n increases.

2.4. *From Sims Causality to Granger Causality*

Following Granger's (1969) approach to causality, we now define:

Definition 3 (*Granger non-causality*). *Y does not cause X in the Granger sense (Y.NCG.X) if, for all* $t = 1, \ldots, T$:

$$f_{0t}\left(x_t|x_{-\varpi}^{t-1}, y_{-\varpi}^{t-1}\right) = f_{0t}\left(x_t|x_{-\varpi}^{t-1}\right)$$

Following GMR, we define a Kullback measure of causality from Y to X, in the Granger sense, by considering the set of all possible p.d.f.s $f_t\left(z_{-\varpi}^t\right)$, $t = 1, 2, \ldots, T$ for which, possibly by contrast with the Data Generating Process (DGP) $f_{0t}\left(z_{-\varpi}^t\right)$, $t = 1, 2, \ldots, T$ there is no causality in the Granger sense from Y to X:

$$HG[Y \nrightarrow X] = \{f_T\,(\cdot)\,;\ Y.NCG.X\}$$

Then, we can define a discrepancy between the DGP and the noncausality hypothesis in the Granger sense by solving the program:

$$\begin{cases} \text{Min}\frac{1}{T}\mathbb{E}_0 \log\left(\frac{f_{0T}\left(z_{-\varpi}^T\right)}{f_T\left(z_{-\varpi}^T\right)}\right) \\ \text{s.t.} \quad f_T(\cdot) \in HG[Y \nrightarrow X] \end{cases} \tag{5}$$

We define our Kullback measure of Granger causality from Y to X, denoted by $CG_{Y\to X}(T)$, as the value of the minimization program (5). We can show that:

Proposition 4. *The value of the program* (5) *is:*

$$CG_{Y\to X}(T) = \frac{1}{T}\sum_{t=1}^{T}\mathbb{E}_0 \log\left(\frac{f_{0t}\left(x_t|x_{-\varpi}^{t-1}, y_{-\varpi}^{t-1}\right)}{f_{0t}\left(x_t|x_{-\varpi}^{t-1}\right)}\right)$$

Then, obviously:

Corollary 3.

$$\begin{aligned} CG_{Y\to X}(T) &\geq 0 \\ CG_{Y\to X}(T) &= 0 \Leftrightarrow Y.NCG.X \end{aligned}$$

Moreover, the comparison of propositions 1, 2, and 4 shows that:

Proposition 5.

$$CG_{Y\to X}(T) = CS_{Y\to X}(T) + CIN_{Y\to X}(T)$$

Then, since all these measures are non-negative, we deduce:

Corollary 4. *Y does not cause X in the Granger sense if and only if the two following conditions are fulfilled:*

(i) Y does not cause X in the Sims sense
(ii) Y does not initiate X

In other words, Proposition 5 sheds some new light on an issue already pointed out by Florens and Mouchart (1982, p. 587) "Granger noncausality still implies, but is not equivalent to, Sims noncausality. Some care has to be taken (..) in order to handle the initial condition properly." Similarly to Theorem 3 in Chamberlain (1982, p. 575), the conjunction of Proposition 4 and 5 shows that the equivalence is restored for large T if condition (R) holds:

Corollary 5. *Under Condition (R):*

$$\lim_{T=\infty} CG_{Y\to X}(T) = \lim_{T=\infty} CS_{Y\to X}(T)$$

3. CAUSALITY MEASURES AND PSEUDO-TRUE VALUES

3.1. General Issue

For the purpose of statistical inference, causality measures have mainly been studied, so far, in the context of stationary Markov processes. Hence, we will maintain throughout the assumption that the process $\{Z_t; t \geq -\varpi\}$ is stationary Markov of order p. This assumption is especially convenient to simplify the expression of the Granger causality measure:

$$CG_{Y\to X}(T) = \mathbb{E}_0 \log\left[f_0\left(x_t|x_{t-p}^{t-1}, y_{t-p}^{t-1}\right)\right] - \frac{1}{T}\sum_{t=1}^{T} \mathbb{E}_0 \log\left[f_{0t}\left(x_t|x_{-\varpi}^{t-1}\right)\right] \quad (6)$$

where $f_0\left(x_t|x_{t-p}^{t-1}, y_{t-p}^{t-1}\right)$ stands for the time invariant transition p.d.f. of this stationary Markov process. It is worth stressing that by contrast, in spite of stationarity, $f_{0t}\left(x_t|x_{-\varpi}^{t-1}\right)$ depends in general on t because the process $\{X_t;\ t \geq -\varpi\}$ is not Markov and thus the number of relevant lagged values in the conditioning information increases with t. In the context of a parametric model, the marginal transition p.d.f. and the expectation of its logarithm may be computed by using the ARMA structure of the process $\{X_t;\ t \geq -\varpi\}$. However, this difficulty seems to have been largely overlooked in the literature. Instead of computing properly the causality measure $CG_{Y\to X}(T)$ in Eq. (6) as the value of the minimization program (5), people would in general prefer to simplify the computation by solving instead:

$$\begin{cases} \text{Min} \dfrac{1}{T} E_0 \log\left(\dfrac{f_{0T}\left(z_{-\varpi}^{T}\right)}{f_T\left(z_{-\varpi}^{T}\right)}\right) \\ \text{s.t.} \quad f_T(\cdot) \in HG_c[Y \nrightarrow X] \end{cases} \quad (7)$$

where $HG_c[Y \nrightarrow X]$ is a strict subset of $HG[Y \nrightarrow X]$ because some of the properties assumed for the DGP have been imposed to the candidate density function $f_T(\cdot)$. Obviously, this approach will lead in general to overestimate the actual level of causality, when the distance between the DGP and the reduced set $HG_c[Y \nrightarrow X]$ is actually also due to some other constraints. Examples of this issue in the extant literature are described below.

3.2. Causality and Markovianity

Most of extant empirical applications of causality measures lie within a Markov framework: the process (X, Y) is assumed to be stationary Markov of some order p. Examples of application include Gaussian VAR(p) models (Geweke, 1982), Qualitative Panel data models (Bouissou, Laffont, & Vuong, 1986) and lattices in physical systems (Schreiber, 2000). All these examples fit within the framework described above if we maintain the assumption that the number $(\varpi + 1)$ of initial values is not smaller than p.

As already mentioned, Geweke (1982, p. 309) is led to "begin by supposing that for purpose of estimation, all lag lengths in the canonical form have been truncated at p." It is a way to acknowledge that he has solved the minimization program (7) with:

$$\begin{aligned} HG_c[Y \nrightarrow X] &= HG\,[Y \nrightarrow X|p] \\ &= \{f_T(\cdot)\,;\, Y.NCG.X \text{ and } Z \sim Mar(p)\} \end{aligned} \tag{8}$$

where the notation $Z \sim Mar(p)$ means that the process $\{Z_t;\ t \geq -\varpi\}$ is stationary Markov of order p. We can show more generally that:

Proposition 6. *If* $Z \sim Mar(p)$, *and* $p \leq q \leq \varpi + 1$, *the value* $CG_{Y\to X}(q)$ *of the program* (7) *with* $HG_c[Y \nrightarrow X] = HG\,[Y \nrightarrow X|q]$ *is:*

$$CG_{Y\to X}(q) = \mathbb{E}_0 \log\left[f_0\left(x_t|x_{t-p}^{t-1}, y_{t-p}^{t-1}\right)\right] - \mathbb{E}_0 \log\left[f_0\left(x_t|x_{t-q}^{t-1}\right)\right]$$

The proof of Proposition 6 is straightforward from Eq. (6) with the Mar(q) assumption in the definition of $HG_c[Y \nrightarrow X]$. Moreover, note that since by stationarity and Markov property the Granger causality measure does not depend on T anymore, we have simplified the notation.

Obviously:

Corollary 6.

$$q \leq q' \leq \varpi + 1 \Rightarrow CG_{Y\to X}(q) \geq CG_{Y\to X}(q') \geq CG_{Y\to X}(T)$$

It is worth noting that $CG_{Y\to X}(q)$ overestimates the actual measure $CG_{Y\to X}(T)$ of causality precisely because it adds a term measuring the amount of non-Markovianity at degree q for the process X. More precisely

Corollary 7. *If $Z \sim Mar(p)$, and $p \leq q \leq \varpi + 1$:*

$$CG_{Y\to X}(q) - CG_{Y\to X}(T) = \frac{1}{T}\sum_{t=1}^{T} \mathbb{E}_0 \log\left(\frac{f_{0t}\left(x_t|x_{-\varpi}^{t-1}\right)}{f_0\left(x_t|x_{t-q}^{t-1}\right)}\right) = M_X(q)$$

where $M_X(q)$ is the value of the minimization program:

$$\begin{cases} \text{Min}\,\frac{1}{T}\mathbb{E}_0 \log\left(\frac{f_{0T}\left(z_{-\varpi}^{T}\right)}{f_T\left(z_{-\varpi}^{T}\right)}\right) \\ s.t. \quad X \sim Mar(q) \end{cases} \tag{9}$$

Recall that $Z \sim Mar(p)$ is the maintained assumption. The reason why it is the markovianity of the process X that is now at stake is the following. Obviously X is Markov of order p when Y does not cause X in the Granger sense (see J. Florens et al., 1993 for necessary and sufficient conditions). However, when looking for the p.d.f.s with noncausality the closest to the DGP, there is no reason to limit ourselves to stochastic processes that are themselves Markov of order p. After all, when Y does cause X, one may sometimes realize that the accuracy loss (in forecasting a future value of X) due to omission of the past values of Y in the conditioning information is not so important when one allows herself to keep a large number of lagged values of X in the conditioning information. In this case, a large value of $CG_{Y\to X}(p)$ may rather be seen as a signal that X is far from being a Markov process (of the small order q considered) rather than evidence of a high degree of causality from Y to X. Actually, Corollary 7 points out the right additive decomposition to assess the trade off between causality and non-Markovianity:

$$CG_{Y\to X}(q) = CG_{Y\to X}(T) + M_X(q) \tag{10}$$

If we think about Kullback–Leibler discrepancy (KL herefafter) as a squared norm in some Hilbert space (see for instance the formula of KL in the case of Gaussian distributions, Kullback (1968, p. 189) or Gouriéroux & Monfort (1995, p. 15), see also the example in the next subsection), equality (10) looks like an application of Pythagoras' theorem. The noncausality property *Y.NCG.X* and the Markov property $X \sim Mar(q)$ (when $Z = (X', Y')' \sim Mar(p)$, $p \leq q$) look like defined by two "orthogonal directions," the squared distances to them being additive.

Overestimation of the causality measure $CG_{Y\to X}(T)$ due to the Markov measure $M_X(q)$ is of course maximum for the choice $q = p$, which is typically the common practice in applications (due to the fact that X is Markov of order p when Y does not cause X). By contrast, since the theory tells us that we should rather consider a model with an infinite number of lags, in practice one would have a large number q.

A possible way to devise a proper asymptotic theory for this practice would be to consider a number q_T of lags going to infinity with T, albeit slower than T (see, e.g., Berk, 1974).[1] Another possible approach would be to resort to ARMA models (see Boudjellaba, Dufour, & Roy, 1992; Dufour, Pelletier, & Renault, 2006 for related discussions). The example of Gaussian transition densities will allow us to assess even further the possible overestimation of causality due to the use of pseudo-true values.

3.3. *The Case of a Parametric Model for a Markov Process*

In this section, we discuss more explicitly the assessment of a causality measure like $CG_{Y\to X}(p)$ as characterized in Proposition 6 above:

$$CG_{Y\to X}(p) = \mathbb{E}_0 \log\left[f_0\left(x_t | x_{t-p}^{t-1}, y_{t-p}^{t-1}\right)\right] - \mathbb{E}_0 \log\left[f_0\left(x_t | x_{t-p}^{t-1}\right)\right]$$

under the maintained assumption that the process (X, Y) is Markov of order p with transition densities defined by a parametric model:

$$f_0\left(x_t, y_t | x_{t-p}^{t-1}, y_{t-p}^{t-1}\right) = f\left(x_t, y_t | x_{t-p}^{t-1}, y_{t-p}^{t-1}; \theta^0\right)$$

where θ^0 stands for the true unknown value of the parameter vector $\theta \in \Theta \subset \mathbb{R}^p$.

3.3.1. *The Case of a Gaussian Process*

It is the case of the Gaussian VAR(p) as studied by Geweke (1982). For the sake of notational simplicity, we will assume throughout that the process X is of dimension 1. Then, the conditional probability distribution of X_t given $(X_{t-p}^{t-1'}, Y_{t-p}^{t-1'})'$ (resp. given X_{t-p}^{t-1}) is the normal distribution with mean $m_t = \mathbb{E}[X_t \mid (X_{t-p}^{t-1'}, Y_{t-p}^{t-1'})']$ (resp. $m_t^* = \mathbb{E}(X_t \mid X_{t-p}^{t-1})$) and variance σ^2 (resp. σ^{*2}) where:

m_t (resp. m_t^*) is the affine regression of X_t on $(X_{t-p}^{t-1'}, Y_{t-p}^{t-1'})'$ (resp. on X_{t-p}^{t-1})

and:

$$\sigma^{*2} = \sigma^2 + Var\left[m_t - m_t^*\right] \tag{11}$$

Then, by virtue of the formula for KL in the case of Gaussian distributions:

$$CG_{Y\to X}(p) = \log\left(\frac{\sigma^*}{\sigma}\right) + \frac{1}{2}\left(\frac{\sigma^2}{\sigma^{*2}} - 1\right) + \frac{Var\left[m_t - m_t^*\right]}{2\sigma^{*2}} = \log\left(\frac{\sigma^*}{\sigma}\right) \tag{12}$$

where the last equality is obtained thanks to Eq. (11). As noted by GMR, this provides a parametric interpretation of the KL causality measure in terms of pseudo-true value. More precisely, we can write:

$$f_0\left(x_t, y_t | x_{t-p}^{t-1}, y_{t-p}^{t-1}\right) = f\left(x_t, y_t | x_{t-p}^{t-1}, y_{t-p}^{t-1}; \theta^0\right)$$

where θ^0 stands for the true unknown value of the parameter vector θ whose components include the coefficients of the affine function $\mathbb{E}[(X_t, Y_t) \,|\, (X_{t-p}^{t-1'}, Y_{t-p}^{t-1'})']$ as well as the parameters to describe the residual variance (including the parameter σ^2 for the residual variance of X_t). Thus, instead of solving (7) over a set of probability distributions defined by Eq. (8), one could have contemplated rather solving the minimization program (7) with:

$$\begin{aligned} HG_c[Y \nrightarrow X] = \{ & f_T(\cdot)\,;\, Y.NCG.X \text{ and} \\ & \exists\theta \in \Theta,\ f\left(x_t, y_t | x_{t-p}^{t-1}, y_{t-p}^{t-1}\right) = f\left(x_t, y_t | x_{t-p}^{t-1}, y_{t-p}^{t-1}; \theta\right)\} \end{aligned} \tag{13}$$

It turns out that Eq. (13) does not add any constraint with respect to Eq. (8). As it is obvious from Eqs. (11) and (12) we actually have:

$$CG_{Y\to X}(p) = \mathbb{E}_0 \log\left[f\left(x_t | x_{t-p}^{t-1}, y_{t-p}^{t-1}; \theta^0\right)\right] - \mathbb{E}_0 \log\left[f\left(x_t | x_{t-p}^{t-1}; \nu(\theta^0)\right)\right] \tag{14}$$

where $\nu(\theta^0)$ defines the KL pseudo-true value of θ, that is the value of θ that makes the transition density $f\left(x_t, y_t | x_{t-p}^{t-1}, y_{t-p}^{t-1}; \theta\right)$ the closest possible (in the KL sense) to the DGP, subject to restrictions defined by Eq. (13). From Eqs. (11) and (12) respectively, we see that $f\left(x_t | x_{t-p}^{t-1}, y_{t-p}^{t-1}; \nu(\theta^0)\right)$ is the normal distribution with mean:

$$m_t^* = \mathbb{E}\left(X_t | X_{t-p}^{t-1}; \theta^0\right)$$

and variance:

$$\sigma^{*2} = (\sigma^0)^2 + Var\left[\mathbb{E}\left(X_t | (X_{t-p}^{t-1'}, Y_{t-p}^{t-1'})'; \theta^0\right) - \mathbb{E}\left(X_t | X_{t-p}^{t-1}; \theta^0\right)\right]$$

Formula (14) explains why Geweke (1982) noticed that the sample counterpart of the Kullback causality measure is nothing but (up to scaling) the likelihood ratio (LR hereafter) test statistic for the null of noncausality. A sample counterpart of the pseudo-true value is the constrained maximum likelihood estimator (MLE) of θ. Of course, due to inequalities of Corollary 6, it may be misleading to test for noncausality by just looking at the sample counterpart of $CG_{Y\to X}(p)$. A reinterpretation of this problem in terms of testing strategy is that, as usual, the LR test does not take properly into account the need to compare models of similar dimensions. The Akaike Information Criterion (AIC) approach put forward in this context by Polasek (1994, 2000) does not fix this issue. We would have a valid comparison between models of similar dimensions if we would have compared a specification Markov of order p for Z (with causality from Y to X) with a specification Markov of order $p\left[1+\frac{\dim(Y)}{\dim(X)}\right]$ for X in isolation.

3.3.2. The General Case

GMR go one step further by proposing more generally to compute causality measures within a given parametric model by using the pseudo-true value. More precisely, they would generally consider:

$$HG_c^*[Y \rightarrow X] = \{f_T(\cdot)\,;\ Y.NCG.X \text{ and } \exists\theta \in \Theta,\ f\left(x_t, y_t | x_{t-p}^{t-1}, y_{t-p}^{t-1}\right) = f\left(x_t, y_t | x_{t-p}^{t-1}, y_{t-p}^{t-1};\ \theta\right)\}$$

instead of

$$HG_c[Y \nrightarrow X] = \{f_T(\cdot)\,;\ Y.NCG.X \text{ and } Z \sim Mar(p)\}$$

As a result, they come up with an alternative causality measuree (see their formula for $\tilde{D}$ on page 384) generalizing the idea of Eq. (14) above:

$$CG^*_{Y\rightarrow X}(p) = \mathbb{E}_0 \log\left[f\left(x_t | x_{t-p}^{t-1}, y_{t-p}^{t-1};\ \theta^0\right)\right] - \mathbb{E}_0 \log\left[f\left(x_t | x_{t-p}^{t-1};\ \nu(\theta^0)\right)\right]$$

However, it is worth realizing that the coincidence between the two definitions of causality measures ($CG_{Y\rightarrow X}(p) = CG^*_{Y\rightarrow X}(p)$) that we found in the former subsection does not generalize beyond the simple Gaussian setting. Obviously, $HG_c^*[Y \nrightarrow X]$ is a strict subset of $HG_c[Y \nrightarrow X]$ and we should find more often than not that:

$$CG^*_{Y\rightarrow X}(p) > CG_{Y\rightarrow X}(p) \tag{15}$$

As already mentioned, GMR show in their Theorem 8 that, under the non-causality hypothesis, the sample counterparts of the two causality measures do not differ by more than a $o_P(1/T)$ term, so that after rescaling by a factor $(2T)$ to compute an LR test statistic, one is led to two asymptotically equivalent test statistics. But once more, this equivalence is valid only under the null hypothesis of noncausality, that is precisely the case when causality measurement is irrelevant.

By contrast , when it is relevant, by tightening her hands within a given parametric model, the econometrician will in general overestimate even more the actual amount of causality, by comparison with only maintaining the Markov (of same order p) assumption for the zero-causality proxy of the DGP. To see that, a simple generalization of the example of the former section featuring now conditional heteroskedasticity is sufficiently compelling. Let us assume now that both X and Y are univariate, $p=2$, and the conditional probability distribution of X_t given $(X_{t-2}^{t-1'}, Y_{t-2}^{t-1'})'$ is the normal distribution with mean m_t and variance σ_t^2 defined by:

$$m_t = c + aX_{t-1} + bY_{t-1} \tag{16}$$

$$\sigma_t^2 = \omega + \alpha\,(X_{t-1} - c - aX_{t-2} - bY_{t-2})^2$$

Obviously the conditional distribution of X_t given X_{t-2}^{t-1} does not belong in general to the parametric model delineated by conditional normality with mean and variance in the parametric specification (16). Therefore:

$$\mathbb{E}_0 \log\left[f\left(x_t | x_{t-2}^{t-1};\ \nu(\theta^0)\right)\right] < \mathbb{E}_0 \log\left[f_0\left(x_t | x_{t-2}^{t-1}\right)\right]$$

which in turns implies Eq. (15). The econometrician who uses an estimator of $CG_{Y\to X}^{*}(p)$ to assess the amount of causality from Y to X will overestimate this amount for two reasons. First, when X is forecasted from its own past, a Markov model of order $p=2$ is not appropriate. A higher order would give a more reliable assessment. Second, even within the set of processes that are Markov of order 2, there is no reason to believe that X in isolation is properly described by a $AR(1) - ARCH(1)$ model conformable to Eq. (16) (with $b=0$). It is well known that the GARCH model is not robust to marginalization (see Nijman & Sentana, 1996).

3.4. *Testing Non-Nested Hypotheses*

The main lesson of this section is that, when wondering whether there is a significant amount of causality from Y to X, one should not tight her hands by assuming that a model that sets the focus on the dynamics of X in isolation should be determined by the model at stake for the joint dynamics of X and Y. The two models should be non-nested. Of course, this comes with an important consequence when it comes to testing. Since, as shown above, the sample counterpart of KL causality measures leads naturally to LR tests, we should resort to the Cox procedure for testing non-nested hypotheses (see, e.g., Cox, 1962; Pesaran, 1974; and Gouriéroux & Monfort, 1994). When causality from Y to X is not precluded, we have in mind a parametric model where the process (X, Y) is Markov of order p with transition densities defined by:

$$f\left(x_t, y_t | x_{t-p}^{t-1}, y_{t-p}^{t-1}\right) = f\left(x_t, y_t | x_{t-p}^{t-1}, y_{t-p}^{t-1}; \theta\right), \quad \theta \in \Theta$$

The corresponding maximum (conditional) log-likelihood function evaluated under this hypothesis, let us call it $H(X|Y)$, is:

$$L_T\left\{\hat{\theta}_T;\ H(X|Y)\right\} = \sum_{t=1}^{T} \log\left[f\left(x_t, y_t | x_{t-p}^{t-1}, y_{t-p}^{t-1}; \hat{\theta}_T\right)\right]$$

where $\hat{\theta}_T$ stands for the (conditional) MLE in this model.

By contrast, when we want to maintain the null hypothesis of (Granger) non-causality from Y to X, we contemplate an asymmetric model in which the process X is Markov of order $q > p$:

$$f\left(x_t, y_t | x_{-\varpi}^{t-1}, y_{-\varpi}^{t-1}\right) = f\left(x_t | x_{t-q}^{t-1}; \lambda\right) f\left(y_t | x_{t-p}^{t}, y_{t-p}^{t-1}; \lambda\right), \quad \lambda \in \Lambda \qquad (17)$$

Note that we have assumed in Eq. (17) that Y_t is independent of Z_{t-r} for $r > p$. Let us call $H(X \mid X)$ this model. It is just an example of a possible way to specify the dynamics of (X, Y) in an asymmetric fashion. For instance, the extant literature on asymmetric VAR (see, e.g., Keating, 2000) would rather assume:

$$f\left(x_t, y_t | x_{-\varpi}^{t-1}, y_{-\varpi}^{t-1}\right) = f\left(x_t | x_{t-q}^{t-1}; \lambda\right) f\left(y_t | x_{t-q}^{t}, y_{t-p}^{t-1}; \lambda\right), \quad \lambda \in \Lambda$$

Even though we will stick to the specification (17) for sake of expositional simplicity, it is important to keep in mind that different specifications are always possible for the factor $f\left(y_t | x_{-\varpi}^{t}, y_{-\varpi}^{t-1}\right)$ which is not the focus of our interest regarding a KL measure of Granger causality from Y to X. The corresponding maximum (conditional) log-likelihood function evaluated under hypothesis $H(X \mid X)$ is:

$$L_T\left\{\hat{\lambda}_T;\ H(X|X)\right\} = \sum_{t=1}^{T}\left\{\log\left[f\left(x_t | x_{t-q}^{t-1}; \hat{\lambda}_T\right)\right] + \log\left[f\left(y_t | x_{t-p}^{t}, y_{t-p}^{t-1}; \hat{\lambda}_T\right)\right]\right\}$$

The usual LR test statistic is defined by:

$$\xi_T^{LR} = 2\left[L_T\left\{\hat{\theta}_T;\ H(X \mid Y)\right\} - L_T\left\{\hat{\lambda}_T;\ H(X \mid X)\right\}\right]$$

Under the null hypothesis $H(X \mid Y)$, the normalized version of ξ_T^{LR} tends to:

$$p \lim_{T=\infty} \frac{1}{2T} \xi_T^{LR} = \mathbb{E}\left[\log\left(f\left(x_t | x_{t-p}^{t-1}, y_{t-p}^{t-1}; \theta^0\right)\right)\right] - \mathbb{E}\left[\log\left(f\left(x_t | x_{t-q}^{t-1}; \tilde{\lambda}(\theta^0)\right)\right)\right]$$

where $\tilde{\lambda}(\theta^0)$ is the pseudo-true value of λ under the maintained hypothesis $H(X \mid Y)$. In other words, with an obvious extension of the notations introduced in the previous subsection we have:

$$p \lim_{T=\infty} \frac{1}{2T} \xi_T^{LR} = CG^*_{Y \to X}(q) \tag{18}$$

Recall that in the particular case of a Gaussian process, we have $CG^*_{Y \to X}(q) = CG_{Y \to X}(q)$. More generally, the message of the result (18) is the following regarding the value added by the introduction in this paper of a new causality measure $CG^*_{Y \to X}(q)$ with $q > p$. A Cox test based on the above LR test statistic (after proper centering and rescaling) will be interpreted as follows. If the Cox test does not succeed to reject the null while q is large in front of p, it means that the VAR(p) model for (X, Y) (or more generally a Markov(p) model) does not do a bad job in forecasting X with a parsimonious model of $2p$ regressors instead of a large number q of regressors taken from the own lagged values of X. In contrast, in the case where $q = p$, the noncausality hypothesis becomes nested within the VAR(p) model and failing to reject means that the causality measure is not sufficiently large for a compelling evidence of causality from Y to X.

However, it must be acknowledged that there is no such thing as a free lunch and both strategies, either taking $q = p$ as Geweke (1982) and GMR or taking q much larger than p as advocated in this paper have their own shortcomings. On the one hand, as discussed above (see also the next section for quantitative evidence), taking $q = p$ may lead the researcher to believe that there is a large amount of causality from Y to X, while it may be rather the non-Markovanity of X that is at stake. On the other hand, taking $q > p$ implies that we are testing for non-nested hypotheses, which comes with a cost, as well explained by Dastoor (1981, p. 115) "we can only accept or reject the hypothesis that is under test, without any implication whatsoever for the alternative."

The bottom line is that the Cox test based on Eq. (18) can only accept or reject the null hypothesis that the forecasting performance of a VAR(p) model for (X, Y) (or more generally a Markov(p) model) is not dominated by the one based on a large number q of regressors taken from the own lagged values of X. This is exactly the aforementioned Hoel's (1947) point of view. We will reject the null when causality from Y to X is not sufficiently strong to improve the forecast accuracy by comparison with the alternative "univariate" forecasting strategy based only on lagged values of X. In other words, the approach is more "model selection" than "hypothesis testing" according to the classification in Pesaran & Weeks (2001, p. 288): "Model selection is more appropriate when the objective is decision making," namely forecasting X in this case. If by contrast we have in mind a hypothesis testing approach that is "better suited to inferential problems where the empirical validity of a theoretical prediction is the primary objective," like the absence of feedback from income to money in the Sims example, we should rather consider the non-nested testing problem the other way round, that is, under the null hypothesis $H(X \mid X)$ defined by Eq. (17) against the alternative of the VAR(p) model for (X, Y). In this case:

$$
\begin{aligned}
p \lim_{T=\infty} \frac{1}{2T} \xi_T^{LR} &= \mathbb{E}\left[\log\left(f\left(x_t | x_{t-p}^{t-1}, y_{t-p}^{t-1}; \tilde{\theta}(\lambda^0)\right)\right)\right] - \mathbb{E}\left[\log\left(f\left(x_t | x_{t-q}^{t-1}; \lambda^0\right)\right)\right] \\
&= -CG_{Y\to X}^{**}(q)
\end{aligned}
$$

where it must be understood that the new causality measure $CG_{Y\to X}^{**}(q)$ is non-negative (it is not the opposite of $CG_{Y\to X}^{*}(q)$) because expectations are now computed under the maintained hypothesis $H(X \mid X)$ with a true value λ^0 and a pseudo-true value $\tilde{\theta}(\lambda^0)$.

4. QUANTITATIVE ASSESSMENT

Consider a Gaussian process (X, Y) with a VAR(1) representation; we take X and Y univariate. We focus on the Granger causality measure from Y to X. The DGP of (X, Y) is given by

$$
\begin{bmatrix} X_t \\ Y_t \end{bmatrix} = A \begin{bmatrix} X_{t-1} \\ Y_{t-1} \end{bmatrix} + \begin{bmatrix} u_t \\ v_t \end{bmatrix}, \quad A = \begin{bmatrix} a & b \\ c & d \end{bmatrix}, \quad \Sigma = Var\left[\begin{pmatrix} u_t \\ v_t \end{pmatrix}\right] = \begin{bmatrix} \sigma_u^2 & \rho\sigma_u\sigma_v \\ \rho\sigma_u\sigma_v & \sigma_v^2 \end{bmatrix} \tag{19}
$$

We can consider a matrix A that can be diagonalized and rewrite it as follows:

$$
\begin{bmatrix} X_t \\ Y_t \end{bmatrix} = M \begin{bmatrix} \lambda_1 & 0 \\ 0 & \lambda_2 \end{bmatrix} M^{-1} \begin{bmatrix} X_{t-1} \\ Y_{t-1} \end{bmatrix} + \begin{bmatrix} u_t \\ v_t \end{bmatrix} \tag{20}
$$

where M is the square (2×2) matrix whose ith column is the m_i eigenvector of A, and λ_i, $i = 1, 2$, is the corresponding ith eigenvalue of A.

This reparametrization is useful for two purposes. First, to easily guarantee a causal VAR process when choosing parameter values, that is, $|\lambda_i| < 1$ (i.e., inside the unit circle), for $i = 1, 2$. Second, to understand how the results change when the persistence of past information (i.e., X_{t-1} and Y_{t-1}) in the DGP changes. More precisely, with

$$\begin{bmatrix} X_t^* \\ Y_t^* \end{bmatrix} = M^{-1} \begin{bmatrix} X_t \\ Y_t \end{bmatrix}$$

we have

$$\begin{bmatrix} X_t^* \\ Y_t^* \end{bmatrix} = \begin{bmatrix} \lambda_1 & 0 \\ 0 & \lambda_2 \end{bmatrix} \begin{bmatrix} X_{t-1}^* \\ Y_{t-1}^* \end{bmatrix} + M^{-1} \begin{bmatrix} u_t \\ v_t \end{bmatrix}$$

with

$$X_t^* = \frac{m_{22}}{Det(M)} X_t - \frac{m_{12}}{Det(M)} Y_t$$

$$Y_t^* = \frac{-m_{21}}{Det(M)} X_t + \frac{m_{11}}{Det(M)} Y_t$$

and similar expressions apply for X_{t-1}^* and Y_{t-1}^*. Therefore, to interpret λ_1 as "mostly about" the persistence of X and λ_2 as "mostly about" the persistence of Y, we conveniently fix M as follows

$$M = \begin{bmatrix} 0.9329 & -0.2492 \\ 0.3601 & 0.9684 \end{bmatrix}, \quad Det(M) = 0.99322$$

Indeed, with this choice of M we obtain that

$$X_t^* = \beta_1 X_{t-1} + \beta_2 Y_{t-1}, \quad \frac{|\beta_1|}{|\beta_2|} > 3.8$$

$$Y_t^* = \beta_3 X_{t-1} + \beta_4 Y_{t-1}, \quad \frac{|\beta_4|}{|\beta_3|} > 2.5$$

such that λ_1 (respectively λ_2), autoregressive coefficient of X_t^* (respectively Y_t^*), is mostly informative about the persistence of X (respectively Y).

Our goal is to study $CG_{Y \to X}$ as computed by a researcher who "wrongly" sticks to GMR and Schreiber (2000) using q lags, with $q \geq p$, for the marginal of X_t instead of the correct measure which takes $\varpi + 1$. Hence, the marginal autoregression for X_t is

$$X_t = \sum_{j=1}^{q} \alpha_j X_{t-j} + \epsilon_t, \quad \mathbb{E}[\epsilon_t] = 0, \quad V[\epsilon_t] = \sigma_\epsilon^2(q) \tag{21}$$

Remark 1. *Notice that here the underlying model for the joint process* (X, Y) *is the following Asymmetric VAR model, where the equation for* Y_t *remains unchanged when compared to the DGP,*

$$X_t = \sum_{j=1}^{q} \alpha_j X_{t-j} + \epsilon_t, \quad \mathbb{E}[\epsilon_t] = 0, \quad V[\epsilon_t] = \sigma_\epsilon^2(q)$$

$$Y_t = \gamma\, X_{t-1} + \delta\, Y_{t-1} + \eta_t, \quad \mathbb{E}[\eta_t] = 0, \quad V[\eta_t] = \sigma_\eta^2$$

or in matrix notation

$$\begin{bmatrix} X_t \\ Y_t \end{bmatrix} = A_1 \begin{bmatrix} X_{t-1} \\ Y_{t-1} \end{bmatrix} + \cdots + A_q \begin{bmatrix} X_{t-q} \\ Y_{t-q} \end{bmatrix} + \begin{bmatrix} \epsilon_t \\ \eta_t \end{bmatrix},$$

where

$$A_1 = \begin{bmatrix} \alpha_1 & 0 \\ \gamma & \delta \end{bmatrix}, \quad A_j = \begin{bmatrix} \alpha_j & 0 \\ 0 & 0 \end{bmatrix} \quad \textit{for } j = 2, \ldots, q, \quad \Sigma_q = \begin{bmatrix} \sigma_\epsilon^2 & \rho_q \sigma_\epsilon \sigma_\eta \\ \rho_q \sigma_\epsilon \sigma_\eta & \sigma_\eta^2 \end{bmatrix}$$

This leads to the following Kullback measure of Granger causality

$$CG_{Y \to X}(q) = \frac{1}{2} \log \frac{\sigma_\epsilon^2(q)}{\sigma_u^2} \tag{22}$$

where we write $\sigma_\epsilon^2(q)$ instead of σ_ϵ^2 to make explicit the dependence of the result on the choice of q. Our interest is on a population measure of Granger causality as a function of λ_1, λ_2, σ_u, σ_v, and ρ for different values of q. This can be derived in closed form solution as shown in the appendix. All the numerical evidence is coded in Mathematica version 10.0.1.0.

Fig. 1 depicts how $CG_{Y \to X}(q)$ changes as q increases, for a fixed configuration of the parameters of the model. Notice that $CG_{Y \to X}(q)$ is decreasing in q, which is consistent with our theoretical finding that if we do not include enough lags of X we end up overestimating the amount of causality. Indeed, the distance between two points is our measure of degree of non-Markovianity. In addition, we see that the bigger jump is attained going from the order of the VAR in the DGP

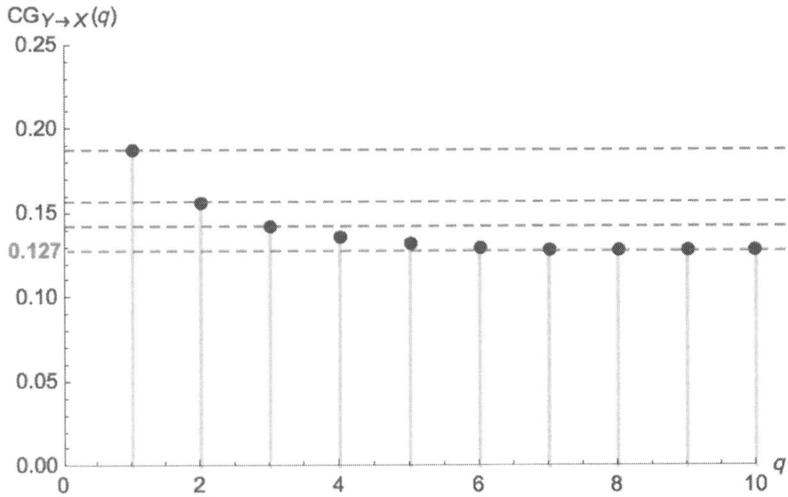

Fig. 1. Comparison of $CG_{Y\to X}(q)$ across q for Fixed Values of the Parameters: $\lambda_1 = -0.6$, $\lambda_2 = 0.9$, $\rho = 0.5$, $\sigma_u = 1$, $\sigma_v = 1$.

$q = p = 1$, to the next order $q = p + 1 = 2$.[2] Finally, it is worth noting that after a finite number of lags ($q = 4$ in this figure) the measure stabilizes. The limit value is about 0.127, which we can interpret as the true value of $CG_{Y\to X}$. This shows that, for all practical purposes, we do not need to include an infinite amount of lags to perform a regression; a finite number of lags, large enough, would be sufficient not to overestimate the amount of causality.

There can be cases in which the amount of overestimation is severe. This is a significant concern as it might lead to wrong conclusions about the amount of causality present in the problem at hand. For instance, in Fig. 2, if we choose $q = p = 1$ we are lead to think that the amount of causality is around 0.20, while the true measure (i.e., for $q > 3$) is close to zero. The magnitude of the causality measure across values of q is displayed in Table 1. Notice that the true amount of causality cannot be exactly zero as in that case, from Corollary 6, we know that $CG_{Y\to X}(1) = CG_{Y\to X}(2) = \cdots = CG_{Y\to X} = 0$.

The intuition in this particular case is as follows. The persistence of X (i.e., λ_1) and the persistence of Y (i.e., λ_2) are of the same order of magnitude, although of opposite signs since if $\lambda_1 = \lambda_2$ there would be no causality, that is, $CG_{Y\to X} = 0$. Since the correlation between u_t and v_t is close to -1, after one period most of the information contained in the past of Y is already contained in the past of X.[3] As a result, we see a huge drop in the amount of causality going from $q = 1$ to $q = 2$. This is consistent with the idea that because X is highly persistent, and given

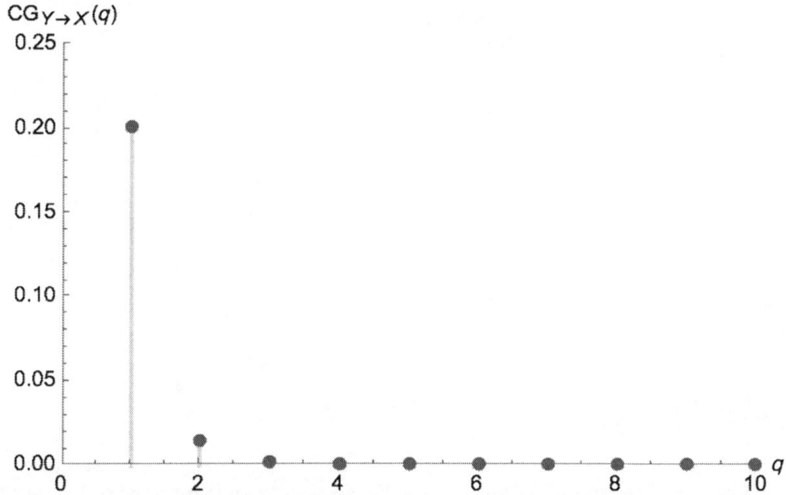

Fig. 2. Comparison of $CG_{Y \to X}(q)$ for $q = 1, 2, \ldots, 10$: $\lambda_1 = -0.8$, $\lambda_2 = 0.8$ $\rho = -0.99$, $\sigma_u = 1$, $\sigma_v = 1$.

Table 1. Value of $CG_{Y \to X}(q)$ for $q = 1, 2, \ldots, 10$.

q	1	2	3	4	5	6	7	8	9	10
$CG_{Y \to X}(q)$	0.2011	0.0146	0.0026	0.0016	0.0015	0.0015	0.0015	0.0015	0.0015	0.0015

that Y does not carry much additional information after one period, the degree of non-Markovianity between $q = 1$ and $q = 2$ is of a considerable size.

To further the analysis on how persistence of the past of X impacts $CG_{Y \to X}(q)$ across values of q, in Fig. 3 we compare $CG_{Y \to X}(1)$, $CG_{Y \to X}(2)$, and $CG_{Y \to X}(3)$ across values of λ_1 for given values of the reminding parameters. The overall effect of λ_1 on $CG_{Y \to X}(q)$ is comprised of two components. On the one hand, the amount of causality increases with the absolute value of the difference between λ_1 and λ_2, that is, $|\lambda_1 - \lambda_2|$. The larger this difference, all else equal, the larger the value of $CG_{Y \to X}(q)$. In particular, when this difference is zero, that is, $\lambda_1 = \lambda_2$, there is no causality.[4] As a result, the amount of causality needs not to be close to zero when λ_1 is low. This is particularly the case here since the persistence of the past of Y (i.e., λ_2) is also small.[5] On the other hand, when there is causality, the amount of overestimation increases with $|\lambda_1 - \lambda_2|$. The difference across $CG_{Y \to X}(q)$ becomes particularly noticeable when going from $q = 1$ to $q = 2$.

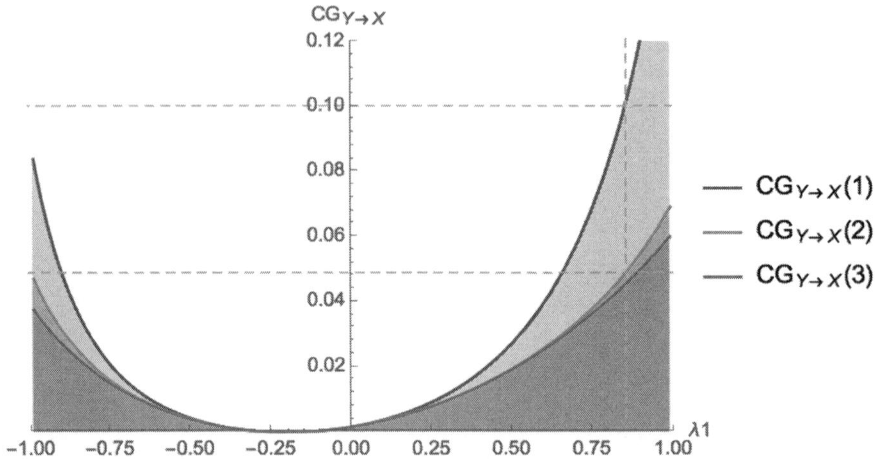

Fig. 3. Comparison of $CG_{Y\to X}(1)$, $CG_{Y\to X}(2)$ and $CG_{Y\to X}(3)$ for Different Values of λ_1, and Fixed Values of the Other Parameters: $\lambda_2 = -0.2$, $\rho = -0.8$, $\sigma_u = 1$, $\sigma_v = 2$.

5. CONCLUDING REMARKS

A common practice in econometrics amounts to assume that, when considering a sufficiently large number of state variables, the joint dynamics can be properly represented as a Markov process. Prominent examples of this practice are the extensive use of VAR processes in macro-econometrics as well as the use of diffusion processes in finance. This paper starts from the observation that, when a joint process (X, Y) is Markov, the statement that Y does not cause X entails two different phenomena: On the one hand, X will be in isolation a Markov process of the same order as (X, Y), and, on the other hand, information about lagged values of Y does not improve the performance of forecasts of X by comparison with what can be done using only past information about X. We argue in this paper that, in the opposite situation where Y does cause X, the two above properties (and their negations) should be disentangled when it comes to measurement of the strength of causality. On the one hand, how far is X to be a Markov process of the same order as (X, Y)? On the other hand, how much can we improve the accuracy of the forecasts of X by using past information about Y?

We note that the extant literature on causality measurement (Geweke, 1982; GMR; Schreiber, 2000) has failed to disentangle these two components and, as a result, may lead to the misleading belief that Y powerfully causes X, whereas we would actually be able to forecast X accurately only from its own past, at the cost of a larger number of lags than by using also the past of Y. Our understanding of the reason why the extant literature has failed to disentangle the two is that when testing for non-causality, the main focus is on size control and, thus, the behavior of the test statistic is essentially studied under the null hypothesis of noncausality when the two above statements are true together. We advocate in this paper an alternative strategy when testing for (non)causality. One would actually consider two non-nested hypotheses: One focused on using Y to help forecasting X, and one focused on using a large number of lags to forecast X from its own past.

The price to pay for testing non-nested hypotheses is that the treatment is not symmetric: "we can only accept or reject the null hypothesis that is under test, without any implication whatsoever for the alternative" (Dastoor, 1981, p. 115). We acknowledge that, as stressed more generally by Pesaran & Weeks (2001), the two ways to perform the Cox test for non-nested hypotheses correspond to two different points of view: Either defining the null hypothesis as the Markov property for (X, Y) puts the emphasis on the usefulness of a multivariate model (including Y) to forecast X, or, conversely, one would test the null that a large number of its own lags is sufficient to describe the dynamics of the X process, which is more a statement about "economic exogeneity" of X with respect to Y. In the former case, failing to reject the null advocates for the multivariate forecast. The issue of interest is more about non-nested comparison via predictive ability, as currently fashionable in the forecasting literature (for a recent illustration, see Noureldin, Shephard, & Sheppard, 2014). In the latter case, the issue that is addressed is in line with the research agenda put forward for instance by Sims (1972) about exogeneity of money. In other words, the first approach corresponds to a measure of forecasting performance, while the second one is more about genuine theoretical causality.

A natural extension of this paper would be to revisit these causality measures between Y and X in a conditional setting given additional state variables Z. Then, one should distinguish direct and indirect causality relationships, paving the way for different intensities of causality relationships at different horizons (see Dufour & Renault, 1998). Then, one should revisit the causality measures at different horizons (see also Dufour & Taamouti, 2010) in order to accommodate two kinds of time lags: time lag for Markov property, and time lag for impact of the cause on the effect.

NOTES

1. We are grateful to a referee for this suggestion.
2. Given that we need to choose the value of five parameters to display this graph, it is difficult to show all possible scenarios. However, it is important to remark that the overall

observed pattern is consistent across different configurations of parameters, beyond the one chosen for this particular figure.

3. This can be easily seen by thinking in terms of impulse response functions.

4. This is clear from Eq. (20). For instance, in Fig. 3, $CG_{Y\to X}(q)=0$ at $\lambda_1=0.2$ since $\lambda_2=0.2$.

5. For completeness, supplementary examples where the past of Y is highly persistent are provided in Appendix A. In addition, Table A1 shows how $CG_{Y\to X}(2)$ changes as a function of σ_u/σ_v for different configurations of parameters that give $CG_{Y\to X}(1)=0.10$.

6. Let $\beta:=[\alpha_1,\ldots,\alpha_q]'$ be a $q\times 1$ vector. The equation for $\sigma_\epsilon^2(q)$ is derived using that $X_t=\beta' Z_q+\epsilon_t$, $\beta'=Cov(X_t,Z_q)Var(Z_q)^{-1}$, and $Var(\beta' Z_q)=Cov(X_t,Z_q)Var(Z_q)^{-1}Cov(Z_q,X_t)$.

REFERENCES

Berk, K. N. (1974). Consistent autoregressive spectral estimates. *The Annals of Statistics*, *2*(3), 489–502.

Boudjellaba, H., Dufour, J.-M., & Roy, R. (1992). Testing causality between two vectors in multivariate autoregressive moving average models. *Journal of the American Statistical Association*, *87*(420) 1082–1090.

Bouissou, M.B., Laffont, J.-J., & Vuong, Q. H. (1986). Tests of noncausality under Markov assumptions for qualitative panel data. *Econometrica*, *54*(2), 395–414.

Chamberlain, G. (1982). The general equivalence of Granger and Sims causality. *Econometrica*, *50*(3), 569–581.

Cox, D. R. (1962). Further results on tests of separate families of hypotheses. *Journal of the Royal Statistical Society. Series B (Methodological)*, *24*(2) 406–424.

Dastoor, N. K. (1981). A note on the interpretation of the Cox procedure for non-nested hypotheses. *Economics Letters*, *8*(2), 113–119.

Dufour, J.-M., Pelletier, D., & Renault, E. (2006). Short run and long run causality in time series: inference. *Journal of Econometrics*, *132*(2), 337–362.

Dufour, J.-M., & Renault, E. (1998). Short run and long run causality in time series: Theory. *Econometrica*, *66*(5), 1099–1125.

Dufour, J.-M., & Taamouti, A. (2010). Short and long run causality measures: Theory and inference. *Journal of Econometrics*, *154*(1), 42–58.

Dufour, J.-M., & Tessier, D. (1993). On the relationship between impulse response analysis, innovation accounting and Granger causality. *Economics Letters*, *42*(4), 327–333.

Fisher, G.R., & McAleer, M. (1981). Alternative procedures and associated tests of significance for non-nested hypotheses. *Journal of Econometrics*, *16*(1), 103–119.

Florens, J.-P., & Mouchart, M. (1982). A note on noncausality. *Econometrica*, *50*(3), 583–591.

Florens, J.-P., Mouchart, M., & Rolin, J. (1993). Noncausality and marginalization of Markov processes. *Econometric Theory*, *9*(02), 241–262.

Geweke, J. (1982). Measurement of linear dependence and feedback between multiple time series. *Journal of the American Statistical Association*, *77*(378), 304–313.

Gouriéroux, C., & Monfort, A. (1994). Testing non-nested hypotheses. *In: Engle, R.F., McFadden, D.L. (Eds.), Handbook of Econometrics*, *4*(Chapter 44), 2583–2637.

Gouriéroux, C., & Monfort, A. (1995). *Statistics and econometric models* (Vol. 1). Cambridge University Press.

Gouriéroux, C., Monfort, A., & Renault, E. (1987). Kullback causality measures. *Annales d'Economie et de Statistique*, *6/7*, 369–410.

Granger, C. W. J. (1969). Investigating causal relations by econometric models and cross-spectral methods *Econometrica*, *37*(3), 424–438.

Hoel, P. G. (1947). On the choice of forecasting formulas. *Journal of the American Statistical Association*, *42*(240), 605–611.

Hsiao, C. (1979). Autoregressive modeling of Canadian money and income data. *Journal of the American Statistical Association*, *74*(367), 553–560.

Hsiao, C. (1981). Autoregressive modelling and money-income causality detection. *Journal of Monetary Economics*, *7*(1), 85–106.

Keating, J. W. (2000). Macroeconomic modeling with asymmetric vector autoregressions *Journal of Macroeconomics*, *22*(1), 1–28.

Kullback, S. (1968). *Information theory and statistics*. Dover Publications, Inc., Mineola, New York.

Nijman, T., & Sentana, E. (1996). Marginalization and contemporaneous aggregation in multivariate GARCH processes. *Journal of Econometrics*, *71*(1/2), 71–87.

Noureldin, D., Shephard, N., & Sheppard, K. (2014). Multivariate rotated ARCH models. *Journal of Econometrics*, *179*(1), 16–30.

Pesaran, M. H. (1974). On the general problem of model selection. *The Review of Economic Studies*, *41*(2), 153–171.

Pesaran, M. H. (1982). Comparison of local power of alternative tests of non-nested regression models. *Econometrica*, *50*(5), 1287–1305.

Pesaran, M. H., & Weeks, M. (2001). Non-nested hypothesis testing: an overview. *A Companion to Theoretical Econometrics* B.H. Baltagi (Ed.) 279–309.

Polasek, W. (1994). *Temporal causality measures based on AIC*. Springer Netherlands.

Polasek, W. (2002). Bayesian causality measures for multiple ARCH models using marginal likelihoods. *In: Technical Report. Institute of Statistics and Econometrics, Univeristy of Basel, Switzerland.*

Schreiber, T. (2000). Measuring information transfer. *Physical Review Letters*, *85*(2), 461–464.

Sims, C. A. (1972). Money, income, and causality. *The American Economic Review*, *62*(4) 540–552.

APPENDIX A: ADDITIONAL FIGURES AND TABLE

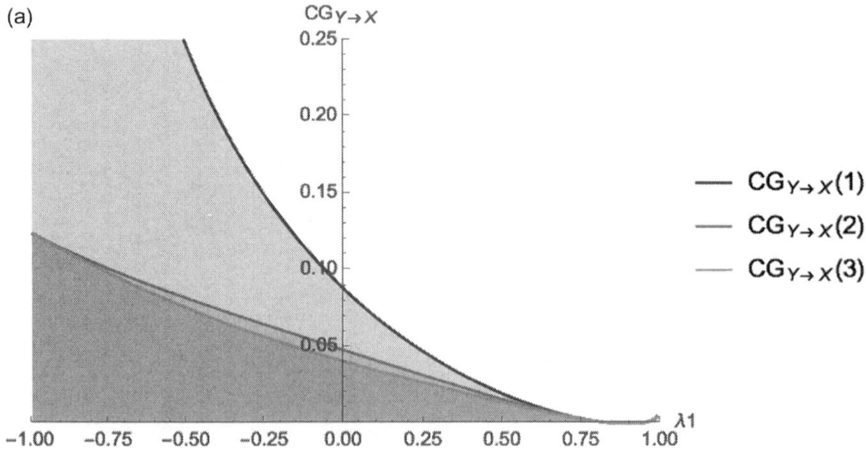

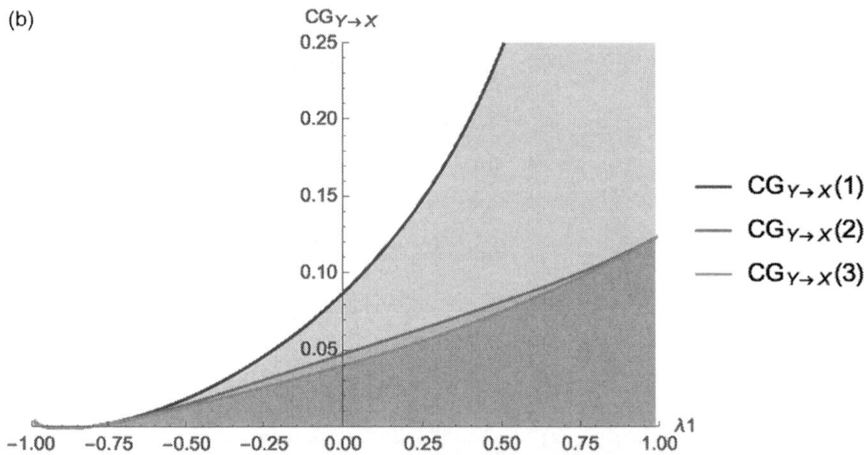

Fig. A1. Comparison of $CG_{Y\to X}(1)$, $CG_{Y\to X}(2)$ and $CG_{Y\to X}(3)$ for different values of λ_1, and fixed values of the other parameters: $\rho = -0.8$, $\sigma_u = 1$, $\sigma_v = 2$. (a) $\lambda_2 = 0.9$ and (b) $\lambda_2 = -0.9$.

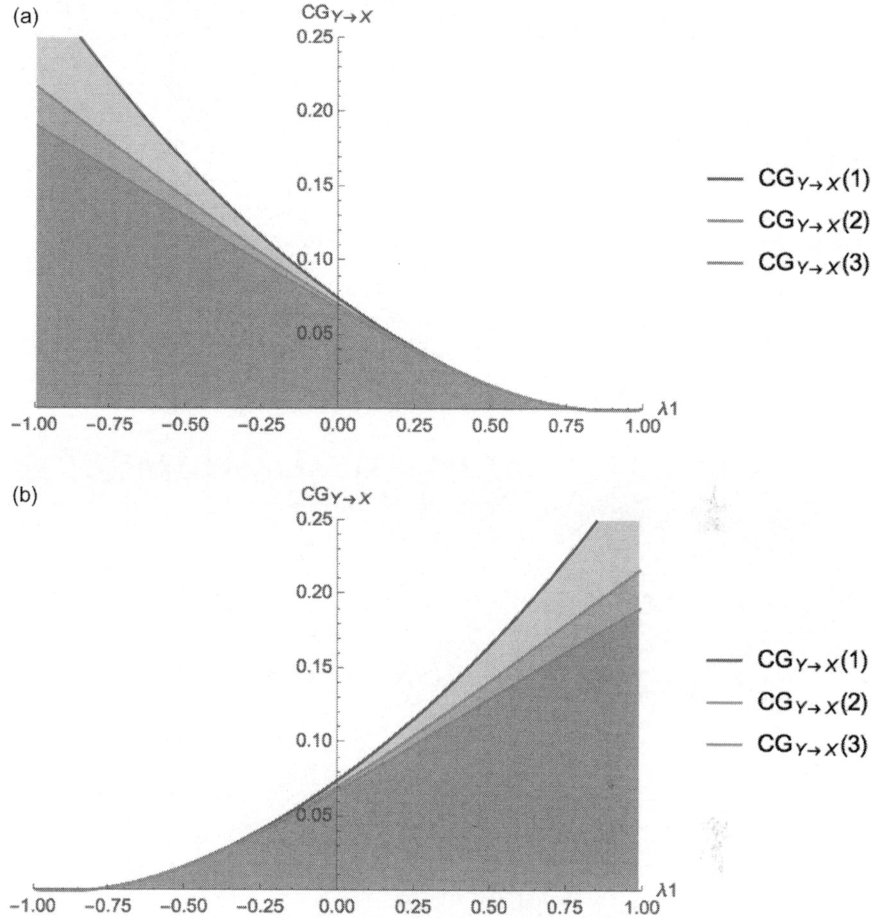

Fig. A2. Comparison of $CG_{Y\to X}(1)$, $CG_{Y\to X}(2)$ and $CG_{Y\to X}(3)$ for Different Values of λ_1, and Fixed Values of the Other Parameters: $\rho = 0.5$, $\sigma_u = 1$, $\sigma_v = 1$. (a) $\lambda_2 = 0.9$ and (b) $\lambda_2 = -0.9$.

Table A1. Analysis of $CG_{Y\to X}(2)$ for $CG_{Y\to X}(1) = 0.10$.

5th Pctl	95th Pctl	Median	σ_u/σ_v
0.05697	0.09999	0.0992	0.1
0.06780	0.09994	0.0967	0.25
0.03823	0.09991	0.0913	0.5
0.02877	0.09929	0.0779	1
0.03406	0.08588	0.0664	2
0.04004	0.07411	0.0622	4
0.00000	0.06823	0.0596	10

Notes: For each value of σ_u/σ_v, $CG_{Y\to X}(2)$ is computed for different configurations of λ_1, λ_2, and ρ, that give $CG_{Y\to X}(1) = 0.10$. The statistics (5th percentile, 95th percentile, and median) are then computed based on these values of $CG_{Y\to X}(2)$.

APPENDIX B: MATHEMATICAL APPENDIX

B.1. Proof of Proposition 1

Consider the following decomposition

$$\begin{aligned}
&\frac{1}{T}\operatorname*{Min}_{f_T\in HS}\mathbb{E}_0\log\left(\frac{f_{0T}\left(z_{-\varpi}^{T}\right)}{f_T\left(z_{-\varpi}^{T}\right)}\right)\\
&=\frac{1}{T}\operatorname*{Min}_{f_T\in HS}\mathbb{E}_0\log\left(\frac{f_0(z_{-\varpi}^{0})f_{0T}\left(x_1^T|z_{-\varpi}^{0}\right)f_{0T}\left(y_1^T|x_{-\varpi}^{T},y_{-\varpi}^{0}\right)}{f(z_{-\varpi}^{0})f_T\left(x_1^T|z_{-\varpi}^{0}\right)f_T\left(y_1^T|x_{-\varpi}^{T},y_{-\varpi}^{0}\right)}\right)\\
&=\frac{1}{T}\operatorname*{Min}_{f_T\in HS}\left\{\mathbb{E}_0\log\left(\frac{f_0\left(z_{-\varpi}^{0}\right)}{f\left(z_{-\varpi}^{0}\right)}\right)\right.\\
&\quad+\mathbb{E}_0\log\prod_{t=1}^{T}\left(\frac{f_{0t}\left(x_t|x_{-\varpi}^{t-1},y_{-\varpi}^{0}\right)}{f_t\left(x_t|x_{-\varpi}^{t-1},y_{-\varpi}^{0}\right)}\right)\\
&\quad\left.+\mathbb{E}_0\log\prod_{t=1}^{T}\left(\frac{f_{0t}\left(y_t|x_{-\varpi}^{T},y_{-\varpi}^{t-1}\right)}{f_t\left(y_t|x_{-\varpi}^{T},y_{-\varpi}^{t-1}\right)}\right)\right\}
\end{aligned}\tag{B.1}$$

Since expectations are by definition computed under the true DGP, we obviously have for any $f_T(\cdot)\in HS$ that each of the three terms in the above decomposition are non-negative. Therefore, the minimization of Eq. (B.1) will obviously lead to set the first two terms to zero, since it is possible to set the denominator equal to the denominator while staying within HS. Then, to fully characterize the solution of Eq. (B.1), we only have to minimize the third term, that is, to maximize:

$$\mathbb{E}_0\left[\log\prod_{t=1}^{T} f_t\left(y_t|x_{-\varpi}^{T}, y_{-\varpi}^{t-1}\right)\right] = \mathbb{E}_0\left[\log\prod_{t=1}^{T} f_t\left(y_t|x_{-\varpi}^{t}, y_{-\varpi}^{t-1}\right)\right]$$

since, by the constraint of non-Sims causality that must be fulfilled by $f_T(\cdot)$, we know that:

$$f_t\left(y_t|x_{-\varpi}^{T}, y_{-\varpi}^{t-1}\right) = f_t\left(y_t|x_{-\varpi}^{t}, y_{-\varpi}^{t-1}\right)$$

By the Law of Iterated Expectations (LIE), the above maximization is equivalent to maximizing

$$\sum_{t=1}^{T} \mathbb{E}_0\mathbb{E}_0\left[\log f_t\left(y_t|x_{-\varpi}^{t}, y_{-\varpi}^{t-1}\right)|x_{-\varpi}^{t}, y_{-\varpi}^{t-1}\right]$$

Finally, by means of the Kullback inequality, it follows that for each t and for a given $(x_{-\varpi}^{t}, y_{-\varpi}^{t-1})$, the conditional expectation is maximized by choosing $f_t\left(y_t|x_{-\varpi}^{t}, y_{-\varpi}^{t-1}\right) = f_{0t}\left(y_t|x_{-\varpi}^{t}, y_{-\varpi}^{t-1}\right)$. Hence, we result follows. ■

B.2. Proof of Proposition 2

Consider the following decomposition

$$\begin{aligned}
&\frac{1}{T}\underset{f_T\in HIN}{\text{Min}}\ \mathbb{E}_0\log\left(\frac{f_{0T}\left(z_{-\varpi}^{T}\right)}{f_T\left(z_{-\varpi}^{T}\right)}\right)\\
&=\frac{1}{T}\underset{f_T\in HIN}{\text{Min}}\ \mathbb{E}_0\log\left(\frac{f_0(z_{-\varpi}^{0})f_{0T}\left(x_1^T|z_{-\varpi}^{0}\right)f_{0T}\left(y_1^T|x_{-\varpi}^{T}, y_{-\varpi}^{0}\right)}{f(z_{-\varpi}^{0})f_T\left(x_1^T|z_{-\varpi}^{0}\right)f_T\left(y_1^T|x_{-\varpi}^{T}, y_{-\varpi}^{0}\right)}\right) \qquad \text{(B.2)}\\
&=\frac{1}{T}\underset{f_T\in HIN}{\text{Min}}\left\{\mathbb{E}_0\log\left(\frac{f_0\left(z_{-\varpi}^{0}\right)}{f\left(z_{-\varpi}^{0}\right)}\right)\right.\\
&\quad+\mathbb{E}_0\log\prod_{t=1}^{T}\left(\frac{f_{0t}\left(x_t|x_{-\varpi}^{t-1}, y_{-\varpi}^{0}\right)}{f_t\left(x_t|x_{-\varpi}^{t-1}, y_{-\varpi}^{0}\right)}\right)\\
&\quad\left.+\mathbb{E}_0\log\prod_{t=1}^{T}\left(\frac{f_{0t}\left(y_t|x_{-\varpi}^{T}, y_{-\varpi}^{t-1}\right)}{f_t\left(y_t|x_{-\varpi}^{T}, y_{-\varpi}^{t-1}\right)}\right)\right\}
\end{aligned}$$

Since expectations are by definition computed under the true DGP, we obviously have for any $f_T(\cdot) \in HIN$ that each of the three terms in the above decomposition are non-negative. Therefore, the minimization of Eq. (B.2) will obviously lead to set the first and third terms to zero, since it is possible to set the denominator equal to the denominator while staying within HIN. Then, to fully characterize the solution of Eq. (B.1), we only have to minimize the second term, that is, to maximize:

$$\mathbb{E}_0\left[\log \prod_{t=1}^{T} f_t\left(x_t | x_{-\varpi}^{t-1}, y_{-\varpi}^{0}\right)\right] = \mathbb{E}_0\left[\log \prod_{t=1}^{T} f_t\left(x_t | x_{-\varpi}^{t-1}\right)\right]$$

since, by the non-Initiation constraint that must be fulfilled by $f_T(\cdot)$, we know that:

$$f_t\left(x_t | x_{-\varpi}^{t-1}, y_{-\varpi}^{0}\right) = f_t\left(x_t | x_{-\varpi}^{t-1}\right)$$

By LIE, the above maximization is equivalent to maximizing

$$\sum_{t=1}^{T} \mathbb{E}_0 \mathbb{E}_0\left[\log f_t\left(x_t | x_{-\varpi}^{t-1}\right) | x_{-\varpi}^{t-1}\right]$$

Finally, by means of the Kullback inequality, it follows that for each t and for a given $x_{-\varpi}^{t-1}$, the conditional expectation is maximized by choosing $f_t\left(x_t | x_{-\varpi}^{t-1}\right) = f_{0t}\left(x_t | x_{-\varpi}^{t-1}\right)$. Hence, the result follows.

■

B.3. Proof of Proposition 4

Consider the following decomposition

$$\frac{1}{T} \underset{f_T \in HG}{\text{Min}}\, \mathbb{E}_0 \log\left(\frac{f_{0T}\left(z_{-\varpi}^{T}\right)}{f_T\left(z_{-\varpi}^{T}\right)}\right) = \frac{1}{T} \underset{f_T \in HG}{\text{Min}}\, \mathbb{E}_0 \log\left(\frac{f_0(z_{-\varpi}^{0}) \prod_{t=1}^{T} f_{0t}\left(z_t | z_{-\varpi}^{t-1}\right)}{f(z_{-\varpi}^{0}) \prod_{t=1}^{T} f_t\left(z_t | z_{-\varpi}^{t-1}\right)}\right) \tag{B.3}$$

$$= \frac{1}{T} \underset{f_T \in HG}{\text{Min}} \left\{ \mathbb{E}_0 \log\left(\frac{f_0\left(z_{-\varpi}^{0}\right)}{f\left(z_{-\varpi}^{0}\right)}\right) + \mathbb{E}_0 \log \prod_{t=1}^{T}\left(\frac{f_{0t}\left(x_t | x_{-\varpi}^{t-1}, y_{-\varpi}^{t-1}\right)}{f_t\left(x_t | x_{-\varpi}^{t-1}, y_{-\varpi}^{t-1}\right)}\right) + \mathbb{E}_0 \log \prod_{t=1}^{T}\left(\frac{f_{0t}\left(y_t | x_{-\varpi}^{t}, y_{-\varpi}^{t-1}\right)}{f_t\left(y_t | x_{-\varpi}^{t}, y_{-\varpi}^{t-1}\right)}\right)\right\}$$

Since expectations are by definition computed under the true DGP, we obviously have for any $f_T(\cdot) \in HG$ that each of the three terms in the above decomposition are non-negative. Therefore, the minimization of Eq. (B.3) will obviously lead to set the first and last terms to zero, since it is possible to set the denominator equal to the denominator while staying within HG. Then, to fully characterize the solution of Eq. (B.3), we only have to minimize the third term, that is, to maximize:

$$\mathbb{E}_0\left[\log \prod_{t=1}^{T} f_t\left(x_t | x_{-\varpi}^{t-1}, y_{-\varpi}^{t-1}\right)\right] = \mathbb{E}_0\left[\log \prod_{t=1}^{T} f_t\left(x_t | x_{-\varpi}^{t-1}\right)\right]$$

since, by the constraint of non-Sims causality that must be fulfilled by $f_T(\cdot)$, we know that:

$$f_t\left(x_t | x_{-\varpi}^{t-1}, y_{-\varpi}^{t-1}\right) = f_t\left(x_t | x_{-\varpi}^{t-1}\right)$$

By LIE, the above maximization is equivalent to maximizing

$$\sum_{t=1}^{T} \mathbb{E}_0 \mathbb{E}_0\left[\log f_t\left(x_t | x_{-\varpi}^{t-1}\right) | x_{-\varpi}^{t-1}\right]$$

Finally, by means of the Kullback inequality, it follows that for each t and for a given $x_{-\varpi}^{t-1}$, the conditional expectation is maximized by choosing $f_t\left(x_t | x_{-\varpi}^{t-1}\right) = f_{0t}\left(x_t | x_{-\varpi}^{t-1}\right)$. Hence, the result follows.

■

B.4. Proof of Corollaries 1, 2 and 3

The proof of these corollaries is obvious from the following lemma (See GMR for a proof of this lemma which corresponds to their Lemma 1).

Lemma 1. *Let X, Y, Z be three random vectors whose joint p.d.f., with respect to a given σ-finite measure, is denoted by $f(X, Y, Z)$. We have:*

(i)

$$\mathbb{E} \log\left(\frac{f(X | Y, Z)}{f(X | Y)}\right) \geq 0$$

(ii) This expectation is equal to zero if and only if, almost surely:

$$f(X | Y, Z) = f(X | Y)$$

B.5. Proof of Proposition 5

We have:

$$CS_{Y\to X} + CIN_{Y\to X} = \frac{1}{T}\mathbb{E}_0 \log\left(\prod_{t=1}^{T} \frac{f_{0t}(y_t \mid x_{-\varpi}^T, y_{-\varpi}^{t-1})}{f_{0t}(y_t \mid x_{-\varpi}^t, y_{-\varpi}^{t-1})} \cdot \frac{f_{0t}(x_t \mid x_{-\varpi}^{t-1}, y_{-\varpi}^0)}{f_{0t}(x_t \mid x_{-\varpi}^{t-1})}\right) \tag{B.4}$$

The numerator of the above product can be rewritten as:

$$\begin{aligned}
& f_0(y_1^T \mid x_{-\varpi}^T, y_{-\varpi}^0) f_0(x_1^T \mid x_{-\varpi}^0, y_{-\varpi}^0) \\
&= f_0(x_1^T, y_1^T \mid x_{-\varpi}^0, y_{-\varpi}^0) \\
&= \prod_{t=1}^{T} f_{0t}(x_t, y_t \mid x_{-\varpi}^{t-1}, y_{-\varpi}^{t-1}) \\
&= \prod_{t=1}^{T} f_{0t}(x_t \mid x_{-\varpi}^{t-1}, y_{-\varpi}^{t-1}) f_{0t}(y_t \mid x_{-\varpi}^t, y_{-\varpi}^{t-1})
\end{aligned}$$

Plugging this result in Eq. (B.4) and noting that one factor cancels out with the denominator, we end up with:

$$CS_{Y\to X} + CIN_{Y\to X} = \frac{1}{T}\mathbb{E}_0 \log\left(\prod_{t=1}^{T} \frac{f_{0t}(x_t \mid x_{-\varpi}^{t-1}, y_{-\varpi}^{t-1})}{f_{0t}(x_t \mid x_{-\varpi}^{t-1})}\right) = CG_{Y\to X}$$

■

B.6. Closed-Form Solution for $CG_{Y\to X}(q)$ in Eq. (22)

We first derive a closed form expression for $\sigma_\epsilon^2(q)$ in terms of population moments of X and Y. Let $Z_q = [X_{t-1}, \ldots, X_{t-q}]'$ then[6]

$$\sigma_\epsilon^2(q) = Var(X_t) - Cov(X_t, Z_q) Var(Z_q)^{-1} Cov(Z_q, X_t) \tag{B.5}$$

Notice that the value of $\sigma_\epsilon^2(q)$ depends on q through Z_q. Hence we have

$$CG_{Y\to X}(q) = \frac{1}{2}\log \frac{\gamma_{XX0} - \begin{bmatrix}\gamma_{XX1} & \cdots & \gamma_{XXq}\end{bmatrix} \Omega_q^{-1} \begin{bmatrix}\gamma_{XX1} \\ \vdots \\ \gamma_{XXq}\end{bmatrix}}{\sigma_u^2} \tag{B.6}$$

where Ω_q is the symmetric matrix of size q whose generic element is:

$$\left(\Omega_q\right)_{ij} = \gamma_{XX|i-j|}$$

To compute γ_{XXh}, $h = 0, 1, 2, \ldots, q$, we use the following recursion formulas:

$$\Gamma(h) = \begin{bmatrix} \gamma_{XXh} & \gamma_{XYh} \\ \gamma_{YXh} & \gamma_{YYh} \end{bmatrix} = A^h \Gamma(0)$$

$$\Gamma(0) = A\Gamma(0)A' + \Sigma$$

solved as

$$Vec\,\Gamma(0) = (Id_4 - A \otimes A)^{-1}\, Vec(\Sigma)$$

where Id_4 is the identity matrix of order 4, and $Vec(C)$ stands for the vectorization of some matrix C.

PART V
ISSUES IN ECONOMETRIC THEORY

A LIKELIHOOD-FREE REVERSE SAMPLER OF THE POSTERIOR DISTRIBUTION

Jean-Jacques Forneron and Serena Ng
Department of Economics, Columbia University, New York, NY, USA

ABSTRACT

This paper considers properties of an optimization-based sampler for targeting the posterior distribution when the likelihood is intractable. It uses auxiliary statistics to summarize information in the data and does not directly evaluate the likelihood associated with the specified parametric model. Our reverse sampler approximates the desired posterior distribution by first solving a sequence of simulated minimum distance problems. The solutions are then reweighted by an importance ratio that depends on the prior and the volume of the Jacobian matrix. By a change of variable argument, the output consists of draws from the desired posterior distribution. Optimization always results in acceptable draws. Hence, when the minimum distance problem is not too difficult to solve, combining importance sampling with optimization can be much faster than the method of Approximate Bayesian Computation that by-passes optimization.

Essays in Honor of Aman Ullah
Advances in Econometrics, Volume 36, 389–415

ISSN: 0731-9053/doi:10.1108/S0731-905320160000036020

Keywords: Approximate Bayesian Computation; indirect inference; importance sampling

JEL classifications: C22; C23

1. INTRODUCTION

Maximum likelihood estimation rests on the ability of a researcher to express the joint density of the data, or the likelihood, as a function of K unknown parameters $\boldsymbol{\theta}$. Inference can be conducted using classical distributional theory once the mode of the likelihood function is determined by numerical optimization. Bayesian estimation combines the likelihood with a prior to form the posterior distribution from which the mean and other quantities of interest can be computed. Though the posterior distribution may not always be tractable, it can be approximated by Monte-Carlo methods provided that the likelihood is available. When the likelihood is intractable but there exists $L \geq K$ auxiliary statistics $\hat{\boldsymbol{\psi}}$ with model analog $\boldsymbol{\psi}(\boldsymbol{\theta})$ that is analytically tractable, one can still estimate $\boldsymbol{\theta}$ by minimizing the difference between $\hat{\boldsymbol{\psi}}$ and $\boldsymbol{\psi}(\boldsymbol{\theta})$.

Increasingly, parametric models are so complex that neither the likelihood nor $\boldsymbol{\psi}(\boldsymbol{\theta})$ is tractable. But if the model is easy to simulate, the mapping $\boldsymbol{\psi}(\boldsymbol{\theta})$ can be approximated by simulations. Estimators that exploit this idea can broadly be classified into two types. One is simulated minimum distance (SMD) estimator, a frequentist approach that is quite widely used in economic analysis. The other is the method of Approximate Bayesian Computation that is popular in other disciplines. This method, ABC for short, approximates the posterior distribution using auxiliary statistics $\hat{\boldsymbol{\psi}}$ instead of the full dataset y. It takes draws of $\boldsymbol{\theta}$ from a prior distribution and keeps the draws that, when used to simulate the model, produce auxiliary statistics that are close to the sample estimates $\hat{\boldsymbol{\psi}}$. Both the ABC and SMD can be regarded as likelihood-free estimators in the sense that the likelihood that corresponds to the structural model of interest is not directly evaluated.

While both the SMD and ABC exploit auxiliary statistics to perform likelihood-free estimation, there are important differences between them. The SMD solves for the $\boldsymbol{\theta}$ that makes $\hat{\boldsymbol{\psi}}$ close to the average of $\boldsymbol{\psi}(\boldsymbol{\theta})$ over many simulated paths of the data. In contrast, the ABC evaluates $\boldsymbol{\psi}(\boldsymbol{\theta})$ for each draw from the prior and accepts the draw only if $\boldsymbol{\psi}(\boldsymbol{\theta})$ is close to $\hat{\boldsymbol{\psi}}$. The ABC estimate is the average over the accepted draws, which is the posterior mean. In Forneron and Ng (2014), we focused on the case of exact identification and used a reverse sampler (RS) to better understand the difference between the two approaches. The RS approximates the posterior distribution by solving a sequence of SMD problems, each using only one simulated path of data. Using stochastic expansions as in Rilstone et al. (1996) and Bao and Ullah (2007), we reported that in the special case when $\boldsymbol{\psi}(\boldsymbol{\theta}) = \boldsymbol{\theta}$ (i.e., the auxiliary model is the assumed model), the SMD has an unambiguous bias advantage over the ABC. But in more general settings, the ABC can, by clever choice of prior, eliminate biases that are inherent in the SMD.

In this paper, we extend the analysis to overidentified models and provide a deeper understanding of the reverse sampler. The RS is shown to be an optimization-based importance sampler that transforms the density from draws of $\boldsymbol{\psi}$ to draws of $\boldsymbol{\theta}$ so that when multiplied by the prior and properly weighted, the draws follow the desired posterior distribution. Section 2 considers the exactly identified case and shows that the importance ratio is the determinant of the Jacobian matrix. Section 3 considers the overidentified case when the dimension of $\boldsymbol{\psi}(\boldsymbol{\theta})$ exceeds that of $\boldsymbol{\theta}$. Because of the need to transform densities of different dimensions, the determinant of the Jacobian matrix is replaced by its volume. Using analytically tractable models, we show that the RS exactly reproduces the desired posterior distribution.

The RS was initially developed as a framework to better understand the different approaches to likelihood-free estimation. While not intended to compete with existing implementations of ABC, the use of optimization in RS turns out to have a property that is of independent interest. Creating a long sequence of ABC draws such that the simulated statistic $\hat{\boldsymbol{\psi}}^b$ and the data $\hat{\boldsymbol{\psi}}$ deviate by no more than δ can take infinite time if δ is set to exactly zero as theory suggests. This has generated interests within the ABC community to control for δ. The RS by-passes this problem because SMD estimation makes $\hat{\boldsymbol{\psi}}^b$ as close to $\hat{\boldsymbol{\psi}}$ as machine precision permits. We elaborate on this feature in Section 4. Of course, the RS is useful only when the SMD objective function is well behaved and easy to optimize, which may not always be the case. But allowing optimization to play a role in ABC can be useful, as independent work by Meeds and Welling (2015) also found.

1.1. Preliminaries

In what follows, we use a "hat" to denote estimators that correspond to the mode (or extremum estimators) and a "bar" for estimators that correspond to the posterior mean. We use (s, S) and (b, B) to denote the (specific, total number of) draws in frequentist and Bayesian-type analyses, respectively. A superscript s denotes a specific draw and a subscript S denotes the average over S draws. These parameters S and B have different roles. The SMD uses S simulations to approximate the mapping $\boldsymbol{\psi}(\boldsymbol{\theta})$, while the ABC uses B simulations to approximate the posterior distribution of the infeasible likelihood.

We assume that the data $\mathbf{y} = (y_1, \ldots, y_T)'$ have finite fourth moments and can be represented by a parametric model with probability measure $\mathcal{P}_\theta$ where $\boldsymbol{\theta} \in \Theta \subset \mathbb{R}^K$, $\boldsymbol{\theta}_0$ is the true value. The likelihood $L(\boldsymbol{\theta}|\mathbf{y})$ is intractable. Estimation of $\boldsymbol{\theta}$ is based on $L \geq K$ auxiliary statistics $\hat{\boldsymbol{\psi}}(\mathbf{y}(\boldsymbol{\theta}_0))$, which we simply denote by $\hat{\boldsymbol{\psi}}$ when the context is clear. The model implies statistics $\boldsymbol{\psi}(\boldsymbol{\theta})$. The classical minimum distance estimator is

$$\hat{\boldsymbol{\theta}}_{\text{CMD}} = \arg\min_\theta J(\hat{\boldsymbol{\psi}}, \boldsymbol{\psi}(\boldsymbol{\theta})) = \bar{g}(\boldsymbol{\theta})'\mathbf{W}\,\bar{g}(\boldsymbol{\theta}), \quad \bar{g}(\boldsymbol{\theta}) = \hat{\boldsymbol{\psi}} - \boldsymbol{\psi}(\boldsymbol{\theta}).$$

Assumption A:

(i) *There exists a unique interior point* $\boldsymbol{\theta}_0 \in \Theta$ *(compact) that minimizes the population objective function* $(\boldsymbol{\psi}(\boldsymbol{\theta}_0) - \boldsymbol{\psi}(\boldsymbol{\theta}))'\mathbf{W}(\boldsymbol{\psi}(\boldsymbol{\theta}_0) - \boldsymbol{\psi}(\boldsymbol{\theta}))$. *The mapping* $\boldsymbol{\theta} \to \boldsymbol{\psi}(\boldsymbol{\theta}) = \lim_{T\to\infty} \mathbb{E}[\hat{\boldsymbol{\psi}}(\boldsymbol{\theta})]$ *is continuously differentiable and injective. The* $L \times K$ *Jacobian matrix* $\boldsymbol{\psi}_\theta(\boldsymbol{\theta}) = \frac{\partial \boldsymbol{\psi}(\boldsymbol{\theta})}{\partial \boldsymbol{\theta}}$ *has full-column rank, and the rank is constant in the neighborhood of* $\boldsymbol{\theta}_0$.

(ii) *There is an estimator* $\hat{\boldsymbol{\psi}}$ *such that* $\sqrt{T}(\hat{\boldsymbol{\psi}} - \boldsymbol{\psi}(\boldsymbol{\theta}_0)) \xrightarrow{d} \mathcal{N}(0, \boldsymbol{\Sigma})$.

(iii) $\mathbf{W}$ *is an* $L \times L$ *positive-definite matrix and* $\mathbf{W}\boldsymbol{\psi}_\theta(\boldsymbol{\theta}_0)$ *has rank K.*

Assumption A ensures global identification and consistent estimation of $\boldsymbol{\theta}$, see Newey and McFadden (1994). In Gourieroux, Monfort, and Renault (1993), the mapping $\boldsymbol{\psi} : \boldsymbol{\theta} \to \boldsymbol{\psi}(\boldsymbol{\theta})$ is referred to as the binding function while in Jiang and Turnbull (2004), $\boldsymbol{\psi}(\boldsymbol{\theta})$ is referred to as a bridge function. When $\boldsymbol{\psi}(\boldsymbol{\theta})$ is analytically intractable, the SMD estimator is

$$\hat{\boldsymbol{\theta}}_{\text{SMD}} = \arg\min_\theta J_S(\hat{\boldsymbol{\psi}}, \hat{\boldsymbol{\psi}}_S(\boldsymbol{\theta})) = \arg\min_\theta \bar{g}_S(\boldsymbol{\theta})'\mathbf{W}\bar{g}_S(\boldsymbol{\theta}). \tag{1}$$

where $S \geq 1$ is the number of simulations,

$$\bar{g}_S(\boldsymbol{\theta}) = \hat{\boldsymbol{\psi}} - \frac{1}{S}\sum_{s=1}^{S} \hat{\boldsymbol{\psi}}^s(\mathbf{y}^s(\boldsymbol{\theta})).$$

Notably, the term $\mathbb{E}[\hat{\boldsymbol{\psi}}(\boldsymbol{\theta})]$ in CMD estimation is approximated by $\frac{1}{S}\sum_{s=1}^{S} \hat{\boldsymbol{\psi}}^s(\mathbf{y}^s(\boldsymbol{\theta}))$. The SMD was first used in Smith (1993). Different SMD estimators can be obtained by suitable choice of the moments $\bar{g}(\boldsymbol{\theta})$, including the indirect inference estimator of Gourieroux et al. (1993), the simulated method of moments of Duffie and Singleton (1993), and the efficient method of moments of Gallant and Tauchen (1996).

The first ABC algorithm was implemented by Tavare, Balding, Griffiths, and Donnelly (1997) and Pritchard, Seielstad, Perez-Lezman, and Feldman (1996) to study population genetics. They draw $\boldsymbol{\theta}^b$ from the prior distribution $\pi(\boldsymbol{\theta})$, simulate the model under $\boldsymbol{\theta}^b$ to obtain data $\mathbf{y}^b$, and accept $\boldsymbol{\theta}^b$ if the vector of auxiliary statistics $\boldsymbol{\psi}(\boldsymbol{\theta}^b)$ deviates from $\hat{\boldsymbol{\psi}}$ by no more than a tuning parameter δ. If $\hat{\boldsymbol{\psi}}$ are sufficient statistics and $\delta = 0$, the procedure produces samples from the true posterior distribution if $B \to \infty$.

The Accept-Reject ABC: For $b = 1, \ldots, B$

(i) Draw ϑ from $\pi(\boldsymbol{\theta})$ and $\boldsymbol{\varepsilon}^b$ from an assumed distribution F_ε.
(ii) Generate $\mathbf{y}^b(\boldsymbol{\varepsilon}^b, \vartheta)$ and $\hat{\boldsymbol{\psi}}^b = \boldsymbol{\psi}(\mathbf{y}^b)$.
(iii) Accept $\boldsymbol{\theta}^b = \vartheta$ if $J_1^b = \left(\hat{\boldsymbol{\psi}}^b - \hat{\boldsymbol{\psi}}\right)' \mathbf{W} \left(\hat{\boldsymbol{\psi}}^b - \hat{\boldsymbol{\psi}}\right) \leq \delta$.

The accept-reject method (hereafter, AR-ABC) simply keeps those draws from the prior distribution $\pi(\boldsymbol{\theta})$ that produces auxiliary statistics which are close to the observed $\hat{\boldsymbol{\psi}}$. As it is not easy to choose δ a priori, it is common in AR-ABC to fix a desired quantile q, repeat the steps $[B/q]$ times. Setting δ to the q-th quantile of the sequence of J_1^b that will produce exactly B draws is analogous to the idea of keeping k-nearest neighbors considered in Gao and Hong (2014).

Since simulating from a noninformative prior distribution is inefficient, the accept-reject sampler can be replaced by one that targets at features of the posterior distribution. There are many ways to target the posterior distribution. We consider the MCMC implementation of ABC proposed in Marjoram et al. (2003) (hereafter, MCMC-ABC).

The MCMC-ABC: For $b = 1, \ldots, B$ with $\boldsymbol{\theta}^b$ given and proposal density $q(\cdot\,|\boldsymbol{\theta}^b)$,

(i) Generate $\vartheta \sim q(\vartheta|\boldsymbol{\theta}^b)$
(ii) Draw errors $\boldsymbol{\varepsilon}^{b+1}$ from F_ε and simulate data $\mathbf{y}^{\mathbf{b+1}}(\boldsymbol{\varepsilon}^{b+1}, \vartheta)$. Compute $\hat{\boldsymbol{\psi}}^{b+1} = \boldsymbol{\psi}(\mathbf{y}^{b+1})$.
(iii) Set $\boldsymbol{\theta}^{b+1}$ to ϑ with probability $\rho_{ABC}(\boldsymbol{\theta}^b, \vartheta)$ and to $\boldsymbol{\theta}^{b+1}$ with probability $1 - \rho_{ABC}(\boldsymbol{\theta}^b, \vartheta)$ where

$$\rho_{ABC}(\boldsymbol{\theta}^b, \vartheta) = \min\left(\mathbb{I}_{\|\hat{\boldsymbol{\psi}}, \hat{\boldsymbol{\psi}}^{b+1}\| \leq \delta} \frac{\pi(\vartheta) q(\boldsymbol{\theta}^b|\vartheta)}{\pi(\boldsymbol{\theta}^b) q(\vartheta|\boldsymbol{\theta}^b)}, 1\right). \qquad (2)$$

The AR and MCMC both produce an approximation to the posterior distribution of $\boldsymbol{\theta}$. It is common to use the posterior mean of the draws $\bar{\boldsymbol{\theta}} = \frac{1}{B}\sum_{b=1}^B \boldsymbol{\theta}^b$ as the ABC estimate. The MCMC-ABC uses a proposal distribution to account for features of the data so that it is less likely to have proposed values with low posterior probability. The tuning parameter δ affects the bias of the estimates. Too small a δ may require making many draws which can be computationally costly.

The ABC samples from the joint distribution of $(\boldsymbol{\theta}^b, \boldsymbol{\psi}^b(\boldsymbol{\varepsilon}^b, \boldsymbol{\theta}^b))$ and then integrates out $\boldsymbol{\varepsilon}^b$. The posterior distribution is thus

$$p(\boldsymbol{\theta}^b|\hat{\boldsymbol{\psi}}) \propto \int p(\boldsymbol{\theta}^b, \hat{\boldsymbol{\psi}}^b(\boldsymbol{\theta}^b, \boldsymbol{\varepsilon}^b)|\hat{\boldsymbol{\psi}})\mathbf{I}_{\|\hat{\boldsymbol{\psi}}-\boldsymbol{\psi}^b\|<\delta} d\boldsymbol{\varepsilon}^b.$$

The indicator function (also the rectangular kernel) equals one if $\|\hat{\boldsymbol{\psi}} - \boldsymbol{\psi}^b\|$ does not exceed δ. The ABC draws are dependent due to the Markov nature of the MCMC-ABC sampler.

Both the SMD and ABC assume that simulations provide an accurate approximation of $\boldsymbol{\psi}(\boldsymbol{\theta})$ and that auxiliary statistics are chosen to permit identification of $\boldsymbol{\theta}$. Creel and Kristensen (in press) suggests a cross-validation method for selecting the auxiliary statistics. For the same choice of $\hat{\boldsymbol{\psi}}$, the SMD finds the $\boldsymbol{\theta}$ that makes the average of the simulated auxiliary statistics close to $\hat{\boldsymbol{\psi}}$. The ABC takes the average of $\boldsymbol{\theta}^b$, drawn from the prior, with the property that each $\boldsymbol{\psi}^b$ is close to $\hat{\boldsymbol{\psi}}$. In an attempt to understand this difference, Forneron and Ng (2014) take as starting point that each $\boldsymbol{\theta}^b$ in the above ABC algorithm can be reformulated as an SMD problem with $S = 1$. We consider an algorithm that solves the SMD problem many times to obtain a distribution for $\boldsymbol{\theta}^b$, each time using one simulated path. The sampler terminates with an evaluation of the prior probability, in contrast to the ABC which starts with a draw from the prior distribution. Hence, we call our algorithm a reverse sampler (hereafter, RS). The RS produces a sequence of $\boldsymbol{\theta}^b$ that are independent optimizers and do not have a Markov structure.

In the next two sections, we explore additional features of the RS. As an overview, the distribution of draws that emerge from SMD estimation with $S = 1$ may not be from the desired posterior distribution. Hence, the draws are reweighted to target the posterior. In the exactly identified case, $\hat{\boldsymbol{\psi}}^b$ can be made exactly equal to $\hat{\boldsymbol{\psi}}$ by choosing the SMD estimate as $\boldsymbol{\theta}^b$. Thus, the RS is simply an optimization-based importance sampler using the determinant of Jacobian matrix as importance ratio. In the overidentified case, the volume of the (rectangular) Jacobian matrix is used in place of the determinant. Additional weighting is given to those $\hat{\boldsymbol{\theta}}^b$ that yields $\hat{\boldsymbol{\psi}}^b$ sufficiently close to $\hat{\boldsymbol{\psi}}$.

2. THE RS: CASE $K = L$

The algorithm for the case of exact identification is as follows. For $b = 1, \ldots, B$

(i) Generate $\boldsymbol{\varepsilon}^b$ from F_ε.
(ii) Find $\boldsymbol{\theta}^b = \arg\min_{\boldsymbol{\theta}} J_1^b(\hat{\boldsymbol{\psi}}^b(\boldsymbol{\theta}, \boldsymbol{\varepsilon}^b), \hat{\boldsymbol{\psi}})$ and let $\hat{\boldsymbol{\psi}}^b = \hat{\boldsymbol{\psi}}^b(\boldsymbol{\theta}^b, \boldsymbol{\varepsilon}^b)$.
(iii) Set $w(\boldsymbol{\theta}^b, \boldsymbol{\varepsilon}^b) = \pi(\boldsymbol{\theta}^b)|\hat{\boldsymbol{\psi}}^b_{\boldsymbol{\theta}}(\boldsymbol{\theta}^b, \boldsymbol{\varepsilon}^b)|^{-1}$.

(iv) Reweigh the $\boldsymbol{\theta}^b$ by $\frac{w(\boldsymbol{\theta}^b)}{\sum_{b=1}^B w(\boldsymbol{\theta}^b)}$.

Like the ABC, the draws $\boldsymbol{\theta}^b$ provides an estimate of the posterior distribution of $\boldsymbol{\theta}$ from which an estimate of the posterior mean

$$\bar{\boldsymbol{\theta}}_{RS} = \sum_{b=1}^{B} \frac{w(\boldsymbol{\theta}^b)}{\sum_{b=1}^B w(\boldsymbol{\theta}^b)} \boldsymbol{\theta}^b$$

can be used as an estimate of $\boldsymbol{\theta}$. Each $\boldsymbol{\theta}^b$ is a function of the data $\hat{\boldsymbol{\psi}}$ and the draws $\boldsymbol{\varepsilon}^b$ that minimizes $J_1^b(\boldsymbol{\psi}(\boldsymbol{\theta}, \boldsymbol{\varepsilon}^b), \hat{\boldsymbol{\psi}})$. The K first-order conditions are given by

$$\mathcal{F}(\boldsymbol{\theta}^b, \boldsymbol{\varepsilon}^b, \hat{\boldsymbol{\psi}}) = \frac{\partial \bar{g}_1(\boldsymbol{\theta}^b, \boldsymbol{\varepsilon}^b, \hat{\boldsymbol{\psi}})}{\partial \boldsymbol{\theta}}' \mathbf{W} \bar{g}_1(\boldsymbol{\theta}^b, \boldsymbol{\varepsilon}^b, \hat{\boldsymbol{\psi}}) = 0 \tag{3}$$

where $\frac{\partial \bar{g}_1(\boldsymbol{\theta}^b, \boldsymbol{\varepsilon}^b, \hat{\boldsymbol{\psi}})}{\partial \boldsymbol{\theta}}$ is the $L \times K$ matrix of derivatives with respect to $\boldsymbol{\theta}$ evaluated at the arguments. It is assumed that, for all b, this derivative matrix has full-column rank K. For SMD estimation, $\frac{\partial \bar{g}_1(\boldsymbol{\theta}^b, \boldsymbol{\varepsilon}^b, \hat{\boldsymbol{\psi}})}{\partial \boldsymbol{\theta}} = \hat{\boldsymbol{\psi}}_{\boldsymbol{\theta}}^b(\boldsymbol{\theta}^b, \boldsymbol{\varepsilon}^b, \hat{\boldsymbol{\psi}})$. This Jacobian matrix plays an important role in the RS.

The importance density denoted $h(\boldsymbol{\theta}^b, \boldsymbol{\varepsilon}^b | \hat{\boldsymbol{\psi}})$ is obtained by drawing $\boldsymbol{\varepsilon}^b$ from the assumed distribution F_ε and finding $\boldsymbol{\theta}^b$ such that $J(\hat{\boldsymbol{\psi}}^b(\boldsymbol{\theta}, \boldsymbol{\varepsilon}^b), \hat{\boldsymbol{\psi}})$ is smaller than a prespecified tolerance. When $K = L$, this tolerance can be made arbitrarily small so that up to numerical precision, $\hat{\boldsymbol{\psi}}^b(\boldsymbol{\theta}^b, \boldsymbol{\varepsilon}^b) = \hat{\boldsymbol{\psi}}$. This density $h(\boldsymbol{\theta}^b, \boldsymbol{\varepsilon}^b | \hat{\boldsymbol{\psi}})$ is related to $p_{\hat{\boldsymbol{\psi}}^b, \boldsymbol{\varepsilon}^b}(\hat{\boldsymbol{\psi}}^b(\boldsymbol{\theta}^b, \boldsymbol{\varepsilon}^b)) \equiv p(\hat{\boldsymbol{\psi}}^b, \boldsymbol{\varepsilon}^b)$ by a change of variable:

$$h(\boldsymbol{\theta}^b, \boldsymbol{\varepsilon}^b | \hat{\boldsymbol{\psi}}) = p(\hat{\boldsymbol{\psi}}^b, \boldsymbol{\varepsilon}^b | \hat{\boldsymbol{\psi}}) \cdot |\hat{\boldsymbol{\psi}}_{\boldsymbol{\theta}}^b(\boldsymbol{\theta}^b, \boldsymbol{\varepsilon}^b)|.$$

Now $p(\boldsymbol{\theta}^b, \hat{\boldsymbol{\psi}}^b | \hat{\boldsymbol{\psi}}) \propto p(\hat{\boldsymbol{\psi}} | \boldsymbol{\theta}^b, \hat{\boldsymbol{\psi}}^b) p(\hat{\boldsymbol{\psi}}^b, \boldsymbol{\varepsilon}^b | \boldsymbol{\theta}^b) \pi(\boldsymbol{\theta}^b)$ and $p(\hat{\boldsymbol{\psi}} | \boldsymbol{\theta}^b, \hat{\boldsymbol{\psi}}^b)$ is constant since $\hat{\boldsymbol{\psi}}^b = \hat{\boldsymbol{\psi}}$. Hence,

$$\begin{aligned} p(\boldsymbol{\theta}^b | \hat{\boldsymbol{\psi}}) &\propto \int \pi(\boldsymbol{\theta}^b) p(\hat{\boldsymbol{\psi}}^b, \boldsymbol{\varepsilon}^b | \hat{\boldsymbol{\psi}}) \mathbb{I}_{\|\hat{\boldsymbol{\psi}} - \hat{\boldsymbol{\psi}}^b\| = 0} d\boldsymbol{\varepsilon}^b \\ &= \int \pi(\boldsymbol{\theta}^b) |\hat{\boldsymbol{\psi}}_{\boldsymbol{\theta}}^b(\boldsymbol{\theta}^b, \boldsymbol{\varepsilon}^b, \hat{\boldsymbol{\psi}})|^{-1} h(\boldsymbol{\theta}^b, \boldsymbol{\varepsilon}^b | \hat{\boldsymbol{\psi}}) \mathbb{I}_{\|\hat{\boldsymbol{\psi}} - \hat{\boldsymbol{\psi}}^b\| = 0} d\boldsymbol{\varepsilon}^b \\ &= \int w(\boldsymbol{\theta}^b, \boldsymbol{\varepsilon}^b) h(\boldsymbol{\theta}^b, \boldsymbol{\varepsilon}^b | \hat{\boldsymbol{\psi}}) d\boldsymbol{\varepsilon}^b \end{aligned}$$

where the weights are, assuming invertibility of the determinant,

$$w(\boldsymbol{\theta}^b, \boldsymbol{\varepsilon}^b) = \pi(\boldsymbol{\theta}^b) |\hat{\boldsymbol{\psi}}_{\boldsymbol{\theta}}^b(\boldsymbol{\theta}^b, \boldsymbol{\varepsilon}^b, \hat{\boldsymbol{\psi}})|^{-1}. \tag{4}$$

Note that, in general, $\frac{w(\boldsymbol{\theta}^b)}{\sum_{b=1}^B w(\boldsymbol{\theta}^b)} \neq \frac{1}{B}$.

In the above, we have used the fact that $\mathbb{I}_{\|\hat{\psi}-\hat{\psi}^b\|=0}$ is 1 with probability one when $K=L$. The Jacobian of the transformation appears in the weights because the draws θ^b are related to the likelihood via a change of variable. Hence, a crucial aspect of the RS is that it reweighs the draws of θ^b from $h(\theta^b, \varepsilon)$. Put differently, the unweighted draws will not, in general, follow the target posterior distribution.

Consider a weighted sample $(\theta^b, w(\theta^b, \varepsilon))$ with $w(\theta^b, \varepsilon^b)$ defined in Eq. (4). The following proposition shows that as $B \to \infty$, RS produces the posterior distribution associated with the infeasible likelihood, which is also the ABC posterior distribution with $\delta = 0$.

Proposition 1. *Suppose that $\hat{\psi}^b : \theta \to \hat{\psi}^b(\theta, \varepsilon^b)$ is one-to-one and the determinant $|\frac{\partial \psi^b(\theta,\varepsilon^b,\hat{\psi})}{\partial \theta}| = |\hat{\psi}^b_\theta(\theta, \varepsilon^b, \hat{\psi})|$ is bounded away from zero around θ^b. For any measurable function $\varphi(\theta)$ such that $\mathbb{E}_{p(\theta|\hat{\psi})}(\varphi(\theta)) = \int \varphi(\theta) p(\theta|\hat{\psi}) d\theta$ exists, then*

$$\frac{\sum_b^B w(\theta^b, \varepsilon^b)\varphi(\theta^b)}{\sum_b^B w(\theta^b, \varepsilon^b)} \xrightarrow{a.s.} \mathbb{E}_{p(\theta|\hat{\psi})}(\varphi(\theta)) .$$

Convergence to the target distribution follows from a strong law of large numbers. Fixing the event $\hat{\psi}^b = \hat{\psi}$ is crucial to this convergence result. To see why, consider first the numerator:

$$\begin{aligned}
\frac{1}{B}\sum_b w(\theta^b, \varepsilon^b)\varphi(\theta^b) &\xrightarrow{a.s.} \iint \varphi(\theta) w(\theta, \varepsilon)\, p(\hat{\psi}^b, \varepsilon^b|\theta) |\hat{\psi}_\theta(\theta, \varepsilon, \hat{\psi})| d\varepsilon^b d\theta \\
&= \iint \varphi(\theta) \left|\hat{\psi}^b_\theta(\theta, \varepsilon, \hat{\psi})\right|^{-1} \pi(\theta) p(\hat{\psi}^b, \varepsilon^b|\theta) \left|\hat{\psi}^b_\theta(\theta, \varepsilon, \hat{\psi})\right| d\varepsilon^b d\theta \\
&= \iint \varphi(\theta)\pi(\theta) p(\hat{\psi}^b, \varepsilon|\theta) d\varepsilon d\theta \\
&= \iint \varphi(\theta)\pi(\theta) p(\hat{\psi}, \varepsilon|\theta) d\varepsilon d\theta \\
&= \int \varphi(\theta)\pi(\theta) L(\hat{\psi}|\theta) d\theta.
\end{aligned}$$

Furthermore, the denominator converges to the integrating constant since $\frac{1}{B}\sum_b w(\theta^b, \varepsilon^b) \xrightarrow{a.s.} \int \pi(\theta) L(\hat{\psi}|\theta) d\theta$. Proposition 1 implies that the weighted average of θ^b converges to the posterior mean. Furthermore, the posterior quantiles produced by the RS tends to those of the infeasible posterior distribution $p(\theta|\hat{\psi})$ as $B \to \infty$. As discussed in Forneron and Ng (2014), the ABC can be presented as an importance sampler. Hence, the accept-reject algorithm in Tavare et al. (1997) and Pritchard et al. (1996), as well as the Sequential Monte-Carlo approach to

ABC in Sisson, Fan, and Tanaka (2007), Toni, Welch, Strelkowa, Ipsen, and Stumpf (2009), and Beaumont, Corneut, Marin, and Robert (2009) are all important samplers. The RS differs in that it is optimization based. It is also developed independently in Meeds andWelling (2015).

We now use examples to illustrate how the RS works in the exactly identified case.

Example 1: Suppose we have one observation $y \sim \mathcal{N}(\theta, 1)$ or $y = \theta + \varepsilon$, $\varepsilon \sim \mathcal{N}(0, 1)$. The prior for θ is $\theta \sim \mathcal{N}(0, 1)$. By drawing, $\theta^b, \varepsilon^b \sim \mathcal{N}(0, 1)$, we obtain $y^b = \theta^b + \varepsilon^b \sim \mathcal{N}(0, 2)$. The ABC keeps $\theta^b | y^b = y$. Since (θ^b, y^b) are jointly normal with covariance of 1, we deduce that $\theta^b | y^b = y \sim \mathcal{N}(y/2, 1/2)$. The exact posterior distribution for θ is $\mathcal{N}(y/2, 1/2)$.

The RS draws $\varepsilon^b \sim \mathcal{N}(0, 1)$ and computes $\theta^b = y - \varepsilon^b$ which is $\mathcal{N}(y, 1)$ conditional on y. The Jacobian of the transformation is 1. Reweighting according to the prior, we have:

$$p_{\text{RS}}(\theta | y) \propto \phi(\theta)\phi(\theta - y) \propto \exp\left(-\frac{1}{2}\left(\theta^2 + (\theta - y)^2\right)\right) \propto \exp\left(-\frac{1}{2}\left(2\theta^2 - 2\theta y\right)\right)$$
$$\propto \exp\left(-\frac{2}{2}(\theta - y/2)^2\right).$$

This is the exact posterior distribution as derived above.

Example 2: Suppose $y = Q(u, \theta)$, $\varepsilon \sim \mathcal{U}_{[0,1]}$ and Q is a quantile function that is invertible and differentiable in both arguments.[1] For a single draw, y is a sufficient statistic. The likelihood-based posterior is

$$p(\theta | y) \propto \pi(\theta) f(y | \theta).$$

The RS simulates $y^b(\theta) = Q(\varepsilon^b | \theta)$ and sets $Q(\varepsilon^b | \theta^b) = y$. Or, in terms of the CDF:

$$\varepsilon^b = F(y | \theta^b)$$

Consider a small perturbation to y holding u^b fixed:

$$0 = dy \frac{dF(y|\theta^b)}{dy} + d\theta^b \frac{dF(y|\theta^b)}{d\theta^b} = dy F'_y(y|\theta^b) + d\theta^b F'_{\theta^b}(y|\theta^b).$$

In the above, $f \equiv F'_y(\cdot)$ is the density of y given θ. The Jacobian is

$$\left|\frac{d\theta^b}{dy}\right| = \left|\frac{F'_y(y|\theta^b)}{F'_{\theta^b}(y|\theta^b)}\right| = \left|\frac{f(y|\theta^b)}{F'_{\theta^b}(y|\theta^b)}\right|.$$

To find the distribution of θ^b conditional on y, assume $F(y,.)$ is increasing in θ:

$$\begin{aligned}\mathbb{P}(\theta^b \le t|y) &= \mathbb{P}\Big(F(y|\theta^b) \le F(y|t)|y\Big)\\ &= \mathbb{P}\left(\varepsilon^b \le F(y|t)|y\right)\\ &= F(y|t).\end{aligned}$$

By construction, $f(\theta|y) = F'_\theta(y|\theta)$.[2] Putting things together,[3]

$$p_{\mathrm{RS}}(\theta|y) \propto \pi(\theta)|F'_\theta(y|\theta)|\left|\frac{f(y|\theta)}{F'_\theta(y|\theta)}\right| = \pi(\theta)f(y|\theta) \propto p(\theta|y).$$

Example 3: Normal Mean and Variance. We now consider an example in which the estimators can be derived analytically, and given in Forneron and Ng (2014). We assume $y_t = \varepsilon_t \sim N(m,\sigma^2)$. The parameters of the model are $\boldsymbol{\theta} = (m,\sigma^2)'$. We consider the auxiliary statistics: $\hat{\boldsymbol{\psi}}(\mathbf{y})' = \left(\bar{y}\ \hat{\sigma}^2\right)$. The parameters are exactly identified.

The MLE of $\boldsymbol{\theta}$ is

$$\hat{m} = \frac{1}{T}\sum_{t=1}^{T} y_t, \quad \hat{\sigma}^2 = \frac{1}{T}\sum_{t=1}^{T}(y_t - \bar{y})^2.$$

We consider the prior $\pi(m,\sigma^2) = (\sigma^2)^{-\alpha}\mathbb{I}_{\sigma^2>0}$, $\alpha > 0$ so that the log posterior distribution is

$$\log p(\boldsymbol{\theta}|\hat{m},\hat{\sigma}^2) \propto \frac{-T}{2}\log(2\pi)\sigma^2 - \alpha\log\sigma^2 - \frac{1}{2\sigma^2}\sum_{t=1}^{T}(y_t - m)^2.$$

Since $\hat{\boldsymbol{\psi}}(\mathbf{y})$ are sufficient statistics, the RS coincides with the likelihood-based Bayesian estimator, denoted B below. This is also the infeasible ABC estimator. We focus discussion on estimators for σ^2 which have more interesting properties. Under a uniform prior, we obtain

$$\begin{aligned}\bar{\sigma}^2_B &= \hat{\sigma}^2\frac{T}{T-5}\\ \hat{\sigma}^2_{\mathrm{SMD}} &= \frac{\hat{\sigma}^2}{\frac{1}{ST}\sum_{s=1}^{S}\sum_{t=1}^{T}(\varepsilon^s_t - \bar{\varepsilon}^s)^2}\end{aligned}$$

Table 1. Properties of the Estimators.

Estimator	Prior	$\mathbf{E}[\hat{\theta}]$	Bias	Variance	MSE
$\hat{\theta}_{ML}$	–	$\sigma^2 \frac{T-1}{T}$	$-\frac{\sigma^2}{T}$	$2\sigma^4 \frac{T-1}{T^2}$	$2\sigma^4 \frac{2T-1}{2T^2}$
$\bar{\theta}_B$	1	$\sigma^2 \frac{T-1}{T-5}$	$\frac{2\sigma^2}{T-5}$	$2\sigma^4 \frac{T-1}{(T-5)^2}$	$2\sigma^4 \frac{T+1}{(T-5)^2}$
$\bar{\theta}_{RS}$	1	$\sigma^2 \frac{T-1}{T-5}$	$\frac{2\sigma^2}{T-5}$	$2\sigma^4 \frac{T-1}{(T-5)^2}$	$2\sigma^4 \frac{T+1}{(T-5)^2}$
$\hat{\theta}_{\text{SMD}}$	–	$\sigma^2 \frac{S(T-1)}{S(T-1)-2}$	$\frac{2\sigma^2}{S(T-1)-2}$	$2\sigma^4 \kappa_1 \frac{1}{T-1}$	$2\sigma^4 \frac{\kappa_1}{T-1} + \frac{4\sigma^4}{(S(T-1)-2))^2}$

where $\kappa_1(S,T) = \frac{(S(T-1))^2(T-1+S(T-1)-2)}{(S(T-1)-2)^2(S(T-1)-4)} > 1$, κ_1 tends to one as S tend to infinity.

$$\hat{\sigma}^2_{\text{RS}} = \sum_{b=1}^{B} \frac{\frac{\hat{\sigma}^2}{[\sum_{t=1}^{T}(\varepsilon_t^b - \bar{\varepsilon}^b)^2/T]^2}}{\sum_{k=1}^{B} \frac{1}{\sum_{t=1}^{T}(\varepsilon_t^k - \bar{\varepsilon}^k)^2/T}}$$

In this example, the RS is also the ABC estimator with $\delta = 0$. It is straightforward to show that the bias reducing prior is $\alpha = 1$ and coincides with the SMD. Table 1 shows that the estimators are asymptotically equivalent but can differ for fixed T.

To highlight the role of the Jacobian matrix in the RS, the top panel of Fig. 2 plots the exact posterior distribution and the one obtained from the RS. They are indistinguishable. The bottom panel shows an incorrectly constructed RS that does not apply the Jacobian transformation. Notably, the two distributions are not the same. Reweighting by the Jacobian matrix is crucial to targeting the desired posterior distribution.

Fig. 1 presents the likelihood-based posterior distribution, along with the likelihood-free ones produced by ABC and the RS-JI (just identified) for one draw of the data. The ABC results are based on the accept-reject algorithm. The numerical results corroborate with the analytical ones: all the posterior distributions are very similar. The RS-JI posterior distribution is very close to the exact posterior distribution. Fig. 1 also presents results for the overidentified case (denoted RS-OI) using two additional auxiliary statistics: $\hat{\boldsymbol{\psi}} = (\bar{y}, \hat{\sigma}_y^2, \hat{\mu}_3/\hat{\sigma}_y^2, \hat{\mu}_4/\hat{\sigma}_y^4)$ where $\mu_k = \mathbb{E}(y^k)$. The weight matrix is diag$(1, 1, 1/2, 1/2)$. The posterior distribution is very close to RS-JI obtained for exact identification. We now explain how the posterior distribution for the overidentified case is obtained.

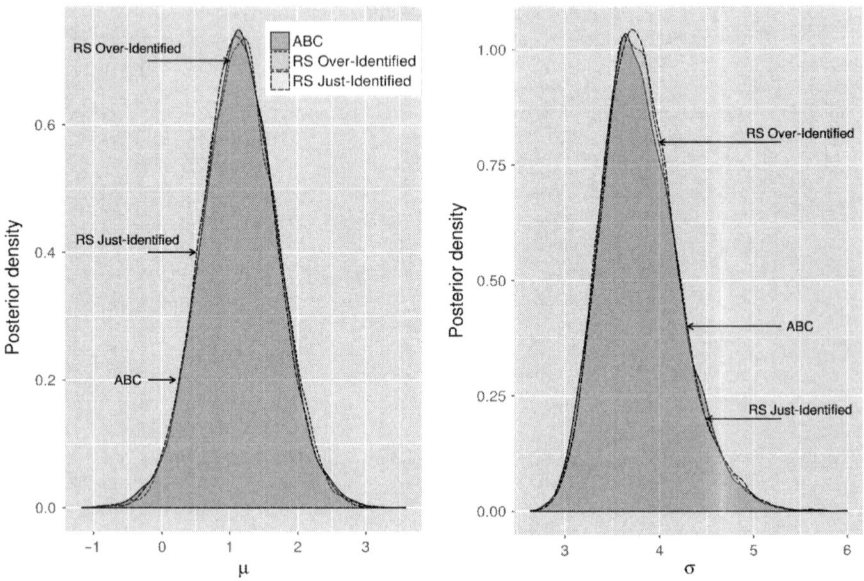

Fig. 1. Normally Distributed Data.

3. THE RS: CASE $L \geq K$

The idea behind the RS is the same when we go from the case of exact to overidentification. The precise implementation is as follows. Let $\mathbb{K}_\delta(\hat{\boldsymbol{\psi}}, \hat{\boldsymbol{\psi}}^b)$ be a kernel function and δ be a tolerance level such that $\mathbb{K}_0(\hat{\boldsymbol{\psi}}, \boldsymbol{\psi}^b) = \mathbb{I}_{\|\hat{\boldsymbol{\psi}}-\hat{\boldsymbol{\psi}}^b\|=0}$.

For $b = 1, \ldots, B$

(i) Generate $\boldsymbol{\varepsilon}^b$ from F_ε.

(ii) Find $\boldsymbol{\theta}^b = \arg\min_{\boldsymbol{\theta}} J_1^b(\hat{\boldsymbol{\psi}}^b, \hat{\boldsymbol{\psi}})$ where $\hat{\boldsymbol{\psi}}^b = \hat{\boldsymbol{\psi}}(\boldsymbol{\theta}, \boldsymbol{\varepsilon}^b)$;

(iii) Set $w(\boldsymbol{\theta}^b, \boldsymbol{\varepsilon}^b) = \pi(\boldsymbol{\theta}^b)\mathrm{vol}\left(\hat{\boldsymbol{\psi}}_{\boldsymbol{\theta}}^b(\boldsymbol{\theta}^b, \boldsymbol{\varepsilon}^b, \hat{\boldsymbol{\psi}})\right)^{-1} \mathbb{K}_\delta(J_1^b(\hat{\boldsymbol{\psi}}^b, \hat{\boldsymbol{\psi}}))$, where $\mathrm{vol}(\hat{\boldsymbol{\psi}}_{\boldsymbol{\theta}}^b) = \sqrt{\left|\hat{\boldsymbol{\psi}}_{\boldsymbol{\theta}}^{b\prime}\hat{\boldsymbol{\psi}}_{\boldsymbol{\theta}}^b\right|}$.

(iv) Reweigh $\boldsymbol{\theta}^b$ by $\frac{w(\boldsymbol{\theta}^b)}{\sum_{b=1}^B w(\boldsymbol{\theta}^b)}$.

We now proceed to explain the two changes: the use of volume in place of determinant in the importance ratio, and the need for $L - K$-dimensional kernel smoothing.

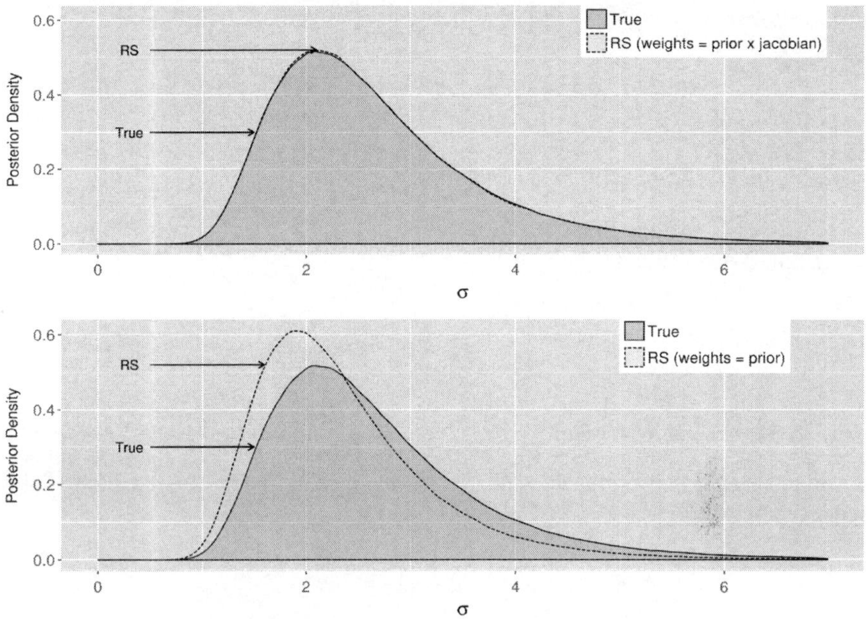

Fig. 2. The Importance of Reweighting in RS.

The usual change of variable formula evaluates the absolute value of the determinant of the Jacobian matrix when the matrix is square. The determinant then gives the infinitesimal dilatation of the volume element in passing from one set of variables to another. The main issue in the case of overidentification is that the determinant of a rectangular Jacobian matrix is not well defined. However, as shown in Ben-Israel (1999), the determinant can be replaced by the volume when transforming from sets of a higher dimension to a lower one.[4] For an $L \times K$ matrix A, its volume, denoted $\text{vol}(A)$, is the product of the (nonzero) singular values of A:

$$\text{vol}(A) = \begin{cases} \sqrt{|A'A|} & L \geq K, \quad \text{rank}(A) = K \\ \sqrt{|AA'|} & L \leq K, \quad \text{rank}(A) = L. \end{cases}$$

Furthermore, if $A = BC$, $\text{vol}(A) = \text{vol}(B)\text{vol}(C)$.

To verify that our target distribution is unaffected by whether we calculate the volume or the determinant of the Jacobian matrix when $K = L$, observe that

$$\hat{\boldsymbol{\psi}}^b_\theta(\boldsymbol{\theta}^b(\hat{\boldsymbol{\psi}}), \boldsymbol{\varepsilon}^b) = \frac{\partial \hat{\boldsymbol{\psi}}^b(\boldsymbol{\theta}^b, \boldsymbol{\varepsilon}^b, \hat{\boldsymbol{\psi}})}{\partial \hat{\boldsymbol{\psi}}} \frac{\partial \hat{\boldsymbol{\psi}}}{\partial \boldsymbol{\theta}^b}. \tag{5}$$

The K first-order conditions defined by Eq. (3) become

$$\mathcal{F}(\boldsymbol{\theta}^b, \boldsymbol{\varepsilon}^b, \hat{\boldsymbol{\psi}}) = \hat{\boldsymbol{\psi}}^b_\theta(\boldsymbol{\theta}^b, \boldsymbol{\varepsilon}^b, \hat{\boldsymbol{\psi}})' \mathbf{W}(\hat{\boldsymbol{\psi}} - \hat{\boldsymbol{\psi}}^b(\boldsymbol{\theta}^b, \boldsymbol{\varepsilon}^b)) = 0. \tag{6}$$

Since $L = K$, $\mathbf{W}$ can be set to an identity matrix I_K. Furthermore, $\boldsymbol{\psi}(\boldsymbol{\theta}^b, \boldsymbol{\varepsilon}) = \hat{\boldsymbol{\psi}}$ since $J_1^b(\boldsymbol{\theta}^b) = 0$ under exact identification. As $\frac{\partial \boldsymbol{\theta}}{\partial \hat{\boldsymbol{\psi}}}$ is a square matrix when $K = L$, we can directly use the fact that $\mathcal{F}_\theta(\boldsymbol{\theta}^b, \boldsymbol{\varepsilon}^b, \hat{\boldsymbol{\psi}})d\boldsymbol{\theta} + \mathcal{F}_\psi(\boldsymbol{\theta}^b, \boldsymbol{\varepsilon}^b, \hat{\boldsymbol{\psi}})d\hat{\boldsymbol{\psi}} = 0$ to obtain the required determinant:

$$|\hat{\boldsymbol{\psi}}^b_\theta(\boldsymbol{\theta}^b, \boldsymbol{\varepsilon}^b, \hat{\boldsymbol{\psi}})|^{-1} = \mathrm{I}_K \cdot \left|\frac{\partial \boldsymbol{\theta}}{\partial \hat{\boldsymbol{\psi}}}\right| = |-\mathcal{F}_\theta(\boldsymbol{\theta}^b, \boldsymbol{\varepsilon}^b, \hat{\boldsymbol{\psi}})^{-1}\mathcal{F}_{\hat{\psi}}(\boldsymbol{\theta}^b, \boldsymbol{\varepsilon}^b, \hat{\boldsymbol{\psi}})|. \tag{7}$$

Now to use the volume result, put $\mathrm{A} = \mathrm{I}_K$, $\mathrm{B} = \frac{\partial \boldsymbol{\theta}}{\partial \hat{\boldsymbol{\psi}}}$ and $\mathrm{C} = \frac{\partial \hat{\boldsymbol{\psi}}}{\partial \boldsymbol{\theta}}$. But A is just a K-dimensional identity matrix. Hence, $\mathrm{vol}(\mathrm{I}_K) = \mathrm{vol}\left(\frac{\partial \boldsymbol{\theta}}{\partial \hat{\boldsymbol{\psi}}}\right)\mathrm{vol}\left(\frac{\partial \hat{\boldsymbol{\psi}}}{\partial \boldsymbol{\theta}}\right)$ which evaluates to

$$\mathrm{vol}\left(\frac{\partial \hat{\boldsymbol{\psi}}}{\partial \boldsymbol{\theta}}\right)^{-1} = \mathrm{vol}\left(\frac{\partial \boldsymbol{\theta}}{\partial \hat{\boldsymbol{\psi}}}\right) \quad \text{or} \quad \left|\frac{\partial \hat{\boldsymbol{\psi}}}{\partial \boldsymbol{\theta}}\right|^{-1} = \left|\frac{\partial \boldsymbol{\theta}}{\partial \hat{\boldsymbol{\psi}}}\right|$$

which is precisely $|\hat{\boldsymbol{\psi}}^b_\theta(\boldsymbol{\theta}, \boldsymbol{\varepsilon}^b)|^{-1}$ as given in Eq. (7).[5] Hence, in the exactly identified case, there is no difference whether one evaluates the determinant or the volume of the Jacobian matrix.

Next, we turn to the role of the kernel function $\mathbb{K}_\delta(\hat{\boldsymbol{\psi}}, \hat{\boldsymbol{\psi}}^b)$. The joint density $h(\boldsymbol{\theta}^b, \boldsymbol{\varepsilon}^b)$ is related to $p_{\hat{\boldsymbol{\psi}}^b, \boldsymbol{\varepsilon}^b}(\hat{\boldsymbol{\psi}}(\boldsymbol{\theta}^b, \boldsymbol{\varepsilon}^b)) = p(\hat{\boldsymbol{\psi}}^b, \boldsymbol{\varepsilon}^b)$ through a change a variable now expressed in terms of volume:

$$h(\boldsymbol{\theta}, \boldsymbol{\varepsilon}^b|\hat{\boldsymbol{\psi}}) = p(\hat{\boldsymbol{\psi}}^b, \boldsymbol{\varepsilon}^b|\hat{\boldsymbol{\psi}}) \cdot \mathrm{vol}\left(\hat{\boldsymbol{\psi}}^b_\theta(\boldsymbol{\theta}^b, \boldsymbol{\varepsilon}^b, \hat{\boldsymbol{\psi}})\right)$$

When $L \geq K$, the objective function $\|\hat{\boldsymbol{\psi}} - \hat{\boldsymbol{\psi}}^b\|_{\mathbf{W}} = J_1^b \geq 0$ measures the extent to which $\hat{\boldsymbol{\psi}}$ deviates from $\hat{\boldsymbol{\psi}}^b$ when the objective function at its minimum. Consider the thought experiment that $J_1^b = 0$ with probability 1, such as enabled by a particular draw of $\boldsymbol{\varepsilon}^b$. Then the arguments above for $K = L$ would have applied. We would still have $p(\boldsymbol{\theta}^b|\hat{\boldsymbol{\psi}}) = \int \pi(\boldsymbol{\theta}^b)p(\hat{\boldsymbol{\psi}}^b, \boldsymbol{\varepsilon}^b|\hat{\boldsymbol{\psi}})\mathbb{I}_{\|\hat{\boldsymbol{\psi}} - \hat{\boldsymbol{\psi}}^b\| = 0}d\boldsymbol{\varepsilon}^b = \int w(\boldsymbol{\theta}^b, \boldsymbol{\varepsilon}^b)h(\boldsymbol{\theta}^b, \boldsymbol{\varepsilon}^b|\hat{\boldsymbol{\psi}})d\boldsymbol{\varepsilon}^b$, except that the weights are now defined in terms of volume. Proposition 1 would then extend to the case with $L \geq K$.

But, in general, $J_1^b \neq 0$ almost surely. Nonetheless, we can use only those draws that yield $J_1^b(\boldsymbol{\theta}^b)$ that are sufficiently close to zero. The more draws we make, the tighter this criterion can be. Suppose there is a symmetric kernel $\mathbb{K}_\delta(\cdot)$

satisfying conditions in Pagan and Ullah (1999, p. 96) for consistent estimation of conditional moments nonparametrically. Analogous to Proposition 1, the volume $\mathrm{vol}(\hat{\boldsymbol{\psi}}^b_\theta(\boldsymbol{\theta}^b, \boldsymbol{\varepsilon}^b, \hat{\boldsymbol{\psi}}))$ is assumed to be bounded away from zero. Then as the number of draws $B \to \infty$, the bandwidth $\delta(B) \to 0$ and $B\delta(B) \to \infty$ with

$$w_{\delta(B)}(\boldsymbol{\theta}^b, \hat{\boldsymbol{\varepsilon}}^b) = \pi(\boldsymbol{\theta}^b)\mathrm{vol}\left(\hat{\boldsymbol{\psi}}^b_\theta(\boldsymbol{\theta}^b, \boldsymbol{\varepsilon}^b, \hat{\boldsymbol{\psi}})\right)^{-1} \mathbb{K}_{\delta(B)}(\hat{\boldsymbol{\psi}}, \hat{\boldsymbol{\psi}}^b), \tag{8}$$

a result analogous to Proposition 1 can be obtained:

$$\begin{aligned}
\frac{1}{B}\sum_b w_{\delta(B)}(\boldsymbol{\theta}^b, \boldsymbol{\varepsilon}^b)\varphi(\boldsymbol{\theta}^b) &\xrightarrow{p} \iint \varphi(\boldsymbol{\theta})w_0(\boldsymbol{\theta}, \boldsymbol{\varepsilon})\mathrm{vol}\left(\hat{\boldsymbol{\psi}}^b_\theta(\boldsymbol{\theta}, \boldsymbol{\varepsilon}^b; \hat{\boldsymbol{\psi}})\right)p(\hat{\boldsymbol{\psi}}, \boldsymbol{\varepsilon}^b|\boldsymbol{\theta})d\boldsymbol{\theta}d\boldsymbol{\varepsilon}^b \\
&= \iint \varphi(\boldsymbol{\theta})\pi(\boldsymbol{\theta})\mathbb{I}_{\|\hat{\boldsymbol{\psi}}-\hat{\boldsymbol{\psi}}^b\|=0}\mathrm{vol}\left(\hat{\boldsymbol{\psi}}^b_\theta(\boldsymbol{\theta}, \boldsymbol{\varepsilon}^b; \hat{\boldsymbol{\psi}})\right)^{-1} p(\hat{\boldsymbol{\psi}}^b, \boldsymbol{\varepsilon}^b|\boldsymbol{\theta})\mathrm{vol}\left(\hat{\boldsymbol{\psi}}^b_\theta(\boldsymbol{\theta}, \boldsymbol{\varepsilon}^b; \hat{\boldsymbol{\psi}})\right)d\boldsymbol{\theta}d\boldsymbol{\varepsilon}^b \\
&= \iint \varphi(\boldsymbol{\theta})\pi(\boldsymbol{\theta})\mathbb{I}_{\|\hat{\boldsymbol{\psi}}-\hat{\boldsymbol{\psi}}^b\|=0}p(\hat{\boldsymbol{\psi}}, \boldsymbol{\varepsilon}^b|\boldsymbol{\theta})d\boldsymbol{\theta}d\boldsymbol{\varepsilon}^b \\
&= \int \varphi(\boldsymbol{\theta})\pi(\boldsymbol{\theta})L(\hat{\boldsymbol{\psi}}|\boldsymbol{\theta})d\boldsymbol{\theta}.
\end{aligned}$$

Similarly, the integrating constant is consistent as $\frac{1}{B}\sum_b w_{\delta(B)}(\boldsymbol{\theta}^b, \boldsymbol{\varepsilon}^b) \xrightarrow{p} \int \pi(\boldsymbol{\theta})L(\hat{\boldsymbol{\psi}}|\boldsymbol{\theta})d\boldsymbol{\theta}$. Hence, the RS still recovers the posterior distribution with the infeasible likelihood. Note that the kernel function was introduced for developing a result analogous to Proposition 1, but no kernel smoothing is required in practical implementation. What is needed for the RS in the overidentified case is B draws with sufficiently small $J_1(\boldsymbol{\theta}^b)$. Hence, we can borrow the idea used in the AR-ABC. Specifically, we fix a quantile q, repeat $[B/q]$ times until the desired number of draws is obtained. Discarding some draws seems necessary in many ABC implementations.

In summary, there are two changes in implementation of the RS in the overidentified case: the volume and the kernel function. Kernel smoothing has no role in the RS when $K = L$. It is interesting to note that while the ABC and RS both rely on the kernel $\mathbb{K}_\delta$ to keep draws close to $\hat{\boldsymbol{\psi}}^b$ in the overidentified case, the nonparametric rate at which the sum converges to the integral are different. The RS uses the first-order conditions $\hat{\boldsymbol{\psi}}^b_\theta(\boldsymbol{\theta}^b, \boldsymbol{\varepsilon}^b)'\mathbf{W}\left(\hat{\boldsymbol{\psi}}^b(\boldsymbol{\theta}^b, \boldsymbol{\varepsilon}^b) - \hat{\boldsymbol{\psi}}\right) = 0$ to indicate which K combinations of $\hat{\boldsymbol{\psi}}^b(\boldsymbol{\theta}^b, \boldsymbol{\varepsilon}^b) - \hat{\boldsymbol{\psi}}$ are set to zero, rendering the dimension of the smoothing problem $L - K$. To see this, note first that each draw $\boldsymbol{\theta}^b$ from the RS is consistent for $\boldsymbol{\theta}_0$ and asymptotically normal as shown in Forneron and Ng (2014). In consequence, the first-order condition (FOC) can be rewritten as:

$\left(\frac{d\psi(\theta)}{d\theta}|_{\theta=\theta_0} + O_p\left(\frac{1}{\sqrt{T}}\right)\right)' \mathbf{W}\left(\hat{\psi}^b(\theta^b, \varepsilon^b) - \hat{\psi}\right) = 0$, or

$$\frac{d\psi(\theta)}{d\theta}|'_{\theta=\theta_0} \mathbf{W}\left(\hat{\psi}^b(\theta^b, \varepsilon^b) - \hat{\psi}\right) = o_p\left(\frac{1}{\sqrt{T}}\right).$$

Since $\frac{d\psi(\theta)}{d\theta}|'_{\theta=\theta_0}\mathbf{W}$ is full rank, there exists a subspace of dimension K such that $\hat{\psi}^b(\theta^b, \varepsilon^b) - \hat{\psi}$ is zero asymptotically. Hence, the kernel smoothing problem is effectively $L - K$ dimensional. The ABC does not use the FOC. Even in the exactly identified case, the kernel smoothing is an $L = K$-dimensional problem. In general, the convergence rate of the ABC is $L \geq K$, the dimension of $\hat{\psi}$.

The following two examples illustrate the properties of the ABC and RS posterior distributions. The first example uses sufficient statistics and the second example does not. Both the ABC and RS achieve the desired number of draws by setting the quantile, as discussed in Section 2.

Example 4: Exponential Distribution. Let $y_1, \ldots, y_T \sim \mathcal{E}(\theta), T = 5, \theta_0 = 1/2$. Now $\hat{\psi} = \bar{y}$ is a sufficient statistic for $y_1, \ldots, y_T$. For a flat prior $\pi(\theta) \propto 1_{\theta \geq 0}$ we have:

$$p(\theta|\bar{y}) \propto p(\theta|y_1, \ldots, y_T) = \theta^T \exp(-\theta^T \bar{y}) \sim \Gamma(T+1, T\bar{y})$$

In the just identified case, we let $u_t^b \sim \mathcal{U}_{[0,1]}$ and $y_t^b = -\log(1 - u_t^b)/\theta^b$. This gives:

$$\hat{\psi}^b = \frac{1}{T}\sum_{t=1}^{T} y_t^b = -\frac{1}{T}\sum_{t=1}^{T}\frac{\log(1-u_t^b)}{\theta^b}.$$

Since $\bar{y}^b = \bar{y}$, the Jacobian matrix is:

$$\hat{\psi}_b(\theta^b) = \frac{d\hat{\psi}^b(\theta)}{d\theta}\bigg|_{\theta^b} = \frac{1}{T}\sum_{t=1}^{T}\frac{\log(1-u_t^b)}{[\theta^b]^2} = -\frac{\bar{y}}{\theta^b}.$$

Hence, for a given T, the weights are: $w(\theta^b, u^b) \propto \mathbb{I}_{\theta^b \geq 0}\frac{\theta^b}{\bar{y}^b} = \frac{\theta^b}{\bar{y}}$. We verified that the numerical results agree with this analytical result.

In the overidentified case, we consider two moments:

$$\hat{\psi}^b = \begin{pmatrix} \bar{y}^b \\ \hat{\sigma}_y^{b,2} \end{pmatrix} = \begin{pmatrix} \frac{1}{T}\sum_{t=1}^{T} y_t^b \\ \frac{1}{T}\sum_{t=1}^{T}(y_t^b)^2 - \left(\frac{1}{T}\sum_{t=1}^{T} y_t^b\right)^2 \end{pmatrix}.$$

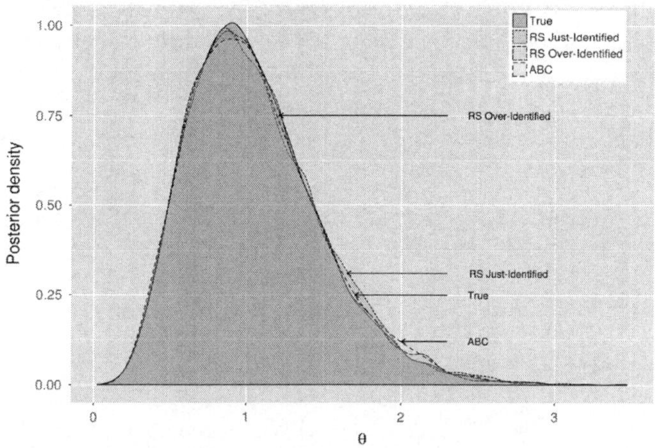

Fig. 3. Exponential Distribution.

Since $\frac{dy_t^b}{d\theta} = \frac{\log(1-u_t^b)}{(\theta^b)^2} = -\frac{y_t^b}{\theta^b}$. If $\delta = 0$, the Jacobian matrix is

$$\hat{\psi}_\theta^b = -\begin{pmatrix} \frac{1}{T}\sum_{t=1}^{T}\frac{y_t^b}{\theta} \\ \frac{2}{\theta^b}\frac{1}{T}\sum_{t=1}^{T}(y_t^b)^2 - \frac{2}{\theta^b}\left[\frac{1}{T}\sum_{t=1}^{T}y_t^b\right]^2 \end{pmatrix} = -\begin{pmatrix} \frac{\bar{y}}{\theta^b} \\ \frac{2(\hat{\sigma}_y)^2}{\theta^b} \end{pmatrix}.$$

The volume to be computed is $\text{vol}(\hat{\psi}_\theta^b) = \sqrt{|\hat{\psi}_\theta^{b\prime}\hat{\psi}_\theta^b|}$, as stated in the algorithm. Even if $\mathbf{W} = \mathrm{I}$, the volume is the determinant of $\hat{\psi}_\theta^b$ in the exactly identified case, plus a term relating to the variance of y^b. We computed $\hat{\psi}_\theta^b$ for draws with $J_1^b \approx 0$ using numerical differentiation[6] and verified that the values are very close to the ones computed analytically for this example.

Fig. 3 depicts a particular draw of the ABC posterior distribution (which coincides with the likelihood-based posterior since the statistics are sufficient), along with two generated by the RS sampler. The first one uses the sample mean as auxiliary statistic and hence is exactly identified. The second uses two auxiliary statistics: the sample mean and the sample variance. For the AR-ABC, we draw from the prior 10 million times and keep the 10,000 nearest draws. This corresponds to a value of $\delta = 0.0135$. For the RS, we draw one million times[7] and keep the 10,000 nearest draws which corresponds to a $\delta = 0.0001$. As for the weight matrix $\mathbf{W}$, if we put $\mathbf{W}_{11} > 0$ and zero elsewhere, we will recover the exactly identified distribution. Here, we intentionally put a positive weight on the variance (which is not a sufficient statistic) to check the effect on the posterior mean. With $\mathrm{W}_{11} = 1/5$ and $\mathrm{W}_{22} = 4/5$, the RS posterior means are 0.7452 and 0.7456 for the just and overidentifed cases. The corresponding values are are 0.7456 and .7474 for the exact posterior and the AR-ABC. They are very similar.

Example 5: ARMA(1,1): For $t = 1, \ldots, T = 200$ and $\boldsymbol{\theta}_0 = (\alpha_0, \theta_0, \sigma_0) = (0.5, 0.5, 1.0)$, the data are generated as

$$y_t = \alpha y_{t-1} + \varepsilon_t + \theta \varepsilon_{t-1}, \quad \boldsymbol{\varepsilon}_t \sim \mathcal{N}(0, \sigma^2).$$

Least squares estimation of the auxiliary model

$$y_t = \phi_1 y_{t-1} + \phi_2 y_{t-2} + \phi_3 y_{t-3} + \phi_4 y_{t-4} + u_t$$

yields $L = 5 > K = 3$ auxiliary parameters

$$\hat{\boldsymbol{\psi}} = (\hat{\phi}_1, \hat{\phi}_2, \hat{\phi}_3, \hat{\phi}_4, \hat{\sigma}_u^2).$$

We let $\pi(\alpha, \theta, \sigma) = \mathbb{I}_{\alpha, \theta \in [-1,1], \sigma \geq 0}$ and $\mathbf{W} = \mathrm{I}_5$ which is inefficient. In this example, $\hat{\boldsymbol{\psi}}$ are not sufficient statistics since y_t has an infinite-order autoregressive representation.

We draw σ from a uniform distribution on $[0, 3]$ since $\mathcal{U}_{[0,\infty]}$ is not a proper density. The weights of the RS are obtained by numerical differentiation. The likelihood-based posterior is computed by MCMC using the Kalman Filter with initial condition $\varepsilon_0 = 0$. As mentioned above, the desired number of draws is obtained by setting the quantile instead of setting the tolerance δ. For the RS, we keep the $1/10 = 10\%$ closest draws corresponding to a $\delta = 0.0007$. The Sequential Monte-Carlo implementation of ABC (SMC-ABC) is more efficient at targeting the posterior than the AR-ABC. Hence, we also compare the RS with SMC-ABC as implemented in the Easy-ABC package of Lenormand, Jabot, and Deffuant (2013).[8] The requirement for 10,000 posterior draws is listed in Table 2.

The difference, both in terms of computation time and number of model simulations, is notable. As shown in Fig. 4, the quality of the approximation is also different, especially for α and σ. The difference can be traced to δ. The δ used for the SMC-ABC is effectively much larger than for the RS. A better approximation requires a smaller δ which implies longer computational time. Alternatively stated, the acceptance rate at a low value of δ is very low. The caveat is that the speed gain is possible only if the optimization problem can be solved in a few iterations and reasonably fast. In practice, there will be a trade-off between the number of draws and the number of iterations in the optimization step as we further explore below.

Table 2. Computation Efficiency.

	AR-ABC	SMC-ABC	RS	Likelihood
Computation time (hours)	63	25	5	0.1
Effective number of draws	100,000,000	36,805,000	10,153,108	
δ	0.0132	0.0283	0.0007	

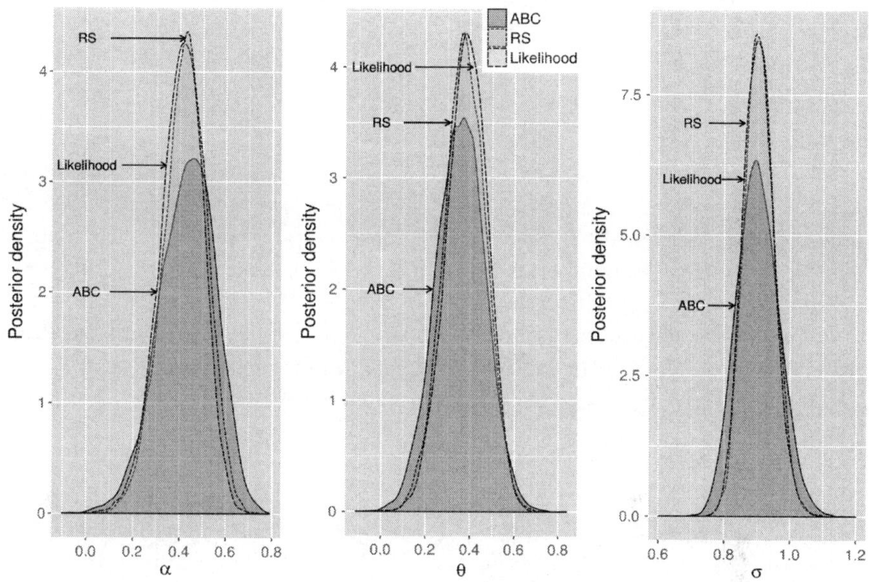

Fig. 4. ARMA Model.

4. ACCEPTANCE RATE

The RS was initially developed in Forneron and Ng (2014) as a framework to help understand frequentist (SMD) and the Bayesian (ABC) way of likelihood-free estimation. But it turns out that the RS has one computation advantage that is worth highlighting. The issue pertains to the low acceptance rate of the ABC.

As noted above, the ABC exactly recovers the posterior distribution associated with the infeasible likelihood if $\hat{\boldsymbol{\psi}}$ are sufficient statistics and $\delta = 0$ as noted in Blum (2010). Of course, $\delta = 0$ is an event of measure zero, and the ABC has an approximation bias that depends on δ. In theory, a small δ is desired. The ABC needs a large number of draws to accurately approximate the posterior and can be computationally costly.

To illustrate this point, consider estimating the mean m in Example 3 with $\sigma^2 = 1$ assumed to be known, and $\pi(m) \propto 1$. All computations are based on the software package R. From a previous draw m^b, a random walk step gives $m^* = m^b + \varepsilon, \varepsilon \sim \mathcal{N}(0,1)$. For small δ, we can assume $m^*|\hat{m} \sim \mathcal{N}(\hat{m}, 1/T)$. From a simulated sample of T observations, we get an estimated mean $\hat{m}^* \sim \mathcal{N}(m^*, 1/T)$. As is typical of MCMC chains, these draws are serially correlated. To see that the algorithm can be stuck for a long time if m^* is far from $\hat{m}$, observe that the event $\hat{m}^* \in [\hat{m} - \delta, \hat{m} + \delta]$ occurs with probability

$$\begin{aligned}\mathbb{P}(\hat{m}^* \in [\hat{m} - \delta, \hat{m} + \delta]) &= \Phi\left(\sqrt{T}(\hat{m} + \delta - m^*)\right) - \Phi\left(\sqrt{T}(\hat{m} - \delta - m^*)\right) \\ &\approx 2\sqrt{T}\delta\phi\left(\sqrt{T}(\hat{m} - m^*)\right).\end{aligned}$$

The acceptance probability $\int_{m^*} \mathbb{P}(\hat{m}^* \in [\hat{m} - \delta, \hat{m} + \delta])dm^*$ is thus approximately linear in δ. To keep the number of accepted draws constant, we need to increase the number of draws as we decrease δ.

This result that the acceptance rate is linear in δ also applies in the general case. Assume that $\hat{\boldsymbol{\psi}}^*(\boldsymbol{\theta}^*) \sim \mathcal{N}(\boldsymbol{\psi}(\boldsymbol{\theta}^*), \Sigma/T)$. We keep the draw if $\|\hat{\boldsymbol{\psi}} - \hat{\boldsymbol{\psi}}^*(\boldsymbol{\theta}^*)\| \leq \delta$. The probability of this event can be bounded above by $\sum_{j=1}^K \mathbb{P}\left(|\hat{\boldsymbol{\psi}}_j - \hat{\boldsymbol{\psi}}_j^*(\boldsymbol{\theta}^*)| \leq \delta\right)$, that is:

$$\begin{aligned}&\sum_{j=1}^K \Phi\left(\frac{\sqrt{T}}{\sigma_j}\left(\hat{\boldsymbol{\psi}}_j + \delta - \boldsymbol{\psi}_j(\boldsymbol{\theta}^*)\right)\right) - \Phi\left(\frac{\sqrt{T}}{\sigma_j}\left(\hat{\boldsymbol{\psi}}_j - \delta - \boldsymbol{\psi}_j(\boldsymbol{\theta}^*)\right)\right) \\ &\quad \approx 2\sqrt{T}\delta \sum_{j=1}^K \frac{\phi}{\sigma_j}\left(\frac{\sqrt{T}}{\sigma_j}\left(\hat{\boldsymbol{\psi}}_j - \boldsymbol{\psi}_j(\boldsymbol{\theta}^*)\right)\right).\end{aligned}$$

The acceptance probability is still at best linear in δ. In general, we need to increase the number of draws at least as much as δ declines to keep the number of accepted draws fixed.

Table 3 shows the acceptance rate for Example 3 for $\boldsymbol{\theta}_0 = (m_0, \sigma_0^2) = (0, 2)$, $T = 20$, and weighting matrix $W = \text{diag}(\hat{\sigma}^2, 2\hat{\sigma}^4)/T, \pi(m, \sigma^2) \propto \mathbb{I}_{\sigma^2 \geq 0}$. The results confirm that for small values of δ, the acceptance rate is approximately linear in δ. Even though in theory, the targeted ABC posterior should be closer to the true posterior when δ is small, this may not be true in practice because of the poor properties of the MCMC chain. At least for this example, the MCMC chain with moderate value of δ provides a better approximation to the true posterior density.

Table 3. Acceptance Probability as a function of δ.

δ	10	1	0.1	0.01	0.001
$\mathbb{P}(\Vert\hat{\boldsymbol{\psi}} - \hat{\boldsymbol{\psi}}^b\Vert_{\mathbf{W}} \leq \delta)$	0.72171	0.16876	0.00182	0.00002	<0.00001

To overcome the low acceptance rate issue, Beaumont, Zhang, and Balding (2002) suggest to use local regression techniques to approximate $\delta = 0$ without setting it equal to zero. The convergence rate is then nonparametric. Gao and Hong (2014) analyzes the estimator of Creel and Kristensen (2013) and finds that to compensate for the large variance associated with the kernel smoothing, the number of simulations need to be larger than $T^{K/2}$ to achieve $\sqrt{T}$ convergence, where K is the number of regressors. Other methods that aim to increase the acceptance rate include the ABC-SMC algorithm of Sisson et al. (2007), Sisson and Fan (2011), as well as the adaptive weighting variant due to Bonassi and West (2015), referred to below as SMC-AW. These methods build a sequence of proposals to more efficiently target the posterior. The acceptance rate still declines rapidly with δ, however.

The RS circumvents this problem because each $\boldsymbol{\theta}^b$ is accepted by virtue of being the solution of an optimization problem, and hence $\hat{\boldsymbol{\psi}} - \hat{\boldsymbol{\psi}}^b(\boldsymbol{\theta}^b)$ is the smallest possible. In fact, in the exactly identified case, $\delta = J_1^b = 0$. Furthermore, the sequence of optimizers are independent, and the sampler cannot be stuck. We use two more examples to highlight this feature.

Example 6: Mixture Distribution. Consider the example in Sisson et al. (2007), also considered in Bonassi and West (2015). Let $\pi(\boldsymbol{\theta}) \propto 1_{\boldsymbol{\theta}\in[-10,10]}$ and

$$x|\boldsymbol{\theta} \sim 1/2\mathcal{N}(\boldsymbol{\theta}, 1) + 1/2\mathcal{N}(\boldsymbol{\theta}, 1/100)$$

Suppose we observe one draw $x = 0$. Then the true posterior is $\boldsymbol{\theta}|x \sim 1/2\mathcal{N}(0, 1) + 1/2\mathcal{N}(0, 1/100)$ truncated to $[-10, 10]$. As in Sisson et al. (2007) and Bonassi and West (2015), we choose three tolerance levels: $(2, 0.5, 0.025)$ for AR-ABC. Fig. 5 shows that the ABC posterior distributions computed using accept-reject sampling with $\delta = 0.025$ are similar to the ones using SMC with and without adaptive weighting. The RS posterior distribution is close to both ABC-SMC and ABC-SMC-AW, and all similar to Figure 3 reported in Bonassi and West (2015). However, they are quite different from the AR-ABC with $\delta = 2$ and 0.5 are 2, showing that the choice of δ is important in ABC.

While the SMC, RS, and AR-ABC sampling schemes can produce similar posterior distributions, Table 4 shows that their computational time differ dramatically. The two SMC algorithms need to sample from a multinomial distribution which

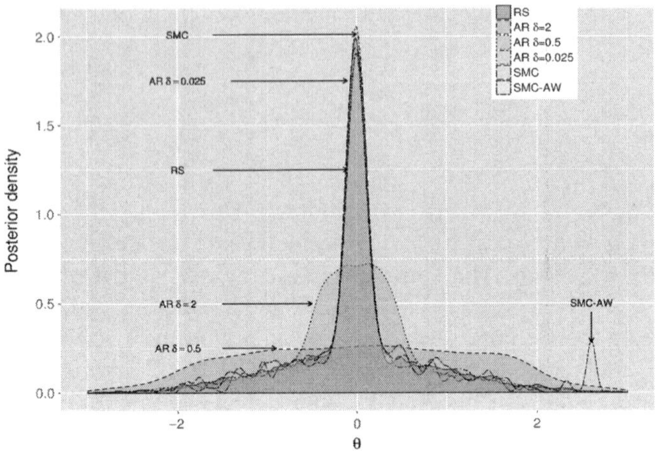

Fig. 5. Mixture Distribution.

Table 4. Computation Time (in Seconds).

RS	AR-ABC			ABC-SMC	
	δ=2	δ=0.5	δ=0.025	Sisson et al.	Bonassi-West
0.0017	0.4973	1.6353	33.8136	190.1510	199.1510

are evidently more time consuming. When $\delta = 0.25$, the AR-ABC posterior distribution is close to the ones produced by the SMC samplers and the RS, but the computational cost is still high. The AR-ABC is computationally efficient when δ is large, but as seen from Fig. 5, the posterior distribution is quite poorly approximated. The RS takes 0.0017 seconds to solve, which is amazingly fast because for this example, the solution is available analytically. No optimization is involved, and there is no need to evaluate the Jacobian because the model is linear. Of course, in cases when the SMD problem is numerically challenging, numerical optimization can be time consuming as well. Our results nonetheless suggest a role for optimization in Bayesian computation; they need not be mutually exclusive. Combining the ideas is an interesting topic for future research.

Example 7: Precautionary Savings. The foregoing examples are simple and serve illustrative purposes. We now consider an example that indeed has an infeasible likelihood. In Deaton (1991), agents maximize expected utility $\mathbb{E}_0\left(\sum_{t=0}^{\infty}\beta^t u(c_t)\right)$ subject to the constraint that assets $a_{t+1} = (1+r)(a_t + y_t - c_t)$ are bounded below by zero, where r is interest rate, y is income and c consumption. The desire for

Table 5. Deaton Model: RS, SMD with $\mathbf{W} = \mathrm{I}$.

	Posterior Mean/Estimate			Posterior SD/SE		
	γ	μ	σ	γ	μ	σ
RS	1.86	99.92	10.48	0.19	0.84	0.37
SMD	1.76	99.38	10.31	0.12	0.60	0.34

precautionary saving interacts with borrowing constraints to generate a policy function that is not everywhere concave, but is a piecewise linear when cash-on-hand is below an endogenous threshold. The policy function can only be solved numerically at assumed parameter values. SMD estimation thus consists of solving the model and simulating S auxiliary statistics at each guess $\boldsymbol{\theta}$. Michaelides and Ng (2000) evaluate the finite sample properties of several SMD estimators using a model with similar features. Since the likelihood for this model is not available analytically. Hence, Bayesian estimation of this model has not been implemented. Here, we use the RS to approximate the posterior distribution.

We generate $T = 400$ observations assuming that $U(c) = \frac{c^{1-\gamma}-1}{1-\gamma}$, $y_t \sim$ i.i.d. $\mathcal{N}(\mu, \sigma^2)$ with $r = 0.05$, $\beta = 10/11$, $\mu = 100, \sigma = 10, \gamma = 2$ as true values. We estimate $\boldsymbol{\theta} = (\gamma, \mu, \sigma)$ and assume (β, r) are known. We use 10 auxiliary statistics:

$$\hat{\boldsymbol{\psi}} = \left(\bar{y}\ \hat{\Gamma}_{yy}(0)\ \hat{\Gamma}_{aa}(0)\ \hat{\Gamma}_{cc}(0)\ \hat{\Gamma}_{cc}(1)\ \hat{\Gamma}_{aa}(1)\ \hat{\Gamma}_{cc}(2)\ \hat{\Gamma}_{aa}(2)\ \hat{\Gamma}_{cy}(0)\ \hat{\Gamma}_{ay}(0)\right)'$$

where $\hat{\Gamma}_{ab}(j) = \frac{1}{T}\sum_{t=1}^{T}(a_t - \bar{a})(b_{t-j} - \bar{b})$. We generate $B = 13,423$ draws and keep the $3,356$ (25%) nearest draws to $\hat{\boldsymbol{\psi}}$. After weighting using the volume of the Jacobian matrix, we have an effective sample size of $1,421$ draws.[9] We use an identity weighting matrix so $J_{RS}(\boldsymbol{\theta}) = \bar{g}(\boldsymbol{\theta})'\bar{g}(\boldsymbol{\theta})$. The Jacobian is computed using finite differences for the RS. As benchmark, we also compute an SMD with $S = 100$, $J_S = \bar{g}_S(\boldsymbol{\theta})'\bar{g}_S(\boldsymbol{\theta})$. In this exercise, the SMD only needs to solve for the policy function once at each step of the optimization. Hence, the binding function can be approximated using simulated data at a low cost. For this example, the programs are coded in PYTHON. The Nelder–Mead method is used for optimization.

Fig. 6 shows the posterior distribution of the RS (blue) along with the SMD distribution (purple) as approximated by $\mathcal{N}(\hat{\boldsymbol{\theta}}_{\text{SMD}}, \hat{\mathbf{V}}_{\mathbf{SMD}}/T)$ according to asymptotic theory. Table 5 shows that the two sets of point estimates are similar. As explained in Forneron and Ng (2014), the SMD uses simulations to approximate the binding function while the RS (and by implication the ABC) uses simulations to approximate the infeasible posterior distribution. In this example, the difference

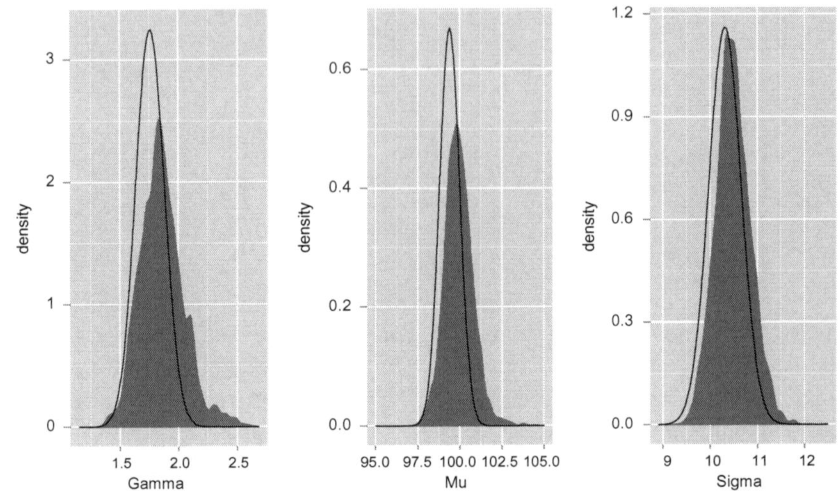

Fig. 6. Deaton Model: RS and SMD. *Notes:* Blue density: RS posterior, Black line: large sample approximation for the SMD estimator (identity weighting matrix).

in bias is quite small. We should note that the RS took well over a day to solve while the SMD took less than three hours to compute. Whether we use our own code for the MCMC-ABC or from packages available, the acceptance rate is too low for the exercise to be feasible.

5. CONCLUSION

This paper studies properties of the RS considered in Forneron and Ng (2014) for likelihood-free estimation. The sampler produce draws from the infeasible posterior distribution by solving a sequence of frequentist SMD problems. We showed that the RS uses the Jacobian matrix as importance ratio. In the overidentified case, the importance ratio can be computed using the volume of the Jacobian matrix. The RS does not suffer from the problem of low acceptance rate that makes the ABC computationally demanding.

NOTES

1. We thank Neil Shephard for suggesting the example.
2. If $F(y, \cdot)$ is decreasing in θ, we have $\mathbb{P}(\theta^b \leq t|y) = 1 - F(y,t)$.
3. An alternative derivation is to note that $t = \mathbb{P}(u \leq t|y) = \mathbb{P}\left(u = F(y,\theta^b) \leq t|y\right) = \mathbb{P}\left(\theta^b \leq F^{-1}(y,t) = t'|y\right)$. Hence, $f(\theta^b|y) = \frac{dt}{dt'} = \frac{1}{(F^{-1})'_\theta(y,t)} = F'_2(y,t)$ as above.

4. From Ben-Israel (2001), $\int_V f(v)dv = \int_U f(\phi(u))\text{vol}(\phi_u(u))du$ for a real-valued function f integrable on V. See also http://www.encyclopediaofmath.org/index.php/Jacobian.

5. Using the implicit function theorem to compute the gradient gives the same result. Since $\hat{\psi}^b = \hat{\psi}$ we have: $\mathcal{F}_\theta = -\hat{\psi}^b_\theta(\theta^b, \varepsilon^b, \hat{\psi})' \text{W} \hat{\psi}^b_\theta(\theta^b, \varepsilon^b, \hat{\psi}) + \sum_j \hat{\psi}^b_{\theta,\theta_j}(\theta^b, \varepsilon^b)\mathbf{W}\left(\hat{\psi} - \hat{\psi}^b(\theta^b, \varepsilon^b, \hat{\psi})\right) = -\hat{\psi}^b_\theta(\theta^b, \varepsilon^b, \hat{\psi})' W \hat{\psi}^b_\theta(\theta^b, \varepsilon^b, \hat{\psi})$. Then $\text{vol}(\mathcal{F}_\theta^{-1}\mathcal{F}_{\hat{\psi}}) = \text{vol}(\mathcal{F}_\theta^{-1})\text{vol}(\mathcal{F}_{\hat{\psi}}) = \text{vol}(\hat{\psi}^b_\theta(\theta^b, \varepsilon^b, \hat{\psi}))^{-1}|\mathbf{W}|^{-1}\text{vol}(\hat{\psi}^b_\theta(\theta^b, \varepsilon^b, \hat{\psi}))^{-1}\text{vol}(\hat{\psi}^b_\theta(\theta^b, \varepsilon^b, \hat{\psi}))^{-1}|\mathbf{W}| = \text{vol}(\hat{\psi}^b_\theta(\theta^b, \varepsilon^b, \hat{\psi}))^{-1}$. Hence, the weights are the same when we only consider the draws where $J_1^b = 0$ which are the draws we are interested in.

6. In practice, since the mapping $\theta \rightarrow \hat{\psi}^b(\theta)$ is not known analytically, the derivatives are approximated using finite differences: $\partial_{\theta_j}\hat{\psi}^b(\theta) \simeq \frac{\hat{\psi}^b(\theta+e_j\varepsilon) - \hat{\psi}^b(\theta-e_j\varepsilon)}{2\varepsilon}$ for $\varepsilon \simeq 0$.

7. This means that we solve the optimization problem one million times. Given that the optimization problem is one dimensional, the one-dimensional R optimization routine *optimize* is used. It performs a combination of the golden section with parabolic interpolations. The optimum is found, up to a given tolerance level (the default is 10^{-4}), over the interval $[0, 10]$.

8. We implemented the SMC-ABC in two ways. First, we use the procedure in Vo, Drovandi, Pettitt, and Pettet (2015) using code generously provided by Christopher Drovandi. We also use the Easy-ABC package in *R* of Lenormand et al. (2013). We thank an anonymous referee for this suggestion.

9. The effective sample size is computed as $1/\sum_{b=1}^{B} w_b^2$ where the weights satisfy $\sum_{b=1}^{B} w^b = 1$.

ACKNOWLEDGMENTS

We thank Christopher Drovandi, Neil Shephard, and two anonymous referees for many helpful comments. The second author would like to thank Aman Ullah for his support and guidance.

REFERENCES

Bao, Y., & Ullah, A. (2007). The second-order bias and mean-squared error of estimators in time series models. *Journal of Econometrics*, *140*(2), 650–669.

Beaumont, M., Corneut, J., Marin, J., & Robert, C. (2009). Adaptive approximate Bayesian computation. *Biometrika*, *96*(4), 983–990.

Beaumont, M., Zhang, W., & Balding, D. (2002). Approximate Bayesian computation in population genetics. *Genetics*, *162*, 2025–2035.

Ben-Israel, A. (1999). The change of variables forumla using matrix volume. *SIAM Journal of Matrix Analysis*, *21*, 300–312.

Ben-Israel, A. (2001). An application of the matrix volume in probability. *Linear Algebra and Applications*, *321*, 9–25.

Blum, M. (2010). Approximate Bayesian computation: A nonparametric perspective. *Journal of the American Statistical Association*, *105*(491), 1178–1187.

Bonassi, F., & West, M. (2015). Sequential Monte Carlo with adaptive weights for approximate Bayesian computation. *Bayesian Analysis*, *10*(1), 171–187.

Creel, M., & Kristensen, D. (2013). Indirect likelihood inference. *mimeo, UCL.*

Creel, M., & Kristensen, D. (in press). On selection of statistics for approximate Bayesian computing or the method of simulated moments. *Computational Statistics and Data Analysis*. Retrieved from http://www.sciencedirect.com/science/article/pii/S016794731500122X

Deaton, A. S. (1991). Saving and liqudity constraints. *Econometrica*, *59*, 1221–1248.

Duffie, D., & Singleton, K. (1993). Simulated moments estimation of Markov models of asset prices. *Econometrica*, *61*, 929–952.

Forneron, J. J., & Ng, S. (2014). The ABC of simulation estimation with auxiliary statistics, arXiv:1501.01265.

Gallant, R., & Tauchen, G. (1996). Which moments to match. *Econometric Theory*, *12*, 657–681.

Gao, J., & Hong, H. (2014). *A computational implementation of GMM*. SSRN Working Paper No. 2503199.

Gourieroux, C., Monfort, A., & Renault, E. (1993). Indirect inference. *Journal of Applied Econometrics*, *85*, 85–118.

Jiang, W., & Turnbull, B. (2004). The indirect method: Inference based on intermediate statistics – A synthesis and examples. *Statistical Science*, *19*(2), 239–263.

Lenormand, M., Jabot, F., & Deffuant, G. (2013). Adaptive approximate Bayesian computation computation for complex models. *Journal of Computational and Graphical Statistics*, *28*(6), 2777–2796.

Marjoram, P., Molitor, J., Plagnol, V., & Tavare, S. (2003). Markov chain Monte Carlo without likelihoods. *Procedings of the National Academy of Science*, *100*(26), 15324–15328.

Meeds, E., & Welling, M. (2015). *Optimization Monte Carlo: Efficient and embarrassingly parallel likelihood-free inference*, arXiv:1506:03693v1.

Michaelides, A., & Ng, S. (2000). Estimating the rational expectations model of speculative storage: A Monte Carlo comparison of three simulation estimators. *Journal of Econometrics*, *96:2*, 231–266.

Newey, W., & McFadden, D. (1994). Large sample estimation and hypothesis testing. *Handbook of econometrics* (Vol. 4, pp. 2111–2234). Amsterdam: North Holland.

Pagan, A., & Ullah, A. (1999). Nonparametric econometrics. *Themes in modern econometrics*. Cambridge: Cambridge University Press.

Pritchard, J., Seielstad, M., Perez-Lezman, A., & Feldman, M. (1996). Population growth of human Y chromosomes: A study of Y chromosome microsatellites. *Molecular biology and evolution*, *16*(12), 1791–1798.

Rilstone, P., Srivastara, K., & Ullah, A. (1996). The second-order bias and mean squared error of nonlinear estimators. *Journal of Econometrics*, *75*, 369–385.

Sisson, S., & Fan, Y. (2011). Likelihood free Markov chain Monte Carlo. In S. Brooks, A. Celman, G. L. Jones, & X.-L. Meng (Eds.), *Handbook of Markov chain Monte Carlo* (pp. 313–335). CRC Press. Retrieved from https://www.crcpress.com/Handbook-of-Markov-Chain-Monte-Carlo/Brooks-Gelman-Jones-Meng/9781420079418. arXiv:10001.2058v1.

Sisson, S., Fan, Y., & Tanaka, M. (2007). Sequential Monte Carlo without likelihood. *Procedings of the National Academy of Science*, *104*(6), 1760–1765.

Smith, A. (1993). Estimating nonlinear time series models using simulated vector autoregressions. *Journal of Applied Econometrics*, *8*, S63–S84.

Tavare, S., Balding, J., Griffiths, C., & Donnelly, P. (1997). Inferring coalescence times from DNA sequence data. *Genetics*, *145*, 505–518.

Toni, T., Welch, D., Strelkowa, N., Ipsen, A., & Stumpf, M. (2009). Approximate Bayesian computation scheme for parameter inference and model selection in dynamic models. *Journal of the Royal Society Inference*, *6*, 187–222.

Vo, R., Drovandi, C., Pettitt, A., & Pettet, G. (2015). Melanoma cell colony expansion parameters revealed by approximate Bayesian computation, eprints.qut.edu/au/83824.

A VECTOR AUTOREGRESSIVE MOVING AVERAGE MODEL FOR INTERVAL-VALUED TIME SERIES DATA

Ai Han[a], Yongmiao Hong[b,c], Shouyang Wang[a], and Xin Yun[a]

[a]*Academy of Mathematics and Systems Science, Chinese Academy of Sciences, Beijing, People's Republic of China*

[b]*Department of Economics and Department of Statistical Sciences, Cornell University, Ithaca, NY, USA*

[c]*Wang Yanan Institute for Studies in Economics (WISE), Xiamen University, People's Republic of China*

ABSTRACT

Modelling and forecasting interval-valued time series (ITS) have received increasing attention in statistics and econometrics. An interval-valued observation contains more information than a point-valued observation in the same time period. The previous literature has mainly considered modelling and forecasting a univariate ITS. However, few works attempt to model a vector process of ITS. In this paper, we propose an interval-valued vector autoregressive moving average (IVARMA) model to capture

Essays in Honor of Aman Ullah

Advances in Econometrics, Volume 36, 417–460

ISSN: 0731-9053/doi:10.1108/S0731-905320160000036021

the cross-dependence dynamics within an ITS vector system. A minimum-distance estimation method is developed to estimate the parameters of an IVARMA model, and consistency, asymptotic normality and asymptotic efficiency of the proposed estimator are established. A two-stage minimum-distance estimator is shown to be asymptotically most efficient among the class of minimum-distance estimators. Simulation studies show that the two-stage estimator indeed outperforms other minimum-distance estimators for various data-generating processes considered.

Keywords: Asymptotic efficiency; interval vector-valued time series; interval-valued data; minimum-distance estimation; vector autoregressive moving average interval models

JEL classifications: C3; C32

1. INTRODUCTION

There has been an increasing attention in modelling and forecasting interval-valued time series (ITS) in statistics and econometrics (e.g. Arroyo, Espínola, & Maté, 2011; Golan & Ullah, 2015; Han, Lai, Wang, & Xu, 2012; Maia, Carvalho, & Ludermir, 2008, and the references therein). ITS examples are not uncommon in practice. For example, in financial markets, a stock price movement during a given trading period forms an interval observation that consists of the maximum and minimum prices in the period. Other well-known examples include daily temperature in meteorology science, as well as the interval blood pressure formed by the systolic and diastolic pressures in medicine. Interval data are also the main interest of 'Symbolic Data Analysis (SDA)' in statistics; see Billard and Diday (2003, 2006) for key references in the field. There are two main advantages of modelling ITS over modelling point-valued time series data. First, an interval observation in a time period contains more information than a point-valued observation in the same time period since it captures both the variation and level characteristics of the underlying process; see He and Hu (2009), González-Rivera and Lin (2013), and Han, Hong, and Wang (2015). Thus, we expect more efficient estimation and powerful inference by using ITS data. Second, due to certain disturbances, point-valued time series might change significantly during a time period, and these variations may be seen as noises and have an undesirable effect on identifying the tendency of a time series. This issue can be addressed by modelling ITS in a lower-frequency set-up. For instance, an ITS sample data collected on a daily basis can characterize the daily range of an interval observation as a measure of volatility (see Parkinson (1980), Rogers and Satchell (1991), Yang and Zhang (2000), and

Chou (2005)). It is less affected by the noises to the point-valued intraday time series data collected in a higher-frequency level, for example, every 5 minutes. The higher-frequency point-valued time series might contain too much noises. For example, it is well known that high-frequency intraday asset price time series may contain non-trivial market microstructure noises.

A large number of studies have documented methods concerning modelling and forecasting a univariate ITS (Arroyo & Maté, 2006; Arroyo et al., 2011; Arroyo, Roque, Maté, & Sarabia, 2007; González-Rivera & Lin, 2013; Han et al., 2015; He & Hu, 2009; Maia & Carvalho, 2011; Maia et al., 2008; Neto & Carvalho, 2008, 2010). Arroyo et al. (2007) proposed the exponential smoothing method and compared it with other interval modelling approaches. They considered that the most straightforward approach is transforming the ITS by a pair of classical time series. Maia et al. (2008) presented several approaches based on autoregressive (AR), autoregressive integrated moving average (ARIMA) and artificial neural network (ANN) models, respectively. González-Rivera and Lin (2013) proposed a constrained regression model for the two boundaries of the ITS that preserves the natural order of the interval in all instances. The fundamental idea of the aforementioned approaches to modelling a univariate ITS is to model a representative bivariate point-valued time series, that is, the midpoint and range, or the two boundaries, of a univariate ITS, based on traditional point-based statistical tools, and then the prediction of the lower and upper bounds of the interval process is accomplished from its midpoint and range forecasts. Han et al. (2015) proposed a new modelling strategy for ITS via a class of autoregressive conditional interval (ACI) models for a univariate ITS. Different from other approaches, the ACI approach proposes a parsimonious model that considers an interval observation as an inseparable unity. Yang and Han (2015) explored the forecasting power of an ACI model for the daily U.S. stock data, and they documented that an interval-based ACI model produces more accurate volatility forecasts than classic point-based linear time series models.

Most of the ongoing efforts on modelling a univariate ITS provide a basis to develop new analytical tools for modelling and forecasting a higher-dimensional ITS system. In multivariate point-valued time series analysis, since the influential work of Sims (1980), the vector autoregressive (VAR) model has become popular for analyzing the cross-dependence dynamics within an economic system. See also Runkle (1991), Pesaran and Shin (1998), Johansen (1988), Blanchard and Watson (1986), Bernanke (1986), and Nakajima (2011). In the field of vector ITS analysis, to the best of our knowledge, few works have considered modelling an ITS vector system. Roque, Maté, Arroyo, and Sarabia (2007) proposed a so-called Multi-Layer Perceptrons model, which may be the first effort on vector ITS modelling. The interval multi-layer perceptrons were applied to electric power demand forecasting, and the comparison with a VAR based on the lower and upper bounds of ITS suggests that the interval method produces better forecasts than the point-based VAR model. Froelich and Salmeron (2014) dealt with multivariate ITS from the perspective of artificial intelligence but not from the perspective of probability and statistics.

In this paper, we propose a parsimonious IVARMA model to investigate the dynamics of an ITS vector system and to forecast a vector ITS. The IVARMA model generalizes the classic vector autoregressive moving average model for a vector of point-valued time series to an interval set-up. This is achieved by extending the work of Han et al. (2015) from a univariate ITS to a multivariate ITS system. To estimate the parameters of an IVARMA model using interval data, a minimum-distance estimation method is proposed, and the asymptotic theory of the proposed estimators is established. A feasible two-stage estimation scheme is shown to be asymptotically most efficient among the class of minimum-distance estimators. Simulation studies confirm that the finite sample performances of the proposed estimators are consistent with the asymptotic theory. An IVARMA model could capture the cross-dependence dynamics among multiple ITS and utilize the richer information contained in a vector ITS. The class of IVARMA models can be seen as a statistical tool for a wide range of applications. For example, in order to model the co-movement of asset prices in commodity markets, such as gold, oil and agricultural commodities (see Sadorsky, 2014), which is an economic phenomenon that is determined by the interaction of various economic factors, the modelling approaches for a univariate ITS might not be suitable. On the other hand, using the traditional VAR methodology that employs the point-valued data might lead to the loss of sample information. In this scenario, the class of IVARMA models, which follows the spirit of ACI models in Han et al. (2015) that considers an ITS observation as a unity, will be more appropriate. Additionally, we allow the case where the lower bound of an interval is larger than the upper bound in order to define the interval residuals in fitting an interval model, and to cover more applications in economics and finance (see detailed discussion after Definition 1).

The remainder of this paper is organized as follows. Section 2 introduces the class of IVARMA models for a vector ITS, and derives some popular point-valued VARMA models as special cases. Section 3 proposes a minimum D_K-distance estimation method. The consistency and asymptotic normality of the proposed estimators are established. Furthermore, an asymptotically most efficient two-stage minimum-distance estimator is proposed. Section 4 presents simulation studies with an interval-based and a bivariate point-based data-generating processes, respectively. The simulation studies show that the two-stage estimator generally outperforms other estimators, and the finite-sample properties of estimators confirm the asymptotic theory. Section 5 concludes the paper. All mathematical proofs are collected in the appendix.

2. THE IVARMA MODEL

In this section, we first introduce an IVARMA model. Then we derive some point-valued VARMA models as special cases of the class of IVARMA models. Following Han et al. (2015), we first define an extended interval vector.

Definition 1 (*Extended Interval Vector*). An extened interval vector Y of size $n \times 1$ is a set of n extended intervals Y_i for $i = 1, \ldots, n$ as $Y = (Y_1, \ldots, Y_n)'$.

For an extended random interval Y_i, see Definition 2.1 in Han et al. (2015) for details. Intuitively, Y_i on a probability space $(\Omega, \mathcal{F}, P)$ is a measurable mapping as $Y_i(\omega) = \left[Y_i^L(\omega), Y_i^R(\omega)\right]$, where $Y_i^L(\omega), Y_i^R(\omega) \in \mathbf{R}$ for all $\omega \in \Omega$. We call it an *extended interval vector* since, following the extension in Han et al. (2015) for the definition of an interval observation, we allow $Y_i^L > Y_i^R$. The regular intervals, for which $Y_i^L \leq Y_i^R$, are covered in this definition. This extension makes our modelling approach suitable for time series analysis. Firstly, one obtains interval-valued model residuals by taking the Hukuhara difference (Hukuhara (1967)) between the original ITS and the fitted intervals, which might be with the reversed order. Secondly, the extension ensures the completeness of the interval space and the consistency among the interval operations. Thirdly, the extended interval covers many real cases. In study of the intra-house inequality, a wage interval of a family unit consists of the wife's and the husband's incomes as Y_i^L and Y_i^R, respectively; in capital asset pricing modelling, Y_i^L and Y_i^R can be the risk-free interest rate and the portfolio return to form an asset price interval. In both cases, $Y_i^L \leq Y_i^R$ is not necessarily true.

Let Y_t denote an $n \times 1$ extended interval vector as $Y_t = (Y_{1t}, \ldots, Y_{nt})'$, where n is a fixed positive integer and each component $\{Y_{it}\}$ is a univariate ITS. Then, we assume that the ITS vector process $\{Y_t\}$ is governed by the following IVARMA model with lag orders of p and q:

$$Y_t = (\alpha^0 + \beta^0 I_0) + \sum_{j=1}^{p} \Phi_j Y_{t-j} + \sum_{j=1}^{q} \Gamma_j \varepsilon_{t-j} + \varepsilon_t, \tag{1}$$

where $I_0 = [-\frac{1}{2}, \frac{1}{2}]$ is a unit interval, $\alpha^0 = (\alpha_1^0, \alpha_2^0, \ldots, \alpha_n^0)'$, and $\beta^0 = (\beta_1^0, \beta_2^0, \ldots, \beta_n^0)'$ are both $n \times 1$ parameter vector,

$$\Phi_j = \begin{pmatrix} \phi_{11}^j & \phi_{12}^j & \cdots & \phi_{1n}^j \\ \phi_{21}^j & \phi_{22}^j & \cdots & \phi_{2n}^j \\ \vdots & \vdots & \ddots & \vdots \\ \phi_{n1}^j & \phi_{n2}^j & \cdots & \phi_{nn}^j \end{pmatrix}, \Gamma_j = \begin{pmatrix} \gamma_{11}^j & \gamma_{12}^j & \cdots & \gamma_{1n}^j \\ \gamma_{21}^j & \gamma_{22}^j & \cdots & \gamma_{2n}^j \\ \vdots & \vdots & \ddots & \vdots \\ \gamma_{n1}^j & \gamma_{n2}^j & \cdots & \gamma_{nn}^j \end{pmatrix}$$

are the $n \times n$ coefficient matrices of the Y_{t-j} and the ε_{t-j}. Note that all parameters in an IVARMA model are scalars. The interval vector $\varepsilon_t = (\varepsilon_{1t}, \varepsilon_{2t}, \ldots, \varepsilon_{nt})'$ is an interval innovation vector with each component ε_{it} being an interval martingale difference sequence (IMDS) with respect to the information set $\{I_{it-1}\}_{i=1}^{n}$ available at time $t-1$, that is, for any i, $E(\varepsilon_{it} \mid I_{1t-1}, I_{2t-1}, \ldots, I_{nt-1}) = [0, 0]$ a.s. The variance of the interval innovation vector $var(\varepsilon_t) = \Sigma$ is an $n \times n$ positive-definite symmetric matrix, and each of its elements is a scalar-valued variance or covariance of the interval innovations, that is, $cov(\varepsilon_{it}, \varepsilon_{jt}) = E\langle s_{\varepsilon_{it}}, s_{\varepsilon_{jt}}\rangle_K$ for $i, j = 1 \ldots n$, and $var(\varepsilon_{it}) = E\langle s_{\varepsilon_{it}}, s_{\varepsilon_{it}}\rangle_K$ for $i = j$, where the second moment of an ITS is an inner product of support functions with respect to a kernel K. See Section 3 for a brief review of these definitions, and see detailed discussion in Han et al. (2015).

The interval operation rules involved in Eq. (1) follow from the definitions in Han et al. (2015): For two extended intervals $A = [A_L, A_R]$, $B = [B_L, B_R]$, and a scalar $\beta \in \mathbf{R}$, we have (i) Addition: $A + B = [A_L + B_L, A_R + B_R]$; (ii) Scalar multiplication: $\beta A = [\beta A_L, \beta A_R]$; (iii) Difference (Hukuhara (1967)): $A -_H B = [A_L - B_L, A_R - B_R]$. The introduction of an extended interval is consistent with the Hukuhara difference operation.

We note that for each i, the specification of the univariate interval process $\{Y_{it}\}$ in Eq. (1) can be seen as an ACIX(p, q, s) model in Han et al. (2015), where p, q, s are the lag orders of the autogressive term, the interval innovation and the vector of exogenous interval variables. In particular, the model for each $\{Y_{it}\}$ in Eq. (1) is with the lag terms of $Y_{jt}(j \neq i)$ being the vector of exogenous interval variables in an ACIX model. On the other hand, when $\Gamma_j = 0$ for $j = 1, 2, \ldots, q$, or there are no MA terms, the IVARMA model becomes an interval vector autogressive model (IVAR):

$$Y_t = (\alpha^0 + \beta^0 I_0) + \sum_{j=1}^{p} \Phi_j Y_{t-j} + \varepsilon_t.$$

This can be viewed as an interval generalization of the popular point-valued vector autoregressive model in time series econometrics.

An IVARMA model can also be expressed compactly as

$$B(L)Y_t = (\alpha^0 + \beta^0 I_0) + A(L)\varepsilon_t, \tag{2}$$

where $B(L) = I_n - \sum_{j=1}^{p} \Phi_j L^j$, $A(L) = I_n + \sum_{j=1}^{q} \Gamma_j L^j$, and L is the lag operator.

We can extend an IVARMA(p, q, n) model by incorporating strictly stationary exogenous explanatory vector ITS:

$$Y_t = (\alpha^0 + \beta^0 I_0) + \sum_{j=1}^{p} \Phi_j Y_{t-j} + \sum_{j=1}^{q} \Gamma_j \varepsilon_{t-j} + \sum_{j=0}^{w} \Psi_j X_{t-j} + \varepsilon_t, \tag{3}$$

where $X_t = (X_{1t}, X_{2t}, \ldots, X_{Jt})'$ is an exogenous stationary ITS vector process, and

$$\Psi_j = \begin{pmatrix} \psi_{11}^j & \psi_{12}^j & \cdots & \psi_{1J}^j \\ \psi_{21}^j & \psi_{22}^j & \cdots & \psi_{2J}^j \\ \vdots & \vdots & \ddots & \vdots \\ \psi_{n1}^j & \psi_{n2}^j & \cdots & \psi_{nJ}^j \end{pmatrix}$$

is the $n \times J$ coefficient matrix of X_{t-j}. Note that we have introduced the term *stationary ITS vector process*. It is defined below, following the definition of the *weak stationarity* of a univariate ITS introduced in Han et al. (2015).

Definition 2 (*Stationary Interval Time Series Vector Process*). For an extended interval time series vector process $\{Y_t = (Y_{1t}, \ldots, Y_{nt})'\}$, if neither the mean vector $E(Y_t)$ nor the autocovariance matrix $E\langle s_{Y_t} - s_{E(Y_t)}, s_{Y_{t-j}} - s_{E(Y_{t-j})}\rangle_K$, for each given j, depends on time t, then Y_t is a weakly stationary ITS vector process.

The class of IVARMA(p, q, n) models can be used to capture the cross-sectional dependence dynamics within an ITS vector system. It is a generalization of the traditional point-valued VARMA(p, q, n) model. Following the interval algorithm, one can obtain a VARMA(p, q, n) model for the midpoint of the ITS vector system by taking the midpoints of boundaries from Eq. (1), namely,

$$Y_t^m = \alpha^0 + \sum_{j=1}^{p} \Phi_j Y_{t-j}^m + \sum_{j=1}^{q} \Gamma_j \varepsilon_{t-j}^m + \varepsilon_t^m,$$

where Y_t^m is an $n \times 1$ point-valued vector $(Y_{1t}^m \ldots Y_{nt}^m)'$ and ε_t^m is an $n \times 1$ point-valued innovation vector $(\varepsilon_{1t}^m \ldots \varepsilon_{nt}^m)'$. Similarly, we can derive a VARMA(p, q, n) model for the range of the ITS vector system by taking the difference between boundaries from Eq. (1), namely,

$$Y_t^r = \beta^0 + \sum_{j=1}^{p} \Phi_j Y_{t-j}^r + \sum_{j=1}^{q} \Gamma_j \varepsilon_{t-j}^r + \varepsilon_t^r,$$

where Y_t^r is a point-valued vector $(Y_{1t}^r \dots Y_{nt}^r)'$ and ε_t^r is point-valued innovation vector $(\varepsilon_{1t}^r \dots \varepsilon_{nt}^r)'$.

Note that the intercept parameter vector α^0 (or β^0) cannot be identified when we use the range (or midpoint) data only. As we shall show in the simulation studies below, using the entirely interval sample to estimate the common parameters yield more efficient parameter estimates than using only the point-valued sample information.

3. ESTIMATION AND EFFICIENCY

In Section 3.1, we will propose a minimum D_K-distance estimation method for an IVARMA model and establish the asymptotic properties of the proposed estimators. A feasible two-stage minimum D_K-distance estimator is proposed in Section 3.2, which is shown to be asymptotically most efficient among a class of minimum-distance estimators.

We firstly review some fundamental concepts concerning the D_K-distance and develop the D_K-distance between two interval vectors. For details of the D_K-distance, see Körner (1997), Körner and Näther (2002) and Han et al. (2015). The D_K-distance between any pair of extended intervals A, B is given as

$$D_K(A,B) = \sqrt{\int_{(u,v)\in \mathbf{S}^0} [s_A(u) - s_B(u)]\,[s_A(v) - s_B(v)]\,dK(u,v)}$$
$$= \sqrt{\langle s_{A-B}, s_{A-B}\rangle_K},$$

where the unit space $\mathbf{S}^0 = \{u \in \mathbf{R}^1, |u| = 1\} = \{1, -1\}$, $s_A(u)$ is the support function which, in the univariate interval context, is defined as $s_A(u) = A_R$ if $u = 1$, $s_A(u) = -A_L$ if $u = -1$ for the unit space $\mathbf{S}^0$. The support function follows a set of operational rules; see Han et al. (2015). The kernel $K(u, v)$ is a symmetric positive-definite function for $u, v \in \mathbf{S}^0$ such as $K(1,1) > 0$, $K(1,-1) = K(-1,1)$ and $K(1,1)K(-1,-1) > K(1,-1)^2$.

Han et al. (2015) have shown that

$$\begin{cases} K(1,1) = \int_0^1 \lambda^2 dW(\lambda), \; K(-1,-1) = \int_0^1 (1-\lambda)^2 dW(\lambda) \\ K(1,-1) = K(-1,1) = \int_0^1 \lambda(\lambda - 1) dW(\lambda), \end{cases}$$

where $W(\lambda)$ is a probability measure on the real Borel space $([0,1], \mathbf{B}([0,1]))$, $0 < \lambda < 1$. This suggests that the choice of kernel K is equivalent to the choice of a certain weighting function $W(\lambda)$. Thus, $D_K^2(A, B)$ includes the information of distances between all pairs of points in intervals A and B with a weighting function $W(\lambda)$ induced by the choice of $K(u, v)$.

It follows that the D_K-distance between two extended interval vectors $Y = (Y_1, \ldots, Y_n)'$ and $X = (X_1, \ldots, X_n)'$ with the same size of n is

$$D_K(X, Y) = \sqrt{\sum_{i=1}^{n} D_K^2(X_i, Y_i)}.$$

The D_K-distance between two interval vectors will be used as the basis to define our objective function for estimating an IVARMA model.

3.1. Minimum D_K-distance Estimation

In this section, we propose a minimum D_K-distance estimator for an IVARMA(p, q, n) model. The proposed estimation method is based on the D_K-distance that measures the distance between two interval vectors, and thus it does not require knowing the distribution of an interval-valued random vector. Similar results could be obtained for a more generalized IVARMAX model that contains exogenous variables. We first impose some regularity conditions.

Assumption 1.
$\{Y_t = (Y_{1t}, \ldots, Y_{nt})'\}$ is a strictly stationary and ergodic stochastic interval time series vector process with $E\|Y_{it}\|_K^4 < \infty$, and it follows an IVARMA(p, q, n) model in Eq. (1). The interval innovation vector ε_t is a vector-valued IMDS with respect to the information set I_{t-1}, and $var(\varepsilon_t) = \Sigma$ is a positive-definite symmetric matrix.

Assumption 2.
Let $A(z) = I_n + \sum_{j=1}^{q} \Gamma_j z^j$, $B(z) = I_n - \sum_{j=1}^{p} \Phi_j z^j$, where $z = (z_1, z_2, \ldots, z_n)$. The roots of $| A(z) | = 0$, $| B(z) | = 0$ lie outside the unit circle $| z | = 1$.

Assumption 3.
(i) The parameter space Θ is a finite-dimensional compact space of $\mathbb{R}^{k\times 1}$, where $\mathbf{k} = (p + q)n^2 + 2n$. (ii) θ^0 is an interior point in Θ and has following form, $\theta^0 = (\theta_1^0, \theta_2^0, \ldots, \theta_n^0)'$ where $\theta_i^0 = (\alpha_i^0, \beta_i^0, \phi_{1i}^1, \ldots, \phi_{1i}^p, \ldots, \phi_{ni}^1, \ldots, \phi_{ni}^p, \gamma_{1i}^1, \ldots, \gamma_{1i}^q, \ldots, \gamma_{ni}^1, \ldots, \gamma_{ni}^q)$.

Assumption 4.
For any $i = 1, \ldots, n$, we assume that the initial values are $Y_{it} = \hat{Y}_{i0}$ for $-p + 1 \leq t \leq 0$, $\varepsilon_{it} = \hat{\varepsilon}_{i0}$ for $-q + 1 \leq t \leq 0$, where there exists a constant $0 < C < \infty$ such that $E \sup_{\theta\in\Theta} \|Y_{i0}\|_K^2 < C$ and $E \sup_{\theta\in\Theta} \|\varepsilon_{i0}\|_K^2 < C$.

Assumption 5.
For any $i=1,\ldots,n$, *the square matrices* $E[\langle s_{\frac{\partial \varepsilon_{it}(\theta)}{\partial\theta}}, s'_{\frac{\partial \varepsilon_{it}(\theta)}{\partial\theta}}\rangle_K]$ *and* $E[\langle s_{\frac{\partial \varepsilon_{it}(\theta)}{\partial\theta}}, s_{\varepsilon_{it}(\theta)}\rangle_K \langle s_{\varepsilon_{it}(\theta)}, s_{\frac{\partial \varepsilon_{it}(\theta)}{\partial\theta}}\rangle_K]$ *are positive definite for all* θ *in a small neighborhood of* θ^0.

The D_K-distance has certain desirable properties, including the suitability for the least-squares estimation of time series models for the conditional mean of an ITS; see Körner (1997) and Körner and Näther (2002). Han et al. (2015) discuss the mean-squared error (MSE) of a univariate interval model with respect to the D_K-distance and derive the conditional mean as its optimal solution. Let $f(I_{t-1})$ denote a measurable interval function of information set I_{t-1}. Then the MSE with respect to D_K of $f(I_{t-1})$ is $MSE_{D_K}=E[D_K^2(Y_{it}, f(I_{t-1}))]=E[D_K^2(Y_{it}-f(I_{t-1}), [0,0])]$, where Y_{it} is a univariate ITS. The conditional mean of a univariate ITS $\{Y_{it}\}$ is the optimal solution of minimizing MSE respect to D_K: $E(Y_{it}|I_{t-1})=\arg\min_{f\in I_{\mathbf{R}}} E[D_K^2(Y_{it}, f(I_{t-1}))]$.

It follows that the parameter estimator for the IVARMA(p,q,n) model can be obtained as a minimizer of a sample analogue of $E[D_K^2(Y_t, f(I_{t-1}))]$, namely,

$$\hat{\theta}=\arg\min_{\theta\in\Theta}\hat{Q}_T(\theta) \tag{4}$$

where

$$\hat{Q}_T(\theta)=\frac{1}{nT}\sum_{t=1}^{T}\sum_{i=1}^{n} q_{it}(\theta) \tag{5}$$

$$q_{it}(\theta)=\|\varepsilon_{it}(\theta)\|_K^2=\langle s_{\varepsilon_{it}(\theta)}, s_{\varepsilon_{it}(\theta)}\rangle_K \tag{6}$$

$$\begin{aligned}\varepsilon_{it}(\theta)=Y_{it}-\Bigg[&(\alpha_i^0+\beta_i^0 I_0)+\sum_{j=1}^{p}\sum_{h=1}^{n}\phi_{ih}^{j}Y_{ht-j}\\&+\sum_{j=1}^{q}\sum_{h=1}^{n}\gamma_{ih}^{j}\varepsilon_{ht-j}(\theta)+\sum_{j=0}^{s}\sum_{h=1}^{J}\psi_{ih}^{j}X_{ht-j}\Bigg]\end{aligned} \tag{7}$$

where $\hat{Q}_T(\theta)$ is the sum of squared interval residual vector with respect to the D_K-distance over the T observations, and $\|\varepsilon_{it}(\theta)\|_K$ in Eq. (6) is the D_K-distance between the i-th interval residual $\varepsilon_{it}(\theta)$ and the zero interval $[0,0]$ with respect to kernel K.

When an IVARMA model becomes an IVAR model:

$$Y_t = (\alpha^0 + \beta^0 I_0) + \sum_{j=1}^{p} \Phi_j Y_{t-j} + \varepsilon_t,$$

the right side in Eq. (7) excludes the terms of $\varepsilon_{it-j}(\theta)$ and can be written as $\varepsilon_{it}(\theta) = Y_{it} - [(\alpha_i^0 + \beta_i^0 I_0) + \sum_{j=1}^{p} \sum_{h=1}^{n} \phi_{ih}^j Y_{ht-j}]$. Interestingly, this is in essence the interval residual for an ACIX$(p, 0, s)$ model. For the i-th ACIX model, the lag terms of $Y_{jt}(j \neq i)$ are treated as exogenous interval variables. It follows from Eqs. (5) and (6) that the minimizer of $\hat{Q}_T(\theta)$ in Eq. (5) of an IVAR model can be obtained by minimizing the sum of $\|\varepsilon_{it}(\theta)\|_K^2$ for each $i = 1, 2, \ldots, n$, respectively, with respect to the same kernel. Analogous to Corollary 3.1 in Han et al. (2015), we can obtain a closed form of the estimator $\hat{\theta}_i$ for parameter vector θ_i^0 in the i-th equation of an IVAR model, namely,

$$\hat{\theta}_i = \sum_{t=1+p}^{T} [\langle s_{Z_{it}}, s'_{Z_{it}} \rangle_K]^{-1} \sum_{t=1+p}^{T} [\langle s_{Z_{it}}, s_{Y_{it}} \rangle_K],$$

where $Z_{it} = ([1,1], I_0, Y_{1t-1}, \ldots, Y_{1t-p}, \ldots, Y_{nt-1}, \ldots, Y_{nt-p})'$. Then the optimal solution of Eq. (4) is $\hat{\theta} = (\hat{\theta}'_1, \ldots, \hat{\theta}'_n)'$. Like in a point-valued VAR model, the parameters in each equation of an IVAR model can be consistently estimated separately.

Now we establish the consistency and asymptotic normality of the proposed estimator.

Theorem 1. (*Consistency*). *Under the Assumptions 1, 2, 3(i) and 4,* $\hat{\theta} \xrightarrow{p} \theta^0$, *as* $T \to \infty$.

Theorem 2. (*Asymptotic Normality*). *Under Assumptions 1–5, as* $T \to \infty$

$$\sqrt{T}(\hat{\theta} - \theta^0) \xrightarrow{L} N(0, M^{-1}(\theta^0) V(\theta^0) M^{-1}(\theta^0)),$$

where $V(\theta^0) = \frac{1}{n^2} E\left[\sum_{i=1}^{n} \frac{\partial q_{it}(\theta^0)}{\partial \theta} \sum_{j=1}^{n} \frac{\partial q_{jt}(\theta^0)}{\partial \theta'}\right]$, $M(\theta^0) = \frac{1}{n} \sum_{i=1}^{n} E\left[\frac{\partial^2 q_{it}(\theta^0)}{\partial \theta \partial \theta'}\right]$, $q_{it}(\theta)$ *is defined as in Eq. (6) and all the derivatives are evaluated at* θ^0.

Now we develop a consistent estimator of the variance-covariance matrix of $\hat{\theta}$.

Theorem 3. (*Asymptotic Variance Estimation*). *Under Assumptions 1–5, as* $T \to \infty$

$$\hat{M}_T(\hat{\theta}) = \frac{1}{nT} \sum_{i=1}^{n} \sum_{t=1}^{T} \frac{\partial^2 q_{it}(\hat{\theta})}{\partial \theta \partial \theta'} \xrightarrow{p} M(\theta^0),$$

$$\hat{V}_T(\hat{\theta}) = \frac{1}{n^2 T} \sum_{t=1}^{T} \left[\sum_{i=1}^{n} \frac{\partial q_{it}(\hat{\theta})}{\partial \theta} \sum_{j=1}^{n} \frac{\partial q_{jt}(\hat{\theta})}{\partial \theta'} \right] \xrightarrow{p} V(\theta^0).$$

And all the derivatives are evaluated at $\hat{\theta}$.

Note that the above asymptotic properties of the minimum D_K-distance estimator hold for any symmetric and positive-definite kernel. A natural question rises: What is the optimal choice of kernel, if any, that yields the most efficient estimator? We will explore the asymptotic efficiency of the minimum D_K-distance estimation in the following section.

3.2. *Efficiency and Two-Stage Minimum-Distance Estimation*

Han et al. (2015) suggested that various choices of kernel K lead to different ways of using the sample information in estimating model parameters. And they proposed an optimal choice of kernel that yields an asymptotically most efficient minimum D_K-distance estimator among a class of minimum-distance estimators for a univariate ITS model. Now we examine the asymptotic efficiency of the proposed minimum-distance estimators for an IVARMA model and derive a feasible asymptotically most efficient two-stage estimator, as shown in Theorems 4 and 5.

We first impose additional conditions in Assumptions 6 and 7.

Assumption 6.
For any $i = 1, 2, \ldots, n$, *the bivariate point process* $\{\varepsilon_{it}^L, \varepsilon_{it}^R\}$ *satisfies* $var[(\varepsilon_{it}^L, \varepsilon_{it}^R)' | I_{t-1}] = \Sigma_i$, *where* ε_{it}^L, ε_{it}^R *are the left and right bounds of the interval innovation* ε_{it}, *respectively, and* Σ_i *is a positive-definite symmetric matrix.*

Assumption 7.
The conditional variance $var(\varepsilon_t | I_{t-1}) = \Sigma^0$, *where* Σ^0 *is a diagonal matrix.*

Under Assumption 6, the conditional variance-covariance of $(\varepsilon_{it}^L, \varepsilon_{it}^R)'$ given I_{t-1} is assumed to be constant for all t, which implies that the interval innovation ε_{it} satisfies conditional homoscedasticity for each i. Assumption 7 assumes that the conditional covariance between ε_{it} and ε_{jt} given I_{t-1} is zero when $i \neq j$. We derive an optimal kernel for our minimum D_K-distance estimator under Assumptions 6 and 7. The optimal choice of kernel in a more general set-up that allows that ε_{it} and ε_{jt} are correlated given I_{t-1}, will be explored in a future study. We emphasize that the asymptotic theory established in Theorems 1–3 (i.e. consistency, asymptotic normality, and consistent estimation of avar($\hat{\theta}$)) holds without Assumptions 6 and 7.

Now we can obtain the optimal kernel for estimating an IVARMA model in Theorem 4.

Theorem 4. (***Optimal Kernel***). *Under Assumptions 1–7, the choice of kernel* $K^{opt}(u,v)$ *with* $K^{opt}(1,1) = n^{-1}\sum_{i=1}^{n} var(\varepsilon_{it}^{L})$, $K^{opt}(-1,1) = K^{opt}(1,-1) = n^{-1}\sum_{i=1}^{n} cov(\varepsilon_{it}^{L}, \varepsilon_{it}^{R})$, *and* $K^{opt}(-1,-1) = n^{-1}\sum_{i=1}^{n} var(\varepsilon_{it}^{R})$ *yields a minimum* D_K*-distance estimator* $\widetilde{\theta}^{opt} = \arg\min_{\theta\in\Theta} \frac{1}{nT}\sum_{i=1}^{n}\sum_{t=1}^{T} D_{K^{opt}}^{2}[Y_t, Z_{it}^{'}(\theta)\theta]$ *which is asymptotically most efficient among all symmetric positive-definite kernels, with the minimum asymptotic variance*

$$\Omega^{opt} = n \| K^{opt} \| \left[\sum_{i=1}^{n} E\left(\left\langle s_{\frac{\partial\varepsilon_{it}}{\partial\theta}}, s_{\frac{\partial\varepsilon_{it}}{\partial\theta}}^{'} \right\rangle_{K^{opt}} \right) \right]^{-1}$$

where $\|K^{opt}\| \equiv K^{opt}(1,1)K^{opt}(-1,-1) - K^{opt}(1,-1)K^{opt}(-1,1)$.

Since K^{opt} depends on the data-generating process (DGP) that is unknown, we consider a two-stage minimum D_K-distance estimation procedure. In the first step, we obtain a consistent minimum D_K-distance estimator $\hat{\theta}$ from an arbitrary choice of kernel. Then, with the estimated residuals $\hat{\varepsilon}_t(\hat{\theta})$ that are based on $\hat{\theta}$, we can construct an estimator for K^{opt}:

$$\hat{K}^{opt} = \frac{1}{nT}\sum_{t=1}^{T} \begin{bmatrix} \sum_{i=1}^{n} [\hat{\varepsilon}_{it}^{L}(\hat{\theta})]^2 & \sum_{i=1}^{n} \hat{\varepsilon}_{it}^{L}(\hat{\theta})\hat{\varepsilon}_{it}^{R}(\hat{\theta}) \\ \sum_{i=1}^{n} \hat{\varepsilon}_{it}^{R}(\hat{\theta})\hat{\varepsilon}_{it}^{L}(\hat{\theta}) & \sum_{i=1}^{n} [\hat{\varepsilon}_{it}^{R}(\hat{\theta})]^2 \end{bmatrix}.$$

This is a consistent estimator for K^{opt} in Theorem 4. In the second step, we estimate the model parameters with $\hat{K}^{opt}$, which attains the minimum asymptotic variance, that is, Ω^{opt} when $T \to \infty$. This is stated in Theorem 5.

Theorem 5. (***Two-Stage Estimation***). *Under Assumptions 1–7, as* $T \to \infty$, *the two-stage minimum* D_K*-distance estimator* $\sqrt{T}(\hat{\theta}^{opt} - \theta^0) \xrightarrow{L} N(0, \Omega^{opt})$ *where* Ω^{opt} *is the minimum asymptotic variance as given in Theorem 4.*

4. SIMULATION

In this section, we investigate the finite-sample properties of the class of proposed minimum D_K-distance estimators via a Monte Carlo study. In particular, we are interested in the relative efficiency between the interval data-based estimators from IVARMA models and the point data-based estimators from VARMA models. We consider an IVARMA(1,1,2) model as the DGP:

$$\begin{cases} Y_{1t} = \alpha_1^0 + \beta_1^0 I_0 + \phi_{11}^1 Y_{1t-1} + \phi_{12}^1 Y_{2t-1} + \gamma_{11}^1 \varepsilon_{1t-1} + \gamma_{12}^1 \varepsilon_{2t-1} + \varepsilon_{1t}, \\ Y_{2t} = \alpha_2^0 + \beta_2^0 I_0 + \phi_{21}^1 Y_{1t-1} + \phi_{22}^1 Y_{2t-1} + \gamma_{21}^1 \varepsilon_{1t-1} + \gamma_{22}^1 \varepsilon_{2t-1} + \varepsilon_{2t}, \end{cases} \tag{8}$$

The initial values of Y_t and ε_t for $t=0$ are both set to be $[0,0]$.

We generate the interval innovation vector ε_t with the following two DGPs, respectively.

DGP 1. Bivariate Point-Valued DGP

The two boundaries of the interval innovation $\varepsilon_{it}=[\varepsilon_{it}^L, \varepsilon_{it}^R]$ for $i=1,2$ follow the parameterizations $\varepsilon_{it}^L = a_{i1}\mu_{it}^0 + \mu_{it}^1$ and $\varepsilon_{it}^R = a_{i2}\mu_{it}^1 + \mu_{it}^2$, where μ_{it}^j follows *i.i.d.* $EXP(1)-1$ for $j=0,1,2, i=1,2$. We set $a_{11}=1, a_{12}=-0.6, a_{21}=1, a_{22}=0.5$, which ensures that the interval innovation vector ε_t satisfies $cov(\varepsilon_{1t}^L, \varepsilon_{1t}^R)=-0.6$ and $cov(\varepsilon_{2t}^L, \varepsilon_{2t}^R)=0.5$ respectively. The interval innovation ε_{it} $(i=1,2)$ is generated via the bivariate distribution with $T=100, 250$ and 500, respectively. For each sample size T, we perform $1,000$ replications. The true parameter vector value $\theta^0=(\alpha_1^0, \beta_1^0, \phi_{11}^1, \phi_{12}^1, \gamma_{11}^1, \gamma_{12}^1, \alpha_2^0, \beta_2^0, \phi_{21}^1, \phi_{22}^1, \gamma_{21}^1, \gamma_{22}^1)'$ for **DGP 1** is set as $\theta^0 = (0.08, -0.03, 0.47, 0.62, -0.234, -0.17, 0.07, 0.4, -0.58, 0.18, -0.28, -0.31)'$.

DGP 2. IVARMA-Based DGP

We first obtain the minimum D_K-distance estimator of the IVARMA(1, 1, 2) model based on the interval-valued data of the S&P 500 and NASDAQ daily price indices from January 3, 1988 to September 18, 2009, with the choice of kernel K with $K(1,1)=K(-1,-1)=5$ and $K(-1,1)=K(1,-1)=3$. The daily raw vector of interval prices is converted to a weakly stationary interval sample by taking the logarithm and Hukuhara difference. We obtain the minimum D_K-distance parameter estimates and use them as the true parameter values for DGP (8). To simulate the innovation vector ε_t in Eq. (8), we first compute the estimated model residuals

$$\begin{cases} \hat{\varepsilon}_{1t} = Y_{1t} - [\hat{\alpha}_1^0 + \hat{\beta}_1^0 I_0 + \hat{\phi}_{11}^1 Y_{1t-1} + \hat{\phi}_{12}^1 Y_{2t-1} + \hat{\gamma}_{11}^1 \hat{\varepsilon}_{1t-1} + \hat{\gamma}_{12}^1 \hat{\varepsilon}_{2t-1}] \\ \hat{\varepsilon}_{2t} = Y_{1t} - [\hat{\alpha}_2^0 + \hat{\beta}_2^0 I_0 + \hat{\phi}_{21}^1 Y_{1t-1} + \hat{\phi}_{22}^1 Y_{2t-1} + \hat{\gamma}_{21}^1 \hat{\varepsilon}_{1t-1} + \hat{\gamma}_{22}^1 \hat{\varepsilon}_{2t-1}] \end{cases} \tag{9}$$

based on the S&P 500 and NASDAQ daily interval data. ε_t is then generated via a naive bootstrapping from $\{\hat{\varepsilon}_t\}_{t=1}^T$ with $T=100, 250$ and 500, respectively. For each sample size T, we perform $1,000$ replications.

Under both DGPs, we conduct minimum D_K-distance estimation with various kernels. Denote $K(1,1)$, $K(-1,1)$ and $K(-1,-1)$ as a, b and c, respectively. The two-stage estimator $\hat{\theta}^{opt}$ is obtained using a preliminary kernel K with $(a,b,c)=(10,8,16)$ in the first stage. We examine the finite-sample properties of the estimators under study by computing the bias, standard deviation (SD), and root-mean-square error (RMSE) for each estimator: $\text{Bias}(\hat{\theta}_i)=\frac{1}{1,000}\sum_{m=1}^{1,000}(\hat{\theta}_i^{(m)}-\hat{\theta}_i^0)$, $\text{SD}(\hat{\theta}_i)=[\frac{1}{1,000}\sum_{m=1}^{1,000}(\hat{\theta}_i^{(m)}-\bar{\theta}_i)^2]^{1/2}$, $\text{RMSE}(\hat{\theta}_i)=[\text{Bias}^2(\hat{\theta}_i)+\text{SD}^2(\hat{\theta}_i)]^{1/2}$, where $\bar{\theta}_i=\frac{1}{1,000}\sum_{m=1}^{1,000}\hat{\theta}_i^{(m)}$, respectively. Since similar patterns are revealed from the

Table 1. Bias, SD and RMSE of Representative Estimators with DGP 1.

$a/b/c$	$Bias(10^{-2})$			$SD(10^{-2})$			$RMSE(10^{-2})$		
	$T=100$	$T=250$	$T=500$	$T=100$	$T=250$	$T=500$	$T=100$	$T=250$	$T=500$
$\hat{\alpha}_2^0$									
$1/1/1$	N/A	N/A	N/A	N/A	N/A	N/A	N/A	N/A	N/A
$1/-1/1$	6.1420	0.6433	1.7894	7.5525	3.6412	2.4629	9.7347	3.6976	3.0443
$1/0/1$	2.7357	2.3477	3.4683	5.8293	3.8548	2.7153	6.4393	4.5135	4.4047
$10/6/10$	0.3882	−1.9981	1.0754	5.9467	3.6197	2.5176	5.9593	4.1346	2.7376
$10/8/16$	−1.1151	2.3709	2.4531	6.6825	3.7835	2.4803	6.7749	4.4650	3.4885
$\hat{\theta}^{opt}$	−1.3788	−3.1668	−1.4700	5.5048	3.4407	2.4766	5.6748	4.6762	2.8800
$\hat{\beta}_2^0$									
$1/1/1$	−10.2639	5.8630	−3.8390	18.1536	9.6045	7.6121	20.8543	11.2526	8.5254
$1/-1/1$	N/A	N/A	N/A	N/A	N/A	N/A	N/A	N/A	N/A
$1/0/1$	32.5379	9.9925	−2.2693	17.7461	9.5676	7.3165	37.0626	13.8344	7.6603
$10/6/10$	11.5196	−11.3105	5.6780	16.2410	11.0888	7.7496	19.9116	15.8395	9.6071
$10/8/16$	11.5196	−11.3105	5.6780	16.2410	11.0888	7.7496	19.9116	15.8395	9.6071
$\hat{\theta}^{opt}$	−5.5801	1.5175	4.5422	13.2200	10.0187	7.4677	14.3494	10.1330	8.7406
$\hat{\phi}_{11}^1$									
$1/1/1$	−4.4757	−1.0961	−0.8687	19.3703	11.5677	7.6234	19.8807	11.6195	7.6727
$1/-1/1$	−3.0226	−1.5869	−0.6967	18.4825	10.3608	7.7212	18.7281	10.4817	7.7525
$1/0/1$	−1.5210	−0.9663	−0.5285	13.3951	8.2285	5.7449	13.4812	8.2850	5.7692
$10/6/10$	−1.6012	−1.2393	−1.1596	17.5912	10.6903	7.0434	17.6639	10.7619	7.1382
$10/8/16$	−3.7068	−1.2242	−1.0563	18.6436	9.9268	6.9565	19.0086	10.0020	7.0362
$\hat{\theta}^{opt}$	−0.1169	−0.3323	0.1050	13.6561	8.0133	5.4040	13.6566	8.0202	5.4050
$\hat{\gamma}_{22}^1$									
$1/1/1$	2.0422	0.6248	0.4778	19.3203	12.6028	9.1633	19.4279	12.6183	9.1757
$1/-1/1$	2.9735	1.2306	0.8318	21.7056	13.7100	8.9021	21.9083	13.7652	8.9409
$1/0/1$	1.3417	0.6969	0.3561	16.3762	10.3837	6.9417	16.4310	10.4071	6.9508
$10/6/10$	1.7097	1.0115	0.3761	16.7713	10.4139	8.0412	16.8582	10.4629	8.0500
$10/8/16$	2.1482	1.1752	1.0508	18.1010	12.2995	8.7178	18.2280	12.3555	8.7809
$\hat{\theta}^{opt}$	0.3594	0.2795	0.1911	14.1346	8.7513	6.5971	14.1392	8.7558	6.5999

Notes:

(a) Bivariate point-valued process with $n=2$:

$$\begin{cases} Y_{1t}^L = \alpha_1^0 - 1/2\beta_1^0 + \phi_{11}^1 Y_{1t-1}^L + \phi_{12}^1 Y_{2t-1}^L + \gamma_{11}^1 \varepsilon_{1t-1}^L + \gamma_{12}^1 \varepsilon_{2t-1}^L + \varepsilon_{1t}^L, \\ Y_{1t}^R = \alpha_1^0 + 1/2\beta_1^0 + \phi_{21}^1 Y_{1t-1}^R + \phi_{22}^1 Y_{2t-1}^R + \gamma_{21}^1 \varepsilon_{1t-1}^R + \gamma_{22}^1 \varepsilon_{2t-1}^R + \varepsilon_{2t}^R, \end{cases}$$

and

$$\begin{cases} Y_{2t}^L = \alpha_2^0 - 1/2\beta_2^0 + \phi_{11}^1 Y_{1t-1}^L + \phi_{12}^1 Y_{2t-1}^L + \gamma_{11}^1 \varepsilon_{1t-1}^L + \gamma_{12}^1 \varepsilon_{2t-1}^L + \varepsilon_{1t}^L, \\ Y_{2t}^R = \alpha_2^0 + 1/2\beta_2^0 + \phi_{21}^1 Y_{1t-1}^R + \phi_{22}^1 Y_{2t-1}^R + \gamma_{21}^1 \varepsilon_{1t-1}^R + \gamma_{22}^1 \varepsilon_{2t-1}^R + \varepsilon_{2t}^R, \end{cases}$$

(b) The kernel K is of the form $K(1,1)=a$, $K(1,-1)=K(-1,1)=b$ and $K(-1,-1)=c$. The value of $a/b/c$ is listed in the first column of the table.

(c) Mixture density for $\varepsilon_{it}=(\varepsilon_{it}^L,\varepsilon_{it}^R)'$ for $i=1,2$ are considered here. $\varepsilon_{it}^L = a_{i1}\mu_{it}^0 + \mu_{it}^1$ and $\varepsilon_{it}^R = a_{i2}\mu_{it}^1 + \mu_{it}^2$, where μ_{it}^j follows *i.i.d.* $EXP(1)-1$ for $j=0,1,2$, $i=1,2$ and $t=1,2,\ldots,T$.$cov(\varepsilon_{1t}^L,\varepsilon_{1t}^R)=-0.6$ and $cov(\varepsilon_{2t}^L,\varepsilon_{2t}^R)=0.5$.

(d) Bias, SD and the standard error of each parameter are computed based on 1,000 bootstrap replications.

Table 2. Bias, SD and RMSE of Representative Estimators under DGP 2.

$a/b/c$	$Bias(10^{-2})$			$SD(10^{-2})$			$RMSE(10^{-2})$		
	$T=100$	$T=250$	$T=500$	$T=100$	$T=250$	$T=500$	$T=100$	$T=250$	$T=500$
$\hat{\alpha}_2^0$									
$1/1/1$	N/A	N/A	N/A	N/A	N/A	N/A	N/A	N/A	N/A
$1/-1/1$	−0.2743	−0.2437	−0.2268	0.5229	0.3393	0.2281	0.5905	0.4178	0.3217
$1/0/1$	−0.2892	−0.2687	−0.2500	0.5016	0.2938	0.2219	0.5790	0.3982	0.3343
$10/6/10$	−0.2518	−0.2544	−0.2505	0.4794	0.2864	0.2154	0.5415	0.3831	0.3304
$10/8/16$	−0.2330	−0.2441	−0.2291	0.4811	0.3126	0.2123	0.5346	0.3966	0.3124
$\hat{\theta}^{opt}$	−0.2310	−0.2350	−0.2216	0.4718	0.2863	0.2009	0.5253	0.3704	0.2991
$\hat{\beta}_2^0$									
$1/1/1$	−2.1086	0.0237	0.0122	0.7813	0.4538	0.3343	2.2487	0.4545	0.3346
$1/-1/1$	N/A	N/A	N/A	N/A	N/A	N/A	N/A	N/A	N/A
$1/0/1$	0.0962	0.0274	0.0067	0.7745	0.4967	0.3435	0.7804	0.4974	0.3435
$10/6/10$	0.0976	0.0250	−0.0010	0.6931	0.4488	0.3068	0.7000	0.4495	0.3068
$10/8/16$	0.0975	0.0275	−0.0146	0.6797	0.4528	0.3101	0.6867	0.4536	0.3104
$\hat{\theta}^{opt}$	0.0208	−0.0224	−0.0009	0.6733	0.4659	0.2986	0.6737	0.4664	0.2986
$\hat{\phi}_{11}^1$									
$1/1/1$	−4.6841	−2.5541	−0.8118	19.0103	14.8832	10.3425	19.5789	15.1008	10.3743
$1/-1/1$	−2.5845	−2.2151	−1.4337	19.0103	12.1470	8.4684	19.1852	12.3473	8.5889
$1/0/1$	−2.6478	−0.9545	−1.1047	15.8698	9.7366	6.9438	16.0892	9.7832	7.0312
$10/6/10$	−1.9635	−1.4768	−1.0915	16.4091	10.5054	7.8689	16.5262	10.6086	7.9443
$10/8/16$	−1.8215	−1.2769	−0.5168	18.7275	11.8519	8.2917	18.8158	11.9205	8.3078
$\hat{\theta}^{opt}$	−1.4160	−0.8032	−0.8089	14.9278	9.3877	6.8935	14.9948	9.4220	6.9408
$\hat{\gamma}_{22}^1$									
$1/1/1$	1.9368	0.8661	0.2419	17.2340	7.9146	6.0589	17.3425	7.9618	6.0637
$1/-1/1$	1.9768	1.6638	0.3899	17.2340	10.6429	7.3764	17.3470	10.7721	7.3867
$1/0/1$	1.5512	0.2347	0.5081	12.8726	7.7909	5.4824	12.9657	7.7944	5.5059
$10/6/10$	1.0473	0.3942	0.4326	10.1101	6.2555	4.4654	10.1642	6.2679	4.4863
$10/8/16$	0.9020	0.3828	−0.2338	10.2883	6.3881	4.4302	10.3277	6.3996	4.4440
$\hat{\theta}^{opt}$	−0.9035	−0.3581	−0.3499	12.0738	6.5249	4.3845	12.1075	6.5291	4.3991

Notes:

(a) IVARMA(1, 1, 2) model:

$$\begin{cases} Y_{1t} = \alpha_1^0 + \beta_1^0 I_0 + \phi_{11}^1 Y_{1t-1} + \phi_{12}^1 Y_{2t-1} + \gamma_{11}^1 \varepsilon_{1t-1} + \gamma_{12}^1 \varepsilon_{2t-1} + \varepsilon_{1t}, \\ Y_{2t} = \alpha_2^0 + \beta_2^0 I_0 + \phi_{21}^1 Y_{1t-1} + \phi_{22}^1 Y_{2t-1} + \gamma_{21}^1 \varepsilon_{1t-1} + \gamma_{22}^1 \varepsilon_{2t-1} + \varepsilon_{2t}, \end{cases}$$

(b) The kernel K is of the form $K(1,1)=a$, $K(1,-1)=K(-1,1)=b$ and $K(-1,-1)=c$. The value of $a/b/c$ is listed in the first column of the table.

(c) Bias, SD and the standard error of each parameter are computed based on 1,000 bootstrap replications.

estimation results of each parameter, we only report the results of $\hat{\alpha}_2^0, \hat{\beta}_2^0, \hat{\phi}_{11}^1, \hat{\gamma}_{22}^1$ in Tables 1 and 2.

Tables 1 and 2 summarize results for bias, SD and RMSE of the above estimators under DGP 1 and DGP 2, respectively. First, Bias, SD and RMSE of each estimator are approaching zero as T increases under both DGPs, which confirms the consistency result in Theorem 1. Note that the two-stage $\hat{\theta}^{opt}$ displays robust efficiency gain over other estimators in terms of RMSE, and the efficiency gain is enormous as T becomes large. This is consistent with the asymptotic efficiency result in Theorem 5. Third, as shown in Han et al. (2015), the minimum D_K estimators from kernels with $(a, b, c) = (1, 1, 1)$ and $(1, -1, 1)$ only utilize the range or midpoint information, respectively, not both of the interval sample. Therefore, they cannot identify α_2^0 and β_2^0, respectively, as shown in Tables 1 and 2. In Section 2, we have shown that VARMA models of the range and midpoint vector processes can consistently estimate common parameters in an IVARMA model. In fact, the estimators from these two kernels are the ordinary least-square estimators for the VARMA models of the range and midpoint processes, respectively. While both kernels provide consistent estimation for model parameters, they are less efficient than the class of minimum D_K-distance estimators based on the entire interval data. This highlights the informational advantages of using interval-valued data.

5. CONCLUSION

There exists a relative large body of ITS modelling in the literature. With interval-valued data, most of the ongoing efforts have been directed to the adaptation of classical point-valued regression models for a univariate ITS. To explore cross-dependence dynamics among multiple ITS, we have proposed a new IVARMA model to capture the dynamics of an ITS vector process. We have proposed a minimum-distance estimation method for an IVARMA model, and established the consistency, asymptotic normality of the proposed estimators. A feasible asymptotically most efficient two-stage minimum-distance estimator is derived, which attains the minimum asymptotic variance-covariance matrix among a class of minimum-distance estimators. Compared to the existing approaches for a univariate ITS modelling, the IVARMA model is more flexible in that it can characterize some cross-sectional dynamics of a multivariate ITS system in a parsimonious way, since we treat an interval observation as an inseparable unity.

The Monte Carlo simulation studies documented significant efficiency gain of the estimators proposed, measured by the average behavior of the root-mean-squared error, when compared with the traditional point-based VARMA models. It was seen that the minimum D_K-distance estimators, and in particular the feasible two-stage estimator that used the entire interval data outperform the estimators for

VARMA models that used the point-based data no matter whether the observed interval vector data are generated from an interval-based DGP or a bivariate point-based DGP.

We now outline some limitations and issues that deserve further research. First, our estimation method does not involve the distribution function of the examined ITS vector system, since this is a rather tricky problem for set-valued variables. Classic order-selection approaches for point-valued time series models, for example, the Akaike information criterion (Akaike (1974)), as well as the likelihood ratio test for specific lags of VAR models in Hamilton (1994), are both based on the distribution information of the point-valued processes. Thus, those point-based approaches cannot be applied directly to the models for ITS. To fix the dilemma between overfitting and underfitting, we need to consider a model selection criterion for IVARMA models, as well as for other interval models, in future research. Second, our IVARMA modelling approach suggests an important avenue for some main concerns in point-valued vector time series analysis. For example, Granger causality analysis for a pair of extended random interval variables can examine whether and how the interval information in one ITS can be useful in forecasting the other. Also, the impulse response function of an IVAR model can be explored to describe how an interval system reacts over time to exogenous impulses, for example, economic shocks. Third, one could consider some flexible extension of point-valued VAR models under an interval set-up, such as structural-IVAR and time-varying parameter IVAR models. Finally, the co-integration theory and vector error-correction modelling for an ITS vector system are also of great interest for further research.

ACKNOWLEDGEMENTS

The authors gratefully acknowledge the NSF of China Grant No. 71201161 and the National Center for Mathematics and Interdisciplinary Sciences, Chinese Academy of Sciences. We benefit from the comments and suggestions by three referees, Ana Colubi, Amos Golan, Carlos Maté, Aman Ullah, and the conference participants at the First International Symposium on Interval Data Modelling – Theory and Applications in Beijing.

REFERENCES

Akaike, H. (1974). A new look at the statistical model identification. *IEEE Transactions on Automatic Control*, *19*(6), 716–723.

Amemiya, T. (1985). *Advanced econometrics*. Cambridge, MA: Harvard University Press.

Andrews, D. W. K. (1992). Generic uniform convergence. *Econometric Theory*, *8*(2), 241–257.

Arroyo, J., Espínola, R., & Maté, C. (2011). Different approaches to forecast interval time series: A comparison in finance. *Computational Economics*, *37*(2), 169–191.

Arroyo, J., & Maté, C. (2006). Introducing interval time series: Accuracy measures. In *Proceedings in Computational Statistics, COMPSTAT 2006* (pp. 1139–1146). Heidelberg: Physica-Verlag.

Arroyo, J., Roque, A. M. S., Maté, C., & Sarabia, A. (2007). Exponential smoothing methods for interval time series. In *Proceedings of the 1st European Symposium on Time Series Prediction* (pp. 231–240).

Bernanke, B. S. (1986). Alternative explanations of the money-income correlation. *Carnegie-Rochester Conference Series on Public Policy*, *25*, 49–99.

Billard, L., & Diday, E. (2003). From the statistics of data to the statistics of knowledge: Symbolic data analysis. *Journal of the American Statistical Association*, *98*, 470–487.

Billard, L., & Diday, E. (2006). *Symbolic data analysis: Conceptual statistics and data mining* (1st edn.). New York, NY: Wiley.

Billingsley, P. (2013). *Convergence of probability measures*. New York, NY: Wiley.

Blanchard, O. J., & Watson, M. W. (1986). *Are business cycles all alike? The American business cycle: Continuity and change* (pp. 123–180). Chicago, IL: University of Chicago Press.

Chou, R. (2005). Forecasting financial volatilities with extreme values: The conditional auto-regressive range (CARR) model. *Journal of Money, Credit and Banking*, *37*(3), 561–582.

Froelich, W., & Salmeron, J. L. (2014). Evolutionary learning of fuzzy grey cognitive maps for the forecasting of multivariate, interval-valued time series. *International Journal of Approximate Reasoning, 55*(6), 1319–1335.

García-Ascanio, C., & Maté, C. (2010). Electric power demand forecasting using interval time series: A comparison between VAR and iMLP. *Energy Policy*, *38*(2), 715–725.

Golan, A., & Ullah, A. (2015). *Interval estimation: An infometrics approach*. Working Paper.

González-Rivera, G., & Lin, W. (2013). Constrained regression for interval-valued data. *Journal of Business & Economic Statistics*, *4*, 473–490.

Hamilton, J. D. (1994). *Time series analysis*. Princeton, NJ: Princeton university press.

Han, A., Hong, Y., & Wang, S. (2015). *Autoregressive conditional models for interval-valued time series data*, Working Paper.

Han, A., Lai, K. K., Wang, S., & Xu, S. (2012). An interval method for studying the relationship between the Australian dollar exchange rate and the gold price. *Journal of Systems Science and Complexity*, *25*(1), 121–132.

He, L. T., & Hu, C. (2009). Impacts of interval computing on stock market variability forecasting. *Computational Economics*, *33*(3), 263–276.

Hukuhara, M. (1967). Intégration des applications measurable dont la valeur est un compact convexe. *Funkcial Ekvac*, *10*, 205–223.

Johansen, S. (1988). Statistical analysis of cointegration vectors. *Journal of Economic Dynamics and Control*, *12*(2), 231–254.

Körner, R. (1997). On the variance of fuzzy random variables. *Fuzzy Sets and Systems*, *92*, 83–93.

Körner, R., & Näther, W. (2002). On the variance of random fuzzy variables. In *Statistical Modeling, Analysis and Management of Fuzzy Data* (pp. 25–42). Heildelberg: Physica-Verlag.

Lee, S. W., & Hansen, B. E. (1994). Asymptotic theory for the GARCH(1, 1) quasi-maximum likelihood estimator. *Econometric Theory*, *10*(01), 29–52.

Lima Neto, E., & Carvalho, F. A. T. (2008). Centre and range method for fitting a linear regression model to symbolic interval data. *Computational Statistics and Data Analysis*, *52*, 1500–1515.

Lima Neto, E., & Carvalho, F. A. T. (2010). Constrained linear regression models for symbolic interval-valued variables, *Computational Statistics and Data Analysis*, *54*, 333–347.

Maia, A. L. S., & Carvalho, F. A. T. (2011). Holt's exponential smoothing and neural network models for forecasting interval-valued time series. *International Journal of Forecasting*, *27*(3), 740–759.

Maia, A. L. S., Carvalho, F. A. T., & Ludermir, T. B. (2008). Forecasting models for interval-valued time series. *Neurocomputing*, *71*(16), 3344–3352.

Nakajima, J. (2011). *Time-varying parameter VAR model with stochastic volatility: An overview of methodology and empirical applications*. Institute for Monetary and Economic Studies, Bank of Japan.

Parkinson, M. (1980). The extreme value method for estimating the variance of the rate of return. *The Journal of Business*, *53*(1), 61–65.

Pesaran, M. H., & Shin, Y. (1988). An autoregressive distributed-lag modelling approach to cointegration analysis. *Econometric Society Monographs*, *31*, 371–413.

Pesaran, M. H., & Shin, Y. (1998). Generalized impulse response analysis in linear multivariate models. *Economics letters*, *58*(1), 17–29.

Rogers, L. C. G., & Satchell, S. E. (1991). Estimating variance from high, low and closing prices. *The Annals of Applied Probability*, *1*(4), 504–512.

Roque, A. M. S., Maté, C., Arroyo, J., & Sarabia, A. (2007). iMLP: Applying multi-layer perceptrons to interval-valued data. *Neural Processing Letters*, *25*, 157–169.

Runkle, D. E. (1991). Liquidity constraints and the permanent-income hypothesis: Evidence from panel data. *Journal of Monetary Economics*, *27*(1), 73–98.

Sadorsky, P. (2014). Modeling volatility and correlations between emerging market stock prices and the prices of copper, oil and wheat. *Energy Economics*, *43*(2), 72–81.

Sargent, T. J. (1987). *Macroeconomic theory*. New York, NY: Academic Press.

Sims, C. A. (1980). Macroeconomics and reality. *Econometrica: Journal of the Econometric Society*, *48*, 1–48.

White, H. (1999). *Asymptotic theory for econometrician*. New York, NY: Academic Press.

Yang, D., & Zhang, Q. (2000). Drift-independent volatility estimation based on high, low, open, and close prices. *The Journal of Business*, *73*(3), 477–491.

Yang, W., & Han, A. (2015). A new approach for forecasting the price range with financial interval-valued time series data. *ASCE-ASME Journal of Risk Uncertainty Engineering Systems, Part B: Mechanical Engineering*, *1*(2), 021004, 1–8. doi:10.1115/1.4028751

APPENDIX

To verify Theorems 1–3, we first establish propositions below. We shall prove several propositions of IARMA(p, q, n) models for simplicity. The proof of IVARMAX(p, q, s, n, J) is analogous.

Proposition 1. *Under Assumptions 1–3, let* $Q(\theta)=\frac{1}{n}\sum_{i=1}^{n} E[q_{it}^{*}(\theta)]$, $q_{it}^{*}(\theta)=\|\varepsilon_{it}(\theta)\|_K^2$. *Then* $Q(\theta)$ *is uniquely minimized at* $\theta=\theta^{0^0}$.

Proof. By Assumption 1, rewrite Eq. (1),

$$Y_{it} = Z_t^T \theta_i^0 + \varepsilon_{it} \tag{A.1}$$

where

$$\begin{aligned} Z_t &= ([1,1], I_0, y_{1t-1}, \ldots, y_{1t-p}, \ldots, y_{nt-1}, \ldots, y_{nt-p}, \varepsilon_{1t-1}, \ldots, \\ &\quad \varepsilon_{1t-q}, \ldots, \varepsilon_{nt-1}, \ldots, \varepsilon_{nt-q})^{\tau}, \\ \theta_i^0 &= (\alpha_i^0, \beta_i^0, \phi_{1i}^1, \ldots, \phi_{1i}^p, \ldots, \phi_{ni}^1, \ldots, \phi_{ni}^p, \gamma_{1i}^1, \ldots, \gamma_{1i}^q, \ldots, \gamma_{ni}^1, \ldots, \gamma_{ni}^q)'. \end{aligned}$$

Then follows that

$$\begin{aligned} Q(\theta) &= \frac{1}{n}\sum_{i=1}^{n} E[q_{it}^{*}(\theta)] = \frac{1}{n}\sum_{i=1}^{n} E\|Y_{it} - Z_t^T(\theta_i)\theta_i\|_K^2 \\ &= \frac{1}{n}\sum_{i=1}^{n} [E\|Z_t^T\theta_i^0 - Z_t^T(\theta)\theta_i\|_K^2 - 2E\langle s_{Z_t^T\theta_i^0 - Z_t^T\theta_i}, s_{\varepsilon_t}\rangle_K + E\|\varepsilon_{it}\|_K^2] \end{aligned}$$

According to Assumption 1 and the linearity of the support function, then follows $E(s_{\varepsilon_{it}} \mid I_{t-1}) = 0$ a.s. So we have

$$E\langle s_{Z_t^T\theta_i^0 - Z_t^T(\theta)\theta_i}, s_{\varepsilon_{it}}\rangle_K = 0.$$

Hence,

$$Q(\theta) = \frac{1}{n}\sum_{i=1}^{n} [E\|Z_t^T\theta_i^0 - Z_t^T(\theta)\theta_i\|_K^2 + E\|\varepsilon_{it}\|_K^2],$$

Let

$$Q_i(\theta_i) = E\|Z_t^T\theta_i^0 - Z_t^T(\theta)\theta_i\|_K^2 + E\|\varepsilon_{it}\|_K^2,$$

which follows that for any $i = 1, 2, \ldots, n$, minimizing $Q_i(\theta_i)$ is equivalent to minimize the first term $E\|Z_t^T\theta_i^0 - Z_t^T(\theta)\theta_i\|_K^2$ and it is straightforward to see that $\theta_i = \theta_i^0$ implies $Z_t^{'}(\theta)\theta = Z_t^{'}\theta^0 a.s.$ So it remain to show $\theta = \theta^0$ is the unique solution for minimizing $Q(\theta)$. Suppose there is another $\tilde{\theta} \in \Theta$ such that $Z_t^{'}\theta^0 = Z_t^{'}(\tilde{\theta})\tilde{\theta}$ $a.s.$, that is, $E(\varepsilon_{it-j}|I_{t-1}) = [0, 0]$ $a.s.$, for $j = 0, 1, \ldots, q$, which contradicts with Assumption 1. Furthermore, because of the arbitrariness of i and the notation of $Q(\theta)$, Proposition 1 is proved. ■

Proposition 2.1. *Let* $Q_T^* = \frac{1}{nT}\sum_{t=1}^{T}\sum_{i=1}^{n}\|\varepsilon_{it}(\theta)\|_K^2$ *and* $Q(\theta) = \frac{1}{n}\sum_{i=1}^{n} E\|\varepsilon_{it}(\theta)\|_K^2$. *Assumptions 1, 2 and 3(i) hold. Then*

$$\sup_{\theta\in\Theta} |Q_T^* - Q(\theta)| \xrightarrow{p} 0$$

Proof. First of all, we consider that

$$\begin{aligned}\sup_{\theta\in\Theta} |Q_T^* - Q(\theta)| &= \sup_{\theta\in\Theta}\left|\frac{1}{n}\sum_{i=1}^{n} Q_i^*(\theta) - \frac{1}{n}\sum_{i=1}^{n} E\|\varepsilon_{it}(\theta)\|_K^2\right| \qquad (A.2)\\ &\leq \sup_{\theta\in\Theta}\frac{1}{n}\sum_{i=1}^{n}|Q_i^*(\theta) - E\|\varepsilon_{it}(\theta)\|_K^2| \\ &\leq \frac{1}{n}\sum_{i=1}^{n}[\sup_{\theta\in\Theta}|Q_i^*(\theta) - E\|\varepsilon_{it}(\theta)\|_K^2|],\end{aligned}$$

where $Q_i^*(\theta) = \frac{1}{T}\sum_{t=1}^{T}\|\varepsilon_{it}(\theta)\|_K^2$. If we can prove that for any $i = 1, 2, \ldots, n$,

$$\sup_{\theta\in\Theta}|Q_i^*(\theta) - Q_i(\theta)| = \sup_{\theta\in\Theta}\left|\frac{1}{T}\sum_{t=1}^{T}\|\varepsilon_{it}(\theta)\|_K^2 - E\|\varepsilon_{it}(\theta)\|_K^2\right| \xrightarrow{p} 0, \qquad (A.3)$$

then follows Proposition 2.1.

According to Andrews (1992, Theorem 3.a), we shall show Proposition 2.1 by verifying (i): Θ is a totally bounded metric space with metric d; (ii) P-WLLN: for any $\theta \in \Theta$ and $i = 1, 2, \ldots, n$, $T^{-1}\sum_{t=1}^{T}\|\varepsilon_{it}(\theta)\|_K^2 - E\|\varepsilon_{it}(\theta)\|_K^2 \xrightarrow{p} 0$; (iii) W-LIP: for any $i = 1, 2, \ldots, n$, $T^{-1}\sum_{t=1}^{T}\|\varepsilon_{it}(\theta)\|_K^2$ satisfies the Lipschitz condition.

(i) is induced directly by Assumption 3. It is straightforward to see whether a) For any $i = 1, 2, \ldots, n$, $\|\varepsilon_{it}(\theta)\|_K^2$ is stationary and ergodic process and b) $E\|\varepsilon_{it}(\theta)\|_K^2 < \infty$ are satisfied in order to prove (ii).

Under the Assumption 2, we can rewrite Eq. (2),

$$\varepsilon_t(\theta) = A^{-1}(L)[B(L)Y_t - C_0] = \sum_{j=0}^{\infty} \pi_j \widetilde{y}_{t-j} \tag{A.4}$$

where $C_0 = (\alpha_0 + \beta_0 I_0)I_n$, $\widetilde{y}_t = Y_t - B^{-1}(1)C_0$, π_j is an $n \times n$ matrix satisfying $\sum_{j=0}^{\infty} \pi_j L^j = A(L)^{-1}B(L)$. Under Assumption 1, definition of inner product with respect to kernel K and the description of ε_t above, we can conclude that for any $i = 1, 2, \ldots, n$, $\|\varepsilon_{it}(\theta)\|_K^2 = \langle s_{\varepsilon_{it}(\theta)}, s_{\varepsilon_{it}(\theta)}\rangle_K$ is a point-valued, stationary and ergodic process following White (1999, Theorem 3.35), which follows (a).

Rewrite Eq. (2), we have

$$A_i(L)\varepsilon_{it}(\theta) = B_i(L)Y_{it} - \sum_{h=1,h\neq i}^{n} B_h(L)y_{ht} - \sum_{h=1,h\neq i} A_h(L)\varepsilon_{ht} - C_0^i,$$

where $A_i(L) = 1 + \sum_{j=1}^{q} \gamma_{ii}^j L^j$, $B_i(L) = 1 - \sum_{j=1}^{p} \phi_{ii}^j L^j$, $B_h(L) = \sum_{j=1}^{p} \phi_{ih}^j L^j$, $A_h(L) = \sum_{j=1}^{q} \gamma_{ih}^j L^j$, and $C_0^i = \alpha_0 + \beta_0 I_0$.

According to Assumption 2, Let z_i be the roots of the MA polynomial equation $|A(z)| = 0$, so we have $|z_i| > 1$, $i = 1, 2, \ldots, q$, that is, all the roots of individual i lie outside the unit circle. Following Sargent (1987, Chapter IX), we have

$$\begin{aligned}
\varepsilon_{it}(\theta) &= A_i^{-1}(L)\left[B_i(L)Y_{it} - \sum_{h=1,h\neq i}^{n} B_h(L)Y_{ht} - \sum_{h=1,h\neq i}^{n} A_h(L)\varepsilon_{ht} - C_0^i\right] \qquad \text{(A.5)}\\
&= \prod_{m=1}^{q}(1-\eta_m L)^{-1}\left[B_i(L)Y_{it} - \sum_{h=1,h\neq i}^{n}(B_h(L)Y_{ht} + A_h(L)\varepsilon_{ht}) - C_0^i\right]\\
&= \sum_{s=0}^{\infty}\left[\sum_{m=1}^{q}(c_m \eta_{m^s})\right]\\
&\quad \times \left[B_i(L)Y_{it-s} - \sum_{h=1,h\neq i}^{n}(B_h(L)Y_{ht-s} + A_h(L)\varepsilon_{ht-s}) - C_0^i\right]
\end{aligned}$$

where $|\eta_m| = |z_m|^{-1} < 1$, $c_m = \eta_m^q[\prod_{j=1,j\neq i}(\eta_m - \eta_j)^{-1}]$. For any $m = 1, 2, \ldots, q$, such that $\sum_{m=1}^{q} c_m = 1$.

Put $\eta = \max_{1\leq m\leq q}\{|\eta_i|\}$ and $\kappa = q \times \max_{1\leq m\leq q}\{|c_m|\}$. Then $0 < \eta < 1$, $0 < \kappa < \infty$. Now we could establish the uniform boundedness of $E|q^*(\theta)|$ over Θ

It follows from Eq. (14) that

$$
\begin{aligned}
E[|q_{it}^{*}(\theta)|] &= E\|\varepsilon_{it}\|_K^2 \le E\sup_{\theta\in\Theta}\|\varepsilon_{it}\|_K^2 \\
&= E\sup_{\theta\in\Theta}\left\|\sum_{s=0}^{\infty}\left[\sum_{m=1}^{q}(c_m\eta_m^s)\right]\right. \\
&\quad \times\left.\left[B_i(L)Y_{it-s}-\sum_{h=1,h\neq i}^{n}(B_h(L)Y_{ht-s}+A_h(L)\varepsilon_{ht-s})-C_0^i\right]\right\|_K^2 \\
&\le E\sup_{\theta\in\Theta}\left\|\sum_{s=0}^{\infty}\left[\sum_{m=1}^{q}(c_m\eta_m^s)\right]\right. \\
&\quad \times\left[Y_{it-s}-\sum_{j=1}^{p}\phi_{ii}^{j}Y_{it-j-s}-\sum_{j=1}^{p}\sum_{h=1,h\neq i}^{n}\phi_{ih}^{j}y_{ht-j-s}\right. \\
&\quad \left.\left.-\sum_{j=1}^{q}\sum_{h=1,h\neq i}^{n}\gamma_{ih}^{j}\varepsilon_{ht-j-s}-C_0^i\right]\right\|_K^2 \\
&\le\left\{\sum_{s=0}^{\infty}\sup_{\theta\in\Theta}\left[\sum_{m=1}^{q}|c_m\eta_m^s|\right]\left(E\|Y_{it-s}\|_K+\sum_{j=1}^{p}\sup_{\theta\in\Theta}|\phi_{ii}^{j}|E\|Y_{it-s-j}\|_K\right.\right. \\
&\quad +\sum_{h=1,h\neq i}^{n}\sum_{j=1}^{p}\sup_{\theta\in\Theta}|\phi_{ih}^{j}|E\|Y_{ht-s-j}\|_K \\
&\quad \left.\left.+\sum_{h=1,h\neq i}^{n}\sum_{j=1}^{q}\sup_{\theta\in\Theta}|\gamma_{ih}^{j}|E\|\varepsilon_{ht-s-j}\|_K+\|C_i^0\|_K\right)\right\}^2 \\
&\le\left\{\sum_{s=0}^{\infty}[\kappa\eta^s]\left(E\|Y_{it-s}\|_K+\sum_{j=1}^{p}\sup_{\theta\in\Theta}|\phi_{ii}^{j}|E\|Y_{it-s-j}\|_K\right.\right. \\
&\quad +\sum_{h=1,h\neq i}^{n}\sum_{j=1}^{p}\sup_{\theta\in\Theta}|\phi_{ih}^{j}|E\|Y_{ht-s-j}\|_K \\
&\quad \left.\left.+\sum_{h=1,h\neq i}^{n}\sum_{j=1}^{q}\sup_{\theta\in\Theta}|\gamma_{ih}^{j}|E\|\varepsilon_{ht-s-j}\|_K+E\|C_i^0\|_K\right)\right\}^2
\end{aligned}
$$

$$\le 2\left[\sum_{s=0}^{\infty}\kappa\eta^{s}(E\|Y_{it}\|_K^2)^{\frac{1}{2}}\right]^2 + 2\left[\sum_{s=0}^{\infty}\kappa\eta^{s}p\delta^{-1}(E\|Y_{it}\|_K^2)^{\frac{1}{2}}\right]^2$$

$$+ 2\left[\sum_{s=0}^{\infty}\kappa\eta^{s}p\delta^{-1}\sum_{h=1,h\neq i}^{n}(E\|Y_{ht}\|_K^2)^{\frac{1}{2}}\right]^2$$

$$+ 2\left[\sum_{s=0}^{\infty}\kappa\eta^{s}\delta^{-1}\sum_{h=1,h\neq i}^{n}\sum_{j=1}^{q}(E\|\varepsilon_{ht-j-s}\|_K^2)^{\frac{1}{2}}\right]^2$$

$$+ 2\left[\sum_{s=0}^{\infty}\kappa\eta^{s}\delta^{-1}\right]^2$$

$$\le 2\left(\frac{\kappa}{1-\eta}\right)^2\left\{\left(C_i + p^2\delta^{-2}C_i + p^2\delta^{-2}\sum_{h=1,h\neq i}^{n}C_h + \delta^{-2}\right)\right.$$

$$\left. + \delta^{-2}\left[\sum_{h=1,h\neq i}^{n}\sum_{j=1}^{q}(E\|\varepsilon_{ht-j-s}\|_K^2)^{\frac{1}{2}}\right]^2\right\}$$

where

$$E\|Y_{it}\|_K^2 < C_i < \infty$$

is ensured by Assumption 1; and

$$\delta^{-1} = \max\left\{\max_{1\le j\le p}\max_{1\le i\le n}\max_{1\le h\le n}\{|\phi_{ih}^{j}|\}, \max_{1\le j\le p}\max_{1\le i\le n}\max_{1\le h\le n}\{|\gamma_{ih}^{j}|\}, |\alpha_0|\right\} < \infty,$$

which is ensured by Assumption 3(i). So, we can conclude that

$$E|q_{it}^{*}| \le E\sup_{\theta\in\Theta}\|\varepsilon_{it}(\theta)\|_K^2 < C_s < \infty \tag{A.6}$$

due to the fact that

$$E\|\varepsilon_{it}(\theta)\|_K^2 - 2\left(\frac{\kappa}{1-\eta}\right)^2\delta^{-2}\left[\sum_{h=1,h\neq i}^{n}\sum_{j=1}^{q}(E\|\varepsilon_{ht-j-s}\|_K^2)^{\frac{1}{2}}\right]^2 \le C_s,$$

where

$$C_s = 2\left(\frac{\kappa}{1-\eta}\right)^2 \left(C_i + p^2\delta^{-2}C_i + p^2\delta^{-2}\sum_{h=1,h\neq i}^{n} C_h + \delta^{-2}\right) < \infty.$$

So, (ii) is proved.

A sufficient condition is provided by Lee and Hansen (1994, Lemma 8.(2)) to verify the W-LIP condition, that is, for any $i = 1, 2, \ldots, n$, the uniform boundedness of the expectation of the vector of derivatives of $q_{it}^*(\theta)$ with respect to θ is finite, namely, $\sup_{\theta\in\Theta} E|\frac{\partial q_{it}^*(\theta)}{\partial\theta}| < \infty$, which we will establish in the following proof.

Following Eq. (10), note that

$$\begin{aligned}\sup_{\theta\in\Theta} E\left|\frac{\partial q_{it}^*(\theta)}{\partial\theta}\right| &= 2\sup_{\theta\in\Theta} E\left|\left\langle s_{\frac{\partial\varepsilon_{it}(\theta)}{\partial\theta}}, s_{\varepsilon_{it}(\theta)}\right\rangle_K\right| \\ &\leq 2\left(\sup_{\theta\in\Theta} E\left\|\frac{\partial\varepsilon_{it}(\theta)}{\partial\theta}\right\|_K^2\right)^{\frac{1}{2}}\left(\sup_{\theta\in\Theta} E\|\varepsilon_{it}(\theta)\|_K^2\right)^{\frac{1}{2}} \end{aligned} \quad \text{(A.7)}$$

where

$$\frac{\partial\varepsilon_{it}(\theta)}{\partial\theta} = -Z_t(\theta) + \sum_{h=1}^{n}\sum_{j=1}^{q}(-\gamma_{hi}^j)\frac{\partial\varepsilon_{ht-j}(\theta)}{\partial\theta}.$$

So, (iii) will be proved if for any $i = 1, 2, \ldots, n$, $\sup_{\theta\in\Theta} E\|\frac{\partial\varepsilon_{it}(\theta)}{\partial\theta}\|_K^2 < \infty$.

For any kernel K satisfying Han et al. (2015, Eq. (2.6)) and any $l = 1, 2, \ldots, n$, we have

$$
\begin{aligned}
&E\sup_{\theta\in\Theta}\left\|\frac{\partial\varepsilon_{it}(\theta)}{\partial\alpha_l^0}\right\|_K^2 \\
&\quad= E\sup_{\theta\in\Theta}\left\|[1,1]+\sum_{h=1}^{n}\sum_{j=1}^{q}\gamma_{ih}^{j}\frac{\partial\varepsilon_{ht-j}(\theta)}{\partial\alpha_l^0}\right\|_K^2 \\
&\quad= E\sup_{\theta\in\Theta}\left[\|1\|_K^2+\left\|\sum_{h=1}^{n}\sum_{j=1}^{q}\gamma_{ih}^{j}\frac{\partial\varepsilon_{ht-j}(\theta)}{\partial\alpha_l^0}\right\|_K^2\right. \\
&\qquad\left.+2\sum_{h=1}^{n}\sum_{j=1}^{q}\gamma_{hi}^{j}\left\langle s_{[1,1]}, s_{\frac{\partial\varepsilon_{ht-j}(\theta)}{\partial\alpha_l^0}}\right\rangle_K\right] \\
&\quad= E\sup_{\theta\in\Theta}\left\{\|1\|_K^2+\left\|\sum_{h=1}^{n}\sum_{j=1}^{q}\gamma_{ih}^{j}\frac{\partial\varepsilon_{ht-j}(\theta)}{\partial\alpha_l^0}\right\|_K^2\right\}<\infty
\end{aligned}
$$

and

$$
\begin{aligned}
&E\sup_{\theta\in\Theta}\left\|\frac{\partial\varepsilon_{it}(\theta)}{\partial\beta_l^0}\right\|_K^2 \\
&\quad= E\sup_{\theta\in\Theta}\left\|I_0+\sum_{h=1}^{n}\sum_{j=1}^{q}\gamma_{ih}^{j}\frac{\partial\varepsilon_{ht-j}(\theta)}{\partial\beta_l^0}\right\|_K^2 \\
&\quad= E\sup_{\theta\in\Theta}\left[\|I_0\|_K^2+\left\|\sum_{h=1}^{n}\sum_{j=1}^{q}\gamma_{ih}^{j}\frac{\partial\varepsilon_{ht-j}(\theta)}{\partial\beta_l^0}\right\|_K^2\right. \\
&\qquad\left.+2\sum_{h=1}^{n}\sum_{j=1}^{q}\gamma_{ih}^{j}\left\langle s_{I_0}, s_{\frac{\partial\varepsilon_{ht-j}(\theta)}{\partial\beta_l^0}}\right\rangle_K\right] \\
&\quad= E\sup_{\theta\in\Theta}\left\{\|I_0\|_K^2+\left\|\sum_{h=1}^{n}\sum_{j=1}^{q}\gamma_{ih}^{j}\frac{\partial\varepsilon_{ht-j}(\theta)}{\partial\beta_l^0}\right\|_K^2\right\}<\infty
\end{aligned}
$$

For any $h = 1, 2, \ldots, n$,

$$
\begin{aligned}
&E \sup_{\theta\in\Theta} \left\| \frac{\partial \varepsilon_{it}(\theta)}{\partial \phi_{ih}^{j}} \right\|_K^2 \\
&= E \sup_{\theta\in\Theta} \left\| \frac{\partial}{\partial \phi_{ih}^{j}} \left[\sum_{s=0}^{\infty} \sum_{m=1}^{q} (c_m \eta_m^s) \left(Y_{it} - \sum_{j=1}^{p} \phi_{ii}^{j} y_{it-j-s} \right.\right.\right. \\
&\qquad \left.\left.\left. - \sum_{h=1,h\neq i}^{n} \sum_{j=1}^{p} \phi_{ih}^{j} y_{ht-j-s} - \sum_{h=1,h\neq i}^{n} \sum_{j=1}^{q} \gamma_{ih}^{j} \varepsilon_{ht-j-s} \right) \right] \right\|_K^2 \\
&= E \sup_{\theta\in\Theta} \left\| \sum_{s=0}^{\infty} \sum_{m=1}^{q} (c_m \eta_m^s) \left[-y_{ht-j-s} - \sum_{h=1,h\neq i}^{n} \sum_{j=1}^{q} \gamma_{ih}^{j} \frac{\partial \varepsilon_{ht-j-s}}{\partial \phi_{ih}^{j}} \right] \right\|_K^2 \\
&= E \sup_{\theta\in\Theta} \left\| \sum_{s=0}^{\infty} \sum_{m=1}^{q} (c_m \eta_m^s) y_{ht-j-s} \right\|_K^2 \\
&= E \left\| \sum_{s=0}^{\infty} \kappa \eta^s Y_{it} \right\|_K^2 \leq \frac{\kappa^2 C_h}{(1-\eta)^2} < \infty.
\end{aligned}
$$

Similarly,

$$
\begin{aligned}
E \sup_{\theta\in\Theta} \left\| \frac{\partial \varepsilon_{it}(\theta)}{\partial \gamma_{ih}^{j}} \right\|_K^2 &= E \sup_{\theta\in\Theta} \| - A(L) \varepsilon_{ht-j}(\theta) \|_K^2 \\
&= E \sup_{\theta\in\Theta} \left\| \sum_{s=0}^{\infty} \sum_{m=1}^{q} (c_m \eta_m^s) [\varepsilon_{ht-j-s}(\theta)] \right\|_K^2 \\
&\leq E \sup_{\theta\in\Theta} \left\| \sum_{s=0}^{\infty} \kappa \eta^s \varepsilon_{it}(\theta) \right\|_K^2 \leq \frac{\kappa^2 C_s}{(1-\eta)^2} < \infty.
\end{aligned}
$$

So we have verified that the inner product of each derivative in $\frac{\partial \varepsilon_{it}(\theta)}{\partial \theta}$ is bounded in expectation, and therefore

$$
\sup_{\theta\in\Theta} E \left\| \frac{\partial \varepsilon_{it}(\theta)}{\partial \theta} \right\|_K^2 \leq E \sup_{\theta\in\Theta} \left\| \frac{\partial \varepsilon_{it}(\theta)}{\partial \theta} \right\|_K^2 < \infty. \tag{A.8}
$$

In sum, Proposition 2.1 is proved according to Eqs. (15)–(17). ■

Proposition 2.2. *Let $\varepsilon_{it}(\theta)$ be defined as Eq. (7). We assume some initual values for $\{Y_{is}\}_{s=-p+1}^{0}$ and $\{\varepsilon_{is}\}_{s=-p+1}^{0}$ with $Y_{is} = \hat{Y}_{i0}, \varepsilon_{is} = \hat{\varepsilon}_{i0}$. Put*

$$Q_T^* = \frac{1}{nT} \sum_{t=1}^{T} \sum_{i=1}^{n} \|\varepsilon_{it}(\theta)\|_K^2$$

and

$$\hat{Q}_T(\theta) = \frac{1}{nT} \sum_{t=1}^{T} \sum_{i=1}^{n} \|\varepsilon_{it}(\hat{\theta})\|_K^2.$$

Assumptions 1, 2 and 3(i) hold. Then

$$\sup_{\theta \in \Theta} |Q_T^* - \hat{Q}_T(\theta)| \xrightarrow{p} 0$$

Proof. If for any $i = 1, 2, \ldots, n$ and any $t = 1, 2, \ldots, T$, $|\|\varepsilon_{it}(\theta)\|_K^2 - \|\hat{\varepsilon}_{it}(\theta)\|_K^2|$ is dominated by a converging sequence that is independent of θ, so that $E \sup_{\theta \in \Theta} \sum_{t=1}^{T} |\varepsilon_{it}(\theta)\|_K^2 - \|\hat{\varepsilon}_{it}(\theta)\|_K^2|$ converges to a finite constant as $T \to \infty$, which follows for any $i = 1, 2, \ldots, n$,

$$\sup_{\theta \in \Theta} \sum_{t=1}^{T} |\|\varepsilon_{it}(\theta)\|_K^2 - \|\hat{\varepsilon}_{it}(\theta)\|_K^2| \xrightarrow{p} 0,$$

then proposition 2.2 will be proved.

So all we need to prove is for any $i = 1, 2, \ldots, n$ and any $t = 1, 2, \ldots, T$, $|\|\varepsilon_{it}(\theta)\|_K^2 - \|\hat{\varepsilon}_{it}(\theta)\|_K^2|$ is dominated by a converging sequence that is independent of θ.

Let

$$\xi_{it} = (\varepsilon_{it}(\theta), \varepsilon_{it-1}(\theta), \ldots, \varepsilon_{it-q+1}(\theta))^{\tau},$$

$$\Upsilon_i = \begin{pmatrix} -\gamma_{ii}^1 & -\gamma_{ii}^2 & \ldots & -\gamma_{ii}^{q-1} & -\gamma_{ii}^q \\ 1 & 0 & \ldots & 0 & 0 \\ \vdots & \vdots & \ddots & \vdots & \vdots \\ 0 & 0 & \ldots & 1 & 0 \end{pmatrix},$$

$$V_{it} = \left(\left[B_i(L)Y_{it} - \sum_{h=1,h\neq i}^{n} B_h(L)Y_{ht} - \sum_{h=1,h\neq i} A_h(L)\varepsilon_{ht} - C_0^i \right], \right.$$

$$\left. [0,0], \ldots, [0,0] \right)^{\tau},$$

then we have

$$\xi_{it} = \Upsilon_i \xi_{it-1} + V_{it}.$$

By recursive substitution, we have

$$\xi_{it} = \Upsilon_i^t \xi_{i0} + \sum_{j=1}^{t-1} \Upsilon_i^{t-j} V_{ij} + V_{it}.$$

Note that

$$\begin{aligned} \varepsilon_{it}(\theta) - \hat{\varepsilon}_{it}(\theta) = & \sum_{j=1}^{q} a_{1j}^{(it)}(\gamma)[\varepsilon_{i1-j}(\theta) - \hat{\varepsilon}_{i0}] \\ & - \sum_{j=1}^{p} a_{11}^{(it-j)}(\gamma) \left[\sum_{m=j}^{p} \phi_{ii}^{m}(Y_{ij-m} - \hat{Y}_{i0}) \right. \\ & \left. - \sum_{h=1,h\neq i}^{n} \left(\sum_{m=j}^{p} \phi_{ih}^{m}(Y_{hj-m} - \hat{Y}_{h0}) + \sum_{m=j}^{q} \gamma_{ih}^{m}(\varepsilon_{hj-m}(\theta) - \hat{\varepsilon}_{h0}) \right) \right] \end{aligned} \tag{A.9}$$

Using Minkowski's and the C_r inequalities, Eq. (18) induces that

$$\begin{aligned} & E \sup_{\theta\in\Theta} \|\hat{\varepsilon}_{it}^2(\theta) - \varepsilon_{it}(\theta)\|_K^2 \\ & \leq 2 \left[\sum_{j=1}^{q} \sup_{\theta\in\Theta} |a_{1j}^{(t)}(\gamma)| \left(E \sup_{\theta\in\Theta} \|\varepsilon_{i1-j}(\theta) - \hat{\varepsilon}_{i0}\|_K^2 \right) \right]^2 \\ & + 6 \left[\sum_{j=1}^{p} \sum_{m=j}^{p} \sup_{\theta\in\Theta} |a_{11}^{(it-j)}(\gamma)\phi_{ii}^{m}| \left(E \sup_{\theta\in\Theta} \|Y_{ij-m} - \hat{Y}_{i0}\|_K^2 \right)^{1/2} \right]^2 \end{aligned}$$

$$+6\left[\sum_{j=1}^{p}\sum_{h=1,h\neq i}^{n}\sum_{m=j}^{p}\sup_{\theta\in\Theta}|a_{11}^{(it-j)}(\gamma)\phi_{ih}^{m}|\left(E\sup_{\theta\in\Theta}\|Y_{hj-m}-\hat{Y}_{h0}\|_K^2\right)^{1/2}\right]^2$$

$$+6\left[\sum_{j=1}^{p}\sum_{h=1,h\neq i}^{n}\sum_{m=j}^{p}\sup_{\theta\in\Theta}|a_{11}^{(it-j)}(\gamma)\gamma_{ih}^{m}|\left(E\sup_{\theta\in\Theta}\|\varepsilon_{hj-m}-\hat{\varepsilon}_{h0}\|_K^2\right)^{1/2}\right]^2$$

By Minkowski's and the C_r inequalities, for any $1\leq h\leq n$, it follows that there exists $0<C_2<\infty$ such that

$$\begin{aligned}\sum_{m=j}^{p}\sup_{\theta\in\Theta}|\phi_{ih}^{m}|\left(E\sup_{\theta\in\Theta}\|Y_{hj-m}-\hat{Y}_{h0}\|_K^2\right)^{1/2}\\ \leq\left(2p\delta^{-1}E\|Y_{ht}\|_K^2+2p\delta^{-1}E\sup_{\theta\in\Theta}\|\hat{Y}_{i0}\|_K^2\right)^{1/2}\\ <C_2.\end{aligned}$$

Secondly, by the Minkowski and the C_r inequalities, for any $1\leq h\leq n$, it follow that there exists $0<C_3<\infty$

$$\begin{aligned}E\left(\sup_{\theta\in\Theta}\|\varepsilon_{h1-j}(\theta)-\hat{\varepsilon}_{i0}\|_K^2\right)^{1/2}&\leq\left(2E\sup_{\theta\in\Theta}\|\varepsilon_{h1-j}(\theta)\|_K^2+2E\sup_{\theta\in\Theta}\|\hat{\varepsilon}_{i0}\|_K^2\right)^{1/2}\\&<C_3.\end{aligned}$$

Thirdly, according to Han et al. (2015, A28), we have

$$\sup_{\theta\in\Theta}|a_{1j}^{(t)}(\gamma)|\leq\phi\lambda^t,$$

$$\text{where}\quad \phi=q\times\max_{1\leq i\leq q}\{\phi_{1i}\phi^{ij}\},\quad\text{and}\quad 0<\lambda=\max_{1\leq i\leq q}\{|\lambda_j|\}<1.$$

In particular, $\sup_{\theta\in\Theta}|a_{11}^{(t)}(\gamma)|\leq\lambda^t$. Then, we have

$$\begin{aligned}&2E\sup_{\theta\in\Theta}\|\hat{\varepsilon}_{it}-\varepsilon_{it}\|_K^2\\&\leq[2+6(n-1)]C_3^2q^2\phi^2\lambda^{2t}+12\left[p(n-1)\delta^{-1}C_2\left(\sum_{i=1}^{p}\lambda^{t-i}\right)\right]^2\end{aligned}$$

$$\leq [2+6(n-1)]C_3^2 q^2 \phi^2 \lambda^{2t} + \frac{12p^2(n-1)^2\delta^2 C_2^2}{(1-\lambda)^2\lambda^{2t}} \leq W_1 \lambda^{2t},$$

where $W_1 = [2+6(n-1)]C_3^2 q^2 \phi^2 + \frac{12p^2(n-1)^2\delta^2 C_2^2}{(1-\lambda)^2\lambda^2}$.

By the triangle and the Cauchy–Schwarz inequalities, for each $\theta \in \Theta$ and $T \to \infty$

$$\begin{aligned}
&E \sup_{\theta\in\Theta} |\hat{Q}_T(\theta) - Q_T^*(\theta)| \\
&\leq E \sup_{\theta\in\Theta} \frac{1}{nT} \sum_{i=1}^{n} \sum_{t=1}^{T} |\|\hat{\varepsilon}_{it}(\theta) - \varepsilon_{it}(\theta) + \varepsilon_{it}(\theta)\|_K^2 - \|\varepsilon_{it}(\theta)\|_K^2| \\
&\leq \frac{1}{nT} \sum_{i=1}^{n} \sum_{t=1}^{T} \left[E \sup_{\theta\in\Theta} \|\hat{\varepsilon}_{it}(\theta) - \varepsilon_{it}(\theta)\|_K^2 + 2E \sup_{\theta\in\Theta} |\langle s_{\hat{\varepsilon}_{it}(\theta)-\varepsilon_{it}(\theta)}, s_{\varepsilon_{it}(\theta)} \rangle_K| \right] \\
&\leq \frac{1}{nT} \sum_{i=1}^{n} \sum_{t=1}^{T} \left\{ E \sup_{\theta\in\Theta} \|\hat{\varepsilon}_{it}(\theta) - \varepsilon_{it}(\theta)\|_K^2 \right. \\
&\quad \left. + \left[E \left(\sup_{\theta\in\Theta} \|\hat{\varepsilon}_{it}(\theta) - \varepsilon_{it}(\theta)\|_K^2 \right)^{\frac{1}{2}} E \left(\sup_{\theta\in\Theta} \|\varepsilon_{it}(\theta)\|_K^2 \right)^{\frac{1}{2}} \right] \right\} \\
&\leq \frac{1}{nT} \sum_{i=1}^{n} \left| W_1 \sum_{t=1}^{T} \lambda^{2t} + 2W_2 \sum_{t=1}^{T} \lambda^t \right| \to 0,
\end{aligned}$$

where $E \sup_{\theta\in\Theta} \|\varepsilon_{it}(\theta)\|_K^2 < \infty$ is proved. So we have

$$P\left(\sup_{\theta\in\Theta} |\hat{Q}_T(\theta) - \hat{Q}_T^*(\theta)| \geq \epsilon \right) \leq \frac{1}{\epsilon} E \sup_{\theta\in\Theta} |\hat{Q}_T(\theta) - \hat{Q}_T^*(\theta)| \to 0$$

as $T \to \infty$. And then we prove Proposition 2.2. ■

Proposition 3.1. *Under Assumptions 1–5. Put*

$$M(\theta) = \frac{1}{n} \sum_{i=1}^{n} E\left[\frac{\partial^2 q_{it}^*(\theta)}{\partial\theta\partial\theta^\tau} \right], \quad \hat{M}_T^*(\theta) = \frac{1}{nT} \sum_{t=1}^{T} \sum_{i=1}^{n} \frac{\partial^2 q_{it}^*(\theta)}{\partial\theta\partial\theta^\tau},$$

where $q_{it}^*(\theta) = \|\varepsilon_{it}(\theta)\|_K^2$. *Then,* $\sup_{\theta\in\Theta} |\hat{M}_T^*(\theta) - M(\theta)| \xrightarrow{p} 0$ *as* $T \to \infty$.

Proof. Analogous to the proof of Proposition 2.1, we will verify conditions (ii) P-WLLN and (iii) W-LIP.

We first verify condition (ii) by showing that $\{\frac{1}{n}\sum_{i=1}^{n}\frac{\partial^2 q_{it}^*(\theta)}{\partial\theta\partial\theta^\tau}\}$ is a stationary and ergodic random matrix process with $E|\frac{\partial^2 q_{it}^*(\theta)}{\partial\theta\partial\theta^\tau}|<\infty$. $\frac{\partial^2 q_{it}^*(\theta)}{\partial\theta\partial\theta'}=2\|\frac{\partial\varepsilon_{it}(\theta)}{\partial\theta}\|_K^2+2\langle s_{\frac{\partial^2\varepsilon_{it}(\theta)}{\partial\theta\partial\theta'}},s_{\varepsilon_{it}(\theta)}\rangle_K$, and we have shown that $\{\varepsilon_{it}(\theta)\}$ is a stationary and ergodic process for all $\theta\in\Theta$. Therefore, $\{\frac{\partial\varepsilon_{it}(\theta)}{\partial\theta}\}$ and $\{\frac{\partial^2\varepsilon_{it}(\theta)}{\partial\theta\partial\theta'}\}$ are both stationary and ergodic for all $\theta\in\Theta$, which implies that $\{\frac{1}{n}\sum_{i=1}^{n}\frac{\partial^2 q_{it}^*(\theta)}{\partial\theta\partial\theta'}\}$ is a stationary and ergodic matrix process. Note that we have

$$
\begin{aligned}
E\sup_{\theta\in\Theta}\left|\frac{1}{n}\sum_{i=1}^{n}\frac{\partial^2 q_{it}^*(\theta)}{\partial\theta\partial\theta'}\right| &\le \frac{2}{n}\sum_{i=1}^{n}E\sup_{\theta\in\Theta}\left\|\frac{\partial\varepsilon_{it}(\theta)}{\partial\theta}\right\|_K^2\\
&\quad+\frac{2}{n}\sum_{i=1}^{n}\left(E\sup_{\theta\in\Theta}\|\frac{\partial^2\varepsilon_{it}(\theta)}{\partial\theta\partial\theta'}\|_K^2\right)^{\frac{1}{2}}\\
&\quad\times\left(E\sup_{\theta\in\Theta}\|\varepsilon_{it}(\theta)\|_K^2\right)^{\frac{1}{2}}
\end{aligned}
\tag{A.10}
$$

by Cauchy–Schwarz inequality. Following Proposition 2.1, $E\sup_{\theta\in\Theta}\|\frac{\partial^2\varepsilon_{it}(\theta)}{\partial\theta_k\partial\theta_l}\|_K^2<\infty$ for any $k,l=1,\ldots,\mathbf{k}$ is induced. Meanwhile, there are $\mathbf{k}^2$ distinct second derivatives of $\frac{\partial^2\varepsilon_{it}(\theta)}{\partial\theta_k\partial\theta_l}$ for different i, each of whose expectations needs to be bounded. Then follows $E|\frac{1}{n}\sum_{i=1}^{n}\frac{\partial^2 q_{it}^*(\theta)}{\partial\theta\partial\theta^\tau}|<\infty$. According to Eq. (19), P-WLLN holds for $\hat{M}_T^*(\theta)$.

The condition (iii) W-LIP holds for $\hat{M}_T^*(\theta)$. $\sup_{\theta\in\Theta}E|\frac{1}{n}\sum_{i=1}^{n}\frac{\partial}{\partial\theta_j}[\frac{\partial^2 q_{it}^*}{\partial\theta_k\partial\theta_l}]|<\infty$ can also be verified for all $j,k,l=1,\ldots,\mathbf{k}$. In together with Assumption 3(i), we have established Proposition 3.1 by (ii) and (iii). ■

Proposition 3.2. *Put* $\hat{M}_T(\theta)=\frac{1}{nT}\sum_{t=1}^{T}\sum_{i=1}^{n}\frac{\partial^2 q_{it}(\theta)}{\partial\theta\partial\theta'}$, *where* $q_{it}(\theta)=\|\hat{\varepsilon}_{it}(\theta)\|_K^2$ *and is computed with the initial values* $\{\hat{Y}_{it}\}_{t=-p+1}^{0}$ *and* $\{\hat{\varepsilon}_{it}(\theta)\}_{t=-q+1}^{0}$. *Suppose Assumptions 1–5 hold. Then*

$$
\begin{aligned}
&\sup_{\theta\in\Theta}|\hat{M}_T^*-\hat{M}_T(\theta)|\\
&=\sup_{\theta\in\Theta}\frac{1}{nT}\left|\sum_{i=1}^{n}\sum_{t=1}^{T}\left(\frac{\partial^2 q_{it}(\theta)}{\partial\theta\partial\theta'}-\frac{\partial^2 q_{it}^*(\theta)}{\partial\theta\partial\theta'}\right)\right|\xrightarrow{p}0 \quad \text{as } T\to\infty.
\end{aligned}
$$

Proof. For any $i=1,2,\ldots,n$, by the triangle and the Cauchy–Schwarz inequalities, it follows that

$$\begin{aligned}
&\frac{1}{2}E\sup_{\theta\in\Theta}\left|\frac{\partial^2 q_{it}(\theta)}{\partial\theta\partial\theta'}-\frac{\partial^2 q^*_{it}(\theta)}{\partial\theta\partial\theta'}\right| \\
&\leq E\sup_{\theta\in\Theta}\left|\left\|\frac{\partial\hat{\varepsilon}_{it}(\theta)}{\partial\theta}\right\|_K^2-\left\|\frac{\partial\varepsilon_{it}(\theta)}{\partial\theta}\right\|_K^2\right| \\
&\quad +E\sup_{\theta\in\Theta}\left|\left\langle s_{\frac{\partial^2\hat{\varepsilon}_{it}(\theta)}{\partial\theta\partial\theta'}}, s_{\hat{\varepsilon}_{it}(\theta)}\right\rangle_K-\left\langle s_{\frac{\partial^2\varepsilon_{it}(\theta)}{\partial\theta\partial\theta'}}, s_{\varepsilon_{it}(\theta)}\right\rangle_K\right| \\
&\leq E\sup_{\theta\in\Theta}\left\|\frac{\partial[\hat{\varepsilon}_{it}(\theta)-\varepsilon_{it}(\theta)]}{\partial\theta}\right\|_K^2+2E\sup_{\theta\in\Theta}\left\|\frac{\partial[\hat{\varepsilon}_{it}(\theta)-\varepsilon_{it}(\theta)]}{\partial\theta}\right\|_K\left\|\frac{\partial\varepsilon_{it}(\theta)}{\partial\theta}\right\|_K \\
&\quad +E\sup_{\theta\in\Theta}\left\|\frac{\partial^2[\hat{\varepsilon}_{it}(\theta)-\varepsilon_{it}(\theta)]}{\partial\theta\partial\theta'}\right\|_K\|\hat{\varepsilon}_{it}(\theta)-\varepsilon_{it}(\theta)\|_K \\
&\quad +E\sup_{\theta\in\Theta}\left\|\frac{\partial^2[\hat{\varepsilon}_{it}(\theta)-\varepsilon_{it}(\theta)]}{\partial\theta\partial\theta'}\right\|_K\|\varepsilon_{it}(\theta)\|_K \\
&\quad +E\sup_{\theta\in\Theta}\left\|\frac{\partial^2\varepsilon_{it}(\theta)}{\partial\theta\partial\theta'}\right\|_K\|\hat{\varepsilon}_{it}(\theta)-\varepsilon_{it}(\theta)\|_K
\end{aligned}$$

We shall show that both $\sum_{t=1}^T\|\frac{\partial[\hat{\varepsilon}_{it}(\theta)-\varepsilon_{it}(\theta)]}{\partial\theta}\|_K^2$ and $\sum_{t=1}^T\|\frac{\partial^2[\hat{\varepsilon}_{it}(\theta)-\varepsilon_{it}(\theta)]}{\partial\theta\partial\theta'}\|_K^2$ converge to finite constants as $T\to\infty$. Due to the proof of Proposition 2.2, we can conclude that

$$\sum_{t=1}^T\|\frac{\partial[\hat{\varepsilon}_{it}(\theta)-\varepsilon_{it}(\theta)]}{\partial\theta}\|_K^2\to D_1 \quad as\ T\to\infty$$

and

$$\sum_{t=1}^T\|\frac{\partial^2[\hat{\varepsilon}_{it}(\theta)-\varepsilon_{it}(\theta)]}{\partial\theta\partial\theta'}\|_K^2\to D_2 \quad as\ T\to\infty.$$

where D_1 and D_2 are finite constants. Combining the previous proof, we have that

$$\sum_{t=1}^T E\sup_{\theta\in\Theta}\left|\frac{\partial^2 q_{it}(\theta)}{\partial\theta\partial\theta'}-\frac{\partial^2 q^*_{it}(\theta)}{\partial\theta\partial\theta'}\right|\to D \quad as\ T\to\infty,$$

for any $i = 1, 2, \ldots, n$, where D is a finite constant. Therefore,

$$E \sup_{\theta\in\Theta} |\hat{M}_T(\theta) - \hat{M}^*_T(\theta)|$$
$$= E \sup_{\theta\in\Theta} \frac{1}{T} \sum_{t=1}^{T} \left| \frac{\partial^2 q_{it}(\theta)}{\partial\theta\partial\theta'} - \frac{\partial^2 q^*_{it}(\theta)}{\partial\theta\partial\theta'} \right| \to 0 \quad as \ T \to \infty.$$

It follows from that

$$P\left(\sup_{\theta\in\Theta} |\hat{M}_T(\theta) - \hat{M}^*_T(\theta)| \geq \epsilon \right) \leq E \sup_{\theta\in\Theta} |\hat{M}_T(\theta) - \hat{M}^*_T(\theta)| \to 0 \quad as \ T \to \infty.$$

These above-mentioned establish Proposition 3.2. ■

Proposition 4.1. *Under Assumptions 1–5. Put* $V(\theta) = \frac{1}{n^2} E\{[\sum_{i=1}^n \frac{\partial q^*_{it}(\theta)}{\partial\theta}][\sum_{i=1}^n \frac{\partial q^*_{it}(\theta)}{\partial\theta'}]\}$, $\hat{V}^*_T(\theta) = \frac{1}{n^2 T} \sum_{t=1}^T [\sum_{i=1}^n \frac{\partial q^*_{it}(\theta)}{\partial\theta}][\sum_{i=1}^n \frac{\partial q^*_{it}(\theta)}{\partial\theta'}]$, *where* $q^*_{it}(\theta) = \|\varepsilon_{it}(\theta)\|^2_K$. *Then,* $\sup_{\theta\in\Theta} |\hat{V}^*_T(\theta) - V(\theta)| \xrightarrow{p} 0$.

Proof. Analogous to the proof of Propositions 2.2 and 3.2, we will verify conditions (ii)P-WLLN and (iii) W-LIP.

We first verify condition (ii) by showing that $\{\frac{1}{n^2}[\sum_{i=1}^n \frac{\partial q^*_{it}(\theta)}{\partial\theta}][\sum_{i=1}^n \frac{\partial q^*_{it}(\theta)}{\partial\theta'}]\}$ is a stationary and ergodic random matrix process with $\frac{1}{n^2} E|[\sum_{i=1}^n \frac{\partial q^*_{it}(\theta)}{\partial\theta}][\sum_{i=1}^n \frac{\partial q^*_{it}(\theta)}{\partial\theta'}]| < \infty$, where

$$\frac{1}{n^2}\left[\sum_{i=1}^{n} \frac{\partial q^*_{it}(\theta)}{\partial\theta}\right]\left[\sum_{i=1}^{n} \frac{\partial q^*_{it}(\theta)}{\partial\theta'}\right]$$
$$= \frac{4}{n^2}\left[\sum_{i=1}^{n} \left\langle s_{\frac{\partial\varepsilon_{it}(\theta)}{\partial\theta}}, s_{\varepsilon_{it}(\theta)} \right\rangle_K\right]\left[\sum_{i=1}^{n} \left\langle s_{\varepsilon_{it}(\theta)}, s_{\frac{\partial\varepsilon_{it}(\theta)}{\partial\theta'}} \right\rangle_K\right]. \quad (A.11)$$

Therefore, $\{\frac{1}{n^2}[\sum_{i=1}^n \frac{\partial q^*_{it}(\theta)}{\partial\theta}][\sum_{i=1}^n \frac{\partial q^*_{it}(\theta)}{\partial\theta'}]\}$ is a stationary and ergodic random matrix process, provided that for all $\theta \in \Theta$, $\{\varepsilon_{it}(\theta)\}$ and $\{\frac{\partial\varepsilon_{it}(\theta)}{\partial\theta}\}$ are both stationary and ergodic shown in the previous proof.

Now we consider $\frac{1}{n^2}E|[\sum_{i=1}^n \frac{\partial q_{it}^*(\theta)}{\partial\theta}][\sum_{i=1}^n \frac{\partial q_{it}^*(\theta)}{\partial\theta'}]|$. Note that

$$\begin{aligned}
&\frac{1}{n^2}E\left|\left[\sum_{i=1}^n \frac{\partial q_{it}^*(\theta)}{\partial\theta}\right]\left[\sum_{i=1}^n \frac{\partial q_{it}^*(\theta)}{\partial\theta'}\right]\right| \le \frac{1}{n^2}\sum_{i=1}^n\sum_{j=1}^n E\left|\frac{\partial q_{it}^*(\theta)}{\partial\theta}\frac{\partial q_{jt}^*(\theta)}{\partial\theta'}\right| \\
&= \frac{4}{n^2}\sum_{i=1}^n\sum_{j=1}^n E\left|\left\langle S_{\frac{\partial\varepsilon_{it}(\theta)}{\partial\theta}}, S_{\varepsilon_{it}(\theta)}\right\rangle_K \left\langle S_{\varepsilon_{jt}(\theta)}, S_{\frac{\partial\varepsilon_{jt}(\theta)}{\partial\theta'}}\right\rangle_K\right| \\
&\le \frac{8}{n^2}\sum_{i=1}^n E\left|\langle S_{\varepsilon_{it}(\theta)}, S_{\varepsilon_{it}(\theta)}\rangle_K \left\langle S_{\frac{\partial\varepsilon_{it}(\theta)}{\partial\theta}}, S_{\frac{\partial\varepsilon_{it}(\theta)}{\partial\theta}}\right\rangle_K\right| \\
&\quad + \frac{4}{n^2}\sum_{i\ne j}^n E\left|\left\langle S_{\frac{\partial\varepsilon_{it}(\theta)}{\partial\theta}}, S_{\varepsilon_{it}(\theta)}\right\rangle_K \left\langle S_{\varepsilon_{jt}(\theta)}, S_{\frac{\partial\varepsilon_{jt}(\theta)}{\partial\theta'}}\right\rangle_K\right| \\
&\le \frac{8}{n^2}\sum_{i=1}^n \left(E\sup_{\theta\in\Theta}\|\varepsilon_{it}(\theta)\|_K^4\right)^{1/2}\left(E\sup_{\theta\in\Theta}\left\|\frac{\partial\varepsilon_{it}(\theta)}{\partial\theta}\right\|_K^4\right)^{1/2} \\
&\quad + \frac{4}{n^2}\sum_{i\ne j}^n \left(E\sup_{\theta\in\Theta}\|\varepsilon_{it}(\theta)\|_K^2\right)^{1/2}\left(E\sup_{\theta\in\Theta}\|\varepsilon_{jt}(\theta)\|_K^2\right)^{1/2} \\
&\quad \times \left(E\sup_{\theta\in\Theta}\left\|\frac{\partial\varepsilon_{it}(\theta)}{\partial\theta}\right\|_K^2\right)^{1/2}\left(E\sup_{\theta\in\Theta}\left\|\frac{\partial\varepsilon_{jt}(\theta)}{\partial\theta}\right\|_K^2\right)^{1/2} \\
&< \infty. \qquad \text{(A.12)}
\end{aligned}$$

where $E\sup_{\theta\in\Theta}\|\varepsilon_{it}(\theta)\|_K^4 < \infty$ and $E\sup_{\theta\in\Theta}\|\frac{\partial\varepsilon_{it}(\theta)}{\partial\theta}\|_K^4 < \infty$ according to Proposition 2.1 and the form of $\frac{\partial\varepsilon_{it}(\theta)}{\partial\theta}$. Hence, (ii)P-WLLN holds for $\hat{V}_T^*(\theta)$ following Eq. (21).

Next condition (iii) holds for $\hat{V}_T^*(\theta)$ is verified by $\sup_{\theta\in\Theta}E|\frac{\partial}{\partial\theta_j}\{[\sum_{i=1}^n \frac{\partial q_{it}(\theta)}{\partial\theta_k}][\sum_{i=1}^n \frac{\partial q_{it}(\theta)}{\partial\theta_l}]\}| < \infty$ for all $j,k,l = 1,\ldots,\mathbf{k}$ analogue with Proposition 2.1. Therefore, conditions (ii) and (iii) hold. In together with Assumption 3(i), we have established Proposition 4.1. ■

Proposition 4.2. *Put* $\hat{V}_T(\theta) = \frac{1}{n^2T}\sum_{t=1}^T[\sum_{i=1}^n \frac{\partial q_{it}(\theta)}{\partial\theta}][\sum_{i=1}^n \frac{\partial q_{it}(\theta)}{\partial\theta'}]$, *where* $q_{it}(\theta) = \|\hat{\varepsilon}_{it}(\theta)\|_K^2$ *and is computed with the initial values* $\{\hat{y}_{it}\}_{t=-p+1}^0$ *and* $\{\hat{\varepsilon}_{it}(\theta)\}_{t=-q+1}^0$. *Suppose Assumptions 1–5 hold. Then*

$$E\sup_{\theta\in\Theta}|\hat{V}_T^* - \hat{V}_T(\theta)| = E\sup_{\theta\in\Theta}\frac{1}{n^2T}\left|\sum_{t=1}^{T}\left[\sum_{i=1}^{n}\frac{\partial q_{it}(\theta)}{\partial\theta}\right]\left[\sum_{i=1}^{n}\frac{\partial q_{it}(\theta)}{\partial\theta'}\right]\right.$$
$$\left.-\sum_{t=1}^{T}\left[\sum_{i=1}^{n}\frac{\partial q_{it}^*(\theta)}{\partial\theta}\right]\left[\sum_{i=1}^{n}\frac{\partial q_{it}^*(\theta)}{\partial\theta'}\right]\right| \to 0,$$

as $T \to \infty$.

Proof. By the triangle inequalities, it follows that

$$\frac{1}{2}E\sup_{\theta\in\Theta}\left|\sum_{i=1}^{n}\frac{\partial q_{it}(\theta)}{\partial\theta}\sum_{j=1}^{n}\frac{\partial q_{jt}(\theta)}{\partial\theta'} - \sum_{i=1}^{n}\frac{\partial q_{it}^*(\theta)}{\partial\theta}\sum_{j=1}^{n}\frac{\partial q_{jt}^*(\theta)}{\partial\theta'}\right|$$
$$\leq \frac{1}{2}\sum_{i=1}^{n}\sum_{j=1}^{n}\left|\frac{\partial q_{it}(\theta)}{\partial\theta}\frac{\partial q_{jt}(\theta)}{\partial\theta'} - \frac{\partial q_{it}^*(\theta)}{\partial\theta}\frac{\partial q_{jt}^*(\theta)}{\partial\theta'}\right|$$

We can verified that $\frac{1}{2}E\sup_{\theta\in\Theta}|\frac{\partial q_{it}^*(\theta)}{\partial\theta}\frac{\partial q_{it}^*(\theta)}{\partial\theta'} - \frac{\partial q_{it}^*(\theta)}{\partial\theta}\frac{\partial q_{it}^*(\theta)}{\partial\theta'}| < \infty$, for any $i, j = 1, 2, \ldots, n$ analogue with Proposition 2.2 and 3.2 by Cauchy–Schwarz inequalities, which yields that $E\sup_{\theta\in\Theta}|\hat{V}_T(\theta) - \hat{V}_T^*(\theta)| \to 0$ as $T \to \infty$. Note that

$$P\left(\sup_{\theta\in\Theta}|\hat{V}_T(\theta) - \hat{V}_T^*(\theta)| \geq \epsilon\right) \leq \frac{1}{\epsilon}E\sup_{\theta\in\Theta}|\hat{V}_T(\theta) - \hat{V}_T^*(\theta)| \to 0 \;\; as \;\; T \to \infty.$$

Proposition 4.2 is verified. ■

Proof of Theorem 1. According to Propositions 2.1 and 2.2, as $T \to \infty$, we have

$$\sup_{\theta\in\Theta}|\hat{Q}_T(\theta) - Q(\theta)| \leq \sup_{\theta\in\Theta}|\hat{Q}_T(\theta) - \hat{Q}_T^*(\theta)| + \sup_{\theta\in\Theta}|\hat{Q}_T^*(\theta) - Q(\theta)| \xrightarrow{p} 0.$$

Meanwhile, $Q(\theta)$ is uniquely minimized at $\theta = \theta^0$ and $Q(\theta)$ is continuous on a compact space Θ, which are ensured by Proposition 1. Theorem 1 is proved by Amemiya (1985, Theorem 4.1.1). ■

Proof of Theorem 2. The first-order derivatives of the minimum D_K-distance problem $\hat{\theta} = \arg_{\theta\in\Theta}\min\hat{Q}_T(\theta)$ satisfy

$$\frac{1}{nT}\sum_{t=1}^{T}\sum_{i=1}^{n}\frac{\partial q_{it}(\hat{\theta})}{\partial\theta} = \frac{1}{nT}\sum_{t=1}^{T}\sum_{i=1}^{n}2\left\langle s_{\frac{\partial\varepsilon_{it}(\hat{\theta})}{\partial\varepsilon_\theta}}, s_{\varepsilon_{it}(\hat{\theta})}\right\rangle_K = 0.$$

where $\frac{\partial \hat{\varepsilon}_{it}(\hat{\theta})}{\partial \theta} = -Z_t(\hat{\theta}) + \sum_{h=1}^{n} \sum_{j=1}^{q} (-\gamma_{hi}^{j}) \frac{\partial \hat{\varepsilon}_{ht-j}(\hat{\theta})}{\partial \theta}$ according to Eq. (10). Since Assumption 3(ii) holds, we take the Taylor expansion of $\frac{1}{nT} \sum_{t=1}^{T} \sum_{i=1}^{n} \frac{\partial q_{it}(\hat{\theta})}{\partial \theta}$ at θ^0,

$$\frac{1}{nT} \sum_{t=1}^{T} \sum_{i=1}^{n} \frac{\partial q_{it}(\hat{\theta})}{\partial \theta} = \frac{1}{nT} \sum_{t=1}^{T} \sum_{i=1}^{n} \frac{\partial q_{it}(\theta^0)}{\partial \theta} + \frac{1}{nT} \sum_{t=1}^{T} \sum_{i=1}^{n} \frac{\partial^2 q_{it}(\widetilde{\theta})}{\partial \theta \partial \theta'} (\hat{\theta} - \theta^0)$$
$$= 0.$$

where $\widetilde{\theta}$ is a segment between θ^0 and $\hat{\theta}$ such that $\lim_{T \to \infty} \widetilde{\theta} = \theta^0$. Note that for $k = 1, \ldots, \mathbf{k}$, the values of $0 < \upsilon_k < 1$ of $\widetilde{\theta}_k = \upsilon_k \theta^0 + (1 - \upsilon_k)\hat{\theta}_k$ are different, where $\widetilde{\theta}_k$ is the kth element of $\widetilde{\theta}$. Then we have

$$\frac{1}{\sqrt{T}} \sum_{t=1}^{T} \left[\frac{1}{n} \sum_{i=1}^{n} \frac{\partial q_{it}(\theta^0)}{\partial \theta} \right] + \frac{1}{T} \sum_{t=1}^{T} \left[\frac{1}{n} \sum_{i=1}^{n} \frac{\partial^2 q_{it}(\widetilde{\theta})}{\partial \theta \partial \theta'} \right] \sqrt{T}(\hat{\theta} - \theta^0) = 0,$$

Now we establish the CLT of $\{\frac{1}{n} \sum_{i=1}^{n} \frac{\partial q_{it}(\theta^0)}{\partial \theta}\}$, which is induced from the initial values and thus is not a stationary process. We first consider the asymptotic property of the unobserved fist-order derivative sequence $\{\frac{1}{n} \sum_{i=1}^{n} \frac{\partial q_{it}^*(\theta^0)}{\partial \theta}\}$. Following Billingsley (1968, Theorem 23.1), $\{\frac{1}{n} \sum_{i=1}^{n} \frac{\partial q_{it}^*(\theta^0)}{\partial \theta}\}$ has the central limit property if the following condition hold: (i) $\{\frac{1}{n} \sum_{i=1}^{n} \frac{\partial q_{it}^*(\theta^0)}{\partial \theta}, \mathcal{F}_t\}$ is a vector of stationary and ergodic martingale difference sequence; (ii) $E|\frac{1}{n^2}[\sum_{i=1}^{n} \frac{\partial q_{it}^*(\theta^0)}{\partial \theta}][\sum_{i=1}^{n} \frac{\partial q_{it}^*(\theta^0)}{\partial \theta}]| < \infty$.

We have shown that $\{q_{it}^*(\theta)\}$ is a stationary and ergodic process, and thus $\{\frac{\partial q_{it}^*(\theta^0)}{\partial \theta}, \mathcal{F}_t\}$ is an adapted stochastic sequence for any $i = 1, 2, \ldots, n$. On the other hand, we have shown that $E(s_{\varepsilon_{it}} | I_{t-1}) = 0$ *a.s.*, therefore

$$E\left(\frac{\partial q_{it}^*(\theta^0)}{\partial \theta} | I_{t-1} \right) = 0,$$

which verifies condition (i).

Assumption 5 implies that $V(\theta^0) = \frac{1}{n^2} \sum_{i=1}^{n} \sum_{j=1}^{n} E[\frac{\partial q_{it}^*(\theta^0)}{\partial \theta} \frac{\partial q_{jt}^*(\theta^0)}{\partial \theta'}]$ is positive definite. We conclude that

$$\frac{1}{\sqrt{T}} \sum_{t=1}^{T} \left[\frac{1}{n} \sum_{i=1}^{n} \frac{\partial q_{it}^*(\theta^0)}{\partial \theta} \right] \xrightarrow{L} N(0, V(\theta^0)). \qquad \text{(A.13)}$$

To derive the limit distribution of the first-order derivatives of the observed criterion function (with initial values), we need to show that $T^{-\frac{1}{2}}\sum_{t=1}^{T}|\frac{\partial q_{it}(\theta^0)}{\partial\theta} - \frac{\partial q_{it}^*(\theta^0)}{\partial\theta}| \xrightarrow{p} 0$. By the triangle and the Cauchy–Schwartz inequalities, when $T\to\infty$, for any i,

$$
\begin{aligned}
&\frac{1}{2}E\sup_{\theta\in\Theta}\frac{1}{\sqrt{T}}\sum_{t=1}^{T}\left|\frac{\partial q_{it}(\theta^0)}{\partial\theta}-\frac{\partial q_{it}^*(\theta^0)}{\partial\theta}\right| \\
&\le \frac{1}{\sqrt{T}}\sum_{t=1}^{T}\left[E\sup_{\theta\in\Theta}\left\|\frac{\partial[\hat{\varepsilon}_{it}(\theta)-\varepsilon_{it}(\theta)]}{\partial\theta}\right\|_K^2\right]^{\frac{1}{2}}\left[E\sup_{\theta\in\Theta}\left\|\hat{\varepsilon}_{it}(\theta)-\varepsilon_{it}(\theta)\right\|_K^2\right]^{\frac{1}{2}} \\
&\quad+\frac{1}{\sqrt{T}}\sum_{t=1}^{T}\left[E\sup_{\theta\in\Theta}\left\|\frac{\partial[\hat{\varepsilon}_{it}(\theta)-\varepsilon_{it}(\theta)]}{\partial\theta}\right\|_K^2\right]^{\frac{1}{2}}\left[E\sup_{\theta\in\Theta}\|\varepsilon_{it}(\theta)\|_K^2\right]^{\frac{1}{2}} \\
&\quad+\frac{1}{\sqrt{T}}\sum_{t=1}^{T}\left[E\sup_{\theta\in\Theta}\left\|\hat{\varepsilon}_{it}(\theta)-\varepsilon_{it}(\theta)\right\|_K^2\right]^{\frac{1}{2}}\frac{1}{\sqrt{T}}\sum_{t=1}^{T}\left[E\sup_{\theta\in\Theta}\left\|\frac{\partial\varepsilon_{it}(\theta)}{\partial\theta}\right\|_K^2\right]^{\frac{1}{2}} \\
&\to 0
\end{aligned}
\tag{A.14}
$$

Meanwhile, when $T\to\infty$,

$$
\begin{aligned}
&P\left(\frac{1}{\sqrt{T}}\sum_{t=1}^{T}\left|\frac{1}{n}\sum_{i=1}^{n}\left(\frac{\partial q_{it}(\theta^0)}{\partial\theta}-\frac{\partial q_{it}^*(\theta^0)}{\partial\theta}\right)\right|\right) \\
&\le\frac{1}{\epsilon\sqrt{T}}\sum_{t=1}^{T}E\left|\frac{1}{n}\sum_{i=1}^{n}\left(\frac{\partial q_{it}(\theta^0)}{\partial\theta}-\frac{\partial q_{it}^*(\theta^0)}{\partial\theta}\right)\right| \\
&\le\frac{1}{\epsilon\sqrt{T}}\sum_{t=1}^{T}\frac{1}{n}\sum_{i=1}^{n}E\left|\frac{\partial q_{it}(\theta^0)}{\partial\theta}-\frac{\partial q_{it}^*(\theta^0)}{\partial\theta}\right|\to 0.
\end{aligned}
\tag{A.15}
$$

By White (1999, Lemma 4.7), we have that

$$
\frac{1}{\sqrt{T}}\sum_{t=1}^{T}\left[\frac{1}{n}\sum_{i=1}^{n}\frac{\partial q_{it}(\theta^0)}{\partial\theta}\right]\xrightarrow{L}N(0,V(\theta^0)). \tag{A.16}
$$

where $V(\theta^0)=\frac{1}{n^2}E[(\sum_{i=1}^{n}\frac{\partial q_{it}^*(\theta^0)}{\partial\theta})(\sum_{i=1}^{n}\frac{\partial q_{it}^*(\theta^0)}{\partial\theta'})]$.

Next, by the triangle inequality, it follows from Propositions 3.1 and 3.2 that

$$\sup_{\theta\in\Theta}|\hat{M}_T(\theta)-M(\theta)|\leq\sup_{\theta\in\Theta}|\hat{M}_T(\theta)-\hat{M}^*_T(\theta)|+\sup_{\theta\in\Theta}|\hat{M}^*_T(\theta)-M(\theta)|\xrightarrow{p}0. \tag{A.17}$$

So, we can conclude that

$$\hat{M}_T^{-1}(\widetilde{\theta})\xrightarrow{p}M^{-1}(\theta^0) \tag{A.18}$$

by Assumption 5 if $T\to\infty$ and $\lim_{T\to\infty}\widetilde{\theta}=\theta^0$. In all, Theorem 2 is established by Eqs. (24) and (25), and Theorem 1. ■

Proof of Theorem 3. By the consistency of $\hat{\theta}$ and Propositions 3.1 and 3.2, as $T\to\infty$, we have

$$|\hat{M}_T(\hat{\theta})-M(\theta^0)|\leq\sup_{\theta\in\Theta}|\hat{M}_T(\hat{\theta})-\hat{M}^*_T(\hat{\theta})|+\sup_{\theta\in\Theta}|\hat{M}^*_T(\hat{\theta})-M(\theta^0)|\xrightarrow{p}0.$$

analogously, according to the consistency of $\hat{\theta}$ and Propositions 4.1 and 4.2, we have

$$|\hat{V}_T(\hat{\theta})-V(\theta^0)|\leq\sup_{\theta\in\Theta}|\hat{V}_T(\hat{\theta})-\hat{V}^*_T(\hat{\theta})|+\sup_{\theta\in\Theta}|\hat{V}^*_T(\hat{\theta})-V(\theta^0)|\xrightarrow{p}0$$

as $T\to\infty$, by triangle inequality. Hence, Theorem 3 is proved by the result that

$$\hat{M}_T^{-1}(\hat{\theta})\hat{V}_T(\hat{\theta})\hat{M}_T^{-1}(\hat{\theta})-M_T^{-1}(\theta^0)V_T(\theta^0)M_T^{-1}(\theta^0)\xrightarrow{p}0$$

under Assumption 5. ■

Proof of Theorem 4. There are two steps in the proof of Theorem 4. We first verify that the asymptotic variance of $\widetilde{\theta}^{opt}$ equals to Ω^{opt} under Assumptions 1–7. Define that Ω_i is 2×2 positive-definite matrix with $\Omega_i(1,1)=var(\varepsilon^L_{it})$, $\Omega_i(2,2)=var(\varepsilon^R_{it})$ and $\Omega_i(1,2)=\Omega_i(2,1)=cov(\varepsilon^L_{it},\varepsilon^R_{it})$. So, we define that

$$\Omega_0=\frac{1}{n}\sum_{i=1}^{n}\Omega_i=\frac{1}{n}\begin{bmatrix}\sum_{i=1}^n var(\varepsilon^L_{it}) & \sum_{i=1}^n cov(\varepsilon^L_{it},\varepsilon^R_{it})\\ \sum_{i=1}^n cov(\varepsilon^L_{it},\varepsilon^R_{it}) & \sum_{i=1}^n var(\varepsilon^R_{it})\end{bmatrix}.$$

The $M(\theta^0)$ and $V(\theta^0)$ established in Theorem 2 have an alternative expression based on the bivariate point process ε_{it}. Note that Assumption 7 assume that $cov(\varepsilon_{it}(\theta), \varepsilon_{jt}(\theta)|I_{t-1}) = 0$ for $i \neq j$. Then we can conclude that $E\langle s_{\varepsilon_{it}}, s_{\varepsilon_{jt}}\rangle_K = 0$ for $i \neq j$. In sum, under conditional homoscedasticity and Assumption 7, there exist δ satisfying $|\delta| < \infty$ and $\delta \neq 0$ such that

$$M(\theta^0) = 2\|K\|\delta^2 E\left[\sum_{i=1}^{n} D_{it}(\theta)K^{-1}\sum_{i=1}^{n} D_{it}^{'}(\theta)\right],$$

$$V(\theta^0) = \frac{4}{n}\|K\|^2\delta^4 E\left[\sum_{i=1}^{n} D_{it}(\theta)K^{-1}\sum_{i=1}^{n}\Omega_i K^{-1}\sum_{i=1}^{n} D_{it}^{'}(\theta)\right].$$

where $D_{it}(\theta)$ contains the left and right bounds of the interval-valued derivatives $\frac{\partial\varepsilon_{it}(\theta)}{\partial\theta}$ and of size $\mathbf{k} \times 2$, which lead to

$$\begin{aligned}
avar(\sqrt{T}\hat{\theta}) &= M^{-1}(\theta^0)V(\theta^0)M^{-1}(\theta^0)\\
&= \frac{1}{n}E^{-1}\left[\sum_{i=1}^{n} D_{it}K^{-1}\sum_{i=1}^{n} D_{it}^{'}\right]\\
&\quad \times E\left[\sum_{i=1}^{n} D_{it}K^{-1}\sum_{i=1}^{n}\Omega_i K^{-1}\sum_{i=1}^{n} D_{it}^{'}\right]\\
&\quad \times E^{-1}\left[\sum_{i=1}^{n} D_{it}K^{-1}\sum_{i=1}^{n} D_{it}^{'}\right]
\end{aligned}$$

Substituting K^{opt} for K induces the following results,

$$\begin{aligned}
avar(\sqrt{T}\tilde{\theta}^{opt}) &= \left[\sum_{i=1}^{n} D_{it}(\theta)(\Omega_0)^{-1}\sum_{i=1}^{n} D_{it}^{'}(\theta)\right]^{-1}\\
&= n\|K^{opt}\|\left[\sum_{i=1}^{n} E^{-1}\left\langle s_{\frac{\partial\varepsilon_{it}(\theta)}{\partial\theta}}, s^{'}_{\frac{\partial\varepsilon_{it}(\theta)}{\partial\theta}}\right\rangle_K\right]^{-1}
\end{aligned}$$

So, we have

$$avar(\sqrt{T}\tilde{\theta}^{opt}) \equiv \Omega^{opt}$$

by substituting K^{opt} for K.

In the second step, we note that the condition that $M^{-1}(\theta^0)V(\theta^0)M^{-1}(\theta^0) - \Omega^{opt}$ is positive semi-definite is equivalent to show that $(\Omega^{opt})^{-1} - M(\theta^0)$

$V^{-1}(\theta^0)M(\theta^0)$ is positive semi-definite. Given the results established in previous proof,

$$
\begin{aligned}
&(\Omega^{opt})^{-1} - M(\theta^0)V^{-1}(\theta^0)M(\theta^0) \\
&= D_0\left(\frac{1}{n}\sum_{i=1}^{n}\Omega_i\right)^{-1} D_0^{'} - (D_0K^{-1}D_0^{'})(D_0K^{-1}\Omega_0K^{-1}D_0^{'})^{-1}(D_0K^{-1}D_0^{'}) \\
&= D_0^{'}(\Omega_0)^{-1/2}G(\Omega_0)^{-1/2}D_0^{'}
\end{aligned}
$$

where $D_0(\theta) = \sum_{i=1}^{n} E[D_{it}(\theta)]$ and

$$G = I - (\Omega_0)^{1/2}K^{-1}D_0^{'}\left(D_0K^{-1}\Omega_0K^{-1}D_0^{'}\right)^{-1}D_0K^{-1}(\Omega_0)^{1/2}$$

is a symmetric idempotent matrix. This completes the proof. ■

To show Theorem 5, we first establish Propositions 5.1 and 5.2.

Proposition 5.1. *Put $\hat{\Sigma}_T^*(\theta) = \frac{1}{nT}\sum_{t=1}^{T}[\nu_{it}(\theta)\nu_{it}^{'}(\theta)]$ and $\Sigma(\theta) = E[\nu_{it}(\theta)\nu_{it}^{'}(\theta)]$, where $\nu_{it} = (\varepsilon_{it}^L(\theta), \varepsilon_{it}^R(\theta))'$ is the bivariate point process form of $\{\varepsilon_{it}(\theta)\}$ that is defined in Eq. (7). Suppose Assumptions 1–3(i) and Assumption 7 hold. Then*

$$\sup_{\theta\in\Theta}|\hat{\Sigma}_T^*(\theta) - \Sigma(\theta)| \xrightarrow{p} 0$$

and $\Sigma(\theta)$ is continuous on Θ.

Proof of Proposition 5.1. Analogous to the proof of Propositions 2.2, 3.2 and 4.2, we will verify condition P-WLLN and W-LIP. Note that

$$
\nu_{it}(\theta) = \begin{cases}
\varepsilon_{it}^L(\theta) = \displaystyle\sum_{s=0}^{\infty}\left[\sum_{m=1}^{q}(c_m\eta_{m^s})\right] \\
\qquad \times \left[B_i(L)Y_{it-s}^L - \displaystyle\sum_{h=1,h\neq i}^{n}(B_h(L)Y_{ht-s}^L + A_h(L)\varepsilon_{ht-s}^L) - C_0^i\right], \\
\varepsilon_{it}^R(\theta) = \displaystyle\sum_{s=0}^{\infty}\left[\sum_{m=1}^{q}(c_m\eta_{m^s})\right] \\
\qquad \times \left[B_i(L)Y_{it-s}^R - \displaystyle\sum_{h=1,h\neq i}^{n}(B_h(L)Y_{ht-s}^R + A_h(L)\varepsilon_{ht-s}^R) - C_0^i\right],
\end{cases}
$$

The matrix point process $\{\nu_{it}(\theta)\nu_{it}^{'}(\theta)\}$ is stationary and ergodic since $\{\varepsilon_{it}(\theta)\}$ is stationary and ergodic process. Note that we show the condition P-WWLN by showing that $E[\varepsilon_{it}^L(\theta)]^2$, $E[\varepsilon_{it}^R(\theta)]^2$ and $E[\varepsilon_{it}^L(\theta)\varepsilon_{it}^R(\theta)]$ is uniformly bounded over Θ. Under the proof of Proposition 2.1, there exists $1 < C_{LL} < \infty$, $1 < C_{RR} < \infty$ and $1 < C_{LR} < \infty$ such that

$$E\sup_{\theta\in\Theta}[\varepsilon_{it}^L(\theta)]^2 < C_{LL} < \infty \quad and \quad E\sup_{\theta\in\Theta}[\varepsilon_{it}^R(\theta)]^2 < C_{RR} < \infty.$$

$$\begin{aligned} E\sup_{\theta\in\Theta}[\varepsilon_{it}^L(\theta)\varepsilon_{it}^R(\theta)] &\le \left(E\sup_{\theta\in\Theta}[\varepsilon_{it}^L(\theta)]^2\right)^{1/2}\left(E\sup_{\theta\in\Theta}[\varepsilon_{it}^R(\theta)]^2\right)^{1/2} \\ &< C_{LR} < \infty. \end{aligned}$$

Note that $E\sup_{\theta\in\Theta}\left|\frac{\partial\varepsilon_{it}^L(\theta)}{\partial\theta}\right|^2 < \infty$, $E\sup_{\theta\in\Theta}\left|\frac{\partial\varepsilon_{it}^R(\theta)}{\partial\theta}\right|^2 < \infty$ and $E\sup_{\theta\in\Theta}\left|\frac{\partial\varepsilon_{it}^L(\theta)\varepsilon_{it}^R(\theta)}{\partial\theta}\right| < \infty$. We can conclude that $\sup_{\theta\in\Theta}E\left|\frac{\partial\varepsilon_{it}^L(\theta)}{\partial\theta}\right|^2 < \infty$, $\sup_{\theta\in\Theta}E\left|\frac{\partial\varepsilon_{it}^R(\theta)}{\partial\theta}\right|^2 < \infty$ and $\sup_{\theta\in\Theta}E\left|\frac{\partial\varepsilon_{it}^L(\theta)\partial\varepsilon_{it}^R(\theta)}{\partial\theta}\right| < \infty$ by triangle and Cauchy–Schwarz inequalities. So W-LIP is verified and we establish Proposition 5.1. ∎

Proposition 5.1. *Put $\hat{\Sigma}_T(\theta) = \frac{1}{nT}\sum_{t=1}^{T}[\hat{\nu}_{it}(\theta)\hat{\nu}_{it}^{'}(\theta)]$, where $\hat{\nu}_{it} = (\hat{\varepsilon}_{it}^L, \hat{\varepsilon}_{it}^R)'$ is computed with initial values $\{\hat{Y}_{it}^L, \hat{Y}_{it}^R\}_{t=-p+1}^0$ and $\{\hat{\varepsilon}_{it}^L, \hat{\varepsilon}_{it}^R\}_{t=-q+1}^0$. Suppose Assumptions 1–4 and 7 hold, then we have*

$$\sup_{\theta\in\Theta}|\hat{\Sigma}_T^*(\theta) - \hat{\Sigma}_T(\theta)| \xrightarrow{p} 0.$$

Proof. The proof of Proposition 5.2 is an analogy to that of Propositions 2.2, 3.2 and 4.2.

$$\begin{aligned} &\varepsilon_{it}^L(\theta) - \hat{\varepsilon}_{it}^L(\theta) \\ &= \sum_{j=1}^{q} a_{1j}^{(it)}(\gamma)[\varepsilon_{i1-j}^L(\theta) - \hat{\varepsilon}_{i0}^L(\theta)] - \sum_{j=1}^{p} a_{11}^{(it-j)}(\gamma)\left[\sum_{m=j}^{p}\phi_{ii}^m(Y_{ij-m}^L - \hat{Y}_{i0}^L)\right. \\ &\quad \left. - \sum_{h=1,h\neq i}^{n}\left(\sum_{m=j}^{p}\phi_{ih}^m(Y_{hj-m}^L - \hat{Y}_{h0}^L) + \sum_{m=j}^{q}\gamma_{ih}^m(\varepsilon_{hj-m}^L(\theta) - \hat{\varepsilon}_{h0}^L(\theta))\right)\right] \end{aligned}$$

By triangle and Cauchy–Schwarz inequalities, we have

$$E \sup_{\theta\in\Theta} |[\varepsilon_{it}^L(\theta)]^2 - [\hat{\varepsilon}_{it}^L(\theta)]^2| \le E \sup_{\theta\in\Theta} [\hat{\varepsilon}_{it}^L(\theta) - \varepsilon_{it}^L(\theta)]^2 + 2E \sup_{\theta\in\Theta} |[\hat{\varepsilon}_{it}^L(\theta) - \varepsilon_{it}^L(\theta)]\varepsilon_{it}^L(\theta)|.$$

Applying the Minkowski's and the C_r inequalities repeatedly, it follows that

$$E \sup_{\theta\in\Theta} [\hat{\varepsilon}_{it}^L(\theta) - \varepsilon_{it}^L(\theta)]^2 \le W_{L1} \quad and \quad E \sup_{\theta\in\Theta} |[\hat{\varepsilon}_{it}^L(\theta) - \varepsilon_{it}^L(\theta)]\varepsilon_{it}^L(\theta)| \le W_{L2}$$

where W_{L1} and W_{L2} are finite constants. And we can obtain

$$E \sup_{\theta\in\Theta} \frac{1}{nT} \sum_{i=1}^{n} \sum_{t=1}^{T} |[\varepsilon_{it}^L(\theta)]^2 - [\hat{\varepsilon}_{it}^L(\theta)]^2| \to 0 \quad as \ T \to \infty.$$

Similarly, $E \sup_{\theta\in\Theta} \frac{1}{nT} \sum_{i=1}^{n} \sum_{t=1}^{T} |[\varepsilon_{it}^R(\theta)]^2 - [\hat{\varepsilon}_{it}^R(\theta)]^2|$ and $E \sup_{\theta\in\Theta} \frac{1}{nT} \sum_{i=1}^{n} \sum_{t=1}^{T} |\varepsilon_{it}^L(\theta)\varepsilon_{it}^R(\theta) - \hat{\varepsilon}_{it}^L(\theta)\hat{\varepsilon}_{it}^R(\theta)|$ converge to zero as $T \to \infty$. ■

Proof of Theorem 5. Since the consistency of $\hat{\theta}$ is established in Theorem 1. According to Propositions 5.1 and 5.2,

$$\begin{aligned} |\hat{\Sigma}_T(\hat{\theta}) - \Sigma(\theta^0)| &\le |\hat{\Sigma}_T(\hat{\theta}) - \hat{\Sigma}_T^*(\hat{\theta})| + |\hat{\Sigma}_T^*(\hat{\theta}) - \Sigma(\theta^0)| \\ &\le \sup_{\theta\in\Theta} |\hat{\Sigma}_T(\hat{\theta}) - \hat{\Sigma}_T^*(\hat{\theta})| + \sup_{\theta\in\Theta} |\hat{\Sigma}_T^*(\hat{\theta}) - \Sigma(\theta^0)| \to 0, \end{aligned} \tag{A.19}$$

as $T \to \infty$. Hence, $\hat{K}^{opt} \xrightarrow{p} K^{opt}$ as $T \to \infty$. And thus the two-stage minimum D_K-distance estimator $\hat{\theta}^{opt}$ is asymptotically efficient. And the Theorem 5 is established. ■

INFERENCE IN NEAR-SINGULAR REGRESSION

Peter C. B. Phillips[a,b,c,d]
[a]Department of Economics, Yale University, New Haven, CT, USA
[b]University of Auckland, Auckland, New Zealand
[c]Singapore Management University, Singapore
[d]University of Southampton, Southampton, UK

ABSTRACT

This paper considers stationary regression models with near-collinear regressors. Limit theory is developed for regression estimates and test statistics in cases where the signal matrix is nearly singular in finite samples and is asymptotically degenerate. Examples include models that involve evaporating trends in the regressors that arise in conditions such as growth convergence. Structural equation models are also considered and limit theory is derived for the corresponding instrumental variable (IV) estimator, Wald test statistic, and overidentification test when the regressors are endogenous. It is shown that near-singular designs of the type considered here are not completely fatal to least squares inference, but do inevitably involve size distortion except in special Gaussian cases. In the endogenous case, IV estimation is inconsistent and both the block Wald test and Sargan overidentification test are conservative, biasing these tests in favor of the null.

Essays in Honor of Aman Ullah
Advances in Econometrics, Volume 36, 461–486

ISSN: 0731-9053/doi:10.1108/S0731-905320160000036022

Keywords: Endogeneity; instrumental variable; singular signal matrix; size distortion; structural equation

JEL classification: C23

1. INTRODUCTION

Near-collinear regressors arise frequently in empirical work in both time series and cross-section data. The case of comoving regressors is particularly well known and has been extensively studied (Park & Phillips, 1988, 1989; Phillips, 1988, 1989, 1995; Sims, Stock, & Watson, 1990; Toda & Phillips, 1993) in the context of time series regression with some unit roots and possibly cointegrated regressors. Related problems of partial identification and weak instrumentation in structural model estimation have also proved to be relevant in applications and have been studied in a large literature following initial research on the asymptotic theory of these models by Phillips (1989) and Staiger and Stock (1997). Earlier important work by Sargan (1958, 1983) also considered some aspects of the impact of nearly unidentified models on estimation and inference. More recent work on common explosive roots has shown that near collinearity can produce inconsistencies even in the presence of extremely strong regressor signals (Phillips & Magdalinos, 2013).

While this research primarily involves parametric models and linear systems of equations, nonlinear regressions are also affected by near-collinearity in the regressors, weak identification, and singularities in the limit theory that can produce inconsistencies and differing rates of convergence (Park & Phillips, 2000). It has recently been discovered that nonparametric kernel regression, an area of econometrics to which Aman Ullah has made many lasting contributions including a foundational text (Pagan & Ullah, 1999), is also affected by singularities and differing convergence rates when the regressors are nonstationary (Li, Phillips, & Gao, 2016; Phillips, Li, & Gao, 2014).

The present work considers analogous problems associated with near-collinear regressors that arise in stationary and trend stationary regression. To illustrate, we study the case of a near-singular signal matrix where there is degeneracy in the limit. Such cases occur in practical econometric work when there are evaporating trends or decay effects in the data that produce asymptotic comovement, as in growth convergence modeling (Phillips & Sul, 2007, 2009). Similar issues can arise when power law time trends such as γt^{α} with unknown parameters (α, γ) need to be estimated (Phillips, 2007; Robinson, 2012) because of the asymptotic collinearity of the regressors such as $(t^{\alpha}, t^{\alpha} \log t)$ that appear in the corresponding linearized system.

We develop stationary asymptotics for estimates and tests in regressions where signal matrix singularities that arise in the limit produce inconsistencies in estimation and failures in central limit theory. We also provide limit theory for instrumental variable (IV) regression and the associated block Wald test statistic and overidentification test when the regressor is endogenous. The limit theory is developed for stationary regressions with martingale difference errors.

This paper relates to other recent work on near-singular regression designs by Knight and Fu (2000), Knight (2008), Caner (2008), and Caner and Yildiz (2012). These papers consider a variety of scenarios where near singularity arises, including large numbers of regressors, instruments or moment conditions, weak instrumentation, and cases of signal matrix asymptotic degeneracy. The analysis in these papers concentrates on cases where there is still consistency in linear regression (or shrinkage estimation methods) and limiting normal asymptotics obtain but at slower rates in certain directions. In such cases, self normalized scaling or rotational scaling effectively leads to overall convergence rates at the slowest directional rate rather than the usual $\sqrt{n}$ or trend regressor rate. A leading example cited in Knight (2008) for such near-collinearity causing slower rates of convergence is linear regression on slowly varying regressors or nonlinear regression involving power trend regressors, which were studied in Phillips (2007).

An important distinction between the present work and this earlier research on near-singular designs is that the near-collinearity considered in the current paper produces more serious failures, involving inconsistencies in regression, absence of an invariance principle, and mixed normal limit theory for appropriately standardized estimates. Nevertheless, a remarkable element of the new findings is that, in spite of the coefficient inconsistency and the breakdown of central limit theory, the near singularity in the regressors is not completely fatal either in the linear regression model or structural equation model. In the linear regression case, the mixed normal limit theory for the coefficient estimates and the use of self normalization in inference leads to a test statistic limit theory that involves a mixture of a chi-square distribution and the squared length of the mixing variate which reduces to the usual chi-squared limit theory in the Gaussian case. The use of conventional least squares tests under near-singular designs of the type considered here will therefore inevitably involve size distortion in non-Gaussian cases. In the structural model case, IV estimation is inconsistent but both the Wald test and Sargan overidentification test are size controlled and conservative.

The remainder of this paper is organized as follows. Section 2 examines a prototypical stationary linear regression model with asymptotically collinear regressors and develops limit theory for the coefficient estimates and block Wald test.

Although the coefficient estimates are generally inconsistent, some linear functions as well as the equation error variance are shown to be consistently estimable. Section 3 develops similar limit theory for instrumental variable estimates and test statistics in the structural model case with endogenous regressors. Section 4 concludes and discusses extensions. Proofs are given in the Appendix.

2. SINGULAR REGRESSION MODELS AND LIMIT THEORY

2.1. A Prototypical Model

We study the linear model

$$y_t = x_t'\beta + u_{0t}, \quad t = 1, \ldots, n \tag{1}$$

where β is an unknown $k \times 1$ vector of parameters and the errors u_{0t} are martingale differences with respect to the filtration $\mathcal{F}_t = \sigma\{u_{0t}, u_{0t-1}, \ldots; x_{t+1}, x_t, \ldots\}$ and with conditional variance $\mathbb{E}\{u_{0t}^2|\mathcal{F}_{t-1}\} = \sigma_{00}$ *a.s.* The regressor x_t in Eq. (1) is assumed to have components with differing asymptotic characteristics that lead to a limiting singular system. In particular, upon transformation by some (unknown) nonsingular matrix $G' = [G_a, G_b]'$ with submatrices G_a, G_b of unknown dimension a priori, the model (1) transforms to the partitioned system

$$y_t = x_t'GG^{-1}\beta + u_{0t} = w_{at}'\alpha_a + w_{bt}'\alpha_b + u_{0t}, \tag{2}$$

with

$$w_t = \begin{bmatrix} w_{at} \\ w_{bt} \end{bmatrix} := G'x_t = \begin{bmatrix} G_a'x_t \\ G_b'x_t \end{bmatrix}, \quad \alpha := \begin{bmatrix} \alpha_a \\ \alpha_b \end{bmatrix} := \begin{bmatrix} G^{a'}\beta \\ G^{b'}\beta \end{bmatrix} =: G^{-1}\beta,$$

involving a k_a-vector of stationary, ergodic variates w_{at} and a k_b-vector w_{bt} which satisfies $\sum_{t=1}^{n} w_{bt}w_{bt}' \rightarrow_{a.s.} \Sigma_{bb}$. Sample moments of the components w_{at} and vector w_{bt} therefore have different orders of magnitude. Let $X' = [x_1, \ldots, x_n]'$, $W' = [w_1, \ldots, w_n]'$, $u_0 = [u_{01}, \ldots, u_{0n}]'$, and $y' = [y_1, \ldots, y_n]$. In observation matrix form, Eq. (2) then takes the form

$$y = X\beta + u_0 = W\alpha + u_0. \tag{3}$$

Upon standardization with the matrix $D_n = \mathrm{diag}\left[\sqrt{n} I_{k_a}, I_{k_b}\right]$ the sample moment matrix $X'X = \sum_{t=1}^{n} x_t x_t'$ satisfies, as shown in Eq. (9),

$$D_n^{-1} G' X' X G D_n^{-1} \rightarrow_{a.s.} \Sigma = \begin{bmatrix} \Sigma_{aa} & 0 \\ 0 & \Sigma_{bb} \end{bmatrix} > 0, \tag{4}$$

leading to

$$\frac{\sum_{t=1}^{n} w_{at} w_{at}'}{\sum_{t=1}^{n} u_{0t}^2} \rightarrow_{a.s.} \frac{\Sigma_{aa}}{\sigma_{00}} \quad \text{and} \quad \frac{\sum_{t=1}^{n} w_{bt} w_{bt}'}{\sum_{t=1}^{n} u_{0t}^2} = O_{a.s}\left(n^{-1}\right).$$

So signal-to-noise ratios differ by an order of magnitude in the directions w_{at} and w_{bt}.

To fix ideas, we henceforth assume that the regressors x_t in Eq. (2) have the partitioned form

$$x_t = \begin{bmatrix} x_{at} \\ x_{bt} \end{bmatrix} = \begin{bmatrix} x_t^0 \\ \Pi x_t^0 + a_t v_t \end{bmatrix}, \tag{5}$$

where $\left(x_t^{0\prime}, v_t'\right)'$ is a $k_a + k_b$ vector of stationary ergodic time series, Π is an unknown constant matrix of dimension $k_b \times k_a$, and a_t is a deterministic sequence with $a_t \rightarrow 0$ as $t \rightarrow \infty$. The regressors x_{at} and x_{bt} may then be interpreted as asymptotically comoving stationary regressors. For instance, when $a_t = 1/t$, we have $x_{bt} = \Pi x_{at} + O_{a.s}\left(\frac{1}{t}\right) \sim \Pi x_{at}$ as $t \rightarrow \infty$. Empirical examples of such cases arise when there is convergence over time between regression components. For instance, modern industrialized economies share many common technologies which can lead over time to convergence in the technology drivers of factor productivity, as illustrated by the convergent transition paths shown in Phillips and Sul (2009) for the contiguous USA states during the twentieth century and the Western OECD economies. In research on the cost of living in metropolitan areas in the USA, Phillips and Sul (2007) found evidence of convergence in certain metropolitan subgroups corresponding to very high, moderate, and low costs of living.

In practical work, the respective dimensions (k_a, k_b) of the components in Eq. (5) will generally be unknown. Nonetheless, as shown below there are consistently estimable functions of the parameter vector β and the error variance is also consistently estimable, which together enable inference on the coefficients, albeit with some size distortion except in the Gaussian case. Evidence of near-collinearity in the regressors may be detected by a variety of methods, including principle component analysis or by direct convergence testing and clustering algorithms such as those developed and applied in Phillips and Sul (2007, 2009).

With this structure the system (1) has the partitioned form

$$y_t = x_{at}' \beta_a + x_{bt}' \beta_b + u_{0t}, \tag{6}$$

where $\beta' = (\beta_a, \beta_b)$ is a conformable partition of β. The block triangular transform matrix

$$G = \begin{bmatrix} I & -\Pi' \\ 0 & I \end{bmatrix}, \quad G^{-1} = \begin{bmatrix} I & \Pi' \\ 0 & I \end{bmatrix} =: \begin{bmatrix} G^{a'} \\ G^{b'} \end{bmatrix} \tag{7}$$

leads to the transformed parametric structure $\alpha = G^{-1}\beta$ written in partitioned form as

$$\begin{bmatrix} \alpha_a \\ \alpha_b \end{bmatrix} = \begin{bmatrix} G^{a'}\beta \\ G^{b'}\beta \end{bmatrix} = \begin{bmatrix} \beta_a + \Pi'\beta_b \\ \beta_b \end{bmatrix}$$

and corresponding regressor structure

$$w_t = G'x_t = \begin{bmatrix} w_{at} \\ w_{bt} \end{bmatrix} = \begin{bmatrix} x_t^0 \\ a_t v_t \end{bmatrix}. \tag{8}$$

Here, $w_{bt} = a_t v_t$ involves a stationary component v_t and an evaporating deterministic trend factor, $a_t = o(1)$ as $t \to \infty$, of the type that arises in the study of growth convergence (Phillips & Sul, 2007, 2009). The regression components (x_{at}, x_{bt}) in the untransformed model (6) are therefore asymptotically collinear because $w_{bt} = a_t v_t = o_{a.s.}(1)$ as $t \to \infty$.

Let $s_t = \left(x_t^{0\prime}, v_t'\right)'$ and $q_t = s_t u_{0t} = \left(q_{xt}', q_{vt}'\right)$, partitioned conformably with s_t. We make the following conditions on these components to facilitate the development of the limit theory.

Assumption A.

(i) u_{0t} *is a martingale difference sequence (mds) with respect to the filtration* $\mathcal{F}_t = \sigma\{u_{0t}, u_{0t-1}, \ldots; s_{t+1}, s_t, \ldots\}$ *and with conditional variance* $\mathbb{E}\left\{u_{0t}^2 | \mathcal{F}_{t-1}\right\} = \sigma_{00}$ *a.s.*
(ii) $r_t = (s_t, u_{0t})'$ *is strictly stationary and ergodic with* $E\left(\|r_t\|^{2+\delta}\right) < \infty$ *for some* $\delta > 0$*, and variance matrix* $\Sigma_{rr} = diag\left[\Sigma_{ss}, \sigma_{00}\right] > 0$.

Assumption B.
a_t *is a deterministic sequence for which either*

(i) $\sum_{t=1}^{\infty} |a_t|^{1+\eta} < \infty$ *for some (possibly small)* $\eta \in (0,1)$*, or*
(ii) $\sum_{t=1}^{\infty} |a_t| < \infty$.

As shown in Lemma 1 in the Appendix, Assumptions A(i) and (ii) ensure that a functional law applies to partial sums of the mds $q_t = \left(q_{xt}', q_{vt}'\right)$, so that $n^{-1/2}\sum_{t=1}^{\lfloor n\cdot \rfloor} q_t \Rightarrow B_q(\cdot)$, with limiting Brownian motion vector B_q and covariance matrix $\Omega_{qq} = \sigma_{00}\Sigma_{ss}$ where $B_q = \left(B'_{q_x}, B'_{q_v}\right)'$ and

$$\Sigma_{ss} = \mathbb{E}\left(s_t s_t'\right) = \begin{bmatrix} \Sigma_{aa} & \Sigma_{av} \\ \Sigma_{va} & \Sigma_{vv} \end{bmatrix} > 0$$

are conformably partitioned with q_t. Assumption B requires absolute summability of the deterministic sequence $\{a_t\}$ in B(ii) or the alternate $(1+\eta)$ absolute summability in B(i). These conditions imply that a_t is an evaporating sequence, so that $a_t \to 0$, and they are sufficient to ensure *a.s.* summability of certain sums that appear in the limit theory such $\sum_{t=1}^{\infty} a_t^2 v_t v_t'$ and $\sum_{t=1}^{\infty} a_t x_t^0 v_t'$ in the following analysis. For example, $a_t = t^{-1}$ satisfies B(i) for any $\eta > 0$, and $a_t = t^{-1}(\log t)^{-1-\epsilon}$ satisfies B(ii) for any $\epsilon > 0$.

Under Assumptions A and B we have the following explicit form for the limit behavior of the standardized signal matrix in Eq. (4)

$$D_n^{-1} G' X' X G D_n^{-1} \to_{a.s.} \Sigma = \begin{bmatrix} \Sigma_{aa} = \mathbb{E}\left(x_t^0 x_t^{0\prime}\right) & 0 \\ 0 & \Sigma_{bb} = \sum_{t=1}^{\infty} a_t^2 v_t v_t' \end{bmatrix}. \quad (9)$$

Observe that the sum $\sum_{t=1}^{\infty} a_t^2 v_t v_t' < \infty$ *a.s.* since

$$\mathbb{E}\left(\sum_{t=1}^{\infty} a_t^2 v_t v_t'\right) = \sum_{t=1}^{\infty} a_t^2 \mathbb{E}\left(v_t v_t'\right) = \Sigma_{vv} \sum_{t=1}^{\infty} a_t^2 < \infty,$$

under both B(i) and (ii). The off-diagonal block in Eq. (9) is a zero matrix because: under B(ii), $\mathbb{E}\left(\sum_{t=1}^{\infty} \left\|x_t^0 v_t'\right\| |a_t|\right) = \mathbb{E}\left(\left\|x_t^0 v_t'\right\|\right) \sum_{t=1}^{\infty} |a_t| < \infty$, in which case $\sum_{t=1}^{\infty} x_t^0 v_t' a_t$ converges almost surely and $n^{-1/2} \sum_{t=1}^{n} x_t^0 v_t a_t = O_{a.s.}\left(n^{-1/2}\right)$; alternatively, under B(i), we have by Hölder's inequality

$$\begin{aligned} \frac{1}{\sqrt{n}} \mathbb{E}\left(\sum_{t=1}^{n} \left\|x_t^0 v_t'\right\| |a_t|\right) &= \mathbb{E}\left(\left\|x_t^0 v_t'\right\|\right) \frac{1}{\sqrt{n}} \sum_{t=1}^{n} |a_t| \\ &\leq \mathbb{E}\left(\left\|x_t^0 v_t'\right\|\right) \frac{n^{\frac{\eta}{1+\eta}}}{\sqrt{n}} \left(\sum_{t=1}^{n} |a_t|^{1+\eta}\right)^{\frac{1}{1+\eta}} \\ &= O\left(\frac{1}{n^{\frac{1}{2} - \frac{\eta}{1+\eta}}}\right) = o(1) \quad \text{for all } \eta \in (0,1), \end{aligned}$$

and then $n^{-1/2} \sum_{t=1}^{n} x_t^0 v_t a_t \to_{L_1} 0$.

The standardized signal matrix therefore has a random limit and no invariance principle applies because $\sum_{t=1}^{\infty} a_t^2 v_t v_t'$ depends on the distribution of v_t. Further,

$$D_n^{-1} W' u_0 = \begin{bmatrix} \frac{1}{\sqrt{n}} \sum_{t=1}^{n} w_{at} u_{0t} \\ \sum_{t=1}^{n} w_{bt} u_{0t} \end{bmatrix} = \begin{bmatrix} \frac{1}{\sqrt{n}} \sum_{t=1}^{n} x_t^0 u_{0t} \\ \sum_{t=1}^{n} a_t v_t u_{0t} \end{bmatrix} \Rightarrow \begin{bmatrix} B_{q_x}(1) \\ Q_v \end{bmatrix}, \tag{10}$$

where $Q_v := \sum_{t=1}^{\infty} a_t v_t u_{0t}$ converges almost surely since $\sum_{t=1}^{m} a_t v_t u_{0t}$ is an L_2 martingale with $\sum_{t=1}^{\infty} a_t^2 \mathbb{E} \left\| v_t v_t' u_{0t}^2 \right\| = \sigma_{00} \mathbb{E} \left\| v_t v_t' \right\| \sum_{t=1}^{\infty} a_t^2 < \infty$. So $D_n^{-1} W' u_0$ converges weakly but does not satisfy an invariance principle, the distribution of the limit component Q_v depending on the distribution of the component variates (v_t, u_{0t}).

2.2. *Near-Singular Least Squares Regression*

The parameter vector β in Eq. (1) is estimated by ordinary least squares regression and the null hypothesis $\mathbb{H}_0 : \beta = 0$ is tested using the Wald statistic $W_n = \hat{\beta}' X' X \hat{\beta} / \hat{\sigma}^2$, where $\hat{\sigma}^2 = n^{-1} y' \left(I_n - X \left(X'X \right)^{-1} X \right) y$ is the usual sample variance of the regression residuals. The limit behavior of the regression components $\left\{ \hat{\beta}, \hat{\sigma}^2, W_n \right\}$ is as follows.

Theorem 1. *Under Assumptions A and B*

(i) $\begin{bmatrix} \hat{\beta}_a - \beta_a \\ \hat{\beta}_b - \beta_b \end{bmatrix} \Rightarrow \begin{bmatrix} -\Pi' \\ I_{k_b} \end{bmatrix} \xi_b$, *where* $\xi_b = \left(\sum_{t=1}^{\infty} a_t^2 v_t v_t' \right)^{-1} \sum_{t=1}^{\infty} a_t v_t u_{0t}$,

(ii) $\hat{\sigma}^2 \to_p \sigma_{00}$,

(iii) $W_n \Rightarrow \chi_{k_a}^2 + \zeta_b' \zeta_b$, *where* $\zeta_b := \Sigma_{bb}^{1/2} \xi_b / \sigma_{00}^{1/2} = \Sigma_{bb}^{-1/2} \sum_{t=1}^{\infty} a_t v_t u_{0t} / \sigma_{00}^{1/2}$.

It follows from (i) that both estimates $\hat{\beta}_a$ and $\hat{\beta}_b$ are inconsistent and converge to random quantities dependent on ξ_b. No invariance principle applies because the distribution of ξ_b depends on the distribution of the data through the inputs $\{v_t, u_{0t}\}_{t=1}^{\infty}$. The limit theory also has degenerate dimension k_b because $\hat{\beta}_a - \beta_a$ is asymptotically proportional to $\hat{\beta}_b - \beta_b$. Thus, the asymptotic singularity in the signal matrix leads to inconsistency in the regression coefficients and degeneracy in their limit distribution. As noted above, the weak signal is in the direction w_{bt} for which the sample excitation matrix $\sum_{t=1}^{n} a_t^2 v_t v_t' \to \sum_{t=1}^{\infty} a_t^2 v_t v_t'$ does not diverge as the sample size $n \to \infty$, leading to the inconsistency and a singular limit distribution that depends on the limit regression coefficient $\xi_b = \left(\sum_{t=1}^{\infty} a_t^2 v_t v_t' \right)^{-1} \sum_{t=1}^{\infty} a_t v_t u_{0t}$ in this direction.

Nonetheless, there are identifiable and estimable functions of the coefficients. In particular, as shown in the proof of (i), the linear combination $\beta_a + \Pi' \beta_b$ is consistently estimated by $\hat{\beta}_a + \Pi'\hat{\beta}_b$ at a $\sqrt{n}$ rate, giving a consistently estimable function of the original coordinates with the normal limit distribution

$$\sqrt{n}\left(\hat{\beta}_a + \Pi'\hat{\beta}_b - \beta_a - \Pi'\beta_b\right) \Rightarrow N\left(0, \sigma_{00}\Sigma_{aa}^{-1}\right). \tag{11}$$

The matrix Π is generally unknown but it can be consistently estimated at an $O(n)$ rate. In particular, if the partition structure of $x_t = \left(x_{at}', x_{bt}'\right)'$ is known, least squares regression of x_{bt} on x_{at} gives $\hat{\Pi} = \left(\sum_{t=1}^{n} x_{bt}x_{at}'\right)\left(\sum_{t=1}^{n} x_{at}x_{at}'\right)^{-1}$ and simple manipulations reveal that $n\left(\hat{\Pi} - \Pi\right) \rightarrow_{a.s.} \left(\sum_{t=1}^{\infty} a_t v_t x_t^{0\prime}\right)\Sigma_{aa}^{-1}$. Then $\hat{\beta}_a + \hat{\Pi}'\hat{\beta}_b$ is consistent for $\beta_a + \Pi'\beta_b$ with the same $\sqrt{n}$ rate of convergence and asymptotic distribution as Eq. (11).

Somewhat curiously, as shown in (ii), the least squares error variance estimate $\hat{\sigma}^2$ is consistent even though the regression coefficients are inconsistent. The reason is that asymptotic collinearity in the regressor vector x_t does not prevent consistency of the residual variance. In particular, the fitted residual is

$$\begin{aligned}\hat{u}_{0t} &= y_t - x_t'\hat{\beta} = u_{0t} - x_t'\left(\hat{\beta} - \beta\right) = u_{0t} - w_t'\left(\hat{\alpha} - \alpha\right)\\ &= u_{0t} - x_t^{0\prime}\left(\hat{\alpha}_a - \alpha_a\right) - a_t v_t\left(\hat{\alpha}_b - \alpha_b\right)\\ &= u_{0t} - w_t' D_n^{-1} D_n\left(\hat{\alpha} - \alpha\right)\end{aligned}$$

and, since $D_n\left(\hat{\alpha} - \alpha\right)$ and $D_n^{-1}W'WD_n^{-1}$ are both $O_p(1)$ from Eqs. (A.1) and (A.3) in the proof of Theorem 1, we find that

$$\begin{aligned}\hat{\sigma}^2 &= \frac{1}{n}\sum_{t=1}^{n}\hat{u}_{0t}^2 = \frac{1}{n}\sum_{t=1}^{n}u_{0t}^2 - \frac{1}{n}\left(\hat{\alpha} - \alpha\right)' D_n\left(D_n^{-1}W'WD_n^{-1}\right)D_n\left(\hat{\alpha} - \alpha\right)\\ &= \frac{1}{n}\sum_{t=1}^{n}u_{0t}^2 + o_p(1) \rightarrow_p \sigma_{00}.\end{aligned}$$

From (iii), W_n is a limiting mixture of a chi-square variate and the squared length of the vector variate ζ_b. No invariance principle holds because ζ_b depends on the data distribution through $\{v_t, u_{0t}\}_{t=1}^{\infty}$. In the general case, there will therefore be some size distortion when conventional chi-square critical values are used in testing. However, in the special case where (v_t, u_{0t}) is Gaussian, then $u_{0t} \sim i.i.d.$ $N(0, \sigma_{00})$ is independent of $\{v_t\}$ because $E(v_t u_{0t}) = 0$ in view of Assumption A(ii). Then $\zeta_b =_d N\left(0, I_{k_b}\right)$ and $\zeta_b'\zeta_b \sim_d \chi_{k_b}^2$, so that $W_n \Rightarrow \chi_k^2$. Thus, the usual limit theory for the test statistic W_n applies when the input variates (v_t, u_{0t}) are Gaussian.

3. SINGULAR STRUCTURAL MODEL AND IV ESTIMATION

3.1. Model Formulation and Limit Theory

We now consider the structural equation case where the regressor x_t in (1) is endogenous. The asymptotic characteristics of x_t are assumed to be the same as those given earlier, so that Eqs. (4) and (5) continue to hold but now $\mathbb{E}(x_t u_{0t}) = \Sigma_{x0} \neq 0$. Let z_t be a $K \times 1$ vector of instruments with $K \geq k+1$, full rank $(K < n)$ observation matrix $Z' = [z_1, \ldots, z_n]$, and corresponding projector $P_Z = Z\left(Z'Z\right)^{-1} Z$. The IV estimator is $\beta_{IV} = \left(X'P_Z X\right)^{-1}\left(X'P_Z y\right)$ and the estimation error has the form

$$\beta_{IV} - \beta = \left(X'P_Z X\right)^{-1} X'P_Z u_0 = \left(G'^{-1} W' P_Z W G^{-1}\right)^{-1} G'^{-1} W' P_Z u_0$$
$$= G\left(W'P_Z W\right)^{-1} W' P_Z u_0, \tag{12}$$

with G and W defined as in Eqs. (7) and (8) and corresponding coefficient estimates $\alpha_{IV} = G^{-1}\beta_{IV}$ with estimation error

$$\alpha_{IV} - \alpha = G^{-1}\left(\beta_{IV} - \beta\right) = \left(W'P_Z W\right)^{-1}\left(W'P_Z u_0\right). \tag{13}$$

We replace Assumption A with the following.

Assumption A′.

(i) *u_{0t} is a martingale difference sequence (mds) with respect to the filtration $\mathcal{F}_t = \sigma\{u_{0t}, u_{0t-1}, \ldots; z_{t+1}, z_t, \ldots\}$ and with conditional variance $\mathbb{E}\left\{u_{0t}^2 | \mathcal{F}_{t-1}\right\} = \sigma_{00}$ a.s.*

(ii) *$r_t = \left(x_t^0, v_t, z_t, u_{0t}\right)'$ is strictly stationary and ergodic with $E\left(\|r_t\|^{2+\delta}\right) < \infty$ for some $\delta > 0$, and variance matrix*

$$\Sigma_{rr} = \begin{bmatrix} \Sigma_{xx} & \Sigma_{xv} & \Sigma_{xz} & \Sigma_{x0} \\ \Sigma_{vx} & \Sigma_{vv} & \Sigma_{vz} & \Sigma_{v0} \\ \Sigma_{zx} & \Sigma_{zv} & \Sigma_{zz} & 0 \\ \Sigma_{0x} & \Sigma_{0v} & 0 & \sigma_{00} \end{bmatrix} > 0$$

with Σ_{xz} having full rank $k_a < K$.

Assumption A′(i) ensures that the orthogonality condition $\mathbb{E}\{z_t u_{0t}\} = 0$ holds, giving instrument validity to z_t, and A′(ii) imposes the partial relevance rank condition that $\text{rank}\left(\Sigma_{zx}\right) = k_a < K$. The full relevance condition $\text{rank}\left[\Sigma_{zx}, \Sigma_{zv}\right] = k$ with respect to x_t, or equivalently the pair $\left(x_t^0, v_t\right)$, is not required in what follows as the regressor singularity dominates the asymptotics.

The parameter vector β in Eq. (1) is estimated by instrumental variables regression using the instruments z_t. The null hypothesis $\mathbb{H}_0 : \beta = 0$ is block tested using the corresponding Wald statistic $\tilde{W}_n = \beta_{IV}' X' P_Z X \beta_{IV} / \tilde{\sigma}^2$, where $\tilde{\sigma}^2 = n^{-1} \tilde{u}' \tilde{u}$ is the usual sample variance of the regression residuals $\tilde{u} = y - X\beta_{IV}$. We also consider the Sargan overidentification test statistic for testing the validity of the instruments. Using the IV residuals

$$\begin{aligned}\tilde{u} &= y - X\beta_{IV} = u_0 - X\left(X'P_Z X\right)^{-1} X' P_Z u_0 \\ &= u_0 - W\left(W' P_Z W\right)^{-1} W' P_Z u_0,\end{aligned}$$

we write the projection

$$P_Z \tilde{u} = \left\{P_z - P_z X\left(X' P_Z X\right)^{-1} X' P_Z\right\} u_0 = \left\{P_z - P_z W\left(W' P_Z W\right)^{-1} W' P_Z\right\} u_0.$$

Then the Sargan test for overidentification has the form

$$\begin{aligned}S_n &= \tilde{u}' P_Z \tilde{u} / \tilde{\sigma}^2 = u_0' \left\{P_z - P_z X\left(X' P_Z X\right)^{-1} X' P_Z\right\} u_0 / \tilde{\sigma}^2 \\ &= u_0' \left\{P_z - P_z W\left(W' P_Z W\right)^{-1} W' P_Z\right\} u_0 / \tilde{\sigma}^2.\end{aligned}$$

The limit behavior of the IV regression components $\left\{\beta_{IV}, \tilde{\sigma}^2, \tilde{W}_n, S_n\right\}$ is given in the following result where $MN(0, V)$ signifies a mixed normal distribution with zero mean and mixing variance matrix V.

Theorem 2. *Under Assumptions A′ and B and using the normalization matrix* $F_n = \operatorname{diag}\left(\sqrt{n} I_{k_a}, \frac{1}{\sqrt{n}} I_{k_b}\right)$ *we have:*

(i) $F_n G^{-1}\left(\beta_{IV} - \beta\right) \Rightarrow MN\left(0, \sigma_{00}\begin{bmatrix}\Sigma_{xz}\Sigma_{zz}^{-1}\Sigma_{zx} & \Sigma_{xz}\Sigma_{zz}^{-1}A_z \\ A_z'\Sigma_{zz}^{-1}\Sigma_{zx} & A_z'\Sigma_{zz}^{-1}A_z\end{bmatrix}^{-1}\right)$, *where* $A_z = \sum_{t=1}^{\infty} a_t z_t v_t'$, *and in partitioned component form*

$$\frac{1}{\sqrt{n}}\begin{bmatrix}\beta_{a,IV} - \beta_a \\ \beta_{b,IV} - \beta_b\end{bmatrix} \Rightarrow \begin{bmatrix}-\Pi' \\ I_{k_b}\end{bmatrix} \times MN\left(0, \sigma_{00} H^{-1}\right), \tag{14}$$

where $H = A_z'\Sigma_{zz}^{-1}A_z - A_z'\Sigma_{zz}^{-1}\Sigma_{zx}\left(\Sigma_{xz}\Sigma_{zz}^{-1}\Sigma_{zx}\right)^{-1}\Sigma_{xz}\Sigma_{zz}^{-1}A_z$.

(ii) $\tilde{\sigma}^2 \to_p \sigma_{00}\left\{1 + \omega_{zz}\right\}$, *where* $\omega_{zz} = \psi_b' H^{-1/2}\left(\sum_{t=1}^{\infty} a_t^2 v_t v_t'\right) H^{-1/2}\psi_b$ *and* $\psi_b \sim_d N\left(0, I_{k_b}\right)$.

(iii) $\tilde{W}_n \Rightarrow \chi_k^2 / \left\{1 + \omega_{zz}\right\}$.

(iv) $S_n \Rightarrow \chi_{K-k}^2 / \left\{1 + \omega_{zz}\right\}$.

3.2. Discussion

As shown in the proof of Theorem 2(i), when the IV signal matrix $W'P_ZW$ is standardized by the matrix $D_n = \text{diag}\left[\sqrt{n}I_{k_a}, I_{k_b}\right]$ that accords with the respective order of the regressors and was used earlier in the least squares regression case, the limiting signal matrix is now degenerate with

$$D_n^{-1}W'P_ZWD_n^{-1} \to_{a.s} \begin{bmatrix} \Sigma_{xz}\Sigma_{zz}^{-1}\Sigma_{zx} & 0 \\ 0 & 0 \end{bmatrix}. \tag{15}$$

Correspondingly, there is limiting degeneracy in the scaled IV error component

$$D_n^{-1}W'P_Zu_0 \Rightarrow \begin{bmatrix} N\left(0, \sigma_{00}\Sigma_{xz}\Sigma_{zz}^{-1}\Sigma_{zx}\right) \\ 0 \end{bmatrix}. \tag{16}$$

These degeneracies that arise with the use of the scaling matrix D_n mean that the limit behavior of the IV estimated coefficients is dominated by divergent components that produce the singularity in Eqs. (15) and (16). Use of the alternate scaling matrix $F_n = \text{diag}\left(\sqrt{n}I_{k_a}, \frac{1}{\sqrt{n}}I_{k_b}\right)$ controls this singularity and enables the development of a nondivergent and nondegenerate limit theory.

Part (i) shows that using F_n the standardized and centred IV estimate $F_nG^{-1}(\beta_{IV} - \beta) = F_n(\alpha_{IV} - \alpha)$ has a mixed normal limit, where the mixing variance matrix depends on the matrix $A_z = \sum_{t=1}^{\infty} a_t z_t v_t'$, which in turn depends on the distribution of (z_t, v_t) and the deterministic sequence (a_t). This random matrix A_z is a measure of the importance of the near-collinearity in the system between the component regressors $x_{at} = x_t^0$ and $x_{bt} = \Pi x_t^0 + a_t v_t$ when the system is estimated using instrumental variables z_t. Importantly, the series $\sum_{t=1}^{\infty} a_t z_t v_t' < \infty$ *a.s.*, so that A_z is a well defined random matrix.

As is apparent from Eq. (14), the individual IV component vectors $\beta_{a,IV}$ and $\beta_{b,IV}$ both have divergent behavior at the $\sqrt{n}$ rate. Hence, the effects of the weak signal arising from the near-collinearity in the regressors that is evident in least squares regression under exogeneity, is exacerbated by endogeneity, even when the instruments are valid, satisfying both orthogonality and strong relevance conditions. Thus, near-collinearity in the presence of endogeneity, even with strong instruments in regression, leads to divergent behavior in the estimates.

On the other hand, as in the case of exogenous x_t and as shown in the proof of (i), there are some estimable components. In particular, the linear combination $\beta_a + \Pi'\beta_b$ is again consistently estimated, here by $\beta_{a,IV} + \Pi'\beta_{b,IV}$ and at a $\sqrt{n}$ rate, giving a consistently estimable function of the original coordinates with the mixed normal limit distribution

$$\sqrt{n}\left(\beta_{a,IV}+\Pi'\beta_{b,IV}-\beta_a-\Pi'\beta_b\right)\Rightarrow MN\left(0,\sigma_{00}H_{\beta\beta}^{-1}\right), \tag{17}$$

where $H_{\beta\beta}=\left[\Sigma_{xz}\Sigma_{zz}^{-1}\Sigma_{zx}-\Sigma_{xz}\Sigma_{zz}^{-1}A_z\left(A_z'\Sigma_{zz}^{-1}A_z\right)^{-1}A_z'\Sigma_{zz}^{-1}\Sigma_{zx}\right]$ and with the mixing matrix A_z again influencing the asymptotics. The matrix Π is generally unknown but, as earlier in the regression model case, it can be consistently estimated at an $O(n)$ rate by least squares regression of x_{bt} on x_{at}. In the same way, the estimate $\hat{\Pi}=\left(\sum_{t=1}^n x_{bt}x_{at}'\right)\left(\sum_{t=1}^n x_{at}x_{at}'\right)^{-1}\rightarrow_{a.s}\Pi$ with limit distribution $n\left(\hat{\Pi}-\Pi\right)\rightarrow_{a.s.}\left(\sum_{t=1}^\infty a_t v_t x_t^{0\prime}\right)\Sigma_{aa}^{-1}$. So, $\beta_{a,IV}+\hat{\Pi}'\beta_{b,IV}$ is again consistent for $\beta_a+\Pi'\beta_b$ with the same $\sqrt{n}$ rate of convergence and asymptotic distribution as Eq. (17).

Part (ii) shows that the usual error variance estimate is inconsistent and asymptotically overestimates σ_{00} by the asymptotic bias expression $\sigma_{00}\omega_{zz}=\psi_b'H^{-1/2}\left(\sum_{t=1}^\infty a_t^2 v_t v_t'\right)H^{-1/2}\psi_b$. As shown in the proof, this asymptotic bias arises in the residual variance estimate from the limit of the following component involving a quadratic form in the estimation error $(\alpha_{IV}-\alpha)$

$$(\alpha_{IV}-\alpha)'F_n\left(\frac{1}{n}F_n^{-1}W'WF_n^{-1}\right)F_n(\alpha_{IV}-\alpha)$$
$$=\left\{\frac{1}{\sqrt{n}}\left(\alpha_{b,IV}-\alpha_b\right)'\right\}\left(\sum_{t=1}^n a_t^2 v_t v_t'\right)\left\{\frac{1}{\sqrt{n}}\left(\alpha_{b,IV}-\alpha_b\right)\right\}+o_p(1).$$

Thus, in contrast to the linear regression case, the estimation error is not negligible when estimating the error variance and produces error variance estimation bias in the limit.

It follows from Part (iii) that the limit distribution of the Wald test of the block hypothesis $H_0:\beta=0$ is a mixed chi-square distribution with degrees of freedom k and scale mixing coefficient $\{1+\omega_{zz}\}^{-1}<1$ *a.s.* In particular, $\tilde{W}_n\Rightarrow\chi_k^2/\{1+\omega_{zz}\}\leq\chi_k^2$. Tail significance in the limit occurs when $\chi_k^2/\{1+\omega_{zz}\}>cv_\alpha$ for the test critical value cv_α and this inequality implies that $\chi_k^2>cv_\alpha$ so that

$$P\left[\tilde{W}_n>cv_\alpha\right]\rightarrow\mathbb{P}\left[\chi_k^2/\{1+\omega_{zz}\}>cv_\alpha\right]<\mathbb{P}\left[\chi_k^2>cv_\alpha\right].$$

Tests based on $\tilde{W}_n$ with the usual χ_k^2 critical value are therefore conservative asymptotically. The reason is that the IV error variance estimate $\tilde{\sigma}^2\Rightarrow\sigma_{00}\{1+\omega_{zz}\}>\sigma_{00}$ so that $\tilde{\sigma}^2$ overestimates σ_{00} and hence the Wald statistic $\tilde{W}_n$ is biased downwards, thereby favoring the null and leading to a conservative test.

This is a curious finding that implies size-controlled tests of $\beta = 0$ exist even when the regression coefficient β cannot be consistently estimated. Lack of asymptotic identifiability means that the equation error variance estimate is larger than the error variance in the limit, which then biases the test in favor of the null hypothesis, thereby reducing power. The impact on test power may be further investigated by doing an asymptotic power analysis for local and distant alternatives in various directions, a topic that is not pursued here.

The mixed normal limit distribution given in Part (i) of Theorem 2 presumes the invertibility of the (conditional) covariance matrix

$$\begin{bmatrix} \Sigma_{xz}\Sigma_{zz}^{-1}\Sigma_{zx} & \Sigma_{xz}\Sigma_{zz}^{-1}A_z \\ A_z'\Sigma_{zz}^{-1}\Sigma_{zx} & A_z'\Sigma_{zz}^{-1}A_z \end{bmatrix} = \begin{bmatrix} \Sigma_{xz} \\ A_z' \end{bmatrix} \Sigma_{zz}^{-1} \left[\Sigma_{zx} \;\; A_z \right]. \tag{18}$$

This matrix is nonsingular if the matrix $[\Sigma_{zx}, A_z]$ has full column rank. By assumption A′(ii) Σ_{zx} has full column rank k_a. The second component in the partition, $A_z = \sum_{t=1}^{\infty} a_t z_t v_t'$, is a random matrix. We take a leading case for analysis. In particular, if $(z_t, v_t) \sim_d i.i.d.\ N\left(0, \operatorname{diag}(\Sigma_{zz}, \Sigma_{vv})\right)$, then

$$A_z = \sum_{t=1}^{\infty} a_t z_t v_t' \sim_d MN\left(0, \Sigma_{zz} \otimes \sum_{t=1}^{\infty} a_t^2 v_t v_t'\right),$$

which is a nondegenerate mixed normal distribution since $\sum_{t=1}^{\infty} a_t^2 v_t v_t' > 0\ a.s.$, and Σ_{zz} is positive definite, by assumption. Deficient rank of Eq. (18) means that $[\Sigma_{zx}, A_z]\, g = \Sigma_{zx} g_a + A_z g_b = 0\ a.s.$ for some $g' = \left(g_a', g_b\right) \neq 0$. That is, $A_z g_b = -\Sigma_{zx} g_a$, a constant vector $a.s.$ Note that $g_b \neq 0$, otherwise $\Sigma_{zx} g_a = 0$ which further implies $g_a = 0$ because Σ_{zx} has full rank by assumption. Since A_z has a full rank mixed normal distribution, it follows that for $g_b \neq 0$ we have $\mathbb{P}\left(A_z g_b = -\Sigma_{zx} g_a\right) = 0$. So the conditional covariance matrix (18) almost surely has full rank.

The final part of Theorem 2 considers the behavior of the Sargan overidentification test statistic for testing the validity of the instruments, showing that the Sargan statistic S_n is distributed in the limit as $\chi^2_{K-k} / \{1 + \omega_{zz}\}$, which is proportional to a chi-squared variate with degrees of freedom $K - k$ corresponding to the degree of overidentification. This limit theory involves the error variance estimation bias through the presence of the scale factor $\{1 + \omega_{zz}\}^{-1}$, which leads to a mixed chi-square limit. Thus, even though the estimates of the structural coefficients are inconsistent, the overidentification test is proportional to chi-square with the usual degrees of freedom. In consequence, like the Wald test, the overidentification test statistic is biased in favor of the null, leading to a conservative test of instrument validity.

4. CONCLUSION AND EXTENSION

In order to explore the implications for inference of asymptotic singularity in stationary regressors, it has been convenient to use the partitioned structure $x_t = (x'_{at}, x'_{bt})'$ given in Eq. (5). This structure leads to a triangular model in which the components of x_t are related according to the linear system $x_{bt} = \Pi x_{at} + a_t v_t$. In practical work, theory may sometimes suggest such a relationship in which variables are asymptotically stationary and co-related. In general, however, near-collinearity in stationary regressors may be suspected without knowledge of a particular functional relation. In such cases, it will be of practical interest to develop methods that enable inference about possible asymptotic singularities when the form of the dependence between the components of x_t is completely unknown. This topic of investigation is now being explored. What is known from the present study is that near-singular designs of the type considered here, while not completely fatal to least squares inference, will inevitably involve size distortion in non-Gaussian cases. With IV estimation in the endogenous case, the block Wald test is size controlled but conservative, biasing the test in favor of the null.

ACKNOWLEDGEMENTS

This paper was written during a cross-Canada rail journey in June 2015. It originated in a Yale Take Home Examination given in the Fall, 2014. The author thanks two referees for helpful comments and acknowledges support of the NSF under Grant SES 12-58258.

REFERENCES

Caner, M. (2008). Nearly-singular design in GMM and generalized empirical likelihood estimators. *Journal of Econometrics*, *144*, 511–523.

Caner, M., & Yildiz, N. (2012). CUE with many weak instruments and nearly-singular design. *Journal of Econometrics, 170*, 422–421.

Hall, P., & Heyde, C. C. (1980). *Martingale limit theory and its application*. New York, NY: Academic Press.

Knight, K. (2008). Shrinkage estimation for nearly singular designs. *Econometric Theory, 24*, 323–337.

Knight, K., & Fu, W. (2000). Asymptotics for lasso-type estimators. *Annals of Statistics, 28*, 1356–1378.

Li, D., Phillips, P. C. B., & Gao, J. (2016). Uniform consistency of nonstationary kernel-weighted sample covariances for nonparametric regression. *Econometric Theory* (forthcoming).

Pagan, A., & Ullah, A. (1999). *Nonparametric econonometrics*. New York, NY: Cambridge University Press.

Park, J. Y., & Phillips, P. C. B. (1988). Statistical inference in regressions with integrated processes: Part 1. *Econometric Theory, 4*, 468–497.

Park, J. Y., & Phillips, P. C. B. (1989). Statistical inference in regressions with integrated processes: Part 2. *Econometric Theory, 5*, 95–131.
Park, J. Y., & Phillips, P. C. B. (2000). Nonstationary binary choice. *Econometrica, 68*, 1249–1280.
Phillips, P. C. B. (1988). Multiple regression with integrated processes. In N. U. Prabhu (Ed.). *Statistical Inference from Stochastic Processes, Contemporary Mathematics, 80*, 79–106.
Phillips, P. C. B. (1989). Partially identified econometric models. *Econometric Theory, 5*, 181–240.
Phillips, P. C. B. (1995). Fully modified least squares and vector autoregression. *Econometrica, 63*, 1023–1078.
Phillips, P. C. B. (2007). Regression with slowly varying regressors and nonlinear trends. *Econometric Theory, 23*, 557–614.
Phillips, P. C. B., Li, D., & Gao, J. (2014). *Estimating smooth structural changes in cointegration models*. Cowles Foundation Discussion Paper, Yale University.
Phillips, P. C. B., & Magdalinos, T. (2013). Inconsistent VAR regression with common explosive roots. *Econometric Theory, 29*, 808–837
Phillips, P. C. B., & Sul, D. (2007). Transition modeling and econometric convergence tests. *Econometrica, 75*, 1771–1855.
Phillips, P. C. B., & Sul, D. (2009). Economic transition and growth. *Journal of Applied Econometrics, 24*, 1153–1185.
Robinson, P. M. (2012). Inference on power law spatial trends. *Bernoulli, 18*, 644–677.
Sargan, J. D. (1958). The estimation of economic relationships using instrumental variables. *Econometrica, 26*, 393–415.
Sargan, J. D. (1983). Identification and lack of identification. *Econometrica, 51*, 1605–1633.
Sims, C. A., Stock, J. H., & Watson, M. W. (1990). Inference in linear time series models with some unit roots. *Econometrica, 58*, 113–144.
Staiger, D., & Stock, J. H. (1997). Instrumental variables regression with weak instruments. *Econometrica, 65*, 557–586.
Toda, H., & Phillips, P. C. B. (1993). Vector autoregressions and causality. *Econometrica, 61*, 1367–1393.

APPENDIX

The following preliminary result is useful:

Lemma 1.

(a) *Under Assumptions A(i), A(ii) and with* $s_t = \left(x_t^{0\prime}, v_t'\right)'$, *partial sums of* $q_t = s_t u_{0t} = \left(q_{xt}', q_{vt}'\right)$, *partitioned conformably with* $s_t = \left(x_t^{0\prime}, v_t'\right)'$, *satisfy the functional law* $n^{-1/2}\sum_{t=1}^{\lfloor n\cdot\rfloor} q_t \Rightarrow B_q(\cdot)$ *with limiting Brownian motion vector* $B_q = \left(B_{q_x}', B_{q_v}'\right)'$, *conformably partitioned with* q_t, *and covariance matrix*

$$\Omega_{qq} = \sigma_{00}\Sigma_{ss} = \sigma_{00}\begin{bmatrix}\Sigma_{aa} & \Sigma_{av}\\ \Sigma_{va} & \Sigma_{vv}\end{bmatrix} > 0.$$

(b) *Under Assumptions A′(i) and A′(ii), partial sums of* $z_t u_{0t}$ *satisfy the functional law* $n^{-1/2}\sum_{t=1}^{\lfloor n\cdot\rfloor} z_t u_{0t} \Rightarrow B_{zu}(\cdot)$ *with limiting Brownian motion* B_{zu} *with covariance matrix* $\sigma_{00}\Sigma_{zz}$.

Proof.

Part (a) The CLT follows from Assumptions A(i) and A(ii) since $n^{-1/2}\sum_{t=1}^{n} q_t$ satisfies the stability and Lindeberg conditions. In particular, the martingale conditional variance matrix $n^{-1}\sum_{t=1}^{n} s_t s_t' \mathbb{E}\left\{u_{0t}^2 | \mathcal{F}_{t-1}\right\} \to_{a.s} \sigma_{00}\Sigma_{ss}$ as $n \to \infty$, ensuring stability. The Lindeberg condition

$$n^{-1}\sum_{t=1}^{n} \mathbb{E}\left[\left\|s_t s_t'\right\| u_{0t}^2 1\left\{\left\|s_t s_t'\right\|^{1/2}|u_{0t}| > \sqrt{n}\epsilon\right\} |\mathcal{F}_{t-1}\right] \to_p 0, \quad \text{for all } \epsilon > 0$$

holds by standard manipulations since

$$1\left\{\left\|s_t s_t'\right\|^{1/2}|u_{0t}| > \sqrt{n}\epsilon\right\} \le 1\left\{\left\|s_t s_t'\right\|^{1/2} > n^{1/4}\epsilon^{1/2}\right\} + 1\left\{|u_{0t}| > n^{1/4}\epsilon^{1/2}\right\},$$

and

$$\begin{aligned} & n^{-1}\sum_{t=1}^{n} \mathbb{E}\left[\left\|s_t s_t'\right\| u_{0t}^2 1\left\{\left\|s_t s_t'\right\|^{1/2}|u_{0t}| > \sqrt{n}\epsilon\right\} |\mathcal{F}_{t-1}\right] \\ & \le n^{-1}\sum_{t=1}^{n} \left\|s_t s_t'\right\| 1\left\{\left\|s_t s_t'\right\|^{1/2} > n^{1/4}\epsilon^{1/2}\right\} \mathbb{E}\left\{u_{0t}^2 | \mathcal{F}_{t-1}\right\} \\ & \quad + n^{-1}\sum_{t=1}^{n} \left\|s_t s_t'\right\| \mathbb{E}\left[u_{0t}^2 1\left\{|u_{0t}| > n^{1/4}\epsilon^{1/2}\right\} |\mathcal{F}_{t-1}\right] \\ & = \sigma_{00} n^{-1}\sum_{t=1}^{n} \left\|s_t s_t'\right\| 1\left\{\left\|s_t s_t'\right\|^{1/2} > n^{1/4}\epsilon^{1/2}\right\} \\ & \quad + \left(n^{-1}\sum_{t=1}^{n} \left\|s_t s_t'\right\|\right) \mathbb{E}\left[u_{01}^2 1\left\{|u_{01}| > n^{1/4}\epsilon^{1/2}\right\} |\mathcal{F}_{0}\right] \\ & \to_{L_1} 0. \end{aligned}$$

The functional law $n^{-1/2}\sum_{t=1}^{\lfloor n\cdot \rfloor} q_t \Rightarrow B_q(\cdot)$ then follows directly by Hall and Heyde (1980, theorem 4.1).

Part (b) The CLT follows in the same way from Assumptions A′(i) and A′(ii): $n^{-1/2}\sum_{t=1}^{n} z_t u_{0t}$ has martingale conditional variance matrix $n^{-1}\sum_{t=1}^{n} z_t z_t' \mathbb{E}\left\{u_{0t}^2 | \mathcal{F}_{t-1}\right\} \to_{a.s} \sigma_{00}\Sigma_{zz}$ as $n \to \infty$, and the Lindeberg condition

$$n^{-1}\sum_{t=1}^{n} \mathbb{E}\left[\left\|z_t z_t'\right\| u_{0t}^2 1\left\{\left\|z_t z_t'\right\|^{1/2}|u_{0t}| > \sqrt{n}\epsilon\right\} |\mathcal{F}_{t-1}\right] \to_p 0, \quad \text{for all } \epsilon > 0$$

holds by the same argument given in part (a). The functional law again follows.

■

Proof of Theorem 1.

Part (i) We start by considering the transformed system (3) and corresponding least squares estimate $\hat{\alpha} = \left(W'W\right)^{-1} W'y$. In view of Eqs. (9) and (10), we have

$$D_n^{-1} W' W D_n^{-1} \rightarrow_{a.s.} \begin{bmatrix} \Sigma_{aa} = \mathbb{E}\left(x_t^0 x_t^{0\prime}\right) & 0 \\ 0 & \Sigma_{bb} = \sum_{t=1}^{\infty} a_t^2 v_t v_t' \end{bmatrix}, \tag{A.1}$$

and

$$D_n^{-1} W' u_0 = \begin{bmatrix} \frac{1}{\sqrt{n}} \sum_{t=1}^{n} w_{at} u_{0t} \\ \sum_{t=1}^{n} w_{bt} u_{0t} \end{bmatrix} \Rightarrow \begin{bmatrix} B_{q_x}(1) \\ Q_v := \sum_{t=1}^{\infty} a_t v_t u_{0t} \end{bmatrix}, \tag{A.2}$$

so that

$$\begin{aligned} D_n\left(\hat{\alpha} - \alpha\right) &= \left[D_n^{-1} W' W D_n^{-1}\right]^{-1} \left[D_n^{-1} W' u_0\right] \\ &\Rightarrow \begin{bmatrix} \Sigma_{aa}^{-1} B_{q_x}(1) \\ \Sigma_{bb}^{-1} \sum_{t=1}^{\infty} a_t v_t u_{0t} \end{bmatrix} =: \begin{bmatrix} \xi_a \\ \xi_b \end{bmatrix}, \end{aligned} \tag{A.3}$$

where $\xi_a \equiv N\left(0, \sigma_{00} \Sigma_{aa}^{-1}\right)$ and $\xi_b = \left(\sum_{t=1}^{\infty} a_t^2 v_t v_t'\right)^{-1} \sum_{t=1}^{\infty} a_t v_t u_{0t}$. Next note that $\hat{\beta} - \beta = G\left(\hat{\alpha} - \alpha\right) = G D_n^{-1} D_n \left(\hat{\alpha} - \alpha\right)$, so that

$$\left(G D_n^{-1}\right)^{-1} \left(\hat{\beta} - \beta\right) = D_n\left(\hat{\alpha} - \alpha\right) \Rightarrow \left(\xi_a', \xi_b'\right)'.$$

Now

$$\begin{bmatrix} \hat{\beta}_a - \beta_a \\ \hat{\beta}_b - \beta_b \end{bmatrix} = G D_n^{-1} D_n \begin{bmatrix} \hat{\alpha}_a - \alpha_a \\ \hat{\alpha}_b - \alpha_b \end{bmatrix} = \begin{bmatrix} \frac{1}{\sqrt{n}} I_{k_a} & -\Pi' \\ 0 & I_{k_b} \end{bmatrix} D_n \begin{bmatrix} \hat{\alpha}_a - \alpha_a \\ \hat{\alpha}_b - \alpha_b \end{bmatrix},$$

so that

$$D_n G^{-1} \begin{bmatrix} \hat{\beta}_a - \beta_a \\ \hat{\beta}_b - \beta_b \end{bmatrix} = D_n \begin{bmatrix} \hat{\alpha}_a - \alpha_a \\ \hat{\alpha}_b - \alpha_b \end{bmatrix} \Rightarrow \begin{bmatrix} \xi_a \\ \xi_b \end{bmatrix}.$$

That is

$$\begin{bmatrix} \sqrt{n} I_{k_a} & \sqrt{n}\Pi' \\ 0 & I_{k_b} \end{bmatrix} \begin{bmatrix} \hat{\beta}_a - \beta_a \\ \hat{\beta}_b - \beta_b \end{bmatrix} \Rightarrow \begin{bmatrix} \xi_a \\ \xi_b \end{bmatrix},$$

It follows that

$$\hat{\beta}_b - \beta_b \Rightarrow \xi_b,$$

$$\sqrt{n}\left(\hat{\beta}_a - \beta_a\right) + \sqrt{n}\Pi'\left(\hat{\beta}_b - \beta_b\right) \Rightarrow N\left(0, \sigma_{00}\Sigma_{aa}^{-1}\right),$$

which leads to

$$\begin{bmatrix} \hat{\beta}_a - \beta_a \\ \hat{\beta}_b - \beta_b \end{bmatrix} = \begin{bmatrix} -\Pi' \\ I_{k_b} \end{bmatrix}\left(\hat{\beta}_b - \beta_b\right) + o_p(1) \Rightarrow \begin{bmatrix} -\Pi' \\ I_{k_b} \end{bmatrix}\xi_b.$$

Hence, both $\hat{\beta}_a$ and $\hat{\beta}_b$ are inconsistent with limits that are random, dependent on $\xi_b = \left(\sum_{t=1}^{\infty} a_t^2 v_t v_t'\right)^{-1} \sum_{t=1}^{\infty} a_t v_t u_{0t}$, and of degenerate dimension k_b because $\hat{\beta}_a - \beta_a$ is asymptotically proportional to $\hat{\beta}_b - \beta_b$. No invariance principle applies because the distribution of ξ_b depends on the distribution of the data.

Part (ii) Note that

$$\begin{aligned} \hat{\sigma}^2 &= n^{-1}u_0'\left(I_n - X\left(X'X\right)^{-1}X'\right)u_0 = \frac{u_0'u_0}{n} \\ &\quad - \frac{1}{n}u_0'XG\left(G'X'XG\right)^{-1}G'X'u_0 \\ &= \frac{u_0'u_0}{n} - \frac{1}{n}u_0'W\left(W'W\right)^{-1}W'u_0 = \frac{u_0'u_0}{n} \\ &\quad - \frac{1}{n}u_0'WD_n^{-1}\left(D_n^{-1}W'WD_n^{-1}\right)^{-1}D_n^{-1}W'u_0 \\ &\rightarrow_p \mathbb{E}\left(u_{0t}^2\right) = \sigma_{00}, \end{aligned}$$

since $n^{-1}u_0'u_0 \rightarrow_{a.s} \mathbb{E}\left(u_{0t}^2\right)$ by the ergodic theorem, $D_n^{-1}W'WD_n^{-1} \rightarrow_{a.s.} \mathrm{diag}\left\{\Sigma_{aa}, \Sigma_{bb}\right\} > 0$ by Eq. (A.1), and $D_n^{-1}W'u_0 = O_p(1)$ by Eq. (A.2). Hence, $\hat{\sigma}^2$ is consistent for σ_{00}.

Part (iii) Under the null $\mathbb{H}_0 : \beta = 0$, we have $\alpha = G^{-1}\beta = 0$ and

$$\begin{aligned} W_n &= \hat{\beta}'X'X\hat{\beta}/\hat{\sigma}^2 = \hat{\beta}'G'^{-1}G'X'XGG^{-1}\hat{\beta}/\hat{\sigma}^2 = \hat{\alpha}'W'W\hat{\alpha}/\hat{\sigma}^2 \\ &= \hat{\alpha}'D_nD_n^{-1}W'WD_n^{-1}D_n\hat{\alpha}/\hat{\sigma}^2 \\ &\Rightarrow \left(\xi_a', \xi_b'\right)\begin{bmatrix} \Sigma_{aa} & 0 \\ 0 & \Sigma_{bb} \end{bmatrix}\begin{bmatrix} \xi_a \\ \xi_b \end{bmatrix}\Big/\sigma_{00} = \left\{\xi_a'\Sigma_{aa}\xi_a + \xi_b'\Sigma_{bb}\xi_b\right\}/\sigma_{00} \\ &= \zeta_a'\zeta_a + \zeta_b'\zeta_b, \end{aligned}$$

where

$$D_n\left(\hat{\alpha}-\alpha\right)\Rightarrow\begin{bmatrix}\xi_a\\ \xi_b\end{bmatrix}=\begin{bmatrix}N\left(0,\sigma_{00}\Sigma_{aa}^{-1}\right)\\ \Sigma_{bb}^{-1}\sum_{t=1}^{\infty}a_t v_t u_{0t}\end{bmatrix},$$

using Eq. (A.3) and setting $\zeta_a := \Sigma_{aa}^{1/2}\xi_a/\sigma_{00}^{1/2} =_d N\left(0, I_m\right)$ and $\zeta_b := \Sigma_{bb}^{1/2}\xi_b/\sigma_{00}^{1/2} = \Sigma_{bb}^{-1/2}\sum_{t=1}^{\infty}a_t v_t u_{0t}/\sigma_{00}^{1/2}$. We deduce that $W_n \Rightarrow \chi^2_{k_a} + \zeta_b'\zeta_b$, a mixture of a chi-square distribution and the squared length of the vector variate ζ_b.

■

Proof of Theorem 2.

Part (i) We start the analysis by considering the behavior of the sample moment matrix of w_t and the instruments z_t, viz.,

$$W'Z=\begin{bmatrix}\sum_{t=1}^{n}x_t^0 z_t'\\ \sum_{t=1}^{n}a_t v_t z_t'\end{bmatrix}.$$

Under Assumption A′(i), A′(ii), and B(ii) $\sum_{t=1}^{n}a_t v_t z_t' \to_{a.s} \sum_{t=1}^{\infty}a_t v_t z_t'$, which is convergent $a.s.$ because $\sum_{t=1}^{\infty}|a_t|\,\mathbb{E}\left\|v_t z_t'\right\| < \infty$. It follows that $n^{-1/2}\sum_{t=1}^{n}a_t v_t z_t' \to_{a.s} 0$ and then

$$\begin{aligned}D_n^{-1}W'P_Z W D_n^{-1} &= \begin{bmatrix}\frac{1}{\sqrt{n}}\sum_{t=1}^{n}x_t^0 z_t'\\ \sum_{t=1}^{n}a_t v_t z_t'\end{bmatrix}\left(\sum_{t=1}^{n}z_t z_t'\right)^{-1}\left[\frac{1}{\sqrt{n}}\sum_{t=1}^{n}z_t x_t^{0\prime}, \sum_{t=1}^{n}a_t z_t v_t'\right]\\ &= \begin{bmatrix}\frac{1}{n}\sum_{t=1}^{n}x_t^0 z_t'\\ \frac{1}{\sqrt{n}}\sum_{t=1}^{n}a_t v_t z_t'\end{bmatrix}\left(\frac{\sum_{t=1}^{n}z_t z_t'}{n}\right)^{-1}\\ &\quad\times\left[\frac{1}{n}\sum_{t=1}^{n}z_t x_t^{0\prime}, \frac{1}{\sqrt{n}}\sum_{t=1}^{n}a_t z_t v_t'\right]\\ &\to_{a.s}\begin{bmatrix}\Sigma_{xz}\Sigma_{zz}^{-1}\Sigma_{zx} & 0\\ 0 & 0\end{bmatrix},\end{aligned}$$

which is singular. Applying the martingale CLT (see Lemma 1) we have $n^{-1/2}\sum_{t=1}^{n}z_t u_{0t} \Rightarrow N\left(0, \sigma_{00}\Sigma_{zz}\right)$, and by ergodicity $n^{-1}\left[\sum_{t=1}^{n}z_t x_t^{0\prime}, \sum_{t=1}^{n}z_t v_t', \ \sum_{t=1}^{n}z_t z_t'\right] \to_{a.s.} \left[\Sigma_{zx}\ \Sigma_{zv}\ \Sigma_{zz}\right]$, which leads to

$$D_n^{-1}W'P_Z u_0 = \begin{bmatrix} \frac{1}{n}\sum_{t=1}^n x_t^0 z_t' \\ \frac{1}{\sqrt{n}}\sum_{t=1}^n a_t v_t z_t' \end{bmatrix} \left(\frac{\sum_{t=1}^n z_t z_t'}{n}\right)^{-1} \left[\frac{1}{\sqrt{n}}\sum_{t=1}^n z_t u_{0t}\right]$$
$$\Rightarrow \begin{bmatrix} \Sigma_{xz} \\ 0 \end{bmatrix} \Sigma_{zz}^{-1} \times N(0, \sigma_{00}\Sigma_{zz}) = \begin{bmatrix} N\left(0, \sigma_{00}\Sigma_{xz}\Sigma_{zz}^{-1}\Sigma_{zx}\right) \\ 0 \end{bmatrix}.$$

Now define $F_n = diag\left(\sqrt{n}I_{k_a}, \frac{1}{\sqrt{n}}I_{k_b}\right)$ and note that

$$F_n^{-1}W'P_Z WF_n^{-1} = \begin{bmatrix} \frac{1}{n}\sum_{t=1}^n x_t^0 z_t' \\ \sum_{t=1}^n a_t v_t z_t' \end{bmatrix} \left(\frac{\sum_{t=1}^n z_t z_t'}{n}\right)^{-1} \left[\frac{1}{n}\sum_{t=1}^n z_t x_t^{0\prime}, \sum_{t=1}^n a_t z_t v_t'\right]$$
$$\rightarrow_{a.s} \begin{bmatrix} \Sigma_{xz}\Sigma_{zz}^{-1}\Sigma_{zx} & \Sigma_{xz}\Sigma_{zz}^{-1}\left(\sum_{t=1}^\infty a_t z_t v_t'\right) \\ \left(\sum_{t=1}^\infty a_t v_t z_t'\right)\Sigma_{zz}^{-1}\Sigma_{zx} & \left(\sum_{t=1}^\infty a_t v_t z_t'\right)\Sigma_{zz}^{-1}\left(\sum_{t=1}^\infty a_t z_t v_t'\right) \end{bmatrix}$$
$$=: \begin{bmatrix} \Sigma_{xz}\Sigma_{zz}^{-1}\Sigma_{zx} & \Sigma_{xz}\Sigma_{zz}^{-1}A_z \\ A_z'\Sigma_{zz}^{-1}\Sigma_{zx} & A_z'\Sigma_{zz}^{-1}A_z \end{bmatrix} = M, \tag{A.4}$$

where $A_z = \sum_{t=1}^\infty a_t z_t v_t'$, which is convergent almost surely because $\sum_{t=1}^\infty |a_t| \mathbb{E}\left\|z_t v_t'\right\| < \infty$ in view of B(ii) and A′(ii). Also

$$F_n^{-1}W'P_Z u_0 = \begin{bmatrix} \frac{1}{n}\sum_{t=1}^n x_t^0 z_t' \\ \sum_{t=1}^n a_t v_t z_t' \end{bmatrix} \left(\frac{\sum_{t=1}^n z_t z_t'}{n}\right)^{-1} \left[\frac{1}{\sqrt{n}}\sum_{t=1}^n z_t u_{0t}\right]$$
$$\Rightarrow \begin{bmatrix} \Sigma_{xz} \\ A_z' \end{bmatrix} \Sigma_{zz}^{-1} \times N(0, \sigma_{00}\Sigma_{zz}) = MN(0, \sigma_{00}M).$$

Note that the matrix variate $A_z = \sum_{t=1}^\infty a_t z_t v_t'$ is independent of the limit of $\left(\frac{1}{n}\sum_{t=1}^n z_t z_t'\right)^{-1/2} \frac{1}{\sqrt{n}}\sum_{t=1}^n z_t u_{0t} \Rightarrow N(0, I_K)$, since this Gaussian limit does not depend on $\{z_t, v_t\}_{t=1}^\infty$. Hence, we have the mixed normal (MN) limit theory

$$F_n(\alpha_{IV} - \alpha) = \left(F_n^{-1}W'P_Z WF_n^{-1}\right)^{-1}\left(F_n^{-1}W'P_Z u_0\right)$$
$$\Rightarrow MN\left(0, \sigma_{00}M^{-1}\right). \tag{A.5}$$

In partitioned form, we have

$$F_n\left(\alpha_{IV}-\alpha\right)=\left\{\sqrt{n}\left(\alpha_{a,IV}-\alpha_a\right),\frac{1}{\sqrt{n}}\left(\alpha_{b,IV}-\alpha_b\right)\right\}$$
$$\Rightarrow MN\left(0,\sigma_{00}\begin{bmatrix}\Sigma_{xz}\Sigma_{zz}^{-1}\Sigma_{zx} & \Sigma_{xz}\Sigma_{zz}^{-1}A_z\\ A_z'\Sigma_{zz}^{-1}\Sigma_{zx} & A_z'\Sigma_{zz}^{-1}A_z\end{bmatrix}^{-1}\right) \tag{A.6}$$

and so $\alpha_{a,IV}\to_p\alpha_a$ but $\alpha_{b,IV}$ diverges at a $\sqrt{n}$ rate. Transforming to the original coordinates, we have

$$\beta_{IV}-\beta=G\left(\alpha_{IV}-\alpha\right)=\begin{bmatrix}I_{k_a} & -\Pi'\\ 0 & I_{k_b}\end{bmatrix}\left(\alpha_{IV}-\alpha\right), \tag{A.7}$$

and then

$$\beta_{IV}-\beta=\begin{bmatrix}\beta_{a,IV}-\beta_a\\ \beta_{b,IV}-\beta_b\end{bmatrix}=G\begin{bmatrix}\alpha_{a,IV}-\alpha_a\\ \alpha_{b,IV}-\alpha_b\end{bmatrix}=GF_n^{-1}F_n\left(\alpha_{IV}-\alpha\right),$$

giving

$$F_nG^{-1}\left(\beta_{IV}-\beta\right)=F_n\left(\alpha_{IV}-\alpha\right)\Rightarrow MN\left(0,\sigma_{00}M^{-1}\right). \tag{A.8}$$

Since $G^{-1}=\begin{bmatrix}I_{k_a} & \Pi'\\ 0 & I_{k_b}\end{bmatrix}$ and $F_n=\operatorname{diag}\left(\sqrt{n}I_{k_a},\frac{1}{\sqrt{n}}I_{k_b}\right)$, we have the partitioned asymptotics

$$\begin{aligned}
&F_nG^{-1}\left(\beta_{IV}-\beta\right)\\
&=\begin{bmatrix}\sqrt{n}I_{k_a} & \sqrt{n}\Pi'\\ 0 & 1/\sqrt{n}\end{bmatrix}\begin{bmatrix}\beta_{a,IV}-\beta_a\\ \beta_{b,IV}-\beta_b\end{bmatrix}\\
&=\begin{bmatrix}\sqrt{n}\left(\beta_{a,IV}-\beta_a\right)+\sqrt{n}\Pi'\left(\beta_{b,IV}-\beta_b\right)\\ \frac{1}{\sqrt{n}}\left(\beta_{b,IV}-\beta_b\right)\end{bmatrix}\\
&\Rightarrow MN\left(0,\sigma_{00}\begin{bmatrix}\Sigma_{xz}\Sigma_{zz}^{-1}\Sigma_{zx} & \Sigma_{xz}\Sigma_{zz}^{-1}A_z\\ A_z'\Sigma_{zz}^{-1}\Sigma_{zx} & A_z'\Sigma_{zz}^{-1}A_z\end{bmatrix}^{-1}\right).
\end{aligned} \tag{A.9}$$

Recall that $\alpha=G^{-1}\beta=\begin{bmatrix}\beta_a+\Pi'\beta_b\\ \beta_b\end{bmatrix}=:\begin{bmatrix}\alpha_a\\ \alpha_b\end{bmatrix}$ so that $\beta_{a,IV}+\Pi'\beta_{b,IV}$ is consistent for $\beta_a+\Pi'\beta_b$ and $\sqrt{n}\left(\beta_{a,IV}-\beta_a\right)+\sqrt{n}\Pi'\left(\beta_{b,IV}-\beta_b\right)$ has a limiting MN distribution, whereas $\beta_{b,IV}-\beta_b$ diverges at the rate

$\sqrt{n}$. More specifically, we have by partitioning the limit covariance matrix in Eq. (A.9) that

$$\sqrt{n}\left(\beta_{a,IV} + \Pi'\beta_{b,IV} - \beta_a - \Pi'\beta_b\right) \Rightarrow MN0, \sigma_{00}H_{\beta\beta}^{-1},$$

where $H_{\beta\beta} = \left[\Sigma_{xz}\Sigma_{zz}^{-1}\Sigma_{zx} - \Sigma_{xz}\Sigma_{zz}^{-1}A_z\left(A_z'\Sigma_{zz}^{-1}A_z\right)^{-1}A_z'\Sigma_{zz}^{-1}\Sigma_{zx}\right]$.

Part (ii) We next consider the IV error variance estimate $\tilde{\sigma}^2 = \frac{1}{n}\tilde{u}'\tilde{u}$, where $\tilde{u} = y - X\beta_{IV} = y - W\alpha_{IV} = u_0 - W\left(W'P_ZW\right)^{-1}W'P_Zu_0$. The estimate can be expanded as follows:

$$\begin{aligned}
\tilde{\sigma}^2 &= \frac{1}{n}u_0'u_0 - \frac{2}{n}u_0'P_ZW\left(W'P_ZW\right)^{-1}W'u_0 \\
&\quad + \frac{1}{n}u_0'P_ZW\left(W'P_ZW\right)^{-1}W'W\left(W'P_ZW\right)^{-1}W'P_Zu_0 \\
&= \frac{1}{n}u_0'u_0 - \frac{2}{n}u_0'P_ZWF_n^{-1}\left(F_n^{-1}W'P_ZWF_n^{-1}\right)^{-1}F_n^{-1}W'u_0 \\
&\quad + \frac{1}{n}u_0'P_ZWF_n^{-1}\left(F_n^{-1}W'P_ZWF_n^{-1}\right)^{-1}F_n^{-1}W'WF_n^{-1} \\
&\quad \times \left(F_n^{-1}W'P_ZWF_n^{-1}\right)^{-1}F_n^{-1}W'P_Zu_0.
\end{aligned}$$

Observe that $n^{-1}u_0'u_0 \rightarrow_{a.s.} \sigma_{00}$, $F_n(\alpha_{IV} - \alpha) \Rightarrow Z_\alpha := MN(0, \sigma_{00}M^{-1})$ in view of Eq. (A.5), and

$$F_n^{-1}W'u_0 = \begin{bmatrix} \frac{1}{\sqrt{n}}\sum_{t=1}^n x_t^0 u_{0t} \\ \sqrt{n}\sum_{t=1}^n a_t v_t u_{0t} \end{bmatrix},$$

so that

$$\begin{aligned}
\frac{1}{n}u_0'P_ZW\left(W'P_ZW\right)^{-1}W'u_0 &= \frac{1}{n}\left(\alpha_{IV} - \alpha\right)'F_nF_n^{-1}W'u_0 \\
&= \frac{1}{\sqrt{n}}\left(\alpha_{IV} - \alpha\right)'F_n\begin{bmatrix} \frac{1}{n}\sum_{t=1}^n x_t^0 u_{0t} \\ \sum_{t=1}^n a_t v_t u_{0t} \end{bmatrix} = O_p\left(\frac{1}{\sqrt{n}}\right).
\end{aligned}$$

Next, note that

$$\frac{1}{n}F_n^{-1}W'WF_n^{-1} = \frac{1}{n}\begin{bmatrix} \frac{1}{n}\sum_{t=1}^n x_t^0 x_t^{0\prime} & \sum_{t=1}^n a_t x_t^0 v_t' \\ \sum_{t=1}^n a_t v_t x_t^{0\prime} & n\sum_{t=1}^n a_t^2 v_t v_t' \end{bmatrix}$$

$$= \begin{bmatrix} \frac{1}{n^2}\sum_{t=1}^n x_t^0 x_t^{0\prime} & \frac{1}{n}\sum_{t=1}^n a_t x_t^0 v_t' \\ \frac{1}{n}\sum_{t=1}^n a_t v_t x_t^{0\prime} & \sum_{t=1}^n a_t^2 v_t v_t' \end{bmatrix}$$

$$= \begin{bmatrix} O_p\left(n^{-1}\right) & O_p\left(n^{-1}\right) \\ O_p\left(n^{-1}\right) & \sum_{t=1}^n a_t^2 v_t v_t' \end{bmatrix}, \quad \text{under A}' \text{ and B(ii).}$$

Alternatively under A′ and B(i), we have

$$\begin{bmatrix} \frac{1}{n^2}\sum_{t=1}^n x_t^0 x_t^{0\prime} & \frac{1}{n}\sum_{t=1}^n a_t x_t^0 v_t' \\ \frac{1}{n}\sum_{t=1}^n a_t v_t x_t^{0\prime} & \sum_{t=1}^n a_t^2 v_t v_t' \end{bmatrix} = \begin{bmatrix} O_p\left(n^{-1}\right) & O_p\left(n^{-1+\eta}\right) \\ O_p\left(n^{-1+\eta}\right) & \sum_{t=1}^n a_t^2 v_t v_t' \end{bmatrix},$$

for some small $\eta > 0$. Using these results we obtain

$$\begin{aligned}
&\frac{1}{n}u_0' P_Z W F_n^{-1}\left(F_n^{-1}W'P_Z W F_n^{-1}\right)^{-1} F_n^{-1}W'WF_n^{-1} \\
&\quad \times \left(F_n^{-1}W'P_Z W F_n^{-1}\right)^{-1} F_n^{-1}W'P_Z u_0 \\
&= (\alpha_{IV}-\alpha)' F_n \left\{\frac{1}{n}F_n^{-1}W'WF_n^{-1}\right\} F_n(\alpha_{IV}-\alpha) \\
&= (\alpha_{IV}-\alpha)' F_n \begin{bmatrix} O_p\left(n^{-1}\right) & O_p\left(n^{-1+\eta}\right) \\ O_p\left(n^{-1+\eta}\right) & \sum_{t=1}^n a_t^2 v_t v_t' \end{bmatrix} F_n(\alpha_{IV}-\alpha) \\
&= \left\{\frac{1}{\sqrt{n}}\left(\alpha_{b,IV}-\alpha_b\right)'\right\}\left(\sum_{t=1}^n a_t^2 v_t v_t'\right)\left\{\frac{1}{\sqrt{n}}\left(\alpha_{b,IV}-\alpha_b\right)\right\} + o_p(1) \\
&\Rightarrow \sigma_{00}\psi_b' H^{-1/2}\left(\sum_{t=1}^\infty a_t^2 v_t v_t'\right) H^{-1/2}\psi_b
\end{aligned}$$

where we use the fact that $\frac{1}{\sqrt{n}}\left(\alpha_{b,IV}-\alpha_b\right) = \frac{1}{\sqrt{n}}\left(\beta_{b,IV}-\beta_b\right) \Rightarrow MN\left(0,\sigma_{00}H^{-1}\right) = \sigma_{00}^{1/2}H^{-1/2}\psi_b$ with $\psi_b = N\left(0, I_{k_b}\right)$ and

$$H = \left[A_z'\Sigma_{zz}^{-1}A_z - A_z'\Sigma_{zz}^{-1}\Sigma_{zx}\left(\Sigma_{xz}\Sigma_{zz}^{-1}\Sigma_{zx}\right)^{-1}\Sigma_{xz}\Sigma_{zz}^{-1}A_z\right].$$

It follows that

$$\tilde{\sigma}^2 = \frac{1}{n}\tilde{u}'\tilde{u} \to_p \sigma_{00}\left\{1 + \omega_{zz}\right\}$$

where $\omega_{zz} = \psi_b' H^{-1/2}\left(\sum_{t=1}^{\infty} a_t^2 v_t v_t'\right) H^{-1/2}\psi_b$, as stated.

Part (iii) The block Wald test is

$$\begin{aligned} W_n &= \beta_{IV}' X' P_Z X \beta_{IV}/\tilde{\sigma}^2 = \beta_{IV}' G'^{-1} G' X' P_Z X G G^{-1}\beta_{IV}/\tilde{\sigma}^2 \\ &= \alpha_{IV}' W' P_Z W \alpha_{IV}/\tilde{\sigma}^2 \\ &= \alpha_{IV}' F_n \left(F_n^{-1} W' P_Z W F_n^{-1}\right) F_n \alpha_{IV}/\tilde{\sigma}^2. \end{aligned}$$

Under the null hypothesis $\mathbb{H}_0 : \beta = \alpha = 0$ we have from Eq. (A.8) that $F_n\alpha_{IV} \Rightarrow N\left(0, \sigma_{00}M^{-1}\right)$, and from Eq. (A.4) that $F_n^{-1}W'P_Z W F_n^{-1} \Rightarrow M$. It follows that

$$\left\{F_n^{-1} W' P_Z W F_n^{-1}\right\}^{1/2} F_n \alpha_{IV}/\sigma_{00}^{1/2} \Rightarrow Z \sim N\left(0, I_k\right),$$

so that

$$W_n \Rightarrow \frac{1}{\{1+\omega_{zz}\}} Z'Z = \chi_k^2/\left\{1+\omega_{zz}\right\},$$

as stated.

Part (iv) The Sargan test for overidentification has the form

$$\begin{aligned} S_n &= \tilde{u}' P_Z \tilde{u}/\tilde{\sigma}^2 = u_0'\left\{P_Z - P_Z X\left(X'P_Z X\right)^{-1} X' P_Z\right\} u_0/\tilde{\sigma}^2 \\ &= u_0'\left\{P_Z - P_Z W\left(W'P_Z W\right)^{-1} W' P_Z\right\} u_0/\tilde{\sigma}^2 \\ &= \zeta_n'\left\{I_K - \left(Z'Z\right)^{-1/2} Z'W\left(W'P_Z W\right)^{-1} W'Z\left(Z'Z\right)^{-1/2}\right\}\zeta_n/\tilde{\sigma}^2, \end{aligned}$$

where $\zeta_n = \left(n^{-1}Z'Z\right)^{-1/2}\left(n^{-1/2}Z'u_0\right) \Rightarrow \zeta \equiv MN\left(0, \sigma_{00}I_K\right) \equiv N(0, \sigma_{00}I_K)$ by the MGCLT in Lemma 1. Note that the limit distribution and random vector ζ is independent of (z_t). Use the earlier finding (A.4) that

$$F_n^{-1} W' P_Z W F_n^{-1} \to_{a.s} \begin{bmatrix} \Sigma_{xz}\Sigma_{zz}^{-1}\Sigma_{zx} & \Sigma_{xz}\Sigma_{zz}^{-1}A_z \\ A_z'\Sigma_{zz}^{-1}\Sigma_{zx} & A_z'\Sigma_{zz}^{-1}A_z \end{bmatrix},$$

where $A_z = \sum_{t=1}^{\infty} a_t z_t v_t'$, and $F_n = \text{diag}\left(\sqrt{n} I_{k_a}, \frac{1}{\sqrt{n}}\right)$. We further note that

$$\begin{aligned}
\left(Z'Z\right)^{-1/2} Z'WF_n^{-1} &= \left(\frac{Z'Z}{n}\right)^{-1/2} \frac{Z'W}{\sqrt{n}} F_n^{-1} \\
&= \left(\frac{Z'Z}{n}\right)^{-1/2} \left[\tfrac{1}{n} \textstyle\sum_{t=1}^{n} z_t x_t^0 \ \sum_{t=1}^{n} a_t z_t v_t'\right] \\
&\to_{a.s} \Sigma_{zz}^{-1/2} \left[\Sigma_{zx}, A_z\right],
\end{aligned}$$

and, defining $Q = \Sigma_{zz}^{-1/2}\left[\Sigma_{zx} \ A_z\right]$, observe that

$$\begin{bmatrix} \Sigma_{xz}\Sigma_{zz}^{-1}\Sigma_{zx} & \Sigma_{xz}\Sigma_{zz}^{-1}A_z \\ A_z'\Sigma_{zz}^{-1}\Sigma_{zx} & A_z'\Sigma_{zz}^{-1}A_z \end{bmatrix} = \begin{bmatrix} \Sigma_{xz} \\ A_z' \end{bmatrix} \Sigma_{zz}^{-1}\left[\Sigma_{zx} \ A_z\right] = Q'Q.$$

We deduce that

$$\begin{aligned}
S_n &= \zeta_n' \left\{ I_K - \left(Z'Z\right)^{-1/2} Z'W\left(W'P_Z W\right)^{-1} W'Z\left(Z'Z\right)^{-1/2} \right\} \zeta_n / \tilde{\sigma}^2 \\
&= \zeta_n' \left\{ I_K - Q\left(Q'Q\right)^{-1} Q' + o_{a.s.}(1) \right\} \zeta_n / \left\{\sigma_{00}\left[1+\omega_{zz}\right] + o_{a.s.}(1)\right\} \\
&\Rightarrow \chi^2_{K-k} / \left\{1+\omega_{zz}\right\},
\end{aligned}$$

since $P_Q = I_K - Q\left(Q'Q\right)^{-1} Q'$ is symmetric and idempotent of rank $K-k$. Hence, the Sargan overidentification test statistic is distributed in the limit as $\chi^2_{K-k}/\left\{1+\omega_{zz}\right\}$, as stated.

■

PART VI
NONPARAMETRIC AND SEMIPARAMETRIC METHODS

MULTIVARIATE LOCAL POLYNOMIAL ESTIMATORS: UNIFORM BOUNDARY PROPERTIES AND ASYMPTOTIC LINEAR REPRESENTATION

Yanqin Fan[a] and Emmanuel Guerre[b]

[a] *Department of Economics, University of Washington, Seattle, WA, USA*

[b] *School of Economics and Finance, Queen Mary, University of London, London, UK*

ABSTRACT

The asymptotic bias and variance of a general class of local polynomial estimators of M-regression functions are studied over the whole compact *support of the* multivariate *covariate under a minimal assumption on the support. The support assumption ensures that the vicinity of the boundary of the support will be visited by the multivariate covariate. The results show that like in the univariate case, multivariate local polynomial estimators have good bias and variance properties near the boundary. For the local polynomial regression estimator, we establish its asymptotic normality near the boundary and the usual optimal uniform convergence rate over the whole support. For local polynomial quantile regression, we establish a uniform linearization result which allows us to obtain similar results to the local*

Essays in Honor of Aman Ullah

Advances in Econometrics, Volume 36, 489–537

ISSN: 0731-9053/doi:10.1108/S0731-905320160000036023

polynomial regression. We demonstrate both theoretically and numerically that with our uniform results, the common practice of trimming local polynomial regression or quantile estimators to avoid "the boundary effect" is not needed.

Keywords: Compact support; boundary effect; pseudo-true value; Newton–Kantorovich Theorem; regression discontinuity design; trimming

JEL classifications: C12; C14; C21

1. INTRODUCTION

Recent work illustrate the practical relevance of correcting the boundary bias of kernel estimators. For example, Hickman and Hubbard (2015) demonstrate that standard kernel procedures used in the estimation of auction models may not be able to uncover important features due to boundary bias. In the context of regression discontinuity design (RDD), estimating the parameters of interest involves the estimation of two conditional expectations or conditional quantiles at the discontinuity point(s), so suffers from the boundary effect if kernel estimators are used. It is well known in the literature that theoretically one must deal with either the small denominator problem or the boundary bias for semiparametric estimators and test statistics involving averages of kernel estimators over all sample points. One way to address boundary effects is to use boundary kernels as applied in Hickman and Hubbard (2015). This solution is simple to implement in the univariate case but can become burdensome in the multivariate case where it may require estimation of the support or the support is of complicated form. See, for instance, Müller and Stadtmüller (1999) or Bouezmarni and Rombouts (2010) for the case of a known support.

Local polynomial estimators are known to have better boundary properties than the popular kernel estimators – their bias order is the same for interior and boundary points. This could alleviate the aforementioned technical and practical problems with kernel estimators. Work in both RDD and semiparametric estimation and inference using local polynomial estimators have started to appear, see, for example, Altonji, Ichimura, and Otsu (2012), Aryal, Gabrielli, and Vuong (2014), Bravo and Jacho-Chávez (2011), Hoderlein, Su, White, and Yang (2016), Qu and Yoon (2015), Su and Ullah (2008), and Su and White (2012) for estimation and inference in semiparametric and nonparametric models; and Hahn, Todd, and Van der Klaauw (2001), Porter (2003), Frandsen, Frölich, and Melly (2012), Imbens and Zajonc (2011), and Oka (2009) for the estimation in RDD. However, these works are either limited to the univariate case or circumvent potential boundary issues by trimming or focusing interest on an inner subset of the covariate support. Notable exceptions are Banerjee (2007) and Kong, Linton, and Xia (2010), who average over the whole support (unit hypercube) of a multivariate covariate to estimate, respectively, regression average derivatives and an additive quantile specification. More theoretical works in this direction are Ruppert and Wand (1994), Gu, Li, and Yang (2015), and Chen and Wu (2013), who deal with pointwise bias and variance expressions for local polynomial regression estimators.

Two important properties of local polynomial estimators are crucial to their successful applications in Econometrics: a precise characterization of their boundary properties including the bias and variance and a uniform asymptotic linear representation. For univariate covariate, boundary bias and variance expressions are well known, see Fan and Gijbels (1996). For multivariate covariate, they become complicated. The only general paper that deals with boundary bias and variance for multivariate covariates is Ruppert and Wand (1994). Under the boundary assumption (A4) of their paper, Ruppert and Wand (1994) establish expressions of bias and variance of local polynomial regression estimators at the boundary points. Specifically, Ruppert and Wand (1994) assumption (A4) considers a boundary point x_∂ belonging to a convex neighborhood $\mathcal{C}$ such that $\inf_{x \in \mathcal{C}} f(x) > 0$, where $f(\cdot)$ is the probability density function (p.d.f.) of the covariate. Imbens and Zajonc (2011) apply results in Ruppert and Wand (1994) in the context of RDD with multiple forcing variables. The local assumption (A4) of Ruppert and Wand (1994) seems difficult to extend to allow for uniform estimation in the neighborhood of the support boundary. The uniform results of Kong et al. (2010) are specific to hypercube supports which, as the half spaces support considered in Gu et al. (2015), may be too restrictive in practice. We propose instead a uniform version of Chen and Wu (2013) which accounts for general boundaries.

As seen from Guerre (2000), what matters for consistent estimation is to have "enough" observations near the estimation location, a condition which involves the geometry of the support in a more subtle way and is flexible enough to cover uniform estimation. The first contribution of this paper is to provide expressions for bias and variance of a general class of multivariate local polynomial estimators of M-regression functions, including both regression and conditional quantile functions under weaker support assumptions than (A4) in Ruppert and Wand (1994). Specifically, our support condition does not require the support of the covariate to be connected and allows it to have holes. Under the new support condition, we show that the asymptotic order of the bias and variance of the local polynomial estimators of M-regression functions are not affected by boundary.

The weaker support condition is made possible by our novel application of the Newton–Kantorovich Theorem[1] to local polynomial estimation. The new approach is in line with White's (1982) approach and uses a pseudo-true value to center the local polynomial estimator. Because the pseudo-true value minimizes the expectation of the objective function and satisfies a key centered score condition, it provides a more natural centering than the partial derivatives of the function to be estimated, as in Fan and Gijbels (1996) or Fan, Heckman, and Wand (1995) and the vast majority of the local polynomial literature. The Newton–Kantorovich Theorem is then used to study the bias, which is defined here as the difference between the pseudo-true value and the partial derivatives. The first-order variance of the estimator can be defined using the usual sandwich formula taken at the pseudo-true value. An interesting finding is that the bias expression may not depend on the estimation method, being for instance identical for regression or quantile local polynomial estimators.

Our results for the bias and variance of multivariate local polynomial estimators have immediate applications in RDD with multiple forcing variables. First, the result for regression could be used to relax Assumption (A4) in Ruppert and Wand (1994) adopted in Imbens and Zajonc (2011) in the context of RDD with multiple forcing variables. In addition, our result for the conditional quantile could be used to extend the estimator of quantile treatment effect in RDD with a univariate forcing variable (see, e.g., Frandsen et al., 2012; Oka, 2009), to allow for multiple forcing variables.

The second contribution of this paper is to establish asymptotic normality and uniform consistency over the whole support for local polynomial estimators of both regression and conditional quantile functions. A simple consistent estimator of the asymptotic variance is also proposed for both models. This requires to establish a new uniform linearization result for local polynomial quantile regression which holds over the whole support. In sharp contrast to Corollary 2, ii) in Masry (1996), which is concerned with multivariate covariates whose support is the entire Euclidean space and is uniformly valid over a compact subset of the support, our results deal directly with multivariate covariates with compact supports and are uniformly valid over the whole supports.

Although the order of bias and variance is not affected by boundary, a qualitative conclusion of our results is that the variance may nevertheless significantly increase near the boundary as well documented in the univariate case. The intuition is that the small denominator problem of the Kernel estimation method is not specific and should affect any nonparametric methods. Estimating a function in a narrow area of the support can only be based on few observations so that a high variance should be effected. Hence, trimming to avoid high estimation variance may make sense in practice. This issue is investigated through a small simulation experiment which considers testing, additive, and single-index specifications. It suggests that although the small denominator problem cannot be completely ruled out for a simple unit square support, the impact of trimming is mostly negative with small potential improvements. This is especially true for testing problems where trimming may decrease the power against some standard alternatives, as well as against more specific boundary alternative which will be poorly detected.

The rest of this paper is organized as follows. The next section introduces the setup, a general class of local polynomial estimators, and the motivating examples. Section 3 presents our results for the asymptotic bias and variance for the class of local polynomial estimators in Section 2. Section 3 establishes asymptotic normality and uniform convergence of the local polynomial regression over the entire support. A uniform linearization result for the local polynomial quantile regression is also derived in Section 4. Section 5 presents results from our simulation experiment. Section 6 offers concluding remarks and Section 7 collects technical proofs.

To close this section, we introduce some notations that will be used throughout the rest of this paper. Let $\lfloor s \rfloor$ be the lower integer part of the real number s, that is the unique integer number such that $\lfloor s \rfloor < s \leq \lfloor s \rfloor + 1$. In what follows, $\|\cdot\|$ stands for the Euclidean or a vector norm and $\mathcal{V}(x,r) = \{z;\, \|z - x\| \leq r\}$ is the closed ball with center x and radius r. When M is a matrix, $\|M\| = \mathrm{Tr}^{1/2}(M'M)$ is the Frobenius norm of M. For symmetric matrices A and B, $A \succeq B$ means that $A - B$ is a positive matrix. The indicator function $\mathbb{I}(X \in A)$ takes value 1 when X lies in A and 0 otherwise.

2. M-REGRESSION, MULTIVARIATE LOCAL POLYNOMIAL ESTIMATION, AND MOTIVATING EXAMPLES

This section first introduces a general multivariate M-regression and its local polynomial estimator. It then reviews several examples including the RDD with multiple forcing variables in Imbens and Zajonc (2011), consistent model specification testing, additive models, and average derivative estimation, where estimation of an M-regression either at the boundary or the entire support is needed.

Consider a univariate-dependent variable Y and a d-dimensional covariate X. We assume that the support of X, denoted as $\mathcal{X}$, is a compact set with a boundary $\mathcal{B}$. Let $\rho(\cdot)$ be a loss function and define the associated M-regression of Y on X as

$$\mu(X) = \arg\min_{\mu \in \mathbb{R}} \mathbb{E}\left[\rho(Y - \mu)|X\right]. \tag{1}$$

It is assumed that $\mu(X)$ is the unique minimizer of $\mathbb{E}\left[\rho(Y - \cdot)|X\right]$. When $\rho(t) = t^2$, $\mu(X)$ is the regression function $\mathbb{E}[Y|X]$ while when $\rho(t) = (1-\alpha)t\mathbb{I}(t \leq 0) - \alpha t\mathbb{I}(t > 0)$ for some $\alpha \in (0,1)$, $\mu(X)$ is the αth quantile of the conditional distribution of Y given X. The αth expectile of Newey and Powell (1987) corresponds to $\rho(t) = (1-\alpha)t^2 I(t \leq 0) + \alpha t^2 I(t > 0)$.

The pth-order local polynomial estimator of $\mu(\cdot)$ in Eq. (1) is defined as follows. Let $U(x)$ be the vector which groups the power $x^{\pi} = x_1^{\pi_1} \times \cdots \times x^{\pi_d}$ for all non-negative integer numbers $\pi_1, \ldots, \pi_d$ with $|\pi| = \pi_1 + \cdots + \pi_d \leq p$ according to the lexicographic order. Let $K(\cdot)$ be a non-negative kernel function and $h > 0$ a bandwidth. The local polynomial estimator of $\mu(x) = \beta_0(x)$ and its partial derivatives

$$\mu^{(\pi)}(x) = \frac{\partial^{|\pi|}\mu(x)}{\partial x_1^{\pi_1} \cdots \partial x^{\pi_d}} = \frac{|\pi|!}{\pi_1! \times \cdots \times \pi_d!}\beta_\pi(x) \tag{2}$$

are denoted as $\hat{\beta}(x; h) = \left(\hat{\beta}_\pi(x; h), |\pi| \leq p\right)'$ with

$$\hat{\beta}(x; h) = \arg\min_{\beta} \sum_{i=1}^{n} \rho\left(Y_i - U(X_i - x)'\beta\right) K\left(\frac{X_i - x}{h}\right), \tag{3}$$

where a suitable convention is used to break possible ties when the minimizer $\hat{\beta}(x; h)$ is not unique as in the case of local polynomial quantile regression.

M-regressions are not only of interest in their own right but also play important roles in other contexts including estimation of average treatment effect parameters, semiparametric models, and consistent model specification testing. Throughout this paper, we use the RDD in Example 1 to illustrate the usefulness of the bias and variance expressions established in Section 3 and Examples 2–4 to demonstrate the usefulness of the uniform results of the type established in this paper in the context of consistent model specification testing and semiparametric estimation involving (weighted) averages of multivariate local polynomial estimators by avoiding fixed trimming of the boundary commonly adopted in existing work.

Example 1: Regression discontinuity design. Suppose that the support $\mathcal{X}$ is partitioned into $\mathcal{X}_0$ and $\mathcal{X}_1$, with boundaries $\mathcal{B}_0$ and $\mathcal{B}_1$. Let $\mathcal{B}_{01} = \mathcal{B}_0 \cap \mathcal{B}_1$ be the frontier between $\mathcal{X}_0$ and $\mathcal{X}_1$. Suppose that individuals with $X = X_1$ in $\mathcal{X}_1$ receive a treatment and let Y_1 be the associated response. Denote (X_0, Y_0) in $\mathcal{X}_0 \times \mathbb{R}$ the control group variables, and

$$\mu_j(x) = \arg\min_{\mu \in \mathbb{R}} \mathbb{E}\left[\rho(Y_j - \mu)|X_j = x\right], \quad x \in \mathcal{X}_j \text{ for } j = 0, 1. \tag{4}$$

Extending the regression setup of Imbens and Zajonc (2011), we define the conditional average treatment effect as

$$\tau(x) = \mu_1(x) - \mu_0(x), \quad x \in \mathcal{B}_{01}. \tag{5}$$

When the treatment has no effect on the conditional parameter $\mu(\cdot)$, $\tau(\cdot) = 0$ and $\tau(\cdot) \neq 0$ otherwise. A potential difficulty with this multivariate setup is that the conditional average treatment effect is a function, as $\mathcal{B}_{01}$ is in general not a singleton. Let $x_k \in \mathcal{B}_{01}$ for $k = 1, \ldots, K$, where K could be fixed or grow with the sample size. Simple summaries of the average treatment effect on the boundary $\mathcal{B}_{01}$ such as

$$\tau_A = \frac{1}{K}\sum_{k=1}^{K} \tau(x_k), \quad \tau_M = \max_{k=1,\ldots,K} \tau(x_k), \quad \tau_m = \min_{k=1,\ldots,K} \tau(x_k), \tag{6}$$

may be of interest. It is also possible to change the discrete set $\{x_1, \ldots, x_K\}$ to the entire frontier $\mathcal{B}_{01}$ but τ_A should be redefined using an integral instead of a discrete sum.

Example 2: Significance testing. Consider the null and alternative hypotheses:

$$H_0 : \mathbb{P}(\mu(X) = 0) = 1, \quad H_1 : \mathbb{P}(\mu(X) = 0) < 1.$$

To avoid boundary issues, trimming is often used to construct test statistics for H_0 versus H_1. Let $\mathcal{X}_c$ be an inner subset of the support $\mathcal{X}$ of X, which is for instance obtained by selecting those x in $\mathcal{X}$ at a distance c from the boundary $\mathcal{B}$, where c is a trimming parameter. The null and alternative hypotheses are

$$H_{0c} : \mathbb{P}\left(\mu(X)\mathbb{I}\left[X \in \mathcal{X}_c\right] = 0\right) = 1,$$
$$H_{1c} : \mathbb{P}\left(\mu(X)\mathbb{I}\left[X \in \mathcal{X}_c\right] = 0\right) < 1.$$

Note that the alternative $H_{1,0} = H_1$ contains all the alternatives H_{1c} with $c > 0$, so that trimming may give a test which is not consistent against the alternatives in H_1 but not in H_{1c}. A possible test statistic is

$$\hat{t}_c^2 = \frac{1}{n}\sum_{i=1}^{n} \hat{\mu}^2(X_i)\mathbb{I}\left[X_i \in \mathcal{X}_c\right], \tag{7}$$

where $\hat{\mu}(X_i)$ is a local polynomial estimator of $\mu(\cdot)$ in Eq. (1). As is well documented in the testing literature, such test statistics can also be applied to residuals to test for more general model specification. The statistic $\hat{t}_c^2$ is an average version of the integral test statistic of Härdle and Mammen (1993) for testing specification of the regression model. A study of the asymptotic behavior of $\hat{t}_0^2$ for a regression null hypothesis with a univariate covariate can be found in Li (2005). A similar test was developed for a linear regression null hypothesis with dependent data by Hjellvik, Yao, and Tjøstheim (1998). It follows from these authors that for some Δ_c and σ_c^2 which depend upon the distribution of the observations,

$$nh^{d/2}\hat{t}_c^2 - h^{-d/2}\Delta_c \xrightarrow{d} \mathcal{N}\left(0, \sigma_c^2\right), \tag{8}$$

under the null. The asymptotic mean $h^{-d/2}\Delta_c$ and variance σ_c^2 can be consistently estimated provided that $h^{-d/2}$ does not diverge too fast, so that Eq. (8) leads to a rejection region: $nh^{d/2}\hat{t}_c^2 - h^{-d/2}\widehat{\Delta}_c \geq \hat{\sigma}_c^2\Phi(1-\alpha)$, where $\Phi(1-\alpha)$ is the standard normal $(1-\alpha)$th quantile.

An alternative approach is Fan and Li (1996), who propose a test statistic which is asymptotically centered, so that $\widehat{\Delta}_c$ is not needed. In our context, this would lead to a test statistic of the form:

$$\widehat{T}_c = \sum_{i=1}^{n} Y_i \hat{\mu}_{-i}(X_i)\mathbb{I}\left[X_i \in \mathcal{X}_c\right], \tag{9}$$

where $\hat{\mu}_{-i}(X_i)$ is a local polynomial leave-one-out estimation of $\mu(X_i)$. But $\widehat{T}_c$ is asymptotically normal under the null $E\left[Y\mu(X)\mathbb{I}\left[X \in \mathcal{X}_c\right]\right] = 0$, which is equivalent to H_{0c} in the regression case but not necessarily for alternative choices of $\rho(\cdot)$, so that Eq. (7) should be preferred for general $\rho(\cdot)$.

Example 3: Additive specification estimation. A useful dimension reduction technique to estimate a function $\mu(\cdot)$ depending upon a high-dimensional covariate is to impose an additive structure on μ. Suppose that $X = \left(X_1', X_2'\right)'$ and that the function $\mu(\cdot)$ of Eq. (1) has an additive decomposition,

$$\mu(X) = m_1(X_1) + m_2(X_2).$$

A popular method for estimating $m_1(\cdot)$ is the marginal integration method of Linton and Nielsen (1995). Let $\mathcal{X}_{2c}$ be an inner subset of the support $\mathcal{X}_2$ of X_2. An estimator of

$$\mu_{1,c}(x_1) = m_1(x_1) + \mathbb{E}\left[m_2(X_2)\mathbb{I}\left(X_2 \in \mathcal{X}_{2c}\right)\right]$$

is

$$\hat{\mu}_{1,c}(x_1) = \frac{\sum_{i=1}^{n} \mathbb{I}\left(X_{2i} \in \mathcal{X}_{2c}\right) \hat{\mu}_{-i}\left(x_1, X_{2i}\right)}{\sum_{i=1}^{n} \mathbb{I}\left(X_{2i} \in \mathcal{X}_{2c}\right)}. \tag{10}$$

In a regression setup, Linton and Nielsen (1995) consider an integral version of Eq. (10) where $\hat{\mu}_{-i}(\cdot,\cdot) = \hat{\mu}(\cdot,\cdot)$ is a standard kernel regression estimator. The role of the trimming set $\mathcal{X}_{2c}$ is to avoid boundary effects. In a quantile setup and for the support $\mathcal{X}_2 = [0,1]^{d_2}$, Kong et al. (2010) show that trimming is not needed when using local polynomial estimation. In both papers, the convergence rate of the additive component is shown to be faster than the ones usually obtained for the estimation of an unrestricted function $\mu(\cdot)$.

Example 4: Average derivative estimation. Another popular dimension reduction approach is based on the single-index specification

$$\mu(X) = g(X'\beta),$$

where β is a d-dimensional vector and $g(\cdot)$ a real-valued function. The slope parameter β can be identified, up to a scaling coefficient, using the average derivatives of $\mu(X)$ since

$$\mathbb{E}\left[\frac{\partial\mu(X)}{\partial X}\right] = \beta\mathbb{E}\left[g^{(1)}(X'\beta)\right],$$

where $g^{(1)}(\cdot)$ is the derivative of $g(\cdot)$. See Härdle and Stoker (1989) or Powell, Stock, and Stoker (1989) for the regression case and Chaudhuri, Doksum, and Samarov (1997) for quantile functions. As seen from Altonji et al. (2012), average derivatives are also of independent interest in microeconometric issues. Direct methods average an estimator of $\partial\mu(X)/\partial X$ over $\mathcal{X}_c$ as in

$$\widehat{M}_c^{(1)} = \frac{1}{\sum_{i=1}^{n}\mathbb{I}[X_i \in \mathcal{X}_c]}\sum_{i=1}^{n}\mathbb{I}[X_i \in \mathcal{X}_c]\,\widehat{\frac{\partial\mu}{\partial X}}(X_i). \tag{11}$$

Chaudhuri, Doksum, and Samarov (1997) consider local polynomial estimators of $\partial\mu(X)/\partial X$ in a quantile setup while Li, Lu, and Ullah (2003), Banerjee (2007), and Altonji et al. (2012) implement local polynomial for regressions. Chaudhuri et al. (1997) use a weighting function instead of trimming and Altonji et al. (2012) consider $\mathcal{X}_c = [0.5, 3.5]$ for a support $\mathcal{X} = [0, 4]$.

3. THE BIAS AND VARIANCE OF MULTIVARIATE LOCAL POLYNOMIAL ESTIMATORS

In this section, we establish results for the asymptotic bias and variance of multivariate local polynomial estimators of an M-regression that are valid uniformly over $\mathcal{X}$. First, we introduce the main assumptions including our new support condition and contrast it with Assumption (A4) in Ruppert and Wand (1994), who use it to develop pointwise results.

3.1. Main Assumptions

A key issue that we have to deal with is that $\hat{\beta}(x;h)$ is an estimator of the pseudo-true value $\bar{\beta}(x;h)$ defined as

$$\bar{\beta}(x;h) = \arg\min_{\beta} \mathbb{E}\left[\rho\left(Y - U(X-x)'\beta\right) K\left(\frac{X-x}{h}\right)\right] \tag{12}$$

and that $\bar{\beta}(x;h)$ may differ from $\beta(x)$, the vector with entries

$$\beta^*_\pi(x) = \begin{cases} 0 & \text{if the partial derivative } \mu^{(\pi)}(x) \text{ does not exist} \\ \beta_\pi(x) \text{ defined in Eq. (2)} & \text{otherwise} \end{cases}.$$

The first goal of this paper is to study the bias term $\left[\bar{\beta}(x;h) - \beta(x)\right]$ over the support $\mathcal{X}$ of X. This will be done under the assumptions introduced below.

Assumption R. *(Loss function $\rho(\cdot)$).*
(i) For each $x \in \mathcal{X}$, $\mu \in \mathbb{R} \mapsto \mathbb{E}\left[\rho(Y-\mu)|X=x\right] = R(\mu|x)$ is twice continuously differentiable with respect to μ. The second order derivative $R^{(2)}(\cdot\,|\,\cdot)$ satisfies, for some $\epsilon > 0$,

$$\inf_{x\in\mathcal{X}} \inf_{\mu\in[\mu(x)-\epsilon,\mu(x)+\epsilon]} R^{(2)}(\mu|x) > 0, \ \sup_{x\in\mathcal{X}} \left|R^{(2)}(\mu(x)|x)\right| < \infty, \text{ and}$$

$$\left|R^{(2)}(\mu|x) - R^{(2)}\left(\mu'|x\right)\right| < C\left|\mu - \mu'\right|$$

for all real numbers μ and μ' in $[\mu(x)-\epsilon, \mu(x)+\epsilon]$. (ii) $\rho(\cdot)$ is continuous and there is a finite collection of intervals (a_j, a_{j+1}) with $\bigcup_{j=0}^{J}(a_j, a_{j+1})$ such that $\rho(\cdot)$ is continuously differentiable with derivative $\rho^{(1)}(\cdot)$ over each (a_j, a_{j+1}). Moreover,

$$\sup_{x\in\mathcal{X}} \mathbb{E}\left[\left(\rho^{(1)}(Y-\mu(X))\right)^2 |X=x\right] < \infty.$$

The functions $(\mu, x) \in \mathbb{R}\times\mathcal{X} \mapsto R^{(2)}(\mu|x)$ and $\mathbb{E}\left[\left(\rho^{(1)}(Y-\mu)\right)^2 |X=x\right]$ are continuous.

Assumption S. *(Smoothness of $\mu(\cdot)$).*
There is a smoothness index $s > 0$ such that either S1 or S2 below holds:

S1: *$s > 1$, $\mu(\cdot)$ is $\lfloor s \rfloor$ times differentiable and for some $L > 0$, the partial derivatives of order π with $|\pi| = \lfloor s \rfloor$ satisfy: for all x, $x' \in \mathcal{X}$,*

$$\left|\mu^{(\pi)}\left(x'\right) - \mu^{(\pi)}(x)\right| \le L\left\|x' - x\right\|^{s-\lfloor s \rfloor}.$$

S2: *s is an integer and $\mu(\cdot)$ is s times continuously differentiable.*

Assumption X. *($\mathcal{X}$-boundary).*
(i) The marginal probability density function $f(\cdot)$ of the d-dimensional X is continuously differentiable and bounded away from 0 on its support $\mathcal{X}$. (ii) There are some κ_0, κ_1 in $(0, 1]$ such that for any $x \in \mathcal{X}$ and all ϵ in $(0, \kappa_0]$, there is a $x' \in \mathcal{X}$ satisfying

$$\mathcal{V}\left(x', \kappa_1 \epsilon\right) \subset \mathcal{V}(x, \epsilon) \cap \mathcal{X}. \tag{13}$$

(iii) $\mathcal{X}$ is a compact subset of $\mathbb{R}^d$.

Assumption K. *(Kernel function).*
The kernel function $K(\cdot)$ is non-negative and Lipschitz, that is, $\left|K(x) - K\left(x'\right)\right| \leq L \left\|x - x'\right\|$ for any x, $x' \in \mathbb{R}^d$. The kernel function $K(\cdot)$ has a compact support and is bounded away from 0 over the unit ball $\mathcal{V}(0, 1)$. The bandwidth $h = h_n \to 0$ as $n \to \infty$.

A brief discussion of the assumptions is in order. Assumption R-(i) is important to ensure that $\mu(x)$ in Eq. (1) and the pseudo-true value $\bar{\beta}(x; h)$ in Eq. (12) are unique as implied by $R^{(2)}(\cdot\,|x) > 0$ and Assumption K. Indeed this implies that the Hessian matrix

$$\frac{\partial}{\partial\beta\partial\beta'}\mathbb{E}\left[\rho\left(Y - U(X - x)'\beta\right) K\left(\frac{X - x}{h}\right)\right]$$

is strictly positive and remains so when $h \to 0$. The additional Lipshitz condition on $R^{(2)}(\cdot|x)$ is used to study $\bar{\beta}(x; h)$ when $h \to 0$. Assumption R-(i) clearly holds when $\rho(t) = t^2$. In the quantile case with α in $(0, 1)$, $\rho(t) = (1 - \alpha)t\mathbb{I}(t \leq 0) - \alpha t\mathbb{I}(t > 0)$ and $R^{(2)}(\mu|x) = f(\mu|x)$, where $f(\cdot\,|x)$ denotes the conditional pdf of Y given $X = x$, so that Assumption R-(i) holds when $\inf_{x\in\mathcal{X}} f(\mu(x)|x) > 0$ as standard in quantile estimation and if $\mu \mapsto f(\mu|x)$ is differentiable or Lipschitz in the vicinity of $\mu(x)$. Assumption R-(ii) is used to study the variance of the local polynomial estimator.

Assumption S describes some smoothness conditions for $\mu(\cdot)$. Assumption S1 is from Chaudhuri (1991) or Masry (1996). It allows for a noninteger smoothness index s as necessary when considering some power functions like $|x|^s$ whose derivatives of order $\lfloor s \rfloor$ can have a singular behavior in the vicinity of the origin. Assumption S2 is slightly stronger and implies Assumption S1 when the support $\mathcal{X}$ of the covariate is compact. Note that it is not assumed that $p < s$ as it is also clear from the definition of the pseudo-true value $\beta_\pi^*(x)$ which allows for $p \geq s$. Indeed, nonexistence of the partial derivative $\mu^{(\pi)}(x)$ in the definition of $\beta_\pi^*(x)$ should be understood as $|\pi| > \lfloor s \rfloor$ under Assumption S1 and as $|\pi| > p$ under Assumption S2. Assumption K is rather standard in local polynomial estimation.

Assumption X is our key support condition. Assumption X-(i, iii) are standard but Assumption X-(ii) seems to be new to the best of our knowledge. Assumption X-(ii) holds for hypercubes $[a, b]^d$ or hyperrectangles, spheres, or supports delimited by smooth boundaries but also for more irregular support shapes. It relaxes the usual intuition of a connected support with no hole and delimited by a smooth boundary. In particular, the support $\mathcal{X}$ of the covariate X does not need to be connected and can have holes. The latter possibility extends Assumption (A4) in Ruppert and Wand (1994), who assume that there is a nontrivial convex set $\mathcal{C} \subset \mathcal{X}$ with nonempty interior containing x. This restricts the shape of $\mathcal{X}$ since there cannot be a sequence of holes with vanishing size converging to x. In sharp contrast, under Assumption X-(ii), the boundary of $\mathcal{X}$ can be very irregular in the vicinity of x with many peaks, as illustrated by an example below. In addition, Assumption X-(ii) is suitable for uniform or global studies of local polynomial estimation, while Ruppert and Wand (1994) only consider pointwise estimation of a regression function $\mu(x)$ for a given x.

The intuition behind Assumption X-(ii) is that a local polynomial estimator performs well provided that there are many observations close to x, say up to a distance $h \to 0$ given by a bandwidth, to estimate $\mu(x)$. This will hold if it is possible to find a sequence of balls in the support $\mathcal{X}$ with a radius proportional to h which will converge to x. The key point here is that these balls do not need to be centered at x, which would be impossible when x is on the boundary of $\mathcal{X}$, but can be centered at an interior point $x' \neq x$ of $\mathcal{X}$. This is the intuitive content of Eq. (13), where ϵ plays the role of a bandwidth. For $\epsilon > 0$ small enough, Eq. (13) means that there is a ball $\mathcal{V}\left(x', \kappa_1 \epsilon\right)$ in the support $\mathcal{X}$ which is also in the vicinity set $\mathcal{V}(x, \epsilon)$ of x. The fact that the constants κ_0 and κ_1 in Eq. (13) do not depend upon x is essential to establish the uniformity results in this paper.

To compare and contrast with Assumption (A4) in Ruppert and Wand (1994), consider the case $d = 2$ for the sake of brevity. Like Assumption (A4) in Ruppert and Wand (1994), Assumption X-(ii) also excludes the support defined below:

$$\mathcal{X}_b = \left\{x = (x_1, x_2) : 0 \leq x_1 \leq 1,\ 0 \leq x_2 \leq x_1^2\right\}$$

due to the origin $o = (0, 0)'$ and the fast decrease of x_2 when $x_1 \to 0$. Indeed balls in $\mathcal{V}(o, \epsilon) \cap \mathcal{X}_b$ have a radius which is of order ϵ^2 and therefore not compatible with Eq. (13). On the other hand, a support like

$$\mathcal{X}_c = \{x = (x_1, x_2) : 0 \leq x_1 \leq 1,\ 0 \leq x_2 \leq b(x_1)\}, \quad \text{with } b(x_1) \geq \underline{b}(x_1),$$

$$\text{where } \underline{b}(x_1) = C \sum_{k=1}^{\infty} |x_1| \mathbb{I}\left(x_1 \in \left[\frac{1}{k + 1/2}, \frac{1}{k}\right]\right) \quad \text{for some } C > 0$$

will satisfy Assumption X-(ii) due to the restriction $b(x_1) \geq \underline{b}(x_1)$ with $\underline{b}(x_1) = C|x_1|$ on $\left[(k+1/2)^{-1}, k^{-1}\right]$. Indeed, it is sufficient to consider, for all $k \geq 1$, those x' with $x'_1 \in \left[(k+1/2)^{-1}, k^{-1}\right]$ and $x'_2 \in \left[0, Ck^{-1}\right]$ and balls $\mathcal{V}\left(x', \epsilon\right)$ in the rectangle $\left[(k+1/2)^{-1}, k^{-1}\right] \times [0, Ck^{-1}]$ to show that Eq. (13) holds. On the other hand, when $b(x_1) = \underline{b}(x_1)$, $\mathcal{X}_c$ does not satisfy Assumption (A4) in Ruppert and Wand (1994), due to the irregular behavior of $\underline{b}(x_1)$ when $x_1 \to 0$. Indeed since $\underline{b}(x_1) = 0$ on all $\left((k+1)^{-1}, (k+1/2)^{-1}\right)$, there is no nontrivial convex set in $\mathcal{X}_c$ which contains the origin o.

3.2. *The Bias*

Under the assumptions introduced in Section 3.1, it is possible to obtain the orders of the bias terms: $\left[\bar{\beta}_\pi(x,h) - \beta_\pi(x)\right]$ uniformly over $x \in \mathcal{X}$, including the boundary of $\mathcal{X}$.

Theorem 1. *Suppose Assumptions K, R, S1, and X hold with $p \geq \lfloor s \rfloor$. Then for all $\pi \in \mathbb{N}^d$ with $|\pi| \leq \lfloor s \rfloor$ and h small enough,*

$$\sup_{x \in \mathcal{X}} \left|\bar{\beta}_\pi(x,h) - \beta_\pi(x)\right| \leq CLh^{s-|\pi|}.$$

Theorem 1 extends existing bias results for x in inner subsets of $\mathcal{X}$. See for instance Chaudhuri (1991) and Guerre and Sabbah (2012) for the quantile case. Theorem 1 therefore shows that, thanks to Assumption X, the order of the bias of the local polynomial estimator is not affected by boundary. This contrasts with Nadaraya–Watson Kernel estimators and is a key reason for preferring local polynomial methods as argued by Fan and Gijbels (1996) for univariate local polynomial regression. The proof of Theorem 1 works by checking that the tentative limit $\beta_\pi(x)$ approximately satisfies the first-order condition of the minimization (12). Since Assumption R ensures that the Hessian of the objective function of Eq. (12) is full-rank, the Newton–Kantorovich Theorem is then used to show that $\bar{\beta}_\pi(x,h) - \beta_\pi(x) = O\left(Lh^{s-|\pi|}\right)$ uniformly over $\mathcal{X}$ as stated in the theorem. As far as we know, this approach is new in the context of local polynomial estimation.

Theorem 2 gives a uniform expansion of $\left[\bar{\beta}_\pi(x,h) - \beta_\pi(x)\right]$ under the stronger smoothness Assumption S2 which allows for a better description of the bias. Theorem 2 also completes Theorem 1 by considering the case where $p \leq s-1 = \lfloor s \rfloor$. Define

$$\Omega_1(x,h) = \int \mathbb{I}\left(x + hz \in \mathcal{X}\right) U(z)U(z)' K(z) dz, \qquad (14)$$

$$\mathrm{Sp}\left(\Omega_1^{-1}(x,h)\right) = \text{ the largest eigenvalue of } \Omega_1^{-1}(x,h),$$

$$b_{p+1}(x,h) = \sum_{\pi \in \mathbb{N}^d : |\pi| = p+1} \kappa_\pi(x,h)\beta_\pi(x), \quad \text{and} \tag{15}$$

$$\kappa_\pi(x,h) = \int \mathbb{I}\,(x + hz \in \mathcal{X})\, z^\pi U(z)K(z)dz.$$

Let e_π be the πth element of the canonical basis, that is, the vector with a 1 in the πth lexicographic position and 0 elsewhere.

Theorem 2. *Suppose Assumptions K, R, S2, and X hold and that p satisfies* $p \leq \lfloor s \rfloor = s - 1$. *Then for all* $\pi \in \mathbb{N}^d$ *with* $|\pi| \leq p$,

$$\bar{\beta}_\pi(x,h) = \beta_\pi(x) + h^{p+1-|\pi|} e_\pi' \Omega_1(x,h)^{-1} b_{p+1}(x,h) + o\left(h^{p+1-|\pi|}\right),$$

uniformly in $x \in \mathcal{X}$ *with* $\max_{x\in\mathcal{X}} \mathrm{Sp}\left(\Omega_1(x,h)^{-1}\right) < \infty$ *and* $\max_{x\in\mathcal{X}} \left\| b_{p+1}(x,h) \right\| < \infty$ *for h small enough.*

A first noticeable fact is that the leading term in the bias expansion in Theorem 2 is independent of the loss function $\rho(\cdot)$. The term $e_\pi' \Omega_1(x,h)^{-1} b_{p+1}(x,h)$ multiplying $h^{p+1-|\pi|}$ is identical to the one obtained for regression local polynomial estimators which has been already studied by Ruppert and Wand (1994) and more recently by Gu et al. (2015). Second, the bias boundary effect is captured through the matrix $\Omega_1(x,h)$ and the vector $\kappa_\pi(x,h)$. When x is an inner point of $\mathcal{X}$, or, more precisely, when $x + hz$ lies in $\mathcal{X}$ for all z in the support of the kernel function, $\Omega_1(x,h) = \Omega_1$ and $\kappa_\pi(x,h) = \kappa_\pi$ with

$$\Omega_1 = \int U(z)U(z)'K(z)dz \quad \text{and} \quad \kappa_\pi = \int z^\pi U(z)K(z)dz, \tag{16}$$

in which case $b_{p+1}(x,h) = b_{p+1}(x)$ with,

$$b_{p+1}(x) = \sum_{\pi \in \mathbb{N}^d : |\pi| = p+1} \kappa_\pi \beta_\pi(x).$$

An important issue is whether the term $e_\pi' \Omega_1(x,h)^{-1} b_{p+1}(x,h)$ in front of $h^{p+1-|\pi|}$ vanishes or not. This has been recently discussed for the regression case and a symmetric kernel $K(\cdot)$ by Gu et al. (2015) and, as noted above, their results can also be applied to a more general $\rho(\cdot)$. When $p + 1 - |\pi|$ is odd, the exact order $h^{p+1-|\pi|}$ holds over the whole support except for those unlikely x such that $b_{p+1}(x,h) = 0$. In this case, Theorem 2 can be used in conjunction with Theorem 4 below to propose an optimal bandwidth for inner x. The situation differs when $p + 1 - |\pi|$ is even. When $K(\cdot)$ is symmetric, $\int z^{\pi_1} z^{\pi_2} K(z)dz = 0$ when $|\pi_1|$

is even and $|\pi_2|$ odd, so that reorganizing the entries of $U(z)$ gives a block-diagonal Ω. As shown by Gu et al. (2015), this implies that $e_\pi' \Omega_1^{-1} b(x) = 0$ when $p+1-|\pi|$ is even. Because $\Omega_1(x,h)$ is not similar to a block-diagonal matrix when x lies on the boundary $\mathcal{B}$, it is unlikely to have $e_\pi' \Omega_1(x,h)^{-1} b(x,h) = 0$ unless the partial derivatives $\mu^{(\pi)}(x)$ take some very specific values. Hence for inner x, the bias has a smaller order $o\left(h^{p+1-|\pi|}\right)$ while for x on the boundary the bias will be $O\left(h^{p+1-|\pi|}\right)$. This shows that the bias can be slightly larger near the boundary. Under some additional regularity conditions, it is possible to show that the bias is $O\left(h^{p+2-|\pi|}\right)$ for inner x.

Let

$$\boldsymbol{R}_{f,\mu}^{(2)}(x) = R^{(2)}(\mu(x)|x) f(x), \quad \kappa_{\pi,j} = \int z_j z^\pi U(z) K(z) dz \quad \text{and}$$

$$\boldsymbol{b}_{p+1}(x) = \sum_{j=1}^{d} \sum_{\pi \in \mathbb{N}^d : |\pi| = p+1} \kappa_{\pi,j} \frac{1}{\boldsymbol{R}_{f,\mu}^{(2)}(x)} \frac{\partial \boldsymbol{R}_{f,\mu}^{(2)}(x)}{\partial x_j} \beta_\pi(x).$$

Proposition 3. *Suppose Assumptions K, R, S2, and X hold and that p satisfies $p \leq \lfloor s \rfloor = s - 1$. Assume in addition that $K(\cdot)$ is symmetric and that $\boldsymbol{R}_{f,\mu}^{(2)}(x)$, $\mu^{(p+1)}(x)$ are continuously differentiable over $\mathcal{X}$. Then if $p+1-|\pi|$ is even and if x is in the interior of $\mathcal{X}$,*

$$\bar{\beta}_\pi(x,h) = \beta_\pi(x) + h^{p+2-|\pi|} e_\pi' \Omega_1^{-1} \left(b_{p+2}(x) + \boldsymbol{b}_{p+1}(x)\right) + o\left(h^{p+2-|\pi|}\right).$$

Proposition 3 suggests that for an even $p+1-|\pi|$, the bias grows from $O\left(h^{p+2-|\pi|}\right)$ for those x at a distance $O(h)$ to the higher order $O\left(h^{p+1-|\pi|}\right)$ when x is a boundary point. As in Gu et al. (2015), Ruppert and Wand (1994) or when $d=1$, it is possible to study the bias for a sequence $x_h = x + hc$ in the interior of $\mathcal{X}$ and x in $\mathcal{B}$ under additional simplifying assumptions on the boundary shape. Note also that the higher-order expansion of Proposition 3 now depends on the choice of $\rho(\cdot)$ through the partial derivatives of $R_{f,\mu}^{(2)}(x)$ in the term $b_{p+1}(x)$ of the expansion.

3.3. The Variance

Consider now the variance of the local polynomial estimator. As is well known, the partial derivative estimators $\hat{\beta}_\pi(x;h)$ converge with a different rate and should be first standardized with the diagonal matrix

$$H = \text{Diag}\left(h^{|\pi|}, |\pi| \leq p\right).$$

Standard arguments as in Huber (1967) then suggest that the variance of $H\left(\hat{\beta}(x,h)-\bar{\beta}(x,h)\right)$ is close to $\overline{V}(x,h)/nh^d$, where $\overline{V}(x,h)$ has the usual sandwich form

$$\overline{V}(x,h)=\overline{\boldsymbol{R}}^{(2)}(x,h)^{-1}\overline{\mathbf{S}}(x,h)\overline{\boldsymbol{R}}^{(2)}(x,h)^{-1}$$

with

$$\begin{aligned}\overline{\boldsymbol{R}}^{(2)}(x,h)&=h^{-d}\mathbb{E}\left[R^{(2)}\left(U(X-x)'\bar{\beta}(x,h)|X\right)U\left(\frac{X-x}{h}\right)\right.\\&\quad\left.\times U\left(\frac{X-x}{h}\right)'K\left(\frac{X-x}{h}\right)\right],\\\overline{\mathbf{S}}(x,h)&=h^{-d}\mathbb{E}\left[\left(\rho^{(1)}\left(Y-U(X-x)'\bar{\beta}(x,h)\right)\right)^2U\left(\frac{X-x}{h}\right)\right.\\&\quad\left.\times U\left(\frac{X-x}{h}\right)'K^2\left(\frac{X-x}{h}\right)\right],\end{aligned}$$

where the superscript "–" indicates dependence on $\bar{\beta}(x,h)$. Since Assumptions R-(i) and X-(i) give, for $\Omega_1(x,h)$ in Eq. (14),

$$\begin{aligned}\overline{\boldsymbol{R}}^{(2)}(x,h)&\succeq Ch^{-d}\mathbb{E}\left[U\left(\frac{X-x}{h}\right)U\left(\frac{X-x}{h}\right)'K\left(\frac{X-x}{h}\right)\right]\\&=C\int U(z)U(z)'K(z)f(x+hz)dz\succeq C\Omega_1(x,h),\end{aligned}$$

and because $\max_{(x,h)\in\mathcal{X}\times[0,\infty)}\mathrm{Sp}\left(\Omega_1(x,h)^{-1}\right)<\infty$ as stated in Theorem 2, $\overline{\boldsymbol{R}}^{(2)}(x,h)$ has an inverse for all $x\in\mathcal{X}$ and $h\geq 0$, so that $\overline{V}(x,h)$ is well defined.

Consider the following approximations for $\overline{V}(x,h)$:

$$V(x,h)=\frac{\mathbb{E}\left[\left(\rho^{(1)}\left(Y-\mu(X)\right)\right)^2|X=x\right]}{\left(R^{(2)}(\mu(x)|x)\right)^2f(x)}\Omega(x,h)^{-1}\quad\text{and}$$

$$V(x)=\frac{\mathbb{E}\left[\left(\rho^{(1)}\left(Y-\mu(X)\right)\right)^2|X=x\right]}{\left(R^{(2)}(\mu(x)|x)\right)^2f(x)}\Omega^{-1},$$

where

$$\Omega_2(x,h) = \int \mathbb{I}(x+hz \in \mathcal{X})\, U(z)U(z)'K^2(z)dz$$
$$\Omega(x,h)^{-1} = \Omega_1(x,h)^{-1}\Omega_2(x,h)\Omega_1(x,h)^{-1}$$
$$\Omega_2 = \int U(z)U(z)'K^2(z)dz, \quad \Omega^{-1} = \Omega_1^{-1}\Omega_2\Omega_1^{-1}$$

and $\Omega_1(x,h)$ and Ω_1 are as in Eqs. (14) and (16), respectively. The next theorem shows that $V(x,h)$ is a suitable approximation for $\overline{V}(x,h)$ over $\mathcal{X}$, while $V(x)$ is a suitable approximation for $\overline{V}(x,h)$ over interior subsets of $\mathcal{X}$.

Theorem 4. *Suppose Assumptions K, R, X hold together with Assumptions S1 or S2. Then* $\max_{x\in\mathcal{X}} \mathrm{Sp}\,(V(x,h)) = O(1)$ *and*

$$\sup_{x\in\mathcal{X}} \left\| \overline{V}(x,h) - V(x,h) \right\| = o(1).$$

Consider a subset $\mathcal{X}_0$ *of* $\mathcal{X}$ *such that* $\bigcup_{x\in\mathcal{X}_0} \mathcal{V}(x,\epsilon) \subset \mathcal{X}$ *for some* $\epsilon > 0$. *Then*

$$\sup_{x\in\mathcal{X}_0} \left\| \overline{V}(x,h) - V(x) \right\| = o(1).$$

Theorem 4 shows that the asymptotic variance $\overline{V}(x,h)$ of $(nh^d)^{1/2}H(\hat{\beta}(x,h) - \bar{\beta}(x,h))$ stays bounded over $\mathcal{X}$ so that the order of $H(\hat{\beta}(x,h) - \bar{\beta}(x,h))$ should be $(nh^d)^{-1/2}$ for all $x \in \mathcal{X}$. Combining this result with Theorem 1 gives that $[\hat{\beta}_\pi(x,h) - \beta_\pi(x)]$ should be of order $((nh^d)^{-1/2} + h^s)/h^{-|\pi|}$ for all π with $|\pi| \leq s$ and for all $x \in \mathcal{X}$ including the boundary, that is, there is no boundary effect for the consistency rate of $\hat{\beta}_\pi(x,h)$.

As shown as Theorem 4, the variance boundary effect arises because the limit of $\Omega(x,h)^{-1}$ may differ from Ω^{-1} when x is close to the boundary as when $x = x_\partial + hc$ where x_∂ lies on the boundary. In the univariate case, Ruppert and Wand (1994) mentioned an increase by a factor 4 when x goes to the boundary and $K(\cdot)$ is a uniform kernel over $[-1,1]$. The situation can be much worse in a multidimensional case since the variance increase due to boundary is not bounded and can be made arbitrarily large by considering a support which is very narrow in the vicinity of some estimation point x. For instance, consider a bivariate covariate $x = (x_1, x_2)'$ and the ray of the unit disk determined by angle $\overline{\theta} > 0$, that is,

$$\mathcal{X}_{\overline{\theta}} = \left\{(x_1,x_2)'; x_1 = r\cos\theta,\ x_2 = r\sin\theta,\ (r,\theta) \in [0,1] \times \left[0,\overline{\theta}\right]\right\}$$

and estimation at the vertex $o=(0,0)$. Suppose that $K(x_1,x_2)=K(r)$ with $\int_0^1 K(r)rdr=1/(2\pi)$ and $U(x)=[1,x_1,x_2]'$. Then for h small enough and $\overline{\theta}$ small, the symmetric $\Omega_j(o,h)$, $j=1,2$ satisfy

$$\Omega_j(o,h)=\begin{bmatrix} \frac{\overline{\theta}}{2\pi} & \left(\overline{\theta}-\frac{\overline{\theta}^3}{6}\right)\int_0^1 rK^j(r)dr & \frac{\overline{\theta}^2}{2}\int_0^1 rK^j(r)dr \\ \times & \left(\overline{\theta}-\frac{\overline{\theta}^3}{3}\right)\int_0^1 r^2K^j(r)dr & \frac{\overline{\theta}^2}{2}\int_0^1 r^2K^j(r)dr \\ \times & \times & \frac{\overline{\theta}^3}{3}\int_0^1 r^2K^j(r)dr \end{bmatrix}+o\left(\overline{\theta}^3\right)$$

which is such $\Omega_j(o,h)$ goes to 0 when $\overline{\theta}\to 0$. Further calculations yield that all the diagonal entries of

$$\Omega(o,h)=\Omega_1(o,h)^{-1}\Omega_2(o,h)\Omega_1(o,h)^{-1}$$

diverge as $1/\overline{\theta}$ diverges suggesting estimation of all derivatives becomes imprecise. In other words, although Assumption X implies that $\Omega(x,h)^{-1}$ stays bounded when x varies over $\mathcal{X}$, this example suggests that $\Omega(x,h)^{-1}$ can be large especially when the boundary takes the shape of such small angle ray with center x. By contrast, the leading bias term $\Omega_1(x,h)^{-1}b_{p+1}(x,h)$ from Theorem 2 is probably less affected by such small denominator problems. Indeed, by Eqs. (14) and (15),

$$\Omega_1(x,h)^{-1}b_{p+1}(x,h)=\sum_{\pi\in\mathbb{N}^d:|\pi|=p+1}\Omega_1(x,h)^{-1}\kappa_\pi(x,h)\beta_\pi(x),$$

and a large $\Omega_1(x,h)^{-1}$ can be compensated by a small $\kappa_\pi(x,h)$.

4. LOCAL POLYNOMIAL REGRESSION AND QUANTILE REGRESSION

In this section, we focus on two specific M-regressions, the local polynomial regression and local polynomial quantile regression. For each case, we establish asymptotic normality and uniform convergence rate. For local polynomial quantile, we first derive a uniform Bahadur representation valid over the whole support of the covariate X. We illustrate its usefulness via Examples 2–4.

4.1. Local Polynomial Regression

Consider a regression model with a heteroscedastic error term,

$$Y_i = m(X_i) + \varepsilon_i, \quad \mathbb{E}\left[\varepsilon_i | X_i\right] = 0, \quad \text{Var}\left(\varepsilon_i | X_i\right) = \sigma^2(X_i), \tag{17}$$

and the quadratic loss function $\rho(t) = t^2$. We shall assume that

Assumption E .
The variables $\left(Y_i, X_i'\right)'$, $i = 1, \ldots, n$, are i.i.d. The conditional p.d.f. of ε_i given X_i denoted as $f(e|x)$ is continuous with respect to e and x. The variance function $\sigma^2(\cdot) = \text{Var}\left(\varepsilon_i | X_i = \cdot\right)$ is bounded away from 0 and continuous over $\mathcal{X}$. Moreover, $\sup_{x\in\mathcal{X}} \mathbb{E}\left[|\varepsilon_i|^{2+\nu} \,|X_i = x\right] < \infty$ for some $\nu > 0$.

For a quadratic loss function $\rho(\cdot)$, the local polynomial regression estimator in Eq. (3) is

$$\begin{aligned}
\hat{\beta}(x, h) &= \left(\sum_{i=1}^{n} U(X_i - x)U(X_i - x)' K\left(\frac{X_i - x}{h}\right)\right)^{-1} \\
&\quad \times \sum_{i=1}^{n} U(X_i - x) Y_i K\left(\frac{X_i - x}{h}\right) \\
&= H^{-1}\left(\sum_{i=1}^{n} U\left(\frac{X_i - x}{h}\right) U\left(\frac{X_i - x}{h}\right)' K\left(\frac{X_i - x}{h}\right)\right)^{-1} \\
&\quad \times \sum_{i=1}^{n} U\left(\frac{X_i - x}{h}\right) Y_i K\left(\frac{X_i - x}{h}\right),
\end{aligned} \tag{18}$$

where H is the diagonal matrix with entries $h^{|\pi|}$. The first entry of $\hat{\beta}(x, h)$, say $\widehat{m}_h(x)$, is an estimator of the regression function $m(x)$, whereas the other entries estimate its partial derivatives. The pseudo-true value $\bar{\beta}(x, h)$ from Eq. (12) can be computed explicitly as

$$\begin{aligned}
\bar{\beta}(x, h) &= \left(\mathbb{E}\left[U\left(\frac{X - x}{h}\right) U\left(\frac{X - x}{h}\right)' K\left(\frac{X - x}{h}\right)\right]\right)^{-1} \\
&\quad \times \mathbb{E}\left[\mu(X) U\left(\frac{X - x}{h}\right) K\left(\frac{X - x}{h}\right)\right].
\end{aligned}$$

The asymptotic variance $V(x,h)$ is

$$V(x,h) = \frac{\sigma^2(x)}{f(x)}\Omega(x,h)^{-1}$$

which can be estimated using

$$\widehat{V}(x,h) = \hat{\sigma}^2(x)\widehat{\Omega}_1(x,h)^{-1}\widehat{\Omega}_2(x,h)\widehat{\Omega}_1(x,h)^{-1},$$

where

$$\widehat{\Omega}_j(x,h) = \frac{1}{nh^d}\sum_{i=1}^{n} U\left(\frac{X_i - x}{h}\right) U\left(\frac{X_i - x}{h}\right) K^j\left(\frac{X_i - x}{h}\right), \quad j = 1,2,$$

$$\hat{\sigma}^2(x) = \frac{\sum_{i=1}^n \left(Y_i - \hat{\beta}_0(x,h)\right)^2 K\left(\frac{X_i - x}{h}\right)}{\sum_{i=1}^n K\left(\frac{X_i - x}{h}\right)},$$

which is consistent but with a large $O(h)$ boundary bias. Note that both $\hat{\beta}(x,h)$ and $\widehat{V}(x,h)$ depend upon an inverse matrix which may not exist. The next lemma shows that $\hat{\beta}(x,h)$ and $\widehat{V}(x,h)$ are well defined with a probability tending to 1.

Lemma 5. *Suppose that Assumptions K and X hold and that $h = h_n \to 0$ with $\log n/(nh^d) = o(1)$. Then, for $j = 1,2$,*

$$\sup_{x\in\mathcal{X}}\left\| \frac{1}{nh^d}\sum_{i=1}^{n} U\left(\frac{X_i - x}{h}\right) U\left(\frac{X_i - x}{h}\right)' K^j\left(\frac{X_i - x}{h}\right) - \int U(z)U'(z)K^j(z)f(x+hz)dz \right\|$$
$$= O_{\mathbb{P}}\left(\left(\frac{\log n}{nh^d}\right)^{1/2}\right) = o_{\mathbb{P}}(1). \quad (19)$$

Moreover, for $j = 1$, the limit matrix has an inverse and

$$\max_{x\in\mathcal{X}} \mathrm{Sp}\left(\left(\int U(z)U'(z)K(z)f(x+hz)dz\right)^{-1}\right) = O(1).$$

The next two propositions show that standard asymptotic normality and uniform convergence results hold over the whole support. Because, as is well-known, the process $(nh^d)^{1/2}H\left(\hat{\beta}(\cdot;h)-\bar{\beta}(\cdot;h)\right)$ is not tight so that convergence in distribution to a Gaussian process cannot hold in usual functional sense, Proposition 6 considers the asymptotic normality of $(nh^d)^{1/2}\widehat{V}(x_n,h)^{-1/2}H\left(\hat{\beta}(x_n;h)-\overline{\beta}(x_n;h)\right)$, where the sequence $\{x_n\}\subset\mathcal{X}$ can go to the boundary of the support $\mathcal{X}$. Note that Proposition 6 also establishes the consistency of the variance estimator $\widehat{V}(x_n,h)$ near the boundary. These asymptotic normality and consistency results imply that each

$$(nh^d)^{1/2}h^{|\pi|}\left(\hat{\beta}_\pi(x_n;h)-\bar{\beta}_\pi(x_n;h)\right)$$

is asymptotically normal and gives an estimate of its asymptotic variance.

Proposition 6. *Suppose that Assumptions E, K, X, and S1 or S2 hold, that $h=h_n\to 0$ with $\log n/(nh^d)=o(1)$ and that $\{x_n\}\subset\mathcal{X}$ is a deterministic sequence. Then*

$$(nh^d)^{-1/2}\widehat{V}(x_n,h)^{-1/2}H\left(\hat{\beta}(x_n;h)-\overline{\beta}(x_n;h)\right)$$

converges in distribution to a standard multivariate normal with

$$\widehat{V}(x_n,h)=V(x_n,h)+o_p(1).$$

Proposition 7. *Suppose that Assumptions E, K, X, and S1 or S2 hold, that $h=h_n\to 0$ with $h^{-d}=O\left(n^{(\nu-2)/\nu}/\log n\right)$. Then*

$$\sup_{x\in\mathcal{X}}\left\|H\left(\hat{\beta}(x;h)-\beta(x)\right)\right\|=O_p\left(\left(\frac{\log n}{nh^d}\right)^{1/2}+h^s\right).$$

Example 1 (Cont'd). In this example, the two different regression functions are estimated using two different and independent samples of observations $\left(X_{ji},Y_{ji}\right)$, $j=0,1$, with the same sample size n and the same bandwidth for the sake of simplicity. The estimator of the average treatment effect in Eq. (5) is then

$$\hat{\tau}_h(x)=\hat{\mu}_{1h}(x)-\hat{\mu}_{2h}(x),\quad x\in\mathcal{B}_{01}$$

Proposition 7 implies that $\hat{\tau}_h(x)$ converges uniformly to $\tau(x)$ over B_{01} with a rate $\left[\left(\log n/(nh^d)\right)^{1/2}+h^s\right]$ extending the pointwise result in Imbens and Zajonc (2011). Proposition 6 easily extends to a vector $\left(\hat{\tau}_h(x_1),\ldots,\hat{\tau}_h(x_K)\right)'$ which will be asymptotically independent. It follows that the estimation $\hat{\tau}_{Ah}$ of the average treatment effect mean τ_A *as in Eq. (6) is asymptotically normal with a bias which can be derived from Theorems 1 and 2 and an asymptotic variance of order* $1/(nh^d)$ obtained by averaging the ones from Proposition 6. Approximation for the asymptotic distribution of $\hat{\tau}_{Mh}$ and $\hat{\tau}_{mh}$ can also be easily obtained under the additional condition that the maximum and minimum of the $\tau(x_k)$'s are achieved for one x_k, *say* x_M and x_m. In this case, $(nh^d)^{1/2}\left(\hat{\tau}_{Mh}-\hat{\tau}_h(x_M)\right)$ and $(nh^d)^{1/2}\left(\hat{\tau}_{mh}-\hat{\tau}_h(x_m)\right)$ are both $o_p(1)$ so that the asymptotic distribution of $(nh^d)^{1/2}\left(\hat{\tau}_{Mh}-\tau_M\right)$ and $(nh^d)^{1/2}\left(\hat{\tau}_{mh}-\tau_m\right)$ are the ones of $(nh^d)^{1/2}\left(\hat{\tau}_h(x_M)-\tau(x_M)\right)$ and $(nh^d)^{1/2}\left(\hat{\tau}_h(x_m)-\tau(x_m)\right)$. Interestingly, under the assumption of no treatment effect, the estimator $\hat{\tau}_h(x)$ is asymptotically unbiased because the same bandwidth is used for the treated and control samples. This may considerably simplify testing.

Examples 2, 3, and 4 (Cont'd). Although Propositions 6 and 7 do not apply to these Examples, the proof of these results suggests that our bias and variance results are sufficient to extend existing results which involve trimming to the bounded support case under Assumption X. For the full support test statistic $\hat{t}_0$ in Eq. (7), establishing that $nh^{d/2}\hat{t}_0$ converges in distribution to a centered normal distribution can be done with minor modifications of the arguments of Hjellvik et al. (1998). Studying the full support marginal integration estimator $\hat{\mu}_{1,0}(x_1)$ in Eq. (10) easily follows from Kong et al. (2010) while the full support average derivatives estimator $\widehat{M}_0^{(1)}$ in Eq. (11) can be studied following Chaudhuri et al. (1997), Li et al. (2003), or Banerjee (2007).

4.2. *Local Polynomial Quantile Regression*

Consider the family of loss functions

$$\rho_\alpha(t) = t\left[\alpha - \mathbb{I}(t \le 0)\right], \quad \alpha \in \left[\underline{\alpha}, \overline{a}\right] \subset (0,1),$$

so that

$$\rho_\alpha^{(1)}(t) = \alpha - \mathbb{I}(t \le 0).$$

For this choice of loss functions, $\hat{\beta}_0(\alpha|x,h) = \hat{\beta}_0(x,h)$ is an estimator of the conditional quantile function $Q(\alpha|x)$ of Y_i given $X_i = x$ and $\hat{\beta}_\pi(\alpha|x,h) = \widehat{\beta}_\pi(x,h)$ estimates the partial derivative $\partial^{|\pi|}Q(\alpha|x)/\partial x^\pi$. We shall use the following standard assumption.

Assumption F .
The variables $\left(Y_i, X_i'\right)_{i=1}^n$ *are i.i.d. The conditional p.d.f. of* Y *given* $X = x$ *denoted as* $f(y|x)$ *is continuous and differentiable with respect to* y

such that $f(y|x) > 0$ *for all* $(x, y) \in \mathcal{X} \times \mathbb{R}$, $\sup_{(x,y)\in\mathcal{X}\times\mathbb{R}} \left|\frac{\partial f(y|x)}{\partial y}\right| < \infty$, *and* $\sup_{(x,y)\in\mathcal{X}\times\mathbb{R}} \left|\frac{\partial f(y|x)}{\partial x}\right| < \infty$.

Under Assumption F, the minimizers $Q(\alpha|x) = \mu(x)$ and $\bar{\beta}(\alpha|x, h) = \overline{\beta}(x, h)$ of Eqs. (1) and (12) are unique. Let $F(\cdot\,|\,\cdot)$ be the cumulative distribution function of Y given X. The functions $R_\alpha^{(1)}(\mu|x)$, $\mathbb{E}\left[\left(\rho_\alpha^{(1)}(Y-\mu)\right)^2 |X = x\right]$, $\mathbb{E}\left[\left(\rho_\alpha^{(1)}(Y - Q(\alpha|x))\right)^2 |X = x\right]$, $R_\alpha^{(2)}(\mu|x)$, $V(\alpha|x, h)$, and $V(\alpha|x)$ are:

$$R_\alpha^{(1)}(\mu|x) = F(\mu|x) - \alpha, \quad R_\alpha^{(2)}(\mu|x) = f(\mu|x),$$

$$\mathbb{E}\left[\left(\rho_\alpha^{(1)}(Y-\mu)\right)^2 |X = x\right] = \mathbb{E}\left[(\mathbb{I}(Y \le \mu) - \alpha)^2 |X = x\right],$$

$$\mathbb{E}\left[\left(\rho_\alpha^{(1)}(Y - Q(\alpha|x))\right)^2 |X = x\right] = \alpha(1-\alpha),$$

$$V(\alpha|x, h) = \frac{\alpha(1-\alpha)}{f^2(Q(\alpha|x)|x)\, f(x)}, \Omega(x, h)^{-1}, \quad \text{and}$$

$$V(\alpha|x) = \frac{\alpha(1-\alpha)}{f^2(Q(\alpha|x)|x)\, f(x)} \Omega^{-1}.$$

Hence, Assumption R follows from Assumption F. Since

$$\frac{1}{f(Q(\alpha|x)|x)} = \frac{\partial Q(\alpha|x)}{\partial \alpha},$$

a possible estimator of the asymptotic variance $V(\alpha|x, h)$ is

$$\widehat{V}(\alpha|x, h) = \alpha(1-\alpha)\left(\frac{\partial \widehat{Q}(\alpha|x)}{\partial \alpha}\right)^2 \Omega(x, h)^{-1},$$

$$\text{where } \frac{\partial \widehat{Q}(\alpha|x)}{\partial \alpha} = \frac{\hat{\beta}_0(\alpha + \eta|x, h) - \hat{\beta}_0(\alpha - \eta|x, h)}{2\eta}, \quad \eta = \eta_n \to 0.$$

An important difference between conditional regression and quantile estimation is that the local polynomial quantile regression is neither explicit nor linear with respect to the Y_i. An additionalstep is needed to show that $\hat{\beta}(\alpha|x, h)$ is asymptotically linear, see, for example, Chaudhuri (1991), Su and Xiao (2009), or Guerre and Sabbah (2012). To this aim, define

$$\begin{aligned}\widehat{S}(\alpha|x,h) &= \frac{1}{(nh^d)^{1/2}} \sum_{i=1}^{n} \left(\mathbb{I}\left(Y_i \le U(X_i - x)'\bar{\beta}(\alpha|x,h)\right) - \alpha\right) \\ &\quad \times U\left(\frac{X_i - x}{h}\right) K\left(\frac{X_i - x}{h}\right), \\ \widehat{J}(\alpha|x,h) &= \frac{1}{nh^d} \sum_{i=1}^{n} f\left(U(X_i - x)'\bar{\beta}(\alpha|x,h)|X_i\right) U\left(\frac{X_i - x}{h}\right) \\ &\quad \times U'\left(\frac{X_i - x}{h}\right) K\left(\frac{X_i - x}{h}\right), \quad \text{and} \\ \overline{J}(\alpha|x,h) &= \mathbb{E}\left[\widehat{J}(\alpha|x,h)\right].\end{aligned}$$

Lemma 5 and Assumption F ensure that $\widehat{J}(\alpha|x,h)$ has an inverse asymptotically. The next linearization proposition is an extension of Guerre and Sabbah (2012, Theorem 2), which allows for estimation location x close or on the boundary of $\mathcal{X}$. Note that under Assumption F, the smoothness index s in Assumption S can be taken greater than 1 as assumed in all the results below.

Proposition 8. *Suppose that Assumptions K, F, X, and S1 or S2 hold for some* $s \ge 1$, *that* $h = h_n \to 0$ *with* $\log n/(nh^d) = o(1)$. *Then*

$$\sup_{(\alpha,x)\in[\underline{\alpha},\overline{\alpha}]\times\mathcal{X}} \left\| H\left(\hat{\beta}(\alpha|x,h) - \bar{\beta}(\alpha|x,h)\right) + \frac{\widehat{J}(\alpha|x,h)^{-1}\widehat{S}(\alpha|x,h)}{(nh^d)^{1/2}} \right\|$$

$$= O_p\left(\left(\frac{\log n}{nh^d}\right)^{\frac{3}{4}}\right) \quad \textit{and}$$

$$\sup_{(\alpha,x)\in[\underline{\alpha},\overline{\alpha}]\times\mathcal{X}} \left\| H\left(\hat{\beta}(\alpha|x,h) - \bar{\beta}(\alpha|x,h)\right) + \frac{\overline{J}(\alpha|x,h)^{-1}\widehat{S}(\alpha|x,h)}{(nh^d)^{1/2}} \right\|$$

$$= O_p\left(\left(\frac{\log n}{nh^d}\right)^{\frac{3}{4}}\right).$$

Approximating $H\left(\hat{\beta}(\alpha|x,h) - \bar{\beta}(\alpha|x,h)\right)$ with $\widehat{J}(\alpha|x,h)^{-1}\widehat{S}(\alpha|x,h)$ as in the first equation gives an approximation similar to that for a local polynomial regression estimator. Using the leading term $\overline{J}(\alpha|x,h)^{-1}\widehat{S}(\alpha|x,h)$ shows that the local polynomial quantile estimator is asymptotically a sum which can be handled with standard limit theorems. A similar result can be established for a larger class of loss functions $\rho(\cdot)$ such as the one used in Newey and Powell (1987). However, the rate $\left(\log n/(nh^d)\right)^{3/4}$ is typical of the quantile check function which is not twice continuously differentiable and better rates hold for smoother $\rho(\cdot)$.

This linearization result is the key tool to establish a Central Limit Theorem and uniform consistency for local polynomial quantile regression. The next two propositions parallel Propositions 6 and 7 for local polynomial regression. Like Theorems 1, 2, and 4, these results show that the boundary effect can be weak for local polynomial quantile regression estimators.

Proposition 9. *Suppose that Assumptions K, F, X, and S1 or S2 hold with* $s \geq 1$, *that* $h = h_n \to 0$ *and* $\eta = \eta_n \to 0$ *with* $\log^3 n/(nh^d) = o(1)$, $h + (\log n/(nh^d))^{1/2} = o(\eta)$ *and that* $\{x_n\} \subset \mathcal{X}$ *is a deterministic sequence. Then*

$$(nh^d)^{-1/2}\widehat{V}(\alpha|x_n, h)^{-1/2} H\left(\hat{\beta}(\alpha|x_n; h) - \overline{\beta}(\alpha|x_n; h)\right)$$

converges in distribution to a multivariate normal with

$$\widehat{V}(\alpha|x_n, h) = V(\alpha|x_n, h) + o_p(1).$$

Proposition 10. *Suppose that Assumptions K, F, X, and S1 or S2 hold, that* $h = h_n \to 0$ *with* $\log^3 n/(nh^d) = o(1)$. *Then*

$$\sup_{(\alpha,x)\in[\underline{\alpha},\overline{\alpha}]\times\mathcal{X}} \left\| H\left(\hat{\beta}(\alpha|x; h) - \beta(\alpha|x; h)\right)\right\| = O_p\left(\left(\frac{\log n}{nh^d}\right)^{1/2} + h^s\right).$$

Example 1 (Cont'd). In the quantile setup, the estimation of the average treatment effect in Eq. (5) becomes

$$\hat{\tau}_h(\alpha|x) = \widehat{Q}_{1h}(\alpha|x) - \widehat{m}_{2h}(\alpha|x), \quad \alpha \in [0, 1], \quad x \in \mathcal{B}_{01}.$$

Proposition 10 yields that $\hat{\tau}_h(\alpha|x)$ converges uniformly to $\tau(\alpha|x)$ over $[\underline{\alpha}, \overline{\alpha}] \times \mathcal{B}_{01}$ with a rate $\left(\log n/(nh^d)\right)^{1/2} + h^s$ extending Imbens and Zajonc (2011) to quantile setup. The indicators in Eq. (6) can be computed for each quantile levels. For a given α, they behave as in the regression case. When α varies in $[\underline{\alpha}, \overline{\alpha}]$, these indicators should be considered as stochastic processes whose asymptotic distribution can be derived using the asymptotic expansion stated in Proposition 8.

Example 2 (Cont'd). Proposition 8 is useful to obtain a suitable approximation of the test statistic $\hat{t}_c^2$. Let $\widetilde{\mu}(x) = \widetilde{Q}(\alpha|x)$ be the leading term of the conditional quantile local polynomial estimator $\hat{\mu}(x) = \widehat{Q}(\alpha|x)$

$$\widetilde{\mu}(x) = \overline{Q}_h(\alpha|x) - e_1' \frac{\overline{J}(\alpha|x,h)^{-1}\widehat{S}(\alpha|x,h)}{(nh^d)^{1/2}}, \tag{20}$$

where $e_1' = [1, 0, \ldots, 0]$ and $\overline{Q}_h(\alpha|x) = e_1'\overline{\beta}\,(\alpha|x;h)$. The "linearized" version of $\hat{t}_c^2$ is

$$\tilde{t}_c^2 = \frac{1}{n}\sum_{i=1}^{n} \widetilde{\mu}^2(X_i)\mathbb{I}\,[X_i \in \mathcal{X}_c]\,.$$

Proposition 8 and the triangular inequality yield that

$$\begin{aligned}
nh^{d/2}\left(\hat{t}_c^2 - \tilde{t}_c^2\right) &= \left(\left(nh^{d/2}\right)^{1/2}\left[\hat{t}_c - \tilde{t}_c\right]\right) \times \left(\left(nh^{d/2}\right)^{1/2}\left[\hat{t}_c + \tilde{t}_c\right]\right) \\
&= \left(nh^{d/2}\right)^{1/2} O_p\left(\left(\frac{\log n}{nh^d}\right)^{\frac{3}{4}}\right) \\
&\quad \times \left(\left(nh^{d/2}\right)^{1/2} 2\hat{t}_c + \left(nh^{d/2}\right)^{1/2} O_p\left(\left(\frac{\log n}{nh^d}\right)^{\frac{3}{4}}\right)\right) \\
&= O_p\left(\left(\frac{\log^3 n}{nh^{2d}}\right)^{\frac{1}{4}}\right) \times \left(\left(nh^{d/2}\right)^{1/2} 2\hat{t}_c + O_p\left(\left(\frac{\log^3 n}{nh^{2d}}\right)^{\frac{1}{4}}\right)\right).
\end{aligned}$$

Consider the null hypothesis. Solving the first-order condition for $\bar{\beta}\,(\alpha|x;h)$ gives $\overline{\beta}\,(\alpha|x;h) = 0$ when $Q(\alpha|x) = 0$ for all x in $\mathcal{X}_c$. As a consequence, $\tilde{t}_c^2$ is a quadratic form similar for the one obtained in the regression framework, but with the centered variables $\mathbb{I}\,(Y_i \le 0) - \alpha$ instead of the regression error terms. It follows that $\tilde{t}_c^2$ will satisfy Eq. (8) with a proper choice of standardizing constants. This gives,

$$nh^{d/2}\left(\hat{t}_c^2 - \tilde{t}_c^2\right) = O_p\left(\left(\frac{\log^3 n}{nh^{3d}}\right)^{\frac{1}{4}}\right),$$

which goes to 0 when $\left(\log^3 n\right)/\left(nh^{3d}\right) \to 0$, a condition which will also ensure that $\hat{t}_c^2$ is asymptotically normal as in Eq. (8) and that normal critical values can be used to perform the test.

Example 3 (Cont'd). Defining a leave-one-out version of the linear $\widetilde{\mu}(x_1, x_2)$ as in Eq. (20) yields for the marginal integration estimator (10) of $\mu_1(x_1)$ and applying

Proposition 8 suggests,

$$\hat{\mu}_{1,c}(x_1) = \frac{\sum_{i=1}^{n} \mathbb{I}(X_{2i} \in \mathcal{X}_{2c})\, \widetilde{\mu}_i(x_1, X_{2i})}{\sum_{i=1}^{n} \mathbb{I}(X_{2i} \in \mathcal{X}_{2c})} + O_p\left(\left(\frac{\log n}{nh^d}\right)^{\frac{3}{4}}\right),$$

with a leading term which can be studied as in Kong et al. (2010), for any $c \geq 0$. The estimator error $\left(nh^{d_1}\right)^{1/2}\left(\hat{\mu}_{1,c}(x_1) - \mu_{1,c}(x_1)\right)$ will satisfies a CLT if the contribution of the linearization remainder term is negligible, yielding the necessary condition,

$$\left(nh^{d_1}\right)^{1/2}\left(\frac{\log n}{nh^d}\right)^{\frac{3}{4}} = \left(\frac{\log^3 n}{nh^{3d-2d_1}}\right)^{\frac{1}{4}} \to 0.$$

Example 4 (Cont'd). The case of the average derivatives estimator is similar to Example 3. However, the contribution of the linearization remainder term must take into account an additional 1/h due to the estimation of a derivative. The $n^{1/2}$ asymptotic normality of the estimator requests a more drastic bandwidth condition,

$$n^{1/2}\frac{1}{h}\left(\frac{\log n}{nh^d}\right)^{\frac{3}{4}} = \left(\frac{\log^3 n}{nh^{3d+4}}\right)^{\frac{1}{4}} \to 0.$$

The asymptotic bias and variance of the estimator can be obtained from Chaudhuri et al. (1997) and our bias and variance results to account for the good boundary properties of the conditional quantile local polynomial estimator.

5. SIMULATION EXPERIMENTS

Our theoretical results have illustrated the good bias and variance boundary properties of local polynomial estimation for general loss functions. The boundary bias has the same order as the minimax bias obtained for worst case specifications. The behavior of the variance is similar, with an order which is not affected by the boundary. However, for the variance, the constant in front of the order may be larger for points close to the boundary than for points away from the boundary. Preventing poor estimation induced by such areas may justify trimming in Examples 2, 3, and 4. The purpose of this section is to use a small simulation experiment.to illustrate how trimming influences inference in various settings.

We will use the setup of Examples 2, 3, and 4. To avoid nonlinearity issues, we will consider the regression model,

$$Y_i = \mu(X_{1i}, X_{2i}) + \varepsilon_i, \quad i = 1, \ldots, 1{,}000,$$

Table 1. Trimming Values Used in the Experiment.

Trimming 1 ($c=0$)	Trimming 2 ($c=0.1$)	Trimming 3 ($c=0.2$)
$(X_{1i}, X_{2i}) \in [0,1]^2$	$(X_{1i}, X_{2i}) \in [0.1, 0.9]^2$	$(X_{1i}, X_{2i}) \in [0.2, 0.8]^2$

where $\left\{[X_{1i}, X_{2i}]'\right\}_{i=1}^{n}$ are i.i.d. Uniform over $[0,1]^2$ and $\{\varepsilon_i\}_{i=1}^{n}$ are i.i.d. centered normal with standard deviation 0.1. The choice of the regression function $\mu(\cdot)$ will vary across examples. The number of replications is 5,000. The regression local polynomial estimators of order 1 (linear) and order 2 (quadratic) will be considered with the kernel:

$$K(x) = \left(1 - x^2\right) \mathbb{I}\left(x \in [-1, 1]\right).$$

Three trimming values will be investigated, see Table 1, where trimming 1 corresponds to no trimming.

5.1. Example 2: Significance Testing

Instead of Eq. (7), the more popular test statistic $\widehat{T}_c$ of Eq. (9) is used. This test statistic can be written as a quadratic form $Y_n' W Y_n$, where the symmetric matrix W depends on the local polynomial estimator, the bandwidth h, and the trimming parameter c. Its variance can be estimated using

$$\hat{\sigma}_c^2 = 2 \sum_{i \le i \ne j \le n} W_{ij}^2 \widehat{\varepsilon}_i^2 \widehat{\varepsilon}_j^2,$$

where the residuals $\widehat{\varepsilon}_i$ are computed from the local polynomial estimation. The considered bandwidths are

$$h^2 \in \{0.01, 0.04, 0.07, 0.10, 0.13, 0.16, 0.19\}.$$

We estimated the 90%, 95%, and 99% critical values by computing the test statistic $\widehat{T}_c / \hat{\sigma}_c$ for each level of trimming and each bandwidth over 5,000 replications of the null model: $\mu(\cdot) = 0$. This did not show specific impact of trimming with simulated critical values reasonably close to their nominal counterparts.

The simulated 90% critical values were used to study the power of the tests using 1,000 replications of the model for the two regression functions below:

$$m_1(x_1, x_2) = 0.1K\left(\frac{x_1}{0.1}\right) - 0.1K\left(\frac{1 - x_2}{0.1}\right) \text{ and}$$

$$m_2(x_1, x_2) = -0.05\cos(6\pi x_1) + 0.05\cos(6\pi x_2).$$

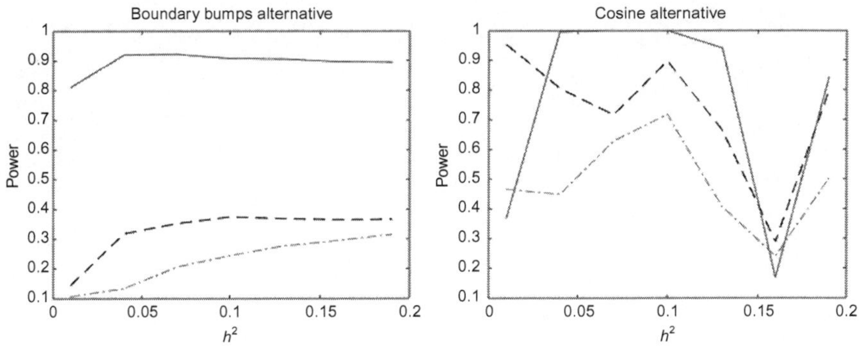

Fig. 1. Power of the Three Trimming 90% Tests as a Function of h^2. Left: Alternative $m_1(\cdot)$. Right: Alternative $m_2(\cdot)$. *Note*: Solid: No trimming. Dash: Trimming 2. Dash-dot: Trimming 3.

The alternative $m_1(\cdot)$ consists of two bumps along the boundaries $x_1 = 0$ and $x_2 = 1$ which are difficult to detect with the trimming tests. On the contrary, the alternative $m_2(\cdot)$ violates the null for most x in the support $[0, 1]^2$. Fig. 1 reports the results of the simulation experiment. As expected the power of the tests against alternative $m_1(\cdot)$ deteriorates with the level of trimming and the test without trimming clearly dominates. The evidence is less clear for alternative $m_2(\cdot)$ which periodicity induces an irregular bandwidth behavior. However, only the test without trimming achieves a power close to 1. Considering a quadratic local polynomial estimator gives a much less powerful test for the considered bandwidths. This surprising finding is however in line with the theoretical results of Guerre and Lavergne (2002) which shows that lower order methods can have good power properties in a minimax framework.

5.2. *Example 3: Additive Specification Estimation*

In this experiment, the regression function is set to $m(x_1) + m\,(x_2)$ with $m(x_1) = \sin(2\pi x_1)$. The local linear smoother $\widehat{\mu}_{1,c}(x_1)$ from Eq. (10) is an estimator of

$$\mu_{1,c}(x_1) = m(x_1) + \mathbb{E}\left[m(X_2)\mathbb{I}\left(X_2 \in [c, 1-c]\right)\right]$$

which includes an expectation term. This term can be removed by imposing an identification restriction such as $m\,(1/2) = 0$. The proposed estimator of $m(x_1)$ is therefore[2]

$$\widehat{m}_c(x_1) = \hat{\mu}_{1,c}(x_1) - \hat{\mu}_{1,c}\,(1/2)\,.$$

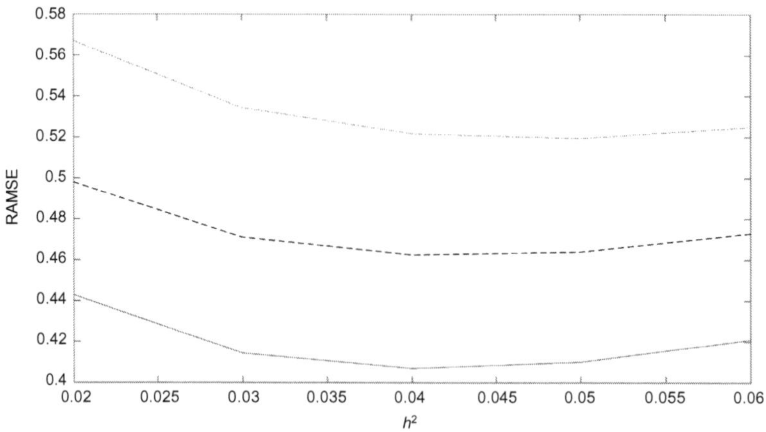

Fig. 2. Square Root Average Mean-Squared Error of $\widehat{m}_c(\cdot)$ as a Function of h^2. *Note*: Solid: No trimming. Dash: Trimming 2. Dash-dot: Trimming 3.

The local linear estimator performs poorly and the reported results are for the local quadratic estimator. The considered bandwidths are smaller than the ones used in Example 1. They are:

$$h^2 \in \{0.02, 0.03, \ldots, 0.06\}.$$

The performance of the estimator is evaluated using the square root average mean-squared error (RAMSE):

$$RAMSE = \left[\frac{1}{11}\sum_{j=0}^{10}\left(\widehat{m}_c\left(\frac{j}{10}\right) - m_c\left(\frac{j}{10}\right)\right)^2\right]^{\frac{1}{2}}.$$

Fig. 2 shows that the estimator without trimming clearly dominates. RAMSE is around 0.40 at best, which is quite big but not surprising since the best bandwidth is $h^2 = 0.04$ implying that only 40 observations are used to estimate each $\mu_{1,c}(j/10)$.

5.3. *Example 4: Average Derivative Estimation*

For this example, a single-index specification is used and the regression function is

$$\mu(x) = \sin^3\left(\frac{\pi}{2}\left(x' - [1/2, 1/2]\right)\beta_0\right), \quad \beta_0' = [1, 1/2].$$

The parameter of interest is $\delta_0 = \beta_{02}/\beta_{01} = 1/2$ which is estimated using a ratio of average derivatives

$$\widehat{\delta}_c = \frac{\sum_{i=1}^{n} \widehat{\partial\mu_i/\partial x_2}(X_i)\mathbb{I}\left[X_i \in \mathcal{X}_c\right]}{\sum_{i=1}^{n} \widehat{\partial\mu_i/\partial x_1}(X_i)\mathbb{I}\left[X_i \in \mathcal{X}_c\right]}.$$

The performance of $\widehat{\delta}_c$ is measured using the square root mean squared error (RMSE). Because estimation of derivatives yields a bigger variance of order $1/(nh^3)$ compared to estimation of a regression for which the variance order is $1/(nh^2)$, the RMSE of $\widehat{\delta}_c$ could be more sensitive than the RAMSE of Example 3 to an increase of the variance near the boundary. The local linear and quadratic regression estimators perform similarly and both are reported here. The considered bandwidths are

$$h^2 \in \{0.015, 0.035, \ldots, 0.135\} \text{ for linear local estimation and}$$
$$h^2 \in \{0.02, 0.07, \ldots, 0.32\} \text{ for local quadratic estimation.}$$

The highest trimming estimator is dominated by lower trimming ones, for both local linear and quadratic estimation. The trimming 1 and 2 estimators behave similarly but trimming 2 seems slightly better than no trimming when looking at the optimal performance. This holds for both local linear and quadratic estimators. Since the bias of the local quadratic estimator is smaller, this behavior suggests that

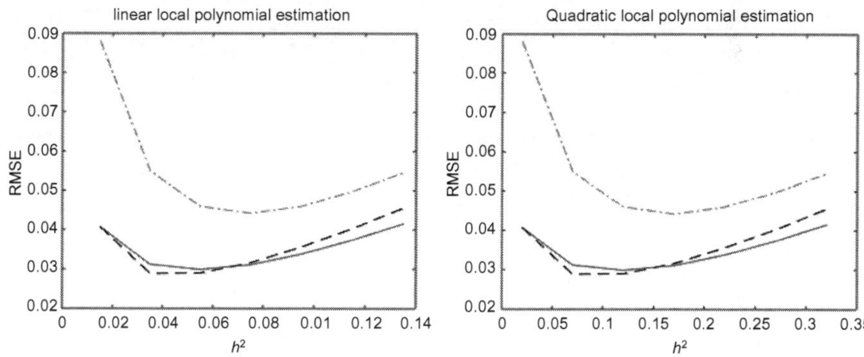

Fig. 3. Square Root Mean-Squared Error for the Three Trimming Estimators as a Function of h^2. Left: Linear Local Polynomial. Right: Quadratic Local Polynomial. *Note*: Solid: No trimming. Dash: Trimming 2. Dash-dot: Trimming 3.

there is an optimal level of trimming possibly due to an increase of variance near the boundary. However, the potential gain seems very small in this experiment (Fig. 3).

6. CONCLUSION

In this paper, we have investigated the boundary and uniform asymptotic properties of multivariate local polynomial estimators of M-regression functions under a weak condition on the *compact* support of the multivariate covariate. This is made possible by a pseudo-true value approach based on a novel application of the Newton–Kantorovich Theorem in our context. Compared with Assumption (A4) in Ruppert and Wand (1994) who use it to establish pointwise boundary properties of local polynomial regression estimators, our support condition allows for more general support shapes, in particular, it allows the support of the covariate to be non-connected and have holes. Compared with the uniform result in Corollary 2, ii) in Masry (1996), our results deal directly with multivariate covariates with compact support and are uniformly valid over the entire support. As such they should be useful in contexts where estimation or testing require (weighted) averages of multivariate nonparametric estimators with compactly supported covariate as in Examples 2–4.

7. PROOF SECTION

Note that Assumption X ensures that for any $h > 0$ small enough, any $x \in \mathcal{X}$, there is a $x_h \in \mathcal{X}$ such that $\mathcal{V}(x_h, \kappa_1 h) \subset \mathcal{V}(x, h) \cap \mathcal{X}$. We will use this equivalent statement of Eq. (13) throughout this section. Also we will use C to denote a generic positive constant whose value may differ in different places.

We start with Lemma 11 which will be used in many proofs below.

Lemma 11. *Under Assumptions K and X, there is a $C > 1$ such that the eigenvalues of $\int U(z)U'(z)K^j(z)f(x+hz)dz$ and $\Omega_j(x,h)$, $j = 1, 2$, are in $[1/C, C]$ for all $x \in \mathcal{X}$ and $h \geq 0$ small enough.*

Proof of Lemma 11. It is sufficient to consider $j = 1$. Since

$$\int U(z)U'(z)K(z)f(x+hz)dz \preceq C\Omega_j(x,h) \preceq C \int U(z)U'(z)K(z)dz,$$

the eigenvalues are in $[0, C]$ for all $x \in \mathcal{X}$ and $h \geq 0$. We now show that the eigenvalues can be bounded from below by $1/C$. Assumptions K and X-(i) give, uniformly in $x \in \mathcal{X}$,

$$\int U(z)U'(z)K(z)f(x+hz)dz \succeq C\Omega(x,h)$$
$$\succeq C\int U(z)U(z)'\,\mathbb{I}\,(x+hz\in\mathcal{X}, z\in\mathcal{V}(0,1))\,dz.$$

Assume that h is small enough. Assumption X-(ii) gives, with $(t-x)/h = z$,

$$\int U(z)U(z)'\,\mathbb{I}\,(x+hz\in\mathcal{X}, z\in\mathcal{V}(0,1))\,dz$$
$$= \int U\left(\frac{t-x}{h}\right)U\left(\frac{t-x}{h}\right)'\,\mathbb{I}\,(t\in\mathcal{V}(x,h)\cap\mathcal{X})\,\frac{dt}{h^d}$$
$$\succeq \int U\left(\frac{t-x}{h}\right)U\left(\frac{t-x}{h}\right)'\,\mathbb{I}\,(t\in\mathcal{V}\,(x_h,\kappa_1 h))\,\frac{dt}{h^d}$$
$$\succeq \int U(z)U(z)'\,\mathbb{I}\left(z\in\mathcal{V}\left(\frac{x_h-x}{h},\kappa_1\right)\right)dz,$$

where $\|(x_h-x)/h\| \le 1$. Hence, the eigenvalues of $\int U(z)U'(z)K(z)f(x+hz)dz$ and $\Omega_j(x,h)$ are larger than

$$\inf_{y\in\mathcal{V}(0,1)}\min_{b:b'b=1} b'\left(\int U(z)U(z)'\,\mathbb{I}\,(z\in\mathcal{V}\,(y,\kappa_1))\,dz\right)b.$$

Suppose now that this lower bound is equal to 0. This implies that there is a sequence $y_n\in\mathcal{V}(0,1)$ and b_n with $b_n'b_n = 1$ such that

$$\int \left(U(z)'b_n\right)^2\mathbb{I}\,(z\in\mathcal{V}\,(y_n,\kappa_1))\,dz\to 0.$$

By compacity and continuity of $(b,y)\mapsto\int\left(U(z)'b\right)^2\mathbb{I}\,(z\in\mathcal{V}\,(y,\kappa_1))\,dz$, this implies that there is a $y\in\mathcal{V}(0,1)$ and b with $b'b=1$ such that

$$\int \left(U(z)'b\right)^2\mathbb{I}\,(z\in\mathcal{V}\,(y,\kappa_1))\,dz = 0.$$

Hence, $U(z)'b=0$, but this is impossible since $b\neq 0$. Hence, the eigenvalues of $\int U(z)U'(z)K(z)f(x+hz)dz$ are in $[1/C, C]$ for all $x\in\mathcal{X}$ and h small enough. ■

7.1. Theorems 1, 2, and Proposition 3

A technical challenge comes from the fact that $\bar{\beta}(x,h)$ is not explicit but defined through Eq. (12). The next lemma is the key tool to study the bias term $\left[\bar{\beta}(x,h)-\beta(x)\right]$ when using the first-order condition which characterizes $\bar{\beta}(x,h)$. In this lemma, D is an integer number and $\|\cdot\|$ stands for the Euclidean norm over $\mathbb{R}^D$ or for the associated operator norm.

Lemma 12. **(*Newton–Kantorovich*).** *Let $\mathcal{F}(\cdot):\mathbb{R}^D\to\mathbb{R}$ be a twice continuously differentiable convex function with a unique minimizer $\bar{\mathbf{b}}$. Suppose that*

1. *There is $\mathbf{b}^*\in\mathbb{R}^D$ such that $\left\|\mathcal{F}^{(1)}(\mathbf{b}^*)\right\|\leq\eta$ and $\left\|\left[\mathcal{F}^{(2)}(\mathbf{b}^*)\right]^{-1}\right\|\leq C_0$;*
2. $\left\|\mathcal{F}^{(2)}(b)-\mathcal{F}^{(2)}\left(b'\right)\right\|\leq C_1\left\|b-b'\right\|$ *for all $b,b'\in\mathbb{R}^D$;*
3. *$C_0^2C_1\eta\leq 1/4$.*

Then $\left\|\mathbf{b}^*-\bar{\mathbf{b}}\right\|\leq 2C_0\eta$.

Proof of Lemma 12. This follows from conclusion 3 in the Newton–Kantorovich Theorem stated in Gragg and Tapia (1974). ■

It is convenient to rescale β with H^{-1} and to set $b=H^{-1}\beta$, where H is a diagonal matrix with entries $h^{|\pi|}$. This gives in particular

$$U(X_i-x)'\beta=U\left(\frac{X_i-x}{h}\right)'H\beta=U\left(\frac{X_i-x}{h}\right)'b.$$

Lemma 12 will be applied for $\bar{\mathbf{b}}=H\bar{\beta}(x;h)=\bar{b}(x;h)$, where $\bar{\beta}(x;h)$ is as in Eq. (12) and we now define a candidate $\mathbf{b}^*$. Define

$$s_p=\begin{cases} s & \text{for the proof of Theorem 1}\\ p & \text{for the proof of Theorem 2}\end{cases},$$

and $b^*(x,h)=\left(b_\pi^*(x,h),|\pi|\leq p\right)'$ with

$$b_\pi^*(x,h)=\begin{cases}\frac{h^{|\pi|}\pi_1!\cdots\pi_d!\mu^{(\pi)}(x)}{|\pi|!} & \text{for } |\pi|\leq\lfloor s_p\rfloor\\ 0 & \text{for } \lfloor s_p\rfloor<|\pi|\leq p\end{cases}.$$

In other words, when proving Theorem 1, $b^*(x,h)$ completes the entries $h^{|\pi|}\mu^{(\pi)}(x)/(\pi_1!\cdots\pi_d!)$, $|\pi|\leq\lfloor s\rfloor$, with entries equal to 0 whereas in the proof of Theorem 2 the entries of $b^*(x,h)$ are all the $h^{|\pi|}\mu^{(\pi)}(x)/\left(\pi_1!\cdots\pi_d!\right)$, $|\pi|\leq p$.

The Taylor formula implies, under Assumptions S and X which implies that $\mathcal{X}$ has no isolated points,

$$\max_{(x,z)\in\mathcal{X}\times\text{Supp}\,K, x+hz\in\mathcal{X}} \left|\mu(x+hz) - U(z)'b^*(x,h)\right| \leq Ch^{s_p}, \tag{21}$$

with $C = C'L$ under Assumption S1.

Define now

$$\boldsymbol{R}_h(b|x) = \int R\left(U(z)'b|x+hz\right) f(x+hz)K(z)dz,$$

where $x+hz$ stands for X. The Lebesgue Dominated Convergence Theorem gives under Assumptions R, X, and K that $b \mapsto \boldsymbol{R}_h(b|x)$ is twice continuously differentiable with first and second derivatives

$$\boldsymbol{R}_h^{(1)}(b|x) = \int R^{(1)}\left(U(z)'b|x+hz\right) U(z) f(x+hz)K(z)dz \quad \text{and}$$

$$\boldsymbol{R}_h^{(2)}(b|x) = \int R^{(2)}\left(U(z)'b|x+hz\right) U(z)U(z)' f(x+hz)K(z)dz.$$

The next lemma shows that the matrix $\boldsymbol{R}_h^{(2)}(b|x)$ satisfies some of the conditions of Lemma 12.

Lemma 13. *Under Assumptions K, R, and X and for $h \leq \kappa_0/\kappa_1$, there is a $C > 1$ such that the eigenvalues of $\boldsymbol{R}_h^{(2)}(b|x)$ are in $[1/C, \infty)$ for all b and all $x \in \mathcal{X}$ and, for all b, b' and all $x \in \mathcal{X}$, $\left\|\boldsymbol{R}_h^{(2)}(b|x) - \boldsymbol{R}_h^{(2)}\left(b'|x\right)\right\| \leq C\left\|b-b'\right\|$.*

Proof of Lemma 13. The bound for $\left\|\boldsymbol{R}_h^{(2)}(b|x) - \boldsymbol{R}_h^{(2)}\left(b'|x\right)\right\|$ follows from Assumption R:

$$\begin{aligned}
&\left\|\boldsymbol{R}_h^{(2)}(b|x) - \boldsymbol{R}_h^{(2)}\left(b'|x\right)\right\| \\
&\leq \int \left|R^{(2)}\left(U(z)'b|x+hz\right) - R^{(2)}\left(U(z)'b'|x+hz\right)\right| \\
&\times \left\|U(z)U(z)'\right\| f(x+hz)K(z)dz \\
&\leq C \int \left|U(z)'\left(b-b'\right)\right| \|U(z)\|^2 f(x+hz)K(z)dz \leq C \\
&\times \int \left\|b-b'\right\| \|U(z)\|^3 f(x+hz)K(z)dz \leq C\left\|b-b'\right\|,
\end{aligned}$$

since the support of $K(\cdot)$ is compact and $f(\cdot)$ is bounded. For the lower bound of the eigenvalues of $\boldsymbol{R}_h^{(2)}(b|x)$, observe

$$\boldsymbol{R}_h^{(2)}(b|x) \succeq C \int U(z)U(z)'K(z)f(x+hz)dz,$$

so that the result follows from Lemma 11.

Let us now return to the proof of Theorems 1 and 2. Equation (12) gives $\bar{\beta}(x;h) = \arg\min_{\beta} \boldsymbol{R}_h\left(H^{-1}\beta|x\right)$ so that $\bar{b}(x;h)$ satisfies the first-order condition:

$$\boldsymbol{R}_h^{(1)}\left(\bar{b}(x;h)|x\right) = 0 \quad \text{for all } x \in \mathcal{X}. \tag{22}$$

We now study $\boldsymbol{R}_h^{(1)}\left(b^*(x;h)|x\right)$ which satisfies:

$$\begin{aligned}\boldsymbol{R}_h^{(1)}\left(b^*(x;h)|x\right) &= \int U(z)R^{(1)}\left(U(z)'b^*(x;h)|x+hz\right) f(x+hz)K(z)dz \\ &= \int U(z)R^{(1)}\left(\mu(x+hz) + U(z)'b^*(x;h) - \mu(x+hz)|x+hz\right) \\ &\quad \times f(x+hz)K(z)dz.\end{aligned}$$

Hence, Eq. (21), Assumption R, and Eq. (1) give, uniformly in $x \in \mathcal{X}$

$$\begin{aligned}\left\|\boldsymbol{R}_h^{(1)}\left(b^*(x;h)|x\right)\right\| &\leq \left\|\int U(z)R^{(1)}\left(\mu(x+hz)|x+hz\right) f(x+hz)K(z)dz\right\| \\ &\quad + C \max_{(x,x+hz,z)\in\mathcal{X}^2\times\text{Supp } K} \left|\mu(x+hz) - U(z)'b^*(x,h)\right| \\ &\leq Ch^{s_p}.\end{aligned}$$

Then Lemma 12 shows that Theorem 1 is proved.

For Theorem 2, recall that $s_p = p$. A Taylor expansion of order $p+1$ gives that uniformly in $x \in \mathcal{X}$

$$\mu(x+hz) - U(z)'b^*(x,h) = h^{p+1} \sum_{|\pi|=p+1} \frac{\pi_1!\cdots\pi_d!}{(p+1)!} z^{\pi}\mu^{(\pi)}(x) + o\left(h^{p+1}\right).$$

Recall that $\boldsymbol{R}^{(2)}_{f,\mu}(x) = R^{(2)}(\mu(x)|x)f(x)$ is bounded away from 0. Hence, Eqs. (22), (1) and standard uniform expansions give, for $\mathbb{I}_{\mathcal{X}}(x+hz) = \mathbb{I}(x+hz \in \mathcal{X})$,

$$
\begin{aligned}
0 = \int & U(z)R^{(1)}\left(\mu(x+hz) + U(z)'\overline{b}(x;h) - \mu(x+hz)|x+hz\right) \\
& \times f(x+hz)K(z)dz = \underbrace{\int U(z)R^{(1)}\left(\mu(x+hz)|x+hz\right) f(x+hz)K(z)dz}_{=0} \\
& + \int \left(\boldsymbol{R}^{(2)}_{f,\mu}(x+hz) + o(1)\right) U(z)(U(z)'\overline{b}(x;h) \\
& - \mu(x+hz))\mathbb{I}_{\mathcal{X}}(x+hz)K(z)dz \\
= & \left(\boldsymbol{R}^{(2)}_{f,\mu}(x) + o(1)\right) \int U(z)U(z)'\left(\overline{b}(x;h) - b^*(x;h)\right)\mathbb{I}_{\mathcal{X}}(x+hz)K(z)dz \\
& + \left(\boldsymbol{R}^{(2)}_{f,\mu}(x) + o(1)\right) \int U(z)\left\{h^{p+1} \sum_{|\pi|=p+1} \frac{\pi_1! \cdots \pi_d!}{(p+1)!} z^{\pi} \mu^{(\pi)}(x)\right\} \\
& \times \mathbb{I}_{\mathcal{X}}(x+hz)K(z)dz + o\left(h^{p+1}\right).
\end{aligned}
$$

Rearranging gives,

$$
\begin{aligned}
\overline{b}(x;h) - b^*(x;h) = h^{p+1} & \left(\int U(z)U(z)'K(z)\mathbb{I}_{\mathcal{X}}(x+hz)dz\right)^{-1} \\
& \times \int U(z)\left\{\sum_{|\pi|=p+1} \frac{\pi_1! \cdots \pi_d!}{(p+1)!} z^{\pi} \mu^{(\pi)}(x)\right\}\mathbb{I}_{\mathcal{X}}(x+hz)K(z)dz \\
& + o\left(h^{p+1}\right),
\end{aligned}
$$

showing that Theorem 2 is proved.

For Proposition 3, performing a Taylor expansion of order $p+2$ and arguing as above gives, for inner x,

$$
\overline{b}(x;h) - b^*(x;h) = \frac{(1+o(1))}{\boldsymbol{R}^{(2)}_{f,\mu}(x)} \Omega^{-1}\boldsymbol{B}(x;h) + o\left(h^{p+2}\right),
$$

where

$$
\begin{aligned}
\boldsymbol{B}(x;h) = & \int U(z) \left\{ h^{p+1} \boldsymbol{R}^{(2)}_{f,\mu}(x+hz) \sum_{|\pi|=p+1} \frac{\pi_1! \cdots \pi_d!}{(p+1)!} z^{\pi} \mu^{(\pi)}(x) \right\} K(z)dz \\
& + \int U(z) \left\{ h^{p+2} \boldsymbol{R}^{(2)}_{f,\mu}(x) \sum_{|\pi|=p+2} \frac{\pi_1! \cdots \pi_d!}{(p+1)!} z^{\pi} \mu^{(\pi)}(x) \right\} K(z)dz \\
& = h^{p+1} \boldsymbol{R}^{(2)}_{f,\mu}(x) b_{p+1}(x) + h^{p+2} \sum_{j=1}^{d} \frac{\partial \boldsymbol{R}^{(2)}_{f,\mu}(x)}{\partial x_j} \mu^{(\pi)}(x) \int z_j z^{\pi} U(z) K(z) dz \\
& + o\left(h^{p+2}\right) + h^{p+2} \boldsymbol{R}^{(2)}_{f,\mu}(x) b_{p+2}(x),
\end{aligned}
$$

This gives the expansion of the proposition since $e'_{\pi} \Omega_1^{-1} b_{p+1}(x) = 0$ by Gu et al. (2015). ■

7.2. *Theorem 4*

Let

$$
\boldsymbol{R}^{(2)}(x,h) = h^{-d} \mathbb{E}\left[R^{(2)}\left(\mu(x)|X\right) U\left(\frac{X-x}{h}\right) U\left(\frac{X-x}{h}\right)' K\left(\frac{X-x}{h}\right) \right],
$$

$$
\boldsymbol{S}(x,h) = h^{-d} \mathbb{E}\left[\left(\rho^{(1)}\left(Y - \mu(X)\right)\right)^2 U\left(\frac{X-x}{h}\right) U\left(\frac{X-x}{h}\right)' K^2\left(\frac{X-x}{h}\right) \right],
$$

Theorems 1 and 2, Eq. (21), give that

$$
\max_{(x,z) \in \mathcal{X} \times \operatorname{Supp} K, x+hz \in \mathcal{X}} \left| U(hz)' \beta(x,h) - \mu(x+hz) \right| = o(1).
$$

Therefore $\max_{x,h} \operatorname{Sp}\left(h^{-d} \mathbb{E}\left[U\left(\frac{X-x}{h}\right) U\left(\frac{X-x}{h}\right)' K^j\left(\frac{X-x}{h}\right)\right]\right) < \infty$, $j = 1, 2$, Assumption R-(ii), and uniform continuity of $\mu(\cdot)$ over $\mathcal{X}$ give when $h \to 0$,

$$
\max_{x \in \mathcal{X}} \left\| \overline{\boldsymbol{R}}^{(2)}(x,h) - \boldsymbol{R}^{(2)}(x,h) \right\| = o(1), \quad \max_{x \in \mathcal{X}} \left\| \overline{\boldsymbol{S}}(x,h) - \boldsymbol{S}(x,h) \right\| = o(1).
$$

A standard change of variable gives

$$\begin{aligned}
\boldsymbol{R}^{(2)}(x,h) &= \int R^{(2)}\left(\mu(x)|x+hz\right) U(z)U(z)' K(z) f(x+hz)dx \\
&= R^{(2)}(\mu(x)|x) f(x)\Omega_1(x,h) + o(1), \\
\boldsymbol{S}(x,h) &= \int \mathbb{E}\left[\left(\rho^{(1)}\left(Y-\mu(X)\right)\right)^2 |X = x+hz\right] U(z)U(z)' K^2(z) f(x+hz)dx \\
&= \mathbb{E}\left[\left(\rho^{(1)}\left(Y-\mu(X)\right)\right)^2 |X = x\right] f(x)\Omega_2(x,h) + o(1),
\end{aligned}$$

uniformly over $\mathcal{X}$ by Assumption R-(ii) and X-(i). Hence, Lemma 11 yields that $\overline{V}(x,h)$ is equal to

$$\begin{aligned}
&\left(R^{(2)}(\mu(x)|x) f(x)\Omega_1(x,h)\right)^{-1} \mathbb{E}\left[\left(\rho^{(1)}\left(Y-\mu(X)\right)\right)^2 |X = x\right] \\
&\qquad \times f(x)\Omega_2(x,h)\left(R^{(2)}(\mu(x)|x) f(x)\Omega_1(x,h)\right)^{-1} + o(1) \\
&= \frac{\mathbb{E}\left[\left(\rho^{(1)}\left(Y-\mu(X)\right)\right)^2 |X = x\right]}{\left(R^{(2)}(\mu(x)|x)\right)^2 f(x)} \Omega(x,h)^{-1} + o(1),
\end{aligned}$$

uniformly over $\mathcal{X}$, that is the first approximation in the theorem. The second approximation follows since $\Omega(x,h) = \Omega$ for all x in subset $\mathcal{X}_0$ of $\mathcal{X}$ as in the theorem provided h is small enough. ■

7.3. *Lemma 5, Propositions 6, and 7*

The proof of these results makes use of the Bernstein inequality, which states that for independent centered real random variables Z_i with $|Z_i| \leq M$,

$$\mathbb{P}\left(\left|\frac{1}{\sqrt{n}}\sum_{i=1}^{n} Z_i\right| \geq t\right) \leq 2\exp\left(-\frac{t^2/2}{\frac{1}{n}\sum_{i=1}^{n}\operatorname{Var}(Z_i) + \frac{1}{3}\frac{Mt}{\sqrt{n}}}\right) \text{ for any } t \geq 0. \quad (23)$$

Proof of Lemma 5. It is sufficient to consider $j = 1$. To prove Eq. (19), it is sufficient to show that for any $\epsilon > 0$ large enough, all π with $|\pi| \leq 2p$, $K_\pi(z) = z^\pi K(z)$ and $r_n = \left(\log n/(nh^d)\right)^{1/2}$,

$$\mathbb{P}\left(\sup_{x\in\mathcal{X}}\left|\frac{1}{nh^d}\sum_{i=1}^{n} K_\pi\left(\frac{X_i - x}{h}\right) - \int K_\pi(z) f(x+hz)dz\right| \geq r_n\epsilon\right) \to 0. \quad (24)$$

By Assumptions K, X and $1/h^d = O(n/\log n)$, there is a $\delta = \delta_n = n^{-a}$ such that

1. There is an integer number $J_n = O(n^b)$, $b > 0$, and some $x_j \in \mathcal{X}$ such that $\mathcal{X} = \bigcup_{j=1}^{J_n} \mathcal{V}_X(x_j, \delta_n)$, where $\mathcal{V}_X(x_j, \delta_n) = \mathcal{V}(x_j, \delta_n) \cap \mathcal{X}$;
2. For all x, x' with $\|x - x'\| \leq \delta_n$ and all i and n, $\left|K_\pi\left(\frac{X_i - x}{h}\right) - K_\pi\left(\frac{X_i - x'}{h}\right)\right| \leq h^d r_n \epsilon/3$;
3. For all $x, x' \in \mathcal{X}$ with $\|x - x'\| \leq \delta_n$ and all n, $\left|\int K_\pi(z) f(x + hz) dz - \int K_\pi(z) f(x' + hz) dz\right| \leq r_n \epsilon/3$.

This gives

$$\begin{aligned}
&\sup_{x \in \mathcal{X}} \left| \frac{1}{nh^d} \sum_{i=1}^n K_\pi\left(\frac{X_i - x}{h}\right) - \int K_\pi(z) f(x + hz) dz \right| \\
&\leq \max_{j=1,\ldots,J_n} \left| \frac{1}{nh^d} \sum_{i=1}^n K_\pi\left(\frac{X_i - x_j}{h}\right) - \int K_\pi(z) f(x_j + hz) dz \right| \\
&\quad + \max_{j=1,\ldots,J_n} \sup_{x \in \mathcal{V}_X(x_j, \delta_n)} \left| \frac{1}{nh^d} \sum_{i=1}^n \left(K_\pi\left(\frac{X_i - x}{h}\right) - K_\pi\left(\frac{X_i - x_j}{h}\right)\right)\right| \\
&\quad + \max_{j=1,\ldots,J_n} \sup_{x \in \mathcal{V}_X(x_j, \delta_n)} \left| \int K_\pi(z) \left(f(x) - f(x_j + hz)\right) dz \right| \\
&\leq \max_{j=1,\ldots,J_n} \left| \frac{1}{nh^d} \sum_{i=1}^n K_\pi\left(\frac{X_i - x_j}{h}\right) - \int K_\pi(z) f(x_j + hz) dz \right| + \frac{2}{3} r_n \epsilon.
\end{aligned}$$

Hence, Eq. (24) holds if

$$\mathbb{P}\left(\max_{j=1,\ldots,J_n} \left| \frac{1}{nh} \sum_{i=1}^n K_\pi\left(\frac{X_i - x_j}{h}\right) - \int K_\pi(z) f(x_j + hz) dz \right| \geq r_n \frac{\epsilon}{3}\right) \to 0.$$

Since an elementary change of variables gives

$$\mathbb{E}\left[\frac{1}{h^d} K_\pi\left(\frac{X_i - x_j}{h}\right)\right] = \int K_\pi(z) f(x_j + hz) dz \text{ and}$$

$$\operatorname{Var}\left(\frac{1}{h^{d/2}} K_\pi\left(\frac{X_i - x_j}{h}\right)\right) \leq \mathbb{E}\left[\frac{1}{h^d} K_\pi^2\left(\frac{X_i - x_j}{h}\right)\right] \leq \frac{C}{h^d},$$

Equation (24) follows from the Bonferoni inequality and Eq. (23) which give

$$
\begin{aligned}
&\mathbb{P}\left(\max_{j=1,\dots,J_n}\left|\frac{1}{nh^d}\sum_{i=1}^{n}K_\pi\left(\frac{X_i-x_j}{h}\right)-\int K_\pi(z)f\left(x_j+hz\right)dz\right|\geq r_n\frac{\epsilon}{3}\right)\\
&\leq\sum_{j=1}^{J_n}\mathbb{P}\left(\left|\frac{1}{\sqrt{n}}\sum_{i=1}^{n}h^{-\frac{d}{2}}K_\pi\left(\frac{X_i-x_j}{h}\right)-\int K_\pi(z)f\left(x_j+hz\right)dz\right|\geq\log^{1/2}n\frac{\epsilon}{3}\right)\\
&\leq 2J_n\exp\left(-\frac{\epsilon^2\log n}{C+C/(nh^d)^{1/2}}\right)\leq 2\exp\left(-\frac{\epsilon^2\log n-b\log n}{C}\right)\to 0,
\end{aligned}
$$

for $\epsilon^2>b$. Hence, Eq. (19) is proved. The existence of the inverse matrix stated in the lemma and the uniform bound for its spectral radius follow from Lemma 11. ■

Proof of Proposition 6. Let

$$
\begin{aligned}
\widehat{M}_n(x,h)&=\frac{1}{nh^d}\sum_{i=1}^{n}U\left(\frac{X_i-x}{h}\right)U'\left(\frac{X_i-x}{h}\right)K\left(\frac{X_i-x}{h}\right)\quad\text{and}\\
M(x,h)&=h^{-d}\mathbb{E}\left[U\left(\frac{X_i-x}{h}\right)U'\left(\frac{X_i-x}{h}\right)K\left(\frac{X_i-x}{h}\right)\right].
\end{aligned}
$$

We first show that $(nh^d)^{1/2}V(x_n,h)^{-1/2}H\left(\hat{\beta}(x_n;h)-\overline{\beta}(x_n;h)\right)$ is asymptotically a standard normal. Observe that

$$
\begin{aligned}
&(nh^d)^{1/2}V(x_n,h)^{-1/2}H\left(\hat{\beta}(x_n;h)-\bar{\beta}\,(x_n;h)\right)\\
&\quad=V(x_n,h)^{-1/2}\widehat{M}_n(x_n,h)^{-1}\frac{\sum_{i=1}^{n}U\left(\frac{X_i-x_n}{h}\right)\xi_i(x_n;h)K\left(\frac{X_i-x_n}{h}\right)}{(nh^d)^{1/2}}\\
&\qquad+V(x_n,h)^{-1/2}\widehat{M}_n(x_n,h)^{-1}\frac{\sum_{i=1}^{n}U\left(\frac{X_i-x_n}{h}\right)\varepsilon_iK\left(\frac{X_i-x_n}{h}\right)}{(nh^d)^{1/2}},
\end{aligned}
$$

where

$$\xi_i(x;h)=m(X_i)-U(X_i-x)'\bar{\beta}(x;h).$$

Since, for all $x\in\mathcal{X}$, $\bar{\beta}(x;h)$ satisfies the first-order condition

$$\mathbb{E}\left[U(X_i-x)\left(m(X_i)-U(X_i-x)'\bar{\beta}(x;h)\right)K\left(\frac{X_i-x}{h}\right)\right]=0,\qquad(25)$$

the variables $U\left(\frac{X_i-x_n}{h}\right)\xi_i(x_n;h)K\left(\frac{X_i-x_n}{h}\right)$ are centered. Moreover, Theorems 1 and 2 together with Eq. (21), Assumptions X-(iii) and K and Lemma 5 give that

$$\begin{aligned}
&\operatorname{Var}\left(h^{-d/2}U(X_i-x)\left(m(X_i)-U(X_i-x)'\overline{\beta}(x;h)\right)K\left(\frac{X_i-x}{h}\right)\right)\\
&=O\left(h^{2s}\right)\int U(z)U(z)'K^2(z)f(x+hz)dz=o(1),
\end{aligned}$$

uniformly in $x\in\mathcal{X}$. Hence,

$$V(x_n,h)^{-1/2}\widehat{M}_n(x_n,h)^{-1}\frac{\sum_{i=1}^n U\left(\frac{X_i-x_n}{h}\right)\xi_i(x_n;h)K\left(\frac{X_i-x_n}{h}\right)}{(nh^d)^{1/2}}=o_p(1),$$

and it is sufficient to show that

$$V(x_n,h)^{-1/2}\widehat{M}_n(x_n,h)^{-1}\frac{\sum_{i=1}^n U\left(\frac{X_i-x_n}{h}\right)\varepsilon_i K\left(\frac{X_i-x_n}{h}\right)}{(nh^d)^{1/2}}\xrightarrow{d}N\left(0,I_d\right).$$

This follows from Theorem 4, Assumption E, and the Lindeberg Central Limit Theorem for triangular arrays. To complete the proof of the proposition, it is now sufficient to show that $\widehat{V}(x_n,h)=V(x_n,h)+o_p(1)$. This follows from Lemma 5 and $\hat{\sigma}^2\left(x_n\right)=\sigma^2\left(x_n\right)+o_p(1)$ as established now. Let

$$\widetilde{\sigma}^2(x)=\frac{\sum_{i=1}^n\left(Y_i-\mu(x)\right)^2K\left(\frac{X_i-x}{h}\right)}{\sum_{i=1}^n K\left(\frac{X_i-x}{h}\right)}\quad\text{and}\quad\overline{\sigma}^2(x)=\frac{\sum_{i=1}^n\sigma^2(X_i)K\left(\frac{X_i-x}{h}\right)}{\sum_{i=1}^n K\left(\frac{X_i-x}{h}\right)}.$$

The asymptotic normality above, Theorems 1 and 2, yields that

$$\begin{aligned}
\left|\hat{\sigma}\left(x_n\right)-\widetilde{\sigma}\left(x_n\right)\right|&\le\left(\frac{\sum_{i=1}^n\left(\hat{\beta}_0(x_n,h)-\mu\left(x_n\right)\right)^2K\left(\frac{X_i-x_n}{h}\right)}{\sum_{i=1}^n K\left(\frac{X_i-x_n}{h}\right)}\right)^{1/2}\\
&=\left|\hat{\beta}_0(x_n,h)-\mu\left(x_n\right)\right|=O_p\left(\frac{1}{(nh^d)^{1/2}}+h^s\right)=o_p(1).
\end{aligned}$$

Let $\delta_i = \varepsilon_i^2 - \sigma^2(X_i)$. Observe that

$$\widetilde{\sigma}^2(x_n) = \overline{\sigma}^2(x_n) + O_p\left(\frac{\sum_{i=1}^n (\mu(X_i) - \mu(x_n))^2 K\left(\frac{X_i - x_n}{h}\right)}{\sum_{i=1}^n K\left(\frac{X_i - x_n}{h}\right)}\right)$$
$$+ O_p\left(\frac{\sum_{i=1}^n \delta_i K\left(\frac{X_i - x_n}{h}\right)}{\sum_{i=1}^n K\left(\frac{X_i - x_n}{h}\right)}\right),$$

with, by uniform continuity of $\mu(\cdot)$ over the compact $\mathcal{X}$ and since $h \to 0$,

$$\frac{\sum_{i=1}^n (\mu(X_i) - \mu(x_n))^2 K\left(\frac{X_i - x_n}{h}\right)}{\sum_{i=1}^n K\left(\frac{X_i - x_n}{h}\right)} = o(1).$$

Let $\mathbb{E}_n[\cdot]$ be the conditional expectation given $X_1, \ldots, X_n$ and $i = \sqrt{-1}$. Then, under Assumption E and assuming w.l.o.g. that $\nu \leq 2$, Assumptions X-(i) and K, and by standard manipulations involving uniform $O(\cdot)$ terms, we have for any t,

$$\left|\mathbb{E}_n\left[\exp\left(it\frac{\sum_{i=1}^n \delta_i K\left(\frac{X_i - x_n}{h}\right)}{\sum_{i=1}^n K\left(\frac{X_i - x_n}{h}\right)}\right)\right]\right| = \left|\prod_{i=1}^n \mathbb{E}_n\left[\exp\left(it\frac{\delta_i K\left(\frac{X_i - x_n}{h}\right)}{\sum_{i=1}^n K\left(\frac{X_i - x_n}{h}\right)}\right)\right]\right|$$
$$= \left|\prod_{i=1}^n \exp\left\{\ln\left(1 - it\mathbb{E}_n\left[\frac{\delta_i K\left(\frac{X_i - x_n}{h}\right)}{\sum_{i=1}^n K\left(\frac{X_i - x_n}{h}\right)}\right]\right.\right.\right.$$
$$\left.\left.\left.+ |t|^{1+\nu/2} O\left(\mathbb{E}_n\left[\left|\frac{\delta_i K\left(\frac{X_i - x_n}{h}\right)}{\sum_{i=1}^n K\left(\frac{X_i - x_n}{h}\right)}\right|^{1+\nu/2}\right]\right)\right)\right\}\right|$$
$$\leq \exp\left(-C|t|^{1+\nu/2}\sum_{i=1}^n \left(\frac{K\left(\frac{X_i - x_n}{h}\right)}{\sum_{i=1}^n K\left(\frac{X_i - x_n}{h}\right)}\right)^{1+\nu/2}\right) = \exp\left(O_p\left((nh)^{-\nu/2}\right)\right) \xrightarrow{p} 1.$$

This implies that

$$\frac{\sum_{i=1}^n \delta_i K\left(\frac{X_i - x_n}{h}\right)}{\sum_{i=1}^n K\left(\frac{X_i - x_n}{h}\right)} \xrightarrow{d} 0 \text{ and then } \xrightarrow{p} 0,$$

so that $\hat{\sigma}^2(x_n) = \overline{\sigma}^2(x_n) + o_p(1)$, with $\overline{\sigma}^2(x_n) = \sigma^2(x_n) + o_p(1)$ by uniform continuity of $\sigma(\cdot)$ over the compact $\mathcal{X}$. Hence, $\hat{\sigma}^2(x_n) = \sigma^2(x_n) + o_p(1)$. ■

Proof of Proposition 7. Let $K_\pi(z) = z^\pi K(z)$,

$$S_n(x;h) = \frac{1}{(nh^d)^{1/2}} \sum_{i=1}^{n} (\xi_i(x;h) + \varepsilon_i)\, K_\pi\left(\frac{X_i - x}{h}\right),$$

$$\xi_i(x;h) = m(X_i) - U\left(\frac{X_i - x}{h}\right)' H\overline{\beta}(x;h).$$

Lemma 5 implies that it is sufficient to show that

$$\sup_{x\in\mathcal{X}} |S_n(x;h)| = O_p\left(\log^{1/2} n\right). \tag{26}$$

Define, for $\eta_i = \varepsilon_i \mathbb{I}(|\varepsilon_i| < \tau_n) - \mathbb{E}[\varepsilon_i \mathbb{I}(|\varepsilon_i| < \tau_n)\,|X_i]$,

$$s_n(x;h) = \frac{1}{(nh^d)^{1/2}} \sum_{i=1}^{n} (\xi_i(x;h) + \eta_i)\, K_\pi\left(\frac{X_i - x}{h}\right).$$

The Chebychev inequality gives, for $\tau_n = C_\tau n^{1/\nu}$,

$$\mathbb{P}\left(\max_{i=1,\dots,n} |\varepsilon_i| \ge \tau_n\right) \le \sum_{i=1}^{n} \mathbb{P}(|\varepsilon_i| \ge \tau_n) \le \frac{\mathbb{E}[|\varepsilon_i|^\nu]}{C_\tau^\nu},$$

which can be made arbitrarily small by increasing C_τ. Arguing as in the proof of Lemma 5 gives, when $\max_{i=1,\dots,n} |\varepsilon_i| \ge \tau_n$ and since $-\mathbb{E}[\varepsilon_i \mathbb{I}(|\varepsilon_i| < \tau_n)\,|X_i] = \mathbb{E}[\varepsilon_i \mathbb{I}(|\varepsilon_i| \ge \tau_n)\,|X_i]$,

$$\begin{aligned}
\sup_{x\in\mathcal{X}} |S_n(x;h) - s_n(x;h)| &= \sup_{x\in\mathcal{X}} \left| \frac{1}{(nh^d)^{1/2}} \sum_{i=1}^{n} \mathbb{E}[\varepsilon_i \mathbb{I}(|\varepsilon_i| \ge \tau_n)\,|X_i]\, K_\pi\left(\frac{X_i - x}{h}\right)\right| \\
&\le \sup_{x\in\mathcal{X}} \frac{1}{(nh^d)^{1/2}} \sum_{i=1}^{n} \mathbb{E}\left[\frac{|\varepsilon_i|^\nu\, \mathbb{I}(|\varepsilon_i| \ge \tau_n)}{\tau_n^{\nu-1}}\Big|X_i\right] \left|K_\pi\left(\frac{X_i - x}{h}\right)\right| \\
&= O_p\left(\frac{(nh^d)^{1/2}}{n^{1-1/\nu}}\right) = o_p\left(\frac{1}{n^{1/2-1/\nu}}\right) = o_p(1),
\end{aligned}$$

since $\nu > 2$ by Assumption E. Therefore, it is sufficient to show that

$$\sup_{x\in\mathcal{X}} |s_n(x;h)| = O_p\left(\log^{1/2} n\right) \tag{27}$$

to prove Eq. (26). Observe that the expectation of the summands in $s_n(x;h)$ is 0 by Eq. (25) and the definition of η_i. Equation (25) also gives

$$H\bar{\beta}(x;h) = \left(\mathbb{E}\left[U\left(\frac{X_i - x}{h}\right)U\left(\frac{X_i - x}{h}\right)' K\left(\frac{X_i - x}{h}\right)\right]\right)^{-1} \times \mathbb{E}\left[U\left(\frac{X_i - x}{h}\right)m(X_i)K\left(\frac{X_i - x}{h}\right)\right]$$

so that Assumption K gives that $\left\| H\left(\bar{\beta}(x;h) - \bar{\beta}\left(x';h\right)\right)\right\| \le Ch^{-1}\left\|x - x'\right\|$ for all $x, x' \in \mathcal{X}$. This also gives, by Eq. (21) which ensures that $\max_{x\in\mathcal{X}} |\xi_i(x;h)| \le C$,

$$\left\|(\xi_i(x;h) + \eta_i)\, K_\pi\left(\frac{X_i - x}{h}\right) - \left(\xi_i\left(x';h\right) + \eta_i\right) K_\pi\left(\frac{X_i - x'}{h}\right)\right\| \le C\frac{\tau_n}{h}\left\|x - x'\right\|,$$

for all $i = 1, \ldots, n$ and all n, all $x, x' \in \mathcal{X}$,

$$\left|s_n(x;h) - s_n\left(x';h\right)\right| \le C\frac{n^{1/2}\tau_n}{h^{d/2+1}}\left\|x - x'\right\|.$$

This together Assumptions K, X and $1/h^d = O\left(n/\log n\right)$, there is a $\delta = \delta_n = n^{-a}$ such that

1. There is an integer number $J_n = O\left(n^b\right)$, $b > 0$, and some $x_j \in \mathcal{X}$ such that $\mathcal{X} = \bigcup_{j=1}^{J_n} \mathcal{V}_X\left(x_j, \delta_n\right)$, where $\mathcal{V}_X\left(x_j, \delta_n\right) = \mathcal{V}\left(x_j, \delta_n\right) \cap \mathcal{X}$;
2. For all x, x' with $\left\|x - x'\right\| \le \delta_n$ and all i and n, $\left|s_n(x;h) - s_n\left(x';h\right)\right| \le 1$.

Hence,

$$\sup_{x\in\mathcal{X}} |s_n(x;h)| \le \max_{j=1,\ldots,J_n}\left|s_n\left(x_j;h\right)\right| + \max_{j=1,\ldots,J_n}\sup_{x\in\mathcal{V}_X\left(x_j,\delta_n\right)}\left|s_n(x;h) - s_n\left(x_j;h\right)\right| \le \max_{j=1,\ldots,J_n}\left|s_n\left(x_j;h\right)\right| + 1.$$

As a consequence, Eq. (27) holds if $\max_{j=1,\ldots,J_n}\left|s_n\left(x_j;h\right)\right| = O_p\left(\log^{1/2} n\right)$. The Bonferoni inequality and Eq. (23) give, using $\max_{x\in\mathcal{X}} |\xi_i(x;h)| \le C$ and

$h^{-d} = O\left(n^{1-2/\nu} \log n\right)$,

$$\mathbb{P}\left(\max_{j=1,\ldots,J_n} \left|s_n\left(x_j;h\right)\right| \geq t\log^{1/2} n\right) \leq \sum_{j=1}^{n} \mathbb{P}\left(\left|s_n\left(x_j;h\right)\right| \geq t\log^{1/2} n\right)$$

$$\leq 2J_n \exp\left(-\frac{t\log n}{C + \left(\frac{h^{-d}\tau_n^2 \log n}{n}\right)^{1/2} t}\right) = \exp\left(-\frac{(t-C)\log n}{C'}\right) \to 0$$

for $t > C$. This ends the proof of Proposition 7. ■

7.4. Propositions 8, 9 and 10

Proof of Proposition 8. Lemma 5, Theorems 1 and 2 which give Eq. (21), imply that the conclusions of Lemmas A.1, A.2 and A.3 in Guerre and Sabbah (2012) are true when $x \in \mathcal{X}$. Hence, the first equation in Proposition 8 follows from minor modifications of the proof of Theorem 2 in Guerre and Sabbah (2012). The second equation follows from $\max_{(\alpha,x)\in[\underline{\alpha},\overline{\alpha}]\times\mathcal{X}} \left\|\widehat{J}(\alpha|x,h) - \overline{J}(\alpha|x,h)\right\| = O_{\mathbb{P}}\left(\left(\log n/(nh^d)\right)^{1/2}\right)$ and $\max_{(\alpha,x)\in[\underline{\alpha},\overline{\alpha}]\times\mathcal{X}} \left\|\widehat{S}(\alpha|x,h)\right\| = O_p\left(\log^{1/2} n\right)$ as established below. ■

Proof of Proposition 10. Theorems 1 and 2 which give Eq. (21) are sufficient to show that the conclusion of Lemma A.3 in Guerre and Sabbah (2012) holds for $x \in \mathcal{X}$, that is

$$\max_{(\alpha,x)\in[\underline{\alpha},\overline{\alpha}]\times\mathcal{X}} \left\|\widehat{S}(\alpha|x,h)\right\| = O_p\left(\log^{1/2} n\right).$$

Hence, Proposition 8 and Lemma 5 give

$$\sup_{(\alpha,x)\in[\underline{\alpha},\overline{\alpha}]\times\mathcal{X}} \left\|(nh^d)^{1/2} H\left(\hat{\beta}(\alpha|x,h) - \overline{\beta}(\alpha|x,h)\right)\right\|$$

$$= O_p\left(\max_{(\alpha,x)\in[\underline{\alpha},\overline{\alpha}]\times\mathcal{X}} \left\|\frac{\widehat{S}(\alpha|x,h)}{(nh^d)^{1/2}}\right\|\right) + O_p\left(\left(\frac{\log n}{nh^d}\right)^{3/4}\right) = O_p\left(\left(\frac{\log n}{nh^d}\right)^{1/2}\right).$$

Hence, Theorems 1 and 2 show that the Proposition is proved. ■

Proof of Proposition 9. As in the proof of Proposition 6, the key issue here is to show that $\widehat{V}\left(\alpha|x_n,h\right) = V\left(\alpha|x_n,h\right) + o_p(1)$, and Lemma 5 shows that is sufficient to show that $\partial\widehat{Q}\left(\alpha|x_n\right)/\partial\alpha$ is consistent. This follows from Proposition 10, the fact that $s \geq 1$ and the choice of η which gives under Assumption F which ensures that $(\alpha, x) \mapsto \partial Q(\alpha|x)/\partial\alpha$ is continuous,

$$\begin{aligned}\frac{\partial \widehat{Q}\,(\alpha|x_n)}{\partial\alpha} &= \frac{\widehat{Q}\,(\alpha+\eta|x_n) - \widehat{Q}\,(\alpha+\eta|x_n)}{2\eta} \\ &= \frac{Q\,(\alpha+\eta|x_n) - Q\,(\alpha+\eta|x_n)}{2\eta} + O_p\left(\frac{1}{\eta}\left(h + \left(\frac{\log n}{nh^d}\right)^{1/2}\right)\right) \\ &= \frac{\partial Q\,(\alpha|x_n)}{\partial\alpha} + o_p(1).\end{aligned}$$

■

NOTES

1. We refer interested readers to Gragg and Tapia (1974) for a complete statement of the Newton–Kantorovich Theorem and to Lemma 7.2 of this paper for the part used in this paper.
2. When $m(x_1) = \sin(2\pi x_1)$, $\mathbb{E}\,[m(X_2)\mathbb{I}\,(X_2 \in [c, 1-c])] = 0$ so that $\hat{\mu}_{1,c}(x_1)$ could also be used. However identifying restrictions such as $m\,(1/2) = 0$ seems to be more popular and does not involve the trimming parameter. Unreported simulation results suggest however that $\hat{\mu}_{1,c}(\cdot)$ may have better performances than $\widehat{m}_c(\cdot)$.

ACKNOWLEDGMENTS

We thank Ruixuan Liu for drawing our attention to Chen and Wu (2013) and Shih-Tang Hwu for pointing out an error in a preliminary draft. All remaining errors are ours. Yanqin Fan is grateful to Aman Ullah for introducing him to nonparametric econometrics and for his continued support throughout his career.

REFERENCES

Altonji, J. G., Ichimura, H., & Otsu, T. (2012). Estimating derivatives in nonseparable models with limited dependent variables. *Econometrica, 80*, 1701–1719.

Aryal, G., Gabrielli, M. F., & Vuong, Q. (2014). *Semiparametric estimation of first-price auction models*. arXiv:1407.7140.

Banerjee, A. N. (2007). A method of estimating the average derivative. *Journal of Econometrics, 136*, 65–88.

Bouezmarni, T., & Rombouts, J. (2010). Nonparametric density estimation for multivariate bounded data. *Journal of Statistical Planning and Inference, 140*, 139–152.

Bravo, F., & Jacho-Chávez, D. T. (2011). Empirical likelihood for efficient semiparametric average treatment effects. *Econometric Reviews, 30*, 1–24.

Chaudhuri, P. (1991). Nonparametric estimates of regression quantiles and their local bahadur representation. *The Annals of Statistics, 11*, 760–777.

Chaudhuri, P., Doksum, K., & Samarov, A. (1997). On average derivative quantile regression. *The Annals of Statistics, 25*, 715–744.

Chen, M.-Y., & Wu, H.-T. (2013). Local linear regression on manifolds and its geometric interpretation. *Journal of the American Statistical Association, 108*, 1421–1434.

Fan, J., & Gijbels, I. (1996). *Local polynomial modelling and its applications.* Chapman & Hall/CRC.

Fan, J., Heckman, N. E., & Wand, M. P. (1995). Local polynomial kernel regression for generalized linear models and quasi-likelihood functions. *Journal of the American Statistical Association, 90*, 141–150.

Fan, Y., & Li, Q. (1996). Consistent model specification tests: Omitted variables and semiparametric functional forms. *Econometrica, 64*, 865–890.

Frandsen, B. R., Frölich, M., & Melly, B. (2012). Quantile treatment effects in the regression discontinuity design. *Journal of Econometrics, 168*, 382—395.

Gragg, W. B., & Tapia, R. A. (1974). Optimal error bounds for the Newton–Kantorovich Theorem. *SIAM Journal on Numerical Analysis, 11*, 10–13.

Gu, J., Li, Q., & Yang, J.-C. (2015). Multivariate local polynomial kernel estimators: Leading bias and asymptotic distribution. *Econometric Reviews, 34*, 979–1010.

Guerre, E. (2000). Design adpative nearest neighbor regression estimation. *Journal of Multivariate Analysis, 75*, 219–244.

Guerre, E., & Lavergne, P. (2002). Optimal minimax rates for nonparametric specification testing in regression models. *Econometric Theory, 18*, 1139–1171.

Guerre, E., & Sabbah, C. (2012). Uniform bias study and Bahadur representation for local polynomial estimators of the conditional quantile function. *Econometric Theory, 28*, 87–129.

Hahn, J., Todd, P., & Van der Klaauw, W. (2001). Identification and estimation of treatment effects with a regression-discontinuity design. *Econometrica, 69*, 201–209.

Härdle, W., & Mammen, E. (1993). Comparing nonparametric versus parametric regression fits. *The Annals of Statistics, 21*, 1926–1947.

Härdle, W., & Stoker, T. H. (1989). Investigating smooth multiple regression by the method of average derivatives. *Journal of the American Statistical Association, 84*, 986–995.

Hickman, B. R., & Hubbard, T. P. (2015). Replacing sample trimming with boundary correction in nonparametric estimation of first-price auctions. *Journal of Applied Econometrics, 30*, 739–762.

Hjellvik, J., Yao, Q., & Tjøstheim, D. (1998). Linearity testing using local polynomial approximation. *Journal of Statistical Planning and Inference, 68*, 295–321.

Hoderlein, S., Su, L., White, H., & Yang, T. T. (2016). Testing for monotonicity in unobservables under unconfoundedness. *Journal of Econometrics, 193*, 183–202.

Huber, P. J. (1967). The behavior of maximum likelihood estimation under nonstandard conditions. *Proceedings of the fifth berkeley symposium on mathematical statistics and probability* (Vol. 1). University of California Press.

Imbens, G. W., & Zajonc, T. (2011). *Regression discontinuity design with multiple forcing variables.* Working Paper.

Kong, E., Linton, O., & Xia, Y. (2010). Uniform Bahadur representation for local polynomial estimates of M-regression and its application to the additive model. *Econometric Theory, 26*, 1529–1564.

Li, C.-S. (2005). Using local linear kernel smoothers to test the lack of fit of nonlinear regression models. *Statistical Methodology, 2*, 267–284.

Li, Q., Lu, X., & Ullah, A. (2003). Multivariate local polynomial regression for estimating average derivatives. *Journal of Nonparametric Statistics, 15*, 607–624.

Linton, O., & Nielsen, J. P. (1995). A Kernel Method of Estimating Structured Nonparametric Regression Based on Marginal Integration. *Biometrika*, 82, 93–100.

Masry, E. (1996). Multivariate local polynomial regression for time series: uniform strong consistency and rates. *Journal of Time Series Analysis, 17*, 571–599.

Müller, H. G., & Stadtmüller, U. (1999). Multivariate boundary kernels and a continuous least squares principle. *Journal of the Royal Statistical Society B, 61*, 439–458.

Newey, W., & Powell, J. L. (1987). Asymmetric least squares estimation and testing. *Econometrica, 55*, 819–847.

Newey, W. K., & Powell, J. L. (1987). Asymmetric least squares estimation and testing. *Econometrica, 55*(4), 819–847.

Oka, T. (2009). *Nonparametric quantile regression with discontinuities*. Working Paper.

Porter, J. (2003). *Estimation in the regression discontinuity model*. Working Paper.

Powell, J. L., Stock, J. H., & Stoker, T. M. (1989). Semiparametric estimation of index coefficients. *Econometrica, 57*, 1403–1430.

Qu, Z., & Yoon, J. (2015). Nonparametric estimation and inference on conditional quantile processes. *Journal of Econometrics, 185*, 1–19.

Ruppert, D., & Wand, M. P. (1994). Multivariate locally weighted least squares regression. *The Annals of Statistics, 22*, 1346–1370.

Su, L., & Ullah, A. (2008). Local polynomial estimation of nonparametric simultaneous equations models. *Journal of Econometrics, 144*, 193–218.

Su, L., & White, H. (2012). Conditional independence specification testing for dependent processes with local polynomial quantile regression. *Advances in Econometrics, 29*, 355–434.

Su, L., & Xiao, Z. (2009). Testing structural change in conditional distribution. Unpublished Manuscript.

White, H. (1982). Maximum likelihood estimation of misspecified models. *Econometrica, 50*, 1–25.

MODEL AVERAGING OVER NONPARAMETRIC ESTIMATORS

Daniel J. Henderson[a] and Christopher F. Parmeter[b]

[a]*Department of Economics, University of Alabama, Tuscaloosa, AL, USA*

[b]*Department of Economics, University of Miami, Miami, FL, USA*

ABSTRACT

It is known that model averaging estimators are useful when there is uncertainty governing which covariates should enter the model. We argue that in applied research there is also uncertainty as to which method one should deploy, prompting model averaging over user-defined choices. Specifically, we propose, and detail, a nonparametric regression estimator averaged over choice of kernel, bandwidth selection mechanism and local-polynomial order. Simulations and an empirical application are provided to highlight the potential benefits of the method.

Keywords: Cross-validation; kernel; local-polynomial; model averaging

JEL classifications: C13; C14; C52

1. INTRODUCTION

Nonparametric kernel methods are praised for their ability to consistently estimate unknown quantities without having to make strict functional form assumptions.

Essays in Honor of Aman Ullah
Advances in Econometrics, Volume 36, 539–560

ISSN: 0731-9053/doi:10.1108/S0731-905320160000036024

These methods have been used across a wide variety of fields and are now becoming commonplace in academia and industry. Proponents argue that the methods avoid arbitrary choice of functional form, but typically fail to acknowledge that many choices made in applied kernel estimation are arbitrary as well. For example, we must choose a weighting function. Typically, we pick a weighting function (kernel) which comes from a probability density: the two most popular being the Epanechnikov and Gaussian kernels. It is often argued that kernel choice is not of much importance, and in small dimensions it often is not, but it can become much more of a factor in higher-dimensional data (e.g., see Table 3.2 in Henderson & Parmeter, 2015, p. 69). We must also choose a kernel estimator. In regression, the dominant estimator of choice is the local-linear least-squares estimator (Fan 1993). However, it has been shown that this estimator does not always perform well (the conditional variance is unbounded) with sparse data (e.g., see Seifert & Gasser, 1996). Therefore, sometimes it is better to use the local-constant least-squares estimator (Nadaraya, 1964; Watson, 1964), noting that it has boundary bias issues (e.g., see Fan & Gijbels, 1996). Finally, we have to make a choice with respect to bandwidth selection. Least-squares cross-validation (Härdle & Marron, 1985) is a popular choice, but it often under smooths (in finite samples) relative to approaches such as AIC_c (Hurvich, Simonoff, & Tsai, 1998).

Researchers tend to rely on asymptotic equivalence to argue for ambivalence of one method over another. That being said, we know that in finite samples that there can be significant differences. However, those differences need not be a problem. It is feasible to combine the estimators to achieve better prediction (e.g., see Cheng, Peng, & Wu, 2007, Choi & Hall, 1998; Seifert & Gasser, 1996, 2000; Yang, 2001, 2004). For example, Liu (2011) combines a local-constant and a local-linear estimator. This is designed to minimize the mean-square error and the weighted integrated mean-square error of the averaging estimator, respectively. His simulations show that significant efficiency gains can be obtained relative to each individual estimator separately.

There is no reason that we must simply look over kernel estimator. In addition to kernel estimator, we can additionally average over the kernel function and bandwidth selector. In this paper, we propose to do just that. Specifically, we propose a model averaging estimator which chooses weights for different estimation procedures. We conjecture that asymptotically this approach will pick a single model (e.g., see Yang, 1999, 2007), but in finite samples it is possible to achieve significant gains over a single alternative when the error variance is not sufficiently small (e.g., see Yang, 2001, 2003). Our Monte Carlo simulations show finite sample gains for the majority of cases over a single estimator (a substantially small error variance often leads to better outcomes for a single estimator). Even in the cases where we do not find gains, it is not obvious *a priori* which estimation combination should be used and hence the approach is still useful in determining a single procedure (e.g., see Yang). We further provide an empirical illustration (by studying the relationship between religiosity and economic growth) which shows positive weights for each type of kernel function, kernel regression estimator and bandwidth selector.

We would like to note that model averaging is a very diverse field and the approach we propose here represents an alternative form of averaging to account for uncertainty for the practitioner. The more common approach to model averaging is to average across models with different covariates, holding fixed the estimation method. Approaches in the parametric realm can be found in, for example, Hansen (2007) or Wan, Zhang, and Zou (2010). The most common approach in the applied literature appears to be Bayesian model averaging (e.g., Raferty, Madigan, & Hoeting, 1997; Raferty, 1997) where authors try to determine which variables are relevant in a regression. For example, Durlauf, Kourtellos, and Tan (2008, 2012) use Bayesian model averaging to determine which theories/variables impact economic growth.

Nonparametric papers that combine estimators include Kotlyarova and Zinde-Walsh (2006, 2007), who look at different density estimators, and Liu (2011), who averages over the local-constant and the local-linear estimator (holding fixed the kernel and method of bandwidth selection). Wang, Zou, and Wan (2012) use model averaging in semiparametric models. Hall and Racine (2015) introduce generalized local-polynomial regression which selects both the bandwidth and the order of the polynomial to conduct local smoothing. Frölich (2004) uses the techniques in Seifert and Gasser (1996, 2000) to study propensity-score matching. Our exact approach is to assume that the regressors which enter the unknown conditional mean are known, relevant and exogenously determined (although these can potentially be relaxed without loss of generality), but we allow uncertainty over the precise nature of how best to estimate the conditional mean. More precisely, we allow for averaging in each dimension of choice faced by a practitioner; namely, the choice of kernel, polynomial order and method of bandwidth selection in order to estimate the conditional mean of the left-hand-side variable given the set of regressors.[1] Averaging over these specific dimensions can produce an estimator which provides finite sample gains relative to a single estimator for recovering the unknown conditional mean. Finally, we emphasize here that we are proposing these methods without a rigorous theoretical treatment (see Section 2.3). We leave that to future research.

The remainder of this paper is organized as follows: Section 2 introduces our model averaging approach. Section 3 details a set of Monte Carlo simulations, while Section 4 gives the empirical illustration. Concluding remarks and areas for future research appear in Section 5.

2. MODEL AVERAGING OVER ESTIMATORS

We consider two different approaches to constructing model weights. Our first approach mimics the time-series nonparametric model averaging estimator of Li, Linton, and Lu (2015). Our second approach to constructing weights follows Liu (2011), who selects the model weights via cross-validation.

Consider data $(y_i, \boldsymbol{x}_i) \in \mathbf{R} \times \mathbf{R}^p$, $p \geq 1$ for estimating the regression function $m(\boldsymbol{x}) = E(y_i|\boldsymbol{x}_i = \boldsymbol{x})$. A nonparametric estimator of the unknown conditional mean is

$$\widehat{m}(\boldsymbol{x}) = \sum_{i=1}^{n} A_i(\boldsymbol{x}) y_i$$

where the weights depend on the location of the data with respect to the point of interest $\boldsymbol{x}$ and a smoothing parameter vector h.

At this stage, the applied researcher is faced with numerous choices before $\widehat{m}(\boldsymbol{x})$ can be obtained. First, the type of weight structure ($A_i(\boldsymbol{x})$) needs to be selected (local-constant, local-linear, local-polynomial). For example, if we were to deploy the local-constant estimator of Nadaraya (1964) and Watson (1964), then our weights take the form

$$A_i(\boldsymbol{x}) = \frac{K_h(\boldsymbol{x}, \boldsymbol{x}_i)}{\sum_{j=1}^{n} K_h(\boldsymbol{x}, \boldsymbol{x}_j)},$$

whereas for the local-linear estimator the weights are

$$A_i(\boldsymbol{x}) = \left[\sum_{i=1}^{n} K_h(\boldsymbol{x}, \boldsymbol{x}_i) \begin{pmatrix} 1 \\ \boldsymbol{x} - \boldsymbol{x}_i \end{pmatrix} (1, (\boldsymbol{x} - \boldsymbol{x}_i)) \right]^{-1} K_h(\boldsymbol{x}, \boldsymbol{x}_i) \begin{pmatrix} 1 \\ \boldsymbol{x} - \boldsymbol{x}_i \end{pmatrix}$$

where $K_h(\boldsymbol{x}, \boldsymbol{x}_i) = \prod_{d=1}^{p} h_d^{-1} k\left(\frac{x_d - x_{di}}{h_d}\right)$ is the product kernel.

Second, the choice of kernel must be provided (Epanechnikov, Triweight, Gaussian). For example, if we were to choose the Gaussian kernel, the (univariate) kernel function takes the form

$$k\left(\frac{x_d - x_{di}}{h_d}\right) = \frac{1}{\sqrt{2\pi}} \exp\left[-\frac{1}{2}\left(\frac{x_d - x_{di}}{h_d}\right)^2\right].$$

while the Epanechnikov kernel takes the form

$$k\left(\frac{x_d - x_{di}}{h_d}\right) = \frac{3}{4}\left[1 - \left(\frac{x_d - x_{di}}{h_d}\right)^2\right] \mathbf{1}\left\{\left|\frac{x_d - x_{di}}{h_d}\right| \leq 1\right\},$$

where $\mathbf{1}\{A\}$ is the indicator function that takes the value 1 if the event A is true.

Finally, the bandwidths (h_d) need to be recovered (rule-of-thumb, plug-in, cross-validation). Choosing the bandwidth via least-squares cross-validation follows from minimization of

$$CV(h) = \sum_{i=1}^{n} [y_i - \widehat{m}_{-i}(\boldsymbol{x}_i)]^2,$$

where $\widehat{m}_{-i}(\boldsymbol{x}_i)$ is the leave-one-out estimator. The AIC_c bandwidth selector is obtained by minimization over

$$AIC_c(h) = \ln\left(\widehat{\sigma}^2\right) + \frac{1 + tr(\mathbf{H})/n}{1 - (tr(\mathbf{H}) + 2)/n},$$

where $\widehat{\sigma}^2 = \sum_{i=1}^{n} [y_i - \widehat{m}(\boldsymbol{x}_i)]^2$ and $tr(\mathbf{H})$ is the trace of the matrix $\mathbf{H}$, an $n \times n$ matrix such that $\widehat{m}(\boldsymbol{x}_i) = Hy$.

Each of these choices will impact the final estimator of $\widehat{m}(\boldsymbol{x})$. Instead of arbitrarily choosing one type from each category, we propose to average the estimates over the set of combinations. Two possible methods for which to pick the weights for the averages are now given (several other possibilities for choosing weights can be found in the review article by Ullah and Wang, 2013).[2]

2.1. *Least-Squares Weights*

We design our model averaging estimator by first estimating $\widehat{m}(\boldsymbol{x})$ for each combination of kernel, bandwidth selection mechanism, and local smoothing technique, calling these estimates $\widehat{m}_s(\boldsymbol{x})$ $(s = 1, 2, \ldots, S)$. We can then construct a model averaged estimator as

$$\widehat{m}(\boldsymbol{x}) = \sum_{s=1}^{S} \widehat{w}_s \widehat{m}_s(\boldsymbol{x}),$$

where w_s is the weight assigned to the sth model. The main advantage of this method is that it is fast to compute. Define

$$\widehat{M} \equiv \begin{pmatrix} \widehat{m}_1(\boldsymbol{x}_1) & \cdots & \widehat{m}_S(\boldsymbol{x}_1) \\ \vdots & \vdots & \vdots \\ \widehat{m}_1(\boldsymbol{x}_n) & \cdots & \widehat{m}_S(\boldsymbol{x}_n) \end{pmatrix},$$

$y \equiv (y_1, \ldots, y_n)'$ and $w \equiv (w_1, \ldots, w_S)'$. The least-squares estimator for the weights is given by $\widehat{w} = (\widehat{M}'\widehat{M})^{-1}\widehat{M}'y$.

It is likely that this approach will over fit the data, leading to good in-sample fit at the expense of poorer out-of-sample predictions. In this case, we can define $\widehat{m}_{s,-i}(\boldsymbol{x}_i)$ to be the leave-one-observation-out estimator of the sth equation and can construct $\widehat{M}_{-i}$ as

$$\widehat{M}_{-1} \equiv \begin{pmatrix} \widehat{m}_{1,-i}(\boldsymbol{x}_1) & \cdots & \widehat{m}_{S,-i}(\boldsymbol{x}_1) \\ \vdots & \vdots & \vdots \\ \widehat{m}_{1,-i}(\boldsymbol{x}_n) & \cdots & \widehat{m}_{S,-i}(\boldsymbol{x}_n) \end{pmatrix}.$$

The least-squares estimator for the weights is given by $\widehat{w}_{-i} = (\widehat{M}'_{-i}\widehat{M}_{-i})^{-1}\widehat{M}'_{-i}y$. This model average estimator is constructed as

$$\widehat{m}(\boldsymbol{x}_i) = \sum_{s=1}^{S} \widehat{w}_{s,-i}\widehat{m}_s(\boldsymbol{x}_i).$$

Given the linearity of $\widehat{m}(\boldsymbol{x}_i)$ with regards to $\widehat{w}$, construction of model averaged gradients is also straightforward. We have

$$\widehat{\beta}(\boldsymbol{x}_i) = \sum_{s=1}^{S} \widehat{w}_{s,-i}\widehat{\beta}_s(\boldsymbol{x}_i),$$

where $\beta_s(\boldsymbol{x}_i)$ is the gradient of the (kernel estimated) conditional mean function evaluated at the point $\boldsymbol{x}_i$.

2.2. *Cross-Validation Weights*

Our second approach to constructing weights follows Liu (2011). He elects to select the model weights using two-step cross-validation. In the first stage, the bandwidths are selected for each estimator, and in the second stage the weights are chosen to minimize the leave-one-out locally weighted estimator. That is, define $\widehat{m}_{s,-i}(\boldsymbol{x}_i)$ to be the leave-one-observation-out sth estimator and $\widehat{m}_{-i}(\boldsymbol{x}_i) = \sum_{s=1}^{S} \widehat{w}_s\widehat{m}_{s,-i}(\boldsymbol{x}_i)$. Then, the weights are selected as

$$\min_{w_s \in \mathcal{W}} n^{-1} \sum_{i=1}^{n} \left[y_i - \widehat{m}_{-i}(\boldsymbol{x}_i)\right]^2.$$

The weighted conditional mean and gradient estimators are then constructed as

$$\widehat{m}(\boldsymbol{x}_i) = \sum_{s=1}^{S} \widehat{w}_s\widehat{m}_s(\boldsymbol{x}_i)$$

and

$$\widehat{\beta}(\boldsymbol{x}_i) = \sum_{s=1}^{S} \widehat{w}_s \widehat{\beta}_s(\boldsymbol{x}_i),$$

respectively.

Note that we do not have to use leave-one-out weights as we use the leave-one-out conditional mean estimator to construct the weights. Further note that each approach (to constructing weights) will differ in finite samples, but we conjecture that they will pick the same estimator asymptotically (e.g., see Yang, 1999, 2007).

2.3. Theoretical Properties

While the exact asymptotic properties of our proposed model averaging estimators are not studied here, there are several existing papers which we can glean results from to inform us on the relative behavior of our approach. First, Liu (2011), in his averaging estimator for the local-constant and local-linear estimators, demonstrates that the weighted average mean-square error is less than the mean-square error of any other linear combination of the local-constant and local-linear estimators, provided that the covariance between the local-linear and local-constant estimators does not explicitly equal the leading mean-square error of either estimator. In this case, the two estimators have identical performance asymptotically and there is no benefit from averaging.[3]

Liu's (2011) imposes nonrestrictive conditions to prove the optimality of the weighted average estimator in terms of mean-square error. More specifically, for our purposes, the kernel function used to smooth the data for both the local-constant and local-linear estimators is required to have bounded support. While this formally rules out use of the Gaussian kernel, it would allow for averaging over the Epanechnikov, biweight, and triweight kernel. Mean-square error optimality of the weighted average estimator across the different kernels should hold in this case.

The more difficult hurdle in extending the theory of Liu (2011) is the averaging across bandwidth selection mechanisms. In the theory provided in Liu (2011), the bandwidths are assumed to be fixed decreasing sequences. However, when using bandwidth selection (data-driven or plug-in), this implicitly makes the bandwidths random, which leads to nonstandard extensions of Liu's (2011) theory. Some work has established the asymptotic properties of kernel estimators with stochastic bandwidths (Boente & Fraiman, 1995, Masry & Fan, 1997, Li & Racine, 2004, Martins-Filho, & Saraiva, 2012). A common condition required is that $\widehat{h}_n/h_n - 1 = o_p(1)$, where $\widehat{h}_n$ is the bandwidth selected in a data-driven fashion. While some work exists which establishes that bandwidths selected via LSCV satisfy this condition (Xia & Li, 2002), to our knowledge, no such precise result exists for AIC_c bandwidth selection (though it is conjectured by Li and Racine 2004, p. 491). We conjecture that extensions of Liu's (2011) theory on the optimality of the averaged estimator holds not only across kernel smoothed estimators, but also across kernel choice and bandwidth selection mechanism as well.

Other theoretical properties for the averaging estimator can be gleaned from the work of Li, Linton, and Lu (2015) and Yang (2003, 2007). Li et al. (2015) establish the asymptotic normality of the least squares weights for their particular averaging estimator, which is a set of univariate, kernel regression estimators of the same order (i.e. all local-constant). While their averaging is for estimators across different covariates, here we are keep the set of covariates fixed. Similar to above, for local-constant and local-linear estimators and for different kernels, the assumptions of Li et al. (2015) hold. As with the extension of the work of Liu (2011), progressing from a fixed bandwidth assumption to a stochastic bandwidth involves non-trivial extensions.

An interesting theoretical possibility to develop for our averaging approach is determining *the* optimal model. Yang (2007) outlines how cross-validation can pick between two models. The primary differences to our framework are that he typically finds that a leave-one-out estimator is often not desirable (and that a larger number of observations should be left out) and that he assumes that under an L_2 loss that one estimator is asymptotically better than the other. While there are known results for comparisons of different kernel functions as well as different kernel estimators, it is feasible that the bandwidth selectors (say LSCV vs. AICc) would be asymptotically equivalent and hence this approach to choosing *the* best model may not work. We leave a more formal development of this potential result for future research.

3. FINITE SAMPLE PERFORMANCE

To investigate the finite sample performance of the two averaging estimators, we perform a simulation study. Our design follows Seifert and Gasser (2000) and Cheng, Peng, and Wu (2007). We consider three differently shaped regression functions:

1. $m(x_i) = 2 - 5x_i + 5\exp\left[-44(x_i - 0.5)^2\right]$,
2. $m(x_i) = 0.3\exp\left[-16(x_i - 0.25)^2\right] + 0.7\exp\left[-64(x_i - 0.75)^2\right]$,
3. $m(x_i) = \sin(5\pi x_i)$.

For all simulations, our covariate x_i is drawn from one of three different distributions: standard normal, uniform on $[0, 1]$ or a mixed normal $0.5N(-1, 1) + 0.5N(1.75, 0.25)$. The random noise ($\varepsilon_i$) is drawn from $N(0, \rho\sigma)$

where $\rho \in \{0.1, 0.5, 1, 2\}$ and $\sigma = \sqrt{0.5}$, 0.1, or 0.5, corresponding to the DGP under study, 1, 2, or 3, respectively. We conduct 1,000 Monte Carlo replications for each DGP, covariate distribution, and ρ combination, varying the sample size from $n = 100$, 200, and 400.

We compare the performance of our two model averaging estimators against eight combinations across kernel choice (Gaussian or Epanechnikov), bandwidth selection mechanism (LSCV or AIC_c) and polynomial order (local-constant or local-linear). We also present statistics of the models selected across our simulations to determine how frequently a given combination is used in the model average. To evaluate the finite sample performance of the estimator with respect to the unknown conditional mean, we compute mean-squared estimation error (MSEE):

$$MSEE = n^{-1} \sum_{i=1}^{n} [m(x_i) - \widetilde{m}(x_i)]^2 ,$$

where $\widetilde{m}(x_i)$ is one of the eight different estimators being studied and $m(x_i)$ is the true data-generating process. We compare relative median MSEE to discern the performance of all the estimators.[4] In this setting, our benchmark estimator is our model average estimator (with weights selected either via least-squares or LSCV) and our comparison group is one of the eight single models. Superior performance of the model average estimator results (at the median) when the MSEE ratio is greater than 1.

Given the large number of simulations, our discussion that follows will focus on a single data-generating process under a single distribution for our covariate. This will allow us to more rigorously discuss our results. We note that the results that follow are qualitatively similar for the other DGPs and covariate generations unless otherwise stated.

3.1. The OLS Criterion

Using the OLS criterion[5] to select the weights, for DGP 1, with our covariate generated as a standard normal, Table 1 displays relative median MSEE across the eight individual estimators. Several observations are immediate. Some estimators perform better than other estimators. For example, the local-constant estimator with bandwidths selected via LSCV and a Gaussian kernel (Model I) often outperforms the model averaged estimator. Note that this is true here, but is not always true for other distributions of the covariate (likely the avoidance of significant boundary bias issues here given the thin tails of X). Note that the performance of this particular estimator is often better when the signal-to-noise ratio is large

Table 1. Relative Simulation Performance of Model Averaging (Least-Squares) Estimators versus Single Models.

		I	II	III	IV	V	VI	VII	VIII
	$n=100$	0.846	1.846	0.977	1.189	2.444	2.972	0.901	1.135
$\rho=0.1$	$n=200$	0.957	2.340	1.017	1.020	3.675	4.655	1.132	1.309
	$n=400$	0.982	2.496	0.990	0.988	4.789	6.190	1.278	1.482
	$n=100$	0.940	1.488	1.064	1.229	1.576	2.023	1.081	1.357
$\rho=0.5$	$n=200$	0.963	1.715	1.006	1.067	2.045	2.777	1.163	1.387
	$n=400$	0.988	1.955	0.999	1.027	2.607	3.506	1.337	1.561
	$n=100$	1.024	1.342	1.134	1.235	1.287	1.579	1.143	1.356
$\rho=1.0$	$n=200$	0.986	1.585	1.030	1.108	1.518	2.051	1.232	1.456
	$n=400$	0.985	1.690	0.990	1.035	1.771	2.506	1.340	1.550
	$n=100$	1.102	1.229	1.155	1.194	1.233	1.317	1.201	1.300
$\rho=2.0$	$n=200$	1.037	1.390	1.062	1.178	1.290	1.537	1.220	1.395
	$n=400$	1.000	1.421	1.002	1.057	1.356	1.800	1.347	1.530

Notes: Each column corresponds to a specific comparison model (estimator, bandwidth selection and kernel): Model (I) LCLS, LSCV, Gaussian; Model (II) LLLS, LSCV, Gaussian; Model (III) LCLS, AICc, Gaussian; Model (IV) LLLS, AICc, Gaussian; Model (V) LCLS, LSCV, Epanechnikov; Model (VI) LLLS, LSCV, Epanechnikov; Model (VII) LCLS, AICc, Epanechnikov; Model (VII) LLLS, AICc, Epanechnikov – DGP 1, X generated as standard normal, 1,000 Simulations.

(ρ is small), as Yang (2003) suggests. As for the remaining estimators, we generally see improved performance for the model averaged estimator, especially when ρ is greater than 0.5. In some cases, the improvement is substantial.

Table 2 presents the proportion of the simulations where a given number of estimators were selected with weight greater than 0.001 via the least-squares criterion. This will give us insight into how many estimators are selected in the averaging setting. We do not see any case where all eight estimators receive non-zero weight. Further still, in only a limited number of cases were seven different estimators averaged over (7 out of a possible 12,000). Parallel to this, few simulations resulted in a singular estimator receiving a weight of unity. The majority of the simulations produced two to four estimators being averaged across.

While Table 2 displays the general tendency of the number of estimators averaged over, it sheds no light on which estimators are being favored. Table 3 gives the proportion of the 1,000 simulations that resulted in the OLS criterion selecting a weight greater than 0.001 for each of the given estimators. Here, we see greater values for estimators which use the Gaussian kernel. In other scenarios, we find the local-linear estimator to be more prevalent. This result actually emphasizes the need for the model averaging technique as the weight devoted to a given estimator/bandwidth selector/kernel function appears to depend on the data generating process.

Table 2. Proportion, Out of 1,000 Simulations, the Number of Models with Weight Greater than 0.001 Are Selected (Least-Squares Selection) – DGP 1, X Generated as Standard Normal.

		1	2	3	4	5	6	7	8
	$n=100$	0.063	0.427	0.317	0.136	0.046	0.010	0.001	0
$\rho=0.1$	$n=200$	0.164	0.535	0.211	0.075	0.014	0.001	0.000	0
	$n=400$	0.310	0.459	0.164	0.057	0.010	0.000	0.000	0
	$n=100$	0.020	0.381	0.324	0.193	0.075	0.006	0.001	0
$\rho=0.5$	$n=200$	0.079	0.499	0.265	0.123	0.032	0.002	0.000	0
	$n=400$	0.189	0.489	0.220	0.083	0.017	0.002	0.000	0
	$n=100$	0.026	0.327	0.327	0.201	0.098	0.019	0.002	0
$\rho=1.0$	$n=200$	0.025	0.433	0.333	0.137	0.064	0.007	0.001	0
	$n=400$	0.108	0.464	0.280	0.126	0.019	0.003	0.000	0
	$n=100$	0.029	0.269	0.277	0.251	0.140	0.032	0.002	0
$\rho=2.0$	$n=200$	0.013	0.361	0.350	0.186	0.075	0.015	0.000	0
	$n=400$	0.037	0.378	0.356	0.177	0.043	0.009	0.000	0

Table 3. Proportion, Out of 1,000 Simulations, that Given Estimator Was Given (Least-Squares) Weight Greater than 0.001.

		I	II	III	IV	V	VI	VII	VIII
	$n=100$	0.871	0.648	0.137	0.410	0.050	0.188	0.104	0.301
$\rho=0.1$	$n=200$	0.973	0.574	0.161	0.203	0.046	0.090	0.072	0.124
	$n=400$	0.993	0.404	0.164	0.163	0.052	0.059	0.065	0.098
	$n=100$	0.855	0.676	0.101	0.498	0.082	0.264	0.114	0.354
$\rho=0.5$	$n=200$	0.946	0.616	0.138	0.259	0.067	0.194	0.109	0.207
	$n=400$	0.976	0.467	0.195	0.191	0.068	0.107	0.098	0.154
	$n=100$	0.767	0.649	0.102	0.594	0.109	0.311	0.156	0.395
$\rho=1.0$	$n=200$	0.930	0.649	0.130	0.350	0.069	0.249	0.148	0.282
	$n=400$	0.939	0.593	0.179	0.202	0.062	0.176	0.142	0.200
	$n=100$	0.638	0.694	0.108	0.682	0.129	0.399	0.173	0.485
$\rho=2.0$	$n=200$	0.804	0.651	0.169	0.464	0.101	0.304	0.192	0.309
	$n=400$	0.878	0.636	0.237	0.276	0.102	0.269	0.174	0.266

Notes: Each column corresponds to a specific single equation model (estimator, bandwidth selection, and kernel): Model (I) LCLS, LSCV, Gaussian; Model (II) LLLS, LSCV, Gaussian; Model (III) LCLS, AICc, Gaussian; Model (IV) LLLS, AICc, Gaussian; Model (V) LCLS, LSCV, Epanechnikov; Model (VI) LLLS, LSCV, Epanechnikov; Model (VII) LCLS, AICc, Epanechnikov; Model (VII) LLLS, AICc, Epanechnikov – DGP 1, X generated as standard normal.

In Table 4, we list the average weight assigned to each estimator across the simulations. The results are related to those in Table 3, but emphasize not only the use of each specific estimator, but also the importance of it in determining the model averaged estimator. The results here are very interesting. We find the weight

Table 4. Average (Least-Squares) Weight Assigned to a Given Estimator across the 1,000 Simulations.

		I	II	III	IV	V	VI	VII	VIII
	$n=100$	0.504	0.276	0.031	0.110	0.001	0.031	0.001	0.048
$\rho=0.1$	$n=200$	0.768	0.164	0.026	0.031	0.001	0.007	0.001	0.004
	$n=400$	0.893	0.065	0.020	0.018	0.001	0.001	0.000	0.000
	$n=100$	0.461	0.270	0.019	0.130	0.003	0.050	0.002	0.065
$\rho=0.5$	$n=200$	0.698	0.179	0.031	0.054	0.001	0.022	0.001	0.013
	$n=400$	0.854	0.075	0.036	0.026	0.002	0.006	0.001	0.001
	$n=100$	0.382	0.284	0.020	0.169	0.004	0.059	0.005	0.076
$\rho=1.0$	$n=200$	0.618	0.205	0.035	0.067	0.003	0.040	0.003	0.029
	$n=400$	0.778	0.125	0.051	0.024	0.002	0.014	0.002	0.004
	$n=100$	0.279	0.291	0.023	0.204	0.007	0.083	0.010	0.102
$\rho=2.0$	$n=200$	0.447	0.250	0.053	0.124	0.006	0.067	0.008	0.043
	$n=400$	0.639	0.174	0.087	0.046	0.004	0.036	0.004	0.010

Notes: Each column corresponds to a specific single equation model (estimator, bandwidth selection, and kernel): Model (I) LCLS, LSCV, Gaussian; Model (II) LLLS, LSCV, Gaussian; Model (III) LCLS, AICc, Gaussian; Model (IV) LLLS, AICc, Gaussian; Model (V) LCLS, LSCV, Epanechnikov; Model (VI) LLLS, LSCV, Epanechnikov; Model (VII) LCLS, AICc, Epanechnikov; Model (VII) LLLS, AICc, Epanechnikov – DGP 1, X generated as standard normal.

devoted to any model with a Gaussian kernel (Models I, II, III and IV) is much larger than that of single equations which used an Epanechnikov kernel (this result is prevalent across each of our data-generating processes). We also see least-squares cross-validation providing more weight than that for the AIC_c bandwidth selector (Models I and II).

3.2. The LSCV Criterion

To determine the performance of our LSCV weight criterion we also consider DGP 1, with identical covariate generation, as before. Table 5 displays relative median MSEE across the eight individual estimators. Again, the local-constant estimator with LSCV bandwidth selector and Gaussian kernel outperforms our model averaged estimator when ρ is not large. For each of the other estimators, the model averaged estimator has superior performance (excluding once case) when ρ is greater than 0.1 and outperforms most others when $\rho > 0.1$.

Table 6 presents the proportion of the simulations where a given number of estimators were assigned weights greater than 0.001 via the LSCV criterion. This will give us insight into how many estimators are favored in the averaging setting. As common to least-squares selection of the weights, it is striking that in none of

Table 5. Relative Simulation Performance of Model Averaging (Cross-Validation) Estimators versus Single Models.

		I	II	III	IV	V	VI	VII	VIII
	$n=100$	0.848	1.851	0.980	1.192	2.451	2.981	0.904	1.138
$\rho=0.1$	$n=200$	0.957	2.340	1.017	1.020	3.675	4.655	1.132	1.309
	$n=400$	0.982	2.496	0.990	0.988	4.789	6.190	1.278	1.482
	$n=100$	0.940	1.488	1.064	1.229	1.576	2.023	1.081	1.357
$\rho=0.5$	$n=200$	0.963	1.715	1.006	1.067	2.045	2.777	1.163	1.387
	$n=400$	0.988	1.955	0.999	1.027	2.607	3.506	1.337	1.561
	$n=100$	1.024	1.342	1.134	1.235	1.287	1.579	1.143	1.356
$\rho=1.0$	$n=200$	0.986	1.585	1.030	1.108	1.518	2.051	1.232	1.456
	$n=400$	0.985	1.690	0.990	1.035	1.771	2.506	1.340	1.550
	$n=100$	1.102	1.229	1.155	1.194	1.233	1.317	1.201	1.300
$\rho=2.0$	$n=200$	1.037	1.390	1.062	1.178	1.290	1.537	1.220	1.395
	$n=400$	1.000	1.421	1.002	1.057	1.356	1.800	1.347	1.530

Notes: Each column corresponds to a specific comparison model (estimator, bandwidth selection, and kernel): Model (I) LCLS, LSCV, Gaussian; Model (II) LLLS, LSCV, Gaussian; Model (III) LCLS, AICc, Gaussian; Model (IV) LLLS, AICc, Gaussian; Model (V) LCLS, LSCV, Epanechnikov; Model (VI) LLLS, LSCV, Epanechnikov; Model (VII) LCLS, AICc, Epanechnikov; Model (VII) LLLS, AICc, Epanechnikov – DGP 1, X generated as standard normal, 1,000 Simulations.

Table 6. Proportion, Out of 1,000 Simulations, the Number of Models with Weight Greater than 0.001 Are Selected (Cross-Validation Selection) – DGP 1, X Generated as Standard Normal.

		1	2	3	4	5	6	7	8
	$n=100$	0.060	0.434	0.327	0.127	0.042	0.009	0.001	0
$\rho=0.1$	$n=200$	0.163	0.535	0.211	0.076	0.014	0.001	0.000	0
	$n=400$	0.310	0.458	0.164	0.058	0.010	0.000	0.000	0
	$n=100$	0.020	0.390	0.350	0.173	0.062	0.004	0.001	0
$\rho=0.5$	$n=200$	0.079	0.502	0.262	0.127	0.028	0.002	0.000	0
	$n=400$	0.189	0.488	0.222	0.079	0.020	0.002	0.000	0
	$n=100$	0.028	0.347	0.330	0.200	0.076	0.018	0.001	0
$\rho=1.0$	$n=200$	0.025	0.442	0.333	0.135	0.056	0.008	0.001	0
	$n=400$	0.107	0.465	0.277	0.129	0.020	0.002	0.000	0
	$n=100$	0.031	0.281	0.311	0.240	0.108	0.027	0.002	0
$\rho=2.0$	$n=200$	0.013	0.369	0.353	0.184	0.073	0.008	0.000	0
	$n=400$	0.037	0.379	0.355	0.178	0.042	0.009	0.000	0

the simulations did all eight estimators receive non-zero weight. Similarly, only six times were seven of the eight estimators, in the 12,000 total simulations, averaged over. The majority of the simulations produced two to four estimators receiving positive weight.

Table 7. Proportion, Out of 1,000 Simulations, that Given Estimator Was Given (Cross-Validation) Weight Greater than 0.001.

		I	II	III	IV	V	VI	VII	VIII
	$n = 100$	0.868	0.647	0.138	0.398	0.051	0.187	0.105	0.294
$\rho = 0.1$	$n = 200$	0.972	0.574	0.163	0.204	0.046	0.091	0.072	0.124
	$n = 400$	0.993	0.403	0.166	0.164	0.052	0.059	0.065	0.098
	$n = 100$	0.855	0.666	0.102	0.474	0.082	0.252	0.115	0.337
$\rho = 0.5$	$n = 200$	0.946	0.615	0.139	0.257	0.067	0.191	0.109	0.205
	$n = 400$	0.980	0.468	0.194	0.191	0.068	0.107	0.097	0.154
	$n = 100$	0.767	0.634	0.102	0.568	0.109	0.302	0.155	0.370
$\rho = 1.0$	$n = 200$	0.931	0.642	0.132	0.342	0.071	0.241	0.148	0.276
	$n = 400$	0.941	0.593	0.181	0.202	0.063	0.174	0.142	0.200
	$n = 100$	0.639	0.663	0.108	0.638	0.129	0.384	0.173	0.468
$\rho = 2.0$	$n = 200$	0.805	0.644	0.169	0.449	0.101	0.298	0.193	0.300
	$n = 400$	0.881	0.635	0.238	0.276	0.102	0.266	0.174	0.264

Notes: Each column corresponds to a specific single equation model (estimator, bandwidth selection and kernel): Model (I) LCLS, LSCV, Gaussian; Model (II) LLLS, LSCV, Gaussian; Model (III) LCLS, AICc, Gaussian; Model (IV) LLLS, AICc, Gaussian; Model (V) LCLS, LSCV, Epanechnikov; Model (VI) LLLS, LSCV, Epanechnikov; Model (VII) LCLS, AICc, Epanechnikov; Model (VII) LLLS, AICc, Epanechnikov – DGP 1, X generated as standard normal.

Table 7, which gives the proportion of the 1,000 simulations that resulted in the LSCV criterion selected a weight greater than 0.001, gives very similar conclusions to that of Table 3. Again, we see greater values for estimators which use the Gaussian kernel, but in other scenarios we find the local-linear estimator to be the dominant determinant of weights.

Table 8 lists the average weight assigned to each estimator across the simulations. Again, we find the weight devoted to any model with a Gaussian kernel to be much larger than that of single equations which used an Epanechnikov kernel (this result is prevalent across each of our data-generating processes). We also see least-squares cross-validation providing more weight than that for the AIC_c bandwidth selector for the Gaussian kernel (Models I and II).

3.3. *Comparison across Weight Selection Criterion*

While we have presented our results independently between least-squares weight selection and least-squares cross-validation weight selection, we can draw comparisons between the relative performance of each method. Both methods were used during the simulations on the same data, thus, by comparing similar cells in Tables 1 and 5, we can determine if one method consistently outperforms another. However, we immediately notice that median MSEE is essentially identical for

Table 8. Average (Cross-Validation) Weight Assigned to a Given Estimator across the 1,000 Simulations.

		I	II	III	IV	V	VI	VII	VIII
	$n=100$	0.498	0.277	0.031	0.107	0.001	0.032	0.001	0.052
$\rho=0.1$	$n=200$	0.766	0.164	0.026	0.031	0.001	0.007	0.001	0.004
	$n=400$	0.893	0.065	0.020	0.019	0.001	0.001	0.000	0.000
	$n=100$	0.461	0.269	0.019	0.128	0.003	0.052	0.002	0.067
$\rho=0.5$	$n=200$	0.698	0.178	0.031	0.053	0.001	0.023	0.001	0.015
	$n=400$	0.857	0.075	0.032	0.026	0.002	0.006	0.001	0.001
	$n=100$	0.382	0.279	0.020	0.163	0.004	0.065	0.006	0.081
$\rho=1.0$	$n=200$	0.619	0.202	0.034	0.067	0.003	0.040	0.003	0.032
	$n=400$	0.779	0.126	0.050	0.024	0.002	0.014	0.002	0.004
	$n=100$	0.279	0.289	0.023	0.189	0.007	0.088	0.010	0.115
$\rho=2.0$	$n=200$	0.447	04850	0.053	0.121	0.006	0.070	0.008	0.047
	$n=400$	0.641	0.174	0.084	0.046	0.004	0.036	0.004	0.010

Notes: Each column corresponds to a specific single equation model (estimator, bandwidth selection and kernel): Model (I) LCLS, LSCV, Gaussian; Model (II) LLLS, LSCV, Gaussian; Model (III) LCLS, AICc, Gaussian; Model (IV) LLLS, AICc, Gaussian; Model (V) LCLS, LSCV, Epanechnikov; Model (VI) LLLS, LSCV, Epanechnikov; Model (VII) LCLS, AICc, Epanechnikov; Model (VII) LLLS, AICc, Epanechnikov – DGP 1, X generated as standard normal.

these two methods (see Tables 1 and 5). This would tend to favor selection of the weights via OLS as their estimation does not involve nonlinear optimization. This is not to say that the methods produce identical weights; compare Tables 2 and 6 or Tables 3 and 7 where there are slight differences in the actual weights assigned to each different estimator. We leave a theoretical discussion of this issue to future research.

4. EMPIRICAL ILLUSTRATION – RELIGIOSITY AND ECONOMIC GROWTH

In this section, we apply our model averaging estimator to the field of economic growth. Specifically, we are going to consider the relationship between religiosity and the growth rate of real gross domestic product per capita. It has been argued (Barro & McCleary, 2003) that religious beliefs (e.g., belief in hell) correlate with economic growth while time spent on religious activities (e.g., church attendance) are negatively correlation with growth. One argument for the former is that religious beliefs can lead to more trust and one argument for the latter is that more time spent on religious activities results in more resources devoted to non-economic activity.

This result has been disputed in the literature. For example, Durlauf, Kourtellos, and Tan (2012) use model averaging techniques and find little evidence that the religiosity variables are relevant predictors of growth. The approach of Durlauf, Kourtellos, & Tan (2012), albeit with a similar name, is quite different from what we plan to do as they are mostly looking to see the relevance of given variables. We are going to take a baseline specification as given and look across estimators. We will therefore avoid direct comparisons with their paper, but note that we obtain the same conclusion regarding the impact of the religiosity variables.

4.1. Data

The data come directly from Durlauf et al. (2012) and can be obtained from the *Journal of Applied Econometrics* data archive. We have an unbalanced panel of countries over three ($T = 3$) time periods: 1965–1974 ($n_1 = 38$), 1975–1984 ($n_2 = 41$), and 1985–1994 ($n_3 = 39$). The left-hand-side variable is the average growth rate of real per capita GDP and is obtained via the Penn World Tables, Version 6.1. The religiosity measures are obtained from both the World Values Survey and the International Social Survey Programme. Monthly church attendance is measured as the population averages of monthly church attendance and belief in hell is measured as the fraction of the population who believe in hell. We further include four dummy variables: two for time (1975–1984 and 1985–1994) and two for region (East Asia and Sub-Sahara Africa). The latter two are obtained from the World Bank.

Notably absent are the traditional Solow variables: initial income, population growth rate, investment share, and schooling. We also ran estimates with these variables included. While the primary conclusions (with respect to the religiosity variables) did not change, it is a bit ridiculous to run a nonparametric regression on 118 sample points with six continuous regressors. These results are available from the authors upon request.

4.2. Results

We consider the same eight estimation strategies we considered in Section 3. We have two different kernel regression estimators, LCLS and LLLS; two different bandwidth selectors, LSCV and AIC_c as well as two different kernel functions, Gaussian and Epanechnikov. Each set of bandwidths are calculated separately (with five multistarts) via the np package (Hayfield & Racine, 2008) in R and are given in Table 9.

The odd numbered columns (I, III, V, and VII) are for the local-constant estimator. Bandwidths near the respective upper bound suggest that a variable is

Table 9. Model Averaging Weights (Both Least-Squares and Cross-Validation) along with Bandwidths for Each Regressor (Monthly Church Attendance, Belief in Hell, Time Dummies, and Region Dummies) for Each Model (Estimator, Bandwidth Selection and Kernel): Model (I) LCLS, LSCV, Gaussian; Model (II) LLLS, LSCV, Gaussian; Model (III) LCLS, AICc, Gaussian; Model (IV) LLLS, AICc, Gaussian; Model (V) LCLS, LSCV, Epanechnikov; Model (VI) LLLS, LSCV, Epanechnikov; Model (VII) LCLS, AICc, Epanechnikov; Model (VII) LLLS, AICc, Epanechnikov.

	I	II	III	IV	V	VI	VII	VIII
Monthly church attendance	1.0411	0.6726	1.2925	10,825,197	1.3769	0.6627	1.3976	4,779,075
Belief in hell	0.4312	0.3827	2,832,599	37,325,896	1,502,907	0.5408	1,788,999	3,744,384
Time dummy (1975–1984)	0.0033	0.0121	0.0565	0.1247	0.0000	0.0612	0.0540	0.1251
Time dummy (1985–1994)	0.1630	0.2494	0.1580	0.2403	0.1630	0.2825	0.1534	0.2412
Region dummy (Asia)	0.0417	0.2057	0.0091	0.0021	0.0095	0.1601	0.0128	0.0021
Region dummy (Africa)	0.4081	0.5000	0.1520	0.2654	0.0249	0.2053	0.0974	0.2646
Weight (Least-squares)	0.0000	0.4240	0.1923	0.0000	0.2192	0.1645	0.0000	0.0000
Weight (Cross-validation)	0.0000	0.4385	0.2032	0.0000	0.2037	0.1546	0.0000	0.0000

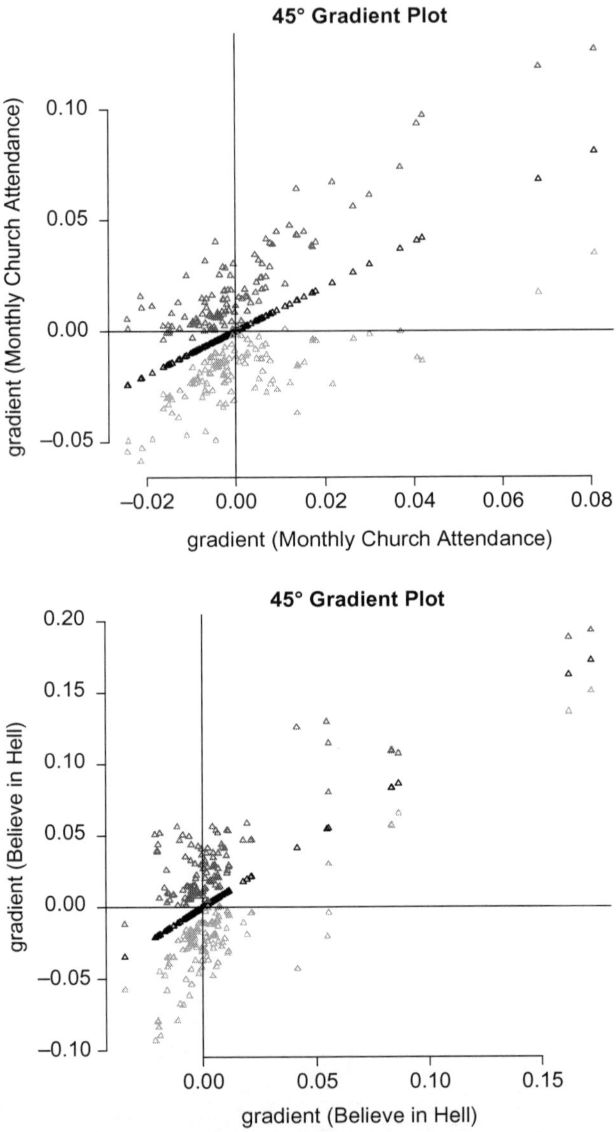

Fig. 1. 45° Plots for Gradients of Religiosity Variables.

irrelevant. For the continuous variables, the upper bound is infinity, while it is 0.5 for the discrete variables. Belief in hell has a large bandwidth in three of those models (III, V, and VII), which brings into question its relevance.

The last two rows of Table 9 give the model weights constructed via the (least-squares) quadratic program and cross-validation function, respectively (as expected, they are quite similar). We see that in each case, we have positive weights for four separate models. What is interesting is that the combination of these weights includes each estimator, bandwidth selector and kernel function. It appears, at least in this small sample, each method helps in the prediction of output growth. We would like to note, even with this small sample and in the absence of the Solow variables, we still have relatively strong predictive power. The R^2 measure, obtained as the squared correlation between the predicted and true left-hand-side values, is equal to 0.6738 for the least-squares weights and 0.7132 for the cross-validation weights.

Regarding the variables of interest, instead of giving a single-point estimate, we plot the entire set of gradients for both monthly church attendance and belief in hell (solely for the least-squares weights as these two sets of figures are not easily distinguishable from one another). Specifically, Fig. 1 gives the 45° plots (Henderson, Kumbhakar, & Parmeter, 2012) for each gradient estimate. The 45° plots are constructed by plotting each of the point estimates for the gradients of a given regressor against themselves (resulting in a 45° line, hence the name). In addition, we plot the upper and lower confidence bounds (90%) for each point estimate.[6] If both the upper and lower bounds lie in the first quadrant, the point estimate is positive and significant. Similarly, if both the upper and lower bounds lie in the third quadrant, the point estimate is negative and significant. All other cases are statistically insignificant.

Fig. 1 shows that nearly all point estimates for each regressor are insignificant. Even in the absence of other controls, we can only find a handful of point estimates (notably in the tails) that are statistically significant. This result is in contrast to that in Barro and McCleary (2003) and more in-line with the results in Durlauf et al. (2012). That being said, this is simply an empirical illustration. A proper study should (at least) include additional controls as well as examine the exogeneity assumption which is being assumed by our estimation procedures.

5. CONCLUDING REMARKS

In this paper, we propose to use model averaging techniques, similar to those used to aggregate forecasts in the time series literature, in order to mitigate the problems in choosing "seemingly" arbitrary choices in the nonparametric kernel literature. Specifically, we suggest to average over the kernel estimator, kernel function, and bandwidth selection mechanism. Our generic model included a few cases, but could be extended to cover any number of different models. For example, we can look at kernels versus splines or single equation versus simultaneous equation models. Our belief is that these approaches may lead to better predicting models as well as more robust results in practice.

Future work could consider comparisons to the literature. For example, under what circumstances would the estimators in Liu (2011) or Hall and Racine (2015) bring improvements over our estimator and vice versa. Further, a rigorous theoretical treatment could be conducted similar to that in Zhang and Yang (2015) or extended, for example, to the treatment effect case as in Rolling and Yang (2014).

NOTES

1. We note that our approach here could easily encompass averaging over different types of nonparametric estimators (spline and series) as well as different covariate choices.

2. There is a large time series literature on combining forecasts which uses similar (as well as additional) techniques (e.g., see the discussion in Section 2.13 of Enders 2015, p. 109).

3. Requiring this type of behavior of the covariance between two different kernel smoothed estimators has appeared in other contexts as well (e.g., Henderson, Li, Parmeter & Yao (2015), in their gradient-based bandwidth selection mechanism, albeit there the comparison is between the local-linear and the local-cubic estimators).

4. We also calculated the mean MSEE over the simulations and these results are available upon request.

5. In the simulations we constrain the weights to be positive and sum to one for descriptive purposes. This is not necessary and it is even possible that we may obtain gains by allowing some of the weights to be negative.

6. The upper and lower bounds are calculated via a wild bootstrap. Specifically, we wild bootstrap the residuals from the "averaged" model and add those to the fitted values from the "averaged" model in order to compute the new left-hand-side variable. These new y values are then used to reconstruct each conditional mean estimate and then the model averaged estimate.

REFERENCES

Barro, R., & McCleary, R. (2003). Religion and economic growth across countries. *American Journal of Sociology, 68*, 760–781.

Boente, G., & Fraiman, R. (1995). Asymptotic distribution of data-driven smoothers in density and regression esiimation under dependence. *Canadian Journal of Statistics, 23*, 383–397.

Cheng, M., Peng, L., & Wu, J.-S. (2007). Reducing variance in univariate smoothing. *The Annals of Statistics, 35*, 522–542.

Choi, E., & Hall, P. (1998). On bias reduction in local linear smoothing. *Biometrika, 85*, 333–345.

Durlauf, S. N., Kourtellos, A., & Tan, C. (2008). Are any growth theories robust? *Economic Journal, 118*, 329–346.

Durlauf, S. N., Kourtellos, A., & Tan, C. (2012). Is god in the details? A reexamination of the role of religion in economic growth. *Journal of Applied Econometrics, 27*, 1059–1075.

Enders, W. (2015). *Applied econometric time series*. New York, NY: Wiley.

Fan, J. (1993). Local linear regression smoothers and their minimax efficiencies. *The Annals of Statistics, 21*, 196–216.

Fan, J., & Gijbels, I. (1996). *Local polynomial modeling and its applications*. London: Chapman and Hall.

Frölich, M. (2004). Finite-sample properties of propensity-score matching and weighting estimators. *Review of Economics and Statistics, 86*, 77–90.

Hall, P., & Racine, J. S. (2015). Infinite-order cross-validated local polynomial regression. *Journal of Econometrics, 185*, 510–525.

Hansen, B. E. (2007). Least squares model averaging. *Econometrica, 75*, 1175–1189.

Härdle, W., & Marron, J. (1985). Optimal bandwidth selection in nonparametric regression function estimation. *The Annals of Statistics, 13*, 1465–1481.

Hayfield, T., & Racine, J. S. (2008). Nonparametric econometrics: The np package. *Journal of Statistical Software, 27*(5), 1–32.

Henderson, D. J., Kumbhakar, S. C., & Parmeter, C. F. (2012). A simple method to visualize results in nonlinear regression models. *Economics Letters, 117*, 578–581.

Henderson, D. J., Li, Q., Parmeter, C. F., & Yao, S. (2015). Gradient-based smoothing parameter selection for nonparametric regression estimation. *Journal of Econometrics, 184*, 233–241.

Henderson, D. J., & Parmeter, C. F. (2015). *Applied nonparametric econometrics*. Cambridge: Cambridge University Press.

Hurvich, C. M., Simonoff, J. S., & Tsai, C.-L. (1998). Smoothing parameter selection in nonparametric regression using an improved Akaike information criterion. *Journal of the Royal Statistical Society, Series B, 60*(2), 271–293.

Kotlyarova, Y., & Zinde-Walsh, V. (2006). Non- and semi-parametric estimation in models with unknown smoothness. *Economics Letters, 93*, 379–386.

Kotlyarova, Y., & Zinde-Walsh, V. (2007). Robust kernel density estimation in models with unknown smoothness. *Journal of Nonparametric Statistics, 19*, 89–101.

Li, D., Linton, O., & Lu, Z. (2015). A flexible semiparametric forecasting model for time series. *Journal of Econometrics, 187*, 345–357.

Li, Q., & Racine, J. S. (2004). Cross-validated local linear nonparametric regression. *Statistica Sinica, 14*, 485–512.

Liu, C.-A. (2011). Averaging estimators for kernel regressions. Working Paper, University of Wisconsin.

Martins-Filho, C., & Saraiva, P. (2012). On asymptotic normality of the local polynomial regression estimator with stochastic bandwidths. *Communications in Statistics - Theory and Methods, 41*, 1052–1068.

Masry, E., & Fan, J. (1997). Local polynomial estimation of regression functions for mixing processes. *Scandinavian Journal of Statistics, 24*, 1965–1979.

Nadaraya, E. (1964). On estimating regression. *Theory of Probability and Its Applications, 9*, 141–142.

Raferty, A. E. (1997). Bayesian model selection in social research (with discussion). *Sociological Methodology, 25*, 111–196.

Raferty, A. E., Madigan, D., & Hoeting, J. A. (1997). Bayesian model averaging for regression models. *Journal of the American Statistical Association, 92*, 179–191.

Rolling, C. A., & Yang, Y. (2014). Model selection for estimating treatment effects. *Journal of the Royal Statistical Society, Series B, 76*, 749–769.

Seifert, B., & Gasser, T. (1996). Finite-sample variance of local polynomials: Analysis and solutions. *Journal of the American Statistical Association, 91*, 267–275.

Seifert, B., & Gasser, T. (2000). Data adaptive ridging in local polynomial regression. *Journal of Computational and Graphical Statistics, 9*, 338–360.

Ullah, A., & Wang, H. (2013). Parametric and nonparametric frequentist model selection and model averaging. *Econometrics, 1*, 157–179.

Wan, A. T. K., Zhang, X., & Zou, G. (2010). Least squares model averaging by Mallows criterion. *Journal of Econometrics, 156*, 277–283.

Wang, H., Zou, G., & Wan, A. T. K. (2012). Model averaging for varying-coefficient partially linear measurement error models. *Electronic Journal of Statistics, 6*, 1017–1039.

Watson, G. S. (1964). Smooth regression analysis. *Sankhya, 26*(15), 175–184.

Xia, Y., & Li, W. K. (2002). Asymptotic behavior of bandwidth selected by the cross-validation method for local polynomial fitting. *Journal of Multivariate Analysis, 83*, 265–287.

Yang, Y. (1999). Model selection for nonparametric estimation. *Statistica Sinica, 9*, 475–499.

Yang, Y. (2001). Adaptive regression by mixing. *Journal of the American Statistical Association, 96*, 574–588.

Yang, Y. (2003). Regression with multiple candidate models: Selecting or mixing. *Statistica Sinica, 13*, 783–809.

Yang, Y. (2004). Aggregating regression procedures to improve performance. *Bernoulli, 10*, 25–47.

Yang, Y. (2007). Consistency of cross validation for comparing regression procedures. *Annals of Statistics, 35*, 2450–2473.

Zhang, Y., & Yang, Y. (2015). Cross-validation for selecting a model selection procedure. *Journal of Econometrics, 187*, 95–112.

SMOOTHNESS: BIAS AND EFFICIENCY OF NONPARAMETRIC KERNEL ESTIMATORS

Yulia Kotlyarova[a], Marcia M. A. Schafgans[b] and Victoria Zinde-Walsh[c,d]

[a]*Department of Economics, Dalhousie University, Halifax, Canada*
[b]*Department of Economics, London School of Economics, London, UK*
[c]*Department of Economics, McGill University, Montréal, Canada*
[d]*CIREQ, Montréal, Canada*

ABSTRACT

For kernel-based estimators, smoothness conditions ensure that the asymptotic rate at which the bias goes to zero is determined by the kernel order. In a finite sample, the leading term in the expansion of the bias may provide a poor approximation. We explore the relation between smoothness and bias and provide estimators for the degree of the smoothness and the bias. We demonstrate the existence of a linear combination of estimators whose trace of the asymptotic mean-squared error is reduced relative to the individual estimator at the optimal bandwidth. We examine the finite-sample performance of a combined estimator that minimizes the trace of the MSE of a linear combination of individual kernel estimators for a multimodal

Essays in Honor of Aman Ullah
Advances in Econometrics, Volume 36, 561–589

ISSN: 0731-9053/doi:10.1108/S0731-905320160000036025

density. The combined estimator provides a robust alternative to individual estimators that protects against uncertainty about the degree of smoothness.

Keywords: Nonparametric estimation; kernel-based estimator; combined estimator

JEL classification: C14

1. INTRODUCTION

Kernel smoothing is now widely used in empirical economic research, facilitated by its introduction in popular statistical packages such as Stata, R, and XploRE. The implementation requires the researcher to select a kernel function, $K(\cdot)$, and a bandwidth parameter, h. It is important to recognize that this selection affects two components of the error of the estimator: the stochastic component associated with the variance and the approximation error coming from the bias. We emphasize the relation each component has to the theoretically imposed, but unknown, smoothness of the underlying functions and propose a more robust way of dealing with this uncertainty. We consider two classes of estimators: one consists of local kernel-based estimators such as univariate and multivariate density, density derivatives, (weighted) conditional moment and (weighted) derivatives of the conditional moment estimators, and the other consists of average kernel-based estimators such as average density, average (weighted) conditional moments, and average (density-weighted) derivatives of the conditional moment estimators.

In kernel estimation, it is assumed that the density and any other relevant functions are in some class of smooth functions. The main theoretical purpose of the various smoothness conditions in the literature is to ensure that the kernel order determines the rate at which the bias of the estimator goes to zero. It enables one to control this rate via the choice of the kernel and bandwidth. For example, the rule-of-thumb plug-in method of bandwidth selection for univariate density estimation in Silverman (1986) assumes that the density has at least two continuous derivatives and specifies the use of a second-order kernel. With enough smoothness, improvements in the rate of the bias are achieved via the use of higher-order kernels (see, e.g., Pagan & Ullah, 1999 for discussion). For local kernel-based estimators, smoothness conditions do not affect the leading term of the stochastic component associated with the variance; it depends on the dimension of the function argument.

The use of higher-order kernels and smoothness requirements is instrumental in allowing one to make claims of a parametric convergence rate for average kernel-based estimators over a range of bandwidth choices. The asymptotic variance of estimators for functionals that involve averaging may have a leading term that decreases at a parametric rate. The dominance of this term does depend on the smoothness of the functions involved in the averaging; to ensure a parametric rate a sufficient number of derivatives may need to exist. For the average density-weighted derivative estimator (ADE) of Powell, Stock, and Stoker (PSS, 1989), for instance, the density of the k covariates is assumed to possess at least $(k+6)/2$ continuous derivatives and a kernel of order $(k+4)/2$ is needed; the (direct) average derivatives estimator of Stoker (1991) necessitates smoothness assumptions both on the density and the conditional moment $E(Y|X)$ (specifically, the existence of at least $k+2$ continuous derivatives) in conjunction with the use of a kernel of order $k+2$.

The expansion of the bias function at a point requires smoothness conditions such that the leading term has a rate that is determined by the kernel order and a remainder term that goes to zero sufficiently fast. In addition, for the existence of a bandwidth that is applicable not just pointwise but also over the whole support of the function being estimated, uniform bounds must apply to the integrals of the derivatives of the functions. Function classes that satisfy such restrictions are defined, for example, in Hasminskii and Ibragimov (1990) for density estimation and, more recently, in Birgé (2014) for density estimation under quadratic loss. The existence of derivatives is not sufficient to ensure appropriate performance of the kernel estimators over the function class. The values of the integrals of the derivatives of the functions are important as well in that they can affect the speed of convergence of the kernel estimators. Multimodal distributions such as mixtures of normals, while satisfying the smoothness assumptions, often exhibit very high values of bounds on the derivatives and their integrals (see, e.g., Marron & Wand, 1992 and Section 2.1 for a theoretical discussion and examples; economic examples where multimodal distributions may arise can be found in Horowitz and Härdle, 1996 and DiNardo, Fortin and Lemieux, 1996).

The finite sample behavior of the kernel estimators exhibits significant variability depending on the actual underlying distribution, reflecting the fact that differentiability alone is no guarantee of a good asymptotic approximation. Finite sample problems are documented in many papers, including, for example, Hansen (2005). Simulations reveal that the root mean-squared error (RMSE) for the ADE with distribution of the regressors given by normal mixtures (which satisfy all smoothness assumptions) can be as much as 4–10 times that obtained under Gaussian density (see Table 1 in Schafgans & Zinde-Walsh, 2010). The root mean integrated squared error (RMISE) for the univariate kernel density estimation of a mixture of normal distribution (or, similarly, for a non-smooth density) was 3–4 times that obtained under Gaussian density (see Table 1 in Kotlyarova & Zinde-Walsh, 2007).

Even in a setting where all derivatives exist, it may be advantageous to assume that the unknown function is in a class of functions with lower smoothness, in particular when the bounds on the derivatives and their integrals may be large. In this paper, we investigate an example of a mixed normal density to illustrate this point by showing that the bias may be poorly represented by the leading term in the asymptotic expansion (based on kernels of order two or four). We demonstrate that the approximation error can be substantial, to the extent that the leading asymptotic term in the bias expansion may provide a totally misleading impression of the bias (up to a wrong sign) even in a sample of 1,000 observations.

Of course, if the unknown function does not possess all the derivatives required in the expansion of the bias function, the rate of the bias may be below the kernel order even asymptotically. In Table A1, we provide formulas for the bias and variance for some commonly used estimators under relaxed smoothness assumptions. They clarify that optimal rates are determined by the kernel order only when there is sufficient smoothness of the functions that drive the bias expansion. For the average kernel-based estimators, in the absence of sufficient smoothness, the term with the parametric rate of convergence may be dominated by terms that depend on the kernel and bandwidth.

Thus, there are two problems: (a) there may be insufficient differentiability of the underlying distributions and (b) even with the existence of derivatives there may be uncertainty about how far to take the expansion of the bias function to obtain the best approximation in a finite sample. Both these problems can be characterized as an uncertainty about the degree of smoothness of the unknown underlying distribution.

In an early paper, Woodroofe (1970) proposed to estimate the smoothness of a density function; his approach was not given much prominence in the research that followed where sufficient differentiability was assumed instead. Schafgans and Zinde-Walsh (2010) recently successfully implemented his approach in the context of ADE. The advantage of this method is that the selection of the bandwidth reflects the estimated smoothness in an adaptive way; the bias approximation can be improved. We continue to explore this method here.

The uncertainty about appropriate smoothness, and thus kernel and bandwidth selection, can be resolved by combining estimators obtained for different kernels and bandwidths. Kotlyarova and Zinde-Walsh (2006) proposed a combined estimator that is adaptive to the unknown smoothness and could achieve the best available (a priori unknown) asymptotic rate. The combined estimator uses a linear (not necessarily convex) combination of various kernel estimators. Schafgans and Zinde-Walsh (2010) made an argument (in the ADE case) that a combined estimator with appropriate selection of tuning parameters can outperform the estimator with optimal bandwidth not only in case of insufficient smoothness (as in Kotlyarova & Zinde-Walsh, 2006) but with sufficient smoothness as well.

In this paper, we pursue the strategy of estimating the leading bias term rate (extending the results of Woodroofe, 1970 and of Schafgans & Zinde-Walsh, 2010 to the general case) and combining estimators with different kernels and bandwidths. A similar analysis applies to extremum estimators; for example, Kotlyarova and Zinde-Walsh (2010) examine a combined estimator for the smoothed maximum score of Horowitz (1992).

We show that even with knowledge of the optimal bandwidth, there always exists a linear combination of estimators that has a smaller trace of the asymptotic mean-squared error ($trAMSE$) than that of the optimal estimator. This result exploits the fact that the distribution of an oversmoothed estimator is dominated by the bias and that one can find weights that will give a zero leading bias term in the linear combination while simultaneously reducing the variance. This result was presented in Schafgans and Zinde-Walsh (2010) for ADE; here we give a general (and corrected) version.

There are various approaches aimed at improving the performance of kernel estimators such as the use of local adaptive bandwidths, bootstrap, binning and twicing kernels. All the estimators obtained via these methods could also be used in a combined estimator.

We discuss the possible inadequacy of using the standard leading $O(h^{\upsilon(K)})$ term as the approximation of the bias in kernel density estimation, with $\upsilon(K)$ denoting the kernel order, by examining an example of a normal mixture density. We explore the properties of the infeasible combined estimator that uses the true bias and demonstrate that it exhibits a performance superior to the infeasible combined estimator that uses the true asymptotic leading term of the bias. This indicates that there may also be estimators of the bias that are superior to the ones that use the leading asymptotic term. We employ two approaches to estimate the bias: one is the approach utilized in Schafgans and Zinde-Walsh (2010) that is based on the strategy of Woodroofe (1970), and the other is a simplified estimator introduced in Kotlyarova and Zinde-Walsh (2007). We estimate the covariances by a bootstrap procedure.

Section 2 introduces the notation and provides the high-level assumptions on the bias and variance of the estimators. Section 2.1 provides a discussion on the bias and introduces the illustrative example of a mixed normal density, while Section 2.2 focuses on the variance and mean-squared error. Section 3 examines the estimation of the smoothness via the rate of the bias; this provides an estimated optimal bandwidth rate. This section also presents the two strategies for estimating the leading bias term. Section 4 demonstrates the existence of a linear combination of kernel estimators with different bandwidths that can provide a smaller $trAMSE$ than that obtainable with the optimal bandwidth. It achieves this goal by automatically removing the asymptotic bias without increasing the asymptotic variance. Implementation of the "combined estimator" requires estimation of biases and covariances. Section 5 introduces the infeasible combined estimator to demonstrate that, indeed, without the approximation error the combined estimator provides a better finite sample performance than that of any individual estimator. We also implement and discuss the feasible combined estimator. Section 6 presents our conclusions. The proofs and tables are in the appendix.

2. CLASSES OF ESTIMATORS AND ASSUMPTIONS

Kernel estimators involve the choice of a kernel function, $K(\cdot)$, and a bandwidth parameter (or vector of parameters), h, with $h \to 0$ as $N \to \infty$. We consider two types of kernel estimators: local kernel-based estimators and average kernel-based estimators. We generically denote them by $\hat{\delta}_N(K, h)$. The distinction between local and average estimators refers to the type of functional, δ_0, that is being estimated. The δ_0 could be defined either locally as the value of the function at a particular point (e.g., density) or as an expectation (such as the average density or the average derivative of the regression function). Examples of such estimators are provided in Table A1.

The kernel function $K: R^k \to R$ is assumed to be of order $v(K) \geq 2$ and satisfies other standard assumptions (see, for example, Pagan & Ullah, 1999). We do not require the kernel to be symmetric. As argued in Kotlyarova and Zinde-Walsh (2007), asymmetric kernel functions may be beneficial in some cases (see also Abadir & Lawford, 2004).

We make two high-level assumptions. The first is an assumption on the convergence of the bias; it generalizes the usual $h^{v(K)}$ rate that may be obtainable with sufficient differentiability.

Assumption 1.
As $N \to \infty$, $h \to 0$ *and* $h = O(N^{-\epsilon})$, *with* $\epsilon > \epsilon_L > 0$,

$$h^{-\bar{v}} bias(\hat{\delta}_N(K, h)) \to \mathcal{B}(K),$$

for some $\bar{v} > 0$, *where the vector* $\mathcal{B}(K) = (\mathcal{B}_1(K), \ldots, \mathcal{B}_\Delta(K))'$ *is such that* $0 < |\mathcal{B}_\ell(K)| < \infty$ *for* $\ell = 1, \ldots, \Delta$ *with* $\Delta = \dim(\delta_0)$.

The bound ϵ_L may be needed to ensure that the rest of the bias expansion converges to zero sufficiently fast.

The second assumption, which differs for local and average kernel-based estimators, is about convergence of the variance, $Var(\hat{\delta}_N(K, h))$.

Assumption 2.
As $N^\omega h^{d(k)} \to \infty$, $h \to 0$, *for some* $\omega \geq 0$, $d(k) \geq 1$,

(a) *for local kernel-based estimators: there is a finite positive-definite matrix* $\Sigma(K)$ *such that*

$$N^{\omega} h^{d(k)} var(\hat{\delta}_N(K,h)) \to \Sigma(K);$$

(b) *for average kernel-based estimators: there exist finite positive definite matrices* $\Sigma_1(K)$ *and* Σ_2 *and* $r > 0$ *such that an expansion for the variance is given by*

$$var(\hat{\delta}_N(K,h)) = N^{-\omega} h^{-d(k)} \left[\Sigma_1(K) + o(h^r)\right] + N^{-1}\left[\Sigma_2 + o(h^r)\right].$$

For kernel density and conditional mean estimators, $\omega = 1$ and $d(k) = k$; for the mth partial derivative $\omega = 1$ and $d(k) = k + m$. The average kernel-based estimators in Table A1 have $\omega = 2$; the parameter $d(k)$ equals k for the average density and $k + 2$ for the ADE.

2.1. *Discussion of the Approximation Error and the Bias*

The convergence rate for the bias, denoted $\bar{v}$ in Assumption 1, typically depends on the order of the kernel and on the smoothness properties of the functions that enter into the definition of δ_0.

To characterize this dependence on smoothness, we consider the following situations. Suppose that a function $\phi(x)$ is not differentiable over some domain $\Omega \subseteq R^k$ but for some $0 < \alpha \leq 1$ satisfies a Holder condition for every $x, x + \Delta x \in \Omega$:

$$|\phi(x + \Delta x) - \phi(x)| \leq \omega_{\phi}(x) \, \|\Delta x\|^{\alpha}.$$

Then we say that ϕ has smoothness order α (fractional) and set $v = \alpha$. If for some function $\phi(x)$ and integer m it can be assumed that all the partial derivatives of order m given by $\partial^m \phi(x)/(\partial^{m_1} x_1 \ldots \partial^{m_k} x_k)$, with $m_1 + \cdots + m_k = m$, are (Holder) continuous, then ϕ has smoothness order no less than m and we set $v = m$.

When v, as defined above, determines the expansion terms in the bias, then Assumption 1 is typically satisfied with $\bar{v}$ given by

$$\bar{v} = \min(v, v(K)).$$

With insufficient smoothness, that is, when $v < v(K)$, the rate at which the bias of the estimator goes to zero is not determined by the choice of the order of the kernel but could be determined by the degree of smoothness of the appropriate functions instead.

For example, for a second-order kernel density estimator it is known that if the second derivative of the density is continuous at x, the bias expansion provides the leading term $h^2\mathcal{B}_2(K)$, with $\mathcal{B}_2(K) = 0.5 f^{(2)}(x) \int u^2 K(u)\, du$. Similarly, for a fourth-order kernel density estimator if the fourth derivative of the density is continuous at x the leading term in the expansion is $h^4\mathcal{B}_4(K)$, with $\mathcal{B}_4(K) = \frac{1}{4!} f^{(4)}(x) \int u^4 K(u)\, du$ (see Pagan & Ullah, 1999). However, if the density function is only twice continuously differentiable, the leading term in the bias expansion of the fourth-order kernel density estimator could be still of order $O(h^2)$.

Our Assumption 1 states that there exists some (possibly unknown) $\bar{v}$ at which the bias is stabilized. This assumption is made by Woodroofe (1970) for the density estimation and is also made in Schafgans and Zinde-Walsh (2010) for ADE to approximate the $bias(\hat{\delta}_N(K,h))$ by $h^{\bar{v}}\mathcal{B}(K)$.

The leading term in the bias expansion provides an approximation for the bias function. If, for any $\varepsilon > 0$, a small enough h provides

$$\left| bias(\hat{\delta}_N(K,h)) - h^{\bar{v}}\mathcal{B}(K) \right| < \varepsilon h^{\bar{v}},$$

then the approximation error goes to zero as $h \to 0$. The approximation is determined by the kernel order if $\bar{v} = v(K)$.

We provide a heuristic discussion of the bias approximation via an illustrative example. The example represents a normal mixture density.[1] Specifically, we consider the normal mixture density, $f(x)$, for the distribution

$$0.5N(0,1) + 0.3N(0.8, 0.01) + 0.2N(1.2, 0.01), \tag{1}$$

(see Fig. 1).

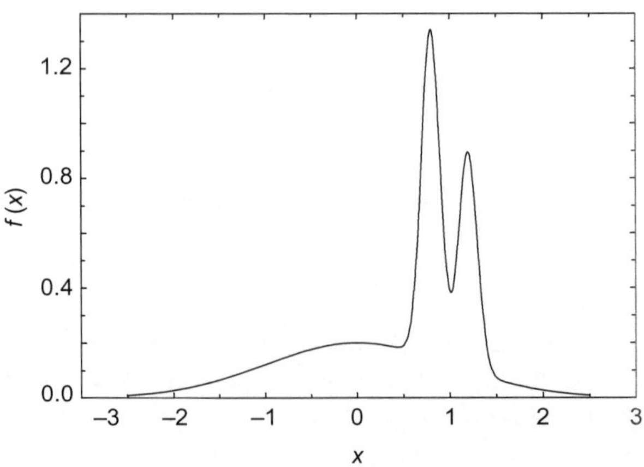

Fig. 1. Density – Mixture of Normal.

For this density all the smoothness conditions are satisfied and the bias should be well estimated by the function of the form $h^{v(K)}\mathcal{B}(K)$ which represents the approximating leading term. We call this expression here "asymptotic bias". In the estimation, we use symmetric polynomial kernel functions of order two, $K_2 = \frac{15}{16}\left(1-u^2\right)^2 I(|u| \leq 1)$, and four, $K_4 = \frac{105}{64}\left(1-u^2\right)^2(1-3u^2)I(|u| \leq 1)$.

Fig. 2 represents the true and asymptotic bias evaluated at the cross-validated bandwidth, h_{cv}, and at multiples of this bandwidth, $c \cdot h_{cv}$, where c takes values between 0.82 and 2.08. The optimal bandwidth is included in this range and the sample size is 1,000. The true bias of our density estimator, $\hat{f}_{K,h}(x)$, is obtained by integration using the true density: $E(\hat{f}_{K,h}(x) - f(x)) = \int_{-1}^{1} K(u)(f(x+uh) - f(x))du$. The "true bias" here is random with the randomness associated with the data-dependent bandwidth; to reflect this randomness we provide values averaged over 100 simulations. The different panels represent different points x_0 at which the bias is evaluated.

As expected, the size of the bias increases with the bandwidth. The bias is lower at points where the density derivatives are small. For example, at $x_0 = 0$ the values and behavior of the bias and asymptotic bias are similar to what one would get for a normal distribution. At points in the vicinity of which the density changes a lot, the bias could be greater by orders of magnitude. We also observe that there is a large discrepancy between the true bias and the asymptotic bias (represented by the dashed line); this discrepancy is particularly striking at the points $x_0 = 0.5$ and $x_0 = 1.5$ where the signs differ.

Next we consider the approximation of the bias by a function of the general form $h^{\bar{v}}\mathcal{B}(K)$ by establishing the value of $\bar{v}$ at different points x_0. We estimate the slope in the regression of $\ln bias(\hat{f}_{K,h}(x))^2$ on $\ln h^2$ as the bandwidth changes. If the leading term of the usual bias expansion of order $O(h^{v(K)})$ provides a good fit, then regressing $\ln bias(\hat{f}_{K,h}(x))^2$ on a constant and on $\ln h^2$ should give a slope value close to $v(K)$ (see Theorem 1); otherwise, the slope is below $v(K)$. We use 10 bandwidths in the range $0.8h_{cv} - 1.25h_{cv}$ and consider four different sample sizes: $N = 500$, $1,000$, $2,000$, and $4,000$. The distribution of the estimated $\bar{v}$ is represented by box-whiskers plots in Fig. 3. The variation exhibited by the box-whiskers comes from evaluating the true bias at cross-validated bandwidths, which vary over our 100 simulations. Each graph corresponds to a different location x_0 and shows four box-whiskers for different sample sizes.

The results for $x_0 = 0, 0.75, 1.0, 1.25$ are insensitive to increasing the range of bandwidths, while the results for $x_0 = 0.5$ and $x_0 = 1.5$ deteriorate when more oversmoothed bandwidths are considered. We truncated the estimates at the kernel order; this trimming had little impact on these graphs. Here, we see that the estimates at points where the density does not change much provide the value of the kernel order (as predicted by the expansions). However, there are points

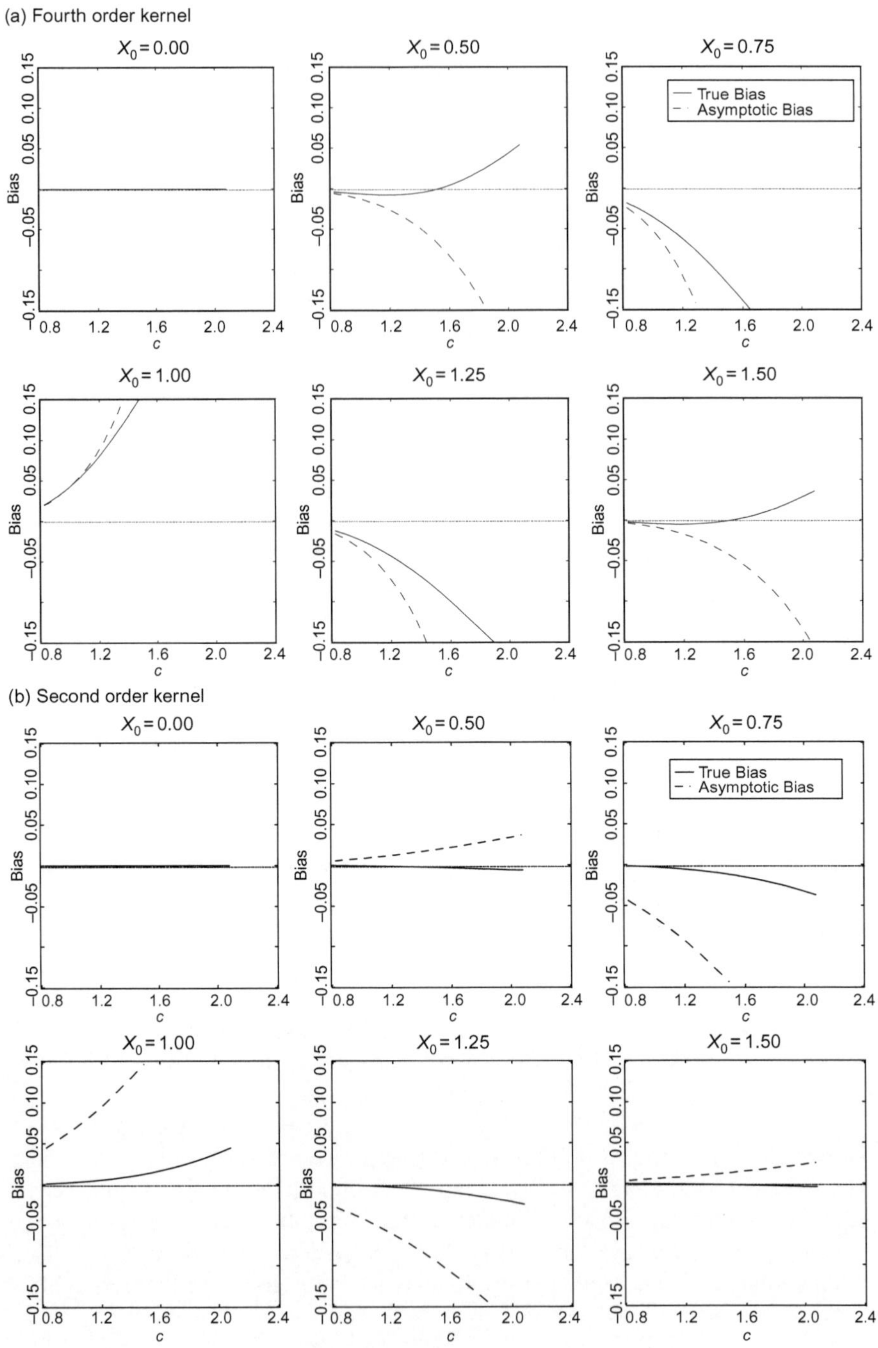

Fig. 2. True and Asymptotic Bias; $h = c \cdot h_{cv}$.

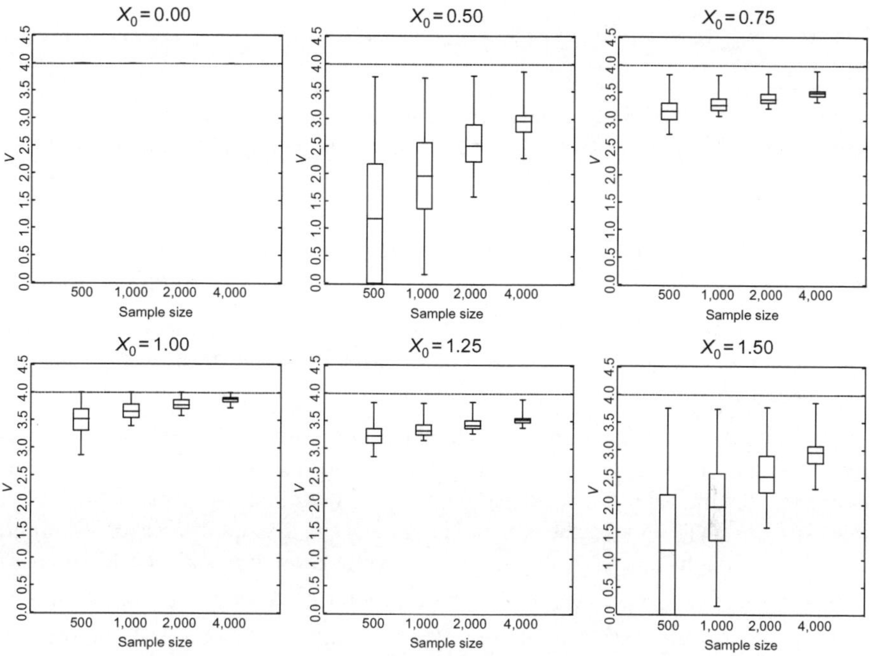

Fig. 3. $\bar{\upsilon}$ Estimates with True Bias – Fourth-Order Kernel.

where the estimates are well below the kernel order. As expected, as the sample size increases, the order of the approximating leading bias term gets closer to the kernel order. For the second-order kernel, the estimates of $\bar{\upsilon}$ were close to the kernel order at all points and any sample size.

It is usual to consider the MISE. Here, focusing on the integrated squared bias, we can conclude that the asymptotic approximation, with the rate determined by the kernel order, may not work. The true bias is smaller than the asymptotic counterpart over a large range of bandwidths. In our example, at the optimal bandwidth for $N = 500$ and the fourth-order kernel, the ratio of the difference between the mean integrated squared asymptotic bias and the mean integrated squared true bias to the mean integrated squared true bias is greater than 1 and equals 1.29. This error is smaller for the second-order kernel and declines as the sample size increases, but it is nevertheless substantial.

The example above represented a known density. In the nonparametric context, the density function is unknown and the assumptions place it in a particular functional class Σ. The bound on quadratic loss (MISE) of estimator $\hat{f}$ of a density function f in the class Σ can then be represented by

$$\inf_{\hat{f}_n} \sup_{f \in \Sigma} E_f \int (\hat{f}_n(x) - f(x))^2 dx.$$

Denote by $C_{m+a}(\Omega)$ the class of functions that satisfy the requirement that the function and all its derivatives up to order m are square integrable, and additionally satisfy for $L < \infty$, $0 < a \leq 1$ the condition

$$\int \left(f^{(m)}(x + \Delta x) - f^{(m)}(x)\right)^2 dx \leq L\,|\Delta x|^a. \quad (2)$$

Hasminskii and Ibragimov (1990) demonstrate that for densities in $\Sigma \subset C_{m+a}(\Omega)$, both the lower and upper bounds on the loss over the general class Σ are $O\left(n^{-\frac{m+a}{2m+2a+1}}\right)$.

For any individual function, the bound in Eq. (2) enters into the error of the bias approximation through expansion up to the mth derivative. Thus, for example, if $m = 2$ and the third derivatives exist almost everywhere and are square integrable, that is, $\int (f^{(3)}(x))^2 dx \leq L$, the actual accuracy of the asymptotic bias approximation depends on the bound L. We compare the value of such bounds for the standard normal function φ, $\int \left(\varphi^{(3)}(x)\right)^2 dx = 0.52893$, to the corresponding one for the normal mixture density considered here, $\int \left(f^{(3)}(x)\right)^2 dx = 7.6743 \times 10^5$. We see that in the case of the mixture the bound is vastly larger. For lower order derivatives, the bounds on the normal mixture are lower, for example, $\int \left(f^{(1)}(x)\right)^2 dx = 16.216$. This indicates that, possibly, it is advantageous to assume lower orders of smoothness for the unknown density. It is not clear how to interpret the numbers that characterize the particular class or evaluate what impact the bounds have. Moreover, there is no test that can establish whether the density belongs to a class Σ.

Thus, even if we were to observe the true bias in a sample, we can see that there would be no reason for us to assume that it is well approximated by terms of order $h^{v(K)}$ at each point. This motivates Assumption 1 on the bias, which is still restrictive but allows one to avoid commitment to a particular density class.

2.2. *Discussion of the Variance and Asymptotic Mean-Square Error*

The conditions that guarantee the high-level Assumption 2 include the existence of various second-order moments and, for some cases, the continuity of conditional moment functions. For kernel density and conditional mean estimators, the asymptotic variance is of the form $(Nh^k)^{-1}\Sigma(K)$; for kernel estimators of the mth partial derivatives of the density it is $(Nh^{k+m})^{-1}\Sigma(K)$.

For the average kernel-based estimators, Assumption 2(b) highlights that there are two possible leading terms. Given sufficient smoothness, averaging can yield a parametric rate of convergence for a range of bandwidths; however, the dominance of the parametric term depends on careful selection of the kernel and the bandwidth. Even when the parametric term dominates, the nonparametric term that depends on the kernel and the bandwidth could be important in finite samples.

The representative results about the estimators are summarized in Table A1. This table lists the rates of the leading terms in the AMSE expansion and the optimal rate that depends on $\bar{v}$ and may differ from the standard rate under insufficient smoothness. For average kernel-based estimators, as for ADE (Schafgans & Zinde-Walsh, 2010), the optimal bandwidth rate is defined so as to balance the bandwidth-dependent part in the expression in Assumption 2(b) with the bias. When the parametric rate is not achievable for such estimators because of lack of smoothness, the bandwidth determines the convergence rate of the estimator.

The optimal bandwidth is defined to have the rate $N^{-\eta(\bar{v})}$, where

$$\eta(\bar{v}) \equiv \frac{\omega}{2\bar{v} + d(k)}. \tag{3}$$

When smoothness holds, $v \geq v(K)$, the order of the kernel determines the asymptotic results that we list from the literature (see, e.g., Pagan & Ullah, 1999 or Li & Racine, 2007). When the smoothness assumption is violated, $v < v(K)$, non-standard results arise. We list (in the notation of this paper) the results from the articles Kotlyarova and Zinde-Walsh (2007) and Schafgans and Zinde-Walsh (2010) for density and ADE; the results for average density and for the conditional mean are obtained in the appendix. Similar results were also obtained for the smoothed maximum score estimator (SMS) in Kotlyarova and Zinde-Walsh (2010). The general conclusion is that with insufficient smoothness standard asymptotic approximations may be misleading.

3. ESTIMATION OF THE RATE OF THE BIAS

From Table A1 we can see that knowledge of $\bar{v}$ would enable one to find the optimal rate of the bandwidth that minimizes the trace of asymptotic MSE. Moreover, as our example demonstrated, it may be advantageous not to commit to specific $\bar{v}$ even under infinite smoothness, as the usual approximation may be poor.

Under Assumptions 1 and 2, $\bar{v}$ can be consistently estimated; this idea was applied by Woodroofe (1970) to density estimation. Denote by h_o some oversmoothed bandwidth. We assume that such a bandwidth can be obtained. For example, it would be provided by an "optimal" plug-in bandwidth computed on the basis of $v(K)$ rather than $\bar{v}$; such a bandwidth would provide oversmoothing if $\bar{v} < v(k)$; to cover the smooth case as well, it could be magnified by some N^{ε} for a small $\varepsilon > 0$. In Schafgans and Zinde-Walsh (2010) the generalized cross-validation bandwidth was used, since it is known to oversmooth in the ADE case.

Define a sequence of bandwidths $\{h_t\}_{t=1}^{H}$ such that $h_t = c_t h_o N^{\gamma_t}$ for some $c_t > 0$ and $0 \leq \gamma_1 < \cdots < \gamma_H$, where γ_H is such that $h_H = c_H h_o N^{\gamma_H} \to 0$. For ADE, for example, if h_o is given by cross-validation that has the rate $N^{-\frac{1}{2\bar{v}+k}}$, select $\gamma_H < \frac{1}{2\bar{v}+k}$. Let $\mathcal{T}$ define a subset of all pairs $\{(h_t, h_{t'}),\ t, t' = 1, \ldots, H \text{ with } t' < t\}$ with cardinality $Q : 2 \leq Q \leq \frac{H(H+1)}{2}$. Our estimator for the smoothness and the associated optimal bandwidth is provided in the next theorem.

Theorem 1. *Under Assumptions 1 and 2, the estimator for* $\bar{v}, \widehat{\bar{v}}$, *given by*

$$\widehat{\bar{v}} = \frac{\sum_{(t,t')\in\mathcal{T}} \ln\left[\left(\hat{\delta}_N(K, h_t) - \hat{\delta}_N(K, h_{t'})\right)^2\right] \cdot \left(\ln h_t{}^2 - \frac{1}{Q}\sum_{(t,t')\in\mathcal{T}} \ln h_t{}^2\right)}{\sum_{(t,t')\in\mathcal{T}} \left(\ln h_t{}^2 - \frac{1}{Q}\sum_{(t,t')\in\mathcal{T}} \ln h_t{}^2\right)^2}, \tag{4}$$

satisfies $\widehat{\bar{v}} - \bar{v} = o_p((\ln N)^{-1})$. *A bandwidth vector with the optimal rate is consistently estimated by* $\widehat{h^{opt}} = cN^{-\eta(\widehat{\bar{v}})}$, *with* $\eta(\bar{v})$ *specified in Eq. (3).*

Proof. The proof requires comparison of the asymptotic bias and variance contribution in the stochastic expansion of the estimator. It is essentially the same as that given in Schafgans and Zinde-Walsh (2010) Theorem 3.3a, the only difference being that a specific γ_H and rate of h^{opt} are used in Schafgans and Zinde-Walsh (2010). ■

4. ASYMPTOTIC EFFICIENCY OF LINEAR COMBINATIONS OF ESTIMATORS

It was argued in Kotlyarova and Zinde-Walsh (2006) that linear combinations of estimators based on different bandwidths and kernels could provide the rate associated with the best of those estimators, which may not be known a priori. Performance is evaluated in terms of minimizing the trace of the asymptotic MSE. Whereas linear combinations of estimators typically used in the literature are convex combinations, we do not restrict the signs of the weights.

In Schafgans and Zinde-Walsh (2010), it was shown that there exists a linear combination of kernel estimators with different bandwidths that asymptotically outperforms the estimator that uses the optimal bandwidth. Theorem 2 provides this result in the general case.

Theorem 2. *Under Assumptions 1 and 2, for any kernel K and given an optimal bandwidth vector* h^{opt} *there exists a set of S bandwidth vectors* $h_1, \ldots, h_S$ *with* *a corresponding set of weights,* $\{a_s\}_{s=1}^S : \sum_{s=1}^S a_s = 1$*, such that for the linear combination* $\sum_{s=1}^S a_s\hat{\delta}_N(K,h_s)$

$$trAMSE\left(\sum_{s=1}^{S} a_s\hat{\delta}_N(K,h_s)\right) < trAMSE(\delta_N(K,h^{opt})). \tag{5}$$

Proof. See the appendix. ■

The proof gives a specific example of a set of bandwidths and weights that satisfy Eq. (5). The proof of this result relies on the fact that with weights of different signs the leading terms in the biases can be eliminated and the weights can be selected in a way that simultaneously reduces the variance. One kernel is examined in the proof; more kernels would allow for more flexibility in the choice of bandwidths. This theorem could be modified (following Schafgans & Zinde-Walsh, 2010) to account for the use of unequal bandwidths for the different components of the vector $\hat{\delta}_N$.

It can be seen from the construction in the proof that a larger number of bandwidth vectors, S, could also allow more flexibility in the choice of the bandwidths.

5. COMBINED ESTIMATOR

Theorem 2 demonstrated the existence of a linear combination of estimators that exhibits superior performance to the estimators based on individual kernel and bandwidth pairs. We now discuss a combined estimator that optimizes the weights in the linear combination.

Consider a set of kernel/bandwidth pairs, $\{(K,h)_s)\}_{s=1}^S$, and corresponding estimators $\{\hat{\delta}_N(K,h)_s)\}_{s=1}^S$. We note that if only one kernel is considered this set is reduced to $\{\hat{\delta}_N(K,h_s))\}_{s=1}^S$.

We define the infeasible combined estimator by the linear combination $\sum_{s=1}^S a_s\hat{\delta}_N(K,h)_s$ that minimizes the trace of the mean-squared error:

$$\hat{\delta}_{N,comb} = \left\{\sum_{s=1}^{S} \hat{a}_s\hat{\delta}_N(K,h)_s;\right.$$

such that

$$\left.(\hat{a}_1,\ldots,\hat{a}_S) = \underset{\Sigma a_s=1}{\arg\min}\, trMSE\left(\sum_{s=1}^{S} a_s\hat{\delta}_N(K,h)_s\right)\right\}.$$

The infeasible combined estimator is based on the true biases, $bias(\hat{\delta}_N(K,h)_s)$, and true covariances, $cov(\hat{\delta}_N(K,h)_{s_1},\hat{\delta}_N(K,h)_{s_2})$. The computation of the feasible combined estimator requires the estimation of the biases, variances and covariances between the different estimators. Below, we provide numerical results for the normal mixture density in Eq. (1).

5.1. Infeasible Combined Estimator

First, we examine an infeasible combined estimator and demonstrate that, in accordance with Theorem 2, it does provide an improvement relative to using individual estimators based on a single bandwidth/kernel pair even when using an optimal bandwidth.

Table 1 presents the results for the normal mixture density example at various points x_0 based on 1,000 simulations. The infeasible combined estimator uses the second- and fourth-order kernels for a range of bandwidths $(0.8h^{opt}, 0.9h^{opt}, h^{opt}, 1.1h^{opt}, 1.2h^{opt})$, where the AMISE minimizing bandwidth h^{opt} is given by $n^{-1/5}\left(\frac{\int K^2(u)du}{\mu_2^2 \int (f^{(2)}(x))^2 dx}\right)^{1/5}$ for the second-order kernel and $n^{-1/9}\left(\frac{72\int K^2(u)du}{\mu_4^2 \int (f^{(4)}(x))^2 dx}\right)^{1/9}$ for the fourth-order kernel, with $\mu_r = \int u^r K(u)du$ for $r = 2, 4$ (Pagan & Ullah, 1999).

Table 1 shows the range of the RMSE over all bandwidth/kernel pairs under consideration and presents the RMSE of the infeasible combined estimator. The table demonstrates that at $N = 2,000$ and $N = 4,000$ the combined estimator performs better than any individual estimator. The gains in RMSE of the combined estimator are strongest at the peak points $x_0 = 0.75$ and $x_0 = 1.25$. The RMISE over the interval $-2 \leq x_0 \leq 2$ also reveals an overall improvement of the combined estimator over the individual estimators. The values of the RMSE highlight the difference in performance in areas where the function greatly fluctuates as opposed to areas where the change is gradual. The results for the combined estimator that utilizes the asymptotic approximation of the bias were generally less encouraging, although with an increased sample size they start to resemble those based on the true bias. This indicates that the asymptotic approximation may work poorly in finite samples.

In order to obtain a feasible combined estimator, it is necessary to estimate the biases and covariances at different bandwidths and kernels. The feasible combined estimator also uses the second- and fourth-order kernel for bandwidths now anchored around the cross-validated bandwidth h_{cv}: $(0.8h_{cv}, 0.9h_{cv}, h_{cv}, 1.1h_{cv}, 1.2h_{cv})$.

5.2. Bias Estimation

Different bias estimators have been used by the authors in the construction of the combined estimators. Kotlyarova and Zinde-Walsh (2007) used a heuristic bias

Table 1. RMSE of the Individual and Infeasible Combined Density Estimators.

	RMSE		
	Indiv. $\hat{f}_{K,h}(x_0)$	Infeasible Combined	
		True bias	Asy. bias
$N = 2,000$			
$x_0 = -1.0$	0.018 – 0.023	0.011	0.011
$x_0 = 0.0$	0.025 – 0.031	0.015	0.015
$x_0 = 0.50$	0.026 – 0.031	0.023	0.024
$x_0 = 0.75$	0.059 – 0.080	0.049	0.064
$x_0 = 1.00$	0.044 – 0.072	0.040	0.040
$x_0 = 1.25$	0.050 – 0.062	0.044	0.049
$x_0 = 1.50$	0.016 – 0.020	0.014	0.016
RMISE over [–2, 2]	0.059 – 0.070	0.046	0.092
$N = 4,000$			
$x_0 = -1.0$	0.014 – 0.018	0.009	0.009
$x_0 = 0.0$	0.019 – 0.024	0.011	0.011
$x_0 = 0.50$	0.019 – 0.023	0.017	0.018
$x_0 = 0.75$	0.047 – 0.064	0.039	0.051
$x_0 = 1.00$	0.033 – 0.057	0.030	0.030
$x_0 = 1.25$	0.038 – 0.049	0.032	0.037
$x_0 = 1.50$	0.012 – 0.014	0.011	0.011
RMISE over [–2, 2]	0.045 – 0.053	0.034	0.043

estimator for the case of kernel density estimators; the bias was estimated as the difference between a given density estimator and the average of the density estimators at the lowest bandwidth. Note that because of the linear structure of the estimator, one cannot use the standard bootstrap to estimate the bias (Hall, 1992, p. 205). For the semiparametric SMS estimator, Kotlyarova and Zinde-Walsh (2010) utilized the fact that an unbiased (Manski's maximum score) estimator was available. Schafgans and Zinde-Walsh (2010) implemented the strategy outlined above of estimating the smoothness parameter $\bar{v}$, and used oversmoothed estimators to find the components of the bias for the various bandwidths.

In our normal mixture example, we employ two estimates of the bias for $\hat{\delta}_{h,K}$. The first estimator, $\widehat{Bias}(dif)$, is the bias estimator of Kotlyarova and Zinde-Walsh (2007) obtained by computing the difference

$$\widehat{Bias}(dif) = \hat{\delta}_{h,K} - \frac{1}{2}\left(\hat{\delta}_{0.8h_{cv},K_2} + \hat{\delta}_{0.8h_{cv},K_4}\right).$$

The second estimator, $\widehat{Bias}(regr)$, is computed in two steps. The first step applies the regression strategy outlined in Section 3 to estimate $\bar{v} : \widehat{\bar{v}}$ is obtained by OLS

Table 2. Estimated $\bar{\upsilon}$ – Mixture of Normal Density.

	$N=2,000$		$N=4,000$	
	K_4	K_2	K_4	K_2
$x_0=-1.0$	2.88	1.80	3.14	1.78
$x_0=0.0$	2.88	1.83	3.06	1.84
$x_0=0.50$	2.98	1.76	3.09	1.81
$x_0=0.75$	3.90	1.93	3.82	1.96
$x_0=1.00$	3.86	1.97	3.90	1.96
$x_0=1.25$	3.77	1.93	3.65	1.93
$x_0=1.50$	2.96	1.83	2.61	1.85

regression of $\ln\left[\left(\hat{\delta}_{h_t}-\hat{\delta}_{h_{cv}}\right)^2\right]$ on $\ln h_t^2$ for the bandwidths selected here as $(1.1h_{cv}, 1.2h_{cv}, 1.3h_{cv}, 1.4h_{cv}, 1.5h_{cv}, 1.6h_{cv})$. The second step computes for given bandwidth h and kernel K

$$\widehat{Bias}(regr)=\left(\frac{h}{h_o}\right)^{\widehat{\bar{\upsilon}}}\left(\hat{\delta}(K,h_o)-\hat{\delta}(K,h_u)\right),$$

with $h_o=2h_{cv}$ and $h_u=0.5h_{cv}$.

For our mixed normal density, the averages of the estimates of $\bar{\upsilon}$ for each kernel at various locations x_0 are given in Table 2. As in Fig. 3, the estimates for $\bar{\upsilon}$ at $x_0=0.75$, 1.0, and 1.25 are close to $\upsilon(K)$, but at other points $\bar{\upsilon}$ is markedly below the order of the kernel. The orders of the approximating leading bias terms do not always get closer to $\upsilon(K)$ as the sample increases.

5.3. *Covariance estimation*

The covariances can be estimated by using plug-in estimators for the leading terms in the asymptotic expansion of the covariances. The covariances were derived for the density, SMS and ADE estimators in the respective papers Kotlyarova and Zinde-Walsh (2007, 2010) and Schafgans and Zinde-Walsh (2010); in this paper, they are provided in the appendix for the cases of the conditional mean and the average density as well. Alternatively, covariances can be estimated by a bootstrap procedure. Bootstrap estimators for the covariances of the local kernel-based estimators are straightforward. Bootstrap estimators for the covariances of average kernel-based estimators, on the other hand, can lead to a significant bias in the nonparametric term in the bias expansion as documented by Cattaneo, Crump, and Jansson (2014) and Kotlyarova, Schafgans, and Zinde-Walsh (2011).[2]

Table 3. RMSE of the Individual and Feasible Combined Density Estimators.

		RMSE			
	Best K/h	Indiv. $\hat{f}_{K,h}(x_0)$	Combined		
			True bias	$\widehat{Bias}(dif)$	$\widehat{Bias}(regr)$
$N=2,000$					
$x_0=-1.0$	$K_4, 1.2h_{cv}$	0.016* – 0.021	0.016*	0.018	**0.016***
$x_0=0.0$	$K_4, 1.2h_{cv}$	0.022* – 0.028*	0.019**	0.026*	**0.022***
$x_0=0.50$	$K_4, 1.2h_{cv}$	0.028* – 0.033	0.026*	**0.031**	0.045
$x_0=0.75$	K_4, h_{cv}	0.065** – 0.088**	0.053**	**0.071****	0.108**
$x_0=1.00$	$K_4, 0.8h_{cv}$	0.044** – 0.074	0.045*	**0.047***	0.076
$x_0=1.25$	K_4, h_{cv}	0.053** – 0.069**	0.047*	**0.062****	0.105*
$x_0=1.50$	$K_4, 1.2h_{cv}$	0.014** – 0.019	0.018	**0.018**	0.025
RMISE over $[-2, 2]$		0.063 – 0.072	0.057	0.067	0.094
$N=4,000$					
$x_0=-1.0$	$K_4, 1.2h_{cv}$	0.015* – 0.019	0.012*	0.017*	**0.016***
$x_0=0.0$	$K_4, 1.2h_{cv}$	0.018** – 0.024*	0.013**	0.021*	**0.018****
$x_0=0.50$	$K_4, 1.2h_{cv}$	0.019* – 0.025*	0.018**	**0.023***	0.028*
$x_0=0.75$	K_4, h_{cv}	0.052** – 0.069**	0.041**	**0.058****	0.095**
$x_0=1.00$	$K_4, 0.8h_{cv}$	0.033** – 0.056*	0.031**	**0.035****	0.053*
$x_0=1.25$	$K_4, 1.0h_{cv}$	0.042** – 0.052**	0.036**	**0.049****	0.073**
$x_0=1.50$	$K_4, 1.2h_{cv}$	0.010* – 0.013	0.014	**0.012**	0.019
RMISE over $[-2, 2]$		0.047 – 0.054	0.039	0.051	0.067

Note: ** Denotes that the estimator is within 10% of true density; * denotes that the estimator is within 15% of true density.
For each point, we indicate in bold the best feasible combination in order to compare the performance of the two bias estimators.

In our normal mixture density example, we will employ the bootstrap estimator for the covariances.

5.4. *Performance of the feasible combined estimator*

The results for the feasible combined estimator for the density at various points x_0 are presented in Table 3. For reference, we present the RMSE of the infeasible combined estimator that makes use of the true bias but estimates the variances.

To make better sense of the ranges of values at different points, we follow Wolfowitz (1949), who in nonparametric estimation of distribution functions proposed a band around the function with width proportional to the values of the function; these bands provide benchmarks for the relative RMSE.

We note that the individual estimators at the cross-validated bandwidth are not the best at the majority of points; in some cases undersmoothed estimators are the best, and in many cases, oversmoothed. In many cases, some estimators are outside of the 10% or even 15% bands. By comparison, combined estimators are typically better than the worst performing individual estimators and are often within the bands. This confirms the claim that the combined estimator is robust with respect to uncertain smoothness.

Of the combined estimators, the heuristic Kotlyarova and Zinde-Walsh (2007) estimator, $\widehat{Bias}(dif)$, seems to outperform the estimator that uses the Woodroofe (1970) and Schafgans and Zinde-Walsh (2010) approach, $\widehat{Bias}(regr)$. This assertion is supported by RMISE results. With sample size 2,000, the RMISE for the feasible combined estimator equals 0.067 using $\widehat{Bias}(dif)$ and 0.094 using $\widehat{Bias}(regr)$; in comparison the RMISE for the infeasible combined estimator equals 0.057. The disparity diminishes as the sample size increases. Improvements in the estimation of the bias would further enhance the performance of the combined estimator as indicated by the combined estimator that uses the true bias instead.[3]

6. CONCLUSIONS

In this paper, we have explored two main issues.

One is the standard notion that the leading term in the asymptotic expansion, which relies on kernel order, provides a good approximation to the bias of a kernel estimator. We argue that the approximation could be poor even when the smoothness assumptions that justify it apply and illustrate this point in an example of density estimation for a normal mixture distribution. Following Woodroofe, we estimate the bias rate. We conclude that this rate could easily differ from the one determined by kernel order even in fairly large samples. We argue that this implies that it may be beneficial not to commit to a bias rate based on the kernel order, or, alternatively to the corresponding smoothness of the underlying functions.

The second point is that the combined estimator could offer significant advantages over an individual estimator that relies on a particular kernel/bandwidth pair, since there is uncertainty about the degree of smoothness and therefore about the appropriate kernel order and the bandwidth. For the example of density here, we show that the infeasible combined estimator outperforms the best of the individual estimators. The usual strategy for the density example here, which is to select a fourth-order kernel at the cross-validated bandwidth, does not dominate; there is significant uncertainty about how best to select an individual estimator and an error could be costly in terms of RMSE. The feasible combined estimator delivers an estimator that is robust with respect to this uncertainty.

NOTES

1. Marron and Wand (1992) examined normal mixtures and discussed the performance of kernel estimators with evaluation of MISE (mean integrated squared error), asymptotic MISE, integrated squared bias and asymptotic integrated squared bias.

2. Cattaneo et al. (2014) demonstrated this fact for the ADE. In the working paper, Kotlyarova et al. (2011) derived a similar result for non-derivative-based estimators, such as the average density and the average density-weighted moments. For all average estimators considered, the leading non-parametric term in the bootstrap estimator is three times the leading non-parametric term of the variance of the estimator. Suggested corrections to the bootstrap estimator are to divide the estimated value by three or to use the bandwidth $h_{var} = 3^{-\frac{1}{d(k)}} h$ in the bootstrap variance estimation (Cattaneo et al., 2014).

3. It may be of interest to compare the performance of the combined estimator to the performance of other MSE/MISE-reducing kernel estimators.

4. The proof in Schafgans and Zinde-Walsh (2010) mistakenly used the root 1/5 which is only applicable in the trivial case where all the biases are zero.

ACKNOWLEDGEMENT

The authors thank the participants of the Advances in Econometrics Conference in honor of Aman Ullah and the participants of the Canadian Economics Association meeting, in particular Heng Chen. We also thank the anonymous referees who provided insightful comments and useful criticism. This work was supported by the Social Sciences and Humanities Research Council of Canada (SSHRC) and by the *Fonds québecois de la recherche sur la société et la culture* (FQRSC).

REFERENCES

Abadir, K. M., & Lawford, S. (2004). Optimal asymmetric kernels. *Economics Letters, 83*, 61–68.

DiNardo, J., Fortin, N. M., & Lemieux, T. (1996). Labor market institutions and the distribution of wages, 1973-1992: A semiparametric approach. *Econometrica, 64*, 1001–1044.

Hall, P. (1992). *The bootstrap and Edgeworth expansion*. New York, NY: Springer-Verlag.

Hansen, B. E. (2005). Exact mean integrated squared error of higher order kernel estimators. *Econometric Theory, 21*, 1031–1057.

Hasminskii, R., & Ibragimov, I. (1990). On density estimation in the view of Kolmogorov's ideas in approximation theory. *The Annals of Statistics, 18*, 999–1010.

Horowitz, J. L. (1992). A smoothed maximum score estimator for the binary response model. *Econometrica, 60*, 505–531.

Horowitz, J. L., & Härdle, W. (1996). Direct semiparametric estimation of single-index models with discrete covariates. *Journal of the American Statistical Association, 91*, 1632–1640.

Kotlyarova, Y., Schafgans, M. M. A., & Zinde-Walsh, V. (2011). *Adapting kernel estimation to uncertain smoothness*. STICERD Paper No. EM/2011/557.

Kotlyarova, Y., & Zinde-Walsh, V. (2006). Non- and semi-parametric estimation in models with unknown smoothness. *Economics Letters, 93*, 379–386.
Kotlyarova, Y., & Zinde-Walsh, V. (2007). Robust kernel estimator for densities of unknown smoothness. *Journal of Nonparametric Statistics, 19*, 89–101.
Kotlyarova, Y., & Zinde-Walsh, V. (2010). Robust estimation in binary choice models. *Communications in Statistics – Theory and Methods, 39*, 266–279.
Li, Q., & Racine, J. (2007). *Nonparametric econometrics: Theory and practice*. Princeton, NJ: Princeton University Press.
Marron, J. S., & Wand, M. P. (1992). Exact mean integrated squared error. *Annals of Statistics, 20*, 712–736.
Pagan, A., & Ullah, A. (1999). *Nonparametric econometrics*. Cambridge: Cambridge University Press.
Powell, J. L., Stock, J. H., & Stoker, T. M. (1989). Semiparametric estimation of index coefficients. *Econometrica, 57*, 1403–1430.
Schafgans, M. M. A., & Zinde-Walsh, V. (2010). Smoothness adaptive average derivative estimation. *Econometrics Journal, 13*, 40–62.
Silverman, B. W. (1986). *Density estimation for statistics and data analysis*. London: Chapman and Hall.
Stoker, T. M. (1991). Equivalence of direct, indirect, and slope estimators of average derivatives. In W. A. Barnett, J. Powell, & G. E. Tauchen (Eds.). *Nonparametric and semiparametric estimation methods in econometrics and statistics*. Cambridge: Cambridge University Press.
Wolfowitz, J. (1949). Non-parametric statistical inference. In Neyman J. (Ed.) *Proceedings of the First Berkeley Symposium on Mathematical Statistics and Probability* (pp. 93–114).
Woodroofe, M. (1970). On choosing a delta sequence. *The Annals of Mathematical Statistics, 41*, 1665–1671.

APPENDIX

In this appendix, we first provide results for the average density and the Nadaraya–Watson estimator. The results confirm that these estimators can satisfy our Assumptions 1 and 2. The covariances, needed for our combined estimator, are provided as well. The results for the covariances can be adapted easily to allow for unequal bandwidths for the different components. This appendix then provides the proof of Theorem 2 and finally a Table on AMSE rates.

A.1. Average Density Estimator

Consider the average density estimator for $f(x)$ with degree of smoothness $\bar{\upsilon}$:

$$\hat{\delta}_N(K,h) = \tfrac{1}{N}\sum_{i=1}^{N} \hat{f}_{(K,h)}(x_i) = \tfrac{1}{N(N-1)} h^{-k} \sum_{i=1}^{N}\sum_{j\neq i}^{N} K\left(\frac{x_i - x_j}{h}\right).$$

We have

$$\begin{aligned} E\left(\hat{\delta}_N(K,h)\right) &= h^{-k} E\left[E\left(K\left(\frac{x_i - x_j}{h}\right)|x_j\right)\right] \\ &= h^{-k} E\left[\int K\left(\frac{x_i - x_j}{h}\right) f(x_i)dx_i\right] \\ &= E\left[\int K(u) f(x_j + uh)du\right] = E(f(x)) + h^{\bar{\upsilon}}\mathcal{B}(K) + o(h^{\bar{\upsilon}}). \end{aligned}$$

The covariance is provided in Lemma 1.

Lemma 1. *Under Assumptions 1 and 2, if* $h_s \to 0$ *and* $N^2 h_s^k \to \infty$ *for* $s = 1, \ldots, S$, *the covariance of* $\hat{\delta}_N(K_{s_1}, h_{s_1})$ *and* $\hat{\delta}_N(K_{s_2}, h_{s_2})$, Γ_{s_1,s_2}, *for* $s_1, s_2 = 1, \ldots, S$ *is*

$$\Gamma_{s_1,s_2} = N^{-2} h_{s_2}^{-k}\left(\Sigma_1(K_{s_1}, K_{s_2}, h_{s_1}, h_{s_2}) + o(1)\right) + (\Sigma_2 + o(1))\, N^{-1},$$

with

$$\begin{aligned} &\Sigma_1(K_{s_1}, K_{s_2}, h_{s_1}, h_{s_2}) = 2E\left[f(x_i)\right]\kappa_2(K_{s_1}, K_{s_2}, h_{s_1}, h_{s_2}); \\ &\kappa_2(K_{s_1}, K_{s_2}, h_{s_1}, h_{s_2}) = \int K_{s_1}(u) K_{s_2}\left(u\frac{h_{s_1}}{h_{s_2}}\right) du; \\ &\Sigma_2 = 4E\left[(f(x_i) - Ef(x_i))^2\right]. \end{aligned}$$

The proof is similar to that derived for the ADE in Schafgans and Zinde-Walsh (2010) and has therefore been omitted.

A.2. *Conditional Mean Estimator*

Consider the Nadaraya–Watson Kernel regression estimator for the model $Y_i = g(X_i) + u_i$:

$$\hat{\delta}_N(K, h, x) = \hat{g}(x) = \frac{\frac{1}{Nh^k}\sum_{i=1}^N K(\frac{X_i - x}{h})Y_i}{\frac{1}{Nh^k}\sum_{i=1}^N K(\frac{X_i - x}{h})}.$$

Following the notation in Li and Racine (2007, p. 61),

$$\hat{g}(x) - g(x) = \frac{\left(\hat{g}(x) - g(x)\right)\hat{f}(x)}{\hat{f}(x)} \equiv \frac{\hat{m}(x)}{\hat{f}(x)} = \frac{\hat{m}_1(x) + \hat{m}_2(x)}{\hat{f}(x)} = \frac{\hat{m}_1(x) + \hat{m}_2(x)}{f(x) + o_p(1)},$$

where

$$\hat{m}_1(x) = \frac{1}{Nh^k}\sum_{i=1}^N (g(X_i) - g(x))K\left(\frac{X_i - x}{h}\right);$$

$$\hat{m}_2(x) = \frac{1}{Nh^k}\sum_{i=1}^N u_i K\left(\frac{X_i - x}{h}\right).$$

Assume $f(x) > 0$, $\hat{g}(x) - g(x) = O_p\left(\frac{\hat{m}(x)}{f(x) + o_p(1)}\right)$ and smoothness of order $\bar{v}$. Since

$$\begin{aligned}
E(\hat{m}_1(x)) &= h^{-k}\left[E\left((g(z) - g(x))K\left(\frac{z - x}{h}\right)\right)\right] \\
&= h^{-k}\left[\int (g(z) - g(x))f(z)K\left(\frac{z - x}{h}\right)dz\right] \\
&= \left[\int f(x + uh)(g(x + uh) - g(x))K(u)du\right] = h^{\bar{v}}\mathcal{B}_m(K, x) + o(h^{\bar{v}}), \\
E(\hat{m}_2(x)) &= 0,
\end{aligned}$$

we have

$$E\left(\hat{\delta}_N(K, h, x)\right) = g(x) + h^{\bar{v}}\mathcal{B}(K, x) + o(h^{\bar{v}}),$$

where $\mathcal{B}(K, x) = \mathcal{B}_m(K, x)/f(x)$. The covariance is provided in Lemma 2.

Lemma 2. *Under Assumptions 1 and 2, if* $h_s \to 0$ *and* $Nh_s^k \to \infty$ *for* $s=1,\ldots,S$, *the covariance of* $\hat{\delta}_N(K_{s_1},h_{s_1})$ *and* $\hat{\delta}_N(K_{s_2},h_{s_2})$, Γ_{s_1,s_2}, *for* $s_1,s_2=1,\ldots,S$ *is*

$$\Gamma_{s_1,s_2}=N^{-1}h_{s_2}^{-k}\left(\Sigma_1(K_{s_1},K_{s_2},h_{s_1},h_{s_2})+o(1)\right),$$

with

$$\Sigma_1(K_{s_1},K_{s_2},h_{s_1},h_{s_2})=\frac{\sigma^2(x)}{f(x)}\kappa_2(K_{s_1},K_{s_2},h_{s_1},h_{s_2});$$

$$\kappa_2(K_{s_1},K_{s_2},h_{s_1},h_{s_2})=\int K_{s_1}(u)K_{s_2}\left(u\frac{h_{s_1}}{h_{s_2}}\right)du.$$

The proof of this lemma has also been left out as it follows readily from Schafgans and Zinde-Walsh (2010).

A.3. *Proof of Theorem 2.*

For this proof, it is sufficient to give a set of bandwidths with a corresponding set of weights, such that the leading bias terms will cancel out and the variance will not inflate. We consider each ith component of $\hat{\delta}_N(K,h_s)$ separately and suppress the subscript i.

We first find, for a given set of bandwidths h_s, $s=1,\ldots,S$, a norm-minimizing set of weights a_s which satisfy the conditions that the weights eliminate the leading bias term and sum to one (the weights are not necessarily non-negative). To do this, we solve

$$\min \Sigma_{s=1}^S a_s^2, \quad \text{subject to } \Sigma_{s=1}^S a_s=1; \quad \Sigma_{s=1}^S a_s h_s^{\bar{v}}=0, \tag{A.1}$$

noting that $\Sigma_{s=1}^S a_s B_i(K)h_s^{\bar{v}}=0$ implies that $\Sigma_{s=1}^S a_s h_s^{\bar{v}}=0$. We denote $h_s^{\bar{v}}$ by b_s; then the Lagrangian is given by

$$\Sigma_{s=1}^S a_s^2-\lambda(\Sigma_{s=1}^S a_s-1)-\theta\Sigma_{s=1}^S a_s b_s.$$

From the FOC, we obtain

$$\lambda=2\Sigma a_s^2;\quad \theta=\frac{2-2S\Sigma a_s^2}{\Sigma b_s};\quad \text{and}\quad a_s=\frac{1}{2}(\lambda+\theta b_s).$$

Denoting Σa_s^2 by ψ, we obtain $a_s=\psi+\frac{1-S\psi}{\Sigma b_s}b_s$. By squaring and summing a_s for $s=1,\ldots,S$, we get

$$\psi=S\psi^2+2\psi(1-S\psi)+(1-S\psi)^2\frac{\Sigma b_s^2}{(\Sigma b_s)^2}.$$

This quadratic equation for ψ has a root of $\frac{1}{S}$ as a solution to the FOC, the other root is $\psi = \frac{\Sigma b_s^2}{S\Sigma b_s^2 - (\Sigma b_s)^2}$. This provides the general form for ψ. [4]

Given these weights, the trace AMSE of a linear combination reduces to the trace of the asymptotic variance of the linear combination that includes the covariance terms. Denote $\hat{\delta}_N(K, h_s)$ by $\hat{\delta}_s$ and let Σ_{ii} denote the ith diagonal element of the matrix $N^{-\omega}\Sigma(K)$ from Assumption 2(a) or $N^{-\omega}\Sigma_1(K)$ from Assumption 2(b), whichever is appropriate. Given the usual bound for covariance via variances we can bound the trace AMSE:

$$
\begin{aligned}
tr\left(Avar\left(\sum_{s=1}^{S} a_s \hat{\delta}_s\right)\right) &= \sum_{s_1,s_2}^{S} a_{s_1} a_{s_2} \sum_{i=1}^{k} Acov(\hat{\delta}_{s_1,i}, \hat{\delta}_{s_2,i}) \\
&\leq \sum_{s_1,s_2}^{S} |a_{s_1} a_{s_2}| \sum_{i=1}^{k} \left|Acov(\hat{\delta}_{s_1,i}, \hat{\delta}_{s_2,i})\right| \\
&\leq \sum_{s_1,s_2}^{S} |a_{s_1} a_{s_2}| \sum_{i=1}^{k} \max_{j=1,2} Avar(\hat{\delta}_{s_j,i}) \\
&= \sum_{s_1,s_2}^{S} |a_{s_1} a_{s_2}| \max_{j=1,2} h_{s_j}^{-d(k)} \sum_{i=1}^{k} \Sigma_{ii}.
\end{aligned}
$$

Next, we substitute the values of the selected bandwidths $h_s = c_{s,i} h_i^{opt}$ to enable us to further bound the trace AMSE using the smallest of all the $c_{s,i}$ by

$$
\sum_{s_1,s_2}^{S} |a_{s_1} a_{s_2}| \left(\min_{j=1,2,i=1,\ldots,k} c_{s_j,i}\right)^{-d(k)} \sum_{i=1}^{k} (h_i^{opt})^{-d(k)} \Sigma_{ii},
$$

as we use the same bandwidths for all components $c_{s,i} h_i^{opt} = c_{s,1} h_1^{opt}$. Note that the optimal bandwidth has components with the same rates that may vary in the constant, since $B_i(K)$ may differ for different i. Using the bound

$$
\begin{aligned}
\Sigma_{s_1,s_2=1}^{S} \left|a_{s_1 i} a_{s_2 i}\right| &\leq S\left(\Sigma_{s_1,s_2=1}^{S} \left|a_{s_1 i}\right|^2\right)^{1/2} \left(\Sigma_{s_1,s_2=1}^{S} \left|a_{s_2 i}\right|^2\right)^{1/2} \\
&= S\psi^{1/2}\psi^{1/2} = S\psi,
\end{aligned}
$$

we finally obtain

$$tr\left(Avar\left(\sum_{s=1}^{S} a_s\hat{\delta}_s\right)\right) \leq \left(\min_{s,i} c_{s,i}\right)^{-d(k)} S\psi \cdot tr\left(Avar\hat{\delta}^{opt}\right).$$

Recall that $\psi = \frac{\Sigma b_s^2}{S\Sigma b_s^2 - (\Sigma b_s)^2}$ and $b_s = h_s^{\bar{v}}$. Superiority of the combination will follow if we can show that there exist $c_{s,i}$ such that

$$(\min c_{s,i})^{-d(k)} S \frac{\Sigma c_{s,i}^{2\bar{v}}}{S\Sigma c_{s,i}^{2\bar{v}} - \left(\Sigma c_{s,i}^{\bar{v}}\right)^2} < 1.$$

Suppose that h_1^{opt} is the largest among the components of the optimal bandwidth; then $c_{s,1}$ is the smallest among $c_{s,i}$ for a fixed s. Recall that, for every i, $c_{s,i}$ is proportional to $c_{s,1}$ with the same coefficient of proportionality: $c_{s,i} = \left(\frac{h_1^{opt}}{h_i^{opt}}\right) c_{s,1}$. Then, it is sufficient to show that

$$(\min c_{s,1})^{-d(k)} S \frac{\Sigma c_{s,1}^{2\bar{v}}}{S\Sigma c_{s,1}^{2\bar{v}} - \left(\Sigma c_{s,1}^{\bar{v}}\right)^2} < 1.$$

Equivalently (dropping subscript 1),

$$\left((\min c_s)^{-d(k)} - 1\right) S\Sigma c_s^{2\bar{v}} + \left(\Sigma c_s^{\bar{v}}\right)^2 < 0. \tag{A.2}$$

To conclude the proof, we show that there exists some S and a set of c_s, $s = 1, \ldots, S$, which satisfies this inequality.

We observe that the left-hand side of Eq. (A.2) is monotone in $d(k)$ and $d(k) \geq 1$. Thus, Eq. (A.2) would hold for any $d(k)$ as long as it holds for $d(k) = 1$. We therefore set $d(k) = 1$. Define $c_s = \beta^{s/\bar{v}}$, $\beta > 1$.

As the sums in Eq. (A.2) are sums of geometric progressions, for the inequality to hold we require that there exist β and S for which

$$\left(\beta^{-\frac{1}{\bar{v}}} - 1\right) S \frac{\beta^{2S+2} - 1}{\beta^2 - 1} + \left(\frac{\beta^{S+1} - 1}{\beta - 1}\right)^2 < 0.$$

Cancelling the common factors, we get the condition that

$$\left(\beta^{-\frac{1}{\bar{v}}} - 1\right) S \frac{\beta^{S+1} + 1}{\beta + 1} + \frac{\beta^{S+1} - 1}{\beta - 1} < 0.$$

This inequality can be rewritten as

$$S\left(1-\beta^{-\frac{1}{\bar{v}}}\right)\left(\beta^{S+2}-\beta^{S+1}+\beta-1\right)-\left(\beta^{S+2}+\beta^{S+1}-\beta-1\right)>0$$

or

$$S\left(\beta^{\frac{1}{\bar{v}}}-1\right)\left(\beta^{S+2}-\beta^{S+1}+\beta-1\right)-\left(\beta^{S+2+\frac{1}{\bar{v}}}+\beta^{S+1+\frac{1}{\bar{v}}}-\beta^{1+\frac{1}{\bar{v}}}-\beta^{\frac{1}{\bar{v}}}\right)>0.$$

Collecting terms yields

$$\begin{aligned}\beta^{S+2+\frac{1}{\bar{v}}}(S-1)-\beta^{S+1+\frac{1}{\bar{v}}}(S+1)+\beta^{1+\frac{1}{\bar{v}}}\,(S+1)-\beta^{\frac{1}{\bar{v}}}\,(S-1)\\ -S\left(\beta^{S+2}-\beta^{S+1}+\beta-1\right)>0.\end{aligned}$$

The term with the highest exponent, $\beta^{S+2+\frac{1}{\bar{v}}}$, has a positive coefficient. We conclude that for any $S>1$, $\bar{v}>0$ there exists a β (possibly large) such that the inequality holds. ■

Indeed, suppose that $\bar{v}=2$. Given $S=5$ the inequality holds with $\beta=3$ (or 2.9). If $\bar{v}=1$, with five bandwidths we can select $\beta=2.2$.

Table A.4. AMSE Rates.

Estimated δ	AMSE Terms	Optimal Bandwidth rate	MSE Rate	
			Smooth $\bar{v} = v(K)$	Non-Smooth $\bar{v} < v(K)$
Density, $\hat{f}_{(K,h)}(x)$ $\frac{1}{Nh^k}\sum_{i=1}^{N} K\left(\frac{X_i - x}{h}\right)$	$h^{2\bar{v}}\mathcal{B}(K)\mathcal{B}(K)^T +$ $(Nh^k)^{-1}\Sigma(K)$	$N^{-\frac{1}{2\bar{v}+k}}$	$N^{-\frac{2v(K)}{2v(K)+k}}$ (PU, 1999)	$h^{2\bar{v}}$ (KZW, 2007)
Conditional Mean $\frac{\frac{1}{Nh^k}\sum_{i=1}^{N} K\left(\frac{X_i - x}{h}\right)Y_i}{\hat{f}_{(K,h)}(x)}$	$h^{2\bar{v}}\mathcal{B}(K)\mathcal{B}(K)^T +$ $(Nh^k)^{-1}\Sigma(K)$	$N^{-\frac{1}{2\bar{v}+k}}$	$N^{-\frac{2v(K)}{2v(K)+k}}$ (PU, 1999)	$h^{2\bar{v}}$ (see A.2.)
Average Density $\frac{1}{N}\sum_{i=1}^{N} \hat{f}_{(K,h)}(X_i)$	$h^{2\bar{v}}\mathcal{B}(K)\mathcal{B}(K)^T +$ $N^{-2}h^{-k}\Sigma_1(K) + N^{-1}\Sigma_2$	$N^{-\frac{2}{2\bar{v}+k}}$	N^{-1}	Either $h^{2\bar{v}}$ or $N^{-2}h^{-k}$ (see A.2.)
ADE (PSS) $-\frac{2}{N}\sum_{i=1}^{N} \frac{\partial \hat{f}_{(K,h)}(X_i)}{\partial x} Y_i$	$h^{2\bar{v}}\mathcal{B}(K)\mathcal{B}(K)^T +$ $N^{-2}h^{-(k+2)}\Sigma_1(K) + N^{-1}\Sigma_2$	$N^{-\frac{2}{2\bar{v}+k+2}}$	N^{-1} (PU, 1999)	Either $h^{2\bar{v}}$ or $N^{-2}h^{-(k+2)}$ (SZW, 2010)

Note: PU, 1999 stands for the reference Pagan and Ullah, 1999; KZW, 2007 stands for Kotlyarova and Zinde-Walsh, 2007; SZW, 2010 stands for Schafgans and Zinde-Walsh, 2010.

A CLASS OF NONPARAMETRIC DENSITY DERIVATIVE ESTIMATORS BASED ON GLOBAL LIPSCHITZ CONDITIONS

Kairat Mynbaev[a], Carlos Martins-Filho[b,c] and Aziza Aipenova[d,e]

[a]*International School of Economics, Kazakh-British Technical University, Almaty, Kazakhstan*

[b]*Department of Economics, University of Colorado at Boulder, Boulder, CO, USA*

[c]*IFPRI, Washington, DC, USA*

[d]*Department of Mechanics and Mathematics, Kazakh National University, Almaty, Kazakhstan*

[e]*Faculty of Engineering and Natural Sciences, Suleyman Demirel University, Almaty, Kazakhstan*

ABSTRACT

Estimators for derivatives associated with a density function can be useful in identifying its modes and inflection points. In addition, these estimators play an important role in plug-in methods associated with bandwidth selection in nonparametric kernel density estimation. In this paper, we extend

Essays in Honor of Aman Ullah
Advances in Econometrics, Volume 36, 591–615

ISSN: 0731-9053/doi:10.1108/S0731-905320160000036026

the nonparametric class of density estimators proposed by Mynbaev and Martins-Filho (2010) to the estimation of m*-order density derivatives. Contrary to some existing derivative estimators, the estimators in our proposed class have a full asymptotic characterization, including uniform consistency and asymptotic normality. An expression for the bandwidth that minimizes an asymptotic approximation for the estimators' integrated squared error is provided. A Monte Carlo study sheds light on the finite sample performance of our estimators and contrasts it with that of density derivative estimators based on the classical Rosenblatt–Parzen approach.*

Keywords: Nonparametric derivative estimation; Lipschitz conditions

AMS-MS classifications: 62G07; 62G20

JEL classifications: C14; C18

1. INTRODUCTION

Let f be a density associated with a real random variable X and $\{X_j\}_{j=1}^n$ be an independent and identically distributed random sample of size n from f. The Rosenblatt–Parzen estimator for the density f evaluated at $x \in \mathbb{R}$ is given by

$$\hat{f}_{RP}(x) = \frac{1}{n} \sum_{j=1}^{n} \frac{1}{h_n} K\left(\frac{x - X_j}{h_n}\right),$$

where $h_n > 0$ is a global bandwidth and K is a kernel on $\mathbb{R}$ satisfying

$$\int_{-\infty}^{+\infty} K(t)dt = 1. \tag{1}$$

If f and K are $m \in \mathbb{N}$ times continuously differentiable, with $f^{(m)}$ and $K^{(m)}$ denoting their mth order derivatives, the most commonly used estimator of $f^{(m)}$ at $x \in \mathbb{R}$ (Bhattacharya, 1967) is given by $\hat{f}_{RP}^{(m)}(x) = \frac{1}{n} \sum_{j=1}^{n} \frac{1}{h_n^{m+1}} K^{(m)}\left(\frac{x-X_j}{h_n}\right)$.

Estimators for $f^{(m)}$ are important in various contexts. They can be used to evaluate the location of modes and inflection points of f, to construct plug-in bandwidths for kernel density estimation of f, and can be applied to the estimation of scores in certain additive models (Härdle & Stoker, 1989). The asymptotic properties of $\hat{f}_{RP}^{(m)}(x)$ have been studied by, among others, Bhattacharya (1967), Schuster (1969), and Silverman (1978). Singh (1977, 1979, 1987) shows that it is possible to reduce bias and improve the mean integrated squared error (MISE) of $\hat{f}^{(m)}_{RP}(x)$ by considering restrictions on the class of kernels K used in its construction. Similar efforts have been undertaken by Muller (1984) and Henderson and Parmeter (2012).

Recently, Mynbaev and Martins-Filho (2010) proposed a class of nonparametric density estimators that attains bias reduction relative to $\hat{f}_{RP}(x)$ by imposing global higher order Lipschitz conditions on f. Usually, the order of the bias for $\hat{f}_{RP}(x)$ is established by requiring that f be r-times ($r \in \mathbb{N}$) differentiable. They show that r-times differentiability is stronger than a Lipschitz order r. Hence, although some smoothness is still required to attain a suitable order for the bias, the constraint on the class of densities containing f is milder than what is traditionally required. In practice, certain discontinuous densities satisfy global Lipschitz conditions of a certain order, but are not differentiable of the same order.[1]

In this paper, we propose a new class of estimators for $f^{(m)}$ by considering m-order derivatives of the kernel density estimators in the class proposed in Mynbaev and Martins-Filho (2010). We provide a full asymptotic characterization of the new density derivative estimators, including uniform consistency, asymptotic normality and give exact convergence rates. An important by-product of our results is an expression and the exact order for the bias for the density estimators proposed in Mynbaev and Martins-Filho (2010). There, they only provide the order of the bound on the absolute bias. This is useful, since it allows for our discussion of optimal bandwidth selection based on the minimization of an asymptotic approximation for the integrated mean-squared error.

Besides this introduction, this paper contains four more sections. The next section provides new estimators for $f^{(m)}$ based on a class of density estimators proposed in Mynbaev and Martins-Filho (2010) and a fundamental integral representation for their bias. The following section provides asymptotic properties of our estimators and discusses optimal bandwidth selection. Then, we provide a small Monte Carlo study that gives some evidence on the small sample properties of our estimators and compares their performance to that of $\hat{f}^{(m)}_{RP}$. Finally, the last section provides a conclusion. All proofs and technical lemmas are collected in the appendix.

2. A CLASS OF ESTIMATORS FOR $f^{(m)}(x)$ AND THEIR BIAS

The properties of nonparametric density estimators are traditionally obtained by imposing smoothness conditions on the underlying density f. Smoothness can be regulated by finite differences, which can be defined as forward, backward, or centered. The corresponding examples of finite first-order differences for a function $f(x)$ are $f(x+h)-f(x)$, $f(x)-f(x-h)$, and $f(x+h)-f(x-h)$, where $h\in\mathbb{R}$. We will focus on centered even-order differences because, as will soon become apparent, the resulting kernels are symmetric. Let $C_{2k}^{l}=\frac{(2k)!}{(2k-l)!l!}$, $l=0,\ldots,2k$, $k\in\mathbb{N}$ be the binomial coefficients, $c_{k,s}=(-1)^{s+k}C_{2k}^{s+k}$, $s=-k$, $\ldots,k$ and

$$\Delta_h^{2k}f(x)=\sum_{s=-k}^{k}c_{k,s}f(x+sh),\qquad h\in\mathbb{R}. \tag{2}$$

For example, taking $k=1,2$ we have $\Delta_h^2 f(x)=[f(x+h)-f(x)]-[f(x)-f(x-h)]$ and $\Delta_h^4 f(x)=[f(x+2h)-f(x+h)]-3[f(x+h)-f(x)]+3[f(x)-f(x-h)]-[f(x-h)-f(x-2h)]$.

We say that a function $f(x):\mathbb{R}\to\mathbb{R}$ satisfies the Lipschitz condition of order $2k$ if for any $x\in\mathbb{R}$ there exist $H(x)>0$ and $\varepsilon(x)>0$ such that $\left|\Delta_h^{2k}f(x)\right|\le H(x)h^{2k}$ for all h such that $|h|\le\varepsilon(x)$. We call $H(x)$ a Lipschitz constant and $\varepsilon(x)$ a Lipschitz radius.[2] For a kernel K, Mynbaev and Martins-Filho (2010) define a class of kernels $\{M_k(x)\}_{k=1,2,3,\ldots}$ where

$$M_k(x)=-\frac{1}{c_{k,0}}\sum_{|s|=1}^{k}\frac{c_{k,s}}{|s|}K\left(\frac{x}{s}\right). \tag{3}$$

K is called a seed kernel for M_k. The main impetus for the definition of $M_k(x)$ is that it allows us to express the bias of our proposed estimator

$$\hat{f}_k(x)=\frac{1}{n}\sum_{j=1}^{n}\frac{1}{h_n}M_k\left(\frac{x-X_j}{h_n}\right)\qquad\text{for } k=1,2,\ldots$$

in terms of centered even-order differences of $f(x)$. Let $\lambda_{k,s}=\frac{(-1)^{s+1}(k!)^2}{(k+s)!(k-s)!}$, $s=1,\ldots,k$ and since $-\frac{c_{k,s}}{c_{k,0}}=-\frac{c_{k,-s}}{c_{k,0}}=\lambda_{k,s}$, $s=1,\ldots,k$, (3) can also be written as $M_k(x)=\sum_{s=1}^{k}\frac{\lambda_{k,s}}{s}\left(K\left(\frac{x}{s}\right)+K\left(-\frac{x}{s}\right)\right)$. It follows by construction that M_k is symmetric, that is, $M_k(x)=M_k(-x)$, $x\in\mathbb{R}$. Since the coefficients $c_{k,s}$ satisfy $\sum_{|s|=0}^{k}c_{k,s}=(1-1)^{2k}=0$, we have $-\frac{1}{c_{k,0}}\sum_{|s|=1}^{k}c_{k,s}=1$ or $\sum_{s=1}^{k}\lambda_{k,s}=\frac{1}{2}$.

Consequently, Eqs. (1) and (3) imply that $\int_{-\infty}^{+\infty}M_k(x)dx=\sum_{s=1}^{k}\frac{\lambda_{k,s}}{s}\left(\int_{-\infty}^{+\infty}K\left(\frac{x}{s}\right)dx+\int_{-\infty}^{+\infty}K\left(-\frac{x}{s}\right)dx\right)=1$, establishing that $\{M_k(x)\}_{k=1,2,\ldots}$ is a class of kernels. Tsybakov (2009) provides several choices for a seed kernel K, but perhaps the most popular would be a Gaussian density. In this case, $\hat{f}_k(x)$ has derivatives of all orders. It should also be noted that when K is symmetric $\hat{f}_1(x)$ is the traditional Rosenblatt–Parzen density estimator. We define a new class of $m=1,2,\ldots$ order nonparametric estimators for $f^{(m)}$ by

$$\hat{f}_k^{(m)}(x) = \frac{1}{n}\sum_{j=1}^{n}\frac{1}{h_n^{m+1}}M_k^{(m)}\left(\frac{x-X_j}{h_n}\right) = \frac{1}{n}\sum_{j=1}^{n}u_j \tag{4}$$

where $u_j = \frac{1}{h_n^{m+1}}M_k^{(m)}\left(\frac{x-X_j}{h_n}\right)$ and

$$M_k^{(m)}(x) = -\frac{1}{c_{k,0}}\sum_{|s|=1}^{k}\frac{c_{k,s}}{|s|s^m}K^{(m)}\left(\frac{x}{s}\right). \tag{5}$$

It follows from the fact that $\{X_j\}_{j=1}^n$ is an independent and identically distributed random sample that

$$E\left(\hat{f}_k^{(m)}(x)\right) = \frac{1}{n}\sum_{j=1}^{n}\frac{1}{h_n^{m+1}}E\left(M_k^{(m)}\left(\frac{x-X_j}{h_n}\right)\right) = \frac{1}{n}\sum_{j=1}^{n}E(u_j) = E(u_1) \tag{6}$$

and

$$\begin{aligned} V\left(\hat{f}_k^{(m)}(x)\right) &= V\left(\frac{1}{n}\sum_{j=1}^{n}\frac{1}{h_n^{m+1}}M_k^{(m)}\left(\frac{x-X_j}{h_n}\right)\right) = \frac{1}{n^2}\sum_{j=1}^{n}V(u_j) \\ &= \frac{V(u_1)}{n} = \frac{1}{n}(E(u_1^2) - E(u_1)^2). \end{aligned} \tag{7}$$

As in the existing literature, restrictions on K and f are needed to obtain a suitable representation for the bias and variance of the density derivative estimators. Hence, we assume that

Assumption 1.

(a) K is symmetric and belongs to the weighted Sobolev space with norm $\|K\|_{W_1^m} = \int_{\mathbb{R}}\left(|K(t)| + |K^{(m)}(t)|\right)|t|dt$.

(b) $\max\left\{|f(s)|, \ldots, |f^{(m-1)}(s)|\right\} = O(s),\ |s| \to \infty.$

Assumption 1 is used to obtain an integral representation for the bias $B(\hat{f}_k^{(m)}(x)) = E(\hat{f}_k^{(m)}(x)) - f^{(m)}(x)$ of $\hat{f}_k^{(m)}(x)$ in terms of centered even order differences of $f^{(m)}(x)$. Most of other results depend on this representation.

Theorem 1. *Under Assumption 1, for any $h_n > 0$, $B(\hat{f}_k^{(m)}(x)) = -\frac{1}{c_{k,0}}\int_{-\infty}^{+\infty}K(t)\Delta_{h_nt}^{2k}f^{(m)}(x)dt$.*

3. ASYMPTOTIC CHARACTERIZATION OF $\hat{f}_k^{(m)}(x)$

3.1. Uniform Consistency and Orders for Bias and Variance

We start our investigation of the asymptotic behavior of $\hat{f}_k^{(m)}(x)$ by providing conditions under which the estimator is asymptotically uniformly unbiased and uniformly consistent. To establish the uniform consistency $\hat{f}_k^{(m)}(x)$, we make the following assumption:

Assumption 2.

(a) The characteristic function ϕ_K *of* K *satisfies* $\int_{\mathbb{R}} |s^m \phi_K(s)| ds < \infty$*; (b)* $f^{(m)}(x)$ *is bounded and uniformly continuous in* $\mathbb{R}$*; (c)* $nh_n^{2m+2} \to \infty$ *as* $n \to \infty$*.*

Theorem 2. *Suppose that Assumption 2(a) and (c) hold. Then,*

$$\lim_{n\to\infty} E\left(\sup_{x\in\mathbb{R}} |\hat{f}_k^{(m)}(x) - E(\hat{f}_k^{(m)}(x))|\right) = 0.$$

Let also Assumption 2(b) hold. Then $\hat{f}_k^{(m)}(x)$ *is uniformly consistent.*

We note that the rate of decay of the bandwidth in Assumption 2(c), needed for the uniform consistency of $\hat{f}_k^{(m)}(x)$, could potentially be relaxed by, for example, limiting uniform consistency to restricted (compact) subsets of $\mathbb{R}$. In the following theorem, we provide exact orders for the bias and variance of the estimators. As a result, it can be promptly verified that the usual rate of decay of h_n implied by $nh_n^{2m+1} \to \infty$ as $n \to \infty$ is sufficient for pointwise consistency. The theorem depends on the following assumption.

Assumption 3.

(a) $f^{(m)}(x)$ *is bounded and continuous in* $\mathbb{R}$*; (b) there exist functions* $H_{2k,m}(x) > 0$ *and* $\varepsilon_{2k}(x) > 0$ *such that*

$$\left|\Delta_h^{2k} f^{(m)}(x)\right| \le H_{2k,m}(x) h^{2k} \quad \text{for all } |h| \le \varepsilon_{2k}(x); \tag{8}$$

(c) $\int_{-\infty}^{\infty} |K(t)| t^{2k} dt < \infty$*.*

Theorem 3. *Suppose that Assumptions 1 and 3 hold. Then, for all* $x \in \mathbb{R}$ *and* $0 < h_n \le \varepsilon_{2k}(x)$

$$\left|B(\hat{f}_k^{(m)}(x))\right| \le c h_n^{2k} \left(H_{2k,m}(x) + \varepsilon_{2k}^{-2k}(x)\right) \tag{9}$$

where the constant c does not depend on x or h_n. Suppose additionally that $\int_{-\infty}^{\infty} |K^{(m)}(t)|^2(1+|t|)dt < \infty$ *and there exist functions* $H_1(x) > 0$ *and* $\varepsilon_1(x) > 0$ *such that*

$$|f(x) - f(x-h)| \leq H_1(x)|h| \quad \text{for all } |h| \leq \varepsilon_1(x). \tag{10}$$

Then, for all $x \in \mathbb{R}$ *and* $0 < h_n \leq \min\{\varepsilon_{2k}(x), \varepsilon_1(x)\}$

$$\begin{aligned} V(\hat{f}_k^{(m)}(x)) &= \frac{1}{nh_n^{2m+1}}\left\{ f(x)\int_{-\infty}^{\infty}\left(M_k^{(m)}(t)\right)^2 dt + R_1(x,h_n) \right. \\ &\quad \left. -h_n[f^{(m)}(x) + R_{2k}(x,h_n,m)]^2 \right\}, \end{aligned} \tag{11}$$

where the residuals satisfy

$$|R_1(x,h_n)| \leq c_1|h_n|(H_1(x) + \varepsilon_1^{-1}(x)), \quad |R_{2k}(x,h_n,m)| \leq c_2 h_n^{2k}(H_{2k,m}(x) + \varepsilon_{2k}^{-2k}(x)) \tag{12}$$

with constants c_1 *and* c_2 *independent of x and* h_n.

3.2. *Integrated Mean-Squared Error and Bandwidth Choice*

We consider optimal choice of bandwidth by minimizing the Integrated Mean Squared Error (IMSE),

$$IMSE(\hat{f}^{(m)}(x)) = \int_{\mathbb{R}}\left(V(\hat{f}^{(m)}(x)) + B(\hat{f}^{(m)}(x))^2\right)dx.$$

The precise value of IMSE, as a function of h_n, is usually impossible to obtain. The common approach is to derive asymptotic approximations of variance and bias, as $h_n \to 0$, and plug those approximations into IMSE to obtain an approximation of type $IMSE \asymp \varphi(h_n)$ where φ depends on h_n, n and some well-defined constants. Then minimization of φ over h_n yields an expression of the optimal h_n as a function of the sample size. This is the approach we take up here. The result we formulate below, when $m=0$, is better than Theorem 8 in Mynbaev and Martins-Filho (2010). In the latter theorem, IMSE is bounded above by $\varphi(h_n)$, while here we obtain the asymptotic expression for IMSE. Our results depend on two auxiliary lemmas that are given in the appendix.

In the next theorem, we derive the exact order of bias, as $h_n \to 0$. The result is stronger than the upper bound Eq. (9) and, correspondingly, it requires stronger conditions. The result is also new for $m=0$ as Mynbaev and Martins-Filho (2010) did not derive the exact order of bias. We need the following assumption.

Assumption 4.
(a) $\int |K(t)||t|^{2k+1}dt = \beta_{2k+1}(K) < \infty$; *(b)* $f^{(m+2k)}$ *is absolutely continuous, bounded and satisfies the following Lipschitz condition: there exist positive functions* $H_{1,m}(x), \varepsilon(x)$ *such that*

$$\left|f^{(m+2k)}(x) - f^{(m+2k)}(x-h)\right| \leq H_{1,m}(x)|h| \quad \text{for all } |h| \leq \varepsilon(x). \tag{13}$$

Theorem 4. *Suppose that Assumptions 1 and 4 hold. Then*

$$B(\hat{f}^{(m)}(x)) = cf^{(m+2k)}(x)h_n^{2k} + O(h_n^{2k+1}G(x)) \tag{14}$$

where $c = (-1)^{k+1}\alpha_{2k}(K)\frac{(k!)^2}{(2k)!}$, $\alpha_{2k}(K) = \int_{\mathbb{R}} K(t)t^{2k}dt$ *and* $G(x) = H_{1,m}(x) + \frac{2\|f^{(m+2k)}\|_C}{\varepsilon(x)}$.

We note that if the Lipschitz condition in Eq. (13) is uniform on $\mathbb{R}$, then we can write $B(\hat{f}^{(m)}(x)) = cf^{(m+2k)}(x)h_n^{2k} + O(h_n^{2k+1})$. In the next theorem, we obtain the optimal bandwidth by minimizing the asymptotic expression for IMSE.

Theorem 5. *In addition to the conditions imposed in Theorem 3 for validity of Eq. (11), let us assume the conditions* $f^{(m)}$, H_1, $\varepsilon_1^{-1} \in L_1$, H_{2k}, $\varepsilon_{2k}^{-2k} \in L_2$ *that provide integrability in x of the right side of Eq. (11). In addition to the conditions of Theorem 4, suppose that* $f^{(m+2k)}$, H, $\frac{1}{\varepsilon} \in L_2$ *which makes sure that the right side of Eq. (14) is square integrable. Then*

$$IMSE = h_n^{4k}\left[c^2\|f^{(m+2k)}\|_{L_2}^2 + O(h_n)\right] + \frac{1}{nh_n^{2m+1}}\left[\|M_k^{(m)}\|_{L_2}^2 + O(h_n)\right]. \tag{15}$$

where c is the constant from Theorem 4. Hence, the function $\varphi(h_n) = c_1h_n^{4k} + c_2\frac{1}{nh_n^{2m+1}}$ *where* $c_1 = c^2\|f^{(m+2k)}\|_{L_2}^2$ *and* $c_2 = \|M_k^{(m)}\|_{L_2}^2$ *approximates IMSE. Minimization of* φ *yields the following optimal bandwidth:*

$$h_{opt} = \left(\frac{(2m+1)c_2}{4knc_1}\right)^{1/(4k+2m+1)}. \tag{16}$$

3.3. Asymptotic Normality

In this section, we state a theorem that gives the asymptotic normality of our estimator under suitable normalization. The proof is omitted as it follows closely the proof of Theorem 9 in Mynbaev and Martins-Filho (2010).

Theorem 6. *Suppose that Assumption 3(a) and (b) hold. Let* $\int_{\mathbb{R}} |K^{(m)}(t)|^{2+\delta} dt < \infty$ *for some* $\delta > 0$. *If* $nh_n \to \infty$ *and* $nh_n^{4k+2m+1} \to 0$, *then*

$$(nh_n^{2m+1})^{1/2}(\hat{f}^{(m)}(x) - f^{(m)}(x)) \xrightarrow{d} N\left(0, f(x)\int_{\mathbb{R}}\left[M_k^{(m)}(t)\right]^2 dt\right). \tag{17}$$

4. MONTE CARLO STUDY

We implement our estimator $\hat{f}_k^{(m)}$ with $k = 1, 2, 3, 4, 8$ for derivatives of order $m = 0, 1, 2$. Our simulations were conducted for four different densities and three different seed kernels (K) to construct M_k. Since the fit quickly worsens as the derivative order grows, we did not consider $m > 2$. Note that if $k = 1$ and the seed K is symmetric, the kernel M_k is just K, so results reported below for $k = 1$ are actually for Rosenblatt–Parzen estimators. Mynbaev and Martins-Filho (2010) demonstrated that increasing k indeed improves estimation (they allowed k to take values 2, 4, 8) of the density. In case of derivative estimation, considering large k is technically more complex because the formula for the optimal bandwidth Eq. (16) requires a derivative of order $2k + m$ of the density.

The four densities to be estimated were proposed in Marron and Wand (1992) and are examples of normal mixtures. They are: (1) Gaussian ($f_1(x) \equiv N(1, 1)$); (2) Bimodal ($f_2(x) \equiv \frac{1}{2}N(-1, \frac{1}{9}) + \frac{1}{2}N(1, \frac{1}{9})$); (3) Separated-Bimodal ($f_3(x) \equiv \frac{1}{2}N(-1.5, \frac{1}{4}) + \frac{1}{2}N(1.5, \frac{1}{4})$), and (4) Trimodal ($f_4(x) \equiv \frac{9}{20}N(-\frac{6}{5}, \frac{9}{25}) + \frac{9}{20}N(\frac{6}{5}, \frac{9}{25}) + \frac{1}{10}N(0, \frac{1}{16})$). These four densities were used by Mynbaev and Martins-Filho (2010) for their simulations. They also considered one more density, whose second derivative is not continuous for all x but satisfies a Lipschitz condition of order 2. We exclude this fifth density from consideration because the optimal bandwidth we apply is not defined for the fifth density unless $m = 0$ and $k = 1$ (this case has already been considered by Mynbaev & Martins-Filho, 2010).

The three seeds we consider are: (1) Gaussian, (2) t distribution with 5 degrees of freedom, and (3) concentrated density. The concentrated density is defined as $\exp(-x^8)/c$, where $c = 2\Gamma(\frac{9}{8})$ is the normalization constant. Fig. 1 provides a graph for the different seeds we use. The motivation for the name of the concentrated density is clear from Fig. 1.

Note that the concentrated density has a flat top and nonexistent tails, while the t distribution is sharper at the top than the Gaussian and has fat tails. We did not use degrees of freedom larger than 5 for the t-distribution to avoid smoothing of the density at the top. The reason to experiment with different seeds was motivated by the fact that even with a very large number of observations ($n = 100,000$) the

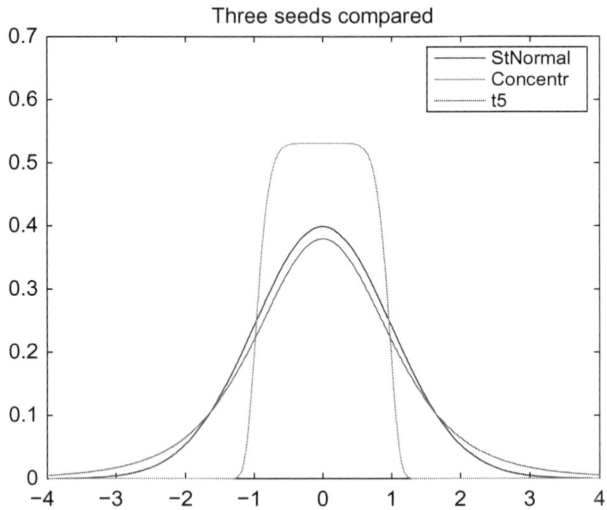

Fig. 1. Comparison of Three Seed Kernels.

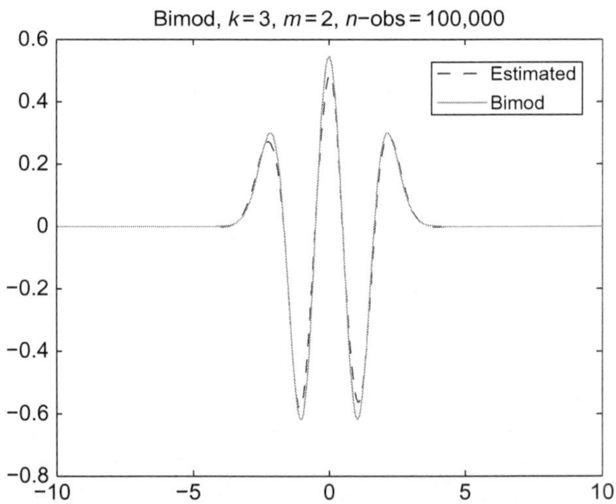

Fig. 2. Estimation of Second Derivative of Bimodal.

differences between the estimated density derivative and the true density derivative at the peaks and troughs of the graph do not vanish (see Fig. 2).

We report first the results for the Gaussian seed and then indicate the variations caused by replacing the seed. For each of the four densities 1,000 samples of size

Table 1. Five Estimators with Optimal Bandwidth h_{opt}.

	Estimators	$f_1(x)$		$f_2(x)$		$f_3(x)$		$f_4(x)$	
		B	MSE	B	MSE	B	MSE	B	MSE
	$n=200$								
$m=0$	$\hat{f}_1$	0.110	0.003	0.121	0.005	0.147	0.007	0.148	0.006
	$\hat{f}_2$	0.107	0.002	0.129	0.004	0.140	0.005	0.158	0.008
	$\hat{f}_3$	0.099	0.002	0.129	0.004	0.142	0.006	0.164	0.008
	$\hat{f}_4$	0.102	0.002	0.125	0.005	0.130	0.006	0.176	0.009
	$\hat{f}_8$	0.099	0.002	0.131	0.005	0.145	0.006	0.184	0.010
$m=1$	$\hat{f}_1$	0.202	0.009	0.338	0.030	0.463	0.060	0.571	0.088
	$\hat{f}_2$	0.177	0.008	0.293	0.026	0.428	0.055	0.666	0.123
	$\hat{f}_3$	0.170	0.009	0.296	0.024	0.455	0.051	0.762	0.170
	$\hat{f}_4$	0.176	0.007	0.301	0.022	0.443	0.052	0.841	0.203
	$\hat{f}_8$	0.178	0.008	0.299	0.025	0.440	0.056	0.931	0.267
$m=2$	$\hat{f}_1$	0.415	0.047	0.978	0.273	1.887	0.999	3.209	3.036
	$\hat{f}_2$	0.041	0.037	0.930	0.258	1.775	0.844	4.185	5.345
	$\hat{f}_3$	0.358	0.037	0.945	0.230	1.792	0.922	5.263	7.547
	$\hat{f}_4$	0.407	0.043	0.928	0.228	1.950	0.980	6.045	10.842
	$\hat{f}_8$	0.413	0.041	1.007	0.273	2.010	1.144	7.372	15.053
	$n=400$								
$m=0$	$\hat{f}_1$	0.086	0.002	0.101	0.003	0.114	0.004	0.111	0.004
	$\hat{f}_2$	0.075	0.002	0.095	0.003	0.107	0.003	0.116	0.004
	$\hat{f}_3$	0.077	0.001	0.093	0.003	0.107	0.003	0.123	0.004
	$\hat{f}_4$	0.077	0.001	0.094	0.002	0.106	0.003	0.128	0.005
	$\hat{f}_8$	0.075	0.001	0.097	0.003	0.106	0.003	0.130	0.005
$m=1$	$\hat{f}_1$	0.159	0.007	0.267	0.020	0.385	0.043	0.459	0.065
	$\hat{f}_2$	0.142	0.005	0.242	0.016	0.334	0.031	0.538	0.085
	$\hat{f}_3$	0.138	0.005	0.246	0.016	0.343	0.032	0.585	0.099
	$\hat{f}_4$	0.136	0.005	0.240	0.015	0.346	0.033	0.629	0.115
	$\hat{f}_8$	0.132	0.006	0.238	0.015	0.350	0.032	0.681	0.135
$m=2$	$\hat{f}_1$	0.343	0.032	0.848	0.194	1.621	0.741	2.840	2.421
	$\hat{f}_2$	0.317	0.027	0.880	0.164	1.514	0.640	3.353	3.252
	$\hat{f}_3$	0.305	0.024	0.773	0.160	1.480	0.604	4.068	4.688
	$\hat{f}_4$	0.326	0.027	0.775	0.151	1.570	0.679	4.924	7.040
	$\hat{f}_8$	0.322	0.025	0.791	0.165	1.534	0.651	5.472	8.532
	$n=600$								
$m=0$	$\hat{f}_1$	0.072	0.002	0.086	0.002	0.098	0.003	0.103	0.003
	$\hat{f}_2$	0.069	0.001	0.083	0.002	0.091	0.002	0.102	0.003
	$\hat{f}_3$	0.064	0.001	0.081	0.002	0.089	0.002	0.101	0.003
	$\hat{f}_4$	0.065	0.001	0.080	0.002	0.091	0.002	0.106	0.003
	$\hat{f}_8$	0.061	0.001	0.079	0.002	0.090	0.002	0.109	0.004
$m=1$	$\hat{f}_1$	0.148	0.006	0.240	0.016	0.348	0.036	0.414	0.050
	$\hat{f}_2$	0.129	0.004	0.210	0.013	0.302	0.025	0.457	0.060
	$\hat{f}_3$	0.124	0.004	0.209	0.012	0.309	0.026	0.501	0.072
	$\hat{f}_4$	0.130	0.004	0.206	0.011	0.305	0.024	0.547	0.084
	$\hat{f}_8$	0.116	0.003	0.205	0.010	0.312	0.027	0.574	0.096
$m=2$	$\hat{f}_1$	0.326	0.030	0.802	0.183	1.471	0.621	2.506	1.976
	$\hat{f}_2$	0.293	0.022	0.695	0.132	1.350	0.508	2.986	2.579
	$\hat{f}_3$	0.271	0.018	0.684	0.126	1.359	0.497	3.475	3.624
	$\hat{f}_4$	0.281	0.019	0.677	0.120	1.329	0.474	4.029	4.733
	$\hat{f}_8$	0.279	0.020	0.687	0.129	1.365	0.519	4.715	6.450

400 were generated. In our first set of simulations, five estimators were obtained for each sample: $\hat{f}_k(x)$ for $k = 1, 2, 3, 4, 8$ where, as stated earlier, $\hat{f}_1(x) = \hat{f}_{RP}(x)$, the Rosenblatt–Parzen estimator. For all estimators, the optimal bandwidth h_{opt} in Eq. (16) was used in our implementation. The usual caveat applies: in practice, this bandwidth is infeasible given that $f(x)$ is unknown. However, in the context of a Monte Carlo study it is desirable since estimation performance is not impacted by the noise introduced through a data-driven bandwidth selection. Table 1 provides average absolute bias (B) and average mean-squared error (MSE) for each density considered for $n = 200, 400, 600$ respectively. We observe the following general regularities. As follows from the theory, increases in the values of k seem to reduce average absolute bias and MSE, but this is not verified for all experiments. Specifically, the step from $k = 3$ to $k = 4$ does not always improve B and MSE in case of higher order derivatives or in case of densities that are more difficult to estimate, i.e, f_3 and f_4. Further, density functions with larger curvature (in increasing order of curvature f_1, f_2, f_3, and f_4) are more difficult to estimate both in terms of bias and MSE for all estimators considered. Our proposed estimators $(\hat{f}_2, \hat{f}_3, \hat{f}_4)$ outperform the Rosenblatt–Parzen estimator both in terms of bias and MSE, except when estimating f_4.

For the other two seeds (concentrated and t distribution), we give a verbal description of the simulation results (full tables are available on request). When we use the concentrated distribution as a seed, the statistics behave the same as one moves right along the table (they worsen when the density curvature increases). The behavior along columns changes. For $m = 0$, the case $k = 1$ is about as good as $k = 2$, except for f_4 when the Rosenblatt–Parzen is the best. In case $m = 1, 2$, the Rosenblatt–Parzen outperforms the others. This is true both for B and MSE. With t distribution with 5 degrees of freedom as a seed, the requirement $\int K(t)t^{2k}dt < \infty$ implied by the definition of the optimal bandwidth limits the value of k: $k \leq 2$. For $m = 1, 2$ our estimator with $k = 2$ outperforms the Rosenblatt–Parzen for all densities, except f_4. For $m = 0$, our estimator is better everywhere.

Finally, if we compare, for fixed k and m, the three seeds, the Gaussian is the best of all, with the margins being the largest for f_4, which is the most difficult to estimate. The Gaussian density seems to strike the right balance between concentration and dispersion.

5. CONCLUSION

We have shown that taking derivatives of order m of the density estimators in the class first proposed by Mynbaev and Martins-Filho (2010) produce estimators for the m-order derivative of the densities that have desirable asymptotic properties.

In particular, these estimators are (uniformly) consistent and asymptotically normally distributed under suitable normalization. In addition, the reduction in the order of the bias, relative to the classical Rosenblatt–Parzen density estimator, first discovered in Mynbaev and Martins-Filho (2010) in the context of density estimation, also manifests itself in the context of derivative estimation. These theoretical results are supported by a small Monte Carlo study, but in agreement with previous simulations we conducted in the case of density estimation, very large values of k seem, in some contexts, to damage finite sample performance as measured by MSE. An interesting extension of this research would be to develop a practical criterion for the selection of k, viz., a criterion for the selection of an optimal density or density derivative estimator in the class we have proposed. We leave such efforts for future studies.

NOTES

1. For an example of one such density, see Mynbaev and Martins-Filho (2010, p. 232).
2. Theorem 1 in Mynbaev and Martins-Filho (2010) obtained expressions for $H(x)$ and $\varepsilon(x)$ for the Gaussian and Cauchy densities.
3. This proof extends the arguments from Besov, Il'in, and Nikolskii (1975, p. 254).
4. Note that since x_0 and $2k$ are fixed, the operator acts on the function g and the result is a function of x.

ACKNOWLEDGMENTS

We thank two anonymous referees for useful comments.

REFERENCES

Besov, O., Il'in, V., & Nikolskii, S. (1975). *Integral representations of functions and imbedding theorems*. VSP BV, Nauka: Moscow.

Bhattacharya, P. K. (1967). Estimation of a probability density function and its derivatives. *Sankhya, 29*, 373–382.

Härdle, W., & Stoker, T. M. (1989). Investigating smooth multiple regression by the method of average derivatives. Journal of the American Statistical Association 20, 986–995.

Henderson, D., & Parmeter, C. (2012). Canonical higher-order kernels for density derivative estimation. *Statistics and Probability Letters, 82*, 1383–1387.

Jennrich, R. I. (1969). Asymptotic properties of non-linear least squares estimators. *The Annals of Mathematical Statistics, 40*(2), 633–643.

Marron, J. S., & Wand, M. P. (1992). Exact mean integrated squared error. *Annals of Statistics, 20*, 712–736.

Muller, H.-G. (1984). Smooth optimum kernel estimators of densities, regression curves and models. *Annals of Statistics, 12*, 766–774.

Mynbaev, K., & Martins-Filho, C. (2010). Bias reduction in kernel density estimation via Lipschitz condition. *Journal of Nonparametric Statistics, 22*, 219–235.

Schuster, E. F. (1969). Estimation of a probability density and its derivatives. *Annals of Mathematical Statistics, 40*, 1187–1196.

Silverman, B. W. (1978). Weak and strong uniform consistency of the kernel estimate of a density and its derivatives. *Annals of Statistics, 6*, 177–184.

Singh, R. (1977). Improvement on some known nonparametric uniformly consistent estimators of derivatives of a density. *Annals of Statistics, 5*, 394–399.

Singh, R. (1979). Mean squared errors of estimates of a density and its derivatives. *Biometrika, 66*, 177–180.

Singh, R. (1987). Mise of kernel estimates of a density and its derivatives. *Statistics and Probability Letters, 5*, 153–159.

Tsybakov, A. B. (2009). *Introduction to nonparametric estimation*. New York, NY: Springer-Verlag.

APPENDIX A: LEMMAS AND PROOFS

Lemma 1. *(a) Let* $\gamma_i = \sum_{s=-k}^{k} c_{k,s} s^i$ *for* $i = 0, \ldots, 2k$. *Then,* $\gamma_0 = \cdots = \gamma_{2k-1} = 0$, $\gamma_{2k} = (-1)^{2k}(2k)!$; *(b) Suppose K has finite moments* $\alpha_l(K)$ *of orders* $l \le 2k$. *Then* M_k *has moments* $\alpha_l(M_k) = 0 < l < 2k$, $\alpha_{2k}(M_k) = -\frac{\gamma_{2k}}{c_{k,0}} \alpha_{2k}(K)$.

Proof. (a) The function $\phi_q(x) = (1-x)^q$ vanishes at $x = 1$ together with all its derivatives of orders $l < q$. For the qth derivative, we have $\phi_q^{(q)}(x) = \left(\frac{d}{dx}\right)^q [\phi_q(x)] = (-1)^q q!$. Now, consider the linear operator $\left(x\frac{d}{dx}\right)$. By induction, for $l < q$ we have $\left(x\frac{d}{dx}\right)^l [\phi_q(x)] = \sum_{j=1}^{l} a_{j,l} x^j \phi_q^{(j)}(x)$, where $a_{j,l}$ are constants and $a_{l,l} = 1$. Now it is easy to see that

$$\left(x\frac{d}{dx}\right)^l [\phi_q(x)]|_{x=1} = \begin{cases} 0 & \text{if } l < q \\ (-1)^q q! & \text{if } l = q \end{cases}. \tag{A.1}$$

Note that by the binomial theorem, $\phi_q(x) = \sum_{m=0}^{q} (-1)^m x^m C_q^m$ and we see that

$$\left(x\frac{d}{dx}\right)^l [\phi_q(x)] = \sum_{m=0}^{q} (-1)^m m^l x^m C_q^m. \tag{A.2}$$

Comparing (A.1) and (A.2) we have

$$\sum_{m=0}^{q} (-1)^m m^l C_q^m = \begin{cases} 0 & \text{if } l < q \\ (-1)^q q! & \text{if } l = q \end{cases}. \tag{A.3}$$

By the definition of $c_{k,s}$ and replacing $s + k$ with m, we have

$$\gamma_i = \sum_{s=-k}^{k} (-1)^{s+k} C_{2k}^{s+k} s^i = \sum_{m=0}^{2k} (-1)^m C_{2k}^m (m-k)^i$$

$$= \sum_{m=0}^{2k} (-1)^m C_{2k}^m \sum_{j=0}^{i} C_i^j m^j (-k)^{i-j} = \sum_{j=0}^{i} C_i^j (-k)^{i-j} \sum_{m=0}^{2k} (-1)^m C_{2k}^m m^j.$$

This identity and (A.3) prove statement (a).[3] b) Replacing $x/s = t$ we have

$$\int_R M_k(x)x^l dx = -\frac{1}{c_{k,0}} \sum_{|s|=1}^{k} \frac{c_{k,s}}{|s|} s^l \int_R K\left(\frac{x}{s}\right)\left(\frac{x}{s}\right)^l dx$$
$$= -\frac{1}{c_{k,0}} \sum_{|s|=1}^{k} s^l c_{k,s} \int_R K(t)\, t^l dx$$
$$= -\frac{1}{c_{k,0}} \sum_{s=-k}^{k} s^l c_{k,s} \alpha_l(K) = -\frac{1}{c_{k,0}} \gamma_l \alpha_l(K)$$

which completes the proof. ■

Lemma 2. *Let* $I(x,g) = \frac{1}{(2k)!}\int_{x_0}^{x}(x-t)^{2k} g(t)dt$ *denote the* $(2k+1)$*-fold integration operator for some fixed* x_0 *and Assumption 1 hold.*[4] *If the density* f *has an absolutely continuous derivative* $f^{(m+2k)}$*, then the bias of* $\hat{f}^{(m)}(x)$ *has the representation*

$$B(\hat{f}^{(m)}(x)) = -\frac{\gamma_{2k}}{c_{k,0}} \frac{f^{(m+2k)}(x_0)}{(2k)!} h^{2k} \alpha_{2k}(K) - \frac{1}{c_{k,0}} \int_{\mathbb{R}} K(t) \Delta_{ht}^{2k} I(x, f^{(m+2k+1)}) dt \tag{A.4}$$

where $\alpha_{2k}(K) = \int_{\mathbb{R}} K(t)t^{2k}dt$ *and* x_0 *is arbitrary.*

Proof. If $g^{(2k)}$ is absolutely continuous, then $g^{(2k+1)}$ is summable and by Taylor's theorem with remainder in integral form one has $g(x) = \sum_{i=0}^{2k} \frac{g^{(i)}(x_0)}{i!}$ $(x-x_0)^i + \frac{1}{(2k)!}\int_{x_0}^{x}(x-t)^{2k} g^{(2k+1)}(t)dt$.

Applying this formula to $g = f^{(m)}$ and recalling our notation for the integration operator, we get

$$f^{(m)}(x) = \sum_{i=0}^{2k} \frac{f^{(m+i)}(x_0)}{i!}(x-x_0)^i + I(x, f^{(m+2k+1)}).$$

In view of Eq. (A.9), we need to consider

$$\Delta_{ht}^{2k} f^{(m)}(x) = \sum_{i=0}^{2k} \frac{f^{(m+i)}(x_0)}{i!} \Delta_{ht}^{2k}(x-x_0)^i + \Delta_{ht}^{2k} I(x, f^{(m+2k+1)}) \tag{A.5}$$

where the difference is applied with respect to the variable x, x_0 being fixed. By Lemma 1

$$\Delta_{ht}^{2k}(x-x_0)^i = \sum_{s=-k}^{k} c_{k,s}(x+sht-x_0)^i = \sum_{s=-k}^{k} c_{k,s} \sum_{j=0}^{i} C_i^j (x-x_0)^{i-j}(sht)^j$$

$$= \sum_{j=0}^{i} C_i^j (x-x_0)^{i-j}(ht)^j \sum_{s=-k}^{k} c_{k,s}s^j = \begin{cases} 0, & i<2k \\ \gamma_{2k}(ht)^{2k}, & i=2k \end{cases} \quad \text{(A.6)}$$

Under Assumption 1, combining Eqs. (A.9), (A.5), and (A.6) we finish the proof of Eq. (A.4):

$$B(\hat{f}^{(m)}(x)) = -\frac{1}{c_{k,0}} \int_{\mathbb{R}} K(t) \left[\frac{f^{(m+2k)}(x_0)}{(2k)!} \gamma_{2k}(ht)^{2k} + \Delta_{ht}^{2k} I(x, f^{(m+2k+1)}) \right] dt$$

$$= -\frac{\gamma_{2k}}{c_{k,0}(2k)!} f^{(m+2k)}(x_0) h^{2k} \int_{\mathbb{R}} K(t) t^{2k} dt$$

$$- \frac{1}{c_{k,0}} \int_{\mathbb{R}} K(t) \Delta_{ht}^{2k} I(x, f^{(m+2k+1)}) dt.$$

■

Theorem 1. Under Assumption 1, we show that $\max\{|K(s)|, |K^{(1)}(s)|, \ldots, |K^{(m-1)}(s)|\} = o\left(\frac{1}{|s|}\right)$ as $|s| \to \infty$. Let $s>0$. It is well-known that the Sobolev space $W_1^m[0,1]$ is embedded in $C^j[0,1]$ for $j=0,1,\ldots,m-1$, that is, with some constant c independent of K one has $\|K^{(j)}\|_{C[0,1]} \leq c\int_0^1 \left(|K(t)| + |K^{(m)}(t)|\right) dt$. Applying this bound to the segment $[s, s+1]$ and using the fact that $|t/s| \geq 1$ for $t \in [s, s+1]$ we get

$$\max_j |K^{(j)}(s)| \leq c \int_s^{s+1} \left(|K(t)| + |K^{(m)}(t)|\right) dt$$

$$\leq \frac{c}{|s|} \int_s^{s+1} \left(|K(t)| + |K^{(m)}(t)|\right) |t| dt.$$

The case of $s<0$ is treated similarly.

Under Assumption 1 $\left|K^{(j)}(t) f^{(m-1-j)}(x-sh_n t)\right| = o\left(\frac{1}{|t|}\right) O(|x-sh_n t|) = o\left(\left|\frac{x-sh_n t}{t}\right|\right) = o(1)$, as $|t| \to \infty$ for $j=0,\ldots,m-1$, $h_n>0$. Therefore, we can integrate by parts, and from Eq. (5) and a change of variables, we obtain

$$
\begin{aligned}
E(\hat{f}_k^{(m)}(x)) = E(u_1) &= \frac{1}{h_n^{m+1}} \int_{-\infty}^{+\infty} M_k^{(m)}\left(\frac{x-t}{h_n}\right) f(t)dt \\
&= \frac{1}{h_n^m} \int_{-\infty}^{+\infty} M_k^{(m)}(l) f(x-h_n l)dl \\
&= -\frac{1}{c_{k,0}} \sum_{|s|=1}^{k} \frac{c_{k,s}}{|s| s^m h_n^m} \int_{-\infty}^{+\infty} K^{(m)}\left(\frac{l}{s}\right) f(x-h_n l)dl \\
&= -\frac{1}{c_{k,0}} \sum_{|s|=1}^{k} \frac{c_{k,s}}{|s| s^m} \left[\frac{s}{h_n^m} K^{(m-1)}\left(\frac{l}{s}\right) f(x-h_n l)\Big|_{-\infty}^{+\infty} \right. \\
&\quad \left. + \frac{s}{h_n^{m-1}} \int_{-\infty}^{+\infty} K^{(m-1)}\left(\frac{l}{s}\right) f^{(1)}(x-h_n l)dl \right] \\
&= -\frac{1}{c_{k,0}} \sum_{|s|=1}^{k} \frac{c_{k,s}}{|s| s^m} \left[\frac{s^2}{h_n^{m-1}} K^{(m-2)}\left(\frac{l}{s}\right) f'(x-h_n l)\Big|_{-\infty}^{+\infty} \right. \\
&\quad \left. + \frac{s^2}{h_n^{m-2}} \int_{-\infty}^{+\infty} K^{(m-2)}\left(\frac{l}{s}\right) f^{(1)}(x-h_n l)dl \right] \\
&= \cdots = -\frac{1}{c_{k,0}} \sum_{|s|=1}^{k} \frac{c_{k,s}}{|s| s^m} \left[\frac{s^m}{h_n} K\left(\frac{l}{s}\right) f^{(m-1)}(x-h_n l)\Big|_{-\infty}^{+\infty} \right. \\
&\quad \left. + \frac{s^m}{h_n} h_n \int_{-\infty}^{+\infty} K\left(\frac{l}{s}\right) f^{(m)}(x-h_n l)dl \right] \\
&= -\frac{1}{c_{k,0}} \sum_{|s|=1}^{k} \frac{c_{k,s}}{|s|} \int_{-\infty}^{+\infty} K\left(\frac{l}{s}\right) f^{(m)}(x-h_n l)dl \\
&= -\frac{1}{c_{k,0}} \left[\sum_{s=-k}^{-1} \frac{c_{k,s}}{-s}(-s) \int_{-\infty}^{+\infty} K(-t) f^{(m)}(x+sh_n t)dt \right. \\
&\quad \left. + \sum_{s=1}^{k} \frac{c_{k,s}}{s} s \int_{-\infty}^{+\infty} K(-t) f^{(m)}(x+sh_n t)dt \right] \\
&= -\frac{1}{c_{k,0}} \sum_{|s|=1}^{k} c_{k,s} \int_{-\infty}^{+\infty} K(-t) f^{(m)}(x+sh_n t)dt. \qquad \text{(A.7)}
\end{aligned}
$$

Hence, from Eqs. (1), (2), and (A.7) we obtain

$$B(\hat{f}^{(m)}(x)) = -\frac{1}{c_{k,0}}\left[\sum_{s=-k}^{-1} c_{k,s}\int_{-\infty}^{+\infty} K(-t)f^{(m)}(x+sh_nt)dt\right.$$

$$\left.+\sum_{s=1}^{k} c_{k,s}\int_{-\infty}^{+\infty} K(-t)f^{(m)}(x+sh_nt)dt\right] - \frac{c_{k,0}}{c_{k,0}}f^{(m)}(x) \quad \text{(A.8)}$$

$$= -\frac{1}{c_{k,0}}\left[\sum_{|s|=1}^{k} c_{k,s}\int_{-\infty}^{+\infty} K(-t)f^{(m)}(x+sh_nt)dt\right.$$

$$\left.+c_{k,0}\int_{-\infty}^{+\infty} K(-t)f^{(m)}(x+0h_nt)dt\right]$$

$$= -\frac{1}{c_{k,0}}\int_{-\infty}^{+\infty} K(-t)\Delta_{h_nt}^{2k}f^{(m)}(x)dt$$

$$= -\frac{1}{c_{k,0}}\int_{-\infty}^{+\infty} K(t)\Delta_{h_nt}^{2k}f^{(m)}(x)dt, \quad \text{(A.9)}$$

where the last equality follows from the symmetry of K. ■

Theorem 2. (a) We denote $\psi_j = \frac{x-X_j}{h_n}$, then we can rewrite Eq. (4) as $\hat{f}_k^{(m)}(x) = \frac{1}{n}\sum_{j=1}^{n}\frac{1}{h_n^{m+1}}M_k^{(m)}(\psi_j)$ and using Eq. (5), we get

$$M_k^{(m)}(\psi_j) = -\frac{1}{c_{k,0}}\sum_{|s|=1}^{k}\frac{c_{k,s}}{|s|s^m}K^{(m)}\left(\frac{\psi_j}{s}\right). \quad \text{(A.10)}$$

Under Assumption 2(a) the inversion theorem for Fourier transforms gives

$$K^{(m)}\left(\frac{\psi_j}{s}\right) = \frac{(-i)^{(m)}}{2\pi}\int_{\mathbb{R}} \exp\left\{\frac{-it\psi_j}{s}\right\} t^m\phi_K(t)dt. \quad \text{(A.11)}$$

Using Eqs. (4), (5), (A.10), and (A.11) and by changing variables of integration, we have

$$\begin{aligned}
\hat{f}_k^{(m)}(x) &= \frac{1}{nh_n^{m+1}} \sum_{j=1}^{n} M_k^{(m)}\left(\frac{x-X_j}{h_n}\right) = \frac{1}{nh_n^{m+1}} \sum_{j=1}^{n} M_k^{(m)}(\psi_j) \\
&= -\frac{(-i)^{(m)}}{2\pi c_{k,0}} \sum_{j=1}^{n} \frac{1}{nh_n^{m+1}} \sum_{|s|=1}^{k} \frac{c_{k,s}}{|s|s^m} \int_{\mathbb{R}} \exp\left\{\frac{-it\psi_j}{s}\right\} t^m \phi_K(t)dt \\
&= -\frac{(-i)^{(m)}}{2\pi c_{k,0}} \sum_{j=1}^{n} \frac{1}{nh_n^{m+1}} \sum_{|s|=1}^{k} \frac{c_{k,s}}{|s|s^m} \int_{\mathbb{R}} \exp\left\{-it\left(\frac{x-X_j}{sh}\right)\right\} t^m \phi_K(t)dt \\
&= -\frac{(-i)^{(m)}}{2\pi c_{k,0}} \sum_{j=1}^{n} \frac{1}{n} \sum_{|s|=1}^{k} c_{k,s} \int_{\mathbb{R}} \exp\{-i\gamma x\} \exp\{i\gamma X_j\} \gamma^m \phi_K(sh_n\gamma)d\gamma \\
&= -\frac{(-i)^{(m)}}{2\pi c_{k,0}} \int_{\mathbb{R}} \exp\{-i\gamma x\} \sum_{j=1}^{n} \frac{1}{n} \exp\{i\gamma X_j\} \sum_{|s|=1}^{k} c_{k,s}\gamma^m \phi_K(sh_n\gamma)d\gamma \\
&= -\frac{(-i)^{(m)}}{2\pi c_{k,0}} \int_{\mathbb{R}} \exp\{-i\gamma x\} \hat{\phi}_n(\gamma)\Delta(\gamma)d\gamma
\end{aligned}$$

where $\hat{\phi}_n(\gamma) = \sum_{j=1}^{n} \frac{1}{n} \exp\{i\gamma X_j\}$ is an unbiased estimator for the characteristic function $\phi_f(t)$ of f and $\Delta(\gamma) = \sum_{|s|=1}^{k} c_{k,s}\gamma^m \phi_K(sh_n\gamma)$. Thus,

$$\begin{aligned}
E(\hat{f}_k^{(m)}(x)) &= -\frac{(-i)^{(m)}}{2\pi c_{k,0}} \int_{\mathbb{R}} \exp\{-i\gamma x\} E\hat{\phi}_n(\gamma)\Delta(\gamma)d\gamma \\
&= -\frac{(-i)^{(m)}}{2\pi c_{k,0}} \int_{\mathbb{R}} \exp\{-i\gamma x\} \phi_f(\gamma)\Delta(\gamma)d\gamma
\end{aligned}$$

so that $|\hat{f}_k^{(m)}(x) - E(\hat{f}_k^{(m)}(x))| \le c \int_{\mathbb{R}} |\hat{\phi}_n(\gamma) - \phi_f(\gamma)| |\exp\{-i\gamma x\}| |\Delta(\gamma)| d\gamma$. But since $|\exp\{-i\gamma x\}| = 1$,

$$\sup_{x\in\mathbb{R}} |\hat{f}_k^{(m)}(x) - E(\hat{f}_k^{(m)}(x))| \le c \int_{\mathbb{R}} |\hat{\phi}_n(\gamma) - \phi_f(\gamma)| |\Delta(\gamma)| d\gamma.$$

with no sup on the right-hand side because it does not depend on x. It follows from Lemma 2.1 of Jennrich (1969) that $\sup|\cdot|$ is measurable, its expectation is well defined and

$$E\left(\sup_{x\in\mathbb{R}} |\hat{f}_k^{(m)}(x) - E\hat{f}_k^{(m)}(x)|\right) \le c \int_{\mathbb{R}} E\left|\hat{\phi}_n(\gamma) - \phi_f(\gamma)\right| |\Delta(\gamma)| d\gamma.$$

Now,

$$E\left(|\hat{\phi}_n(\gamma)-\phi_f(\gamma)|\right)=E\left(\left|\frac{1}{n}\sum_{j=1}^{n}\exp\{i\gamma X_j\}-E(\exp\{i\gamma X_j\})\right|\right)$$
$$=E(\,|Y_1+iY_2|\,)=E|Y_1|+E|Y_2|=E[(Y_1^2+Y_2^2)]^{\frac{1}{2}}$$
$$\leq[E(Y_1^2+Y_2^2)]^{\frac{1}{2}}\leq(EY_1^2)^{\frac{1}{2}}+(EY_2^2)^{\frac{1}{2}}$$

where

$$\begin{cases} Y_1=\frac{1}{n}\sum\limits_{j=1}^{n}(\cos(\gamma X_j)-E(\cos(\gamma X_j))) \\ Y_2=\frac{1}{n}\sum\limits_{j=1}^{n}(\sin(\gamma X_j)-E(\sin(\gamma X_j))). \end{cases}$$

Using the i.i.d. assumption, it is easy to see that

$$EY_1^2=\frac{1}{n^2}\sum_{j=1}^{n}\left[E\cos^2(\gamma X_j)-(E\cos(\gamma X_j))^2\right]$$
$$=\frac{1}{n^2}\sum_{j=1}^{n}V\left(\cos(\gamma X_j)\right)=\frac{1}{n}\,[V(\cos(\gamma X_1)]$$
$$EY_2^2=\frac{1}{n^2}\sum_{j=1}^{n}\left[E\sin^2(\gamma X_j)-(E\sin(\gamma X_j))^2\right]$$
$$=\frac{1}{n^2}\sum_{j=1}^{n}V\left(\sin(\gamma X_j)\right)=\frac{1}{n}\,[V(\sin(\gamma X_1))]$$

Consequently, $(EY_1^2)^{\frac{1}{2}}+(EY_2^2)^{\frac{1}{2}}=\left(\frac{1}{n}V(\cos(\gamma X_1)\right)^{\frac{1}{2}}+\left(\frac{1}{n}V(\sin(\gamma X_1)\right)^{\frac{1}{2}}$. Since $E\cos^2(\gamma X_1)\leq 1$ and $E\sin^2(\gamma X_1)\leq 1$, $V(\cos(\gamma X_1))^{\frac{1}{2}}=\left[E\cos^2(\gamma X_1)\right.$ $\left.-(E\cos(\gamma X_1))^2\right]^{\frac{1}{2}}\leq\left[E\cos^2(\gamma X_1)+E\cos^2(\gamma X_1)\right]^{\frac{1}{2}}\leq\sqrt{2}$. $V(\sin(\gamma X_1))^{\frac{1}{2}}$ $=\left[E\sin^2(\gamma X_1)-(E\sin(\gamma X_1))^2\right]^{\frac{1}{2}}\leq\left[E\sin^2(\gamma X_1)+E\sin^2(\gamma X_1)\right]^{\frac{1}{2}}$ $\leq\sqrt{2}$. $(EY_1^2)^{\frac{1}{2}}+(EY_2^2)^{\frac{1}{2}}=\frac{2\sqrt{2}}{\sqrt{n}}$. Hence, $E\left(\left|\hat{\phi}_n(\gamma)-\phi_f(\gamma)\right|\right)\leq\frac{2\sqrt{2}}{\sqrt{n}}$ and

$$\int_{\mathbb{R}}|\Delta(\gamma)|d\gamma\leq\sum_{|s|=1}^{k}|c_{k,s}|\int_{\mathbb{R}}|\gamma^m||\phi_K(sh_n\gamma)|d\gamma$$
$$\leq\frac{1}{h_n^{m+1}}\sum_{|s|=1}^{k}\frac{|c_{k,s}|}{s^{m+1}}\int_{\mathbb{R}}|t^m\phi_K(t)|dt=\frac{c}{h_n^{m+1}}\int_{\mathbb{R}}|t^m\phi_K(t)|dt.$$

Finally, $E\left(\sup_{x\in\mathbb{R}}|\hat{f}_k^{(m)}(x) - E\hat{f}_k^{(m)}(x)|\right) \leq \frac{c}{h_n^{m+1}\sqrt{n}}\int_{\mathbb{R}}|t^m\phi_K(t)|dt$ which tends to zero as $n \to \infty$ under Assumption 2(c) ($nh_n^{2m+2} \to \infty$). Further, by Markov's inequality

$$P\left(\sup_x |\hat{f}_k^{(m)}(x) - E(\hat{f}_k^{(m)}(x))| > \varepsilon\right) \to 0 \tag{A.12}$$

as $n \to \infty$ for all $\varepsilon > 0$. Therefore, $\sup_{x\in\mathbb{R}}|\hat{f}_k^{(m)}(x) - E\hat{f}_k^{(m)}(x)| \xrightarrow{p} 0$. Note that

$$\sup_{x\in\mathbb{R}}|\hat{f}_k^{(m)}(x) - f^{(m)}(x)| \leq \sup_{x\in\mathbb{R}}|\hat{f}_k^{(m)}(x) - E\hat{f}_k^{(m)}(x)| + \sup_{x\in\mathbb{R}}|E\hat{f}_k^{(m)}(x) - f^{(m)}(x)|.$$

The first term on the right-hand side of the inequality is uniformly $o_p(1)$ from Eq. (A.12). The second term tends to zero by Eq. (A.7), Assumption 2(b) and Theorem 5 (for the case where $m=0$) in Mynbaev and Martins-Filho (2010). We have $\lim_{n\to\infty}\sup_{x\in\mathbb{R}}|\hat{f}_k^{(m)}(x) - f^{(m)}(x)| = 0$. Consequently, $\hat{f}_k^{(m)}(x)$ is uniformly consistent. ■

Theorem 3. Assumption 3(c) implies for any $N > 0$

$$\int_{|t|>N}|K(t)|\,dt \leq \int_{|t|>N}|K(t)|\left|\frac{t}{N}\right|^{2k}dt \leq N^{-2k}\int_{-\infty}^{\infty}|K(t)|\,t^{2k}dt. \tag{A.13}$$

Then, using Eq. (A.9) and Assumption 3(b), we have

$$\begin{aligned}
\left|B(\hat{f}_k^{(m)}(x))\right| &= \left|\frac{1}{c_{k,0}}\right|\left|\int_{-\infty}^{\infty}K(t)\Delta_{h_nt}^{2k}f^{(m)}(x)dt\right| \\
&\leq c_1\left(\int_{|h_nt|\leq\varepsilon_{2k}(x)} + \int_{|h_nt|>\varepsilon_{2k}(x)}\right)|K(t)||\Delta_{h_nt}^{2k}f^{(m)}(x)|dt \\
&\leq c_2\left[H_{2k,m}(x)\int_{|h_nt|\leq\varepsilon_{2k}(x)}|K(t)|(h_nt)^{2k}dt\right. \\
&\quad\left. + \sup_{x\in\mathbb{R}}|f^{(m)}(x)|\int_{|h_nt|>\varepsilon_{2k}(x)}|K(t)|dt\right].
\end{aligned}$$

It remains to apply Eqs. (A.13) and (8) to obtain Eq. (9).

Now, we proceed with derivation of Eq. (11). According to Eq. (7) we need to evaluate $E(u_1^2)$ and $E(u_1)^2$. By Eqs. (6) and (9),

$$Eu_1 = E(\hat{f}_k^{(m)}(x)) = f^{(m)}(x) + B(\hat{f}_k^{(m)}(x)) = f^{(m)}(x) + R_{2k}(x, h_n, m) \qquad \text{(A.14)}$$

where $R_{2k}(x, h_n)$ satisfies Eq. (12). Now, $E(u_1^2) = \left(\frac{1}{h_n^{m+1}}\right)^2 \int_{\mathbb{R}} \left[M_k^{(m)}\left(\frac{x-t}{h_n}\right)\right]^2$ $f(t)dt = \frac{1}{h_n^{2m+1}} \int_{\mathbb{R}} \left[M_k^{(m)}(t)\right]^2 f(x - h_n t)dt$. Consider

$$\begin{aligned}
&\int_{\mathbb{R}} \left[M_k^{(m)}(t)\right]^2 f(x - h_n t)dt - f(x) \int_{\mathbb{R}} \left[M_k^{(m)}(t)\right]^2 dt \\
&\quad = \int_{\mathbb{R}} \left[M_k^{(m)}(t)\right]^2 [f(x - h_n t) - f(x)]\, dt
\end{aligned}$$

Then, similarly to Eq. (A.13), we have

$$\int_{|t|>N} \left|M_k^{(m)}(t)\right|^2 dt \le \int_{|t|>N} \left|M_k^{(m)}(t)\right|^2 \left|\frac{t}{N}\right| dt \le N^{-1} \int_{-\infty}^{\infty} \left|M_k^{(m)}(t)\right|^2 |t| dt. \qquad \text{(A.15)}$$

Using Eqs. (10) and (A.15), we have

$$\begin{aligned}
&\left|\int_{-\infty}^{\infty} \left(M_k^{(m)}(t)\right)^2 (f(x - h_n t) - f(x))dt\right| \\
&\le \left(\int_{|h_n t| \le \varepsilon_1(x)} + \int_{|h_n t| > \varepsilon_1(x)}\right) \left|M_k^{(m)}(t)\right|^2 |f(x - h_n t) - f(x)|\, dt \\
&\le H_1(x) \int_{|h_n t| \le \varepsilon_1(x)} \left|M_k^{(m)}(t)\right|^2 |(h_n t)| dt + \sup_{x \in \mathbb{R}} |f(x)| \int_{|h_n t| > \varepsilon_1(x)} \left|M_k^{(m)}(t)\right|^2 dt.
\end{aligned}$$

Then using Eq. (10), we get

$$\int_{\mathbb{R}} \left[M_k^{(m)}(t)\right]^2 f(x - h_n t)dt = f(x) \int_{\mathbb{R}} \left[M_k^{(m)}(t)\right]^2 dt + R_1(x, h_n) \qquad \text{(A.16)}$$

where $R_1(x, h_n)$ satisfies Eq. (12).

Now we show that $\int_{\mathbb{R}} \left[M_k^{(m)}(t)\right]^2 dt < \infty$. From Eq. (5), we have $M_k^{(m)}(x) = \sum_{|s|=1}^k a_s K^{(m)}\left(\frac{x}{s}\right)$, where $a_s = -\frac{1}{c_{k,0}} \frac{c_{k,s}}{|s|} s^{(-m)}$. Hence, by Hölder's inequality

$$\begin{aligned}
\int_{\mathbb{R}} \left(M_k^{(m)}(x)\right)^2 dx &= \int_{\mathbb{R}} \sum_{|s|,|t|=1}^{k} a_s a_t K^{(m)}\left(\frac{x}{s}\right) K^{(m)}\left(\frac{x}{t}\right) dx \\
&\leq \sum_{|s|,|t|=1}^{k} |a_s a_t| \int_{\mathbb{R}} \left|K^{(m)}\left(\frac{x}{s}\right)\right| \left|K^{(m)}\left(\frac{x}{t}\right)\right| dx \\
&\leq \sum_{|s|,|t|=1}^{k} |a_s a_t| \left(\int_{\mathbb{R}} \left|K^{(m)}\left(\frac{x}{s}\right)\right|^2 dx\right)^{\frac{1}{2}} \left(\int_{\mathbb{R}} \left|K^{(m)}\left(\frac{x}{t}\right)\right|^2 dx\right)^{\frac{1}{2}} \\
&= c_1 \left(\int_{\mathbb{R}} \left|K^{(m)}(t)\right|^2 dt\right) < \infty
\end{aligned}$$

because $K^{(m)} \in L_2(\mathbb{R})$.

Note that Eq. (11) is a consequence of Eqs. (A.14) and (A.16). In addition, if $f(x) \neq 0$ and for small h_n we can rewrite Eq. (11) as

$$V(\hat{f}_k^{(m)}(x)) = \frac{1}{nh_n^{2m+1}} \left[f(x) \int_{\mathbb{R}} \left(M_k^{(m)}(t)\right)^2 dt + O(h_n)\right]. \tag{A.17}$$

■

Theorem 4. By Eq. (7) in Mynbaev and Martins-Filho (2010) $\left|\Delta_h^{2k} g(x)\right| \leq h^{2k} \sup_{|x-t| \leq k|h|} |g^{(2k)}(t)|$. It is easy to verify that $\left(\frac{d}{dx}\right)^{2k} I(x, g) = \int_{x_0}^x g(t)dt$. Hence, using the last equation and the preceding inequality, we have

$$\begin{aligned}
\left|\Delta_{ht}^{2k} I(x, f^{(m+2k+1)})\right| &\leq (ht)^{2k} \sup_{|x-y| \leq k|ht|} \left|\left(\frac{d}{dy}\right)^{2k} I(y, f^{(m+2k+1)})\right| \\
&= (ht)^{2k} \sup_{|x-y| \leq k|ht|} \left|\int_{x_0}^{y} f^{(m+2k+1)}(z)dz\right|.
\end{aligned}$$

Next, given that x_0 is arbitrary, we set $x_0 = x$ and use Eq. (A.6) and Assumption 4(b) to obtain

$$\begin{aligned}
\left|\Delta_{ht}^{2k} I(x, f^{(m+2k+1)})\right| &\leq (ht)^{2k} \sup_{|x-y| \leq k|ht|} \left|f^{(m+2k)}(y) - f^{(m+2k)}(x)\right| \\
&\leq \begin{cases} |ht|^{2k+1} k H_{1,m}(x) & \text{if } k|ht| \leq \varepsilon(x), \\ 2(ht)^{2k} \| f^{(m+2k)} \|_C & \text{if } k|ht| > \varepsilon(x). \end{cases}
\end{aligned}$$

It follows that

$$\left|\int_{\mathbb{R}} K(t)\Delta_{ht}^{2k} I(x, f^{(m+2k+1)})dt\right| \le kh_n^{2k+1} H_{1,m}(x) \int_{k|ht|\le\varepsilon(x)} |K(t)||t|^{2k+1}dt$$

$$+ 2h_n^{2k} \| f^{(m+2k)} \|_C$$

$$\times \int_{k|ht|>\varepsilon(x)} |K(t)|t^{2k}dt.$$

In the first integral on the right expand the domain of integration; in the second one use the inequality $1 < k|ht|/\varepsilon(x)$ and then expand the domain. The outcome is

$$\left|\int_{\mathbb{R}} K(t)\Delta_{ht}^{2k} I(x, f^{(m+2k+1)})dt\right| \le kh_n^{2k+1} H_{1,m}(x)\beta_{2k+1}(K)$$

$$+ 2kh_n^{2k+1} \| f^{(m+2k)} \|_C \frac{1}{\varepsilon(x)} \beta_{2k+1}(K)$$

$$\le kh_n^{2k+1}\beta_{2k+1}(K)\left[H_{1,m}(x) + \frac{2\| f^{(m+2k)}\|_C}{\varepsilon(x)}\right].$$

This equation and Eq. (A.4) prove the theorem. ■

Theorem 5. Under the conditions imposed, Eq. (A.17) implies

$$\int_{\mathbb{R}} V(\hat{f}^{(m)}(x))dx = \frac{1}{nh_n^{2m+1}}\left[\int_{\mathbb{R}} f(x)dx \| M_k^{(m)} \|_{L_2}^2 + O(h_n)\right],$$

while Eq. (14) gives $\int_{\mathbb{R}} \left[B(\hat{f}^{(m)}(x))\right]^2 dx = h^{4k}\left[c^2 \| f^{(m+2k)} \|_{L_2}^2 + O(h)\right]$. Summing the last two equations we get Eq. (15). The rest is obvious and

$$h_{opt} = \left\{\frac{2m+1}{4kn\gamma_{2k}^2} \frac{\int [M_k^{(m)}(t)]^2 dt}{\int [f^{(m+2k)}]^2 dt (\int K(t)t^{2k}dt)^2} \left(\frac{(2k)!}{k!}\right)^4\right\}^{\frac{1}{4k+2m+1}}. \quad \text{(A.18)}$$

■

LOCAL POLYNOMIAL DERIVATIVE ESTIMATION: ANALYTIC OR TAYLOR?

Jeffrey S. Racine

Department of Economics and Graduate Program in Statistics, McMaster University, Hamilton, Canada

Department of Economics and Finance, La Trobe University, Melbourne, Australia

Info-Metrics Institute, American University, Washington, DC, USA

Rimini Center for Economic Analysis, Rimini, Italy

ABSTRACT

Local polynomial regression is extremely popular in applied settings. Recent developments in shape-constrained nonparametric regression allow practitioners to impose constraints on local polynomial estimators thereby ensuring that the resulting estimates are consistent with underlying theory. However, it turns out that local polynomial derivative estimates may fail to coincide with the analytic derivative of the local polynomial regression estimate which can be problematic, particularly in the context of shape-constrained estimation. In such cases, practitioners might prefer to instead use analytic derivatives along the lines of those proposed in the local constant setting by Rilstone and Ullah (1989). Demonstrations and applications are considered.

Keywords: Nonparametric; smoothing; constrained estimation

JEL classification: C14

Essays in Honor of Aman Ullah
Advances in Econometrics, Volume 36, 617–633

ISSN: 0731-9053/doi:10.1108/S0731-905320160000036027

1. INTRODUCTION

Local polynomial regression has emerged as a dominant method for nonparametric estimation and inference. The local linear variant was proposed by Stone (1977) and Cleveland (1979); see Fan (1992) and Fan and Gijbels (1996) for an extensive treatment of the local polynomial estimator. Local estimators are nowadays being used in the context of shape-constrained estimation and inference; see Hall and Huang (2001), Du, Parmeter, and Racine (2013), and Lee, Tu, and Ullah (2014) by way of illustration. However, one feature of local polynomial estimators that may not be widely appreciated is that the local polynomial derivative estimator does not, in general, coincide with the analytic derivative of the local polynomial regression estimator in finite-sample settings. This can cause problems, particularly in the context of shape-constrained estimation. The problem arises when the object of interest is the regression function itself and constraints are to be imposed on derivatives of the regression function, however the regression estimate and derivative estimate are not internally consistent, that is, the derivative of the local polynomial regression estimate does not coincide with the local polynomial derivative estimate. In such cases, the 'analytic' derivative of the regression estimate is required, otherwise the shape-constrained estimate may fail to satisfy the constraints imposed, which would be troubling for the practitioner. As well, the divergence between the local polynomial derivative estimate and the analytic derivative of the local polynomial regression estimate may be cause for concern in settings other than shape constrained estimation.

In this paper, we derive the relationship between the two derivative estimators, demonstrate conditions under which they are equal, consider a measure of divergence between the two, and alert practitioners to the pitfalls associated with using local polynomial smoothers in a shape-constrained framework and elsewhere.

2. LOCALLY WEIGHTED REGRESSION

Consider a model of the form

$$y_i = g(x_i) + \epsilon_i, \quad i = 1, \dots, n,$$

where $g(x) = E(Y|X = x)$ is an unknown but smooth conditional mean function evaluated at the value $X = x$, ϵ_i is a stochastic error term, and n the number of sample realizations. To fix ideas, we restrict attention to the single predictor case in what follows (extensions to the multiple predictor case will hopefully be obvious to the reader).

A fairly broad class of nonparametric kernel regression estimators of $g(x)$ can be written as a linear combination of locally weighted y_i, that is,

$$\hat{g}(x) = \sum_{i=1}^{n} W\left(\frac{x_i - x}{h}\right) y_i, \tag{1}$$

where $W((x_i - x)/h)$ is a local weight function, examples of which will be given shortly. Local weights will be used below, with the defining feature being that observations lying close to the point x will receive higher weight than those lying far from x. Having selected a kernel function, the bandwidth h controls the amount of weight given to each sample realization. For notational simplicity we shall write $W_i(x) = W((x_i - x)/h)$ in what follows, hence we can succinctly express this class of locally weighted estimators as $\hat{g}(x) = \sum_{i=1}^{n} W_i(x) y_i$. Estimators of the form (1) include the local constant estimator (Nadaraya, 1965; Watson, 1964), the Priestley–Chao estimator (Priestley & Chao, 1972), the Gasser–Müller estimator (Gasser & Muller, 1979), and the local polynomial estimator (Cleveland, 1979; Fan, 1992; Stone, 1977), among others. The most popular estimators, among practitioners, are the local constant estimator (Nadaraya, 1965; Watson, 1964) and the local linear variant of Fan's (1992) local polynomial estimator, the latter being dominant in applied settings.

2.1. *Shape-Constrained Locally Weighted Regression*

Shape-constrained nonparametric regression is sometimes required. When imposing shape constraints on local estimators of the form (1) derivative estimates may be necessary (i.e. derivatives of $g(x)$ with respect to x). For the local constant estimator, the analytic derivative of $\hat{g}(x)$ has been studied by Rilstone and Ullah (1989). For the local polynomial estimator, derivatives are delivered by the estimation procedure itself, that is, the local linear estimator delivers estimators of $g(x)$ and $g'(x)$, the local quadratic estimators of $g(x)$, $g'(x)$, and $g''(x)$ and so forth. To impose shape constraints, one can introduce n weights p_i, $i = 1, \ldots, n$, in the class of estimators given in Eq. (1) as follows:

$$\hat{g}(x|p) = \sum_{i=1}^{n} W_i(x) y_i p_i. \tag{2}$$

Shape constraints of the form

$$l(x) \leq \frac{d^j}{dx^j} \hat{g}(x|p) \leq u(x), \tag{3}$$

for arbitrary $l(\cdot)$, $u(\cdot)$ and j, are obtained by solving a nonlinear program to obtain the p_i (hence $\hat{g}(x|p)$) satisfying the constraint (3); see Hall and Huang (2001) and Du et al. (2013) for further details. When $j = 0$ the constraint is on the conditional mean $g(x)$, when $j = 1$ on its first derivative, etc. For constraints such as monotonicity and concavity, we require the jth derivative of Eq. (2) which involves the jth derivative of $W_i(x)$ with respect to x, that is,

$$\frac{d^j}{dx^j}\hat{g}(x|p) = \sum_{i=1}^{n} W_i^{(j)}(x) y_i p_i \tag{4}$$

where $W_i^{(j)}(x) = \frac{d^j}{dx^j} W_i(x)$. From Eq. (4) it is evident that imposing constraints on derivatives necessitates computation of analytic derivatives, that is, ones that coincide with the derivative of the estimator $\hat{g}(x|p)$. Though we consider the single-predictor setting here by way of illustration, shape restrictions can be imposed in the multiple predictor setting; see Du et al. (2013) for illustrations. We now turn to the local constant and local linear derivative estimators as they play a central role in what follows.

2.2. *Local Constant Derivative Estimation*

We first consider the local constant derivative estimator studied by Rilstone and Ullah (1989) as it nicely illustrates the role played by the analytic derivative. The local constant (Nadaraya, 1965; Watson, 1964) estimator of $g(x)$ is obtained as $\arg\min_a \mathcal{S}$, where $\mathcal{S}$ is given by the locally weighted sum of squares,

$$\mathcal{S} = \sum_{i=1}^{n} (y_i - a)^2 \, K(z_i),$$

where $K(z_i) \equiv K((x_i - x)/h)$ is a kernel function such as the Gaussian or Epanechnikov weight function, which yields the local constant estimator

$$\hat{g}(x) = \frac{\sum_{i=1}^{n} K(z_i) y_i}{\sum_{i=1}^{n} K(z_i)} = \sum_{i=1}^{n} W_i(x) y_i,$$

where the local weights for this estimator are of the form $W_i(x) = K(z_i)/\sum_{i=1}^{n} K(z_i)$. The local constant estimator of the first derivative of $g(x)$ is the analytic derivative of $\hat{g}(x)$ with respect to x, that is,

$$\hat{\beta}(x) = \frac{d}{dx}\hat{g}(x) = \sum_{i=1}^{n} \frac{d}{dx} W_i(x) y_i = \sum_{i=1}^{n} W_i'(x) y_i$$

and was studied by Rilstone and Ullah (1989). The local constant estimator, however, is known to suffer from so-called 'boundary bias'. In applied settings, local polynomial estimation is often preferred as it possesses the same bias in the interior of the support as it does at the boundaries, unlike its local constant peer. The local linear variant is dominant in applied settings, so we consider the local linear estimator by way of illustration.

2.3. *Local Linear Taylor-Based Derivative Estimation*

Assuming that the second derivative of $E[Y|x]$ exists, then in a small neighbourhood of a point x, by Taylor approximation we can write $E[Y|x_0] \approx E[Y|x] + (\partial E[Y|x]/\partial x)(x_0 - x) = a + b(x_0 - x)$. The problem of estimating $g(x) \equiv E[Y|x]$ is equivalent to the local linear regression problem of estimating the intercept a. The problem of estimating the derivative $\beta(x) \equiv \partial E[Y|x]/\partial x$ is equivalent to the local linear regression problem of estimating the slope b. The local linear estimators of a and b, denoted by $\hat{a}$ and $\hat{b}$, are obtained as $\arg\min_{a,b} \mathcal{S}$ where $\mathcal{S}$ is given by the locally weighted sum of squares

$$\mathcal{S} = \sum_{i=1}^{n} (y_i - a - b(x_i - x))^2 K(z_i).$$

In this univariate predictor setting, the local linear regression estimator $\hat{g}(x) = \hat{a}$ can be shown to be

$$\hat{g}(x) = \frac{\sum_{i=1}^{n} (S_2(x) - S_1(x)(x_i - x)) K(z_i) y_i}{S_2(x) S_0(x) - S_1^2(x)} = \frac{\sum_{i=1}^{n} C_i(x) y_i}{D(x)} = \sum_{i=1}^{n} W_i(x) y_i, \tag{5}$$

where

$$S_j(x) = \sum_{i=1}^{n} (x_i - x)^j K(z_i),$$

while the local linear (i.e. Taylor-based) derivative estimator, $\hat{\beta}(x)=\hat{b}$, can be shown to be

$$\hat{\beta}(x)=\frac{\sum_{i=1}^{n}\left(S_0(x)(x_i-x)-S_1(x)\right)K(z_i)y_i}{D(x)}=\frac{\sum_{i=1}^{n}E_i(x)y_i}{D(x)}=\sum_{i=1}^{n}B_i(x)y_i. \tag{6}$$

See Fan and Gijbels (1996) for further details.

2.4. *Local Linear Analytic Derivative Estimation*

An alternative derivative estimator, the 'analytic' derivative of $\hat{g}(x)$ which we denote by $\hat{\beta}^a(x)$, is obtained by taking the derivative of $\hat{g}(x)$ defined in Eq. (5), and is given by

$$\hat{\beta}^a(x)=\sum_{i=1}^{n}W_i'(x)y_i, \tag{7}$$

where $W_i'(x)$ is the derivative of $W_i(x)$ from Eq. (5) with respect to x and is given by

$$\begin{aligned}W_i'(x)&=\frac{D(x)C_i'(x)-C_i(x)D'(x)}{D(x)^2}\\&=\frac{D(x)R_{1,i}(x)K(z_i)+D(x)R_{2,i}(x)K'(z_i)-C_i(x)R_3(x)}{D(x)^2}\\&=\frac{R_{1,i}(x)K(z_i)+R_{2,i}(x)K'(z_i)}{D(x)}-W_i(x)\frac{R_3(x)}{D(x)},\end{aligned}$$

where

$$\begin{aligned}R_{1,i}(x)&=T_2(x)-T_1(x)(x_i-x)+S_1(x)\\R_{2,i}(x)&=S_2(x)-S_1(x)(x_i-x)\\R_3(x)&=T_2(x)S_0(x)+S_2(x)T_0(x)-2S_1(x)T_1(x),\end{aligned}$$

and where $T_j(x)$ is given below.

To obtain this result, we note that

$$\begin{aligned}C_i'(x)&=\frac{d}{dx}\left[\left(S_2(x)-S_1(x)(x_i-x)\right)K(z_i)\right]\\&=\left(T_2(x)-T_1(x)(x_i-x)+S_1(x)\right)K(z_i)+\left(S_2(x)-S_1(x)(x_i-x)\right)K'(z_i).\end{aligned}$$

Note that when $j \geq 1$, we have

$$T_j(x) = S_j'(x) = \sum_{i=1}^{n} \frac{d}{dx}(x_i - x)^j K(z_i)$$
$$= \sum_{i=1}^{n} \left((x_i - x)^j K'(z_i) - j(x_i - x)^{j-1} K(z_i)\right),$$

while, when $j = 0$,

$$S_0(x) = \sum_{i=1}^{n} K(z_i),$$

hence

$$T_0(x) = S_0'(x) = \sum_{i=1}^{n} K'(z_i).$$

Finally,

$$D'(x) = \frac{d}{dx}\left[S_2(x)S_0(x) - S_1^2(x)\right]$$
$$= T_2(x)S_0(x) + S_2(x)T_0(x) - 2S_1(x)T_1(x).$$

Therefore, $D(x)C_i'(x) - C_i(x)D'(x)$ is seen to be

$$D(x)\left\{(T_2(x) - T_1(x)(x_i - x) + S_1(x))\, K(z_i) + (S_2(x) - S_1(x)(x_i - x))\, K'(z_i)\right\}$$
$$- C_i(x)\left\{T_2(x)S_0(x) + S_2(x)T_0(x) - 2S_1(x)T_1(x)\right\}.$$

As it turns out, the Taylor-based and analytic local linear derivative estimators given in Eqs. (6) and (7), respectively, may not coincide. We now turn to an assessment of the degree to which they may differ and the conditions under which they are equal.

2.5. *Assessing Divergence between Analytic and Taylor Derivative Estimates*

From the definition of the local linear Taylor-based and analytic derivatives, we see that

$$\begin{aligned}\hat{\beta}(x) &= \sum_{i=1}^{n} B_i(x) y_i + \left(\hat{\beta}^a(x) - \sum_{i=1}^{n} W_i'(x) y_i\right) \\ &= \hat{\beta}^a(x) - \sum_{i=1}^{n} \left(B_i(x) - W_i'(x)\right) y_i.\end{aligned}$$

Observe that when $h \to \infty$, $K(z_i) = K(0) = c_0$, $T_0(x) = 0$, $T_1(x) = -nc_0$, $T_2(x) = -2c_0 \sum_{i=1}^{n} (x_i - x)$, $S_0(x) = nc_0$, $S_1(x) = c_0 \sum_{i=1}^{n} (x_i - x)$, and $S_2(x) = c_0 \sum_{i=1}^{n} (x_i - x)^2$. Then

$$\begin{aligned}R_{1,i}(x) &= T_2(x) - T_1(x)(x_i - x) + S_1(x) \\ &= -c_0 \sum_{i=1}^{n} (x_i - x) + nc_0(x_i - x), \\ R_{2,i}(x) &= S_2(x) - S_1(x)(x_i - x) \\ &= c_0 \sum_{i=1}^{n} (x_i - x)^2 - c_0(x_i - x) \sum_{i=1}^{n} (x_i - x), \\ R_3(x) &= T_2(x)S_0(x) + S_2(x)T_0(x) - 2S_1(x)T_1(x) \\ &= -2nc_0^2 \sum_{i=1}^{n} (x_i - x) + 2nc_0^2 \sum_{i=1}^{n} (x_i - x) = 0,\end{aligned}$$

hence

$$\begin{aligned}W_i'(x) &= \frac{R_{1,i}(x) K(z_i)}{D(x)} \\ &= \frac{-c_0^2 \sum_{i=1}^{n} (x_i - x) + nc_0^2(x_i - x)}{D(x)} \\ &= \frac{E_i(x)}{D(x)} \\ &= B_i(x),\end{aligned}$$

hence

$$\lim_{h\to\infty} \hat{\beta}(x) = \hat{\beta}^a(x),$$

that is, as h increases the analytic and local linear derivatives will converge. Otherwise, they may differ, sometimes substantially so. Though it is common to think of $h \to 0$ as $n \to \infty$ being a requirement for consistent local estimation, this is not always the case. For instance, it is known that $h \to \infty$ is appropriate when using the local constant estimator in the presence of an irrelevant predictor, or when using the local linear estimator when the underlying data-generating process (DGP) is in fact linear, or when the DGP is analytic and one uses a data-driven choice of polynomial order; see Hall, Li, and Racine (2007) and Hall and Racine (2015) for details. In such cases, when cross-validation appropriately selects a large value of h, the divergence will not arise.

The divergence metric

$$\|\hat{\beta}(x) - \hat{\beta}^a(x)\| / \|\hat{\beta}(x)\| \tag{8}$$

could serve as a useful measure of the degree to which these derivative estimates diverge, where $\|.\|$ denotes Euclidean norm. The divergence between the local polynomial derivative estimate and the analytic derivative of the local polynomial regression estimate discussed above is present in multiple predictor settings as well, and Eq. (8) could be use element-wise as a divergence metric.

Before proceeding, some comments on the estimation of higher order derivatives are in order. One might suspect that, when estimating higher order derivatives, the divergence between the derivative estimates would increase. However, in order to estimate higher order derivatives in the local polynomial setting, we would need to increase the order of the polynomial used, and in general the size of the bandwidth increases with the order of the polynomial, other things equal. But this depends on the underlying DGP as well, as discussed in Hall & Racine (2015), so there is no guarantee that the problem will be exacerbated when estimating higher order derivatives, but it almost certainly will manifest itself to some extent.

2.6. Related Nonparametric Estimators

In addition to the local polynomial estimators (Fan & Gijbels, 1996) considered above, there exist a range of nonparametric regression estimators including series estimators (Newey, 1997), regression splines (de Boor, 2001) and partitioning estimators (Cattaneo & Farrell, 2013). Series estimators and splines are 'global' in nature, while partitioning estimators use least-squares polynomial approximations within each partition or 'cell'. For the above estimators, derivatives are obtained analytically. See, by way of illustration, Cattaneo and Farrell (2013, p. 130) whose 'estimator of $\partial^m \mu(x)$ is $\partial^m \hat{\mu}(x)$' ($\mu(x)$ is our $g(x)$). Given that these approaches employ analytic estimators of derivatives by default, there is no mismatch arising between the analytic and conventional derivative estimator. The mismatch uncovered herein is a by-product of the nature of the local weighting used in local polynomial estimation.

The issue at hand is whether, in applied settings, any such divergence between the Taylor-based and analytic derivatives arises when conducting local polynomial estimation and, if so, what impact it might have. We now consider a simple illustration that will serve to highlight this divergence.

3. DEMONSTRATION: THE PRESTIGE DATA

We consider the 'Prestige' data taken from the R package 'car' (Fox & Weisberg, 2011) and use variables 'income' (average income of incumbents, in thousands of dollars, in 1971) and the logarithm of 'prestige' (the Pineo-Porter prestige score for occupation, from a social survey conducted in the mid-1960s, collected by Census Canada). This dataset contains $n = 102$ observations. We conduct local linear estimation with least-squares cross-validation for bandwidth selection using the R package np (Hayfield & Racine, 2008). The cross-validated bandwidth using a second-order Gaussian kernel is $h = 3.48$ thousand dollars. The local linear estimate $\hat{g}(x)$ is presented in Fig. 1.

The local linear Taylor-based derivative $\hat{\beta}(x)$ is presented in Fig. 2 along with the analytic derivative $\hat{\beta}^a(x)$ and that obtained by numerical differentiation of $\hat{g}(x)$ itself, denoted as $\Delta\hat{g}(x)/\Delta x$. The inclusion of the numerical derivative is to verify that the analytic derivative coincides with the derivative of $\hat{g}(x)$. For a fairly large range of income, Fig. 2 reveals the substantial discrepancy between the Taylor-based and analytic derivative estimates. The value of the divergence metric given in Eq. (8) is $\|\hat{\beta}(x) - \hat{\beta}^a(x)\| / \|\hat{\beta}(x)\| = 0.102$.

Close inspection of Figs. 1 and 2 reveal that the regression function $\hat{g}(x)$ is non-monotonic for large values of income (i.e. $\hat{g}(x)$ falls slightly, while a close examination of Fig. 2 reveals that for high levels of income, the analytic/numeric derivatives assume negative values). In addition, the Taylor-based estimate is substantially higher than the analytic derivative over much of the support, that is, it overstates the actual derivative of $\hat{g}(x)$.

Suppose, by way of illustration, that we required a monotonic estimate $\hat{g}(x)$, and imposed monotonicity on the resulting regression function, that is, we imposed $\hat{g}'(x|p) \geq 0$. The resulting shape constrained estimator is presented in Fig. 3, and the unconstrained and constrained derivative estimates are presented in Fig. 4.

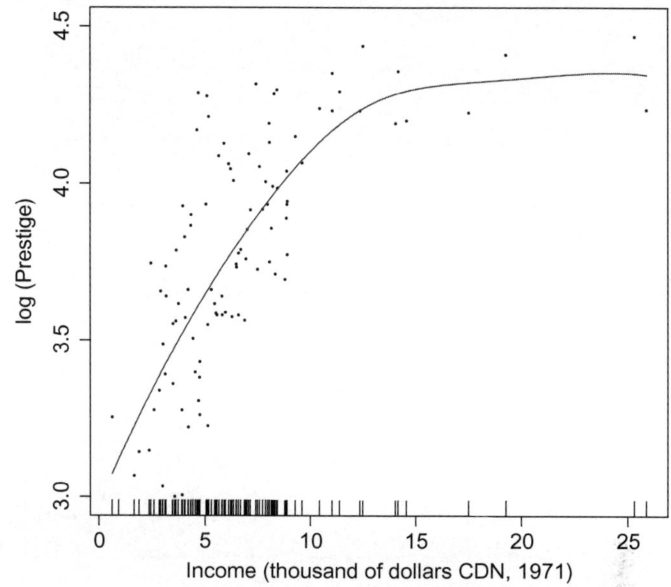

Fig. 1. Local Linear Regression, Prestige Data.

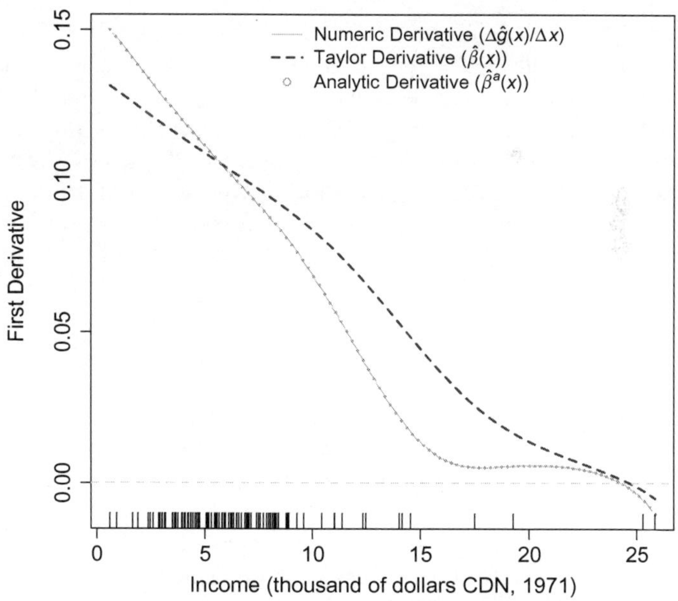

Fig. 2. Taylor versus Analytic Derivatives.

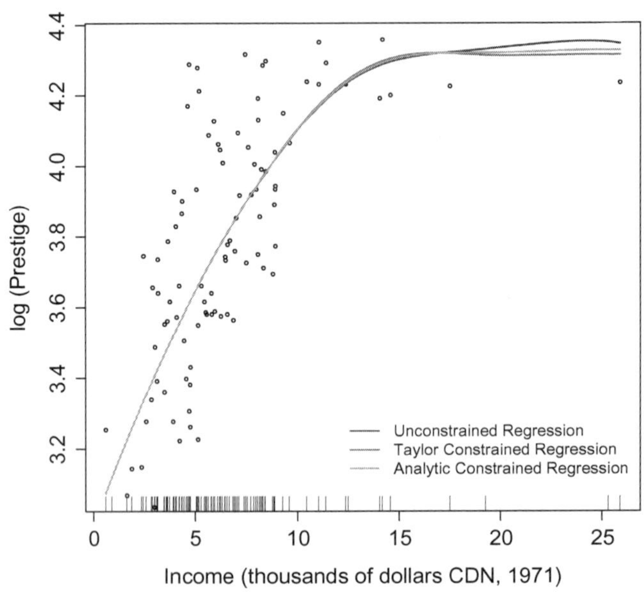

Fig. 3. Constrained Local Linear Regression.

Close inspection of Fig. 3 reveals a rather curious artefact of using the Taylor-based derivative to impose monotonicity, namely that the Taylor-based shape-constrained estimate is non-monotone in income. This is most unwelcome as we imposed monotonicity on the resulting estimate. The analytic-based shape constrained estimate is, of course, monotonic. This simple illustration demonstrates the pitfalls of using local polynomial derivatives in settings where one requires the derivative of $\hat{g}(x)$, not just a consistent estimator of $\beta(x) = d\, g(x)/dx$.

3.1. Implications for Inference

The use of Taylor-based derivatives for shape-constrained estimation is not the only illustration of the potential pitfalls associated with local polynomial estimation, and the use of analytic derivatives might also be germane for inference and prediction. For instance, nonparametric tests of significance may involve imposing the null $H_0: \beta(x) = 0$ almost everywhere, with rejection of the null implying, for instance, predictability in the conditional mean in a time-series setting. But given that the Taylor-based derivative estimates may fail to correspond to the conditional mean estimate, the outcome of the test may be misleading when it comes to testing

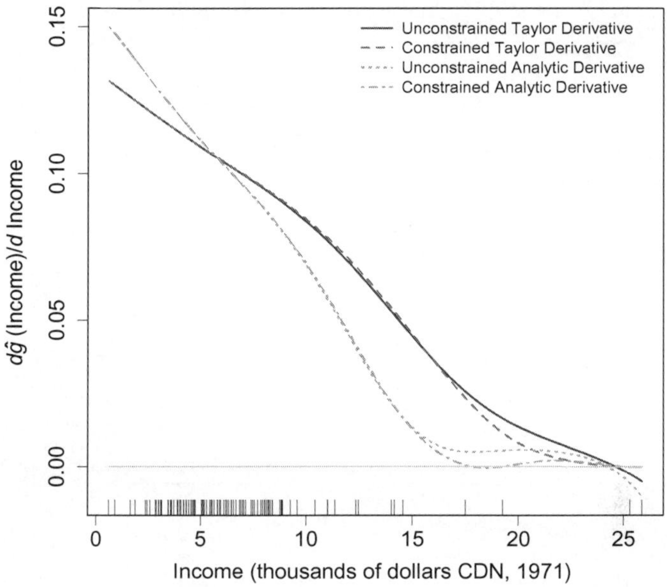

Fig. 4. Constrained and Unconstrained Derivatives for the Prestige Dataset.

for predictability in the conditional mean of a series. By way of illustration, suppose one wanted to test for a function being monotone increasing and suppose that the unrestricted function was monotone increasing. But if the derivative estimate possesses the incorrect sign (as happens in the Prestige illustration above) this may well affect both size and power of the test.

4. FINITE-SAMPLE COMPARISON OF ANALYTIC- AND TAYLOR-BASED DERIVATIVES

The question naturally arises, 'why not simply always use the analytic derivatives?' This is certainly a reasonable query. One would expect that the analytic derivatives are less biased in finite-sample than the Taylor-based ones given the results presented above. The issue is whether, from a square error loss perspective, the use of analytic derivatives over its Taylor-based peer can be justified in general.

To address this issue, we consider a Monte-Carlo simulation in which the data is generated from

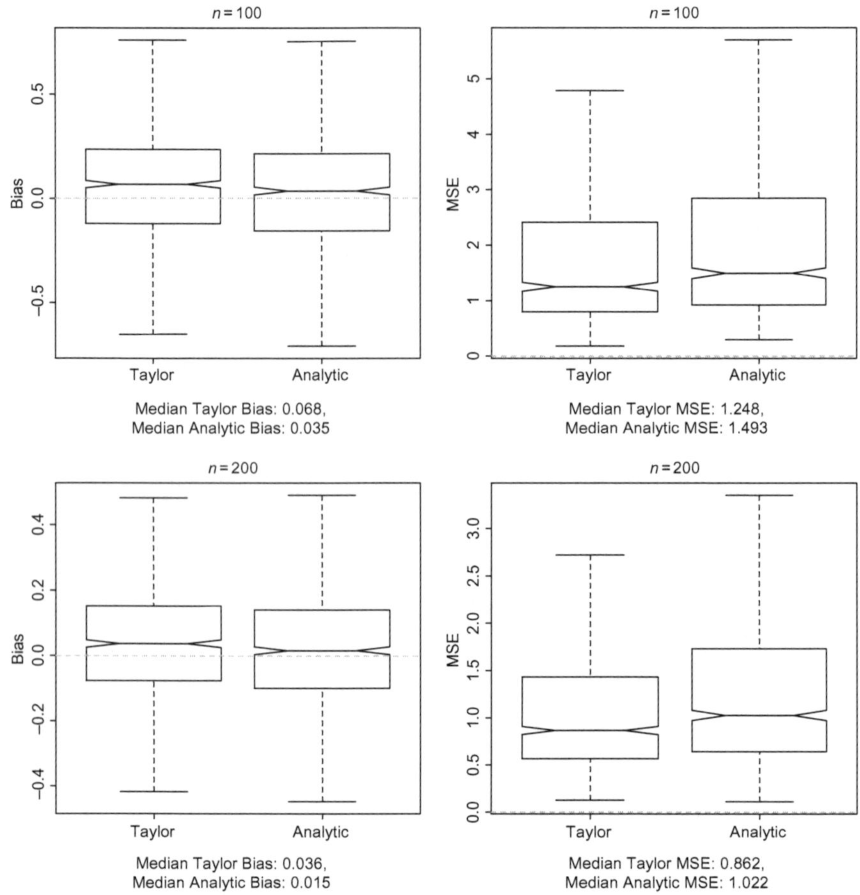

Fig. 5. Boxplots of Bias (Left Figures) and MSE (Right Figures) of the Analytic (Right Boxplot in Each Figure) and Taylor-Based (Left Boxplot in Each Figure) Derivative Estimates, $\sigma = 0.25$, $n = 100, 200$.

$$y = \sin(2\pi x) + \epsilon, \tag{9}$$

where $x \sim U[0, 1]$ and $\epsilon \sim N(0, \sigma^2)$ with $\sigma = 0.25, 0.50$. We consider $M = 1,000$ Monte Carlo draws from this data-generating process. Here, $g'(x) = 2\pi \cos(2\pi x)$, and we compare the analytic and Taylor-based estimates. We present boxplots of the bias and MSE of the estimator where each is averaged pointwise over the empirical support of the data. Results are presented in Figs. 5 and 6 for samples of size

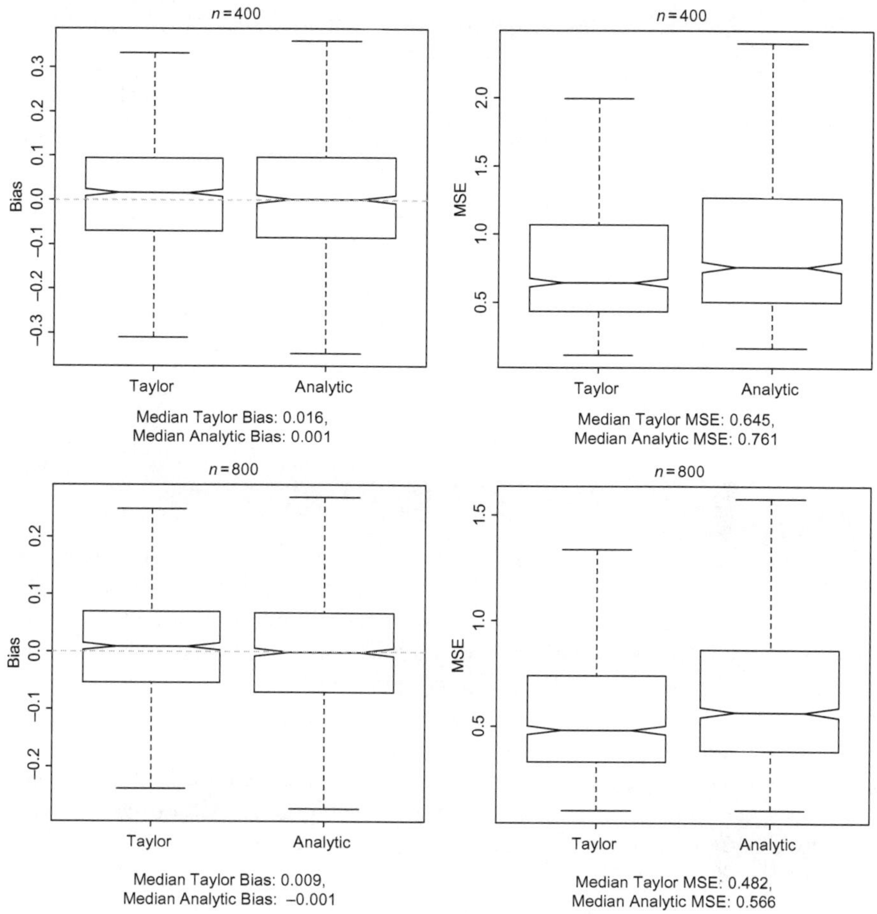

Fig. 6. Boxplots of Bias (Left Figures) and MSE (Right Figures) of the Analytic (Right Boxplot in Each Figure) and Taylor-Based (Left Boxplot in Each Figure) Derivative Estimates, $\sigma = 0.25$, $n = 400, 800$.

$n = 100$, 200, 400 and 800 and $\sigma = 0.25$. Median bias and MSE are summarized in Table 1 for the above sample sizes and for $\sigma = 0.25, 0.50$.

Figs. 5 and 6 reveal that the analytic derivatives display less bias than the Taylor-based ones, while the median bias tends towards zero for both approaches as n increases. However, the analytic derivatives display higher MSE for all n, so from an MSE perspective using analytic derivatives may not be warranted in general.

Table 1. Median Bias and MSE of the Analytic and Taylor-Based Derivative Estimates.

n	σ	Bias		MSE	
		Analytic	Taylor	Analytic	Taylor
100	0.25	0.035	0.068	1.493	1.248
200	0.25	0.015	0.036	1.022	0.862
400	0.25	0.001	0.016	0.761	0.645
800	0.25	−0.001	0.009	0.566	0.482
100	0.50	0.072	0.145	2.802	2.438
200	0.50	0.036	0.072	2.024	1.716
400	0.50	0.040	0.069	1.377	1.210
800	0.50	0.020	0.036	1.042	0.882

5. SUMMARY

We consider the impact of using local polynomial Taylor-based derivative estimates for shape-constrained estimation, and caution practitioners that these derivatives may be internally inconsistent with the estimated regression function. However, in cases where internal consistency is required, an option is to instead use analytic derivatives. Such derivatives possess lower bias than their Taylor-based counterparts, however they also are less efficient from the mean square error perspective so their use as a general replacement for Taylor-based derivatives cannot be justified, at least not from a square error perspective. For shape-constrained estimation and other uses that require internal consistency between the regression function and derivative estimates, analytic derivatives cannot be avoided.

ACKNOWLEDGEMENTS

I would like to express my deepest gratitude to Aman Ullah for his encouragement and guidance over the course of my education and career. I would also like to acknowledge Chris Parmeter for his encouragement and feedback, and with whom previous work and discussions provided the groundwork for this paper, and to thank Carlos Ordas Criado for the illustrative example used herein. Finally, I would like to gratefully acknowledge support from the Natural Sciences and Engineering Research Council of Canada (NSERC:www.nserc.ca), the Social Sciences and Humanities Research Council of Canada (SSHRC:www.sshrc.ca), and the Shared Hierarchical Academic Research Computing Network (SHARCNET:www.sharcnet.ca).

REFERENCES

Cattaneo, M. D., & Farrell, M. H. (2013). Optimal convergence rates, Bahadur representation, and asymptotic normality of partitioning estimators. *Journal of Econometrics, 174*, 127–143.

Cleveland, W. S. (1979). Robust locally weighted regression and smoothing scatterplots. *Journal of the American Statistical Association, 74*, 829–836.

de Boor, C. (2001). *A practical guide to splines*. New York, NY: Springer.

Du, P., Parmeter, C. F., & Racine, J. S. (2013). Nonparametric kernel regression with multiple predictors and multiple shape constraints. *Statistica Sinica, 23*(3), 1343–1372.

Fan, J. (1992). Design-adaptive nonparametric regression. *Journal of the American Statistical Association, 87*, 998–1004.

Fan, J., & Gijbels, I. (1996). *Local polynomial modelling and its applications*. London: Chapman and Hall.

Fox, J., & Weisberg, S. (2011). *An R companion to applied regression* (2nd ed.). Thousand Oaks, CA: Sage. Retrieved from http://socserv.socsci.mcmaster.ca/jfox/Books/Companion

Gasser, T., & Müller, H.-G. (1979). Kernel estimation of regression functions. In *Smoothing techniques for curve estimation* (pp. 23–68). New York, NY: Springer-Verlag.

Hall, P. G., & Racine, J. S. (2015). Infinite order cross-validated local polynomial regression. *Journal of Econometrics, 185*(2), 510–525.

Hall, P., & Huang, H. (2001). Nonparametric kernel regression subject to monotonicity constraints. *Annals of Statistics, 29*, 624–647.

Hall, P., Li, Q., & Racine, J. S. (2007). Nonparametric estimation of regression functions in the presence of irrelevant regressors. *The Review of Economics and Statistics, 89*, 784–789.

Hayfield, T., & Racine, J. S. (2008). Nonparametric econometrics: The np package. *Journal of Statistical Software, 27*(5). Retrieved from http://www.jstatsoft.org/v27/i05/

Lee, T., Tu, Y., & Ullah, A. (2014). Nonparametric and semiparametric regressions subject to monotonicity constraints: Estimation and forecasting. *Journal of Econometrics, 182*, 196–210.

Nadaraya, E. A. (1965). On nonparametric estimates of density functions and regression curves. *Theory of Applied Probability, 10*, 186–190.

Newey, W. K. (1997). Convergence rates and asymptotic normality for series estimators. *Journal of Econometrics, 79*, 147–168.

Priestley, M. B., & Chao, M. T. (1972). Nonparametric function fitting. *Journal of the Royal Statistical Society, 34*, 385–392.

Rilstone, P., & Ullah, A. (1989). Nonparametric estimation of response coefficients. *Communications in Statistics – Theory and Methods, 18*(7), 2615–2627.

Stone, C. J. (1977). Consistent nonparametric regression. *Annals of Statistics, 5*, 595–645.

Watson, G. S. (1964). Smooth regression analysis. *Sankhya, 26:15*, 359–372.

A SIMPLE CONSISTENT NONPARAMETRIC ESTIMATOR OF THE LORENZ CURVE

Yu Yvette Zhang[a], Ximing Wu[a], and Qi Li[b,c]
[a]*Department of Agricultural Economics, Texas A&M University, College Station, TX, U.S.A.*
[b]*Department of Economics, Texas A&M University, College Station, TX, U.S.A.*
[c]*Department of Economics, Tsinghua University, Beijing, People's Republic of China*

ABSTRACT

We propose a nonparametric estimator of the Lorenz curve that satisfies its theoretical properties, including monotonicity and convexity. We adopt a transformation approach that transforms a constrained estimation problem into an unconstrained one, which is estimated nonparametrically. We utilize the splines to facilitate the numerical implementation of our estimator and to provide a parametric representation of the constructed Lorenz curve. We conduct Monte Carlo simulations to demonstrate the superior performance of the proposed estimator. We apply our method to estimate the Lorenz curve of the U.S. household income distribution and calculate the Gini index based on the estimated Lorenz curve.

Essays in Honor of Aman Ullah
Advances in Econometrics, Volume 36, 635–653

ISSN: 0731-9053/doi:10.1108/S0731-905320160000036028

Keywords: Lorenz curve; spline estimation; monotonicity; convexity; Gini index

JEL classifications: C14; C52; D63

1. INTRODUCTION

The Lorenz curve is an important tool of economic analysis. For instance, the Lorenz curve of an income distribution describes the proportion of total income assumed by the bottom u proportion of the population, where $u \in [0, 1]$. The Gini index, a popular measure of economic inequality, is closely related to the Lorenz curve: The value of Gini index equals twice the area between a Lorenz curve and the 45° line of a unit square, which corresponds to a completely egalitarian distribution. Lorenz curve is also useful for the testing of stochastic dominance. If Lorenz curve A is everywhere above Lorenz curve B, then the corresponding distribution A stochastically dominates distribution B. For general overviews of the Lorenz curve and its applications in economics, see, for example, Chotikapanich (2008) and Silber (1999, Chapters 10 and 11).

Consider a positive random variable Y with a distribution function $F : R^+ \to [0, 1]$. Throughout this study, we assume that F is strictly monotone with a quantile function $Q(u) = F^{-1}(u)$ and continuously differentiable with a density function $f(y) = F'(y)$. The Lorenz curve can be constructed as follows:

$$L(u) = \frac{\int_0^u Q(t)dt}{\int_0^1 Q(t)dt} = \frac{\int_0^u Q(t)dt}{\mu}, \quad u \in [0, 1],$$

where $\mu = \int ydF(y) < \infty$ is the population mean.

The Lorenz curve has the following properties:

1. $0 \le L(u) \le u$ for all $u \in [0, 1]$.
2. $L(0) = 0$ and $L(1) = 1$.
3. $L'(u) > 0$ for all $u \in [0, 1]$.
4. $L''(u) > 0$ for all $u \in [0, 1]$.

In other words, the Lorenz curve resides below the 45° of the unit square and is monotonically increasing and strictly convex (except for a completely egalitarian distribution). Throughout the text, for simplicity, we shall use convexity in the place of strict convexity. For a detailed treatment of the properties of the Lorenz curve, see, for example, Gastwirth (1972).

Analogous to the empirical distribution function, the empirical Lorenz curve can be constructed from data in a straightforward manner. Consider $\{Y_i\}_{i=1}^n$ an *i.i.d.* sample from distribution F and $\{Y_{(i)}\}_{i=1}^n$ its corresponding order statistics arranged in the ascending order. Define

$$s_i \equiv s(u_i) = \frac{\sum_{j=1}^{i} Y_{(j)}}{\sum_{j=1}^{n} Y_{(j)}} \quad \text{and} \quad u_i = \frac{i}{n}, \quad i = 1, \ldots, n. \tag{1}$$

Similar to the empirical distribution function, $s(u) \xrightarrow{p} L(u)$ as $n \to \infty$ uniformly for $u \in [0, 1]$ under very mild regularity conditions. Although the empirical Lorenz curve can be easily constructed, it suffers from the drawbacks that it is not a smooth function and does not allow easy portability (like the empirical distribution function, its parametrization requires the entire sample of data). Luo (2013) presents a kernel-based estimator that yields a smoothed empirical Lorenz curve. However, this kernel estimator, like the empirical Lorenz curve, lacks portability.

This study concerns the estimation of the Lorenz curve. There exists in the literature two general approaches of estimation. The parametric approach assumes some parametric forms, often out of mathematical convenience. Parametric Lorenz curves usually satisfy its theoretical properties and converge at root-N rates. Their limitations include the lack of flexibility and possible misspecification errors. Sarabia (2008) reviews parametric estimation of Lorenz curves. In contrast, the nonparametric approach employs smoothing techniques to encourage flexibility (see, e.g., Ryu & Slottje, 1996, for series-based estimators, Luo, 2013, for kernel-based estimators, and Cowell & Victoria-Fester, 2008, for semiparametric estimations of the Lorenz curves and robustness issues). This advantage, however, is gained at the price of slower convergence rates and oftentimes violations to the theoretical properties of the Lorenz curve. There is also a small literature that utilizes the Dirichlet distribution in the estimation of Lorenz curves (Chotikapanich, & Griffiths, 2002; Hasegawa & Kozumi, 2003).

The goal of this study is to propose a flexible nonparametric estimator of the Lorenz curve that satisfies all its theoretical properties. We adopt a transformation approach, in the spirit of Ramsay (1998), to incorporate the theoretical constraints. This approach transforms a constrained estimation problem into an unconstrained one. We model the unconstrained component using nonparametric methods to gain flexibility. In particular, we use the spline method in our nonparametric modeling. This approach facilitates the numerical implementations of the proposed estimator. In addition, it provides the convenience of portability such that the resultant Lorenz curve, albeit nonparametrically constructed, is parametrized by a small number of parameters.

The rest of this paper is organized as follows. Section 2 provides a brief review of the relevant literature. Section 3 presents our alternative estimator and Section 4 proposes a nonparametric estimator of the proposed method. Sections 5 and 6 report Monte Carlo simulations and an empirical application. The last section concludes the paper. Some technical details are provided in the appendix.

2. ESTIMATION OF LORENZ CURVES: A BRIEF REVIEW

There exists a sizable literature on the estimation of the Lorenz curve. Chotikapanich (2008) and Silber (1999, Chapters 10 and 11) offer excellent overviews of this literature. In this section, we provide a brief review of some commonly used estimators of the Lorenz curve.

In terms of modeling strategy, there are generally two possibilities: the direct and the indirect approaches. The direct approach models the Lorenz curve, usually via statistical fitting of the empirical Lorenz curves. In contrast, the indirect approach first models some related subject such as the density, distribution, or quantile function and then constructs its corresponding Lorenz curve.

Regardless of the modeling strategy, either the parametric or nonparametric method can be used to estimate the Lorenz curve. Kakwani and Podder (1973) propose a parsimonious Lorenz curve as follows:

$$L(u) = u \exp\left(-h(1-u) + \mu\right), \tag{2}$$

which provides reasonable fits to some commonly used income distributions. Basmann, Hayes, Johnson, and Slottje (1990) generalize model (2) to provide enhanced flexibility. Their model takes the form

$$L(u) = u^{au+b} \exp\left(-g(1-u^2) - h(1-u) + \mu\right). \tag{3}$$

Both Models (2) and (3), via a logarithm transformation, can be estimated by OLS based on the empirical Lorenz coordinates (1).

Ryu and Slottje (1996) propose two nonparametric estimators of the Lorenz curve. Their first estimator takes the indirect approach. A two-step procedure is suggested. First, the quantile function is approximated by a J-th degree exponential polynomial series:

$$Q(u) \approx \exp\left(\sum_{j=0}^{J} a_j u^j\right). \tag{4}$$

This approach is equivalent to approximating the logarithm of a quantile function by polynomials and can be easily implemented by OLS. Denote the estimated coefficients by $\hat{a} = (\hat{a}_0, \ldots, \hat{a}_J)$. The Lorenz curve is then constructed as

$$\hat{L}(u_i) = \frac{1}{n\hat{\mu}} \sum_{k=1}^{i} \exp\left(\sum_{j=0}^{J} \hat{a}_j u_k^j \right), \quad i = 1, \ldots, n, \tag{5}$$

where $\hat{\mu}$ is the sample average.

Ryu and Slottje (1996) also propose a direct estimator of the Lorenz curve based on the Bernstein polynomials. This estimator is given by

$$\hat{L}(u) = \sum_{j=0}^{J} L(j/J) \binom{J}{j} u^j (1-u)^{J-j}. \tag{6}$$

In practice, the unknown Lorenz curve $L(j/J)$ is replaced by its empirical counterpart given in Eq. (1).

By construction, the direct estimators (2) and (3) satisfy all theoretical properties of the Lorenz curve. They are, however, vulnerable to misspecification errors because of their parametric nature. In contrast, the two nonparametric estimators converge to the true Lorenz curve asymptotically under some mild regularity conditions, but they are not without their limitations. The exponential polynomial estimator (5) does not guarantee convexity because the exponential polynomial approximation to a quantile function, given in Eq. (4), is not necessarily monotonically increasing. Furthermore, it is based on the modeling of the quantile function; an optimal approximation to the quantile function may not be optimal for the Lorenz curve. Lastly, the Bernstein estimator (6) enjoys favorable theoretical properties: it preserves the properties of $L(\cdot)$ such as monotonicity and convexity (see Ryu & Slottje, 1996, for details). We note that, however, this estimator essentially interpolates data and suffers from a rather slow convergence rate. Our experiments indicate that a considerably large number of parameters are required to obtain performance comparable to that of other estimators with a more economical parametrization.

3. AN ALTERNATIVE ESTIMATOR

Aiming to avoid the limitations of the existing methods discussed above, in this section, we propose an alternative estimator that: (i) estimates the Lorenz curve directly; (ii) allows flexible functional forms; and (iii) complies with all theoretical properties of the Lorenz curve. The key innovation of our estimator is to employ integral transformations to transform a constrained problem into an unconstrained one. Subsequently, nonparametric method is applied to the unconstrained component to obtain flexibility.

Our estimator is inspired by the monotone spline estimator of Ramsay (1998). Suppose that one is interested in modeling a strictly monotonic relationship $y = g(x)$ with $g'(x) > 0$ for $x \in R^+$. Ramsay (1998) suggests the following parametrization:

$$g(x) = \int_0^x \exp(r(t))dt.$$

It follows that $g'(x) = \exp(r(x)) > 0$. One advantage of Ramsay's (1998) approach is that the resultant estimates satisfy the monotonicity constrain globally. This approach has been used to model monotonic relationships implied by economic theories; see, for example, Zhang, Gu, and Li (2011) and Liu, Zhang, and Li (2015) on the modeling of monotone bidding processes of auctions.

To further impose convexity, we propose the following model:

$$g(x) = \int_0^x \exp\left(\int_0^s r(t)dt\right) ds.$$

We then have

$$g'(x) = \exp\left(\int_0^x r(t)dt\right) > 0, \quad g''(x) = g'(x)r(x).$$

Thus, for convexity, we can choose $r(\cdot)$ such that $r(x) > 0$ for all x.

We therefore advocate the following parameterization of a Lorenz curve:

$$L(u) = \frac{\int_0^u \exp\left(\int_0^s r(t)dt\right) ds}{\int_0^1 \exp\left(\int_0^s r(t)dt\right) ds}, \quad u \in [0, 1], \tag{7}$$

with

$$r(\cdot): [0, 1] \to R^+,$$

where the denominator ensures that $L(1) = 1$. It can be verified that all four properties of the Lorenz curve listed in Section 1 are satisfied.

We next suggest an economic interpretation of $r(\cdot)$ related to income mobility, which is inspired by Basmann, Hayes, and Slottje (1991). Let $E(u)$ designate the logarithmic derivative of $L(u)$, that is,

$$E(u) = uL'(u)/L(u).$$

Basmann et al. (1991) note that $E(u)$ satisfies the Bernoulli differential equation

$$uE'(u) - \{I(u) + 1\}\, E(u) + E^2(u) = 0,$$

where $I(u)$ is the logarithmic derivative of $L'(u)$. It follows that

$$I(u) = uE'(u)/E(u) + \{E(u) - 1\}\,.$$

Basmann et al. (1991) suggest that $I(u)$ reflects the relative difficulty in moving up the income graduation (as captured by the Lorenz curve) and therefore can be viewed as a "mobility function." For the proposed estimator, note that

$$r(u) = L''(u)/L'(u). \tag{8}$$

Thus, $r(\cdot)$ is the relative curvature of the Lorenz curve. In the spirit of Basmann et al. (1991), r can be interpreted as a mobility function, or more precisely an "immobility function" of the underlying distribution. By construction, it is strictly positive on $u \in [0, 1]$. Therefore, our estimation strategy has an interesting economic interpretation in that we transform the modeling of Lorenz curve to that of its associated mobility function.

We plot in Fig. 1 the density and mobility function (8) of the standard exponential and log-normal distributions. The exponential density is infinite at zero and downward sloping on its entire range. Its mobility function is also infinite at origin and descends quickly. Its slope, however, eventually becomes positive at the right end of the distribution. Intuitively, it is most difficult to escape extreme poverty under an exponential distribution that peaks at origin. The difficulty of moving up the distribution then decreases along the distribution until one gets to the right tail of the distribution, where it again becomes difficult to further move up. In contrast, the log-normal density is finite at origin; it increases until it peaks at $\exp(\mu - \sigma^2)$ and then decreases. Interestingly, its mobility function has a symmetric U shape, which tends to infinity at both ends of the distribution. The symmetry of its mobility function is consistent with the fact that the log-normal distribution is Lorenz symmetric in the sense that it is symmetric about the anti-diagonal of the unit square.

4. NONPARAMETRIC ESTIMATION

We now proceed to the statistical estimation of the proposed model. To ensure convexity, we further write $r(t) = h(m(t))$, where $h(\cdot): R \to R^+$ and $m(\cdot): R \to R$. The parametrization (7) thus transforms a constrained problem (modeling of $g(\cdot)$) into an unconstrained one (modeling of $m(\cdot)$), enforcing the convexity of the thus constructed Lorenz curve.

To obtain flexibility, we model $m(\cdot)$ nonparametrically. Kernel smoothing and spline approximation are two commonly used nonparametric methods. In this study, we adopt the spline estimator out of the consideration of portability: despite its nonparametric nature, the spline estimator admits a parametric representation which facilitates subsequent model manipulation and analysis, especially when sample size is large. In addition, our estimator (7) entails numerical evaluation of a nested integration. It is computationally expensive to implement this estimator if $m(\cdot)$ is modeled by a kernel smoother.

The spline estimation is essentially a series estimation with piecewise polynomial basis functions. For instance, the truncated power series, a commonly used spline basis, are given by

$$1, t, \ldots, t^k, (t - z_1)_+^k, \ldots, (t - z_J)_+^k,$$

where $t_+ = \max(t, 0)$ and $z = \{z_1 < \cdots < z_J\} \in \mathcal{T}$, the support of t, are the so-called *knots* of spline functions. A spline approximation to a smooth function, $m(t) : \mathcal{T} \to R$, consists of a linear combination of spline basis:

$$m_k(t; z) = \beta_0 + \beta_1 t + \cdots + \beta_k t^k + \sum_{j=1}^{J} b_j (t - z_j)_+^k. \tag{9}$$

Generally, the k-th order global polynomials determine the overall shape of the curve, while the piecewise polynomials characterize local deviations from the "baseline" curve and thus facilitate flexibility. One important advantage of the spline basis relative to the power series is its robustness against potentially untamed oscillations associated with high order power series. Spline estimators with a small k and a relatively large J are customarily used to achieve both robustness and flexibility.

Given a spline approximation to $m(\cdot)$, next we need to specify $h(\cdot)$ such that $h(m(t)) > 0$ to ensure the convexity of the resultant Lorenz curve. In principle, any specification satisfying $h(t) > 0$ for all t suffices, such as $h(t) = \exp(t)$, $h(t) = t^2$ or $h(t) = |t|$. For the proposed estimator (7), we advocate the quadratic specification $h(t) = t^2$. Since the square of (piecewise) power series remains power series, it follows that the inner integration of Eq. (7) admits an analytical solution and thus avoids nested integration by numerical methods, which is difficult and numerically rather expensive. We provide in the appendix an algorithm to numerically evaluate

$$s(u; \theta) \equiv \int_0^u \exp\left(\int_0^s m_k^2(t; z) dt\right) ds, \tag{10}$$

where $\theta = (\beta_0, \ldots, \beta_k, b_1, \ldots, b_J)$ and $m_k(\cdot; z)$ is given by Eq. (9). We stress that the choice of quadratic specification is based on computation consideration. We have experimented with the exponential specification $h(t) = \exp(t)$. The results are essentially identical to those from quadratic $h(t)$. However the computation time increases substantially because it now involves expensive nested numerical integration in iterations.

Our estimator of Lorenz curve is then defined by the following minimization problem:

$$\min_{\theta} \sum_{i=1}^{n} (s_i - s(u_i; \theta))^2,$$

where s_i, given in Eq. (1), is the empirical Lorenz curve evaluated at u_i, $i = 1, \ldots, n$. It turns out that the parametrization (10) considerably simplifies the implementation of the proposed estimator, which can be solved by the method of nonlinear least squares. As is suggested by a referee, one can use alternative objective function such as the minimum absolute deviation, which is more robust to possible outliers. This alternative, however, significantly complicates the estimation and inference. Nonetheless, we report in the next section simulation results in terms of both sum of residual squares and sum of absolute residuals. The proposed estimator dominates its competitors according to either criterion.

The practical implementation of spline estimations entails the selection of its polynomial order k and a vector of knots z. For a general treatment of spline specification and estimation, see, for example, Ruppert, Wand, and Carroll (2003). Low-ordered spline basis, for example, $k = 1, 2$, or 3, is often used. It is known that a k-th order spline series is $(k - 1)$ times differentiable. Our estimator is at least twice differentiable regardless of the smoothness of $r(\cdot)$ due to the presence of double integration in its construction. For simplicity, in our simulations and empirical application below we use the linear splines.

Equally-spaced knots or equal-percentile knots are two commonly used principles of knot placement. In our case, the Lorenz curve depicts the relationship between cumulative income share, s, against population share, u, which is uniform on [0, 1]. Therefore the two principles are equivalent. The number of knots can be determined by data driven methods that balance the trade-off between the goodness of fit and model parsimony. For instance, one can use the information criterion (such as the Akaike Information Criterion or Bayesian Information Criterion) or the method of cross validation.

We conclude this section with a discussion of the covariance matrix of Lorenz curve. Similar to the empirical CDF's, the empirical Lorenz curves are not independently distributed. Beach and Davidson (1983) derive the asymptotic covariance matrix of a vector of Lorenz curve coordinates. Let $s = (s_1, \ldots, s_n)'$ be a vector of Lorenz curve associated with accumulated income shares $u = (u_1 < u_2 < \cdots < u_n)' \in (0, 1)$. Denote the corresponding quantiles by $\xi_i = \min\{x : u_i \leq F(x)\}, i = 1, \ldots, n$. Define the truncated mean $\mu_i = E[x | x \leq \xi_i]$, the corresponding Lorenz curves can be written as $s_i = u_i \mu_i / \mu, i = 1, \ldots, n$.

Next let $u_{n+1} = 1$, it follows that $\mu_{n+1} = \mu$. Define

$$\nu = (u_1 \mu_1, \ldots, u_{n+1} \mu_{n+1})'$$

The covariance matrix of ν, denoted by Ω, is then given by

$$\Omega_{ij} = u_i \left\{ \sigma_i^2 + (1 - u_j)(\xi_i - \mu_i)(\xi_j - \mu_j) + (\xi_i - \mu_i)(\mu_j - \mu_i) \right\}, \quad 1 \leq i \leq j \leq n + 1$$

where $\sigma_i^2 = E[(x - \mu_i)^2 | x \leq \xi_i], i = 1, \ldots, n + 1$. Define $G_1 = \mathrm{diag}(1/\mu)$, an n-dimensional diagonal matrix and $G_2 = (-u_1 \mu_1/\mu^2, \ldots, -u_n \mu_n/\mu^2)'$. Denote by $G = [G_1 | G_2]$ the $n \times (n + 1)$ dimensional gradient of s with respect to ν. We then have the covariance matrix of s given by

$$V = G \Omega G'$$

In practice, we replace V with its sample analog. In particular, we set, for $i = 1, \ldots, n$

$$u_i = i/n, \quad \hat{\xi}_i = Y_{(i)}$$

$$\hat{\mu}_i = \frac{1}{i} \sum_{j=1}^{i} Y_{(j)}, \quad \hat{\sigma}_i^2 = \frac{1}{i} \sum_{j=1}^{i} (Y_{(j)} - \hat{\mu}_j)^2$$

and $\hat{V}$ is calculated accordingly.

Our estimator is then given by the following weighted quadratic objective function:

$$\min_{\theta} (s - s(u; \theta))' \hat{V}^{-1} (s - s(u; \theta))$$

Lastly, we advocate regulating $\hat{V}$ to avoid numerical instability due to sampling variation. For a general treatment of regulated or penalized spline estimations, see, for example, Ruppert et al. (2003). In the simulations below, we use instead $\tilde{V} = \hat{V} + I_n/\sqrt{n}$ as the weighting matrix, which is found to provide satisfactory performance. Here, I_n is an identity matrix of dimension n.

5. SIMULATIONS

We use Monte Carlo experiments to explore the numerical performance of the proposed shape-restricted spline estimator (S-Spline hereafter). Following Ryu and Slottje (1996), we consider three distributions that are commonly used to model income distributions: the log-normal distribution, the Gamma distribution, and the Generalized Beta distribution of type II (GB2), whose density function is given by

$$f(x) = \frac{a(x/b)^{ap-1}}{bB(p,q)(1+(x/b))^{p+q}}, \quad x > 0.$$

In particular, we consider the standard log-normal distribution, a Gamma distribution with the shape parameter being 3, and a GB2 distribution with $a = 5.0573, b = 13.5815, p = 0.2961, q = 0.6708$ (as given by McDonald, 1984).

For comparison, we also consider the four commonly used estimators of the Lorenz curve described in Section 2. The estimator by Basmann et al. (1990) (BHJS hereafter) is parametrized by five parameters. To facilitate comparison, we restrict the number of parameters for all nonparametric estimators to be the same. In particular, we set the order of the exponential polynomial estimator (Exp-Poly hereafter) and the Bernstein estimator (Bern hereafter) to be five, and use a linear spline basis with knots $z = (1/4, 1/2, 3/4)$ for S-Spline. The estimator by Kakwani and Podder (1973) (KP hereafter) is a special case of BHJS with two parameters and is included for completeness.

We consider three sample sizes: $n = 50, 100$, and 200; each experiment is repeated 1,000 times. We gauge the estimation performance by the Mean Square Error (MSE) evaluated at a 99-point equally spaced grid $(0.01, 0.02, \ldots, 0.99)$:

$$\text{MSE} = \frac{1}{99}\sum_{i=1}^{99}\left(s_0(i/100) - \hat{s}(i/100)\right)^2,$$

where $s_0(\cdot)$ is the true Lorenz curve calculated from the underlying distribuiton and $\hat{s}(\cdot)$ is its estimate. Table 1 reports the average and median MSE across all repetitions for each experiment. In all experiments, the proposed estimator outperforms the others, often by considerable margins. Some remarks are in order.

- KP, a restricted case of BHJS, is dominated by BHJS. BHJS provides the second best overall performance, plausibly due to its flexible parametrization and theoretical consistency. Nevertheless, it is strictly dominated by S-Spline in all experiments.
- Exp-Poly provides satisfactory results for the log-normal distribution, but is severely biased for the Gamma and GB2 distributions. In all three cases,

Table 1. Simulation Results (KP: Kakwani and Podder (1973) Estimator; BHJS: Basmann et al. (1990) Estimator; Exp-Poly: Exponential Polynomial Estimator of Ryu and Slottje (1996); Bern: Bernstein Estimator of Ryu and Slottje (1996); S-Spline: Shape-Restricted Spline Estimator of the Current Study).

		KP	BHJS	Exp-Poly	Bern	S-Spline
			Log-normal			
$n=50$	Mean MSE	6.35	2.55	1.64	7.01	1.54
	Median MSE	5.80	1.87	1.62	6.80	0.81
$n=100$	Mean MSE	6.10	2.21	1.64	6.37	0.84
	Median MSE	5.77	1.90	1.65	6.15	0.46
$n=200$	Mean MSE	6.04	1.99	1.66	5.99	0.41
	Median MSE	5.91	1.81	1.66	5.97	0.22
			Gamma			
$n=50$	Mean MSE	1.08	0.50	6.95	1.66	0.33
	Median MSE	0.64	0.30	6.85	1.52	0.19
$n=100$	Mean MSE	0.88	0.34	6.92	1.47	0.16
	Median MSE	0.61	0.21	6.87	1.39	0.09
$n=200$	Mean MSE	0.77	0.26	6.98	1.40	0.09
	Median MSE	0.62	0.17	6.99	1.36	0.06
			GB2			
$n=50$	Mean MSE	2.74	1.14	5.73	2.43	0.73
	Median MSE	1.71	0.69	5.59	2.23	0.44
$n=100$	Mean MSE	2.34	0.89	5.70	2.13	0.41
	Median MSE	1.61	0.55	5.58	2.01	0.25
$n=200$	Mean MSE	2.15	0.78	5.64	1.99	0.23
	Median MSE	1.76	0.52	5.52	1.92	0.14

Note: All figures have been multiplied by 1,000 to improve readability.

the performance does not seem to improve with sample size. We conjecture its subpar performance might be associated with the following reasons: (i) this estimator approximates the underlying quantile function rather than the Lorenz curve; (ii) the approximation is based on (exponential) power series, which suffers from possible oscillations and can be sensitive to extreme values; (iii) the resultant Lorenz curve estimate is not necessarily convex.

- Despite its appealing theoretical properties, Bern suffers from a rather slow convergence rate, as is evident in our simulations. In contrast, S-Spline not only provides better results, but also converges faster. For instance, under the log-normal distributions, the average MSE of Bern improves from 7.01 with $n=50$ to 5.99 with $n=200$, by 15%; while that of S-Spline improves from 1.54 to 0.41 by 73%.

Since Exp-Poly, Bern and S-Spline are nonparametric estimators, we next explore their performance under data-driven specification of tunning parameters. In particular, we use the Bayesian Information Criterion (BIC) to select the order of polynomials for Exp-Poly and Bern and the number of knots for S-Spline. The simulation results are reported in Table 2. In addition to the MSE's, we also report the median number of parameters selected by each estimator. The results suggest that

Table 2. Simulation Results (Exp-Poly: Exponential Polynomial Estimator of Ryu and Slottje (1996); Bern: Bernstein Estimator of Ryu and Slottje (1996); S-Spline: Shape-Restricted Spline Estimator of the Current Study; K: Number of Parameters).

		Exp-Poly	Bern	S-Spline
		Log-normal		
$n=50$	Mean MSE	1.23	2.90	1.47
	Median MSE	1.13	1.61	0.80
	Median K	3	12	3
$n=100$	Mean MSE	1.02	1.22	0.77
	Median MSE	0.99	0.62	0.43
	Median K	3	19	3
$n=200$	Mean MSE	0.86	0.50	0.38
	Median MSE	0.86	0.19	0.22
	Median K	3	17	4
		Gamma		
$n=50$	Mean MSE	6.52	0.63	0.31
	Median MSE	6.32	0.32	0.19
	Median K	3	12	3
$n=100$	Mean MSE	6.23	0.29	0.19
	Median MSE	6.25	0.09	0.09
	Median K	3	20	4
$n=200$	Mean MSE	6.20	0.13	0.09
	Median MSE	6.12	0.03	0.05
	Median K	3	15	4
		GB2		
$n=50$	Mean MSE	4.70	0.98	0.62
	Median MSE	4.52	0.33	0.34
	Median K	3	12	3
$n=100$	Mean MSE	4.59	0.45	0.33
	Median MSE	4.59	0.19	0.18
	Median K	3	17	3
$n=200$	Mean MSE	4.54	0.18	0.28
	Median MSE	4.52	0.08	0.14
	Median K	3	15	4

Note: MSE's multiplied by 1,000 to improve readability.

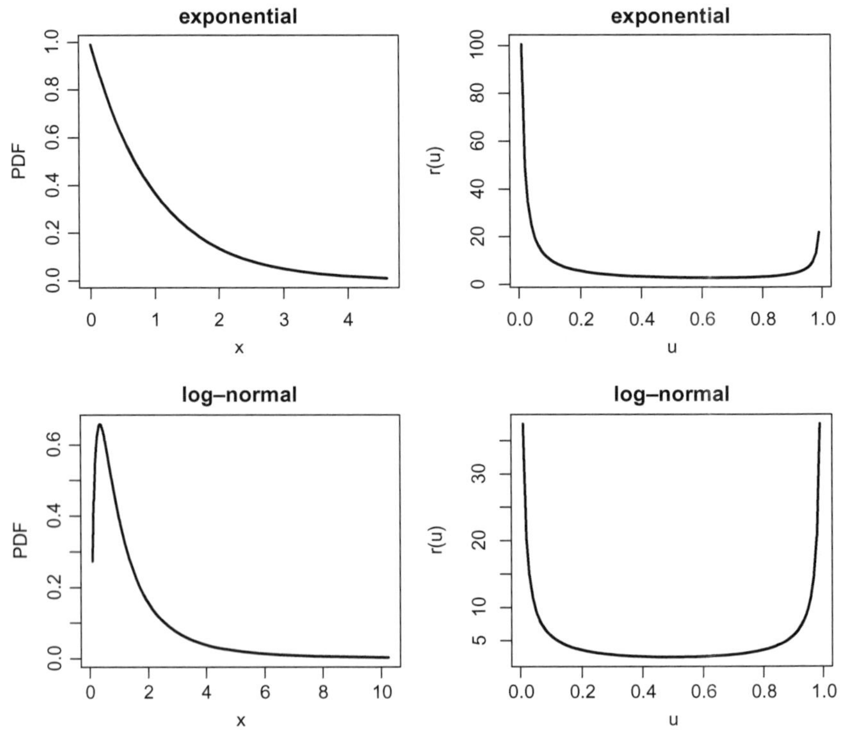

Fig. 1. Density and Mobility Functions of the Standard Exponential Distribution (Top) and the Standard Log-Normal Distribution (Bottom).

all three estimators perform better under data-driven selection of tunning parameters than under fixed specification as is reported in Table 1. Again, S-Spline is seen to provide the best overall performance and clearly dominates the other two estimators under small or modest sample size. Only modest improvement is observed for Exp-Poly, suggesting its rigidity. In contrast, Bern improves substantially. But this improvement comes at the price of a considerably larger number of parameters; for instance, the median number of parameters is 12 for the experiments on log-normal distributions when $n = 50$. As is discussed above, this is because Bern effectively interpolates the data.

6. EMPIRICAL EXAMPLE

In this section, we apply the proposed estimator of Lorenz curve to a real income dataset. Our data consist of observations of U.S. household income, extracted from

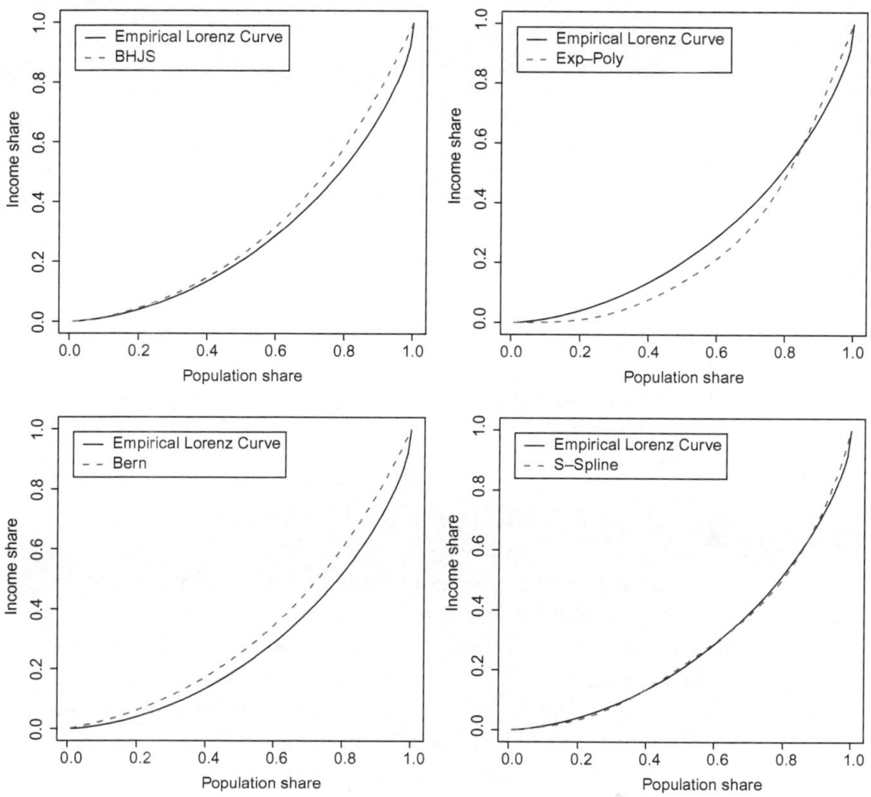

Fig. 2. Estimated and Empirical Lorenz Curve.

the Current Population Survey March Supplement of Year 2013. We include only households with positive income, resulting in a sample of 200,452 households. We construct the empirical Lorenz curve of this sample and use 99 points of this curve, evaluated at $(0.01, 0.02, \ldots, 0.99)$ of the population share, in our estimation. We also consider the four other estimators and use the same specifications as in the previous section. Since KP is clearly dominated by BHJS, we do not report its results in this application. The estimated Lorenz curves are plotted in Fig. 2, along with the underlying empirical Lorenz curve. The graphs suggest that S-Spline provides a superior fit relative to its competitors.

We next report in the top panel of Table 3 some summary statistics of the estimation error $e_i = s_0(i/100) - \hat{s}(i/100), i = 1, \ldots, 99$, with s_0 and $\hat{s}$ being the empirical Lorenz curve and its estimate. The results confirm the superior performance of S-Spline demonstrated in Fig. 2. Lastly, we compare the Gini index calculated from

Table 3. Estimation Results.

	sample	BHJS	Exp-Poly	Bern	S-Spline
Mean of e_i^2		.0018	.0025	.0034	.0012
Mean of $\lvert e_i \rvert$		.0307	.0450	.0505	.0071
Max. of $\lvert e_i \rvert$		.0895	.0736	.0996	.0438
Gini	.4419	.3710	.5028	.3744	.4440

Note: $e_i = s_0(i/100) - \hat{s}(i/100), i = 1, \ldots, 99$.

the full sample of more than 200,000 observations to those obtained from the estimated Lorenz curves. The results are reported in the last row of Table 3. The sample Gini is 0.4419 and that based on the Lorenz curve with S-Spline is 0.4440. In contrast, all other estimates show considerable biases.

7. CONCLUDING REMARKS

In this study, we have proposed an estimator of the Lorenz curve that is both flexible and consistent with all theoretical properties of the Lorenz curve. The proposed estimator is easy to implement and satisfies the theoretical constraints globally. Our Monte Carlo simulations and empirical example demonstrate excellent performance of the estimator. We expect the new estimator to be a useful addition to the toolbox of researchers in the areas of income distribution, inequality and welfare analysis. We conjecture that statistical inference can be conducted along the line of nonlinear least squares or nonlinear penalized spline estimation in conjunction with the results by Beach and Davidson (1983). Another possibility is the likelihood approach adopted by Chotikapanich and Griffiths (2002) and Hasegawa and Kozumi (2003). Formal inference with the Lorenz curves using the proposed estimator will be a topic of interest for future research.

REFERENCES

Basmann, R., Hayes, K., Johnson, J., & Slottje, D. (1990). A general functional form for approximating the Lorenz curve. *Journal of Econometrics*, *43*, 77–90.

Basmann, R., Hayes, K., & Slottje, D. (1991). The Lorenz curve and the mobility function. *Economics Letters*, *35*, 105–111.

Beach, C., & Davidson, R. (1983). Distribution-free statistical inference with Lorenz curves and income shares. *Review of Economic Studies*, *50*, 723–735.

Chotikapanich, D. (2008). *Modeling income distributions and Lorenz curves*, New York, NY: Springer.

Chotikapanich, D., & Griffiths, W. (2002). Estimating Lorenz curves using a Dirichlet distribution. *Journal of Business and Economic Statistics*, *20*, 290–295.

Cowell, F., & Victoria-Fester, M. (2008). Modelling Lorenz curves: Robust and semiparametric issues. In D. Chotikapanich (Ed.), *Modeling income distributions and Lorenz curves*. New York, NY: Springer.

Gastwirth, J. (1972). The estimation of the Lorenz curve and Gini index. *The Review of Economics and Statistics*, *54*, 306–316.

Hasegawa, H., & Kozumi, H. (2003). Estimation of Lorenz curves: A Bayesian nonparametric approach. *Journal of Econometrics*, *115*, 277–291.

Kakwani, N., & Podder, N. (1973). On the estimation of Lorenz curve from grouped observations. *International Economic Review*, *14*, 278–292.

Liu, W., Zhang, Y., & Li, Q. (2015). A semiparametric varying-coefficient model of monotone auction bidding processes. *Empirical Economics*, *48*, 313–335.

Luo, S. (2013). *New non-parametric methods for income distributions*. Dissertation, Georgia State University.

McDonald, D. (1984). Some generalized functions for the size distribution of income. *Econometrica*, *52*, 647–665.

Ramsay, J. (1998). Estimating smooth monotone functions. *Journal of the Royal Statistical Society: Series B*, *60*, 365–375.

Ruppert, D., Wand, W., & Carroll, R. (2003). *Semiparametric regression*. Cambridge: Cambridge University Press.

Ryu, H. & Slottje, D. (1996). Two flexible functional form approaches for approximating the Lorenz curve. *Journal of Econometrics*, *72*, 251–274.

Sarabia, J. (2008). Parametric Lorenz curve: Models and applications. In D. Chotikapanich (Ed.). *Modeling income distributions and Lorenz curves*. New York, NY: Springer.

Silber, J. (1999). *Handbook of income inequality measurement*. New York, NY: Springer.

Zhang, Y., Gu, J., & Li, Q. (2011). Nonparametric panel estimation of online auction process. *Empirical Economics*, *40*, 51–68.

APPENDIX

In this appendix, we present an algorithm to numerically evaluate the integration (10). An *R*-code implementing the estimation procedure is available from the authors upon request. For simplicity, we consider the case of linear splines with

$$m_1(t;z) = \beta_0 + \beta_1 t + \sum_{j=1}^{J} b_j (t - z_j)_+. \tag{A.1}$$

Generalizations to higher order splines are straightforward.

Define ($\alpha_0 = \beta_0, a_0 = \beta_1$) and ($\alpha_j = \beta_0 - \sum_{i=1}^{j} b_i z_i, a_j = \beta_1 + \sum_{i=1}^{j} b_i$) for $j = 1, \ldots, J$. It follows that

$$m_1(t;z) = \begin{cases} \alpha_0 + a_0 t, & \text{if } 0 \le t \le z_1 \\ \alpha_1 + a_1 t, & \text{if } z_1 < t \le z_2 \\ \vdots & \\ \alpha_J + a_J t, & \text{if } z_J < t \le 1 \end{cases}.$$

Define $h(\alpha, a; s_1, s_2) = \int_{s_1}^{s_2} (\alpha + at)^2 dt = (\alpha^2 t + \alpha a t^2 + \frac{a^2}{3} t^3)|_{s_1}^{s_2}$. Let z_0=0 and $h_0 = h(\alpha_0, a_0; z_0, z_1)$, $h_1 = h(\alpha_1, a_1; z_1, z_2)$,..., $h_J = h(\alpha_J, a_J; z_J, 1)$. Next define $J(s) = \max\{j : z_j \le s, j = 1, \ldots, J\}$. We then have

$$\int_0^s m_1^2(t;z)dt = \sum_{j=0}^{J(s)-1} h_j + h(\alpha_{J(s)}, a_{J(s)}; z_{J(s)}, s) \equiv H_{J(s)-1} + h(\alpha_{J(s)}, a_{J(s)}; z_{J(s)}, s).$$

Finally, for an arbitrary $u \in [0, 1]$, we have

$$\int_0^u \left\{ \exp\left(\int_0^s m_1^2(t;z)dt \right) \right\} ds = \sum_{j=0}^{J(u)-1} \int_{z_j}^{z_{j+1}} \exp\left(\sum_{i=0}^{j} H_i \right) ds$$
$$+ \int_{z_{J(u)}}^{u} \exp\left(\sum_{i=0}^{J(u)} H_i + h(\alpha_{J(u)}, a_{J(u)}; z_{J(u)}, s) \right) ds = \sum_{j=0}^{J(u)-1} (z_{j+1} - z_j) \exp\left(\sum_{i=0}^{j} H_i \right)$$
$$+ \exp\left(\sum_{i=0}^{J(u)} H_i \right) \int_{z_{J(u)}}^{u} \exp\left(h(\alpha_{J(u)}, a_{J(u)}; z_{J(u)}, s) \right) ds.$$

Although direct evaluation of *nested* integration, as required in Eq. (7), is difficult and computationally expensive, we have shown that our procedure only requires numerical evaluation of the following *single-layer* integration:

$$\int_{z^*}^{u} \exp\left(h(s)\right) ds.$$

where z^* is the largest element of the knots that is smaller than u and $h(\cdot)$ is a simple power series. This quantity can be easily and accurately evaluated by a standard numerical integration routine.